ENGLISH LETTER SYMBOLS

L	linear contrast
ln	natural logarithm
MS	mean square
n, n_i, N_i	number of cases in a sample
N	total number of cases
$N(0, 1)$	read "normally distributed with $\mu = 0$, $\sigma^2 = 1$"
p	general symbol for probability; in binomial, probability of success
q	Studentized range statistic; in binomial, probability of failure
r, r_{XY}	correlation coefficient
r'	Fisher's transformation of r
$r_b; r_{pb}; r_t$	biserial; point-biserial; and tetrachoric correlation coefficient
r_S	Spearman's rank-order correlation coefficient
$R, R_{0.123}$	multiple correlation coefficient
$r_{01.234}$	partial correlation coefficient
$r_{0(1.234)}$	semipartial correlation coefficient
$R^*, R^*_{0.123}$	population multiple correlation coefficient
$R^2_{\alpha, \beta, \alpha\beta}$	R^2 using predictors associated with variables A, B, and the AB interaction
s^2	pooled sample variance
s, s_X	standard deviation
s_D	standard deviation of difference scores
$s_{\overline{X}}; s_{\overline{X}_1 - \overline{X}_2}$	standard error of mean; standard error of mean differences
$s_{Y \cdot X}$	standard error of estimate
s_X^2	variance of X
SS_A	sum of squares for variable A
SS_{error}	error sum of squares
SS_{AB}	interaction sum of squares
$SS_{regression}$	sum of squares due to regression (i.e., accounted for by predictors)
$SS_{residual}$	sum of squares not accounted for by predictors
t	Student's t statistic
t'	t statistic with heterogeneous variances; Bonferroni t statistic
t_d	Dunnett's t statistic
T	Wilcoxon's matched-pairs signed-ranks statistic
T_j	total for treatment j
W	Kendall's coefficient of concordance
W_r	critical width for range tests
W_S	Wilcoxon's rank-sum statistic
$\overline{X}, \overline{X}_i$	sample mean
$\overline{X}_h$	harmonic mean
$\hat{Y}, \hat{Y}_i$	predicted value of Y
z	normal deviate (also called standard score)

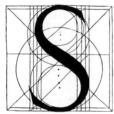# STATISTICAL METHODS
FOR PSYCHOLOGY

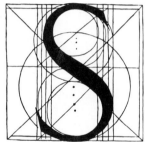

STATISTICAL METHODS
FOR PSYCHOLOGY

THIRD EDITION

DAVID C. HOWELL
UNIVERSITY OF VERMONT

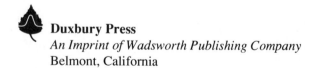

Duxbury Press
An Imprint of Wadsworth Publishing Company
Belmont, California

Duxbury Press
An Imprint of Wadsworth Publishing Company
A division of Wadsworth, Inc.

To Cathy, Barbara, Lynda, and Stephanie

Library of Congress Cataloging-in-Publication Data
Howell, David C.
    Statistical methods for psychology/David C. Howell.—3rd ed.
    p. cm.
    Includes bibliographical references and index.
    ISBN 0-534-92955-9
    1. Psychology—Statistical methods.   I. Title.
    [DNLM: 1. Psychometrics—methods. BF 39 H859s]
BF39.H69   1992
519.5'02415—dc20
DNLM/DLC for Library of Congress   91-24097   CIP

International Student Edition ISBN: 0-534-97217-9

Printed in the United States of America
        95 96—10 9 8 7

 This book is printed on recycled, acid-free paper.

Assistant Editor: Marcia Cole
Production Editor: S. London
Manufacturing Coordinator: Marcia A. Locke
Text and Cover Designer: S. London
Cover Photographer: Digital Art, West Light Backgrounds
Typesetter: Asco Trade Typesetting Ltd.
Cover Printer: Henry N. Sawyer, Inc.
Printer and Binder: Arcata Graphics Halliday

The cover image is taken from a drawing by Leonardo da Vinci, entitled "The Human Proportions Reconstructed According to Vitruvius." The "S" is part of the alphabet from *Da Divina Proportione*, Venice 1509, written by Pacioli Luca and illustrated by Leonardo da Vinci. Used with permission of the Boston Public Library.

CONTENTS

7 HYPOTHESIS TESTS APPLIED TO MEANS   159

8 POWER   204

9 CORRELATION AND REGRESSION   220

10   ALTERNATIVE CORRELATIONAL TECHNIQUES   265

11   SIMPLE ANALYSIS OF VARIANCE   286

17 LOG-LINEAR ANALYSIS   576

18 NONPARAMETRIC AND DISTRIBUTION-FREE STATISTICAL TESTS   609

PREFACE

This third edition of *Statistical Methods for Psychology*, like the previous editions, surveys statistical techniques commonly used in psychology, education, and the behavioral and social sciences. Although it is designed for students at the intermediate level or above, it does not assume that students have had either a previous course in statistics or a course in mathematics beyond high-school algebra. Those students who have had an introductory course in statistics will find that the early material provides a good review. The book is suitable for either a one-term or a full-year course, and I have used it successfully for both. Since I have found that students, and faculty, frequently refer back to the book from which they originally learned statistics, I have included material that will make the book a useful reference for future use. The instructor who wishes to omit this material will have no difficulty doing so.

My intention in writing this book was to explain the material at an intuitive level. This should not be taken to mean that the material is "watered down," but only that the emphasis is on *conceptual understanding*. The fact that a student can derive the sampling distribution of *t*, for example, does not mean that he or she understands how that distribution is to be used. My aim has been to concentrate on the *meaning* of a sampling distribution and to show the role it plays in the general theory of hypothesis testing. In my opinion this approach allows students to gain a better understanding of the way a particular test works and of the interrelationships among tests than would a more technical approach.

The third edition contains several new features that make the book more appealing to the student and more relevant to the actual process of data analysis:

1. Even more actual examples from the research literature are included.

2. Some early chapters have been rearranged in response to suggestions from reviewers.

3. Some further elaboration of the material on probability is included.

4. Examples of statistical output from Minitab, EXECUSTAT, EcStatic, SPSS^X, BMDP, JMP, and SAS computer packages are used. These examples have been expanded considerably from previous editions.

5. Where appropriate, computer calculations are relied on, in recognition of the fact that very few practicing psychologists still calculate complex statistics by hand. Despite the emphasis on using computers to perform calculations in some

circumstances, this book has not been turned into a "cookbook" of computer analyses.

6. A major revision of Chapter 12 on multiple comparison procedures brings it up to date. This revision broadens the concept of Bonferroni procedures. It also reflects the reality that most experiments in the literature contain relatively few groups, whereas most presentations of this material assume the existence of many groups. The chapter also now includes a discussion of trend analysis.

7. MANOVA procedures have been introduced in the analysis of repeated-measures designs, and ways of handling violations of the sphericity assumption are discussed more completely.

8. The discussion of the analysis of residuals in multiple regression is more extensive, and the presentation of regression diagnostics is more complete.

9. An entirely new chapter (Chapter 17) on log-linear models and their use in the behavioral sciences has been added.

This edition shares with the second edition two underlying themes that are more or less independent of the statistical hypothesis tests that are the main content of the book.

1. The first theme is the importance of looking at the data before jumping in with a hypothesis test. With this in mind, I discuss, in detail, plotting data, looking for outliers, and checking assumptions. (Graphical displays are used even more than in the second edition.) I try to do this with each data set as soon as I present it, even though the data set may be intended as an example of a sophisticated statistical technique. As examples, see pages 305–306, 486–488.

2. The second theme is the importance of the relationship between the statistical test to be employed and the theoretical questions being posed by the experiment. To emphasize this relationship, I use real examples in an attempt to make the student understand the purpose behind the experiment and the predictions made by the theory. For this reason I sometimes use one major example as the focus for an entire section, or even a whole chapter. For example, interesting data on the moon illusion from a well-known study by Kaufman and Rock (1962) are used in several forms of the t test (pages 170–171, 175–176), and all of Chapter 12 is organized around an important study of morphine addiction by Siegel (1975). Chapter 17 on log-linear models is built around Pugh's (1983) study of the "blame-the-victim" strategy in prosecutions for rape.

Although no one would be likely to call this book controversial, I have felt it important to express opinions on a number of controversial issues. After all, the controversies within statistics are part of what make it an interesting discipline. For example, I have argued that the underlying measurement scale is not as important as some have suggested, and I have recommended that the Newman–Keuls test and modified Bonferroni procedures are probably the most useful techniques for making multiple comparisons in the general case. I do not expect every instructor to agree with me on every point, and he or she has the opportunity to present an opposing view in class. At the same time, it seems to me that it is unfair and frustrating to the student to present a large number of multiple comparison procedures (which I do), and then to walk away and leave that student with no recommendation about which procedure is best for his or her problem.

A solutions manual, and data disks for Macintosh, and PC are available for instructors.

This book owes much to many people who have contributed in a variety of ways. I owe thanks to my colleagues at the University of Vermont; at the University of Durham, England, where I spent a sabbatical year working on the first edition of the book; and at the University of Bristol, England, where I worked on the second edition. I am indebted to many students and colleagues for their comments and suggestions. In particular, I want to thank my colleague Bruce Compas, whose data I have used so liberally, and those students who contributed their own data to this effort: Lisa Conti, Janet Gross, David King, Helen Klemchuk, Gina Mireault, Dale Swartzentruber, and Barry Wagner. Tim Heckman read the entire manuscript and checked all of the calculations. Ken Fajil also did error checking.

Several instructors who have used the book offered useful suggestions, in particular Kenneth Barry of Colorado State University and Karl Wuensch of East Carolina University. Many reviewers read the manuscript and provided valuable feedback:

Mary J. Allen
California State College

Carl Bassi
Vanderbilt University

Bernard Beins
Ithaca College

Kathleen Bloom
University of Waterloo

Barbara Bulman-Fleming
University of Waterloo

Stanley Cohen
West Virginia University

Ralph B. D'Agostino
Boston University

Kathleen M. Donovan
University of Central Oklahoma

Janis W. Driscoll
University of Colorado at Denver

Bert F. Green
Johns Hopkins University

George F. Hilton
Pacific Union College

Raymond F. Koopman
Simon Fraser University

Neal A. Kroll
University of California

Jacqueline Oler
Drexel University

Daniel Ozer
Boston University

John Polich
University of California, San Diego

Joseph L. Rodgers
University of Oklahoma

Douglas Rosenthal
Colorado State University

J. E. Keith Smith
University of Michigan

John E. Stecklein
University of Minnesota

Robert Strahan
Iowa State University

Ellen P. Susman
Metropolitan State College of Denver

Hoben Thomas
Pennsylvania State University

Jeff Witmer
University of Florida

Dominic J. Zerbolio
University of Missouri

I would also like to thank my editor, Michael Payne, and production editor, Susan London, for all that they have done.

Most of all I want to thank my wife, Cathy. She offered substantive criticism, worked all of the examples and exercises, wrote the index, and hunted out errors and inconsistencies with relish.

I am indebted to PWS-KENT, the University of California Press, The SAS Institute, the McGraw-Hill Book Company, NCSS, and Someware in Vermont for permission to illustrate computer examples and exercises by means of Minitab®, EXECUSTAT®, BMDP, the SAS® System and JMP®, SPSS^X®, NCSS®, and EsStatic® software, respectively. Information about the SPSS® Batch System is available from SPSS, Inc. I am also indebted to B. J. Winer and William Winkler for permission to use numerical examples from their work. Finally, I want to thank the Institute of Mathematical Statistics, the Biometric Society, the American Statistical Society, and the *Biometrika* Trustees for permission to reproduce tables from their journals.

Finally, I would like to take the novel step of supplying an Internet address. Those with access to the Internet, Bitnet, or many other electronic networks are welcome to offer suggestions or comments and to pose questions about material in the book. Within the limits of what time I have available, I would be happy to respond. My Internet address is D_Howell@uvmvax.uvm.edu.

David C. Howell
Burlington, Vermont

Basic Concepts

Objectives *To examine the kinds of problems presented in this book and the issues involved in selecting a statistical procedure.*

Contents

Stress is something that we are all forced to deal with throughout life. It arises in our daily interactions with those around us, in our interactions with the environment, in the face of an impending exam, and, for many students, in the realization that they are required to take a statistics course. Although most of us learn to respond and adapt to stress, the learning process is often slow and painful. This preamble leads to a description of a somewhat hypothetical research project, which in turn illustrates a number of important statistical concepts.

A group of educators has put together a course designed to teach high-school students how to manage stress. They need an outside investigator, however, who can tell them how well the course is working and, in particular, whether students who take the course have fewer problems with stress, and handle it better, than do students who have not taken the course. For the moment we will assume that we are charged with the task of designing an evaluation of their program. The experiment that we design will not be complete, but it will illustrate some of the issues involved in designing and analyzing experiments and some of the statistical concepts with which you must be familiar.

1.1 Important terms

Although the program in stress management was designed for high-school students, it clearly would be impossible to apply it to the population of all high-school students in the country. First of all, there are far too many such students. Moreover, it makes no sense to apply a program to everyone until we know if it is a useful program. Instead of dealing with the entire population of high-school students, we will draw a sample of students from that population and apply the program to them. But we will not draw just any old sample. We will attempt to draw a **random sample**. To do this, we follow a particular set of procedures to ensure that each and every element of the population has an equal chance of being selected. Having drawn our sample of students, we will **randomly assign** half the subjects to a group that will receive the stress-management program and half to a group that will not receive the program.

Random sample

Randomly assign

This description has already brought out several concepts that need further elaboration; namely, a population, a sample, a random sample, and random assignment. A **population** is the entire collection of events (students' scores, people's incomes, rats' running speeds, etc.) in which you are interested. Thus, if you are interested in the stress-management scores of all high-school students in the United States, then the collection of all high-school students' stress scores would form a population—in this case, a population of many millions of elements. If, on the other hand, you were interested in the stress scores of high-school seniors only in Fairfax, Vermont (a town of fewer than 2000 inhabitants), the population would consist of only about 60 elements.

Population

The point is that a population can range from a relatively small set of numbers, which can be collected easily, to a large but finite set of numbers, which would be impractical to collect in their entirety, to an infinite set of numbers, such as the set of all possible cartoon drawings that students could theoretically produce, which would be impossible to collect. Unfortunately for us, the populations we are interested in are usually very large. The practical consequence is that we seldom if ever measure entire populations. Instead, we are forced to draw only a **sample** of observations from that population and to use that sample to infer something about the characteristics of the population.

Sample

Assuming that the sample is truly random, we not only can estimate certain characteristics of the population but can also have a very good idea of how accurate our estimates are. To the extent that the sample is not random, our estimates may or may not be meaningful, since the sample may or may not accurately reflect the entire population. Studies based on nonrandom samples may lack **external validity**. A sample drawn from a small town in Nebraska would not produce a valid estimate of the percentage of the population of the United States that is Hispanic—nor would a sample drawn solely from the American Southwest.

External validity

Before going on, let us clear up one point that tends to confuse many people. The problem is that one person's sample might be another person's population. For example, if I were to conduct a study on the effectiveness of this book as a teaching instrument, one class's scores on an examination might be considered by me to be a sample, albeit a nonrandom one, of the population of scores for all students using, or potentially using, this book. The class instructor, on the other hand, is probably not terribly concerned about this book, but instead cares only about his or her own students. He or she would regard the same set of scores as a population. In turn, someone interested in the teaching of statistics might regard my population (everyone using my book) as a nonrandom sample from a larger population (everyone using any textbook in statistics). Thus, the definition of a population depends on what you are interested in studying.

The fact that I have used nonrandom samples here to make a point should not lead you to think that randomness is not important. On the contrary, it is the cornerstone of most statistical procedures. As a matter of fact, the relevant population could be defined as the collection of elements from which samples have been randomly drawn. But this leads to a major theoretical problem. In our stress study, for example, it is highly unlikely that we could seriously consider drawing a truly random sample of U.S. high-school students and administering the stress-management program to them. How then are we going to take advantage of methods and procedures based on the assumption of random sampling? This question has no clear answer other than to realize the limitations of our methodology and to draw our conclusions accordingly. To the extent that we think that our sample is not representative of U.S. high-school students, we must limit our interpretation of the results.

Random assignment
Internal validity

While we are dealing with random selection of subjects, we must consider the related concept of random assignment. Whereas random selection concerns the *source* of our data and is important in terms of generalizing the results of our study to the whole population, **random assignment** of subjects (once selected) to treatment groups is fundamental to the integrity, or **internal validity**, of our experiment. It helps ensure that our results mean what we think they mean (which, for example, would not be the case if we put all our timid subjects in one group and our more self-confident subjects in the other).

Variable

Having dealt with the selection of subjects and their assignment to treatment groups, it is time to consider the data that will result. Because we want to study the ability of subjects to deal with stress, and because the response to stress is a function of many variables, a critical aspect of planning the study involves selecting the variables to be studied. A **variable** is a property of an object or event that can take on different values. For example, hair color is a variable because it is a property of an object (hair) and can take on different values (brown, yellow, red, gray, etc.). With respect to our evaluation, such things as self-confidence, social support (the degree to which help is available from people around you), gender, degree of personal control, and treatment group are all relevant variables, and each element of the population takes on *one* value of each variable. We can further discriminate between **discrete variables**, such as gender or high-school class, which take on only a limited number of values, and **continuous variables**, such as age and self-esteem score, which can assume, at least in theory, any value between the lowest and highest points on the scale.[†] As you will see, this distinction plays an important role in the way we treat data.

Discrete variables

Continuous variables

Measurement data
Quantitative data

Closely related to the distinction between discrete and continuous variables is the distinction between measurement and categorical data. By **measurement data** (sometimes called **quantitative data**) we mean the results of any sort of measurement—for example, grades on a test, people's weights, scores on a scale of self-esteem, and so on.

[†] Actually, a continuous variable is one in which *any* value between the extremes of the scale (e.g., 32.48...) is possible. In practice, however, we treat a variable as continuous whenever it can take on many different values, and we treat it as discrete whenever it can take on only a few different values.

In all cases, some sort of instrument (in its broadest sense) has been used to measure something.

**Categorical data,
Frequency data,
Qualitative data**

On the other hand, **categorical data** (also known as **frequency data** or **qualitative data**) are illustrated in such statements as, "There are 34 females and 26 males in our study" or "Fifteen people were classed as 'highly anxious,' 33 as 'neutral,' and 12 as 'low anxious.'" Here we are categorizing things, and our data consist of frequencies for each category (hence the name categorical data). Several hundred subjects might be involved in our study, but the results (data) would consist of only two or three numbers—the number of subjects falling in each category. In contrast, if instead of sorting people with respect to high, medium, and low anxiety, we had assigned them each a score based on some a more-or-less continuous scale of anxiety, we would be dealing with measurement data, and the data would consist of scores for each subject on that variable. Note that in both situations the variable is labeled *anxiety*. As with most distinctions, the one between measurement and categorical data can be pushed too far. The distinction is useful, however, and the answer to the question of whether a variable is a measurement or a categorical one is almost always clear in practice.

In statistics, we also dichotomize the concept of a variable in an additional way.

**Independent
variables
Dependent
variables**   *is measured*

We speak of **independent variables** (those that are manipulated by the experimenter) and **dependent variables** (those that are not under the experimenter's control—the data). In our example, group membership is an independent variable, since we control it. We decide what the treatments will be and who will receive each treatment. The data—such as self-esteem scores, age, personal control, and so on—are the dependent variables. Basically, the study is about the independent variables, and the results of the study (the data) are the dependent variables. Independent variables may be either quantitative or qualitative, whereas dependent variables are generally, but certainly not always, quantitative.[†]

1.2   DESCRIPTIVE AND INFERENTIAL STATISTICS

Returning to our intervention program for stress, once we have chosen the variables to be measured and the schools have administered the program to the subjects, we are left with a collection of raw data—the scores. There are two primary divisions of the field of statistics that are concerned with the use we make of these data.

**Descriptive
statistics**

Whenever our purpose is merely to describe a set of data, we are employing **descriptive statistics**. For example, one of the first things that we would want to do with our data is to graph them, to calculate means (averages) and other measures, and to look for extreme scores or oddly shaped distributions of scores. These procedures are called descriptive statistics because they are primarily aimed at describing the data. The field of descriptive statistics was once looked down on as a rather uninteresting field populated primarily by those who drew distorted-looking graphs for such publi-

[†] Many people have difficulty remembering which is the dependent variable and which is the independent variable. Notice that both "dependent" and "data" start with a "d."

**Exploratory data
analysis (EDA)**

cations as *Time* magazine. In the last 15 years, however, John Tukey has developed what he calls exploratory statistics, or **exploratory data analysis (EDA)**. He has shown the necessity of paying close attention to the data and examining them in detail before invoking more technically involved procedures. In this book, we will spend some time considering exploratory methods and Tukey's general orientation toward data.

After we have described our data in detail and are satisfied that we understand what the numbers have to say on a superficial level, we will be particularly interested in what is called **inferential statistics**. In fact, most of this book will deal with inferential statistics. In designing our experiment, we acknowledged that it was not possible to measure the entire population, and therefore we drew samples from that population. Our basic questions, however, deal with the population itself. We might want to ask, for example, about the average self-esteem score for an entire population of students who could have taken our program, even though all that we really have is the average score for the sample of students who actually went through the program.

Inferential statistics -
*inferring something
about a population
based on a sample*

A measure, such as the average self-esteem score, that refers to an entire population is called a **parameter**. That same measure, when it is calculated from a sample of data that we have collected, is called a **statistic**. Parameters are the *real* entities of interest, and the corresponding statistics are *guesses* at reality. Although most of what we will do in this book deals with sample statistics (or guesses, if you prefer), keep in mind that the reality of interest is the corresponding population parameter. We want to *infer* something about the characteristics of the population (parameters) from what we know about the characteristics of the sample (statistics). In a similar vein, we are particularly interested in knowing whether the average self-esteem score of a population of students enrolled in our program is higher, or lower, than the average self-esteem score of students not enrolled. Again we are dealing with the area of inferential statistics, since we are inferring characteristics of populations from characteristics of samples.

**Parameter
Statistic**

1.3 MEASUREMENT SCALES

The topic of measurement scales is one that some writers think is crucial and others think is irrelevant. Although this book will tend to side with the latter group, it is important that you have some familiarity with the general issue. (You do not have to agree with something to think that it is worth studying. After all, evangelists claim to know a great deal about sin.) An additional benefit of this discussion is that you will begin to realize that statistics as a subject is not merely a cut-and-dried set of facts, but rather is a set of facts put together with a variety of interpretations and opinions.

Probably the foremost leader of those who see measurement scales as crucial to the choice of statistical procedures was S. S. Stevens.[†] Basically, Stevens defined four

---

[†]Chapter 1 in Stevenss' *Handbook of Experimental Psychology* (1951) is an excellent reference for anyone wishing to examine the substantial mathematical issues underlying his position.

types of scales: nominal, ordinal, interval, and ratio. These scales are distinguished on the basis of the relationships assumed to exist between items having different scale values.

Nominal scales

Nominal scales

In a sense, **nominal scales** are not really scales at all; they do not scale items along any dimension, but rather label them. Variables such as gender and political-party affiliation are nominal variables. Such categorical data are usually measured on a nominal scale, since we merely assign category labels (e.g., male or female; Republican, Democrat, or Independent) to observations. A numerical example of a nominal scale is the set of numbers assigned to football players. Frequently, these numbers have no meaning other than that they are convenient labels to distinguish the players from one another. Letters or pictures of animals could just as easily be used.

Ordinal scales

Ordinal scale

The simplest true scale is an **ordinal scale**, which orders people, objects, or events along some continuum. An excellent example of such a scale is the ranks in the Navy. A commander is lower in prestige than a captain, who in turn is lower than a rear admiral. However, there is no reason to think that the *difference* in prestige between a commander and a captain is the same as that between a captain and a rear admiral. An example from psychology would be the Holmes and Rahe (1967) scale of life stress. Using this scale, you count (sometimes with differential weightings) the number of changes (marriage, moving, new job, etc.) that have occurred during the past 6 months of a person's life. Someone who has a score of 20 is presumed to have experienced more stress than someone with a score of 15, and the latter in turn is presumed to have experienced more stress than someone with a score of 10. Thus, people are ordered, in terms of stress, by the number of changes in their recent lives. This is another example of an ordinal scale, because nothing is implied about the differences between points on the scale. We do not assume, for example, that the difference between 10 and 15 points represents the same difference in stress as the difference between 15 and 20 points. Distinctions of that sort must be left to interval scales.

Interval scales

Interval scale

With an **interval scale**, we have a measurement scale in which we can legitimately speak of differences between scale points. A common example is the Fahrenheit scale of temperature, where a 10-point difference has the same meaning anywhere along the scale. Thus, the difference in temperature between 10° F and 20° F is the same as the difference between 80° F and 90° F. Notice that this scale also satisfies the properties of the two preceding ones. What we do not have with an interval scale, however, is the ability to speak meaningfully about ratios. Thus, we cannot say, for example, that 40° F is half as hot as 80° F, or twice as hot as 20° F. We have to use ratio scales for that purpose. (In this regard, it is worth noting that when we perform perfectly legitimate conversions from one interval scale to another—for example, from the Fahrenheit to the Celsius scale of temperature—we do not even keep the same ratios. Thus, the ratio between 40° and 80° on a Fahrenheit scale is different from the ratio between 4.4° and 26.7° on a Celsius scale, although the temperatures are comparable. This highlights the arbitrary nature of ratios when dealing with interval scales.)

RATIO SCALES

Ratio scale

A **ratio scale** is one that has a *true* zero point. Notice that the zero point must be a true zero point and not an arbitrary one, such as 0° F or even 0° C. (A true zero point is the point corresponding to the absence of the thing being measured. Since 0° F and 0° C do not represent the absence of temperature or molecular motion, they are not true zero points.) Examples of ratio scales are the common physical ones of length, volume, time, and so on. With these scales, we not only have the properties of the preceding scales but we also can speak about ratios. We can say that in physical terms 10 seconds is twice as long as 5 seconds, that 100 lbs is one-third as heavy as 300 lbs, and so on.

You might think that the kind of scale with which we are working would be obvious. Unfortunately, especially with the kinds of measures we collect in the social sciences, this is rarely the case. Consider for a moment the situation in which an anxiety questionnaire is administered to a group of high-school students. If you were foolish enough, you might argue that this is a ratio scale of anxiety. You would maintain that a person who scored 0 had no anxiety at all and that a score of 80 reflected twice as much anxiety as did a score of 40. Although most people would find this position ridiculous, with certain questionnaires you might be able to build a reasonable case. Someone else might argue that it is an interval scale and that, although the zero point was somewhat arbitrary (the student receiving a 0 was somewhat anxious but your questions failed to detect it), equal differences in scores represent equal differences in anxiety. A more reasonable stance might be to say that the scores represent an ordinal scale: a 95 reflects more anxiety than an 85, which in turn reflects more than a 75, but equal differences in scores do not reflect equal differences in anxiety. For an excellent and readable discussion of measurement scales, see Hays (1981, pp. 59–65).

As an example of a form of measurement that has a scale that depends on its use, consider the temperature of a house. We generally speak of Fahrenheit temperature as an interval scale. We have just used it as an example of one, and there is no doubt that, to a physicist, the difference between 62° F and 64° F is exactly the same as the difference between 72° F and 74° F. If we are measuring temperature as an index of *comfort*, rather than as an index of molecular activity however, the same numbers no longer form an interval scale. To a person sitting in a room at 62° F, a jump to 64° F would be distinctly noticeable (and welcome). The same cannot be said about the difference between room temperatures of 72° F and 74° F. This points up the important fact that *it is the underlying variable that we are measuring (e.g., comfort), not the numbers themselves, that is important in defining the scale.* As a scale of *comfort*, degrees Fahrenheit do not form an interval scale.

Since there usually is no unanimous agreement concerning the measurement scale employed, it is up to the individual user of statistical procedures to decide which scale best fits the data. All that can be asked of the user is that he or she think about the problem carefully before coming to a decision, and not simply assume that the standard answer is necessarily the best answer.

THE ROLE OF MEASUREMENT SCALES

I stated earlier that writers disagree about the importance assigned to measurement scales. Some authors have ignored the problem totally, whereas others have organized whole textbooks around the different scales. A reasonable view is that the central issue is the absolute necessity of separating in our minds the numbers we collect from the objects or events to which they refer. Such an argument was made for the example of room temperature, where the scale (interval or ordinal) depended on whether we were interested in measuring some physical attribute of temperature or its effect on people (i.e., comfort). A difference of 2° F is the same, *physically*, anywhere on the scale, but a difference of 2° F when a room is already warm may not *feel* as large as does a difference of 2° F when a room is relatively cool. In other words, we have an interval scale of the physical units but no more than an ordinal scale of comfort.

Because statistical tests use numbers without considering the objects or events to which those numbers refer, we may carry out any of the standard mathematical operations (addition, multiplication, etc.) regardless of the nature of the underlying scale. An excellent, entertaining, and highly recommended paper on this point is one by Lord (1953), entitled "On the Statistical Treatment of Football Numbers," in which he argues that these numbers can be treated in any way you like because, "The numbers do not remember where they came from" (p. 751).

The problem arises when it is time to interpret the results of some form of statistical manipulation. At that point, we must ask whether the statistical results are related in any meaningful way to the objects or events in question. Here we are no longer dealing with a statistical issue, but with a methodological one. No *statistical* procedure can tell us whether the fact that one group received higher scores than another on an anxiety questionnaire reveals anything about group differences in underlying anxiety levels. Moreover, to be satisfied because the questionnaire provides a ratio scale of anxiety *scores* (a score of 50 is twice as large as a score of 25) is to lose sight of the fact that we set out to measure anxiety, which may not increase in an orderly way with increases in scores. Our statistical tests can apply only to the numbers that we obtain, and the validity of statements about the objects or events that we think we are measuring hinges primarily on our knowledge of those objects or events, not on the measurement scale. We do our best to ensure that our measures relate as closely as possible to what we want to measure, but our results are ultimately only the numbers we obtain and our faith in the relationship between those numbers and the underlying objects or events.[†]

From the preceding discussion, the apparent conclusion—and the one accepted in

---

[†] As Cohen (1965) has pointed out, "Thurstone once said that in psychology we measure men by their shadows. Indeed, in clinical psychology we often measure men by their shadows while they are dancing in a ballroom illuminated by the reflections of an old-fashioned revolving polyhedral mirror" (p. 102).

this book—is that the underlying measurement scale is not crucial in our choice of statistical techniques. Obviously, a certain amount of common sense is required in interpreting the results of these statistical manipulations. Only a fool would conclude that a painting that was judged as excellent by one person and contemptible by another ought therefore to be classified as mediocre.

1.4   USING COMPUTERS

In the not too distant past, most statistical analyses were done on desktop or hand calculators, and textbooks were written accordingly. Methods have changed, however, and most calculations are now done by computers—either large mainframes or desktop microcomputers. (In fact, the distinction between mainframes and microcomputers is quickly becoming blurred.)

This book, particularly this edition, attempts to deal with the increased availability of computers by incorporating them into the discussion. The level of computer involvement increases substantially as the book proceeds and as computations become more laborious. For the simpler procedures, the calculational formulas are important in defining the concept. For example, the formula for a standard deviation or a t test defines and makes meaningful what a standard deviation or a t test actually is. In those cases hand calculation is emphasized even though examples of computer solutions are also given. Later in the book, when we discuss multiple regression or log-linear models, for example, the formulas become less informative. The formula for deriving regression coefficients with five predictors, or the formula for estimating expected frequencies in a complex log-linear model, would not reasonably be expected to add to your understanding of such statistics. In those situations we will rely almost exclusively on computer solutions.

At present many statistical software packages are available to the typical researcher or student conducting statistical analyses. Whereas a few year ago we would have broken those into mainframe packages and microcomputer packages, we no longer make that distinction. Almost all the major mainframe packages are now available for microcomputers, doing virtually the same analyses. The most important large statistical packages, which will carry out nearly every analysis that statisticians have invented, are the BMDP series, Minitab®, SAS®, SPSS^{X}©, and SYSTAT. These are highly reliable and relatively easy-to-use packages, and one or more of them is generally available in any college or university computer center. Many examples of their use are scattered throughout this book. Each has its own set of supporters (my preference may become obvious as we go along), but they are all excellent. Choosing among them hinges on subtle differences.

In addition to the "heavyweight" packages, many smaller programs are available for microcomputers, especially for computers running the MS-DOS operating system.[†] The smaller packages are often easier to use, more interactive, faster running,

---

[†] The MS-DOS operating system generally refers to computers that are labelled "IBM compatible," whether they were manufactured by IBM or one of the company's many high-quality competitors.

and expensive. Although such packages may not perform every conceivable analysis or produce as many different statistics in the process of running any one analysis, they are extremely useful in exploring a data set, testing major hypotheses, and generally helping you to understand your data. A good example of such a program, and one I single out because it is both very comprehensive and currently more-or-less free, is called MYSTAT. MYSTAT is a subset of SYSTAT, and is a fairly complete program in its own right. Its MS-DOS version is not as easy to learn as some programs because it does not operate off the standard menu structure that many microcomputer users have come to expect, but it is an excellent package.

Somewhat less statistical software is available for the Apple Macintosh than for the MS-DOS machines. However, several good packages, including the very complete SYSTAT, STATVIEW, JMP, and, for analysis of variance, SuperAnova, are on the market. MYSTAT is also available for the Macintosh; this version is very easy to use.

A number of statistical graphics packages produce excellent graphs. Graphs are extremely useful for getting a feel for the data, as you will see in Chapter 2. Most of these packages are expensive, but they are often available on college and university computer systems. An excellent combined graphics and statistical analysis package with an inexpensive student edition is EXECUSTAT. Acceptable graphics can also be created within the major programs, particularly Minitab, SAS, and SPSS^X.

One of the important distinctions that relates to using computer packages for statistical analyses concerns the way instructions are passed to the program. In the days of mainframe computers, instructions were passed via "command-line statements." For example, one line might contain the name of the procedure to be used, the next line might contain the list of variables to be included, and so forth. That structure has largely been carried over into statistical packages running under MS-DOS, although there are exceptions. On the other hand, programs written for the Macintosh, and new ones being written to operate under Windows^{TM}, use "pull-down menus." Here you generally use a mouse, although equivalent keyboard commands often exist, to select the analysis, to select the variables, to specify which variables are independent variables, and so on. This is by far the easier system.

For this book I have used the command-line approach. First of all, it applies to a higher percentage of users. Second, there is no simple way of specifying pull-down commands that would mean anything to people using a different statistical package. Third, it is usually relatively easy to translate a command-line instruction into the appropriate pull-down steps. I would be surprised if this created any serious problems for students using pull-down menus. Such menus are sufficiently self-explanatory that I suspect that 5 years from now most analyses will rely on them.

An advantage of the pull-down approach, aside from ease of use, is that it tends to be much more interactive. You look at a set of data, calculate some descriptive statistics, plot the data, transform the data on the basis of what you have seen, call up inferential analyses, modify those analyses on the basis of the results, and so on. With command-line input you generally lay out everything in advance and then run it all at once. Although there is nothing to stop you from working in a step-by-step approach with command lines, and in fact it is advisable to do so, command-line input encourages people to run their analyses less interactively.

In speaking about statistical packages, we should mention the widely available spreadsheets such as Excel, Lotus 1-2-3®, Quattro® Pro, and Wingz. Not only are these programs capable of performing a number of statistical calculations, but they also produce reasonably good graphics and are an excellent way of carrying out hand calculations. They force you to go about your calculations logically, at the same time retaining all intermediate steps for later examination. Statisticians often criticize such programs for the accuracy of their results with very large samples or with samples of unusual data, but they are extremely useful for small- to medium-sized problems.

For anyone interested in statistical computing or graphics, the major computer magazines review statistical software about every other year. Excellent reviews can be found in *PC Magazine* and *MacWorld*. In addition, public domain and shareware programs are available from bulletin boards and from distributors who sell software by the disk.

1.5 THE PLAN OF THE BOOK

Our original example, the examination of the effects of a program of stress management, offers an opportunity to illustrate the book's organization. In the process of running the study, we will be collecting data on many variables. One of the first things we will do with these data is to plot them, to look at the distribution for each variable, to calculate means and standard deviations, and so on. These techniques will be discussed in Chapter 2.

Following an exploratory analysis of the data, we will apply several inferential procedures. For example, we will want to compare the mean score on a scale of coping skills for a group who received stress-management training with the mean score for a group who did not receive such training. Techniques for making these kinds of comparisons will be discussed in Chapters 7, 11, 12, 13, 14, 16, and 18, depending on the complexity of our experiment, the number of groups to be compared, and the degree to which we are willing to make certain assumptions about our data.

We might also want to ask questions dealing with the relationships between variables rather than the differences among groups. For example, we might like to know whether a person's level of behavior problems is related to his score on self-esteem, or whether a person's coping scores can be predicted from variables such as her self-esteem and social support. Techniques for asking these kinds of questions will be considered in Chapters 9, 10, 15 and 17, depending on the type of data we have and the number of variables involved.

Figure 1.1 provides an organizational scheme that distinguishes among the various procedures on the basis of a number of dimensions, such as the type of data, the questions we wish to ask, and so on. The dimensions should be self-explanatory. This diagram is not meant to be a guide for choosing a statistical test. Rather, it is intended to give you a sense of how the book is organized.

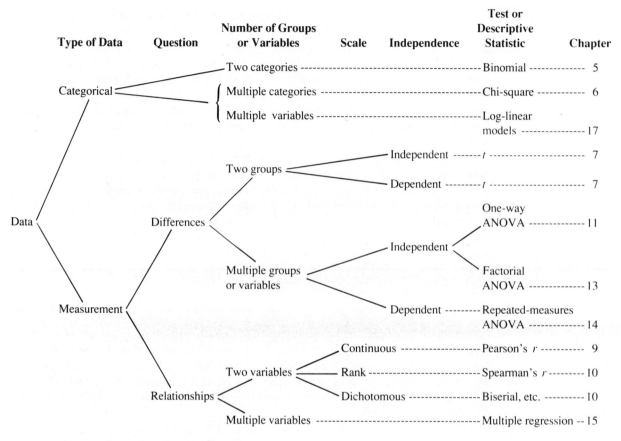

FIGURE 1.1 Decision tree

KEY TERMS

Random sample (1.1)
Randomly assign (1.1)
Population (1.1)
Sample (1.1)
External validity (1.1)
Random assignment (1.1)
Internal validity (1.1)
Variable (1.1)
Discrete variables (1.1)
Continuous variables (1.1)
Measurement data (1.1)
Quantitative data (1.1)
Categorical data (1.1)

Frequency data (1.1)
Qualitative data (1.1)
Independent variables (1.1)
Dependent variables (1.1)
Descriptive statistics (1.2)
Exploratory data analysis (EDA) (1.2)
Inferential statistics (1.2)
Parameter (1.2)
Statistic (1.2)
Nominal scales (1.3)
Ordinal scale (1.3)
Interval scale (1.3)
Ratio scale (1.3)

EXERCISES

1.1   Under what conditions would the entire student body of your college or university be considered a population?

1.2   Under what conditions would the entire student body of your college or university be considered a sample?

1.3   If the student body of your college or university were considered to be a sample, as in Exercise 1.2, would this sample be random or nonrandom? Why?

1.4   Why would choosing names from a local telephone book not produce a random sample of the residents of that city? Who would be underrepresented and who would be overrepresented?

1.5   Give two examples of independent variables and two examples of dependent variables.

1.6   Write a sentence describing an experiment in terms of an independent and a dependent variable.

1.7   Give three examples of continuous variables.

1.8   Give three examples of discrete variables.

1.9   Give an example of a study in which we are interested in estimating the average score of a population.

1.10   Give an example of a study in which we do not care about the actual numerical value of a population average, but wish to know whether the average of one population is greater than the average of a different population.

1.11   Give three examples of categorical data.

1.12   Give three examples of measurement data.

1.13   Give an example in which the thing we are studying could be either a measurement or a categorical variable.

1.14   Give one example of each kind of measurement scale.

1.15   Give an example of a variable that might be said to be measured on a ratio scale for some purposes and on an interval or ordinal scale for other purposes.

1.16   We trained rats to run a straight-alley maze by providing positive reinforcement with food. On trial 12 a rat lay down and went to sleep halfway through the maze. What does this say about the measurement scale when speed is used as an index of learning?

1.17   What does Exercise 1.16 say about speed used as an index of motivation?

1.18   Give two examples of studies in which our primary interest is in looking at relationships between variables.

1.19   Give two examples of studies in which our primary interest is in looking at differences among groups.

CHAPTER TWO

DESCRIBING AND EXPLORING DATA

OBJECTIVES *To show how data can be reduced to a more interpretable form by using graphical representation and measures of central tendency and dispersion.*

CONTENTS

B y itself, a collection of raw data is no more exciting or informative than a pile of junk mail. Whether the data have been neatly arranged in rows on a data collection form or have been scribbled on the back of an out-of-date announcement torn from a bulletin board, a collection of numbers is still just a collection of numbers. The numbers must be put into some sort of logical organization if they are to be interpretable.

As an illustration we can examine some data collected by Wagner and his colleagues (Wagner, Compas, and Howell, 1987) concerning student attitudes toward events in their lives. This study presented college students with 210 potentially stressful life events, both negative and positive (e.g., death of parent, breakup of an important relationship, admission to graduate school) and asked them to indicate whether the event had happened to them in the past 6 months and to rate on a 9-point scale how desirable or undesirable it was. One of the items was "attending class," something that all students do. This item had 74 ratings, one for each student. It should be apparent that we will not learn very much by looking at a jumble of 74 numbers, other than gaining some vague subjective impression that people generally found attending class desirable or undesirable. We must first organize the data and then reduce them to a few numbers that carry most of the relevant information.

2.1 PLOTTING DATA

One of the simplest ways to reorganize data to make them more intelligible is to plot them in some sort of graphical form. Data can be represented graphically in several common ways.

FREQUENCY DISTRIBUTIONS

Frequency distribution

As a first step, we might wish to make a **frequency distribution** of the data. In our example, we would count the number of times each of the nine numerical ratings was given by Wagner's subjects. The results are shown in Table 2.1. From the distribution shown in Table 2.1, it is clear that there is a wide distribution of opinion on the desirability of attending class, with responses ranging from 2 to 9. Interestingly, the bulk of the responses pile up on the "desirable" side of neutral. The most common value is a 7 ("quite desirable"), which was assigned by 25 subjects.

TABLE 2.1
Frequency distribution of ratings of the desirability of attending class

	Rating (X)	Frequency (f)
Extremely undesirable	1	0
	2	1
	3	4
	4	8
	5	9
	6	15
	7	25
	8	7
Extremely desirable	9	2
(Missing)		(3)

HISTOGRAMS

Histogram

It might be easier to understand the data if we graphed them as a series of vertical bars, with the height of each bar representing the frequency of the rating and the width of each bar representing the width of the interval containing the underlying subjective ratings. Such a graph is called a **histogram**. A histogram for our data is presented in Figure 2.1.

The histogram has one interesting feature that generalizes to other methods of plotting distributions. If we arbitrarily define the width of an interval to be one unit, then the *area* of any interval or set of intervals is equal to the number of scores falling within that region. Furthermore, the total area within the histogram is equal to N, the sample size (number of scores). The same general statement, with appropriate changes in wording, can be made about many distributions we plot. This is the reason that we repeatedly refer to the "area under the curve"—*area and number* (or *percentage*) of scores are interchangeable concepts. If we arbitrarily define the total area under the curve to be 1.00, then the area within a particular segment of the histogram becomes equivalent to the proportion (or percentage) of scores falling within that segment.

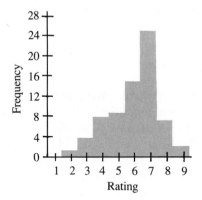

FIGURE 2.1
Histogram of 71 ratings of the desirability of attending class

GROUPING DATA

In the preceding discussion of frequency distributions and histograms, we assumed that the data are discrete, with only relatively few different values (the integers 1 through 9). But Wagner et al. also counted the number of potentially important life events that the subject checked as having happened to him or her in the past 6 months. (This measure was part of preliminary work on developing an improved scale of stressful life events.) A student's total score could range from 0 to 210; the actual scores ranged from 39 to 121. Each individual score value generally was obtained by only a few subjects (if any), and it would not be very instructive for us to present a standard frequency distribution or histogram, as in the top half of Table 2.2, because it would be very flat and spread out. What is more useful is to group the data into adjacent 10-point intervals (30–39, 40–49, ..., 120–129) and to plot that distribution, as shown in the bottom of Table 2.2 and in Figure 2.2.

For the grouped data in Table 2.2, the intervals have been listed on the left. In this case, I have reported the upper and lower boundaries of the intervals as whole integers for the simple reason that it makes the table easier to read. You should realize, **Real lower limit, Real upper limit** however, that the true limits of the interval (known as the **real lower limit** and the **real upper limit**) are decimal values falling halfway between the top of one interval and the bottom of the next. Thus, for example, the 40–49 interval has real limits of 39.5 to 49.5, since any value falling above 39.5 or below 49.5 would be rounded up or down into that interval. (Students often become terribly worried about what we would do with a score of exactly 19.500000 that sat right on the breakpoint between two intervals. Don't worry about it. First, it is very unlikely to happen. Second, you can always flip a coin. Third, there are many more important things to worry about. This is one of those nonissues that makes people think that the study of statistics is confusing, or boring, or both.)

TABLE 2.2
Frequency distri-
bution of number of
stressful life events

Raw Data (Partial)		Raw Data (Partial)	
Number of Reported Events X	Frequency Y	Number of Reported Events X	Frequency Y
...		60	1
39	1	61	1
40	0	62	2
41	1	63	0
42	1	64	3
43	0	65	2
44	0	66	0
45	0	67	1
46	1	68	3
...		69	2
58	1	...	
59	1	121	1

Grouped Data

Interval (Events) X	Midpoint (Events)	Frequency Y	Cumulative Frequency
30– 39	34.5	1	1
40– 49	44.5	3	4
50– 59	54.5	3	7
60– 69	64.5	15	22
70– 79	74.5	14	36
80– 89	84.5	17	53
90– 99	94.5	10	63
100–109	104.5	5	68
110–119	114.5	5	73
120–129	124.5	1	74

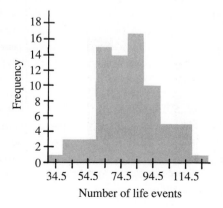

FIGURE 2.2
Histogram of
life-events data

Midpoints

In the second column of the lower half of Table 2.2 are the **midpoints** of the intervals. These are just the average of the upper and lower limits and are presented for convenience. When we plot the data, we will plot the points as if they all fell at the midpoint of their respective intervals.

In the third column are the frequencies with which scores fell in each interval. Thus, for example, three people reported between 40 and 49 stressful life events. The distribution presented in Table 2.2 is shown as a histogram in Figure 2.2.

Questions are often asked about the optimal *number* of intervals to use when grouping data. Although this question has no one right answer, somewhere around 10 intervals is usually reasonable. In the previous example, we used 10 intervals because the numbers naturally broke that way. In general, it is best to use natural breaks in the number system when practical (e.g., 0–9, 10–19, ..., or 100–119, 120–139, 140–159, ...) rather than to break up the range into exactly 10 arbitrarily defined intervals. If setting other kinds of limits makes the data easier to interpret, however, then that method should be used. It is more important to present data clearly than to follow a predefined set of rules.

Bar graph

At first glance, histograms resemble a similar graphic called a **bar graph**. The difference between the two is that a histogram has at least an ordinal variable on the X-axis, increasing from left to right. A bar graph has a categorical variable on the X-axis, and the values of that variable do not usually increase along any continuum. For example, you might plot per capita income on the Y-axis against region of the country (Northeast, Southwest, Midwest, etc.) on the X-axis. In a bar graph, the bars are often separated from one another by spaces, whereas in a histogram they are adjoining. The bar graph in Figure 2.3 illustrates the difference between histograms and bar graphs. This graph is from a paper by Zemsky (1989) in which he examined the breadth of study in a typical liberal arts education. He examined course enrollment at 30 institutions and classed those universities as providing substantial experience in a domain (i.e., humanities, social sciences, and math/science) if 80% of their students

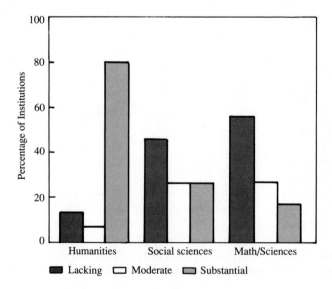

FIGURE 2.3
Bar graph showing experience by domain

took four or more courses in the domain, as providing moderate experience if 87.5% of the students took at least three courses in the domain, and as lacking experience if more than 12.5% of their students took fewer than three courses in the domain. The results are somewhat disturbing to those who believe in a liberal arts education, with substantial experience predominating only in the humanities, and a plurality of institutions being classed as lacking in both social sciences and math/sciences.

CUMULATIVE DISTRIBUTIONS

The distributions that we have discussed have been concerned with the frequency of observations at each score or within each interval. An alternative way of looking at data is in terms of a distribution that records the number of scores falling at *or below* each score or interval. For example, you can see from Table 2.2 that one student reported between 30 and 39 stressful events, and an additional three students reported between 40 and 49. Thus, 1 + 3 = 4 students reported 49 or fewer events. Similarly, 4 + 3 = 7 students reported 59 or fewer events. A distribution that plots **cumulative frequencies** is called a **cumulative distribution**; an example of such a distribution is shown in the right column in the bottom of Table 2.2 and is plotted in Figure 2.4.

Cumulative frequencies, Cumulative distribution

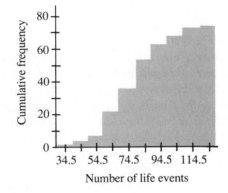

FIGURE 2.4
Cumulative distribution of life-events data

STEM-AND-LEAF DISPLAYS

Although both histograms and frequency distributions are commonly used methods of presenting data, each has drawbacks. Histograms usually portray grouped data, thus losing the actual numerical values of the individual scores within each interval. Frequency distributions, on the other hand, retain the value of the individual observations but often are difficult to use when they do not summarize the data sufficiently. An alternative approach that avoids both of these problems is known as a **stem-and-leaf display**. These are so easy to construct and so useful that I often use them as a quick tallying tool.

Stem-and-leaf display

Exploratory data analysis (EDA)

As part of his general approach to data analysis, known as **exploratory data analysis (EDA)**, Tukey (1977) developed a variety of methods for displaying data in visually meaningful ways. One of the simplest of these is a stem-and-leaf display. If you think

Leading digits,
Most significant
digits,
Stem
Trailing digits
Least significant
digits,
Leaves

of the previous example of number of stressful life events reported, you can imagine a bunch of scores in the 40s, another in the 50s, another in the 60s, and so on. We refer to the tens' digits, 4, 5, 6, . . . , as the **leading digits** (sometimes called the **most significant digits**) in these scores. These leading digits form the **stem**, or vertical axis, of the display. Within the set of 3 scores that were in the 40s, we had one 41, one 42, and one 46 (refer to Table 2.2). Here the units' digits, 1, 2, and 6, are called the **trailing digits** (or **least significant digits**), and they form the **leaves** of the display—the horizontal elements. Some of the raw data from the life-events example are presented in Figure 2.5 along with the entire stem-and-leaf display that results.[†]

Raw Data	Stem	Leaf
39	3	9
41 42 46	4	126
52 58 59	5	289
60 61 62 62 64	6	012244455788899
64 64 65 65 67	7	22335677888889
68 68 68 69 69	8	00111224555567789
. . .	9	0012245579
	10	00123
	11	23478
	12	1

FIGURE 2.5
Stem-and-leaf display
of life-events data

In the raw data column of Figure 2.5, you can see, for example, that there was one 60, one 61, two 62s, no 63s, three 64s, two 65s, no 66s, one 67, three 68s, and two 69s. Thus, opposite the stem 6, we find one 0, one 1, two 2s, and so on. By looking at the display, we can reconstruct the original data perfectly. This presentation thus has the virtue of giving us a full frequency distribution. At the same time, the stem-and-leaf display itself is also just a peculiarly drawn histogram turned on its side. A comparison of Figure 2.2 with Figure 2.5 makes the last point clear.

One apparent drawback of this simplest of stem-and-leaf displays is that for some data it might lead to a grouping that is too coarse for our purposes. If, for example, all the scores were between 30 and 59, we would be left with a stem having only three levels. Tukey solved this problem by using the stem 4* to represent the interval 40–44, and 4. to represent the interval 45–49. A similar system applies to the other intervals. Still other conventions handle different kinds of groupings. We will not go into them here, but you can refer to excellent discussions in Velleman and Hoaglin (1981), Tukey (1977), and Hoaglin, Mosteller, and Tukey (1983).

Stem-and-leaf displays can be particularly useful for comparing two different distributions. This is accomplished by plotting the two distributions on opposite sides of the stem. Figure 2.6 shows the actual distribution of numerical grades of males and females in a course on experimental methods that included a substantial statistics

---

[†] It is not always true that the tens' digit forms the stem and the units' digit forms the leaves. For example, if the data ranged from 100 to 1000, the hundreds' digit would form the stem, the tens' digit would form the leaves, and the units' digit would be ignored.

component. In this example I have used 6* to represent the stem for all values between 60 and 64, and 6. to represent the stem for all values between 65 and 69. The same is true for each decade. The code at the bottom of the table shows that 4* 1 represents 41, not 4.1 or 410.

Males		Females
	3*	
6	3.	
	4*	1
	4.	
	5*	
	5.	
2	6*	03
	6.	568
44444432200	7*	0144
88888755	7.	555556666788899
44322210000	8*	0000011112222233444
7666666555	8.	55666666666666677888888899
422	9*	000000000133
	9.	56
	Code 4* 1 = 41	

FIGURE 2.6
Grades (percentage) for an actual course in experimental methods, plotted separately by gender

ALTERNATIVE METHODS OF PLOTTING DATA

In the preceding sections, we dealt with only a few of the available ways of plotting data. Data can be plotted in an almost unlimited number of other ways, some of which are quite ingenious and informative. Other examples are shown in Figures 2.7, and 2.8, and Table 2.3. They were chosen as examples because they illustrate how displays can be used to reveal interesting features of the data, and to encourage creative approaches to presenting data.

Figure 2.7 shows a comparison of the causes of death among Vermont residents in 1900 and 1981. Notice that the various causes have been ordered from bottom to top in terms of decreasing order of magnitude. From this figure, it is immediately apparent that whereas almost a third of the deaths in 1900 were attributable to a high rate of infant mortality and to tuberculosis, neither of those sources contributed noticeably to death rates in 1981. On the other hand, cancer and heart disease, which together accounted for 60% of all deaths in 1981, played a much-reduced role in 1900, accounting for less than 15% of all deaths.

Figure 2.8 shows the distribution by age and gender of the populations of Mexico, Spain, the United States, and Sweden. This presentation clearly portrays differences between countries in terms of their age distributions (e.g., compare Mexico and Sweden). By plotting males and females back to back, we can also see the effects of gender differences in life expectancy: the older-age groups in all four countries contain more females than males.

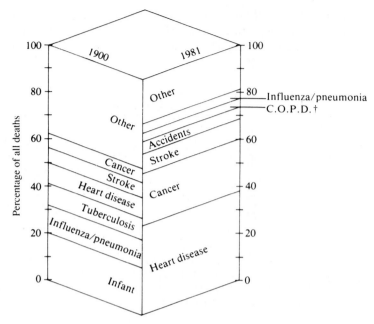

FIGURE 2.7
Major causes of death in Vermont, 1900 and 1981 (From 1981 Annual Report of Vital Statistics in Vermont. Vermont Department of Health, 1982.)

†Chronic obstructive pulmonary disease

Table 2.3 comes from a paper by Achenbach, McConaughy, and C. T. Howell (1987). In this study the authors were trying to assess the magnitude of the correlation between parents' and teachers' reports of behavior problems in children. At the same time, they wanted to indicate to the reader the source of each correlation. The histogram was created by using two-digit numbers to fill out the frequencies for each interval, with the numbers themselves referring to the numbered references at the end of the paper. This original and creative arrangement of data conveys a large amount of information in a small space.

The field of graphical presentation of data has received considerable attention recently, and several excellent books and papers on the subject have been published. The interest goes along with the current emphasis on exploring and understanding data before jumping in with your favorite statistical test. An excellent introduction to the problems of plotting data can be found in a very entertaining paper, "How to Display Data Badly," by Wainer (1984). Wainer not only presents some marvelously confusing, misleading, and silly graphics, but he does so in a way that teaches a great deal about how to do the job well. Tufte's (1983) fascinating book on meaningful ways of plotting data will certainly dispel the belief that graphical techniques are dependent on the use of computer graphics. Some wonderful graphs from the 18th and 19th centuries are at least the equal of anything done recently. Other important discussions of graphical techniques can be found in Chambers, Cleveland, Kleiner, and Tukey (1983), Cleveland and McGill (1984), and Wainer and Thissen (1981).

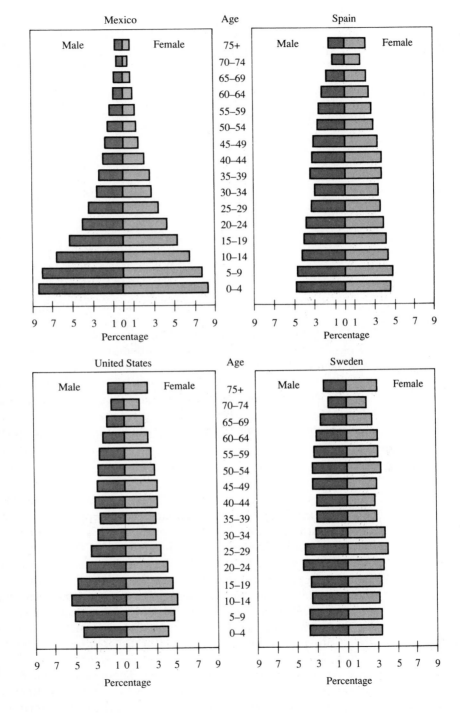

FIGURE 2.8
Population, by gender and age, for selected countries, 1970 (From Social Indicators, 1976. U.S. Department of Commerce. U.S. Government Printing Office, 1977.)

TABLE 2.3
Distribution of correlation coefficients from Achenbach, McConaughy, and C. T. Howell (1987)

						r				
−.10	.00	.10	.20	.30	.40	.50	.60	.70	.80
							1		
							2	12	
						5	11	13	
						21	16	13	
						24	30	19	
						29	38	26	5
						45	57	26	6
					21	45	82	30	13
					38	59	88	42	46
					60	67	90	43	78
					60	72	96	56	79
			16		69	79	104	57	82
			16		72	80	104	64	82
			59	16	73	85	112	72	104
	80		83	72	85	104	114	86	117

The use of graphical representation is increasing rapidly. Not only are many new books on the topic available, but many computer programs are beginning to emphasize the use of graphics. This is especially true of most of the new statistical programs being written for the Apple Macintosh, such as JMP and StatView. EXECUSTAT, for MS-DOS machines, is another package that blends graphics and statistical procedures. Many people are beginning to use graphics heavily to supplement, and even to replace, some of the more traditional "heavy-duty" statistical techniques.

DESCRIBING DISTRIBUTIONS

The scores that were illustrated in Figure 2.2 have a more or less regularly shaped distribution, rising to a maximum and then dropping away again rather smoothly. Not all distributions are like this, however, and it is important to understand the terms used to describe different distributions. Consider the two hypothetical distributions **Symmetric** shown in Figures 2.9a and 2.9b. Both of these distributions are called **symmetric** because they have the same shape on either side of the center. The distribution shown **Normal distribution** in Figure 2.9a is what we will later refer to as the **normal distribution**. The distribution **Bimodal** in Figure 2.9b is referred to as **bimodal**, because it has two peaks. The term *bimodal* is used to refer to any distribution that has two predominant peaks, whether or not these peaks are exactly the same height. (If a distribution has only one major peak, it is **Unimodal** called **unimodal**.)

Next consider Figures 2.9c and 2.9d. These two distributions are obviously not symmetric. The distribution in Figure 2.9c has a tail going to the left, whereas the one **Negatively skewed** in Figure 2.9d has a tail going to the right. We say that the former is **negatively skewed**, **Positively skewed** and the latter is **positively skewed**. (*Hint*: It may help to remember which is which if you notice that the long tail of a negatively skewed distribution points to the negative, or small, numbers, and the long tail of a positively skewed distribution points to the

Skewness   positive, or large, ones.) Although there are statistical measures of the degree of asymmetry or **skewness**, they are not commonly used in the social sciences.

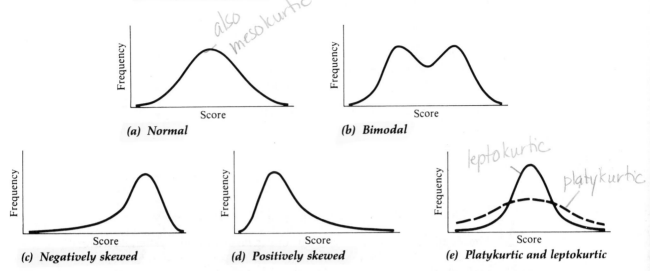

also
mesokurtic

leptokurtic

platykurtic

(a) Normal   *(b) Bimodal*

(c) Negatively skewed   *(d) Positively skewed*   *(e) Platykurtic and leptokurtic*

FIGURE 2.9 Shapes of frequency distributions: **(a)** normal, **(b)** bimodal, **(c)** negatively skewed, **(d)** positively skewed, **(e)** platykurtic (dashed curve) and leptokurtic (solid curve)

Kurtosis

Platykurtic
Leptokurtic
Mesokurtic

The last characteristic of a distribution that we will examine is kurtosis, which is illustrated in Figure 2.9e. **Kurtosis** has a specific mathematical definition, but basically it refers to the degree to which scores congregate in the tails of the distribution. A distribution that has a large number of high and low scores (relative to the mean) is referred to as a heavy-tailed or (**platykurtic**) distribution. A distribution that is relatively thin in the tails is called a **leptokurtic** distribution. Distributions whose tails are neither too thick nor too thin, such as the normal distribution, are called **mesokurtic**.

An interesting example of a positively skewed distribution is shown in Figure 2.10. These data were generated by Bradley (1963), who instructed subjects to press a button as quickly as possible whenever a small light came on. Notice that most of the data points are smoothly distributed between roughly 7 and 17 hundredths of a second, but that a small but noticeable cluster of points lies between 30 and 70 hundredths, trailing off to the right. This second cluster of points was obtained primarily from trials on which the subject missed the button on the first try. Their inclusion in the data significantly affects the distribution's shape. An experimenter who had such a collection of data might seriously consider eliminating times greater than some maximum (e.g., 25 hundredths of a second) on the grounds that these times are more a reflection of the accuracy of a psychomotor response than they are a measure of the speed of that response. It is speed that concerns us here.

We need relatively large samples of data before we can have a very good idea about the shape of a distribution—especially its kurtosis. With sample sizes of around 30, the best that we can reasonably expect to see is whether the data tend to pile up in the middle of the distribution and trail off in both extremes, or whether they are markedly skewed in one direction or another.

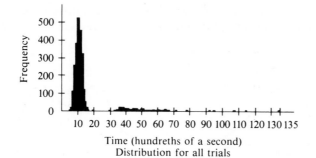

FIGURE 2.10
Frequency distribu-
tion of reaction-time
scores

USING COMPUTER PROGRAMS TO DISPLAY DATA

Almost all statistics texts—and this one is no exception—generally assume that data analyses will be carried out by hand with the help of a standard calculator. This is probably the best approach to teaching, but it is nonetheless true that more and more analyses are carried out today by computer programs. It is therefore important for you to be familiar with reading and interpreting the results of computer printouts. For that reason, most chapters in this book include samples of computer solutions for examples previously analyzed by hand. (If you have no interest in computer solutions, you can omit these examples without disrupting the flow or your understanding of the rest of the text.)

In the early chapters, many of these solutions will be obtained using Minitab, because it is one of the easiest general-purpose programs to use and is widely available. With the printout you will find the instructions required to produce those results. For those of you who want to explore the really powerful features of Minitab, Ryan, Joiner, and Ryan (1985) provide a good discussion. For more complex analyses later in the book, examples of printouts from the BMDP, SAS, and SPSS[X] statistical packages will be provided. Those of you who have these or other programs are encouraged to enter the examples and run the analyses. It is really not important which program you use, but it is extremely helpful to know that you can generate results similar to those given here.

Exhibit 2.1 shows a histogram and a stem-and-leaf display for the life-events data as produced by Minitab. Note that the raw data (number of events reported for each subject) are entered first, in any order, using the SET command. (The "MTB>" and "DATA>" are "prompts," supplied by Minitab, requesting input of either a command or data. Only the first few scores are shown to illustrate the use of the SET command, but the full set of observations could be reconstructed from the stem-and-leaf display.) Minitab chooses its own intervals for the histogram (in this case, 34.5–44.5, 44.5–54.5, ..., and 114.5–124.5) and lists each interval's midpoint (rounded). Since Minitab has chosen intervals that are different from ours, it produces a different (though still correct) histogram from the one shown in Figure 2.2.

EXHIBIT 2.1
EXHIBIT 2.1
Minitab program for
obtaining histogram
and stem-and-leaf
display for
life-events data

```
MTB  > SET THE FOLLOWING DATA IN COLUMN C1
DATA > 39 69 81 95 41 69 ...
DATA > END
MTB  > HISTOGRAM ON THE DATA IN COLUMN C1

Histogram of C1      N = 74

Midpoint   Count
      40       3   ***
      50       2   **
      60       9   *********
      70      12   ************
      80      18   ******************
      90      15   ***************
     100       9   *********
     110       3   ***
     120       3   ***

MTB  > STEM AND LEAF ON THE DATA IN COLUMN C1

Stem-and-leaf of C1        N = 74
Leaf Unit = 1.0

      1       3   9
      3       4   12
      4       4   6
      5       5   2
      7       5   89
     14       6   0122444
     22       6   55788899
     26       7   2233
     36       7   5677888889
    (8)       8   00111224
     30       8   555567789
     21       9   001224
     15       9   5579
     11      10   00123
      6      10
      6      11   234
      3      11   78
      1      12   1

MTB  > STOP
```

Depth

The stem-and-leaf display is equivalent to ours, although an additional column on the left contains cumulative frequencies (often referred to as **depth**) running inward from each end. The number in parentheses is the frequency (noncumulative) for the interval that contains the middle value. From this display we can see, for example, that 7 people had scores *less* than or equal to 59 events, 11 people had scores *greater* than or equal to 100 events, and 8 people fell in the interval containing the middle value.

So far in our discussion, we have seen how data may be organized and presented in the form of distributions, and we have discussed a number of ways in which distributions can be characterized—symmetry or lack thereof (skewness), kurtosis, and modality (e.g. unimodal vs. bimodal). As useful as this information might be in certain circumstances, it is inadequate in others. We still have only a vague idea whether the subjects generally liked or disliked attending class, and we do not even know the average number of stressful life events reported. Moreover, we do not know how much agreement there was among subjects, either in their opinions concerning attending class or in their numbers of reported life events. To obtain this knowledge, we must reduce the data to a set of measures that carry the information we need. The questions to be asked refer to the location, or central tendency, and to the dispersion, or variability, of the distribution along the underlying scale. Measures of these characteristics will be considered in Sections 2.3 and 2.4.

2.2   NOTATION

Any discussion of statistical techniques requires a notational system for expressing mathematical operations. It is thus surprising that no standard notational system has been adopted. Although several attempts to formulate a general policy have been made, the fact remains that no two textbooks use exactly the same notation.

The notational systems commonly used range from the very complex to the very simple. The more complex systems gain precision at the expense of easy intelligibility, whereas the simpler systems gain intelligibility at the expense of precision. Since the loss of precision is usually minor when compared with the gain in comprehension, in this book we will adopt an extremely simple system of notation.

NOTATION OF VARIABLES

The general rule is that a variable as a whole will be represented by an uppercase letter, often X or Y. An individual value of that variable will then be represented by the letter and a subscript. Suppose for example that we have the following five scores on the length of time (in seconds) that third-grade children can hold their breath:

$$45 \quad 42 \quad 35 \quad 23 \quad 52$$

This set of scores will be referred to as X. The first number of this set (45) can be referred to as X_1, the second (42) as X_2, and so on. When we wish to refer to a single score without specifying which one, we will refer to X_i, where i can take on any value between 1 and 5. In practice, the use of subscripts is often a distraction, and they are generally omitted if no confusion will result.

SUMMATION NOTATION

Sigma (Σ)

One of the most common symbols in statistics is the uppercase Greek letter **sigma** (Σ), which is the standard notation for summation. It is readily translated as "add up, or sum, what follows." Thus, ΣX_i, is read "sum the X_is." To be perfectly correct, the notation for summing all N values of X is

$$\sum_{i=1}^{N} X_i$$

which translates to "sum all of the X_is from $i = 1$ to $i = N$." In practice we seldom need to specify what is to be done this precisely, and in most cases all subscripts are dropped and the notation for the sum of the X_i is simply ΣX.

Several extensions of the simple case of ΣX must be noted and thoroughly understood. One of these is ΣX^2, which is read as "sum the squared values of X" (i.e., $45^2 + 42^2 + 35^2 + 23^2 + 52^2$). Another common expression, when data are available on two variables (X and Y), is ΣXY, which mean "sum the products of the corresponding values of X and Y." The use of these and other terms will be illustrated in the following example.

Imagine a simple experiment in which we record the anxiety scores (X) of five students and also record the number of days during the last semester that they missed a test because they were absent from school (Y). The data and simple summation operations on them are illustrated in Table 2.4. Some of these operations have been discussed already and others will be discussed in the next few chapters.

TABLE 2.4
Illustration of operations involving summation notation

	Anxiety Score	Tests Missed				
	(X)	(Y)	X^2	Y^2	$X - Y$	XY
	10	3	100	9	7	30
	15	4	225	16	11	60
	12	1	144	1	11	12
	9	1	81	1	8	9
	10	3	100	9	7	30
Sum	56	12	650	36	44	141

$$\Sigma X = (10 + 15 + 12 + 9 + 10) = 56$$

$$\Sigma Y = (3 + 4 + 1 + 1 + 3) = 12$$

$$\Sigma X^2 = (10^2 + 15^2 + 12^2 + 9^2 + 10^2) = 650$$

$$\Sigma Y^2 = (3^2 + 4^2 + 1^2 + 1^2 + 3^2) = 36$$

$$\Sigma(X - Y) = (7 + 11 + 11 + 8 + 7) = 44$$

$$\Sigma XY = (10)(3) + (15)(4) + (12)(1) + (9)(1) + (10)(3) = 141$$

$$(\Sigma X)^2 = 56^2 = 3136$$

$$(\Sigma Y)^2 = 12^2 = 144$$

$$(\Sigma(X - Y))^2 = 44^2 = 1936$$

$$(\Sigma X)(\Sigma Y) = (56)(12) = 672$$

Examining Table 2.4 reveals another set of operations involving parentheses, such as $(\Sigma X)^2$. *The general rule, which always applies, is to perform operations within parentheses before performing operations outside parentheses.* Thus, for $(\Sigma X)^2$, we sum the values of X and *then* we square the result, as opposed to ΣX^2, for which we square the Xs before we sum. You should verify for yourself that ΣX^2 is not equal to (written $\neq$) $(\Sigma X)^2$ using simple numbers such as 2, 3, and 4.

DOUBLE SUBSCRIPTS

A common notational device is to use two or more subscripts to specify exactly which value of X you have in mind. Suppose for example that we were given the data shown in Table 2.5. If we want to specify the entry in the ith row and jth column, we will denote this as X_{ij}. Thus, the score on the third trial of Day 2 is $X_{2,3} = 13$. Some notational systems use

$$\sum_{i=1}^{2} \sum_{j=1}^{5} X_{ij}$$

which translates as "sum the X_{ij}s where i takes on values 1 and 2 and j takes on all values from 1 to 5." You should be aware of this system of notation, since some other textbooks use it. In this book, however, the simpler, but less precise, ΣX is used where possible, with ΣX_{ij} used only when absolutely necessary, and $\Sigma\Sigma X_{ij}$ never appearing.

TABLE 2.5
Sample data

		Trial					
		1	2	3	4	5	Total
Day	1	8	7	6	9	12	42
	2	10	11	13	15	14	63
	Total	18	18	19	24	26	105

You must thoroughly understand notation if you are to learn even the most elementary statistical techniques. You should study Table 2.4 until you fully understand all the procedures involved.

RULES OF SUMMATION

Three additional rules for using the summation sign (Σ) will be extremely helpful in following the text discussion. The demonstration of these rules is left to you, since their application can be illustrated with simple examples.

1. $\Sigma(X - Y) = \Sigma X - \Sigma Y$
2. $\Sigma(X + C) = \Sigma X + nC$ (where n is the number of elements that you sum and C represents any constant.[†]
3. $\Sigma CX = C\Sigma X$

(The notation ΣCX means "multiply every value of X by the constant C and then sum the results.")

2.3   MEASURES OF CENTRAL TENDENCY

Measures of central tendency,
Measures of location

The phrase **measures of central tendency**, or sometimes **measures of location**, refers to the set of measures that deals with where on the scale the distribution is centered. The three major measures of central tendency are the mode, median, and mean.

[†]A constant is any number that does not change its value within a given situation (as opposed to a variable, which does). Constants are most often represented by the letters C and k, but other symbols may be used as well.

THE MODE

Mode (Mo)

The **mode (Mo)** is simply the most common score—the score obtained from the largest number of subjects. Thus, the mode is the value of X that corresponds to the highest point on the distribution. In the example used in Figure 2.1, this value is 7, since more people rated attending class as 7, "somewhat desirable," than rated it any other value.

If two *adjacent* ratings occur with equal (and greatest) frequency, a common convention is to take an average of the two values and call that the mode. If two *nonadjacent* ratings occur with nearly equal (and greatest) frequency, we say that the distribution is bimodal and most likely report both modes.

THE MEDIAN

Median (Mdn)

The **median (Mdn)** is the point that corresponds to the score that lies in the middle of the distribution when the data are arranged in increasing or decreasing numerical order—in other words, it is the point that divides the distribution in half. For example, for the numbers

$$3 \quad 5 \quad 7 \quad 8 \quad 15$$

the middle of the distribution is at 7, and 7 would be called the median. Suppose, however, that there were an even number of scores—for example,

$$3 \quad 5 \quad 7 \quad 8 \quad 14 \quad 15$$

Here the middle of the distribution is halfway between 7 and 8. In this case, the average (7.5) of the two middle scores (7 and 8) is commonly taken as the median.[†]

Median location

A term that we shall need shortly is the **median location**. The median location of N numbers is defined as

$$\text{Median location} = \frac{N + 1}{2}$$

Thus, for five numbers the median location $= (5 + 1)/2 = 3$, which means that the median is located at the third position in an ordered series. For 12 numbers, the median location $= (12 + 1)/2 = 6.5$, and thus the median is the average of the sixth and the seventh numbers.

For the stressful-life-events data (see Table 2.2) the median location $= (74 + 1)/2 = 37.5$. A little work will show that, if the data were arranged in increasing or decreasing order, the 37 and 38 scores would both be 80, which is thus the median. For the data on class attendance (Table 2.1), there are 71 (nonmissing) scores and the median location is 36. We can tell from the histogram in Figure 2.1 that the 36 score is a 6, and thus 6 is the median of this distribution.

[†]The definition of the median is something over which statisticians love to argue. The definition given here, in which the median is defined as a *point* on a distribution of numbers, is the one that most critics prefer. It is also in line with the common observation that the median is the 50th percentile. On the other hand, many people are perfectly happy to say that the median is either the middle *number* in an ordered series (if N is odd), or the average of the middle two numbers (if N is even). I think that there are more interesting things to fight about than the precise definition of the median.

THE MEAN

Mean

The most common measure of central tendency, and one that needs little explanation, is the **mean**, or what is generally meant by the word *average*. The mean is the total of the scores divided by the number of scores, and the *sample* mean is usually designated as $\overline{X}$ (read "X bar"):

$$\overline{X} = \frac{\Sigma X}{N}$$

[The mean of a population is calculated in the same way but is denoted by μ (the lower case Greek letter mu).] As an illustration, the mean of the numbers 3, 5, 12, 5 is

$$\frac{3 + 5 + 12 + 5}{4} = \frac{25}{4} = 6.25$$

RELATIVE ADVANTAGES AND DISADVANTAGES OF THE MODE, MEDIAN, AND MEAN

Only when the distribution is symmetric will the mean and median be equal, and only when the distribution is symmetric and unimodal will all three measures be the same. In all other cases—including almost all situations dealing with samples rather than with populations—we must choose which measure of central tendency to use. A set of rules governing when to use a particular measure of central tendency would be convenient, but no such clearly defined rules exist. If we are to choose intelligently among the three measures, we need some idea of the strengths and weaknesses of each measure.

THE MODE   As we said, the mode is the most commonly occurring score. By definition, then, it is a score that actually occurred. By contrast, the mean and sometimes the median—because they are not, strictly speaking, scores, but rather points on a distribution—may be values that never appear in the data. The mode also has the obvious advantage of representing the largest number of people.

A disadvantage of the mode is clearly illustrated if we were to ask students to report the number of cigarettes they smoke in a week. The modal value would probably be 0, because most students do not smoke at all, but that value is not a good measure of the smoking behavior that actually does occur.

THE MEDIAN   The major advantage of the median, an advantage it shares with the mode, is that within a fixed number of scores it is unaffected by extreme scores at one or the other end of the distribution. Thus, the medians of both

5   8   9   15   16

and

0   8   9   15   206

are 9. Many experimenters find this characteristic extremely useful in studies in which aberrant scores occur occasionally but have no particular significance. For example, the average trained rat can run down a short runway in approximately 1 to 2 seconds. Every once in a while, this same rat will inexplicably stop halfway down, scratch himself, poke his nose at the photocells, and lie down and go to sleep. In this instance, it is of no practical significance whether he takes 30 seconds or 10 minutes to get to the other end—it may even depend on when the experimenter gives up and pokes him with a pencil. If we ran a rat through three trials per day, and his times were 1.2, 1.3, and 20.0 seconds, these values would have the same meaning to us as would times of 1.2, 1.3, and 136.5 seconds. Obviously, however, the rat's daily mean would be different in the two cases. It is this problem that frequently induces experimenters to work with the median, rather than the mean, time per day.

In contrast to the mean, the median has another point in its favor which those writers who get excited over measurement scales are likely to point out. Calculating the median does not require even the vaguest assumptions about the interval properties of the scale. With the numbers

$$5 \quad 8 \quad 11$$

the object represented by the number 8 is in the middle, no matter how close or distant it is from the objects represented by 5 and 11. When we say that the *mean* is 8, however, we may imply to the reader, if not to ourselves, that the underlying distance between objects 5 and 8 is the same as the underlying distance between objects 8 and 11. Whether or not this assumption is reasonable is up to the experimenter. I suggested in Chapter 1 that the *calculation* of a statistic does not depend on the underlying scale, although the *interpretation* often does. From this point of view, the median may be an attractive statistic.

THE MEAN   Of the three principal measures of central tendency, the mean is by far the most common. It would not be an exaggeration to say that, for many people, "statistics" is (unfortunately) nearly synonymous with "the study of the mean."

As already noted, certain disadvantages are associated with the mean. It is influenced by extreme scores, its value may not actually exist in the data, and its interpretation in terms of the underlying variable being measured requires at least some faith in the interval properties of the data. You might be inclined to politely suggest that if the mean has all of the disadvantages I have just attributed to it, then maybe it should be quietly forgotten and allowed to slip into oblivion along with statistics like the "critical ratio"—a statistical concept that hasn't been heard from in years. The mean, however, is made of sterner stuff.

The mean has several important advantages that far outweigh its disadvantages. Probably the most important of these, from a historical point of view, is that it can easily be manipulated algebraically. Whatever its faults, in large part this accounts for its widespread application. The mean has other important advantages (unbiasedness and efficiency) that we will discuss later in the chapter, after we have examined the principle of estimation.

One characteristic that statisticians often use in determining the "goodness" of a measure of central tendency is the degree to which it is close, in some sense, to the individual observations that it is supposed to represent. If we were to define a statistic to be a good estimate of central tendency if the sum of the deviations of the individual data points from that statistic is a minimum (is as small as possible), then our best measure of central tendency is the median. In other words, the sum of the absolute deviations (i.e., ignoring plus and minus signs) from the median is less than the sum of the absolute deviations from any other point. That might seem to be a perfectly logical definition of a good estimate of central tendency. At least it is a commonsensical one. However, a second definition that is even more appealing to statisticians is one expressed in terms of *squared* deviations rather than absolute deviations. If we look for the statistic for which the sum of the squared deviations is a minimum, that statistic is the mean. This is not the place to go into why statisticians prefer to worry about the sum of squared rather than absolute deviations—the arguments are beyond the scope of this book. You should know, however, that the fact that the sum of the squared deviations around the mean is less than the sum of the squared deviations around any other point is fundamental to the explanation of why the mean plays a more important role than the median in statistical procedures. It is a "good fit" to the data.

OBTAINING MEASURES OF CENTRAL TENDENCY USING MINITAB

For small sets of data, it is reasonable to compute measures of central tendency by hand. With larger sample sizes or with data sets that have many variables, however, it is much simpler to let a computer program do the work. (It is also more fun.) Minitab is ideally suited to this purpose; as mentioned, it is easy to use, versatile, and widely available.

Suppose that, as part of a large study on teaching effectiveness, we asked each of 15 students in a class to record the number of different annoying mannerisms exhibited by the instructor (e.g., dropping chalk, losing chalk, being excessively neat in arranging lecture notes, pacing, alternating standing and sitting, and all of those other activities

EXHIBIT 2.2

Minitab program for obtaining measures of central tendency on annoying mannerisms

```
MTB  > SET THE FOLLOWING DATA IN COLUMN C1
DATA > 12 18 19 15 18 14 17 20 18 15 17 11 23 19 10
DATA > END
MTB  > MEAN OF THE DATA IN COLUMN C1
     MEAN    =        16.400
MTB  > MEDIAN OF THE DATA IN COLUMN C1
     MEDIAN  =        17.000
MTB  > HISTOGRAM OF THE DATA IN COLUMN C1

Histogram of C1     N = 15

Midpoint   Count
      10      1   *
      11      1   *
      12      1   *
      13      0
      14      1   *
      15      2   **
      16      0
      17      2   **
      18      3   ***
      19      2   **
      20      1   *
      21      0
      22      0
      23      1   *

MTB  > SAVE 'MANNER.MIN'

Worksheet saved into file: MANNER.MIN
MTB  > STOP
```

whose counting helps get you to the end of the lecture). These data are illustrated in Exhibit 2.2, with those commands that are required to produce the three common measures of central tendency. Note that we can obtain the mean and median directly, but to get the mode we need to produce a histogram (or stem-and-leaf display) and then look for the most frequently appearing interval.

From Exhibit 2.2 we can see that the mean (16.4), median (17), and mode (18) are all about the same, and that the distribution is fairly smooth, though flat, but is slightly negatively skewed. We can also see from the histogram that there is considerable disagreement among the students concerning the number of annoying mannerisms exhibited by the instructor. This dispersion on either side of the mean will be discussed next. The SAVE command is used to save these data in a Minitab system file so that they do not need to be reentered for future analyses. The exact convention for naming the file (MANNER. MIN) will vary from one computer installation to another.

2.4   MEASURES OF VARIABILITY

In Section 2.3 we considered several measures relating to the center of a distribution. However, an average value for a distribution (whether it be the mode, median, or mean) does not tell the whole story. We need some additional measure (or measures) to indicate the degree to which individual observations are clustered about—or deviate from—that average value. Two distributions may have the same mean but different degrees of dispersion of scores around those means. In one distribution, the average may reflect the general location of most of the scores. In the other distribution, the scores may be distributed over a wide range of values, and the "average" may be some sort of bad compromise. Probably everyone has had experience with examinations on which all students received approximately the same grade and with examinations on which the scores ranged from excellent to dreadful. Measures referring to the differences between these two types of situations are what we have in mind

Variability, Dispersion

when we speak of **variability** or **dispersion** around the median, mode, or any other point. In general, we will be referring specifically to variability around the mean.

As an example of a situation in which differences in variability from one group to another might be expected, consider the case in which two sections of a computer science class are given the same exam. One section is told that the exam will account for 20% of their final grade, whereas the other section is told that it will account for 90%. It is reasonable to expect that the two sections will have roughly the same mean. "Pressure" has a facilitory effect on the performance of some people and a disruptive effect on the performance of others, however, so we might expect more variability among students in the section for whom the exam accounts for 90% of the final grade.

As a second illustration, consider the following two sets of data. Twenty rats from each of two strains have been deposited individually on the bottom of a circular box. The floor has been laid off in a grid, and the number of squares into which each rat stepped in a 30-second interval has been counted. This is a commonly used index of exploratory behavior; it is called the "open field test." We are interested in whether animals in Strain X differ more from each other (are more variable) in the exploratory behavior they exhibit than do animals in Strain Y. This is not as foolish a study as you might at first suspect. Strains of rats that show highly consistent behavior (are less variable) are, for some purposes, particularly suitable experimental animals, because using them ensures there will be less random variability in the data. The mean level of exploratory behavior is of no interest to us, and in fact the two strains have the same means:

Strain X: 5 4 4 6 6 4 6 4 5 6 4 4 6 5 5 6 6 4 6 4
Strain Y: 5 1 8 7 4 8 8 1 5 1 5 5 7 7 7 1 5 7 5 3

We could plot the distributions of these scores to illustrate the differences between the strains. The two distributions are shown in Figure 2.11 as back-to-back histograms, where the x-axis is frequency and the y-axis in the activity score (Back-to-back histograms and similar graphical displays, as illustrated in Figures 2.8 and 2.11, are particularly useful for quickly comparing two distributions. They deserve to be used much more often than they currently are.)

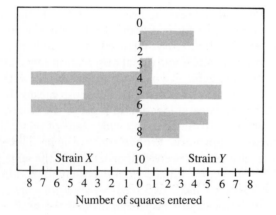

FIGURE 2.11
Distribution of scores for rat strains X and Y in terms of the number of grid squares entered

Although it is apparent that rats of Strain Y differ from each other more than do those of Strain X, some sort of measure is needed to reflect this difference in variability. A number of measures could be used, and we will consider them in turn, starting with the simplest.

RANGE

Range

The **range** is a measure of distance—namely, the distance from the lowest to the highest score. For our data, the range for Strain X is $(6 - 4) = 2$, and for Strain Y is $(8 - 1) = 7$. The range is an exceedingly common measure and is illustrated in everyday life by such statements as, "The price of hamburger fluctuates over an 80¢ range from \$1.89 to \$2.69 per pound." The range suffers, however, because it ignores almost all the distribution and is calculated from the extreme values, or, if the values are *unusually* extreme, on what are commonly called *outliers*. The range also has the undesirable property of being dependent on the sample size because the more values that you have, the farther apart the largest and smallest of those values are likely to be. The importance of this last fact will become apparent when we consider certain multiple comparison procedures in Chapter 12.

INTERQUARTILE RANGE AND OTHER RANGE STATISTICS

Interquartile range

The **interquartile range**, which is closely related to the H-spread (to be discussed shortly), represents an attempt to circumvent the problem of the range being heavily dependent on extreme scores. An interquartile range is obtained by discarding the upper and lower 25% of the distribution and taking the range of what remains. As such, it is the range of the middle 50% of the observations. We can calculate the interquartile range for the exploratory behavior of our rats by omitting the lowest five scores and the highest five scores and determining the range of the remainder. In this case, the range for Strain X would still be $6 - 4 = 2$. For Strain Y, however, the range would now be $7 - 4 = 3$.

The interquartile range plays an important role in a useful graphical method known as a boxplot. This method will be discussed later in this chapter.

In many ways, the interquartile range suffers from problems that are just the opposite of those encountered with the range. Specifically, it discards too much of the data set. If we want to know if one strain is more variable than another, it does not make much sense to toss out those scores that are most extreme and thus vary the most from the mean.

There is nothing sacred about the idea of eliminating the upper and lower 25% of the distribution before calculating the range. In fact, we can eliminate any percentage we wish as long as we can justify to ourselves and to others what we are doing. What we really want is to eliminate those scores that we think are likely to be accidents, without eliminating the variability that we seek to study. Samples that have had a certain percentage (e.g., 10%) of the values in each tail removed are called **trimmed samples** and statistics calculated on such samples are called **trimmed statistics** (e.g., *trimmed means* or *trimmed ranges*).

Trimmed samples
Trimmed statistics

THE AVERAGE DEVIATION

At first glance, it would seem that if we want to measure how scores are dispersed around the mean (i.e., deviate from the mean), then the most logical thing to do would be to obtain all the deviations (i.e., $X_i - \overline{X}$) and average them. We might expect that the more widely the scores are dispersed, the greater the deviations, and therefore the greater the average of the deviations. Consider the exploratory-behavior data for Strain X and Strain Y from the previous example. These data, with the deviation of each score from the mean, are shown in Table 2.6. Observe that if you calculate the average of these deviations,

$$\frac{\Sigma(X - \overline{X})}{N} \quad \text{or} \quad \frac{\Sigma(Y - \overline{Y})}{N}$$

the sum is zero. The deviations below the mean are balanced by those above the mean. The sum of the deviations around the mean *always* will be zero, making the average zero. As a result, this measure is not a satisfactory measure of dispersion.

TABLE 2.6
Exploratory-behavior data for strains X and Y

	Strain X		Strain Y	
	X	$X - \overline{X}$	Y	$Y - \overline{Y}$
	5	0	5	0
	4	−1	1	−4
	4	−1	8	3
	6	1	7	2
	6	1	4	−1
	4	−1	8	3
	6	1	8	3
	4	−1	1	−4
	5	0	5	0
	6	1	1	−4
	4	−1	5	0
	4	−1	5	0
	6	1	7	2
	5	0	7	2
	5	0	7	2
	6	1	1	−4
	6	1	5	0
	4	−1	7	2
	6	1	5	0
	4	−1	3	−2
Mean raw score	5		5	
Total deviations		0		0
Average deviation		0		0

THE MEAN ABSOLUTE DEVIATION

If you think about the difficulty we encountered when we tried to get some useful information out of the average deviations, you might well be led to suggest that we could solve the whole problem by taking the absolute values of the deviations—that is, by dropping the signs. This proposal makes sense because we want to know *how much* scores deviate from the mean, and at the moment we are not particularly concerned with whether they are above or below it. The measure thus obtained is a perfectly legitimate one and even has a name—the **mean absolute deviation (m.a.d.)**:

Mean absolute deviation (m.a.d.)

$$\text{m.a.d.} = \frac{\Sigma |X - \overline{X}|}{N}$$

— add up all of the $X - \overline{X}$ but ignore the signs

The vertical lines in the equation indicate that we are taking the absolute deviations. The sum of the absolute deviations is divided by N (the number of scores) to yield an average (mean) deviation.

For the data from the two strains of rats, we can easily calculate the mean absolute deviations by ignoring the sign of the differences shown in Table 2.6. For Strain X, m.a.d. is $16/20 = 0.80$; for Strain Y, it is $38/20 = 1.9$. Thus, the m.a.d. reflects the differences in dispersion, being larger with greater dispersion.

For all its simplicitly and intuitive appeal, the mean absolute deviation has not played an important role in statistics. Instead, much more useful measures, the variance and the standard deviation, are normally used.

The Variance

Sample variance (s^2)

Population variance (σ^2)

The measure considered in this section, the **sample variance (s^2)**, represents a different approach to the problem that the deviations themselves average to zero. [When referring to the **population variance**, we use σ^2 (lowercase Greek sigma squared).] In this case we take advantage of the fact that the square of a negative number is positive and sum the *squared* deviations rather than the deviations themselves. Since we want an average, we next divide this sum by a function of N, the number of scores. As a matter of fact, we divide it not by N itself, but by $(N - 1)$. We use $N - 1$ as a divisor *for the sample variance* because, as we shall see shortly, it leaves us with a sample variance that is a better estimate of the population variance. (The population variance would be calculated by dividing the sum of the squared deviations by N rather than $N - 1$. However, we rarely calculate a population variance; we almost always estimate it from the sample variance.) The sample variance is denoted s^2, or, to be more specific s_X^2, where the subscript (X in this case) indicates the variable whose variance we seek.

For our example,

Strain X:

$$
\begin{aligned}
s_X^2 &= \frac{\Sigma(X - \overline{X})^2}{N - 1} \\
&= \frac{(5 - 5)^2 + (4 - 5)^2 + \cdots + (4 - 5)^2}{20 - 1} \\
&= \frac{16}{20 - 1} \\
&= 0.84
\end{aligned}
$$

Strain Y:

$$
\begin{aligned}
s_Y^2 &= \frac{\Sigma(Y - \overline{Y})^2}{N - 1} \\
&= \frac{(5 - 5)^2 + (1 - 5)^2 + \cdots + (3 - 5)^2}{20 - 1} \\
&= \frac{1\text{'}6}{20 - 1} \\
&= 6.11
\end{aligned}
$$

From this example we see that the variances reflect the difference in dispersion. Strain Y, which is much more dispersed than Strain X, has a variance of 6.11, whereas Strain X has a variance of only 0.84.

Although the variance is an exceptionally important concept and is one of the most commonly used statistics, it does not have the direct intuitive interpretation we would like. Because it is based on *squared* deviations, the result is given in terms of squared units. Thus, Strain Y has a mean of 5 units and a variance of 6.11 squared units. Squared units are awkward things to talk about. Fortunately, the solution to this problem is simple—we take the square root of the variance.

Standard deviation

Standard deviation (s)

The **standard deviation (s)** is the positive square root of the variance. The s (or, occasionally, S.D.) is written with a subscript identifying the variable if necessary.

$$s_X = \sqrt{\frac{\Sigma(X - \overline{X})^2}{N - 1}} = \sqrt{s_X^2}$$

For our example,

$$s_X = \sqrt{s_X^2}$$
$$= \sqrt{0.84}$$
$$= 0.92$$
$$s_Y = \sqrt{s_Y^2}$$
$$= \sqrt{6.11}$$
$$= 2.47$$

[again, if we are calculating the standard deviation for a whole population,

$$\sigma = \sqrt{\sigma^2}$$
$$= \sqrt{\frac{\Sigma(X - \mu)^2}{N}}$$

Notice that because we are dealing with a population we use the population mean (μ).]

Look at the formula for the sample standard deviation. You can see that the standard deviation, like the mean absolute deviation, is basically a measure of the average of the deviations of each score from the mean. Granted, these deviations have been squared, summed, and so on; but at heart they are still deviations. Furthermore, even though we have divided by $N - 1$ instead of N, we have still obtained something very much like a mean, or average, of these deviations. Thus, we can say without too much distortion that subjects in Strain X deviate, on the average, 0.92 units from the mean, whereas subjects in Strain Y deviate, on the average, 2.47 units from the mean. This rather loose way of thinking about the standard deviation as a sort of average deviation goes a long way toward giving it meaning without doing serious injustice to the concept. (The standard deviation will be about 20% larger than the mean absolute deviation for reasonable sample sizes.)

A different way of assigning meaning to the standard deviation is to think in terms of how many scores fall within one standard deviation of the mean. For a variety of distributions, we can say that approximately two-thirds of the observations lie within one standard deviation of the mean (for a normal distribution, to be discussed in Chapter 4, it is almost exactly two-thirds). Although this rule has exceptions (especially for badly skewed distributions), it is still handy. If someone told you that for traditional jobs the mean starting annual salary for college graduates this year is expected to be $21,000 with a standard deviation of $2000, you would probably not be far off if you concluded that about two-thirds of the graduates who take these jobs will earn between $19,000 and $23,000 this year.

A third characteristic of the standard deviation is that for many distributions it is usually about one-fifth or one-sixth of the range. Although this is not a particularly useful way of interpreting the standard deviation, it is a handy way of checking your work. If a glance at the data shows that the range is about 20, and you have just calculated $s_X = 15$, this strongly suggests that you check your work. Your calculation may be right, but it is probably not. On the other hand, if you find that $s_X = 3.8$, you have at least a reasonable answer.

COMPUTATIONAL FORMULAS FOR THE VARIANCE AND STANDARD DEVIATION

Although correct, the previous expressions for the variance and standard deviation are incredibly unwieldy given any reasonable set of data. They are also prone to rounding error, because they usually involve squaring fractional deviations. They are excellent definitional formulas, but we will now consider a more practical set of calculational formulas. While fewer and fewer people actually calculate variances by hand (as opposed to pressing the s^2 button on their calculator), the computational formula is not only useful in its own right, but it will reappear in later chapters in what you might think of as unrelated settings.

The definitional formula was

$$s_X^2 = \frac{\Sigma(X - \overline{X})^2}{N - 1}$$

A more practical, and algebraically equivalent, computational formula is

$$s_X^2 = \frac{\Sigma X^2 - \dfrac{(\Sigma X)^2}{N}}{N - 1}$$

Similarly, for the sample standard deviation,

$$s_X = \sqrt{\frac{\Sigma X^2 - \dfrac{(\Sigma X)^2}{N}}{N - 1}}$$

Applying the computational formula for the variance of our example, we obtain

$$s_X^2 = \frac{\Sigma X^2 - \dfrac{(\Sigma X)^2}{N}}{N - 1}$$

$$= \frac{(5^2 + 4^2 + \cdots + 6^2 + 4^2) - \dfrac{100^2}{20}}{19}$$

$$= \frac{516 - \dfrac{100^2}{20}}{19} = \frac{516 - 500}{19} = \frac{16}{19}$$

$$= 0.84$$

and

$$s_Y^2 = \frac{\Sigma Y^2 - \dfrac{(\Sigma Y)^2}{N}}{N - 1}$$

$$= \frac{(5^2 + 1^2 + \cdots + 5^2 + 3^2) - \dfrac{100^2}{20}}{19}$$

$$= \frac{616 - \dfrac{100^2}{20}}{19} = \frac{616 - 500}{19} = \frac{116}{19}$$

$$= 6.11$$

Notice that these answers are the same as those we obtained earlier.

THE INFLUENCE OF EXTREME VALUES ON THE VARIANCE AND STANDARD DEVIATION

The variance and standard deviation are very sensitive to extreme scores. To put this differently, extreme scores play a disproportionate role in determining the variance. Consider a set of data that range from roughly 0 to 10, with a mean of 5. From the definitional formula for the variance, you will see that a score of 5 (the mean) contributes nothing to the variance, because the deviation score is 0. A score of 6 contributes $1/(N - 1)$ to s^2, since $(X - \overline{X})^2 = (6 - 5)^2 = 1$. A score of 10, however, contributes $25/(N - 1)$ units to s^2, since $(10 - 5)^2 = 25$. Thus, although 6 and 10 deviate from the mean by 1 and 5 units, respectively, their relative contributions to the variance are 1 and 25. This is what we mean when we say that large deviations are disproportionately represented. You might keep this in mind the next time you use a measuring instrument that is "OK because it is unreliable only at the extremes." It is just those extremes that may have the greatest effect on the interpretation of the data.

THE COEFFICIENT OF VARIATION

One of the most common things we do in statistics is to compare the means of two or more groups, or even two or more variables. Comparing the variability of those groups or variables, however, is also a legitimate and worthwhile activity. Suppose, for example, that we have two competing tests for assessing long-term memory. One of the tests typically produces data with a mean of 15 and a standard deviation of 3.5. The second, quite different, test produces data with a mean of 75 and a standard deviation of 10.5. All other things being equal, which test is better for assessing long-term memory? We might be inclined to argue that the second test is better, in that we want a measure on which there is enough variability that we are able to study differences among people. However, keep in mind that the two tests also differ substantially in their means, and this difference must be taken into account.

If you think for a moment about the fact that the standard deviation is based on deviations from the mean, it seems logical that one could more easily deviate substantially from a large mean than from a small one. For example, if you rate teaching effectiveness on a 7-point scale with a mean of 3, it would be impossible to have a deviation greater than 4. On the other hand, on a 70-point scale with a mean of 30, deviations of 10 or 20 would be common. Somehow we need to take into account the greater opportunity for large deviations in the second case when we compare the variability of our two measures. In other words, when we look at the standard deviation, we must keep in mind the magnitude of the mean as well.

The simplest way to compare standard deviations on measures that have quite different means is simply to scale the standard deviation by the magnitude of the mean. This is what we do with the **coefficient of variation (CV)**.[†] We will define that coefficient as simply the standard deviation divided by the mean.

Coefficient of variation (CV)

$$CV = \frac{\text{Standard deviation}}{\text{Mean}} = \frac{s_X}{\overline{X}}$$

To return to our memory-task example, for the first measure, CV = 3.5/15 = 0.233. For the second measure, CV = 10.5/75 = 0.14. In this case the coefficient of variation for the first measure is about two-thirds larger than for the second. If I could be convinced that the larger coefficient of variation in the first measure was not attributable simply to sloppy measurement, I would be inclined to choose the first measure over the second.

To take a second example, Katz, Lautenschlager, Blackburn, and Harris (1990) asked students to answer a set of multiple-choice questions from the Scholastic Aptitude Test (SAT). One group read the relevant passage and answered the questions.

[†] I want to thank Andrew Gilpin (personal communication, 1990) for reminding me of the usefulness of the coefficient of variation. It is a meaningful statistic that is often overlooked.

Another group answered the questions without having read the passage on which they were based—sort of like taking a multiple-choice test on Mongolian history without having taken the course. The data follow:

	Passage	No Passage
Mean	69.6	46.6
S.D.	10.6	6.8
CV	0.152	0.146

The ratio of the two standard deviations is $10.6/6.8 = 1.56$, meaning that the Passage group had a standard deviation that was over 50% larger than the No Passage group. On the other hand, the coefficients of variation are virtually the same for the two groups, suggesting that any difference in variability between the groups can be explained by the higher scores in the first group. (Incidentally, chance performance would have produced a mean of 20 with a standard deviation of 4. Even without reading the passage, students score well above chance levels just by intelligent guessing.)

In using the coefficient of variation, it is important to keep in mind the nature of the variable that you are measuring. If its scale is arbitrary, you might not want to put too much faith in the coefficient. But perhaps you don't want to put too much faith in the variance either. This is a place where a little common sense is particularly useful.

THE MEAN AND VARIANCE AS ESTIMATORS

I pointed out in Chapter 1 that we generally calculate measures such as the mean and variance to use as *estimates* of the corresponding values in the populations. Characteristics of samples are called statistics and are designated by Roman letters (e.g., $\overline{X}$). Characteristics of populations are called parameters and are designated by Greek letters. Thus, the population mean is symbolized by μ (mu). In general, then, we use statistics as estimates of parameters.

If the purpose of obtaining a statistic is to use it as an estimator of a parameter, then it should come as no surprise that our choice of a statistic (and even how we define it) is based partly on how well that statistic functions as an estimator of the parameter in question. In fact, the mean is usually preferred over other measures of central tendency because of its performance as an estimator of μ. The variance (s^2) is defined as it is specifically because of the advantages that accrue when s^2 is used to estimate the population variance (σ^2).

Several properties of estimators are of particular interest to statisticians and heavily influence the choice of the statistics we compute. These properties are those of sufficiency, unbiasedness, efficiency, and resistance. They are discussed here simply to give you a feel for why some measures of central tendency and variability are regarded as more important than others. It is not critical that you have a thorough understanding of estimation and related concepts, but you should have a general appreciation of the issues involved.

Sufficient statistic

SUFFICIENCY   A **sufficient statistic** contains (makes use of) all of the information in a sample that is relevant to the parameter being estimated. The mean is a sufficient statistic because we average all the observations. The mode, however, uses only the most common observations, ignoring all others, and the median uses only the middle one, again ignoring the values of other observations. Sufficiency is one of the reasons we emphasize the mean as our measure of central tendency. Similarly, the variance is based on all the data points, whereas the range is based on only the maximum and minimum points. By our definition, the range is not a sufficient estimator of the spread of the population.

UNBIASEDNESS   Suppose we have a population for which we somehow know the mean (μ)—say, for example, the heights of all basketball players in the NBA. If we were to draw one sample from that population and calculate the sample mean ($\overline{X}_1$), we would expect $\overline{X}_1$ to be reasonably close to μ, particularly if N is large. So if the average height in this population is 7 feet ($\mu = 7.0$), we would expect a sample of, say, 10 players to have an average height of *approximately* 7 feet as well ($\overline{X}_1 \simeq 7$; the symbol $\simeq$ means "approximately equal"). Now suppose we draw another sample and obtain its mean ($\overline{X}_2$); the subscript is used here to differentiate the means of successive samples. This mean would probably also be reasonably close to μ, but we would not expect it to be equal to μ, or to $\overline{X}_1$. If we were to keep repeating this procedure and drawing sample means ad infinitum, we would find that the *average of the sample means*

Expected value

would be equal to μ. Thus, we say that the **expected value** (i.e., the long-range average) of an unlimited number of samples) of the sample mean is equal to μ, the population mean. An estimator with an expected value that is equal to the parameter to be esti-

Unbiased estimator

mated is called an **unbiased estimator**. Unbiasedness is an important property for a statistic to possess. The sample mean is an unbiased estimator of the population parameter (μ). Furthermore, because of the way that we have defined the sample variance (s^2), it is an unbiased estimate of the population variance (σ^2). By and large, unbiased estimators are like unbiased people—they are nicer to work with than biased ones are.

Efficiency

EFFICIENCY   Estimators are also characterized in terms of **efficiency**. Suppose that the population is symmetric, and thus the values of the mean and median are equal. Now suppose that we want to estimate the mean of this population (or, equivalently, its median). If we drew many samples and calculated their means, we would find that the means ($\overline{X}$s) clustered relatively closely around μ. The medians of the same samples, however, would cluster more loosely around μ. This greater spread around the median happens even though the median is also an unbiased estimator in this situation. The fact that the sample means cluster more closely around μ than do the sample medians (for a constant sample size) indicates that the mean is more *efficient* as an estimator (in fact, it is the most efficient estimator) of μ. Since the mean is more likely to be closer to μ (i.e., to be a more accurate estimate) than is the median, it is a better statistic to use to estimate μ.

Although it should be obvious that *efficiency* is a relative term (a statistic is more or less efficient than some other statistic), statements that such and such a statistic is "efficient" are common. In this usage of the term, we really mean that the statistic is more efficient than all other statistics as an estimate of the parameter in question. Both the sample mean, as an estimate of μ, and the sample variance, as an estimate of σ^2, are efficient estimators in this sense. The fact that both the mean and variance are sufficient, unbiased, and efficient is the major reason they play such an important role in statistics. These two statistics will form the basis for most of the procedures discussed in the remainder of this book.

RESISTANCE   The last property of an estimator to be considered concerns the degree to which the estimator is influenced by the presence of outliers. Recall that the median is relatively uninfluenced by outliers, whereas the mean can drastically change with the inclusion of one or two extreme scores. In a very real sense we can say that the median "resists" the influence of these outliers, whereas the mean does not. This

Resistance   property is called the **resistance** of the estimator. In recent years, considerably more attention has been placed on developing resistant estimators; these should soon start filtering down to the level of everyday data analysis.

THE SAMPLE VARIANCE AS AN ESTIMATOR OF THE POPULATION VARIANCE

The sample variance offers an excellent example of what was said in the discussion of unbiasedness. You may recall that I earlier sneaked in the divisor of $N - 1$ instead of N for the calculation of the variance and standard deviation. Now is the time to explain why.

There are a number of ways to explain why sample variances require $N - 1$ as the denominator. Perhaps the simplest is phrased in terms of what has been said about the sample variance (s^2) as an unbiased estimate of the population variance (σ^2). Assume for the moment that we have an infinite number of samples (each containing N observations) from one population and that we know the population variance. Suppose further that we are foolish enough to calculate sample variances as

$$\frac{\Sigma(X - \overline{X})^2}{N}$$

(Note the denominator.) If we take the average of these samples' variances, we find

$$\text{Average } \frac{\Sigma(X - \overline{X})^2}{N} = E\left[\frac{\Sigma(X - \overline{X})^2}{N}\right] = \frac{(N - 1)\sigma^2}{N}$$

where $E[\ ]$ is read as "the expected value of (whatever is in brackets)."

This last point can be illustrated by a simple example. Suppose we have a population that consists of only the three numbers 1, 2, and 3. Since this is the entire population, we can calculate μ and σ^2 exactly: $\mu = 2$ and $\sigma^2 = 0.667$. (Remember that if, *and only if*, we have the entire population instead of a sample, $\sigma^2 = \Sigma(X - \mu)^2/N$.) Only nine *different* samples of $N = 2$ could possibly be drawn from this population, and if we sample randomly, each of these nine possible samples is equally likely to occur. It is a simple matter to list them and to compute the mean and variance of each sample. For our example, we will calculate s^2 using both N and $N - 1$ as the denominator.

The data and the calculations are presented in Table 2.7. Notice that, as predicted, the mean of the sample means is equal to μ and the mean of the sample variances, using $N - 1$ as the denominator, is equal to σ^2. Furthermore, the average of $\Sigma(X - \overline{X})^2/N$ (the *biased* statistic) is

$$E\left(\frac{\Sigma(X - \overline{X})^2}{N}\right) = \frac{(N - 1)\sigma^2}{N} = \frac{1}{2}(\sigma^2) = \frac{1}{2}(0.667) = 0.333$$

The expected value of $\Sigma(X - \overline{X})^2/N$ is not σ^2, which we hoped to estimate. Rather, it is $\sigma^2(N - 1)/N$. Thus, when we use N in the denominator, we estimate the wrong thing and have a biased estimate of σ^2. This result provides us with a basis for an unbiased estimate of σ^2, however. If

$$E\left[\frac{\Sigma(X - \overline{X})^2}{N}\right] = \frac{(N - 1)\sigma^2}{N}$$

then simple algebra will show that

$$E\left[\frac{\Sigma(X - \overline{X})^2}{N} \cdot \frac{N}{N - 1}\right] = \sigma^2$$

and thus

$$E\left[\frac{\Sigma(X - \overline{X})^2}{N - 1}\right] = \sigma^2$$

This last equation is our standard definitional formula for the variance. It shows us not only how to find an estimate of σ^2, but also that this estimate is unbiased.

TABLE 2.7
Results of sampling from a very small population

Sample		$\overline{X}$	s^2 (Using $N - 1$)	s^2 (Using N)
1	1	1.0	0.00	0.00
1	2	1.5	0.50	0.25
1	3	2.0	2.00	1.00
2	1	1.5	0.50	0.25
2	2	2.0	0.00	0.00
2	3	2.5	0.50	0.25
3	1	2.0	2.00	1.00
3	2	2.5	0.50	0.25
3	3	3.0	0.00	0.00
Average		2.0	0.667	0.333

DEGREES OF FREEDOM

Degrees of freedom (df)

The foregoing discussion is very much like saying that we divide by $N - 1$ *because it works*. Although some people find this an acceptable rationale, others do not— they wish to know why it works. To explain this, we must first consider **degrees of freedom (df)**. Assume that you have in front of you the three numbers 6, 8, and 10.

Their mean is 8. You are now informed that you may change any of these numbers, as long as the mean is kept constant at 8. How many numbers are you free to vary? If you think that you are free to vary all three numbers, you are wrong. If you change all three of them in some haphazard fashion, the mean almost certainly will not equal 8. Only two of the numbers can be *freely* changed if the mean is to remain constant. For example, if you change the 6 to a 7 and the 10 to a 13, the remaining number is determined; it must be 4 if the mean is to be 8. If you had 50 numbers and were given the same instructions, you would be free to vary only 49 of them; the 50th would be determined.

Now let us go back to the formulas for the population and sample variances and see why we lost one degree of freedom in calculating the sample variances.

$$\sigma^2 = \frac{\Sigma(X - \mu)^2}{N} \qquad s^2 = \frac{\Sigma(X - \overline{X})^2}{N - 1}$$

In the case of σ^2, μ is known and does not have to be estimated from the data. Thus, no *df* are lost and the denominator is N. In the case of s^2, however, μ is not known and must be estimated from the sample mean ($\overline{X}$). Once you have estimated μ from $\overline{X}$, you have fixed it for purposes of estimating variability. Thus, you lose that degree of freedom that we discussed, and you have only $N - 1$ *df* left ($N - 1$ scores free to vary). We lose this one degree of freedom *whenever* we estimate a mean. It follows that the denominator (the number of scores on which our estimate is based) should reflect this restriction. For an interesting geometrical interpretation of degrees of freedom, see Walker (1940).

2.5   BOXPLOTS: GRAPHICAL REPRESENTATIONS OF DISPERSION AND EXTREME SCORES

**Boxplots,
Box-and-whisker
plots**

Earlier in this chapter, we saw how stem-and-leaf displays can be used to represent the data in several meaningful ways at the same time. Such displays combine the data into something much like a histogram while retaining the individual values of the observations. In addition to the stem-and-leaf display, Tukey developed other ways of looking at data, one of which gives greater prominence to the dispersion of the data. This is the method known as **boxplots**, or, sometimes, **box-and-whisker plots**.

The data in Table 2.8 were taken from a study by Nurcombe et al. (1984) comparing duration of hospitalization of normal- and low-birthweight infants; they represent preliminary data on the length of hospitalization of 38 normal-birthweight infants. Data on three infants are missing for this particular variable and are represented by an asterisk (*). (The asterisks are included to emphasize that we should not just ignore missing data.) Because the data vary from 1 to 10, with two exceptions, all of the leaves are zeros. The zeros really just fill in space to produce a histogram-type distribution. Examination of the data as plotted in the stem-and-leaf display reveals that the distribution is positively skewed, with a mode of 3 days. At the bottom of the stem you will see the entry "HI" and the values "20" and "33." These are extreme values (outliers) and are set off in this way to highlight their existence. Whether they are large enough to make us suspicious is one of the questions a boxplot is designed to address. The last line of the stem-and-leaf display indicates the number of missing observations.

TABLE 2.8
Data and stem-and-leaf display on length of hospitalization of normal-birthweight infants (in days)

Data			Stem-and-Leaf
2	1	7	1 000
1	33	2	2 000000000
2	3	4	3 00000000000
3	*	4	4 0000000
3	3	10	5 00
9	2	5	6 0
4	3	3	7 0
20	6	2	8
4	5	2	9 0
1	*	*	10 0
3	3	4	HI 20,33
2	3	4	
3	2	3	Missing = 3
2	4		

To understand how a boxplot is constructed, we need to invoke a number of concepts we have already discussed and then add a few more. Earlier in this chapter, we defined the median location of a set of N scores as $(N + 1)/2$. When the median location is a whole number, then the median is simply the value that occupies that location in an ordered arrangement of data. When the median location is a decimal number, the median is the average of the two values on either side of that location. For the data in Table 2.8, the median location is $(38 + 1)/2 = 19.5$. Counting down from the top or up from the bottom, we find the 19th and 20th values are 3. Thus, the median in also 3.

To construct a boxplot, we take what amounts to the medians of each half of the display and call these points the **hinges**. Hinges are closely related to the first and third quartile (often designated Q_1 and Q_3), which are the values that cut off the lowest and highest 25% of the distributions. (The difference between the hinges and the quartiles is minor and tends to vanish with large sample sizes. Most people ignore the distinction entirely, as will we.) To calculate the hinges we first need to obtain the **hinge location**, which is defined as

Hinges

Hinge location

$$\text{Hinge location} = \frac{\text{Median location} + 1}{2}$$

If the median location were a fractional value, the fractional part would be dropped in computing the hinge location. Thus, for the data on hospital stay, the hinge location is $(19 + 1)/2 = 10$, and the hinges are located at the 10th score from the bottom and the 10th score from the top. These values are 2 and 4, respectively. For data sets without tied scores, or for large samples, the hinges will bracket the middle 50% of the scores.

H-spread

Inner fence

Adjacent values

To complete the concepts required for understanding boxplots, we need to consider three more terms: H-spread, inner fences, and adjacent values. The **H-spread** is simply the range between the two hinges, and as such is basically just the interquartile range. For our data, the H-spread is $4 - 2 = 2$. An **inner fence** is a point that falls 1.5 times the H-spread above or below the appropriate hinge. Because the H-spread is 2 for our data, the inner fence is $2 \times 1.5 = 3$ points farther out than the hinges. Because our hinges are the values 2 and 4, the inner fences will be at $2 - 3 = -1$ and $4 + 3 = 7$. **Adjacent values** are those values in the data that are no more extreme (no farther from the median) than are the inner fences. Because the smallest value we have is 1, that is the closest to the lower inner fence and is the lower adjacent value. The higher inner fence is 7 and, because we have a 7 in our data, that will be the higher adjacent value. The calculations for all the terms we have just defined are shown in the upper part of Figure 2.12.

Median location $= (N + 1)/2 = (38 + 1)/2 = 19.5$
Median $= 3$
Hinge location $=$ (median location[†] $+ 1)/2 = (19 + 1)/2 = 10$
Lower hinge $=$ 10th lowest score $= 2$
Upper hinge $=$ 10th highest score $= 4$
H-spread $=$ upper hinge $-$ lower hinge $= 4 - 2 = 2$
H-spread $\times 1.5 = 2(1.5) = 3$
Lower fence $=$ lower hinge $- 1.5$ (hinge spread) $= 2 - 3 = -1$
Upper fence $=$ upper hinge $+ 1.5$ (hinge spread) $= 4 + 3 = 7$
Lower adjacent value $=$ smallest value $\geq$ lower fence $= 1$
Upper adjacent value $=$ largest value $\leq$ upper fence $= 7$

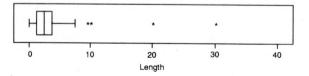

FIGURE 2.12
Calculations and boxplots for data from Table 2.8

[†] Drop any fractional elements.

Inner fences and adjacent values sometimes confuse people. Think of a herd of cows in a field or a group of children on a playground. The fence around the field or playground represents the inner fence in the boxplot. The cows or children closest to *but inside* the fence are the adjacent values. Don't worry about the cows who have escaped and are outside the fence. We'll come to them later.

Now we are ready to draw the boxplot. First, we draw and label a scale that covers the entire range of the obtained values, as shown at the bottom of Figure 2.12. We then draw a rectangular box from one hinge to the other, with a vertical line representing the location of the median. Next, we draw lines, called **whiskers**, from the hinges out to the adjacent values. Finally we plot the location of all points more extreme than the adjacent values.

Whiskers

From Figure 2.12 we can see several important things. First, the central portion of the distribution is reasonably symmetric. This is indicated by the fact that the median lies in the center of the box and was also apparent from the stem-and-leaf display. We can also see that the distribution is positively skewed—the whisker on the right is substantially longer than the one on the left. This was apparent from the stem-and-leaf display, although not so clearly. Finally, we see that we have four points (denoted by asterisks) that lie beyond the inner fences. We will label these points as **outliers**. The term *outlier* is often loosely used to mean "extreme values", but we will use it here to mean those values that are sufficiently extreme to lie beyond the inner fences.) The stem-and-leaf display did not show the position of the outliers nearly so graphically as does the boxplot.

Outliers

Outliers deserve special attention. An outlier could represent an error in measurement, in data recording, or in data entry, or it could represent a legitimate value that just happens to be extreme. For example, a normal-birthweight infant might have been born with a physical defect that required extended hospitalization. Since these are actual data, it was possible to go back to hospital records and look more closely at the four extreme cases. It turned out that the two most extreme scores were attributable to errors in data entry and were readily correctable. The other two extreme scores were caused by physical problems of the infants. Here the project staff had to decide whether the problems were severe enough to cause the infants to be dropped from the study (both were retained as subjects). The two corrected values were 3 and 5 (instead of 33 and 20, respectively); the new boxplot based on the corrected data is

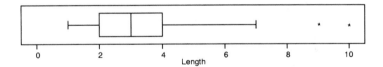

This boxplot is identical to the one shown in Figure 2.12 except for the spacing and the two largest values. (Verify for yourself that the corrected data set indeed yields this boxplot.)

It should now be evident that boxplots are extremely useful tools for examining data with respect to dispersion. They are particularly handy for screening data for errors and for highlighting potential problems before subsequent analyses are carried out. In the remainder of the book, boxplots are presented as a visual guide to the data. It is a good idea to make up a few boxplots of your own. The first one will take a while, the second will not be too bad, and the third will be easy and quick.

A word of warning: Different statistical computer programs may vary in the ways they define the various elements in boxplots. [See Frigge, Hoagland, and Iglewicz (1989) for an extensive discussion of this issue.] You may find two different programs that produce slightly different boxplots for the same set of data. They may even identify different outliers. However, boxplots are normally used as informal heuristic devices, and subtle differences in definition are rarely, if ever, a problem. I mention the potential discrepancies here simply to explain why analyses that you do on the data in this book may come up with slightly different results.

2.6   DOTPLOTS FOR REPRESENTING DISPERSION

Dotplot

Another way of examining data for dispersion, for outliers, and for skewness is with dotplots. A **dotplot** is an extremely simple representation of the data which can easily be created with pencil and paper or with a simple plotting program. Although a dotplot does not convey all of the information a boxplot does, it is considerably easier to create and interpret and offers its own unique perspective on the data.

An example of a dotplot for the data on length of hospitalization (see Table 2.8) is presented in Figure 2.13. Along the x-axis of this figure are the values of the dependent variable (length of stay). To keep things in perspective, the x-axis has been truncated at 10, and values of X greater than 10 (33 and 20) have been shown as being off the graph.

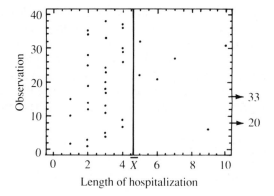

FIGURE 2.13
Dotplot of length of hospitalization data from Table 2.8

To create the plot, we simply start at the bottom of the y-axis and move up as we come to each observation. Each data point is represented by a dot corresponding to the (usually arbitrary) observation number (Y) and the dependent variable (X). Thus, the first observation from Table 2.8 is a 2, and it is plotted at the point (2, 1); the sixth observation is a 9, and it is plotted at (9, 6); and so on. If we read from the bottom to the top of this figure, we will see the individual observations in turn. Their position on the x-axis will correspond to the length of hospitalization for that person.

The vertical line corresponds to the mean (4.65). This line really highlights the skewness in the data. Notice that the majority of the points are located to the left of the mean. Those points that are on the right tend to be very much to the right, representing large deviations.

Data are usually recorded in a more-or-less random order, depending on the order in which they were collected. We would not normally expect systematic changes in data over time; we expect later subjects to be pretty much like earlier subjects. However, if we notice that as we move up the dotplot the data tend to move to the right or to become more dispersed, that should signal us to examine our data and our procedures, looking carefully for changes in subjects, in procedures, in the way that data are recorded, and so on. If we just record data in the order in which they come in, systematic changes are not welcome. They usually indicate that something we did not expect is going on.

Dotplots can be created using standard graphics packages such as EXECUSTAT, either by plotting the data against the observation number, if such exists, or by requesting a one-dimensional plot with "jittering" or "dithering." Jittering is a technique of displacing points vertically or horizontally by a small amount so that overlapping points do not hide one another.

Cleveland (1984) has proposed using dotplots somewhat differently. He suggests using dotplots when the identity of the individual data points is important. For example, he examined a number of journals in the social sciences and calculated the percentage of area in each article that was devoted to graphs. He then displayed the "graph percentage" along the X-axis and the journal titles along the Y-axis, with journals arranged in order of increasing graph percentage. This presentation not only makes clear the differences among journals in terms of the percentage of the area of each article that is devoted to graphical information, but it also identifies the journal. Refer to Cleveland's article for an interesting argument on why dotplots are better in this situation than bar graphs.

2.7 OBTAINING MEASURES OF DISPERSION USING MINITAB

Earlier we saw how to use Minitab to calculate measures of central tendency. We can also use Minitab to calculate measures of dispersion, as shown in Exhibit 2.3, which is based on our previous data on annoying mannerisms of instructors (Exhibit 2.2). Note that the simple DESCRIBE command supplies nearly all the statistics we need. The BOXPLOT command generates a boxplot.

EXHIBIT 2.3
Minitab program for obtaining measures of dispersion on annoying mannerisms

```
MTB  > SET THE FOLLOWING DATA IN COLUMN C1
DATA > 12 18 19 15 18 14 17 20 18 15 17 11 23 19 10
DATA > END
MTB  > MEAN OF THE DATA IN COLUMN C1
      MEAN    =    16.400
MTB  > MEDIAN OF THE DATE IN COLUMN C1
      MEDIAN  =    17.000
MTB  > HISTOGRAM OF THE DATA IN COLUMN C1

Histogram of C1      N = 15

Midpoint    Count
      10        1    *
      11        1    *
      12        1    *
      13        0
      14        1    *
      15        2    **
      16        0
      17        2    **
      18        3    ***
      19        2    **
      20        1    *
      21        0
      22        0
      23        1    *
```

EXHIBIT 2.3 (Cont.)

```
MTB  > DESCRIBE COLUMN C1

          N       MEAN     MEDIAN    TRMEAN    STDEV    SEMEAN
   C1     15      16.400   17.000    16.385    3.562    0.920

          MIN     MAX      Q1        Q3
   C1     10.000  23.000   14.000    19.000

MTB  > BOXPLOT ON DATA IN COLUMN C1


                              -------------------
         --------------------|        +        |---------------------
                              -------------------
         --+----------+----------+----------+----------+----------+----C1
         10.0       12.5       15.0       17.5       20.0       22.5

MTB  > STOP
```

2.8 PERCENTILES, QUARTILES, AND DECILES

Quartiles

A distribution has many properties besides its location and dispersion. We saw one of these briefly when we considered boxplots, where **quartiles** were defined as those values that divide the distribution into fourths. Thus, the first quartile cuts off the lowest 25%, the second quartile cuts off the lowest 50%, and the third quartile cuts off the lowest 75%. (Note that the second quartile is also the median.) If we wish to examine finer gradations of the distribution, we can look at **deciles**, which divide the distribution up into tenths, with the first decile cutting off the lowest 10%, the second decile cutting off the lowest 20%, and so on. Finally, most of you have had experience with **percentiles**, which are values that divide the distribution into hundredths. Thus, the 81st percentile is that point on the distribution below which 81% of the scores lie.

Deciles

Percentiles

Quantiles, Fractiles

Quartiles, deciles, and percentiles are the three most common examples of a general class of statistics known by the generic name of **quantiles**, or, sometimes, **fractiles**. We will not have much to say about quantiles in this book, but they are usually covered extensively in more introductory texts (e.g., Howell, 1989). They also play an important role in many of the techniques of exploratory data analysis advocated by Tukey.

2.9 THE EFFECT OF LINEAR TRANSFORMATIONS ON DATA

Frequently, we wish to transform data in one way or another. For instance, we may wish to convert feet into inches, inches into centimeters, degrees Fahrenheit into degrees Celsius, test grades based on 79 questions to grades based on a 100-point scale, four- to five-digit incomes into one- to two-digit incomes, and so on. Fortunately, all of these transformations fall within a set called **linear transformations**, in which we multiply each X by some constant (possibly 1) and add a constant (possibly 0).

Linear transformations

$$X_{new} = bX_{old} + a$$

where a and b are our constants. (Transformations that use exponents, logs, trigonometric functions, etc., are not linear transformations.) An example of a linear transformation is the formula for converting degrees Celsius to degrees Fahrenheit:

$$F = 9/5(C) + 32$$

As long as we content ourselves with linear transformations, a set of simple rules defines the mean and variance of the observations on the new scale in terms of their means and variances on the old one:

1. Adding (or subtracting) a constant to (or from) a set of data adds (or subtracts) that same constant to (or from) the mean:

$$\text{For } X_{new} = X_{old} \pm a: \qquad \overline{X}_{new} = \overline{X}_{old} \pm a$$

2. Multiplying (or dividing) a set of data by a constant multiplies (or divides) the mean by the same constant:

$$\text{For } X_{new} = bX_{old}: \qquad \overline{X}_{new} = b\overline{X}_{old}$$

$$\text{For } X_{new} = X_{old}/b: \qquad \overline{X}_{new} = \overline{X}_{old}/b$$

3. Adding or subtracting a constant to (or from) a set of scores leaves the variance and standard deviation unchanged:

$$\text{For } X_{new} = X_{old} \pm a: \qquad s^2_{new} = s^2_{old}$$

4. Multiplying (or dividing) a set of scores by a constant multiplies (or divides) the variance by the square of the constant and the standard deviation by the constant:

$$\text{For } X_{new} = bX_{old}: \qquad s^2_{new} = b^2 s^2_{old} \qquad \text{and} \qquad s_{new} = bs_{old}$$

$$\text{For } X_{new} = X_{old}/b: \qquad s^2_{new} = s^2_{old}/b^2 \qquad \text{and} \qquad s_{new} = s_{old}/b$$

The following example illustrates these rules. In each case, the constant used is 3.

Addition of a constant:

Old Data	$\overline{X}$	s^2	s	New Data	$\overline{X}$	s^2	s
4 8 12	8	16	4	7 11 15	11	16	4

Multiplication by a constant:

Old Data	$\overline{X}$	s^2	s	New Data	$\overline{X}$	s^2	s
4 8 12	8	16	4	12 24 36	24	144	12

REFLECTION AS A TRANSFORMATION   A very common and useful transformation concerns reversing the ordering of a scale. For example, assume that we asked subjects to indicate on a 5-point scale the degree to which they agree or disagree with each of several items. To prevent the subjects from simply checking the same point on the scale all the way down the page without thinking, we phrase half of our questions

Reflection

in the positive direction and half in the negative direction. Thus, given a 5-point scale where 5 represents "strongly agree" and 1 represents "strongly disagree," a 4 on "I hate movies" would be comparable to a 2 on "I love plays." If we want the scores to be comparable, we need to rescore the negative items (for example), converting a 5 to a 1, a 4 to a 2, and so on. This procedure is called **reflection** and is quite simply accomplished by a linear transformation. We merely write

$$X_{new} = 6 - X_{old}$$

The constant (6) is just the largest value on the scale plus 1. It should be evident that when we reflect a scale, we also reflect its mean but have no effect on its variance or standard deviation. This is true by rule 3 in the preceding list.

Deviation scores
Centering

Standard scores,
Standardization

STANDARDIZATION   One common linear transformation often employed to rescale data involves subtracting the mean from each observation. Such transformed observations are called **deviation scores**, and the transformation itself is often referred to as **centering**, since we are centering the mean at 0. Centering is most often used in regression, which is discussed later in the book. An even more common transformation involves dividing the deviation scores by the standard deviation. Such scores are called **standard scores**, and the process is referred to as **standardization**. Basically, standardized scores are simply transformed observations that are measured in standard deviation units. Thus, for example, a standardized score of 0.75 is a score that is 0.75 standard deviations above the mean; a standardized score of -0.43 is a score that is 0.43 standard deviations below the mean. I will have much more to say about standardized scores when we consider the normal distribution in Chapter 3. I mention them here specifically to show that we can compute standardized scores regardless of whether or not we have a normal distribution (defined in Chapter 3). People often think of standardized scores as being normally distributed, but there is absolutely no requirement that they be.

KEY TERMS

Frequency distribution (2.1)

Histogram (2.1)

Real lower limit (2.1)

Real upper limit (2.1)

Midpoints (2.1)

Cumulative frequencies (2.1)

Cumulative distribution (2.1)

Stem-and-leaf display (2.1)

Exploratory data analysis (EDA) (2.1)

Leading digits (2.1)

Most significant digits (2.1)

Stem (2.1)

Trailing digits (2.1)

Least significant digits (2.1)

Leaves (2.1)

Symmetric (2.1)

Normal distribution (2.1)

Bimodal (2.1)

Unimodal (2.1)

Negatively skewed (2.1)

Positively skewed (2.1)

Skewness (2.1)

EXERCISES

Some of the following exercises suggest that you use Minitab to obtain certain results. If you do not have Minitab available, you can easily substitute any other computer program. If you do not have access to computer facilities, you can simply skip those exercises.

Some of the exercises refer to a large data set that is listed in Appendix Data Set. These data come from an actual research study (Howell & Huessy, 1981, 1985), which is described at the beginning of Appendix Data Set.

2.1 Children differ from adults in that they tend to recall stories in terms of a sequence of actions rather than in terms of an overall plot. This means that their descriptions of a movie are filled with the phrase "and then...." An experimenter with supreme patience asked 50 children to tell her about a given movie. Among other variables, she counted the number of "and then..." statements. The data follow:

18   15   22   19   18   17   18   20   17   12   16   16   17   21   23   18   20   21   20

20   15   18   17   19   20   23   22   10   17   19   19   21   20   18   18   24   11   19

31   16   17   15   19   20   18   18   40   18   19   16

(a) Plot an ungrouped frequency distribution for these data.

(b) What is the general shape of the distribution?

2.2   Make a histogram for the data in Exercise 2.1 using a reasonable number of intervals.

2.3   What difficulty would you encounter in making a stem-and-leaf display of the data in Exercise 2.1?

2.4   As part of the study described in Exercise 2.1, the experimenter obtained the same kind of data for adults. The data follow:

10 12 5 8 13 10 12 8 7 11 11 10 9 9 11 15 12 17 14 10 9

8 15 16 10 14 7 16 9 1 4 11 12 7 9 10 3 11 14 8 12 5 10

9 7 11 14 10 15 9

(a) What can you tell just by looking at these numbers? Do children and adults seem to recall stories in the same way?

(b) Plot an ungrouped frequency distribution for these data using the same scale on the axes as you used for the children's data in Exercise 2.1.

(c) Overlay the frequency distribution from (b) on the one from Exercise 2.1.

2.5   Use a back-to-back histogram (see Figures 2.8 and 2.11) to compare the data from Exercises 2.1 and 2.4.

2.6   Make a cumulative frequency distribution for the data in Exercise 2.1.

2.7   Make a cumulative frequency distribution for the data in Exercise 2.4.

2.8   Create a positively skewed set of data and plot it.

2.9   Create a bimodal set of data and plot it.

2.10 The output in Exhibit 2.4 comes from applying Minitab to the data in Exercise 2.1. Compare the printout to the results you obtained in Exercises 2.2 and 2.3.

EXHIBIT 2.4

```
MTB  > SET THE FOLLOWING DATA IN C1

DATA > 18 15 22 19 18 17 18 ...
DATA > END

MTB  > NAME C1 'AndThen'

MTB  > HISTOGRAM FOR 'AndThen'                    MTB  > STEM-AND-LEAF FOR 'AndThen'

Histogram of AndThen    N = 50                    Stem-and-Leaf of AndThen      N = 50
                                                  Leaf Unit = 1.0
Midpoint    Count
   12         3    ***                               2    1   01
   16        13    *************                      3    1   2
   20        27    ***************************         6    1   555
   24         5    *****                              16    1   6666777777
   28         0                                      (17)   1   88888888889999999
   32         1    *                                  17    2   0000000111
   36         0                                        7    2   2233
   40         1    *                                    3    2   4
                                                        2    2
                                                        2    2
                                                        2    3   1
                                                        1    3
                                                        1    3
                                                        1    3
                                                        1    4   0
```

2.11 Use Minitab or a similar statistical program to produce a histogram and stem-and-leaf display for the data in Exercise 2.4.

2.12 Create a set of data with one extreme score (a number considerably larger than the rest) and see how Minitab or a similar statistical package responds when you ask for a histogram.

2.13 What would you predict to be the shape of the distribution of the number of movies attended per month for the next 200 people you meet?

2.14 Draw a histogram for the data for GPA in Appendix Data Set using reasonable intervals.

2.15 Create a stem-and-leaf display for the ADDSC score in Appendix Data Set.

2.16 In a hypothetical experiment, Harris, Peabody, and Smith (1999) rated 10 Europeans and 10 North Americans on a 12-point scale of musicality. The data for the Europeans were

$$10 \quad 8 \quad 9 \quad 5 \quad 10 \quad 11 \quad 7 \quad 8 \quad 2 \quad 7$$

Using X for this variable,
(a) what are X_3, X_5, and X_8?
(b) calculate ΣX.
(c) write the summation notation for (b) in its most complex form.

2.17 The data for the North Americans (Y) in Exercise 2.16 were

$$9 \quad 9 \quad 5 \quad 3 \quad 8 \quad 4 \quad 6 \quad 6 \quad 5 \quad 2$$

Using Y for this variable,
(a) what are Y_1 and Y_{10}?
(b) calculate ΣY.

2.18 Using the data from Exercise 2.16,
(a) calculate $(\Sigma X)^2$ and ΣX^2.
(b) calculate $\Sigma X/N$, where $N =$ the number of scores.
(c) What do you call what you calculated in (b)?

2.19 Using the data from Exercise 2.17,
(a) calculate $(\Sigma Y)^2$ and ΣY^2.
(b) calculate

$$\frac{\Sigma Y^2 - \dfrac{(\Sigma Y)^2}{N}}{N - 1}$$

(c) calculate the square root of the answer for (b).
(d) What are the units of measurement for (b) and (c)?

2.20 Using the data from Exercises 2.16 and 2.17,
(a) calculate ΣXY.
(b) calculate $\Sigma X \Sigma Y$.
(c) calculate

$$\frac{\Sigma XY - \dfrac{\Sigma X \Sigma Y}{N}}{N - 1}$$

(You will come across these calculations again in Chapter 9.)

2.21 Use the data from Exercises 2.16 and 2.17 to show that
(a) $\Sigma(X + Y) = \Sigma X + \Sigma Y$.
(b) $\Sigma XY \neq \Sigma X \Sigma Y$.
(c) $\Sigma CX = C\Sigma X$, where C is a constant (e.g., 3).
(d) $\Sigma X^2 \neq (\Sigma X)^2$.

2.22 Calculate the mode, median, and mean for the data in Exercise 2.1.

2.23   Calculate the mode, median, and mean for the data in Exercise 2.4.

2.24   Compare the answers you gave for Exercises 2.22 and 2.23. What do they indicate about story-telling behavior in adults and children?

2.25   Make up a set of data for which the mean is greater than the median.

2.26   Make up a positively skewed set of data. Does the mean fall above or below the median?

2.27   Make up a unimodal set of data for which the mean and median are equal but are different from the mode.

2.28   A group of 15 rats running a straight-alley maze required the following number of trials to perform at a predetermined criterion level:

Trials required to reach criterion: 18   19   20   21   22   23   24

Number of rats (frequency):   1   0   4   3   3   3   1

Calculate the mean and median number of the required number of trials for this group.

2.29   Given the following set of data, demonstrate that subtracting a constant (e.g., 5) from every score reduces all measures of central tendency by that constant:

$$8 \quad 7 \quad 12 \quad 14 \quad 3 \quad 7$$

2.30   Given the following set of data, show that multiplying each score by a constant multiplies all measures of central tendency by that constant:

$$8 \quad 3 \quad 5 \quad 5 \quad 6 \quad 2$$

2.31   Create a sample of 10 numbers that has a mean of 8.6. How does this illustrate the point we discussed about degrees of freedom?

2.32   The printout in Exhibit 2.5 comes from applying Minitab to the data in Exercise 2.1. Compare these answers to those obtained in Exercise 2.22. As you can see, Minitab does not have a command for the mode (nor for the variance); how could you determine them?

EXHIBIT 2.5

```
MTB > RETRIEVE 'EX2-10.DAT'
   WORKSHEET SAVED 12/30/1990

Worksheet retrieved from file:  ex2-10.dat

MTB > PRINT C1
C1
   18    15    22    19    18    17    18    20    17    12    16    16    17
   21    23    18    20    21    20    20    15    18    17    19    20    23
   22    10    17    19    19    21    20    18    18    24    11    19    31
   16    17    15    19    20    18    18    40    18    19    16

MTB > NAME C1 'AndThen'

MTB > DESCRIBE 'AndThen'

                 N       MEAN     MEDIAN     TRMEAN      STDEV     SEMEAN
AndThen         50     18.900     18.000     18.568      4.496      0.636

               MIN        MAX         Q1         Q3
AndThen     10.000     40.000     17.000     20.000

MTB > MODE 'AndThen'
* ERROR * Name not found in dictionary

MTB > STOP
```

2.33   The output in Exhibit 2.6 was produced by a statistical package named EXECUSTAT, applied to the data on ADDSC and GPA in Appendix Data Set. (These data are also on your instructor's disk, should you wish to use them. They are named ADD. dat.) How do these answers on measures of central tendency compare to what you would predict from the answers to Exercises 2.14 and 2.15?

EXHIBIT 2.6
Summary statistics
for DATASET

	ADDSC	GPA
Sample size	88	88
Mean	52.6023	2.45625
Median	50	2.635
Mode	50	3
Geometric mean	51.148	2.26679
Variance	154.311	0.742063
Std. deviation	12.4222	0.861431
Coeff. of variation	23.6153	35.071
Std. error	1.32421	0.0918288
Minimum	26	0.67
Maximum	85	4
Range	59	3.33
Lower quartile	44.5	1.75
Upper quartile	60.5	3
Interquartile range	16	1.25
Skewness	0.402304	- 0.352333
Std. skewness	1.5769	- 1.38994
Kurtosis	0.0205969	- 0.64949

2.34 Why would it not make any sense to calculate the mean for GENDER or ENGL in Appendix Data Set? If we did go ahead and compute the mean for GENDER, what would the value of the mean minus 1 represent?

2.35 Figure 2.14 was produced by EXECUSTAT for the data on GPA in Appendix Data Set. Compare this figure to the answer to Exercise 2.14.

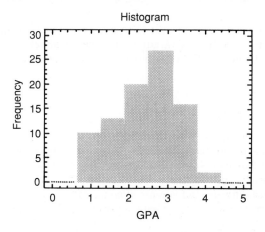

FIGURE 2.14
Histogram for grade
point average

2.36 In one or two sentences, describe what the graphic in Figure 2.14 has to say about the grade point averages for the students in our sample.

2.37 Calculate the range, variance, and standard deviation for the data in Exercise 2.1.

2.38 Calculate the range, variance, and standard deviation for the data in Exercise 2.4.

2.39 Compare the answers to Exercises 2.37 and 2.38. Is the standard deviation for children substantially greater than that for adults?

2.40 In Exercise 2.1, what percentage of the scores fall within plus or minus two standard deviations from the mean?

2.41 In Exercise 2.4, what percentage of the scores fall within plus or minus two standard deviations from the mean?

2.42 Given the following set of data, demonstrate that adding or subtracting a constant to each score does not change the standard deviation. (What happens to the mean when a constant is added or subtracted?)

$$5 \quad 4 \quad 2 \quad 3 \quad 4 \quad 9 \quad 5$$

2.43 Given the data in Exercise 2.42, show that multiplying or dividing by a constant multiplies or divides the standard deviation by that constant. How is this related to what happens to the mean under similar conditions?

2.44 Using the results demonstrated in Exercises 2.42 and 2.43, transform the following set of data to a new set that has a standard deviation of 1.00:

$$5 \quad 8 \quad 3 \quad 8 \quad 6 \quad 9 \quad 9 \quad 7$$

2.45 Use your answers to Exercises 2.42 and 2.43 to modify your answer to Exercise 2.44 such that the new set of data has a mean of 0 and a standard deviation of 1.00. (*Note*: The solution of Exercises 2.44 and 2.45 will be elaborated further in Chapter 3.)

2.46 What would we call the set of data that results from Exercise 2.45? How would you interpret the values for the first two observations?

2.47 Create two sets of scores that have equal ranges but different variances.

2.48 Create a boxplot for the data in Exercise 2.1.

2.49 Create a boxplot for the data in Exercise 2.4.

2.50 Create a boxplot for the variable ADDSC in Appendix Data Set.

2.51 Compute the coefficient of variation to compare the variability of children and adults in Exercises 2.1 and 2.4.

2.52 For the data in Appendix Data Set, the GPA has a mean of 2.456 and a standard deviation of 0.8614. Compute the coefficient of variation as defined in this chapter. Compare that answer to the value given in Exercise 2.33. Why do the answers disagree?

COMPUTER DATA PROBLEM

Throughout the book you will find exercises in almost every chapter that refer to sets of data that your instructor has available on a disk. These data sets are generally too large or cumbersome to be entered by hand into a file. The exercises associated with them also require more computation than you would care to do by hand. They are designed to be analyzed using standard computer software, and you are often asked to run an analysis several different ways to compare results. This is easy to do with a computer, whereas it would be very difficult to do by hand.

Since I do not know what software you have available, I may occasionally request analyses that may not be possible for you. That should occur only rarely, if ever. Everything requested here can be done using BMDP, Minitab, SAS, or SPSS^x. Other large programs, such as MYSTAT, JMP, and StatView, should also do most of what is requested here, if not all of it. Smaller packages may have difficulty in a few places (e.g., complex repeated-measures analysis of variance) but will do everything else.

2.53 Your instructor has a large data set named BadCancr.dat. These data have been deliberately corrupted by entering errors into a perfectly good data set (named Cancer.dat). The purpose of this corruption was to give you experience in detecting and correcting the kinds of errors that appear almost every time we attempt to use a newly entered data set. Every error in here is one that I and almost everyone I know have come across countless times. Some of them are so extreme that most statistical packages will not run until they are corrected. Others are logical errors that will allow the program to run, producing meaningless results. (No college student will be 10 years old or receive a score of 15 on a 10-point quiz.)

The variables in this set are described in the Appendix Computer Exercises for the file Cancer.dat. That description tells where each variable should be found and the range of its legitimate values. You can use any statistical package available to read the data. Standard error messages will identify some of the problems, visual inspection will identify others, and computing descriptive statistics and/or plotting the data will help identify the rest. In some cases the appropriate correction will be obvious. In other cases you will just have to delete the offending values. When you have cleaned the data, use your program to compute a final set of descriptive statistics on each of the variables.

This problem will take a fair amount of time. I have found that it is best to have students work in pairs.

CHAPTER THREE

THE NORMAL DISTRIBUTION

OBJECTIVES *To develop the concept of the normal distribution and show how it can be used to draw inferences about observations.*

CONTENTS

Normal distribution

B y now it should be apparent that we are very much concerned with distributions —distributions of data, hypothetical distributions of populations, and sampling distributions (which will be introduced in Chapter 4). Of all the possible forms that distributions can take, the class known as the **normal distribution** is by far the most important for our purposes.

Before discussing the normal distribution, however, it is worth a short digression to explain why we are so interested in distributions in general. The critical factor is that there is an important link between distributions and probabilities. If we know something about the distribution of events (or of sample statistics), we know something about the probability that one of those events (or statistics) is likely to occur. To see the issue in its simplest form, take the lowly pie chart. (This is the only pie chart you will see in this book.)

The pie chart shown in Figure 3.1 is taken from a U.S. Department of Justice report on probation and parole. It shows the status of all individuals who have been convicted of a criminal offense. From this figure you can see that 9% were in jail, 19% were in prison, 61% were on probation, and the remaining 11% were on parole. You can also see that the percentages in each category are directly reflected in the percentage of area of the pie that each wedge occupies. The area taken up by each segment is directly proportional to the percentage of individuals in that segment. Moreover, if we declare that the total area of the pie is 1.00 unit, the area of each segment is equal to the proportion of observations falling in that segment.

It is easy to go from speaking about areas to speaking about probabilities. The concept of probability will be examined in Chapter 5; but even without a precise definition of probability we can make an important point about areas of a pie chart. For now simply think of probability in its common everyday usage: the likelihood that some event will occur. From this perspective it is logical to conclude that, because 19% of those convicted of a federal crime are currently in prison, if we were to randomly draw the name of one person from a list of convicted individuals, the probability is .19 that the individual would be in prison. To put this in slightly different terms, if 19% of the area of the pie is allocated to prison, then the probability that a person would fall in that segment is .19.

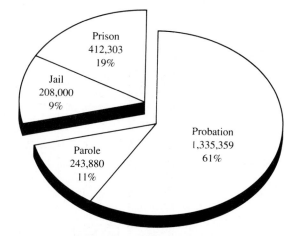

FIGURE 3.1
Pie chart showing persons under correctional super-vision, by type of supervision, on December 31, 1982

Note: The prison data are from the U.S. Department of Justice, Bureau of Justice Statistics, *Prisoners in 1982*, Bulletin NCJ-87933 (Washington, D.C.: U.S. Government Printing Office, 1983). The jail data are from the U.S. Department of Justice, Bureau of Justice Statistics, *Jail Inmates 1982*. Bulletin NCJ-87161 (Washington, D.C.: U.S. Department of Justice, February 1983). The parole data and the probation data are from the annual Uniform Parole Reports and National Probation Reports surveys.

This pie chart also allows us to explore the addition of areas. It should be clear that if 19% are in prison and 9% are in jail, $19 + 9 = 28\%$ are incarcerated. In other words, we can find the percentage of individuals in one or another of several categories just by adding the percentages for each category. The same thing holds in terms of areas; we can find the percentage of incarcerated individuals by adding the areas devoted to prison and to jail. And finally, if we can find percentages by adding areas, we can also find probabilities by adding areas. Thus, the probability of being incarcerated is the probability of being in one of the two segments associated with incarceration, which we can get by summing the two areas (or their associated probabilities).

Data can be presented in other ways besides pie charts, and one of the simplest is a histogram or its closely related cousin, the bar chart (both discussed in Chapter 2). Figure 3.2 shows Figure 3.1 redrawn as a bar chart. Although this figure does not contain any new information, it has two advantages over the pie chart. First of all, it is easier to compare categories, because the only thing we need to look at is the height of the bars; we do not have to compare the lengths of two different arcs in different orientations. The second advantage is that the bar chart is visually more like the common distributions we will deal with, in that the various levels or categories are spread out along the horizontal dimension and the percentages in each category are shown along the vertical dimension. Here again you can see that the various areas of the distribution are related to probabilities. Furthermore, you can see that we can meaningfully sum areas the same way we did in the pie chart. When we move to more common distributions, particularly the normal distribution, the principles of areas, percentages, probabilities, and the addition of areas or probabilities carry over almost without change.

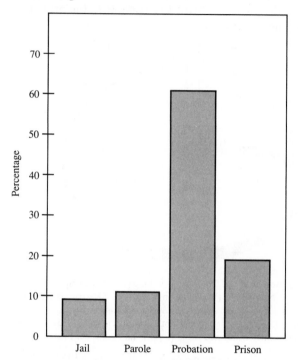

FIGURE 3.2
Bar chart showing persons under correctional supervision by type of supervision

As stated earlier, the normal distribution is one of the most important distributions we will encounter. There are several reasons for this:

1. Many of the dependent variables we commonly deal with are assumed to be normally distributed in the population; that is, we frequently assume that if we were to obtain the whole population of observations, the resulting distribution would closely resemble the normal distribution.

2. If we assume that a variable is at least approximately normally distributed, then the techniques discussed in this chapter allow us to make a number of inferences (either exact or approximate) about values of that variable.

3. The theoretical distribution of the hypothetical set of sample means obtained by drawing an infinite number of samples from a specified population can be shown to be approximately normal under a wide variety of conditions. Such a distribution is called the sampling distribution of the mean and is discussed and used extensively in later chapters.

4. Most of the statistical procedures we will employ have, somewhere in their derivation, an assumption that the population of observations is normally distributed.

To introduce the normal distribution, we will look at one additional data set that is approximately normal (and would be normal if we had more observations). The data were collected using the Achenbach Youth Self-Report form (Achenbach, 1991b). This frequently used measure of behavior problems produces scores on a number of different dimensions. The dimension we are going to look at is Total Behavior Problems, which represents the total number of behavior problems reported by the child, weighted by the severity of the problem. (Examples of Behavior Problem categories are "Argues," "Impulsive," "Shows off," and "Teases.") Figure 3.3 is a histogram of data from 309 junior-high-school students. A higher score represents more behavior problems. You can see that this distribution has a center very near 50 and is fairly symmetrically distributed on either side of that value, with the scores ranging between about 25 and 75. The standard deviation of this distribution is approximately 10. The distribution is not perfectly smooth—it has some bumps and valleys—but overall it is fairly smooth, rising in the center and falling off at the ends. (The actual mean and standard deviation for this particular sample are 50.98 and 10.42, respectively.)

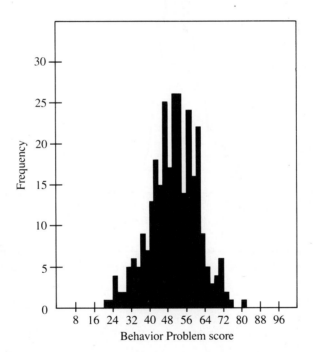

FIGURE 3.3
Histogram showing distribution of Total Behavior Problems scores

One thing you might note from this distribution is that if you add the frequencies of people falling in the intervals 52–53, 53–54, and 55–56, you will find that approximately 65 people obtained a score between 52 and 56. Because there are 309 observations in this sample, 65/309 = 21% of the observations fell in this interval. This illustrates the comments made earlier on the addition of areas.

If we take this same set of data and represent it by a frequency polygon rather than a histogram, we obtain Figure 3.4. All the information in this figure was in Figure 3.3.

I have merely connected the tops of the bars in the histogram and then erased the bars themselves. Why waste an artist's time by putting in a figure that has nothing new to offer? The reason is simply that I want you to see the transition from a histogram, which you see nearly every time you open a newspaper or a magazine, to a line graph. The next transition from there to the smoothed curves you will see in the rest of the book (e.g., Figure 3.5) is straightforward. The major difference between the line graph (frequency polygon) and the smoothed curve is that the latter is a stylized version that leaves out the bumps and valleys.

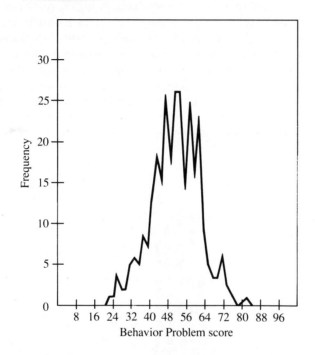

FIGURE 3.4
Frequency polygon showing distribution of Total Behavior Problems scores

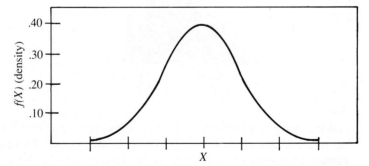

FIGURE 3.5
Characteristic normal distribution with values of X on the abscissa and density on the ordinate

Now we are ready to go to the normal distribution. First we will consider it in the abstract, and then we will take a concrete example using the Achenbach Youth Self-Report Total Behavior Problem scores from Figures 3.3 and 3.4.

The distribution shown in Figure 3.5 is a characteristic normal distribution. It is a

Abscissa
Ordinate

symmetric, unimodal distribution, frequently referred to as "bell shaped," and has limits of $\pm \infty$. The **abscissa** (or horizontal axis) represents different possible values of X, and the **ordinate** (or vertical axis) shows the density and is related to (but not the same as) the frequency or probability of the occurrence of X. The concept of density will be discussed in further detail in Chapter 5.

The normal distribution has a long history. It was originally investigated by DeMoivre (1667–1754), who was interested in its use in describing the results of games of chance (gambling). The distribution was defined precisely by Pierre-Simon Laplace (1749–1827), a French astronomer and mathematician, and put in its more usual form by Carl Friedrich Gauss (1777–1855), a German mathematician and astronomer. Both Laplace and Gauss were interested in the distribution of errors in astronomical observations. In fact, the normal distribution is often referred to as the Gaussian distribution and as the "normal law of error." Adolph Quetelet (1796–1874), a Belgian astronomer, was the first to apply the distribution to social and biological data. He collected chest measurements of Scottish soldiers and heights of French soldiers. He found that both sets of measurements were approximately normally distributed. Quetelet interpreted the data to indicate that the mean of this distribution was the ideal at which nature was aiming and that observations to either side of the mean represented error (a deviation from nature's ideal). (For 5'8" males like myself it is somehow comforting to think of a 6'2" football player as nature's mistake.) Although we no longer think of the mean as nature's ideal, this is a useful way to conceptualize variability around the mean. In fact, we still use the word *error* to refer to deviations from the mean. The English scientist Sir Francis Galton (1822–1911) carried Quetelet's ideas further and gave the normal distribution a central role in psychological theory—especially the theory of mental abilities.

Mathematically, the normal distribution is defined as

$$f(X) = \frac{1}{\sigma \sqrt{2\pi}} (e)^{-(X-\mu)^2/2\sigma^2}$$

where π and e are constants ($\pi = 3.1416$ and $e = 2.7183$), and μ and σ are the mean and standard deviation, respectively, of the distribution. Given that μ and σ are known, the ordinate $[f(X)]$ for any value of X is obtained simply by substituting μ, σ, and X in the equation and solving the equation. This is not nearly as difficult as it looks, but in practice it is unlikely that you will ever have to make the calculations. The cumulative form of this distribution is tabled, and we can simply read the information we need from the table.

Those of you who have had a course in calculus may recognize that the area under the curve between any two values of X (say from X_1 to X_2), and thus the probability that a randomly drawn score will fall within that interval, could be found by integrating the function over the range from X_1 to X_2. Those of you who have not had such a course can take comfort from the fact that tables are readily available in which this work has already been done—or by using the tables we can easily do the work ourselves. Such a table appears in Appendix z.

You might wonder at this point why anyone would want to table such a distribution in the first place. Just because a distribution is common (or at least commonly assumed) doesn't automatically suggest a reason for wanting an appendix telling all about it. The reason is quite simple. By using Appendix z, we can readily calculate the probability that a score drawn at random from the population will have a value lying between any two specified points (X_1 and X_2). Thus by using statistical tables we can make probability statements that answer a variety of questions.

3.1   THE STANDARD NORMAL DISTRIBUTION

Standard normal distribution

A problem arises when we try to table the normal distribution, however, because the distribution depends upon the values of the mean and standard deviation (μ and σ) of the distribution. Thus to do the job right, we would have to make up a different table for every possible combination of the values of μ and σ. Solving this problem is quite simple. What we actually have in the table is the **standard normal distribution**, which has a mean of 0 and a standard deviation and variance of 1. Such a distribution is often designated as $N(0, 1)$, where N refers to the fact that it is normal, 0 is the value of μ, and 1 is the value of σ^2. [Thus the more general expression is $N(\mu, \sigma^2)$.] Given the standard normal distribution in the appendix and a set of rules for transforming any normal distribution to standard form, and vice versa, we can use Appendix z to find the areas under any normal distribution.

Consider the distribution shown in Figure 3.6. This distribution has a mean of 50 and a standard deviation of 10 (variance of 100). It represents the distribution of *an entire population* of Total Behavior Problem scores from the Achenbach Youth Self-Report form, of which the data in Figures 3.3 and 3.4 are a sample. If we knew something about the areas under the curve in Figure 3.6, we could say something about the probability of various values of Behavior Problem scores and could identify, for example, those scores that are so high that they are obtained by only 5% or 10% of the population.

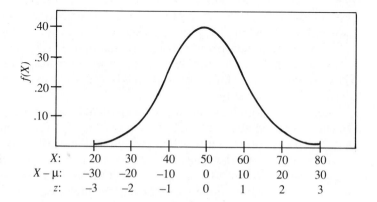

FIGURE 3.6
Normal distribution with various transformations on the abscissa

Because the only tables of the normal distribution that are readily available are those of the *standard* normal distribution, before we can answer questions about the probability that an individual will get a score above some particular value, we must first transform the distribution in Figure 3.6 (or at least specific points along it) to a standard normal distribution; that is, we want to be able to say that a score of X_i from $N(50, 100)$ (i.e., a normal distribution with a mean of 50 and a variance of 100) is comparable to a score of z_i from $N(0, 1)$. Then anything that is true of z_i is also true of X_i, and z and X are comparable variables.

From Chapter 2 we know that subtracting a constant from each score in a set of scores reduces the mean of the set by that constant. Thus, if we subtract 50 (the mean) from all of the values for X, the new mean will be $50 - 50 = 0$. [More generally, the distribution of values of $(X - \mu)$ has a mean of 0.] The effect of this transformation is shown in the second set of values for the abscissa in Figure 3.6. We are halfway there since we now have the mean down to 0, although the standard deviation (σ) is still 10. We also know from Chapter 2 that if we divide all values of a variable by a constant (e..g, 10), we divide the standard deviation by that constant. Thus, if we divide $(X - \mu)$ by 10, the standard deviation will now be $10/10 = 1$, which is just what we wanted. We will call this transformed distribution z and can define it, on the basis of what we have done, as

$$z = \frac{X - \mu}{\sigma}$$

For our particular case, where $\mu = 50$ and $\sigma = 10$,

$$z = \frac{X - \mu}{\sigma} = \frac{X - 50}{10}$$

The third set of values (labeled z) for the abscissa in Figure 3.6 shows the effect of this transformation. Notice that aside from a linear transformation[†] of the numerical values, the data have not been changed in any way. The distribution has the same shape, and the observations stand in the same relation to each other as they did before the transformation. It should not come as a great surprise that changing the unit of measurement does not change the shape of the distribution or the relative standing of observations. Whether we measure the quantity of soft drinks that people consume per week in ounces or in milliliters really makes no difference in the relative standings of people. It just changes the numerical values on the abscissa. It is important to realize exactly what converting X to z has accomplished. A score that used to be 60 is now 1; that is, a score that used to be one standard deviation (10 points) above the mean remains one standard deviation above the mean but is now given a new value of 1. A score of 45, which was 0.5 standard deviation *below* the mean, is now given the value of -0.5, and so on. In other words, a **z score** represents the number of standard deviations that X_i is above or below the mean—a positive z score being above the mean and a negative z score being below the mean.

z score

The equation for z is completely general. We can transform any distribution to a distribution of z scores simply by applying this equation. However, keep in mind the

---

[†]A linear transformation involves only multiplication (or division) of X by a constant and/or adding (or subtracting) a constant to X. Such a transformation leaves the relationship among the values unaffected. In other words, it does not distort values at one part of the scale more than values at another part. Changing units from inches to centimeters is a good example of a linear transformation.

point that was just made. The *shape* of the distribution is unaffected by the transformation. That means that *if the distribution was not normal before it was transformed, it will not be normal afterward.* Some people believe that they can "normalize" (in the sense of producing a normal distribution) their data by transforming them to z. It just won't work.

3.2 USING THE TABLES OF THE STANDARD NORMAL DISTRIBUTION

As I have mentioned, the standard normal distribution is extensively tabled. Such a table can be found in Appendix z, part of which is reproduced in Table 3.1. To see how we can use this table, consider the normal distribution represented in Figure 3.7. This might represent the standardized distribution of the Behavior Problem scores as seen in Figure 3.6. Suppose we wish to know how much of the area under the curve is above one standard deviation from the mean, if the total area under the curve is taken to be 1.00. We have already seen that z scores represent standard deviations from the mean, and thus we know that we want to find the area above $z = 1$.

Only the positive half of the normal distribution is tabled. Because the distribution is symmetric, any information given about a positive value of z applies equally to the corresponding negative value of z. In Table 3.1 we find the row corresponding to $z = 1.00$. Reading across that row, we can see that the area from the *mean to $z = 1$* is 0.3413, that the area in the *larger portion* is 0.8413, and that the area in the *smaller portion* is 0.1587. (If you visualize the distribution being divided into the segment below $z = 1$ [the unshaded part of Figure 3.7] and the segment above $z = 1$ [the shaded part], the meaning of the terms *larger portion* and *smaller portion* becomes obvious.) Thus the answer to our original question is 0.1587. Because we already have equated the terms *area* and *probability*, we can now say that if we sample a child at random from the population of children and if Behavior Problem scores are normally distributed, then the probability that the child will score more than one standard deviation above the mean of the population (i.e., above 60) is .1587. Because the distribution is symmetric, we also know that the probability that a child will score more than one standard deviation *below* the mean of the population is also .1587.

Now suppose that we want the probability that the child will be more than one standard deviation (10 points) from the mean *in either direction*. Finding this probability is a simple matter of summing areas. Because we know that the normal distribution is symmetric, then the area below $z = -1$ will be the same as the area above $z = +1$. We already know that the areas we are interested in are each 0.1587. Then the total area outside $z = \pm 1$ must be $0.1587 + 0.1587 = 0.3174$. The converse is also true. If the area outside $z = \pm 1$ is 0.3174, then the area between $z = +1$ and $z = -1$ is equal to $1 - 0.3174 = 0.6826$. Thus the probability that a child will score between 40 and 60 is .6826.

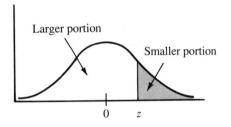

TABLE 3.1
Normal distribution
(portion of Appendix z)

z	Mean to z	Larger Portion	Smaller Portion	z	Mean to z	Larger Portion	Smaller Portion
0.00	0.0000	0.5000	0.5000	0.45	0.1736	0.6736	0.3264
0.01	0.0040	0.5040	0.4960	0.46	0.1772	0.6772	0.3228
0.02	0.0080	0.5080	0.4920	0.47	0.1808	0.6808	0.3192
0.03	0.0120	0.5120	0.4880	0.48	0.1844	0.6844	0.3156
0.04	0.0160	0.5160	0.4840	0.49	0.1879	0.6879	0.3121
0.05	0.0199	0.5199	0.4801	0.50	0.1915	0.6915	0.3085
...	...	...	...	...	...	...	...
0.97	0.3340	0.8340	0.1660	1.42	0.4222	0.9222	0.0788
0.98	0.3365	0.8365	0.1635	1.43	0.4236	0.9236	0.0764
0.99	0.3389	0.8389	0.1611	1.44	0.4251	0.9251	0.0749
1.00	0.3413	0.8413	0.1587	1.45	0.4265	0.9265	0.0735
1.01	0.3438	0.8438	0.1562	1.46	0.4279	0.9279	0.9721
1.02	0.3461	0.8461	0.1539	1.47	0.4292	0.9292	0.0708
1.03	0.3485	0.8485	0.1515	1.48	0.4306	0.9306	0.0694
1.04	0.3508	0.8508	0.1492	1.49	0.4319	0.9319	0.0681
1.05	0.3531	0.8531	0.1469	1.50	0.4332	0.9332	0.0668
...	...	...	...	...	...	...	...
1.95	0.4744	0.9744	0.0256	2.40	0.4918	0.9918	0.0082
1.96	0.4750	0.9750	0.0250	2.41	0.4920	0.9920	0.0080
1.97	0.4756	0.9756	0.0244	2.42	0.4922	0.9922	0.0078
1.98	0.4761	0.9761	0.0239	2.43	0.4925	0.9925	0.0075
1.99	0.4767	0.9767	0.0233	2.44	0.4927	0.9927	0.0073
2.00	0.4772	0.9772	0.0228	2.45	0.4929	0.9929	0.0071
2.01	0.4778	0.9778	0.0222	2.46	0.4931	0.9931	0.0069
2.02	0.4783	0.9783	0.0217	2.47	0.4932	0.9932	0.0068
2.03	0.4788	0.9788	0.0212	2.48	0.4934	0.9934	0.0066
2.04	0.4793	0.9793	0.0207	2.49	0.4936	0.9936	0.0064
2.05	0.4798	0.9798	0.0202	2.50	0.4938	0.9938	0.0062

To extend this procedure, consider the situation in which we want to know the probability that a score will be between 30 and 40. A little arithmetic will show that this is simply the probability of falling between 1.0 standard deviation below the mean and 2.0 standard deviations below the mean. This situation is diagrammed in Figure 3.8. (*Hint:* It is always wise to draw simple diagrams such as Figure 3.8. They eliminate many errors and make clear the area(s) for which you are looking.)

From Appendix z we know that the area from the mean to $z = -2.0$ is 0.4772 and from the mean to $z = -1.0$ is 0.3413. The difference in these two areas must represent the area between $z = -2.0$ and $z = -1.0$. This area is $0.4772 - 0.3413 = 0.1359$. Thus the probability that Behavior Problem scores drawn at random from a normally distributed population will be between 30 and 40 is .1359.

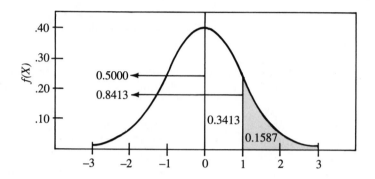

FIGURE 3.7
Illustrative areas under the normal curve

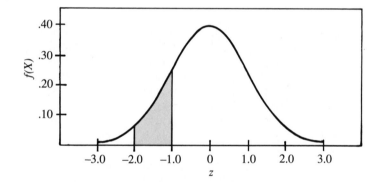

FIGURE 3.8
Area between 1.0 and 2.0 standard deviations below the mean

3.3 SETTING PROBABLE LIMITS ON AN OBSERVATION

For a final example, consider the situation in which we want to identify limits within which we have some specified degree of certainty that a given child sampled at random will fall. In other words, we want to make a statement of the form "If I draw a child at random from this population, 95% of the time her score will lie between ____ and ____." From Figure 3.9 you can see the limits we want—the limits that include 95% of the scores in the population.

If we are looking for the limits within which 95% of the scores fall, we also are looking for the limits beyond which the remaining 5% of the scores fall. To rule out this remaining 5%, we want to find that value of z that cuts off 2.5% at each end ("tail") of the distribution. (We would not need to use symmetric limits, but we typically do because they usually make the most sense and produce the shortest interval.) From Appendix z we see that these values are $z = \pm 1.96$. Thus we can say that 95% of the

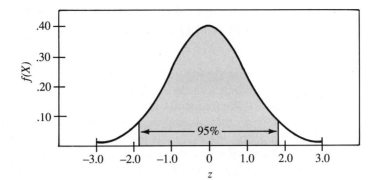

FIGURE 3.9
Values of z that enclose 95% of the Behavior Problem scores

time a child's score sampled at random will fall between 1.96 standard deviations above the mean and 1.96 standard deviations below the mean.

Because we generally want to express our answers in terms of raw Behavior Problem scores rather than z scores, we must do a little more work. To obtain the raw score limits, we simply work the formula for z backward, solving for X instead of z. Thus if we want to state the limits within which 95% of the population falls, we want to find those scores that are 1.96 standard deviations above or below the mean of the population. This can be written as

$$z = \frac{X - \mu}{\sigma}$$

$$\pm 1.96 = \frac{X - \mu}{\sigma}$$

$$X - \mu = \pm 1.96\sigma$$

$$X = \mu \pm 1.96\sigma$$

where the values of X corresponding to ($\mu + 1.96\sigma$) and ($\mu - 1.96\sigma$) represent the limits we seek. For our example the limits would be

Limits $= 50 \pm (1.96)(10) = 50 \pm 19.6 = 30.4$ and 69.6

Thus the probability is .95 that a child's score (X) chosen at random would be between 30.4 and 69.6. We may not be very interested in low scores, because they don't represent problems. But anyone with a socre of 69.6 is a problem to someone. Only 2.5% of children score that high or higher.

What we have just discussed is closely related to, but not quite the same as, what we will later consider under the heading of confidence limits. The major difference is that here we knew the population mean and were trying to estimate where a single observation (X) would fall. When we discuss confidence limits in Chapter 7, we will have a sample mean (or some other statistic) and will want to set limits that have a .95 probability of bracketing the population mean (or some other relevant parameter). You do not need to know anything about confidence limits at this point. I simply mention the issue to forestall any confusion in the future.

3.4   MEASURES RELATED TO z

Standard scores

We have already seen that the z formula can be used to convert a distribution with any mean and variance to a distribution with a mean of 0 and a standard deviation (and variance) of 1. We frequently refer to such transformed scores as **standard scores**. There are, however, other transformational scoring systems with particular properties, some of which people use every day without realizing what they are.

A good example of such a scoring system is the common IQ. The raw scores from an IQ test are routinely transformed to a distribution with a mean of 100 and a standard deviation of 15 (or 16 in the case of the Binet). Knowing this, you can readily convert an individual's IQ (e.g., 120) to his position in terms of standard deviations above or below the mean (i.e., you can calculate his z score). Because IQ scores are more or less normally distributed, you can then convert z into a percentile measure by using Appendix z.

Some other common examples are the nationally administered examinations, such as the SAT. In these cases the raw scores are transformed by the producers of the test and are reported as coming from a distribution with a mean of 500 and a standard deviation of 100 (at least when the tests were first developed). Such a scoring system is easy to devise. We start by converting raw scores to z scores (on the basis of the raw score mean and standard deviation). We then convert the z scores to the particular scoring system we have in mind. Thus

$$\text{New score} = \text{New S.D.}(z) + \text{New mean}$$

where z represents the z score corresponding to the individual's raw score. For the SAT,

$$\text{New score} = 100(z) + 500$$

KEY TERMS

Normal distribution (introduction)

Abscissa (introduction)

Ordinate (introduction)

Standard normal distribution (3.1)

z score (3.1)

Standard scores (3.4)

EXERCISES

3.1   Assume that the following data represent a population with $\mu = 4$ and $\sigma = 1.63$:

$$X = 1 \quad 2 \quad 2 \quad 3 \quad 3 \quad 3 \quad 4 \quad 4 \quad 4 \quad 4 \quad 5 \quad 5 \quad 5 \quad 6 \quad 6 \quad 7$$

(a) Plot the distribution as given.

(b) Convert the distribution in (a) to a distribution of $X - \mu$.

(c) Convert the distribution in (b) to a distribution of z.

3.2   Using the distribution in Exercise 3.1, calculate z scores for $X = 2.5$, 6.2, and 9. (Use μ and σ as given.) Interpret these results.

3.3   Suppose we want to study the errors found in the performance of a simple task. We take a piggy bank containing approximately $10 in pennies and ask a large number of subjects to count the pennies. We find that the mean number of pennies reported is 975 with a standard deviation of 15. Assume that the distribution of counts is normal.

(a) What percentage of the counts will lie between 960 and 990?

(b) What percentage of the counts will lie below 975?

(c) What percentage of the counts will lie below 990?

3.4   Using the example from Exercise 3.3,

(a) what two values of X (the count) would encompass the middle 50% of the results?

(b) 75% of the counts would be less than _____.

(c) 95% of the counts would be between _____ and _____.

3.5   The head of my department has just finished counting the pennies, and he claims that there are only 950 pennies in the pile. Is this count a reasonable answer if he was counting conscientiously? Why or why not?

3.6   A set of reading scores for fourth-grade children has a mean of 25 and a standard deviation of 5. A set of scores for ninth-grade children has a mean of 30 and a standard deviation of 10. Assume that the distributions are normal.

(a) Draw a rough sketch of these data, putting both groups in the same figure.

(b) What percentage of fourth graders score better than the average ninth grader?

(c) What percentage of the ninth graders score worse than the average fourth grader? (We will come back to the idea behind these calculations when we study power in Chapter 8.)

3.7   Under what conditions would the answers to (b) and (c) of Exercise 3.6 be equal?

3.8   A certain diagnostic test is indicative of problems only if a child scores at or below the 10th percentile. If the mean score is 150 with a standard deviation of 30 and if scores are normally distributed, what would the diagnostically meaningful cutoff be?

3.9   A dean must distribute salary raises for next year. She has decided that the mean raise is to be $2000, the standard deviation of raises is to be $400, and the distribution is normal.

(a) The highest 10% of the faculty will have a raise equal to or greater than $_____.

(b) The 5% of the faculty who have not done anything useful in years will receive no more than $_____ each.

3.10 We have sent out everyone in a large introductory psychology course to check whether people use seat belts. Each has been told to look at 100 cars and to count the number of people wearing seat belts. The number found by any given student is considered that student's score. The mean score for the class is 30 with a standard deviation of 7.

(a) Diagram this distribution, assuming that the counts are normally distributed.

(b) A student who has done very little work all year has reported finding 50 users (out of 100). Do we have reason to suspect that the student just made up a number rather than actually counting?

3.11 Several years ago a friend produced a diagnostic test of language problems. A score on her scale is obtained simply by counting the number of language constructions (e.g., plural, negative, passive) that the child produces correctly in response to specific prompts from the person administering the test. The test has a mean of 48 and a standard deviation of 7. Parents have trouble understanding the meaning of a score on this scale, and my friend wants to convert the scores to a mean of 80 and a standard deviation of 10 (to make them more like the kinds of grades parents are used to). How should she go about this task?

3.12   Unfortunately, the whole world is not built upon the principle of a normal distribution. In the example in Exercise 3.11, the real distribution is badly skewed because most children do not have language problems and therefore produce all constructions correctly.
  (a) Diagram how this distribution might look.
  (b) How would you go about finding the cutoff for the bottom 10% if the distribution is not normal?

3.13   Make up a sample of data that are markedly skewed, and demonstrate that using the normal distribution to find the theoretical cutoff for the top 15% of the scores is misleading.

3.14   Make up a simple set of data that are at least reasonably normal. What percentage of the scores lie beyond 1.5 standard deviations from the mean, and how does this result compare to the theoretical value?

3.15   Assuming that the Behavior Problem scores discussed in this chapter come from a population with a mean of 50 and a standard deviation of 10, what would be a diagnostically meaningful cutoff if you wanted to identify children who score in the highest 2% of the population?

CHAPTER FOUR

SAMPLING DISTRIBUTIONS AND HYPOTHESIS TESTING

OBJECTIVES *To lay the groundwork for the procedures discussed in this book by examining the general theory of hypothesis testing and describing specific concepts as they apply to all hypothesis tests.*

CONTENTS

In chapter 2 we examined a number of different statistics and saw how they might be used to describe a set of data or to represent the frequency of the occurrence of some event. Although the description of the data is important and fundamental to any analysis, it is not sufficient to answer many of the most interesting problems we encounter. In a typical experiment, we might treat one group of people in a special way and wish to see whether their scores differ from the scores of people in general. Or we might offer a treatment to one group but not to a control group and wish to compare the means of the two groups on some variable. Descriptive statistics will not tell us, for example, whether the difference between a sample mean and a hypothetical population mean, or the difference between two obtained sample means, is small enough to be explained by chance alone or whether it represents a true difference that might be attributable to the effect of our experimental treatment(s).

Statisticians frequently use phrases such as "variability due to chance" or "sampling error" and assume that you know what they mean. Probably you do; but if you do not, you are headed for confusion in the remainder of this book unless we spend a minute clarifying the meaning of these terms. We will begin with a simple example.

In Chapter 3 we considered the distribution of Total Behavior Problems scores from Achenbach's Youth Self-Report form. As you may recall, Total Behavior Problems scores are normally distributed in the population (i.e., the complete population of such scores would be normally distributed) with a population mean (μ) of 50 and a population standard deviation (σ) of 10. We know that children show different levels of problem behaviors and therefore have different scores, and that if we took a sample of children their sample mean would probably not equal exactly 50. One sample might have a mean of 49.1, whereas a second might have one of 52.3. The actual sample mean would depend on the particular children who happened to be included in it. This expected variability from sample to sample is what we mean when we speak of "variability due to chance." We are referring to the fact that statistics (in this case, means) obtained from samples naturally vary from one sample to another.

Sampling error   Along the same lines, the phrase **sampling error** is often used in this context as a synonym for variability due to chance. It indicates that the value of a sample statistic probably will be in error (i.e., will deviate from the parameter that it is estimating) as a result of the particular observations that happened to be included in the sample. In this context, "error" does not imply carelessness or mistakes. In the case of behavior problems, one random sample might happen to include an unusually obnoxious child, whereas another sample might happen to include an unusual number of relatively well-behaved children.

4.1   TWO SIMPLE EXAMPLES INVOLVING BEHAVIOR PROBLEMS AND RUDE MOTORISTS

One of the useful scales included on Achenbach's Youth Self-Report form is the Total Behavior Problems score, which, for a population of normal children, as I have said, has a mean of 50 and a standard deviation of 10. Suppose we have a sample of five children who we know to have been under a considerable amount of stress at home because of parental divorce, and we want to study this sample to see if children who are under high levels of stress also show an elevated level of behavior problems. Suppose further that these five children filled out the Youth Self-Report form, and the mean for this sample truned out to be 56, which is a full 6 points above the mean of a population of normal children. What we really want to know is whether the difference between 56 and 50 is small enough to be attributable to the chance variation we would normally expect if the scores were sampled from normal children, or whether the difference is sufficiently large to lead us to conclude that the population of children from which we sampled has a mean higher than the mean of a population of normal children. Put another way, we want to test the hypothesis that the mean of the population from which we sampled (μ) is 50 against the alternative hypothesis that μ is greater than 50. The answer to this specific question will be discussed in detail in Chapter 7. Here we are concerned only with general issues involved in the approach to such question.

A second example comes from a study by Doob and Gross (1968), who investigated the influence of perceived social status. They found that if an old, beat-up (low-status) car failed to start when a stoplight turned green, 84% of the time the driver of the second car in line honked the horn. However, when the stopped car was an expensive, high-status car, only 50% of the time did the following driver honk. These results could be explained in one of two ways:

1. The difference between 84% in one sample and 50% in a second sample is attributable to sampling error (random variability among samples), and therefore we cannot conclude that perceived social status influences horn-honking behavior.

2. The difference between 84% and 50% is large, a difference not attributable to sampling error (random variability among samples), and therefore people are less likely to honk at drivers of high-status cars.

Although the statistical calculations required to answer this question are different from those used to answer the behavior problem (because that one dealt with means and this one deals with proportions), the underlying logic is fundamentally the same.

Hypothesis testing These examples of behavior problems and horn-honking behavior are two of the kinds of questions that fall under the heading of **hypothesis testing**. This chapter presents the theory of hypothesis testing as generally as possible, without becoming involved in the specific techniques or properties of any particular test.

The theory of hypothesis testing is so important in all that follows that a thorough understanding of it is essential. Many students who have had one or more courses in statistics and know how to run a number of different statistical tests still do not have a basic knowledge of what it is they are doing. As a result they have difficulty interpreting statistical tables and must learn every new procedure in a step-by-step, rote fashion. This chapter is designed to avoid that difficulty by presenting the theory in its most general sense, without using any formulas. You can learn the formulas later, after you understand why you might want to use them. Professional statisticians might fuss over the looseness of the definitions, but any looseness will be set right in subsequent chapters. Others may object that we are considering hypothesis testing before we consider the statistical procedures that produce the test. That is precisely the intent. The material covered here cuts across all statistical tests and can be discussed independently of them. By separating the material in this way, you are free to concentrate on the underlying principles without worrying about the mechanics of calculation.

The important issue in hypothesis testing is to find some way of deciding whether we are looking at a small chance fluctuation from a true underlying mean of 50, to use the behavior problem example, or whether the deviation from 50 is large enough to suggest that stressed children present, on average, more behavior problems than normal children. To answer this kind of question, we have to use what are called **sampling**

Sampling distributions **distributions,** which tell us specifically what degree of sample-to-sample variability we can expect by chance as a function of sampling error.

4.2   SAMPLING DISTRIBUTIONS

The most basic concept underlying all statistical tests is that of the sampling distribution of a statistic. It is fair to say that if we did not have sampling distributions, we would not have any statistical tests. Roughly speaking, sampling distributions tell us what values we might (or might not) expect to obtain for a particular statistic under a set of predefined conditions (e.g., what the obtained mean of five children might be *if* the true mean of the population from which those children come is 50.0). As such, sampling distributions provide the opportunity to evaluate the likelihood (given the value of a sample statistic) of whether or not such predefined conditions actually exist.

Basically, the sampling distribution of a statistic can be thought of as the distribution of values obtained for that statistic over repeated sampling (i.e., running the experiment, or drawing samples, an unlimited number of times). Although sampling distributions are almost always derived mathematically, it is easier to understand what they represent if we consider how they could, in theory, be derived empirically with a simple sampling experiment.

We will take as an illustration the sampling distribution of the mean, because it is the most easily understood and relates directly to the example of behavior problems. The **sampling distribution of the mean** is nothing but the distribution of the means of an infinite number of random samples drawn under certain specified conditions (e.g., under the condition that the true mean of our population is 50 and the standard deviation is 10). Suppose that we have a population with a known mean ($\mu = 50$). Further suppose that we draw a very large number (theoretically an infinite number) of random samples from this population, each sample consisting of five scores. For each sample we will calculate its mean, and when we finish drawing all of the samples, we will plot the distribution of these means. Such a distribution would be a sampling distribution of the mean and might look like the one presented in Figure 4.1. We can see from this figure that sample means between 48 and 52, for example, are likely to occur when we sample five children at random. We can also see that it is extremely unlikely that we would draw from this population a sample of five observations that has a sample mean as high as 70, although there is some (quite small) probability of doing so. The fact that we know the kinds of values to expect for the mean of a sample drawn from this population is now going to allow us to turn the question around and ask if an obtained sample mean can be taken as evidence in favor of the hypothesis that we actually are sampling from this population.

Sampling distribution of the mean

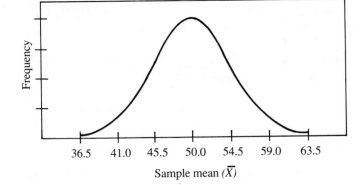

FIGURE 4.1
Distribution of sample means of behavior problems, each based on $N = 5$ scores

4.3 HYPOTHESIS TESTING

We do not go around obtaining sampling distributions, either mathematically or empirically, simply because they are interesting to look at. We have important reasons for doing so. The usual reason is that we want to test some hypothesis. As mentioned before, I have found that a random sample of five highly stressed children has a mean behavior problem score of 56. I would like to test the hypothesis that such a sample mean could reasonably have arisen had I drawn my sample from a population in which $\mu = 50$. This is another way of saying that I want to know whether the mean behavior problem score of stressed children is different from the mean behavior problem score of normal children. The only way I can test such a hypothesis is to have some idea of the probability of obtaining a sample mean of 56 *if* I were actually sampling observations from a population in which $\mu = 50$. The answer to this question is precisely what a sampling distribution is designed to provide.

Suppose that we obtained (constructed) the sampling distribution of the mean for samples of five children from a population whose mean μ is 50. (This is actually the distribution plotted in Figure 4.1). Suppose further that we then determined from that distribution the probability of a sample mean as high as 56. For the sake of argument, suppose that this probability is .15. My reasoning can then go as follows: "If I in fact did sample from a population with $\mu = 50$, the probability of obtaining a sample mean as high as 56 is .15—a fairly likely event. Because a sample mean this high is often obtained from a population with a mean of 50, I have no reason to doubt that this sample came from such a population."

On the other hand, suppose that I obtained a sample mean of 62 and that I calculated from the sampling distribution that the probability of a sample mean as high as 62 was only .004. My argument can then go like this: "If I in fact did sample from a population with $\mu = 50$ the probability of obtaining a sample mean as high as 62 is only .004—an unlikely event. Because a sample mean this high is unlikely to be obtained from such a population, I can reasonably conclude that this sample probably came from some other population (one whose mean is not 50)."

It is important to realize precisely what has been done in this example, because the logic is typical of most tests of hypotheses. The actual test consisted of several stages:

Research hypothesis

1. I wished to test the hypothesis, often called the **research hypothesis**, that children under stress are more likely than normal children to exhibit behavior problems.

Null hypothesis (H_0)

2. I set up the hypothesis (called the **null hypothesis, H_0**) that the sample was in fact drawn from a population whose mean, denoted μ_0, equals 50. This is the hypothesis that stressed children do not differ from normal children in terms of behavior problems.

3. I then obtained the sampling distribution of the mean under the assumption that H_0 (the null hypothesis) is true (i.e., I obtained the sampling distribution of the mean from a population with $\mu_0 = 50$).

4. I obtained a random sample of children under stress.

5. Given the sampling distribution I calculated the probability of a mean *at least as large* as my actual sample mean.

6. On the basis of this probability, I made a decision. I either rejected or failed to reject H_0. Because H_0 states that $\mu = 50$, rejection of H_0 represents a belief that $\mu > 50$, although the actual value of μ remains unspecified.

The preceding discussion is oversimplifed in the sense that we would generally prefer to test the research hypothesis that children under stress are *different from* (rather than just *higher than*) other children, but we will return to this point shortly. It is also oversimplified in the sense that in practice we also would need to take into account (either directly or by estimation) the value of σ^2, the population variance, and N, the sample size. However, the logic of the approach is representative of the logic of most, if not all, statistical tests. In each case we begin with a research hypothesis, set up the null hypothesis, construct the sampling distribution of the particular statistic on the assumption that H_0 is true, collect some data, compare the sample statistic to that distribution, and reject or retain H_0 depending upon the probability, under H_0, of a sample statistic as extreme as the one we have obtained.

4.4   THE NULL HYPOTHESIS

As we have seen, the concept of the null hypothesis plays a crucial role in testing hypotheses. Students are frequently puzzled by the fact that we set up a hypothesis that is directly counter to what we hope to show. For example, if we hope to demonstrate the research hypothesis that college students do not come from a population with a mean self-confidence score of 100, we immediately set up the null hypothesis that they do. Or, if we hope to demonstrate the validity of a research hypothesis that the means (μ_1 and μ_2) of the populations from which two samples are drawn are different, we state the null hypothesis that the population means are equal (or, equivalently, that $\mu_1 - \mu_2 = 0$). (The phrase "null hypothesis" is most easily seen in this second example, in which it refers to the hypothesis that the difference between the two populations means is zero, or null.) We use the null hypothesis for several reasons. The philosophical argument known as the *method of contradiction*, used by R. A. Fisher when he first introduced the concept, is that we can never prove a hypothesis to be true but we can sometimes prove one to be false. Observing that 3000 people have two arms does not prove the statement, "Every person has two arms." Finding one person with one arm or no arms, however, does disprove the statement beyond any shadow of doubt. Although one might argue with Fisher's basic position—and many people have—the null hypothesis retains its dominant place in statistics.

A second and more practical reason for employing the null hypothesis is that it provides a starting point for any statistical test. Consider the case in which you wish to show that the mean self-confidence score of college students is greater than 100. Suppose further that you were granted the privilege of proving the truth of some hypothesis. What hypothesis are you going to test? Should you test the hypothesis that $\mu = 101$, or maybe that $\mu = 112$; or how about $\mu = 113$? The point is that you do not have a *specific* hypothesis in mind, and without one you cannot construct the sampling distribution that you need. If, however, you start by assuming $H_0 : \mu = 100$, you can immediately set about obtaining the sampling distribution for $\mu = 100$ and then, with luck, reject that hypothesis and conclude that the mean score of college students is greater than 100, which is what you wanted to show in the first place.

STATISTICAL CONCLUSIONS

When the data differ markedly from what we would expect if the null hypothesis were true, we simply reject the null hypothesis and there is no particular disagreement about what our conclusions mean—we conclude that the null hypothesis is false. The interpretation is murkier and more problematic, however, when the data do not lead us to reject the null hypothesis. How are we to interpret a nonrejection? Shall we say that we have "proved" the null hypothesis to be true? Or shall we claim that we can "accept" the null, or that we shall "retain" it, or that we shall "withhold judgment"?

The problem of how to interpret a nonrejected null hypothesis has plagued students in statistics courses for over 50 years, and it will probably continue to do so. The idea that if something is not false then it must be true is too deeply ingrained in common sense to be dismissed lightly.

The one thing on which all statisticians agree is that we can never claim to have "proved" the null hypothesis. As was pointed out, the fact that the next 3000 people we meet all have two arms certainly does not prove the null hypothesis that all people have two arms. In fact we know that many perfectly normal people in the world have fewer than two arms. Failure to reject the null hypothesis often means that we have not collected enough data.

The issue is easier to understand if we use a concrete example. In Chapter 2 we considered an ongoing study by Wagner, Compas, and Howell (1987) designed to evaluate the effectiveness of a program for teaching high-school students to deal with stress. If this study should find that students who participate in such a program had significantly fewer stress-related problems than did students in a control group who did not have the program, then we can, without much debate, conclude that the program was effective. However, if the groups did not differ at some predetermined level of statistical significance, what could we conclude?

We know we cannot conclude from a nonsignificant difference that we have proved that the mean of a population of scores of treatment subjects is the same as the mean of a population of scores of control subjects. The two treatments may in fact lead to subtle differences that we were not able to identify conclusively with our small sample of observations.

Fisher's position was that a nonsignificant result is an inconclusive result. For Fisher, the choice was between rejecting a null hypothesis and suspending judgment. He would have argued that a failure to find a significant difference between conditions could result from the fact that the students who participated in the program handled stress only *slightly* better than did control subjects, or that they handled it only slightly less well, or that there was no difference between the groups. For Fisher, a failure to reject H_0 merely means that our data are insufficient to allow us to choose among these three alternatives; therefore, we must suspend judgment.

A slightly different approach was taken by Neyman and Pearson (1933). They took a much more pragmatic view of the results of an experiment. In our example, Neyman and Pearson would be concerned with the problem faced by the school board, who must decide whether to continue spending money on this stress-management program. The school board would probably not be impressed if we told them that our study was inconclusive and then asked them to give us money to continue operating the program until we had sufficient data to state confidently whether or not the program was beneficial (or harmful). In the Neyman–Pearson position, one either rejects or *accepts* the null hypothesis. When we say that we "accept" a null hypothesis, however, we do not mean that we take it to be proven as true. We simply mean that we will *act as if* it is true, at least until we have more adequate data. Whereas given a nonsignificant result, the ideal school board from Fisher's point of view would continue to support the program until we finally were able to make up our minds, the school board with a Neyman–Pearson perspective would conclude that the available evidence is that the program is not worth supporting and would cut off our funding.

This discussion of the Neyman–Pearson position has been much oversimplified, but it does contain the central issue of their point of view. The debate between Fisher on the one hand and Neyman and Pearson on the other was a lively (and not always civil) one, and present practice contains elements of both viewpoints. Most statisticians prefer to use phrases such as "retain the null hypothesis" and "fail to reject the null hypothesis" because these make clear the tentative nature of a nonrejection. These phrases have a certain Fisherian ring to them. On the other hand, the emphasis on Type II errors (discussed in Section 4.6) is clearly an essential feature of the Neyman–Pearson school. If you are going to choose between two alternatives (accept or reject), then you have to be concerned with the probability of falsely accepting as well as that of falsely rejecting the null hypothesis. Since Fisher would never accept a null hypothesis in the first place, he did not need to worry much about the probability of accepting a false one.

4.5 USING THE NORMAL DISTRIBUTION TO TEST HYPOTHESES

Much of the discussion so far has dealt with statistical procedures that you do not yet know how to use. As mentioned earlier in the chapter, the separation of theory and technique was done deliberately to emphasize the point that the logic and the calculations behind a test are two separate issues. However, we now can use what we already know about the normal distribution to test some simple hypotheses. In the process we can deal with a number of fundamental issues.

One of the important uses of the normal distribution is in testing hypotheses. It can be used to test hypotheses either about individual observations or, more commonly, about sample statistics such as the mean. In this chapter we will deal with individual observations, leaving the question of testing sample statistics until later chapters.

Because we are dealing with only single observations, the sampling distribution invoked here will be the distribution of individual scores (rather than the distribution of means). The basic logic is the same, and we are using an example of individual scores only because it simplifies the explanation and is something with which you have already had experience.

To take a simple example, assume that we know that the mean rate of finger tapping of normal healthy adults is 100 taps in 20 seconds, with a standard deviation of 20, and that tapping speeds are normally distributed in the population. Assume further that we know that the tapping rate is slower among people with certain neurological problems. (In fact, tapping speeds are an important diagnostic indicator of neurological damage, although the difference in rates between left and right hands is more important than the absolute rate.) Finally suppose that an individual who taps at a rate of 70 taps in 20 seconds has just been sent to us. Is his score sufficiently below the mean for us to assume that he did not come from a population of neurologically healthy people? This situation is diagrammed in Figure 4.2, in which the arrow indicates the location of our piece of data (the person's score).

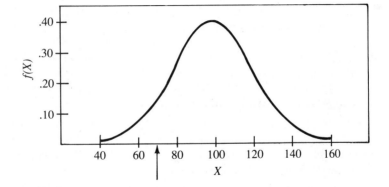

FIGURE 4.2
Location of a person's score on a distribution of scores of neurologically healthy people

The logic of the solution to this problem is the same as the logic of hypothesis testing in general. We will begin by assuming that the individual's score comes from the population of healthy scores. This is the null hypothesis (H_0). If H_0 is true, we automatically know the mean and standard deviation of the population from which he was supposedly drawn (100 and 20, respectively). With this information we are in a position to calculate the probability that a score *as low as* his would be obtained from this population. If the probability is very low, we can reject H_0 and conclude that he did not come from the healthy population. On the other hand, if the probability is not particularly low, then the data represent a reasonable result under H_0, and we would have no reason to doubt its validity and thus no reason to doubt that the person is healthy. Keep in mind that we are not interested in the probability of a score *equal to* 70 (which, because the distribution is continuous, would be infinitely small) but rather with the probability that the score would be as low as (i.e., less than or equal to) 70.

The individual had a score of 70. What we want to know is the probability of obtaining a score *at least as low as* 70 if H_0 were true. This probability is something we already know how to find—it is the area below 70 in Figure 4.2. All we have to do is convert the 70 to a z score and then refer to Appendix z.

$$z = \frac{X - \mu}{\sigma} = \frac{70 - 100}{20} = \frac{-30}{20} = -1.5$$

From Appendix z we can see that the probability of a z score of -1.5 or below is .0668. (This is shown in the table opposite $z = 1.50$ and under the column headed "Smaller Portion.")

At this point we have to become involved in the decision-making aspects of hypothesis testing. We must decide if an event with a probability of .0668 is sufficiently unlikely to cause us to reject H_0. Here we will fall back on arbitrary conventions that have been established over the years. The rationale for these conventions will become clearer as we go along, but keep in mind that they are merely conventions. One convention calls for rejecting H_0 if the probability under H_0 is less than or equal to .05 ($p \leqslant .05$), whereas another convention—more conservative with respect to the probability of rejecting H_0—calls for rejecting H_0 when the probability under H_0 is less than or equal to .01. These values of .05 and .01 are often referred to as the **rejection level**, or **significance level**, of the test. Whenever the probability obtained under H_0 is less than or equal to our predetermined significance level, we will reject H_0. Another way of stating this is to say that any outcome whose probability under H_0 is less than or equal to the significance level falls in the **rejection region**, since such an outcome leads us to reject H_0. For the purpose of setting a standard level of rejection for this book, we will use the .05 level of significance, keeping in mind that some people would consider this level too lenient. When we come to Chapter 8 it will be more apparent why this particular level was chosen over the alternatives.[†] For our particular example we have obtained a probability value of .0668, which is obviously greater than .05. Because we have specified that we will not reject H_0 unless the probability of the data under H_0 less than .05, we must conclude that we have no reason to decide that the person did not come from a population of healthy people. More specifically, we conclude that a finger-tapping rate of 70 could reasonably have come from a population of scores with a mean equal to 100 and standard deviation equal to 20. It is important to stress that we have not shown that this person is healthy, only that we have insufficient reason to believe that he is not. It may be that he is just acquiring the disease and therefore is not as different from normal as is usual for his condition. Or maybe he has the disease at an advanced stage but just happens to be an unusually fast tapper. This example shows why we can never say that we have proved the null

Rejection level, Significance level

Rejection region

[†]The particular view of hypothesis testing described here is the classical one that a null hypothesis is rejected if its probability is less than the predefined significance level and not rejected if its probability is greater than the significance level. Currently, a substantial body of opinion holds that such cut-and-dried rules are inappropriate and that more attention should be paid to the probability value itself. In other words, the classical approach (using a .05 rejection level) would declare $p = .051$ and $p = .150$ to be (equally) "nonsignificant" and $p = .048$ and $p = .00003$ to be (equally) "significant." The alternative view would think of $p = .051$ as "nearly significant" or "marginally significant" ("marginal significance" often refers to $.10 \geqslant p \geqslant .05$) and would think of $p = .0003$ as "very significant." Although this view has much to recommend it, it is not wholeheartedly adopted here. However, most computer programs do print out exact probability levels, and those values, when interpreted judiciously, can be useful. The difficulty comes in defining what is meant by "interpreted judiciously."

hypothesis. We can conclude only that this person does not tap sufficiently slowly for his illness, if he is ill, to be statistically detectable.

Alternative hypothesis (H_1)

Current statistical practice most closely follows the Neyman–Pearson approach, which emphasizes more than Fisher did the fact that we also have an **alternative hypothesis (H_1)** that is contradictory to the null hypothesis (H_0). Thus, if the null hypothesis is

$$H_0: \mu = 100$$

then the alternative hypothesis could be

$$H_1: \mu \neq 100$$

or

$$H_1: \mu < 100$$

or

$$H_1: \mu > 100$$

We will have more to say about these alternative hypotheses shortly.

4.6 TYPE I AND TYPE II ERRORS

Whenever we reach a decision with a statistical test, there is always a chance that our decision was the wrong one. Although this is true of almost all decisions, statistical or otherwise, the statistician has one point in her favor that other decision makers normally lack. She not only makes a decision by some rational process, but she can also specify the probability of that decision being in error. In everyday life we make a decision with only the subjective feeling that we probably made the right choice. (I once had an excellent student who lived under the constant feeling that whatever his choice, it was probably the wrong one.) The statistician on the other hand can state quite precisely the probability that she erroneously rejected H_0 in favor of the alternative hypothesis (H_1) when in fact H_0 was true. This ability to specify the probability of error follows directly from the logic of hypothesis testing.

Consider the finger-tapping example, this time ignoring the person's score. The situation is diagrammed in Figure 4.3, in which the distribution is the distribution of scores from healthy subjects and the shaded portion represents the lowest 5% of the distribution. The actual score that cuts off the lowest 5% is called the critical value.

Critical values

Critical values are those values of X (the variable) that describe the boundary, or boundaries, of the rejection region(s). For this particular example the critical value is 67.[†]

[†]The value of 67 is obtained by solving for that value of X that produces $z = -1.65$ (the cutoff obtained from the tables of the normal distribution).

$$-1.65 = \frac{X - 100}{20}$$

$$-33 = X - 100$$

$$X = 67$$

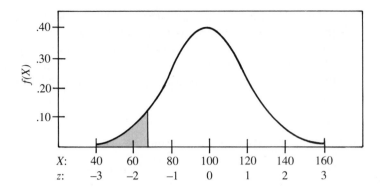

FIGURE 4.3
Lowest 5% of scores
from clinically
healthy people

If we have a decision rule that says to reject H_0 whenever an outcome falls in the lower 5% of the distribution, we will reject H_0 whenever an individual's score falls in the shaded area, that is, whenever a score as low as his has a probability of .05 or less of coming from the population of healthy scores. Yet by the very nature of our procedure, 5% of the scores from healthy people will themselves fall in the shaded portion. Thus, if we actually have sampled a person who is healthy, we stand a 5% chance of his score being in the shaded tail of the distribution, causing us to erroneously reject the null hypothesis. This kind of error (rejecting H_0 when in fact it is true) is called a **Type I error**, and its probability is designated as **α (alpha)**, the size of the rejection region. In the future whenever we represent a probability by α, we will be referring to the probability of a Type I error.

Type I error, α (alpha)

You might feel that a 5% chance of making an error is too great a risk to take, and suggest that we make our criterion much more stringent—for example, by rejecting only the lowest 1% of the distribution. This is a perfectly legitimate procedure, but realize that the more stringent you make your criterion, the more likely you are to make another kind of error—failing to reject H_0 when it is in fact false and H_1 is true. This type of error is called a **Type II error**, and its probability is symbolized by **β (beta)**.

Type II error, β (Beta)

The major difficulty in terms of Type II errors stems from the fact that if H_0 is false, we almost never know what the true distribution (the distribution under H_1) would look like for the population from which our data came. We know only the distribution of scores under H_0. Put in the present context, this is to say that we know the distribution of scores from healthy people but not from nonhealthy people. It may be that people suffering from some neurological disease tap, on average, considerably more slowly than healthy people, or it may be that they tap, on average, only a little more slowly. This situation is illustrated in Figure 4.4, in which the distribution labeled H_0 represents the distribution of scores from healthy subjects (the set of observations expected under the null hypothesis), and the distribution labeled H_1 represents our hypothetical distribution of nonhealthy scores (the distribution under H_1). Remember that the curve H_1 is only hypothetical. We really do not know the location of the non-healthy distribution, other than that it is lower (slower speeds) than the distribution H_0. (I have arbitrarily drawn it with a mean of 80 and a standard deviation of 20.)

The darkly shaded portion in the top half of Figure 4.4 represents the rejection region. Any observation falling in that area (i.e., to the left of about 67) would lead to rejection of the null hypothesis. If the null hypothesis is true, we know that our observation will fall in this area, and we will thus make a Type I error, 5% of the time.

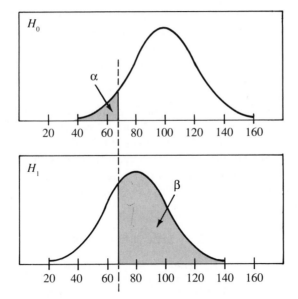

FIGURE 4.4
Areas corresponding to α and β for tapping-speed example

The lightly shaded portion in the bottom half of Figure 4.4 represents the probability (β) of a Type II error. This is a situation in which a person was actually drawn from the nonhealthy population but his score was not sufficiently low to cause us to reject H_0.

In the particular situation illustrated in Figure 4.4, we can calculate β by using the normal distribution to calculate the probability of obtaining a score *greater than* 67 (the critical value) if $\mu = 80$ and $\sigma = 20$. The actual calculation is not important for your understanding of β, and, because this chapter was designed specifically to avoid calculation, I will simply state that this probability (i.e., the area labeled β) is .74. Thus, for this example, 74% of the time when we have a person who is actually nonhealthy (i.e., H_1 is actually true), we will make a Type II error by failing to reject H_0 when it is false—as medical diagnosticians we leave a lot to be desired.

From Figure 4.4 you can see that if we were to reduce the level of α (the probability of a Type I error) from .05 to .01 by moving the rejection region to the left, it would reduce the probability of Type I errors, but it would increase the probability of Type II errors. Setting α at .01 would mean that $\beta = .908$. Thus, there is obviously room for debate over what level of significance to use. The decision rests primarily on your opinion about the relative importance of Type I and Type II errors for the type of study you are conducting. If it is important to avoid Type I errors (such as telling someone that he has a disease when he does not), then you would set a stringent (i.e., small) level of α. If on the other hand you want to avoid Type II errors (telling someone to go home and take an aspirin when in fact he needs immediate treatment), then you might set a fairly high level of α. (Setting α at .20 in this example would reduce β to .44.) Unfortunately, in practice most people choose an arbitrary level of α, such as .05 or .01, and simply ignore β. In some cases this is probably all that you can do. In other cases, however, much more can be done, as we will see in Chapter 8.

I will stress again that Figure 4.4 is hypothetical. I could draw that figure only because I arbitrarily decided that tapping speeds of nonhealthy people were normally distributed with a mean of 80 and a standard deviation of 20. In most everyday situations we do not know the mean and variance of that distribution and can make only educated guesses, thus providing only crude estimates of β. In practice, we can select a value of μ under H_1 that represents the *minimum* difference we would like to be able to detect, since larger differences will have even smaller βs. We will return to this problem in Chapter 8.

From this discussion of Type I and Type II errors, we can summarize the decision-making process with a simple table. Table 4.1 presents the four possible outcomes of an experiment. The cells of this table should be self-explanatory. Notice that the cell in the upper right contains a concept (power) that we have not yet discussed. The **power** of a test is the probability of rejecting H_0 when it is actually false. Because the probability of *failing* to reject a false H_0 is β, then power must equal $1 - \beta$. We will discuss power in more detail in Chapter 8.

Power

TABLE 4.1
Possible outcomes of the decision-making process

	True State of the World	
Decision	H_0 **True**	H_0 **False**
Reject H_0	Type I error $p = \alpha$	Correct decision $p = 1 - \beta = $ Power
Fail to Reject H_0	Correct decision $p = 1 - \alpha$	Type II error $p = \beta$

4.7 ONE- AND TWO-TAILED TESTS

In our example we knew that nonhealthy subjects tapped more slowly than healthy individuals, and therefore we decided to reject H_0 only if a subject tapped too slowly. However, suppose our subject had tapped 180 times in 20 seconds. Although this observation would be exceedingly unlikely in a healthy subject, it did not fall in the rejection region that we just established, which consisted solely of low rates. As a result we find ourselves in the position of not rejecting H_0 in the face of a piece of data that is very unlikely, but not in the direction expected.

How can we protect ourselves against this type of situation (if protection is thought necessary). The answer is to specify, before we run the experiment, that we are going to reject a given percentage (say 5%) of the *extreme* outcomes—both those that are extremely high and those that are extremely low. But if we reject the lowest 5% and the highest 5%, then we would in fact reject H_0 a total of 10% of the time when it is actually true—that is, $\alpha = .10$. Statisticians are rarely willing to work with α as high as .10 and prefer to see it set no higher than .05. The only way to accomplish this is to reject the lowest 2.5% and the highest 2.5%, making a total of 5%.

One-tailed test, Directional test

The situation in which we reject H_0 for only the lowest (or for only the highest) tapping speeds is referred to as a **one-tailed**, or **directional**, **test**, since we make a prediction of the direction in which the individual will differ from the mean and our rejection

**Two-tailed test,
Nondirectional test**

region is located in only one tail of the distribution. When we reject extremes in either tail, we have what is called a **two-tailed**, or **nondirectional**, **test**. Keep in mind, however, that although we gain something with a two-tailed test (the ability to reject the null hypothesis for extreme scores in either direction), we also lose something. A score that would fall in the rejection region of a one-tailed test may not fall in the rejection region of the corresponding two-tailed test, because now we reject only 2.5% in each tail.

In the finger-tapping example, the decision between a one- and a two-tailed test might seem reasonably clear-cut. We know that people with a given disease tap more slowly, and therefore we care only about rejecting H_0 for slow scores—high scores have no diagnostic importance. (Maybe the person is one of those annoying, fidgety types who spends his time tapping on everything in sight and therefore taps rapidly because he has had an unusual amount of practice.) In many other situations, however, we do not know which tail of the distribution is important (or if both are), and we need to guard against extremes in either tail. This situation might arise when we are considering a campaign to persuade children to brush their teeth more often. We might find that the campaign led to an increase in the desired behavior. On the other hand, we might find that kids hate to be told to brush their teeth and therefore brush even less frequently just to spite us. In either case we would want to reject H_0.

In general, two-tailed tests are far more common than one-tailed tests. There are several reasons for this. First of all the investigator may have no idea what the data will look like and therefore has to be prepared for any eventuality. Although this situation is rare, it does occur in some exploratory work.

Another common reason for preferring two-tailed tests is that the investigator is reasonably sure that the data will come out one way, but wishes to cover himself in the event that he is wrong. This type of situation arises more often than you might think. (Carefully formed hypotheses have an annoying habit of being phrased in the wrong direction, for reasons that seem so obvious after the event.) A frequent question that arises when the data may come out the other way around is, "Why not plan to run a one-tailed test and then, if the data come out the other way, just change your test to a two-tailed test?" This kind of question arises from people who have no intention of being devious, but just haven't thought through the logic of what they are suggesting. If you start an experiment with the extreme 5% of the left-hand tail as your rejection region and then turn around and reject any outcome that happens to fall in the extreme 2.5% of the right-hand tail, then you are really working at the 7.5% level. In this situation you will reject 5% of the outcomes in one direction (assuming that the data fell in the desired tail), and you are also willing to reject 2.5% of the outcomes in the other direction (when the data are in the unexpected direction). There is no denying that 5% + 2.5% = 7.5%. To put this another way, would you be willing to flip a coin for an ice cream cone when I have called "heads" but have also reserved the right to switch to "tails" after I saw how the coin landed? Or, would you think it fair of me to shout "2 out of 3" when the first coin came up in your favor? You would object to both of these strategies. This is the reason the choice between a one- and a two-tailed test is made before the data are collected. It is also one of the reasons that two-tailed tests are usually chosen.

Although the preceding discussion argues in favor of two-tailed tests and although in this book we generally will confine ourselves to such procedures, no hard and fast rules exist. The final decision depends upon what you already know about the relative severity of different kinds of errors. It is important to keep in mind that with respect to a given tail of a distribution the difference between a one- and a two-tailed test is that the latter just uses a different cutoff. A two-tailed test at $\alpha = .05$ is more liberal than a one-tailed test at $\alpha = .01$.[†]

If you have a sound grasp of the logic of testing hypotheses by using sampling distributions, the remainder of the course will be relatively simple. For any new statistic you encounter, you need ask only two basic questions:

1. How and with which assumptions is it calculated?

2. What does its sampling distribution look like under H_0?

If you know the answers to these two questions, you can carry out your test by calculating the test statistic for the data at hand and comparing that statistic to the sampling distribution. Because the relevant sampling distributions are tabled in the appendices, all you really need to know is which test is appropriate for a particular situation and how to calculate its test statistic.

4.8 TEST STATISTICS AND THEIR SAMPLING DISTRIBUTIONS

Although we have been discussing the sampling distribution of the mean, the entire discussion would have been essentially the same had we dealt instead with the median, the variance, the range, or any other statistic you care to consider. (Technically, the shape of these distributions would be different, but we are deliberately ignoring such issues in this chapter.) The statistics just mentioned are usually referred to as **sample statistics** because they are used to describe a sample. A whole different class of statistics, called **test statistics**, or **inferential statistics**, is associated with specific statistical procedures and each has its own sampling distribution. Test statistics are statistics such as t, F, χ^2, and so on, which you may have run across in the past. If you are not familiar with them, don't worry—we will consider them separately in later chapters. (As I have mentioned, I put this chapter where I did because I did not want anyone

Sample statistics

**Test statistics,
Inferential statistics**

[†] One of the reviewers of this argument phrased the case for two-tailed tests even more strongly. "It is my (minority) belief that what an investigator *expects to be true* has absolutely no bearing *whatsoever* on the issue of one- versus two-tailed tests. Nature couldn't care less what psychologists' theories predict, and will often show patterns/trends in the opposite direction. Since our goal is to know the truth (not to prove we are astute at predicting), our tests must always allow for testing *both* directions. I say *always* do two-tailed tests, and if you are worried about β, jack the sample size up a bit to offset the loss in power" (Bradley, D., personal communication, 1983). I am personally inclined toward his point of view. Nature is notoriously fickle—or else we are notoriously inept at prediction. On the other hand, a second reviewer (Rodgers, personal communication, 1986) takes exception to this position. While acknowledging that Bradley's point is well considered, Rodgers argues, "To generate a theory about how the world works that implies an expected direction of an effect, but then to hedge one's bet by putting some (up to $\frac{1}{2}$) of the rejection region in the tail other than that predicted by the theory, strikes me as both scientifically dumb and slightly unethical.... Theory generation and theory testing are much closer to the proper goal of science than truth searching, and running one-tailed tests is quite consistent with those goals." Obviously, there is room for disagreement on this issue.

to worry about technical issues yet. This chapter will show that the sampling distributions for test statistics are obtained and used in essentially the same way as the sampling distribution of the mean.

As an illustration, consider the sampling distribution of the statistic t, which will be discussed in Chapter 7. For those students who have never heard of the t test, it is sufficient to say that it is often used, among other things, to answer the question of whether two samples were drawn from populations with the same means. Let μ_1 and μ_2 represent the means of the population from which the two samples were drawn. The null hypothesis is that the difference between the two population means is zero—in other words,

$$H_0: \mu_1 - \mu_2 = 0 \quad (\text{or } \mu_1 = \mu_2)$$

If you were extremely patient, you could empirically obtain the sampling distribution of t when H_0 is true by drawing an infinite number of pairs of samples, all from one population (in which case H_0 must be true because μ_1 and μ_2 are the same thing), calculating t for each pair of samples (by methods discussed later), and plotting the resulting values of t. The resulting distribution is the sampling distribution of t when H_0 is true. If we collected a sample of data that produced a particular value of t, we would test the null hypothesis by comparing our sample t to the sampling distribution of t. We would reject the null hypothesis if our t did not look like the kinds of t values that the sampling distribution tells us to expect when the null hypothesis is true.

The preceding paragraph could be rewritten substituting chi-square, F, or any other test statistic in place of t, with only minor changes dealing with how the statistic is calculated. Thus, we see that all sampling distributions can be obtained in basically the same way (calculate and plot an infinite number of statistics by sampling from a known population when H_0 is true). Once you understand this fact, you can view the remainder of the book largely as the elaboration of methods for calculating the desired statistic and ascertaining the characteristics of the appropriate sampling distribution.

KEY TERMS

Sampling error (introduction)

Hypothesis testing (4.1)

Sampling distributions (4.1)

Sampling distribution of the mean (4.2)

Research hypothesis (4.3)

Null hypothesis (H_0) (4.3)

Rejection level (4.5)

Significance level (4.5)

Rejection region (4.5)

Alternative hypothesis (H_1) (4.5)

Critical values (4.6)

Type I error (4.6)

α (alpha) (4.6)

Type II error (4.6)

β (beta) (4.6)

Power (4.6)

One-tailed test (4.7)

Directional test (4.7)

Two-tailed test (4.7)

Nondirectional test (4.7)

Sample statistics (4.8)

Test statistics (4.8)

Inferential statistics (4.8)

EXERCISES

4.1   Suppose someone told you that last night's NHL hockey game resulted in a score of 26 to 13. You would probably decide that he had misread the paper and was discussing something other than a hockey-game score. In effect, you have just tested and rejected a null hypothesis.
(a) What was the null hypothesis?
(b) Outline the hypothesis-testing procedure that you applied.

4.2   Assume that you found that, during the past year, you spent about $2.00 for lunch each day, give or take a quarter or so.
(a) Draw a rough sketch of this distribution of daily expenditures.
(b) If, without looking at the bill, you pay for your lunch with a $5.00 bill and receive $2.75 in change, should you worry that you were overcharged?
(c) Explain the logic of your answer to (b). Include in your answer the null hypothesis (H_0) and the alternative hypothesis (H_1).

4.3   Imagine that you have just invented a statistical test called the "mode test" for testing whether the mode of a population is some value (e.g., 100). The statistic (M) is calculated as

$$M = \frac{\text{Sample mode}}{\text{Sample range}}$$

Describe how you could obtain the sampling distribution of M. (*Note*: This is a fictitious statistic.)

4.4   In the Exercise 4.3, what would we call M in the terminology given in this chapter?

4.5   Describe a situation in daily life in which we routinely test hypotheses without realizing we are doing so.

4.6   Define "sampling error."

4.7   What is the difference between a "distribution" and a "sampling distribution"?

4.8   Give two examples of research hypotheses and state the corresponding null hypotheses.

4.9   What would be a Type I error in Exercise 4.2?

4.10 What would be a Type II error in Exercise 4.2?

4.11 Why might you want to adopt a one-tailed test in Exercise 4.2? Which tail would you choose? What would happen if you chose the wrong tail?

4.12 Describe what we mean by the rejection region and the critical value using the example in Exercise 4.2.

4.13 A recently admitted class of graduate students at a large state university has a mean Graduate Record Exam verbal score of 650 with a standard deviation of 50. (The scores are reasonably normally distributed.) One of the students, who just happens to have a mother on the board of trustees, was admitted with a GRE score of 490. Should the local newspaper editor, who loves scandals, write a scathing editorial?

4.14 Why is such a small standard deviation reasonable in Exercise 4.13?

4.15 Why might (or might not) the GRE scores be normally distributed for the restricted sample (admitted students) in Exercise 4.13?

COMPUTER EXERCISE

4.16 On the data disk is a file named RandUnif.dat. This file contains 10,000 random numbers sampled from a uniformly distributed population having values between 0 and 100. (A uniform distribution is one in which all possible values are equally likely; a histogram of such a distribution would be flat.) The data are arrayed as a 1000 × 11 matrix, meaning that there are 1000 rows with 11 entries per row. The first 10 entries per row are random numbers, and the 11th entry is a variable to be described later.

(a) Using any statistical package, read these data as 1000 cases of 10 variables $(X_1, \ldots, X_{10})$ and plot a histogram or stem-and-leaf display of X_1. This distribution will not be completely flat, even though it came from a uniform distribution. Why might this be? (We are plotting only one of the possible variables because it represents 1000 values from this population. You could modify the programs that follow to read and plot all 10,000 values, but this would be more trouble than it is worth.)

(b) Now plot the sampling distribution of the mean of a sample of 10 numbers. This is easily done by computing the mean of the 10 numbers in each row and then drawing a histogram of these means. We will have more to say about the sampling distribution of the mean in Chapter 7, but examine this distribution here to understand how such a distribution can be derived and roughly what it looks like.

(c) Draw a histogram of the sampling distribution of some other statistic, such as the minimum, maximum, or range of 10 values.

On the disk I have given you the critical commands to carry out (a) and (c) for BMDP, Minitab, SPSS^x, and SAS in files named Random1.BMD, Random1.Min, Random1.SPX, and Random1.SAS, respectively. Other programs would use similar commands. You can modify these programs to do (b) and to produce cleaner or more elaborate output. As with all the programs given in this book, these may require minor modification for your particular computer system. This is most likely to be true for the way in which data files are identified. I have not given programs for statistical packages that run with pull-down menus for reasons given in Chapter 1. They are usually very straightforward.

Basic Concepts of Probability

OBJECTIVES *To develop the concept of probability, present some basic rules for manipulating probabilities, and introduce the binomial distribution and its role in hypothesis testing.*

CONTENTS

I n Chapter 3 we began using the concept of probability. For example, we saw that about 95% of children have behavior problem scores between 30 and 70. Thus, we concluded that if we chose a child at random, the probability that he or she would score between 30 and 70 is .95. When we introduced inferential statistics in Chapter 4, we relied heavily on statements of probability. There we made statements of the form, "If this hypothesis is correct, the probability is only .015 that we would have obtained the data that we actually obtained." If we are to rely on statements of probability, then it is important to explain what we mean by probability and to understand a few basic rules for computing and manipulating probabilities. That is the purpose of this chapter.

The material covered in this chapter has been selected for one of two reasons. Either it applies directly to understanding material presented in the rest of the book, or it allows you to make simple calculations of probabilities that are likely to be useful to you. Material that does not satisfy one of these qualifications has been deliberately omitted. Thus, for example, we will not consider such things as the probability of drawing the queen of hearts, given that 14 cards, including the four of hearts, have already been drawn. Nor will we consider the probability that your desk light will burn out in the next 25 hours of use, given that it has already lasted 250 hours.

Students interested in these topics are encouraged to take a course in probability theory, in which such material can be covered in depth.

5.1 PROBABILITY

Analytic view

The concept of probability can be defined in several different ways; there is not even general agreement about what the word *probability* means. The oldest and most common definition of a probability is what is called the **analytic view.** I have a bag of caramels hidden in my desk drawer. (It is hidden because I have learned not to trust my colleagues.) This bag contains 85 light caramels, which I like, and 15 dark ones, which I save for candy-grubbing colleagues. Being hungry, I reach into the bag and grab a caramel at random. What is the probability that I will pull out a light-colored caramel? Since 85 out of 100 caramels are light and since I am sampling at random, the probability (*p*) of drawing a light caramel is $85/100 = .85$. This example illustrates one definition of probability:

> If an event can occur in *A* ways and can fail to occur in *B* ways, and if all possible ways are equally likely (e.g., each caramel has an equal chance of being drawn), then the probability of its occurrence is $A/(A + B)$, and the probability of its failing to occur is $B/(A + B)$.

Since there are 85 ways of drawing a light caramel (one for each of the 85 light caramels) and 15 ways of selecting a dark caramel, $A = 85$, $B = 15$, and $p(A) = 85/(85 + 15) = .85$.

Relative-frequency view

Sample with replacement

An alternative view of probability is the **relative-frequency view.** Suppose we keep drawing caramels from this bag, noting the color on each draw. In conducting this sampling study, we **sample with replacement;** that is, we replace each caramel before we draw the next one. If we made a very large number of draws, we would find that (approximately) 85% of the draws would result in a light caramel. Thus, we might define probability as the limit[†] of the relative frequency of occurrence of the desired event that we approach as the number of draws increases.

Subjective probability

A third concept of probability is the concept of **subjective probability.** By this definition, probability represents an individual's subjective belief in the likelihood of the occurrence of an event. Thus, for example, the assertion, "I think this intervention program is very likely to work" is a subjective statement of degree of belief, which probably has little to do with the long-range relative frequency of the occurrence of successful interventions, and in fact may have no mathematical basis whatsoever. This is not to say, however, that such a view of probability is not legitimate. Subjective probabilities play an extremely important role in human decision making and govern

---

[†]The word *limit* refers to the fact that, as we sample more and more caramels, the proportion of light will get closer and closer to some value. After 100 draws, the proportion of light caramels might be .84; after 1000 draws the proportion might be .852; after 10,000 it might be .8496, and so on. Notice that the answer is coming closer and closer to $p = .8500000\ldots$ The value that is being approached is called the limit.

all aspects of our behavior. At the same time, statistical decisions, as we will make them, can generally be stated using more traditional approaches, although even here the *interpretation* of these probabilities has a strong subjective component.

Although the particular definition of probability that a person prefers may be important to him or her, any of the definitions will lead to essentially the same result in terms of hypothesis testing (although those who favor subjective probabilities may not agree with the general hypothesis-testing orientation). In fact, most people use the different approaches interchangeably. When we say that the probability of losing at Russian roulette is one-sixth, we are referring to the fact that only one of the gun's six cylinders has a bullet in it. When we buy a particular car because *Consumer Reports* says that that brand has a good repair record, we are responding to the fact that a high proportion of these cars have been relatively trouble-free. When we say that the probability of the Yankees winning the pennant is high, we are stating our subjective belief in the likelihood of that event. But when we reject some hypothesis because there is a very low probability that the data would have been obtained if the hypothesis had been true, it is not important which view of probability we hold.

5.2 BASIC TERMINOLOGY AND RULES

Event

The basic datum for a probability theorist is called an **event.** Statisticians use the word *event* to cover just about anything. An event can be the occurrence of a king when dealing cards, a score of 36 on a scale of likability, a classification as "female" to the next person appointed to the Supreme Court, or the mean of a sample. Whenever you speak of the probability of something happening, the something is called an event. When we conduct the simple experiment of flipping a coin, the event is the outcome of that flip—either a head or a tail. When we draw caramels out of a bag, the possible events are light and dark caramels. When we investigate grades students receive in a course, the possible events are the letters A, B, C, D, and F.

Independent

Two events are said to be **independent** when the occurrence or nonoccurrence of one event has no effect on the occurrence or nonoccurrence of another. Thus, the voting behavior of two randomly chosen subjects would normally be assumed to be independent, especially with a secret ballot, since how one person votes could not be expected to influence how another votes. The voting behavior of two members of the same family, however, would probably not represent independent events, since people in a family usually share many beliefs and attitudes.

Throughout this book independence is mentioned frequently. For example, in Chapter 7 we will see how to compare the means of two independent samples. In this case the samples will be considered independent if the subjects in one sample are different from the subjects in a second sample. If you are in an experimental group that recalls textual material 10 minutes after reading it, and someone else is in a group that recalls the same material 24 hours after reading it, it is reasonable to assume that whether you recall well or badly has no effect on whether that other person recalls well or badly. In fact, your recall should be independent of other people in your own group as well.

In Chapter 7 we will also consider situations in which observations are definitely *not* independent. In an experiment similar to the one just mentioned, the *same* subjects might be asked to recall material after 10 minutes and again after 24 hours. If you do well on such tasks, both your 10-minute recall and your 24-hour recall will be better than average. If you did not pay attention to the material as it was being presented, you would be expected to do poorly under both retention intervals. Here observations in the two sets of data are not independent, and our statistical test will change accordingly.

Mutually exclusive   Two events are said to be **mutually exclusive** if the occurrence of one event precludes the occurrence of the other. Thus, college-class membership (first year, sophomore, junior, or senior) is mutually exclusive because one person cannot be a member of more than one class. To relate this concept to an experimental situation in psychology, when we sort a list of possible ways to cope with stressful situations, we might establish a set of categories such as problem-focused strategies and emotion-focused strategies. If a response can fall in only one of the two categories, then we would say that the categories are mutually exclusive. If a response could be viewed as falling in one, or the other, *or both*, then the categories are not mutually exclusive. (We could get around this possibility be adding a third category labeled problem-*and*-emotion-focused strategies, because now the ambiguous strategy has its own distinct category.)

Exhaustive   A set of events is said to be **exhaustive** if it includes all possible outcomes. Thus, the four college classes are exhaustive in relation to full-time undergraduates, who have to fall into one of these categories if only to please the registrar's office. At the same time, the classes are not exhaustive in relation to total university enrollments, which include graduate students, medical students, nonmatriculated students, hangers-on, and so forth.

We did not set up exhaustive categories in the coping example because it is reasonable to expect that a subject might propose a strategy that meets none of our categories. Here we would have to add the category "none of the above" to make our list exhaustive.

As you already know or could deduce from the definitions of probability, probabilities range between 0 and 1. If some event has a probability of 1, then it is certain to occur. If its probability is 0, it is certain not to occur. The closer the probability is to either of those extremes, the more likely or unlikely is the occurrence of the event.

BASIC LAWS OF PROBABILITY

Two important theorems, often referred to as the additive and multiplicative laws, are central to any discussion of probability.

THE ADDITIVE LAW   To illustrate the additive law, we will complicate the earlier example by eating 55 of the light caramels and replacing them with wooden cubes. We now have 30 light caramels, 15 dark caramels, and 55 rather tasteless wooden cubes. Given these frequencies, we know from the analytic definition of probability that $p(\text{light}) = 30/100 = .30$, $p(\text{dark}) = 15/100 = .15$, and $p(\text{wooden}) = 55/100 = .55$. But what is the probability that I will draw a caramel, either light *or* dark, rather than a

Additive law of probability

wooden cube? Here we need the **additive law of probability**:

> Given a set of mutually exclusive events, the probability of occurrence of one event *or* another is equal to the sum of their separate probabilities.[†]

Thus $p(\text{light or dark}) = p(\text{light}) + p(\text{dark}) = .30 + .15 = .45$. Notice that we have imposed the restriction that the events must be mutually exclusive, meaning that the occurrence of one event precludes the occurrence of the other. About half the population of this country are female and about half the population have traditionally feminine names. The probability that a person chosen at random will be female *or* will have a feminine name, however, is obviously not $.50 + .50 = 1.00$. The two events are not mutually exclusive. By contrast, the probability that a girl born in Vermont in 1987 was named Ashley or Sarah, the two most common girls' names, equals $p(\text{Ashley}) + p(\text{Sarah}) = .044 + .032 = .076$.

Later in this chapter we will ask a judge to make a decision about a collection of wines. There we will be interested in the probability of 8 or more correct decisions out of a total of 10 trials. We will be using the additive law by calculating the probability of 8 or more correct decisions as the sum of the probabilities of 8, 9, and 10 decisions.

In Chapter 3 we saw how to calculate areas between two points on the distribution or beyond a given point. In these calculations we were essentially using the additive law, because the probability of a value of z greater than 1.96 can be conceived of as the sum of the probabilities of all the possible z values greater than 1.96. I am fudging a bit here because the normal distribution is a continuous distribution and we have to use calculus to find the total area above 1.96 (an infinite number of z values above $z = 1.96$ are possible). But even though we use calculus instead of simple paper-and-pencil addition, we are still using the additive law of probabilities.

THE MULTIPLICATIVE LAW   Now we will go back to the original bag of caramels, in which $p(\text{light}) = .85$ and $p(\text{dark}) = .15$. Suppose that I draw two caramels, replacing the first before drawing the second. What is the probability that I will draw a light one the first time *and* a light one the second [$p(\text{light, light})$]? Here we need to invoke the

Multiplicative law of probability

multiplicative law of probability:

> The probability of the *joint* occurrence of two or more independent events is the product of their individual probabilities.

Thus $p(\text{light, light}) = p(\text{light}) \times p(\text{light}) = .85 \times .85 = .7225$. Similarly, the probability of a light caramel followed by a dark one is $p(\text{light, dark}) = p(\text{light}) \times p(\text{dark}) = .85 \times .15 = .1275$. Notice that the multiplicative law is restricted to independent events, meaning that the occurrence of one event has no effect on the occurrence or nonoccurrence of the other. Because of this restriction, the multiplicative law would not work for our female with feminine name example. Gender and name are not independent, so it would be wrong to state that $p(\text{female with feminine name}) = .50 \times .50 = .25$.

[†] If the events are not mutually exclusive but could occur simultaneously, then the probability of the occurrence of one or the other is the sum of their individual probabilities *minus* the probability of their joint occurrence.

In Chapter 6 we will use the multiplicative law to answer questions about the independence of two variables. An example from Chapter 6 will help illustrate a specific use of this law. In a study to be discussed there, Geller, Witmer, and Orebaugh (1976) wanted to test the (null) hypothesis that what someone did with a supermarket flier was independent of whether or not the flier contained a request not to litter. Part of the solution involves calculating the probability that a flier would contain a message about littering *and* would be found in a trash can. *If* we assume that these two events are independent, then the multiplicative law tells us that the p(message, trash) = p(message) $\times$ p(trash). In their study, 49% of the fliers contained a message, so the probability that a flier chosen at random would contain the message is .49. Similarly, 6.8% of the fliers were later found in the trash, giving p(trash) = .068. Therefore, if the two events are independent, p(message, trash) = .49 $\times$ .068 = .033. (In fact, 4.5% of the fliers with messages were found in the trash, which is a bit higher than we would expect if the ultimate disposal of the flier was independent of the message. What does this tell you about the efficacy of messages?)

Finally, we return to our caramels and use a simple example to illustrate both the additive and multiplicative laws. What is the probability that over two trials (sampling with replacement) I will draw one light caramel and one dark one, *ignoring the order in which they are drawn?* First we use the multiplicative rule to calculate

$$p(\text{light, dark}) = .85 \times .15 = .1275$$

$$p(\text{dark, light}) = .15 \times .85 = .1275$$

Since these two outcomes satisfy our requirement (and since they are the only ones that do), we now need to know the probability that one or the other of these outcomes will occur. These two events are mutually exclusive, so we can apply the additive rule

$$p(\text{light, dark}) + p(\text{dark, light}) = .1275 + .1275 = .2550$$

Thus, the probability of obtaining one caramel of each color over two draws is .2550—that is, the event will occur approximately one-quarter of the time.

JOINT AND CONDITIONAL PROBABILITIES

Two types of probability play an important role in discussions of probability: joint probability and conditional probability. Both of these types of probability have already been used without being pointed out.

Joint probability

A **joint probability** is the probability of the co-occurrence of two or more events. For example, the probability that a flier would *both* contain a message about littering and be found in the trash is a joint probability, as is the probability that a flier would both contain a message about littering and be found stuffed behind the Raisin Bran. Given two events, their joint probability is denoted $p(A, B)$, just as we used p(message, trash). If those events are independent, then the probability of their joint occurrence can be found by using the multiplicative law, as we have just seen. If they are not independent, the probability of their joint occurrence is more complicated to compute and will differ from what it would be if the events were independent.

Conditional probability

A **conditional probability** is the probability that one event will occur *given* that some other event has occurred. The probability that a person will contract AIDS given that he or she is an intravenous drug user is a conditional probability. The probability that a flier will be thrown in the trash given that it contained a message about littering is another example. A third example is the phrase that occurs repeatedly throughout this book: "If the null hypothesis is true, then the probability of obtaining a result such as this is . . . ." Here I have substituted the word *if* for *given*, but the meaning is the same.

With two events, A and B, the conditional probability of A given B is denoted as $p(A|B)$. For example, $p(\text{trash}|\text{message})$.

Suppose that a radio station sampled 100 people, 20 of whom had children. They found that 30 of the people sampled used seatbelts, and that 15 of those with children used them. The results are shown in Table 5.1

TABLE 5.1
The relationship between parenthood and seatbelt use.

Parenthood	Wear Seatbelt	Do Not Wear Seatbelt	Total
Have children	15	5	20
Have no children	15	65	80
Total	30	70	100

The probability that a person sampled at random will use a seatbelt is $30/100 = .30$, whereas the conditional probability of using seatbelts given that you have children is $15/20 = .75$. Do not confuse joint and conditional probabilities. The probability that you have one child who is 3 years old and one who is 6 is a joint probability. The probability that you have a 6-year-old child *given* that you have a 3-year-old child is a conditional probability. This conditional probability is higher than the joint probability, partly because if you have a 3-year-old you are at least in the right age group also to have a 6-year-old.

To take another example, the probability that you have been drinking alcoholic beverages and that you have an accident is a joint probability. This probability is not very high because relatively few people are drinking at any one time and relatively few people have accidents. The probability that you have been drinking *given that* you have an accident, however, is a conditional probability. At night, this conditional probability approaches .50, since nearly half of all automobile accidents at night in the United States involve alcohol. Notice that both $p(\text{drinking}|\text{accident})$ and $p(\text{accident}|\text{drinking})$ are conditional probabilities involving alcohol and automobile accidents. These two probabilities are nowhere near equal; both, however, are higher than the **unconditional probability** of an accident [$p(\text{accident})$].

Unconditional probability

5.3 DISCRETE VERSUS CONTINUOUS VARIABLES

In Chapter 1, I made a distinction between discrete and continuous variables. From a mathematician's perspective, a discrete variable is one that can take on a countable number of different values, whereas a continuous variable is one that can take on an infinite (uncountable) number of different values. For example, the number of people attending a specific Bach concert is a discrete variable because we can actually count the number of people entering the hall, and there is no such thing as a fractional person. The distance between two people in a study of personal space, however, is a continuous variable because the distance could be 2 feet, or 2.8 feet, or 2.8173765814 feet. Although the distinction given here is technically correct, common usage is somewhat different.

In practice, when we speak of a discrete variable we *usually* mean a variable that takes on one of a relatively small number of possible values (e.g., number of siblings). A variable that can take on one of many possible values is generally treated as a continuous variable. Thus, we usually think of an IQ score as a continuous variable even though we recognize that IQ scores are always rounded to whole units and you will not find someone with an IQ of 105.317.

The distinction between discrete and continuous variables is reintroduced here because the *distributions* of the two kinds of variables are treated differently in probability theory. With discrete variables, we can speak of the probability of a specific outcome. With continuous variables, on the other hand, we need to speak of the probability of obtaining a value that falls within a specific *interval*. You saw an example of this earlier when I said that the area under the normal distribution greater than 1.96 can be thought of as being computed by the additive law, but that since we have a continuous distribution we cannot simply add individual probabilities. The probability of $z = 1.967543 \ldots$ is really not defined. If we actually cared about such a probability, we would have to find the probability of an observation falling in an interval, such as the one between 1.9675 and 1.9676. With discrete variables, however, we do not have such a problem.

The distinction between the way we work with continuous variables and the way we work with discrete variables is important. As we have just seen, with continuous variables we do not speak of the probability of a specific outcome; rather, we speak of the probability that an observation will fail within a particular interval. And to do so, we, or at least those who make up the tables we will use, work with calculus to compute those intervals. But with discrete variables we can and do speak of the probability of particular events, and formulas for calculating those individual probabilities are available. You will see a bit of how we work with discrete variables in Section 5.4, and considerably more of it in Section 5.7, on the binomial distribution.

5.4   PROBABILITY DISTRIBUTIONS FOR DISCRETE VARIABLES

An interesting example of a discrete probability distribution is shown in Figure 5.1. The data plotted in this figure come from a study by Campbell, Converse, and Rodgers (1976), who asked 2164 respondents to rate on a scale of 1 to 5 the importance they attached to various aspects of their lives (1 = extremely important, 5 = not at all important). Figure 5.1 presents the distribution of responses for three of these aspects.

The possible values of X (the rating) are presented on the abscissa, and the relative frequency (or probability) of people choosing that response is plotted on the ordinate. From Figure 5.1 you can see that the distributions of responses to questions about health, friends, and savings are quite different. The probability that a person chosen at random will consider his or her health extremely important is .70, whereas the probability that the same person will consider a large bank account extremely important is only .16. (So much for stereotypic conceptions of the American Dream, at least in 1976.)

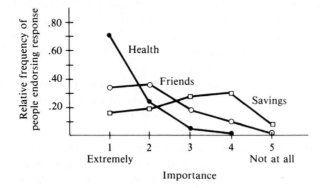

FIGURE 5.1
Distributions of importance ratings of three aspects of life

5.5 PROBABILITY DISTRIBUTIONS FOR CONTINUOUS VARIABLES

When we move from discrete to continuous probability distributions, things become slightly more complicated. We dealt with a continuous distribution when we considered the normal distribution in Chapter 3. Recall that we labeled the ordinate of the distribution "density" and spoke in terms of intervals rather than specific outcomes. Now we need to elaborate on those points.

Figure 5.2 shows the approximate distribution of the age at which children first learn to walk. (This figure is based on data from Hindley, Filliozat, Klackenberg, Nicolet-Meister, and Sand, 1966.) The mean is approximately 14 months, the standard deviation is approximately 3 months, and the distribution is positively skewed. Notice that in this figure the ordinate is labeled "density," whereas in Figure 5.1 it referred to "probability." **Density** is not synonymous with probability; it is probably best thought of as merely the height of the curve at different values of X. The reason for changing the label on the ordinate is that we are now dealing with a continuous distribution rather than a discrete one. If you think for a moment, you will realize that although the highest point of the curve is at 14 months, the probability that a child picked at random will first walk at *exactly* 14 months (i.e., 14.000000000000 ... months) is infinitely small—statisticians would argue that it is in fact zero. Similarly, the probability of first walking at 14.000000000001 months is also infinitely small. This suggests

Density

that it does not make any sense to speak of the probability of any *specific* outcome. On the other hand, we know that many children start walking at *approximately* 14 months, and it does make sense to speak of the probability of obtaining a score falling within some specified interval. For example, we might be interested in the probability that an infant will start walking at 14 months plus or minus two weeks. Such an interval is shown in Figure 5.3. If we arbitrarily define the total area under the curve to be 1, then the shaded area between points *a* and *b* in Figure 5.3 will be equal to the probability that an infant chosen at random will begin walking at this time. Similarly, the (smaller) area between *c* and *d* represents the probability that a child will begin walking at 18 months plus or minus two weeks. Those of you who are familiar with calculus will recognize that if we know the form of the equation that describes this distribution (i.e., if we know the equation for the curve), then we simply need to integrate the function over the interval from *a* to *b*. Calculus is not required, however, because the distributions we will work with usually are adequately approximated by other distributions that have already been presented in tables. You have already had experience with such an approximation with regard to the normal distribution in Chapter 3.

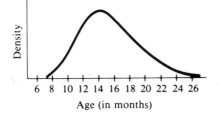

FIGURE 5.2
Age at which a child first walks unaided

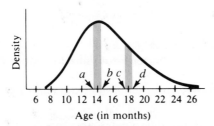

FIGURE 5.3
Probability of first walking during 1-month intervals centered on 14 and 18 months

5.6 PERMUTATIONS AND COMBINATIONS

We will set continuous distributions aside until they are needed again in Chapter 7 and beyond. For now, we will concentrate on two discrete distributions (the binomial and the multinomial) that can be used to develop the chi-square test in Chapter 6. First we must consider the concepts of permutations and combinations, which are required for a discussion of those distributions.

Combinatorics

The special branch of mathematics dealing with the number of ways in which objects can be put together (e.g., the number of different ways of forming a three-person committee with five people available) is known as **combinatorics**. Although not many instances in this book require a knowledge of combinatorics, there are enough of them to make it necessary to briefly define the concepts of permutations and combinations and to give formulas for their calculation.

PERMUTATIONS

We will start with a simple example that is easily expanded into a more useful and relevant one. Assume that four people have entered a lottery for ice-cream cones. The names are placed in a hat and drawn. The person whose name is drawn first wins a double-scoop cone, the second wins a single-scoop cone, the third wins just the cone, and the fourth wins nothing. Assume that the people are named Aaron, Barbara, Cathy, and David, abbreviated A, B, C, and D. The following orders in which the names are drawn are all possible.

A B C D	B A C D	C A B D	D A B C
A B D C	B A D C	C A D B	D A C B
A C B D	B C A D	C B A D	D B A C
A C D B	B C D A	C B D A	D B C A
A D B C	B D A C	C D A B	D C A B
A D C B	B D C A	C D B A	D C B A

Permutation

Each of these 24 orders represents a **permutation** (ordering) of four names taken four at a time. If we represent the number of permutations (orderings) of N things taken r at a time as P_r^N, then

$$r = X \text{ (from lecture)} \qquad P_r^N = \frac{N!}{(N-r)!}$$

N factorial

where the symbol $N!$ is read N **factorial** and represents the product of all integers from N to 1. [In other words, $N! = N(N-1)(N-2)(N-3)\ldots(1)$.] By definition, $0! = 1$.

For our example of drawing four names for four entrants,

$$P_4^4 = \frac{4!}{(4-4)!} = \frac{4!}{0!} = \frac{4 \cdot 3 \cdot 2 \cdot 1}{1} = 24$$

which agrees with the number of listed permutations.

Now, few people would get very excited about winning a cone without any ice cream in it, so let's eliminate that prize. Then out of the four people, only two will win on any drawing. The order in which those two winners are drawn is still important, however, because the first person whose name is drawn wins a larger cone. In this case, we have four names but are drawing only two out of the hat (since the other two are both losers). Thus, we want to know the number of permutations of four names taken two at a time. (P_2^4). We can easily write down these permutations and count them:

$$
\begin{array}{cccc}
\text{A B} & \text{B A} & \text{C A} & \text{D A} \\
\text{A C} & \text{B C} & \text{C B} & \text{D B} \\
\text{A D} & \text{B D} & \text{C D} & \text{D C}
\end{array}
$$

Or we can calculate the number of permutations directly:

$$
P_2^4 = \frac{4!}{(4-2)!} = \frac{4 \cdot 3 \cdot 2 \cdot 1}{2} = 12
$$

Here there are 12 possible orderings of winners, and the ordering makes an important difference—it determines not only who wins, but also which winner receives the larger cone.

Now we will take a more useful example involving permutations. Suppose we are designing an experiment studying physical attractiveness judged from slides. We are concerned that the order of presentation of the slides is important. Given that we have six slides to present, in how many different ways can these be arranged? This again is a question of permutations, because the ordering of the slides is important. More specifically, we want to know the permutations of six slides taken six at a time. Alternatively, suppose we have six slides, of which any given subject is going to see only four. Now how many orders can be used? This is a question about the permutations of six slides taken four at a time.

For the first problem, in which subjects are presented with all six slides, we have

$$
P_6^6 = \frac{6!}{(6-6)!} = \frac{6!}{0!} = \frac{6 \cdot 5 \cdot 4 \cdot 3 \cdot 2 \cdot 1}{1} = 720
$$

and thus there are 720 different ways of arranging six slides. For the second problem, where we have six slides but show only four to any one subject, we have

$$
P_4^6 = \frac{6!}{(6-4)!} = \frac{6!}{2!} = \frac{6 \cdot 5 \cdot 4 \cdot 3 \cdot 2 \cdot 1}{2 \cdot 1} = 360
$$

If we want to present all possible arrangements to each subject, we need 360 trials, a result that may be sufficiently large to lead us to modify our design.

COMBINATIONS

To return to the ice-cream lottery, suppose we now decide that we will award only single-dip cones to the two winners. We will still draw the names of two winners out of a hat, but we will no longer care which of the two names was drawn first—the result AB is for all practical purposes the same as the result BA because in each case Aaron and Barbara win a cone. When the order in which names are drawn is no longer important, we are no longer interested in permutations. Instead, we are now interested **Combinations** in what are called **combinations.** We want to know the number of possible combinations of winning names, but not the order in which they were drawn.

We can enumerate these combinations as

$$
\begin{array}{cc}
\text{A B} & \text{B C} \\
\text{A C} & \text{B D} \\
\text{A D} & \text{C D}
\end{array}
$$

There are six of them. In other words, out of four people, we could compile six different sets of winners. (If you look back to the previous enumeration of permutations of winners, you will see that we have just combined outcomes containing the same names.)

Normally, we do not want to enumerate all possible combinations just to find out how many of them there are. To calculate the number of *combinations* of N things taken r at a time (C_r^N), we will define

$$C_r^N = \frac{N!}{r!(N-r)!}$$

For our example,
$$C_2^4 = \frac{4!}{2!(4-2)!} = \frac{4 \cdot 3 \cdot 2 \cdot 1}{2 \cdot 1 \cdot 2 \cdot 1} = 6$$

Let's return to the example involving slides to be presented to subjects. When we were dealing with permutations, we worried about the way in which each set of slides was arranged; that is, we worried about all possible orderings. Suppose we no longer care about the order of the slides within sets, but we need to know how many different sets of slides we could form if we had six slides but took only four at a time. This is a question of combinations.

For six slides taken four at a time, we have

$$C_4^6 = \frac{6!}{4!(6-4)!} = \frac{\overset{3}{6} \cdot 5 \cdot 4 \cdot 3 \cdot 2 \cdot 1}{4 \cdot 3 \cdot 2 \cdot 1 \cdot 2 \cdot 1} = 15$$

If we wanted every subject to get a different set of four slides but did not care about the order within a set, we would need 15 subjects.

5.7   THE BINOMIAL DISTRIBUTION

Binomial distribution

We now have all the information on probabilities and combinations that we need for understanding one of the most common probability distributions—the **binominal distribution**. This distribution will be discussed briefly, and you will see how it can be used to test simple hypotheses.

Bernoulli trial

The binomial distribution deals with situations in which each of a number of independent trials results in one of two mutually exclusive outcomes. Such a trial is called a **Bernoulli trial** (after a famous mathematician of the same name). The most common example of a Bernoulli trial is flipping a coin, and the binomial distribution could be used to give us the probability of, for example, 3 heads out of 5 tosses of a coin. The binomial distribution is an example of a discrete, rather than a continuous, distribution, since one can flip coins and obtain 3 heads or 4 heads, but not, for example, 3.897 heads.

Mathematically, the binomial distribution is defined as

$$p(X) = C_X^N p^X q^{(N-X)} = \frac{N!}{X!(N-X)!} p^X q^{(N-X)}$$

where

$p(X)$ = The probability of X successes

N = The number of trials

p = The probability of a success on any one trial

$q = (1 - p)$ = The probability of a failure on any one trial

C_X^N = The number of combinations of N things taken X at a time

The notation has been changed from r to X because the symbol X is used to refer to data. Whether we call something r or X is arbitrary; the choice is made for convenience or intelligibility.

Success, failure

The words **success** and **failure** are used as arbitrary labels for the two alternative outcomes. We will require that the trials be independent of one another, meaning that the result of trial$_i$ has no influence on trial$_j$.

To illustrate the application of this formula, suppose we are interested in studying the art of wine tasting. As part of our study, we ask a judge to taste two glasses of wine and pick the more expensive (and presumably the better) one. This task is repeated 10 times, each time with a different pair of wines. Assume for the moment that our wine taster really does not know the first thing about wines. He is just choosing at random and trying to put on a good show. Assuming that there are no extraneous factors to bias the judge's decision (such as a tendency to choose the paler-colored wine), then on each trial the probability of his being correct (i.e., correctly identifying the more expensive wine) is .50, since there are only two wines to choose from. Now suppose we want to know the probability that our judge will somehow manage to make 9 (X) correct choices out of 10 (N) trials. The probability of being correct on any one trial is denoted p and equals .50, whereas the probability of being incorrect on any one trial is denoted q and also equals .50. Then we have

$$p(X) = \frac{N!}{X!(N-X)!} p^X q^{(N-X)}$$

$$p(9) = \frac{10!}{9!1!}(.50^9)(.50^1)$$

But

$$10! = 10 \cdot 9 \cdot 8 \cdots 2 \cdot 1 = 10 \cdot 9!$$

so

$$p(9) = \frac{10 \cdot 9!}{9!1!}(.50^9)(.50^1)$$

$$= 10(.001953)(.50) = .0098$$

Thus, the probability of making 9 correct choices out of 10 trials with $p = .50$ is remote, occurring approximately 1 time out of every 100 tasting sessions.

This simple example incorporates what you have already learned about joint probabilities, additive and multiplicative laws, and combinations (permutations are not involved in the binominal distribution). We are concerned with the probability of obtaining 9 correct choices (and 1 incorrect choice) out of 10 trials. One outcome that satisfies our criterion would be nine corrects followed by one incorrect, and the probability of this particular outcome is the joint probability:

$$p(C, C, C, C, C, C, C, C, C, I) = (.50^9)(.50^1) = p^X q^{(N-X)}$$

This illustrates the application of the multiplicative law. A number of other outcomes also include exactly nine correct choices (e.g., $C, C, C, C, C, C, C, C, I, C$), and the additive law tells us that we can sum the probabilities of each of these to obtain the total probability we seek. We could enumerate all possible $9 : 1$ splits, calculate their probabilities, which will be

$$p^X q^{(N-X)}$$

in each case, and sum. It is easier, however, to calculate the number of ways we could select 9 correct choices out of 10 trials, and multiply

$$p^X q^{(N-X)}$$

by that number. This is where the formula for combinations comes in, because we really want to know the number of combinations of 10 things taken nine at a time without regard to the order of those nine things. This value is

$$C_X^N = C_9^{10} = 10$$

and thus our final answer is

$$(C_9^{10})(p^9 q^1) = \frac{10!}{9!1!}(.5^9)(.5^1) = 10(.00098) = .0098$$

As a second example, the probability of 6 correct choices out of 10 trials is the probability of any one such outcome $(p^6 q^4)$ times the number of possible $6 : 4$ outcomes (C_6^{10}). Thus,

$$p(6) = \frac{N!}{X!(N-X)!} p^X q^{(N-X)}$$

$$= \frac{10!}{6!4!}(.5^6)(.5^4)$$

$$= \frac{10 \cdot 9 \cdot 8 \cdot 7 \cdot 6!}{6!4 \cdot 3 \cdot 2 \cdot 1}(.5^{10})$$

$$= \frac{5040}{24}(.000976)$$

$$= .2050$$

PLOTTING BINOMIAL DISTRIBUTIONS

You will notice that the probability of six correct choices is greater than the probability of nine of them. This is what we would expect, since we are assuming that our judge is operating at random and would be right about as often as he is wrong. If we were to calculate the probabilities for each outcome between 0 and 10 correct out of 10, we would find the results shown in Table 5.2. Observe from this table that the sum of those probabilities is 1, reflecting the fact that all possible outcomes have been considered.

TABLE 5.2
Binomial distribution
for $p = .50$, $N = 10$

Number Correct	Probability
0	.001
1	.010
2	.044
3	.117
4	.205
5	.246
6	.205
7	.117
8	.044
9	.010
10	.001
	1.000

Now that we have calculated the probabilities of the individual outcomes, we can plot the distribution of the results, as has been done in Figure 5.4. Although this distribution resembles many of the distributions we have seen, it differs from them in two important ways. First, notice that the ordinate has been labeled "probability" instead of "frequency." This is because Figure 5.4 is not a frequency distribution at all, but rather is a probability distribution. This distinction is important. With frequency, or relative frequency, distributions, we were plotting the obtained outcomes of some experiment—that is, we were plotting real data. Here we are not plotting real data; instead, we are plotting the probability that some event or another will occur.

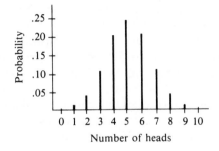

FIGURE 5.4
Binomial distribution
when $N = 10$ and
$p = .50$

To reiterate a point made earlier, the fact that the ordinate represents probabilities instead of densities (as in the normal distribution) reflects the fact that the binomial distribution deals with discrete rather than continuous outcomes. With a continuous distribution such as the normal distribution, the probability of any specified individual outcome is near 0. With a discrete distribution, however, the data fall into one or another of relatively few categories, and probabilities for individual events can be obtained easily. In other words, with discrete distributions we deal with the probability of individual events, whereas with continuous distributions we deal with the probability of intervals of events.

The second way this distribution differs from many others we have discussed is that although it is a sampling distribution, it is obtained mathematically rather than empirically. The values on the abscissa represent statistics (the number of success as obtained in a given experiment) rather than individual observations or events. We have already discussed sampling distributions in Chapter 4, and what we said there applies directly to what we will consider in this chapter.

THE MEAN AND VARIANCE OF A BINOMIAL DISTRIBUTION

In Chapter 2 we saw that it is possible to describe a distribution in many ways—we can discuss its mean, its standard deviation, its skewness, and so on. From Figure 5.4 we can see that the distribution for the outcomes for our judge is symmetric. This will always be the case for $p = q = .50$, but not for other values of p and q. Furthermore, the mean and standard deviation of any binomial distribution are easily calculated:

$$\text{Mean} = Np$$

$$\text{Variance} = Npq$$

$$\text{Standard deviation} = \sqrt{Npq}$$

For example, Figure 5.4 shows the binomial distribution when $N = 10$ and $p = .50$. The mean of this distribution is $10(.5) = 5$ and the standard deviation is

$$\sqrt{10(.5)(.5)} = \sqrt{2.5} = 1.58$$

We will see shortly that being able to specify the mean and standard deviation of any binomial distribution is exceptionally useful when it comes to testing hypotheses. First, however, it is necessary to point out two more considerations.

In the wine-tasting example, we dealt with a judge who was choosing at random ($p = q = .50$). Had we chosen to use a different judge—one who had a higher or lower probability of being correct on any one trial—the arithmetic would have been the same but the results would have been different. For purposes of illustration, three distributions obtained with different values of p are plotted in Figure 5.5.

For the distribution on the left of Figure 5.5, the judge chose the more expensive wine at slightly greater than chance levels and had a probability of .60 of being correct on any given trial. The distribution in the middle represents the results expected from a judge who had a probability of only .30 of being correct on each trial. The distribution on the right represents the behavior of a judge with a nearly unerring ability to choose the *wrong wine*. On each trial, this judge had a probability of only .05 of being correct. From these three distributions, you can see that, for a given number of trials, as p and q depart more and more from .50, the distributions become more and more skewed although the mean and standard deviation are still Np and $\sqrt{Npq}$, respectively. Moreover, it is important to point out (although it is not shown in Figure 5.5, in which N is always 10) that as the number of trials increases, the distribution approaches normal, regardless of the values of p and q. As a rule of thumb, as long as both Np and Nq are greater than about 5, the distribution is sufficiently normal for most purposes.

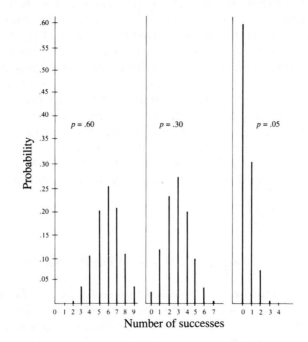

FIGURE 5.5
Binomial distributions
for $N = 10$ and
$p = .60, .30,$ and $.05$

5.8   USING THE BINOMIAL DISTRIBUTION TO
TEST HYPOTHESES

Many of the situations for which the binomial distribution is useful in testing hypotheses are handled equally well by the chi-square test, discussed in Chapter 6. For that reason, this discussion will be limited to those cases for which the binominal distribution is particularly useful.

In the previous sections, we dealt with the situation in which a person was judging wines, and we saw how to calculate the distribution of possible outcomes and their probabilities over $N = 10$ trials. Now suppose we turn the question around and ask whether the available data from a set of wine-tasting trials can be taken as evidence that our judge really can identify expensive wines at better than chance levels.

For example, suppose we have had our judge make eight comparisons of an inexpensive wine with an expensive one, and the judge has been correct on seven out of eight trials. Do these data indicate that she is operating at a better than chance level? Put another way, are we likely to have seven out of eight correct choices if the judge is really operating by blind guessing?

Following the procedure outlined in Chapter 4, we can begin by stating our research hypothesis as the hypothesis that the judge knows a good wine when she tastes it (at least that is presumably what we set out to demonstrate). In other words, the research hypothesis (H_1) is that her performance is at better than chance levels $(p > .50)$. (We have chosen a one-tailed test merely to simplify the example; in general, we would prefer to use a two-tailed test.) The null hypothesis is that the judge's behavior does not differ from chance $(H_0: p = .50)$. The sampling distribution of the number of correct choices out of eight trials, given that the null hypothesis is true, is provided by the binomial distribution with $p = .50$. Rather than calculate the probability of each of the possible number of correct choices (as we did in Figure 5.5, for example), all we need to do is calculate the probability of seven correct choices and the probability of eight correct choices, since we want to know the probability of our judge doing *at least* as well as she did if she were choosing randomly.

Letting N represent the number of trials (eight) and X represent the number of correct trials, the probability of seven correct trials out of eight is given by

$$p(X) = C_X^N p^X q^{N-X}$$

$$p(7) = C_7^8(.5)^7(.5)^1$$

$$= \frac{8!}{7!1!}(.5)^7(.5)^1 = 8(.0078)(.5) = 8(.0039) = .0312$$

Thus, the probability of making seven correct choices out of eight by chance is .0312. But we know that we test null hypotheses by asking questions of the form, "What is the probability of *at least* this many correct choices if H_0 is true?" In other words, we need to sum $p(7)$ and $p(8)$:

$$p(8) = C_8^8 p^8 q^0 = 1(.0039)(1) = .0039$$

Then

$$\begin{aligned} p(7) &= .0312 \\ + p(8) &= .0039 \\ \hline p(7 \text{ or } 8) &= .0351 \end{aligned}$$

Here we see that the probability of at least seven correct choices is approximately .035. Earlier, we said that we will reject H_0 whenever the probability of a Type I error (α) is less than or equal to .05. Since we have just determined that the probability of making at least seven correct choices out of eight is only .035 if H_0 is true (i.e., if $p = .50$), we will reject H_0 and conclude that our judge is performing at better than chance levels. In other words, her performance is better than we would expect if she were just guessing.

THE SIGN TEST

Sign test

Another example of the use of the binomial to test hypotheses is one of the simplest tests we have: the **sign test**. Although the sign test is very simple, it is also very useful in a variety of settings. Suppose we hypothesize that when people know each other they tend to be more accepting of individual differences. As a test of this hypothesis, we asked a group of first-year male students matriculating at a small college to rate 12 target subjects (also male) on physical appearance (higher scores represent greater attractiveness). At the end of the first semester, when students have come to know one another, we again ask them to rate those same 12 targets. Assume we obtain the data in Table 5.3.

TABLE 5.3
Median ratings of physical appearance at the beginning and end of the semester

Target	1	2	3	4	5	6	7	8	9	10	11	12
First	12	21	10	8	14	18	25	7	16	13	20	15
Second	15	22	16	14	17	16	24	8	19	14	28	18
Gain	3	1	6	6	3	−2	−1	1	3	1	8	3

The gain score in this table was computed by subtracting the first score obtained at the beginning of the semester from the second score, obtained at the end of the semester. Notice that in 10 of the 12 cases the score at the end of the semester was higher than at the beginning. In other words, the sign was positive. (The sign test gets its name from the fact that we look at the sign, but not the magnitude, of the difference.)

Consider the null hypothesis in this example. If familiarity does not affect ratings of physical appearance, we would not expect a systematic change in ratings (assuming that no other variables are involved). Ignoring tied scores, which we don't have anyway, we would expect that by chance about half the ratings would increase and half the ratings would decrease over the course of the semester. Thus, under H_0, p(higher) = p(lower) = .50. The binomial can now be used to compute the probability of obtaining at least 10 out of 12 improvements if H_0 is true:

$$p(10) = \frac{12!}{10!2!}(.5^{10})(.5^2) = .0161$$

$$p(11) = \frac{12!}{11!1!}(.5^{11})(.5^1) = .0029$$

$$p(12) = \frac{12!}{12!0!}(.5^{12})(.5^0) = .0002$$

From these calculations we see that the probability of at least 10 improvements = .0161 + .0029 + .0002 = .0192 if the null hypothesis is true and ratings are unaffected by familiarity. Because this probability is less than our traditional cutoff of .05, we will reject H_0 and conclude that ratings of appearance have increased over the course of the semester. (Although variables other than familiarity could explain this difference, at the very least our test has shown that there is a significant difference to be explained.)

5.9   THE MULTINOMIAL DISTRIBUTION

Multinomial distribution

The binomial distribution we have just examined is a special case of a more general distribution, the **multinomial distribution**. In binomial distributions, we deal with events that can have only one of two outcomes—a coin could land heads or tails, a wine could be judged as more expensive or less expensive, and so on. In many situations, however, an event can have more than two possible outcomes—a roll of a die has six possible outcomes; a maze might present three choices (right, left, and center); political opinions could be classified as For, Against, or Undecided. In these situations, we must invoke the more general multinomial distribution.

If we define the probability of each of k events (categories) as $p_1, p_2, \ldots, p_k$ and wish to calculate the probability of exactly X_1 outcomes of $event_1$, X_2 outcomes of $event_2$, $\ldots, X_k$ outcomes of $event_k$, this probability is given by

$$p(X_1, X_2, \ldots, X_k) = \frac{N!}{X_1! X_2! \cdots X_k!} p_1^{X_1} p_2^{X_2} \cdots p_k^{X_k}$$

where N has the same meaning as in the binomial. Note that when $k = 2$ this is in fact the binomial distribution, where $p_2 = 1 - p_1$ and $X_2 = N - X_1$.

As a brief illustration, suppose we had a die with two black sides, three red sides, and one white side. If we roll this die, the probability of a black side coming up is $2/6 = .333$, the probability of a red is $3/6 = .500$, and the probability of a white is $1/6 = .167$. If we roll the die 10 times, what is the probability of obtaining exactly four blacks, five reds, and one white? This probability is given as

$$p(4, 5, 1) = \frac{10!}{4!5!1!}(.333^4)(.500^5)(.167^1)$$

$$= 1260(.333^4)(.500^5)(.167^1) = 1260(.000064)$$

$$= .081$$

At this point, this is all we will say about the multinomial. It will appear again in Chapter 6, when we discuss chi-square, and forms the basis for some of the other tests you are likely to run into in the future.

KEY TERMS

Analytic view (5.1)

Relative-frequency view (5.1)

Sample with replacement (5.1)

Subjective probability (5.1)

Event (5.2)

Independent (5.2)

Mutually exclusive (5.2)

Exhaustive (5.2)

Additive law of probability (5.2)

Multiplicative law of probability (5.2)

Joint probability (5.2)

Conditional probability (5.2)

Unconditional probability (5.2)

Density (5.5)

Combinatorics (5.6)

Permutation (5.6)

N factorial (5.6)

Combinations (5.6)

Binomial distribution (5.7)

Bernoulli trial (5.7)

Success (5.7)

Failure (5.7)

Sign test (5.8)

Multinomial distribution (5.9)

EXERCISES

5.1　Give an example of an analytic, a relative-frequency, and a subjective view of probability.

5.2　Assume that you have bought a ticket for the local fire department lottery and that your brother has bought two tickets. You have just read that 1000 tickets have been sold.
(a) What is the probability that you will win the grand prize?
(b) What is the probability that your brother will win?
(c) What is the probability that you *or* your brother will win?

5.3　Assume the same situation as in Exercise 5.2, except that a total of only 10 tickets were sold and that there are two prizes.
(a) Given that you don't win first prize, what is the probability that you will win second prize? (The first prize-winning ticket is not put back in the hopper.)
(b) What is the probability that your brother will win first prize and you will win second prize?
(c) What is the probability that you will win first prize and your brother will win second prize?
(d) What is the probability that the two of you will win the first and second prizes?

5.4　Which parts of Exercise 5.3 deal with joint probabilities?

5.5　Which parts of Exercise 5.3 deal with conditional probabilities?

5.6　Make up a simple example of a situation in which you are interested in joint probabilities.

5.7　Make up a simple example of a situation in which you are interested in conditional probabilities.

5.8　In some homes, a mother's behavior seems to be independent of her baby's, and vice versa. If the mother looks at her child a total of 2 hours each day, and the baby looks at the mother a total of 3 hours each day, and if they really do behave independently, what is the probability that they will look at each other at the same time?

5.9　In Exercise 5.8, assume that both the mother and child are asleep from 8:00 P.M. to 7:00 A.M. What would the probability be now?

5.10　Give an example of a common continuous distribution for which we have some real interest in the probability that an observation will fall within some specified interval.

5.11　Give an example of a continuous variable that we routinely treat as if it were discrete.

5.12　Give two examples of discrete variables.

5.13　A graduate-admissions committee has finally come to realize that it cannot make valid distinctions among the top applicants. This year, the committee rated all 300 applicants and randomly chose 10 from those in the top 20%. What is the probability that any particular applicant will be admitted (assuming you have no knowledge of her or his rating)?

5.14　With respect to Exercise 5.13,
(a) what is the conditional probability that the person will be admitted given that she has the highest faculty rating among the 300 students?
(b) what is the conditional probability given that she has the lowest rating?

5.15   Using Appendix Data Set,

   (a) what is the probability that a person drawn at random will have an ADDSC score greater than 50 if the scores are normally distributed with a mean of 52.6 and a standard deviation of 12.4?

   (b) what percentage of the sample actually exceeded 50?

5.16   Using Appendix Data Set,

   (a) what is the probability that a male will have an ADDSC score greater than 50 if the scores are normally distributed with a mean of 54.3 and a standard deviation of 12.9?

   (b) what percentage of the male sample actually exceeded 50?

5.17   Using Appendix Data Set, what is the empirical probability that a person will drop out of school given that he or she has an ADDSC score of at least 60? Here we do not need to assume normality.

5.18   How might you use conditional probabilities to determine if an ADDSC cutoff score in Appendix Data Set of 66 is predictive of whether or not a person will drop out of school?

5.19   Using Appendix Data Set scores, compare the conditional probability of dropping out of school given an ADDSC score of at least 60, which you computed in Exercise 5.17, with the unconditional probability that a person will drop out of school regardless of his or her ADDSC score.

5.20   In a five-choice task, subjects are asked to choose the stimulus that the experimenter has arbitrarily determined to be correct; the 10 subjects can guess only on the first trial. Plot the sampling distribution of the number of correct choices on trial 1.

5.21   Refer to Exercise 5.20. What would you conclude if 6 of 10 subjects were correct on trial 1?

5.22   Refer to Exercise 5.20. What is the minimum number of correct choices on a trial necessary for you to conclude that the subjects as a group are no longer performing at chance levels?

5.23   In a study of human cognition, we want to look at recall of different classes of words (nouns, verbs, adjectives, and adverbs). Each subject will see one of each. We are afraid that there may be a sequence effect, however, and want to have different subjects see the different classes in a different order. How many subjects will we need if we are to have one subject per order?

5.24   Refer to Exercise 5.23. Assume we have just discovered that, because of time constraints, each subject can see only two of the four classes. The rest of the experiment will remain the same, however. Now how many subjects do we need? (*Warning*: Do not actually try to run an experiment like this unless you are sure you know how you will analyze the data.)

5.25   In a learning task, a subject is presented with five buttons. He must learn to press a certain three of them in a predetermined order. What chance does that subject have of pressing correctly on the first trial?

5.26   An ice-cream shop has six different flavors of ice cream, and you can order any combination of any number of them (but only one scoop of each flavor). How many different ice-cream cone combinations could they truthfully advertise? (We do not care if the Oreo Mint is above or below the Raspberry-Pistachio. Each cone must have at least one scoop of ice cream—an empty cone doesn't count.)

5.27   We are designing a study in which six external electrodes will be implanted on a rat's brain. The six-channel amplifier in our recording apparatus blew two channels when the research assistant took it home to run her stereo. How many different ways can we record from the brain? (It makes no difference what signal goes on which channel.)

5.28   In a study of knowledge of current events, we give a 20-item true–false test to a class of college seniors. One of the not-so-alert students gets 11 answers right. Do we have any reason to believe that he has done anything other than guess?

5.29 This question is not an easy one, and requires putting together material in Chapters 3, 4, and 5. Suppose we make up a driving test that we have good reason to believe should be passed by 60% of all drivers. We administer it to 30 drivers, and 22 pass it. Is the result sufficiently large to cause us to reject H_0 ($p = .60$)? This problem is too unwieldy to be approached by solving the binomial for $X = 22, 23, \ldots, 30$. But you do know the mean and variance of the binomial, and something about its shape. With the aid of a diagram of what the distribution would look like, you should be able to solve the problem.

5.30 Make up a simple experiment for which a sign test would be appropriate.
(a) Create reasonable data and run the test.
(b) Draw the appropriate conclusion.

CATEGORICAL DATA AND CHI-SQUARE

OBJECTIVES *To present the chi-square test as a procedure for testing hypotheses when the data are categorical.*

CONTENTS

I n Chapter 5 we examined the use of the binomial distribution to test simple hypotheses. In those cases, we were limited to situations in which an individual event had one of only two possible outcomes, and we merely asked whether, over repeated trials, one outcome occurred significantly more often than the other.

In this chapter we will expand the kinds of situations that we can evaluate. We will deal with the case in which a single event can have two *or more* possible outcomes, and then with the case in which we have two variables and we want to test null hypotheses concerning their independence. For both of these situations, the appropriate statistical test will be the chi-square (χ^2) test.

Chi-square (χ^2)

The term **chi-square (χ^2)** has two distinct meanings in statistics, a fact that leads to some confusion. In one meaning, it is used to refer to a particular mathematical distribution that exists in and of itself without any necessary referent in the outside world. In the second meaning, it is used to refer to a statistical test that has a resulting test statistic distributed in approximately the same way as the χ^2 distribution. When you hear someone refer to chi-square, they usually have this second meaning in mind. [The test itself was developed by Karl Pearson (1900) and is often referred to as **Pearson's chi-square** to distinguish it from other tests that also produce a χ^2 statistic—for example, Friedman's test, discussed in Chapter 18, and the likelihood ratio tests discussed at the end of this chapter.] You need to be familiar with both meanings of the term, however, if you are to use the test correctly and intelligently, and if you are to understand many of the other statistical procedures that follow.

Pearson's chi-square

6.1   THE CHI-SQUARE DISTRIBUTION

Chi-square distribution (χ^2)

The **chi-square (χ^2) distribution** is the distribution defined by

$$f(\chi^2) = \frac{1}{2^{k/2}\Gamma(k/2)} \chi^{2[(k/2)-1]} e^{-(\chi^2)/2}$$

This is a rather messy-looking function and most readers will be pleased to know that they will not have to work with it in any arithmetic sense. We do need to consider some of its features, however, to understand what the distribution of χ^2 is all about. The first thing that should be mentioned, if only in the interest of satisfying healthy curiosity, is that the term $\Gamma(k/2)$ in the denominator, called a **gamma function**, is related to what we normally mean by *factorial*. In fact, when the argument of gamma $(k/2)$ is an integer, then $\Gamma(k/2) = [(k/2) - 1]!$. We need gamma functions in part because arguments are not always integers.

Gamma function

A second and more important feature of this equation is that the distribution has only one parameter (k). Everything else is either a constant or else the value of χ^2 for which we want to find the ordinate $[f(\chi^2)]$. Whereas the normal distribution was a two-parameter function, with μ and σ as parameters, χ^2 is a one-parameter function with k as the only parameter. When we move from the mathematical to the statistical world, k will become our degrees of freedom. (We often signify the degrees of freedom by subscripting χ^2. Thus, χ^2_3 is read "chi- square with three degrees of freedom." Alternatively, some authors write it as $\chi^2(3)$).

Figure 6.1 shows the plots for several different χ^2 distributions, each representing a different value of k. From this figure it is obvious that the distribution changes markedly with changes in k, becoming more symmetric as k increases. It is also apparent that the mean and variance of each χ^2 distribution increase with increasing values of k and are directly related to k. It can be shown that in all cases

$$\text{Mean} = k$$

$$\text{Variance} = 2k$$

FIGURE 6.1
χ^2 distributions for $df = 1, 2, 4,$ and 8

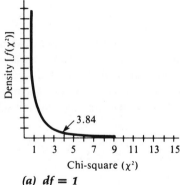

(a) df = 1

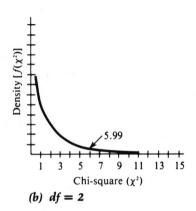

(b) df = 2

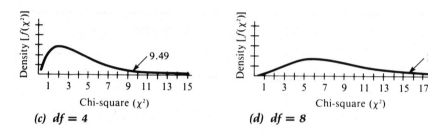

FIGURE 6.1 (Cont.)   *(c) df = 4*   *(d) df = 8*

6.2 STATISTICAL IMPORTANCE OF THE CHI-SQUARE DISTRIBUTION

The χ^2 distribution is a mathematical distribution that exists independently of any particular set of statistical procedures. It would have no place in this book, however, if it was not somehow relevant to at least one statistical procedure. In fact, the χ^2 distribution is related to many of the statistics to be covered in this book, of which the chi-square test is only one.

CHI-SQUARE AND z

Assume we have a normal population with known mean (μ) and variance (σ^2). From this distribution we will sample one observation (X), calculate

$$z^2 = \frac{(X - \mu)^2}{\sigma^2}$$

record z^2, and repeat the procedure an infinite number of times. Assume we finish this task; we can then plot the distribution of z^2, and we will find that this distribution looks exactly like the χ^2 distribution on 1 *df*. In fact,

$$\chi_1^2 = z^2$$

To carry the example further, assume that instead of sampling one score at a time from our normal population, we sampled N scores at a time. For each individual observation we calculated z^2, and then we calculated Σz^2, summing over the sample of N observations. Again we repeat this procedure an infinite number of times and plot the resulting values of Σz^2. The resulting distribution will be distributed as χ^2 on N *df*:

$$\chi_N^2 = \sum_{i=1}^{N} z_i^2 = \sum \frac{(X_i - \mu)^2}{\sigma^2}$$

Since we have just seen that z_i^2 is itself distributed as χ^2, this last equation reveals an important property of χ^2: the sum of N independent values of χ^2 is itself distributed as χ^2. In this case, the degrees of freedom will equal the sum of the degrees of freedom for the separate χ^2s. We will use this property of χ^2 in Section 7.8.

Two important restrictions on the previous two equations are the requirements that the observations be sampled independently of one another and be sampled from a normal population. These restrictions will be referred to again when we discuss the chi-square test.

The usefulness of these relationships probably is not immediately apparent, but a full discussion of their value must await a discussion of the chi-square test. The most important point to be made here is that the last two equations tell us what would happen *if* we were to draw an infinite number of samples under the specified conditions. In other words, we do not ever have to take on the Herculean task of drawing vast numbers of samples, because we already know what the resulting distribution would look like. This is true of most of the sampling distributions we will discuss in this book.

CHI-SQUARE AND VARIANCE

One of the important but little discussed uses of χ^2 deals with its relationship to population and sample variances. This relationship forms the basis of many of our most important statistical tests and helps to explain several of the restrictions we place on the use of these tests.

Assume for the moment that we have a normally distributed population with a known variance (σ^2). From this population, we draw an infinitely large number of samples of N observations each and calculate the sample variance (s^2) for each sample. We could then plot the sampling distribution of the variance—the distribution of sample variances. You can see such a distribution plotted in Figure 7.4. This distribution would bear a direct linear relationship to the distribution of χ^2:

$$\chi^2_{N-1} = \frac{(N-1)s^2}{\sigma^2}$$

Turning this around, we have

$$s^2 = \frac{\chi^2 \sigma^2}{N-1}$$

Since the fraction $\sigma^2/(N-1)$ is a constant for any given population variance and sample size, the distribution of s^2 will differ by only a constant from the distribution of χ^2. In other words, the sampling distribution of the variance has a χ^2 distribution. Keep in mind that we have assumed that we are dealing with normal distributions. (For a more thorough treatment of this topic see Hays, 1981, pp. 308–313.)

We have just seen something that will become important later concerning the sample variance. We already know that s^2 is an unbiased estimate of σ^2, meaning that *on the average s^2 will equal σ^2*. We now know that the distribution of s^2 resembles that of χ^2, which we know to be skewed. This means that although the average s^2 will equal

σ^2, more than half the time our particular value of s^2 will be smaller than σ^2, no matter how things average out in the end. This fact will have important implications when we discuss t tests in Chapter 7.

6.3 THE CHI-SQUARE TEST—ONE-WAY CLASSIFICATION

Chi-square test
Goodness-of-fit test

So far we have confined our discussion to the χ^2 distribution, examining its relationship to certain important statistics. We now turn to what is commonly referred to as the **chi-square test**, which is based on the χ^2 distribution. We will first examine the test as it is applied to one-dimensional tables (often called a **goodness-of-fit test**) and then as applied to two-dimensional tables (contingency tables).

Consider the situation in which we ask 100 people to taste two brands of coffee and state their preferences. Assume for the sake of an example that 65 people preferred Brand A and 35 people preferred Brand B. We will represent the total number of people by N, and the number choosing one brand by X. Then the number choosing the other brand must be $N - X$. The data might be tabled as follows:

Choosing Brand A	Choosing Brand B	Total
X	$N - X$	N
65	35	100

The question we want to answer with our data is, "Do people in general prefer one brand of coffee over the other?" In other words, do the obtained frequencies in favor of each coffee differ from the 50:50 split that would be expected by chance if the coffees were indistinguishable, or if they were distinguishable but the coffee-drinking public was evenly divided in its preference? To answer this question, we will employ the chi-square test. We already know that

$$\chi_1^2 = z^2 = \frac{(X - \mu)^2}{\sigma^2}$$

where X is sampled from a normal population with mean $= \mu$ and variance $= \sigma^2$. We also know that if people are selecting coffees at random, the number of people (X) selecting a particular brand of coffee can be viewed as coming from a binomial distribution with mean $= Np$ and variance $= Npq$. Furthermore, we know that, for reasonable sample sizes, the binomial is approximately normal. These facts allow us to substitute the mean and variance of the binomial into the preceding equation, arriving at

$$\chi_1^2 = z^2 = \frac{(X - Np)^2}{Npq}$$

χ^2 as defined in this equation would be distributed exactly as the distribution of χ^2 if N were infinitely large (and therefore if the binomial distribution were exactly normal). For reasonable sample sizes, the binomial distribution we are sampling from would be approximately normal, and the result of this equation would very closely approximate the χ^2 distribution.

A much more common way to write the formula for χ^2 is to let O_i represent the **observed frequencies** (e.g., 65 and 35) and E_i represent the **expected frequencies** for the ith category (brand). For example, O_1 will be the number of people choosing Brand A, and O_2 will be the number of people choosing Brand B. Expanding the preceding formula by some not-so-obvious algebra, we obtain

$$\chi_1^2 = \frac{(X - Np)^2}{Np} + \frac{(N - X - Nq)^2}{Nq}$$

Substituting O_i and E_i in this equation, we obtain

$$\chi^2 = \frac{(O_1 - E_1)^2}{E_1} + \frac{(O_2 - E_2)^2}{E_2}$$

or, dropping the subscripts as being self-evident,

$$\chi^2 = \sum \frac{(O - E)^2}{E}$$

This last formula is the one commonly given for the chi-square test. The advantage of the earlier one using Np and Nq is that it makes explicit the source of the expected frequencies and serves as a reminder that in the two-category case the test is based on the binomial distribution and the restrictions that go with it. The nice thing about the last equation is that it is completely general. Although it was developed on the basis of the binomial, we can now use it as the formula for all situations to which the chi-square test applies, whether or not that case is also an example of the binomial.

PLACE LEARNING IN RATS

The following example is based on one of the most famous experiments in animal learning, conducted by Tolman, Ritchie, and Kalish (1946). At the time of the original study, Tolman was engaged in a theoretical debate with Clark Hull and the latter's students on whether a rat in a maze learns a discrete set of motor responses (Hull) or forms some sort of cognitive map of the maze and responds on the basis of that map (Tolman). In a simple and ingenious experiment, Tolman and his colleagues first taught a rat to run down a starting alley of a maze into a large circular area. From this circular area, another alley exited straight *across* from the entrance but then turned and ended up in a goal box, which was actually to the right of the circular area. After the rats had learned the task ("go to the circular area and exit straight across"), Tolman changed the task by making the original exit alley into a dead end and by adding several new alleys, one of which pointed in the direction of the original goal box. The maze is shown in Figure 6.2, with the original alley drawn with solid lines and the new alleys drawn with dotted lines. Thus, the rat had several choices, one of which included the original alley and one of which included a new alley that pointed directly toward the goal. If Hull were correct, the rat would have learned a stimulus–response sequence during the first part of the experiment and should therefore continue to make that same set of responses, thus entering the now dead-end alley. If

Tolman were right and the rat learned a cognitive map of the situation, then the rat should enter the alley on the *right* because it knows that the food is "over there to the right." Since Tolman was the one who published the study, you can probably guess how it came out—the rats chose the alley on the right. But we still need some way of testing whether the preference for the alley on the right was due to chance or whether the data support a general preference for the right alley.

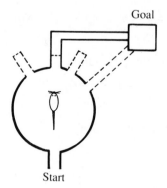

FIGURE 6.2
Schematic view of Tolman's maze

For the sake of this example, I have modified the study slightly to include only two alleys in part 2 of the experiment (Tolman et al. used 18). Let A represent the original exit and let B represent the alley on the right. The choices for the 32 rats in the study are as follows (these are not Tolman's original data; his data showed an even more dramatic difference):

	Alley Chosen		
	A	B	Total
Observed	9	23	32
Expected	16	16	32

The first line of this table contains the observed number of rats entering each alley. This row sums to 32 because there were 32 rats in the experiment. We will take as our null hypothesis (H_0) for this test the hypothesis that the rats showed no preference for either of the two alleys. (Hull predicted that the rats would favor Alley A, whereas Tolman predicted that they would favor Alley B. We are testing the null hypothesis that they do not favor either alley.) In other words, H_0 states that there is no difference between p (probability of choosing Alley A) and q (probability of choosing Alley B) and therefore that $p = q = .50$. In terms of expected values, this means that, under H_0, we would expect half of the 32 rats to choose Alley A and half to choose Alley B. These expected frequencies are shown in the second row of the table. Since Tolman et al. used 32 *different* rats, the observations should be independent; there is no reason to expect that one rat's behavior should influence another rat's behavior. (Contrast this to a study using the same rat 32 times, in which case we would have strong reservations about the independence of the observations.)

From our formula for the chi-square test, we can calculate

$$\chi^2 = \sum \frac{(O - E)^2}{E}$$

$$= \frac{(9 - 16)^2}{16} + \frac{(23 - 16)^2}{16} = \frac{-7^2}{16} + \frac{7^2}{16} = \frac{98}{16}$$

$$= 6.125$$

THE TABLED CHI-SQUARE DISTRIBUTION

Now that we have obtained a value of χ^2, we must refer it to the χ^2 distribution to determine the probability of a value of χ^2 at least this extreme.

Tabled distribution of χ^2

The **tabled distribution of χ^2**, like that of most other statistics, differs in a very important way from the *tabled* standard normal distribution, as was pointed out in Chapter 3. Since some people seem to have difficulty appreciating this difference and understanding the use of statistical tables, we will use a simple illustration. Consider the distribution of χ^2 for 1 *df* shown in Figure 6.1. Although it is certainly true that we could construct a table of exactly the same form as that for the standard normal distribution, allowing us to determine what percentage of the values are greater than any arbitrary value of χ^2, this would be tremendously time-consuming and wasteful. We would have to make up a new table for every reasonable number of degrees of freedom. It is not uncommon to want up to 30 *df*, which would require 30 separate tables, each the size of Appendix z. Such a procedure would be particularly wasteful since most users would need only a small fraction of each of these tables. If we wish to reject H_0 at the .05 level, all that we really care about is whether or not our value of χ^2 is greater or less than the value of χ^2 that cuts off the upper 5% of the distribution. Thus, for our particular purposes, all we need to know is the 5% cutoff point for each *df*. Other people might want the 2.5% cutoff, 1% cutoff, and so on, but it is hard to imagine wanting the 17% values, for example. Thus, tables of χ^2 such as the one given in Appendix χ^2, which is reproduced in part in Table 6.1, are designed to supply only those values that might be of general interest.

TABLE 6.1   Areas under the χ^2 distribution

df	.995	.990	.975	.950	.900	.750	.500	.250	.100	.050	.025	.010	.005
1	0.00	0.00	0.00	0.00	0.02	0.10	0.45	1.32	2.71	3.84	5.02	6.63	7.88
2	0.01	0.02	0.05	0.10	0.21	0.58	1.39	2.77	4.61	5.99	7.38	9.21	10.60
3	0.07	0.11	0.22	0.35	0.58	1.21	2.37	4.11	6.25	7.82	9.35	11.35	12.84
4	0.21	0.30	0.48	0.71	1.06	1.92	3.36	5.39	7.78	9.49	11.14	13.28	14.86
5	0.41	0.55	0.83	1.15	1.61	2.67	4.35	6.63	9.24	11.07	12.83	15.09	16.75
6	0.68	0.87	1.24	1.64	2.20	3.45	5.35	7.84	10.64	12.59	14.45	16.81	18.55
7	0.99	1.24	1.69	2.17	2.83	4.25	6.35	9.04	12.02	14.07	16.01	18.48	20.28
8	1.34	1.65	2.18	2.73	3.49	5.07	7.34	10.22	13.36	15.51	17.54	20.09	21.96
9	1.73	2.09	2.70	3.33	4.17	5.90	8.34	11.39	14.68	16.92	19.02	21.66	23.59
...	...	...	...	...	...	...	...	...	...	...	...	...	...

Look for a moment at Table 6.1. Down the leftmost column you will find the degrees of freedom. In each of the other columns, you will find the critical values of χ^2 cutting off the percentage of the distribution labeled at the top of that column. Thus, for example, you will see that for 2 df a χ^2 of 5.99 cuts off the upper 5% of the distribution. (Note the shaded entry in Table 6.1).

Returning to our example, we have found a value of $\chi^2 = 6.125$ on 1 df. From Table 6.1 or Appendix χ^2, we see that, with 1 df, a χ^2 of 3.84 cuts off the upper 5% of the distribution. Since our obtained value $(\chi^2_{obt}) = 6.125$ is more than $\chi^2_{.05} = 3.84$, we reject the null hypothesis.[†] We therefore conclude that the obtained frequencies differ from the expected frequencies more than would be predicted by chance. In other words, Tolman's rats chose Alley B at greater than chance levels.

Because the logic of hypothesis testing is extremely important to an understanding of statistics, I will risk beating a dead horse by considering what we have done from a different angle. The equation for the chi-square test states that regardless of which hypothesis is true, if we take the obtained frequency, subtract the *true* value of the expected frequency, square the difference, divide by the *true* value of the expected frequency, and then sum the results over all categories, the answer will be distributed as χ^2—that is, only 5% of the time will we obtain a value of χ^2 greater than 3.84 with 1 df. The null hypothesis in effect states that the *true* value of E, in this example, is $(32)(.50) = 16$ for each alley. As a result, we took 16 as the expected frequency and proceeded accordingly. To the extent that H_0 is false, we have inserted the wrong expected value, and our result will not be distributed as χ^2 (i.e., over an infinite number of replications of the experiment, the resulting obtained values of χ^2 will not have a χ^2 distribution). Thus, given the obtained values of χ^2, the null hypothesis that the probability of choosing each of the two alleys is .50 is not tenable.

Extension to the Multicategory Case

Multicategory case

In the example of place learning in rats we had a situation in which the data fell into one of two categories. We can easily extend this to the **multicategory case**, in which data can be classified into three or more categories, the number being signified by k. When we leave the two-category case, however, we also leave the binomial distribution and must consider our data as coming from a multinomial distribution. Aside from an increase in the difficulty of the derivation, which we will not be concerned with anyway, the nature of the test and its application are left unchanged. Since we have more than two categories, we will have to let $p_1, p_2, \ldots, p_k$ replace p and q, and let $X_1, X_2, \ldots, X_2$ replace X and $N - X$. These are minor changes, however, and with these in mind we can rewrite our earlier equation for chi-square as

$$\chi^2 = \sum \frac{(X_i - Np_i)^2}{Np_i} = \sum \frac{(O - E)^2}{E}$$

[†]Notice that here the subscripts for χ^2 (i.e., obt and .05) do not refer to the degrees of freedom but instead designate either the obtained value of χ^2 or the value of χ^2 that cuts off the largest 5% of the distribution. When we wish to designate both the degrees of freedom and the area of the distribution to which the value refers, we write something like $\chi^2_{.05}(1) = 3.84$.

We will again lose 1 *df* (since the frequency of one of the categories is determined by knowing N and the frequencies in the other categories). Thus, the result will be distributed as χ^2 on $k - 1$ *df*.

As an example, we can expand the place learning problem to allow for multiple alleys running off the circular area. We will let Alley A be the one that was originally correct and now has a dead end. Alley D will be the one on the right, which the rats would be expected to choose if they were trying to go to the place where the goal box had previously been. Alleys B and C are located midway between the other two. Suppose we obtained the following data:

	Alley Chosen			
	A	B	C	D
Observed	4	5	8	15
Expected	8	8	8	8

Here you can see that approximately half of the rats chose the alley that Tolman would have predicted they would choose, whereas only four animals chose Alley A, which is the one that Hull's "response-learning" hypothesis would have predicted.

As in the first example, we have 32 animals. But this time we have four alleys. If the rats were responding at random—that is, if the null hypothesis were true—we would expect one-quarter of them to choose each alley. This leads to an expected frequency of eight for each alley shown in the preceding table. Our calculations for the chi-square test are the same as those followed in the earlier example, except that this time we will sum over four categories instead of two:

$$\chi^2_3 = \sum \frac{(O - E)^2}{E}$$

$$= \frac{(4 - 8)^2}{8} + \frac{(5 - 8)^2}{8} + \frac{(8 - 8)^2}{8} + \frac{(15 - 8)^2}{8}$$

$$= 9.25$$

From Appendix χ^2, we see that for $k - 1 = 3$ *df*, $\chi^2_{.05} = 7.82$. Our value of 9.25 is greater than 7.82, and once again we will reject H_0. Again, we have shown that our rats are not choosing at random. They are choosing the alley that leads to the correct place at greater-than-chance levels.

The thoughtful reader might ask why we analyzed the data this way rather than lumping Alleys A, B, and C together into one category labeled "wrong alley." There is no particularly convincing statistical answer to this question other than to say that it depends on what you know about the behavior of your animals and what you expect the data to look like. In our example, the fact that about as many rats chose one of the three wrong alleys as chose the right one does not seem as relevant as the fact that about three times as many rats chose Alley D as chose any one of the other alleys. (If you were to collapse back to "right" and "wrong," the *expected* frequency for "wrong" would be 24, because there are three wrong alleys and only one right one.)

6.4   CHI-SQUARE AS A TEST OF THE INDEPENDENCE OF TWO VARIABLES

In Section 6.3 we examined the situation in which one independent variable (Alley) was being considered. A second and more important use of chi-square deals with the situation in which we have two variables and want to determine whether these variables are *independent* of one another. For example, we might wish to know whether preference for a political party is independent of gender, whether presence or absence of illness is independent of presence or absence of immunization, or whether preference for different types of music is independent of age. Any two variables can be examined in this way, as long as data on each variable can be classified into categories.

Independence of two variables

Contingency table

When we wish to ask about the **independence of two variables**, the data are cast in what is commonly referred to as a **contingency table**. Thus, to evaluate the relationship between attention deficit disorder (ADD) and gender, for example, we would make up a table in which gender appears along one dimension and ADD appears along the other:

	Female	Male
ADD		
Non-ADD		

Cell

In each **cell** we will enter numbers that represent frequency data; the number of male and female ADDs and Non-ADDs.

We use the same underlying procedures as were involved in the earlier examples. The only difference is in the way we obtain the expected frequencies, and you will see that even here we are simply extending what we already know.

THE ZEIGARNIK EFFECT

As an example of testing the independence of two variables, and an extreme one at that, let's consider a study by Lewis and Franklin (1944), based on an earlier study by Zeigarnik (1927). Zeigarnik originally presented subjects with a number of separate tasks, some of which she unobtrusively interrupted, preventing their completion. At the end of the session, subjects were asked to list all of the tasks on which they had worked, and Zeigarnik found substantially better recall of uncompleted tasks than completed tasks. Lewis and Franklin wished to examine whether the presence or absence of the so-called Zeigarnik effect depended on the subject's perception of the tasks. They divided 24 subjects into two groups. Subjects in Group SI (self-involved) were told that the tasks were measures of ability. Subjects in Group TO (task-oriented) were told that they were simply helping the experimenter standardize the tasks. Subjects were then presented with the tasks one at a time; some of the tasks were interrupted before completion, and the subjects were later asked to recall all of the tasks.

Lewis and Franklin hoped to reject the null hypothesis that whether a subject showed greater recall of uncompleted versus completed tasks was independent of which group the subject was in. They hoped to find support for the research hypothesis that recall was dependent on group membership.

The data are presented in Table 6.2, where the cell entries represent the number of subjects in each group recalling more uncompleted (or completed) tasks. Thus, for example, in Group TO, 10 subjects recalled more uncompleted tasks than completed ones, and two subjects recalled more completed tasks than uncompleted ones.

The only change that must be made in our formula for chi-square concerns the fact that the data are arrayed along two dimensions instead of one. This means that we will have to refer to X_{ij} and p_{ij} instead of X_i and p_i. In the new designation, i indicates the number of the row and j the number of the column. Thus, X_{12} is the score in row 1 and column 2, which is a 2. We can now write

$$\chi^2 = \sum \frac{(X_{ij} - Np_{ij})^2}{Np_{ij}} = \sum \frac{(O - E)^2}{E}$$

TABLE 6.2
Data for the Lewis and Franklin (1944) study

	Greater Recall		
	Uncompleted Tasks	Completed Tasks	
Group TO	10	2	12
Group SI	1	11	12
	11	13	24

CALCULATING EXPECTED FREQUENCIES

The only remaining problem is calculating the expected frequencies—NP_{ij}. From Chapter 5 we know that the probability of the *joint* occurrence of two *independent* events is the product of the probabilities of their separate occurrence. Thus, the probability of a head on both of two trials is the probability of a head on the first trial times the probability of a head on the second trial [$p = (.5)(.5) = .25$].

If the variables in Table 6.2 are independent, then the probability that a subject is classified as a member of cell$_{11}$ (TO, Uncompleted) is equal to the probability of her being a member of row 1 times the probability of her being a member of column 1. The probability for row 1 is 12/24, since 12 of the 24 subjects are in row 1. The probability for column 1 is 11/24, since 11 of the 24 subjects are in that column. Given these individual probabilities, then, if the events are independent, the probability that the subject is in row 1 *and* column 1 (cell$_{11}$) is

$$p_{11} = \left(\frac{12}{24}\right)\left(\frac{11}{24}\right)$$

Although this calculation for one cell suggests that our calculations will involve a great deal of arithmetic, in fact they will not. First, remember that we want Np_{ij}, not just p_{ij}. Second, N is the total number of subjects in the experiment, which in this case is 24. Thus,

$$Np_{11} = (24)\left(\frac{12}{24}\right)\left(\frac{11}{24}\right) = \frac{(12)(11)}{24} = 5.5$$

Row total (RT),
Column total (CT),
Grand total (N)

If we let the abbreviations RT, CT, and N stand for **row total, column total,** and **grand total,** where it is understood that the particular row or column total in question is the one corresponding to the row or column of the cell whose expected frequency we seek, then

$$E_{ij} = Np_{ij} = \frac{(RT_i)(CT_j)}{N}$$

It is important to realize that this equation derives directly from the assumption that the two variables are independent and in essence represents the statement of the null hypothesis (H_0). In other words, these are the frequencies we would expect *if* the null hypothesis were true.

CALCULATING CHI-SQUARE

Given the expected frequencies, we can now analyze the data in Table 6.2 by means of a chi-square contingency analysis. Both the observed and expected frequencies appear in Table 6.3.

TABLE 6.3 Observed and expected frequencies for the Lewis and Franklin (1944) study

	Observed Frequencies			Expected Frequencies		
	Uncompleted Tasks	Completed Tasks		Uncompleted Tasks	Completed Tasks	
Group TO	10	2	Group TO	5.5	6.5	12
Group SI	1	11	Group SI	5.5	6.5	12
	11	13		11	13	24

The calculation of χ^2 follows directly now that we have obtained the expected frequencies:

$$\chi^2 = \sum \frac{(O - E)^2}{E}$$

$$= \frac{(10 - 5.5)^2}{5.5} + \frac{(2 - 6.5)^2}{6.5} + \frac{(1 - 5.5)^2}{5.5} + \frac{(11 - 6.5)^2}{6.5}$$

$$= \frac{(4.5)^2}{5.5} + \frac{(-4.5)^2}{6.5} + \frac{(-4.5)^2}{5.5} + \frac{(4.5)^2}{6.5}$$

$$= 13.594$$

DEGREES OF FREEDOM

Before we can compare our χ^2 value with the value in Table 6.1, we must know the degrees of freedom. For analyzing contingency tables, the degrees of freedom are always given by

$$df = (R - 1)(C - 1)$$

where R is the number of rows and C is the number of columns.

For our example with two rows and two columns, we have $(2 - 1)(2 - 1) = 1\ df$. Although it may seem strange that we have $1\ df$ whether we have two categories or four cells, it should be apparent that given only one entry, and the row and column totals, the rest of the entries are completely determined.

EVALUATING CHI-SQUARE

The critical value of χ^2 for $1\ df$ is 3.84 (see Appendix χ^2). Since our obtained value of χ^2 (χ^2_{obt}) is 13.594, we reject the null hypothesis and conclude that there is a relationship between the orientation of the subject toward the task and the types of tasks she is able to recall. If the tasks are seen as measures of ability, the subject has a strong tendency to recall those that she completed. On the other hand, if the subject has no personal involvement with the tasks, the uncompleted tasks are more often recalled.

CORRECTING FOR CONTINUITY

Yates' correction for continuity

Many books advocate that for simple 2×2 tables such as Tables 6.2 and 6.3, we should employ what is called **Yates' correction for continuity**, especially when the expected frequencies are small. (The correction merely involves reducing the absolute value of each numerator by 0.5 units before squaring.) There is an extensive literature on the pros and cons of Yates' correction, with firmly held views on both sides. Although I recommended that you not use the correction in most cases, it is important to understand what all the fuss is about.

A glance back at Figure 6.1 will show that χ^2 is a continuous function, with all values of χ^2 along the abscissa possible. If you go back to the Lewis and Franklin example, however, you will discover that there is no way to rearrange the data, *keeping the marginal totals constant*, to come up with a slightly different χ^2 (e.g., 13.596). With finite sample sizes the obtained distribution of χ^2 for the chi-square test is discrete (especially for small samples), whereas the theoretical χ^2 distribution is continuous. This leads to a certain mismatch when we attempt to evaluate a χ^2 statistic against the χ^2 distribution.

The mismatch led Yates (1934) to devise a correction to be applied in the case of a 2×2 contingency table. The result of this correction is that the probability of the corrected χ^2, taken from χ^2 tables, is quite close to the *true* probabilities calculated on the basis of the individual probabilities of all possible tables *with those marginal totals* (the R_i and C_j). Yates' correction in fact accomplishes his goal quite nicely, and it is recommended whenever it makes sense to calculate a probability given that the marginal totals really are fixed. Unfortunately, to speak about **fixed marginals** implies that if you repeated the experiment, the individual cell totals might well change but you would arrive at the same marginal totals.[†] This situation rarely exists, and when it does not exist it makes little sense to ask what the probability of the data would be if we assumed that it did. For this reason (the unreasonableness of a fixed-marginal assumption), many papers have argued against the use of Yates' correction (Bradley, Bradley, McGrath, & Cutcomb, 1979; Camilli & Hopkins, 1978, 1979; Overall, 1980). Furthermore, for the cases in which either only one or neither marginal total is fixed, the uncorrected chi-square provides a good approximation to the true probabilities—certainly a better approximation than is provided by Yates' correction.

THE SPECIAL CASE OF 2 × 2 TABLES

In this book I have deliberately avoided discussing formulas that apply to special cases when the general formula will accomplish the same thing. It is usually easier to do a tiny bit more work on calculations than it is to remember another formula. In the case of a 2 × 2 table, however, there is a formula that allows you to skip the calculation of expected frequencies, and in fact allows you to calculate χ^2 on a calculator without ever writing down intermediate results.

Suppose we imagine a 2 × 2 table with the cells and marginal totals labeled as follows:

A	B	$A + B$
C	D	$C + D$
$A + C$	$B + D$	N

Then
$$\chi^2 = \frac{N(AD - BC)^2}{(A + B)(C + D)(A + C)(B + D)}$$

Using the data from Lewis and Franklin (1944), we have

10	2	12
1	11	12
11	13	24

$$\chi^2 = \frac{N(AD - BC)^2}{(A + B)(C + D)(A + C)(B + D)}$$

[†] As an example of a table with fixed marginals, imagine that we designed a study to present a subject with handwriting samples from 10 physicians and 10 dentists (fixed row marginals = 10 and 10). We told him to sort them into piles on the basis of his judgment as to whether each sample came from a physician or a dentist. If we constrain the judge's sorting by saying that each pile must contain 10 samples, our column totals will also be fixed at 10 and 10.

$$\chi^2 = \frac{24(110 - 2)^2}{(12)(12)(11)(13)}$$

$$\chi^2 = 13.594$$

This is the same value of χ^2 as we obtained in the previous calculations.

Students often have trouble with this formula because they forget which letter refers to which cell of the table. So do I. But notice what you are doing. You are multiplying diagonal cells and then subtracting one product from the other. It does not even matter which you subtract from which, since you are going to square the result anyway. Next you multiply this squared term by N and divide by the product of all the marginal totals. Moreover, if you become really confused and divide when you should have multiplied, or vice versa, you will generally obtain such an outlandish answer that you will know something is wrong.

6.5   CHI-SQUARE FOR LARGER CONTINGENCY TABLES

The Lewis and Franklin example involved two variables (task orientation and type of material recalled), each of which had two levels. We referred to this design as a 2×2 contingency table; it is a special case of the more general $R \times C$ designs, where, again, R and C represent the number of rows and columns. As an example of a larger contingency table, consider the study by Geller, Witmer, and Orebaugh (1976) mentioned in Chapter 5. These authors were studying littering behavior and were interested, among other things, in whether a message about not littering would be effective if placed on the handbills that are often given out in supermarkets advertising the daily specials. To oversimplify a fairly complex study, two of Geller's conditions involved passing out handbills in a supermarket. Under one condition (Control), the handbills contained only a listing of the daily specials. In the other condition (Message), the handbills also included the notation, "Please don't litter. Please dispose of this properly." At the end of the day, Geller and his students searched the store for handbills. They recorded the number that were found in trashcans; the number that were left in shopping carts, on the floor, and various places where they didn't belong (denoted litter); and the number that could not be found and were apparently removed from the premises. The data obtained under the two conditions are shown in Table 6.4, and are taken from a larger table reported by Geller et al. Expected frequencies are shown in parentheses and were obtained exactly as they were in the previous example $[E = (RT_i)(CT_j)/N]$.

The calculation of χ^2 is carried out just as it was earlier:

$$\chi^2 = \sum \frac{(O - E)^2}{E}$$

$$= \frac{(41 - 61.66)^2}{61.66} + \frac{(385 - 343.98)^2}{343.98} + \cdots + \frac{(499 - 478.64)^2}{478.64}$$

$$= 25.79$$

TABLE 6.4
Data from the Geller, Witmer, and Orebaugh (1976) study (expected frequencies in parentheses)

Instructions	Location		
	Trashcan	Litter	Removed	
Control	41 (61.66)	385 (343.98)	477 (497.36)	903
Message	80 (59.34)	290 (331.02)	499 (478.64)	869
	121	657	976	1772

There are 2 *df* for Table 6.4, since $(R - 1)(C - 1) = (2 - 1)(3 - 1) = 2$. The critical value of $\chi^2_{.05} = 5.99$. Our value of 25.79 is larger than 5.99, so we are led to reject H_0 and to conclude that the location in which the handbills were left depended on the instructions given. In other words, Instructions and Location are not independent. From the data it is evident that when subjects were asked not to litter, a higher percentage of handbills were thrown in the trashcan or taken out of the store, and fewer were left lying in shopping carts or on floors and shelves.

COMPUTER ANALYSES

Chi-square statistics can be produced by computer programs in two different ways. The easiest, though least common, way is to use a program in which you enter the cell totals and ask for χ^2 to be computed. This can be done easily in Minitab; a sample Minitab printout is shown in Exhibit 6.1 for the data in Table 6.4.

EXHIBIT 6.1
Minitab analysis of Geller et al. (1976) data

```
MTB  > READ DATA INTO C1-C3
DATA > 41 385 477
DATA > 80 290 499
DATA > END
        2 ROWS READ
MTB  > CHISQUARE ON DATA IN C1-C3

Expected counts are printed below observed counts

              C1          C2          C3        Total
     1        41         385         477         903
            61.66      343.98      497.36

     2        80         290         499         869
            59.34      331.02      478.64

  Total      121         675         976        1772

ChiSq  =    6.923   +   4.893   +   0.834   +
            7.194   +   5.084   +   0.866   =  25.794

df = 2

MTB > STOP
```

The second way of generating chi-square is to enter the raw data and have the software compute the cell totals and then χ^2. This way is more common, because we usually enter a data set into a file and then ask for a variety of statistics to be computed. For example, suppose we enter the raw data for the Lewis and Franklin study referred to earlier. We will code the TO group as 1 and the SI group as 2. Similarly, those subjects who recall more uncompleted tasks will be coded 1, and those who recalled more completed tasks will be coded 2. Then the data would look like this:

Group: 1 1 1 1 1 1 1 1 1 1 1 1 2 2 2 2 2 2 2 2 2 2 2 2

Recall: 1 1 1 1 1 1 1 1 1 1 2 2 1 2 2 2 2 2 2 2 2 2 2 2

(Many programs would allow you to enter alphanumeric information instead of just numeric, so you could code recall tasks as T or S if you wished. I prefer to use numeric coding throughout.) Exhibit 6.2 contains an SPSS^X program and the corresponding printout for the data shown here. The Statistics command requests (1) chi-square, (2) phi, and (3) the contingency coefficient.

EXHIBIT 6.2
SPSS^X analysis of Lewis and Franklin (1944) data

```
Title          'Analysis of Lewis and Franklin data.'
File Handle    Data/Name = '[D_Howell.book] Lewfrank.dat'
Data List      File = Data/ Group 1 Recall 3
Value Labels
               Group (1) 'Task Oriented' (2) 'Self-Involved'/
               Recall (1) 'Uncompleted' (2) 'Completed'
Crosstabs      Tables = Group By Recall
Statistics     1 2 3
Finish
```

GROUP by RECALL   Page 1 of 1

		RECALL		
	Count	Uncompleted 1	Completed 2	Row Total
GROUP	-------	-----------	---------	
	1	10	2	12
Task Oriented				50.0
	2	1	11	12
Self-Involved				50.0
	Column	11	13	24
	Total	45.8	54.2	100.0

Chi-Square	Value	DF	Significance
Pearson	13.59441	1	.00023
Continuity Correction	10.74126	1	.00105
Likelihood Ratio	15.40667	1	.00009
Mantel-Haenszel test for linear association	13.02797	1	.00031

Minimum Expected Frequency   5.500

Statistic	Value	ASE1	T-value	Approximate Significance	
Phi	.75262			.00023	*1
Cramer's V	.75262			.00023	*1
Contingency Coefficient	.60134			.00023	*1

*1   Pearson chi-square probability

Number of Missing Observations: 0

Exhibit 6.2 contains several statistics we have not yet discussed. The three of them at the end (phi, Cramer's V, and the contingency coefficient) will be discussed later in this chapter. Under the Chi-Square heading are several statistics that have a chi-square distribution. The first entry is labeled Pearson. That is the standard (Pearson's) chi-square, and it is the statistic we seek. The next entry is χ^2 corrected for continuity. Because that correction is meaningful only when both sets of marginal totals are fixed (Recall is a random variable, not under the control of the experimenter, and replications of the experiment would produce different column totals), we will ignore that statistic as being inappropriate. The likelihood ratio is an alternative, and related, test on contingency tables and its statistic is distributed as χ^2. This test will be discussed shortly. The Mantel–Haenszel test is generally used when we have three or more variables. For example, if the Lewis and Franklin experiment had been conducted on several distinct populations of subjects and we wanted to do the same analysis but control for population differences, their test would be appropriate. For our situation the standard Pearson chi-square is more appropriate, and we will ignore the Mantel–Haenszel test. Each of the statistics listed under Chi-Square is automatically produced by SPSS^X whenever you request chi-square, regardless of whether some may be inappropriate for the problem at hand.

SMALL EXPECTED FREQUENCIES

One of the most important requirements for using the chi-square test concerns the size of the expected frequencies. We have already met this requirement briefly in discussing corrections for continuity. Before defining more precisely what we mean by *small*, we should examine why a **small expected frequency** causes so much trouble. There are two ways of explaining the difficulty, and they are so closely related that it is difficult to speak about one without invoking the other.

First, consider the basic fact that we are using a mathematical distribution to approximate the distribution of the statistic resulting from a chi-square test. As you should recall, in deriving the test we first showed that when we sampled observations from a normal population, $\chi^2 = \Sigma z^2$. We then used this relationship to show that Σz^2 could be converted into our familiar chi-square statistic, invoking the binomial (or multinomial) distribution in the process. We were allowed to use the binomial (or multinomial) because these distributions approach the normal when Np is large. Notice that we have invoked the assumption of normality in the process. Neither the binomial nor the multinomial, however, produce anywhere near normal distributions for small values of Np (e.g., see Figure 5.5). This means that we will have violated the assumption of **normality** for small expected frequencies (i.e., for small values of Np).

Suppose we look at the problem from a different angle. If only a few values of χ^2_{obt} are possible, then the χ^2 distribution cannot provide a reasonable approximation to the distribution of our statistic. We cannot fit a discrete distribution having relatively few values with a continuous one. Those cases that result in only a few possible values of χ^2_{obt}, however, are the ones with small expected frequencies. (This is directly analogous to the fact that if you flip a coin only three times, there are only four possible values for the number of heads, and the resulting sampling distribution certainly can-

Small expected frequency

Normality

not be satisfactorily approximated by the normal distribution.) If you take a fixed set of marginal totals for any 2×2 table, select the marginal totals so as to have at least one small expected frequency, and then construct all possible data tables for that set of marginals, it will be immediately obvious what the problem is.

We have seen that difficulties arise when we have small expected frequencies, but the question of how small is small remains. Those conventions that do exist are conflicting and have only minimal claims to preference over one another. Probably the most common is to require that all expected frequencies should be at least five. This is a conservative position and I occasionally violate it. Bradley et al. (1979) ran a computer-based sampling study. They used tables ranging in size from 2×2 to 4×4 and found that for those applications likely to arise in practice, the actual percentage of Type I errors rarely exceed .06, even for *total* samples sizes as small as 20, unless the row or column marginal totals are drastically skewed. Camilli and Hopkins (1979) demonstrated that even with quite small expected frequencies, the test produces few Type I errors in the 2×2 case as long as the total sample size is greater than or equal to eight; but they, and Overall (1980), point to the extremely low power to reject a false H_0 that such tests possess. With small sample sizes, power is more likely to be a problem than inflated Type I error rates.

6.6 SUMMARY OF THE ASSUMPTIONS OF CHI-SQUARE

Assumptions of χ^2

Because of the widespread misuse of chi-square still prevalent in the literature, it is important to pull together in one place the underlying **assumptions of χ^2**. For a thorough discussion of the misuse of χ^2, see the paper by Lewis and Burke (1949) and the subsequent rejoinders to that paper. These articles are not yet out of date, although it has been over 40 years since they were written. A more recent discussion of many of the issues raised by Lewis and Burke (1949) can be found in Delucchi (1983).

THE ASSUMPTION OF INDEPENDENCE

At the beginning of this chapter, we assumed that observations were independent of one another. The word *independence* has been used in two different ways in this chapter, and it is important to keep these two uses separate. A basic assumption of χ^2 deals with the independence of *observations* and is the assumption, for example, that one subject's choice among brands of coffee has no effect on another subject's choice. This is what we are referring to when we speak of an assumption of independence. We also spoke of the independence of *variables* when we discussed contingency tables. In this case, independence is what is being tested, whereas in the former use of the word it is an assumption.

It is not uncommon to find cases in which the assumption of independence of observations is violated, usually by having the same subject respond more than once. A typical illustration of the violation of the independence assumption occurred when a former student categorized the level of activity of each of five animals on each of four days. When he was finished, he had a table similar to this:

	Activity		
High	Medium	Low	Total
10	7	3	20

This table looks legitimate until you realize that there were only five animals, and thus each animal was contributing four tally marks toward the cell entries. If an animal exhibited high activity on Day 1, it is likely to have exhibited high activity on other days. The observations are not independent, and we can make a better-than-chance prediction of one score knowing another score. This kind of error is easy to make, but it is an error nevertheless. The best guard against it is to make certain that the total of all observations (*N*) equals precisely the number of subjects in the experiment.

NORMALITY

We discussed the assumption of normality (and therefore continuity) at length when we spoke of small expected frequencies. Nothing more needs to be said here.

INCLUSION OF NONOCCURRENCES

Although the requirement that nonoccurrences be included has not yet been mentioned specifically, it is inherent in the derivation. It is probably best explained by an example. Suppose that out of 20 students from rural areas, 17 were in favor of having daylight savings time (DST) all year. Out of 20 students from urban areas, only 11 were in favor of DST on a permanent basis. We want to determine if significantly more rural students than urban students are in favor of DST. One *erroneous* method of testing this would be to set up the following data table on the number of students favoring DST:

	Rural	Urban	Total
Observed	17	11	28
Expected	14	14	28

Nonoccurrences

We could then compute $\chi^2 = 1.29$ and fail to reject H_0. This data table, however, does not take into account the *negative* responses, which Lewis and Burke (1949) call **nonoccurrences**. In other words, it does not include the numbers of rural and urban students *opposed* to DST. Look back at our original derivation of chi-square. Note that we began with the formula for the binomial, which included $N - X$ and Nq as well as X and Np. These values must also be taken into account in our analysis. Therefore, the data should really be cast in the form of a contingency table:

	Rural	Urban	
Yes	17	11	28
No	3	9	12
	20	20	40

Now $\chi^2 = 4.29$, which is significant at $\alpha = .05$ resulting in an entirely different interpretation of the results.

Perhaps a more dramatic way to see why we need to include nonoccurrences can be shown by assuming that 17 out of *2000* rural students and 11 out of 20 urban students preferred DST. Consider how much different the interpretation of the two tables would be. Certainly, our analysis must reflect the difference between the two data sets, which would not be the case if we failed to include nonoccurrences.

Failure to take the nonoccurrences into account not only invalidates the test, but also reduces the value of χ^2, leaving you less likely to reject H_0. Again, you must be sure that the total (N) equals the number of subjects in the study.

6.7   ONE- AND TWO-TAILED TESTS

People are often confused as to whether chi-square is a one- or a two-tailed test. This confusion results from the fact that there are different ways of defining what we mean by a one- or a two-tailed test. If we think of the sampling distribution of χ^2, we can argue that χ^2 is a one-tailed test because we reject H_0 only when our value of χ^2 lies in the extreme right tail of the distribution. On the other hand, if we think of the underlying data on which our obtained χ^2 is based, we could argue that we have a two-tailed test. If, for example, we were using chi-square to test the fairness of a coin, we would reject H_0 if it produced too many heads *or* if it produced too many tails, since either event would lead to a large value of χ^2.

The preceding discussion is not intended to start an argument over semantics (it does not really matter whether you think of the test as one-tailed or two); rather, it is intended to point out one of the weaknesses of the chi-square test, so that you can take this into account. The weakness is that the test, as normally applied, is nondirectional. To take a simple example, consider the situation in which you wish to show that increasing amounts of quinine added to an animal's food make it less appealing. You take 90 rats and offer them a choice of three bowls of food that differ in the amount of quinine that has been added. You then count the number of animals selecting each bowl of food. Suppose the data are

Amount of Quinine		
Small	Medium	Large
39	30	21

The computed value of χ^2 is 5.4, which, on 2 *df*, is not significant at $p < .05$.

The important fact about the data is that any of the six possible configurations of the same frequencies (such as 21, 30, 39) would produce the same value of χ^2, and you receive no credit for the fact that the configuration you obtained is precisely the one that you predicted. Thus, you have made a *multi-tailed* test when in fact you have a specific prediction of the direction in which the totals will be ordered. One solution to this problem is to decide *before running the experiment* that you will automatically fail to reject H_0, regardless of the value of χ^2, unless the ordering of the frequencies fits with your prediction. This means that a priori you have a probability of only one-sixth of even calculating χ^2, since the other five-sixths of the outcomes, if H_0 is true, will be in the wrong direction. Since you have restricted yourself to rejecting H_0 only if the one particular order appears (out of six possible orders), you can now evaluate χ^2 at the $6(\alpha) = 6(.05) = .30$ level. If the H_0 is true, the probability of a Type I error will be $(1/6)(.30) = .05$, which is what you originally intended. In this instance, we would reject H_0 for this example.

It should be apparent that we do not have to restrict ourselves to the limited case in which only one particular ordering will lead to a test. For example, we might set the criterion as, The frequency of *small* must be less than the other two frequencies. In this case, we are allowing 2/6 of the possible outcomes and can enter the χ^2 table at $\alpha = .15$. It is important to keep in mind, however, that the admissible orders must be specified a priori, and that H_0 may never be rejected for other orders, regardless of how extreme the frequencies are. For a discussion of alternative ways of handling ordered categories, see Delucchi (1983).

6.8   LIKELIHOOD RATIO TESTS

Likelihood ratios

An alternative approach to analyzing categorical data is based on **likelihood ratios**. These procedures are introduced here for two reasons. First, there is a basis for believing that these tests are less affected by small sample sizes than the usual Pearson chi-square test that we have been considering when there are two or more degrees of freedom; for very large sample sizes, the two tests are equivalent. Second, these tests are heavily used in log-linear models for analyzing contingency tables, which will be discussed in Chapter 17. Log-linear models are particularly important when we want to analyze multidimensional contingency tables. Such models are being used more and more, and you should be exposed at least minimally to such methods.

Without going into detail, the general idea of a likelihood ratio can be described quite simply. Suppose we collect data and calculate the probability or likelihood of the data occuring given that the null hypothesis is true. We also calculate the likelihood that the data would occur under some alternative hypothesis (the hypothesis for which the data are most probable). If the data are much more likely for some alternative hypothesis than for H_0, we would be inclined to reject H_0. However, if the data are almost as likely under H_0 as they are for some other alternative, we would be inclined to retain H_0. Thus, the likelihood ratio (the ratio of these two likelihoods) forms a basis for evaluating the null hypothesis.

Using likelihood ratios, it is possible to devise tests, frequently referred to as "maximum likelihod χ^2," for analyzing both one-dimensional arrays and contingency tables. For the development of these tests, see Mood (1950) or Mood and Graybill (1963).

For the one-dimensional goodness-of-fit case,

$$\chi^2_{(C-1)} = 2 \sum O_i \ln\left(\frac{O_i}{E_i}\right)$$

where O_i and E_i are the observed and expected frequencies for each cell and ln denotes the natural logarithm (logarithm to the base e). This value of χ^2 can be evaluated using the standard table of χ^2 on $C - 1$ degrees of freedom.

For analyzing contingency tables, we can use essentially the same formula,

$$\chi^2_{(R-1)(C-1)} = 2 \sum O_{ij} \ln\left(\frac{O_{ij}}{E_{ij}}\right)$$

where O_{ij} and E_{ij} are the observed and expected frequencies in each cell. The expected frequencies are obtained just as they were for the standard Pearson chi-square test. This statistic is evaluated with respect to the χ^2 distribution on $(R - 1)(C - 1)$ degrees of freedom.

As an illustration of the use of the likelihood ratio test for contingency tables, consider the data found in the Lewis and Franklin (1944) study. The cell and marginal frequencies follow:

	Uncompleted Tasks	Completed Tasks	
Task Oriented	10	2	12
Self-Involved	1	11	12
	11	13	24

$$\chi^2 = 2 \sum O_{ij} \ln\left(\frac{O_{ij}}{E_{ij}}\right)$$

$$= 2\left[10 \ln\left(\frac{10}{5.5}\right) + 2 \ln\left(\frac{2}{6.5}\right) + \ln\left(\frac{1}{5.5}\right) + 11 \ln\left(\frac{11}{6.5}\right) \right]$$

$$= 2[10(0.59784) + 2(-1.17866) + (-1.70475) + 11(0.52609)]$$

$$= 15.4067$$

This answer agrees with the likelihood ratio statistic found in Exhibit 6.2. It is a χ^2 on 1 df, and since it exceeds $\chi^2_{.05} = 3.84$, it will lead to rejection of H_0.

6.9   MEASURES OF ASSOCIATION

A chi-square test is designed primarily to test a null hypothesis. When the data are in the form of a contingency table, the test tells us whether or not the two variables that serve as the basis of classification for that table are independent. But assuming that the test is significant, it still does not tell us much about the degree of relationship between the two variables—only that they are not independent.

For example, the contingency tables in Tables 6.5 and 6.6 will both lead to a significant chi-square test, but they clearly represent different degrees of relationship between the variables. (The examples are fictitious, but the numbers are reasonable.) In Table 6.5, females are somewhat more likely than males to identify as smokers. In Table 6.6, regardless of recent changes in the status of women, women are decidedly more likely to be the primary shopper for food for the family. Although the χ^2 statistics are different in these two situations, the difference in the magnitude of χ^2 is not a useful measure of association. (For example, doubling every number in one of these examples will double the magnitude of χ^2, but it will obviously not change the relative magnitude of the differences among cells.) However, a number of statistics have been developed to address the question of the degree of relationship between variables. These coefficients are generally referred to as **measures of association**. Although none is entirely satisfactory as a measure, you should be familiar with the most common of them. The three coefficients we will consider are based on the χ^2 statistic and are very easy to calculate.

Measures of association

TABLE 6.5
The relationship between smoking and gender

	Smoking Behavior		
	Nonsmoker	Smoker	
Male	400	100	500
Female	350	150	500
	750	250	1000

TABLE 6.6
The relationship between the primary shopper and gender

	Primary Food Shopper		
	Yes	No	
Female	400	100	500
Male	100	400	500
	500	500	1000

CONTINGENCY COEFFICIENT (*C*)

Contingency coefficient (*C*)

When data appear in the form of a contingency table of any dimension, one of the commonly employed coefficients is the **contingency coefficient (*C*)**. For all tables, *C* is defined as

$$C = \sqrt{\frac{\chi^2}{\chi^2 + N}}$$

Several difficulties arise with this coefficient. The first is rather obvious; namely, because N is always greater than 0, C can never equal 1. More important, however, the maximum value of C is dependent on the dimensions of the table from which it is computed. Thus, for a 2×2 table, $C_{max} = 0.707$; for a 3×3, $C_{max} = 0.816$; and so on. In general, $C_{max} = \sqrt{(k-1)/k}$, where k is the smaller of R (the number of rows) or C (the number of columns). This limitation of C_{max} makes interpreting C problematic. Although some have suggested using C/C_{max} as a measure of association, the statistical justification for this is not apparent. The contingency coefficient has long held an important place in statistical procedures and it will probably not be completely replaced in the near future, but it does have important, and better, competitors.

PHI (ϕ)

Phi (ϕ)

In the case of 2×2 tables, a correlation coefficient that we will consider in Chapter 10 serves as a good measure of association. This coefficient is called **phi(ϕ)**, and it represents the correlation between two variables, each of which is a dichotomy (i.e., takes on one of two distinct values). If we coded Gender as 1 or 2, for male and female, and coded Smoking as 1 for nonsmoker and 2 for smoker, and then correlated the two variables (see Chapters 9 and 10), the result would be phi. An easier way to calculate ϕ for these data is by the relation

$$\phi = \sqrt{\frac{\chi^2}{N}}$$

CRAMÉR'S PHI (ϕ_c)

The difficulty with phi is that it applies only to 2×2 tables, and therefore is not of any use with larger contingency tables. A way around this problem was suggested by Cramér (1946), who proposed

$$\phi_c = \sqrt{\frac{\chi^2}{N(k-1)}}$$

Cramér's ϕ_C
Cramér's V

where N is the sample size and k is again defined as the smaller of R and C.

Cramér's ϕ_C, often known as **Cramér's V** (I suspect because mainframe computer line printers do not usually print Greek characters), can be seen as a simple extension of phi. Note that when $k = 2$, it *is* phi. Unlike the contingency coefficient, the maximum value is 1 regardless of the dimensions of the table.

If I were going to retain only one measure of association, it would be Cramer's ϕ_C. It is not constrained by the size of the table; it reduces to phi for 2×2 tables; and, especially with 2×2 tables, it has a certain reasonable interpretation.

For Tables 6.5 and 6.6 given at the beginning of this section, $\chi^2 = 13.333$ and 360, respectively. Then $\phi_c = .12$ and 0.60. If you think of these as coefficients with a possible range of 0 to $+1.00$, you can see that they clearly reflect the differences apparent in the two tables.

ODDS RATIOS

Odds ratio

A useful statistic, especially for 2×2 tables, that makes clear the degree to which one variable influences another is the **odds ratio**. Odds ratios have the distinct advantage of being unaffected by sample size and by unequal row or column totals.

A good example of the use of an odds ratio is cited in a paper by Rosenthal (1990), who was actually using the data for a different purpose. An important study of the beneficial effects of small daily doses of aspirin on reducing heart attacks in men was reported in 1988. Many physicians were administered aspirin or a placebo, and the incidence of heart attacks was recorded. The data follow in Table 6.7.

TABLE 6.7
The effect of aspirin on the incidence of heart attacks

	Heart Attack	**No Heart Attack**	
Aspirin	104	10,933	11,037
Placebo	189	10,845	11,034
	293	21,778	22,071

For these data, 0.94% of people in the aspirin group and 1.71% of those in the control group suffered a heart attack during the course of the study, a difference of 0.77 percentage points. Instead of simply looking at percentages, we can look at the odds in favor of heart attacks over no heart attacks. The odds of having a heart attack given that you were in the aspirin group are equal to the number of people in that group that had a heart attack divided by the number who did not have a heart attack, which equals $104/10,933 = .0095125$. If you were in the control group, the odds of you having a heart attack are $189/10,845 = .0174274$. Both of these odds are quite low. However, if we form a ratio of these two odds, the ratio is $.0174274/.0095125 = 1.83$. This means that a person in the control group is 1.83 times as likely to have a heart attack as is a person in the aspirin group. Put in the reverse, you are about half as likely to have a heart attack if you take an aspirin a day than if you don't take an aspirin. That effect is impressive concerning something as serious as a heart attack. Odds ratios are often a clear and effective way of presenting data in 2×2 tables. Although it is possible to expand such ratios to deal with larger tables, the interpretation is far from clear.

KAPPA (κ)—A MEASURE OF AGREEMENT

Kappa(κ)

An important statistic that is not based on chi-square but that does use contingency tables is **kappa(κ)**, commonly known as Cohen's kappa (Cohen, 1960). This statistic measures interjudge agreement and is often used when we wish to examine the reliability of ratings.

Suppose we asked a judge with considerable clinical experience to interview 30 adolescents and classify them as exhibiting (1) no behavior problems, (2) internalizing behavior problems (e.g., withdrawn), and (3) externalizing behavior problems (e.g., acting out). Anyone reviewing our work would be concerned with the reliability of our measure—how do we know that this judge was doing any better than flipping a coin? As a check we ask a second judge to go through the same process and rate the same adolescents. We then set up a contingency table showing the agreements and disagreements between the two judges. Suppose the data are those shown in Table 6.8.

TABLE 6.8
Interjudge agreement on behavior problems

		Judge I		
Judge II	No Problem	Internalizing	Externalizing	
No Problem	15 (10.67)	2	3	20
Internalizing	1	3 (1.20)	2	6
Externalizing	0	1	3 (1.07)	4
	16	6	8	30

Ignore the values in parentheses for the moment. In this table, Judge I classified 16 adolescents as exhibiting no problems, as shown by the total in column 1. Of those 16, Judge II agreed that 15 had no problems, but also classed 1 of them as exhibiting internalizing problems and 0 as exhibiting externalizing problems. The entries on the diagonal (15, 3, 3) represent agreement between the two judges, whereas the off-diagonal entries represent disagreement.

Percentage of agreement

The simplest approach to these data is to calculate the **percentage of agreement**. For this statistic all we need to say is that out of 30 total cases, there were 21 cases (15 + 3 + 3) where the judges agreed. Then 21/30 = 0.70 = 70% agreement. This measure has problems, however. The majority of the adolescents in our sample exhibit no behavior problems, and both judges are (correctly) biased toward a classification of No Problem and away from the other classifications. The probability of No Problem for Judge I would be estimated as 16/30 = .53. The probability of No Problem for Judge II would be estimated as 20/30 = .67. If the two judges operated independently, the probability that they would both class a case as No Problem is .54. × .67 = .36, which for 30 judgments would mean that .36 × 30 = 10.67 agreements on No Problem alone, purely by chance.

Cohen (1960) proposed a chance-corrected measure of agreement known as kappa. To calculate kappa we first need to calculate the expected frequencies for each of the diagonal cells assuming that judgments are independent. We calculate these the same way we calculate the standard chi-square test. For example, the expected frequency of both judges assigning a classification of No Problem is (20 × 16)/30 = 10.67. For Internalizing it is (6 × 6)/30 = 1.2, and for Externalizing it is (4 × 8)/30 = 1.07. These values are shown in parentheses in the table.

We will now define kappa as

$$\kappa = \frac{\Sigma f_O - \Sigma f_E}{N - \Sigma f_E}$$

where f_O represents the observed frequencies on the diagonal and f_E represents the expected frequencies on the diagonal. Thus, $\Sigma f_O = 15 + 3 + 3 = 21$ and $\Sigma f_E = 10.67 +$

$1.20 + 1.07 = 12.94$. Then

$$\kappa = \frac{21 - 12.94}{30 - 12.94} = \frac{8.06}{17.06} = .47$$

Notice that this coefficient is considerably lower than the 70% agreement figure that we calculated above. Instead of 70% agreement, we have 47% agreement *after correcting for chance.*

If you examine the formula for kappa, you can see the correction that is being applied. In the numerator we subtract, from the number of agreements, the number of agreements that we would expect merely by chance. In the denominator we reduce the total number of judgments by that same amount. We then form a ratio of the two chance-corrected values.

Cohen and others have developed statistical tests for the significance of kappa. However, its significance is often not the issue. If kappa is low enough for us to even question its significance, the lack of agreement among our judges is a serious problem.

KEY TERMS

Chi-square (χ^2) (introduction)

Pearson's chi-square (introduction)

Chi-square distribution (χ^2) (6.1)

Gamma function (6.1)

Chi-square test (6.3)

Goodness-of-fit test (6.3)

Observed frequencies (6.3)

Expected frequencies (6.3)

Tabled distribution of χ^2 (6.3)

Multicategory case (6.3)

Independence of two variables (6.4)

Contingency table (6.4)

Cell (6.4)

Row total (RT) (6.4)

Column total (CT) (6.4)

Grand total (N) (6.4)

Yates' correction for continuity (6.4)

Fixed marginals (6.4)

Small expected frequency (6.5)

Normality (6.5)

Assumptions of χ^2 (6.6)

Nonoccurences (6.6)

Likelihood ratios (6.8)

Measures of association (6.9)

Contingency coefficient (C) (6.9)

Phi (ϕ) (6.9)

Cramér's ϕ_C (6.4)

Cramér's V (6.4)

Odds ratio (6.9)

Kappa (κ) (6.9)

Percentage of agreement (6.9)

EXERCISES

6.1   The chairperson of a psychology department suspects that some of her faculty are more popular with students than are others. There are three sections of introductory psychology, taught at 10:00 A.M., 11:00 A.M., and 12:00 P.M. by Professors Anderson, Klatsky, and Kamm. The number of students who enroll for each is

Professor Anderson	Professor Klatsky	Professor Kamm
32	25	10

State the null hypothesis, run the appropriate chi-square test, and interpret the results.

6.2 From the point of view of designing a valid experiment (as opposed to the arithmetic of calculation), there is an important difference between Exercise 6.1 and the examples used in this chapter. The data in Exercise 6.1 will not really answer the question the chairperson wants answered. What is the problem and how could the experiment be improved?

6.3 You have a theory that if you ask subjects to sort one-sentence characteristics of people (e.g., "I eat too fast") into five piles ranging from "not at all like me" to "very much like me," the percentage of items placed in each of the five piles will be approximately 10, 20, 40, 20, and 10. You have one of your friend's children sort 50 statements, and you obtain the following data:

$$8 \quad 10 \quad 20 \quad 8 \quad 4$$

Do these data support your hypothesis?

6.4 To what population does the answer to Exercise 6.3 generalize? (*Hint*: From what population of observations might these observations be thought to be randomly sampled?)

6.5 In a classic study by Clark and Clark (1939), African-American children were shown black dolls and white dolls and were asked to select the one with which they wished to play. Out of 252 children, 169 chose the white doll and 83 chose the black doll. What can we conclude about the behavior of these children?

6.6 Hraba and Grant (1970) repeated the Clark and Clark (1939) study referred to in Exercise 6.5. The studies were not exactly equivalent, but the results were interesting. Hraba and Grant found that out of 89 African-American children, 28 chose the white doll and 61 chose the black doll. Run the appropriate chi-square test on their data and interpret the results.

6.7 Combine the data from Exercises 6.5 and 6.6 into a two-way contingency table and run the appropriate test. How does the question that the two-way classification addresses differ from the questions addressed by Exercises 6.5 and 6.6?

6.8 From the Minitab output in Exhibit 6.3, verify the results in Exercise 6.7. Does Minitab use Yates' correction?

EXHIBIT 6.3

```
MTB  >  READ DATA INTO C1 AND C2
DATA >  169 83
DATA >  28 61
DATA >  END
        2 ROWS READ
MTB  >  CHISQ ON DATA IN C1 AND C2

Expected counts are printed below observed counts

              C1        C2      Total
       1     169        83       252
            145.58    106.42

       2      28        61        89
             51.42     37.58

Total        197       144       341

ChiSq  =  3.766   +   5.153  +
          10.664  +  14.590  =  34.173

df = 1

MTB  >  STOP
```

6.9   Community mental health centers tend to see clients who have a variety of problems, but some centers seem to see more people who have one kind of problem than people who have others. Out of the last 100 clients seen by each of three centers, (A, B, and C), a count has been made of those classed as having social-adjustment problems, problems with living, and other problems. The data follow:

Mental Health Center

	A	B	C	
Social Adjustment	50 *43.33*	40 *43.33*	40 *43.33*	130
Problems with Living	26 *26.67*	34 *26.67*	20 *26.67*	80
Other Problems	24 *30*	26 *30*	40 *30*	90
	100	100	100	300

(a) What null hypothesis would the chi-square test on this table actually test?
(b) Run the appropriate analysis.
(c) Interpret the results.

6.10   Use the data in Exercise 6.9 to demonstrate how chi-square varies as a function of sample size.
(a) Cut each cell entry in half and recompute chi-square.
(b) What does your answer to (a) say about the role of the sample size in hypothesis testing?

6.11   In discussing the correction for continuity, we referred to the idea of *fixed marginals*, meaning that a replication of the study would produce the same row and/or column totals. Give an example of a study in which
(a) no marginal totals are fixed.
(b) one set of marginal totals is fixed.
(c) both sets of marginal totals (row and column) could reasonably be considered to be fixed. (This is a hard one.)

6.12   Howell and Huessy (1981) used a rating scale to classify children in a second-grade class as showing or not showing behavior commonly associated with attention deficit disorder (ADD). They then classified these same children again when they later were in fourth and fifth grades. When the children reached the end of the ninth grade, the researchers examined school records and noted which children were enrolled in remedial English. In the following data, all children who were ever classified as exhibiting behavior associated with ADD have been combined into one group (labeled ADD):

	Remedial English	Nonremedial English	
Normal	22	187	209
ADD	19	74	93
	41	261	302

Does behavior during elementary school discriminate class assignment during high school?

6.13   In Exercise 6.12 children were classified as those who never showed ADD behavior and those who showed ADD behavior at least once in the second, fourth, or fifth grade. If we do not collapse across categories, we obtain the following data:

	Never	2nd	4th	2nd & 4th	5th	2nd & 5th	4th & 5th	2nd, 4th, & 5th
Remedial	22	2	1	3	2	4	3	4
Nonrem.	187	17	11	9	16	7	8	6

(a) Run the chi-square test.

(b) What would you conclude, ignoring the small expected frequencies?

(c) How comfortable do you feel with these small expected frequencies? If you are not comfortable, how might you handle the problem?

6.14 Apply the special formula for use with 2×2 contingency tables to the data in Exercise 6.12.

6.15 Stress has long been known to influence physical health. Visintainer, Volpicelli, and Seligman (1982) investigated the hypothesis that rats given 60 trials of inescapable shock would be less likely later to reject an implanted tumor than would rats who had received 60 trials of escapable shock or 60 no-shock trials. They obtained the following data:

	Inescapable Shock	Escapable Shock	No Shock	
Reject	8	19	18	45
No Reject	22	11	15	48
	30	30	33	93

What could the authors conclude from the results?

6.16 Darley and Latané (1968) asked subjects to participate in a discussion carried on over an intercom. Aside from the experimenter to whom they were speaking, subjects thought that there were zero, one, or four other people (bystanders) also listening over intercoms. Partway through the discussion, the experimenter feigned serious illness and asked for help. Darley and Latané noted how often the subject sought help for the experimenter as a function of the number of supposed bystanders. The data follow:

		Sought Assistance		
		Yes	No	
	0	11	2	13
Number of Bystanders	1	16	10	26
	4	4	9	13
		31	21	52

What could Darley and Latané conclude from the results?

6.17 In a study similar to the one in Exercise 6.16, Latané and Dabbs (1975) had a confederate enter an elevator and then "accidentally" drop a handful of pencils. They then noted whether bystanders helped pick them up. The data tabulate helping behavior by the gender of the bystander:

Gender of Bystander

	Female	Male	
Help	300	370	670
No Help	1003	950	1953
	1303	1320	2623

What could Latané and Dabbs conclude from the data? (Note that collapsing over gender, only about one-quarter of the bystanders helped. That is not relevant to the question, but it is an interesting finding that could easily be missed by routine computer-based analyses.)

6.18   In a study of eating disorders in adolescents, Gross (1985) asked each of her subjects whether they would prefer to gain weight, lose weight, or maintain their present weight. (*Note*: Only 12% of the girls in Gross's sample were actually more than 15% above their normative weight—a common cutoff for a label of "overweight.") When she broke down the data for girls by race (African-American versus white), she obtained the following results (other races have been omitted because of small sample sizes):

	Reducers	Maintainers	Gainers	
White	352	152	31	535
African-American	47	28	24	99
	399	180	55	634

(a) What conclusions can you draw from these data?

(b) Ignoring race, what conclusion can you draw about adolescent girls' attitudes toward their own weight?

6.19   Use the likelihood ratio approach to analyze the data in Exercise 6.12.

6.20   Use the likelihood ratio approach to analyze the data in Exercise 6.13.

6.21   It would be possible to calculate a one-way chi-square test on the data in row 2 of the table in Exercise 6.13? What hypothesis would you be testing if you did that? How would that hypothesis differ from the one you tested in Exercise 6.13?

6.22   Suppose we asked a group of 40 subjects whether they liked Monday Night Football, made them watch a game, and then asked them again. We would record the data as follows:

	Pro	Con	
Before	30	10	40
After	15	25	40
	45	35	80

Would chi-square calculated on such a table be appropriate? Why or why not?

6.23   As an alternative approach to the data in Exercise 6.22, you might note that after watching the game 20 people switched from Pro to Con and 5 people switched from con to pro. Thus, you can run a one-way chi-square test on the $20 + 5 = 25$ subjects who changed their opinion. [This is a test suggested by McNemar (1969)].

(a) Run the test.

(b) Explain how this tests the null hypothesis that you wanted to test.

6.24 The post office is interested in evaluating the speed of mail delivery. They mail letters to Washington, D.C., from a variety of distances and record the number of days it takes for the mail to arrive. The data follow:

	Distance			
Days to Deliver	**50 miles**	**150 miles**	**300 miles**	**3000 miles**
1	5	10	15	5
2	10	10	5	5
3 or more	15	5	10	10

(a) Run the chi-square test.

(b) Interpret the results.

6.25 From the SPSS[x] computer printout in Exhibit 6.4,

(a) verify the answer to Exercise 6.24a.

(b) interpret all the entries in the upper left-most cell.

(c) interpret the value for "significance."

EXHIBIT 6.4

Row Pct Col Pct Total Pct	50 MILES 1	150 MILES 2	300 MILES 3	3000 MILES 4	Row Total
DAYS					
1 ONE	5 14.3 16.7 4.8	10 28.6 40.0 9.5	15 42.9 50.0 14.3	5 14.3 25.0 4.8	35 33.3
2 TWO	10 33.3 33.3 9.5	10 33.3 40.0 9.5	5 16.7 16.7 4.8	5 16.7 25.0 4.8	30 28.6
3 THREE OR MORE	15 37.5 50.0 14.3	5 12.5 20.0 4.8	10 25.0 33.3 9.5	10 25.0 50.0 9.5	40 38.1
Column Total	30 28.6	25 23.8	30 28.6	20 19.0	105 100.0

CHI - SQUARE	D.F.	SIGNIFICANCE	MIN E. F.	CELLS WITH E. F. < 5
12. 89583	6	0. 0447	5. 714	NONE

NUMBER OF MISSING OBSERVATIONS = 0

6.26 A psychologist is interested in the relationship between depression and marital status. On the basis of a scale that he has devised, he classified single, divorced, and married males as depressed or nondepressed.

	Single	Divorced	Married
Depressed	10	10	15
Nondepressed	25	10	35

Calculate Cramér's ϕ_C and interpret the results.

6.27 Calculate the contingency coefficient for the data in Exercise 6.26 and interpret it. What is C_{max} for these data?

6.28 The relationship between financial security and income is not always as clear as one might suspect. An experimenter has obtained the following data on reported financial security for four groups of individuals who differ on net income. The cell entries are the number of respondents falling into each category.

Income

Security	Below $10,000	Below $20,000	Below $40,000	Above $40,000
Secure	5	10	20	10
Insecure	15	10	10	15

(a) Calculate Cramér's ϕ_C on these data.
(b) Calculate the contingency coefficient on these data.
(c) Interpret the results.

6.29 Another psychologist argued that it would have been more appropriate to offer a third response alternative in Exercise 6.28. She reran the study adding a *neutral* category, and her data look like this:

Income

Security	Below $10,000	Below $20,000	Below $40,000	Above $40,000	
Secure	4 3.67	5 4.89	5 7.33	8 6.11	22
Neutral	1 3.83	5 5.11	15 7.67	2 6.39	23
Insecure	10 7.5	10 10	10 15	15 12.5	45
	15	20	30	25	90

(a) Calculate Cramér's ϕ_C.
(b) Calculate a contingency coefficient.
(c) Interpret the results.

6.30 Can you compare the contingency coefficients you computed in Exercises 6.28 and 6.29?

6.31 Create a data file for Exercise 6.29 that resembles the one we used to generate Exhibit 6.2. Then use any statistical package to calculate χ^2. If your package allows calculation of Cramér's ϕ_C, generate that as well. How do your answers compare to those you obtained in Exercise 6.29?

6.32 Compute the odds and the odds ratio for the data in Exercise 6.12. What do these values mean?

6.33 Compute the odds in favor of seeking assistance for each of the groups in Exercise 6.16. Interpret the results.

6.34 Dabbs and Morris (1990) examined archival data from military records to study the relationship between high testosterone levels and antisocial behavior in males. Out of 4016 men in the Normal Testosterone group, 10.0% had a record of adult delinquency. Out of 446 men in the High Testosterone group, 22.6% had a record of adult delinquency. Is this relationship significant?

6.35 What is the odds ratio in Exercise 6.34? How would you interpret it?

6.36 In the study described in Exercise 6.34, 11.5% of the Normal Testosterone group and 17.9% of the High Testosterone group had a history of childhood delinquency.
(a) Is there a significant relationship between these two variables?
(b) Interpret this relationship.
(c) How does this result expand on what we already know from Exercise 6.34?

6.37 In a study examining the effects of individualized care of youths with severe emotional problems, Burchard and Schaefer (1990, personal communication) proposed to have caregivers rate the presence or absence of specific behaviors for each of 40 adolescents on a given day. To check for rater reliability, they asked two raters to rate each adolescent. The following hypothetical data represent reasonable results for the behavior of "extreme verbal abuse."

	Rater A		
Rater B	Presence	Absence	
Presence	12	2	14
Absence	1	25	26
	13	27	40

(a) What is the percentage of agreement for these raters?
(b) What is Cohen's kappa?
(c) Why is kappa noticeably less than the percentage of agreement?
(d) Modify the raw data, keeping N at 40, so that the two statistics move even farther apart. How did you do this?

COMPUTER EXERCISES

6.38 In a data set named Mireault.dat and described in Appendix Data Set, Mireault (1990) collected data from college students on the effects of the death of a parent. Leaving the critical variables aside for a moment, let's look at the distribution of students. The data set contains information on the gender of the students and the college (within the university) in which they were enrolled.
(a) Use any statistical package to tabulate Gender against College.
(b) What is the chi-square test on the hypothesis that College enrollment is independent of Gender?
(c) Interpret the results.

6.39 When we look at the variables in Mireault's data, we will want to be sure that there are not systematic differences of which we are ignorant. For example, if we found that the gender of the parent who died was an important variable in explaining some outcome variable, we would not like to later discover that the gender of the parent who died was in some way related to the gender of the subject, and that the effects of the two variables were confounded.

(a) Run a chi-square test on these two variables.

(b) Interpret the results.

(c) What would it mean to our interpretation of the relationship between gender of the parent and some other variable (e.g., subject's level of depression) if the gender of the parent is itself related to the gender of the subject?

CHAPTER SEVEN

HYPOTHESIS TESTS APPLIED TO MEANS

OBJECTIVES *To introduce the t test as a procedure for testing hypotheses with measurement data, and to show how it can be used with several different designs.*

CONTENTS

I n Chapters 5 and 6, we considered tests dealing with frequency (categorical) data. In those situations, the results of any experiment can usually be represented by a few subtotals—the frequency of occurrence of each category of response. In this and subsequent chapters, we will deal with a different type of data, that which I have previously termed measurement or quantitative data.

In analyzing measurement data, our interest can focus either on differences between groups of subjects or on the relationship between two or more variables. The question of relationships between variables will be postponed until Chapters 9, 10, 15, and 16. This chapter will be concerned with the question of differences, and the statistic we will be most interested in will be the sample mean.

Low-birthweight (LBW) infants (who are often premature) are considered to be at risk for a variety of developmental difficulties. As part of an example we will return to later, suppose we took 25 LBW infants in an experimental group and 31 LBW infants in a control group and, when these children were 2 years old, obtained a measure of cognitive ability. Suppose that we found that the LBW infants in the experimental group had a mean score of 117.2, whereas those in the control group had a mean score of 106.7. Is the observed mean difference sufficient evidence for us to conclude that 2-year-old LBW children in the experimental group generally score higher, on average, than do 2-year-old LBW control children? We will answer this particular question later; I mention the problem here to illustrate the kind of question we will discuss in this chapter.

7.1   SAMPLING DISTRIBUTION OF THE MEAN

As you should recall from Chapter 4, the sampling distribution of a statistic is the distribution of values we would expect to obtain for that statistic if we drew an infinite number of samples from the population in question and calculated the statistic on each sample. Because we are concerned in this chapter with sample *means*, we need to know something about the **sampling distribution of the mean**. Fortunately, all the important information about the sampling distribution of the mean can be summed up in one very important theorem: the central limit theorem. The **central limit theorem** is a factual statement about the distribution of means. In an extended form it states:

Sampling distribution of the mean

Central limit theorem

> Given a population with mean μ and variance σ^2, the sampling distribution of the mean (the distribution of sample means) will have a mean equal to μ (i.e., $\mu_{\overline{X}} = \mu$), a variance ($\sigma_{\overline{X}}^2$) equal to σ^2/N, and a standard deviation ($\sigma_{\overline{X}}$) equal to $\sigma/\sqrt{N}$. The distribution will approach the normal distribution as N, the *sample size*, increases.[†]

This is one of the most important theorems in statistics. It not only tells us what the mean and variance of the sampling distribution of the mean must be for any given sample size, but also states that as N increases, the shape of this sampling distribution approaches normal, *whatever* the shape of the parent population. The importance of these facts will become clear shortly.

The rate at which the sampling distribution of the mean approaches normal is a function of the shape of the parent population. If the population is itself normal, the sampling distribution of the mean will be normal regardless of N. If the population is symmetric but nonnormal, the sampling distribution of the mean will be nearly normal even for small sample sizes, especially if the population is unimodal. If the population is markedly skewed, sample sizes of 30 or more may be required before the means closely approximate a normal distribution.

To illustrate the central limit theorem, suppose we have an infinitely large population of random numbers evenly distributed between 0 and 100. This population will have what is called a **uniform distribution**—every value between 0 and 100 will be equally likely. The distribution of this population is shown in Figure 7.1. In this case, the mean (μ) is known to be equal to one-half of the range (50), the standard deviation (σ) is known to be equal to 28.87 (the range divided by the square root of 12), and the variance (σ^2) is thus 833.33.

Uniform distribution

Now suppose we drew 5000 samples of size 5 ($N = 5$) from this population and plotted the resulting sample means. Such sampling can be easily accomplished with a

---

[†] The central limit theorem can be found stated in a variety of forms. The simplest form merely says that the sampling distribution of the mean approaches normal as N increases. The more extended form given here includes all the important information about the sampling distribution of the mean.

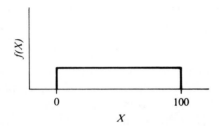

FIGURE 7.1
Uniform distribution
with $\mu = 50$,
$\sigma = 28.87$

simple computer program; the results of just such a procedure are presented in Figure 7.2a. From Figure 7.2a it is apparent that the distribution of means, although not exactly normal, is at least peaked in the center and trails off toward the extremes. If you were to go to the effort of calculating the mean and variance of this distribution, you would find that they are extremely close to $\mu = 50$ and $\sigma_{\bar{X}}^2 = \sigma^2/N = 833.33/5 = 166.67$. Any discrepancy between the actual values and those predicted by the central limit theorem is attributable to rounding error and to the fact that we did not draw an infinite number of samples.

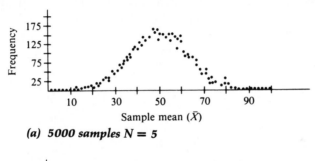

(a) **5000 samples N = 5**

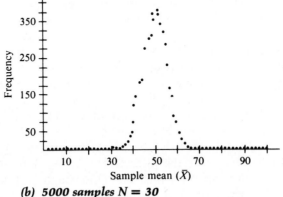

FIGURE 7.2
Computer-generated
sampling distribu-
tions of the mean

(b) **5000 samples N = 30**

Now suppose we repeated the entire procedure, only this time drawing 5000 samples, each with 30 observations. Again I have actually done this, and the results are plotted in Figure 7.2b. Here you see that just as the central limit theorem predicted, the distribution is approximately normal, the mean is again at $\mu = 50$, and the variance has been reduced to $833.33/30 = 27.78$.

7.2   TESTING HYPOTHESES ABOUT MEANS—σ KNOWN

From the central limit theorem, we know all the important characteristics of the sampling distribution of the mean. (We know its shape, its mean, and its standard deviation.) On the basis of this information, we are in a position to begin testing hypotheses about means. But first it might be well to go back to something we discussed with respect to the normal distribution. In Chapter 4 we saw that we could test a hypothesis about the population from which a single score (in that case a finger-tapping score) was drawn by calculating

$$z = \frac{X - \mu}{\sigma}$$

and then, if the population is normally distributed, by obtaining the probability of a value of z as low as the one obtained by using the tables of the standard normal distribution. We ran a one-tailed test on the null hypothesis that the tapping rate (70) of a single individual was drawn at random from a normally distributed population of healthy subjects' tapping rates with a mean of 100 and a standard deviation of 20. We did this by calculating

$$z = \frac{X - \mu}{\sigma}$$

$$= \frac{70 - 100}{20} = \frac{-30}{20}$$

$$= -1.5$$

and then using Appendix z to find the area below $z = -1.5$.[†] This value is 0.0668. Thus, approximately 7% of the time we would expect a score as low as this if we were sampling from a healthy population. Since this probability was not less than our preselected significance level of $\alpha = .05$, we could not reject the null hypothesis. The tapping rate for the person we examined was not an unusual rate for healthy individuals. Although in this example we were testing a hypothesis about a single observation, the same logic applies to testing hypotheses about sample means. The only difference is that instead of comparing an observation to a distribution of observations, we will compare a mean to a distribution of means.

In most situations in which we test a hypothesis about a population mean, we don't have any knowledge about the variance of that population. (This is the main reason we have t tests, which are the main focus of this chapter.) However, in a limited number of situations we do know σ. A discussion of testing a hypothesis when σ is known provides a good transition from what we already know about the normal distribution to what we want to know about t tests. An example of behavior problem scores on the Achenbach Child Behavior Checklist (CBCL) Achenbach (1991a) is a useful exam-

---

[†]Recall that the normal distribution is symmetric, and thus there are no entries for negative values of z. The "smaller portion" for $z = -1.5$ is the same as the "smaller portion" for $z = +1.5$.

ple for this purpose, because we know both the mean and the standard deviation for the population of Total Behavior Problems scores ($\mu = 50$ and $\sigma = 10$). We also know that a random sample of children under stress had a mean score of 56.0, and we want to test the null hypothesis that these five children are a random sample from a population of normal children (i.e., normal with respect to their general level of behavior problems). In other words, we want to test $H_0: \mu = 50$ against the alternative $H_1: \mu \neq 50$.

Because we know the mean and standard deviation of the population of general behavior problem scores, we can use the central limit theorem to obtain the sampling distribution when the null hypothesis is true. The central limit theorem states that if we obtain the sampling distribution of the mean from this population, it will have a mean of 50, a variance of $\sigma^2/N = 10^2/5 = 100/5 = 20$, and a standard deviation

Standard error   (usually referred to as the **standard error**)[†] of $\sigma/\sqrt{N} = 4.47$. This distribution is diagrammed in Figure 7.3. The arrow in Figure 7.3 represents the location of the sample mean.

FIGURE 7.3
Sampling distribution of the mean for samples of $N = 5$ drawn from a population with $\mu = 50$ and $\sigma = 10$

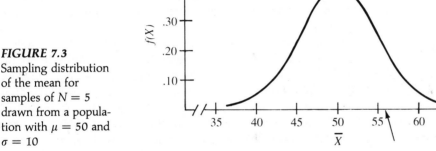

Because we know that the sampling distribution is normally distributed with a mean of 50 and a standard error of 4.47, we can find areas under the distribution by referring to tables of the standard normal distribution. Thus, for example, because two standard errors is $2(4.47) = 8.94$, the area to the right of $\overline{X} = 58.94$ is simply the area under the normal distribution greater than two standard deviations above the mean.

For our particular situation, we first need to know the probability of a sample mean greater than or equal to 56, and thus we need to find the area above $\overline{X} = 56$. We can calculate this in the same way we did with individual observations, with only a minor change in the formula for z:

$$z = \frac{X - \mu}{\sigma} \quad \text{becomes} \quad z = \frac{\overline{X} - \mu}{\sigma_{\overline{X}}}$$

[handwritten: symbol for standard deviation of sampling dist.]

[†]The standard deviation of any sampling distribution is normally referred to as the *standard error* of that distribution. Thus, the standard deviation of means is called the standard error of the mean (symbolized by $\sigma_{\overline{X}}$), whereas the standard deviation of differences between means, which will be discussed shortly, is called the standard error of differences between means and is symbolized by $\sigma_{\overline{X}_1 - \overline{X}_2}$. Minor changes in terminology, such as calling a standard deviation a standard error, are not really designed to confuse students. They just have that effect.

which can also be written as

$$\frac{\overline{X} - \mu}{\dfrac{\sigma}{\sqrt{N}}}$$

For our data this becomes

$$\frac{56 - 50}{4.47} = \frac{6}{4.47} = 1.34$$

Notice that the equation for z used here is in the same form as our earlier formula for z. The only differences are that X has been replaced by $\overline{X}$ and σ has been replaced by $\sigma_{\overline{X}}$. These differences occur because we are now dealing with a distribution of means, and thus the data points are now means, and the standard deviation in question is now the standard error of the mean (the standard deviation of means). The formula for z continues to represent (1) a point on a distribution, minus (2) the mean of that distribution, all divided by (3) the standard deviation of the distribution. Now rather than being concerned specifically with the distribution of $\overline{X}$, we have re-expressed the sample mean in terms of z scores and can now answer the question with regard to the standard normal distribution.

From Appendix z we find that the probability of a z as large as 1.34 is .0901. Because we want a two-tailed test of H_0, we need to double the probability to obtain the probability of a deviation as large as 1.34 standard errors *in either direction* from the mean. This is 2(.0901) = .1802. Thus, with a two-tailed test (that stressed children have a mean behavior problem score that is different in either direction from that of normal children) at the .05 level of significance, we would not reject H_0 because the obtained probability is greater than .05. We would conclude that we have no evidence that stressed children show more or fewer behavior problems than other children.

can't use double chart (only for t-test)

7.3   TESTING A SAMPLE MEAN WHEN σ IS UNKNOWN—THE ONE-SAMPLE t TEST

The preceding example was chosen deliberately from among a fairly limited number of situations in which the population standard deviation (σ) is known. In the general case, we rarely know the value of σ and usually have to estimate it by way of the *sample standard deviation* (s). When we replace σ with s in the formula, however, the nature of the test changes. We can no longer declare the answer to be a z score and evaluate it using tables of z. Instead, we will denote the answer as t and evaluate it using tables of t, which are different than tables of z. The reasoning behind the switch from z to t is really rather simple, although many texts ignore it. The basic problem that requires this change to t is related to the sampling distribution of the sample variance.

THE SAMPLING DISTRIBUTION OF s^2

Because the *t* test uses s^2 as an estimate of σ^2, it is important that we first look at the sampling distribution of s^2. This sampling distribution gives us some insight into the problems we are going to encounter. We saw in Chapter 2 that s^2 is an *unbiased* estimate of σ^2, meaning that with repeated sampling the average value of s^2 will equal σ^2. Although an unbiased estimator is a nice thing, it is not everything. The problem is that the shape of the sampling distribution of s^2 is positively skewed, especially for small samples. (In fact, it is related to the chi-square distribution, as we saw in Chapter 6.) An example of a computer-generated sampling distribution of s^2 ($\sigma^2 = 138.89$) is shown in Figure 7.4. Because of the skewness of this distribution, an *individual* value of s^2 is more likely to underestimate σ^2 than to overestimate it, especially for small samples. (s^2 remains unbiased because when it overestimates σ^2 it does so to such an extent as to balance the more numerous, but less drastic, underestimates.) Because of this skewness, the resulting value of *t* is likely to be larger than the value of *z* that we would have obtained had σ been known and used.

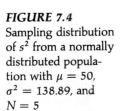

FIGURE 7.4
Sampling distribution of s^2 from a normally distributed population with $\mu = 50$, $\sigma^2 = 138.89$, and $N = 5$

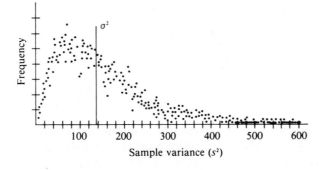

THE *t* STATISTIC

We are going to take the formula that we just developed for *z*,

$$z = \frac{\overline{X} - \mu}{\sigma_{\overline{X}}} = \frac{\overline{X} - \mu}{\dfrac{\sigma}{\sqrt{N}}} = \frac{\overline{X} - \mu}{\sqrt{\dfrac{\sigma^2}{N}}}$$

and substitute *s* for σ to give $t = \dfrac{\overline{X} - \mu}{s_{\overline{X}}} = \dfrac{\overline{X} - \mu}{\dfrac{s}{\sqrt{N}}} = \dfrac{\overline{X} - \mu}{\sqrt{\dfrac{s^2}{N}}}$

Since we know that for any particular sample, s^2 is more likely than not to be smaller than the appropriate value of σ^2, we can see that the *t* formula is more likely than not to produce a larger answer (in absolute terms) than we would have obtained if we had solved for *t* using the true but unknown value of σ^2 itself. As a result, it would not be fair to treat the answer as a *z* score and use the table of *z*. To do so would give us too many "significant" results—that is, we would make more than 5% Type I errors. (For example, when we were calculating z, we rejected H_0 at the .05 level of significance whenever z exceeded ± 1.96. If we create a situation in which H_0 is true, repeatedly draw samples of $N = 6$, and use s^2 in place of σ^2, we will obtain a value of ± 1.96 or greater more than 10% of the time.

The solution to our problem was supplied by William Gossett, who worked for the Guinness Brewing Company and wrote under the pseudonym of Student because the brewery would not allow him to publish under his own name. Gossett showed that if the data are sampled from a normal distribution, using s^2 in place of σ^2 would lead to a particular sampling distribution, now generally known as **Student's t distribution**. As a result of Gossett's work, all we have to do is substitute s^2, denote the answer as t, and evaluate t with respect to its own distribution, much as we evaluated z with respect to the normal distribution. The t distribution is tabled in Appendix t and examples of the actual distribution of t for various sample sizes are shown graphically in Figure 7.5.

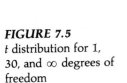

Student's t distribution

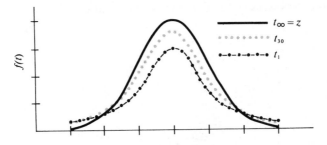

FIGURE 7.5
t distribution for 1, 30, and ∞ degrees of freedom

As you can see from Figure 7.5, the distribution of t varies as a function of the degrees of freedom, which for the moment we will define as one less than the number of observations in the sample. From what we know about χ^2, this is to be expected, since the distribution of χ^2, and thus the distribution of s^2, is also a function of the degrees of freedom. As $N \Rightarrow \infty$, $p(s^2 < \sigma^2) \Rightarrow p(s^2 > \sigma^2)$. Since the skewness of the sampling distribution of s^2 disappears as the number of degrees of freedom increases, the tendency for s to underestimate σ will also disappear. Thus, for an infinitely large number of degrees of freedom, t will be normally distributed and equivalent to z.

The test of one sample mean against a known population mean, which we have just performed, is based on the assumption that the sample was drawn from a normally distributed population. This assumption is required primarily because the t was derived assuming that the mean and variance are independent, which they are with a normal distribution. In practice, however, our t statistic can be referred to the t distribution whenever the sample size is sufficiently large to produce a normal sampling distribution of the mean.

DEGREES OF FREEDOM

I have mentioned that the t distribution is a function of the degrees of freedom (df). For the one-sample case, $df = N - 1$; the one degree of freedom has been lost because we used the sample mean in calculating s^2. To be more precise, we obtained the variance (s^2) by calculating the deviations of the observations from their own mean ($X - \overline{X}$), rather than from the population mean ($X - \mu$). Because the sum of the deviations about the mean [$\Sigma(X - \overline{X})$] is always zero, only $N - 1$ of the deviations are free to vary (the Nth deviation is determined if the sum of the deviations is to be zero). Because s^2 is based on $N - 1$ *df*, we have $N - 1$ degrees of freedom for *t*.

PSYCHOMOTOR ABILITIES OF LOW-BIRTHWEIGHT INFANTS

An example drawn from an actual study of low-birthweight (LBW) infants will be useful at this point because that same general study can serve to illustrate both this particular *t* test and other *t* tests to be discussed later in the chapter. Nurcombe et al. (1984) reported on an intervention program for the mothers of LBW infants. These infants present special problems for their parents because they are (superficially) unresponsive and unpredictable, in addition to being at risk for physical and developmental problems. The intervention program was designed to make mothers more aware of their infant's signals and more responsive to their needs, with the expectation that this would decrease later developmental difficulties often encountered with LBW infants. The study included three groups of infants: an LBW experimental group, an LBW control group, and a normal-birthweight (NBW) group. Mothers of infants in the last two groups did not receive the intervention treatment.

One of the dependent variables used in this study was the Psychomotor Development Index (PDI) of the Bayley Scales of Infant Development. This scale was first administered to all infants in the study when they were 6 months old. Because we would not expect to see differences in psychomotor development between the two LBW groups as early as 6 months, it makes some sense to combine the data from the two groups and ask whether LBW infants in general are significantly different from the normative population mean of 100 usually found with this index.

The data for the LBW infants on the PDI are presented in Table 7.1. To the right of the data are a stem-and-leaf display and a boxplot. These two displays are important for examining the general nature of the distribution of the data and for searching for the presence of outliers.

From the stem-and-leaf display, we can see that the data, although not exactly normally distributed, at least are not badly skewed. Given our sample size (56), it is reasonable to assume that the sampling distribution of the mean would be reasonably normal. One interesting and unexpected finding that is apparent from the stem-and-leaf display is the prevalence of certain scores. For example, there are five scores of 108, but no other scores between 104 and 112. Similarly, there are six scores of 120, but no other scores between 117 and 124. Notice also that, with the exception of six scores of 89, there is a relative absence of odd numbers. A complete analysis of the data requires that we at least notice these oddities and try to track down their source. It would be worthwhile to examine the scoring process to see whether there is a reason why scores often tended to fall in bunches. It is probably an artifact of the way raw scores are converted to scale scores, but it is worth checking. (In fact, if you check the scoring manual, you will find that these peculiarities are to be expected.) The fact that Tukey's exploratory data analysis (EDA) procedures lead us to notice these pecu-

TABLE 7.1
Data for LBW infants
on Psychomotor
Development Index
(PDI)

Raw Data				Stem-and-Leaf Display	
96	120	112	100	Stem	Leaf
125	96	86	124		
89	104	116	89	8*	3
127	89	89	124	8.	6 6 9 9 9 9 9 9
102	104	120	102	9*	2 2 2 2 2 2
112	92	92	102	9.	5 6 6 6 6 8 8
120	124	83	116	10*	0 0 0 2 2 2 2 4 4 4
108	96	108	96	10.	8 8 8 8 8
92	108	108	95	11*	2 2 2
120	86	92	100	11.	6 6 7
104	100	120	120	12*	0 0 0 0 0 0 4 4 4
89	92	102	98	12.	5 6 7
92	98	100	108		
89	117	112	126		

Boxplot

```
|----|----|----|----|----|----|----|----|----|----|
```
Mean = 104.125
S.D. = 12.584
N = 56

```
----------  |======|======|  -----------
```

liarities is one of the great virtues of these methods. Finally, from the boxplot we can see that there are no serious outliers we need to worry about, which makes our task noticeably easier.

From the data in Table 7.1, we can see that the mean PDI score for our LBW infants is approximately 104. The norms for the PDI indicate that the population mean should be 100. Given the data, a reasonable first question concerns whether the mean of our LBW sample departs significantly from a population mean of 100. The t test is designed to answer this question.

From our formula for t and from the data, we have

$$t = \frac{\overline{X} - \mu}{s_{\overline{X}}} = \frac{\overline{X} - \mu}{s/\sqrt{N}}$$

$$= \frac{104.125 - 100}{12.584/\sqrt{56}} = \frac{4.125}{1.682}$$

$$= 2.45$$

This value will be a member of the t distribution on $56 - 1 = 55$ df if the null hypothesis is true—that is, if the data were sampled from a population with $\mu = 100$.

A t value of 2.45 in and of itself is not particularly meaningful unless we can evaluate it against the sampling distribution of t. For this purpose, the critical values of t are presented in Appendix t. This table differs in form from the table of the normal distribution (z) because instead of giving the area above and below each specific value of t, which would require too much space, the table instead gives those values of t that cut off particular critical areas—for example, the .05 and .01 levels of significance. Also, in contrast to z, a different t distribution is defined for each possible number of degrees of freedom. Since we want to work at the two-tailed .05 level, we will want to know the value of t that cuts off $5/2 = 2.5\%$ in each tail. These critical values are generally denoted $t_{\alpha/2}$ or, in this case, $t_{.025}$. From the table of the t distribution in Appendix t, an abbreviated version of which is shown in Table 7.2, we find that the critical value of $t_{.025}$ (rounding to 50 *df* for purposes of the table) = 2.009. (This is sometimes written as $t_{.025}(50) = 2.009$ to indicate the degrees of freedom.) Because the obtained value of t, written t_{obt}, is greater than $t_{.025}$, we will reject H_0 at $\alpha = .05$, two-tailed, that our sample came from a population of observations with $\mu = 100$. Instead, we will conclude that our sample of LBW children differed from the general population of children on the PDI. In fact, their mean was significantly *above* the normative population mean. This points out the advantage of using two-tailed tests, since we would have expected this group to score below the normative mean. (This might also suggest that we check our scoring procedures to make sure we are not systematically overscoring our subjects. In fact, however, a number of other studies using the Bayley have reported similarly high means.)

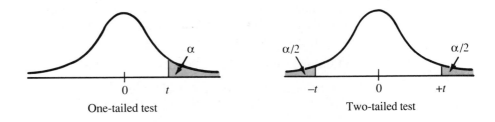

One-tailed test   Two-tailed test

TABLE 7.2
Percentage points of
the *t* distribution

	Level of Significance for One-Tailed Test								
	.25	.20	.15	.10	.05	.025	.01	.005	.0005
	Level of Significance for Two-Tailed Test								
df	.50	.40	.30	.20	.10	.05	.02	.01	.001
1	1.000	1.376	1.963	3.078	6.314	12.706	31.821	63.657	63.662
2	0.816	1.061	1.386	1.886	2.920	4.303	6.965	9.925	31.599
3	0.765	0.978	1.250	1.638	2.353	3.182	4.541	5.841	12.924
4	0.741	0.941	1.190	1.533	2.132	2.776	3.747	4.604	8.610
5	0.727	0.920	1.156	1.476	2.015	2.571	3.365	4.032	6.869
6	0.718	0.906	1.134	1.440	1.943	2.447	3.143	3.707	5.959
7	0.711	0.896	1.119	1.415	1.895	2.365	2.998	3.499	5.408
8	0.706	0.889	1.108	1.397	1.860	2.306	2.896	3.355	5.041
9	0.703	0.883	1.100	1.383	1.833	2.262	2.821	3.250	4.781
10	0.700	0.879	1.093	1.372	1.812	2.228	2.764	3.169	4.587
...	...	...	...	...	...	...	...	...	...
30	0.683	0.854	1.055	1.310	1.697	2.042	2.457	2.750	3.646
40	0.681	0.851	1.050	1.303	1.684	2.021	2.423	2.704	3.551
50	0.679	0.849	1.047	1.299	1.676	2.009	2.403	2.678	3.496
100	0.677	0.845	1.042	1.290	1.660	1.984	2.364	2.626	3.390
∞	0.674	0.842	1.036	1.282	1.645	1.960	2.326	2.576	3.291

Source: The entries in this table were computed by the author.

THE MOON ILLUSION

It may be useful to consider a second example, this one taken from a classic paper by Kaufman and Rock (1962) on the moon illusion. Kaufman and Rock concluded that the commonly observed fact that the moon near the horizon appears larger than does the moon at its zenith (highest point overhead) could be explained on the basis of the greater *apparent* distance of the moon when it is at the horizon. As part of a very complete series of experiments, the authors initially sought to estimate the moon illusion by asking subjects to adjust a variable "moon" that appeared to be on the horizon so as to match the size of a standard "moon" that appeared at its zenith, or vice versa. (In these measurements, they used not the actual moon but an artificial one created with special apparatus.) One of the first questions we might ask is whether there really is a moon illusion—that is, whether a larger setting is required to match a horizon moon or a zenith moon. The following data for 10 subjects are taken from Kaufman and Rock's paper and represent the ratio of the diameter of the variable and standard moons. A ratio of 1.00 would indicate no illusion, whereas a ratio other than 1.00 would represent an illusion. (For example, a ratio of 1.50 would mean that the horizon moon appeared to have a diameter 1.50 times the diameter of the zenith moon.) Evidence in support of an illusion would require that we reject $H_0: \mu = 1.00$ in favor of $H_1: \mu \neq 1.00$.

Obtained ratio: 1.73   1.06   2.03   1.40   0.95   1.13   1.41   1.73   1.63   1.56

For these data, $N = 10$, $\overline{X} = 1.463$, and $s = 0.341$. A t test on $H_0: \mu = 1.00$ is given by

$$t = \frac{\overline{X} - \mu}{s_{\overline{X}}} = \frac{\overline{X} - \mu}{\dfrac{s}{\sqrt{N}}}$$

$$= \frac{1.463 - 1.000}{\dfrac{0.341}{\sqrt{10}}} = \frac{0.463}{0.108}$$

$$= 4.29$$

From Appendix t, with $10 - 1 = 9$ df for a two-tailed test at $\alpha = .05$, the critical value of $t_{.025}(9) = \pm 2.262$. The obtained value of t was 4.29. Since $4.29 > 2.262$, we can reject H_0 at $\alpha = .05$ and conclude that the true mean ratio under these conditions is not equal to 1.00. In fact, it is greater than 1.00, which is what we would expect on the basis of our experience. (It is always comforting to see science confirm what we have all known since childhood, but in this case the results also indicate that Kaufman and Rock's experimental apparatus performs as it should.)

USING MINITAB TO RUN ONE-SAMPLE t TESTS

When you have a large data set, it is often convenient to use a program such as Minitab to compute t values. Exhibit 7.1 shows how Minitab can be used to obtain a one-sample t test and confidence limits for the moon-illusion data. (Confidence limits will be discussed in Section 7.8; for now you can ignore them.) Notice that Minitab's results agree, within rounding error, with those we obtained by hand. Notice also that Minitab computes the exact probability of a Type I error (the ***p* level**), rather than comparing t to a tabled value. Thus, whereas we concluded that the probability of a Type I error was *less than* .05, Minitab reveals that the actual probability is .0020. Most computer programs operate in this way.

***p* level**

EXHIBIT 7.1
Minitab for
one-sample t tests
and confidence limits

```
MTB  > SET THE FOLLOWING DATA IN COLUMN C1
DATA > 1.73 1.06 2.03 1.40 0.95 1.13 1.41 1.73 1.63 1.56
DATA > END
MTB  > TTEST AGAINST MU = 1.00 FOR DATA IN COLUMN C1

TEST OF MU = 1.000 VS MU N.E. 1.000

         N   MEAN   STDEV   SE MEAN      T    P VALUE
C1      10   1.463   0.341    0.108    4.30    0.0020

MTB  > T INTERVAL FOR 95 PERCENT CONFIDENCE INTERVAL FOR DATA IN COLUMN C1

         N   MEAN   STDEV   SE MEAN    95.0 PERCENT C.I.
C1      10   1.463   0.341    0.108    (1.219,   1.707)

MTB  > T INTERVAL FOR 99 PERCENT CONFIDENCE INTERVAL FOR DATA IN COLUMN C1

         N   MEAN   STDEV   SE MEAN    99.0 PERCENT C.I.
C1      10   1.463   0.341    0.108    (1.113,   1.813)

MTB  > STOP
```

7.4   HYPOTHESIS TESTS APPLIED TO MEANS—TWO MATCHED SAMPLES

In Section 7.3 we considered the situation in which we had one sample mean ($\overline{X}$) and wished to test to see whether it was reasonable to believe that such a sample mean would have occurred if we had been sampling from a population with some specified mean (often denoted μ_0). Another way of phrasing this is to say that we were testing to determine whether the mean of the population from which we sampled (call it μ_1) was equal to some particular value given by the null hypothesis (μ_0). In this section we will consider the case in which we have two **matched samples** (often called **repeated measures**, when the same subjects respond on two occasions, or **related samples**, correlated samples, paired samples, or dependent samples) and wish to perform a test on the difference between their two means. In this case we want what is sometimes called the **matched-sample *t* test**.

Matched samples,
Repeated measures,
Related samples

Matched-sample *t*
test

As an example of the analysis of matched (related) samples, we will consider the intervention study of LBW infants referred to earlier. Part of the study on LBW infants involved collecting data on the Bayley Mental Development Index (MDI) when the children were 6, 12, and 24 months old. Previous work on such children would suggest that the MDI scores for the control group of nonintervention LBW children might decline noticeably between 6 and 24 months of age. The data for the

TABLE 7.3 Data and difference scores on Mental Development Index (MDI) for the LBW control group at 6 and 24 months of age

	MDI—6 Months	MDI—24 Months	Difference (D)	Stem-and-Leaf Display	
				Stem	Leaf
	124	114	−10	−3.	5 8
	94	88	−6	−3*	
	115	102	−13	−2.	5 5
	110	127	17	−2*	0
	116	104	−12	−1.	6
	139	104	−35	−1*	0 2 2 3 4 4 4
	116	91	−25	−0.	5 6 9
	110	96	−14	−0*	2 2 3
	129	104	−25	0*	2 3 4
	120	106	−14	0.	7 9 9 9
	105	91	−14	1*	4
	88	102	14	1.	7 7
	120	104	−16	2*	3
	120	100	−20	2.	8
	116	114	−2		
	105	109	4	2*	3 = 23
	100	109	9		
	91	119	28		
	129	91	−38		
	84	81	−3		
	91	114	23		
	116	119	3		
	100	102	2		
	113	111	−2		
	89	80	−9		
	102	119	17		
	110	119	9		
	116	123	7		
	124	119	−5		
	126	114	−12		
	123	132	9		
Mean	111.00	106.71	−4.29		
S.D.	13.85	12.95	16.04		
N	31	31	31		

Boxplot

control group at 6 and 24 months, and the differences between them, are shown in Table 7.3, with the stem-and-leaf display and the boxplot on the difference scores. Because these data represent pairs of scores from each child, the two sets of scores are related rather than independent. Therefore, the appropriate test for a change in the mean score over time is the matched-sample *t* test. Before carrying out that test, however, let's look more closely at the data.

From the stem-and-leaf display in Table 7.3, we can see that the distribution is slightly, but not markedly, skewed. This display highlights the large variability in the difference scores. Two children showed a decrease (negative difference score) of over 30 points, whereas two other children increased their scores by at least 20 points. This substantial variability does not invalidate the *t* test, but it does suggest that the question of whether the MDI *means* decrease may not be the only one we should be asking. In fact, although we will not do so here, it may be more important to try to explain the large variability in difference scores—why do some children show so much improvement while others show so much deterioration? (For example, using the techniques to be discussed in Chapter 9, you might plot the degree of change against initial score level.) The boxplot again illustrates the symmetrical nature of the distribution and does not indicate the presence of any outliers. Although large positive and negative scores occur here, they do not qualify as outliers because they are not uniquely large—the large standard deviation of the difference scores has already been discussed.

We want a *t* test on the difference between the 6- and 24-month means for these matched samples. We will designate the first set of scores as X_1 and the second set as X_2. The null hypothesis we want to test is the hypothesis that the mean (μ_1) of the population of scores from which the first set of data was drawn is equal to the mean (μ_2) of the population from which the second set of data was drawn. In others words, we want to test

$$H_0: \mu_1 = \mu_2 \qquad \text{(or, equivalently, } H_0: \mu_1 - \mu_2 = 0\text{)}$$

Note that we have no interest in the values of μ_1 and μ_2 themselves; only in whether they are equal. Note also that we will be testing this null hypothesis using data from matched samples.

DIFFERENCE SCORES

Difference scores

Although it would seem most obvious to view the data as representing two samples of scores, one set obtained at 6 months and the other at 24 months, it is also possible, and very profitable, to transform the data into one set of scores—the set of differences between X_1 and X_2 for each subject. These differences are called **difference scores** and are indicated in the third column of Table 7.3. These scores are often represented by *D* (for difference) and can be thought of as the degree of improvement or decrement between the two testing times. If in fact the MDI scores of LBW children do not in general decrease over time (i.e., if H_0 is true), the average score would not change from session to session. By chance, some subjects would happen to have a higher score on X_2 than on X_1 and some would have a lower score, but *on the average* there would be no difference. If we now think of our data as being the column of difference scores, the null hypothesis becomes the hypothesis that the mean of a population of difference scores (denoted μ_D) equals zero. Since it can be shown that $\mu_D = \mu_1 - \mu_2$, then we can write $H_0: \mu_D = \mu_1 - \mu_2 = 0$. But now we can see that we are testing a hypothesis using *one* sample of data (the sample of difference scores), and we already know how to do that from Section 7.3.

THE t STATISTIC

We are now at precisely the same place we were with the one-sample t test when we had a sample of data and a null hypothesis ($\mu = 0$). The only difference is that in this case the data are difference scores, and the mean and standard deviation are based on the differences. Recall that t was defined as the difference between a sample mean and a population mean, divided by the standard error of the mean. Then we have

$$t = \frac{\overline{D} - 0}{s_{\overline{D}}} = \frac{\overline{D} - 0}{\frac{s_D}{\sqrt{N}}}$$

where $\overline{D}$ and $s_{\overline{D}}$ are the mean and standard deviation of the difference scores and N is the number of difference scores (the number of *pairs*, not the number of raw scores). For our data

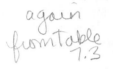
again from Table 7.3

$$t = \frac{\overline{D} - 0}{\frac{s_D}{\sqrt{N}}} = \frac{-4.29 - 0}{\frac{16.04}{\sqrt{31}}} = \frac{-4.29}{2.88} = -1.49$$

DEGREES OF FREEDOM

The degrees of freedom for the matched-sample case are the same as they were for the one-sample case. Since we are working with the difference scores, N will be equal to the number of differences (or the number of *pairs* of observations, or the number of *independent* observations, all of which amount to the same thing). Since the variance of these difference scores (s_D^2) is used as an estimate of the variance of a population of difference scores (σ_D^2), and since this sample variance is obtained using the sample mean ($\overline{D}$), we will lose one *df* to the mean and have $N - 1$ *df*.

Because we have 31 difference scores in this example, we will have 30 degrees of freedom. From Appendix t we find that for a two-tailed test at the .05 level of significance, $t_{.025}(30) = \pm 2.042$. Our obtained value of t (-1.49) is smaller than the critical value; thus we will not reject H_0. We have no reason to doubt that our difference scores were sampled from a population of difference scores where $\mu_D = 0$. In practical terms, this means that we have not shown that the control group of LBW infants exhibited a decreasing level of performance over time. Although this finding is very positive from the point of view of the children involved (who are, after all, the important people!), it makes it more difficult to show later that the intervention program is useful. An intervention program looks best when you can show that people who do *not* receive it *deteriorate* over time, whereas those who *do* receive it stay the same or even *improve*.

THE MOON ILLUSION REVISITED

As a second example, we will return to the work by Kaufman and Rock (1962) on the moon illusion. An important hypothesis about the source of the moon illusion was put forth by Holway and Boring (1940), who suggested that the illusion was due to the fact that when the moon was on the horizon, the observer looked straight at it with eyes level, whereas when it was at its zenith, the observer had to elevate his eyes as well as his head. Holway and Boring proposed that this difference in the elevation of the eyes was the cause of the illusion. Kaufman and Rock thought differently. To test Holway and Boring's hypothesis, Kaufman and Rock devised an apparatus that allowed them to present two artificial moons (one at the horizon and one at the zenith) and to control whether the subjects elevated their eyes to see the zenith moon. In one case, the subject was forced to put his head in such a position as to be able to see the zenith moon with eyes level. In the other case, the subject was forced to see the zenith moon with eyes raised. (The horizon moon was always viewed with eyes level.) In both cases, the dependent variable was the ratio of the perceived size of the horizon moon to the perceived size of the zenith moon (a ratio of 1.00 would represent no illusion). If Holway and Boring were correct, there should have been a greater illusion (larger ratio) in the eyes-elevated condition than in the eyes-level condition, although the moon was always perceived to be in the same place, the zenith. The actual data for this experiment are given in Table 7.4.

TABLE 7.4
Magnitude of the moon illusion when zenith moon is viewed with eyes level and with eyes elevated

Subject	Eyes Elevated	Eyes Level	Difference (*D*)
1	1.65	1.73	-0.08
2	1.00	1.06	-0.06
3	2.03	2.03	0.00
4	1.25	1.40	-0.15
5	1.05	0.95	0.10
6	1.02	1.13	-0.11
7	1.67	1.41	0.26
8	1.86	1.73	0.13
9	1.56	1.63	-0.07
10	1.73	1.56	0.17

$$\bar{D} = 0.019$$
$$s_D = 0.137$$
$$s_{\bar{D}} = 0.043$$

In this example, we want to test the *null* hypothesis that the means are equal under the two viewing conditions. Because we are dealing with related observations (each subject served under both conditions), we will work with the difference scores and test $H_0: \mu_D = 0$. Using a two-tailed test at $\alpha = .05$, the alternative hypothesis is $H_1: \mu_D \neq 0$.

From the formula for a t test on related samples, we have

$$t = \frac{\bar{D} - \mu}{s_{\bar{D}}} = \frac{\bar{D} - 0}{\dfrac{s_D}{\sqrt{N}}}$$

$$= \frac{0.019 - 0}{\dfrac{0.137}{\sqrt{10}}} = \frac{0.019}{0.043}$$

$$= 0.44$$

From Appendix t, we find that $t_{.025}(9) = \pm 2.262$. Since $t_{\text{obt}} = 0.44$ is less than 2.262, we will fail to reject H_0 and will decide that we have no evidence to suggest that the illusion is affected by the elevation of the eyes.[†] (In fact, these data also include a second test of Holway and Boring's hypothesis since they would have predicted that there would not be an illusion if subjects viewed the zenith moon with eyes level. On the contrary, the data reveal a considerable illusion under this condition. A test of the significance of the illusion with eyes level can be obtained by the methods discussed in the previous section, and the illusion is in fact significant.)

MATCHED SAMPLES

In many, but certainly not all, situations in which we will use the matched-sample t test, we will have two sets of data from the same subjects. For example, we might ask each of 20 people to rate their level of anxiety before and after donating blood. Or we might record ratings of level of disability made using two different scoring systems for each of 20 handicapped individuals in an attempt to see whether one scoring system leads to generally lower assessments than does the other. In both examples, we would have 20 sets of numbers, two numbers for each person, and would expect these two sets of numbers to be related (or, in the terminology we will later adopt, to be correlated). Consider the blood-donation example. People differ widely in level of anxiety. Some seem to be anxious all of the time no matter what happens, and others just take things as they come and do not worry about anything. Thus, there should be a relationship between an individual's anxiety level before donating blood and her anxiety level after donating blood. In other words, if we know what a person's anxiety score was before donation, we can make a reasonable guess what it was after donation. Similarly, some people are severely handicapped whereas others are only mildly hand-

---

[†] A glance at Appendix t will reveal that a t less than 1.96 (the critical value for z) will never be significant at $\alpha = .05$, regardless of the number of degrees of freedom. Moreover, unless you have at least 50 degrees of freedom, t values less than 2.00 will not be significant, often making it unnecessary for you even to bother looking at the table of t.

icapped. If we know that a particular person received a high assessment using one scoring system, it is likely that he also received a relatively high assessment using the other system. The relationship between data sets does not have to be perfect—it probably never will be. The fact that we can make better-than-chance predictions is sufficient to classify two sets of data as matched or related.

In the two preceding examples, I chose situations in which each person in the study contributed two scores. Although this is the most common way of obtaining related samples, it is not the only way. For example, a study of marital relationships might involve asking husbands and wives to rate their satisfaction with their marriage, with the goal of testing to see whether wives are, on average, more or less satisfied than husbands. Here each individual would contribute only one score, but the couple as a unit would contribute a pair of scores. It is reasonable to assume that if the husband is very dissatisfied with the marriage, his wife is probably also dissatisfied, and vice versa, thus causing their scores to be related.

Many experimental designs involve related samples. They all have one thing in common, and that is the fact that knowing one member of a pair of scores tells you something—maybe not much, but something—about the other member. Whenever this is the case, we say that the samples are matched.

MISSING DATA

Ideally, with matched samples we have a score on each variable for each case or pair of cases. If a subject participates in the pretest, she also participates in the posttest. If one member of a couple provides data, so does the other member. When we are finished collecting data, we have a complete set of paired scores. Unfortunately, experiments do not usually work out as cleanly as we would like.

Suppose, for example, that we want to compare scores on a checklist of children's behavior problems completed by mothers and fathers. Most of the time both parents will complete the form. But there might be 10 cases where the mother sent in her form but the father did not, and 5 cases where we have a form from the father but not from the mother. The normal procedure in this situation is to eliminate the 15 pairs of parents where we do not have complete data, and then run a matched-sample *t* test on the data that remain. This is the way almost everyone would analyze the data. There is an alternative, however, that allows us to use all of the data if we are willing to assume that data are missing at random and not systematically.

Bohj (1978) proposed an ingenious test in which you basically compute a matched-sample *t* for those cases in which both scores are present, then compute an additional independent group *t* between the scores of mothers without fathers and fathers without mothers, and finally combine the two *t* statistics. This combined *t* can then be evaluated against special tables. These tables are available in Wilcox (1986), and approximations to critical values of this combined statistic are discussed briefly in Wilcox (1987a). This test is sufficiently awkward that you would not use it simply because you are missing two or three observations. But it can be extremely useful when quite a few pieces of data are missing. For a more extensive discussion, see Wilcox (1987b).

USING MINITAB FOR t TESTS ON MATCHED SAMPLES

To use Minitab with matched samples, we simply read in the data on the two observations for each subject and then use Minitab to compute a column of difference scores (e.g., LET C3 = C2 − C1). We then apply the TTEST procedure to these differences. Since this is basically the same approach we used in Exhibit 7.1, it will not be repeated here.

7.5   HYPOTHESIS TESTS APPLIED TO MEANS— TWO INDEPENDENT SAMPLES

One of the most common uses of the t test involves testing the difference between the means of two independent groups. We might wish to compare the mean number of trials needed to reach criterion on a simple visual discrimination task for two groups of rats—one raised under normal conditions and one raised under conditions of sensory deprivation. Or we might wish to compare the mean levels of retention of a group of college students asked to recall active declarative sentences and a group asked to recall passive negative sentences. Or we might place subjects in a situation in which another person needed help; we could compare the latency of helping behavior when subjects were tested alone and when they were tested in groups.

In conducting any experiment with two independent groups, we would most likely find that the two sample means differed by some amount. The important question, however, is whether this difference is sufficiently large to justify the conclusion that the two samples were drawn from different populations—that is, using the example of helping behavior, is the mean of the population of latencies from singly tested subjects different from the mean of the population of latencies from group-tested subjects? Before we consider a specific example, however, we will need to examine the sampling distribution of differences between means and the t test that results from it.

DISTRIBUTION OF DIFFERENCES BETWEEN MEANS

Sampling distribution of differences between means

When we are interested in testing for a difference between the mean of one population (μ_1) and the mean of a second population (μ_2), we will be testing a null hypothesis of the form $H_0: \mu_1 - \mu_2 = 0$ or, equivalently, $\mu_1 = \mu_2$. Because the test of this null hypothesis involves the difference between independent sample means, it is important that we digress for a moment and examine the **sampling distribution of differences between means**. Suppose that we have two populations labeled X_1 and X_2 with means μ_1 and μ_2 and variances σ_1^2 and σ_2^2. We now draw pairs of samples of size N_1 from population X_1 and of size N_2 from population X_2, and record the means and the difference between the means for each pair of samples. Because we are sampling independently from each population, the sample means will be independent. (Means are

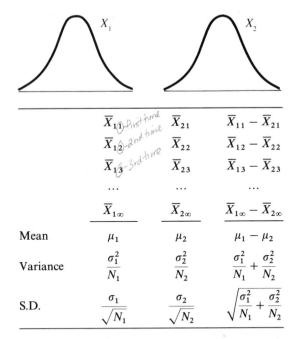

	$\overline{X}_{11}$ First time	$\overline{X}_{21}$	$\overline{X}_{11} - \overline{X}_{21}$
	$\overline{X}_{12}$ 2nd time	$\overline{X}_{22}$	$\overline{X}_{12} - \overline{X}_{22}$
	$\overline{X}_{13}$ 3rd time	$\overline{X}_{23}$	$\overline{X}_{13} - \overline{X}_{23}$
	...	...	...
	$\overline{X}_{1\infty}$	$\overline{X}_{2\infty}$	$\overline{X}_{1\infty} - \overline{X}_{2\infty}$
Mean	μ_1	μ_2	$\mu_1 - \mu_2$
Variance	$\dfrac{\sigma_1^2}{N_1}$	$\dfrac{\sigma_2^2}{N_2}$	$\dfrac{\sigma_1^2}{N_1} + \dfrac{\sigma_2^2}{N_2}$
S.D.	$\dfrac{\sigma_1}{\sqrt{N_1}}$	$\dfrac{\sigma_2}{\sqrt{N_2}}$	$\sqrt{\dfrac{\sigma_1^2}{N_1} + \dfrac{\sigma_2^2}{N_2}}$

FIGURE 7.6
Hypothetical set of means and mean differences when sampling from two populations

Variance sum law

paired only in the trivial and presumably irrelevant sense of being drawn at the same time.) Since we are only supposing, we might as well go all the way and suppose that we repeated this procedure an infinite number of times. The results are presented schematically in Figure 7.6. In the lower portion of this figure, the first two columns represent the sampling distributions of $\overline{X}_1$ and $\overline{X}_2$, and the third column represents the sampling distribution of mean differences $(\overline{X}_1 - \overline{X}_2)$. It is this third column we are most interested in, since we are concerned with testing differences between means. The mean of this distribution can be shown to equal $\mu_1 - \mu_2$. The variance of this distribution of differences is given by what is commonly called the **variance sum law**, a limited form of which states

> The variance of a sum or difference of two *independent* variables is equal to the sum of their variances.[†]

We know from the central limit theorem that the variance of the distribution of $\overline{X}_1$ is σ_1^2/N_1 and the variance of the distribution of $\overline{X}_2$ is σ_2^2/N_2. Since the variables (sample

---

[†] The complete form of the law omits the restriction that the variables must be independent and states that the variance of their sum or difference is

$$\sigma_{X_1 \pm X_2}^2 = \sigma_1^2 + \sigma_2^2 \pm 2\rho\sigma_1\sigma_2$$

where the notation $\pm$ is interpreted as plus when we are speaking of their sum and as minus when we are speaking of their difference. The term ρ (rho) in this equation is the correlation between the two variables (to be discussed in Chapter 9) and is equal to zero when the variables are independent. (The fact that $\rho \neq 0$ when the variables are not independent was what forced us to treat the related sample case separately.)

means) are independent, the variance of the difference of these two variables is the sum of their variances. Thus

$$\sigma^2_{\bar{X}_1 - \bar{X}_2} = \sigma^2_{\bar{X}_1} + \sigma^2_{\bar{X}_2} = \frac{\sigma^2_1}{N_1} + \frac{\sigma^2_2}{N_2}$$

Having found the mean and variance of a set of differences between means, we know most of what we need to know. The general form of the sampling distribution of mean differences is presented in Figure 7.7.

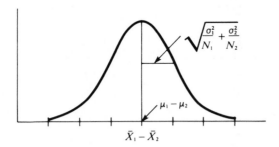

FIGURE 7.7
Sampling distribution
of mean differences

The final point to be made about this distribution concerns its shape. An important theorem in statistics states that the sum or difference of two independent normally distributed variables is itself normally distributed. Because Figure 7.7 represents the difference between two sampling distributions of the mean, and because we know that the sampling distribution of means is at least approximately normal for reasonable sample sizes, the distribution in Figure 7.7 must itself be at least approximately normal.

THE t STATISTIC

**Standard error of
differences between
means**

Given the information we now have about the sampling distribution of mean differences, we can proceed to develop the appropriate test procedure. Assume for the moment that knowledge of the population variances (σ^2_i) is not a problem. We have earlier defined z as a statistic (a point on the distribution) minus the mean of the distribution, divided by the standard error of the distribution. Our statistic in the present case is $(\bar{X}_1 - \bar{X}_2)$, the observed difference between the sample means. The mean of the sampling distribution is $(\mu_1 - \mu_2)$, and, as we saw, the **standard error of differences between means**[†] is

$$\sigma_{\bar{X}_1 - \bar{X}_2} = \sqrt{\frac{\sigma^2_1}{N_1} + \frac{\sigma^2_2}{N_2}}$$

[†]Remember that the standard deviation of any sampling distribution is called the standard error of that distribution.

Thus we can write
$$z = \frac{(\overline{X}_1 - \overline{X}_2) - (\mu_1 - \mu_2)}{\sigma_{\overline{X}_1 - \overline{X}_2}}$$

$$= \frac{(\overline{X}_1 - \overline{X}_2) - (\mu_1 - \mu_2)}{\sqrt{\dfrac{\sigma_1^2}{N_1} + \dfrac{\sigma_2^2}{N_2}}}$$

The critical value for $\alpha = .05$ is $z = \pm 1.96$ (two-tailed), as it was for the one-sample tests discussed earlier.

The preceding formula is not particularly useful except for the purpose of showing the origin of the appropriate t test, since we rarely know the necessary population variances. (Such knowledge is so rare that it is not even worth imagining cases in which we would have it, although a few do exist.) We can circumvent this problem just as we did in the one-sample case, by using the sample variances as estimates of the population variances. This, for the same reasons discussed earlier for the one-sample t, means that the result will be distributed as t rather than z.

$$t = \frac{(\overline{X}_1 - \overline{X}_2) - (\mu_1 - \mu_2)}{s_{\overline{X}_1 - \overline{X}_2}} = \frac{(\overline{X}_1 - \overline{X}_2) - (\mu_1 - \mu_2)}{\sqrt{\dfrac{s_1^2}{N_1} + \dfrac{s_2^2}{N_2}}}$$

Since the null hypothesis is generally the hypothesis that $\mu_1 - \mu_2 = 0$, we will drop that term from the equation and write

$$t = \frac{(\overline{X}_1 - \overline{X}_2)}{s_{\overline{X}_1 - \overline{X}_2}} = \frac{(\overline{X}_1 - \overline{X}_2)}{\sqrt{\dfrac{s_1^2}{N_1} + \dfrac{s_2^2}{N_2}}}$$

POOLING VARIANCES

[handwritten margin note: can use when sample sizes are equal or unequal]

Although the equation for t that we have just developed is appropriate when the sample sizes are equal, it requires some modification when the sample sizes are unequal. This modification is designed to improve the estimate of the population variance. One of the assumptions required in the use of t for two independent samples is that $\sigma_1^2 = \sigma_2^2$ (i.e., the samples come from populations with equal variances, regardless of the truth or falsity of H_0). The assumption is required regardless of whether N_1 and N_2 are equal. Such an assumption is often reasonable. We frequently begin an experiment with two groups of subjects who are equivalent and then do something to one (or both) group(s) that will raise or lower the scores by an amount equal to the effect of the experimental treatment. In such a case, it often makes sense to assume that the variances will remain unaffected. (Recall that adding or subtracting a constant—here, the treatment effect—to or from a set of scores has no effect on its variance.) Since the population variances are assumed to be equal, this common variance can be represented by the symbol σ^2, without a subscript.

In our data we have two estimates of σ^2, namely s_1^2 and s_2^2. It seems appropriate to obtain some sort of an average of s_1^2 and s_2^2 on the grounds that this average should

Weighted average

be a better estimate of σ^2 than either of the two separate estimates. We do not want to take the simple arithmetic mean, however, because doing so would give equal weight to the two estimates, even if one were based on considerably more observations. What we want is a **weighted average**, in which the sample variances are weighted by their degrees of freedom $(N_i - 1)$. If we call this new estimate s_p^2 then

$$s_p^2 = \frac{(N_1 - 1)s_1^2 + (N_2 - 1)s_2^2}{N_1 + N_2 - 2}$$

The numerator represents the sum of the variances, each weighted by their degrees of freedom, and the denominator represents the sum of the weights or, equivalently, the degrees of freedom for s_p^2.

Pooled variance estimate

The weighted average of the two sample variances is usually referred to as a **pooled variance estimate** (a rather inelegant name, but reasonably descriptive). Having defined the pooled estimate (s_p^2), we can now write

$$t = \frac{(\overline{X}_1 - \overline{X}_2)}{s_{\overline{X}_1 - \overline{X}_2}}$$

$$= \frac{(\overline{X}_1 - \overline{X}_2)}{\sqrt{\dfrac{s_p^2}{N_1} + \dfrac{s_p^2}{N_2}}} = \frac{(\overline{X}_1 - \overline{X}_2)}{\sqrt{s_p^2 \left(\dfrac{1}{N_1} + \dfrac{1}{N_2}\right)}}$$

Notice that both this formula for t and the one we have just been using involve dividing the difference between the sample means by an estimate of the standard error of the difference between means. The only difference concerns the way in which this standard error is estimated. When the sample sizes are equal, it makes absolutely no difference whether or not you pool variances; the answer will be the same. When the sample sizes are unequal, however, pooling can make quite a difference.[†]

Degrees of Freedom

Two samples variances (s_1^2 and s_2^2) have gone into calculating t. Each of these variances is based on squared deviations about their corresponding sample means, and therefore each sample variance has $N_i - 1$ *df*. Across the two samples, therefore, we will have $(N_1 - 1) + (N_2 - 1) = N_1 + N_2 - 2$ *df*. Thus, the t for two independent samples will be based on $N_1 + N_2 - 2$ degrees of freedom.

use this formula

Differences Between Two Groups of Low-Birthweight Children at Age 24 Months

For the sake of continuity, we will again draw an example from the study of low-birthweight (LBW) infants to illustrate that we can ask different kinds of questions of

---

[†] Notice the way in which the denominator is written in the last equation. This same form of expression will occur often in our discussions of the analysis of variance.

the same data set, and that these questions lead to different types of *t* tests. (As you will see when we come to the analysis of variance, there are better ways of analyzing the complete data set for this experiment; but the individual *t* tests used here do answer legitimate questions.)

The major purpose of the study was to show that a group of LBW infants whose mothers received the training program performed better than did LBW infants whose mothers did not receive the program. The difference between these two groups was expected to become evident by the time the children were 2 years old. In Table 7.5 you will find the Bayley Mental Development Index (MDI) scores for the two groups

TABLE 7.5 Data from the experimental and control LBW groups at 24 months (MDI scores)

LBW—Experimental	LBW—Control	Stem-and-Leaf		
		Experimental	Stem	Control
96	114		8*	0 1
127	88		8.	8
127	102		9*	1 1 1
137	127		9.	6
114	104	8 6	10*	0 2 2 2 4 4 4
119	104		10.	6 9 9
109	91	9 9 6 9 9 9 9	11*	1 4 4 4
109	96	4 4 2 2 2	11.	9 9 9 9 9
143	104	9 9 7 6	12*	3
109	106		12.	7
116	91	7 7 7	13*	2
114	102		13.	
143	104	7 7	14*	
109	100	3 3		
117	114			
127	109	Code 8 ∗ ∣ 0 = 80		
112	109			
112	119			
98	91			
137	81			
112	114			
109	119			
119	102			
106	111			
109	80			
	119			
	119			
	123			
	119			
	114			
	132			

	LBW—Experimental	LBW—Control
Mean	117.20	106.71
S.D.	12.682	12.954
Variance	160.833	167.806
N	25	31

collected at 24 months, along with a back-to-back stem-and-leaf display. From this display, you can see that the experimental group seems to score somewhat higher than does the control group. The data from the experimental group are positively skewed to some degree, but not seriously enough to cause us undue concern. Boxplots for each group did not reveal any problems with outliers or skewness, and have been omitted.

Before we consider any statistical test, and ideally even before the data are collected, we must specify several features of the test. First we must specify the null and alternative hypotheses:

$$H_0: \mu_1 = \mu_2$$

$$H_1: \mu_1 \neq \mu_2$$

The alternative hypothesis is bidirectional (we will reject H_0 if $\mu_1 < \mu_2$ or if $\mu_1 > \mu_2$), and thus we will use a two-tailed test. For the sake of consistency with other examples in this book, we will let $\alpha = .05$. It is important to keep in mind, however, that there is nothing particularly sacred about any of these decisions. Given the null hypothesis as stated, we can now calculate t:

$$t = \frac{(\overline{X}_1 - \overline{X}_2)}{s_{\overline{X}_1 - \overline{X}_2}}$$

$$= \frac{(\overline{X}_1 - \overline{X}_2)}{\sqrt{\dfrac{s_p^2}{N_1} + \dfrac{s_p^2}{N_2}}}$$

Because we are testing H_0, $\mu_1 - \mu_2 = 0$, the $\mu_1 - \mu_2$ term has been dropped from the equation. When we pool our variances, we obtain

$$s_p^2 = \frac{(N_1 - 1)s_1^2 + (N_2 - 1)s_2^2}{N_1 + N_2 - 2}$$

$$= \frac{24(160.833) + 30(167.806)}{25 + 31 - 2} = \frac{3859.992 + 5034.180}{54} = 164.707$$

Notice that the pooled variance is slightly closer in value to s_2^2 than to s_1^2 because of the greater weight given s_2^2 in the formula. Then

$$t = \frac{(117.20 - 106.71)}{\sqrt{\dfrac{164.707}{25} + \dfrac{164.707}{31}}} = \frac{10.49}{\sqrt{11.901}} = \frac{10.49}{3.450} = 3.04$$

For this example, we have $N_1 - 1 = 24$ df for the experimental group and $N_2 - 1 = 30$ df for the control group, making a total of $N_1 - 1 + N_2 - 1 = 54$ df. From the sampling distribution of t in Appendix t, $t_{.025}(54) \simeq \pm 2.007$ (with linear interpolation). Since the value of t_{obt} far exceeds $t_{\alpha/2}$, we will reject H_0 (at $\alpha = .05$) and conclude that there is a difference between the means of the populations from which our observations were drawn. In other words, we will conclude (statistically) that $\mu_1 \neq \mu_2$ and (practically) that $\mu_1 > \mu_2$. In terms of the experimental variables, at 2 years of age the infants whose mothers received the training program performed better on the MDI than did those whose mothers did not receive the program. Although this is only one of many measures collected on these children, it does suggest that the program was successful, at least in part.

7.6   HETEROGENEITY OF VARIANCE: THE BEHRENS–FISHER PROBLEM

Homogeneity of variance

We have already seen that one of the assumptions underlying the t test for two independent samples is the assumption of **homogeneity of variance** ($\sigma_1^2 = \sigma_2^2 = \sigma^2$). To be more specific, we can say that *when* H_0 is true and *when* we have homogeneity of variance, then, pooling the variances, the ratio

$$t = \frac{\overline{X}_1 - \overline{X}_2}{\sqrt{\dfrac{s_p^2}{N_1} + \dfrac{s_p^2}{N_2}}}$$

is distributed as t on $N_1 + N_2 - 2\ df$. If we have homogeneity of variance there is no difficulty, and the techniques discussed in this section are not needed. When we do not have homogeneity of variance, however, this ratio is not, strictly speaking, distributed as t. This leaves us with a problem, but fortunately a solution (or a number of competing solutions) exists.

First of all, unless $\sigma_1^2 = \sigma_2^2 = \sigma^2$, it makes no sense to pool (average) variances because the reason we were pooling variances in the first place was that we assumed them to be estimating the same quantity. For the case of **heterogeneous variances**, we will first dispense with pooling procedures and define

Heterogeneous variances

$$t' = \frac{\overline{X}_1 - \overline{X}_2}{\sqrt{\dfrac{s_1^2}{N_1} + \dfrac{s_2^2}{N_2}}}$$

where s_1^2 and s_2^2 are taken to be heterogeneous variances. As noted above, the expression that I have just denoted as t' is *not* necessarily distributed as t on $N_1 + N_2 - 2\ df$. If we knew what the sampling distribution of t' actually looked like, there would be no problem. Fortunately, although there is no universal agreement, we know at least the approximate distribution of t'.

THE BEHRENS–FISHER PROBLEM AND ALTERNATIVE SOLUTIONS FOR THE SAMPLING DISTRIBUTION OF t'

One of the first attempts to find the exact sampling distribution of t' was begun by Behrens and extended by Fisher, and the general problem of heterogeneity of vari-

Behrens–Fisher problem

ance has come to be known as the **Behrens–Fisher problem**. Based on this work, the Behrens–Fisher distribution of t' was derived and is presented in a table in Fisher and Yates (1953). However, because this table covers only a few degrees of freedom, it is not particularly useful for most purposes.

To provide a more practical approach to the problem, Cochran and Cox (1957) presented a method of approximating the critical values of the Behrens–Fisher distribution. This method requires that we solve for the critical value of t' against which to compare t'_{obt}:

$$t'_{\alpha/2} = \frac{t_1 \dfrac{s_1^2}{N_1} + t_2 \dfrac{s_2^2}{N_2}}{\dfrac{s_1^2}{N_1} + \dfrac{s_2^2}{N_2}}$$

where t_1 and t_2 are the critical values ($t_{\alpha/2}$) of t for $N_1 - 1$ and $N_2 - 1$ df, respectively.

An alternative solution was developed apparently independently by Welch (1938) and by Satterthwaite (1946). It is based on a different approach to the problem. The **Welch–Satterthwaite solution** is particularly important because we will refer back to it when we discuss the analysis of variance. Using this method, t' is viewed as a legitimate member of the t distribution, but for an unknown number of degrees of freedom. The problem then becomes one of solving for the appropriate df, denoted $\boldsymbol{df'}$:

Welch–Satterthwaite solution

$\boldsymbol{df'}$

$$df' = \frac{\left(\dfrac{s_1^2}{N_1} + \dfrac{s_2^2}{N_2}\right)^2}{\dfrac{\left(\dfrac{s_1^2}{N_1}\right)^2}{N_1 - 1} + \dfrac{\left(\dfrac{s_2^2}{N_2}\right)^2}{N_2 - 1}}$$

The degrees of freedom (df') are then taken to the nearest integer.[†] The advantage of this approach is that df' is bounded by the smaller of $N_1 - 1$ and $N_2 - 1$ at one extreme and $N_1 + N_2 - 2$ at the other. More specifically,

$$\text{Min}(N_1 - 1, N_2 - 1) \leq df' \leq (N_1 + N_2 - 2)$$

Because the critical value of t decreases as df increases, we can first evaluate t' as if df' were at its minimum. If the difference is significant, it will certainly be significant for the true df'. If the difference is not significant, we can then evaluate t' at its maximum $N_1 + N_2 - 2$. If it is not significant at this point, no reduction in the degrees of freedom (by more accurate calculation of df') would cause it to be significant. Thus, the only

---

[†] Welch (1947) later suggested that letting

$$df' = \left[\frac{\left(\dfrac{s_1^2}{N_1} + \dfrac{s_2^2}{N_2}\right)^2}{\dfrac{\left(\dfrac{s_1^2}{N_1}\right)^2}{N_1 + 1} + \dfrac{\left(\dfrac{s_2^2}{N_2}\right)^2}{N_2 + 1}}\right] - 2$$

might be a more accurate solution, although the difference will usually be negligible.

time we actually need to calculate df' is when the value of t' would not be significant for $\text{Min}(N_1 - 1, N_2 - 1)$ df but would be significant for $N_1 + N_2 - 2$ df.

In this book we will rely primarily on the Welch–Satterthwaite approximation. It has the distinct advantage of applying easily to problems that arise in the analysis of variance, and it is not noticeably more awkward than the Cochran and Cox solution.

TESTING FOR HETEROGENEITY OF VARIANCE

How do we know whether we even have heterogeneity of variance to begin with? Since we obviously do not know σ_1^2 and σ_2^2 (if we did we would not be solving for t), we must in some way test their difference by using our two sample variances (s_1^2 and s_2^2).

A number of solutions have been put forth for testing for heterogeneity of variance. One of the simpler ones was advocated by Levene (1960), who suggested replacing each value of X either by its absolute deviation from the group mean—$d_{ij} = |X_{ij} - \overline{X}_j|$—or by its squared deviation—$(X_{ij} - \overline{X}_j)^2$—where i and j represent the ith subject in the jth group. He then proposed running a standard two-sample t test on the d_{ij}s. This test makes intuitive sense, because if there is greater variability in one group, the absolute, or squared, values of the deviations will be greater. If t is significant, we would then declare the two groups to differ in their variances. An alternative approach was proposed by O'Brien (1981), who suggested replacing X_{ij} by a transformed value that he called r_{ij}:

$$r_{ij} = \frac{(N_j - 1.5)N_j(X_{ij} - \overline{X}_j)^2 - 0.5s_j^2(N_j - 1)}{(N_j - 1)(N_j - 2)}$$

and then running a t test on the r_{ij}. Rejection of the null hypothesis of homogeneity of variance would result whenever t is significant.

The procedures just described are suggested as replacements for the more traditional F test, which is a ratio of the larger sample variance to the smaller. This F has been shown by many people to be severely affected by nonnormality of the data, and probably should not be used. The F test is, however, still computed and printed by many of the large computer packages. Since you will come across it on computer printout, I will explain it briefly, but I do not recommend it.

Let

$$F = \frac{s_L^2}{s_S^2}$$

where s_L^2 and s_S^2 represent the larger and smaller of the two variances, respectively. This statistic (F) is distributed as the F distribution on $N_1 - 1$ and $N_2 - 1$ df. The F distribution is presented in Appendix F and will be discussed in more detail later. To use the table, you simply enter it at the column corresponding to the df for the numerator and the row corresponding to the df for the denominator. The cell entries correspond to the upper-tail critical values for $\alpha = .05, .025,$ and 01. Since we want a two-tailed test (we want to reject H_0 whenever $\sigma_1^2 \neq \sigma_2^2$), these α levels should be doubled in the situation described here. Thus, for a two-tailed test at $\alpha = .05$, we would use the critical value shown at $\alpha = .025$.

EATING DISORDERS

An example involving heterogeneous variances can be found in an extensive study of eating disorders in adolescents by Gross (1985). Among other things, Gross examined subjects who had a disorder known as bulimia. "Simple bulimia" is a psychological eating disorder involving uncontrollable eating (often called binge eating), coupled with the knowledge that the eating is abnormal and an associated state of dysphoria (feeling bad). In many cases, but not all, binge eating is followed by intentional vomiting or the use of laxatives. When this behavior is present, the disorder is labeled "bulimia with purging." As one of many variables, Gross investigated whether there was a weight difference between people classified in the two categories of bulimia. Although Gross's actual data are not available, the data given in Table 7.6 were generated to have the same means and variances as she reported for her subjects. Fictional data have been provided because they are necessary for the application of O'Brien's test for homogeneity of variance. The dependent variable shown on the left of Table 7.6 is the mean percentage deviation of an individual's actual weight from the normal weight for her height and build. Notice that the mean for both groups is quite close to normal—that is, the mean percentage deviation is near zero. If we ignored the unequal variances and simply pooled them, we would obtain $t = 1.87$, a nonsignificant result at $\alpha = .05$.

TABLE 7.6
Typical raw scores and transformed data for bulimia study

	Original Data (X_{ij})		Transformed Data (r_{ij})	
	Simple	Purging	Simple	Purging
	24.01	10.23	385.87	127.18
	14.50	−6.20	98.63	28.86
	−5.00	−6.13	92.96	28.03
	7.71	−1.88	7.61	−0.19
	35.25	1.83	966.13	6.15
	−22.18	−10.79	738.28	102.59
	−5.13	4.87	95.57	32.85
	−13.27	16.56	327.46	316.50
	9.11	−15.82	18.59	234.04
	2.54	1.04	2.08	2.39
	...	...	...	...
Mean	4.61	−0.83	219.04	79.21
Variance	219.04	79.21	65432.73	8144.20
N	49	32	49	32

Our first step in dealing with these data involves testing for heterogeneity of variance. This is done using the values on the right of Table 7.6, which have been obtained with O'Brien's transformation. In Table 7.6 notice that the means of the transformed values (r_{ij}) are equal to the variances of the original values (X_{ij}), reflecting the fact that the t test we are about to apply on the means of the *transformed* values is actually comparing the variances of the original values. From the means and variances given in the table, we can compute a t test of the null hypothesis that the data were sampled from populations with equal variances. Since the variances of the r_{ij} are themselves heterogeneous (one is about eight times the other), we will not pool variances.

$$t = \frac{\overline{X}_1 - \overline{X}_2}{\sqrt{\dfrac{s_1^2}{N_1} + \dfrac{s_2^2}{N_2}}} = \frac{219.04 - 79.21}{\sqrt{\dfrac{65432.73}{49} + \dfrac{8144.20}{32}}} = 3.51$$

A t of 3.51 would be significant even for a few degrees of freedom, so we do not need to worry about a more precise computation of df'. Thus, we will reject $H_0: \sigma_1^2 = \sigma_2^2$ and declare the variances to be heterogeneous. As a result, we will not pool the variances but will instead solve for t':

$$t' = \frac{\overline{X}_1 - \overline{X}_2}{\sqrt{\dfrac{s_1^2}{N_1} + \dfrac{s_2^2}{N_2}}} = \frac{4.61 - (-0.83)}{\sqrt{\dfrac{219.04}{49} + \dfrac{79.21}{32}}} = \frac{5.44}{\sqrt{6.9455}} = \frac{5.44}{2.635} = 2.064$$

In this particular case, the result would be significant even for the minimum possible value of $df'(=N_1 - 1 = 31)$, because the critical value for $t_{.025}(31) = \pm 2.04$. For purposes of our example, however, we can go ahead and calculate df':

$$df' = \frac{\left(\dfrac{s_1^2}{N_1} + \dfrac{s_2^2}{N_2}\right)^2}{\dfrac{\left(\dfrac{s_1^2}{N_1}\right)^2}{N_1 - 1} + \dfrac{\left(\dfrac{s_2^2}{N_2}\right)^2}{N_2 - 1}} = \frac{\left(\dfrac{219.04}{49} + \dfrac{79.21}{32}\right)^2}{\dfrac{\left(\dfrac{219.04}{49}\right)^2}{48} + \dfrac{\left(\dfrac{79.21}{32}\right)^2}{31}}$$

$$= \frac{6.9455^2}{\dfrac{4.4702^2}{48} + \dfrac{2.4753^2}{31}} = \frac{48.2400}{0.4163 + 0.1976} = 78.58$$

We will take df' to the nearest integer, which is 79, and for 79 df the critical value (obtained from more extensive tables than the one found in Appendix t) is 1.99. Because $t'_{obt} = -2.04$ exceeds ± 1.99, we will reject H_0 and conclude that there is a significant difference between the two groups. The simple bulimics are about 5.5 percentage points heavier than the purging bulimics. Notice that df' happens to be equal, after rounding, to its maximum possible value $(N_1 + N_2 - 2)$. This illustrates that just because variances are heterogeneous does not necessarily mean that df' must be less than its maximum.

THE ROBUSTNESS OF t

Robust

I mentioned that the t test is what is described as **robust**, meaning that it is more or less unaffected by moderate departures from the underlying assumptions. For the t test for two independent samples, we have two major assumptions and one side condition that must be considered. The two assumptions are those of normality of the sampling distribution of differences between means and homogeneity of variance. The side condition is the condition of equal sample sizes versus unequal sample sizes. Although we have just seen·how the problem of heterogeneity of variance can be handled by special procedures, it is still relevant to ask what happens if we use the standard approach even with heterogeneous variances.

Box (1953), Norton (1953), Boneau (1960), and many others have investigated the effects of violating, both independently and jointly, the underlying assumptions of t. The general conclusion to be drawn from these studies is that for equal sample sizes, violating the assumption of homogeneity of variance produces very small effects—the nominal value of $\alpha = .05$ is most likely within ± 0.02 of the true value of α. By this we mean that if you set up a situation with unequal variances *but with H_0 true* and proceed to draw (and compute t on) a large number of pairs of samples, you will find that somewhere between 3% and 7% of the sample t values actually exceed $\pm t_{.025}$. This level of inaccuracy is not intolerable. The same kind of statement applies to violations of the assumption of normality, provided that the true populations are roughly the same shape, or else both are symmetric. If the distributions are markedly skewed (especially in opposite directions), serious problems arise unless their variances are fairly equal.

With unequal sample sizes, however, the results are more difficult to interpret. In Boneau's study, for example, sample variances were pooled in all cases, since this is probably the most common procedure in practice (although it is incorrect for heterogeneous variances). Boneau found that when there was heterogeneity of variance *and* unequal sample sizes, the actual and normative probability values differed considerably. Keep in mind, however, that Boneau was pooling variances and evaluating t on $N_1 + N_2 - 2 \, df$. We do not know what would have happened had he solved for t' and then evaluated t' on df' degrees of freedom. We do know, however, that had he done so it would be reasonable to expect that the test would have proven to be robust since the Welch–Satterthwaite solution does not require the homogeneity assumption.

The investigator who has collected data that she thinks may violate one or more of the underlying assumptions should refer to the article by Boneau (1960). This article is quite readable and contains an excellent list of references to other work in the area. A good summary of alternative procedures can be found in Games, Keselman, and Rogan (1981). Alternative nonparametric approaches are discussed in Chapter 18 of this book. When assumptions are violated, these nonparametric approaches often have greater power than t (Blair & Higgins, 1980, 1985).

7.7 HETEROGENEITY OF VARIANCE AS AN EXPERIMENTAL FINDING

We have been speaking of heterogeneity of variance as if it were something to be avoided, or at least treated with caution, and have generally ignored the fact that it might be a meaningful result in its own right. Although statistical analyses generally deal with means, and view variability only as something that makes interpreting means more difficult, there is much to be said for the variance as a measure of the effect of an experimental manipulation. Consider, for example, an individual who wishes to investigate the effects of a tutorial system of teaching, as opposed to the more traditional lecture method. He takes two groups of students, drawn at random from the population of available students, teaches one group by a tutorial method and the other by a traditional system of lectures, and finally administers some sort of examination at the end of the year. We will assume that an examination that is fair to both groups can be devised. The data from this hypothetical experiment are given in Table 7.7.

TABLE 7.7
Data for two alternative teaching methods

	Tutorial	Lecture
Mean	86.5	85.1
Variance	61.4	19.75
N	20	20

The difference between the means is obviously trivial, and not even worth testing. (Who would even care if a difference of such a small magnitude were to be statistically significant?) If our investigator were to conclude, however, that there were no differences between the two methods, he would be missing the most interesting result displayed by these data. Notice that the variance for the tutorial group is more than three times the variance for the lecture group. If a test, such as O'Brien's, rejected the null hypothesis of homogeneity of variance, we would be led to conclude that the tutorial method is very good for some students and very bad for others. The lecture method, on the other hand, seems to strike a neutral position for all. This finding is very likely of more interest than any differences that might appear between the means. Psychologists would do well to pay more attention to experimental manipulations that influence the variance. In fact, O'Brien (1981) was particularly concerned with that aspect of the problem in his paper.

TESTING FOR HETEROGENEITY OF NONINDEPENDENT VARIANCES

The tests for the difference between two sample variances to which we have just referred apply only to variances of independent samples. Suppose, however, that we had N subjects perform the same task on two successive days and wished to compare the variances for the two days. Because the same subjects are involved, the variances will not be independent. If we let $F = s_L^2/s_S^2$ and let r stand for the correlation between the two sets of scores, then it can be shown that

$$t = \frac{(F-1)\sqrt{(N-2)}}{2\sqrt{F(1-r^2)}}$$

is distributed as t on $N - 2$ *df* and is a test of $H_0: \sigma_1^2 = \sigma_2^2$. For the ingenious derivation of this technique, see Pitman (1939) or Snedecor and Cochran (1967).

It is of more than passing interest that we have methods for testing the differences between variances. The social sciences have a long tradition of being concerned with differences between means to the exclusion of other types of differences that might exist. In many cases this is justifiable; but we must not forget that the variance can also provide insight into the results of experimental manipulations.

COMBINING THE RESULTS OF SEVERAL EXPERIMENTS

Meta-analysis

In recent years there has been heightened interest in combining the results of significance tests from a number of related studies. This has derived in part from the growing interest in **meta-analysis**, which is concerned with drawing inferences about an area of research from the results of many different studies. For example, Smith (1980) collected and analyzed all the studies she could find concerning gender bias in counseling, and reported that the combined weight of all those studies did not lead to the conclusion that gender bias did in fact exist in that area. A good introduction to meta-analysis can be found in Glass, McGaw, and Smith (1981).

Suppose the experimenter finds that the results for each of several experiments are in the predicted direction, but that not one of them reaches statistical significance. The obvious question that then arises concerns the probability of obtaining this joint set of results if H_0: $\mu_1 = \mu_2$ is in fact true.

A number of schemes for combining results exist, but only the basic ones will be discussed here. A more extensive discussion of the problem of combining data can be found in Rosenthal (1978). Very sophisticated procedures in this area have been developed by Hedges—see, for example, Hedges (1982).

The simplest solution employs the binomial distribution, but it requires at least five separate experiments on no more than two groups. Starting with the logical statement that if H_0 is true, for any given experiment $p(\overline{X}_1 < \overline{X}_2) = p(\overline{X}_1 > \overline{X}_2) = .50$ [or for the one-sample case, $p(\overline{X} < \mu) = p(\overline{X} > \mu) = .50$], one can then ask, "What is the probability of finding r out of k experiments with $\overline{X}_1 > \overline{X}_2$?" This question is easily answered by using the binomial distribution.

A second solution, which is not constrained by the experimental design or the number of experiments, focuses on the significance level (p value) for each result. This solution is based on the fact that a probability can be converted to χ^2 on 2 df.

$$\chi_2^2 = -2 \log_e p$$

Since we have already seen that the sum of k independent chi-square variables is itself distributed as χ^2 with df equal to the sum of the separate degrees of freedom, then for k experiments

$$\chi_{2k}^2 = -2 \sum \log_e p_i$$

will be distributed as χ^2 on $2k$ df. Thus, if we could obtain the exact probability level $[p(t \geq t_{\text{obt}})]$ for each experiment, we could then take the natural logarithms of these probabilities, sum them, multiply by negative 2, and evaluate this result against $\chi_{.05}^2$ on $2k$ df. The only problem with this approach is that we need the actual probabilities. Since most computer programs now print out these probabilities, this problem is not as great as it once was.

The last method we will discuss is the simplest, although it applies only when t is used as the statistical test. Winer (1971) has shown that

$$z = \frac{\sum t_i}{\sqrt{\sum \dfrac{df_i}{df_i - 2}}}$$

is distributed as the standard normal deviate when each $df_i > 10$. To take a simple example, suppose we have run five experiments, each on 20 df, and obtained the following values of t:

Experiment:	1	2	3	4	5
t	1.28	0.50	2.01	1.60	1.70

Each experiment is independent of the others, and all test the same general hypothesis. Then

$$z = \frac{(1.28 + 0.50 + 2.01 + 1.60 + 1.70)}{\sqrt{\dfrac{5(20)}{18}}} = \frac{7.09}{\sqrt{5.56}} = 3.01$$

From the distribution of z, we find that $p(z \geq 3.01) = .0013$. Thus, we can reject H_0 at this level of significance and conclude that $\mu_1 > \mu_2$.

All of these tests require the assumption that the separate experiments are independent and that they test the same general hypothesis. A discussion of combining the results of nonindependent tests can be found in Strube (1985).

Although the techniques discussed in this section play a useful role in statistical analyses, this role should not be overemphasized. In some areas of research a difference, no matter how small, is important; but in many more areas small differences are not only unimportant, but in fact simply add confusion to the literature. We will have considerably more to say about this in later chapters when we consider ways of assessing the magnitude of an experimental effect. Simply because a difference has *statistical* significance does not mean it necessarily has *practical* significance. *Significance and importance are two entirely different concepts.*

7.8 CONFIDENCE INTERVALS

The earlier data on the moon illusion offer an excellent example of a case in which we are particularly interested in estimating the true value of μ—in this case, the true ratio of the perceived size of the horizon moon to the perceived size of the zenith moon. The sample mean ($\overline{X}$), as you already know, is an unbiased estimate of μ. When we have

Point estimate,
Interval estimates

Confidence limits
Confidence interval

one specific estimate of a parameter, we call this a **point estimate**. There are also **interval estimates**, which are attempts to set limits that have a high probability of encompassing the true (population) value of the mean [the mean (μ) of a whole population of observations]. What we want, then, are **confidence limits** on μ. These limits enclose what is called a **confidence interval**. In Chapter 3, we saw how to set "probable limits" on an *observation*. A similar line of reasoning will apply here, where we attempt to set confidence limits on a *parameter*.

If we want to set limits that are likely to include μ given the data at hand, what we really want is to ask how large, or small, μ actually could be without causing us to reject H_0 if we ran a t test on the obtained sample mean. In other words, if μ were quite small (or quite large), we would have been unlikely to obtain the sample data. For a whole range of values for μ, however, we would expect data like those we obtained. We want to calculate what those values of μ are.

Any easy way to see what we are doing is to start with the formula for t:

$$t = \frac{\overline{X} - \mu}{s_{\overline{X}}} = \frac{\overline{X} - \mu}{\dfrac{s}{\sqrt{N}}}$$

Because we have collected the data, we already know $\overline{X}$, s, and N ($\overline{X} = 1.463$, $s = 0.341$, $N = 10$). We also know that the critical two-tailed value for t at $\alpha = .05$ is $t_{.025}(9) = \pm 2.262$. We will substitute these values in the formula for t and solve for μ:

$$t = \frac{\overline{X} - \mu}{\dfrac{s}{\sqrt{N}}}, \qquad \pm 2.262 = \frac{1.463 - \mu}{\dfrac{0.341}{\sqrt{10}}} = \frac{1.463 - \mu}{0.108}$$

Rearranging to solve for μ, we have

$$\mu = \pm 2.262(0.108) + 1.463 = \pm 0.244 + 1.463$$

Using the $+0.244$ and -0.244 separately to obtain the upper and lower limits for μ, we have

$$\mu_{\text{upper}} = +0.244 + 1.463 = 1.707$$

$$\mu_{\text{lower}} = -0.244 + 1.463 = 1.219$$

and thus we can write the 95% confidence limits as 1.219 and 1.707 and the confidence interval as

$$\text{CI}_{.95} = 1.219 \le \mu \le 1.707$$

Testing a null hypothesis about any value of μ outside these limits would lead to rejection of H_0. The general expression is

$$\text{CI}_{.95} = \overline{X} \pm t_{.05/2}(s_{\overline{X}}) = \overline{X} \pm t_{.025}\frac{s}{\sqrt{N}}$$

We have a 95% confidence interval because we used the two-tailed critical value of t at $\alpha = .05$. For the 99% limits we would take $t_{.005} = \pm 3.250$. Then the 99% confidence interval is

$$\text{CI}_{.99} = \overline{X} + t_{.005}(s_{\overline{X}}) = 1.463 \pm 3.250(0.108) = 1.112 \le \mu \le 1.814$$

We can now say that the probability is 0.95 that the interval 1.219 to 1.707 includes the true mean ratio for the moon illusion, whereas the probability is .99 that the interval 1.112 to 1.814 includes μ. Note that neither confidence interval computed includes the value of 1.00, which represents no illusion. We already knew this for the 95% confidence interval because we had rejected that null hypothesis when we ran our t test at that significance level.

Many statisticians would object to the statement of a confidence limit as it is written here. They would argue that *before* the experiment is run and the calculations are made, an interval *of the form*

$$\overline{X} \pm t_{.025}(s_{\overline{X}})$$

has a probability of .95 of encompassing μ. μ is a fixed (though unknown) quantity, however, and once the data are in, the specific interval 1.219 to 1.707 either includes the value of μ ($p = 1.00$) or it does not ($p = .00$). Put in slightly different form,

$$\overline{X} \pm t_{.025}(s_{\overline{X}})$$

is a *random variable*, but the specific interval 1.219 to 1.707 is not a random variable and therefore does not have a probability associated with it. Many would maintain that it is perfectly reasonable to say that my confidence is .95 that if you were to tell me the true value of μ, it would be found to lie between 1.219 and 1.707. Not everyone would agree with this position, however.

I should add another word about the interpretation of confidence limits. Statements of the form $p(1.219 < \mu < 1.707) = .95$ are not interpreted in the usual way. The parameter μ is not a variable—it does not jump around from experiment to experiment. Rather, μ is a constant, and the *interval* is what varies from experiment to experiment. Thus, we can think of the parameter as a stake and the experimenter, in computing confidence limits, as tossing rings at it. Ninety-five percent of the time, a ring of specified width will encircle the parameter; 5% of the time, it will miss. A confidence statement is a statement of the probability that the ring has been on target; it is *not* a statement of the probability that the target (parameter) landed in the ring.

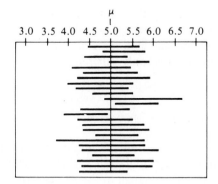

FIGURE 7.8
Confidence intervals computed on 25 samples from a population with $\mu = 5$

A graphic demonstration of confidence limits is shown in Figure 7.8. To generate this figure, I drew 25 samples of $N = 4$ from a population with a mean (μ) of 5. For every sample, a 95% confidence limit on μ was calculated and plotted. For example, the limits produced from the first sample were approximately 4.46 and 5.72, whereas those for the second sample were 4.83 and 5.80. Since in this case we know that the value of μ equals 5, I have drawn a vertical line at that point. Notice that the limits for samples 12 and 14 do not include $\mu = 5$. We would expect that 95% confidence limits would encompass μ 95 times out of 100. Therefore, two misses out of 25 seems reasonable. Notice also that the confidence intervals vary in width. This variability can be explained by the fact that the width of an interval is a function of the standard deviation of the sample, and some samples have larger standard deviations than others.

CONFIDENCE LIMITS ON $\mu_1 - \mu_2$

In addition to setting confidence limits for a single population mean, it is sometimes useful to set confidence limits on the difference between μ_1 and μ_2. The logic for setting these confidence limits is the same as for doing so in the one-sample case. The calculations are the same except that we use the *difference* between the means and the standard error of differences between means in place of the mean and the standard error of the mean. Thus, for the 95% confidence limits on $\mu_1 - \mu_2$, we have

$$CI_{.95} = (\overline{X}_1 - \overline{X}_2) \pm t_{.025} s_{\overline{X}_1 - \overline{X}_2}$$

For the comparison of the LBW experimental and control groups at 24 months, we have

$$CI_{.95} = (117.20 - 106.71) \pm 2.01 \sqrt{\frac{164.707}{25} + \frac{164.707}{31}}$$

$$= 10.49 \pm 2.01(3.450)$$

$$= 10.49 \pm 6.934$$

$$= 3.556 \leq (\mu_1 - \mu_2) \leq 17.424$$

The probability is .95 that an interval such as 3.556 to 17.424 encloses the true difference between MDI scores for theoretical populations of experimental and control LBW subjects. Notice that our calculations and interpretation are the same as they were in the previous example. The only difference is that we have replaced $\overline{X}$ with $(\overline{X}_1 - \overline{X}_2)$ and $s_{\overline{X}}$ with $s_{\overline{X}_1 - \overline{X}_2}$.

CONFIDENCE LIMITS ON σ^2

While we are examining confidence limits, it might be useful to consider the method of setting confidence limits on a population variance. When I presented the set of difference scores representing the change in the scores from children at ages 6 to 24 months, I noted that there was a surprising amount of variability in those data, and suggested that it might be important to examine the sources of that variability. If we want to worry about the variance, it would be useful to have confidence limits on σ^2.

If we let $\chi^2_{1-\alpha/2}$ and $\chi^2_{\alpha/2}$ be the critical values from a table of χ^2 for $N - 1$ df, these would be $\chi^2_{.975}$ and $\chi^2_{.025}$ for $\alpha = .05$. Both of these χ^2 values are on $N - 1$ df. We can then write the formula for the 95% confidence interval on σ^2 as

$$\frac{s^2}{\chi^2_{.025}/df} \leq \sigma^2 \leq \frac{s^2}{\chi^2_{.975}/df}$$

From Table 7.3, $N = 31$ and $s^2 = 16.04^2 = 257.28$. From Appendix χ^2, $\chi^2_{.025}(30) = 46.98$ and $\chi^2_{.975}(30) = 16.79$. Then

$$\frac{s^2}{\chi^2_{.025}/df} \le \sigma^2 \le \frac{s^2}{\chi^2_{.975}/df}$$

$$\frac{257.28}{46.98/30} \le \sigma^2 \le \frac{257.28}{16.79/30}$$

$$\frac{257.28}{1.566} \le \sigma^2 \le \frac{257.28}{0.560}$$

$$164.29 \le \sigma^2 \le 459.70$$

Thus, our confidence limits are 164.29 and 459.70. The probability is .95 that limits formed in this way include the true value of σ^2. Notice that these limits are rather wide. Unless our samples are quite large or s^2 is quite small, it is not possible to be very precise about our estimates of σ^2.

7.9   RUNNING TWO-SAMPLE t TESTS USING SPSS^x

Exhibit 7.2 shows how to use SPSS^x to analyze the data from Table 7.5. You can see that SPSS^x runs both the pooled and nonpooled t test. The F value given is the F test for homogeneity of variance. Note that with the nonpooled t (separate variance estimates), SPSS^x computes df' and uses it to find the probability value. (Minitab TWOSAMPLE does the same thing.)

EXHIBIT 7.2
SPXX^x analysis of data from Table 7.5

Title	'Comparison of MDI at 24 months for LBW groups'
File Handle	Data/Name = 'LBW.dat.'
Data List	File = Data/Group 1 MDI 3-5
Value Labels	Group (1) 'LBW-Exp' (2) 'LBW-Control'/
t-test	Groups = Group (1,2)/
	Variables = MDI
Option	4

t-tests for independent samples of GROUP

GROUP 1 - GROUP EQ 1: LBW-Exp
GROUP 2 - GROUP EQ 2: LBW-Control

Variable	Number of Cases	Mean	Standard Deviation	Standard Error
MDI				
GROUP 1	25	117.2000	12.682	2.536
GROUP 2	31	106.7097	12.954	2.327

		Pooled Variance Estimate			Separate Variance Estimate		
F Value	2-tail Prob.	t Value	Degrees of Freedom	2-tail Prob.	t Value	Degrees of Freedom	2-tail Prob.
1.04	.925	3.04	54	.004	3.05	51.95	.004

KEY TERMS

Sampling distribution of the mean (7.1)	Weighted average (7.5)
Central limit theorem (7.1)	Pooled variance estimate (7.5)
Uniform distribution (7.1)	Homogeneity of variance (7.6)
Standard error (7.2)	Heterogeneous variances (7.6)
Student's t distribution (7.3)	Behrens–Fisher problem (7.6)
p level (7.3)	Welch–Satterthwaite solution (7.6)
Matched samples (7.4)	df' (7.6)
Repeated measures (7.4)	Robust (7.6)
Related samples (7.4)	Meta-analysis (7.7)
Matched-sample t test (7.4)	Point estimate (7.8)
Difference scores (7.4)	Interval estimates (7.8)
Sampling distribution of differences between means (7.5)	Confidence limits (7.8)
	Confidence interval (7.8)
Variance sum law (7.5)	
Standard error of differences between means (7.5)	

EXERCISES

7.1 Using your local telephone book (or any other source of more or less random numbers), plot the distribution of the first 100 least significant (rightmost) digits.

7.2 Repeat Exercise 7.1, except calculate and plot the means for 25 samples of five least significant digits. (Group the means into appropriate intervals.)

7.3 Compare the means and standard deviations for the distribution of digits in Exercise 7.1 and the sampling distribution of the mean in Exercise 7.2. Do these answers agree with what the central limit theorem would lead you to expect?

7.4 In 1979 the 238 students from North Dakota who took the verbal portion of the SAT exam had a mean score of 525. The standard deviation was not reported.
  (a) Is this result consistent with the idea that the SAT has a mean of 500 and a standard deviation of 100?
  (b) Would you have rejected H_0 had you been looking for evidence that SAT scores in general have been declining over the years from a mean of 500?

7.5 Why do the data in Exercise 7.4 not really speak to the issue of whether American education in general is in a terrible state?

7.6 In 1979 the 2345 students from Arizona who took the math portion of the SAT had a mean score of 524. Is this consistent with the notion of a population mean of 500 if we assume that $\sigma = 100$?

7.7 Why does the answer to Exercise 7.6 differ substantially from the answer to Exercise 7.4 even though the means are virtually the same?

7.8   It is commonly assumed that GREs produce scores with a mean of 500. In October 1981 the mean verbal score of 5701 college seniors and nonenrolled college graduates in the biological sciences was 503 with a standard deviation of 104.
   (a) Is our common belief about the mean of the GRE justified, at least for the biological sciences?
   (b) What, if anything, are the *practical* implications of your answer to (a)?

7.9   What are the null hypothesis (H_0) and the alternative hypothesis (H_1) in Exercise 7.8?

7.10 Would it have made sense to run a one-tailed test for Exercise 7.8?

7.11 If you rejected the null hypothesis in Exercise 7.8, was that an important finding? Why or why not?

7.12 In a large corporation, the mean salary for all males with 3 to 5 years of experience was $28,000. Salaries (expressed in thousands) for a random sample of 10 women also having 3 to 5 years of experience were

$$24 \quad 27 \quad 31 \quad 21 \quad 19 \quad 26 \quad 30 \quad 22 \quad 15 \quad 36$$

Is there evidence of different salary levels for males and females?

7.13 Although most of the salaries for women in Exercise 7.12 were less than $28,000, you could not reject H_0. Why not?

7.14 Compute 95% confidence limits on μ for the data in Exercise 7.4.

7.15 Compute 95% confidence limits on μ for the data in Exercise 7.8.

7.16 How did your approaches to Exercises 7.14 and 7.15 differ?

7.17 Katz, Lauténschlager, Blackburn, and Harris (1990) examined the performance of 28 students, who answered multiple choice items on the SAT without having read the passages to which the items referred. The mean score (out of 100) was 46.6, with a standard deviation of 6.8. Random guessing would have been expected to result in 20 correct answers.
   (a) Were these students responding at better-than-chance levels?
   (b) If performance is significantly better than chance, does it mean that the SAT test is not a valid predictor of future college performance?

7.18 For 6 months we worked with a group of 15 severely retarded individuals in an attempt to teach them self-care skills through imitation. For a second 6-month period, we used physically guided practice with the same individuals. For each 6-month session, we collected ratings on the level of required assistance (high = bad) for each person. The data for each individual follow:

Subject:	1	2	3	4	5	6	7	8	9	10	11	12	13	14	15
Imitation:	14	11	19	8	4	9	12	5	14	17	18	0	2	8	6
Physical guidance:	10	13	15	5	3	6	7	9	16	10	13	1	2	3	6

Was required assistance reduced in the second 6-month period?

7.19 Does the study described in Exercise 7.18 clearly indicate the relative quality of the two approaches? Why or why not?

7.20 How could we improve the study described in Exercise 7.18?

7.21 Construct 95% confidence limits on the true mean difference between the treatments described in Exercise 7.18.

7.22 As part of a program to reduce smoking, a national organization ran an advertising campaign to convince people to quit or reduce their smoking. To evaluate the effectiveness of their campaign, they had 15 subjects record the average number of cigarettes smoked per day in the week before and the week after exposure to the advertisement. The data follow:

Subject:	1	2	3	4	5	6	7	8	9	10	11	12	13	14	15
Before:	45	16	20	33	30	19	33	25	26	40	28	36	15	26	32
After:	43	20	17	30	25	19	34	28	23	41	26	40	16	23	34

Run the appropriate *t* test. *matched pairs* $t = \dfrac{\bar{D} - 0}{s_D / \sqrt{N}}$ *Ho = the ads were not effective.*

7.23   Assume that the data in Exercise 7.22 were instead: $df = N-1$

Subject:	1	2	3	4	5	6	7	8	9	10	11	12	13	14	15
Before:	45	16	20	33	30	19	33	25	26	40	28	36	15	26	32
After:	59	35	30	40	20	10	20	20	36	46	10	25	8	35	46
	-14	-19	-10	-7	10	9	13	5	-10	-6	18	11	7	-9	-14
	196	361	100	49	100	81	169	25	100	36	324	121	49	81	196

Run the appropriate *t* test.

7.24   Draw conclusions (of which a careful experimenter would approve) from Exercises 7.22 and 7.23 and compare them.

7.25   Give an example of an experiment in which using related samples would be ill-advised because of carryover effects.

7.26   Using the data for the first 20 subjects in Appendix Data Set, test the hypothesis that English grades generally are higher than the overall GPA.

7.27   In the study referred to in Exercise 7.17, Katz et al. (1990) compared the performance on SAT items of a group of 17 students who were answering questions about a passage after having read the passage with the performance of a group of 28 students who had not seen the passage. The mean and standard deviation for the first group were 69.6 and 10.6, whereas for the second group they were 46.6 and 6.8.
(a) What is the null hypothesis?
(b) What is the alternative hypothesis?
(c) Run the appropriate *t* test.
(d) Interpret the results.

7.28   Suppose we redesigned the study described in Exercise 7.18 to have *different* subjects serve under the imitation and physical guidance conditions. We obtained the following data:

Imitation:	14	11	19	8	4	9	12	5	14	17	18	0	2	8	6
Physical guidance:	10	14	5	8	1	10	13	14	0	1	4	2	3	4	14

What would you conclude?

7.29   What is the most obvious problem with the data in Exercise 7.28 in terms of finding a significant difference?

7.30   Why was the experimental design (repeated measures) used in Exercise 7.18 able to produce a statistically significant difference when there was not a significant difference for Exercise 7.28?

7.31   We randomly assigned nine children to each of two groups. One group was given training in creative problem solving and the other was not. All children were then given a series of problems and asked to generate possible solutions. The number of solutions generated by each subject was:

Training:	12	16	19	8	10	13	9	15	14
No training:	15	5	11	8	9	5	6	11	10

(a) State the null hypothesis.
(b) State a reasonable alternative hypothesis.
(c) Run the appropriate t test.
(d) Interpret the results.

7.32 What is the role of random assignment in Exercise 7.31?

7.33 In a comparison of different programs advocated by two organizations concerned with weight loss, 20 subjects were enrolled in Program A and 20 in Program B. The amount of weight lost in the next 6 months by those subjects who completed the program was:

Program A:	25	21	18	20	22	30						
Program B:	15	17	9	12	11	19	14	18	16	10	5	13

Run the appropriate t test after considering the group variances.

7.34 Assume that the following data were obtained in the study described in Exercise 7.33:

Program A:	25	21	8	20	12	30						
Program B:	15	17	9	12	11	19	14	18	16	10	15	13

Calculate and evaluate t after considering the two sample variances.

7.35 In Exercise 7.34, are the means the most important statistics? What might be considered more important?

7.36 Much has been made of the concept of experimenter bias, which refers to the fact that even the most conscientious experimenters tend to collect data that come out in the desired direction (they see what they want to see). Suppose we use students as experimenters. All the experimenters are told that subjects will be given caffeine before the experiment, but one-half of the experimenters are told that we expect caffeine to lead to good performance and one-half are told that we expect it to lead to poor performance. The dependent variable is the number of simple arithmetic problems the subjects can solve in 2 minutes. The data obtained are:

[handwritten above Expectation good row: 361 225 484 169 324 225 400 625 484]

Expectation good:	19	15	22	13	18	15	20	25	22	
Expectation poor:	14	18	17	12	21	21	24	14		

[handwritten annotations near Expectation poor row: 196 324 289 144 441 441 576 196]

[handwritten equations to the right:]
$$t = \frac{(\bar{X}_1 - \bar{X}_2)}{\sqrt{S_p^2 \left(\frac{1}{N_1} + \frac{1}{N_2} \right)}}$$
$$S_p^2 = \frac{(N_1 - 1)S_1^2 + (N_2 - 1)S_2^2}{N_1 + N_2 - 2}$$
$$df = N_1 + N_2 - 2.$$

What can you conclude?

7.37 Calculate 95% confidence limits on $\mu_1 - \mu_2$ for the data in Exercise 7.36.

7.38 Calculate 95% confidence limits on $\mu_1 - \mu_2$ for the data in Exercise 7.34.

7.39 Using the data in Appendix Data Set, run a t test to compare ADDSC scores of males and females.

7.40 Using the data in Appendix Data Set, compare GPAs for students having ADDSC scores of 65 or less with those having ADDSC scores of 66 or more.

7.41 What does your answer to Exercise 7.40 tell you about the predictive utility of the ADDSC score?

7.42 An experimenter examining decision making asked 10 children to solve as many problems as they could in 10 minutes. One group (5 subjects) was told that this was a test of their innate problem-solving ability; a second group (5 subjects) was told that this was just a time-filling task. The data follow:

Innate ability:	4	5	8	3	7
Time-filling task:	11	6	9	7	9

[handwritten note in left margin beside 7.36: $H_0 = $ exp. do not only see what they want to see]

7.43 A second investigator repeated the experiment described in Exercise 7.42 and obtained the same results. However, she thought that it would be more appropriate to record the data in terms of minutes per problem (e.g., 4 problems in 10 minutes = 10/4 = 2.5 problems/minute). Thus, her data were:

| **Innate ability:** | 2.50 | 2.00 | 1.25 | 3.33 | 1.43 |
| **Time-filling task:** | 0.91 | 1.67 | 1.11 | 1.43 | 1.11 |

Analyze and interpret these data with the appropriate t test.

7.44 What does a comparison of Exercises 7.42 and 7.43 show you?

COMPUTER EXERCISES

7.45 Use any statistical package with the data set named ADD.dat to test the null hypothesis that the population mean for IQ is 100.

7.46 Use any statistical package to test the difference between the means of ENGG and GPA in the ADD data set. Why would you expect beforehand that the variances of these two variables will differ?

7.47 In Chapter 4 (Exercise 4.16) you used a data file named RandUnif.dat to plot the sampling distribution of the mean for samples of size 10. Go back and modify the program you used there to take means of samples of size 2, 4, 6, 8, and 10 (e.g., Mean2 = (X1 + X9)/2; Mean4 = X3 + X5 + X7 + X9)/4; Mean6 = (X2 + X3 + X5 + X6 + X9 + X10)/6, etc. The variables you choose to average are arbitrary.) Have your program plot the distributions for these new variables. Do the results agree with the results you would have predicted from the central limit theorem? (*Hint*: The mean of the population is 50, and the standard deviation is 28.868.)

7.48 Research on clinical samples (i.e., people referred for diagnosis or treatment) has suggested that children who experience the death of a parent may be at risk for developing depression or anxiety in adulthood. Mireault (1990) collected data on 140 college students who had experienced the death of a parent, 182 students from two-parent families, and 59 students from divorced families. The data are found in the file Mireault.dat and are described in Appendix: Computer Exercises.
(a) Use any statistical program to run t tests to compare the first two groups on the Depression, Anxiety, and Global Symptom Index T scores from the Brief Symptom Inventory (Derogatis, 1983).
Are these three t tests independent of one another? [*Hint*: To do this problem you will have to ignore or delete those cases in Group 3 (the Divorced group). Your instructor or the appropriate manual will explain how to do this for the particular software that you are using.]

7.49 It is commonly reported that women show more symptoms of anxiety and depression than men. Would the data from Mireault's study support this hypothesis?

7.50 Now run separate t tests to compare Mireault's Group 1 versus Group 2, Group 1 versus Group 3, and Group 2 versus Group 3 on the Global Symptom Index. (This is *not* a good way to compare the three group means, but it is being done here because it leads to more appropriate analyses in Chapter 12.)

7.51 It is instructive to observe the actual values of t that result from situations in which the null hypothesis is, or is not, true. You have a data file named RandNorm.dat, which contains 10,000 random numbers drawn from one normally distributed population with a mean of 50 and a standard deviation of 10. This file has the same structure as RandUnif.dat, which we have used before. You need to change only the file name in the earlier programs.

(a) Read 100 cases from this file. Using Group as a grouping variable, run t tests between groups for each X_i. If different students read different sections of the file or delete an arbitrary number of cases from the file before beginning, then you can pool data across students to produce a small empirical sampling distribution of t.

(b) Part (a) was done with a true null hypothesis. Now add a small constant (2.5) to each value of X for one of the groups in a set. For example, "If Group = 2 then X1 = X1 + 2.5." Now run a t test comparing the two groups. Repeat the test for other variables, again pooling results across students. How often was the null hypothesis actually rejected when it was false?

(c) In (b) you added 2.5, which was one-quarter of a standard deviation, to X1, making the null hypothesis false by that amount. Repeat (b) using constants of 5.0 and then 10.0 (one-half a standard deviation and one standard deviation, respectively). What effect do the larger constants have on the frequency with which you reject the null hypothesis? (We will make more of this in Chapter 8.)

[*Hint*: Each program has a different way of specifying how to use only part of the data. For BMDP, add CASES = 100. to the /INPUT paragraph. For Minitab, the easiest thing to do is just to delete rows (Del 101 : 1000 c1-c11). For SAS, add OBS = 100 to the INFILE statement. Finally, for SPSS^X, use N OF CASES 50 after the DATA LIST statement.]

CHAPTER EIGHT

POWER

OBJECTIVES *To introduce the concept of the power of a statistical test and to show how we can calculate the power of a variety of statistical procedures.*

CONTENTS

Until recently, most applied statistical work as it is actually carried out in analyzing experimental results was primarily concerned with minimizing (or at least controlling) the probability of a Type I error (α). When proceeding to design experiments, people tend to ignore the very important fact that there is a probability (β) of another kind of error, Type II errors. Whereas Type I errors deal with the problem of *finding* a difference that is not there, Type II errors concern the equally serious problem of not finding a difference that is there. When we consider the substantial cost in time and money that goes into a typical experiment nowadays, we could argue that it is remarkably short-sighted of experimenters not to recognize that they may, from the start, have only a small chance of finding the effect they are looking for, even if such an effect does exist in the population.

There are very good historical reasons why investigators have tended to ignore Type II errors. Until recently, many textbooks avoided the problem altogether, and those books that did discuss the material did so in ways that were not easily understood by the average reader (noncentrality parameters and power curves with strange things on the abscissa can be puzzling at first). Cohen, however, discussed the problem very clearly and lucidly in several publications. Cohen (1988) presented a thorough and rigorous treatment of the material. In Welkowitz, Ewen, and Cohen (1991), the material is treated in a slightly simpler way through the use of an approximation technique. Their approach is the one adopted in this chapter. You should have no difficulty with either of these sources, or for that matter with any of the many excellent papers Cohen has published on a wide variety of topics not necessarily directly related to this particular one.

Power

Speaking in terms of Type II errors is a rather negative way of approaching the problem, since it keeps reminding us that we might make a mistake. The more positive approach would be to speak in terms of **power**, which is defined as the probability of correctly rejecting a false H_0. Thus, power $= 1 - \beta$. A more powerful experiment is one that has a better chance of rejecting a false H_0 than does a less powerful experiment.

In this chapter we will take the approach of Welkowitz, Ewen, and Cohen (1991) and work with an approximation to the true power of a test. This approximation is an excellent one, especially in light of the fact that we do not really care whether the power is .85 or .83, but rather whether it is near .80 or nearer to .30.[†] For expository purposes we will assume for the moment that we are interested in testing one sample mean against a specified population mean, although the approach immediately generalizes to testing other hypotheses.

8.1   FACTORS AFFECTING THE POWER OF A TEST

As might be expected, power is a function of several variables. It is a function of (1) α, the probability of a Type I error, (2) the true alternative hypothesis (H_1), (3) the sample size, and (4) the particular test to be employed. With the exception of the relative power of independent versus matched samples, we will avoid this last relationship on the grounds that when the test assumptions are met, the majority of the procedures discussed in this book can be shown to be the uniformly most powerful tests of those available to answer the question at hand.

THE BASIC CONCEPT

I will briefly review what I covered in Chapter 4. Consider the two distributions in Figure 8.1. The distribution to the left (labeled H_0) represents the sampling distribution of the mean when the null hypothesis is true and $\mu = \mu_0$. The heavily shaded right tail of this distribution represents α, the probability of a Type I error, assuming that we are using a one-tailed test (otherwise it represents $\alpha/2$). This area contains the means that would result in significant values of t. The second distribution (H_1) represents the sampling distribution of the statistic when H_0 is false and the true mean $= \mu_1$. It is readily apparent that even when H_0 is false, many of the sample means (and therefore the corresponding values of t) will nonetheless fall to the left of the critical value, causing us to fail to reject a false H_0, thus committing a Type II error. The probability of this error is indicated by the lightly shaded area in Figure 8.1 and is labeled β. When H_0 is false and the test statistic falls to the right of the critical value,

---

[†]Cohen (1988) takes a more detailed approach; rather than working with an approximation, he works with more exact probabilities. That approach requires much more extensive tables but produces answers very close to the ones we get with an approximation.

we will correctly reject a false H_0. The probability of doing this is what we mean by *power*, and is shown in the unshaded area of the H_1 distribution.[†]

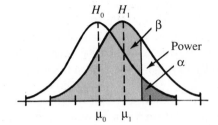

FIGURE 8.1
Sampling distribution of $\overline{X}$ under H_0 and H_1

POWER AS A FUNCTION OF α

With the aid of Figure 8.1, it is easy to see why we say that power is a function of α. If we are willing to increase α, our cutoff point moves to the left, thus simultaneously decreasing β and increasing power, although with a corresponding rise in the probability of a Type I error.

POWER AS A FUNCTION OF H_1

The fact that power is a function of the true alternative hypothesis [more precisely $(\mu_0 - \mu_1)$, the difference between the mean under $H_0(\mu_0)$ and the mean under H_1 (μ_1)] is illustrated by comparing Figures 8.1 and 8.2. In Figure 8.2 the distance between μ_0 and μ_1 has been increased, and this has resulted in a substantial increase in power. This is not particularly surprising, since all that we are saying is that the chances of finding a difference depend on how large the difference actually is.

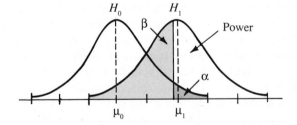

FIGURE 8.2
Effect on β of increasing $\mu_0 - \mu_1$

POWER AS A FUNCTION OF N AND σ^2

The relationship between power and sample size (and between power and σ^2) is only a little subtler. Since we are interested in means or differences between means, we are interested in the sampling distribution of the mean. We know that the variance of the

---

[†]The magnitude of power is proportional to the graphically presented area under the curve when standardized data are used in the graphs.

sampling distribution of the mean decreases as either N increases or σ^2 decreases, since $\sigma_{\bar{X}}^2 = \sigma^2/N$. Figure 8.3 illustrates what happens to the two sampling distributions (H_0 and H_1) as we increase N or decrease σ^2, relative to Figure 8.2. Figure 8.3 also shows that, as $\sigma_{\bar{X}}^2$ decreases, the overlap between the two distributions is reduced with a resulting increase in power. Notice that the two means (μ_0 and μ_1) remain unchanged.

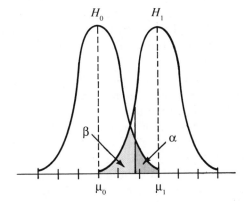

FIGURE 8.3
Effect on β of decrease in standard error of the mean

If an experimenter concerns himself with the power of a test, then he is most likely interested in those variables governing power that are easy to manipulate. Since N is more easily manipulated than is either σ^2 or the difference ($\mu_0 - \mu_1$), and since tampering with α produces undesirable side effects in terms of increasing the probability of a Type I error, discussions of power are generally concerned with the effects of varying sample size.

8.2 EFFECT SIZE

As we saw in Figures 8.1 through 8.3, power depends on the degree of overlap between the sampling distributions under H_0 and H_1. Furthermore, this overlap is a function of both the distance between μ_0 and μ_1 and the standard error. One measure, then, of the degree to which H_0 is false would be the distance from μ_1 to μ_0 expressed in terms of the number of standard errors. The problem with this measure, however, is that it includes the sample size (in the computation of the standard error), when in fact we will usually wish to solve for the power associated with a given N or else for that value of N required for a given level of power. For this reason we will take as our distance

Effect size (d)   measure, or **effect size (d)**,

$$\mathbf{d} = \frac{\mu_1 - \mu_0}{\sigma}$$

ignoring the sign of $\mathbf{d}$, and incorporating N later. Thus, $\mathbf{d}$ is a measure of the degree to which μ_1 and μ_0 differ in terms of the standard deviation of the parent population. We see that $\mathbf{d}$ is estimated independently of N, simply by estimating μ_1, μ_0, and σ.

ESTIMATING THE EFFECT SIZE

The first task is to estimate **d**, since it will form the basis for future calculations. This can be done in three ways:

1. *Prior research.* On the basis of past research, we can often get at least a rough approximation of **d**. Thus, we could look at sample means and variances from other studies and make an informed guess at the values we might expect for $\mu_1 - \mu_0$ and for σ. In practice, this task is not as difficult as it might seem, especially when you realize that a rough approximation is far better than no approximation at all.

2. *Personal assessment of which difference is important.* In many cases, an investigator is able to say, I am interested in detecting a difference of at least 10 points between μ_1 and μ_0. The investigator is essentially saying that differences less than this have no important or useful meaning, whereas greater differences do. Here we are given the value of $\mu_1 - \mu_0$ directly, without needing to know the particular values of μ_1 and μ_0. All that remains is to estimate σ from other data. As an example, the investigator might say that she is interested in finding a procedure that will raise scores on the GRE by 40 points above normal. We already know that the standard deviation for this test is 100. Thus, $\mathbf{d} = \frac{40}{100} = .40$. If our hypothetical experimenter says instead that she wants to raise scores by four-tenths of a standard deviation, she would be giving us **d** directly.

3. *Use of special conventions.* When we encounter a situation in which there is no way we can estimate the required parameters, we can fall back on a set of conventions proposed by Cohen (1988). Cohen more or less arbitrarily defined three levels of **d**:

Effect Size	d	Percentage of Overlap
Small	.20	85
Medium	.50	67
Large	.80	53

Thus, in a pinch, the experimenter can simply decide whether she is after a small, medium, or large effect and set **d** accordingly. However, this solution should be chosen *only* when the other alternatives are not feasible. The right-hand column of this table is labeled Percentage of Overlap, and it records the degree to which the two distributions shown in Figure 8.1 overlap. Thus, for example, when $\mathbf{d} = 0.50$, two-thirds of the two distributions overlap (Cohen, 1988).

It may strike you as peculiar that the investigator is being asked to define the difference she is looking for before the experiment is conducted. Most people would respond by saying, "I don't know how the experiment will come out. I just wonder whether there will be a difference." Although many experimenters speak in this way (the author is no virtuous exception), you should question the validity of this statement. Do we really not know, at least vaguely, what will happen in our experiments; if not, why are we running them? Although there is occasionally a legitimate I-wonder-what-would-happen-if experiment, in general, "I do not know" translates to "I have not thought that far ahead."

RECOMBINING THE EFFECT SIZE AND *N*

δ (delta)

We decided to split the sample size from the effect size to make it easier to deal with *N* separately. We now need a method for combining the effect size with the sample size. We use the statistic δ **(delta)**

$$\delta = \mathbf{d}[f(N)]$$

to represent this combination where the particular function of *N* $[f(N)]$ will be defined differently for each individual test. The convenient thing about this system is that it will allow us to use the same table of δ for power calculations for all the statistical procedures to be considered.

8.3   POWER CALCULATIONS FOR THE ONE-SAMPLE *t*

We will first examine power calculations for the one-sample *t* test. In the preceding section we saw that δ is based on **d** and some function of *N*. For the one-sample *t*, that function will be $\sqrt{N}$, and δ will then be defined as

$$\delta = \mathbf{d}\sqrt{N}$$

Given δ as defined here, we can immediately determine the power of our test from the table of power in Appendix Power.

Assume that a clinical psychologist wants to test the hypothesis that people who seek treatment for psychological problems have higher IQs than the general population. She wants to use the IQs of 25 randomly selected clients and is interested in finding the power of detecting a difference of 5 points between the mean of the general population and the mean of the population from which her clients are drawn. Thus, $\mu_1 = 105$, $\mu_0 = 100$, and $\sigma = 15$.

$$\mathbf{d} = \frac{105 - 100}{15} = 0.33$$

then

$$\delta = \mathbf{d}\sqrt{N} = 0.33\sqrt{25} = 0.33(5)$$
$$= 1.65$$

Although the clinician expects the sample means to be above average, she plans to use a two-tailed test at $\alpha = .05$ to protect against unexpected events. From Appendix Power, for $\delta = 1.65$ with $\alpha = .05$ (two-tailed), power is between .36 and .40. By crude linear interpolation, we will say that power = .38. This means that, if H_0 is false and μ_1 is really 105, only 38% of the time will our clinician find a significant difference between her *sample* mean and that specified by H_0. This is a rather discouraging result, since it means that if the true mean is 105, 62% of the time our clinician will make a Type II error.

Since our experimenter was intelligent enough to examine the question of power before she began her experiment, all is not lost. She still has the chance to make changes that will lead to an increase in power. She could, for example, set α at .10, thus increasing power to approximately .50, but this is probably unsatisfactory. (Journal editors, for example, generally hate to see α set at any value greater than .05.)

ESTIMATING REQUIRED SAMPLE SIZE

Alternatively, the investigator could increase her sample size, thereby increasing power. How large an N does she need? The answer depends on what level of power she desires. Suppose she wishes to set power at .80. From Appendix Power, for power = .80, δ must equal 2.80. Thus, we have δ and can simply solve for N:

$$\delta = \mathbf{d}\sqrt{N}$$

$$N = \left(\frac{\delta}{\mathbf{d}}\right)^2 = \left(\frac{2.80}{0.33}\right)^2 = 8.48^2$$

$$= 71.91$$

Since clients generally come in whole lots, we will round off to 72. Thus, if the experimenter wants to have an 80% chance of rejecting H_0 when $\mathbf{d} = 0.33$ (i.e., when $\mu_1 = 105$), she will have to use the IQs for 72 randomly selected clients. Although this may be more clients than she can test easily, the only alternative is to settle for a lower level of power.

You might wonder why we selected power = .80; with this degree of power, we still run a 20% chance of making a Type II error. The answer lies in the notion of practicality. Suppose, for example, that we had wanted power = .95. A few simple calculations will show that this would require a sample of $N = 119$. For power = .99, you would need approximately 159 subjects. These may well be unreasonable sample sizes for this particular experimental situation, or for the resources of the experimenter. Remember that increases in power are generally bought by increases in N and, at high levels of power, the cost can be very high. If you are taking data from data tapes supplied by the Bureau of the Census, that is quite different from studying teenage college graduates.

NONCENTRALITY PARAMETERS

Noncentrality parameter

δ is what most textbooks refer to as a **noncentrality parameter**. The concept is relatively simple, and well worth considering. First, we know that

$$t = \frac{X - \mu}{s} \quad \text{or} \quad \frac{\overline{X} - \mu}{s/\sqrt{N}}$$

is distributed around zero regardless of the truth or falsity of any null hypothesis, *as long as μ is the true mean* of the distribution from which the Xs were sampled. If H_0 states that $\mu = \mu_0$ (some specific value of μ) *and H_0 is true*, then

$$t = \frac{\overline{X} - \mu_0}{s/\sqrt{N}}$$

will also be distributed around zero. If H_0 is false and $\mu \neq \mu_0$, however, then

$$t = \frac{\overline{X} - \mu_0}{s/\sqrt{N}}$$

will not be distributed around zero because in subtracting μ_0, we have been subtracting the wrong population mean. In fact, the distribution will be centered at the point

$$\delta = \frac{\mu_1 - \mu_0}{\sigma/\sqrt{N}}$$

This shift in the mean of the distribution from zero to δ is referred to as the *degree of noncentrality*, and δ is the noncentrality parameter.

The question of power becomes the question of how likely we are to find a value of the noncentral (shifted) distribution that is greater than the critical value that t would have under H_0. In other words, even though larger-than-normal values of t are to be expected because H_0 is false, we will occasionally obtain small values by chance. The percentage of these values that happen to lie below $t_{.05}$ is β, the probability of a Type II error. As we know, we can easily obtain power from β; power $= 1 - \beta$.

Cohen's contribution can be seen as splitting the noncentrality parameter (δ) into two parts—sample size and effect size. One part (**d**) depends solely on parameters of the populations, whereas the other depends on sample size. Thus, Cohen has separated parametric considerations (μ_0, μ_1 and σ), about which we can do relatively little, from sample characteristics (N), over which we have more control. Although this produces no basic change in the underlying theory, it makes the concept easier to understand and use.

8.4   POWER CALCULATIONS FOR DIFFERENCES BETWEEN TWO INDEPENDENT MEANS

When we wish to test the difference between two independent means, the treatment of power is very similar to our treatment of the case that we used for only one mean. In Section 8.3 we obtained **d** by taking the difference between μ under H_1 and μ under H_0 and dividing by σ. In testing the difference between two independent means, we will do basically the same thing, although this time we will work with mean differences. Thus, we want the difference between the two population means ($\mu_1 - \mu_2$) under H_1 minus the difference ($\mu_1 - \mu_2$) under H_0, divided by σ. (Recall that we assume $\sigma_1^2 =$

$\sigma_2^2 = \sigma^2$.) In all usual applications, however, $(\mu_1 - \mu_2)$ under H_0 is zero, so we can drop that term from our formula. Thus,

$$\mathbf{d} = \frac{(\mu_1 - \mu_2) - (0)}{\sigma} = \frac{\mu_1 - \mu_2}{\sigma}$$

where the numerator refers to the difference to be expected under H_1 and the denominator represents the standard deviation of the populations. In the case of two samples, we must distinguish between experiments involving equal Ns and those involving unequal Ns. We will treat these two cases separately.

EQUAL SAMPLE SIZES

Assume we wish to test the difference between two treatments and either expect that the difference in population means will be approximately 5 points or else are interested only in finding a difference of at least 5 points. Further assume that from past data we think that σ is approximately 10. Then

$$\mathbf{d} = \frac{\mu_1 - \mu_2}{\sigma} = \frac{5}{10} = 0.50$$

Thus, we are expecting a difference of one-half of a standard deviation between the two means.

First we will investigate the power of an experiment with 25 observations in each of two groups. We will define δ in the two-sample case as

$$\delta = \mathbf{d}\sqrt{\frac{N}{2}}$$

where N = the number of cases *in any one sample* (there are $2N$ cases in all). Thus,

$$\delta = (0.50)\sqrt{\frac{25}{2}} = 0.50\sqrt{12.5} = 0.50(3.54)$$

$$= 1.77$$

From Appendix Power, by interpolation for $\delta = 1.77$ with a two-tailed test at $\alpha = .05$, power = .43. Thus, if our investigator actually runs this experiment with 25 subjects, and if her estimate of δ is correct, then she has a 43% chance of actually rejecting H_0.

We next turn the question around and ask how many subjects would be needed for power = .80. From Appendix Power, this would require $\delta = 2.80$.

$$\delta = \mathbf{d}\sqrt{\frac{N}{2}}$$

$$\frac{\delta}{\mathbf{d}} = \sqrt{\frac{N}{2}}$$

$$\left(\frac{\delta}{\mathbf{d}}\right)^2 = \frac{N}{2}$$

$$N = 2\left(\frac{\delta}{d}\right)^2$$

$$= 2\left(\frac{2.80}{0.50}\right)^2 = 2(5.6)^2$$

$$= 62.72$$

N refers to the number of subjects per sample, so for power $= .80$, we need 63 subjects per sample for a total of 126 subjects.

UNEQUAL SAMPLE SIZES

We just dealt with the case in which $N_1 = N_2 = N$. However, experiments commonly have two samples of unequal sizes. This obviously presents difficulties when we try to solve for δ, since we need one value for N. What value can we use?

With reasonably large and nearly equal samples, a conservative approximation can be obtained by letting N equal the smaller of N_1 and N_2. This is not satisfactory, however, if the sample sizes are small or if the two Ns are quite different. For those cases we need a more exact solution.

One seemingly reasonable (but incorrect) procedure would be to set N equal to the arithmetic mean of N_1 and N_2. This method would weight the two samples equally, however, when in fact we know that the variance of means is proportional not to N, but to $1/N$. The measure that takes this relationship into account is not the arithmetic

Harmonic mean ($\overline{X}_h$)   mean but the harmonic mean. The **harmonic mean ($\overline{X}_h$)** of k numbers $(X_1, X_2, \ldots, X_k)$ is defined as

$$\overline{X}_h = \frac{k}{\sum \dfrac{1}{X_i}}$$

Thus for two samples sizes (N_1 and N_2),

$$\overline{N}_h = \frac{2}{\dfrac{1}{N_1} + \dfrac{1}{N_2}} = \frac{2N_1 N_2}{N_1 + N_2}$$

We can then use $\overline{N}_h$ in our calculation of δ.

As an example, assume we want to test the hypothesis that as a result of a change in the textbook, the mean grade for this year's statistics class is different from that of the last 2 years' classes. The classes have been graded on the same system, so that we have comparable measures for the 3 years. There have been 20 students each year. We are interested in an effect size (**d**) of 0.30. We will calculate the effective sample size (the sample size to be used in calculating δ) as

$$\overline{N}_h = \frac{2(40)(20)}{40 + 20} = \frac{1600}{60} = 26.667$$

We see that the *effective* sample size is less than the arithmetic mean of the two individual sample sizes. In other words, this study has the same power as it would have had we run it with 26.667 subjects per group for a total of 53.333 subjects.

To continue,

$$\delta = \mathbf{d}\sqrt{\frac{\overline{N_h}}{2}} = 0.30\sqrt{\frac{26.667}{2}} = 0.30\sqrt{13.333}$$

$$= 1.10$$

For $\delta = 1.10$, power $= .20$.

In this case the power is too low to inspire much confidence in the study. If H_0 is true, we have a 5% chance of rejecting H_0 (a Type I error); if it is false (to the degree specified), we have only a 20% chance of rejecting H_0 (a correct decision). It seems that we stand to retain H_0 almost regardless of its truth or falsity.

If it were possible for us to increase sample sizes (such as by including subjects from more years), it obviously would be desirable to do so. Suppose we could magically produce an additional 20 subjects and add these to the smaller group, making $N_1 = N_2 = N$. With $N = 40$,

$$\delta = \mathbf{d}\sqrt{\frac{N}{2}} = 0.30\sqrt{\frac{40}{2}} = 1.34$$

Power $\simeq .27$

Although this increase in power is not dramatic, it is better than nothing. On the other hand, consider the effect of adding those 20 subjects to the larger group. Then $N_1 = 20$ and $N_2 = 60$.

$$\overline{N_h} = \frac{2(20)(60)}{20 + 60} = 30$$

$$\delta = 0.30\sqrt{\frac{30}{2}} = 0.30\sqrt{15} = 1.16$$

Power $= .21$

In this case, adding 20 subjects increased power by only .01 (as opposed to the increase of .07 when they were added to the smaller group).

This discussion points out an important principle: For a fixed number of subjects, power is maximized by setting $N_1 = N_2$. This suggests the general strategy of balancing sample sizes in designing experiments. When unequal sample sizes are unavoidable, the smaller group should be as large as possible relative to the larger group.

8.5   POWER CALCULATIONS FOR MATCHED-SAMPLE t

When we want to test the difference between two matched samples, the problem becomes a bit more difficult and an additional parameter must be considered. For this reason, the analysis of power for this case is frequently impractical. However, the general solution to the problem illustrates an important principle of experimental design, and thus justifies close examination.

We define **d** as

$$\mathbf{d} = \frac{\mu_1 - \mu_2}{\sigma_{X_1 - X_2}}$$

where $\mu_1 - \mu_2$ represents the expected mean difference (the expected mean of the difference scores). The problem arises because $\sigma_{X_1 - X_2}$ is the standard deviation not of the populations of X_1 and X_2, but of difference scores drawn from these populations. Although we might be able to make an intelligent guess at σ_{X_1} or σ_{X_2}, we probably have no idea about $\sigma_{X_1 - X_2}$.

All is not lost, however; it is possible to calculate $\sigma_{X_1 - X_2}$ on the basis of a few assumptions. The variance sum law (discussed in Chapter 7, p. 179) gives the variance for a sum or difference of two variables. Specifically,

$$\sigma_{X_1 \pm X_2}^2 = \sigma_{X_1}^2 + \sigma_{X_2}^2 \pm 2\rho\sigma_{X_1}\sigma_{X_2}$$

If we make the general assumption of homogeneity of variance ($\sigma_{X_1}^2 = \sigma_{X_2}^2 = \sigma^2$), for the difference of two variables we have

$$\sigma_{X_1 - X_2}^2 = 2\sigma^2 - 2\rho\sigma^2 = 2\sigma^2(1 - \rho)$$
$$\sigma_{X_1 - X_2} = \sigma\sqrt{2(1 - \rho)}$$

where ρ (rho) is the correlation in the population between X_1 and X_2 and can take on values between 1 and -1. It is positive for almost all situations in which we are likely to want a matched-sample t.

Assuming for the moment that we can estimate ρ, the rest of the procedure is the same as that for the one-sample t. We define

$$\mathbf{d} = \frac{\mu_1 - \mu_2}{\sigma_{X_1 - X_2}}$$

and

$$\delta = \mathbf{d}\sqrt{N}$$

We then estimate $\sigma_{X_1 - X_2}$ as $\sigma\sqrt{2(1 - \rho)}$, and refer the value of δ to the tables.

As an example, assume that we want to see whether people's test performance is better in the morning than it is at night. We administer the Wechsler Adult Intelligence Scale (WAIS) to a sample of 30 subjects late one night, send them to bed, and read-minister the test the next morning. (A better experimental design would be to have one-half of the subjects tested in the morning first and one-half tested at night first, but this would have no effect on the power of the test.) We will make the rather naive assumption that there is no carryover effect from one administration to the next. Suppose we want to evaluate the power for finding a difference as great as 3 IQ points. From any standard text on psychometric measurement, we can obtain an estimate of the correlation between the scores on the two sessions. This is nothing but the short-term reliability of the test, and a reasonable value for the reliability is .92. We also would find that the standard deviation for this test is set at 15. Thus

$$\sigma_{X_1 - X_2} = \sigma \sqrt{2(1 - \rho)} = 15\sqrt{2(1 - .92)} = 15\sqrt{2(.08)}$$
$$= 6.0$$

$$\mathbf{d} = \frac{\mu_1 - \mu_2}{\sigma_{X_1 - X_2}} = \frac{3}{6} = 0.50$$

$$\delta = \mathbf{d}\sqrt{N} = 0.50\sqrt{30} = 2.74$$

Power $= .78$

Suppose, on the other hand, that we had used a less reliable test, for which $\rho = .50$. We will assume that σ remains unchanged. Then

$$\sigma_{X_1 - X_2} = 15\sqrt{2(1 - .50)} = 15\sqrt{2(.5)} = 15\sqrt{1} = 15$$

$$\mathbf{d} = \frac{\mu_1 - \mu_2}{\sigma_{X_1 - X_2}} = \frac{3}{15} = 0.20$$

$$\delta = 0.20\sqrt{30} = 1.10$$

Power $= .20$

We see that as ρ drops, so does power. When $\rho = 0$, our two variables are not correlated and thus the matched-sample case has been reduced to the independent-sample case. The important point here is that for practical purposes the minimum power for the matched-sample case occurs when $\rho = 0$ and we have independent samples. Thus, for all situations in which we are even remotely likely to use matched samples (when we expect a positive correlation between X_1 and X_2), the matched-sample design is more powerful than the corresponding independent-groups design. This illustrates one of the main advantages of designs using matched samples.

Remember that we are using an approximation procedure to calculate power. Essentially, we are assuming the sample sizes are sufficiently large that the t distribution is closely approximated by z. If this is not the case, then we have to take account of the fact that a matched-sample t has only one-half as many df as the corresponding independent-sample t, and the power of the two designs will not be quite equal when $\rho = 0$. This is not usually a serious problem.

8.6 POWER CONSIDERATIONS IN TERMS OF SAMPLE SIZE

Our discussion of power illustrates that reasonably large sample sizes are almost a necessity if one is to run experiments with any decent chance of rejecting H_0 when it is in fact false and the effect is small. As an illustration, a few calculations show that if we want to have power $= .80$ and if we accept Cohen's admittedly arbitrary definitions for small, medium, and large effects, our samples may not be small. Table 8.1 presents the total Ns required (at power $= .80$, $\alpha = .05$) for small, medium, and large effects for the tests we have been discussing. These figures indicate that power (at least a substantial amount of it) is an expensive commodity, especially for small effects. We could argue that this is a good thing, because otherwise the literature would contain many more small (trivial?) results than it already does; however, this assertion is unlikely to comfort most experimenters. The general rule is either to look for big effects or to use large samples. An interesting article on the power of published experiments is Cohen (1962).

TABLE 8.1
Total sample sizes required for power = .80, α = .05, two-tailed

Effect Size	d	One-Sample t	Two-Sample t
Small	.20	196	784
Medium	.50	32	126
Large	.80	13	49

KEY TERMS

Power (introduction)

Effect size (d) (8.2)

δ (delta) (8.2)

Noncentrality parameter (8.3)

Harmonic mean ($\bar{X}_h$) (8.4)

EXERCISES

8.1 Over the past 10 years, a small New England college has been able to hold the mean SAT score of its incoming class (and, by inference, the mean score of the population from which it draws) at 520 with a standard deviation of 80. A major competitor would like to demonstrate that standards have slipped and the college is now really drawing from a population of students with a mean score of 500. They plan to run a t test on the mean SAT score of next fall's entering class.
(a) What is the effect size in question?
(b) What is the value of δ if the size of next fall's class is 100?
(c) What is the power of the test?

8.2 Diagram the situation described in Exercise 8.1 along the lines of Figure 8.2.

8.3 In Exercise 8.1 what sample sizes would be needed to raise power to .70, .80, and .90?

8.4 Unbeknownst to the competition, the college in Exercise 8.1 has started a major campaign to increase the SAT scores of their new students. They are hoping to show a 30-point gain in the mean SAT score for next year. If 100 students enroll next fall, what is the power of a t test used to test the significance of any increase?

8.5 Diagram the situation described in Exercise 8.4 along the lines of Figure 8.2.

8.6 A physiological psychology laboratory has been studying avoidance behavior in rabbits for several years and has published numerous papers on the topic. It is clear from this research that the mean response latency for a particular task is 5.8 seconds with a standard deviation of 2 seconds (based on many hundreds of rabbits). Now the investigators wish to induce lesions in certain areas in the rabbits' amygdalae and then demonstrate poorer avoidance conditioning in these animals (i.e., that the rabbits will repeat a punished response sooner). They expect latencies to decrease by about 1 second, and they plan to run a one-sample t test (of $\mu_0 = 5.8$).
(a) How many subjects do they need to have at least a 50 : 50 chance of success?
(b) How many subjects do they need to have at least a 80 : 20 chance of success?

8.7 Suppose that the laboratory referred to in Exercise 8.6 decided not to run one group and compare it against $\mu_0 = 5.8$, but instead to run two groups (one with and one without lesions). They still expect the same degree of difference.
(a) How many subjects do they need (overall) if they are to have power $= .60$?
(b) How many subjects to they need (overall) if they are to have power $= .90$?

8.8 A research assistant ran the experiment described in Exercise 8.7 without first carrying out any power calculations. He tried to run 20 subjects in each group, but he accidentally tipped over a rack of cages and had to void 5 subjects in the experimental group. What is the power of this experiment?

8.9 We have just conducted a study comparing cognitive development of low- and normal-birth-weight babies who have reached 1 year of age. Using a scale we devised, we found that the sample means of the two groups were 25 and 30, respectively, with a pooled standard deviation of 8. Assume that we wish to replicate this experiment with 20 subjects in each group. If we assume that the true means and standard deviations have been estimated exactly, what is the a priori probability that we will find a significant difference in our replication?

8.10 Run the t test on the original data in Exercise 8.9. What, if anything, does your answer to this question indicate about your answer Exercise 8.9?

8.11 Two graduate students recently completed their dissertations. Each used a t test for two independent groups. One found a significant t using 10 subjects per group. The other found a significant t of the same magnitude using 45 subjects per group. Which result impresses you the most?

8.12 Draw a diagram (analogous to Figure 8.1) to defend your answer to Exercise 8.11.

8.13 Make up a simple two-group example to demonstrate that for a total of 30 subjects power increases as the sample sizes become more nearly equal.

8.14 A beleaguered Ph.D. candidate has the impression that he must find significant results if he wants to defend his dissertation successfully. He wants to show a difference in social awareness, as measured by his own scale, between a normal group and a group of ex-delinquents. He has a problem, however. He has data to suggest that the normal group has a true mean of 38, and he has 50 of those subjects. He has access to 100 high-school graduates who have been classed as delinquent in the past. Or, he has access to 25 high-school dropouts who have a history of delinquency. He suspects that the high-school graduates come from a population with a mean of approximately 35, whereas the dropout group comes from a population with a mean of approximately 30. He can use only one of these groups. Which should he use?

8.15 Generate a table analogous to Table 8.1 for power $= .80$, $\alpha = .01$, two-tailed.

8.16 Generate a table analogous to Table 8.1 for power $= .60$, $\alpha = .05$, two-tailed.

8.17 Assume that we want to test a null hypothesis about a single mean at $\alpha = .05$, one-tailed. Further assume that all necessary assumptions are met. Could there be a case in which we would be more likely to reject a true H_0 than to reject a false one? (In other words, can power ever be less than α?)

8.18 If $\sigma = 15$, $N = 25$, and we are testing $H_0: \mu = 100$ versus $H_1: \mu > 100$, what value of the mean under H_1 would result in power being equal to the probability of a Type II error? (*Hint*: Try sketching the two distributions; which areas are you trying to equate?)

COMPUTER EXERCISES

8.19 In Chapter 7 you ran a number of t tests based on random data. In the first case the null hypothesis was true. In later cases the null hypothesis had been made false by the addition of a constant equal to 0.25, 0.50, or 1.00 standard deviations.

(a) Calculate the power of a two-tailed t test at $\alpha = .05$ for each of these situations.

(b) Do your results correspond to the results you would have predicted in part (a)?

8.20 (a) For the data referred to in Exercise 8.19, calculate what **d** would have to be for power to equal .80 with $N = 50$ cases. (Recall that these data were originally sampled from a normal distribution with a mean of 50 and a standard deviation of 10. Any constant you add would only change the mean, not the standard deviation.)

(b) From the answer to (a), calculate the constant you would have to add to one of the variables to produce the necessary **d**.

(c) Now add the constant found in part (b), draw a number of samples (perhaps pooling across students), and determine an estimate of the empirical power of the design. Is it approximately .80?

8.21 Now return to Exercise 7.51, where one group had a constant of 2.5 added to it.

(a) Using a total of 50 cases, repeat the steps that you went through then, calculating t values for X1 as the dependent variable. Then repeat with X2, X3, ..., X10 as the dependent variables. Pool results across students.

(b) Repeat (a), this time using sample sizes of 200.

(c) Do the differences in the rate of rejection of H_0 change appropriately as you increase the sample sizes? Do they correspond to what calculations of power would lead you to predict?[†]

[†] In this particular case there is a small problem with pooling across students. With the larger sample sizes, there will be considerable overlap among the samples used by different students, meaning that the different t tests will not be independent. However, the effect of this should be minor compared to the differences we find as we increase N.

CHAPTER NINE

CORRELATION AND REGRESSION

OBJECTIVES *To introduce the concepts of correlation and regression and to begin looking at how relationships between variables can be represented.*

CONTENTS

Relationships, Differences

In Chapter 7 we dealt with testing hypotheses concerning differences between sample means. In this chapter we will begin examining questions concerning relationships between variables. Although you should not make too much of the distinction between **relationships** and **differences** (if treatments have *different* means, then means are *related* to treatments), the distinction is useful in terms of the interests of the experimenter and the structure of the experiment. When we are concerned with differences between means, the experiment usually consists of a few quantitative or qualitative levels of the independent variable (e.g., Treatment A and Treatment B) and the experimenter is interested in showing that the dependent variable differs from one treatment to another. When we are concerned with relationships, however, the independent variable (X) usually has many quantitative levels and the experimenter is interested in showing that the dependent variable is some *function* of the independent variable.

Correlation, Regression

This chapter will deal with two interwoven topics: **correlation** and **regression**. Statisticians commonly make a distinction between these two techniques. Although the distinction is frequently not followed in practice, it is important enough to consider briefly. In problems of simple correlation and regression, the data consist of two observations from each of N subjects, one observation on each of the variables under consideration. If we were interested in the correlation between running speed in a maze (Y) and number of trials to reach some criterion (X) (both common measures of learning), we would obtain a running-speed score and a trials-to-criterion score from each subject. Similarly, if we were interested in the regression of running speed (Y) on the number of food pellets per reinforcement (X), each subject would have scores corresponding to his speed and the number of pellets he received. The difference between these two situations illustrates the statistical distinction between correlation and regression. In both cases, Y is a **random variable**, beyond the experimenter's control. In the former case, X is also a random variable, since the number of trials to criterion is beyond his control. Put another way, a replication of the experiment would leave us with different values of X. In the latter case, however, X is a **fixed variable** and would remain constant across replications, since the values of X are determined by the experimenter.

Random variable

Fixed variable

To most statisticians, the word *regression* is reserved for those situations in which the value of X is *fixed* or specified by the experimenter before the data are collected. In these situations, no sampling error is involved in X, and repeated replications of the experiment will involve the same X values. The word *correlation* is used to describe the situation in which both X and Y are random variables. In this case, the Xs, as well as the Ys, vary from one replication to another and thus sampling error is involved in both variables. This distinction is basically the distinction between what are called **linear-regression models** and **bivariate-normal models**. We will consider the distinction between these two models in more detail in Section 9.7.

Linear-regression models,

Bivariate-normal models

As mentioned earlier, the distinction between the two models, although appropriate on statistical grounds, tends to break down in practice. A more pragmatic distinction—the one adopted here—relies on the interest of the experimenter. If the purpose of the research is to allow **prediction** of Y on the basis of knowledge about X, we will speak of regression. If, on the other hand, the purpose is merely to obtain a statistic expressing the degree of relationship between the two variables, we will speak of correlation. Although it is possible to raise legitimate objections to this distinction, it has the advantage of describing the different ways in which these two procedures are used in practice.

Prediction

Having differentiated between correlation and regression, we will now proceed to treat the two techniques together, since they are so closely related. The general problem then becomes one of developing an equation to predict one variable from knowledge of the other and of obtaining a measure of the degree of this relationship. The only restriction we will impose for the moment is that the relationship between X and Y be linear. Curvilinear relationships will not be considered, although in Chapter 15 we will see how they can be handled by closely related procedures.

9.1 SCATTER DIAGRAMS

**Scatter diagram,
Scatterplot,
Scattergram**

When we collect measures on two variables for the purpose of examining the relationship between these variables, one of the most useful techniques for gaining some insight into this relationship is a **scatter diagram** (also called a **scatterplot** or **scattergram**). Examples of four such diagrams appear in Figure 9.1. In a scatter diagram, every experimental subject in the study is represented by a point in two-dimensional space, the coordinates of this point (X_i, Y_i) being the individual's (or object's) scores on variables X and Y, respectively.

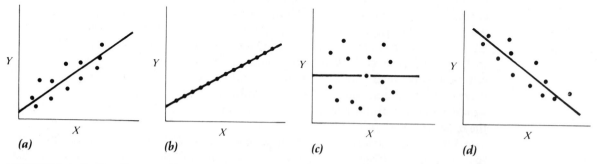

FIGURE 9.1 Scatter diagrams illustrating various degrees of relationship

**Predictor
Criterion**

In preparing a scatter diagram, the **predictor** variable is traditionally represented on the abscissa, or x-axis, and the **criterion** variable on the ordinate, or y-axis. If the eventual purpose of the study is to predict one variable from knowledge of the other, the distinction is obvious: the criterion variable is the one to be predicted, whereas the predictor variable is the one from which the prediction is made. If the problem is simply one of obtaining a correlation coefficient, the distinction may be obvious (incidence of cancer would be dependent on amount smoked rather than the reverse, and thus incidence would appear on the ordinate), or it may not (neither running speed nor number of correct choices—common dependent variables in a learning study— are obviously in a dependent position relative to the other). Where the distinction is not obvious, it is irrelevant which variable is labeled X and which Y.

Consider the four hypothetical scatter diagrams in Figure 9.1. Figure 9.1a represents a case in which the relationship between X and Y is relatively strong; although the relationship is not perfect, it is generally true that as X increases Y also increases.

Perfect relationship

Figure 9.1b illustrates the case of a **perfect relationship**. Every increase in X is accompanied by an exactly proportional increase in Y, so all the points fall on a straight line.

No relationship

Figure 9.1c shows a situation in which there is **no relationship** between X and Y; there is no systematic tendency for Y to vary with X, and the value of X tells us nothing about the corresponding value of Y. Finally, Figure 9.1d represents a relatively strong

**Negative
relationship**

negative relationship between X and Y. (In fact, the degree of relationship, although not its direction, is the same as that shown in Figure 9.1a; the points have merely been rotated 90°.) In this situation, an increase in X corresponds to a general decrease in Y.

Regression lines

The lines superimposed on Figures 9.1a through 9.1d represent those straight lines that best fit the data—the way in which this line is "best" will be defined shortly. These lines are what we will call the **regression lines** of Y predicted on the basis of X (abbreviated Y on X), and they represent our best prediction of Y_i for a given value of X_i, where i represents the ith value of X or Y. Given any specified value of X, the corresponding height of the regression line represents our best prediction of Y (designated $\hat{Y}$, and read "Y hat"). In other words, we can draw a vertical line from X_i to the regression line. We can then move horizontally to the y-axis and read off $\hat{Y}_i$.

Correlation (r)

The degree to which the points cluster about the regression line (in other words, the degree to which the actual values of Y agree with the predicted values) is related to the **correlation (r)** between X and Y. Correlation coefficients range between 1 and -1. In Figure 9.1a the points cluster reasonably closely about the line and the correlation is high ($r = .81$). In Figure 9.1b the points fall exactly on the line and the correlation is perfect ($r = 1.00$). In Figure 9.1c the points do not cluster at all around the line and the correlation is zero ($r = .00$). And in Figure 9.1d the degree of clustering is the same as in Figure 9.1a, but the relationship is negative so the correlation is negative ($r = -.81$).

An alternative approach to interpreting scatter diagrams can be seen in Figures 9.2 and 9.3. These figures are based on data from the Achenbach Teacher Report form, Achenbach (1991a), which is a rating form for behavior problems. (The data have been modified somewhat for purposes of this example.) Figure 9.2 plots the relationship between the teacher's rating of the degree to which the child exhibits behavior appropriate to the situation and the teacher's rating of how much the child is learning. All ratings are on 7-point scales. The dots with circles around them represent coincident points for two children. Figure 9.3 plots the degree to which the teacher rates the child as happy and the degree to which he shows appropriate behavior.

In these figures the vertical and horizontal grid lines divide both axes at their means. For example, the vertical line in Figure 9.2 divides those children who were below the mean on appropriate behavior from those who were above the mean. Similarly, the horizontal line separates those children who were below the mean on the learning variable from those who were above it. In both cases the variable we would

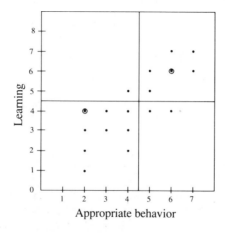

FIGURE 9.2

Relationship between learning and adaptive behavior in normal boys, ages 12–16

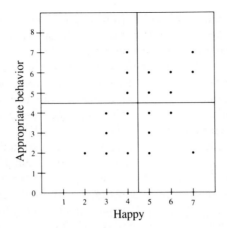

FIGURE 9.3
Relationship between
happiness and
appropriate behavior
in normal boys, ages
12–16

be most likely to think of as the dependent variable is plotted on the *y*-axis, and
the likely independent variable on the *x*-axis. Admittedly, the choice is somewhat
arbitrary.

If there were a strong positive relationship between learning and appropriate behavior, for example, we would expect that most of the children who were high (above
the mean) on one variable would be high on the other. Likewise, most of those who
were below the mean on one variable should be below it on the other. Such an idea
can be represented by a simple table in which we count the number of children who
were above the mean on both variables, the number below the mean on both variables,
and the number above the mean on one and below it on the other. Such a table is
shown in Table 9.1 for the data in Figures 9.2 and 9.3.

TABLE 9.1
Examining scatter
diagrams by division
into quadrants

(a) Appropriate Behavior versus Learning (Figure 9.2)

		Appropriate Behavior	
		Above Mean	Below Mean
Learning	Above Mean	7	1
	Below Mean	2	10

(b) Happy versus Appropriate Behavior (Figure 9.3)

		Happy	
		Above Mean	Below Mean
Appropriate Behavior	Above Mean	6	3
	Below Mean	5	6

With a strong positive relationship between the two variables, we would expect
most of the data points in Table 9.1 to fall in the "Above-Above" and "Below-Below"
cells, with only a smattering in the Above-Below" and "Below-Above" cells. On the

other hand, if the two variables are not related to each other, we would expect to see approximately equal numbers of data points in the four cells of the table (or quadrants of the scatter diagram). From Table 9.1 we see that for the relationship between appropriate behavior and learning, 17 out of the 20 children fall in the cells associated with a positive relationship between the variables. In other words, if they are below the mean on one variable, they are generally below the mean on the other, and vice versa. Only 3 of the children break this pattern. However, for the data plotted in Figure 9.3, Table 9.1 shows us that only 12 children are on the same side of the mean on both variables, whereas 5 children are below the mean on Appropriate Behavior but above it on Happy, and 3 children show the opposite pattern.

These two examples illustrate in a simple way the interpretation of scatter diagrams and the relationship between variables. In the first case there is a strong positive relationship between the variables. In the second case the relationship, although positive, is considerably weaker. This result is reflected in the correlation between the variables. For Figure 9.2 the correlation is .78, whereas the correlation among the data points in Figure 9.3 is .38. (Keep in mind that I have used small samples for ease of discussion, and these correlations might well be different if larger samples had been used. This is especially true because I hunted around to find somewhat extreme examples and may have managed to find unrepresentative ones. We will address the issue of the unreliability of sample results in later chapters.)

9.2   THE RELATIONSHIP BETWEEN STRESS AND HEALTH

Wagner, Compas, and Howell (1988) investigated the relationship between stress and mental health in first-year college students. Using a scale they developed to measure the frequency, perceived importance, and desirability of recent life events, they created a measure of negative events weighted by the reported frequency and the respondent's subjective estimate of the impact of each event. This served as their measure of the subject's perceived social and environmental stress. They also asked students to complete the Hopkins Symptom Checklist, assessing the presence or absence of 57 psychological symptoms. The stem-and-leaf displays and boxplots for the stress and symptom measures are shown in Table 9.2.

Before we consider the relationship between these variables, we need to study the variables individually. The stem-and-leaf displays for both variables show that the distributions are unimodal but are slightly positively skewed. Except for a few extreme values, there is nothing about either variable that should disturb us, such as extreme skewness or bimodality. Note that there is a fair amount of variability in each variable. This variability is important, because if we want to show that different stress scores are associated with differences in symptoms, it is important to have these differences in the first place.

The boxplots in Table 9.2 reveal the presence of outliers on both variables. (The "2" is used to indicate the presence of two overlapping data points.) The existence of outliers should alert us to potential problems that these scores might cause. The first thing we might do is to check the data to see whether these few subjects were responding in unreasonable ways—for example, do they report the occurrence of all sorts of unlikely life events or symptoms, making us question the legitimacy of their responses? (Difficult as it may be to believe, some subjects have been known to treat psychological experiments with something less than the respect and reverence they deserve!) The second thing to check is whether the same subject produced outlying data points on both variables. This would suggest that this subject's data, although legitimate, might have a disproportionate influence on the resulting correlation. The third thing to do is to make a scatterplot of the data, again looking for the undue influence of particular extreme data points. (Such a scatterplot will appear later in Figure 9.4, p. 231) Finally, we can run our analyses including and excluding extreme points to see what differences appear in the results. If you carry out each of these steps on the data, you will find nothing to suggest that the outliers we have identified influenced the resulting correlation or regression equation in any important way. However, these steps are important precursors to any good analysis—if only because they give us greater faith in our final result. A more extensive discussion of techniques for examining data to be used in regression analyses will be found in Chapter 15 when we discuss multiple regression.

TABLE 9.2
Description of data
on the relationship
between stress and
mental health

Stem-and-Leaf for Stress		Stem-and-Leaf for Symptoms	
0*	01222234	5.	8
0.	556677888899	6*	112234
1*	011122222223333444444	6.	55668
1.	5556666777888999	7*	00012334444
2*	0001111223333334	7.	57788899
2.	556778999	8*	00011122233344
3*	012233444	8.	5666677888899
3.	56677778	9*	0111223344
4*	23444	9.	556679999
4.	55	10*	0001112224
		10.	567799
HI	57, 74	11*	112
		11.	78
		12*	11
Code:	2.$\vert$5 = 25	12.	57
		13*	1
		HI	135, 135, 147, 186
		Code:	5.$\vert$8 = 58

Boxplot for Stress

```
      0     10    20    30   40     50    60    70
      |---------|---------|---------|---------|---------|---------|----
                                    *
         ------------ -----------------        *         *
                    |------ |----------|
```

Boxplot for Symptoms

```
   50    60    70    80    90    100   110   120   130   140   150        180
   |---------|---------|---------|---------|---------|---------|---------|---------|---------|-----/  /--|-----
                      ------------------                                          *              *
                            |-------- |-----------|-----------------------------2
```

9.3   THE COVARIANCE

Covariance (cov_{XY} or s_{XY})

The correlation coefficient we seek to compute on the data in Table 9.3 is itself based on a statistic called the **covariance (cov_{XY} or s_{XY})**. The covariance is basically a number that reflects the degree to which two variables vary together.

TABLE 9.3
Data on stress and symptoms for 10 representative subjects

Subject	Stress (X)	Symptoms (Y)
1	30	99
2	27	94
3	9	80
4	20	70
5	3	100
6	15	109
7	5	62
8	10	81
9	24	74
10	34	121
...	...	...

$$\Sigma X = 2297 \qquad \Sigma Y = 9705$$

$$\Sigma X^2 = 67489 \qquad \Sigma Y^2 = 923787$$

$$\overline{X} = 21.467 \qquad \overline{Y} = 90.701$$

$$s_X = 13.096 \qquad s_Y = 20.266$$

standard deviation

$$\Sigma XY = 222576$$

$$N = 107$$

(handwritten annotations in right margin:)

$$\frac{\Sigma X^2 - \frac{(\Sigma X)^2}{N}}{N-1}$$

$$\frac{67489 - 5276209}{107}$$

$$8106$$

To define the covariance mathematically, we can write

$$\text{cov}_{XY} = \frac{\Sigma(X - \overline{X})(Y - \overline{Y})}{N - 1}$$

From this equation it is apparent that the covariance is similar in form to the variance. If we changed all the Ys in the equation to Xs, we would have s_X^2; if we changed the Xs to Ys, we would have s_Y^2.

Some insight into the meaning of the covariance can be gained by considering what we would expect to find in the case of a positive correlation, such as in the data in Table 9.3. In this situation, high stress scores will be paired with high symptom scores. Thus, for a stressed subject with many problems, both $(X - \overline{X})$ and $(Y - \overline{Y})$ will be positive and their product will be positive. For a subject experiencing little stress and few problems, both $(X - \overline{X})$ and $(Y - \overline{Y})$ will be negative, but their product will again be positive. Thus, the sum of $(X - \overline{X})(Y - \overline{Y})$ will be large and positive, giving us a large positive covariance.

Next consider the case of a strong negative relationship. Here, large positive values of $(X - \overline{X})$ most likely will be paired with large negative values of $(Y - \overline{Y})$, and vice versa. Thus, the sum of products of the deviations will be large and negative, indicating a high negative relationship.

Finally, consider a situation in which there is no relationship between X and Y. In this case, a positive value of $(X - \overline{X})$ will be paired sometimes with a positive value and sometimes with a negative value of $(Y - \overline{Y})$. The result is that the products of the deviations will be positive about one-half of the time and negative about one-half of the time, producing a near-zero sum and indicating no relationship between the variables. For a given set of data, it is possible to show that the cov_{XY} will be at its positive maximum whenever X and Y are perfectly positively correlated ($r = 1.00$), and at its negative maximum whenever they are perfectly negatively correlated ($r = -1.00$). When the two variables are perfectly uncorrelated ($r = 0.00$) the cov_{XY} will be zero.

For computational purposes a simple expression for the covariance is given by

$$\text{cov}_{XY} = \frac{\Sigma XY - \dfrac{\Sigma X \Sigma Y}{N}}{N - 1}$$

For the full data set represented in Table 9.3, the covariance is

$$\text{cov}_{XY} = \frac{222576 - \dfrac{(2297)(9705)}{107}}{106} = \frac{222576 - 208340.05}{106}$$

$$= 134.301$$

9.4 THE PEARSON PRODUCT-MOMENT CORRELATION COEFFICIENT (r)

What we said about the covariance might suggest that we could use it as a measure of the degree of relationship between two variables. An immediate difficulty arises, however, in that the absolute value of cov_{XY} is also a function of the standard deviation of X and Y. Thus, a $\text{cov}_{XY} = 134$, for example, might reflect a high degree of correlation when the standard deviations are small, but a low degree of correlation when the standard deviations are high. To resolve this difficulty, we will divide the covariance by the size of the standard deviations and make this our estimate of correlation. Thus, we will define

$$r = \frac{\text{cov}_{XY}}{s_X s_Y}$$

Since the maximum value of cov_{XY} can be shown to be $\pm s_X s_Y$, it follows that the limits on r are ± 1.00. One interpretation of r, then, is that it is a measure of the degree to which the covariance approaches its maximum.

An equivalent way of writing the preceding equation would be to replace the variances and covariances by their computational formulas and then simplify by cancellation. This leaves us with

$$ r = \frac{N\Sigma XY - (\Sigma X)(\Sigma Y)}{\sqrt{[N\Sigma X^2 - (\Sigma X)^2][N\Sigma Y^2 - (\Sigma Y)^2]}} $$

Recall that $(\Sigma X)^2$ represents the square of the sum of X, and ΣX^2 represents the sum of the squared values of X. This was the standard computational formula for r when hand calculations were the rule, but it is used less often today.

There is yet a third formula for r; it is algebraically equivalent to the other two but has the advantage of using the terminology commonly used when speaking of regression—especially multiple regression—and the analysis of variance. If we define the **Sum of squares** **sum of squares** of X as

$$ SS_X = \Sigma(X - \bar{X})^2 = \Sigma X^2 - \frac{(\Sigma X)^2}{N} $$

and the sum of squares of Y as

$$ SS_Y = \Sigma(Y - \bar{Y})^2 = \Sigma Y^2 - \frac{(\Sigma Y)^2}{N} $$

Sum of products   and if we define the **sum of products** of X and Y as

$$ SP_{XY} = \Sigma(X - \bar{X})(Y - \bar{Y}) = \Sigma XY - \frac{(\Sigma X)(\Sigma Y)}{N} $$

then we can define r as

$$ r = \frac{SP_{XY}}{\sqrt{SS_X SS_Y}} $$

The nice thing about sums of squares and products is that they lead directly to variances and covariances. Thus,

$$ s_X^2 = \frac{SS_X}{N - 1} \quad \text{and} \quad cov_{XY} = \frac{SP_{XY}}{N - 1} $$

It is important to become familiar with sums of squares and their relation to variances and covariances. Later in this chapter, and especially in Chapters 11 through 16, we will make extensive use of sums of squares, so it will be worthwhile for you to spend a few moments making certain you understand what they represent.

From Table 9.3 and subsequent calculations, we know that $s_X = 13.096$, $s_Y = 20.266$, and $cov_{XY} = 134.301$. Then the correlation between X and Y is given by

$$ r = \frac{cov_{XY}}{s_X s_Y} $$

$$ r = \frac{134.301}{(13.096)(20.266)} = .506 $$

This coefficient must be interpreted cautiously; do not attribute meaning to it that it does not possess. Specifically, $r = .506$ should *not* be interpreted to mean that there is 50.6% of a relationship (whatever that might mean) between stress and symptoms. The correlation coefficient is simply a point on the scale between -1 and 1, and the closer it is to either of those limits the stronger is the relationship between the two variables. For a more specific interpretation, we can speak in terms of r^2, which will be discussed shortly. It is important to emphasize that the sign of the correlation merely reflects the direction of the relationship and, possibly, the arbitrary nature of the scale. Changing a variable from "number of items correct" to "number of items incorrect" would reverse the sign of the correlation, but it would have no effect on its absolute value.

ADJUSTED r

Correlation coefficient in the population, ρ (rho)

The formulas we have just considered all produce a correlation for the data in our sample. However, this correlation is not an unbiased estimate of the **correlation coefficient in the population**, denoted (ρ) **rho**. To see why this would be the case, imagine two pairs of points—for example, (23, 18) and (40, 66). (I pulled those numbers out of the air.) If you plot these points and fit a line to them, the line will fit perfectly. You most likely learned that in elementary school when you discovered that two points determine a straight line. Since the line fits perfectly, the correlation will be 1.00, even though the points were chosen at random. Clearly, that correlation of 1.00 does not mean that the correlation in the population from which those points were drawn is 1.00 or anywhere near it. The point here is that when the number of observations is small, the sample correlation will be a biased estimate of the population correlation coefficient. To correct for this we can compute what is known as the **adjusted correlation coefficient (r_{adj})**:

Adjusted correlation coefficient (r_{adj})

$$r_{adj} = \sqrt{1 - \frac{(1 - r^2)(N - 1)}{N - 2}}$$

This is a relatively unbiased estimate of the population correlation coefficient.

In the example we have been using, the sample size is reasonably large. Therefore we would not expect a great difference between r and r_{adj}. We know that $r = .506$ and $N = 107$. Then

$$r_{adj} = \sqrt{1 - \frac{(1 - .506^2)(106)}{105}} = .499$$

When we discuss multiple regression, which involves multiple predictors of Y, in Chapter 15, we will see that this equation for the adjusted correlation will continue to hold. The only difference will be that the denominator will be $N - p - 1$, where p stands for the number of predictors. (That is where the $N - 2$ came from in this equation.)

Unless we are explicitly talking about an estimate of the population correlation coefficient, we will continue to use the sample correlation (r) as our primary statistic. In other words, the statistic we normally report and around which we build hypothesis tests is r rather than r_{adj}.

9.5 THE REGRESSION LINE

We have just seen that there is a reasonable degree of relationship between stress and psychological symptoms. We can obtain a better idea of what this relationship is like by looking at a scatterplot of the two variables and the regression line for predicting symptoms (Y) on the basis of stress (X). The scatterplot is shown in Figure 9.4, where the best-fitting line for predicting Y on the basis of X has been superimposed. (The numbers "3" and "4" represent overlapping data points.) We will see shortly where this line came from, but notice first the way in which the symptom scores increase linearly with increases in stress scores. Our correlation coefficient told us that such a relationship existed, but it is easier to appreciate just what it means when you see it presented graphically. Notice also that the degree of scatter of points about the regression line remains about the same as you move from low values of stress to high values, although, with a correlation of approximately .50, the scatter is fairly wide. We will discuss scatter in more detail when we consider the assumptions on which our procedures are based.

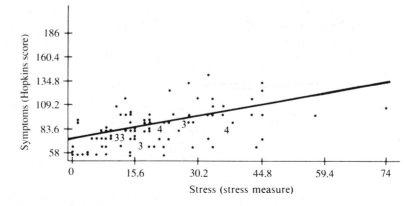

FIGURE 9.4
Scatterplot of symptoms as a function of stress

As you may remember from high school, the equation of a straight line is an equation of the form $Y = bX + a$. For our purposes, we will write the equation as

$$\hat{Y} = bX + a$$

where

$\hat{Y}$ = the predicted value of Y

Slope

b = the **slope** of the regression line (the amount of difference in $\hat{Y}$ associated with a one-unit difference in X)

Intercept

a = the **intercept** (the value of $\hat{Y}$ when $X = 0$)

X is simply the value of the predictor variable. Our task will be to solve for those values of a and b that will produce the best-fitting linear function. In other words, we want to use our existing data to solve for the values of a and b such that the regression

Errors of prediction

Residual

line (the values of $\hat{Y}$ for different values of X) will come as close as possible to the actual obtained values of Y. But how are we to define the phrase "best fitting?" The most logical way would be in terms of **errors of prediction**—that is, in terms of the $(Y - \hat{Y})$ deviations. Since $\hat{Y}$ is the value of the symptom variable that our equation would predict for a given level of stress, and Y is a value that we actually obtained, $(Y - \hat{Y})$ is an error of prediction, usually called the **residual**. We want to find the line (the set of $\hat{Y}$s) that minimizes such errors. We cannot just minimize the *sum* of the errors, however, because for an infinite variety of lines—any line that goes through the point $(\overline{X}, \overline{Y})$—that sum will always be zero. Instead, we will look for that line that minimizes the sum of the squared errors—that minimizes $\Sigma(Y - \hat{Y})^2$. (Note that I said much the same thing in Chapter 2 when I was discussing the variance. There I was discussing deviations from the mean, and here I am discussing deviations from the regression line—sort of a floating or changing mean. These two concepts—errors of prediction and variance—have much in common, as we shall see.)[†]

To obtain the optimal values of a and b, we will begin with the expression to be minimized $[\Sigma(Y - \hat{Y})^2]$. Substituting $bX + a$ for $\hat{Y}$, we obtain

$$\sum (Y - \hat{Y})^2 = \sum [Y - (bX + a)]^2 = \sum (Y - bX - a)^2$$

As already said, we want to find those values of a and b for which $\Sigma(Y - \hat{Y})^2$ is a minimum. Students who have taken a course in calculus will recognize at once that if we take the partial derivatives of this expression with respect to a and b separately, set these derivatives equal to zero, and solve, we will obtain the desired values for a and b. Students who do not know calculus can simply take the next few equations on faith.

$$\sum (Y - \hat{Y})^2 = \sum (Y - bX - a)^2$$
$$= \sum (Y^2 + b^2X^2 + a^2 - 2aY - 2bXY + 2abX)$$

The derivative with respect to a is

$$\frac{d(Y - \hat{Y})^2}{da} = \sum (2a - 2Y + 2bX)$$
$$= 2Na - 2\sum Y + 2b \sum X$$

Setting this equal to zero,

$$2Na - 2\sum Y + 2b \sum X = 0$$
$$Na + b \sum X = \sum Y$$

The derivative with respect to b is

$$\frac{d(Y - \hat{Y})^2}{db} = \sum (2bX^2 - 2XY + 2aX) = 2b \sum X^2 - 2 \sum XY + 2a \sum X$$

Setting this equal to zero,

[†] For those who are interested, Rousseeuw and Leroy (1987) present a good discussion of alternative criteria that could be minimized, often to good advantage.

$$2b \sum X^2 - 2 \sum XY + 2a \sum X = 0$$

$$b \sum X^2 + a \sum X = \sum XY$$

The equations that we have derived,

$$\left(Na + b \sum X = \sum Y\right) \quad \text{and} \quad \left(b \sum X^2 + a \sum X = \sum XY\right)$$

Normal equations   are called the **normal equations**—although they do not have anything to do with the normal distribution. From the normal equations, it is a simple matter to solve for a and b. Solving for a, we obtain

$$Na + b \sum X = \sum Y$$

$$a = \frac{\Sigma Y - b\Sigma X}{N} = \bar{Y} - b\bar{X}$$

To solve for b, we begin with the normal equation

$$b \sum X^2 + a \sum X = \sum XY$$

Substituting from our equation for a and simplifying, we obtain

$$b = \frac{N\Sigma XY - \Sigma X \Sigma Y}{N\Sigma X^2 - (\Sigma X)^2} = \frac{\text{cov}_{XY}}{s_X^2}$$

We now have solutions for a and b in terms of the original variables. To indicate that our solution was designed to minimize errors in predicting Y from X (rather than the other way around), the constants are sometimes denoted as $a_{Y \cdot X}$ and $b_{Y \cdot X}$. When no confusion would arise, the subscripts are usually omitted.[†]

Suppose, however, that we now wanted to predict X from the value of Y. The constants $a_{Y \cdot X}$ and $b_{Y \cdot X}$ are not suitable for that purpose, since they have been derived so as to minimize error in predicting Y. Although we could begin all over again starting with

$$\hat{X} = bY + a$$

and minimizing $\Sigma(X - \hat{X})^2$, a much simpler solution is to interchange the symbols X and Y in our equations for a and b.

As an example of the calculation of regression coefficients, consider the data in Table 9.3. From that table we know that $\bar{X} = 21.467$, $\bar{Y} = 90.701$, and $s_X = 13.096$. We also know that $\text{cov}_{XY} = 134.301$. Thus,

$$b = \frac{\text{cov}_{XY}}{s_X^2} = \frac{134.301}{13.096^2} = 0.7831$$

$$a = \bar{Y} - b\bar{X} = 90.701 - (0.7831)(21.467) = 73.891$$

$$\hat{Y} = bX + a = (0.7831)(X) + 73.891$$

[†] An interesting alternative formula for b can be written as $b = r \, (s_Y/s_X)$. This shows explicitly the relationship between the correlation coefficient and the slope of the regression line. Note that when $s_Y = s_X$, b will equal r. Can you think of a case where this would happen? (*Answer*: When both variables are standardized.)

We have already seen the scatter diagram with the regression line for Y on X superimposed in Figure 9.4.

A word is in order about actually plotting the regression line. To plot the line, you can simply take any two values of X (preferably at opposite ends of the scale), calculate $\hat{Y}$ for each, mark these coordinates on the figure, and connect them with a straight line. You can use three points as a check for accuracy. For our data, we have

$$\hat{Y}_i = (0.7831)(X_i) + 73.891$$

When $X_i = 0$,

$$\hat{Y}_i = 0.7831(0) + 73.891 = 73.891$$

and when $X_i = 50$,

$$\hat{Y}_i = 0.7831(50) + 73.891 = 113.046$$

The line then passes through the points $(X = 0, Y = 73.891)$ and $(X = 50, Y = 113.046)$, as is shown in Figure 9.4. Actually, an even easier procedure is to pass the line through the points $(0, a)$ and $(\overline{X}, \overline{Y})$, provided that these points are far enough apart to lead to a sufficient degree of accuracy in drawing the line. It is safer to calculate them as we first did, however, because that is a good way to pick up major errors.

If you calculate both regression lines (Y on X and X on Y), it will be apparent that the two are not coincident. They do intersect at the point $(\overline{X}, \overline{Y})$, but they have different slopes. The fact that they are different lines reflects the fact that they were designed for different purposes—one minimizes $\Sigma(Y - \hat{Y})^2$ and the other minimizes $\Sigma(X - \hat{X})^2$. They both go through the point $(\overline{X}, \overline{Y})$ because a person who is *average* on one variable would be expected to be *average* on the other, but only when the correlation between the two variables is ± 1.00 will the lines be coincident.

INTERPRETATIONS OF REGRESSION

In certain situations the regression line is useful in its own right. For example, a college admissions officer might be interested in an equation for predicting college performance on the basis of high-school grade point average (although she would most likely want to include multiple predictors in ways to be discussed in Chapter 15). Similarly, a farm manager might be interested in predicting milk production based on the nutrient value of the feed she is recommending.

In most applications of regression in psychology, however, we are not particularly interested in making an actual prediction. Although we might be interested in knowing the relationship between family income and educational achievement, it is unlikely that we would take any particular child's family-income measure and use that to predict her educational achievement. We are usually much more interested in general principles than in individual predictions. A regression equation, however, can in fact tell us something meaningful about these general principles, even though we may never use it actually to form a prediction for a specific case.

INTERCEPT   We have defined the intercept as that value of $\hat{Y}$ when X equals zero. As such, it has meaning in some situations and not in others, primarily depending on whether or not $X = 0$ is near or within the range of values of X used to derive the estimate of the intercept. If, for example, we took a group of overweight people and looked at the relationship between self-esteem (Y) and weight loss (X) (assuming that it is linear), the intercept would tell us what level of self-esteem to expect for an individual who lost 0 pounds. Often, however, there is no meaningful interpretation of the intercept other than a mathematical one. If we are looking at the relationship between self-esteem (Y) and actual weight (X) for adults, it is obviously foolish to ask what someone's self-esteem would be if he weighed 0 pounds. The intercept would appear to tell us this, but it represents such an extreme extrapolation from available data as to be meaningless. (In this case, a nonzero intercept would suggest a lack of linearity over the wider range of weight from 0 to 300 pounds, but we probably are not interested in nonlinearity in the extremes anyway.)

SLOPE   We have defined the slope as the change in $\hat{Y}$ for a one-unit change in X. As such it is a measure of the predicted *rate of change* in Y. By definition, then, the slope is often a meaningful measure. If we are looking at the regression of income on years of schooling, the slope will tell us how much of a difference in income would be associated with each additional year of school. Similarly, if an engineer knows that the slope relating fuel economy in miles per gallon (mpg) to weight of the automobile is 0.01, then if she can assume a causal relationship between mpg and weight, she knows that for every pound that she can reduce the weight of the car she will increase its fuel economy by 0.01 mpg. Thus, if the manufacturer replaces a 30-pound spare tire with one of those useless 20-pound temporary ones, the car will gain 0.1 mpg.

Although we rarely work with standardized data (data that have been transformed so as to have a mean of zero and a standard deviation of one on each variable), it is worth considering what b would represent if the data for each variable were standardized separately. In that case, a difference of one unit in X or Y would represent a difference of one standard deviation. Thus, if the slope were 0.75, for standardized data, we would be able to say that a one standard deviation increase in X will be reflected in three-quarters of a standard deviation increase in $\hat{Y}$. When speaking of the slope coefficient for standardized data, we often refer to the **standardized regression coefficient** as **β (beta)** to differentiate it from the coefficient for nonstandardized data (b). We will return to the idea of standardized variables when we discuss multiple regression. (What would the intercept be if the variables were standardized?)

Standardized regression coefficient, β (beta)

CORRELATION AND BETA   What we have just seen with respect to the slope for standardized variables is directly applicable to the correlation coefficient. Recall that r is defined as $\text{cov}_{XY}/s_X s_Y$, whereas b is defined as cov_{XY}/s_X^2. If the data are standardized, $s_X = s_Y = s_X^2 = 1$, and the slope and the correlation coefficient will be equal. Thus, one interpretation of the correlation coefficient is that it is equal to what the slope would be if the variables were standardized. A derivative interpretation of $r = .80$, for example, is that one standard deviation difference in X is associated *on the average* with an eight-tenths of a standard deviation difference in Y. In some situations such an interpretation can be meaningfully applied.[†]

[†] An interesting geometric interpretation of the correlation coefficient can be found in Marks (1982).

A NOTE OF CAUTION   What has just been said about the interpretation of b and r must be tempered with a bit of caution. To say that a one-unit difference in family income is associated with 0.75 units difference in academic achievement is not to be interpreted to mean that raising family income for Mary Smith will automatically raise her academic achievement. In other words, we are not speaking about cause and effect. We can say that people who score higher on the income variable also score higher on the achievement variable without in any way implying causation or suggesting what would happen to a given individual if her family income were to increase. Family income is associated (in a correlational sense) with a host of other variables (e.g., attitudes toward education, number of books in the home, access to a variety of environments) and there is no reason to expect all of these to change merely because income changes. Those who argue that eradicating poverty will lead to a wide variety of changes in people's lives often fall into such a cause-and-effect trap. Eradicating poverty is certainly a worthwhile and important goal, but the correlations between income and educational achievement *may* be totally irrelevant to the issue.

9.6 THE ACCURACY OF PREDICTION

The fact that we can fit a regression line to a set of data does not mean that our problems are solved. On the contrary, they have only begun. The important point is not whether a straight line can be drawn through the data (you can always do that) but whether that line represents a reasonable fit to the data—in other words, whether our effort was worthwhile.

Before discussing errors of prediction, however, it is instructive to consider the situation in which we wish to predict Y without any knowledge of the value of X.

THE STANDARD DEVIATION AS A MEASURE OF ERROR

As mentioned earlier, the data plotted in Figure 9.4 represent the number of symptoms shown by students (Y) as a function of the number of stressful life events (X). Assume that you are now given the task of predicting the number of symptoms that will be shown by a particular individual, but that you have no knowledge of the number of stressful life events he or she has experienced. Your best prediction in this case would be the mean number of symptoms ($\overline{Y}$) (averaged across all subjects), and the error associated with your prediction would be the standard deviation of Y (s_Y), since your prediction is the mean and s_Y deals with deviations around the mean. Examining s_Y we know that it is defined as

$$s_Y = \sqrt{\frac{\Sigma(Y - \overline{Y})^2}{N - 1}}$$

or, in terms of the variance,

$$s_Y^2 = \frac{\Sigma(Y - \overline{Y})^2}{N - 1}$$

The numerator is the sum of squared deviations from $\overline{Y}$ (the point you would have predicted in this example) and is what we have referred to as the sum of squares of Y (SS_Y). The denominator is simply the degrees of freedom. Thus, we can write

$$s_Y^2 = \frac{SS_Y}{df}$$

THE STANDARD ERROR OF ESTIMATE

Now suppose we wish to make a prediction about symptoms for a student who has a specified number of stressful life events. If we had an infinitely large sample of data, our prediction for symptoms would be the mean of those values of Y that were obtained by all students who had that particular value of stress. We do not have an infinite sample, however, so we will use the regression line. (If all of the assumptions that we will discuss shortly are met, the expected value of the Y scores associated with each specific value of X would lie on the regression line.) In our case, we know the relevant value of X and the regression equation, and our best prediction would be $\hat{Y}$. In line with our previous measure of error (the standard deviation), the error associated with the present prediction will again be a function of the deviations of Y about the predicted point, but in this case the predicted point is $\hat{Y}$ rather than $\overline{Y}$. Specifically, a measure of error can now be defined as

$$s_{Y \cdot X} = \sqrt{\frac{\Sigma(Y - \hat{Y})^2}{N - 2}} = \sqrt{\frac{SS_{error}}{df}}$$

Standard error of estimate

Residual variance, Error variance

and again the sum of squared deviations are taken about the prediction ($\hat{Y}$). The sum of squared deviations about $\hat{Y}$ is often denoted SS_{error} because it is a sum of squared errors of prediction.[†] The statistic $s_{Y \cdot X}$ is called the **standard error of estimate**. It is denoted as $s_{Y \cdot X}$ to indicate that it is the standard deviation of Y predicted from X. It is the most common (although not always the best) measure of the error of prediction. Its square, $s_{Y \cdot X}^2$, is called the **residual variance** or **error variance**, and it can be shown to be an unbiased estimate of the corresponding parameter ($\sigma_{Y \cdot X}^2$) in the population. We have $N - 2$ df because we lost two degrees of freedom in estimating our regression line. (Both a and b were estimated from sample data.)

Conditional distribution

I have suggested that if we had an infinite number of observations, our prediction for a given value of X would be the mean of the Ys associated with that value of X. This idea helps us appreciate what $s_{Y \cdot X}$ is. If we had the infinite sample and calculated the variances for the Ys at each value of X, the average of those variances would be the residual variance, and its square root would be $s_{Y \cdot X}$. The set of Ys corresponding to a specific X is called a **conditional distribution** of Y because it is the distribution of Y scores for those cases that meet a certain condition with respect to X. We say that these standard deviations are conditional on X because we calculate them from Y values corresponding to specific values of X. On the other hand, our usual standard deviation of Y (s_Y) is not conditional on X because we calculate it using all values of Y, regardless of their corresponding X values.

[†]It is also frequently denoted $SS_{residual}$ because it represents variability that remains *after* we use X to predict Y.

One way to obtain the standard error of estimate would be to calculate $\hat{Y}$ for each observation and then to find $s_{Y \cdot X}$ directly, as has been done in Table 9.4. Finding the standard error using this technique is hardly the most enjoyable way to spend a winter evening. Fortunately, a much simpler procedure exists. It not only provides a way of obtaining the standard error of estimate, but also leads directly into even more important matters.

TABLE 9.4
Direct calculation of standard error of estimate

Subject	Stress (X)	Symptoms (Y)	$\hat{Y}$	$Y - \hat{Y}$
1	30	99	97.383	1.617
2	27	94	95.034	−1.034
3	9	80	80.938	−0.938
4	20	70	89.552	−19.552
5	3	100	76.239	23.761
6	15	109	85.636	23.364
7	5	62	77.806	−15.806
8	10	81	81.721	−0.721
9	24	74	92.684	−18.684
10	34	121	100.515	20.485
...	...	...	...	...

$$\Sigma(Y - \hat{Y}) = 0$$

$$\Sigma(Y - \hat{Y})^2 = 32388.049$$

$$s_{Y \cdot X}^2 = \frac{\Sigma(Y - \hat{Y})^2}{N - 2} = \frac{32388.049}{105} = 308.458 \qquad s_{Y \cdot X} = \sqrt{308.458} = 17.563$$

r^2 AND THE STANDARD ERROR OF ESTIMATE

Sums of squares (SS)

In much of what follows, we will abandon the term *variance* in favor of **sums of squares (SS)**. As you should recall, a variance is a sum of squared deviations from the mean (generally known as a sum of squares) divided by the degrees of freedom. The problem with variances is that they are not additive unless they are based on the same *df*. Sums of squares are additive regardless of the degrees of freedom and thus are much easier measures to use.[†]

We earlier defined the residual or error variance as

$$s_{Y \cdot X}^2 = \frac{\Sigma(Y - \hat{Y})^2}{N - 2} = \frac{SS_{error}}{N - 2}$$

Since we are now speaking in terms of sums of squares, we can drop the denominator and simply write

$$SS_{error} = \sum (Y - \hat{Y})^2$$

[†] Later in the book when I wish to speak about a variance-type measure but do not want to specify whether it is a variance, a sum of squares, or whatever, I will use the vague, wishy-washy term *variation*.

With considerable algebraic manipulation, it is possible to express SS_{error} as

$$SS_{error} = SS_Y(1 - r^2)$$

Thus, we have shown that the sum of squares for residual error is a function of the sum of squares for the original values of Y and the correlation between X and Y. All other things being equal, the larger the correlation, the smaller the SS_{error}. This makes sense because the more highly X and Y are correlated, the better we can predict Y and thus the less error we will have.

If we divide SS_{error} by $N - 1$, we obtain

$$\frac{SS_{error}}{N - 1} = s_Y^2(1 - r^2)$$

Multiplying by $(N - 1)/N - 2$, we obtain

$$s_{Y \cdot X}^2 = \frac{SS_{error}}{N - 2} = s_Y^2(1 - r^2)\frac{N - 1}{N - 2}$$

$$s_{Y \cdot X} = s_Y\sqrt{(1 - r^2)\frac{N - 1}{N - 2}}$$

For large samples the fraction $(N - 1)/(N - 2)$ is essentially 1, and we can thus write the equation as it is normally found in most statistics texts:

$$s_{Y \cdot X}^2 = s_Y^2(1 - r^2)$$

or

$$s_{Y \cdot X} = s_Y\sqrt{1 - r^2}$$

Keep in mind, however, that for small samples these equations are only an approximation and $s_{Y \cdot X}^2$ will overestimate the error variance by the fraction $(N - 1)/(N - 2)$. For samples of any size, however, $SS_{error} = SS_Y(1 - r^2)$. This particular formula is going to play a role throughout the rest of the book, especially in Chapters 15 and 16.

ERRORS OF PREDICTION AS A FUNCTION OF r

Now that we have obtained an expression for the standard error of estimate in terms of r, it is instructive to consider how this error decreases as r increases. In Table 9.5, we see the magnitude of the standard error relative to the standard deviation of Y (the error to be expected when X is unknown) for selected values of r.

TABLE 9.5
The standard error of estimate as a function of r

r	$s_{Y \cdot X}$	r	$s_{Y \cdot X}$
.00	s_Y	.60	$0.800s_Y$
.10	$0.995s_Y$	.70	$0.714s_Y$
.20	$0.980s_Y$	.80	$0.600s_Y$
.30	$0.954s_Y$	.866	$0.500s_Y$
.40	$0.917s_Y$	.90	$0.436s_Y$
.50	$0.866s_Y$	.95	$0.312s_Y$

The values in Table 9.5 are somewhat sobering in their implications. With a correlation of .20, the standard error of our estimate is fully 98% of what it would be if X were unknown. This means that if the correlation is .20, using $\hat{Y}$ as our prediction rather than $\bar{Y}$ (i.e., taking into account) reduces the standard error by only 2%. Even more discouraging is that if r is .50, as it is in our example, the standard error of estimate is still 87% of the standard deviation. To reduce our error to one-half of what it would be without knowledge of X requires a correlation of .866, and even a correlation of .95 reduces the error by only about two-thirds. All of this is not to say that there is nothing to be gained by using a regression equation as the basis of prediction; but only that the predictions should be interpreted with a certain degree of caution.

r^2 AS A MEASURE OF PREDICTABLE VARIABILITY

From the preceding equation expressing residual error in terms of r^2, it is possible to derive an extremely important interpretation of the correlation coefficient. We have already seen that

$$SS_{error} = SS_Y(1 - r^2)$$

Expanding and rearranging, we have

$$SS_{error} = SS_Y - SS_Y(r^2)$$

$$r^2 = \frac{SS_Y - SS_{error}}{SS_Y}$$

In this equation, $SS_Y[= \Sigma(Y - \bar{Y})^2]$ is the sum of squares of Y and represents the totals of

1. The part of the sum of squares of Y that is related to $X[SS_Y(r^2)]$
2. The part of the sum of squares of Y that is independent of $X(SS_{error})$

In the context of our example, we are talking about that part of the number of symptoms people exhibited that is related to how many stressful life events they had experienced, and that part that is related to other things. SS_{error} is the sum of squares of Y that is independent of X and is a measure of the amount of error remaining even after we use X to predict Y. These concepts can be made clearer with a second example.

Suppose we were interested in studying the relationship between amount of cigarette smoking (X) and age at death (Y). As we watch people die off over time, we notice several things. First, we see that not all die at precisely the same age. There is variability in age at death regardless of smoking behavior, and this variability is measured by $SS_Y = \Sigma(Y - \bar{Y})^2$. We also notice that some people smoke more than others. This is variability in smoking regardless of age at death and is measured by $SS_X = \Sigma(X - \bar{X})^2$. We further find that cigarette smokers tend to die earlier than nonsmokers, and heavy smokers earlier than light smokers. Thus, we write a regression equation to predict Y from X. Since people differ in their smoking behavior, they will also differ in their *predicted* life expectancy ($\hat{Y}$), and we will label this variability $SS_{\hat{Y}} = \Sigma(\hat{Y} - \bar{\hat{Y}})^2 = \Sigma(\hat{Y} - \bar{Y})^2$. This last measure is variability in Y that is directly attributable to variability in X, since different values of $\hat{Y}$ arise from different values of X and the same values of $\hat{Y}$ arise from the same value of X—that is, $\hat{Y}$ does not vary unless X varies.

We have one last source of variability, and this is the variability in the life expectancy of those people who smoke exactly the same amount. This is measured by SS_{error} and is the variability in Y that cannot be explained by the variability in X (since these people do not differ in the amount they smoke). These several sources of variability (sums of squares) are summarized in Table 9.6.

TABLE 9.6
Sources of variance in regression for study of smoking and life expectancy

SS_X = variability in amount smoked = $\Sigma(X - \overline{X})^2$
SS_Y = variability in life expectancy = $\Sigma(Y - \overline{Y})^2$
$SS_{\hat{Y}}$ = variability in life expectancy directly attributable to variability in
      smoking behavior = $\Sigma(\hat{Y} - \overline{Y})^2$
SS_{error} = variability in life expectancy that cannot be attributed to variability in
      smoking behavior = $\Sigma(Y - \hat{Y})^2 = SS_Y - SS_{\hat{Y}}$

If we considered the absurd extreme in which all of the nonsmokers die at exactly age 72 and all of the smokers smoke precisely the same amount and die at exactly age 68, then all of the variability in life expectancy is directly predictable from variability in smoking behavior. If you smoke you will die at 68, and if you don't you will die at 72. Here $SS_{\hat{Y}} = SS_Y$, and $SS_{error} = 0$.

As a more realistic example, assume smokers tend to die earlier than nonsmokers, but within each group there is a certain amount of variability in life expectancy. This is a situation in which some of SS_Y is attributable to smoking ($SS_{\hat{Y}}$) and some is not (SS_{error}). What we want to be able to do is to specify what *percentage* of the overall variability in life expectancy is attributable to variability in smoking behavior. In other words, we want a measure that represents

$$\frac{SS_{\hat{Y}}}{SS_Y} = \frac{SS_Y - SS_{error}}{SS_Y}$$

As we have seen, that measure is r^2. In other words,

$$r^2 = \frac{SS_{\hat{Y}}}{SS_Y}$$

This interpretation of r^2 is extremely useful. If, for example, the correlation between amount smoked and life expectancy were an unrealistically high .80, we could say that $.80^2 = 64\%$ of the variability in life expectancy is directly predictable from the variability in smoking behavior. (Obviously, this is an outrageous exaggeration of the real world.) If the correlation were a more likely $r = .10$, we would say that $.10^2 = 1\%$ of the variability in life expectancy is related to smoking behavior, whereas the other 99% is related to other factors.

Phrases such as "accounted for by," "attributable to," "predictable from," and "associated with" are *not* to be interpreted as statements of cause and effect. Thus, you could say, "I can predict 10% of the variability of the weather by paying attention to twinges in the ankle that I broke last year—when it aches we are likely to have rain, and when it feels fine the weather is likely to be clear." This does not imply that sore ankles cause rain, or even that rain itself causes sore ankles. For example, it might be that your ankle hurts when it rains because low barometric pressure, which is often associated with rain, somehow affects ankles.

From this discussion it should be apparent that r^2 is easier to interpret as a measure of correlation than is r, since it represents the degree to which the variability in one measure is attributable to variability in the other measure. I recommend that you always square correlation coefficients to get some idea of whether you are talking about anything important. In our symptoms-and-stress example, $r^2 = .50^2 = .256$. Thus, about one-quarter of the variability in symptoms can be predicted from variability in stress. That strikes me as an impressive level of prediction, given all the other factors that influence psychological symptoms. Darlington (1990) has argued for the use of r instead of r^2 as representing the magnitude of an effect. A strong argument in this direction was also made by Ozer (1985), whose paper is well worth reading. In addition, Rosenthal and Rubin (1982) have shown that even small values of r^2 can be associated with powerful effects. (See Chapter 10).

9.7   ASSUMPTIONS UNDERLYING REGRESSION AND CORRELATION

We have derived the standard error of estimate and other statistics without making any assumptions concerning the population(s) from which the data were drawn. Nor do we need such assumptions to use $s_{Y \cdot X}$ as an unbiased estimator of $\sigma_{Y \cdot X}$. If we are to use $s_{Y \cdot X}$ in any meaningful way, however, we will have to introduce certain parametric assumptions. To understand why, consider the data plotted in Figure 9.5. Notice the four statistics labeled $s^2_{Y \cdot 1}$, $s^2_{Y \cdot 2}$, $s^2_{Y \cdot 3}$, and $s^2_{Y \cdot 4}$. These represent the variance of the points around the regression line in each **array** of X. (The residual variance of Y conditional on X). As mentioned earlier, the average of these variances, weighted by the degrees of freedom for each array, would be $s^2_{Y \cdot X}$, the residual or error variance. If

Array

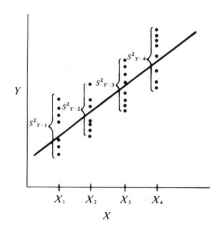

FIGURE 9.5
Scatter diagram
illustrating regression
assumptions

Homogeneity of variance in arrays

$s^2_{Y \cdot X}$ is to have any practical meaning, it must be representative of the various terms of which it is an average. This leads us to the assumption of **homogeneity of variance in arrays**, which is nothing but the assumption that the variance of Y for each value of X is constant (in the population). This assumption will become important when we apply tests of significance using $s^2_{Y \cdot X}$.

Normality in arrays

One further assumption that will be necessary when we come to testing hypotheses is that of **normality in arrays**. We will assume that in the population the values of Y corresponding to any specified value of X—that is, the conditional array of Y for X_i—are normally distributed around $\hat{Y}$. This assumption is directly analogous to the normality assumption we made with the t test—that each treatment population was normally distributed around its own mean—and we make it for similar reasons.

To anticipate what we will discuss in Chapter 11, note that our assumptions of homogeneity of variance and normality in arrays are equivalent to the assumptions of homogeneity of variance and normality of populations that we will make in discussing the analysis of variance. In Chapter 11 we will assume that the treatment populations from which data were drawn are normally distributed and all have the same variance. If you think of the levels of X in Figure 9.5 as representing different experimental conditions, you can see the relationship between the regression and analysis of variance assumptions.

The assumptions of normality and homogeneity of variance in arrays are associated with the regression model, where we are dealing with fixed values of X. On the other hand, when our interest is centered on the correlation between X and Y, we are dealing with the bivariate model, in which X and Y are both random variables. In this case, we are primarily concerned with using the sample correlation (r) as an estimate of the correlation coefficient in the population (ρ). Here we will replace the regression model assumptions with the assumption that we are sampling from a bivariate normal distribution.

The bivariate normal distribution looks roughly like the pictures you see each fall of surplus wheat piled in the main street of some midwestern town. The way the grain pile falls off on all sides resembles a normal distribution. (If there were no correlation between X and Y, the pile would look as though all the grain were dropped in the center of the pile and spread out symmetrically in all directions. When X and Y are correlated the pile is elongated, as when grain is dumped along a street and spreads out to the sides and down the ends.) Imagine that the pile had actually been dumped on top of a huge scattergram, with the main axis of the pile oriented along the regression line. If you sliced the pile on a line corresponding to any given value of X, you would see that the cut end is a normal distribution. You would also have a normal distribution if you sliced the pile along a line corresponding to any given value of Y.

Conditional distributions

These are called **conditional distributions** because the first represents the distribution of Y given (conditional on) a specific value of X, whereas the second represents the distribution of X conditional on a specific value of Y. If, instead, we looked at *all* the values of Y regardless of X (or all values of X regardless of Y), we would have what is

Marginal distribution

called the **marginal distribution** of Y (or X). For a bivariate normal distribution, both the conditional and the marginal distributions will be normally distributed. (Recall that for the regression model we assumed only normality of Y in the arrays of X— what we now know as conditional normality of Y. For the regression model, there is no assumption of normality of the conditional distribution of X or of the marginal distributions.)

9.8 CONFIDENCE LIMITS ON Y

Although the standard error of estimate is useful as an overall measure of error, it is not a good estimate of the error associated with any single prediction. When we wish to predict a value of Y for a given subject, the error in our estimate will be smaller when X is near $\overline{X}$ than when X is far from $\overline{X}$. (For an intuitive understanding of this, consider what would happen to the predictions for different values of X if we rotated the regression line slightly around the point $\overline{X}$, $\overline{Y}$.) If we wish to predict Y on the basis of X for a new member of the population (someone who was not included in the original sample), the standard error of our prediction is given by

$$s'_{Y \cdot X} = s_{Y \cdot X} \sqrt{1 + \frac{1}{N} + \frac{(X_i - \overline{X})^2}{(N-1)s_X^2}}$$

where $(X_i - \overline{X})$ is the deviation of the individual's X score from the mean of X. This leads to the following confidence limits on Y:

$$\text{CI}(Y) = \hat{Y} \pm (t_{\alpha/2})(s'_{Y \cdot X})$$

This equation will lead to elliptical confidence limits around the regression line, which are narrowest for $X = \overline{X}$ and become wider as $|X - \overline{X}|$ increases.

To take a specific example, assume that we wanted to set confidence limits on the number of symptoms (Y) experienced by a student with a stress score of 10—a fairly low level of stress. We know that

$$s_{Y \cdot X} = 17.563$$
$$s_X^2 = 171.505$$
$$\overline{X} = 21.467$$
$$\hat{Y} = 0.7831(10) + 73.890 = 81.721$$
$$t_{.025} = 1.984$$
$$N = 107$$

Then

$$s'_{Y \cdot X} = s_{Y \cdot X} \sqrt{1 + \frac{1}{N} + \frac{(X_i - \overline{X})^2}{(N-1)s_X^2}}$$

$$s'_{Y \cdot X} = 17.563 \sqrt{1 + \frac{1}{107} + \frac{(10 - 21.467)^2}{(106)(171.505)}}$$

$$= 17.563(1.0166) = 17.854$$

Then
$$CI(Y) = \hat{Y} \pm (t_{\alpha/2})(s'_{Y \cdot X})$$
$$= 81.721 \pm 1.984(17.854)$$
$$= 81.721 \pm 35.423$$
$$= 46.298 \le Y \le 117.144$$

The confidence interval is 46.298 to 117.144, and the probability is .95 that an interval computed in this way will include the level of symptoms reported by an individual whose stress score is 10. That interval is wide, but it is not nearly as large as the 95% confidence interval of $50.5 \le Y \le 130.9$ that we would have had if we had not used X—that is, if we had just based our confidence interval on the obtained values of Y (and s_Y) rather than making it conditional on X.

9.9 A COMPUTER EXAMPLE SHOWING GRADES AS A FUNCTION OF IQ

To illustrate a typical solution to a correlation and regression problem, consider the data in Table 9.7. These data are from a random sample of 30 cases from a study by Howell and Huessy (1981) and represent the relationship between (IQ) scores on the Otis–Lennon Mental Abilities Test, administered while subjects were in fifth to eighth grade, and grade point average (GPA) in ninth grade. The computer printout of this analysis is presented in Exhibit 9.1. The analysis was carried out using the SPSS^X REGRESSION procedure.

TABLE 9.7
Data from Howell and Huessy (1981)

IQ	GPA	IQ	GPA	IQ	GPA
102	2.75	115	4.00	111	3.00
108	4.00	92	2.23	95	1.50
109	2.25	95	3.00	106	3.75
118	3.00	90	2.50	83	0.67
79	1.67	106	2.75	81	1.50
88	2.25	85	2.75	112	3.00
100	2.50	95	2.75	85	1.75
92	3.50	97	2.67	115	3.75
131	3.75	93	2.00	86	1.00
83	2.75	81	2.00	85	2.50

Exhibit 9.1 illustrates a number of things we have already discussed. The means and standard deviations are found in the middle of the exhibit, and these numbers are roughly what you might expect. (A mean GPA of 2.586 is reasonable, as is a standard deviation of 0.847. Similarly, we would expect IQ scores to have a mean somewhere around 100 with a standard deviation of about 15, and that is what we have.) Below those values you see the correlation matrix, showing that the correlation between IQ and GPA is .701, a respectable correlation. Moving further down the exhibit, you find

the multiple correlation. A multiple correlation (to be discussed in Chapter 15) represents the correlation between a dependent variable (Y) and multiple independent variables or predictors (X_j). When there is only one independent variable, the multiple correlation reduces to a simple correlation. This section of the output gives us additional information aside from the fact that the multiple correlation is .701, which is what we already knew. Note that the adjusted correlation coefficient (the relatively unbiased estimate of the population correlation) is given as a squared value. We can take the square root of this statistic (.688) as r_{adj}. From the analysis of variance section, we see a test on the hypothesis that the correlation coefficient in the population is 0. We will discuss this in Section 9.10, but the significance level for the F is given as .0000, meaning that the first nonzero digits come beyond the fourth decimal place. Therefore, we can reject the null hypothesis as significant at $\alpha = .05$. In the next section of the printout we see the regression equation. It can be written as

EXHIBIT 9.1
SPSS^x output from
Howell and Huessy
(1981)

File Handle   GPADAT/Name = 'GPA.dat'
Data List   File = GPADAT
               /ID 1-2 IQ 4-6 GPA 8-11 (2)
Variable Labels ID 'Subject ID Number'
               IQ 'Otis-Lennon IQ'
               GPA 'Grade Point Average in Ninth Grade'
Regression   Descriptive = Defaults N
               /Variables = IQ GPA
               /Dependent = GPA /Enter

* * * * * MULTIPLE REGRESSION * * * *

Listwise Deletion of Missing Data

	Mean	Std Dev	Label
IQ	97.267	13.279	OTIS-LENNON IQ
GPA	2.586	.847	GRADE POINT AVERAGE IN NINTH GRADE

N of Cases = 30

Correlation:

	IQ	GPA
IQ	1.000	.701
GPA	.701	1.000

* * * * MULTIPLE REGRESSION * * * *

Equation Number 1   Dependent Variable . . GPA GRADE POINT AVERAGE IN NINTH GRADE

Variable(s) Entered on Step Number
   1 . . IQ   OTIS-LENNON IQ

Multiple R   .70113
R Square   .49158
Adjusted R Square   .47342
Standard Error   .61470

Analysis of Variance

	DF	Sum of Squares	Mean Square
Regression	1	10.22955	10.22955
Residual	28	10.57995	.37786

F = 27.07265   Signif F = .0000

- - - - - - - - - - - - - - - - Variables in the Equation - - - - - - - - - - - - - - - - -

Variable	B	SE B	BETA	T	Sig T
IQ	.044725	.008596	.701128	5.203	.0000
(Constant)	-1.763950	.843587		-2.091	.0457

$$\hat{Y}_i = 0.044725X_i - 1.76395$$

The standardized regression coefficient β (the coefficient for standardized data) is given as .701128. With only one predictor variable, you already know (see p. 233) that the correlation coefficient and the standardized regression coefficient are equal. Here you see confirmation of that. Finally, we see a test of significance on the regression coefficients. We will discuss these tests in Section 9.10.

9.10   HYPOTHESIS TESTING

In this chapter we have seen how to calculate r as an estimate of the relationship between two variables and how to calculate the slope (b) as a measure of the rate of change of Y as a function of X. In addition to estimating r and b, we often wish to perform a significance test on the null hypothesis that the corresponding population parameters equal zero. The fact that a value of r or b calculated from a sample is not zero is not in itself evidence that the corresponding parameters in the population are also nonzero.

TESTING THE SIGNIFICANCE OF r

The most common hypothesis that we test for a sample correlation is that the correlation between X and Y in the population, denoted ρ (rho), is zero. This is a meaningful test because the null hypothesis being tested is really the hypothesis that X and Y are linearly independent. Rejection of this hypothesis leads to the conclusion that they are not independent and that there is some relationship between them.

It can be shown that when $\rho = 0$, for large N, r will be approximately normally distributed around zero with a standard error that can be estimated by

$$s_r = \sqrt{\frac{1 - r^2}{N - 2}}$$

Since the distribution of r is approximately normal (for $\rho = 0$) and its standard error is estimable, we can set up the ratio

$$t = \frac{r - \rho}{s_r} = \frac{r}{\sqrt{\dfrac{1 - r^2}{N - 2}}} = \frac{r\sqrt{N - 2}}{\sqrt{1 - r^2}}$$

which is distributed as t on $N - 2$ df. Returning to the example in Exhibit 9.1, $r = .701$ and $N = 30$. Thus,

$$t = \frac{.701\sqrt{28}}{\sqrt{1 - .701^2}} = \frac{.701\sqrt{28}}{\sqrt{.509}} = 5.201$$

This value of t is significant at $\alpha = .05$ (two-tailed), and we can thus conclude that there is a significant relationship between IQ and GPA. In other words, we can conclude that differences in IQ are associated with differences in grade point average, although this does not necessarily imply a causal association.

In Chapter 7 we saw a brief mention of the F statistic, about which we will have much more to say in Chapters 11–16. You should know that any t statistic on d degrees of freedom can be squared to produce an F statistic on 1 and d degrees of freedom. Many statistical packages use the F statistic instead of t to test hypotheses. In this case you simply take the square root of that F to obtain the t statistics we are discussing here. (From Exhibit 9.1 we find an F of 27.07265. The square root of this is 5.203, which agrees within rounding error with the t we have just computed for this test.)

As a second example, if we go back to our data on stress and psychological symptoms in Table 9.2, and the accompanying text, we find $r = .506$ and $N = 107$. Thus,

$$t = \frac{.506\sqrt{105}}{\sqrt{1 - .506^2}} = \frac{.506\sqrt{105}}{\sqrt{.744}} = 6.011$$

Here again we will reject $H_0: \rho = 0$. We will conclude that there is a significant relationship between stress and symptoms. Differences in stress are associated with differences in reported psychological symptoms.

TESTING THE SIGNIFICANCE OF b

If you think about the problem for a moment, you will realize that a test on b is equivalent to a test on r. If it is true that X and Y are related, then it must also be true that Y varies with X—that is, that the slope is nonzero. This suggests that a test on b will produce the same answer as a test on r, and we could dispense with a test for b altogether. However, since regression coefficients play an important role in multiple regression, and since in multiple regression a significant correlation does not necessarily imply a significant slope for each predictor variable, the exact form of the test will be given here.

We will represent the parametric equivalent of b (the slope we would compute if we had X and Y measures on the whole population) as b^*.[†]

It can be shown that b is normally distributed about b^* with a standard error approximated by

$$s_b = \frac{s_{Y \cdot X}}{s_X \sqrt{N - 1}}$$

Thus, if we wish to test the hypothesis that the true slope of the regression line in the population is zero, we can simply form the ratio

$$t = \frac{b - b^*}{s_b} = \frac{b}{\dfrac{s_{Y \cdot X}}{s_X \sqrt{N - 1}}} = \frac{(b)(s_X)(\sqrt{N - 1})}{s_{Y \cdot X}}$$

which is distributed as t on $N - 2$ df.

[†] Many textbooks use β instead of b^*, but that would lead to confusion in Chapter 15.

For our sample data on stress and psychological symptoms, $b = .7831$, $s_X = 13.096$, and $s_{Y \cdot X} = 17.563$. Thus

$$t = \frac{(.7831)(13.096)(\sqrt{106})}{17.563} = 6.012$$

which is the same answer we obtained when we tested r. Since $t_{obt} = 6.012$ and $t_{.025}(105) = 1.984$, we will reject H_0 and conclude that our regression line has a non-zero slope. In other words, higher levels of reported stress lead to higher predictions of symptoms.

From what we know about the sampling distribution of b, it is possible to set up confidence limits on b^*,

$$CI(b^*) = b \pm t_{\alpha/2}\left[\frac{s_{Y \cdot X}}{s_X \sqrt{N-1}}\right]$$

where $t_{\alpha/2}$ is the two-tailed critical value of t on $N - 2$ df.

For our data, the 95% confidence limits are

$$CI(b^*) = 0.7831 \pm \frac{1.984(17.563)}{13.096\sqrt{106}}$$

$$= 0.7831 \pm 0.2584 = 0.525 \le b^* \le 1.042$$

Thus, the chances are 95 out of 100 that the limits 0.525 and 1.042 encompass the true value of b^*. [As you may recall, I pointed out in Chapter 7 that many statisticians would object to this last statement as phrased, because a set of specific limits (0.525 to 1.042) is not a random variable and therefore does not really have a probability associated with it. It either encloses the parameter or it does not. However, I also pointed out that as a statement of subjective probability, this declaration is a reasonable one.] Note that the confidence limits do not include zero. This is in line with the results of our t test, which rejected H_0: $b^* = 0$.

TESTING THE DIFFERENCE BETWEEN TWO INDEPENDENT bs

Suppose we have two sets of data on the relationship between smoking and life expectancy. One set is made up of females, and the other of males. We have two separate data sets rather than one large one because we do not want our results to be contaminated by normal differences in life expectancy between males and females. Suppose further that we obtained the following data:

	Males	Females
b	−0.40	−0.20
$s_{Y \cdot X}$	2.10	2.30
s_X^2	2.50	2.80
N	101	101

It is apparent that for our data the regression line for males is steeper than the regression line for females. If this difference is significant, it means that males decrease their life expectancy more than do females for any given increment in the amount they smoke. If this were true, it would be an important finding, and we are therefore interested in testing the difference between b_1 and b_2.

The t test for differences between two independent regression coefficients is directly analogous to the test of the difference between two independent means. If H_0 is true $(b_1^* = b_2^*)$, the sampling distribution of $b_1 - b_2$ is normal with a mean of zero and a standard error of

$$s_{b_1 - b_2} = \sqrt{s_{b_1}^2 + s_{b_2}^2}$$

This means that the ratio

$$t = \frac{b_1 - b_2}{\sqrt{s_{b_1}^2 + s_{b_2}^2}}$$

is distributed as t on $N_1 + N_2 - 4$ df. We already know that the standard error of b is estimated by

$$s_b = \frac{s_{Y \cdot X}}{s_X \sqrt{N - 1}}$$

and therefore can write

$$s_{b_1 - b_2} = \sqrt{\frac{s_{Y \cdot X_1}^2}{s_{X_1}^2 (N_1 - 1)} + \frac{s_{Y \cdot X_2}^2}{s_{X_2}^2 (N_2 - 1)}}$$

where $s_{Y \cdot X_1}^2$ and $s_{Y \cdot X_2}^2$ are the error variances for the two samples. As was the case with means, if we assume homogeneity of error variances, we can pool these two estimates, weighting each by its degrees of freedom:

$$s_{Y \cdot X}^2 = \frac{(N_1 - 2)(s_{Y \cdot X_1}^2) + (N_2 - 2)(s_{Y \cdot X_2}^2)}{N_1 + N_2 - 4}$$

For our data,

$$s_{Y \cdot X}^2 = \frac{99(2.10^2) + 99(2.30^2)}{101 + 101 - 4} = 4.85$$

Substituting this pooled estimate into the equation, we obtain

$$s_{b_1 - b_2} = \sqrt{\frac{s_{Y \cdot X}^2}{s_{X_1}^2 (N_1 - 1)} + \frac{s_{Y \cdot X}^2}{s_{X_2}^2 (N_2 - 1)}}$$

$$= \sqrt{\frac{4.85}{(2.5)(100)} + \frac{4.85}{(2.8)(100)}} = 0.192$$

Given $s_{b_1 - b_2}$, we can now solve for t

$$t = \frac{b_1 - b_2}{s_{b_1 - b_2}} = \frac{(-0.40) - (-0.20)}{0.192} = -1.04$$

on 198 *df*. Since $t_{.025}(198) = \pm 1.97$, we would fail to reject H_0 and would therefore conclude that we have no reason to doubt that life expectancy decreases as a function of smoking at the same rate for males as for females.

It is worth noting that although H_0: $b^* = 0$ is equivalent to H_0: $\rho = 0$, it does not follow that H_0: $b_1^* - b_2^* = 0$ is equivalent to H_0: $\rho_1 - \rho_2 = 0$. If you think about it for a moment, it should be apparent that two scatter diagrams could have the same regression line ($b_1^* = b_2^*$) but different degrees of scatter around that line, hence ($\rho_1 \neq \rho_2$). The reverse also holds—two different regression lines could fit their respective sets of data equally well.

TESTING THE DIFFERENCE BETWEEN TWO INDEPENDENT *rs*

When we test the difference between two independent *rs*, a minor difficulty arises. When $\rho \neq 0$, the sampling distribution of *r* is not approximately normal (it becomes more and more skewed as $\rho \Rightarrow \pm 1.00$), and its standard error is not easily estimated. The same holds for the difference $r_1 - r_2$. This raises an obvious problem, but the solution was provided by R. A. Fisher.

Fisher (1921) showed that if we transform *r* to

$$r' = (0.5) \log_e \left| \frac{1 + r}{1 - r} \right|$$

then r' is approximately normally distributed around ρ' (the transformed value of ρ) with standard error

$$s_{r'} = \frac{1}{\sqrt{N - 3}}$$

(Fisher labeled his statistic "z," but "r'" is often used to avoid confusion with the standard normal deviate.) We can now test the null hypothesis that $\rho_1 - \rho_2 = 0$ by converting each *r* to r' and solving for

$$z = \frac{r_1' - r_2'}{\sqrt{\dfrac{1}{N_1 - 3} + \dfrac{1}{N_2 - 3}}}$$

Note that our test statistic is *z* rather than *t*, since our standard error does not rely on statistics computed from the sample (other than *N*) and is therefore a parameter.

Appendix r' presents the values of r' for different values of *r*, which eliminates the need to solve the equation for r'.

To take a simple example, assume that for a sample of 53 males, the correlation between number of packs of cigarettes smoked per day and life expectancy was .50. For females, the correlation was .40. (These are unrealistically high values for *r*, but they better illustrate the effects of the transformation.) The question of interest is, Are these two coefficients significantly different, or are the differences in line with what we would expect when sampling from the same bivariate population of *X*, *Y* pairs?

	Males	**Females**
r	.50	.40
r'	.549	.424
N	53	53

$$z = \frac{.549 - .424}{\sqrt{\dfrac{1}{53 - 3} + \dfrac{1}{53 - 3}}} = \frac{.125}{\sqrt{\dfrac{2}{50}}} \quad \frac{.125}{\dfrac{1}{5}} = 0.625$$

Since $z_{obt} = .625$ is less than $z_{.025} = \pm 1.96$, we fail to reject H_0 and conclude that with a two-tailed test at $\alpha = .05$, we have no reason to doubt that the correlation between smoking and life expectancy is the same for males as it is for females.

TESTING THE HYPOTHESIS THAT ρ EQUALS ANY SPECIFIED VALUE

Now that we have discussed the concept of r', we are in a position to test the null hypothesis that ρ is equal to any value, not just to zero. Although we seldom wish to test null hypotheses of this type, the ability to do so allows us to establish confidence limits on ρ, a more interesting procedure.

As we have seen, for any value of ρ, the sampling distribution of r' is approximately normally distributed around ρ' (the transformed value of ρ) with a standard error of $1/\sqrt{N - 3}$. From this it follows that

$$z = \frac{r' - \rho'}{\sqrt{\dfrac{1}{N - 3}}}$$

is a standard deviate. Thus, if we want to test the null hypothesis that a sample r of .30 (with $N = 103$) came from a population where $\rho = .50$, we proceed as follows

$$r = .30 \qquad r' = .310$$

$$\rho = .50 \qquad \rho' = .549$$

$$N = 103 \qquad s_{r'} = 1/\sqrt{N - 3} = 0.10$$

$$z = \frac{.310 - .549}{0.10} = \frac{-.239}{0.10} = -2.39$$

Since $z_{obt} = -2.39$ is more extreme than $z_{0.025} = \pm 1.96$, we reject H_0 at $\alpha = .05$ (two-tailed) and conclude that our sample did not come from a population where $\rho = .50$.

CONFIDENCE LIMITS ON ρ

We can easily establish confidence limits on ρ by solving the equation for ρ instead of z. To do this, we first solve for confidence limits on ρ', and then convert ρ' to ρ.

$$z = \frac{r' - \rho'}{\sqrt{\dfrac{1}{N - 3}}}$$

therefore

$$\frac{1}{\sqrt{N - 3}}(z) + r' = \rho'$$

and thus

$$\mathrm{CI}(\rho') = r' \pm z_{\alpha/2}\frac{1}{\sqrt{N - 3}}$$

For our stress example, $r = .506$ ($r' = .556$) and $N = 107$, so the 95% confidence limits are

$$\mathrm{CI}(\rho') = .556 \pm 1.96\frac{1}{\sqrt{104}}$$

$$= .556 \pm 1.96(0.098) = .556 \pm .192$$

$$= .364 \le \rho' \le .748$$

Converting from ρ' back to ρ and rounding.

$$.350 \le \rho \le .635$$

Thus, the limits are $\rho = .350$ and $\rho = .635$. The probability is .95 that limits obtained in this way encompass the true value of ρ. Note that $\rho = 0$ is not included within our limits, thus offering a simultaneous test of H_0: $\rho = 0$, should we be interested in that information.

TESTING THE DIFFERENCE BETWEEN TWO NONINDEPENDENT rs

Occasionally we come across a situation in which we wish to test the difference between two correlations that are not independent. Such a case arises when we correlate two variables at Time 1 and then again at some later point (Time 2), and we want to ask whether there has been a significant change in the correlation over time. As another example, Reilly, Drudge, Rosen, Loew, and Fischer (1985) administered two intelligence tests (the WISC-R and the McCarthy) to first-grade children, and then administered the Wide Range Achievement Test (WRAT) to those same children 2 years later. They obtained, among other findings, the following correlations:

	WRAT	WISC-R	McCarthy
WRAT	1.00	.80	.72
WISC-R		1.00	.89
McCarthy			1.00

Note that the WISC-R and the McCarthy are highly correlated but that the WISC-R correlates somewhat more highly with the WRAT (reading) than does the McCarthy. It is of interest to ask whether this difference is significant, but to answer that question requires a test on nonindependent correlations.

When we have two correlations that are not independent—as these are not, since the tests were based on the same 26 children—we must take into account this lack of independence. Specifically, we must incorporate a term representing the degree to which the two tests are themselves correlated. Hotelling (1931) proposed the traditional solution, but a better test was devised by Williams (1959) and endorsed by Steiger (1980). This latter test takes the form

$$t = (r_{12} - r_{13}) \sqrt{\frac{(N-1)(1+r_{23})}{2\frac{(N-1)}{(N-3)}|R| + \frac{(r_{12}+r_{13})^2}{4}(1-r_{23})^3}}$$

where

$$|R| = (1 - r_{12}^2 - r_{13}^2 - r_{23}^2) + (2r_{12}r_{13}r_{23})$$

This ratio is distributed as t on $N - 3$ df. In this equation, r_{12} and r_{13} refer to the correlation coefficients whose difference is to be tested, and r_{23} refers to the correlation between the two predictors. $|R|$ is the determinant of the 3×3 matrix of intercorrelations, but you can calculate it as shown without knowing anything about determinants.

For our example, let

$$r_{12} = \text{correlation between the WISC-R and the WRAT} = .80$$

$$r_{13} = \text{correlation between the McCarthy and the WRAT} = .72$$

$$r_{23} = \text{correlation between WISC-R and the McCarthy} = .89$$

$$N = 26$$

then

$$|R| = (1 - .80^2 - .72^2 - .89^2) + (2)(.80)(.72)(.89) = .075$$

$$t = (.80 - .72) \sqrt{\frac{(25)(1+.89)}{2\frac{25}{23}(.075) + \frac{(.80+.72)^2}{4}(1-.89)^3}}$$

$$= 1.36$$

A value of $t_{obt} = 1.36$ on 23 df is not significant, giving support to the argument that the tests are equally effective in predicting third-grade children's performance on the reading scale of the WRAT.

9.11 CORRELATION COEFFICIENTS AS DATA

We generally think of raw data as being in the form of traditional measures such as time, distance, or number of items recalled. Occasionally, however, the data are more derived measures such as means, variances, and correlation coefficients. Melzer (1975), for example, asked subjects to estimate people's IQs on the basis of certain quantitative cues. For each subject, she obtained the correlation between the subject's estimate and the true IQ. For one of her analyses, she had two groups of 33 subjects, and therefore two sets of 33 correlation coefficients. She wanted to test, by t, the hypothesis that the mean coefficients were different for the two groups. A difficulty arose from the fact that the correlations were in the neighborhood of .80 and .90, and thus the distribution of r about ρ would be very badly skewed. The solution was to convert individual rs to values of r' and to run the t test on r'.

The use of r' instead of r is recommended whenever data are in the form of correlations. It ensures an approximately normal sampling distribution of $\bar{r}'$ (and thus $\bar{r}'_1 - \bar{r}'_2$) and further ensures homogeneity of variance, something that would not occur if the true values of ρ_1 and ρ_2 were quite different.[†]

9.12   THE ROLE OF ASSUMPTIONS IN CORRELATION AND REGRESSION

There is considerable confusion in the literature concerning the assumptions underlying the use of correlation and regression techniques. Much of the confusion stems from the fact that the correlation and regression models, although they lead to many of the same results, are based on different assumptions. Confusion also arises because statisticians tend to make all their assumptions at the beginning and fail to point out that some of these assumptions are not required for certain purposes.

Linearity of regression

Curvilinear

The major assumption that underlies both the linear-regression and bivariate-normal models and all our interpretations is that of **linearity of regression**. We assume that whatever the relationship between X and Y, it is a linear one—meaning that the line that best fits the data is a straight one. We will later refer to measures of **curvilinear** (nonlinear) relationships, but standard discussions of correlation and regression assume linearity unless otherwise stated. (We do occasionally fit straight lines to curvilinear data, but we do so on the assumption that the line will be sufficiently accurate for our purpose—although the standard error of prediction might be poorly estimated.)

As mentioned earlier, whether or not we make various assumptions is a function of what we wish to do. If our purpose is simply to describe data, no assumptions are necessary. The regression line and r best describe the data at hand, without the necessity of any assumptions about the population from which the data were sampled.

If our purpose is to assess the degree to which variance in Y is linearly attributable to variance in X, we again need make no assumptions. This is true because s_Y^2 and $s_{Y \cdot X}^2$ are both unbiased estimators of their corresponding parameters independent of any underlying assumptions, and

---

[†] The accuracy of this procedure can be improved by incorporating a correction discussed by Fisher (1935, p. 205).

$$\frac{SS_Y - SS_{error}}{SS_Y}$$

is algebraically equivalent to r^2.

If we want to set confidence limits on b or Y, or if we want to test hypotheses about b^*, we will need to make the assumptions of homogeneity of variance and normality in arrays of Y. The assumption of homogeneity of variance is necessary to ensure that $s_{Y \cdot X}^2$ is representative of the variance of each array, and the assumption of normality is necessary because we use the standard normal distribution.

If we want to use r to test the hypothesis that $\rho = 0$, or if we wish to establish confidence limits on ρ, we will have to assume that the (X, Y) pairs are a random sample from a bivariate-normal distribution.

9.13 FACTORS THAT AFFECT THE CORRELATION

The correlation coefficient can be substantially affected by characteristics of the sample. Two such characteristics are the restriction of the range (or variance) of X and/or Y and the use of heterogeneous subsamples.

THE EFFECT OF RANGE RESTRICTIONS

Range restrictions

A common problem concerns restrictions on the range over which X and Y vary. The effect of such **range restrictions** is to alter the correlation between X and Y from what it would have been if the range had not been so restricted. Depending on the nature of the data, the correlation may either rise or fall as a result of such restriction, although most commonly r is reduced.

With the exception of very unusual circumstances, restricting the range of X will increase r only when the restriction results in eliminating some curvilinear relationship. For example, if we correlated reading ability with age, where age ran from 0 to 70 years, the data would be decidedly curvilinear (flat to about age 4, rising to about 17 years of age and then leveling off) and the correlation, which measures *linear* relationships, would be relatively low. If however, we restricted the range of ages to 5 to 17 years, the correlation would be quite high, since we would have eliminated those values of Y that were not varying linearly as a function of X.

The more usual effect of restricting the range of X or Y is to reduce the correlation. This problem is especially pertinent in the area of test construction, since here criterion measures (Y) may be available for only the higher values of X. Consider the hypothetical data in Figure 9.6. This figure represents the relation between college GPAs and scores on some standard achievement test (such as the SAT) for a hypothetical sample of students. In the ideal world of the test constructor, all people who took the exam would then be sent on to college and receive a GPA, and the correlation between achievement test scores and GPAs would be computed. As can be seen from Figure 9.6, this correlation would be reasonably high. In the real world, however, not everyone is admitted to college. Colleges take only the more able students, whether this classification be based on achievement test scores, high-school performance, or whatever. This means that GPAs are available mainly for students who had relatively high scores on the standardized test. Suppose this has the effect of allowing us to evaluate the relationship between X and Y for only those values of X that are greater than 400. For the data in Figure 9.6, the correlation will be relatively low, not because the test is worthless, but because the range has been restricted. In other words, when we use the entire sample of points in Figure 9.6, the correlation is .65. However, when we restrict the sample to those students having test scores of at least 400, the correlation drops to only .43. (This is easier to see if you cover up all data points for $X < 400$.)

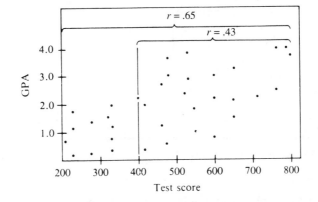

FIGURE 9.6
Hypothetical data
illustrating effect of
restricted range

We must take into account the effect of range restrictions whenever we see a validity coefficient based on a restricted sample. The coefficient might be inappropriate for the question at hand. Essentially, what we have done is to ask how well a standardized test predicts a person's suitability for college, but we have answered that question by referring only to those people who were actually admitted to college.

THE EFFECT OF HETEROGENEOUS SUBSAMPLES

Heterogeneous subsamples

Another important consideration in evaluating the results of regression analyses deals with **heterogeneous subsamples**. This point can be illustrated with a simple example.

Consider our hypothetical study of smoking and life expectancy, in which we plot the data for males and females separately to eliminate contamination from differences in life expectancy normally found between the genders. Assume that the results are represented as shown in Figure 9.7; the data have been exaggerated to make the point more vividly. The ellipses are used to represent the clustering of data points. It is apparent that for both males and females there is a high relationship between smoking and life expectancy. If we group the data into one large sample, however, the relationship deteriorates appreciably. The fact that the correlation is lower for the combined sample has nothing whatsoever to do with the relationship between smoking and life expectancy; rather, it reflects the relationship between gender and life expectancy. [On the other hand, Miller and Gerstein (1983) presented data that suggested that differ-ences in life expectancy between males and females can be attributed largely to differ-ences in smoking behavior.] The point to be made here with respect to heterogeneous subsamples is that in combining data from several sources, experimenters must be very careful not to include variance attributable to irrelevant variables.

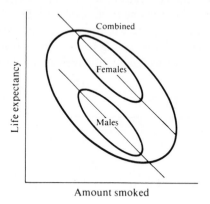

FIGURE 9.7
Illustration of effect of heterogeneous subsamples

9.14   POWER CALCULATION FOR PEARSON'S r

Consider the problem of the individual who wishes to demonstrate a relationship between television violence and aggressive behavior. Assume that he has surmounted all the very real problems associated with designing this study and has devised a way to obtain a correlation between the two variables. He believes that the correlation coefficient in the population (ρ) is approximately .30. (This correlation may seem small but it is impressive when you consider all the variables involved in aggressive be-havior. This value is in line with the correlation obtained in a real study by Eron, Huesmann, Lefkowitz, and Walden, 1972.) Our experimenter wants to conduct a study to find such a correlation but wants to know something about the power of his study before proceeding. Power calculations are easy to make in this situation.

We begin by defining

$$\mathbf{d} = \rho_1 - \rho_0 = \rho_1 - 0 = \rho_1$$

where ρ_1 is the correlation in the population defined by H_1—in this case, .30. We next define

$$\delta = \mathbf{d}\sqrt{N-1} = \rho_1\sqrt{N-1}$$

For a sample of size 50,

$$\delta = .30\sqrt{50-1} = 2.1$$

From Appendix Power, for $\delta = 2.1$, power = .56.

A power coefficient of .56 does not please the experimenter, so he casts around for a way to increase power. He wants power = .80. From Appendix Power, we see that this will require $\delta = 2.8$. Therefore,

$$\delta = \rho_1 \sqrt{N-1}$$

Squaring both sides,

$$2.8 = .30 \sqrt{N-1}$$

$$2.8^2 = .30^2(N-1)$$

$$\left(\frac{2.8}{.30}\right)^2 + 1 = N = 88$$

Thus, to obtain power = .80, the experimenter will have to collect data on nearly 90 subjects.

KEY TERMS

Relationships (introduction)

Differences (introduction)

Correlation (introduction)

Regression (introduction)

Random variable (introduction)

Fixed variable (introduction)

Linear-regression models (introduction)

Bivariate-normal models (introduction)

Prediction (introduction)

Scatter diagram (9.1)

Scatterplot (9.1)

Scattergram (9.1)

Predictor (9.1)

Criterion (9.1)

Perfect relationship (9.1)

No relationship (9.1)

Negative relationship (9.1)

Regression lines (9.1)

Correlation (r) (9.1)

Covariance (cov_{XY} or s_{XY}) (9.3)

Sum of squares (9.4)

Sum of products (9.4)

Correlation coefficient in the population ρ (rho) (9.4)

Adjusted correlation coefficient (r_{adj})

Slope (9.5)

Intercept (9.5)

Errors of prediction (9.5)

Residual (9.5)

Normal equations (9.5)

Standardized regression coefficient β (beta) (9.5)

Standard error of estimate (9.6)

Residual variance (9.6)

Error variance (9.6)

Conditional distribution (9.6)

Sum of squares (SS) (9.6)

Array (9.7)

Homogeneity of variance in arrays (9.7)

Normality in arrays (9.7)

Conditional distributions (9.7)

Marginal distribution (9.7)

Linearity of regression (9.12)

Curvilinear (9.12)

Range restrictions (9.13)

Heterogeneous subsamples (9.13)

EXERCISES

9.1   The State of Vermont is divided into 10 Health Planning Districts, which correspond roughly to counties. The following data for 1980 represent the percentage of births of babies under 2500 grams (Y), the fertility rate for females younger than 18 or older than 34 years of age (X_1), and the percentage of births to unmarried mothers (X_2) for each district.[†]

District	Y	X_1	X_2
1	6.1	43.0	9.2
2	7.1	55.3	12.0
3	7.4	48.5	10.4
4	6.3	38.8	9.8
5	6.5	46.2	9.8
6	5.7	39.9	7.7
7	6.6	43.1	10.9
8	8.1	48.5	9.5
9	6.3	40.0	11.6
10	6.9	56.7	11.6

(a) Make a scatter diagram of Y and X_1.

(b) Draw on your scatter diagram (by eye) the line that appears to best fit the data.

9.2   Calculate the correlation between Y and X_1 in Exercise 9.1.

9.3   Calculate the correlation between Y and X_2 in Exercise 9.1.

9.4   Use a t test to test $H_0: \rho = 0$ for the answers to Exercises 9.2 and 9.3.

9.5   Draw scatter diagrams for the following sets of data. Note that the same values of X and Y are involved in each set.

	1		2		3	
X	Y	X	Y	X	Y
2	2	2	4	2	8
3	4	3	2	3	6
5	6	5	8	5	4
6	8	6	6	6	2

Calculate the covariance for each set.

9.6   Calculate the correlation for each data set in Exercise 9.5. How can the values of Y in Exercise 9.5 be rearranged to produce the smallest possible positive correlation?

9.7   The following data represent the percentage of voluntary homework problems completed by each of 20 students and their final grade at the end of the course (converted to a 100-point scale).

Problems:	50	60	80	70	90	40	100	85	90	80
Grade:	75	75	90	80	85	60	98	95	95	80

Problems:	50	95	40	80	85	95	70	40	80	30
Grade:	75	90	60	50	70	85	75	60	80	55

Plot the data points.

[†] Both X_1 and X_2 are known to be risk factors for low birthweight.

9.8   Compute the correlation between amount of homework completed and final grade in Exercise 9.7. Interpret this correlation.

9.9   Is the correlation you obtained in Exercise 9.8 significant?

9.10   Assume that a set of data contains a slightly curvilinear relationship between X and Y (the best-fitting line is slightly curved). Would it ever be appropriate to calculate r on these data?

9.11   An important developmental question concerns the relationship between severity of cerebral hemorrhage in low-birthweight infants and cognitive deficit in the same children at age 5 years.
(a) Suppose we expect a correlation of .20 and are planning to use 25 infants. How much power does this study have?
(b) How many infants would be required for power to be .80?

9.12   From the data in Exercise 9.1, compute the regression equation for predicting the percentage of births of infants under 2500 grams (Y) on the basis of fertility rate for females younger than 18 or older than 34 years of age (X_1). (X_1 is known as the "high-risk fertility rate.")

9.13   Calculate the standard error of estimate for the regression equation from Exercise 9.12.

9.14   Calculate confidence limits on $b*$ for Exercise 9.12.

9.15   If as a result of ongoing changes in the role of women in society, the age at which women tend to bear children rose such that the high-risk fertility rate defined in Exercise 9.12 jumped to 70, what would you predict for incidence of babies with birthweights less than 2500 grams?

9.16   Should you feel uncomfortable making a prediction if the rate in Exercise 9.15 were 70? Why or why not?

9.17   Compute a regression equation for predicting grade for the data in Exercise 9.7.

9.18   Compute a regression equation for predicting homework problems from grade for the data in Exercise 9.7.

9.19   Using the data in Table 9.2 and the computed coefficients, predict the number of symptoms for a stress score of 8.

9.20   Calculate confidence limits on $b*$ for Exercise 9.17.

9.21   The mean stress score for the data in Table 9.2 was 21.467. What would your prediction for symptoms be for someone who had that stress score? How does this compare to $\overline{Y}$?

9.22   Calculate and plot the 95% confidence interval in $\hat{Y}$ for predicting psychological symptoms—you can overlay the confidence limits on Figure 9.4.

9.23   Within a group of 200 faculty members who have been at a well-known university for less than 15 years (i.e., since before the salary curve levels off) the equation relating salary (in thousands of dollars) to years of service is $\hat{Y} = 0.9X + 15$. For 100 administrative staff at the same university, the equation is $\hat{Y} = 1.5X + 10$. Assuming that all differences are significant, interpret the meaning of these equations. How many years must pass before an administrator and a faculty member earn roughly the same salary?

9.24   In 1886, Sir Francis Galton, an English scientist, spoke about "regression toward mediocrity," which we more charitably refer to today as regression toward the mean. The basic principle is that those people at the ends of any continuum (e.g., height, IQ, or musical ability) tend to have children who are closer to the mean than they are. Use the concept of r as the regression coefficient (slope) with standardized data to explain Galton's idea.

9.25   You want to demonstrate a correlation between the number of days per year on which a person goes downhill skiing and his or her rating of mental health. You are interested in finding such a correlation only if the true correlation is at least .40. What are your chances of finding a significant sample correlation if you use 30 subjects?

9.26   In Exercise 9.25 how many subjects would you need for power = .80?

EXHIBIT 9.2

(a) Minitab *Output*

The regression equation is
Grade = 43.2 + 0.475 Problems

Predictor	Coef	Stdev	t-ratio	p
Constant	43.156	7.531	5.73	0.000
Problems	0.4751	0.1023	4.64	0.000

s = 9.702   R-sq = 54.5%   R-sq(adj) = 52.0%

Analysis of Variance

SOURCE	DF	SS	MS	F	p
Regression	1	2030.3	2030.3	21.57	0.000
Error	18	1694.2	94.1		
Total	19	3724.6			

Unusual Observations

Obs.	Problems	Grade	Fit	Stdev.Fit	Residual	St.Resid
14	80	50.00	81.16	2.38	-31.16	-3.31R

R denotes an obs. with a large st. resid.

(b) SPSS[X] *Output*

**** MULTIPLE REGRESSION ****

Correlation:

	PROBLEMS	GRADE
PROBLEMS	1.000	.738
GRADE	.738	1.000

Equation Number 1   Dependent Variable . .   GRADE

Variable(s) Entered on Step Number 1 . .   PROBLEMS

Multiple R	.73832
R Square	.54512
Adjusted R Square	.51985
Standard Error	9.70172

Analysis of Variance

	DF	Sum of Squares	Mean Square
Regression	1	2030.32821	2030.32821
Residual	18	1694.22179	94.12343

F = 21.57091   Signif F = .0002

- - - - - - - - - - - - - - - - Variable in the Equation - - - - - - - - - - - - - - - - - -

Variable	B	SE B	Beta	T	Sig T
PROBLEMS	.475097	.102294	.738323	4.644	.0002
(Constant)	43.155642	7.530918		5.730	.0000

9.27   Exhibit 9.2 contains the Minitab and SPSS[X] computer printout for the data in Exercise 9.7.
(a) What information do you find on the Minitab output that is not on the SPSS[X] output?
(b) What information do you find on the SPSS[X] output that is not on the Minitab output?
(*Note*: You can ignore the reference to "multiple" regression; with one predictor, multiple regression and simple regression are the same thing.)

9.28   In the study by Katz, Lauténschlager, Blackburn, and Harris (1990) used in Exercises 7.17 and 7.27, we saw that students who were answering reading comprehension questions on the SAT without first reading the passages performed at better-than-chance levels. This does not necessarily mean that the SAT is not a useful test. Katz et al. went on to calculate the correlation between the actual SAT Verbal scores on their subjects' admissions applications and performance on the 100-item test. For those subjects who had read the passage, the correlation was .68 ($N = 17$). For those who had not read the passage, the correlation was .51 ($N = 28$).

(a) Were these correlations significantly different?

(b) What would you conclude from these data?

9.29 Katz et al. replicated their experiment using subjects whose SAT Verbal scores showed considerably more within-group variance than had those in the first study. In this case the correlation for the group that read the passage was .88 ($N = 52$), whereas for the nonreading group it was .72 ($N = 74$). Were these correlations significantly different?

9.30 What conclusions can you draw from the difference between the correlations in Exercises 9.28 and 9.29?

9.31 Make up your own example along the lines of the "smoking versus life expectancy" example given on p. 240 to illustrate the relationship between r^2 and accountable variation.

COMPUTER EXERCISES

9.32 Using the data from Mireault (1990) in the file Mireault.dat, is there a relationship between how well a student performs in college (as assessed by GPA) and that student's psychological symptoms (as assessed by GSIT)?

9.33 (a) Using the data referred to in Exercise 9.32, calculate the correlations among all of the Brief Symptom Inventory subscales. (*Hint*: Virtually all statistical programs are able to calculate these correlations in one statement. You don't have to calculate each one individually.)

(b) What does the answer to (a) tell us about the relationships among the separate scales?

9.34 Compas, Howell, Phares, Williams, and Ledoux (1989) found a significant relationship between parental symptomatology and adolescents' behavior problems. The data set Cancer.dat is taken from a related study.

(a) Calculate the regression of adolescent behavior problems (using TotBPT) on the *father's* GSIT score.

(b) Interpret the regression equation and the associated significance tests.

(c) Interpret the correlation coefficient.

(d) Perform a similar regression using data from mothers.

(e) Interpret the results.

9.35 Refer to the results in Exercise 9.34. Compas et al. (1989) actually found that the relationship depended on both the gender of the parent and the gender of the child. Why could we not *meaningfully* run such an analysis here?

9.36 (a) For the results of Exercise 9.34, with pencil and paper calculate the confidence limits on the correlation between mother's symptoms and the adolescent's behavior problems.

(b) What do the limits found in (a) tell you about your confidence in the correlation coefficient that you have computed?

(c) What do the limits found in (a) tell you about the significance of the correlation coefficient?

9.37 One of the assumptions lying behind our use of regression is the assumption of homogeneity of variance in arrays. One way to examine the data for violations of this assumption is to calculate predicted values of Y and the corresponding residuals ($Y - \hat{Y}$). If you plot the residuals against the predicted values, you should see a more or less random collection of points. The vertical dispersion should not increase or decrease systematically as you move from right to left, nor should there be any other apparent pattern.

Create the scatterplot for the data from Cancer.dat. Most computer packages let you request this plot. If not, you can easily generate the appropriate variables by first determining the regression equation and then feeding that equation back into the program in a "compute statement." (e.g., "set Pred = 0.256*GSIT + 4.65," and "set Resid = TotBPT − Pred".)

CHAPTER TEN

ALTERNATIVE CORRELATIONAL TECHNIQUES

OBJECTIVES *To discuss correlation and regression with regard to dichotomous variables and ranked data, and to present measures of association between categorical variables.*

CONTENTS

T he Pearson product-moment correlation coefficient (r) is only one of many available correlation coefficients. It generally applies to those situations in which the relationship between two variables is basically linear, where both variables are measured on a more or less continuous scale, and where some sort of normality and homogeneity of variance assumptions can be made. As this chapter will point out, r can be meaningfully interpreted in other situations as well, although for those cases it is given a different name and most people fail to recognize it for what it actually is.

In this chapter we will discuss a variety of coefficients that apply to different kinds of data. For example, the data might represent rankings, one or both of the variables might be dichotomous, or the data might be categorical. Depending on the assumptions we are willing to make about the underlying nature of our data, different coefficients will be appropriate in different situations. Some of these coefficients will turn out to be calculated as if they were Pearson rs, and some will not. The important point is that they all represent attempts to obtain some measure of the relationship between two variables and fall under the general heading of *correlation* rather than *regression*.

Correlational measures

Measures of association

When we speak of relationships between two variables without any restriction on the nature of these variables, we have to distinguish between **correlational measures** and **measures of association**. When at least some sort of order can be assigned to the levels of each variable, such that higher scores represent more (or less) of some quantity, then it makes sense to speak of correlation. We can speak meaningfully of increases in one variable being correlated with increases in another variable. In many situations, however, different levels of a variable do not represent an orderly increase or decrease in some quantity. For example, we could sort people on the basis of their membership in different campus organizations, and then on the basis of their views on some issue. We might then find that there is in fact an association between people's views and their membership in organizations, and yet neither of these variables represents an ordered continuum. In cases such as this, the coefficient we will compute is not a correlation coefficient. We will instead speak of it as a measure of association.

There are three basic reasons we might be interested in calculating any type of coefficient of correlation. The most obvious, but not necessarily the most important, reason is to obtain an estimate of ρ, the correlation in the population. Thus, someone interested in the **validity** of a test actually cares about the true correlation between his test and some criterion and approaches the calculation of a coefficient with this purpose in mind. This use is the one for which the alternative techniques are least satisfactory, although they can serve this purpose.

Validity

A second use of correlation coefficients occurs with such techniques as multiple regression and factor analysis. In this situation, the coefficient is not in itself an end product; rather, it enters into the calculation of further statistics. For these purposes, many of the coefficients to be discussed are satisfactory.

The final reason for calculating a correlation coefficient is to use its square as a measure of the variation in one variable accountable for by variation in the other variable. Here again, the coefficients to be discussed are in many cases satisfactory for this purpose.

10.1   POINT-BISERIAL CORRELATION (r_{pb})

Dichotomy

Frequently, variables are measured in the form of a **dichotomy**, such as male–female, homeowner–nonhomeowner, pass–fail, and so on. Ignoring for the moment that these variables are seldom measured quantitatively (a minor problem), it is quite apparent that they are not measured continuously. There is no way we can assume a normal distribution of obtained scores on the dichotomous variable. If we wish to use r as a measure of relationship between variables, we obviously have a problem, since for r to have certain desirable properties as an estimate of ρ, we need to assume at least an approximation of normality in the joint (bivariate) population of X and Y.

The difficulty over the quantitative measurement of X turns out to be trivial for dichotomous variables. If X represents married versus unmarried, for example, then we can legitimately score married as 0 and unmarried as 1, or vice versa. (In fact, *any* two values will do. Thus all married persons could be given a score of 82 on X, whereas all unmarried persons might receive a score of 23, without affecting the correlation in the least.) We generally use 0 and 1 for the simple reason that this makes the arithmetic easier. Given such a system of quantification, it should be apparent that the sign of the correlation will depend solely on the arbitrary way in which we choose to assign 0 and 1 and is therefore meaningless for most purposes.

If we set aside until the end of the chapter the problem of r as an estimate of ρ, things begin to look brighter. For any other purpose, we can proceed as usual to calculate the Pearson coefficient (r), although we will label it the **point-biserial coefficient (r_{pb})**. Thus, algebraically, $r_{pb} = r$, where one variable is dichotomous and the other is roughly continuous and more or less normally distributed in arrays.

CALCULATING r_{pb}

Most textbooks give several special formulas for r_{pb}. All of these formulas, however, are derived from Pearson's original formula and will not be given here. Scoring the dichotomous variable as 0, 1 and calculating a Pearson r (which we now label r_{pb}) is sufficient, completely accurate, and in fact quite easy with a 0,1 variable.

An example of the calculation of r_{pb} is given in Table 10.1; the hypothetical data represent the relationship between marital status (0 = married, 1 = unmarried) and income (in thousands of dollars). The scatter diagram for these data is given in Figure 10.1. In this figure, coincident points have been plotted as if they were adjacent, and the regression line of Y on X has been superimposed. Notice that the regression line

TABLE 10.1
Calculations of r_{pb} for hypothetical data on marital status and income

Marital Status X	Income X		
		$\Sigma X = 14$	$\Sigma Y = 330$
		$\Sigma X^2 = 14$	$\Sigma Y^2 = 4478$
0	15	$\overline{X} = 0.56$	$\overline{Y} = 13.2$
0	17	$s_X^2 = 0.257$	$s_Y^2 = 5.083$
0	14		
0	13	$s_X = 0.507$	$s_Y = 2.255$
0	17		$\overline{Y}_0 = 14.64$
0	11		$\overline{Y}_1 = 12.07$
0	19		
0	14		
0	15	$\Sigma XY = 169$	
0	12	$\text{cov}_{XY} = -0.658$	
0	14		
1	11	$r = \dfrac{\text{cov}_{XY}}{S_X S_Y}$	
1	10		
1	11	$= \dfrac{-0.658}{(0.507)(2.255)}$	
1	12		
1	13	$= -.576$	
1	10		
1	14	$r_{pb} = -.576$	
1	15		
1	12	$r_{pb}^2 = .332$	
1	13		
1	11		
1	12		
1	12		
1	13		

passes through the mean of each array. Thus, when $X = 0$, $\hat{Y}$ is the mean income of the married subjects in the sample (14.64), and when $X = 1$, $\hat{Y}$ is the mean income of the unmarried subjects (12.07). These values are shown in Table 10.1 as $\bar{Y}_0$ and $\bar{Y}_1$, respectively. The fact that the regression line passes through the two Y means will assume more relevance when we later consider eta squared (η^2), where the regression line is deliberately drawn so as to pass through several array means.

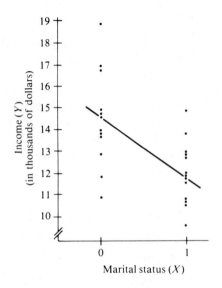

FIGURE 10.1
Scatter diagram for data from Table 10.1

From Table 10.1 you can see that the correlation between marital status and income is $-.576$. We can ignore the sign of this correlation, since the decision about whether married or unmarried subjects should be scored as 1 is arbitrary. A negative coefficient indicates that the mean of the group coded 1 is less than the mean of the group coded 0, whereas a positive correlation indicates the reverse. We can still interpret r^2 as usual, however, and say that 33.2% of the variability in income can be accounted for by marital status. This does not mean that a change in marital status would automatically lead to a change in income. We are not speaking here of a cause-and-effect relationship. As a group, married subjects tend to be older, they tend to have more stable jobs, and so on, and it is these other variables that most likely cause the higher income levels. The label " marital status" is really serving as an index of all of these other, more causal, variables.

Another interesting fact illustrated in Figure 10.1 concerns the equation for the regression line. Recall that the intercept is the value of $\hat{Y}$ when $X = 0$. In this case, $X = 0$ for married subjects and $\hat{Y} = 14.64$. In other words, the mean income of married subjects is the intercept. Moreover, the slope of the regression line is defined as the change in $\hat{Y}$ for a one-unit change in X. Since a one-unit change in X changes it from 0 (married) to 1 (unmarried), and $\hat{Y}$ changes from the mean income of married subjects to the mean income of unmarried subjects, the slope (-2.57) will represent the difference in the two means. We will return to this idea in Chapter 16, but it is important to notice it here in a simple context.

THE RELATIONSHIP BETWEEN r_{pb} AND t

The relationship between t and r_{pb} is very important. It can be shown, although the proof will not be given until we discuss the analysis of variance, that

$$r_{pb}^2 = \frac{t^2}{t^2 + df}$$

where t is obtained from the t test of the difference (for example, between incomes of married and unmarried subjects) and df = the degrees of freedom for t, namely, $N_1 + N_2 - 2$. For example, if we were to run a t test on the difference in incomes between married and unmarried subjects, using a t test for two independent groups with unequal sample sizes,

$$s_p^2 = \frac{(N_1 - 1)s_1^2 + (N_2 - 1)s_2^2}{N_1 + N_2 - 2} = \frac{10(5.455) + 13(2.071)}{23} = 3.542$$

and

$$t = \frac{14.64 - 12.07}{\sqrt{\dfrac{3.542}{11} + \dfrac{3.542}{14}}}$$

$$= 3.389$$

With 23 df, the difference between the two groups is significant. We now calculate

$$r_{pb}^2 = \frac{t^2}{t^2 + df} = \frac{3.389^2}{3.389^2 + 23} = .333$$

$$r_{pb} = \sqrt{.333} = .577$$

which, within rounding error and the arbitrary positive sign, agrees with the more direct calculation.

What is important about the equation linking r_{pb}^2 and t is that it first of all demonstrates that the distinction between relationships and differences is not as clear-cut as you might at first think. More important, we can use r_{pb}^2 and t together to obtain a rough estimate of the practical, as well as the statistical, significance of a difference. Thus $t = 3.389$ is evidence in favor of the experimental hypothesis that the two groups differ in mean income. At the same time, r_{pb}^2 (which is a function of t) tells us that marital status accounts for 33% of the variation in income. Finally, the equation shows us how to calculate r from the research literature when only t is given, and vice versa.

TESTING THE SIGNIFICANCE OF r_{pb}

A test of r_{pb} against the null hypothesis H_0: $\rho = 0$ is simple to construct. Since r_{pb} is a Pearson product-moment coefficient, it can be tested in the same way as r. Namely,

$$t = \frac{r_{pb}\sqrt{N - 2}}{\sqrt{1 - r_{pb}^2}}$$

on $N - 2$ df. Furthermore, since this equation can be derived directly from the definition of r_{pb}^2, the t (-3.389) obtained here is the same (apart from its sign) as a t test between the two levels of the dichotomous variable. This makes sense when you realize that a statement that married and unmarried people differ in income is the same as saying that income varies with (is correlated with or changes as a function of) marital status.

10.2   BISERIAL CORRELATION (r_b)

Biserial correlation coefficient (r_b)

In discussing point-biserial correlation, we began to consider dichotomous variables. A dichotomy can be either (1) discrete, or true, or (2) continuous, or artificial. Examples of discrete, or true, dichotomies are male versus female, group I versus group II, alive versus dead, and so on. In these situations, an individual is clearly in one category or another and we generally do not think of an underlying continuum between the two categories. Continuous, or artificial, dichotomies are those in which we would assume that there is an underlying continuum, but that individuals are assigned to a particular category on the basis of whether they exceed some arbitrary criterion. Thus, people are classified as passing or failing a test on the basis of their performance, although everyone would admit that some people fail abysmally, others barely fail, others barely pass, and a few pass brilliantly. Other examples are adult versus child, tall versus short, and drunk versus sober. If we are willing to assume an underlying continuity that is normally distributed, then for some purposes a better estimate of ρ is given by the **biserial correlation coefficient (r_b)**, although its calculation is more cumbersome.

CALCULATING r_b

The two coefficients r_{pb} and r_b computed on the same data will never agree except when $r_b = 0$. The relationship between them is known, however, and allows us to obtain r_b from r_{pb} whenever necessary.

$$r_b = \frac{r_{pb} \sqrt{p_1 p_2}}{y}$$

This equation contains several terms that need to be defined. The term p_1 refers to the proportion of subjects who fall in category 1 of the dichotomized variable; p_2 is the proportion falling in category 2. The y represents the ordinate of the normal distribution at the point of the distribution cutting off p_1 percent of the area on one side and p_2 percent on the other.

Although it is difficult to believe that marital status represents a normally distributed continuum, we will assume that it does for the purposes of an example. (Certainly, many of the variables that marital status indexes are continuous.)

From Table 10.1 we see that $11/25 = 44\%$ of our subjects were married, and 56% were unmarried. From Appendix z we see that $z = 0.15$ divides the normal distribution into two parts, with 44% of the area in one and 56% of the area in the other. Appendix z also gives the ordinate at $z = 0.15$ as 0.3945. Knowing these values we can calculate

$$r_b = \frac{r_{pb}\sqrt{p_1 p_2}}{y} = \frac{(-.576)\sqrt{(.44)(.56)}}{0.3945} = -\frac{0.2859}{0.3945}$$

$$= -.725$$

Thus, whereas the point-biserial correlation is $-.576$, the biserial correlation is $-.725$. If we were to calculate the value $\sqrt{p_1 p_2}/y$ for different values of p_1, we would find that as p_1 (and therefore p_2) departs from .50, the difference between r_{pb} and r_b increases. Even at the point at which $p_1 = p_2 = .50$, r_{pb} is equal to only about 80% of r_b.

LIMITS ON r_b

One embarrassing difficulty arises with r_b. Under certain conditions, r_b may exceed 1.00, a very unsatisfactory result. The usual explanation for this phenomenon is that one or the other of the variables—most likely the continuous one (McNemar, 1969)—is platykurtic or bimodal. The following data, for example, at least appear to satisfy all reasonable assumptions other than normality in arrays; but $r_b = 1.056$.

X:	0	0	0	0	0	0	1	1	1	1	1	1
Y:	5	6	6	7	7	7	8	8	8	9	9	10

r_{pb} equals a more reasonable .843.

A general rule is to use r_{pb} whenever the data represent a true dichotomy or whenever the underlying distribution of the dichotomous variable is not fairly certain to be normally distributed, and to use r_b only when you are quite sure that a normally distributed underlying dichotomy is present. Whenever there is any doubt, r_{pb} is preferred. In addition, r_{pb} will be the coefficient of choice when computing an intercorrelation matrix for use in a multiple regression or a factor analysis problem. In actual practice the biserial correlation is seldom used. I include it here primarily for reference purposes.

10.3   THE PHI COEFFICIENT (ϕ)

Occasionally, we come across data in which both variables are measured as true dichotomies. For example, we might be interested in the relationship between gender and employment, where individuals are scored as either employed or unemployed. Similarly, we might be interested in the relationship between employment status (employed–unemployed) and whether an individual has been arrested for drunken driving. As a final example, we might wish to know the correlation between smoking

ϕ (phi) coefficient

(smokers versus nonsmokers) and death by cancer (versus death by other causes). Unless we are willing to make special assumptions concerning the underlying continuity of our variables, the most appropriate correlation coefficient is the **ϕ (phi) coefficient**. This is the same ϕ that we considered briefly in Chapter 6.

CALCULATING ϕ

Table 10.2 contains hypothetical data on the relationship between smoking and cancer; both variables have been scored as 0,1 variables—an individual smoked or did not, and died of cancer or did not.

TABLE 10.2
Calculation of ϕ for hypothetical data on smoking and cancer

X:	0 = Smoker
	1 = Nonsmoker

Y:	0 = Died of cancer
	1 = Died of other causes

X: 0 0 0 0 0 0 0 0 0 0 1 1 1 1 1 1 1 1 1 1
Y: 0 1 0 0 1 0 0 0 1 1 0 1 1 1 1 0 1 1 1 0

$\Sigma X = 10 \qquad s_X = 0.513$

$\Sigma Y = 11 \qquad s_Y = 0.510$

$\Sigma XY = 7$

$N = 20$

$$\text{cov}_{XY} = \frac{\Sigma XY - \dfrac{\Sigma X \Sigma Y}{N}}{N-1} = \frac{7 - \dfrac{10(11)}{20}}{19} = 0.079$$

$$\phi = r = \frac{\text{cov}_{XY}}{s_X s_Y} = \frac{0.079}{(0.513)(0.510)}$$

$$= .302$$

$$\phi^2 = .091$$

The appropriate correlation coefficient is the ϕ coefficient, which is equivalent to Pearson's r calculated on these data. Again, special formulas exist for those people who can be bothered to remember them, but they will not be considered here. The simplicity of calculating Pearson's r for these data becomes apparent when you realize that ΣX and ΣX^2 are simply the number of individuals who were scored as 1 on variable X. The same holds for ΣY and ΣY^2. Moreover, ΣXY is simply the number of individuals scored as 1 on both variables. It does not really require a desk calculator to obtain these quantites.

SIGNIFICANCE OF ϕ

The appropriate test of ϕ against $H_0: \rho = 0$ is a chi-square test, since $N\phi^2$ is distributed as χ^2 on 1 df. For our data,

$$\chi^2 = N\phi^2 = 20(.302)^2 = 1.82$$

which, on 1 df, is not significant. We would therefore conclude that we have no evidence in this small sample to indicate a relationship between smoking and cancer.

THE RELATIONSHIP BETWEEN ϕ AND χ^2

The data in Table 10.2 could be recast in another form, as shown in Table 10.3. The two tables (10.2 and 10.3) contain the same information; they merely display it differently. You will immediately recognize Table 10.3 as a contingency table. From it, you could compute a value of χ^2 to test the null hypothesis that the variables are independent. In doing so, you would obtain a χ^2 of 1.82—which, on 1 df, is not significant.

TABLE 10.3
Calculation of χ^2 for hypothetical data on smoking and cancer (expected frequencies in parentheses)

	Cancer (0)	Other (1)	
Smoker (0)	6 (4.5)	4 (5.5)	10
Nonsmoker (1)	3 (4.5)	7 (5.5)	10
	9	11	20

$$\chi^2 = \frac{(6 - 4.5)^2}{4.5} + \frac{(4 - 5.5)^2}{5.5} + \frac{(3 - 4.5)^2}{4.5} + \frac{(7 - 5.5)^2}{5.5}$$

$$= 1.818$$

It should be apparent that in calculating ϕ and χ^2, we have been asking the same question in two different ways: not surprisingly, we have come to the same conclusion. When we calculated ϕ and tested it for significance, we were asking whether there was any correlation (relationship) between X and Y. When we ran a chi-square on Table 10.3, we were also asking whether the variables are related (correlated). Since these questions are the same, we would hope that we would come to the same answer, which we did. On the one hand, χ^2 relates to the statistical significance of a relationship. On the other, ϕ measures the degree or magnitude of that relationship.

It will come as no great surprise that there is a linear relationship between ϕ and χ^2. From the fact that $\chi^2 = N\phi^2$,

$$\phi = \sqrt{\frac{\chi^2}{N}}$$

For our example,

$$\phi = \sqrt{\frac{1.82}{20}} = \sqrt{.091} = .302$$

which agrees with our previous calculation.

ϕ^2 AS A MEASURE OF THE PRACTICAL SIGNIFICANCE OF χ^2

The fact that we can go from χ^2 to ϕ means that we have one way of evaluating the practical significance (importance) of the relationship between two dichotomous variables. For example, suppose that in a study based on 1000 subjects we found a χ^2 of 4.5 for the relationship between two dichotomous variables (political party affiliation and attitude toward research involving animals). Since on 1 df, $\chi^2_{.05} = 3.84$, we would reject H_0 and conclude that the variables were not independent. We can convert χ^2 to ϕ^2,

$$\phi^2 = \chi^2/N = 4.5/1000 = .0045$$
$$\phi = \sqrt{\phi^2} = \sqrt{.0045} = .067$$

and treat ϕ or ϕ^2 as a rough index of the degree of association between the variables.

Rosenthal and Rubin (1982) have argued that psychologists and others in the "softer sciences" are too ready to look at a small value of r^2 and call an effect unimportant. They maintain that very small values of r^2 can in fact be associated with important effects. It is easiest to state their case with respect to ϕ, which is why their work is discussed here.

Rosenthal and Rubin pointed to a large-scale evaluation (called a meta-analysis) of over 400 studies of the efficacy of psychotherapy. The authors, Smith and Glass (1977), reported an effect equivalent to a correlation of .32 between presence or absence of psychotherapy and presence or absence of improvement, by whatever measure. A reviewer subsequently squared this correlation ($r^2 = .1024$) and deplored the fact that psychotherapy accounted for only 10% of the variability in outcome. Rosenthal and Rubin pointed out that if we took 100 people in a control group and 100 people in a treatment group, and dichotomized them as improved or not improved, a correlation of $\phi = .32$ would correspond to a $\chi^2 = 20.48$. This can be seen by computing

$$\phi = \sqrt{\chi^2/N}$$
$$\phi^2 = \chi^2/N$$
$$.1024 = \chi^2/200$$
$$\chi^2 = 20.48$$

Such a χ^2 would result from a contingency table in which 66 of the 100 subjects in the treatment group improved whereas only 34 of the 100 subjects in the control group improved. (You can easily demonstrate this for yourself by computing χ^2 on such a table.) That is a dramatic difference in improvement rates.

More recently, Rosenthal (1990) has pointed to a well-known study of (male) physicians who took a daily dose of either aspirin or a placebo to reduce heart attacks. (We considered this study briefly in Chapter 6, but for a different purpose.) This study was terminated early because the review panel considered the results so clearly in favor of the aspirin group that it would have been unethical to continue to give the control group a placebo. But, said Rosenthal, what was the correlation between aspirin and heart attacks that was so dramatic as to cut short such a study? Would you believe $\phi = .034$ ($\phi^2 = .0011$)?

I include Rosenthal's work to make the point that one does not require large values of r^2 (or ϕ^2) to have an important effect. Small values in certain cases can be quite impressive. For further examples, see Rosenthal (1990). For another way of looking at such effects, see the section on odds ratios in Section 6.9.

10.4 TETRACHORIC CORRELATION (r_t)

Tetrachoric coefficient (r_t)

Just as we saw with the biserial r, situations may arise in which we are willing to assume an underlying continuity of the dichotomous variables and to assume that the traits measured by these variables are normally distributed. In this case, the **tetrachoric coefficient (r_t)** is appropriate. The difficulty with r_t centers on the fact that its calculation is extremely laborious unless special tables are used. In addition, its standard error is very large relative to the standard error of r. This last point means that r_t is a poor estimator of ρ unless N is very large. In those situations in which you think it is desirable to calculate r_t, see McNemar (1969). Since r_t is rarely used in practice, we will not cover its calculation here.

10.5 SPEARMAN'S CORRELATION COEFFICIENT FOR RANKED DATA (r_s)

In some experiments, the data naturally occur in the form of ranks. For example, we might ask judges to rank objects in order of preference under two different conditions, and wish to know the correlation between the two sets of rankings. Usually we are most interested in these correlations when we wish to assess the reliability of some ranking procedure.

A similar procedure, which has frequently been recommended in the past, is to rank sets of measurement data when we have serious reservations about the nature of the underlying scale of measurement. In this case, we are substituting ranks for raw scores. Although we could seriously question the necessity of ranking measurement data (for reasons mentioned in the discussion of measurement scales in Section 1.3 of Chapter 1), this is nonetheless a fairly common procedure.

Spearman's correlation coefficient for ranked data (r_s), Spearman's rho

Whether data naturally occur in the form of ranks (as, for example, when a judge orders 20 paintings in terms of preference) or whether ranks have been substituted for raw scores, an appropriate correlation coefficient is **Spearman's correlation coefficient for ranked data (r_s)**. (This statistic is sometimes referred to as **Spearman's rho**.)

CALCULATING r_s

The easiest way to calculate r_s is by applying Pearson's original formula to the ranked data. Alternative formulas do exist, although whether they are simpler is a matter for debate. One such formula is given here because it is extremely common (although you may well think it is a nuisance):

$$r_s = 1 - \frac{6\Sigma D^2}{N(N^2 - 1)}$$

where D is defined as the difference between the X and Y ranks assigned to each subject.

It is important that you understand the origin of this equation, since the derivation leads to an assumption that is almost never mentioned. It is well known that the sum of the first N integers equals $N(N + 1)/2$. [Thus $1 + 2 + 3 = 3(4)/2 = 6$.] Similarly, the sum of the squares of the first N integers equals $N(N + 1)(2N + 1)/6$. If we ask a judge to rank a set of 10 items from 1 to 10, *allowing no ties,* her data must consist of the integers 1 to 10. If another judge ranked the same set of items, again allowing no ties, her data would also consist of the integers 1 to 10. Since this is the case, ΣX and ΣY in Pearson's formula can be replaced by $N(N + 1)/2$, and ΣX^2 and ΣY^2 can be replaced by $N(N + 1)(2N + 1)/6$. In this way we can derive the previous equation.

Notice the stipulation in the preceding paragraph that there be no tied ranks. If we do have ties, ΣX^2 and ΣY^2 do not equal $N(N + 1)(2N + 1)/6$, and the shortcut equation is wrong. This fact is seldom mentioned, although it has not gone completely unnoticed, and a cumbersome correction procedure has been developed. A much simpler procedure is to calculate Pearson's r using the ranks in the first place rather than to calculate r_s, and then patch up r_s to obtain what you would have had if you had calculated r to begin with. Since r_s is seldom calculated on huge samples and since the correction procedure itself is far more bothersome than calculating r, using a shortcut equation seems rather silly when ranks are tied, and indeed even when they are not.

THE SIGNIFICANCE OF r_s

Recall that in Chapter 9 we imposed normality and homogeneity assumptions in order to provide a test on the significance of r (or to set confidence limits). With ranks, the data clearly cannot be normally distributed. There is no generally accepted method for calculating the standard error of r_s for small samples. As a result, computing confidence limits on r_s is not practical. Numerous textbooks contain tables of critical values of r_s, but for $N \geq 28$ these tables are themselves based on approximations. For $N > 10$, r_s can be tested in the same manner as τ, to be discussed next (Kendall, 1948). Keep in mind in this connection that a typical judge has difficulty ranking a large number of items, and therefore in practice N is usually small when we are using r_s.

RANKING DATA

Ranking

Students occasionally experience difficulty in **ranking** a set of measurement data, and this section is intended to present the method briefly. Assume we have the following set of data, which have been arranged in increasing order:

5   8   9   12   12   15   16   16   16   17

The lowest value (5) is given the rank of 1. The next two values (8 and 9) are then assigned ranks 2 and 3. We then have two tied values (12) that must be ranked. If they were untied, they would be given ranks 4 and 5, so we split the difference and rank them both 4.5. The sixth number (15) is now given rank 6. Three values (16) are tied for ranks 7, 8, and 9; the mean of these ranks is 8. Thus, all are given ranks of 8. The last value is 17, which has rank 10. The data and their corresponding ranks are given below.

X:	5	8	9	12	12	15	16	16	16	17
Ranks:	1	2	3	4.5	4.5	6	8	8	8	10

10.6   KENDALL'S TAU COEFFICIENT (τ)

Kendall's τ

A serious competitor to Spearman's r_S is **Kendall's τ**. Whereas Spearman treated the ranks as scores and calculated the correlation between the two sets of ranks, Kendall based his statistic on the number of *inversions* in the rankings. Suppose for a moment that we asked two judges to rank three objects and obtained the following data:

	Object		
	A	B	C
Judge 1	1	2	3
Judge 2	1	3	2

Notice that when the objects are listed in the order of rankings given by Judge 1, there is an inversion of the ranks given by Judge 2 (rank 3 appears before rank 2). (If there were a perfect ordinal relationship between these two sets of ranks, we would not expect to find any inversions.) Inversions of this form are the basis for Kendall's statistic.

CALCULATING τ

To extend the example, assume that our judges were asked to rank 10 items and produced the following data:

	Object									
	A	B	D	C	E	H	J	G	F	I
Judge 1	1	2	3	4	5	6	7	8	9	10
Judge 2	2	1	5	3	4	6	7	9	8	10

Notice that the objects have been ordered by the ranks given by one of the judges and that lines have been drawn to connect comparable rankings. (Lines are not drawn when two judges give an object the same rank.)

The easiest way to calculate the number of inversions is to count the number of intersections of the lines. In this example, there are four intersections and therefore four inversions.

Kendall defined

$$\tau = 1 - \frac{2(\text{Number of inversions})}{\text{Number of pairs of objects}}$$

It is well known that the number of pairs of N objects is given by $N(N-1)/2$. Thus

$$\tau = 1 - \frac{2(\text{Number of inversions})}{N(N-1)/2}$$

For our example,

$$\tau = 1 - \frac{2(4)}{(10)(9)/2} = 1 - \frac{8}{45} = 1 - .178$$

$$= .822.$$

The interpretation of τ is more straightforward than was the interpretation of r_S calculated on the same data. If $\tau = .82$, we can state that if a pair of objects are sampled at random, the probability that the two judges will rank these objects in the same order is .82 higher than the probability that they will rank them in the reverse order.

When there are tied rankings, the calculation of τ must be modified. For the appropriate correction for ties, see Hays (1981, p. 602 ff).

Significance of τ

Unlike r_S, a test on the statistical significance of τ is easily obtained. It can be shown that the standard error of τ is given by

$$s_\tau = \sqrt{\frac{2(2N+5)}{9N(N-1)}}$$

Thus

$$z = \frac{\tau}{\sqrt{\frac{2(2N+5)}{9N(N-1)}}}$$

is a standard normal deviate and can be referred to Appendix z. For our example, $z = 0.822$ and $N = 10$. Therefore,

$$z = \frac{.822}{\sqrt{\frac{2(25)}{9(10)(9)}}} = \frac{.822}{\sqrt{\frac{50}{810}}} = 3.31$$

which is significant at well beyond $\alpha = .05$.

10.7 ESTIMATING ρ AND THE CHOICE AMONG COEFFICIENTS

When we have two or more statistics that appear to be measuring the same thing (estimating the same parameter), we usually choose between them on the basis of such characteristics as unbiasedness and efficiency. Thus, we chose $SS_X/(N-1)$ rather than SS_X/N as our estimate of σ_X^2 because the former was unbiased whereas the latter was not. Similarly, we chose the standard deviation over the mean absolute deviation partly because the former was more efficient.

When it comes to choosing among correlation coefficients, the issue is not as simple as it might first appear. We first have to decide just what parameter we want to estimate.

To look first at the standard treatment of the problem, consider that two variables (X and Y) represent a bivariate-normal distribution in the population. Thus X and Y are both continuous variables. We generally signify the correlation in the population between these two variables as ρ, but to be more specific we will label it ρ_{biv}, where the subscript *biv* indicates that this is the correlation from a bivariate normal distribution. Now suppose we drew a sample from this population. We could calculate a number of different correlation coefficients from the data. We could compute the usual Pearson r. Alternatively, we could dichotomize one variable and calculate r_b or r_{pb}. Furthermore, we could dichotomize both variables and calculate r_t or ϕ. Finally, we could convert our raw data to ranks and calculate r_S or τ. Suppose we calculated all of these coefficients and then repeated the whole procedure an infinite number of times, thus generating the sampling distribution of each statistic around the true value of ρ_{biv}.

The general conclusions from the results of carrying out this procedure are straightforward. We would find, as expected, that r is the best estimate of ρ_{biv}. Among the more derivative coefficients, we would find that τ was the next best (though not an unbiased) estimate of ρ_{biv}. We would also find that r_S is only slightly less good, that r_b is better than r_{pb}, and that r_t is better than ϕ.

The preceding paragraph may look as if it has answered our original question, but in fact it has not. It has answered the question only when the variables have a bivariate-normal distribution in the population, and when, at least in theory, we could measure these variables on a continuous scale. But suppose we were interested in correlating group membership (drug–no drug) with speed of learning. If a subject must be a member of one group or the other, there is no way that X can be thought of as a continuous variable, or that X and Y can have a bivariate-normal distribution in the population. In this case, it becomes meaningless to speak of ρ_{biv} as the parameter; and the value of r_{pb} as an estimate of ρ_{biv} is totally irrelevant. The parameter we really want to estimate is ρ_{pb}, the point-biserial correlation in the population. In this case, r_{pb} is a better estimator of the parameter than is r_b. With the appropriate changes in wording, the same kind of statement can be made for ϕ.

An interesting issue arises when we consider r_S and τ. If we think of the population consisting of bivariate pairs of ranks, we have a choice as to what we mean by the relevant parameter. Suppose we define two parameters, ρ_S and ρ_τ, corresponding to the calculation of Spearman's rank-order correlation and τ in the population. It turns out that τ is a better estimate of ρ_τ than r_S is of ρ_S. For this reason, there is a great deal to recommend a preference for τ over r_S when we want to correlate ranks.

The choice among coefficients also hinges on the interests of the experimenter and on the kinds of decisions he wants to make on the basis of his data. An interesting illustration of this is that Guilford and Fruchter (1973) use pass–fail on a test as an example of a variable for which r_{pb} is appropriate, whereas most books use this as an example for a variable that has an underlying normal distribution.

In most situations with dichotomous variables where prediction (or percentage of accountable variance) is our primary goal, the coefficients r_{pb} and ϕ are more appropriate in practice than are r_b or r_t, although some exceptions doubtlessly occur. For this reason, when we discuss multiple regression, we will invariably use r_{pb} and ϕ for dichotomous variables without pausing to consider the underlying nature of these variables.

10.8   KENDALL'S COEFFICIENT OF CONCORDANCE (W)

All of the statistics we have been concerned with in this chapter have dealt with the relationship between two sets of scores (X and Y). But suppose that instead of having two judges rank a set of objects, we had six judges doing the ranking. What we need is some measure of the degree to which the six judges agree. Such a measure is afforded by **Kendall's coefficient of concordance (W)**.

Kendall's coefficient of concordance (W)

Suppose, as an example, that we asked six judges to rank order the pleasantness of eight colored patches, and obtained the data in Table 10.4. If all of the judges had agreed that Patch B was the most pleasant, they would all have assigned it a rank of 1, and the column total for that patch across six judges would have been 6. Similarly, if A had been ranked second by everyone, its total would have been 12. Finally, if every judge assigned the highest rank to Patch G, its total would have been 48. In other words, the column totals would have shown considerable variability.

On the other hand, if the judges showed maximal disagreement, each column would have had some high ranks and some low ranks assigned to it, and the column totals

TABLE 10.4
Judges' rankings of pleasantness of colored patches

Judges		A	B	C	D	E	F	G	H
					Colored Patches				
1		1	2	3	4	5	6	7	8
2		2	1	5	4	3	8	7	6
3		1	3	2	7	5	6	8	4
4		2	1	3	5	4	7	8	6
5		3	1	2	4	6	5	7	8
6		2	1	3	6	5	4	8	7
	Σ	11	9	18	30	28	36	45	39

would have been roughly equal. Thus, the variability of the column totals, given disagreement (or random behavior) among judges, would be low.

Kendall used the variability of the column totals in deriving his statistic. He defined W as the ratio of the variability among columns to the maximum possible variability.

$$W = \frac{\text{Variance of column totals}}{\text{Maximum possible variance of column totals}}$$

Since we are dealing with ranks, we know what the maximum variance of the totals will be. Thus, we can define

$$W = \frac{12\Sigma T_j^2}{k^2 N(N^2 - 1)} - \frac{3(N + 1)}{N - 1}$$

where T_j represents the column totals, N = the number of items to be ranked, and k = the number of judges doing the ranking. For the data in Table 10.4,

$$\Sigma T_j^2 = 11^2 + 9^2 + 18^2 + 30^2 + 28^2 + 36^2 + 45^2 + 39^2 = 7052$$

$$W = \frac{12\Sigma T_j^2}{k^2 N(N^2 - 1)} - \frac{3(N + 1)}{N - 1}$$

$$= \frac{12(7052)}{6^2(8)(63)} - \frac{3(9)}{7} = \frac{84624}{18144} - \frac{27}{7} = 4.664 - 3.857$$

$$= .807$$

As you can see from the definition of W, it is not a standard correlation coefficient. It does have an interpretation in terms of a familiar statistic, however, in that it can be viewed as a function of the average Spearman correlation between all possible pairs of rankings. Specifically,

$$\bar{r}_S = \frac{kW - 1}{k - 1}$$

For our data,

$$\bar{r}_S = \frac{kW - 1}{k - 1} = \frac{6(.807) - 1}{5} = .768$$

Thus, if we took all possible pairs of rankings and computed r_S for each, the average r_S would be .768.

Hays (1981) recommends reporting W but converting to $\bar{r}_S$ for interpretation. Indeed, it is hard to disagree with that recommendation, since no intuitive meaning attaches to W itself. W does have the advantage of being bounded by zero and one, whereas $\bar{r}_S$ does not, but it is difficult to attach much practical meaning to the statement that the variance of column totals is 80.7% of the maximum possible variance. Whatever its faults, $\bar{r}_S$ seems preferable.

A test on the null hypothesis that there is no agreement among judges is possible under certain conditions. If $k \geq 7$, the quantity

$$\chi_{N-1}^2 = k(N - 1)W$$

is approximately distributed as χ^2 on $N - 1$ degrees of freedom. Such a test is seldom used, however, since W is usually calculated in those situations in which we seek a level of agreement substantially above the minimum level required for significance, and we rarely have seven or more judges.

KEY TERMS

Correlational measures (introduction)

Measures of association (introduction)

Validity (introduction)

Dichotomy (10.1)

Point-biserial coefficient (r_{pb}) (10.1)

Biserial correlation coefficient (r_b) (10.2)

ϕ (phi) coefficient (10.3)

Tetrachoric coefficient (r_t) (10.4)

Spearman's correlation coefficient for ranked data (r_S) (10.5)

Spearman's rho (10.5)

Ranking (10.5)

Kendall's τ (10.6)

Kendall's coefficient of concordance (W) (10.8)

EXERCISES

10.1   Some people think that they do their best work in the morning, whereas others claim that they do their best work at night. We have dichotomized 20 office workers into morning or evening people (0 = morning, 1 = evening) and have obtained independent estimates of the quality of work they produced on some specified *morning*. The ratings were based on a 100-point scale and appear below.

Peak time of day:
0 0 0 0 0 0 0 0 0 0 0 0 1 1 1 1 1 1 1

Performance rating:
65 80 55 60 55 70 60 70 55 70 40 70 50 40 60 50 40 50 40 60

(a) Plot these data and fit a regression line.
(b) Calculate r_{pb} and test it for significance.
(c) Interpret the results.

10.2   Because of a fortunate change in work schedules, we were able to reevaluate the subjects referred to in Exercise 10.1 for performance on the same tasks in the *evening*. The data are given below.

Peak time of day:
0 0 0 0 0 0 0 0 0 0 0 0 0 1 1 1 1 1 1 1

Performance rating:
40 60 40 50 30 40 50 50 20 30 40 50 30 30 50 50 40 50 40 60

(a) Plot these data and fit a regression line.
(b) Calculate r_{pb} and test it for significance.
(c) Interpret the results.

10.3   Compare the results you obtained in Exercises 10.1 and 10.2. What can you conclude?

10.4   Why would it not make sense to calculate a biserial correlation on the data in Exercises 10.1 and 10.2?

10.5   Perform a t test on the data in Exercise 10.1 and show the relationship between this value of t and r_{pb}.

10.6   A graduate-school admissions committee is concerned about the relationship between an applicant's GPA in college and whether or not the individual eventually completes the requirements for a doctoral degree. They first looked at the data on 25 randomly selected students who entered the program 7 years ago, assigning a score of 1 to those who completed the Ph.D. program, and of 0 to those who did not. The data follow.

GPA:

| 2.0 | 3.5 | 2.75 | 3.0 | 3.5 | 2.75 | 2.0 | 2.5 | 3.0 | 2.5 | 3.5 | 3.25 | 3.0 |

Ph.D.:

| 0 | 0 | 0 | 0 | 0 | 0 | 0 | 0 | 1 | 1 | 1 | 1 | 1 |

GPA:

| 3.0 | 2.75 | 3.25 | 3.0 | 3.33 | 2.5 | 2.75 | 2.0 | 4.0 | 3.0 | 3.25 | 2.5 |

Ph.D.:

| 1 | 1 | 1 | 1 | 1 | 1 | 1 | 1 | 1 | 1 | 1 | 1 |

(a) Plot the data.
(b) Calculate r_{pb}.
(c) Calculate r_b.
(d) Is it reasonable to look at r_b in this situation? Why or why not?

10.7   Compute the regression equation for the data in Exercise 10.6. Show that the line defined by this equation passes through the means of the two groups.

10.8   In terms of the data in Exercise 10.7, what do the slope and the intercept represent?

10.9   Assume that the committee in Exercise 10.6 decided that a GPA-score cutoff of 3.00 would be appropriate. In other words, they classed everyone with a GPA of 3.00 or higher as acceptable and those with a GPA below 3.00 as unacceptable. They then correlated this with completion of the Ph.D. program.
(a) Rescore the data in Exercise 10.6 as indicated.
(b) Run the correlation.
(c) Test this correlation for significance.

10.10 Visualize the data in Exercise 10.9 as fitting into a contingency table.
(a) Compute chi-square on this table.
(b) Show the relationship between chi-square and ϕ.

10.11 An investigator is interested in the relationship between alcoholism and a childhood history of attention deficient disorder ADD. He has collected the following data, where a 1 represents the presence of the relevant problem.

ADD:

| 0 | 1 | 0 | 0 | 1 | 1 | 0 | 0 | 0 | 1 | 0 | 0 | 1 | 0 | 0 | 1 |

Alcoholism:

| 0 | 1 | 0 | 0 | 0 | 1 | 0 | 0 | 0 | 1 | 1 | 0 | 0 | 0 | 0 | 1 |

ADD:

| 1 | 1 | 0 | 0 | 0 | 0 | 0 | 0 | 0 | 1 | 0 | 0 | 1 | 0 | 0 | 0 |

Alcoholism:

| 0 | 1 | 0 | 0 | 0 | 0 | 0 | 0 | 0 | 1 | 0 | 0 | 1 | 0 | 1 | 0 |

(a) What is the correlation between these two variables?

(b) Is the relationship significant?

10.12   An investigator wants to arrange the 15 items on her scale of language impairment on the basis of the order in which language skills appear in development. Not being entirely confident that she has selected the correct ordering of skills, she asks another professional to rank the items from 1 to 15 in terms of the order in which he thinks they should appear. The data are given below.

Investigator:

1	2	3	4	5	6	7	8	9	10	11	12	13	14	15

Consultant:

1	3	2	4	7	5	6	8	10	9	11	12	15	13	14

(a) Use Pearson's formula (r) to calculate Spearman's r_S.

(b) Rerun the calculation in (a) using the other formula for r_S given in the text.

10.13   For the data in Exercise 10.12,

(a) compute Kendall's τ.

(b) test τ for significance.

10.14   In a study of diagnostic processes, entering clinical graduate students are shown a 20-minute videotape of children's behavior and asked to rank-order 10 behavioral events on the tape in the order of the importance each has for a behavioral assessment. The data are then averaged to produce an average rank ordering for the entire class. The same thing was then done using experienced clinicians. The data follow.

Experienced clinicians:	1	3	2	7	5	4	8	6	9	10
New students:	2	4	1	6	5	3	10	8	7	9

Use Spearman's r_S to measure the agreement between experienced and novice clinicians.

10.15   Rerun the analysis on Exercise 10.14 using Kendall's τ.

10.16   Assume in Exercise 10.14 that there were five entering clinical students. They produced the following data:

Student 1:	1	4	2	6	5	3	9	10	7	8
Student 2:	4	3	2	5	7	1	10	8	6	9
Student 3:	1	5	2	6	4	3	8	10	7	9
Student 4:	2	5	1	7	4	3	10	8	6	9
Student 5:	2	5	1	4	6	3	9	7	8	10

Calculate Kendall's W and $\bar{r}_S$ for these data as a measure of agreement. Interpret your results.

COMPUTER EXERCISES

10.17   Using Mireault's data (Mireault.dat), calculate the point-biserial correlation between Gender and the Depression T score. Compare the relevant aspects of this question to the results you obtained in Exercise 7.49. (See "The Relationship Between r_{pb} and t" within Section 10.1.)

10.18   In Exercise 7.48 using Mireault.dat we compared the responses of students who had lost a parent and students who had not lost a parent in terms of their responses on the Global

Symptom Index T score (GSIT), among other variables. An alternative analysis would be to use a clinically meaningful cutoff on the GSIT, classifying anyone over that score as a clinical case (showing a clinically significant level of symptoms) and everyone below that score as a noncase. Derogatis (1983) has suggested a score of 63 as the cutoff (e.g., if GSIT > 63 then ClinCase $= 1$; else ClinCase $= 0$).

(a) Use any statistical package to create the variable of ClinCase, as defined by Derogatis. Then cross-tabulate ClinCase against Group. Compute chi-square and Cramer's ϕ.

(b) How does the answer to (a) compare to the answers obtained in Chapter 7?

(c) Why might we prefer this approach (looking at case versus noncase) over the procedure adopted in Chapter 7?

(*Hint*: When using BMDP, you will want to use BMDP4F. Minitab will use the "Tables" command; SAS will require Proc Freq; and SPSS^X will use CrossTabs. The appropriate manuals will help you set up the commands.)

10.19 Repeat the analysis shown in Exercise 10.18, only this time cross-tabulate ClinCase against Gender.

(a) Compare this answer with the results of Exercise 10.17.

(b) How does this analysis differ from the one in Exercise 10.17 on roughly the same question?

CHAPTER ELEVEN

SIMPLE ANALYSIS OF VARIANCE

OBJECTIVES *To introduce the analysis of variance as a procedure for testing differences among two or more means.*

CONTENTS

Analysis of variance (ANOVA)

The **analysis of variance (ANOVA)** has long enjoyed the status of being the most used (some would say abused) statistical technique in psychological research. The popularity and usefulness of this technique can be attributed to two sources. First, the analysis of variance, like *t*, deals with differences between or among sample means; unlike *t*, it imposes no restriction on the number of means. Instead of asking whether two means differ, we can ask whether three, four, five, or *k* means differ. The analysis of variance also allows us to deal with two or more independent variables simultaneously, asking not only about the individual effects of each variable separately but also about the interacting effects of two or more variables.

This chapter will be concerned with the underlying logic of the analysis of variance (which is really quite simple) and with the analysis of results of experiments employing only one independent variable. We will also examine a number of related topics that are most easily understood in the context of a **one-way** (one-variable) **analysis**. Subsequent chapters will deal with comparisons among individual sample means, with the

One-way analysis

analysis of experiments involving two or more independent variables, and with designs in which repeated measurements are made on each subject.

11.1   THE GENERAL APPROACH

Many features of the analysis of variance can be best illustrated by a simple example, so we will begin with a study by M. W. Eysenck (1974) on recall of verbal material as a function of the level of processing. The data we will use have the same group means and standard deviations as those reported by Eysenck, but the individual observations are fictional.

Craik and Lockhart (1972) proposed as a model of memory that the degree to which verbal material is remembered by the subject is a function of the degree to which it was processed when it was initially presented. Thus, for example, if you are trying to memorize a list of words, repeating a word to yourself (a low level of processing) would not lead to as good recall as thinking about the word and trying to form associations between that word and some other word. Eysenck (1974) was interested in testing this model and, more important, in looking to see whether it could help to explain reported differences between young and old subjects in their ability to recall verbal material. An examination of Eysenck's data on age differences will be postponed until Chapter 13; we will concentrate here on differences due to the level of processing.

Eysenck randomly assigned 50 subjects between the ages of 55 and 65 years to one of five groups—four incidental-learning groups and one intentional-learning group. (Incidental learning is learning in the absence of the expectation that the material will later need to be recalled.) The Counting group was asked to read through a list of words and simply count the number of letters in each word. This involved the lowest level of processing, since subjects did not need to deal with each word as anything more than a collection of letters. The Rhyming group was asked to read each word and think of a word that rhymed with it. This task involved considering the sound of each word, but not its meaning. The Adjective group had to process the words to the extent of giving an adjective that could reasonably be used to modify each word on the list. The Imagery group was instructed to try to form vivid images of each word. This was assumed to require the deepest level of processing of the four incidental conditions. None of these four groups were told that they would later be asked for recall of the items. Finally, the Intentional group was told to read through the list and to memorize the words for later recall. After subjects had gone through the list of 27 items three times, they were given a sheet of paper and asked to write down all of the words they could remember. If learning involves nothing more than being exposed to the material (the way most of us read a newspaper or, heaven forbid, a class assignment), then the five groups should have shown equal recall—after all, they all saw all of the words. If the level of processing of the material is important, then there should have been noticeable differences among the group means. The data are presented in Table 11.1.

TABLE 11.1
Number of words recalled as a function of level of processing

	Counting	Rhyming	Adjective	Imagery	Intentional	Total
	9	7	11	12	10	
	8	9	13	11	19	
	6	6	8	16	14	
	8	6	6	11	5	
	10	6	14	9	10	
	4	11	11	23	11	
	6	6	13	12	14	
	5	3	13	10	15	
	7	8	10	19	11	
	7	7	11	11	11	
Total	70	69	110	134	120	503
Mean	7.00	6.90	11.00	13.40	12.00	10.06
S.D.	1.83	2.13	2.49	4.50	3.74	4.01
Variance	3.33	4.54	6.22	20.27	14.00	16.058

THE NULL HYPOTHESIS

Eysenck was interested in testing the null hypothesis that the level of recall was equal under the five conditions. In other words, if μ_1 represents the population mean for all subjects who could potentially be tested under the counting condition, μ_2 represents the population mean corresponding to the rhyming condition, and so on up to μ_5 (for the intentional condition), then the null hypothesis is

$$H_0: \mu_1 = \mu_2 = \mu_3 = \mu_4 = \mu_5$$

The five hypothetical populations of recall scores are illustrated in Figure 11.1. The analysis of variance is a technique for using differences in sample means to draw inferences about the presence or absence of differences in population means. The null hypothesis could be false in a number of ways (e.g., all means could be different from each other, the first two could be equal to each other but different from the last three, and so on), but for now we are going to be concerned only with whether the null hypothesis is completely true or is false. In Chapter 12 we will deal with the problem of whether subsets of means are equal or different.

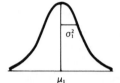 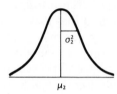 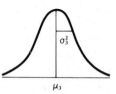 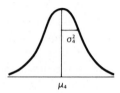 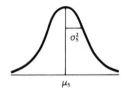

FIGURE 11.1 Graphical representation of populations of recall scores

THE ASSUMPTION OF NORMALITY

For reasons that will become clear when we do our final test of significance, we will make the assumption that recall scores are normally distributed around μ_j for each population. This is no more than the assumption that the distributions in Figure 11.1 are normally distributed. As with t, this assumption is more concerned with the sampling distribution of the mean than with the distribution of observations. Moreover, even substantial departures from normality may, under certain conditions, have remarkably little influence on the final result.

THE ASSUMPTION OF HOMOGENEITY OF VARIANCE

Our second major assumption will be that each of our populations of scores has the same variance, specifically

$$\sigma_1^2 = \sigma_2^2 = \sigma_3^2 = \sigma_4^2 = \sigma_5^2$$

Error variance

Here we will use the notation σ_e^2 to indicate the common value held by the five variances. The subscript e is an abbreviation for *error*; this variance is the **error variance**—the variance unrelated to any treatment differences. Homogeneity of variance would be expected to occur if the effect of a treatment is to add a constant to everyone's score—if, for example, everyone who thought of adjectives in Eysenck's study recalled five more words than they would otherwise have recalled. As we will later see, under certain conditions the assumption of homogeneity of variance can be relaxed without substantially damaging the final result.

THE ASSUMPTION OF INDEPENDENCE OF OBSERVATIONS

Our third important assumption is that the observations are all independent of one another. Thus, for any two observations within an experimental treatment, we assume that knowing how one of these observations stands relative to the treatment (or population) mean tells us nothing about the other observation. This is one of the important reasons why subjects are randomly assigned to groups. Violation of the independence assumption can have serious consequences for an analysis [see Kenny & Judd (1986)].

11.2   THE LOGIC OF THE ANALYSIS OF VARIANCE

The logic underlying the analysis of variance is really very simple, and once you understand it the rest of the discussion will make considerably more sense. Consider for a moment the effect of our three major assumptions—normality, homogeneity of variance, and the independence of observations. By making the first two of these assumptions we have said that the five distributions represented in Figure 11.1 have the same shape and dispersion. As a result, the only way left for them to differ is in terms of their means. (Recall that the normal distribution is a two-parameter distribution.)

We will begin by making no assumption concerning H_0—it may be true or false. For any one treatment, the variance of the 10 scores in that group would be an estimate of the variance of the population from which the scores were drawn. Because we have assumed that all populations have the same variance, it is also one estimate of the common population variance σ_e^2. If you prefer, you can think of

$$\sigma_1^2 \doteq s_1^2, \qquad \sigma_2^2 \doteq s_2^2, \qquad \ldots, \qquad \sigma_5^2 \doteq s_5^2$$

where $\doteq$ is read as "is estimated by". Because of our homogeneity assumption, all these are estimates of σ_e^2. For the sake of increased reliability, we can pool the five estimates by taking their mean, if $n_1 = n_2 = \cdots = n_5 = n$, and thus

$$\sigma_e^2 \doteq s^2 = \bar{s}_j^2 = \sum s_j^2/k$$

MS$_{\text{error}}$

MS$_{\text{within}}$

where k = the number of treatments (in this case, five).[†] This gives us one estimate of the population variance that we will later refer to as **MS$_{\text{error}}$** (read "mean square error"), or, sometimes, **MS$_{\text{within}}$**. It is important to note that this estimate does not depend on the truth or falsity of H_0, since s_j^2 is calculated on each sample separately. For the data from Eysenck's study, our pooled estimate of σ_e^2 will be

$$\sigma_e^2 \doteq (3.33 + 4.54 + 6.22 + 20.27 + 14.00)/5 = 9.67$$

Now let us assume that H_0 is true. If this is the case, then our five samples of 10 cases can be thought of as five independent samples from the same population (or, equivalently, from five identical populations), and we can produce another possible estimate of σ_e^2. Recall from Chapter 7 that the central limit theorem states that the variance of means drawn from the same population equals the variance of the population divided by the sample size. If H_0 is true, the sample means have been drawn from the same population (or identical ones, which amounts to the same thing), and therefore

$$\frac{\sigma_e^2}{n} \doteq s_{\bar{X}}^2$$

where n is the size of each sample. Thus, we can reverse the usual order of things and calculate the variance of our sample means ($s_{\bar{X}}^2$) to obtain a second estimate of σ_e^2:

$$\sigma_e^2 \doteq n s_{\bar{X}}^2$$

MS$_{\text{treatment}}$

This term is referred to as **MS$_{\text{treatment}}$**, often abbreviated as MS$_{\text{treat}}$; we will return to it shortly.

We now have two estimates of the population variance (σ_e^2). One of these estimates (MS$_{\text{error}}$) is independent of the truth or falsity of H_0. The other (MS$_{\text{treatment}}$) is an estimate of σ_e^2 only as long as H_0 is true (only as long as the conditions of the central limit theorem are met; namely, that the means are drawn from one population). Thus, if the two estimates agree, we will have support for the truth of H_0, and if they disagree, we will have support for the falsity of H_0.[‡]

[†] If the sample sizes were not equal, we would still average the five estimates, but in this case we would weight each estimate by the number of degrees of freedom for each sample—just as we did in Chapter 7—although here we have more groups.

[‡] Students often have trouble with the statement that "means are drawn from the same population" when we know in fact that they are often drawn from logically distinct populations. It seems silly to speak of means of males and females as coming from one population when we know that these are really two different populations of people. However, if the population of scores for females is exactly the same as the population of scores for males, then we can legitimately speak of these as being the identical (or the same) populations of *scores*, and we can behave accordingly.

Before we define *agreement* between two estimates, let us consider two other simple examples that have been constructed to have more or less ideal results under the conditions H_0: true and H_0: false. (In practice, data are never as neat as this.)

THE CASE OF A TRUE H_0

We have chosen data from three groups to resemble data that might be drawn from one normally distributed population with a mean (μ) of 5 and a variance (σ_e^2) of 10. The data are presented in Table 11.2a, where the notation $\overline{X}$. denotes the grand mean and $\overline{s}_j^2$ denotes the mean of the sample variances. From this table we can see that the average variance within each treatment is 9.250, a respectable estimate of $\sigma_e^2 = 10$. The variance of the group means is

$$\frac{(6.333 - 5.333)^2 + (4.333 - 5.333)^2 + (5.333 - 5.333)^2}{3 - 1} = \frac{1 + 1 + 0}{2} = 1.00$$

and since we know H_0 to be true,

$$\frac{\sigma_e^2}{n} \doteq s_{\overline{X}}^2$$

$$\sigma_e^2 \doteq n(s_{\overline{X}}^2) = 9(1) = 9$$

This value is also reasonably in agreement with σ_e^2 and with our other estimate based on the variability within treatments. Since these two estimates are in agreement, we would conclude that we have no reason to doubt the truth of H_0.

THE CASE OF A FALSE H_0

Next we consider an example where we know H_0 to be false. By adding constants to the data in Table 11.2a, I produced the data in Table 11.2b, which might have come about by sampling Treatment 1 scores from a population that is $N(8, 10)$,[†] treatment 2 scores from $N(4, 10)$, and Treatment 3 scores from $N(4, 10)$. This represents a substantial departure from H_0.

In Table 11.2b notice that the variance within each treatment remains unchanged, since adding or subtracting a constant has no effect on the variance. This illustrates my earlier statement that the variance within groups is independent of the truth or falsity of the null hypothesis. The variance among the treatment means, however, has increased substantially, reflecting the difference among the population means. In this case, the estimate of σ_e^2 based on the sample means is $9(6.333) = 57$, a value that is way out of line with the estimate of 9.25 given by the variance within groups. The logical conclusion would be that $s_{\overline{X}}^2$ is estimating not merely the population variance (σ_e^2), but σ_e^2 plus the variance of the population means themselves. (In fact, we know this to be the case, since the data have been deliberately manufactured for this purpose.)

[†] Recall from Chapter 3 that $N(8, 10)$ denotes a distribution that is normally distributed with a mean of 8 and a variance of 10.

TABLE 11.2
Illustration of MS_{error} and MS_{treat} with true and false null hypotheses

(a) Representative Data for Case Where H_0: True

	Treatment 1	Treatment 2	Treatment 3	
	3	1	5	
	6	4	2	
	9	7	8	
	6	4	8	
	3	1	2	
	12	10	8	
	6	4	5	
	3	1	2	
	9	7	8	
$\overline{X}_j$	6.333	4.333	5.333	$\overline{X}. = 5.333$
s_j^2	10.000	10.000	7.750	$\bar{s}_j^2 = 9.250$

$$s_{\overline{X}}^2 = \frac{\Sigma(\overline{X}_j - \overline{X}.)^2}{k - 1} = 1.000$$

$$\bar{s}_j^2 = \frac{10.00 + 10.00 + 7.75}{3} = 9.25$$

$$MS_{error} = \bar{s}_j^2 = 9.25$$

$$MS_{treat} = ns_{\overline{X}}^2 = 9(1) = 9$$

(b) Representative Data for Case Where H_0: False

	Treatment 1	Treatment 2	Treatment 3	
	5	0	5	
	8	3	2	
	11	6	8	
	8	3	8	
	5	0	2	
	14	9	8	
	8	3	5	
	5	0	2	
	11	6	8	
$\overline{X}_j$	8.333	3.333	5.333	$\overline{X}. = 5.666$
s_j^2	10.000	10.000	7.750	$\bar{s}_j^2 = 9.250$

$$s_{\overline{X}}^2 = \frac{\Sigma(\overline{X}_j - \overline{X}.)^2}{k - 1} = 6.333$$

$$\bar{s}_j^2 = \frac{10.00 + 10.00 + 7.75}{3} = 9.25$$

$$MS_{error} = \bar{s}_j^2 = 9.25$$

$$MS_{treat} = ns_{\overline{X}}^2 = 9(6.333) = 57$$

SUMMARY OF THE LOGIC OF THE ANALYSIS OF VARIANCE

From the preceding discussion, we can concisely state the logic of the analysis of variance. To test H_0, we calculate two estimates of the population variance—one that is independent of the truth or falsity of H_0, and another that is dependent on H_0. If the two estimates agree, we have no reason to reject H_0. If they disagree sufficiently, we conclude that underlying treatment differences must have contributed to our second estimate, inflating it and causing it to differ from the first. Therefore, we reject H_0.

VARIANCE ESTIMATION

Treatment effect

We will return later to the theory underlying the analysis of variance, but it might be helpful at this point to state without proof the two values that we are really estimating. We will first define the **treatment effect**, denoted τ_j, as $(\mu_j - \mu)$, the difference between the mean of treatment$_j$ (μ_j) and the grand mean (μ), and we will define σ_τ^2 as the variance of the true populations' means ($\mu_1, \mu_2, \ldots, \mu_5$).[†]

$$\sigma_\tau^2 = \frac{\Sigma(\mu_j - \mu)^2}{k - 1} = \frac{\Sigma\tau_j^2}{k - 1}$$

Expected value

In addition, recall that we defined the **expected value** of a statistic [written $E(\ )$] as its long-range average—the average value that statistic would assume over repeated sampling, and thus our best guess as to its value on any particular trial. With these two concepts we can state

$$E(\text{MS}_{\text{error}}) = \sigma_e^2$$

$$E(\text{MS}_{\text{treat}}) = \sigma_e^2 + n\sigma_\tau^2$$

where σ_e^2 is the variance within each population and σ_τ^2 is the variance of the population means (μ_j).

Now, if H_0 is true and $\mu_1 = \mu_2 = \cdots = \mu_5 = \mu$, then $\sigma_\tau^2 = 0$,

$$E(\text{MS}_{\text{error}}) = \sigma_e^2$$

and

$$E(\text{MS}_{\text{treat}}) = \sigma_e^2 + n(0) = \sigma_e^2$$

and thus

$$E(\text{MS}_{\text{error}}) = E(\text{MS}_{\text{treat}})$$

Keep in mind that these are expected values; rarely in practice will the two sample-based mean squares be equal.

[†] Technically, σ_τ^2 is not actually a variance, since, having the actual parameter (μ), we should be dividing by k instead of $k - 1$. Nonetheless, we lose very little by thinking of it as a variance, as long as we keep in mind precisely what we have done. This point will reappear when we discuss ways of estimating the magnitude of an experimental effect.

If H_0 is false, however, the σ_τ^2 will not be zero, but some positive number. In this case,

$$E(MS_{error}) < E(MS_{treat})$$

since MS_{treat} will contain a nonzero term representing the true differences among the μ_j.

To illustrate, we can return to the example in Table 11.2b. For these data, $\sigma_e^2 = 10$ and $\mu_1 = 8$, $\mu_2 = 4$, $\mu_3 = 4$. The variance of the μ_j, denoted σ_τ^2, is found to be $\Sigma(\mu_j - \mu)^2/(k - 1) = 5.33$. Thus,

$$MS_{error} = 9.25 \qquad E(MS_{error}) = \sigma_e^2 = 10.00$$

$$MS_{treat} = 57.00 \qquad E(MS_{treat}) = \sigma_e^2 + n\sigma_\tau^2 = 10 + 9(5.33) = 58.00$$

Here we can see the way in which MS_{treat} reflects the falsity of H_0.

11.3   CALCULATIONS IN THE ANALYSIS OF VARIANCE

At this point we will return to the example from Eysenck to illustrate the calculations used in the analysis of variance. The data have been reproduced in Table 11.3, with the resulting computations, which we will discuss in detail.

SUM OF SQUARES

Sums of squares

In the analysis of variance much of our computation deals with **sums of squares**. As we saw in Chapter 9, a sum of squares is merely the sum of the squared deviations about the mean $[\Sigma(X - \overline{X})^2]$ or, more often, some multiple of that. Sums of squares have the advantage of being additive, whereas mean squares and variances are additive only if they happen to be based on the same number of degrees of freedom. When we first defined the sample variance, we saw that

$$s_X^2 = \frac{\Sigma(X - \overline{X})^2}{n - 1} = \frac{\Sigma X^2 - (\Sigma X)^2/n}{n - 1}$$

Here, the numerator is the *sum of squares* of X and the denominator is the degrees of freedom.

TOTALS

Although we have been speaking in terms of treatment *means*, we will actually carry out our calculations in terms of treatment *totals*. This distinction is one of convenience rather than substance, however, since totals are linearly related to means. If two groups of the same size have different means, they obviously have different totals.

TABLE 11.3
Data and computations for example from Eysenck (1974)

(a) Data

	Counting	Rhyming	Adjective	Imagery	Intentional	Total	
	9	7	11	12	10		
	8	9	13	11	19		
	6	6	8	16	14		
	8	6	6	11	5		
	10	6	14	9	10		
	4	11	11	23	11		
	6	6	13	12	14		
	5	3	13	10	15		
	7	8	10	19	11		
	7	7	11	11	11		
Total (T_j)	70	69	110	134	120	503	$= \Sigma X$
Mean	7.00	6.90	11.00	13.40	12.00	10.06	
S.D.	1.83	2.13	2.49	4.50	3.74	4.01	
Variance	3.33	4.54	6.22	20.27	14.00	16.058	

(b) Computations

$$SS_{total} = \sum X^2 - \frac{(\Sigma X)^2}{N} = (9^2 + 8^2 + \cdots + 11^2) - \frac{503^2}{50}$$

$$= 5847 - 5060.18 = 786.82$$

$$SS_{treat} = \frac{\Sigma T_j^2}{n} - \frac{(\Sigma X)^2}{N} = \frac{(70^2 + 69^2 + 110^2 + 134^2 + 120^2)}{10} - \frac{503^2}{50}$$

$$= 5411.7 - 5060.18 = 351.52$$

$$SS_{error} = SS_{total} - SS_{treat} = 786.82 - 351.52 = 435.30$$

(c) Summary Table

Source	df	SS	MS	F
Treatments	4	351.52	87.88	9.08
Error	45	435.30	9.67	
Total	49	786.82		

When we go from using means to using totals, we need to make only minor changes in our computational formulas. We saw earlier that

$$\sigma_e^2 \doteq n s_{\bar{X}}^2$$

In other words, we multiply the variance of means by n to produce an estimate of σ_e^2. If we are to work with totals, their variances will be not $s_{\bar{X}}^2$, but rather s_T^2, where the subscript T refers to *totals*. It is not difficult to show that

$$\sigma_e^2 \doteq \frac{s_T^2}{n}$$

The proof of this lies in the fact that a total is n times the mean ($\overline{X} = \Sigma X/n; \ n\overline{X} = \Sigma X$), and when we multiply by a constant we multiply the variance by the square of the constant. Thus,

$$s_T^2 = n^2 s_{\overline{X}}^2$$

$$\frac{s_T^2}{n^2} = s_{\overline{X}}^2$$

and therefore

$$\sigma_e^2 \doteq ns_{\overline{X}}^2 = \frac{ns_T^2}{n^2} = \frac{s_T^2}{n}$$

Thus, we will divide the variance of totals by n to produce an estimate of σ_e^2.

Note carefully that n appears in the denominator when we use totals. As will be apparent in the next several chapters, strange-looking divisors keep appearing in formulas for sums of squares. These formulas are readily understood if you keep in mind that the divisors are directly analogous to n in the previous equation. In each case, we are merely dividing by the number of observations on which the total is based, so as eventually to convert a variance of totals into an estimate of σ_e^2.

TERMINOLOGY

Correction factor (CF)

In Table 11.3a we see the observations, the individual treatment totals (T_j), the grand total (ΣX), and what is sometimes called the **correction factor (CF)** for Eysenck's data. The correction factor is always equal to $(\Sigma X)^2/N$ and is frequently denoted as CF. The notation T_j will be used to represent the total of the jth treatment throughout the discussion of the analysis of variance. Although it would be somewhat more correct to speak of the jth treatment total as $\Sigma_{i=1}^{n} X_{ij}$, such a notational system can become exceedingly awkward. In later analyses, where there is more than one independent variable, T_j can be extended to T_{row} and T_{column} without confusion and without any loss of generality.

Since these actual data points are fictitious (although the means and variances are not), there is little to be gained by examining the distribution of observations within individual groups—the data were actually drawn from a normally distributed population. With real data, however, it is important to examine these distributions first to make sure that they are not seriously skewed or bimodal and, even more important, that they are not skewed in different directions. Even for this example, it is useful to examine the individual group variances as a check on the assumption of homogeneity of variance. Although the variances are not as similar as we might like (the variance for imagery is noticeably larger than the others), they do not appear to be so drastically different as to cause concern. As we will see later, the analysis of variance is robust against violations of assumptions, especially when we have the same number of observations in each group.

Table 11.3b shows the calculations required to perform a one-way analysis of variance. These calculations require some elaboration.

SS_{total}

The SS_{total} (read "sum of squares total") represents the sum of squares of all the observations, regardless of which treatment produced them. It is always calculated as the sum of all the squared observations, minus the sum of the observations squared over N:

$$SS_{total} = \sum X^2 - \frac{(\Sigma X)^2}{N}$$

We saw this term in earlier chapters; it was defined as $\Sigma(X - \overline{X})^2$, which is algebraically equivalent to the definition given here.

SS_{treat}

The SS_{treat} term is a measure of differences due to treatments and is directly related to the variability of treatment totals. To calculate SS_{treat}, simply square and sum each treatment total, divide by the number of observations on which each total is based (in this case n) and subtract $(\Sigma X)^2/N$. To gain a better appreciation of exactly what SS_{treat} represents, we will write the formula for it somewhat differently:

$$SS_{treat} = \frac{\Sigma T_j^2}{n} - \frac{(\Sigma X)^2}{N} = \frac{\Sigma T_j^2}{n} - \frac{(\Sigma T_j)^2}{nk}$$

$$= \frac{\Sigma T_j^2 - \frac{(\Sigma T_j)^2}{k}}{n} = \frac{\Sigma(T_j - \overline{T})^2}{n}$$

From this last equation, we can see that SS_{treat} represents the sum of squared deviations of the treatment totals about the mean of the totals $(\overline{T})$, divided by n. The n in this case is the same divisor that we discussed in connection with the central limit theorem. Its purpose is eventually to produce an estimate of σ_e^2 rather than of σ_T^2. In all the sums of squares we are to discuss in this book, the same general principle applies.

GENERAL RULE FOR CALCULATING ANY SUM OF SQUARES

In conjunction with our discussion of SS_{treat}, it is now possible to state a general rule for calculating any sum of squares (SS); with the possible exception of those that we will later calculate by subtraction:

For any SS, square the relevant totals, divide by the number of observations on which each total is based, sum the results, and subtract $\Sigma X^2/N$.

There are only a handful of exceptions; they deal with the case of more than one independent variable with unequal numbers of subjects in the different treatment combinations. Otherwise, this rule will allow you to calculate any SS in any problem, no matter how complex the experimental design. This rule applies in the case of SS_{total} as well, although there the divisor is 1 and is not usually shown.

SS_{error}

In practice, SS_{error} is obtained by subtraction. Since it can be easily shown that

$$SS_{total} = SS_{treat} + SS_{error}$$

then it must also be true that

$$SS_{error} = SS_{total} - SS_{treat}$$

This is the procedure presented in Table 11.3. An alternative approach is available, however. As you will recall from earlier discussions, we seek a term that is not influenced by differences among treatments, and therefore a term that represents the variability within each of the five treatments separately. To this end, we could calculate a sum of squares within the counting treatment ($SS_{within\ Counting}$) and a similar term for the SS within each of the other treatments.

$$SS_{within\ Counting} = (9^2 + 8^2 + \cdots + 7^2) - \frac{70^2}{10}$$

$$= 520 - 490 = 30.00$$

$$SS_{within\ Rhyming} = (7^2 + 9^2 + \cdots + 7^2) - \frac{69^2}{10}$$

$$= 517 - 476.1 = 40.90$$

$$SS_{within\ Adjective} = (11^2 + 13^2 + \cdots + 11^2) - \frac{110^2}{10}$$

$$= 1266 - 1210 = 56.00$$

$$SS_{within\ Imagery} = (12^2 + 11^2 + \cdots + 11^2) - \frac{134^2}{10}$$

$$= 1978 - 1795.6 = 182.40$$

$$SS_{within\ Intentional} = (10^2 + 19^2 + \cdots + 11^2) - \frac{120^2}{10}$$

$$= 1566 - 1440 = \underline{126.00}$$

$$SS_{error} = 435.30$$

When we sum these individual terms, we obtain 435.30, which agrees with the answer we obtained in Table 11.3.

THE SUMMARY TABLE

Summary table
Table 11.3c shows the **summary table** for the analysis of variance. It is called a summary table for the rather obvious reason that it summarizes a series of calculations, making it possible to tell at a glance what the data have to offer.

SOURCES OF VARIATION   The first column of the summary table contains the sources of variation—the word variation being synonymous with the phrase "sum of squares." As can be seen from the table, there are three sources of variation: the variation due to treatments (variation among treatment means), the variation due to error (variation within the treatments), and the total variation. These sources reflect the fact that we have partitioned the total sum of squares into two portions, one representing variability within the individual groups and the other representing variability among the several groups.

DEGREES OF FREEDOM   The degrees of freedom column in Table 11.3c represents the allocation of the total number of degrees of freedom between the two sources of variation. With 49 df overall (i.e., $N - 1$), four of these are associated with differences among treatments and the remaining 45 are associated with variability within the treatment groups. The calculation of df is probably the easiest part of our task. The
df_{total}
df_{treat}
df_{error}
total degrees of freedom (df_{total}) are always $N - 1$, where N is the total number of observations. The degrees of freedom between treatments (df_{treat}) are always equal to $k - 1$, where k is the number of treatments. The degrees of freedom for error (df_{error}) are most easily thought of as what is left over and are obtained by subtracting df_{treat} from df_{total}. However, they can be calculated more directly as the sum of the degrees of freedom within each treatment.

Rather than learning a set of equations for calculating degrees of freedom (a most unsatisfactory undertaking), it is important only that you understand the rationale underlying the allocation of df. SS_{total} is the sum of N squared deviations around one point—the grand mean. The fact that we have taken deviations around this one (estimated) point has cost us 1 df, leaving us with $N - 1$ df. SS_{treat} is the sum of k deviations around one point (again the grand mean), and again we have lost 1 df in estimating this point, leaving us with $k - 1$ df. SS_{error} represents N deviations about k points (the k treatment means), losing us k df and leaving $N - k = k(n - 1)$ df.

To put this in a slightly different form, the total variability is based on N scores and therefore has $N - 1$ df. The variability of treatment means is based on k scores (means or total) and therefore has $k - 1$ df. The variability within any one treatment is based on n scores, and thus has $n - 1$ df, but since we sum k of these within-treatment terms, we will have k times $n - 1 = k(n - 1)$ df.

MEAN SQUARES   We will now go to the MS column in Table 11.3c. (There is little to be said about the column labeled SS; it simply contains the sums of squares obtained in Table 11.3b.)

The column of mean squares contains our two estimates of σ_e^2. These values are obtained by dividing the sums of squares by their corresponding df. Thus, $351.52/4 = 87.88$ and $435.30/45 = 9.67$. We typically do not calculate a MS_{total}, since we have no use for it. If we were to do so, this term would equal $786.82/49 = 16.058$, which, as you can see from Table 11.3a, is the variance of all N observations, regardless of treatment.

Although it is true that mean squares are variance estimates, it is important to keep in mind what variances these terms are estimating. Thus, MS_{error} is an estimate of the population variance, regardless of the truth or falsity of H_0, and is actually the average of the variances within each group when the sample sizes are equal.

$$MS_{error} = (3.33 + 4.54 + 6.22 + 20.27 + 14.00)/5 = 9.67$$

However, MS_{treat} is not the variance of treatment means or totals but rather is the variance of those means (or totals) corrected by n to produce an estimate of the population variance (σ_e^2).

THE F STATISTIC   The last column in Table 11.3c, labeled F, is the most important one in terms of testing the null hypothesis. F is obtained by dividing MS_{treat} by MS_{error}. There is a precise way and a sloppy way to explain why this ratio makes sense, and we will start with the latter. As said earlier, MS_{error} is an estimate of the population variance (σ_e^2). I also said that MS_{treat} is an estimate of the population variance (σ_e^2) *if* H_0 is true, but not if it is false. If H_0 is true, then MS_{error} and MS_{treat} are both estimating the same thing, and as such they should be approximately equal. If this is the case, the ratio of one to the other will be approximately 1, give or take a certain amount for sampling error. Thus, all we have to do is to compute our ratio and determine whether it is close enough to 1 to indicate support for the null hypothesis.

So much for the informal way of looking at F. A more precise approach starts with the *expected mean squares* for error and treatments. From earlier in the chapter, we know

$$E(MS_{error}) = \sigma_e^2$$

$$E(MS_{treat}) = \sigma_e^2 + n\sigma_\tau^2$$

If we now form the ratio

$$\frac{E(MS_{treat})}{E(MS_{error})} = \frac{\sigma_e^2 + n\sigma_\tau^2}{\sigma_e^2}$$

the only time this ratio would have an expectation of 1 is when $\sigma_\tau^2 = 0$—that is, when H_0 is true and $\mu_1 = \cdots = \mu_5$.[†] When $\sigma_\tau^2 > 0$, the expectation will be greater than 1.

The question that remains, however, is, How large a ratio will we accept without

---

[†] As an aside, note that the expected value of F is not precisely 1 under H_0, although

$$\frac{E(MS_{treat})}{E(MS_{error})} = 1$$

if $\sigma_\tau^2 = 0$. To be exact, under H_0

$$E(F) = \frac{df_{error}}{df_{error} - 2}$$

For all practical purposes, nothing is sacrificed by thinking of F as having an expectation of 1 under H_0 and greater than 1 under H_1 (the alternative hypothesis).

rejecting H_0 when we use not *expected* values but mean squares, which are obtained from data and are therefore subject to sampling error? The answer to this question lies in the fact that we can show that the ratio

$$F = \frac{MS_{treat}}{MS_{error}}$$

is distributed as F on $k - 1$ and $k(n - 1)$ df. This is the same F distribution as that discussed earlier in conjunction with testing the ratio of two variances (which in fact is what we are doing here). Note that the degrees of freedom represent the df associated with the numerator and denominator, respectively.

For our example, $F = 9.08$. We have 4 df for the numerator and 45 df for the denominator, and can enter the F table (Appendix F) with these values. From Appendix F, the critical values for $\alpha = .05$ and $\alpha = .01$ for 4 and 45 df are, with linear interpolation, $F_{.05}(4, 45) = 2.58$ and $F_{.01}(4, 45) = 3.78$. Thus, whether we had chosen to work at $\alpha = .05$ or $\alpha = .01$, we would reject H_0 and conclude that there were significant differences among the treatment means.

CONCLUSIONS

On the basis of a significant value of F, we have rejected the null hypothesis that the treatment means in the population are equal. Strictly speaking, this conclusion indicates that at least one of the population means is different from at least one other mean, but we don't know exactly which means are different from which other means. We will pursue that topic in Chapter 12. It is evident from an examination of the data in Table 11.3, however, that increased processing of the material is associated with increased levels of recall. For example, a strategy that involves associating images with items to be recalled leads to nearly twice as good recall as does merely counting the letters in the items. Results such as these give us important hints about how to go about learning any material, and highlight the poor recall to be expected from passive studying. Good recall, whether it be of lists of words or of complex statistical concepts, requires active and "deep" processing of the material, which is in turn facilitated by noting associations between the to-be-learned material and other material.

11.4 THE STRUCTURAL MODEL

Structural model

Although we will not develop the statistical theory of the analysis of variance in detail, some insight into the underlying **structural model** on which the analysis is based is essential. For the student who wishes a more complete understanding of the theory, Winer (1962, 1971) covers this material in more depth but at a reasonably readable level. The model we are interested in states that

$$X_{ij} = \mu + \tau_j + e_{ij}$$

where

$$X_{ij} = \text{the observation for the } i\text{th subject in the } j\text{th treatment}$$

$$\mu = \text{the grand mean}$$

$$\tau_j = \text{the treatment effect associated with the } j\text{th treatment}$$
$$(\tau_j = \mu_j - \mu)$$

and

$$e_{ij} = \text{the unit of error associated with the } i\text{th subject in the } j\text{th treatment}$$

Regardless of the truth or falsity of H_0,

$$\mu = (\mu_1 + \mu_2 + \cdots + \mu_k)/k$$

and

$$\tau_j = \mu_j - \mu$$

In our equation for X_{ij}, we have a model that states that an observation is based on three components. One component (μ) is constant over all observations and treatments. The second component (τ_j) is constant *within* a treatment, but not between treatments. The third component (e_{ij}) varies across all observations and treatments. This model is really no more than a way of expressing a very simple idea. If you are a 69-inch-tall male, your height can be represented as the mean height of the population (66 inches), plus the difference between the mean height of all males and the mean height of the population ($+2$ inches), plus the difference between you and the "average male" ($+1$ inch). Letting X designate your height, we can represent it as

If we add the restriction that the e_{ij} are normally distributed about zero independently of τ_j (which is to say that male heights are normally distributed around μ_{male} and female heights are normally distributed around μ_{female}), then it is possible from this simple model to derive the analysis of variance described previously. It is important to note, however, just what restrictions we have made. To assume that the e_{ij} are normally distributed is to assume that the populations are normally distributed, since within a treatment the only variable part of the model is e_{ij}. Furthermore, to assume that τ_j and e_{ij} are independent is equivalent to the assumption of homogeneity of variance—that variability does not change as a function of treatments. As we examine more complex experimental designs in the analysis of variance, the models will also become more complex. Differences among models, however, are quantitative rather than qualitative—we will add more terms, but the basic idea will remain the same.

The model we are discussing leads directly to the statement made earlier that $SS_{total} = SS_{treat} + SS_{error}$, and this in turn produces the analysis of variance. To prove this, we will start with the basic model

$$X_{ij} = \mu + \tau_j + e_{ij}$$

If we substitute the relevant statistics in place of the parameters, we obtain

$$X_{ij} = \overline{X}. + (\overline{X}_j - \overline{X}.) + (X_{ij} - \overline{X}_j)$$

where $\overline{X}.$ represents the grand mean. This expression is an identity, as is readily seen by removing the parentheses and collecting terms. Subtracting $\overline{X}.$ from both sides, we have

$$(X_{ij} - \overline{X}.) = (\overline{X}_j - \overline{X}.) + (X_{ij} - \overline{X}_j)$$

This equation states that the deviation of a subject's score from the grand mean is equal to the deviation of his group's mean from the grand mean plus the deviation of his score from the group mean, and again is an identity. These last two equations are illustrated geometrically in Figure 11.2. If we square both sides of the equation, we obtain

$$(X_{ij} - \overline{X}.)^2 = (\overline{X}_j - \overline{X}.)^2 + (X_{ij} - \overline{X}_j)^2 + 2(\overline{X}_j - \overline{X}.)(X_{ij} - \overline{X}_j)$$

Summing this expression over subjects (i) and treatments (j) produces

$$\sum\sum_{ij}(X_{ij} - \overline{X}.)^2 = \sum\sum_{ij}(\overline{X}_j - \overline{X}.)^2 + \sum\sum_{ij}(X_{ij} - \overline{X}_j)^2 + 2\sum\sum_{ij}(\overline{X}_j - \overline{X}.)(X_{ij} - \overline{X}_j)$$

The last term will be zero and will drop out, leaving

$$\sum\sum_{ij}(X_{ij} - \overline{X}.)^2 = \sum\sum_{ij}(\overline{X}_j - \overline{X}.)^2 + \sum\sum_{ij}(X_{ij} - \overline{X}_j)^2$$

But within any treatment $(\overline{X}_j - \overline{X}.)$ is a constant, and as a result we have

$$\sum\sum_{ij}(X_{ij} - \overline{X}.)^2 = n\sum_j(\overline{X}_j - \overline{X}.)^2 + \sum\sum_{ij}(X_{ij} - \overline{X}_j)^2$$

$$SS_{total} \qquad = \qquad SS_{treat} \qquad + \qquad SS_{error}$$

Thus we have shown not only that the total sum of squares is completely partitioned into SS_{treat} and SS_{error}, but also that all of this can be derived on the basis of our underlying structural model using simple algebra. From here, we could proceed to obtain our mean squares and F.

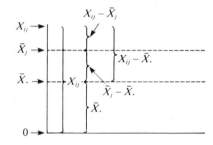

FIGURE 11.2
Geometric representation of the analysis of variance model

11.5   UNEQUAL SAMPLE SIZES

Most experiments are originally designed with the idea of collecting the same number of observations in each treatment. Frequently, however, things do not work out that way. Subjects fail to arrive for testing, or are eliminated because they fail to follow instructions. Animals occasionally become ill during an experiment from causes that have nothing to do with the treatment. There is even a case in the literature in which an animal was eliminated from the study for repeatedly biting the experimenter (Sgro & Weinstock, 1963). Moreover, studies conducted on intact groups, such as school classes, have to contend with the fact that such groups nearly always vary in size.

If the sample sizes are not equal, the analysis discussed earlier is not appropriate without modification. For the case of one independent variable, however, this modification is relatively minor.

Earlier we defined

$$SS_{treat} = \frac{\Sigma T_j^2}{n} - \frac{(\Sigma X)^2}{N}$$

We were able to divide each of the T_j^2 (and therefore ΣT_j^2) by n, because n was common to all treatments. If the sample sizes differ, however, and we define n_j as the number of subjects in the jth treatment ($\Sigma n_j = N$), we can rewrite the expression as

$$SS_{treat} = \Sigma \left(\frac{T_j^2}{n_j} \right) - \frac{(\Sigma X)^2}{N}$$

which, when all n_j are equal, reduces to the original equation.

To appreciate what this formula does, we can speak in terms of means rather than totals, in which case the formula is equivalent to

$$SS_{treat} = \Sigma n_j (\overline{X}_j - \overline{X}.)^2$$

(The proof of this expression is not difficult, and it is left to you.) This last expression shows us that with unequal ns, the deviation of each treatment mean from the grand mean is weighted by the sample size. Thus, the larger the size of one sample relative to the others, the more it will contribute to SS_{treat}.

EFFECTS OF THC ON ACTIVITY IN RATS

The following example illustrates the calculation of a one-way analysis of variance with unequal sample sizes. At the same time, it provides a second example of many of the ideas already presented.

The nucleus accumbens is a forebrain structure that has been shown to be involved in locomotor activity in rats. Systemic administrations of low doses of tetrahydrocannabinol (THC, the major active ingredient in marijuana) is known to increase locomotor activity, whereas high doses lead to a decrease in activity. In an attempt to examine whether THC is acting within the nucleus accumbens to produce its effects on activity, Conti and Musty (1984) bilaterally injected either a placebo, or 0.1, 0.5, 1, or 2 micrograms (μg) of THC into the nucleus accumbens of rats. The investigators recorded the activity level of animals before and after the injection. Activity was recorded by placing the animal in a test chamber and suspending the chamber on rubber mounts. The vibrations of the chamber as the animal moved around were transduced by an accelerometer and converted to activity units, which were read off a meter. These units, then, were arbitrary, a point that will become relevant when we consider transformations. Conti and Musty took as their dependent variable the rat's activity for 10 minutes after the injection as a proportion of the rat's activity in the 10 minutes before the injection. Since animals generally decrease their activity as they become accustomed to an apparatus, most ratios were less than 1. However, it was expected that those rats with intermediate levels of THC would decrease their activity less (exhibit a higher postinjection $\div$ preinjection ratio) than would those with either low or high levels. (Intermediate levels were expected to lead to the greatest activity, because very low doses should be insufficient to produce an effect and high doses should lead to decreases in activity.)

The data for this study are presented in Table 11.4a. The decimal points have been omitted from the proportions for ease of calculation, but this will have no effect on the results—all sums of squares will be affected equally and the resulting F value will be the same as it would be if the decimals were used. Table 11.4b shows boxplots for the individual groups. Although there are too few data points to say much about the shape of the distributions, it would appear that there is a slight negative skewness in all the groups, as judged by the location of the median within the box. The fact that the skewness is in the same direction for all groups and that it is not serious suggests that we can go ahead and run an analysis of variance.

TABLE 11.4
Data and calculations from study by Conti and Musty (1984)

(a) Data

	Control	0.1 μg	0.5 μg	1 μg	2 μg	All Groups
	30	60	71	33	36	
	27	42	50	78	27	
	52	48	38	71	60	
	38	52	59	58	51	
	20	28	65	35	29	
	26	93	58	35	34	
	8	32	74	46	24	
	41	46	67	32	17	
	49	63	61		50	
	49	44			53	
Total	340	508	543	388	381	2160
Mean	34.00	50.80	60.33	48.50	38.10	45.96
S.D.	14.30	18.39	11.07	18.32	14.46	17.62
n	10	10	9	8	10	47

TABLE 11.4 (Cont.)

(b) Boxplots

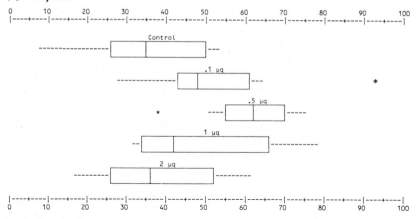

(c) Computations

$$SS_{total} = \sum X^2 - \frac{(\sum X)^2}{N} = (30^2 + 27^2 + \cdots + 53^2) - \frac{2160^2}{47}$$

$$= 113,556 - 99,268.085 = 14,287.91$$

$$SS_{treat} = \sum \left(\frac{T_j^2}{n_j} \right) - \frac{(\sum X)^2}{N} = \frac{340^2}{10} + \cdots + \frac{388^2}{8} + \frac{381^2}{10} - \frac{2160^2}{47}$$

$$= 103,461.50 - 99,268.085 = 4193.41$$

$$SS_{error} = SS_{total} - SS_{treat} = 14,287.91 - 4193.41 = 10,094.50$$

(d) Summary Table

Source	df	SS	MS	F
Treatments	4	4193.43	1048.35	4.36
Error	42	10,094.50	240.35	
Total	46	14,287.91		

There are two noticeable outliers, one in the 0.1-μg group and one in the 0.5-μg group. Outliers of this kind are very common with activity measures and can sometimes have a noticeable effect on the data. We might, for example, expect them to inflate drastically the variances of those two groups. However, a glance at the standard deviations in Table 11.4 shows that this did not happen, and the variances are remarkably homogeneous. With more serious outliers, we might reject the use of the standard analysis of variance and choose either to run a nonparametric test (described in Chapter 18) or to use a transformation of the data, to be discussed later in this chapter. For now, however, we will apply a standard analysis of variance to these data.

The calculations, as just described, are shown in Table 11.4c. From the summary table in Table 11.4d, you can see that there is a significant treatment effect: our obtained F was 4.36, whereas $F_{.05}(4, 42) = 2.61$. Thus, we will reject the null hypothesis that there are equal degrees of activity under the five drug levels. From inspection of the data, it is clear that the medium doses of THC have the greatest effect, with high and low doses resulting in less activity. (In Chapter 12, we will consider methods for making specific comparisons among individual means.)

EQUALLY WEIGHTED MEANS

The analysis we have just discussed is the most common form of the analysis of variance with unequal sample sizes. In this procedure we defined SS_{treat} as

$$SS_{treat} = \sum n_j(\overline{X}_j - \overline{X}.)^2$$

$$= \sum \frac{T_j^2}{n_j} - \frac{(\Sigma X)^2}{N}$$

In this formula we weight each squared deviation of the group mean from the grand mean by the sample size (n_j). This is the analysis that most people use and the one that is reported by most computer programs. However, if sample sizes are missing at random and really have nothing to do with the treatments themselves, one might well ask why we would wish to weight one cell mean more heavily than another.

An alternative analysis that weights cells equally is available. In fact, we will spend more time on such an analysis in Chapter 13. In this chapter I will just outline the procedures used, leaving a discussion until Chapters 13 and 16.

What we will do if we want to weight cells equally is to calculate an average sample size and then use the "equal-n" formula, replacing n by this average n. First we need to define the harmonic mean of the sample sizes. With k samples having sample sizes n_j, the harmonic mean of the n_j is defined as

$$\overline{n}_h = \frac{k}{\dfrac{1}{n_1} + \dfrac{1}{n_2} + \cdots + \dfrac{1}{n_k}}$$

We then define SS_{treat} just as we did above, except that we replace n_j with $\overline{n}_h$. Specifically,

$$SS_{treat} = \sum \overline{n}_h(\overline{X}_j - \overline{X}.)^2$$

The rest of the analysis is the same. However, SS_{treat} and SS_{error} will not sum to SS_{total}.

11.6 VIOLATIONS OF ASSUMPTIONS

As we have seen, the analysis of variance is based on the assumptions of normality and homogeneity of variance. In practice, however, the analysis of variance is a very robust statistical procedure, and the assumptions frequently can be violated with relatively minor effects. This is especially true for the normality assumption. For studies dealing with this problem, see Box (1953, 1954a, 1954b), Boneau (1960), and Bradley (1964).

In general, if the populations can be assumed to be symmetric, or at least similar in shape (e.g., all negatively skewed), and if the largest variance is no more than four times the smallest, the analysis of variance is most likely to be valid. It is important to note, however, that heterogeneity of variance and unequal sample sizes do not mix. If you have reason to anticipate unequal variances, make every effort to keep your sample sizes as equal as possible.

In Chapter 7 we considered several tests (Levene, 1960; Brown & Forsythe, 1974; O'Brien, 1981) used for testing for heterogeneity of variance. These tests are essentially t tests on the deviations (absolute or squared) of observations from the sample means or medians. If one group has a larger variance than another, then the deviations of scores from the mean or median will also, on average, be larger than for a group with a smaller variance. Thus, a significant t test on the absolute values of the deviations represents a test on group variances. Each of those tests can be readily extended to the case of more than two groups in obvious ways. The only difference is that with multiple groups the t test on the deviations would be replaced by an analysis of variance on those deviations. Wilcox (1987b) reports that this test appears to be conservative.

If you are not willing to ignore the heterogeneity or nonnormality in your data, there are alternative ways of handling the problem. Box (1954a) has shown that with unequal variances the appropriate F distribution against which to compare F_{obt} is a regular F with altered degrees of freedom. If we define the true critical value of F (adjusted for heterogeneity of variance) as F'_α, then Box has shown that

$$F_\alpha(1, n - 1) \geq F'_\alpha \geq F_\alpha[k - 1, k(n - 1)]$$

In other words, the true critical value of F lies somewhere between the critical value of F on 1 and $(n - 1)$ df and the critical value of F on $(k - 1)$ and $k(n - 1)$ df. This latter limit is the critical value we would use if we met the assumptions of normality and heterogeneity of variance. Box suggested a conservative test by comparing F_{obt} to $F_\alpha(1, n - 1)$. If this leads to a significant result, then the means are significantly different regardless of the equality, or inequality, of variances. (For those of you who raised your eyebrows when I cavalierly declared the variances in Eysenck's study to be "close enough," it is comforting to know that even Box's conservative approach would lead to the conclusion that the groups are significantly different: $F_{.05}(1, 9) = 5.12$, whereas our obtained F was 9.08.)

The only difficulty with Box's approach is that it is extremely conservative. There are, however, alternative methods. Box (1954a) presented formulas for estimating the actual number of degrees of freedom to use in evaluating F. [These formulas may be found in Myers (1979).] A different approach is one proposed by Welch (1951), which we will consider in the next section.

Wilcox (1987b) has argued that in practice variances frequently differ by more than a factor of four, which is often considered a reasonable limit on heterogeneity. He has some strong opinions concerning the consequences of heterogeneity of variance. He recommends Welch's procedure with samples having different variances, especially when the sample sizes are unequal. Tomarken and Serlin (1986) have investigated the robustness and power of Welch's procedure and a procedure proposed by Brown and Forsythe (1974). They have shown Welch's test to perform well under several conditions. The Brown and Forsythe test also has advantages in certain situations. The

Tomarken and Serlin paper is a good reference for those concerned with heterogeneity of variance.

THE WELCH PROCEDURE

Kohr and Games (1974) and Keselman, Games, and Rogan (1979) have investigated alternative approaches to the treatment of samples with heterogeneous variances (including the one suggested by Box) and have shown that a procedure proposed by Welch (1951) has considerable advantages in terms of both power and protection against Type I errors, at least when sampling from normal populations. The formulas and calculations are somewhat awkward, but not particularly difficult, and you should use them whenever a test, such as O'Brien's (discussed in Chapter 7), indicates heterogeneity of variance—especially when you have unequal sample sizes.

Define

$$w_k = \frac{n_k}{s_k^2}$$

$$\overline{X}'_. = \frac{\Sigma w_k \overline{X}_k}{\Sigma w_k}$$

Then

$$F'' = \frac{\dfrac{\Sigma w_k (\overline{X}_k - \overline{X}'_.)^2}{k - 1}}{1 + \dfrac{2(k - 2)}{k^2 - 1} \Sigma \left(\dfrac{1}{n_k - 1}\right)\left(1 - \dfrac{w_k}{\Sigma w_k}\right)^2}$$

This statistic (F'') is approximately distributed as F on $k - 1$ and df' degrees of freedom, where

$$df' = \frac{k^2 - 1}{3 \Sigma \left(\dfrac{1}{n_k - 1}\right)\left(1 - \dfrac{w_k}{\Sigma w_k}\right)^2}$$

Obviously these formulas are messy, but they are not impossible to use. If you collect all of the terms (such as w_k) first and then work systematically through the problem, you should have no difficulty. (Formulas like this are actually very easy to implement if you have access to any spreadsheet program on a microcomputer.) When you have only two groups, it is probably easier to fall back on a t test with heterogeneous variances, using the approach (also attributable to Welch) taken in Chapter 7.

11.7   TRANSFORMATIONS

In the preceding section we considered one approach to the problem of heterogeneity of variance—calculate F'' on the heterogeneous data and evaluate it against the usual

F distribution on an adjusted number of degrees of freedom. This procedure has been shown to work well when samples are drawn from normal populations. But little is known about its behavior with nonnormal populations. An alternative approach is to transform the data to a form that yields homogeneous variances and to then run a standard analysis of variance on the transformed values.

Most people find it difficult to accept the idea of transforming data. It somehow seems dishonest to decide that you do not like the data you have and therefore to change them into data you like better or, even worse, to throw out some of them and pretend they were never collected. When you think about it, however, there is really nothing unusual about transforming data. We frequently transform data without thinking about it. We sometimes measure the *time* it takes a rat to run through a maze, but then look for group differences in running *speed*, which is the reciprocal of time (a nonlinear transformation). We measure sound in terms of physical energy, but then report it in terms of decibels, which represents a logarithmic transformation. We ask a subject to adjust the size of a test stimulus to match the size of a comparison stimulus, and then take the radius of the test patch setting as our dependent variable—but the *radius* is a function of the square root of the *area* of the patch, and we could just as legitimately use area as our dependent variable. On some tests, we calculate the number of items that a student answered correctly, but then report scores in percentiles—a decidedly nonlinear transformation. Who is to say that speed is a "better" measure than time, that decibels are better than energy levels, that radius is better than area, or that a percentile is better than the number correct? Consider the study by Conti and Musty on the effects of THC on locomotor activity. In what way could their electrically transduced measure of test-chamber vibration be called the "natural" measure of activity? More important, when they took postinjection activity as a percentage of preinjection activity as their dependent variable, did you leap out of your chair and cry "Foul!" because they had used a transformation? Of course you didn't—but it was a transformation nonetheless.

As pointed out earlier in this book, our dependent variables are only convenient and imperfect indicators of the underlying variables we wish to study. No sensible experimenter ever started out with the serious intention of studying, for example, the "number of stressful life events" that a subject reports. The real purpose of such experiments has always been to study *stress*, and the number of reported events is merely a convenient measure of stress. In fact, stress probably does not vary in a linear fashion with number of events. It is quite possible that it varies exponentially—you can take a few stressful events in stride, but once you have a few on your plate additional ones start having greater and greater effects. If this is true, the number of events raised to some power—for example, $Y = (\text{number of events})^2$—might be a more appropriate variable.

The point of this fairly extended, but necessary, digression is that you must be flexible. You should not place blind faith in your original numbers; you must be willing to consider possible transformations. Tukey probably had the right idea when he called these calculations "reexpressions" rather than "transformations." You are merely reexpressing what the data have to say in other terms.

If you are willing to accept that it is permissible to transform one set of measures into another—for example, $Y_i = \log(X_i)$ or $Y_i = \sqrt{X_i}$—then many possibilities become available for modifying our data to fit more closely the underlying assumptions of our statistical tests. The nice thing about most of these transformations is that when we transform the data to meet one assumption, we often come closer to meeting other assumptions as well. Thus, a square root transformation not only may help us equate group variances but, because it compresses the upper end of a distribution more than it compresses the lower end, it may also have the effect of making positively skewed distributions more nearly normal in shape.

A word is in order about reporting transformed data. Although it is legitimate and proper to run a statistical test, such as the analysis of variance, on the transformed values, we often report means in the units of the untransformed scale. This is especially true when the original units are intrinsically meaningful. Suppose we recorded the improvement in students' reading ability in grade-level equivalents (in months). We might run our analysis on the logarithm of improvement. However, teachers in school systems everywhere are accustomed to seeing improvement in terms of grade-level equivalents, and it is not very informative to report the mean improvement in logarithmic units—even if you include a long discussion of the arbitrary nature of your measuring scales. The best approach is to convert all data to logs (assuming you have chosen to use a logarithmic transformation), find the mean of those log values, and then take the antilog to convert that mean back to the original units. This converted mean almost certainly will not equal the mean of the original values, but it is this converted mean that should be reported.

In this chapter we will consider only the most common transformations, because they are the ones that will be most useful to you. Excellent discussions of the whole approach to transformations can be found in Tukey (1977) and Hoaglin. Mosteller, and Tukey (1983). Although these presentations are framed in the language of exploratory data analysis, you should not have much difficulty following them if you invest a modest amount of time in learning the terminology.

LOGARITHMIC TRANSFORMATION

The logarithmic transformation is useful whenever the standard deviation is proportional to the mean. It is also useful when the data are markedly positively skewed. The easiest way to appreciate why both of these statements are true is to recall what logarithms do. [Remember that a logarithm is a power—$\log_{10}(25)$ is the power to which 10 must be raised to give 25; therefore, $\log_{10}(25) = 1.39794$ because $10^{1.39794} = 25$.] If we take the numbers 10, 100, and 1000, their logs are 1, 2, and 3. Thus, the distance between 10 and 100, in log units, is now equivalent to the distance between 100 and 1000. In other words, the right side of the distribution (more positive values) will be compressed more than the left side will be. This not only means that positively skewed distributions tend toward symmetry; it also means that if a set of relatively large numbers has a large standard deviation whereas a set of small numbers has a small standard deviation, taking logs will reduce the standard deviation of the sample with large numbers more than it will reduce the standard deviation of the sample with small numbers.

Table 11.5 contains an example from the study by Conti and Musty (1984) referred to earlier. In this case, however, to have a more useful variable for the discussion, I have reported the activity units (on an arbitrary scale) for each animal over the 10-minute postinjection period rather than, as before, expressing them as a percentage of baseline activity. From the data in Table 11.5 you can see that the variances are unequal: the larger is nearly eight times the smaller. This is partly a function of the well-established fact that drugs tend to increase variability as well as means. Not only are the variances unequal, but the standard deviations appear to be proportional to the means. This is easily seen on the top of Figure 11.3a, where I have plotted the standard deviations on the ordinate and the means on the abscissa. There is clearly a linear relationship between these two statistics ($r = .88$). This linearity suggests that a logarithmic transformation might be useful. In Table 11.5b the data have been transformed to logarithms to the base 10. (I could have used any base and still had the same

TABLE 11.5
Original and log-transformed data on activity

(a) *Original Data*

	Control	0.1 μg	0.5 μg	1 μg	2 μg
	130	93	510	229	144
	94	444	416	475	111
	225	403	154	348	217
	105	192	636	276	200
	92	67	396	167	84
	190	170	451	151	99
	32	77	376	107	44
	64	353	192	235	84
	69	365	384		284
	93	422			293
Mean	109.40	258.60	390.56	248.50	156.00
					$r = .88$
S.D.	58.50	153.32	147.68	118.74	87.65
Variance	3421.82	23,506.04	21,809.78	14,098.86	7682.22

(b) *Log Data*

	Control	0.1 μg	0.5 μg	1 μg	2 μg
	2.11	1.97	2.71	2.36	2.16
	1.97	2.65	2.62	2.68	2.04
	2.35	2.60	2.19	2.54	2.34
	2.02	2.28	2.80	2.44	2.30
	1.96	1.83	2.60	2.22	1.92
	2.28	2.23	2.65	2.18	2.00
	1.50	1.89	2.58	2.03	1.64
	1.81	2.55	2.28	2.37	1.92
	1.84	2.56	2.58		2.45
	1.97	2.62			2.47
Mean	1.981	2.318	2.557	2.353	2124
					$r = -.33$
S.D.	0.241	0.324	0.197	0.208	0.268
Variance	0.058	0.105	0.039	0.043	0.072

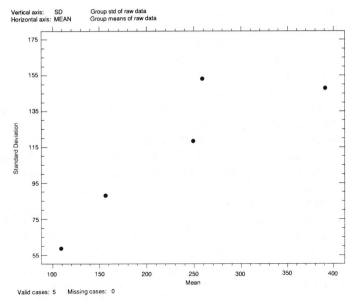

(a) *Relationship Between Means and Standard Deviations for Raw Data*

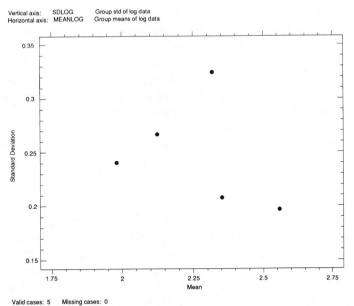

FIGURE 11.3
The relationship between means and standard deviations for original and transformed values of data in Table 11.5

(b) *Relationship Between Means and Standard Deviations of Log-Transformed Data*

effect. I chose base 10 because of its greater familiarity.) Here the means and the standard deviations are no longer correlated, as can be seen on the lower half of Figure 11.3b ($r = -.33$: nonsignificant). We have broken up the proportionality between the mean and the standard deviation, and the largest group variance is now less than three times the smallest.

An analysis of variance could now be run on these transformed data. In this case, we would find $F(4, 42) = 7.24$, which is clearly significant. Conti and Musty chose to run their analysis of variance on the percentage measures, as we saw earlier, both for theoretical reasons and because that is standard practice in this area of research. A case might be made, however, that a logarithmic transformation of the original units might be a more appropriate one for future analyses, especially if problems occur with respect to either the shapes of the distributions or heterogeneity of variance.

As noted earlier, it makes no difference what base you use for a logarithmic transformation. Regardless of the base, however, there are problems when the original values (X_i) are negative or near zero, since logs are defined for only positive numbers. In this case, it is permissible to add a constant to X before taking the log. In general, when you have near-zero values, you should use $\log(X_i + 1)$ instead of $\log(X_i)$.

SQUARE-ROOT TRANSFORMATION

When the data are in the form of counts (e.g., number of bar presses), the mean is often proportional to the *variance* rather than to the standard deviation. In this case, $Y = \sqrt{X}$ is sometimes useful for stabilizing variances and decreasing skewness. If the values of X are fairly small (i.e., less than 10), then $Y = \sqrt{X + 0.5}$ or $Y = \sqrt{X} + \sqrt{X + 1}$ are often better for stabilizing variances. For the Conti and Musty data, the mean correlates nearly as well with the variance as it does with the standard deviation [since standard deviations and variances are themselves highly correlated if the range of values is not large (in this case $r_{s \cdot s^2} = .99$)]. Therefore, you might want to investigate how a square-root transformation affects the data.

RECIPROCAL TRANSFORMATION

When you have a distribution with very large values in the positive tail, a reciprocal transformation may dramatically reduce the importance of those extreme values. For example, animals in a maze often seem to forget their job and stop to sniff at all the photocells and such that they find along the way. Once an animal has been in the maze for 30 seconds, it does not matter to us if he takes another 300 seconds to complete the run. One approach was referred to in Chapter 2—that if there are several trials per day, you might take the daily median time as your measure. An alternative approach is to use all of the data but to take the reciprocal of time (i.e., speed), because it has the effect of nearly equating long times. Suppose that we collected the following times:

10   11   13   14   15   45   450

The reciprocals of these times are

$$0.100 \quad 0.091 \quad 0.077 \quad 0.071 \quad 0.067 \quad 0.022 \quad 0.002$$

Notice that the differences among the longer times are much reduced from what they were in the original units. Moreover, the outliers will have considerably less effect on the size of the standard deviation than they had before the transformation. Similar kinds of effects are found when we apply reciprocal transformations to reaction times, where long reaction times probably indicate less about information-processing speeds than they do about the fact that the subject was momentarily not paying attention or missed the response key that she was supposed to hit.

THE ARCSINE TRANSFORMATION

In Chapter 5 we saw that for the binomial distribution, $\mu = p$ and $\sigma^2 = pq/N$. In this case, then, the variance is a direct function of the mean. Suppose that for some experiment our dependent variable was the proportion of items recalled correctly. Then each item can be thought of as a Bernoulli trial with probability p of being correct (and probability $1 - p$ of being incorrect), and the whole set of items can be thought of as a series of Bernoulli trials. In other words, the results would have a binomial distribution where the variance is dependent on the mean. If this is so, groups with different means would have different variances, and we would have a problem. For this situation, the arcsine transformation is often helpful. The usual form of this transformation is $Y = 2 \, \text{arcsine} \sqrt{p}$. In this case p is the proportion correct and Y will be twice the angle whose sine equals the square root of p. The arcsine transformation can be obtained with most calculators and is presented in any handbook of statistical tables.

Both the square-root and arcsine transformations are suitable when the variance is proportional to the mean. There is, however, a difference between them. The square-root transformation compresses the upper tail of the distribution, whereas the arcsine transformation stretches out both tails relative to the middle. Normally the arcsine is more helpful when you are dealing with proportions.

TRIMMED SAMPLES

Heavy-tailed distributions

Rather than transforming each of your raw scores to achieve homogeneity of variance or normality, an alternative approach with **heavy-tailed distributions** (relatively flat distributions that have an unusual number of observations in the tails) is to use trimmed samples. In Chapter 2 *a trimmed sample* was defined as a sample from which a fixed percentage of the extreme values in each tail has been removed. Thus, with 40 cases, a 5% trimmed sample will be the sample with two of the observations in each tail eliminated. When comparing several groups, as in the analysis of variance, you would trim each sample by the same amount.

Winsorized samples

Closely related to trimmed samples are **Winsorized samples**, in which the trimmed values are replaced by the most extreme value remaining in each tail. Thus, a 10% Winsorization of

$$3 \quad 7 \quad 12 \quad 15 \quad 17 \quad 17 \quad 18 \quad 19 \quad 19 \quad 19$$

$$20 \quad 22 \quad 24 \quad 26 \quad 30 \quad 32 \quad 32 \quad 33 \quad 36 \quad 50$$

would replace the two lowest values (3 and 7) by 12s and the two highest values (36 and 50) by 33s, leaving

$$12 \quad 12 \quad 12 \quad 15 \quad 17 \quad 17 \quad 18 \quad 19 \quad 19 \quad 19$$

$$20 \quad 22 \quad 24 \quad 26 \quad 30 \quad 32 \quad 32 \quad 33 \quad 33 \quad 33$$

[The variance and any test statistics calculated on this sample would be based on $(N - 1 - 4)$ *df*, because we trimmed off four values and replaced them with pseudo-values, and it is not really fair to pretend that those pseudovalues are real data.] Experiments with samples containing an unusual number of outliers may profit from trimming and/or "Winsorizing". When you run an analysis of variance on trimmed data, however, you should base the MS_{error} on the variance of the corresponding Winsorized sample and not on the variance of the trimmed sample. A fairly readable study of the effect of applying *t* tests (and, by extension, the analysis of variance) to trimmed samples was conducted by Yuen and Dixon (1973): you should read it before running such analyses.

WHEN TO TRANSFORM AND HOW TO CHOOSE A TRANSFORMATION

You should not get the impression that transformations should be applied routinely to all of your data. As a rule of thumb, "If it's not broken, don't fix it." If your data are reasonably distributed (i.e., are more or less symmetrical and have few if any outliers) and if your variances are reasonably homogeneous, there is probably nothing to be gained by applying a transformation. If you have markedly skewed data or heterogeneous variances, however, some form of transformation may be useful. Furthermore, it is perfectly legitimate to shop around. If a logarithmic transformation does not do what you want (stabilize the variances or improve shape), then consider the square-root (or cubed-root) transformation. If you have near-zero values and $Y = \sqrt{X + 0.5}$ does not work, try $Y = \sqrt{X} + \sqrt{X + 1}$. The only thing that you should *not* do is to try out every transformation, looking for one that gives you a significant result. (You are trying to optimize the *data*, not the resulting *F*.) Finally, if you are considering using transformations, it would be a good idea to look at Tukey (1977) or Hoaglin, Mosteller, and Tukey (1983).

11.8   FIXED VERSUS RANDOM MODELS

We have not said anything about the levels of our independent variable; we have simply spoken of "treatments." In fact, if you think about it, we could obtain the levels of the treatment variable in at least two different ways; we could deliberately select them or we could sample them at random. The way in which the levels are derived has implications for the generalizations we might draw from our study.

Assume that we were hired as consultants by the Food and Drug Administration (FDA) and asked to run a study to compare the four most popular pain relievers. We will have four treatment levels (corresponding to the four pain relievers) that were selected by the FDA. If we chose to **replicate** the study (run it over again to verify our results), we would use exactly the same levels (drugs). In a sense, the treatment levels actually used have exhausted the levels of interest. The important point here is that the levels are in fact *fixed* in the sense that they do not change randomly from one replication of the study to another. The analysis of such an experiment is referred to as a **fixed-model analysis of variance**.

Replicate

Fixed-model analysis of variance

Now assume that we are hired by the FDA again, but this time they merely tell us to compare a number of pain relievers to see whether "one brand is as good as the next." In this case, it would make sense to select *randomly* the pain relievers to be compared from the population of all available pain relievers. Here the treatment levels are the result of a random process, and the population of interest with respect to pain relievers is quite large (probably over 100). Moreover, if we replicated this study we would again choose the brands randomly, and would most likely have a whole new set of brands to compare. Because of the process by which treatment levels are obtained, we speak of treatments as a random variable and of the analysis as a **random-model analysis of variance**.

Random-model analysis of variance

We will have more to say about fixed and random models as we go on. The important point at this time is that in a fixed model, the treatment levels are deliberately selected and would remain constant from one replication to another. In our example of a fixed model, we actually set out to compare, for example, Bayer Aspirin with Anacin. In a random model, treatment levels are obtained by a random process and would be expected to vary across replications. In our example of a random model, we were studying *pain relievers*, and the ones that we happened to use were just random samples of pain relievers in general. For a one-way analysis of variance, the distinction is not particularly critical (except when we deal with the magnitude of an effect, as discussed in Section 11.9), but it will become quite important when we use more complex designs.

11.9 MAGNITUDE OF EXPERIMENTAL EFFECT

The fact that an analysis of variance has produced a significant F simply tells us that there are differences among the means of treatments that cannot be attributed to error. It says nothing about whether these differences are of any practical importance. For this reason, we must look beyond the value of F to define an additional measure reflecting the "importance" of the difference. This raises the immediate question of what we mean by *importance* and how this quality is to be measured. At this point, we can only answer generally that our measure of importance will be a term analogous to r^2. In other words, we will measure importance by calculating how much of the overall variability can be attributed to the treatment effect. Later in this chapter and in Chapter 13, we will return to the question of whether "importance" can be defined more clearly.

Magnitude of the experimental effect

At last count, there were at least six measures of the **magnitude of the experimental effect**—all different and most claiming to be less biased than some other measure. In this section we will focus on only the two most common measures (η^2 and ω^2), since they have the strongest claim to our attention.

ETA-SQUARED (η^2)

Eta-squared is probably the oldest measure of the strength of an experimental effect. Although it is certainly not the best, it has several points to recommend it. As you will

Eta-squared (η^2)

see, **eta-squared (η^2)** has a certain intuitive appeal. Moreover, it forms a strong link between the traditional analysis of variance and multiple regression, as we will see in Chapter 16.

In many textbooks, eta (η) is defined as the correlation coefficient associated with

Curvilinear regression

curvilinear regression—that is, regression where the best-fit line is not a straight line. Suppose that we propose to use Eysenck's data from Table 11.3 and to calculate the correlation between the recall scores and the treatment levels counting, rhyming, adjective, imagery, and intentional. The first criticism that would be raised is that the names counting, ..., intentional are merely labels for treatments and bear no relationship to anything. This would be true even if we called them treatments 1, 2, ..., 5. True enough, but that will not stop us. The next objection raised might be that the treatments are not ordered on any particular underlying scale, and therefore we would not know in what order to place them if we were to plot the data. Again, true enough, and again that will not stop us. Someone might even argue that the regression might not be linear. True again, but we can get around this problem by calling the coefficient η instead of r. Having cavalierly brushed aside all the objections, we set about plotting the data anyway, as shown in Figure 11.4. (The numbers 2, 3, and 4, in Figure 11.4 indicate the number of overlapping data points.) As you may recall from high school (but probably do not), a kth-order polynomial will exactly fit $k + 1$ points, which means that if we did try to fit a fourth-order polynomial to the five points represented by the treatment *means*, it would fit perfectly. We do not particularly care what the equation would look like, but we can represent the line (as in Figure 11.4) simply by connecting the array means.

Recall from Chapter 9 that r can be calculated in more than one way. One definition, in terms of parameters, is

$$\rho = \frac{\sigma_Y^2 - \sigma_{Y.X}^2}{\sigma_Y^2}$$

where

$$\sigma_Y^2 = \frac{\Sigma(Y_{ij} - \mu_Y)^2}{N}$$

and

$$\sigma_{Y.X}^2 = \frac{\Sigma(Y_{ij} - \hat{Y}_j)^2}{N}$$

Here $\hat{Y}_j$ = the predicted value for subjects in group$_j$ (who would all have the same prediction because they all have the same value of X_j).

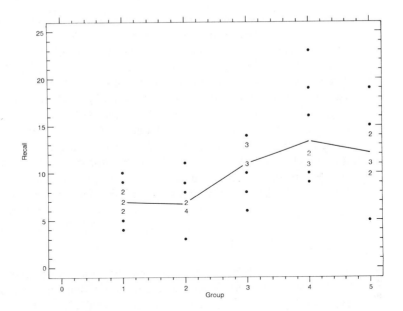

FIGURE 11.4
Scatter diagram of
data in Table 11.3

If we are concerned solely with our data rather than with generalizing to the population, then the data represent the population of interest and $\bar{Y} = \mu_Y$. Furthermore, since the regression line passes through the array means, for each array $\hat{Y}_j = \bar{Y}_j$. These simplifications leave us with

$$\eta^2 = \frac{\Sigma(Y_{ij} - \bar{Y})^2 - \Sigma(Y_{ij} - \bar{Y}_j)^2}{\Sigma(Y_{ij} - \bar{Y})^2}$$

$$= \frac{SS_{total} - SS_{error}}{SS_{total}}$$

$$\eta^2 = \frac{SS_{treat}}{SS_{total}}$$

& make the answer into a % (the % tells us the amount of variation accounted for by the ind. variable)

We have now defined η^2 in terms of the sums of squares of our analysis of variance. Applying η^2 to Eysenck's data in Table 11.3, we have

$$\eta^2 = \frac{SS_{treat}}{SS_{total}} = \frac{351.52}{786.82} = .447$$

The equation for η^2 provides a simple way to estimate the maximum squared correlation between the independent variable and the dependent variable. Its derivation also points out the fact that it can be treated as any other squared correlation coefficient, indicating the proportion of the variation accounted for by the independent variable. For Eysenck's data, 44.7% of the variation in recall scores can be attributed to differences in the instructions given to the groups, and therefore, presumably, to the depth to which the items were processed. This is an unusually large amount of explained variation, reflecting the extreme nature of the group differences.

It is important to realize that η^2 assumes that the regression line passes through the individual treatment means. When the data are treated as a population, the assumption is correct. When the data are treated as a sample from some larger population, however, bias is introduced. Since these means are really sample means, they are subject to sampling error, and η^2 will be biased upward—whatever the *true* regression line through the population means, it probably will not pass exactly through each sample mean, and thus we have underestimated $\sigma_{Y.X}^2$. Although all measures we discuss will be biased, η^2 is the most biased. Thus, although it has the advantage of simplicity and is intuitively appealing, we will generally prefer to use a less biased estimate when our interest is in making general statements about our variables. If we are interested in making statements about only our particular set of data, or if we just want a rough idea of the magnitude of effect, then η^2 is a perfectly good measure.

OMEGA-SQUARED (ω^2)

Omega-squared (ω^2)

An alternative, and for most purposes better, method of assessing the magnitude of the experimental effect is **omega-squared (ω^2)**. This statistic has been discussed by Hays (1963, 1973) and developed more extensively by Fleiss (1969), Vaughan and Corballis (1969), and Dodd and Schultz (1973). The approach essentially relies on the underlying structural model for its justification.

Our estimate of ω^2 (designed $\hat{\omega}^2$) will depend on whether we are using a random or a fixed model, as previously defined. We will first consider the solution for use with a random model, since this is somewhat easier to see.

RANDOM MODEL   We will start from the following random model:

$$x_{ij} = \mu + \tau_j + e_{ij}$$

where the treatment effects (τ_j) are a random variable. We have already seen that in this case

$$E(\text{MS}_{\text{error}}) = \sigma_e^2$$

$$E(\text{MS}_{\text{treat}}) = \sigma_e^2 + n\sigma_\tau^2$$

We will define

$$\omega^2 = \frac{\sigma_\tau^2}{\sigma_\tau^2 + \sigma_e^2}$$

In other words, ω^2 is defined as the ratio of the treatment variance to the sum of the treatment and error variances. Although we cannot measure σ_τ^2 and σ_e^2 directly, it is easy to estimate them (the estimates being represented by $\hat{\sigma}_\tau$ and $\hat{\sigma}_e$). If we drop the expectation notation, include the notation for estimation, and rearrange terms, we get

$$\hat{\sigma}_e^2 = \text{MS}_{\text{error}}$$

$$\hat{\sigma}_\tau^2 = \frac{\text{MS}_{\text{treat}} - \text{MS}_{\text{error}}}{n}$$

If we let $\hat{\omega}^2$ represent our estimate of ω^2,

$$\hat{\omega}^2 = \frac{\hat{\sigma}_\tau^2}{\hat{\sigma}_\tau^2 + \hat{\sigma}_e^2} = \frac{\dfrac{MS_{treat} - MS_{error}}{n}}{\dfrac{MS_{treat} - MS_{error}}{n} + MS_{error}}$$

$$\hat{\omega}^2 = \frac{MS_{treat} - MS_{error}}{MS_{treat} + (n-1)MS_{error}}$$

tells us how much variance can be attributed to treatment effects

For the data in Table 11.3, pretending that treatment levels were sampled at random (which clearly was not the case),

$$\hat{\omega}^2 = \frac{MS_{treat} - MS_{error}}{MS_{treat} + (n-1)MS_{error}} = \frac{87.88 - 9.67}{87.88 + 9(9.67)}$$

$$\hat{\omega}^2 = .447$$

We can now say that 44.7% of the variance in this study can be attributed to treatment effects. This happens, more or less by chance, to be the same value that we found for η^2 (this does not usually happen).

FIXED MODEL   When we use the fixed model, the situation is slightly more complicated. This derivation requires only simple algebra, but those who want to skip it can do so by jumping to the final equation. We will define $\hat{\omega}^2$ as $\hat{\sigma}_\tau^2/(\hat{\sigma}_\tau^2 + \hat{\sigma}_e^2)$, but our estimate of σ_τ^2 is different. When we discussed expected mean squares, we said that

$$E(MS_{treat}) = \sigma_e^2 + \frac{n\Sigma\tau_j^2}{k-1} = \sigma_e^2 + n\sigma_\tau^2$$

where $\tau_j = \mu_j - \mu$. In fact, with a fixed model we have exhausted our treatment populations and $\Sigma\tau_j^2/k$—not $\Sigma\tau_j^2/(k-1)$—is equal to σ_τ^2. (Remember, when we actually have the entire population, we obtain our variance by dividing by the number of observations, not the degrees of freedom, since nothing has to be estimated.) In other words, $\Sigma\tau_j^2/(k-1)$ should not really be denoted as σ_τ^2, although we use this notation by convention. If we really want an estimate of $\sigma_\tau^2 = \Sigma\tau_j^2/k$, we have to manipulate our $E(MS_{treat})$.
    Define

$$\Theta_\tau^2 = \frac{\Sigma\tau_j^2}{k-1} \qquad \text{and} \qquad \sigma_\tau^2 = \frac{\Sigma\tau^2}{k} = \frac{k-1}{k}(\Theta_\tau^2)$$

Now σ_τ^2 is our measure of variance among treatment means.

$$E(MS_{treat}) = \sigma_e^2 + \frac{n\Sigma\tau_j^2}{k-1} = \sigma_e^2 + n\Theta_\tau^2 = \sigma_e^2 + n\left(\frac{k}{k-1}\right)\sigma_\tau^2$$

We can then arrive at an estimate of σ_τ^2:

$$\sigma_\tau^2 = \frac{(k-1)(MS_{treat} - \sigma_e^2)}{nk}$$

Since $E(\mathrm{MS}_{\mathrm{error}}) = \sigma_e^2$,

$$\sigma_\tau^2 = \frac{(k-1)(\mathrm{MS}_{\mathrm{treat}} - \mathrm{MS}_{\mathrm{error}})}{nk}$$

Since σ_τ^2 is our estimate of treatment variance, we again define

$$\omega^2 = \frac{\sigma_\tau^2}{\sigma_\tau^2 + \sigma_e^2}$$

Replacing σ_τ^2 and σ_e^2 by their estimates, we obtain

$$\hat{\omega}^2 = \frac{\hat{\sigma}_\tau^2}{\hat{\sigma}_\tau^2 + \hat{\sigma}_e^2}$$

$$= \frac{\dfrac{(k-1)(\mathrm{MS}_{\mathrm{treat}} - \mathrm{MS}_{\mathrm{error}})}{nk}}{\dfrac{(k-1)(\mathrm{MS}_{\mathrm{treat}} - \mathrm{MS}_{\mathrm{error}})}{nk} + \mathrm{MS}_{\mathrm{error}}}$$

$$\hat{\omega}^2 = \frac{(k-1)(\mathrm{MS}_{\mathrm{treat}} - \mathrm{MS}_{\mathrm{error}})}{(k-1)\mathrm{MS}_{\mathrm{treat}} - (k-1)\mathrm{MS}_{\mathrm{error}} + nk\,\mathrm{MS}_{\mathrm{error}}}$$

$$= \frac{\mathrm{SS}_{\mathrm{treat}} - (k-1)\mathrm{MS}_{\mathrm{error}}}{\mathrm{SS}_{\mathrm{treat}} + [k(n-1) + 1]\mathrm{MS}_{\mathrm{error}}}$$

$$= \frac{\mathrm{SS}_{\mathrm{treat}} - (k-1)\mathrm{MS}_{\mathrm{error}}}{\mathrm{SS}_{\mathrm{treat}} + k(n-1)\mathrm{MS}_{\mathrm{error}} + \mathrm{MS}_{\mathrm{error}}}$$

$$\hat{\omega}^2 = \frac{\mathrm{SS}_{\mathrm{treat}} - (k-1)\mathrm{MS}_{\mathrm{error}}}{\mathrm{SS}_{\mathrm{total}} + \mathrm{MS}_{\mathrm{error}}}$$

Applying this equation to our data from Table 11.3, we have

$$\hat{\omega}^2 = \frac{351.52 - 4(9.67)}{786.82 + 9.67} = \frac{312.84}{796.49} = .393$$

The estimate of ω^2 in this case (.393) is somewhat less than the estimate for the random model, although they are of about the same magnitude. When we have only one independent variable, we are usually using a fixed model, so this last solution is the one we normally adopt. When we investigate more complex designs, however, we will be using random variables more often.

We have discussed two measures of the degree of association between the dependent and independent variables; one of them, omega-squared, has two forms, depending on the underlying model. These are only three of the many approaches that have been suggested. In general, ω^2 is probably the best measure. Fowler (1985) presents evidence on the bias of six different estimates, and ω^2, as defined for the fixed model, performs quite well. (Fowler presents a somewhat less biased estimator, but the improvement in bias is slight and the work entailed is much greater, so you are probably better off staying with ω^2.) A point worth noting is that one measure that partially

Squared intraclass correlation

corrects η^2 for bias is closely related to what is called the **squared intraclass correlation**, which has been put forward as yet another measure of the magnitude of effect. In fact, the intraclass correlation is nothing but ω^2 for the random model; it thus provides a link between the traditional η^2 and the newer, more appropriate ω^2.

Aside from their concern about whether one statistic is more or less biased than another, researchers have raised questions regarding the interpretation of magnitude of effect measures in general. Rosenthal and Rubin (1982) present an interesting argument that quite small values of r^2 (the squared correlation coefficient) can represent important and dramatic effects. O'Grady (1982) presents several arguments for why magnitude-of-effect measures may not be good measures of whatever it is we mean by "importance." Even an important variable may, for several reasons, account for small percentages of variation, and, more commonly, a large value of η^2 may simply mean that we have studied a trivial variable (such as the difference in height between elementary-school children and college students). (Even if not for what O'Grady says about the magnitude of effect, his excellent paper is worth reading for what it has to say about the psychometric and methodological considerations behind all the studies psychologists run.) Lane and Dunlap (1978) raise some important reservations about the routine reporting of magnitude measures and their interpretation in light of the fact that journals mainly publish studies with significant results. Finally, Cohen (1973) outlines some important considerations in the calculation and interpretation of magnitude measures. Although Cohen is primarily concerned with factorial designs (to be discussed in Chapter 13), the philosophy behind his comments is relevant even here. All the papers just cited are clear and readable, and I recommend them.

11.10   POWER

Estimating power in the analysis of variance is a straightforward extension of the power analysis for t, although the notation is different. We will define a statistic, phi prime (ϕ'), estimating the expected differences among the μ_j, derive a second statistic, phi (ϕ), which is a function of n and ϕ', and then calculate power from tables of the **noncentral F distribution**. A more complete treatment of power can be found in Cohen (1988) and Koele (1982).

Noncentral F distribution

We already know that

$$\frac{E(\text{MS}_{\text{treat}})}{E(\text{MS}_{\text{error}})} = \frac{\sigma_e^2 + n\Sigma\tau_j^2/(k-1)}{\sigma_e^2}$$

If H_0 is true, $\Sigma\tau_j^2 = 0$ and the ratio $F = \text{MS}_{\text{treat}}/\text{MS}_{\text{error}}$ will be distributed as the usual (central) F distribution. If H_0 is false, this ratio will depart from the central F distribution by a factor of

$$\frac{n\Sigma\tau_j^2}{\sigma_e^2(k-1)}$$

In other words, the $E(F)$ will be approximately equal to

$$1 + \frac{n\Sigma\tau_j^2}{\sigma_e^2(k-1)}$$

rather than approximately equal to $df_{\text{error}}/(df_{\text{error}} - 2)$.[†]

Noncentrality parameter

One common approach is to define a **noncentrality parameter**, lambda (λ):

$$\lambda = \frac{n\Sigma\tau_j^2}{\sigma_e^2}$$

which is a measure of the differences among population means. It is then possible to develop tables of the noncentral F distribution in terms of λ as our noncentrality parameter.

Most tables, however, are set up differently, based on

$$\phi = \frac{\lambda}{\sqrt{k}} = \sqrt{\frac{n\Sigma\tau_j^2}{k\sigma_e^2}}$$

as the noncentrality parameter. The problem with both approaches is that they make it difficult to separate n from the rest of the elements of the equation, thereby making it more difficult to calculate required sample sizes. To circumvent this difficulty, we will define

$$\phi' = \sqrt{\frac{\Sigma\tau_j^2}{k\sigma_e^2}}$$

and then define

$$\phi = \phi'\sqrt{n}$$

The first problem concerns the estimate of ϕ. Since $\tau = \mu_j - \mu$, we will have to estimate the various values of μ_j, or at least the differences $(\mu_j - \mu)$. This can be done either on the basis of past research or on the basis of deciding what minimum differences would be considered important.

Suppose we wish to investigate differences in IQ among different types of students. We plan to take 15 students classified by their teachers as currently unmanageable, 15 classified as potentially unmanageable, and 15 classified as normal. We have some reason to expect (or hope for) mean IQs of 95, 100, and 105 for the three groups, respectively. Then

$$\mu = \frac{\Sigma\mu_j}{k} = \frac{(95 + 100 + 105)}{3} = 100$$

and

$$\sum \tau_j^2 = \sum (\mu_j - \mu)^2 = (95 - 100)^2 + (100 - 100)^2 + (105 - 100)^2 = 50$$

In this particular case, we will have no trouble estimating σ_e^2, since we know that the variance of IQ scores $= 15^2 = 225$. (This is why I chose IQ scores for this example.) In other cases, we might have to go back to our own previous data or to data in the

[†] See the footnote on page 300.

literature for our estimate. Once we have this estimate, we are in a position to estimate ϕ':

$$\phi' = \sqrt{\frac{\Sigma \tau_j^2}{k\sigma_e^2}} = \sqrt{\frac{50}{3(225)}} = 0.272$$

Each of our samples contains 15 students, so $n = 15$.

$$\phi = \phi'\sqrt{n} = 0.272\sqrt{15} = 1.054$$

To use the table of the noncentral F distribution, we must enter it with ϕ, f_t, and f_e, where f_t is the df for treatments and f_e is the df for error. For our example, $f_t = 2$ and $f_e = 3(15 - 1) = 42$. Thus, we enter the table with $\phi = 1.05$, $f_t = 2$, and $f_e = 42$. Since this table (Appendix ncF) does not contain all possible values of ϕ, f_t, and f_e, we will either have to interpolate or else to round off to the nearest value. For purposes of illustration, we will round off every value in the conservative direction. Thus, we will take $\phi = 1.0$, $f_t = 2$, and $f_e = 30$. The entry in the table for $F(f_t, f_e; \phi) = F(2, 30; 1.0)$ is .71 for $\alpha = .05$. This entry is β, the probability of a Type II error. Since power $= 1 - \beta$, the power for our proposed experiment is $1 - .71 = .29$.

If we wish to have a greater degree of power, the most obvious approach is to increase our sample size. To calculate the required sample sizes, we simply need to work the problem backwards. Suppose that we desire power $= .80$. Then $\beta = .20$, and we simply need to find that value of ϕ for which $\beta = .20$. A minor complication arises because we cannot enter Appendix ncF without f_e, and we cannot calculate f_e without knowing n. This is not a serious problem, however, because whether f_e is 30, 50, 180, or whatever will not make any really important difference in the tables. We will therefore make the arbitrary decision that $f_e = \infty$, since we already know that it will have to be greater than 30. With $f_t = 2$, $f_e = \infty$, and $\beta = .20$, we find from the table that ϕ will have to be 1.8.

Given

$$\phi = \phi'\sqrt{n}$$

then

$$n = \phi^2/\phi'^2$$

$$= 1.8^2/0.272^2$$

$$= 43.79 \approx 44 \text{ per group}$$

Thus, we would need 44 students per group to have an 80% chance of rejecting H_0 if it is false to the extent that we believe it to be.

For those readers who were disturbed by our arbitrary setting of $f_e = \infty$, it might be instructive to calculate the power if $n = 44$.

$$\phi = 0.272\sqrt{44} = 1.8$$

$$f_t = 2$$

$$f_e = 3(43) = 129$$

From Appendix ncF for $F(2,129; 1.80)$, we see that β is between .24 (for $f_e = 30$) and

.20 (for $f_e = \infty$). Thus, our power is between .76 and .80, which is close enough for our purposes. Alternatively, Winer (1971) provides charts for calculating n given ϕ, but using these charts requires visual interpolation, so this approach will lead to no greater accuracy than will the one given here. After all, considering the guesswork that has gone into estimating ϕ', who are we to be concerned whether the power is .78 or .79?

Cohen (1988) made several interesting proposals for estimating ϕ without having to specify $(\mu_j - \mu)$; see his book for a thorough discussion of the techniques. We will discuss one very simple approach proposed by Cohen. If we let η^2 represent the percentage of variation accounted for by the treatment effect, Cohen shows that

$$\phi' = \sqrt{\frac{\eta^2}{1 - \eta^2}}$$

Thus, if we have 15 subjects in each of three treatments and expect (or hope for) treatment differences to account for 25% of the variation,

$$\phi' = \sqrt{0.25/(1 - 0.25)} = 0.577$$
$$\phi = \phi'\sqrt{n} = 0.577\sqrt{15} = 2.236$$

With $f_t = 2$, $f_e = 42$, and $\phi = 2.24$, at $\alpha = .05$, power is somewhere around .92.

As an additional aid, but one to be used with reluctance, Cohen has defined a small effect as $\phi' = 0.10$, a medium effect as $\phi' = 0.25$, and a large effect as $\phi' = 0.40$. These are only crude and rather arbitrary guidelines, although they can be useful when all else fails.

Koele (1982) presents methods for calculating the power of random models. Random models present particular problems because they generally have a low level of power. For these models, two random processes are involved—random sampling of subjects and random sampling of treatment levels. As Koele phrased it, "Not only should there be many observations per level, but also many levels per treatment [independent variable]. Experiments that have random factors with only two or three levels must be considered as absurd as t tests on samples with two or three observations" (p. 516). This is important advice to keep in mind when you are considering random models. We will say more about this problem in Chapter 13.

11.11   COMPUTER ANALYSES

Exhibit 11.1 contains abbreviated copies of computer output for the analysis of variance performed on the data in Table 11.4. The first output is from BMDP2V, the second is from SPSS^X, the third is from Minitab, and the fourth is from the SAS system. Although the BMDP and SAS programs generate very complete printouts and use the preferred method to handle unequal ns in complex designs, the Minitab and SPSS^X programs are slightly easier to use. (The Minitab output is particularly nice because it plots confidence limits on the means of each group. The placement of those limits is a good way of comparing the groups visually if you were remiss and did not create boxplots of the data before you began.) You can see that the results agree with those that we calculated by hand and with each other. Also notice, in the BMDP printout, the line in the summary table labeled "MEAN." This is a test on the null hypothesis that the grand mean of all 47 scores is zero. Since we knew that all the numbers had to be positive, the fact that this test is significant does not come as a surprise. In fact, the test on the mean is usually of absolutely no interest and can be ignored. On a few occasions it is meaningful, however, such as when the data represent the degree of positive or negative change and we are interested in knowing whether the mean change, irrespective of treatment group, is greater or less than zero. When we have equal sample sizes, the sum of squares for the "MEAN" will be equal to the correction factor $[(\Sigma X)^2/N]$. (When we have unequal ns, it will not be exactly equal to the correction factor, but [for those readers who are curious] it will be equal to the correction factor that we would have if we ran the "unweighted means solution" from Chapter 13.) I have included the SAS printout in part because it looks different from the results of using the other packages. The form of the printout reflects the approach to the analysis of variance discussed in Chapter 16.

EXHIBIT 11.1
BMDP, SPSS[x], Minitab, and SAS solutions for data in Table 11.4

(a) BMDP

BMDP2V - ANALYSIS OF VARIANCE AND COVARIANCE WITH REPEATED MEASURES.
COPYRIGHT 1977, 1979, 1981, 1982, 1983, 1985, 1987, 1988, 1990
       by BMDP Statistical Software, Inc.

PROGRAM INSTRUCTIONS

/Problem	Title is 'Bmdp2v Analysis of Conti"s Data'.
/Input	Variables are 2.
	Format is '(F1.0, 1X, F2.0)'.
	File = 'Conti.dat'.
/Variable	Names are Group, Activity.
/Design	Dependent is Activity.
	Group is Group.
/End	

PROBLEM TITLE IS
BMDP2V ANALYSIS OF CONTI"S DATA

CELL MEANS FOR 1-ST DEPENDENT VARIABLE
- - - - - - - - - - - - - - - - - - - -

						MARGINAL
Group =	*1	*2	*3	*4	*5	
Activity	34.0000	50.80000	60.33333	48.50000	38.10000	45.95745
Count	10	10	9	8	10	47

STANDARD DEVIATIONS FOR 1-ST DEPENDENT VARIABLE
- - - - - - - - - - - - - - - - - - - -

Group =	*1	*2	*3	*4	*5
Activity	14.29841	18.38961	11.06797	18.32251	14.45645

ANALYSIS OF VARIANCE FOR 1-ST DEPENDENT VARIABLE - ACTIVITY

	SOURCE	SUM OF SQUARES	D.F.	MEAN SQUARE	F	TAIL PROB.
	MEAN	100166.43316	1	100166.43316	416.76	0.0000
	Group	4193.41489	4	1048.35372	4.36	0.0049
1	ERROR	10094.50000	42	240.34524		

EXHIBIT 11.1 (Cont.)

(b) SPSS[X]

Title	'SPSSX Analysis of Conti Data'
File Handle	Data / Name - ' [D_Howell.book]Conti.dat'
Data List	File = Data/ Group 1 Activity 3-4
Value Labels	Group (1) 'Control' (2) '.1 mg' (3) '.5mg'
(4) '1 mg' (5) '2 mg'	
Oneway	Activity by Group (1, 5)
Statistics	1

```
------------------------ O N E W A Y ------------------------
```

Variable ACITIVITY
By Variable GROUP

ANALYSIS OF VARIANCE

SOURCE	D.F.	SUM OF SQUARES	MEAN SQUARES	F RATIO	F PROB.
BETWEEN GROUPS	4	4193.4149	1048.3537	4.3619	.0049
WITHIN GROUPS	42	10094.5000	240.3452		
TOTAL	46	14287.9149			

GROUP	COUNT	MEAN	STANDARD DEVIATION	STANDARD ERROR	95 PCT CONF INT FOR MEAN
Grp 1	10	34.0000	14.2984	4.5216	23.7715 TO 44.2285
Grp 2	10	50.8000	18.3896	5.8153	37.6449 TO 63.9551
Grp 3	9	60.3333	11.0680	3.6893	51.8257 TO 68.8409
Grp 4	8	48.5000	18.3225	6.4780	33.1820 TO 63.8180
Grp 5	10	38.1000	14.4564	4.5715	27.7585 TO 48.4415
TOTAL	47	45.9574	17.6240	2.5707	40.7828 TO 51.1321

(c) Minitab

```
MTB  > read 'Lisa.dat' C1 C2
      47 ROWS READ

MTB  > Oneway on Data in C2 by Groups in C1
```

ANALYSIS OF VARIANCE ON C2

SOURCE	DF	SS	MS	F	p
C1	4	4193	1048	4.36	0.005
ERROR	42	10095	240		
TOTAL	46	14288			

```
                                        INDIVIDUAL 95 PCT CI'S FOR MEAN
                                        BASED ON POOLED STDEV
LEVEL    N     MEAN    STDEV      ----+---------+---------+---------+--
   1    10    34.00    14.30      (------*-----)
   2    10    50.80    18.39                   (------*-----)
   3     9    60.33    11.07                        (------*------)
   4     8    48.50    18.32                   (------*-------)
   5    10    38.10    14.46        (-----*------)
                                   ----+---------+---------+---------+--
POOLED STDEV =  15.50              30        45        60        75
MTB  > stop
```

(d) SAS

```
Option Linesize = 80;

Data;
    Infile 'Conti.dat';
    Input Group Activity;
Run;

Proc GLM;
    Class Group;
    Model Activity = Group;
Run;
```

EXHIBIT 11.1 (Cont.)   **(d) SAS (Cont.)**

GENERAL LINEAR MODELS PROCEDURE
Class Level Information

Class	Levels	Values
GROUP	5	1 2 3 4 5

Number of observations in data set = 47

General Linear Models Procedure

Dependent Variable: ACTIVITY

Source	DF	Sum of Squares	Mean Square	F Value	Pr > F
Model	4	4193.4148936	1048.3537234	4.36	0.0049
Error	42	10094.5000000	240.3452381		
Corrected Total	46	14287.9148936			

R-Square	C.V.	Root MSE	ACTIVITY Mean
0.293494	33.73354	15.503072	45.95744681

Dependent Variable: ACTIVITY

Source	DF	Type I SS	Mean Square	F Value	Pr > F
GROUP	4	4193.4148936	1048.3537234	4.36	0.0049

Source	DF	Type III SS	Mean Square	F Value	Pr > F
GROUP	4	4193.4148936	1048.3537234	4.36	0.0049

KEY TERMS

Analysis of variance (ANOVA) (introduction)

One-way analysis (introduction)

Error variance (11.1)

MS_{error} (11.2)

MS_{within} (11.2)

$MS_{treatment}$ (11.2)

Treatment effect (11.2)

Expected value (11.2)

Sums of squares (11.3)

Correction factor (CF) (11.3)

SS_{total} (11.3)

SS_{treat} (11.3)

SS_{error} (11.3)

Summary table (11.3)

df_{total} (11.3)

df_{treat} (11.3)

df_{error} (11.3)

Structural model (11.4)

Heavy-tailed distributions (11.7)

Winsorized samples (11.7)

Replicate (11.8)

Fixed-model analysis of variance (11.8)

Random-model analysis of variance (11.8)

Magnitude of the experimental effect (11.9)

Eta-squared (η^2) (11.9)

Curvilinear regression (11.9)

Omega-squared (ω^2) (11.9)

Squared intraclass correlation (11.9)

Noncentral F distribution (11.10)

Noncentrality parameter (11.10)

EXERCISES

11.1   To investigate maternal behavior of laboratory rats, we separate the rat pup from the mother and record the time required for the mother to retrieve the pup. We run the study with 5-, 20-, and 35-day-old pups. We move the pups a fixed distance from the mother and record the retrieval time in seconds. The data are given below; there are six pups per group.

$\Sigma X^2 = 1899$ $\Sigma X = 103$

3079   133

16799   253

5 days: 15   10   25   15   20   18 $\bar{X} = 17.17$ $s^2\ 77.04$ $T_{..} = 489$

20 days: 30   15   20   25   23   20 $\bar{X}\ 22.17$ $s^2\ 123.31$ $T_{..}^2 = 15777$

35 days: 40   35   50   43   45   40 $\bar{X}\ 42.17$ $s^2\ 426.06$

$N = 18$

Run a one-way analysis of variance on the data.

11.2   You have a hypothesis that in restaurants the person paying the bill (Host) orders a less expensive meal than does his or her partner (Guest). To avoid confusing the issue, you chose only same-sex pairs and recorded the price of the meal for only one of the people in each pair. Subjects were assigned to groups on the basis of whether or not each subject eventually picked up the bill. The dependent variable was the cost of the entrée.

$N = 10$

$T_{..} = 98.25$ $n = 5$

$T_{..}^2 =$

976.82

Host: 9.50   8.75   10.25   9.00   9.25 $\Sigma X = 46.75$ $\Sigma X^2 = 438.44$

$n = 5$ **Guest:** 10.75   9.50   8.50   10.50   12.25 $\Sigma X = 51.5$ $\Sigma X^2 = 538.38$

(a) Run the analysis of variance on these groups.
(b) Run an independent t test on the data and compare the results to those you obtained in (a).
(c) Why was it necessary to ensure that you had data on only one member of each pair? (Answer with respect to what you know about t.)

11.3   It might be predicted that consumer buying behavior would vary with the location of the product in the store, even if the product in question elicits a high degree of brand loyalty. We therefore look at the purchases of well-known and unknown brands of candy bars when they are in their usual place behind the counter and when they are prominently displayed next to the cash register. The dependent variable is the number of bars of each brand sold per day. (We will ignore for now the fact that this design might be better analyzed by techniques to be discussed in Chapter 13.)

Known/usual:	15	23	18	16	25	29	17
Known/prominent:	24	14	15	19	30	26	18
Unknown/usual:	10	5	8	13	6	10	12
Unknown/prominent:	15	13	10	17	18	11	15

(a) Run a one-way analysis of variance.
(b) Now run a one-way analysis of variance on treatments 1 and 3 combined versus treatments 2 and 4 combined. What question are you answering?

11.4   Refer to Exercise 11.1. Assume that for reasons beyond our control, neither the data for the last pup in the 5-day group nor those data for the last two pups in the 35-day group could be used. Rerun the analysis of variance using the remaining data.

11.5   Refer to Exercise 11.2. Suppose that we collected two additional data points for the Host group. The data now look like this:

$n = 7$ **Host:**   9.50   8.75   10.25   9.00   9.25   11.75   9.00 $\Sigma X = 67.5$ $\Sigma X^2 = 657.5$ $s^2 = 1.1$

$n = 5$ **Guest:** 10.75   9.50   8.50   10.50   12.25 $\Sigma X = 51.5$ $\Sigma X^2 = 538.38$ $s^2 = 1.98$

$N = 12$ $T_{..} = 119$

$T_{..}^2 = 11951.68$

(a) Rerun the analysis of variance.

(b) Run an independent t without pooling the variances.

(c) Run an independent t after pooling the variances.

(d) For (b) and (c), which of these values of t corresponds (after squaring) to the F in (a)?

11.6 Calculate η^2 and ω^2 for the data in Exercise 11.2. Would you assume a fixed or a random model?

11.7 Would you assume that the experimental design in Exercise 11.1 represents a fixed or a random model?

11.8 Some words in a prose passage are particularly important for the meaning of the passage, whereas other words do not affect the meaning substantially. You have a hypothesis that good readers read primarily the important (key) words, and therefore that if only these words were capitalized, a passage could be read more rapidly. You define three groups and have each read the same passage. For group Normal, the passage is printed normally. For group Random, a random set of words is capitalized. For group Key, key words are capitalized. The dependent variable is the time to read the passage (in seconds).

Group	n	Mean	S.D.
Normal	10	30.2	6.21
Random	10	38.3	7.55
Key	10	25.6	5.75

(a) Run the analysis of variance and draw whatever conclusions are warranted.

(b) Point out at least one major failing in the design of this experiment that is related to the hypothesis that good readers look for key words.

(c) What does rejection of H_0 mean in this case?

11.9 Suppose that the data in Exercise 11.8 had shown a standard deviation of 20.75 for group Key. What could you conclude and why? *Something wrong w̄ homogeneity of variance*

11.10 What would you conclude in Exercise 11.8 if the means and standard deviations were the same but the ns were each 5 instead of 10?

11.11 The computer printout in Exhibit 11.2 is from a BMDP analysis of the data in Exercise 11.1.

(a) Compare the results with those you obtained in Exercise 11.1.

(b) What does the sum of squares labeled "MEAN" represent?

EXHIBIT 11.2

BMDP2V - ANALYSIS OF VARIANCE AND COVARIANCE WITH REPEATED MEASURES

PROGRAM CONTROL INFORMATION

/ PROBLEM	TITLE IS 'BMDP2V ANALYSIS OF DATA IN EXERCISE 11.1'.
/ INPUT	VARIABLES ARE 2.
	FORMAT IS '(F2.0,F3.0)'.
	CASES ARE 18.
	FILE = 'DATA.DAT'.
/ VARIABLES	NAMES ARE GROUP, SCORE.
/ DESIGN	DEPENDENT IS SCORE.
	GROUPS ARE GROUP.
/ END	

PROBLEM TITLE . . . . . . BMDP2V ANALYSIS OF DATA IN EXERCISE 11.1

CELL MEANS FOR 1-ST DEPENDENT VARIABLE

				MARGINAL
GROUP =	*1.0000	*2.0000	*3.0000	
SCORE	17.16667	22.16667	42.16667	27.16667
COUNT	6	6	6	18

EXHIBIT 11.2 (Cont.)   STANDARD DEVIATIONS FOR 1-ST DEPENDENT VARIABLE

GROUP =	*1.0000	*2.0000	*3.0000
SCORE	5.11534	5.11534	5.11534

ANALYSIS OF VARIANCE FOR 1-ST DEPENDENT VARIABLE - SCORE

	SOURCE	SUM OF SQUARES	DEGREES OF FREEDOM	MEAN SQUARE	F	TAIL PROB.
	MEAN	13284.5000	1	13284.5000	507.69	0.0000
	GROUP	2100.0000	2	1050.0000	40.13	0.0000
1	ERROR	392.5000	15	26.1667		

11.12   The computer printout in Exhibit 11.3 is from an SPSS^X analysis of the data in Exercise 11.3.

(a) Compare these results with those you obtained in Exercise 11.3.

(b) How do you interpret the column labeled "F PROB."?

EXHIBIT 11.3

TITLE	'ANALYSIS OF DATA 'IN EXERCISE 11.3'
FILE HANDLE	DATA/NAME = 'EX11-3.DAT'
DATA LIST	FILE = DATA/GROUP 1-2 SCORE 3-5
ONEWAY	SCORE BY GROUP(1,4)

------------------------------------- O N E W A Y -------------------------------------

VARIABLE: SCORE

ANALYSIS OF VARIANCE

SOURCE	D.F.	SUM OF SQUARES	MEAN SQUARES	F	F PROB.
BETWEEN GROUPS	3	655.1429	218.3810	10.778	0.0001
WITHIN GROUPS	24	486.2857	20.2619		
TOTAL	27	1141.4286			

11.13   Write an appropriate statistical model for Exercise 11.1.

11.14   Write an appropriate statistical model for Exercise 11.2.

11.15   Write an appropriate statistical model for Exercise 11.3. Save it for later use in Chapter 13.

11.16   When F is less than 1, we usually write "<1" rather than the actual value. What meaning can be attached to an F appreciably less than 1? Can we speak intelligently about an F "significantly" less than 1? Include $E(MS)$ in your answer.

11.17   Howell and Huessy (1981) classified children as exhibiting (or not exhibiting) attention deficit disorder (ADD) -related behaviors in second, fourth, and fifth grade. The subjects were then sorted on the basis of the year(s) in which the individual was classed as exhibiting such behavior. They then looked at GPA for these children when the latter were in high school. The data are given in terms of mean GPA per group.

	Never ADD	Second Only	Fourth Only	Second and Fourth
Mean GPA	2.6774	1.6123	1.9975	2.0287
S.D.	0.9721	1.0097	0.7642	0.5461
n	201	13	12	8

$N = 272$

S^2 .7723   1.6646   .0927   .3462.

$T_{..} = 664.$
89

	Fifth Only	Second and Fifth	Fourth and Fifth	Second, Fourth, and Fifth
Mean	1.7000	1.9000	1.8986	1.4225
S.D.	0.8788	1.0318	0.3045	0.5884
n	14	9	7	8

$\Sigma X\ 23.8$ $\Sigma X\ 17.1$ $\Sigma X\ 13.2902$ $\Sigma X\ 11.38$

Run the analysis of variance and draw the appropriate conclusion.

11.18 Rerun the analysis in Exercise 11.17, leaving out the Never ADD group. In what way does this analysis clarify the interpretation of the data?

11.19 Employ Welch's procedure for heterogeneous variances to the original data in Table 7.7 and compare your answer with one given in Chapter 7.

11.20 Would a logarithmic transformation or no transformation be more appropriate for the data in Table 11.3? (*Hint:* You may have to apply the transformation to determine the answer.)

11.21 Apply a square-root transformation to the data in Table 11.5.

11.22 Run the analysis of variance for the transformed data you obtained in Exercise 11.21.

11.23 Calculate η^2 and ω^2 for the data in Exercise 11.17.

11.24 Darley and Latané (1968) recorded the speed with which subjects summoned help for a person in trouble. Subjects thought either that they were the only one listening to the person (Group 1, $n = 13$), that one other person was listening (Group 2, $n = 26$), or that four other people were listening (Group 3, $n = 13$). The dependent variable was the speed with which the person summoned help ($= 1/\text{time} \times 100$). The mean speed scores for the three groups were 0.87, 0.72, and 0.51, respectively. The MS_{error} was 0.053. Reconstruct the analysis of variance summary table. (*Hint:* Compute group totals first.) What can you conclude?

11.25 In Exercise 11.24 the data were transformed from their original units (time). What effect would this have on the shape of the distributions?

11.26 Would a transformation of the data in Table 11.3 (Eysenck's data) be useful in terms of equalizing the variances? What transformation would you suggest applying, if any?

COMPUTER EXERCISES

11.27 In Exercise 7.50 you had data on students who had lost a parent through death, who came from a divorced household, or who grew up with two parents. You then ran three separate t tests comparing those groups.
   (a) Now reanalyze those data using an analysis of variance with GSIT as the dependent variable.
   (b) How does your answer to this question differ from your answer in Chapter 7?

Use the following material to answer Exercises 28–31.
Introini-Collison and McGaugh (1986) examined the hypothesis that hormones normally produced in the body can play a role in memory. Specifically, they looked at the effect of post-training injections of epinephrine on retention of a previously learned discrimination. To over-simplify the experiment, they first trained mice to escape mild shock by choosing the left arm of a Y maze. Immediately after training they injected the mice with either 0.0, 0.3, or 1.0 mg/kg of

epinephrine. (The first group was actually injected with saline.) They predicted that low doses of epinephrine would facilitate retention, whereas high doses would inhibit it.

Either 1 day, 1 week, or 1 month after original training, each mouse was again placed in the Y maze, but this time was required to run to the right arm of the maze to escape shock. Presumably the stronger the memory of the original training, the more it would interfere with the learning of this new task and the more errors the subjects would make.

There are two data sets for this experiment, and they are described in Appendix Computer Exercises. The original study used 18 animals in the three dosage groups tested after 1 day, and 12 animals in each group tested after intervals of 1 week and 1 month. Hypothetical data that closely reproduce the original results are contained in Epinuneq.dat, although for our purposes there are data only for 7 subjects in the 1.0 mg/kg dose at the 1 month test. A second data set was created with 12 observations in each of the 9 cells, and is called Epineq.dat. In both cases the need to create data that were integers led to results that are slightly conservative relative to the actual data, but the conclusions with respect to H_0 are the same.

11.28 On the reasonable assumption that there are no important differences from one interval to the next, combine the data by ignoring the Interval variable and run the analysis of variance on Dosage. Use the data in Epinuneq.dat. (You will have 42 observations for the 0.0 and 0.3 mg/kg dose and 37 subjects for the 1.0 mg/kg dose.)

11.29 Use the data in Epinuneq.dat to run three separate one-way analyses of variance, one at each retention interval. In each case, test the null hypothesis that the three dosage means are equal. Have your statistical package print out the means and standard deviations of the three dosage groups for each analysis. (*Hint*: For BMDP programs you can use the USE statement in /Transform. For Minitab it is easiest just to copy subsets of cases to different columns and run the analyses on those columns. For SAS, Proc GLM will allow you to use BY INTERVAL, if you have first sorted by Interval. For SPSS[X] use a Select If.)

11.30 Now run a separate analysis testing the hypothesis that the three Interval means are equal. In this case you will simply ignore Dosage.

11.31 Rerun Exercise 11.29, this time using Epineq.dat. (The results will differ somewhat because the data are different.) Calculate the average of the three error terms (MS_{error}) and show that this is equal to the average of the variances within each of the nine groups in the experiment. Save this value to use in Chapter 13.

CHAPTER TWELVE

MULTIPLE COMPARISONS AMONG TREATMENT MEANS

OBJECTIVES *To extend the analysis of variance by examining ways of making comparisons within a set of means.*

CONTENTS

A significant F in an analysis of variance is simply an indication that not all the population means are equal. It does not tell us which means are different from which other means. As a result, the overall analysis of variance often raises more questions than it answers. We now face the problem of examining differences among individual means, or sets of means, for the purpose of isolating significant differences or testing specific hypotheses. We want to be able to make statements of the form $\mu_1 = \mu_2 = \mu_3$, and $\mu_4 = \mu_5$, but the first three means are different from the last two, and all of them are different from μ_6.

Many different techniques for making comparisons among means are available; here we will consider the most common and useful ones. A thorough, discussion of this topic can be found in Miller (1981), and in Hochberg and Tamhane (1987), and Toothaker (1991). The papers by Games (1978a, 1978b) are also helpful, as is the paper by Games and Howell (1976) on the treatment of unequal sample sizes.

12.1   ERROR RATES

The major issue in any discussion of multiple-comparison procedures is the question of the probability of Type I errors. Most differences among alternative techniques result from different approaches to the question of how to control these errors.[†] The problem is in part technical; but it is really much more a subjective question of how you want to define the error rate and how large you are willing to let the maximum possible error rate be.

We can distinguish three basic ways of specifying error rates, or the probability of Type I errors. In doing so, we shall use the terminology that has become more or less standard since an extremely important unpublished paper by Tukey in 1953. (See also Ryan, 1959; O'Neil & Wetherill, 1971.)

ERROR RATE PER COMPARISON (*PC*)

Error rate per comparison (*PC*)

We have used the **error rate per comparison (*PC*)** in the past and it requires little elaboration. It is the probability of making a Type I error on any given comparison. If, for example, we make a comparison by running a t test between two groups and we reject the null hypothesis because our t exceeds $t_{.05}$, then we are working at a per comparison error rate of .05.

ERROR RATE PER EXPERIMENT (*PE*)

Error rate per experiment (*PE*)

The **error rate per experiment (*PE*)** is the *number* of Type I errors we expect to make in any given experiment if the null hypothesis is true. For example, assume that we give a group of males and a group of females 50 words and ask them to give us as many associations to these words as possible in 1 minute. For each word, we then test (at $\alpha = .05$), whether there is a significant difference in the number of associations given by male and female subjects. Assume that H_0 is always true. Since we have run 50 more or less independent t tests, each at $\alpha = .05$, we expect that an average of $50(.05) = 2.5$ tests will be declared "significant" by chance. Thus, the error rate per experiment is 2.5, whereas the error rate per comparison is .05. Unlike the other two types of error rate we are considering, the error rate per experiment is a frequency, not a probability.

FAMILYWISE ERROR RATE (*FW*)

When we have completed running a set of comparisons among our group means, we will arrive at a set (often called a *family*) of conclusions. For example, the family might

[†] Some authors choose among tests on the basis of power and are concerned with the probability of finding any or all significant differences among pairs of means (any-pairs power and all-pairs power). In this chapter, however, we will focus on the probability of Type I errors and the way in which different test procedures deal with these error rates.

consist of the statements

$$\mu_1 < \mu_2$$

$$\mu_3 < \mu_4$$

$$\mu_1 < (\mu_3 + \mu_4)/2$$

Familywise error rate (FW)

The probability that this family of conclusions will contain *at least* one Type I error is called the **familywise error rate (FW)**.[†] Many of the procedures we will examine are specifically directed at controlling the FW error rate, and even those procedures that are not intended to control FW are still evaluated with respect to what the level of FW is likely to be.

In an experiment in which only one comparison is made, all three error rates will be the same. As the number of comparisons increases, however, the three rates diverge. If we let α' represent the error rate for any one comparison and c represent the number of comparisons, then

Error rate per comparison (PC): $\alpha = \alpha'$

Error rate per experiment (PE): $\alpha = c\alpha'$

Familywise error rate (FW): $\alpha = 1 - (1 - \alpha')^c$

(if comparisons are independent)

If the comparisons are not independent, the first two error rates remain unchanged, but the familywise rate is affected. In most situations, however, $1 - (1 - \alpha')^c$ still represents a reasonable approximation to FW. It is worth noting that the limits on FW are $PC \leqslant FW \leqslant PE$, and in most reasonable cases FW is in the general vicinity of PE.

THE NULL HYPOTHESIS AND ERROR RATES

We have been speaking as if the null hypothesis in question were what is usually called the *complete null hypothesis* ($\mu_1 = \mu_2 = \mu_3 = \cdots = \mu_k$). In fact, this is the null hypothesis tested by the overall analysis of variance. In many experiments, however, nobody is seriously interested in the complete null hypothesis; rather, people are concerned about a few more restricted null hypotheses, such as ($\mu_1 = \mu_2 = \mu_3, \mu_4 = \mu_5, \mu_6 = \mu_7$), with differences among the various subsets. If this is the case, the problem becomes more complex, and it is not always possible to specify FW without knowing the pattern of population means. We will need to take this into account in designating the error rates for the different tests we shall discuss.

[†]This error rate is frequently referred to, especially in older sources, as the "experimentwise" error rate. However, Tukey's term "familywise" has become more common. In more complex analyses of variance, the experiment often may be thought of as comprising several different families of comparisons.

A PRIORI VERSUS POST HOC COMPARISONS

It is often helpful to distinguish between **a priori comparisons**, which are chosen before the data are collected, and **post hoc comparisons**, which are planned after the experimenter has collected the data, looked at the means, and noted which of the latter are far apart and which are close together. To take a simple example, consider a situation in which you have five means. In this case, there are 10 comparisons involving pairs of means (e.g., $\overline{X}_1$ versus $\overline{X}_2$, $\overline{X}_1$ versus $\overline{X}_3$, and so on). Assume that the complete null hypothesis is true but that by chance two of the means are far enough apart to lead us erroneously to reject H_0: $\mu_i = \mu_j$. In other words, the data contain one Type I error. If you have to plan your single comparison in advance, you have a probability of .10 of hitting on the 1 comparison out of 10 that will involve the Type I error. If you look at the data first, however, you are certain to make a Type I error, assuming that you are not so dim that you test anything other than the largest difference. In this case, you are implicitly making all 10 comparisons in your head, even though you perform the arithmetic for only the largest one. In fact, for some post hoc tests, we will adjust the error rate as if you literally made all 10 comparisons.

This simple example demonstrates that if comparisons are planned in advance (and are a subset of all possible comparisons), the probability of a Type I error is smaller than if the comparisons are arrived at on a post hoc basis. It should not surprise you, then, that we will treat a priori and post hoc comparisons separately.

SIGNIFICANCE OF THE OVERALL F

Some controversy surrounds the question of whether one should insist that the overall F on groups be significant before conducting multiple comparisons between individual group means. In the past, the general advice was that without a significant group effect, individual comparisons were inappropriate. In fact, the rationale underlying the error rates for Fisher's least significant difference test, to be discussed in Section 12.4, required overall significance.

Current thinking, however, is that overall significance is not necessary. First of all, the hypotheses tested by the overall test and a multiple-comparison test are quite different, with quite different levels of power. For example, the overall F actually distributes differences among groups across the number of degrees of freedom for groups. This has the effect of diluting the overall F in the situation where several group means are equal to each other but different from some other mean. Second, requiring overall significance will actually change the FW, making the multiple-comparison tests conservative. The tests were designed, and their significance levels established, without regard to the overall F.

Wilcox (1987a) has considered this issue and suggested that "there seems to be little reason for applying the (overall) F test at all" (p. 36). That position may be a bit extreme, but it does emphasize the point. And perhaps it is not all that extreme. If you accept the position that typical multiple-comparison procedures do not require a significant overall F, and I do, then you will examine group differences regardless of the value of that F. Why, then, do we even need that F except to provide a sense of closure?

12.2   MULTIPLE COMPARISONS IN A SIMPLE EXPERIMENT ON MORPHINE TOLERANCE

In discussing the various procedures, it will be helpful to have a data set to which each of the approaches can be applied. We will take as an example a hypothetical study similar to an important experiment on morphine tolerance by Siegel (1975). Although the data are fictitious and a good deal of liberty has been taken in describing the conditions, the means (and the significance of the differences among means) are the same as those in Siegel's paper. It will be necessary to describe this study in some detail, but the example is worth the space required. It will be to your advantage to take the time to understand the hypotheses and the treatment labels.

Morphine is a drug that is frequently used to alleviate pain. Repeated administrations of morphine, however, lead to morphine tolerance, in which morphine has less and less of an effect (pain reduction) over time. A common experimental task that demonstrates morphine tolerance involves placing a rat on an uncomfortably warm surface. When the heat becomes too uncomfortable, the rat will lick its paws, and the latency of the paw-lick is used as a measure of the rat's sensitivity to pain. A rat who has received a morphine injection typically shows a longer paw-lick latency, indicating a reduced pain sensitivity. The development of morphine tolerance is indicated by a progressive shortening of paw-lick latencies (indicating increased sensitivity) with repeated morphine injections.

Siegel noted that there are a number of situations involving drugs other than morphine in which *conditioned* (learned) drug responses are opposite in direction to the unconditioned (natural) effects of the drug. For example, an animal injected with atropine will usually show a marked decrease in salivation. If, however, after repeated injections of atropine, physiological saline (which should have no effect whatsoever) is suddenly injected (*in the same physical setting*), the animal will show an *increase* in salivation. It is as if the animal were compensating for the anticipated effect of atropine. In such studies, it appears that a learned compensatory mechanism develops over trials and counterbalances the effect of the drug.

Siegel theorized that such a process might help to explain morphine tolerance. He reasoned that if you administered a series of pretest trials in which the animal was injected with morphine and placed on a warm surface, morphine tolerance would develop. Thus, if you again injected the subject with morphine on a subsequent test trial, the animal would be as sensitive to pain as would be a naive animal (one who had never received morphine). Siegel further reasoned that if on the test trial you instead injected the animal with physiological saline *in the same test setting*, the conditioned hypersensitivity that results from the repeated administration of morphine would not be counterbalanced by the presence of morphine, and the animal would show very short paw-lick latencies. Siegel also reasoned that if you gave the animal repeated morphine injections in one setting but then tested it in a *new* setting, the new setting would not elicit the conditioned compensatory hypersensitivity to counterbalance the morphine. As a result, the animal would respond as would an animal who was being injected for the first time.

Our version of Siegel's experiment is based on the prediction just outlined. The experiment involved five groups of rats. Each group received four trials, but the data for the analysis come from only the critical fourth (test) trial. The groups are designated by indicating the treatment on the first three trials and then the treatment on the fourth trial. Group M-M received morphine on the first three trials in the test setting and then again on the fourth trial in the same test setting. This is the standard morphine-tolerant group, and we would expect to see normal levels of pain sensitivity. Group M-S received morphine (in the test setting) on the first three trials but then received saline on the fourth trial. These animals would be expected to be hypersensitive to the pain stimulus because the conditioned hypersensitivity would not be balanced by any compensating effects of morphine. Group M(cage)-M (abbreviated Mc-M) received morphine on the first three trials in their home cage but then received morphine on the fourth trial in the standard test setting, which was new to them. For this group, cues originally associated with morphine injection were not present on the test trial, and therefore, according to Siegel, the animals should not exhibit morphine tolerance on that trial. The fourth group (group S-M) received saline on the first three trials (in the test setting) and morphine on the fourth trial. These animals would be expected to show the least sensitivity to pain because there has been no opportunity for morphine tolerance to develop. Finally, group S-S received saline on all four trials. If Siegel is correct, group S-M should show the longest latencies (indicating least sensitivity), whereas group M-S should show the shortest latency (most sensitivity). Group Mc-M should resemble group S-M, because cues associated with group Mc-M's first three trials would not be present on the test trial. Groups M-M and S-S should be intermediate. Whether group M-M will be equal to group S-S will depend on the rate at which morphine tolerance develops. The pattern of anticipated results is

$$\text{S-M} = \text{Mc-M} > \text{M-M} ? \text{S-S} > \text{M-S}$$

The "?" indicates no prediction. The dependent variable is the latency (in seconds) of paw-licking.

TABLE 12.1
Data and analysis on morphine tolerance

(a) *Data*

	M-S	M-M	S-S	S-M	Mc-M
	3	2	14	29	24
	5	12	6	20	26
	1	13	12	36	40
	8	6	4	21	32
	1	10	19	25	20
	1	7	3	18	33
	4	11	9	26	27
	9	19	21	17	30
Total	32	80	88	192	232
Mean	4.00	10.00	11.00	24.00	29.00
S.D.	3.16	5.13	6.72	6.37	6.16

TABLE 12.1 (Cont.)

(b) Summary Table

Source	df	SS	MS	F
Treatment	4	3497.60	874.40	27.33*
Error	35	1120.00	32.00	
Total	39	4617.60		

*$p < .05$

The results of this experiment are presented in Table 12.1a, and the overall analysis of variance is presented in Table 12.1b. Notice that the group variances are more or less equal (a test for heterogeneity of variance was not significant), and there are no obvious outliers. The overall analysis of variance is clearly significant, indicating differences among the five treatment groups.

12.3 A PRIORI COMPARISONS

As we have seen, a priori comparisons (also called contrasts) are planned before the data have been collected. There are several different kinds of a priori comparison procedures, and we will discuss them in turn.

MULTIPLE t TESTS

One of the simplest methods of running preplanned comparisons is to use individual t tests between pairs of groups. In running individual t tests, if the assumption of homogeneity of variance is tenable, we usually replace the individual variances, or the pooled variance estimate, with MS_{error} from the overall analysis of variance and evaluate the t on df_{error} degrees of freedom. When the variances are heterogeneous but the samples sizes are equal, we do not use MS_{error}, but instead use the individual sample variances and evaluate t on $2(n-1)$ degrees of freedom. Finally, when we have heterogeneity of variance and unequal sample sizes, we use the individual variances and correct the degrees of freedom using the Welch–Satterthwaite approach (see Chapter 7). (For an evaluation of this approach, albeit for a slightly different test statistic, see Games and Howell, 1976.)

The indiscriminant use of multiple t tests is typically brought up as an example of a terrible approach to multiple comparisons. In some ways, this is an unfair criticism. It *is* a terrible thing to jump into a set of data and lay waste all around you with t tests on each and every pair of means that looks as if it might be interesting. The familywise error rate will be outrageously high. However, if you have only one or two comparisons to make and if those comparisons were truly planned in advance, (you cannot cheat and say, "Oh well, I would have planned to make them if I had thought about it"), the t-test approach has much to recommend it. With only two comparisons, for example, the maximum FW would be approximately 0.10 if each comparison were run at $\alpha = .05$, and would be approximately 0.02 if each comparison were run at $\alpha = .01$.

If we had actually conducted the study on morphine tolerance described previously, we would probably not use multiple t tests simply because too many important comparisons should be considered. (In fact, we would probably use one of the post hoc procedures for making all pairwise comparisons.) For the sake of an example, however, consider two fundamental comparisons that were clearly predicted by the theory and that can be tested easily with a t test. The theory predicted that a rat who had received three previous morphine trials and was then tested in the same environment using a saline injection would show greater pain sensitivity than would an animal who had always been tested using saline. This involves a comparison of group M-S with group S-S. Furthermore, the theory predicted that group Mc-M would show less sensitivity to pain than would group M-M, since the former would be tested in an environment different from the one in which it had previously received morphine. Because the sample variances are similar and the sample sizes are equal, we will use MS_{error} as the pooled variance estimate and will evaluate the result on df_{error} degrees of freedom.

Our general formula for t will then be

$$t = \frac{\overline{X}_1 - \overline{X}_2}{\sqrt{\dfrac{MS_{error}}{n} + \dfrac{MS_{error}}{n}}} = \frac{\overline{X}_1 - \overline{X}_2}{\sqrt{\dfrac{2MS_{error}}{n}}}$$

Substituting the data from our example, group M-S versus group S-S would be

$$\overline{X}_{M\text{-}S} = 4.00 \qquad \overline{X}_{S\text{-}S} = 11.00 \qquad MS_{error} = 32.00$$

$$t = \frac{\overline{X}_{M\text{-}S} - \overline{X}_{S\text{-}S}}{\sqrt{\dfrac{2MS_{error}}{n}}} = \frac{4.00 - 11.00}{\sqrt{\dfrac{2(32.00)}{8}}} = \frac{-7}{\sqrt{8}} = -2.47$$

And Group Mc-M versus group M-M would be

$$\overline{X}_{Mc\text{-}M} = 29.00 \qquad \overline{X}_{M\text{-}M} = 10.00 \qquad MS_{error} = 32.00$$

$$t = \frac{\overline{X}_{Mc\text{-}M} - \overline{X}_{M\text{-}M}}{\sqrt{\dfrac{2MS_{error}}{n}}} = \frac{29.00 - 10.00}{\sqrt{\dfrac{2(32.00)}{8}}} = \frac{19.00}{\sqrt{8}} = 6.72$$

Both of these obtained values of t would be evaluated against $t_{.05}(35) = 2.03$, and both would lead to rejection of the corresponding null hypothesis. We can conclude that with two groups of animals tested with saline, the group that had previously received morphine in the same situation will show a heightened sensitivity to pain. We can also conclude that changing the setting in which morphine is given significantly reduces, if it does not eliminate, the conditioned morphine-tolerance effect. Since we have tested two null hypotheses, each with $\alpha = .05$ per comparison, the FW will approach .10.

LINEAR CONTRASTS

Linear contrasts

The use of individual t tests is a special case of a much more general technique involving the use of what are known as **linear contrasts**. In particular, t tests allow us to compare one group with another group, whereas linear contrasts allow us to compare one group *or set of groups* with another group or set of groups. Although we can use the calculational procedures of linear contrasts with post hoc tests as well as with a priori tests, they are discussed here under a priori tests because that is where they are most commonly used.

Linear combination   To define linear contrasts, we must first define a **linear combination**. A linear combination of means takes the form

$$L = a_1\overline{X}_1 + a_2\overline{X}_2 + \cdots + a_k\overline{X}_k = \sum a_j\overline{X}_j$$

This equation simply states that a linear combination is a weighted sum of treatment means. If, for example, the a_j were all equal to 1, L would just be the sum of the means. If, on the other hand, the a_j were all equal to $1/k$, then L would be the mean of the means.

When we impose the restriction that $\Sigma a_j = 0$, a linear combination becomes what is called a linear contrast. With the proper selection of the a_j, a linear contrast may be very useful. As an example, consider three means ($\overline{X}_1$, $\overline{X}_2$, and $\overline{X}_3$). Letting $a_1 = 1$, $a_2 = -1$, and $a_3 = 0$, $\Sigma a_j = 0$,

$$L = (1)(\overline{X}_1) + (-1)(\overline{X}_2) + 0(\overline{X}_3) = \overline{X}_1 - \overline{X}_2$$

In this case, L is simply the difference between the means of group 1 and group 2. If, on the other hand, we let $a_1 = 1/2$, $a_2 = 1/2$, and $a_3 = -1$, then

$$L = \left(\frac{1}{2}\right)(\overline{X}_1) + \left(\frac{1}{2}\right)(\overline{X}_2) + (-1)(\overline{X}_3) = \frac{\overline{X}_1 + \overline{X}_2}{2} - X_3$$

in which case L represents the difference between the mean of the third treatment and the average of the means of the first two treatments.

SUM OF SQUARES FOR CONTRASTS   One of the advantages of linear contrasts is that they can be converted to sums of squares very easily and can represent the sum of squared differences between the means of sets of treatments. If we let

$$L = a_1\overline{X}_1 + a_2\overline{X}_2 + \cdots + a_k\overline{X}_k = \sum a_j\overline{X}_j$$

it can be shown that

$$SS_{contrast} = \frac{nL^2}{\Sigma a_j^2}$$

is a component of the overall SS_{treat} on 1 *df*, where n represents the number of scores per treatment. [†][Notice that we are working with means rather than with totals. This equation would be incorrect if it were applied to totals, in which case the right side of the equation would be $L^2/(n\Sigma a_j^2)$.]

Suppose we have three treatments such that

$$n = 10 \qquad \overline{X}_1 = 1.5 \qquad \overline{X}_2 = 2.0 \qquad \overline{X}_3 = 3.0$$

[†] For unequal sample sizes using means,

$$SS_{contrast} = \frac{L^2}{\Sigma(a_j^2/n_j)}$$

For the overall analysis of variance,

$$SS_{treat} = \frac{15^2 + 20^2 + 30^2}{10} - \frac{65^2}{30} = 11.67$$

Suppose we wanted to compare the average of treatments 1 and 2 with treatment 3. Let $a_1 = 1$, $a_2 = 1$, $a_3 = -2$. Then

$$L = \Sigma a_j \overline{X}_j = (1)(1.5) + (1)(2.0) + (-2)(3.0) = -2.5$$

$$SS_{contrast} = \frac{nL^2}{\Sigma a_j^2} = \frac{10(-2.5)^2}{6} = \frac{62.5}{6}$$

$$= 10.42$$

This sums of squares is a component of the overall SS_{treat} on 1 df. We have 1 df because we are really comparing two means (the mean of the first two treatments with the mean of the third treatment). Now suppose we obtain an additional linear contrast comparing treatment 1 with treatment 2.

Let $a_1 = 1$, $a_2 = -1$, and $a_3 = 0$. Then

$$L = \sum a_j \overline{X}_j = (1)(1.5) + (-1)(2.0) + (0)(3.0) = -0.5$$

$$SS_{contrast} = \frac{nL^2}{\Sigma a_j^2} = \frac{10(-0.5)^2}{2} = \frac{2.5}{2}$$

$$= 1.25$$

This $SS_{contrast}$ is also a component of SS_{treat} on 1 df. In addition, because of the particular contrasts that we chose to run,

$$SS_{treat} = SS_{contrast_1} + SS_{contrast_2}$$

$$11.67 = \quad 10.42 \quad + \quad 1.25$$

and thus the two contrasts account for all of the SS_{treat} and all of the df attributable to treatments.

THE CHOICE OF COEFFICIENTS   In the previous example, it should be reasonably clear why we chose the coefficients we did. They weight the treatment means in what seems to be a logical way to perform the contrast in question. Suppose, however, that we have five groups and wished to compare the first three with the last two. We need a set of coefficients (a_j) that will accomplish this task and for which $\Sigma a_j = 0$. The simplest rule is to form the two sets of treatments and to assign as weights to one set the number of treatment groups in the other set, and vice versa. One arbitrary set of coefficients is then given a minus sign. For example, take the means

$$\overline{X}_1 \quad \overline{X}_2 \quad \overline{X}_3 \quad \overline{X}_4 \quad \overline{X}_5$$

We want to compare $\overline{X}_1$, $\overline{X}_2$, and $\overline{X}_3$ combined with $\overline{X}_4$ and $\overline{X}_5$ combined. The first set contains three means, so for $\overline{X}_4$ and $\overline{X}_5$ the $a_j = 3$. The second set contains two means, and therefore for $\overline{X}_1$, $\overline{X}_2$, and $\overline{X}_3$ the $a_j = 2$. We will let the 3s be negative. Then we have

Means:	$\overline{X}_1$	$\overline{X}_2$	$\overline{X}_3$	$\overline{X}_4$	$\overline{X}_5$	
a_j:	2	2	2	-3	-3	$\Sigma a_j = 0$

Then $\Sigma a_j \overline{X}_j$ reduces to $2(\overline{X}_1 + \overline{X}_2 + \overline{X}_3) - 3(\overline{X}_4 + \overline{X}_5)$.

If we have different numbers of subjects in the several groups, we need to obtain our coefficients somewhat differently. Essentially, all we are going to do is average the scores on each of the two sides of the contrast and then subtract one side from the other. Suppose, for example, that we had the following groups and sample sizes:

Group:	1	2	3	4
n_j:	9	10	8	10

Suppose further that we wish to compare groups 1 and 2 combined with groups 3 and 4 combined. The mean of groups 1 and 2 would be

$$\frac{9\overline{X}_1 + 10\overline{X}_2}{9 + 10} = \frac{9\overline{X}_1}{19} + \frac{10\overline{X}_2}{19}$$

and the mean of groups 3 and 4 would be

$$\frac{8\overline{X}_3 + 10\overline{X}_4}{8 + 10} = \frac{8\overline{X}_3}{18} + \frac{10\overline{X}_4}{18}$$

We can then subtract the combined mean of groups 3 and 4 from the combined mean of groups 1 and 2. What this really means is that we are using weights of

$$[9/19 \quad 10/19 \quad -8/18 \quad -10/18]$$

Note that these coefficients meet the requirement that $\Sigma a_j = 0$. If we wanted to compare groups 1 and 2, we would simply use coefficients of $[1 \quad -1 \quad 0 \quad 0]$. Similarly, to compare groups 3 and 4, the coefficients would be $[0 \quad 0 \quad 1 \quad -1]$. In order to have orthogonal contrasts with unequal ns, we must meet the restriction that $\Sigma a_j b_j / n_j = 0$. If you work out the arithmetic, you will find that these contrasts do in fact meet that requirement and the contrasts are orthogonal.

One final word about coefficients. You can save yourself a lot of arithmetic if you divide through by a common factor. For example, suppose that the steps we took had left us with

$$a_j = 2 \quad 2 \quad -2 \quad -2$$

You can divide through by 2 and have

$$a_j = 1 \quad 1 \quad -1 \quad -1$$

which simplifies the arithmetic considerably. In a similar vein, we could use fractional coefficients, which make it clearer that we are really averaging sets of means, but there the arithmetic is more cumbersome, and it is easier to work with whole numbers.

THE TEST OF SIGNIFICANCE   We have seen that linear contrasts can be easily converted to sums of squares on one degree of freedom. These sums of squares can be treated exactly like any other sums of squares. They can be converted to mean squares by dividing by the number of degrees of freedom (in this case, one) and can then produce an F by being divided by MS_{error}. Since all contrasts have one degree of freedom, and since division by 1 will not change anything, $SS_{contrast} = MS_{contrast}$ and

$$F = \frac{MS_{contrast}}{MS_{error}} = \frac{nL^2/(\Sigma a_j^2)}{MS_{error}} = \frac{nL^2}{\Sigma a_j^2 MS_{error}}$$

This F will have one and df_{error} degrees of freedom.

For our example, suppose we had planned (a priori) to compare the two groups receiving saline on trial 4 with the three groups receiving morphine on trial 4. We also planned to compare group Mc-M with group M-M, and group M-S with group S-S, for the same reasons given in the discussion of individual t tests. Finally, we planned to compare group M-M with group S-S to see whether morphine tolerance developed to such an extent that animals who always received morphine were no different after only four trials from animals who always received saline.

Groups:	M-S	M-M	S-S	S-M	Mc-M		
Means:	4.00	10.00	11.00	24.00	29.00		
			Coefficient			Σa_j^2	$L = \Sigma a_j \overline{X}_j$
a_j	-3	2	-3	2	2	30	81
b_j	0	-1	0	0	1	2	19
c_j	-1	0	1	0	0	2	7
d_j	0	1	-1	0	0	2	-1

$$SS_{contrast_1} = \frac{n(\Sigma a_j \overline{X}_j)^2}{\Sigma a_j^2} = \frac{8(81)^2}{30} = \frac{52488}{30} = 1749.60$$

$$F = \frac{MS_{contrast}}{MS_{error}} = \frac{1749.6}{32.00} = 54.675$$

$$SS_{contrast_2} = \frac{n(\Sigma b_j \overline{X}_j)^2}{\Sigma b_j^2} = \frac{8(19)^2}{2} = \frac{2888}{2} = 1444.00$$

$$F = \frac{MS_{contrast}}{MS_{error}} = \frac{1444.00}{32.00} = 45.125$$

$$SS_{contrast_3} = \frac{n(\Sigma c_j \overline{X}_j)^2}{\Sigma c_j^2} = \frac{8(7)^2}{2} = \frac{392}{2} = 196.00$$

$$F = \frac{MS_{contrast}}{MS_{error}} = \frac{196.00}{32.00} = 6.125$$

$$SS_{contrast_4} = \frac{n(\Sigma d_j \overline{X}_j)^2}{\Sigma d_j^2} = \frac{8(-1)^2}{2} = \frac{8}{2} = 4.00$$

$$F = \frac{MS_{contrast}}{MS_{error}} = \frac{4.00}{32.00} = 0.125$$

Each of these F values can be evaluated against $F_{.05}(1, 35) = 4.12$. As expected, the first three contrasts are significant. The fourth contrast, comparing M-M with S-S, is not significant, indicating that complete morphine tolerance seems to develop in as little as four trials. Note that contrasts 2 and 3 test the same hypotheses that we tested using individual t tests—and, as you should recall, when there is one df between groups, $F = t^2$. If you take the square root of the Fs for these two contrasts, they will equal 6.72 and 2.47, which are precisely the values we obtained for t earlier. This simply illustrates the fact that t tests are a special case of linear contrasts.

With four contrasts, we have an FW approaching .20. This error rate is uncomfortably high, although some experimenters would accept it, especially for a priori contrasts. One way of reducing the error rate would be to run each comparison at a more stringent level of α; for example, $\alpha = .01$. Another alternative would be to use a different a priori procedure, Dunn's test, which amounts to almost the same thing as the first alternative but is conducted in a more precise manner. We will consider Dunn's test after we briefly discuss a special type of linear contrast, called orthogonal contrasts. Yet a third way to control FW is to run fewer contrasts. For example, the comparison of M-M with S-S is probably not very important. Whether complete tolerance develops on the fourth trial or on the sixth or seventh trial is of no great theoretical interest. By eliminating that contrast, we could reduce the maximum FW to .15. You should never choose to run contrasts the way you eat peanuts or climb mountains—just because they are there. In general, if a contrast is not important, do not run it.

ORTHOGONAL CONTRASTS

Orthogonal contrasts

Linear contrasts as they have been defined allow us to test a series of hypotheses about treatment differences. There are ways of forming sets of contrasts, called **orthogonal contrasts**, that are particularly useful for a number of reasons. Orthogonality is not as important as used to be thought, but nonetheless, such contrasts do deserve serious attention.

What sets orthogonal contrasts apart from plain old everyday contrasts is the fact that whether or not one contrast shows a significant difference between two groups (or sets of groups) says nothing about whether or not another orthogonal contrast will be significant—the two contrasts address independent questions. The second feature of these contrasts is that because they are orthogonal, the sum of the sums of squares for the set of contrasts is equal to SS_{treat} and thus these contrasts account for all the variation among treatment means.

From a calculational point of view, what sets orthogonal contrasts apart from other types of contrasts we might choose is the relationship between the coefficients for one contrast and the coefficients for other contrasts in the set.

ORTHOGONAL COEFFICIENTS   Given sample sizes are equal, for contrasts to be orthogonal the coefficients must meet the following criteria:

1. $\Sigma a_j = 0$

2. $\Sigma a_j b_j = 0$

where a_j and b_j are the sets of coefficients for different contrasts. Furthermore, for the $SS_{contrast}$ to sum to SS_{treat}, we need to add a third criterion:

3. Number of comparisons = number of *df* for treatments

The first restriction has been discussed already; it results in the contrast being a sum of squares. The second restriction ensures that the contrasts are independent of (or orthogonal to) one another, and thus that we are summing nonoverlapping components. The third restriction says nothing more than that if you want the parts to sum to the whole, you need to have all the parts.

At first glance, it would appear that finding sets of coefficients satisfying the requirement $\Sigma a_j b_j = 0$ would require that we either undertake a frustrating process of trial and error or else solve a set of simultaneous equations. In fact, a simple rule exists for finding orthogonal sets of coefficients; although the rule will not find all possible sets, it will lead to most of them. The rule for forming the coefficients visualizes the process of breaking down SS_{treat} in terms of a tree diagram. The overall *F* for five treatment deals with all five treatment means simultaneously. That is the trunk of the tree. If we then compare the combination of treatments 1 and 2 with the combination of treatments 3, 4, and 5, we have formed two branches of our tree, one representing treatments 1 and 2 and the other representing treatments 3, 4, and 5. As discussed earlier, the value of a_j for the treatment means on the left will be equal to the number of treatments on the right, and vice versa, with one of the sets being negative. Thus, the coefficients are $(3, 3, -2, -2, -2)$ for the five treatments, respectively.

Now that we have formed two limbs or branches of our tree, we can never compare treatments on one limb with treatments on another limb, although we can compare treatments on the same limb. Thus, comparing treatment 3 with the combination of treatments 4 and 5 is an example of a legitimate comparison. The coefficients in this case would be $(0, 0, 2, -1, -1)$. Treatments 1 and 2 have coefficients of 0 because they are not part of this comparison. Treatment 3 has a coefficient of 2 since it is compared with two other treatments. Treatments 4 and 5 received coefficients of -1 since they are compared with one other treatment. The negative signs can be arbitrarily assigned to either side of the comparison.

The previous procedure could be carried on until we have exhausted all possible sets of comparisons. This will occur when we have made as many comparisons as there are *df* for treatments. As a result of this procedure, we might arrive at the comparisons and coefficients shown in Figure 12.1. To show that these coefficients are orthogonal,

FIGURE 12.1
Tree diagram illustrating orthogonal partition of SS_{treat}

		Coefficients				
(1, 2, 3, 4, 5)						
↙ ↘						
(1, 2) vs. (3, 4, 5)		3	3	-2	-2	-2
↙ ↘ ↙ ↘		1	-1	0	0	0
(1) vs. (2) (3) vs. (4, 5)		0	0	2	-1	-1
↙ ↘						
(4) vs. (5)		0	0	0	1	-1

we need to show only that all *pairwise* products of the coefficients sum to zero. For example,

$$\sum a_j b_j = (3)(1) + (3)(-1) + (-2)(0) + (-2)(0) + (-2)(0) = 0$$

and $\qquad \sum a_j c_j = (3)(0) + (3)(0) + (-2)(2) + (-2)(-1) + (-2)(-1) = 0$

Thus, we see that the first and second and the first and third contrasts are both independent. Similar calculations will show that all the other contrasts are also independent of one another.

These coefficients will lead to only one of many possible sets of orthogonal contrasts. If we had begun by comparing treatment 1 with the combination of treatments 2, 3, 4, and 5, the resulting set of contrasts would have been entirely different. It is important for the experimenter to decide what contrasts she considers important, and to plan accordingly.

The actual computation of F with orthogonal contrasts is the same as when we are using nonorthogonal contrasts. Because of this, there is little to be gained by working through an example here. It would be good practice, however, for you to create a complete set of orthogonal contrasts and to carry out the arithmetic. You can check your answers by showing that the sum of the sums of squares equals SS_{treat}.

BONFERRONI t (DUNN'S TEST)

Dunn's test,
Bonferroni t

Bonferroni
inequality

I suggested earlier that one way to control the familywise error rate when using linear contrasts is to use a more conservative level of α for each comparison. The proposal that you might want to use $\alpha = .01$ instead of $\alpha = .05$ was based on the fact that our statistical tables are set up that way. (We do not usually have critical values of t for α between .05 and .01.) A more formal way of controlling FW fairly precisely by manipulating the per comparison error rate can be found in a test proposed by Dunn (1961), which is particularly appropriate when you want to make only a few of all possible comparisons. Although this test had been known for a long time, Dunn was the first person to formalize it and to present the necessary tables, and it is sometimes referred to as **Dunn's test**. It also goes under the name **Bonferroni t**. The Bonferroni t test is based on what is known as the **Bonferroni inequality**, which states that the probability of the occurrence of one *or more* events can never exceed the sum of their individual probabilities. This means that when we make three comparisons, each with a probability $= \alpha$ of a Type I error, the probability of *at least* one Type I error can never exceed .15. In more formal terms, if c represents the number of comparisons and α' represents the probability of a Type I error for each comparison, then FW is less than or equal to $c\alpha'$. From this it follows that if we set $\alpha' = \alpha/c$ for each comparison, where α = the desired maximum FW, then

$$FW \leq c\alpha' = c\left(\frac{\alpha}{c}\right) = \alpha$$

Furthermore, the error rate per experiment will be equal to α. Dunn (1961) used this inequality to design a test in which each comparison is run at $\alpha' = \alpha/c$, leaving the FW for the set of comparisons $\leq \alpha$. This can be accomplished by using the standard t-test procedure but referring the result to modified t tables.

The problem you immediately encounter when you attempt to run each comparison at $\alpha' = \alpha/c$ is that you do not have the necessary statistical tables. If you want to run each of three comparisons at $\alpha' = \alpha/c = .05/3 = .0167$, you do not have tables of critical values of t at $\alpha = .0167$. Dunn's major contribution was to provide such tables.

For the Bonferroni t test on pairwise comparisons of means (i.e., comparing one mean with one other mean) define

$$t' = \frac{\overline{X}_i - \overline{X}_j}{\sqrt{\dfrac{s^2}{n} + \dfrac{s^2}{n}}} = \frac{\overline{X}_i - \overline{X}_j}{\sqrt{\dfrac{2s^2}{n}}} = \frac{\overline{X}_i - \overline{X}_j}{\sqrt{\dfrac{2MS_{error}}{n}}}$$

and evaluate t' against the critical value of t' taken from Dunn's tables in Appendix t'. The only difference between t' and a standard t is the tables used in the evaluation. With unequal sample size but homogeneous variance, replace the ns in the leftmost equation with n_i and n_j. With heterogeneity of variance, see the solution by Games and Howell later in this chapter.

To write a general expression that allows us to test any comparison of means, pairwise or not, let

$$L = \sum a_j \overline{X}_j \qquad \text{and} \qquad t' = \frac{L}{\sqrt{\dfrac{\Sigma a_j^2 MS_{error}}{n}}}$$

This represents the most general form for the Bonferroni t, and it can be shown that if L is *any* linear combination (not necessarily even a linear contrast, requiring $\Sigma a_j = 0$), then FW with c comparisons is at most α (Dunn, 1961). To put it most simply, the Bonferroni t runs a regular t test but evaluates the result against a modified critical value of t (t') that has been chosen so as to limit FW.[†]

A variation on the Bonferroni t test was proposed by Rosenthal and Rubin (1984). Their proposal involves an a priori decision of which contrasts are of primary interest and which are of secondary interest. Alpha is then divided up accordingly, assigning larger values of α to the most important tests and smaller values to the least important ones. This test increased power for those contrasts of greatest interest at the expense of more subsidiary hypotheses. The Rosenthal and Rubin paper is quite readable; it is followed by a paper by de Cani (1984) that presents objections to the proposal.

When we considered linear contrasts, we ran four comparisons, which had an FW of nearly .20. (Our test of each of those contrasts involved an F statistic but, since each contrast involves 1 df, we can go from t to F and vice versa by means of the relationship $t = \sqrt{F}$.) If we wish to run those same comparisons but to keep FW at a maximum of .05, we can use the Bonferroni t test. In each case, we will solve for t' and refer that to Dunn's tables. Taking the pairwise tests first, the calculations follow.

Mc-M versus M-M:

$$t' = \frac{\overline{X}_i - \overline{X}_j}{\sqrt{\dfrac{2MS_{error}}{n}}} = \frac{29.00 - 10.00}{\sqrt{\dfrac{(2)(32.00)}{8}}} = \frac{19}{\sqrt{8}} = 6.72$$

[†]Note the similarity between the right side of the equation and our earlier formula for F with linear contrasts. The resemblance is not accidental: one is just the square of the other.

S-S versus M-S:

$$t' = \frac{\overline{X}_i - \overline{X}_j}{\sqrt{\dfrac{2MS_{error}}{n}}} = \frac{11.00 - 4.00}{\sqrt{\dfrac{(2)(32.00)}{8}}} = \frac{7}{\sqrt{8}} = 2.47$$

M-M versus S-S:

$$t' = \frac{\overline{X}_i - \overline{X}_j}{\sqrt{\dfrac{2MS_{error}}{n}}} = \frac{10.00 - 11.00}{\sqrt{\dfrac{(2)(32.00)}{8}}} = \frac{-1}{\sqrt{8}} = -0.35$$

The calculations for the more complex contrast, letting the $a_j = 2, 2, 2, -3, -3$ as before, follow.

S-M, Mc-M, and M-M versus S-S and M-S:

$$t' = \frac{\Sigma a_j \overline{X}_j}{\sqrt{\dfrac{\Sigma a_j^2 MS_{error}}{n}}} = \frac{(2)(24) + \cdots + (-3)(4)}{\sqrt{\dfrac{(30)(32.00)}{8}}} = \frac{81}{\sqrt{120}} = 7.39$$

From Appendix t', with $c = 4$ and $df_{error} = 35$, we find by interpolation $t'_{.05}(35) = 2.64$. In this case, the first and last contrasts are significant, but the other two are not. Whereas we earlier rejected the hypothesis that groups S-S and M-S were sampled from populations with the same mean, using the more conservative Bonferroni t test we are no longer able to reject that hypothesis. Here we cannot conclude that prior morphine injections lead to hypersensitivity to pain. The difference in conclusions between the two procedures is a direct result of our use of the more conservative familywise error rate. If we wish to concentrate on per comparison error rates, ignoring FW, then we evaluate each t (or F) against the critical value at $\alpha = .05$. On the other hand, if we are primarily concerned with controlling FW, as we usually should be, then we evaluate each t, or F, at a more stringent level. The difference is not in the arithmetic of the test; it is in the critical value we choose to use. The choice is up to the experimenter.

MULTISTAGE BONFERRONI PROCEDURES

The Bonferroni multiple-comparison procedure has a number of variations. Although these are covered here in the context of the analysis of variance, they can be applied equally well whenever we have multiple hypothesis tests for which we wish to control the familywise error rate. These procedures have the advantage of setting a limit on the FW error rate at α against any set of possible null hypotheses, as does the Tukey HSD, while at the same time being less conservative than Tukey's test when our interest is in a specific subset of contrasts. In general, however, multistage procedures would not be used as a substitute when making all pairwise comparisons among a set of means.

As you saw, the Bonferroni test is based on the principle of dividing up FW for a family of contrasts among each of the individual contrasts. Thus, if we want FW to be .05 and we want to test four contrasts, we test each one at $\alpha = .05/4 = .0125$. The multistage tests follow a similar principle, the major difference being in the way they choose to partition α.

HOLM AND LARZELERE AND MULAIK TESTS   Both Holm (1979) and Larzelere and Mulaik (1977) have proposed a multistage test that adjusts the denominator (c) in $\alpha' = \alpha/c$ depending upon the number of null hypotheses remaining to be tested. Holm's test is generally referred to when speaking about the analysis of variance, whereas the Larzelere and Mulaik test is best known as a test of significance for a large set of correlation coefficients. The logic of the two tests is the same.

In the Holm procedure we calculate values of t' just as we did with the Bonferonni t test. For the equal n case, we compute

$$t' = \frac{\overline{X}_i - \overline{X}_j}{\sqrt{\dfrac{2MS_{error}}{n}}}$$

For the unequal n case, or when we are concerned about heterogeneity of variance, we compute

$$t' = \frac{\overline{X}_i - \overline{X}_j}{\sqrt{\dfrac{\dfrac{s_i^2}{n_i} + \dfrac{s_j^2}{n_j}}{2}}}$$

We calculate t' for all contrasts of interest and then arrange the t' values in increasing order without regard to sign. This ordering can be represented as $|t'_1| \leq |t'_2| \leq |t'_3| \leq \cdots \leq |t'_c|$, where c is the total number of contrasts to be tested.

The first significance test is carried out by evaluating t_c against the critical value in Dunn's table corresponding to c contrasts. In other words, t_c is evaluated at $\alpha' = \alpha/c$. If this largest t' is significant, then we test the next largest t' (t'_{c-1}) against the critical value in Dunn's tables corresponding to $c - 1$ contrasts. Thus, t'_{c-1} is evaluated at $\alpha' = \alpha/(c - 1)$. The same procedure continues for $t'_{c-2}, t'_{c-3}, t'_{c-4}, \ldots$ until the test returns a nonsignificant result. At that point we stop testing. Holm has shown that such a procedure continues to keep $FW \leq \alpha$.

To illustrate the use of Holm's test, consider our example on morphine tolerance. With the standard Bonferonni t test, we evaluated four contrasts with the following results, arranged by increasing magnitude of t':

Contrast	Order (i)	t'	t'_{crit}
M-M vs. S-S	1	$t' = -0.35$	2.03
S-S vs. M-S	2	$t' = 2.47$	2.35*
Mc-M vs. M-M	3	$t' = 6.72$	2.52*
S-M, Mc-M vs. S-S, M-S	4	$t' = 7.39$	2.64*

*$p < .05$

If we were using Dunn's test, each of these t's would be evaluated against t' at $\alpha = .0125$, which is 2.64. For Holm's test we vary the critical value in stages, depending on the number of contrasts that have not been tested. This number is indexed by

"Order (*i*)" in the table on page 352. These critical values are presented in the right-hand column above. They were taken, with interpolation, from Dunn's tables for $c = i$ and 35 degrees of freedom. For example, the critical value of 2.35 corresponds to the entry in Dunn's tables for $c = 2$ and $df = 35$. For the smallest t', the critical value came from the standard Student t distribution (Appendix t).

From this table you can see that the test on the complex contrast S-M, Mc-M vs. S-S, M-S required a t' of 2.64 or above to reject H_0. Since t' was 7.39, the difference was significant. The next largest t' was 6.72 for Mc-M vs. M-M, and that was also significant, exceeding the critical value of 2.52. The contrast S-S vs. M-S is tested as if there were only two contrasts in the set, and thus t' must exceed 2.35 for significance. Again this test is significant. If it had not been, we would have stopped at this point. But since it was, we continue and test M-M vs. S-S, which is not significant. Because of the increased power of Holm's test over the Bonferonni t test, we have rejected one null hypotheses (S-S vs. M-S) that was not rejected by the Bonferonni.

LARZELERE AND MULAIK TEST   Larzelere and Mulaik (1977) proposed a test equivalent to Holm's test, but their primary interest was in using that test to control *FW* when examining a large set of correlation coefficients. As you might suspect, something that controls error rates in one situation will tend to control them in another. I will consider the Larzelere and Mulaik test with respect to correlation coefficients because such an example will prove useful to those who conduct research that yields large numbers of such coefficients. However, as you will see when you look at the calculations, the test would be applied in the same way whenever you have a number of test statistics with their associated probability values. If you had never heard of Larzelere and Mulaik, you could still accomplish the same thing with Holm's test. However, the different calculational approach is instructive.

Compas, Howell, Phares, Williams, and Giunta (1989) investigated the relationship between daily stressors, parental levels of psychological symptoms, and adolescent behavior problems [as measured by Achenbach's Youth Self-Report Form (YSR) and by the Child Behavior Checklist (CBCL)]. The study represented an effort to try to understand risk factors for emotional/behavioral problems in adolescents. Among the analyses of the study was the set of intercorrelations between these variables at Time 1. These correlations are presented in Table 12.2.

TABLE 12.2
Correlations among behavioral and stress measures

	(1)	(2)	(3)	(4)	(5)	(6)	(7)
Mother							
(1) Stress	1.00	.69	.48	.37	−.02	.30	.03
(2) Symptoms		1.00	.38	.42	.12	.39	.19
Father							
(3) Stress			1.00	.62	.07	.22	.07
(4) Symptoms				1.00	.00	.24	.20
Adolescent							
(5) Stress					1.00	.11	.44
(6) CBCL						1.00	.23
(7) YSR							1.00

Most standard correlation programs print out a t statistic for each of these correlations. However, we know that with 21 hypothesis tests, the probability of a Type 1 error based on that standard t test, if all null hypotheses were true, would be high. It would still be high if only a reduced set of them were true. For this reason we will apply the modified Bonferroni test proposed by Larzelere and Mulaik. There are two ways to apply this test to this set of correlations. For the first method we could calculate a t value for each coefficient, based on

$$t = \frac{r\sqrt{(N-2)}}{\sqrt{(1-r^2)}}$$

(or take the t from standard computer printout) and then proceed exactly as we did for the Holm procedure. Alternatively, we could operate directly on the two-tailed p values associated with the t test on each correlation. These p values can be calculated using commonly available programs, or they can be taken from standard computer printouts. For purposes of an example, I will use the p-value approach.

Table 12.3 shows the correlations to be tested from Table 12.2 as well as the associated p values, which have been arranged in increasing numerical order. (Note that the sign of the correlation is irrelevant—only the absolute value matters.)

TABLE 12.3
Significance tests for correlations in Table 12.2

Pair	i	Correlation	p value	$\alpha/(k-i+1)$
1 vs. 2	1	.69	.0000	.00238*
3 vs. 4	2	.62	.0000	.00250*
1 vs. 3	3	.48	.0000	.00263*
5 vs. 7	4	.44	.0000	.00278*
2 vs. 4	5	.42	.0000	.00294*
2 vs. 6	6	.39	.0001	.00313*
2 vs. 3	7	.38	.0001	.00333*
1 vs. 4	8	.37	.0002	.00357*
1 vs. 6	9	.30	.0028	.00385*
4 vs. 6	10	.24	.0179	.00417
6 vs. 7	11	.23	.0236	.00455
3 vs. 6	12	.22	.0302	.00500
4 vs. 7	13	.20	.0495	.00556
2 vs. 7	14	.19	.0618	.00625
2 vs. 5	15	.12	.2409	.00714
5 vs. 6	16	.11	.2829	.00833
3 vs. 5	17	.07	.4989	.01000
3 vs. 7	18	.07	.4989	.01250
1 vs. 7	19	.03	.7724	.01667
1 vs. 5	20	−.02	.8497	.02500
4 vs. 5	21	.00	1.0000	.05000

The right-hand column gives the value of α' required for significance. For example, if we consider 21 contrasts to be of interest, $\alpha' = \alpha/(k-i+1) = .05/21 = .00238$. By the time we have rejected the first four correlations and wish to test the fifth largest, we are going to behave as if we want a Bonferonni t on just the $k - i + 1 = 21 - 5 + 1 = 17$ correlations. This correlation will be tested at $\alpha' = \alpha/(k - i + 1) = .05/17 = .00294$.

Each correlation coefficient is tested for significance by comparing the p value associated with that coefficient with the entry in the final column. For example, for the largest correlation coefficient out of a set of 21 coefficients to be significant, it must have a probability (under H_0: $\rho = 0$) less than .00238. Since the probability for $r = .69$ is given as .0000 (there are no nonzero digits until the sixth decimal place), we can reject H_0 and declare that correlation to be significant.

Having rejected H_0 for the largest coefficient, we then move down to the second row, comparing the obtained p value against $p = .00250$. Again we reject H_0 and move on to the third row. We continue this procedure until we find a row at which the obtained p value in column 4 exceeds the critical p value in column 5. At that point we declare that correlation to be nonsignificant and stop testing. All correlations below that point are likewise classed as nonsignificant. For our data, those correlations equal to or greater than .30 are declared significant, and those below .30 are nonsignificant. The significant correlations are indicated with an asterisk in the table.

Had we used a standard Bonferroni test, we would have set $\alpha' = .05/21 = .0024$, and a correlation less than .37 would not have been significant. In this particular case the multistage test made only a small difference. But often the difference is substantial in terms of the number of coefficients that are declared significant.

SHAFFER'S MODIFIED SEQUENTIALLY REJECTIVE PROCEDURE   Shaffer (1986) proposed a modification of the Larzelere and Mulaik and the Holm procedures that takes advantage of the fact that rejection of some hypotheses logically excludes certain others. For example, if we have three means and reject H_0: $\mu_1 = \mu_2$, then we know that it is not possible for H_0: $\mu_1 = \mu_3$ and $\mu_2 = \mu_3$ to *both* be true. Thus, we could reduce even further the denominator used to calculate α', allowing a more generous α' for many comparisons.

The only problem with Shaffer's procedure is the difficulty of calculating the number of logically possible null hypotheses remaining. Because of this difficulty, I will not discuss this test further here. Interested readers are encouraged to consult Shaffer's paper.

12.4 POST HOC COMPARISONS

There is much to recommend the use of linear contrasts and the Bonferroni t test when comparisons can be specified a priori, especially if the desired number of comparisons is small. However, many experiments involve many hypotheses[†] and/or hypotheses that are arrived at only after the data have been examined. In this situation, a number of a posteriori or post hoc techniques are available.

[†] If there are many hypotheses to be tested, regardless of whether they were planned in advance, the procedures discussed here are usually more powerful than is the Bonferroni t test.

FISHER'S LEAST SIGNIFICANT DIFFERENCE PROCEDURE

Fisher's least significant difference (LSD)

One of the oldest methods for making post hoc comparisons is known as **Fisher's least significant difference (LSD)** test (also known as Fisher's protected *t*). The only difference between the post hoc LSD procedure and the a priori multiple *t* test procedure discussed earlier is that the LSD requires a significant *F* for the overall analysis of variance. When the complete null hypothesis is true, the requirement of a significant overall *F* ensures that the familywise error rate will equal α. Unfortunately, if the complete null hypothesis is *not* true but some other more limited null hypothesis involving several means is true, the overall *F* no longer affords protection for *FW*. For this reason, many people recommend that you not use this test, although Carmer and Swanson (1973) have shown it to be the most powerful of the common post hoc multiple-comparison procedures. If your experiment involves three means, the LSD procedure is a good one because *FW* will stay at α, and you will gain the added power of using standard *t* tests. (The *FW* error rate will be α with three means because if the complete null hypothesis is true, you have a probability equal to α of making a Type I error with your overall *F*, and any subsequent Type I errors you might commit with a *t* test will not affect *FW*. If the complete null is not true but a more limited one is, with three means there can be only one null difference among the means and, therefore, only one chance of making a Type I error, again with a probability equal to α.) You should generally be reluctant to use the LSD for more than three means unless you have good reason to believe that there is at most one true null hypothesis hidden in the means.

THE STUDENTIZED RANGE STATISTIC

Studentized range statistic (q)

Because many of the post hoc tests are based on the Studentized range statistic or special variants of it, we will consider this statistic before proceeding. The **Studentized range statistic (q)** is defined as

$$q_r = \frac{\overline{X}_l - \overline{X}_s}{\sqrt{\dfrac{MS_{error}}{n}}}$$

where $\overline{X}_l$ and $\overline{X}_s$ represent the largest and smallest of a set of treatment means and *r* is the number of treatments in the set. You probably have noticed that the formula for *q* is very similar to the formula for *t*. Thus

$$q_r = \frac{\overline{X}_l - \overline{X}_s}{\sqrt{\dfrac{MS_{error}}{n}}} \quad \text{and} \quad t = \frac{\overline{X}_i - \overline{X}_j}{\sqrt{\dfrac{2(MS_{error})}{n}}}$$

The only difference between *q* and a *t* test on the difference between the largest and smallest means is that the formula for *t* has a "$\sqrt{2}$" in the denominator. Thus, *q* is a linear function of *t* and we can always go from *t* to *q* by the relation

$$q = t\sqrt{2}$$

The real difference comes from the fact that the tables of q (Appendix q) are set up to allow us to adjust the critical value of q for the number of means involved, as will become apparent shortly. When there are only two treatments, whether we solve for t or q is irrelevant as long as we use the corresponding tables.

When we have only two means or when we wish to compare two means chosen *at random* from the set of available means, t is an appropriate test.[†] Suppose, however, that we looked at a set of means and deliberately selected the largest and smallest means for testing. It is apparent that we have drastically altered the probability of a Type I error. Given that H_0 is true, the largest and smallest means certainly have a greater chance of being called "significantly different" than do means that are adjacent in an ordered series of means. This is the point at which the Studentized range statistic becomes useful. It was designed for just this purpose.

To use q, we first rank the means from smallest to largest. We then take into account the number of steps between the means to be compared. For adjacent means, no change is made and $q_{.05} = t_{.05}\sqrt{2}$. For means that are not adjacent, however, the critical value of q increases, growing in magnitude as the number of intervening steps between means increases.

As an example of the use of q, consider the data on morphine tolerance. The means are

$$\overline{X}_1 \quad \overline{X}_2 \quad \overline{X}_3 \quad \overline{X}_4 \quad \overline{X}_5$$

$$4 \quad\;\; 10 \quad 11 \quad 24 \quad 29$$

with $n = 8$, $df_{error} = 35$, and $MS_{error} = 32.00$. The largest mean is 29 and the smallest is 4, and there are a total (r) of 5 means in the set (in the terminology of most tables, we say that these means are $r = 5$ steps apart).

$$q_5 = \frac{\overline{X}_l - \overline{X}_s}{\sqrt{\dfrac{MS_{error}}{n}}} = \frac{29 - 4}{\sqrt{\dfrac{32.00}{8}}} = \frac{25}{\sqrt{4}} = 12.5$$

Notice that r is not involved in the calculation. It is involved, however, when we go to the tables. From Appendix q, for $r = 5$ and $df_{error} = 35$, $q_{.05}(5, 35) = 4.07$. Since $12.5 > 4.07$, we will reject H_0 and conclude that there is a significant difference between the largest and smallest means.

An alternative to solving for q_{obt} and referring q_{obt} to the sampling distribution of q would be to solve for the smallest difference that would be significant and then to compare our actual difference with the minimum significant difference. This approach is frequently taken by post hoc procedures. Since

$$q_r = \frac{\overline{X}_l - \overline{X}_s}{\sqrt{\dfrac{MS_{error}}{n}}}$$

[†] With only two means we obtain all of the information we need from the F in the analysis of variance table and would have no need to run any contrast.

then

$$\overline{X}_l - \overline{X}_s = q_{.05}(r, df_{\text{error}}) \sqrt{\frac{MS_{\text{error}}}{n}}$$

where $\overline{X}_l - \overline{X}_s$ is the minimum difference between two means that will be found to be significant.

We know that with five means, $q_{.05}(5, 35) = 4.07$. Then, for our data,

$$\overline{X}_l - \overline{X}_s = 4.07 \sqrt{\frac{32.00}{8}} = 8.14$$

Thus, a difference in means equal to or greater than 8.14 would be judged significant, whereas a smaller difference would not. Since the difference between the largest and smallest means in the example is 25, we would reject H_0.

Although q could be used in place of an overall F (i.e., instead of running the traditional analysis of variance, we would test the difference between the two extreme means), there is rarely an occasion to do so. In most cases, F is more powerful than q. However, where you expect several control group means to be equal to each other, but different from an experimental treatment mean (i.e., $\mu_1 = \mu_2 = \mu_3 = \mu_4 \neq \mu_5$), q might well be the more appropriate statistic.

Although q is seldom a good substitute for the overall F for treatments, it is a very important statistic when it comes to making multiple comparisons among individual treatment means. It forms the basis for the next several tests.

THE NEWMAN–KEULS TEST

Newman–Keuls test

The Newman–Keuls is a controversial test, for reasons that will become clear shortly. However, it is important to discuss it here if only because it is an excellent example of a whole class of multiple-comparison procedures. The basic goal of the **Newman–Keuls test** is to sort all the treatment means into subsets of treatments. These subsets will be homogeneous in the sense that they do not differ among themselves, but they do differ from other subsets.

We will again use the data on morphine tolerance and will start by arranging the treatment means in ascending order from smallest to largest. We will designate these means as $\overline{X}_1 \ldots \overline{X}_5$, *where the subscript now refers to the position of that mean in the ordered series.* For the data in our example,

	Treatment			
M-S	M-M	S-S	S-M	Mc-M
$\overline{X}_1$	$\overline{X}_2$	$\overline{X}_3$	$\overline{X}_4$	$\overline{X}_5$
4	10	11	24	29

We will define the *range* of means as the number of steps in an ordered series between those means. Adjacent means will be defined as being two steps apart, means that have one other mean intervening between them will have a range of three, and so on. In general, the range between $\overline{X}_i$ and $\overline{X}_j = i - j + 1$ (for $i > j$).

If we wished to test the difference $\overline{X}_5 - \overline{X}_1$, the range would be $5 - 1 + 1 = 5 = r$. For this example, we have $r = 5$ and 35 df for error, and thus (from Appendix q) would require $q_{obt} \geq 4.07$ if the difference is to be significant. Given this information, we could now solve for the smallest difference that would be judged significant. As we saw previously, this critical difference would be 8.14. Thus, when the means are five steps apart, a difference of at least 8.14 is required for significance.

If we were only concerned with means that are four steps apart (e.g., $\overline{X}_4 - \overline{X}_1$ or $\overline{X}_5 - \overline{X}_2$), then $r = 4$, $df = 35$, and $q_{.05}(4, 35) = 3.815$ (by linear interpolation). Thus, the minimum difference that would be significant is

$$\overline{X}_l - \overline{X}_s = q_{.05}(4, 35)\sqrt{\frac{MS_{error}}{n}} = 3.815\sqrt{\frac{32.00}{8}} = 3.815(2) = 7.63$$

Thus, four-step differences greater than 7.63 will be classified as significant.[†]

This procedure will be repeated for all ranges possible with our data. If we define W_r as the smallest width or difference between means r steps apart that will be significant, then

$$W_r = q_{.05}(r, df)\sqrt{\frac{MS_{error}}{n}}$$

For our example,

$$W_2 = q_{.05}(2, 35)\sqrt{\frac{MS_{error}}{n}} = 2.875(2) = 5.75$$

$$W_3 = q_{.05}(3, 35)\sqrt{\frac{MS_{error}}{n}} = 3.465(2) = 6.93$$

$$W_4 = q_{.05}(4, 35)\sqrt{\frac{MS_{error}}{n}} = 3.815(2) = 7.63$$

$$W_5 = q_{.05}(5, 35)\sqrt{\frac{MS_{error}}{n}} = 4.07(2) = 8.14$$

The Newman–Keuls test employs the values of W_r and a set of rules that are designed to control FW and to prevent inconsistent conclusions. If we did not adopt a set of rules governing the tests that will be made and the order of the testing, we would lose complete control of FW and, in addition, we might find ourselves making contradictory statements. For example, if three means are ordered $\overline{X}_1$, $\overline{X}_2$, and $\overline{X}_3$, it would be embarrassing if we found that $\overline{X}_1$ was different from $\overline{X}_2$, but not from $\overline{X}_3$ (since $\overline{X}_3$ is larger than $\overline{X}_2$).

To make the procedure systematic, we will adopt an approach similar to the one used by Winer (1962). We will form a matrix with treatment means on the rows and columns, and differences between means as the cell entries. Such a matrix is presented

---

[†] The Newman–Keuls is sometimes referred to as a layered test because it adjusts the critical difference as a function of the number of means contained within a subset of means. This is in contrast to the Tukey HSD and Scheffé tests (to be described shortly), which essentially use a constant critical difference for all contrasts.

in Table 12.4a for the data in Table 12.1. The dashed lines in this table connect differences between means r steps apart with values of r and W_r. Thus, any values along a dashed line that are greater than the corresponding value of W_r are *potentially* significant.

TABLE 12.4
Newman–Keuls test applied to data in Table 12.1

(a) Difference Between Means

			M-S	M-M	S-S	S-M	Mc-M		
			$\overline{X}_1$	$\overline{X}_2$	$\overline{X}_3$	$\overline{X}_4$	$\overline{X}_5$		
			4	10	11	24	29	r	W_r
M-S	$\overline{X}_1$	4	—	6	7	20	25	5	8.14
M-M	$\overline{X}_2$	10		—	1	14	19	4	7.63
S-S	$\overline{X}_3$	11			—	13	18	3	6.93
S-M	$\overline{X}_4$	24				—	5	2	5.75
Mc-M	$\overline{X}_5$	29					—		

(b) Pattern of Significant Difference

			M-S	M-M	S-S	S-M	Mc-M
			$\overline{X}_1$	$\overline{X}_2$	$\overline{X}_3$	$\overline{X}_4$	$\overline{X}_5$
			4	10	11	24	29
M-S	$\overline{X}_1$	4		*	*	*	*
M-M	$\overline{X}_2$	10				*	*
S-S	$\overline{X}_3$	11				*	*
S-M	$\overline{X}_4$	24					
Mc-M	$\overline{X}_5$	29					

We now start in the upper right corner and test along the first row until we reach a difference that is not significant. The upper right entry is 25, which represents a five-step difference. Since $25 > 8.14$, this difference is significant, and an asterisk is placed in the corresponding cell of Table 12.4b. Moving to the left, we find an entry of 20, which represents a difference of four steps. We thus compare 20 against $W_4 = 7.63$, and again reject H_0. Once again, we place an asterisk in the corresponding cell of Table 12.4b. Moving farther to the left, we find the entry of 7, which represents a three-step difference and is significant since $7 > W_3$. Again we place an asterisk in Table 12.4b. When we come to the far left, we find that a two-step difference of 6 is also significant ($6 > 5.75$), and thus enter an asterisk in the matrix.

When we either reach a point at which a difference is not significant or else exhaust a row, we move to the next row. We now start working from right to left across the second row, but stop under one of three conditions: (1) we exhaust the row; (2) we reach a nonsignificant difference; or (3) we reach a column at which a nonsignificant difference was found in an earlier row.

In row 2, $19 > 7.63$, $14 > 6.93$, but $1 < 5.75$. Thus, we place two asterisks in Table 12.4b and continue to the next row. In row 3, both differences are significant, since

$18 > 6.93$ and $13 > 5.75$. Going to row 4, our one difference is not significant $(5 < 5.75)$.

The resulting pattern of significant differences is given in Table 12.4b. Here we can see that group M-S is different from all other groups, groups M-M and S-S are different from groups S-M and Mc-M but not from each other, and groups S-M and Mc-M do not differ. These results can be represented graphically by writing down the treatments and underlining homogeneous subsets. Thus,

M-S	M-M	S-S	S-M	Mc-M
4	10	11	24	29

Treatments not underlined by a common line differ significantly from each other. This pattern of results would appear to confirm Siegel's theory, since the group that received three morphine injections and then was switched to saline (M-S) showed hypersensitivity, whereas the group that received morphine in an environment different from the test environment (Mc-M) was no different from the group that had not previously received morphine (S-M). The other two groups were intermediate, as the theory would predict. Notice that these results differ from those we obtained using the Bonferroni t test, even though both tests attempt to limit FW. The differences are due partly to the different approaches of the two tests and partly to the fact that the Newman–Keuls is actually a less conservative test, as will be discussed shortly. (It does not always hold FW at α.)

UNEQUAL SAMPLE SIZES AND HETEROGENEITY OF VARIANCE   The Newman–Keuls procedure (and the Tukey procedures that follow) were designed primarily for the case of equal sample sizes ($n_1 = n_2 = \cdots = n_k = n$). Frequently, however, experiments do not work out as planned, and we find ourselves with unequal numbers of observations and want to carry out a Newmann–Keuls or a related test on the means. Although little work has been done on this topic with respect to the Newmann–Keuls itself, work has been done on the problem with respect to the Tukey HSD test (see particularly Games & Howell, 1976; Keselman & Rogan, 1977; Games, Keselman, & Rogan, 1981). Because the problems would be the same in the two tests, it is reasonable to generalize from the latter findings. One solution, known as the Tukey–Kramer approach, is to replace $\sqrt{\mathrm{MS_{error}}/n}$ with

$$\sqrt{\frac{\dfrac{\mathrm{MS_{error}}}{n_i} + \dfrac{\mathrm{MS_{error}}}{n_j}}{2}}$$

This procedure has been proposed in conjunction with the Tukey HSD, to be discussed in Section 12.5. An alternative, and generally preferable, test was proposed by Games and Howell (1976). The Games and Howell procedure uses what was referred to as the Behrens–Fisher approach to t tests in Chaper 7. The authors suggest that a critical difference between means (i.e., W_r) be calculated for every pair of means using

$$W_r = \overline{X}_i - \overline{X}_j = q_{.05}(r, df') \sqrt{\dfrac{\dfrac{s_i^2}{n_i} + \dfrac{s_j^2}{n_j}}{2}}$$

where $q_{.05}(r, df')$ is taken from the tables of the Studentized range statistic on

$$df' = \dfrac{\left(\dfrac{s_i^2}{n_i} + \dfrac{s_j^2}{n_j}\right)^2}{\dfrac{\left(\dfrac{s_i^2}{n_i}\right)^2}{n_i - 1} + \dfrac{\left(\dfrac{s_j^2}{n_j}\right)^2}{n_j - 1}}$$

degrees of freedom. This is basically the solution referred to earlier in the discussion of multiple t tests, although here we are using the Studentized range statistic instead of t. This solution is laborious, but the effort involved is still small compared to that of designing the study and collecting the data. The need for special procedures arises from the fact that the analysis of variance and its attendant contrasts are vulnerable to violations of the assumption of homogeneity of variance, especially when the sample sizes are unequal. If there is no serious problem with heterogeneity of variance and if the n_i are nearly equal, then you are probably safe calculating the harmonic mean of the sample sizes $[\bar{n}_h = k/\Sigma(1/n_i)]$ and using that in place of n in the standard approach. Moreover, regardless of the sample sizes, if the sample variances are nearly equal you may replace s_i^2 and s_j^2 in the formula for W_r with MS_{error} from the overall analysis of variance. And regardless of the sample size, if the variances are heterogeneous you should probably use the Games and Howell procedure.

FAMILYWISE ERROR RATE   Although the Newman–Keuls procedure was designed to control the familywise error rate, it does not control it completely. In fact, under certain conditions, the error rate can be quite high. If the *complete* null hypothesis is true (i.e., if $\mu_1 = \mu_2 = \cdots = \mu_k$), then the Newman–Keuls sets $FW = .05$, assuming that this is our chosen significance level. With, for example, five means, our first test will compare μ_1 with μ_5, and since we use the Studentized range statistic, the probability of a Type I error will be .05. If we do not find a difference, we stop testing and thus do not have another chance to make a Type I error. If we do find a difference, we have already made a Type I error (since the complete null hypothesis is true), and FW is not affected by how many more errors we make. (It is the probability of *at least* one Type I error.) Suppose, however, that some other state of affairs is true. For example, suppose $\mu_1 \neq \mu_2 = \mu_3 \neq \mu_4 = \mu_5$. Then our first test is likely to be significant, since $\mu_1 \neq \mu_5$. Now, however, there are two true null hypotheses to be tested and we have a probability of .05 of making a Type I error on each. Therefore, FW will be about $1 - (1 - .05)^2$, which is approximately .10. In general, the *maximum FW* for the Newman–Keuls is approximately α times the maximum number of null hypotheses that could be true, which is equal to the number of pairs involving different means.

Therefore,
$$FW_{max} \simeq \begin{cases} \dfrac{\alpha k}{2} & \text{if } k \text{ is even} \\[2ex] \dfrac{\alpha(k-1)}{2} & \text{if } k \text{ is odd} \end{cases}$$

This means that with three means $FW = .05$ because there is at most one true null hypothesis to be falsely declared "significant," whereas with four or five means $FW \simeq$ .10 (there are *at most* two true null hypotheses).

12.5 TUKEY'S TESTS

Tukey$_a$ test, HSD (honestly significant difference) test

Much of the work on multiple comparisons has been based on the original work of Tukey, and two important tests bear his name. The **Tukey$_a$ test**, also called the **HSD (honestly significant difference) test**, is similar to the Newman–Keuls, except that q_{HSD} is always taken as the maximum value of q_r. In other words, if there are five means, *all* differences are tested as if they were five steps apart. The effect is to fix the familywise error rate at α against all possible null hypotheses, not just the complete null hypothesis, although with a loss of power. The Tukey HSD is the favorite pairwise test for many people because of the control it exercises over α.

Tukey$_b$ test, WSD (wholly significant difference) test

An alternative test, called the **Tukey$_b$ test**, or the **WSD (wholly significant difference) test**, is a compromise, being less conservative than the HSD test. In this procedure, q_{WSD} is taken as the mean of the value of q_r for the Newman–Keuls and the value of q_{HSD} for the HSD test. In other words, if there are k means and we want to test two means that are r steps apart,

$$q_{WSD} = \frac{q_k + q_r}{2}$$

With this modification, the Tukey WSD proceeds in the same manner as the Newman–Keuls. For a complete discussion, see Ryan (1959).

If we apply the Tukey HSD to the data on morphine tolerance, we apply a critical value of $W_r = 8.14$ to all differences. Thus, we declare all mean differences $(\overline{X}_i - \overline{X}_j)$ to be significant if they exceed 8.14 and to be not significant if they are less than 8.14. For our data, the differences between $\overline{X}_{M\text{-}M}$ and $\overline{X}_{M\text{-}S} = 10 - 4 = 6$, and the difference between $\overline{X}_{S\text{-}S}$ and $\overline{X}_{M\text{-}S} = 11 - 4 = 7$. The Newman–Keuls declared these differences to be significant, but the Tukey HSD would declare them not significant because 6 and 7 are less than 8.14. On this basis, we would represent the set of homogeneous means as

M-S	M-M	S-S	S-M	Mc-M
4	10	11	24	29

rather than

This leads to quite a different interpretation of the results, since the group that was switched from morphine to saline (M-S) can no longer be declared significantly more sensitive to pain than is the group that had never received morphine (S-S) or the group that always received it (M-M). (Similar conclusions would result if we used the Tukey WSD procedures.)

If you read the references cited in this chapter, you will find that the Tukey HSD is generally regarded as the best procedure for controlling FW when you are making all pairwise comparisons among many group means. The reason for this is that the Tukey HSD allows you to keep the maximum FW at your desired value (e.g., .05) no matter how many means you have and no matter what the true null hypothesis (or hypotheses) is. The Newman–Keuls, on the other hand, was designed to keep $FW = .05$ against the complete null hypothesis. More will be said on this topic later. I would certainly recommend Tukey's test if you have six or more means or if you are determined to keep a tight rein on FW.

12.6   THE SCHEFFÉ TEST

The post hoc tests we have considered all primarily involve pairwise comparisons of means, although they can be extended to more complex contrasts. One of the best-known tests, which is both broader and more conservative, was developed by Scheffé. The **Scheffé test**, which uses the F distribution rather than the Studentized range statistic, sets the familywise error rate at α against all possible linear contrasts, not just pairwise contrasts. If we let

Scheffé test

$$L = \sum a_j \overline{X}_j \qquad \text{and} \qquad SS_{contrast} = \frac{nL^2}{\Sigma a_j^2}$$

then

$$F = \frac{nL^2}{\Sigma a_j^2 MS_{error}}$$

Scheffé has shown that if F_{obt} is evaluated against $(k - 1)F_{\alpha}(k - 1, df_{error})$—rather than against $F_{\alpha}(1, df_{error})$—the FW is at most α. (Note that all that we have done is to calculate F on a standard linear contrast, but we have evaluated that F against a modified critical value. Although this test has the advantage of holding constant FW for all possible linear contrasts—not just pairwise ones—it pays a price; it has the least power of all the tests we have discussed. Partly to overcome this objection, Scheffé proposed that people may prefer to run his test at $\alpha = .10$. He further showed that the test is much less sensitive than the Tukey HSD for pairwise differences but is more sensitive than the Tukey HSD for complex comparisons (Scheffé, 1953, 1959). In general, the Scheffé test should never be used to make a set of solely pairwise comparisons, nor should it normally be used for a priori comparisons. The test was specifically designed as a post hoc test (as were the Newman–Keuls and Tukey tests), and its use on a limited set of comparisons that were planned before the data were collected would generally be foolish.

12.7   DUNNETT'S TEST FOR COMPARING ALL TREATMENTS WITH A CONTROL

Dunnett's test

In some experiments the important comparisons are between one control treatment and each of several experimental treatments. In this case, the most appropriate test is **Dunnett's test**. This test is more powerful (in this situation) than are any of the other tests we have discussed that seek to hold the familywise error rate at or below α.

We will let t_d represent the critical value of a modified t statistic. This statistic is found in tables supplied by Dunnett (1955, 1964) and is reproduced in Appendix t_d. We can either run a standard t test between the appropriate means (using MS_{error} as our variance estimate and evaluating the t against the tables of t_d) or solve for a critical difference between means. For a difference between means $\overline{X}_c$ and $\overline{X}_j$ (where $\overline{X}_c$ represents the mean of the control group) to be significant, the difference must exceed

$$\text{Critical value } (\overline{X}_c - \overline{X}_j) = t_d \sqrt{\frac{2MS_{error}}{n}}$$

Applying this test to our data, letting group S-S from Table 12.1 be the control group,

$$\text{Critical value } (\overline{X}_c - \overline{X}_j) = t_d \sqrt{\frac{2(32.00)}{8}}$$

We enter Appendix t_d with $k = 5$ means and $df_{error} = 35$. The resulting value of $t_d = 2.56$.

$$\text{Critical value } (\overline{X}_c - \overline{X}_j) = 2.56 \sqrt{\frac{2(32.00)}{8}} = 2.56(2.828) = 7.24$$

Thus, whenever the difference between the control group mean (group S-S) and one of the other group means exceeds ± 7.24, that difference will be significant. The $k - 1$ statements we will make concerning this difference will have an FW of $\alpha = .05$.

$$\text{S-S versus M-S} = 11 - 4 = 7$$

$$\text{S-S versus M-M} = 11 - 10 = 1$$

$$\text{S-S versus S-M} = 11 - 24 = -13$$

$$\text{S-S versus Mc-M} = 11 - 29 = -18$$

Since we have a two-tailed test (t_d was taken from two-tailed tables), the sign of the difference is irrelevant. The last two differences exceed ± 7.24 and are therefore declared to be significant.

In the case in which the groups have unequal sample sizes or heterogeneous variances, a test on the difference in treatment means is given by the same general procedure we used with the Newman–Keuls.

12.8 COMPARISON ON DUNNETT'S TEST AND THE BONFERRONI t

Since the Bonferroni t test allows the experimenter to make any a priori test, it is reasonable to ask what would happen if we decided a priori to apply that test to the differences between the control mean and the experimental treatment means. If we did this for our data, we would find that the required critical difference would be 7.47 instead of the 7.24 required for Dunnett's test. Thus, we would have a less powerful test, since a larger difference is needed for rejection of H_0. Both the Bonferroni t and Dunnett's test are based on inequalities of the form $FW \leq \alpha$, but Dunnett's test uses a sharper inequality (Miller, 1981). To put this rather crudely, in Dunnett's case there is more of the *equal to* and less of the *less than* involved in the relationship between FW and α. For this reason, it is a more powerful test whenever you want simply to compare one treatment (it does not really have to be called a "control" treatment) with each of the others.

12.9 COMPARISON OF THE ALTERNATIVE PROCEDURES

Since the multiple-comparison techniques we have been discussing were designed for different purposes, there is no truly fair basis on which they can be compared. There is something to be gained, however, from summarizing their particular features and comparing the critical differences they require for the same set of data. Table 12.5 lists the tests, the error rate most commonly associated with them, the kinds of comparisons they are primarily designed to test, and the type of test (range test, F test, or t—modified or not in each case).

TABLE 12.5
Comparison of alternative multiple-comparison procedures

Test	Error Rate[#]	Comparison	Type	A Priori/ Post Hoc
1. Individual t tests	PC	Pairwise	t	A priori
2. Linear contrasts	PC	Any contrasts	F	A priori
3. Bonferroni t	PE or FW	Any contrasts	t[‡]	A priori
4. Holm; Larzelere and Mulaik	FW	Any contrasts	t[‡]	A priori
5. Fisher's LSD	FW[†]	Pairwise	t	Post hoc
6. Newman–Keuls	FW[†]	Pairwise	Range	Post hoc
7. Tukey$_a$ (HSD)	FW	Pairwise[∞]	Range[‡]	Post hoc
8. Tukey$_b$ (WSD)	FW?	Pairwise[∞]	Range[‡]	Post hoc
9. Scheffé test	FW	Any contrasts	F[‡]	Post hoc
10. Dunnett's test	FW	With control	t[‡]	Post hoc

[#] PC = per comparison; PE = per experiment; FW = familywise
[†] Against complete H_0
[‡] Modified
[∞] Tukey$_a$ and Tukey$_b$ can be used for all contrasts, but are poor in this case.

If we compare the tests in terms of the critical values they require, we are being somewhat unfair to the a priori tests. To say that the Bonferroni t test, for example, requires a large critical value when making all possible pairwise comparisons is not really doing the test justice, since it was designed to make relatively few individual comparisons and not to be limited to pairwise contrasts. With this word of caution, Table 12.6 compares the critical differences (W_r) for each test. Linear contrasts have been omitted because they are not appropriate to the structure of the table, and the critical values for pairwise comparisons would be the same as for the individual t tests. Dunnett's test has also been omitted because it does not fit with the structure of the table.

TABLE 12.6
Comparison of critical differences for alternative procedures

	W_2	W_3	W_4	W_5
Individual t tests	5.74	5.74	5.74	5.74
Bonferroni t test[‡]	7.47	7.47	7.47	7.47
Holm[*]	5.74	6.64	7.13	7.47
Newman–Keuls	5.75	6.93	7.63	8.14
Tukey$_a$ (HSD)	8.14	8.14	8.14	8.14
Tukey$_b$ (WSD)	6.95	7.54	7.89	8.14
Scheffé test	9.21	9.21	9.21	9.21

[‡] Assuming only four pairwise contrasts are desired
[*] Assuming significance at each preceding level

12.10   WHICH TEST?

Choosing the most appropriate multiple-comparison procedure for your specific situation is not easy. Many tests are available, and they differ in a number of ways. The choice is a bit easier if we consider the two extreme cases first.

If you have planned your test in advance and you want to run only one comparison, I would suggest that you run a standard t test (correcting for heterogeneity of variance if necessary), or if you have a complex comparison, a linear contrast. You might even use this procedure for two planned comparisons if you are willing to accept a maximum $FW \simeq .10$. If you have several a priori contrasts to run, not just pairwise, the multistage Bonferroni t proposed by Holm does a good job of controlling FW while at the same time maximizing power. If you run a large number of groups. (e.g., six or more) then I recommend Tukey's HSD test for making all pairwise comparisons.

If your experiment falls somewhere between these two situations (you have between three and five groups and either you want to make all pairwise comparisons or you have more than two preplanned comparisons), I recommend the Newman–Keuls (or the Tukey HSD for those who prefer to be very cautious). Many people have criticized the Newman–Keuls for allowing FW to exceed α drastically under certain conditions, but their arguments generally start with, "If you have 10 groups and . . . ." However, when I was looking for an example for this chapter, I spent literally $4\frac{1}{2}$ hours thumbing through journals. Not only did I *never* find a study with 10 independent groups, I never found one with 6 independent groups.[†] Moreover, by far the greatest number of studies involved three groups. Just because the Newman–Keuls has a high error rate with 10 groups is no reason why it should not be used with 3 groups, especially since in that case it has an *FW* of .05 (because there could be at most one set of equal population means).

In selecting among the various alternative tests, it is proper and appropriate to compare the critical differences required by each test for the conditions imposed by the experimental design, and then to choose the test with the smallest critical difference. The choice will be independent of the actual data observed and is therefore both theoretically sound and desirable (Keselman, 1974).

12.11   TREND ANALYSIS

The analyses we have been discussing are concerned with identifying differences among group means, whether these comparisons represent complex contrasts among groups or simple pairwise comparisons. Suppose, however, that the groups defined by the independent variable are ordered along some continuum. An example might be a study of the beneficial effects of aspirin in preventing heart disease. We could ask subjects to take daily doses of 1, 2, 3, 4, or 5 grains of aspirin, where 1 grain is equivalent to what used to be called "baby aspirin" and 5 grains is the standard tablet. In this study we would not be concerned so much with whether a 4-grain dose was better than a 2-grain dose, for example, as with whether the beneficial effects of aspirin increase with increasing the dosage of the drug. In other words, we are concerned with the "trend" in effectiveness rather than multiple comparisons among specific means.

To continue with the aspirin example, consider two possible outcomes. In one outcome we might find that the effectiveness increases linearly with dosage. In this case the more aspirin you take, the greater the effect, at least within the range of dosages tested. A second, alternative, finding might be that effectiveness increases with dosage up to some point, but then the curve relating effectiveness to dosage levels off and perhaps even decreases. This would be either a "quadratic" relationship or a relationship with both linear and quadratic components. It would be important to discover such relationships because they would suggest that there is some optimal dose, with low doses being less effective and high doses adding little, if anything, to the effect.

Typical linear and quadratic functions are illustrated in Figure 12.2. (They were produced using JMP on a Macintosh.) It is difficult to characterize quadratic functions neatly because the shape of the function depends both on the sign of the coefficient of X^2 and on the sign of X (the curve changes direction when X passes from negative to positive, and for positive values of X the curve rises if the coefficient is

[†] There are many cases in which the same subjects were tested over a large number of trials, but these do not yield independent sets of data; they will be discussed in Chapter 14.

positive and falls if it is negative). Also included in Figure 12.2 is a function with both linear and quadratic components. Here you can see that the curvature imposed by a quadratic function is superimposed upon a rising linear trend.

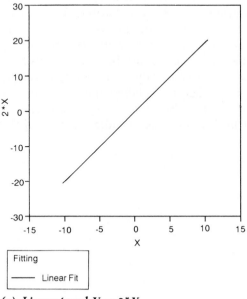

(a) *Linear trend* $Y = 2*X$

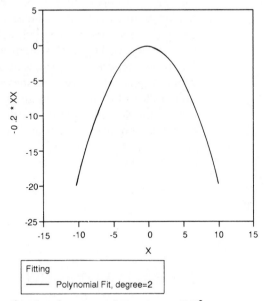

(b) *Quadratic trend* $Y = (-0.2)*X^2$

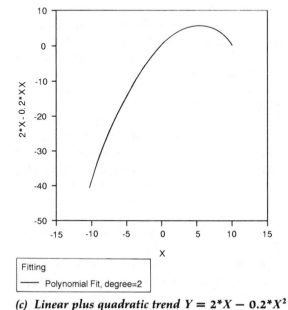

(c) *Linear plus quadratic trend* $Y = 2*X - 0.2*X^2$

FIGURE 12.2   Typical linear and quadratic functions

Tests of trend differ in an important way from the comparison procedures we have been discussing. In all of the previous examples, the independent variable was generally qualitative. Thus, for example, we could have written down the groups in the morphine-tolerance example in any order we chose. Moreover, the F or t values for the contrasts depended only on the numerical value of the means, not on which particular groups went with which particular means. In the analysis we are now considering, F or t values will depend on both the group means and the particular ordering of those means. To put this slightly differently using the aspirin example, a Newman–Keuls test between the largest and the smallest mean will not be affected by which group happens to have each mean. However, in trend analysis the results would be quite different if the 1-grain and 5-grain groups had the smallest and largest means than if the 4- and 2-grain groups had the smallest and largest means, respectively. (A similar point was made in Section 6.7 in discussing the nondirectionality of the chi-Square test.)

BORING IS ATTRACTIVE

A useful example of trend analysis comes from a study by Langlois and Roggman (1990), which examined the question of what makes a human face attractive. They approached the problem from both an evolutionary and a cognitive perspective. Modern evolutionary theory would suggest that average values of some trait would be preferred to extreme ones, and cognitive theory suggests that both adults and children respond to prototypes of objects more positively than to objects near the extremes on any dimension. A prototype, by definition, possesses average values of the object along important dimensions. (A prototype of a cat is one that is not too tall or too short, not too fat or too thin, and doesn't purr too loudly or too quietly.)

Langlois and Roggman took facial photographs of 336 males and 214 females. They then created five groups of composite photographs by computer-averaging the individual faces. Thus, for one group the computer averaged 32 randomly selected same-gender faces, producing a quite recognizable face with average width, height, eyes, nose length, and so on. For the other groups the composite faces were averaged over either 2, 4, 8, 16, or 32 individual faces. An example of composite faces can be seen in Figure 12.3. The label Composite will be used to represent the five different groups. That is not an ideal name for the independent variable, but neither I nor the study's authors have a better suggestion. Within each group of composite photographs were three male and three female faces, but we will ignore gender for this example. (There were no significant gender differences, and the overall test on group differences is not materially affected by ignoring that variable.)

FIGURE 12.3 Composite faces. Faces from left to right represent the six different composite sets. Faces from top to bottom represent composite levels of 4 faces, 8 faces, 16 faces, and 32 faces.

Langlois and Roggman presented different groups of subjects with composite faces and asked them to rate the attractiveness of the faces on a 1–5 scale, where 5 represents "very attractive." The individual data points in their analysis were actually the means averaged across raters for the six different composites in each condition. The data are given in Table 12.7. These data are fictional, but they have been constructed to have the same mean and variance as those reported by Langlois and Roggman, so the overall F and the tests on trend will be the same as those they reported. A standard one-way analysis of variance on these data would produce the following summary table:

Source	df	SS	MS	F
Composite	4	2.1704	0.5426	3.13*
Error	25	4.3281	0.1731	
Total	29	6.4985		

*$p < .05$

TABLE 12.7

	Group 1	Group 2	Group 3	Group 4	Group 5
	2.201	1.893	2.906	3.233	3.200
	2.411	3.102	2.118	3.505	3.253
	2.407	2.355	3.226	3.192	3.357
	2.403	3.644	2.811	3.209	3.169
	2.826	2.767	2.857	2.860	3.291
	3.380	2.109	3.422	3.111	3.290
Total	15.628	15.870	17.340	19.110	19.560
Mean	2.6047	2.6450	2.8900	3.1850	3.2600

From the summary table it is apparent that there are significant differences among the five groups, but it is not clear how these differences are manifested. One way to examine these differences would be to plot the group means as a function of the number of individual pictures that were averaged to create the composite. An important problem that arises if we try to do this concerns the units on the abscissa. We could label the groups as "2, 4, 8, 16, and 32," on the grounds that these values correspond to the number of elements over which the average was taken. However, it seems unlikely that rated attractiveness would increase directly with those values. We might expect that a picture averaged over 32 items would be more attractive than one averaged over 2 items, but I doubt that it would be 16 times more attractive. But notice that each value of the independent variable is a power of 2. In other words, the values of 2, 4, 8, 16, and 32 correspond to 2^1, 2^2, 2^3, 2^4, and 2^5. (Put another way, taking the $\log_2$ of 2, 4, 8, 16, and 32 would give us 1, 2, 3, 4, and 5.) For purposes of analyzing these data, I am going to represent the groups with the numbers 1 to 5 and refer to these as measuring the degree of the composite. (If you don't like my approach, and there is certainly room to disagree, be patient and we will soon see a solution using unequally spaced values of the independent variable. The example will be simpler statistically if the units on the abscissa are evenly spaced.) The group means using my composite measure on the abscissa are plotted in Figure 12.4, using EXECUSTAT, where you can see that the rated attractiveness does increase with increasing levels of Composite.

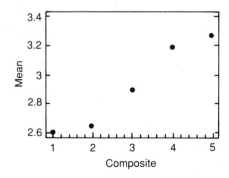

FIGURE 12.4
Scatterplot of mean versus composite group

Our first question asks whether a nonhorizontal straight line provides a significant fit to the data. A glance at Figure 12.4 would suggest that this is the case. We will then follow that question by asking whether systematic residual (nonerror) variance remains in the data after fitting a linear function, and, if so, if this residual variance can be explained by a quadratic function.

To run a trend analysis, we will return to the material we discussed under the headings of linear and orthogonal contrasts. (Don't be confused by the use of the word *linear* in the last sentence. We will use the same approach when it comes to fitting a quadratic function. Linear in this sense simply means that we will form a linear combination of coefficients and means, where nothing is raised to a power.)

In Section 12.3 we defined a linear contrast as

$$L = a_1 \overline{X}_1 + a_2 \overline{X}_2 + a_3 \overline{X}_3 + \cdots + a_k \overline{X}_k = \sum a_j \overline{X}_j$$

The only difference between what we are doing here and what we did earlier will be in the coefficients we use. In the case in which there are equal numbers of subjects in the groups and the values on the abscissa are equally spaced, the coefficients for linear, quadratic, and higher-order functions are easily tabled and are found in Appendix Polynomial. From Appendix Polynomial we find that for five groups the linear and quadratic coefficients are

Linear:	-2	-1	0	1	2
Quadratic:	2	-1	-2	-1	2

We will not be using the cubic and quartic coefficients shown in the appendix, but their use will be evident from what follows. Notice that like any set of orthogonal linear coefficients, the requirements that $\Sigma a_j = 0$, and $\Sigma a_i b_j = 0$ are met.

As you should recall from Section 12.3, we calculate a sum of squares for the contrast as

$$SS_{contrast} = \frac{nL^2}{\Sigma a_j^2}$$

In our case,

$$L_{linear} = (-2)2.6047 + (-1)2.6450 + (0)2.8900 + (1)3.1850 + (2)3.2600$$

$$= 1.8506$$

$$SS_{linear} = \frac{nL^2}{\Sigma a_j^2} = \frac{6(1.8506^2)}{10}$$

$$= 2.0548$$

Like all contrasts, this contrast has a single degree of freedom, and therefore $SS_{linear} = MS_{linear}$. As you probably suspect from what you already know, we can convert this mean square for the contrast to an F by dividing by MS_{error}:

$$F = \frac{MS_{\text{linear}}}{MS_{\text{error}}}$$

$$F = \frac{2.0548}{0.1731}$$

$$= 11.8706$$

This is an F on 1 and 24 degrees of freedom, and from Appendix F we find that $F_{.05}(1, 24) = 4.26$. Since the F for the linear component (11.87) exceeds 4.26, we will reject H_0 and conclude that there is a significant linear trend in our means. In other words, we will conclude that attractiveness varies linearly with increasing levels of Composite.

It is conceivable that we could have a significant linear trend in our data and still have residual variance that can be explained by a higher-order term. For example, it is possible that we might have both linear and quadratic, or linear and cubic, components. In fact, it would be reasonable to expect a quadratic component in addition to a linear one, because it seems unlikely that judged attractiveness will keep increasing indefinitely as we increase the number of individual photographs we average to get the composite. There will presumably be some diminishing returns.

The next step is to ask if the residual variance remaining after we fit the linear component is significantly greater than the error variance that we already know is present. If SS_{linear} accounted for virtually all of $SS_{\text{Composite}}$, there would be little or nothing left over for higher-order terms to explain. On the other hand, if SS_{linear} was a relatively small part of $SS_{\text{Composite}}$, then it would make sense to look for higher-order components. From our previous calculations we obtain

$$SS_{\text{residual}} = SS_{\text{Composite}} - SS_{\text{linear}}$$

$$= 2.1704 - 2.0548$$

$$= 0.1156$$

$$df_{\text{residual}} = df_{\text{Composite}} - df_{\text{linear}}$$

$$= 4 - 1$$

$$= 3$$

$$MS_{\text{residual}} = \frac{SS_{\text{residual}}}{df_{\text{residual}}}$$

$$= \frac{0.1156}{3}$$

$$= 0.0385$$

$$F_{\text{residual}} = \frac{MS_{\text{residual}}}{MS_{\text{error}}}$$

$$= \frac{0.0385}{0.1731}$$

$$< 1$$

Since F for the residual is less than 1, we know automatically that it is not significant. This tells us that there is no significant variability left to be explained over and above that accounted for by the linear component. We would, therefore, normally stop here. However, for purposes of an example I will go ahead and calculate the quadratic component. The calculations will be shown without discussion, because the discussion would essentially be the same as above with the word *quadratic* substituted for *linear*.

$$L_{\text{quadratic}} = (2)2.6047 + (-1)2.6450 + (-2)2.8900 + (-1)3.1850 + (2)3.2600$$

$$= 0.1194$$

$$\text{SS}_{\text{quadratic}} = \frac{nL^2}{\Sigma b_j^2}$$

$$\text{SS}_{\text{quadratic}} = \frac{6(0.1194^2)}{14}$$

$$= 0.0061$$

$$F = \frac{\text{MS}_{\text{quadratic}}}{\text{MS}_{\text{error}}}$$

$$= \frac{0.0061}{0.1731}$$

$$< 1$$

As our test on the residual suggested, there is no significant quadratic component on our plot of the group means. Thus there is no indication, over the range of values used in this study, that the means are beginning to level off. Therefore, we would conclude from these data that attractiveness increases linearly with Composite, at least given the definition of Composite used here.

A word of caution is in order at this point. You might be tempted to go ahead and apply the cubic and quartic coefficients that you find in Appendix Polynomial. You might also observe that having done this, the four sums of squares ($\text{SS}_{\text{linear}}, \ldots, \text{SS}_{\text{quartic}}$) will sum to $\text{SS}_{\text{Composite}}$, and be very impressed that you have accounted for all of the sums of squares between groups. Before you get too impressed, think about how proud you would be if you showed that you could draw a straight line that exactly fit two points. The same idea applies here. Regardless of the data, you know before you begin that a polynomial of order $k - 1$ will exactly fit k points. That is one reason why I was not eager to go much beyond fitting the linear components to the data at hand. A quadratic was stretching things a bit. Moreover, if you were to fit a fourth-order polynomial and found that the quartic component was significant, what would you have to say about the results? A linear or quadratic component would make some sense, but a quartic component could not be explained by any theory I know.

UNEQUAL INTERVALS

In the preceding section we assumed that the levels of the independent variable are equally spaced along some continuum. In fact, I actually transformed the independent variable into a scale called Composite to fulfill that requirement. It is possible to run a trend analysis when we do not have equal intervals, and the arithmetic is the same. The only problem comes when we try to obtain the trend coefficients, because we cannot take our coefficients from Appendix Polynomial unless the intervals are equal.

In what follows I show how to derive polynomial coefficients for linear trend with unequal intervals. Calculating quadratic coefficients is not too difficult, and a good explanation can be found in Keppel (1973). For higher-order polynomials the calculations are more laborious, but a description of the process can be found in Robson (1959). In this example we will solve for those coefficients that would apply if we used the previous example but coded the independent variable as 2, 4, 8, 16, and 32— the number of individual photographs that were averaged to produce the composite photographs for each group.

First we will define the coefficients (a_j) as a function of both X and a dummy variable we will label α. Thus, $a_j = \alpha + X_j$. These values are shown in Table 12.8.

TABLE 12.8
Calculation of linear coefficients

X_j	$\alpha + X_j$	a_j
2	$\alpha + 2$	-10.4
4	$\alpha + 4$	-8.4
8	$\alpha + 8$	-4.4
16	$\alpha + 16$	3.6
32	$\alpha + 32$	19.6

The center column of this table contains the combined function of α and X. But recall that one of the requirements we imposed on our coefficients is that $\Sigma a_j = 0$. Therefore, $\Sigma(\alpha + X_j) = 0$. If we sum the second column and set it equal to 0, we get

$$5\alpha + 62 = 0$$

$$\alpha = \frac{-62}{5} = -12.4$$

Substituting $\alpha = -12.4$ in $a_j = \alpha + X_j$, we obtain the entries in the third column. You should satisfy yourself that these coefficients really do sum to 0.

We can now repeat the calculations we carried out to find SS_{linear}, although this time we will use the coefficients that we calculated in Table 12.8.

$$SS_{contrast} = \frac{nL^2}{\Sigma a_j^2}$$

Therefore,

$$L_{linear} = (-10.4)2.6047 + (-8.4)2.6450 + (-4.4)2.8900 + (3.6)3.1850 + (19.6)3.2600$$

$$= 13.3391$$

$$SS_{linear} = \frac{6(13.3391^2)}{595.2}$$

$$= 1.7938$$

From the earlier analysis, we know that $MS_{error} = 0.1731$. Because we again have one degree of freedom for our contrast, $MS_{linear} = SS_{linear}$. Therefore,

$$F = \frac{MS_{linear}}{MS_{error}}$$

$$= \frac{1.7938}{0.1731}$$

$$= 10.36$$

This F is on 1 and 24 degrees of freedom, for which $F_{.05}(1, 24) = 4.26$. Again we reject the null hypothesis and conclude that there is a linear relationship between judged attractiveness and the number of individual photographs that were averaged to produce the composite. Thus, however we treat our independent variable, we get the same result in this particular case. You should be able to see that if we test the residual sum of squares remaining after fitting a linear trend, this residual will not be significant and we will have no reason to test the quadratic component. (For those who wish to test the quadratic component for practice, the coefficients are 90, 33, -57, -141, and 75.)

Trend analysis can be carried out using any of the major statistical packages. For SPSS^X you would simply use

ONEWAY DEPVAR BY GROUP (1,5)/

POLYNOMIAL $= 2$

The program will compute the relevant sums of squares using the Group coding as the metric.

For SAS you can use the GLM procedure, adding the statements

Contrast 'Linear' Group -2 -1 0 1 2;

Contrast 'Quadratic' Group 2 -1 -2 -1 2;

With unequal spacing of the independent variable (Group), you need to supply the appropriate coefficients.

In BMDP the easiest way to calculate polynomial contrasts is to use BMDP1V and include

/Design Dependent is DepVar.

Independent is Group.

Contrast is -2 -1 0 1 2.

Contrast is 2 -1 -2 -1 2.

For unequal intervals you would substitute the appropriate coefficients.

KEY TERMS

Error rate per comparison (*PC*) (**12.1**)	**Familywise error rate (*FW*) (12.1)**
Error rate per experiment (*PE*) (**12.1**)	**A priori comparisons (12.1)**
	Post hoc comparisons (12.1)
	Linear contrasts (12.3)

Linear combination (12.3)

Orthogonal contrasts (12.3)

Dunn's test (12.3)

Bonferroni t (12.3)

Bonferroni inequality (12.3)

Fisher's least significant difference (LSD) (12.4)

Studentized range statistic (q) (12.4)

Newman–Keuls test (12.4)

Tukey$_a$ test (12.5)

HSD (honestly significant difference) test (12.5)

Tukey$_b$ test (12.5)

WSD (wholly significant difference) test (12.5)

Scheffé test (12.6)

Dunnett's test (12.7)

EXERCISES

12.1 Assume that the data that follow represent the effects of food and/or water deprivation on behavior in a learning task. Treatments 1 and 2 represent control conditions in which the animal received ad lib food and water (1) or else food and water twice per day (2). In treatment 3 animals were food deprived, in treatment 4 they were water deprived, and in treatment 5 they were deprived of both food and water. The dependent variable is the number of trials to reach a predetermined criterion. Assume that before running our experiment we decided that we wanted to compare the combined control groups (treatments 1 and 2) with the combined experimental groups, the control groups with each other, the singly deprived treatments with the doubly deprived treatment, and the singly deprived treatments with each other.

Ad Lib Control	Two per Day Control	Food Deprived	Water Deprived	Food and Water Deprived
18	20	6	15	12
20	25	9	10	11
21	23	8	9	8
16	27	6	12	13
15	25	11	14	11
90	120	40	60	55

(a) Analyze the data using linear contrasts.

(b) Show that the contrasts are orthogonal.

(c) Show that the sums of squares for the contrasts sum to SS_{treat}.

12.2 Using the data from Exercise 11.1, compute the linear contrasts for 5 versus (20 and 35) days and 20 versus 35 days, using $\alpha = .05$ for each contrast.

12.3 What would be the per comparison, per experiment, and familywise error rates in Exercise 12.2? (*Hint*: Are the contrasts orthogonal?)

12.4 Compute F for the linear contrast on the two groups in Exercise 11.2. Is this a waste of time? Why or why not?

12.5 Compute the Studentized range statistic for the two groups in Exercise 11.2, and show that it is equal to $t\sqrt{2}$ (where t is taken from Exercise 11.2b).

12.6   Compute the Fs for the following linear contrasts in Exercise 11.3. Save the results for use in Chapter 13.
  (a) 1 and 2 versus 3 and 4
  (b) 1 and 3 versus 2 and 4
  (c) 1 and 4 versus 2 and 3
  (d) What questions do the contrasts in (a), (b), and (c) address?

12.7   Run the Bonferroni t test on the data for Exercise 11.1 using the contrasts supplied in Exercise 12.2. Set the maximum FW at .05.

12.8   Repeat Exercise 12.7 using Holm's multistage test.

12.9   Apply Holm's multistage test to Exercise 12.1.

12.10   Run a Newman–Keuls test on the example given in Table 11.3a and interpret the results.

12.11   Calculate the two Tukey tests on the data in the example in Table 11.3a, and compare your results to those you obtained for Exercise 12.8.

12.12   Consider the following data for five groups:

Group	1	2	3	4	5
$\overline{X}_j$	10	18	19	21	29
n_j	8	5	8	7	9
s_j^2	7.4	8.9	8.6	7.2	9.3

Run a Newman–Keuls test on these data.

12.13   Run Tukey's WSD and HSD procedures on the data in Exercise 12.12.

12.14   Use the Scheffé test on the data in Exercise 12.12 to compare groups 1, 2, and 3 (combined) with groups 4 and 5 (combined). Then compare group 1 with groups 2, 3, and 4 (combined). (*Hint*: You will need to go back to the section in which unequal sample sizes are discussed in conjunction with Table 12.2.).

12.15   Apply the Newman–Keuls procedure to the THC data from Table 11.4. What is the maximum FW for this procedure?

12.16   Apply Dunnett's test to the data in Table 11.4.

12.17   How could Minitab (for example) be used to run the Bonferroni t test on the data in Exercise 12.7?

12.18   The Holm test and Shaffer's test are referred to as modified sequentially rejective procedures. Why?

12.19   Fit linear and quadratic trend components to the Conti and Musty (1984) data in Table 11.4. The control condition received 0 μg of THC. For purposes of this example, assume that there were 10 subjects in all groups. The linear coefficients (calculated with unequal spacing on the independent variable) are $[-0.72 \quad -0.62 \quad -0.22 \quad 0.28 \quad 1.28]$. The quadratic coefficients are $[0.389 \quad 0.199 \quad -0.362 \quad -0.612 \quad 0.387]$.

COMPUTER EXERCISES

12.20   Use any statistical package to compute Fisher's LSD procedure on all three pairs of means (even though the overall F was not significant) for GSIT from Mireault's data (Mireault.dat). (This is based on the analysis of variance in Exercise 11.27.) Compare these results with the individual t tests that you ran for Exercise 7.50. Interpret the results.

12.21 Use any statistical package to apply the Newman–Keuls, Tukey, and Scheffé procedures to the data from Introini-Collison and McGaugh (1986), described in the exercises for Chapter 11. Do these analyses for both Epineq.dat and Epinuneq.dat. Do *not* combine across the levels of the interval variable.

12.22 In Exercise 12.21 it would not have made much of a difference whether we combined the data across the three intervals or not. Under what conditions would you expect that it would make a big difference?

12.23 Using the data in Epineq.dat, compute both the linear and quadratic trend tests on the three drug dosages. Do this separately for each of the three intervals. (*Hint*: The linear coefficients are $[-0.597110 \quad -0.183726 \quad 0.780836]$, and the quadratic coefficients are $[0.556890 \quad -0.795557 \quad 0.238667]$.)

12.24 Interpret the results in Exercise 12.23.

CHAPTER THIRTEEN

FACTORIAL ANALYSIS OF VARIANCE

OBJECTIVES *To discuss the analysis of variance for the case of two or more independent variables.*

CONTENTS

I n the last two chapters, we dealt with a one-way analysis of variance in which we had only one independent variable. In this chapter, we will extend the analysis of variance to the treatment of experimental designs involving two or more independent variables. For purposes of simplicity, we will be concerned primarily with experiments involving two or three variables, although the techniques discussed can be extended to more complex designs.

In Chapter 11 we considered a study by Eysenck (1974) in which he asked subjects to recall lists of words to which they had been exposed under one of several different conditions. In that example, we were interested in determining whether recall was related to the level at which material was processed initially. Eysenck's study was actually more complex. He was interested in whether level-of-processing notions could explain differences in recall between older and younger subjects. If older subjects do not process information as deeply, they might be expected to recall fewer items than would younger subjects, especially in conditions that entail greater processing. This

Factors study now has two independent variables, which we shall refer to as **factors**: Age and

Two-way factorial design

Factorial design

Recall Condition (hereafter referred to simply as Condition). The experiment thus is an instance of what is called a **two-way factorial design**.

An experimental design in which every level of every factor is paired with every level of every other factor is called a **factorial design**. In other words, a factorial design is one in which we include all *combinations* of the levels of the independent variables. In the factorial designs discussed in this chapter, we will consider only the case in which different subjects serve under each of the treatment combinations. For instance, in our example, one group of younger subjects will serve in the counting condition, a different group of younger subjects will serve in the rhyming condition, and so on. Since we have 10 combinations of our two factors (5 recall Conditions $\times$ 2 Ages), we will have 10 different groups of subjects. When the research plan calls for the *same* subject to be included under more than one treatment combination, we will speak of **repeated-measures designs**. Repeated-measures designs will be discussed in Chapter 14.

Repeated-measures designs

Factorial designs have several important advantages over one-way designs. First, they allow greater generalizability of the results. Consider Eysenck's study for a moment. If we were to run a one-way analysis using the five Conditions with only the older subjects, as in Chapter 11, then our results would apply only to older subjects. When we use a factorial design with both older and younger subjects, we are able to determine whether differences between Conditions apply to younger subjects as well as older ones. We are also able to determine whether age differences in recall apply to all tasks, or whether younger (or older) subjects excel on only certain kinds of tasks. Thus, factorial designs allow for a much broader interpretation of the results, and at the same time give us the ability to say something meaningful about the results for each of the independent variables separately.

Interaction

The second important feature of factorial designs is that they allow us to look at the **interaction** of variables. We can ask whether the effect of Condition is independent of Age or whether there is some interaction between Condition and Age. For example, we would have an interaction if younger subjects showed much greater (or smaller) differences among the five recall conditions than did older subjects. Interaction effects are often among the most interesting results we obtain.

A third advantage of a factorial design is its economy. Since we are going to average the effects of one variable across the levels of the other variable, a two-variable factorial will require fewer subjects than would two one-ways for the same degree of power. Essentially, we are getting something for nothing. Suppose we had no reason to expect an interaction of Age and Condition. Then, with 10 old subjects and 10 young subjects in each Condition, we would have 20 scores for each of the five conditions. If we instead ran a one-way with young subjects and then another one-way with old subjects, we would need twice as many subjects overall for each of our experiments to have the same power to detect Condition differences—that is, each experiment would have to have 20 subjects per condition, and we would have two experiments.

Factorial designs are labeled by the number of factors involved. A factorial design with two independent variables, or factors, is called a two-way factorial, and one with three factors is called a three-way factorial. An alternative method of labeling designs is in terms of the number of levels of each factor. Eysenck's study had two levels of Age and five levels of Condition. As such, it is a **2 × 5 factorial**. A study with three factors, two of them having three levels and one having four levels, would be called a

2 × 5 factorial

$3 \times 3 \times 4$ factorial. The use of such terms as "two-way" and "2×5" are both common ways of designating designs, and both will be used throughout this book.

In much of what follows, we will concern ourselves primarily with the two-way analysis. Higher-order analyses follow almost automatically once you understand the two-way, and many of the related problems we will discuss are most simply explained in terms of two factors. For the moment, we will also limit our discussion to fixed—as opposed to random—models, as these were defined in Chapter 11.

NOTATION

Cell

Consider a hypothetical experiment with two variables, A and B. A design of this type is illustrated in Table 13.1. The number of levels of A is designated by a, and the number of levels of B is designated by b. Any combination of one level of A and one level of B is called a **cell**, and the number of observations per cell is denoted n, or, more precisely, n_{ij}. The total number of observations is $N = \Sigma n_{ij} = abn$. When any confusion might arise, an individual observation (X) can be designated by three subscripts, X_{ijk}, where the subscript i refers to the number of the row (level of A), the subscript j refers to the number of the column (level of B), and the subscript k refers to the kth observation in the ijth cell. Thus, X_{234} is the fourth subject in the cell corresponding to the second row and the third column. Totals for the individual levels of A are denoted T_{A_i}, and for the levels of B are denoted T_{B_j}. The cell totals are designated T_{ij}. The grand total is symbolized by GT or ΣX. Needless subscripts are often a source of confusion, and whenever possible they will be omitted.

TABLE 13.1
Representation of factorial design

	B_1	B_2	$\cdots$	B_b	
A_1	X_{111}	X_{121}		X_{1b1}	
	X_{112}	X_{122}		X_{1b2}	
	$\cdots$	$\cdots$		$\cdots$	
	X_{11n}	X_{12n}		X_{1bn}	
	T_{11}	T_{12}		T_{1b}	T_{A_1}
A_2	X_{211}	X_{221}		X_{2b1}	
	X_{212}	X_{222}		X_{2b2}	
	$\cdots$	$\cdots$		$\cdots$	
	X_{21n}	X_{22n}		X_{2bn}	
	T_{21}	T_{22}		T_{2b}	T_{A_2}
$\cdots$					$\cdots$
A_a	X_{a11}	X_{a21}		X_{ab1}	
	X_{a12}	X_{a22}		X_{ab2}	
	$\cdots$	$\cdots$		$\cdots$	
	X_{a1n}	X_{a2n}		X_{abn}	
	T_{a1}	T_{a2}		T_{ab}	T_{A_a}
	T_{B_1}	T_{B_2}	$\cdots$	T_{B_b}	$GT = \Sigma X$

The notation outlined here will be used throughout the discussion of the analysis of variance, and it is important that you understand it thoroughly before proceeding. The advantage of the present system is that it is easily generalized to more complex designs. Thus, if subjects recalled at three different times of day, it should be self-evident to what T_{time_1} refers.

13.1   AN EXTENSION OF THE EYSENCK STUDY

As mentioned earlier, Eysenck actually conducted a study varying Age as well as Recall Condition. The study included 50 subjects in the 18-to-30–year age range, as well as 50 subjects in the 55-to-65–year age range. The data in Table 13.2 have been created to have the same means and standard deviations as those reported by Eysenck. The table contains all the calculations for a standard analysis of variance, and we will discuss each of these in turn. Before beginning the analysis, it is important to note that the data themselves are approximately normally distributed with acceptably equal variances. The boxplots are not given in the table because the individual data points are artificial, but for real data it is well worth your effort to compute them. You can tell from the cell and marginal totals that recall appears to increase with greater processing, and younger subjects seem to recall more items than do older subjects. Notice also that the difference between younger and older subjects seems to depend on the task, with greater differences for those tasks that involve deeper processing. We will have more to say about these results after we consider the analysis itself.

It will avoid confusion later if I take the time here to define two important terms. As I have said, we have two factors in this experiment—Age and Condition. If we look at the differences between older and younger subjects, *ignoring the particular conditions*, we are dealing with what is called the **main effect** of Age. Similarly, if we look at differences among the five conditions, ignoring the Age of the subjects, we are dealing with the main effect of Conditions.

Main effect

An alternative method of looking at the data would be to compare older and younger subjects for only the data from the Counting task, for example. Or we might compare older and younger subjects on the Intentional task. Finally, we might compare the means on the five conditions for only the older subjects. In each of these three examples we are looking at the effect of one factor for the data at only *one* level of the other factor. When we do this, we are dealing with a **simple effect**—the effect of one factor at one level of the other factor. A main effect, on the other hand, is that of a factor *ignoring* the other factor. If we say that tasks that involve more processing lead to better recall, we are speaking of a main effect. If we say that for younger subjects tasks that involve more processing lead to better recall, we are speaking about a simple effect. We will have considerably more to say about simple effects and their calculation shortly. For now, it is important only that you understand the terminology.

Simple effect

CALCULATIONS

The calculations for the sums of squares appear in Table 13.2b. Many of these calculations should be familiar, since they resemble the procedures used with a one-way. For

TABLE 13.2
Data and computations for example from Eysenck (1974)

(a) Data

	Counting	Rhyming	Adjective	Imagery	Intentional	T_{A_i}
			Recall Conditions			
Old	9	7	11	12	10	
	8	9	13	11	19	
	6	6	8	16	14	
	8	6	6	11	5	
	10	6	14	9	10	
	4	11	11	23	11	
	6	6	13	12	14	
	5	3	13	10	15	
	7	8	10	19	11	
	7	7	11	11	11	
	70 *520*	69 *57*	110 *1266*	134 *1978*	120 *1566*	503
Young	8	10	14	20	21	
	6	7	11	16	19	
	4	8	18	16	17	
	6	10	14	15	15	
	7	4	13	18	22	
	6	7	22	16	16	
	5	10	17	20	22	
	7	6	16	22	22	
	9	7	12	14	18 *3789*	
	7 *441*	7 *612*	11 *2300*	19 *358*	21	
	65	76	148	176	193	658
T_{C_j}	135	145	258	310	313	$1161 = \Sigma X$

(b) Calculations

$$\sum X^2 = 16{,}147 \quad (\sum X)^2/N = 1161^2/100 = 13{,}479.21$$

$$\text{SS}_{\text{total}} = \sum X^2 - (\sum X)^2/N = 16{,}147 - 13{,}479.21 = 2667.79$$

$$\text{SS}_A = \frac{\sum T_A^2}{nc} - \frac{(\Sigma X)^2}{N} = \frac{503^2 + 658^2}{50} - \frac{1161^2}{100}$$

$$= 13{,}719.46 - 13{,}479.21 = 240.25$$

$$\text{SS}_C = \frac{\sum T_C^2}{na} - \frac{(\Sigma X)^2}{N} = \frac{135^2 + 145^2 + 258^2 + 310^2 + 313^2}{20} - \frac{1161^2}{100}$$

$$= 14{,}994.15 - 13{,}479.21 = 1514.94$$

$$\text{SS}_{\text{cells}} = \frac{\sum T_{ij}^2}{n} - \frac{(\Sigma X)^2}{N} = \frac{70^2 + 69^2 + \cdots + 176^2 + 193^2}{10} - \frac{1161^2}{100}$$

$$= 15{,}424.70 - 13{,}479.21 = 1945.49$$

$$\text{SS}_{AC} = \text{SS}_{\text{cells}} - \text{SS}_A - \text{SS}_C$$

$$= 1945.49 - 240.25 - 1514.94 = 190.30$$

$$\text{SS}_{\text{error}} = \text{SS}_{\text{total}} - \text{SS}_{\text{cells}} = 2667.79 - 1945.49 = 722.30$$

TABLE 13.2 (Cont.)   *(c) Summary Table*

Source	df	SS	MS	F
A (Age)	1	240.25	240.250	29.94*
C (Condition)	4	1514.94	378.735	47.19*
AC	4	190.30	47.575	5.93*
Error	90	722.30	8.026	
Total	99	2667.79		

*$p < .05$

example, SS_{total} is computed the same way it was in Chapter 11, which is the same way it is always computed. We sum all of the squared observations and subtract $(\Sigma X)^2/N$, the correction factor.

The sum of squares for the Age factor (SS_A) is nothing but the SS_{treat} that we would obtain if this were a one-way analysis of variance without the Condition factor. In other words, we simply sum the squared Age totals, divide by the number of observations on which each Age total is based ($= nc$), and subtract the correction factor. The same thing can be said for SS_C, except that here we ignore the presence of the Age variable.

You will note that ΣT_A^2 is divided by nc and ΣT_C^2 is divided by na, where A and C represent Age and Condition, respectively. If you try to remember these denominators as formulas, you will be wasting your time. The denominators represent the number of scores per total, and nothing more. They are exactly analogous to the denominator (n) we used in the one-way when we wanted to turn a variance of totals into an estimate of σ_e^2. The only difference is that in a one-way, n represented the number of observations per treatment, and here it represents the number of observations per cell—since c cells are involved with each Age level, there must be nc observations for each Age total (T_{A_i}).

After more than 20 years of teaching this material, I have concluded that confusion about denominators in the analysis of variance is innate. In fact, such confusion probably is a result of people trying to memorize formulas. *Whenever you square any total, divide that square by the number of observations on which the total was based.* Above all, never try to memorize formulas for denominators. They exist only so that textbook writers have a way of writing equations precisely.

SS_{cells} Having obtained SS_{total}, SS_A, and SS_C, we come to an unfamiliar term, SS_{cells}. This term represents the variability of the individual cell totals and is in fact only a dummy term; it will not appear in the summary table. It is calculated just like any other sum of squares. We take the *cell totals*, square and sum them, divide by the number of observations per total, and subtract the correction factor. Although it might not be readily apparent why we want this term, its usefulness will become clear when we calculate a sum of squares for the interaction of Age and Condition. (It may be easier to understand the calculation of SS_{cells} if you think of it as what you would have if you viewed this as a study with 10 "groups" and calculated SS_{treat}.)

The SS_{cells} is a measure of how much the cell totals (and thus the cell means) differ. Two cell totals may differ for any of three reasons, other than sampling error: (1)

because they come from different levels of A; (2) because they come from different levels of C; (3) because of an interaction between A and C. We already have a measure of how much the cells differ, since we know SS_{cells}. SS_A tells us how much of this difference can be attributed to differences in Age, and SS_C tells us how much can be attributed to differences in Condition. Whatever cannot be attributed to Age or Condition must be attributable to the interaction between Age and Condition (SS_{AC}). Thus SS_{cells} has been partitioned into its three constituent parts—SS_A, SS_C, and SS_{AC}. To obtain SS_{AC}, we simply subtract SS_A and SS_C from SS_{cells}. Whatever is left over is SS_{AC}. In our example,

$$SS_{AC} = SS_{cells} - SS_A - SS_C$$
$$= 1945.49 - 240.25 - 1514.94 = 190.30$$

All that we have left to calculate is the sum of squares due to error. Just as in the one-way analysis, we will obtain this by subtraction. The total variation is represented by SS_{total}. Of this total, we know how much can be attributed to A, C, and AC. What is left over represents unaccountable variation or error. Thus

$$SS_{error} = SS_{total} - (SS_A + SS_C + SS_{AC})$$

However, since $SS_A + SS_C + SS_{AC} = SS_{cells}$, it is simpler to write

$$SS_{error} = SS_{total} - SS_{cells}$$

This provides us with our sum of squares for error, and we now have all of the necessary sums of squares for our analysis.

A more direct, but tiresome, way to calculate SS_{error} exists, and it makes explicit just what the error sum of squares is measuring. SS_{error} represents the variation within each cell, and as such can be calculated by obtaining the sum of squares for each cell separately. For example,

$$SS_{cell_{11}} = 9^2 + 8^2 + \cdots + 7^2 - \frac{70^2}{10} = 30.0$$

We could perform a similar operation on each of the remaining cells, obtaining

$$SS_{cell_{11}} = 30.0$$
$$SS_{cell_{12}} = 40.9$$
$$\cdots \qquad \cdots$$
$$\frac{SS_{cell_{25}}}{SS_{error}} = \frac{64.1}{722.30}$$

The sum of squares within each cell is then summed over the 10 cells to produce SS_{error}. Although this is the hard way of computing an error term, it demonstrates that SS_{error} is in fact the sum of within-cell variation.

Table 13.2c shows the summary table for the analysis of variance. The source column and the sum of squares column are fairly obvious from what has already been said. Note, however, that we could organize the summary table somewhat differently, although we would seldom do so in practice. Thus, we could have

Source	df		SS
Between cells	9		1945.49
A		1	240.25
C		4	1514.94
AC		4	190.30
Within cells	90		722.30
(Error)			
Total	99		2667.79

This alternative summary table makes it clear that we have partitioned the total variation into variation among the cell totals and variation within the cells. The former is then further partitioned into A, C, and AC.

Returning to Table 13.2c, look at the degrees of freedom. The calculation of df is straightforward. The total degrees of freedom (df_{total}) are always equal to $N - 1$. The degrees of freedom for Age and Condition are the number of levels of the variable minus 1. Thus, $df_A = a - 1 = 1$ and $df_C = c - 1 = 4$. The number of degrees of freedom for any interaction is simply the product of the degrees of freedom for the components of that interaction. Thus, $df_{AC} = df_A \times df_C = (a - 1)(c - 1) = 1 \times 4 = 4$. These three rules apply to *any* analysis of variance, no matter how complex. The degrees of freedom for error can be obtained either by subtraction ($df_{error} = df_{total} - df_A - df_C - df_{AC}$), or by realizing that the error term represents variability within each cell. Since each cell has $n - 1$ df, and since there are ac cells, then $df_{error} = ac(n - 1) = 2 \times 5 \times 9 = 90$.

Just as with the one-way analysis of variance, the mean squares are again obtained by dividing the sums of squares by the corresponding degrees of freedom. This same procedure is used in any analysis of variance.

Finally, to calculate F, we divide each MS by MS_{error}. Thus, for Age, $F_A = MS_A/MS_{error}$; for Condition, $F_C = MS_C/MS_{error}$; and for AC, $F_{AC} = MS_{AC}/MS_{error}$. To appreciate why MS_{error} is the appropriate divisor in each case, we will digress briefly in a moment and consider the underlying structural model and the expected mean squares. First, however, we need to consider what the results of this analysis tell us.

INTERPRETATION

From the summary table in Table 13.2c, you can see that there were significant effects for Age, Condition, and their interaction. In conjunction with the cell totals, it is clear that younger subjects recall more items overall than do older subjects. It is also clear that those tasks that involve greater depth of processing lead to better recall overall than do tasks involving less processing. This is in line with the differences we found in Chapter 11. The significant interaction tells us that the effect of one variable depends on the level of the other variable. For example, differences between older and younger subjects on the easier tasks such as counting and rhyming are less than age differences on those tasks, such as imagery and intentional, that involve greater depths of processing. Another view is that differences among the five conditions are less extreme for the older subjects than they are for the younger ones.

These results support Eysenck's hypothesis that older subjects do not perform as well as younger subjects on tasks that involve a greater depth of processing of information, but perform about equally with younger subjects when the task does not involve much processing. These results do not mean that older subjects are not *capable* of processing information as deeply. Older subjects simply may not make the effort that younger subjects do. Whatever the reason, however, they do not perform as well on those tasks.

13.2 STRUCTURAL MODELS AND EXPECTED MEAN SQUARES

Recall that in discussing a one-way analysis of variance, we employed the structural model

$$X_{ij} = \mu + \tau_j + e_{ij}$$

where $\tau_j = \mu_j - \mu$ represented the effect of the jth treatment. In a two-way design, we have two "treatment" variables (call them A and B) and their interaction. These can be represented in the model by α, β, and $\alpha\beta$, producing a slightly more complex model. This model can be written as

$$X_{ijk} = \mu + \alpha_i + \beta_j + \alpha\beta_{ij} + e_{ijk}$$

where

$X_{ijk} =$ any observation

$\mu =$ the grand mean

$\alpha_i =$ the effect of Factor $A_i = \mu_{A_i} - \mu; \Sigma\alpha_i = 0$

$\beta_j =$ the effect of Factor $B_j = \mu_{B_j} - \mu; \Sigma\beta_j = 0$

$\alpha\beta_{ij} =$ the interaction effect of Factor A_i and Factor B_j

$\quad = \mu - \mu_{A_i} - \mu_{B_j} + \mu_{ij}; \Sigma_i\alpha\beta_{ij} = \Sigma_j\alpha\beta_{ij} = 0$

$e_{ijk} =$ the unit of error associated with observation X_{ijk}

$\quad = N(0, \sigma_e^2)$

From this model it can be shown that with fixed variables the expected mean squares are those given in Table 13.3. It is apparent that the error term is the proper denominator for each F ratio, since the $E(MS)$ for any effect contains only one term other than σ_e^2.

TABLE 13.3
Expected mean squares for two-way analysis of variance (fixed)

Source	E(MS)
A	$\sigma_e^2 + nb\sigma_\alpha^2$
B	$\sigma_e^2 + na\sigma_\beta^2$
AB	$\sigma_e^2 + n\sigma_{\alpha\beta}^2$
Error	σ_e^2

Consider for a moment the test of the effect of Factor A:

$$\frac{E(\text{MS}_A)}{E(\text{MS}_{\text{error}})} = \frac{\sigma_e^2 + nb\sigma_\alpha^2}{\sigma_e^2}$$

If H_0 is true, then $\mu_{A_1} = \mu_{A_2} = \mu$, and σ_α^2 will be 0. In this case, F will have an expectation of approximately 1 and will be distributed as the standard F distribution. If H_0 is false, however, σ_α^2 will not be 0 and F will have an expectation greater than 1 and will not follow the central F distribution. The same logic applies to tests on the effects of B and AB.

13.3   INTERACTIONS

One of the major benefits of factorial designs is that they allow us to examine the interaction of variables. Indeed, in many cases, the interaction term may well be of greater interest than are the main effects (the effects of factors taken individually). Consider, for example, the study by Eysenck. The means are plotted in Figure 13.1 for each age group separately. Here you can see clearly what I referred to in the interpretation of the results when I said that the differences due to Conditions were greater for younger subjects than for older ones. The fact that the two lines are not parallel is what we mean when we speak of an interaction. If Condition differences were the same for the two Age groups, then the lines would be parallel—whatever differences between Conditions existed for younger subjects would be equally present for older subjects. This would be true regardless of whether younger subjects were generally superior to older subjects or whether the two groups were comparable. Raising or lowering the entire line for younger subjects would change the main effect of Age, but it would have no effect on the interaction.

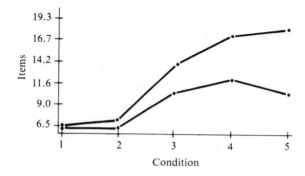

FIGURE 13.1
Cell means for data in
Table 13.2

It may make the situation clearer if you consider several plots of cell means that represent the presence or absence of an interaction. In Figure 13.2 the first three plots represent the case in which there is no interaction. In all three cases the lines are parallel, even when they are not straight. Another way of looking at this is to say that the difference between B_1 and B_2 (the effect of Factor B) at A_1 is the same as it is at A_2 and at A_3. In the second set of three plots, the lines clearly are not parallel. In the first, one line is flat and the other rises. In the second, the lines actually cross. In the third, the lines do not cross, but they move in opposite directions. In every case, the effect of B is *not* the same at the different levels of A. Whenever the lines are (significantly) nonparallel, we say that we have an interaction.

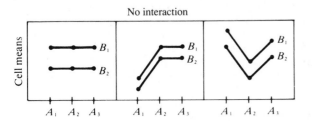
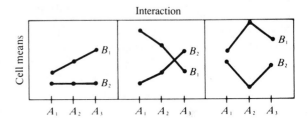

FIGURE 13.2 Illustration of possible noninteractions and interactions

Many people will argue that if you find a significant interaction the main effects should be ignored. It is not reasonable, however, automatically to exclude interpretation of main effects in the presence of *any* significant interaction. In the Eysenck study, we had a significant interaction, but for both younger and older subjects the tasks that involved greater processing led to greater recall. The fact that this effect was more pronounced in the younger group does not negate the fact that it was also clearly present in the older subjects. Here it is perfectly legitimate to speak about the main effect of Condition, even in the presence of an interaction. However, had the younger group shown better recall with more demanding tasks whereas the older group had shown poorer recall, then it might actually not be of interest whether the main effect of Condition was significant or not, and we would instead concentrate on discussing the simple effects of difference among Conditions for the younger and older subjects separately. (Interactions in which group differences reverse their sign at some level of the other variable—that is, when the lines cross—are sometimes referred to as **"disordinal" interactions**.) In general, the interpretation depends on common sense. If the main effects are clearly meaningful, then it makes sense to interpret them, whether or not an interaction is present. However, if the main effect does not really have any meaning, then it should be ignored.

"Disordinal" interactions

13.4   SIMPLE EFFECTS

I earlier defined a simple effect as the effect of one factor (independent variable) at one level of the other factor—for example, the differences among Conditions for the younger subjects. The analysis of simple effects can be an important technique for analyzing data that contain significant interactions. In a very real sense, it allows us to "tease apart" interactions.

I will use the Eysenck data to illustrate how to calculate and interpret simple effects. Table 13.4 shows the cell totals and the summary table reproduced from Table 13.2. The table also contains the calculations involved in obtaining all the simple effects.

TABLE 13.4
Illustration of calculation of simple effects (data taken from Table 13.2)

(a) Cell Totals (n = 10)

	Counting	Rhyming	Adjective	Imagery	Intentional	Totals
Older	70	69	110	134	120	503
Younger	65	76	148	176	193	658
Totals	135	145	258	310	313	1161

(b) Calculations

Conditions at Each Age

$$SS_{C \text{ at Old}} = \frac{70^2 + 69^2 + \cdots + 120^2}{10} - \frac{503^2}{50}$$

$$= 5411.70 - 5060.18 = 351.52$$

$$SS_{C \text{ at Young}} = \frac{65^2 + 76^2 + \cdots + 193^2}{10} - \frac{658^2}{50}$$

$$= 10{,}013.00 - 8659.28 = 1353.72$$

Age at Each Condition

$$SS_{A \text{ at Counting}} = \frac{70^2 + 65^2}{10} - \frac{135^2}{20}$$

$$= 912.50 - 911.25 = 1.25$$

$$SS_{A \text{ at Rhyming}} = \frac{69^2 + 76^2}{10} - \frac{145^2}{20}$$

$$= 1053.70 - 1051.25 = 2.45$$

$$SS_{A \text{ at Adjective}} = \frac{110^2 + 148^2}{10} - \frac{258^2}{20}$$

$$= 3400.40 - 3328.20 = 72.2$$

$$SS_{A \text{ at Imagery}} = \frac{134^2 + 176^2}{10} - \frac{310^2}{20}$$

$$= 4893.20 - 4805.00 = 88.20$$

$$SS_{A \text{ at Intentional}} = \frac{120^2 + 193^2}{10} - \frac{313^2}{20}$$

$$= 5164.9 - 4898.45 = 266.45$$

TABLE 13.4 (Cont.)   **(c) Summary Tables**

Overall Analysis

Source	df	SS	MS	F
A (Age)	1	240.25	240.250	29.94*
C (Condition)	4	1514.94	378.735	47.19*
AC	4	190.30	47.575	5.93*
Error	90	722.30	8.026	
Total	99	2667.79		

$*p < .05$

Simple Effects

Source	df	SS	MS	F
Conditions				
C at Old	4	351.52	87.88	10.95*
C at Young	4	1353.72	338.43	42.15*
Age				
A at Counting	1	1.25	1.25	<1
A at Rhyming	1	2.45	2.45	<1
A at Adjective	1	72.20	72.20	9.00*
A at Imagery	1	88.20	88.20	10.99*
A at Intentional	1	266.45	266.45	33.20*
Error	90	722.30	8.03	

$*p < .05$

The first summary table in Table 13.4c reveals significant effects due to Age, Condition, and their interaction. We already discussed these results earlier in conjunction with the original analysis. As I said there, the presence of an interaction means that there are different Condition effects for the two Ages, and there are different Age effects for the five Conditions. It thus becomes important to ask whether our general Condition effect really applies for older as well as younger subjects, and whether there really are Age differences under all Conditions. The analysis of these simple effects is found in Table 13.4b and the bottom table in Table 13.4c. I have shown all possible simple effects for the sake of completeness of the example, but in general you should examine only those effects in which you are interested.

CALCULATION

In Table 13.4b you can see that $SS_{C\,at\,Old}$ is calculated in the same way as any sum of squares. We simply calculate SS_C using only the data for the older subjects. If we consider only those data, the five Condition totals are 70, 69, 110, 134, and 120. Thus, the sum of squares will be

$$SS_{C \text{ at Old}} = \frac{(\Sigma T_{C \text{ at Old}}^2)}{n} - \frac{(\Sigma T_{\text{Old}})^2}{cn}$$

$$= \frac{70^2 + 69^2 + 110^2 + 134^2 + 120^2}{10} - \frac{503^2}{50} = 351.52$$

The other simple effects are calculated in the same way, by ignoring all data in which you are not at the moment interested. Notice that the sum of squares for the simple effect of Condition for older subjects (351.52) is the same value as that we obtained in Chapter 11 when we ran a one-way analysis of variance on only the data from older subjects.

The degrees of freedom for the simple effects are calculated in the same way as for the corresponding main effects. This makes sense because the number of means we are comparing remains the same. Whether we use all of the subjects or only part of them, we are still comparing five conditions and have $5 - 1 = 4$ df for Conditions.

To test the simple effects, we use the error term from the overall analysis (MS_{error}). The expected mean squares are presented in Table 13.5, and they make it clear why this is the appropriate error term. The expected mean square for each simple effect contains only one effect other than error (e.g., $n\sigma_{\alpha \text{ at } \beta_j}^2$), whereas MS_{error} is an estimate of error variance (σ_e^2). In fact, the only difference between what I have done in Table 13.4 and what I would do if I ran a standard one-way analysis of variance on the Old subjects' data (which is the way I usually calculate sums of squares for simple effects when I use a computer) is the error term. MS_{error} continues to be based on all the data because it is a better estimate with more degrees of freedom.

TABLE 13.5
Expected mean squares for simple effects

Source	E(MS)
Simple Effects of A	
A at B_1	$\sigma_e^2 + n\sigma_{\alpha \text{ at } \beta_1}^2$
A at B_2	$\sigma_e^2 + n\sigma_{\alpha \text{ at } \beta_2}^2$
A at B_3	$\sigma_e^2 + n\sigma_{\alpha \text{ at } \beta_3}^2$
Simple Effects of B	
B at A_1	$\sigma_e^2 + n\sigma_{\beta \text{ at } \alpha_1}^2$
B at A_2	$\sigma_e^2 + n\sigma_{\beta \text{ at } \alpha_2}^2$
Error	σ_e^2

INTERPRETATION

From the column labeled F in the bottom table in Table 13.4c, it is evident that differences due to Conditions occur for both ages although the sum of squares for the older subjects is only about one-quarter of what it is for the younger ones. With regard to the Age effects, however, no differences occur on the lower-level tasks of counting and rhyming, but differences do occur on the higher-level tasks. In other words, differences between age groups show up on only those tasks involving higher levels of processing. This is basically what Eysenck set out to demonstrate.

The present example has shown that we can employ tests on simple effects to clarify significant main effects and interactions. Simple effects can also contribute to the interpretation of nonsignificant main effects. Examine the data illustrated in Figure 13.3. In this figure the main effects of both A and B will be nonsignificant, and in fact both SS_A and SS_B will be 0. This does not mean that A and B are not important, however. If we calculated the simple effects, we could find that they are all significant.

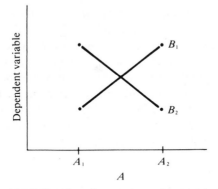

FIGURE 13.3
Illustration of significant simple effects with no main effects

In general, we seldom look at simple effects unless significant interaction is present. However, this practice must be governed by common sense. It is not difficult to imagine data for which an analysis of simple effects would be warranted even in the face of a nonsignificant interaction, or to imagine studies in which the simple effects are the prime reason for conducting the experiment.

Among the points we should emphasize in our discussion of simple effects is that the experimenter must examine her data carefully. Plotting the data and considering what they mean is an important, if not the *most* important, part of an appropriate analysis of any set of data.

ADDITIVITY OF SIMPLE EFFECTS

All sums of squares in the analysis of variance (other than SS_{total}) represent a partitioning of some larger sum of squares, and the simple effects are no exception. The simple effect of Condition at each level of Age represents a partitioning of SS_C and $SS_{A \times C}$, whereas the effects of Age at each level of Condition represent a partitioning of SS_A and $SS_{A \times C}$. Thus

$$\sum SS_{C \text{ at } A} = 351.52 + 1353.72 = 1705.24$$

$$SS_C + SS_{A \times C} = 1514.94 + 190.30 = 1705.24$$

and

$$\sum SS_{A \text{ at } C} = 1.25 + 2.45 + 72.20 + 88.20 + 266.45 = 430.55$$

$$SS_A + SS_{A \times C} = 240.25 + 190.30 = 430.55$$

A similar additive relationship holds for the degrees of freedom. The fact that the sums of squares for simple effects sum to the combined sums of squares for the corresponding main effect and interaction affords us a quick and simple check on our calculations.

ERROR RATES

In testing simple effects, keep in mind that we are generally working with an error rate per comparison of α. In the present example, we have calculated seven Fs, each at $\alpha = .05$. This means that we have a per-experiment error rate of .35, and a familywise error rate that approaches .35. (If the Fs were independent, FW would actually be .30.) This is an uncomfortably high error rate and is not one to be recommended without careful consideration. As a general rule, it is important to balance the gain to be expected from testing all simple effects against the danger to be incurred from an unpleasantly high error rate. In practice, you will usually find that only a few of the possible simple effects are of a priori interest, and only these few should be tested.

13.5   ANALYSIS OF VARIANCE APPLIED TO MATERNAL ADAPTATION

In several places in the book, I have referred to a study by Nurcombe et al. (1984) on low-birthweight (LBW) infants. One of the purposes of that study was to train mothers of LBW infants to improve their ability to cope with the problems that such infants present. The investigators' hypothesis was that mothers in the LBW-Experimental group would show greater maternal adaptation than would mothers in the LBW-Control group. In fact, it was hoped that the LBW-Experimental group would adapt as successfully as the normal-birthweight (NBW) group. The authors of the study also thought that the mothers who had less education might benefit more from the intervention than would more highly educated mothers. If this were true, the LBW-Control versus LBW-Experimental difference would be larger for the low-education group than for the high-education group, leading to an interaction.

The data and the calculations are presented in Table 13.6. These data are a subset of the real data, representing only the first eight subjects in each group. (The results agree with the results obtained on the full data set.) Notice that there is a significant Group effect and a significant Education effect [as indicated by the asterisks (*) following the F values in Table 13.6c], but there is no interaction. (When F is less than 1 we normally write "$F < 1$" rather than give the actual value.) The lack of an interaction means that Group differences do not depend on Education level, which runs counter to our experimental hypothesis. We would conclude from this analysis that both the amount of education and the presence or absence of the intervention program had an effect on maternal adaptation.

TABLE 13.6
Maternal adaptation as a function of group (G) and education (E) (Lower scores represent better adaptation.)

(a) Data

Education	Group			Totals
	LBW-Experimental	LBW-Control	NBW	
High-School Education or Less	14	25	18	
	20	19	14	
	22	21	18	
	13	20	20	
	13	20	12	
	18	14	14	
	13	25	17	
	14	18	17	
	$\overline{127}$	$\overline{162}$	$\overline{130}$	419
More Than High-School Education	11	18	16	
	11	16	20	
	16	13	12	
	12	21	14	
	12	17	18	
	13	10	20	
	17	16	12	
	13	21	13	
	$\overline{105}$	$\overline{132}$	$\overline{125}$	362
Group totals	$\overline{232}$	$\overline{294}$	$\overline{255}$	$\overline{781}$

(b) Calculations

$$SS_{total} = \sum X^2 - \frac{(\Sigma X)^2}{N} = 14^2 + \cdots + 13^2 - \frac{781^2}{48}$$

$$= 13{,}363 - 12{,}707.52 = 655.48$$

$$SS_{cells} = \frac{\Sigma T_{ij}^2}{n} - \frac{(\Sigma X)^2}{N} = \frac{127^2 + \cdots + 125^2}{8} - \frac{781^2}{48}$$

$$= 12{,}918.375 - 12{,}707.52 = 210.86$$

$$SS_{error} = SS_{total} - SS_{cells}$$

$$= 655.48 - 210.86 = 444.62$$

$$SS_E = \frac{\Sigma T_E^2}{ng} - \frac{(\Sigma X)^2}{N} = \frac{419^2 + 362^2}{(8)(3)} - \frac{781^2}{48}$$

$$= 12{,}775.21 - 12{,}707.52 = 67.69$$

$$SS_G = \frac{\Sigma T_G^2}{ne} - \frac{(\Sigma X)^2}{N} = \frac{232^2 + 294^2 + 255^2}{(8)(2)} - \frac{781^2}{48}$$

$$= 12{,}830.31 - 12{,}707.52 = 122.79$$

$$SS_{EG} = SS_{cells} - SS_E - SS_G$$

$$= 210.86 - 67.69 - 122.79 = 20.38$$

TABLE 13.6 (Cont.)

(c) Summary Table

Source	df	SS	MS	F
E	1	67.69	67.69	6.39*
G	2	122.79	61.40	5.80*
E × G	2	20.38	10.19	< 1
Error	42	444.62	10.59	
Total	47	655.48		

*$p < .05$

13.6 MULTIPLE COMPARISONS

All the multiple-comparison procedures discussed in Chapter 12 are applicable to the analysis of factorial designs. Thus, we can test the differences among the five Condition means in the Eysenck example using the Bonferroni t test, the Newman–Keuls test, and so on. Keep in mind, however, that we must interpret the "n" that appears in formulas in Chapter 12 to be the number of observations on which each treatment mean or total was based. Since the Condition totals are based on ($a \times n$) observations, that is the value that you would enter into the formulas, not n.

On rare occasions, it is relevant to compare the individual cell means rather than the means attributable to the main effects. (Be sure this is really what you want to do. People often ask me how to do it, but when I ask them why they want to, they quickly discover that they really do not want to do that after all.) If you do want to compare cell means, just treat the various cell totals as if they came from a large one-way design, and operate accordingly. In others words, for the Eysenck study you could compare the mean of younger subjects in the Counting condition with the mean of the older subjects in the Adjective condition, for example, by acting as if you had a one-way design with 10 groups. You could then use the standard multiple-comparison procedures.[†] The problem with this approach is that if you did find a difference between the two specified cells, you could not tell whether the difference was due to the different conditions, the different ages, or a combination of the two factors. Here Age and Condition are confounded. That is why you would adopt such a procedure only in particular circumstances.

13.7 POWER ANALYSIS FOR FACTORIAL EXPERIMENTS

Calculating power for fixed-variable factorial designs is basically the same as it was for one-way designs. In the one-way design, we defined

---

[†] For a much more complete discussion of the use of multiple-comparison techniques with factorial designs, see Keppel (1973).

$$\phi' = \sqrt{\frac{\Sigma\tau_j^2}{k\sigma_e^2}}$$

and

$$\phi = \phi'\sqrt{n}$$

where $\Sigma\tau_j^2 = \Sigma(\mu_j - \mu)^2$, k = the number of treatments, and n = the number of observations in each treatment. In the two-way and higher-order designs we have more than one "treatment," but this does not alter the procedure in any important way. If we let $\alpha_i = \mu_i - \mu$, and $\beta_j = \mu_j - \mu$, where μ_i represents the parametric mean of Treatment A_i (across all levels of B) and μ_j represents the parametric mean of Treatment B_j (across all levels of A), then we can define the following terms:

$$\phi'_\alpha = \sqrt{\frac{\Sigma\alpha_j^2}{a\sigma_e^2}}$$

$$\phi_\alpha = \phi'_\alpha\sqrt{nb}$$

and

$$\phi'_\beta = \sqrt{\frac{\Sigma\beta_j^2}{b\sigma_e^2}}$$

$$\phi_\beta = \phi'_\beta\sqrt{na}$$

Examining these formulas will reveal that to calculate the power against a null hypothesis concerning A, we act as if variable B did not exist. To calculate the power of the test against a null hypothesis concerning B, we similarly act as if variable A did not exist.

Calculating the power against the null hypothesis concerning the interaction follows the same logic. We define

$$\phi'_{\alpha\beta} = \sqrt{\frac{\Sigma\alpha\beta_{ij}^2}{ab\sigma_e^2}} \quad \text{and then} \quad \phi_{\alpha\beta} = \phi'_{\alpha\beta}\sqrt{n}$$

where $\alpha\beta_{ij}$ is defined as for the underlying structural model ($\alpha\beta_{ij} = \mu - \mu_i - \mu_j + \mu_{ij}$). Given ϕ we can simply obtain the power of the test just as we did for the one-way design.

Calculating power for the random model is more complicated, and for the mixed model (to be discussed shortly) requires a set of rather unrealistic assumptions. To learn how to obtain estimates of power with these models, see Winer (1971, p. 334).

In certain situations, the two-way factorial is more powerful than are two separate one-way designs, in addition to the other advantages that accrue to factorial designs. Consider two hypothetical experimental studies, where the number of subjects per teaching method are held constant across different designs.

In Experiment 1, an investigator wishes to examine the efficacy of three different teaching methods. She has introduced all three methods in each of four schools. Our experimenter is faced with two choices. She can run a one-way analysis on the three teaching methods, ignoring the Schools variable entirely, or she can run a 3 × 4 two-way factorial analysis on the three methods and four schools. In this case, the two-way has more power than the one-way. In the one-way, we would ignore any differences among schools and the interaction of Schools with Methods, and these would go toward increasing the error term. In the two-way, we take into account differences that can be attributed to Schools and to the interaction between Methods and Schools, thus removing them from the error term. The error term for the two-way would thus be smaller than for the one-way, giving us greater power.

For Experiment 2, consider the experimenter who had originally planned to apply her three methods in only one school. Her error term would not be inflated by differences among Schools and the interaction of Schools with Methods, since she has used only one school. If she now *expanded* her study to include several schools, SS_{total} would increase to account for additional effects due to Schools and the interaction of Methods with Schools, but the error term would remain constant because the extra variation would be accounted for by the extra terms. Since the error term would remain constant, she would have no increase in power in this situation over the power she would have had in her original study, except for an increase in N.

As a general rule, a factorial design is more powerful than a one-way design only when the extra factors can be thought of as refining or purifying the error term. In other words, when extra factors or variables account for variance that would normally be incorporated into the error term, the factorial design is more powerful. Otherwise, all other things being equal, it is not, although it still possesses the advantage of allowing us to examine interaction terms and simple effects.

EXPECTED MEAN SQUARES FOR FIXED, RANDOM, AND MIXED MODELS

Although fixed and random models led to the same F test when we were discussing the one-way analysis of variance, this is not the case in more complex designs. Since the denominator in an F ratio is a function of the type of model we are considering, when we come to the factorial designs we find that MS_{error} is not always the appropriate denominator for F.

Mixed-model designs

Sampling fraction

Recall that a variable is defined as a *fixed* variable if we *select* the levels of that variable, and as a *random* variable if we obtain the levels by random sampling. Designs that consist of one or more fixed variables and one or more random variables are referred to as **mixed-model designs**. The difference between a fixed and a random term in any design becomes clearer if we first define a sampling fraction. The **sampling fraction** for a variable is the ratio of the number of levels of a given variable that *actually* are used to the potential number of levels that *could have been* used. We will use lowercase letters to represent the number of levels used and uppercase letters to represent the potential number of levels available.

As pointed out in Chapter 12, for a *fixed* variable the population of levels is limited to the levels actually used. This means that if variable A is fixed, $a = A$ and $a/A = 1$. For a fixed variable, the sampling fraction is always 1. For a random variable, however, this is not the case, because the number of potential levels is generally very large, and a would be very much smaller than A, meaning that $a/A = 0$ for all practical purposes. From this discussion, we can write:

Variable	Sampling fraction
A (fixed)	$a/A = 1$
A (random)	$a/A = 0$
B (fixed)	$b/B = 1$
B (random)	$b/B = 0$
Subjects (random)	$n/N = 0$

We will always treat *subjects* as if they were sampled at random from a large population.

Although it is possible to have sampling fractions between 0 and 1—as, for example, when the variable is a high-school class, which has only four possible levels—these rarely occur in practice. When the number of potential levels is small, that variable is almost always treated as a fixed variable anyway. When peculiar sampling fractions do arise, the investigator will have to work out the $E(MS)$ for herself and is usually advised to design her experiment so that the factor is fixed.

Given the concept of a sampling fraction, it is possible to define the expected mean squares for all models. These are given in Table 13.7 for a two-way factorial.

TABLE 13.7
Expected mean squares for all models of a two-way factorial

Source	$E(MS)$
A	$(1 - n/N)\sigma_e^2 + n(1 - b/B)\sigma_{\alpha\beta}^2 + nb\sigma_\alpha^2$
B	$(1 - n/N)\sigma_e^2 + n(1 - a/A)\sigma_{\alpha\beta}^2 + na\sigma_\beta^2$
AB	$(1 - n/N)\sigma_e^2 + n\sigma_{\alpha\beta}^2$
Error	$(1 - n/N)\sigma_e^2$

Each $E(MS)$ in this table contains the term

$$\left(1 - \frac{n}{N}\right)\sigma_e^2$$

Since subjects are almost always assumed to be chosen at random (at least we look around innocently and pretend that they are), and since the population of potential subjects is huge, n/N vanishes and we are left with σ_e^2 for the first term under each $E(MS)$. Similar reasoning applies to the other terms in Table 13.7, where, for example, $1 - a/A$ is 0 for fixed effects and 1 for random effects. If we substitute values of 0 and 1 for fixed and random effects, we arrive at the results presented in Table 13.8.

TABLE 13.8
Expected mean squares for fixed, random, and mixed models

	Fixed	Random	Mixed	
Source	A fixed B fixed	A random B random	A random B fixed	A fixed B random
A	$\sigma_e^2 + nb\sigma_\alpha^2$	$\sigma_e^2 + n\sigma_{\alpha\beta}^2 + nb\sigma_\alpha^2$	$\sigma_e^2 + nb\sigma_\alpha^2$	$\sigma_e^2 + n\sigma_{\alpha\beta}^2 + nb\sigma_\alpha^2$
B	$\sigma_e^2 + na\sigma_\beta^2$	$\sigma_e^2 + n\sigma_{\alpha\beta}^2 + na\sigma_\beta^2$	$\sigma_e^2 + n\sigma_{\alpha\beta}^2 + na\sigma_\beta^2$	$\sigma_e^2 + na\sigma_\beta^2$
AB	$\sigma_e^2 + n\sigma_{\alpha\beta}^2$	$\sigma_e^2 + n\sigma_{\alpha\beta}^2$	$\sigma_e^2 + n\sigma_{\alpha\beta}^2$	$\sigma_e^2 + n\sigma_{\alpha\beta}^2$
Error	σ_e^2	σ_e^2	σ_e^2	σ_e^2

It is clear from Table 13.8 that the expected mean squares are heavily dependent on the underlying structural model. This in turn means that the denominators for our F ratios will also depend on the model we adopt.

Consider first the usual fixed model. From Table 13.8 we can see that $\mathrm{MS_{error}}$ will always form a suitable test term, since the other $E(\mathrm{MS})$s differ from $E(\mathrm{MS_{error}})$ only by the parameter in question. Thus, for example,

$$\frac{E(\mathrm{MS}_A)}{E(\mathrm{MS_{error}})} = \frac{\sigma_e^2 + nb\sigma_\alpha^2}{\sigma_e^2}$$

will have an expectation appreciably greater than 1 only if $\sigma_\alpha^2 \neq 0$.

For the random model, it is apparent from the expected mean squares that $\mathrm{MS_{error}}$ is not appropriate for testing the main effects. For example, consider

$$\frac{E(\mathrm{MS}_A)}{E(\mathrm{MS_{error}})} = \frac{\sigma_e^2 + n\sigma_{\alpha\beta}^2 + nb\sigma_\alpha^2}{\sigma_e^2}$$

This ratio would have an expectancy appreciably greater than 1 if either σ_α^2 or $\sigma_{\alpha\beta}^2$ were greater than 0, and a significant F would not indicate which H_0 should be rejected. However, the interaction term does provide us with a proper test, since

$$\frac{E(\mathrm{MS}_A)}{E(\mathrm{MS}_{AB})} = \frac{\sigma_e^2 + n\sigma_{\alpha\beta}^2 + nb\sigma_\alpha^2}{\sigma_e^2 + n\sigma_{\alpha\beta}^2}$$

would have an expectation of approximately 1 unless σ_α^2 were greater than 0. In this case, a significant F would have an unequivocal interpretation. Thus, to test the two main effects we would use MS_{AB} as our denominator.

Even with the random model, $\mathrm{MS_{error}}$ does serve as the test term against the null hypothesis concerning the interaction, as is obvious from the ratio

$$\frac{E(\mathrm{MS}_{AB})}{E(\mathrm{MS_{error}})} = \frac{\sigma_e^2 + n\sigma_{\alpha\beta}^2}{\sigma_e^2}$$

where a significant F would occur only if $\sigma_{\alpha\beta}^2$ is greater than 0 (except for Type I errors).

For the mixed models, the situation is more complex, since one main effect will be tested against $\mathrm{MS_{error}}$ and the other against MS_{AB}. The interaction will again be tested against $\mathrm{MS_{error}}$. These tests can be illustrated for the case in which A is random and B is fixed.

$$\frac{E(\mathrm{MS}_A)}{E(\mathrm{MS_{error}})} = \frac{\sigma_e^2 + nb\sigma_\alpha^2}{\sigma_e^2}$$

$$\frac{E(\mathrm{MS}_B)}{E(\mathrm{MS}_{AB})} = \frac{\sigma_e^2 + n\sigma_{\alpha\beta}^2 + na\sigma_\beta^2}{\sigma_e^2 + n\sigma_{\alpha\beta}^2}$$

$$\frac{E(\mathrm{MS}_{AB})}{E(\mathrm{MS_{error}})} = \frac{\sigma_e^2 + n\sigma_{\alpha\beta}^2}{\sigma_e^2}$$

Notice that in a mixed model it is the *fixed* term that is tested against MS interaction and the *random* term that is tested against $\mathrm{MS_{error}}$. Although this looks backward, it follows from what we have said about the role of the sampling fraction.

POOLING ERROR TERMS

In both the random and mixed models, we often find that an important variable is tested against $MS_{interaction}$. Since interactions usually have relatively few degrees of freedom as compared with MS_{error}, this may result in a substantial loss in power, turning what might otherwise be a significant result into a nonsignificant one.

One way out of this difficulty lies in first showing that there is no evidence to cause us to doubt that $\sigma_{\alpha\beta}^2 = 0$, and then dropping the interaction term from the model. If this is possible, we may now pool MS_{AB} and MS_{error}, forming a new error term, and use this to test the main effects.

We started out with the model

$$X_{ijk} = \mu + \alpha_i + \beta_j + \alpha\beta_{ij} + e_{ijk}$$

If there is no interaction between A and B, the model is unnecessarily complicated by the inclusion of $\alpha\beta_{ij}$. We might therefore begin by testing the null hypothesis $H_0: \sigma_{\alpha\beta}^2 = 0$. To reduce the risk of a Type II error, this test should be run at a relatively high level of α—for example, $\alpha = .25$. If we cannot reject H_0 at this level, we can then be reasonably confident about deleting $\alpha\beta_{ij}$ from our model, leaving

$$X_{ijk} = \mu + \alpha_i + \beta_j + e_{ijk}$$

The effect of deleting $\alpha\beta_{ij}$ from the model is to delete all terms of the form $n\sigma_{\alpha\beta}^2$ from the table of expected mean squares (Table 13.8), with the result that both MS_{AB} and MS_{error} will now be estimates of σ_e^2. We can then form a new test by combining the error and interaction mean squares as $MS_{residual}$.

$$MS_{residual} = \frac{SS_{AB} + SS_{error}}{df_{AB} + df_{error}}$$

This new term, on $(df_{AB} + df_{error})$ degrees of freedom, is now used to test the main effects.

Although we might run a preliminary test on the interaction at $\alpha = .25$, we would not declare the interaction to be significant (in terms of our final conclusions about the data) unless we could also reject H_0 at $\alpha = .05$. In other words, our two tests represent two different strategies (accepting versus rejecting H_0), and our levels of α must reflect these differing strategies.

The entire procedure of pooling mean squares is usually relevant only for the random and mixed models. For fixed models, the MS_{error} is always an appropriate error term.

13.8 MAGNITUDE OF EXPERIMENTAL EFFECTS

As with the one-way design, it is both possible and desirable to calculate the magnitude of effect associated with each independent variable. The easiest, but also the most biased, way to do this is to calculate η^2. Here we would simply take the relevant sum of squares and divide by the SS_{total}. Thus, the magnitude of effect for variable A is SS_A/SS_{total} and for variable B is SS_B/SS_{total}, whereas the magnitude of effect for the interaction is SS_{AB}/SS_{total}.

The main difficulty with η^2 is that it is a biased estimate of the true magnitude of effect in the population. To put this somewhat differently, η^2 is a very good descriptive statistic, but a poor inferential statistic.

Although $\hat{\omega}^2$ also is biased, the bias is much less than for η^2. In addition, the statistical theory underlying $\hat{\omega}^2$ allows us to differentiate between fixed and random variables and to act accordingly.

Developing $\hat{\omega}^2$ for two-way and higher-order designs is basically an extension of what we have already done with the one-way. We begin with the set of expected mean squares, derive estimates of σ_α^2, σ_β^2, $\sigma_{\alpha\beta}^2$, and σ_e^2, and then form ratios of each of these components to the total variance. We will begin with the purely random model because of its greater simplicity.

RANDOM MODEL

From Table 13.8 we know that for the completely random model,

$$E(\text{MS}_{error}) = \sigma_e^2$$

and thus

$$\hat{\sigma}_e^2 = \text{MS}_{error}$$

Further,

$$E(\text{MS}_{AB}) = \sigma_e^2 + n\sigma_{\alpha\beta}^2$$

$$n\sigma_{\alpha\beta}^2 = E(\text{MS}_{AB}) - \sigma_e^2$$

Substituting estimates for parameters

$$n\hat{\sigma}_{\alpha\beta}^2 = \text{MS}_{AB} - \hat{\sigma}_e^2$$

and substituting our estimate of $\hat{\sigma}_e^2$, we arrive at

$$\hat{\sigma}_{\alpha\beta}^2 = \frac{\text{MS}_{AB} - \text{MS}_{error}}{n}$$

For variance estimates on main effects, we have

$$E(\text{MS}_A) = \sigma_e^2 + n\sigma_{\alpha\beta}^2 + nb\sigma_\alpha^2$$

$$nb\hat{\sigma}_\alpha^2 = \text{MS}_A - \hat{\sigma}_e^2 - n\hat{\sigma}_{\alpha\beta}^2$$

Substituting we have

$$nb\hat{\sigma}_\alpha^2 = \text{MS}_A - \text{MS}_{error} - \text{MS}_{AB} + \text{MS}_{error}$$

and therefore

$$\hat{\sigma}_\alpha^2 = \frac{\text{MS}_A - \text{MS}_{AB}}{nb}$$

Similarly,

$$\hat{\sigma}_\beta^2 = \frac{\text{MS}_B - \text{MS}_{AB}}{na}$$

To summarize these terms and illustrate their use, I will apply them to the results from Table 13.2, the summary table of which is reproduced here for convenience[†]:

Source	df	SS	MS	F
A (Age)	1	240.25	240.250	29.94*
C (Condition)	4	1514.94	378.735	47.19*
AC	4	190.30	47.575	5.93*
Error	90	722.30	8.026	
Total	99	2667.79		

*$p < .05$

We will let α represent the effect of Age and β represent the effect on Condition. Then we have

$$\hat{\sigma}_\alpha^2 = \frac{MS_A - MS_{AC}}{nc} = \frac{240.250 - 47.575}{(10)(5)} = 3.854$$

$$\hat{\sigma}_\beta^2 = \frac{MS_C - MS_{AC}}{na} = \frac{378.735 - 47.575}{(10)(2)} = 16.558$$

$$\hat{\sigma}_{\alpha\beta}^2 = \frac{MS_{AC} - MS_{error}}{n} = \frac{47.575 - 8.026}{10} = 3.955$$

$$\hat{\sigma}_e^2 = MS_{error} \qquad\qquad\qquad = 8.026$$

We will now define our estimate of the magnitude of the effect of A as

$$\hat{\omega}_A^2 = \frac{\hat{\sigma}_\alpha^2}{\sigma_{total}^2} = \frac{\hat{\sigma}_\alpha^2}{\sigma_\alpha^2 + \hat{\sigma}_\beta^2 + \hat{\sigma}_{\alpha\beta}^2 + \hat{\sigma}_e^2} = \frac{3.854}{32.393} = .12$$

Similarly,

$$\hat{\omega}_C^2 = \frac{\hat{\sigma}_\beta^2}{\sigma_{total}^2} = \frac{\hat{\sigma}_\beta^2}{\sigma_\alpha^2 + \hat{\sigma}_\beta^2 + \hat{\sigma}_{\alpha\beta}^2 + \hat{\sigma}_e^2} = \frac{16.558}{32.393} = .51$$

and

$$\hat{\omega}_{AC}^2 = \frac{\hat{\sigma}_{\alpha\beta}^2}{\sigma_{total}^2} = \frac{\hat{\sigma}_{\alpha\beta}^2}{\sigma_\alpha^2 + \hat{\sigma}_\beta^2 + \hat{\sigma}_{\alpha\beta}^2 + \hat{\sigma}_e^2} = \frac{3.955}{32.393} = .12$$

Although these equations could be expressed in many different ways by substituting the actual estimators and simplifying, there is little point in doing so. Once the four estimates are obtained, the calculation of $\hat{\omega}^2$ is straightforward.

[†] No one would seriously consider that Eysenck sampled the levels of his variables at random. I am treating this as a random model simply for purposes of illustration.

FIXED MODEL

Next we will consider the completely fixed model, and we will run across the same difficulty that we encountered in the one-way analysis of variance—namely, that the quantity

$$\frac{\Sigma \alpha_i^2}{a - 1}$$

is neither a population variance nor an unbiased estimate of one when we have measured the entire population of treatment levels. For a fixed model, we have exhausted the population of treatment levels, and thus we have to make some adjustment to this quantity if we want to estimate the variance of means of treatments.

Returning to the general case of an $A \times B$ factorial, we will let the terms

$$\theta_\alpha^2 = \sum \alpha_i^2/(a - 1)$$
$$\theta_\beta^2 = \sum \beta_j^2/(b - 1)$$
$$\theta_{\alpha\beta}^2 = \sum \alpha\beta_{ij}^2/(a - 1)(b - 1)$$

reserving σ_α^2, σ_β^2, and $\sigma_{\alpha\beta}^2$ as variances with denominators a, b, and ab respectively (e.g., $\sigma_\alpha^2 = \Sigma \alpha_i^2/a$).

Modifying the $E(\text{MS})$ from Table 13.8 to reflect our new, and more exact, terminology, the expected means squares for the fixed model become

$$E(\text{MS}_A) = \sigma_e^2 + nb\theta_\alpha^2 = \sigma_e^2 + \frac{nb\Sigma\alpha_i^2}{a - 1}$$

$$= \sigma_e^2 + \frac{nba}{a - 1}\left(\frac{\Sigma\alpha_i^2}{a}\right) = \sigma_e^2 + \frac{nba}{a - 1}\sigma_\alpha^2$$

$$E(\text{MS}_B) = \sigma_e^2 + na\theta_\beta^2 = \sigma_e^2 + \frac{nab}{b - 1}\sigma_\beta^2$$

$$E(\text{MS}_{AB}) = \sigma_e^2 + n\theta_{\alpha\beta}^2 = \sigma_e^2 + \frac{nab}{(a - 1)(b - 1)}\sigma_{\alpha\beta}^2$$

$$E(\text{MS}_{\text{error}}) = \sigma_e^2$$

As before, $\hat{\sigma}_e^2 = \text{MS}_{\text{error}}$. Since

$$E(\text{MS}_A) = \sigma_e^2 + \frac{nba\sigma_\alpha^2}{a - 1} \qquad \text{then} \qquad \hat{\sigma}_\alpha^2 = \frac{(\text{MS}_A - \text{MS}_{\text{error}})(a - 1)}{nab}$$

By a similar line of reasoning, we obtain

$$\hat{\sigma}_\beta^2 = \frac{(\text{MS}_B - \text{MS}_{\text{error}})(b - 1)}{nab}$$

and

$$\hat{\sigma}_{\alpha\beta}^2 = \frac{(\text{MS}_{AB} - \text{MS}_{\text{error}})(a - 1)(b - 1)}{nab}$$

The approach adopted here again defines

$$\hat{\omega}_A^2 = \frac{\hat{\sigma}_\alpha^2}{\sigma_{\text{total}}^2} = \frac{\hat{\sigma}_\alpha^2}{\hat{\sigma}_\alpha^2 + \hat{\sigma}_\beta^2 + \hat{\sigma}_{\alpha\beta}^2 + \hat{\sigma}_e^2}$$

The other terms ($\hat{\omega}_B^2$ and $\hat{\omega}_{AB}^2$) are defined in a similar fashion.[†] A little algebraic manipulation will show that the denominator in the last expression is equivalent to $(\text{SS}_{\text{total}} + \text{MS}_{\text{error}})/(nab)$ and that the numerators for the variance effects are

Effect	Numerator
A	$[\text{SS}_A - (a-1)\text{MS}_{\text{error}}]/nab$
B	$[\text{SS}_B - (b-1)\text{MS}_{\text{error}}]/nab$
AB	$[\text{SS}_{AB} - (a-1)(b-1)\text{MS}_{\text{error}}]/nab$

Notice that in each case the multiplier for MS_{error} is the degrees of freedom for the effect in question. Thus, the calculations are quite simple. As an example, we will again use the data in Table 13.2, with A and C representing Age and Condition.

For the main effect of Age,

$$\hat{\omega}_A^2 = \frac{\text{SS}_A - (a-1)\text{MS}_{\text{error}}}{\text{SS}_{\text{total}} + \text{MS}_{\text{error}}} = \frac{240.25 - (1)8.026}{2667.79 + 8.026} = .09$$

Similarly, for Condition and $A \times C$,

$$\hat{\omega}_C^2 = \frac{\text{SS}_C - (c-1)\text{MS}_{\text{error}}}{\text{SS}_{\text{total}} + \text{MS}_{\text{error}}} = \frac{1514.94 - (4)8.026}{2667.79 + 8.026} = .55$$

$$\hat{\omega}_{AC}^2 = \frac{\text{SS}_{AC} - (a-1)(c-1)\text{MS}_{\text{error}}}{\text{SS}_{\text{total}} + \text{MS}_{\text{error}}} = \frac{190.30 - (1)(4)8.026}{2667.79 + 8.026} = .06$$

We can now conclude that for Eysenck's study, 9% of the total variation is attributable to the main effect of Age, 55% to the main effect of the Condition, and 6% to their interaction. Thus, we can see that a total of 70% of the variation is attributable to the treatment effects. You might be inclined to think that if only 6% of the variation can be attributable to the interaction, it is probably not very important. I would argue with this interpretation. A great deal of variability in this study results from the dramatic effect of Condition. When we calculate our estimates of the percentage of accountable variation, variability due to Condition is part of the denominator. What we have computed is the *relative contribution* of the interaction of the two factors—and, relative to Condition, it really is not all that impressive. This is like saying that the Columbia River is not much of a river because relative to the Mississippi and the Amazon, it is pretty small. When you interpret a magnitude of effect measurement, you have to keep in mind the other factors that are included in the model. On the other hand, a small value for ω^2 should at least make you stop and think about whether you are dealing with a difference that is of any practical significance. The value of ω^2 for an

[†] See Dwyer (1974) for an alternative definition.

effect may be small because other factors in the experiment are inflating the overall variability, or it may be small because you are dealing with a trivial, although significant, effect. It is important to consider both alternatives.

MIXED MODEL

Following the principles we used to obtain variance components for the fixed and random models, it is not difficult to work out the terms for a mixed model. The actual derivation of these is left to you, although Table 13.9 contains the final results. This table is modified from Tables 1 and 2 of Vaughan and Corballis (1969). In the left column of this table, the designations A_f, B_f, and C_f represent fixed terms, whereas the designations A_r, B_r, and C_r represent random variables. As usual, the lowercase letters represent the number of levels of that variable. Variance components for the three-way factorial (which we shall discuss shortly) have been included for the sake of completeness. On the basis of the variance components given in Table 13.9, you should be able to derive the variance components for any factorial design, given the expected mean squares.

For most calculations of $\hat{\omega}^2$, the numerator is the variance component for the term in question, whereas the denominator is the sum of all components. Depending on the interests of the experimenter, however, other denominators are possible. In this context, a paper by Cohen (1973) is highly recommended. Although that paper deals with $\hat{\eta}^2$ instead of $\hat{\omega}^2$, the generalization is straightforward. The overriding consideration in determining the appropriate denominator is that the experimenter must think about what he is doing, and not simply apply a formula he finds in this or any other book.

TABLE 13.9
Estimates of variance components in one-way, two-way, and three-way designs

Model	Variance Component
A_f	$\sigma_\alpha^2 = (a-1)(\mathrm{MS}_A - \mathrm{MS}_e)/na$
	$\sigma_e^2 = \mathrm{MS}_e$
A_r	$\sigma_\alpha^2 = (\mathrm{MS}_A - \mathrm{MS}_e)/n$
	$\sigma_e^2 = \mathrm{MS}_e$
$A_f B_f$	$\sigma_\alpha^2 = (a-1)(\mathrm{MS}_A - \mathrm{MS}_e)/nab$
	$\sigma_\beta^2 = (b-1)(\mathrm{MS}_B - \mathrm{MS}_e)/nab$
	$\sigma_{\alpha\beta}^2 = (a-1)(b-1)(\mathrm{MS}_{AB} - \mathrm{MS}_e)/nab$
	$\sigma_e^2 = \mathrm{MS}_e$
$A_r B_f$	$\sigma_\alpha^2 = (\mathrm{MS}_A - \mathrm{MS}_e)/nb$
	$\sigma_\beta^2 = (b-1)(\mathrm{MS}_B - \mathrm{MS}_{AB})/nab$
	$\sigma_{\alpha\beta}^2 = (\mathrm{MS}_{AB} - \mathrm{MS}_e)/n$
	$\sigma_e^2 = \mathrm{MS}_e$
$A_r B_r$	$\sigma_\alpha^2 = (\mathrm{MS}_A - \mathrm{MS}_{AB})/nb$
	$\sigma_\beta^2 = (\mathrm{MS}_B - \mathrm{MS}_{AB})/na$
	$\sigma_{\alpha\beta}^2 = (\mathrm{MS}_{AB} - \mathrm{MS}_e)/n$
	$\sigma_e^2 = \mathrm{MS}_e$

TABLE 13.9 (Cont.) $A_f B_f C_f$

$$\sigma_\alpha^2 = (a-1)(\text{MS}_A - \text{MS}_e)/nabc$$
$$\sigma_\beta^2 = (b-1)(\text{MS}_B - \text{MS}_e)/nabc$$
$$\sigma_\gamma^2 = (c-1)(\text{MS}_C - \text{MS}_e)/nabc$$
$$\sigma_{\alpha\beta}^2 = (a-1)(b-1)(\text{MS}_{AB} - \text{MS}_e)/nabc$$
$$\sigma_{\alpha\gamma}^2 = (a-1)(c-1)(\text{MS}_{AC} - \text{MS}_e)/nabc$$
$$\sigma_{\beta\gamma}^2 = (b-1)(c-1)(\text{MS}_{BC} - \text{MS}_e)/nabc$$
$$\sigma_{\alpha\beta\gamma}^2 = (a-1)(b-1)(c-1)(\text{MS}_{ABC} - \text{MS}_e)/nabc$$
$$\sigma_e^2 = \text{MS}_e$$

$A_r B_f C_f$

$$\sigma_\alpha^2 = (\text{MS}_A - \text{MS}_e)/nbc$$
$$\sigma_\beta^2 = (b-1)(\text{MS}_B - \text{MS}_{AB})/nabc$$
$$\sigma_\gamma^2 = (c-1)(\text{MS}_C - \text{MS}_{AC})/nabc$$
$$\sigma_{\alpha\beta}^2 = (\text{MS}_{AB} - \text{MS}_e)/nc$$
$$\sigma_{\alpha\gamma}^2 = (\text{MS}_{AC} - \text{MS}_e)/nb$$
$$\sigma_{\beta\gamma}^2 = (b-1)(c-1)(\text{MS}_{BC} - \text{MS}_{ABC})/nabc$$
$$\sigma_{\alpha\beta\gamma}^2 = (\text{MS}_{ABC} - \text{MS}_e)/n$$
$$\sigma_e^2 = \text{MS}_e$$

$A_r B_r C_f$

$$\sigma_\alpha^2 = (\text{MS}_A - \text{MS}_{AB})/nbc$$
$$\sigma_\beta^2 = (\text{MS}_B - \text{MS}_{AB})/nac$$
$$\sigma_\gamma^2 = (c-1)(\text{MS}_C - \text{MS}_{AC} - \text{MS}_{BC} + \text{MS}_{ABC})/nabc$$
$$\sigma_{\alpha\beta}^2 = (\text{MS}_{AB} - \text{MS}_e)/nc$$
$$\sigma_{\alpha\gamma}^2 = (\text{MS}_{AC} - \text{MS}_{ABC})/nb$$
$$\sigma_{\beta\gamma}^2 = (\text{MS}_{BC} - \text{MS}_{ABC})/na$$
$$\sigma_{\alpha\beta\gamma}^2 = (\text{MS}_{ABC} - \text{MS}_e)/n$$
$$\sigma_e^2 = \text{MS}_e$$

$A_r B_r C_r$

$$\sigma_\alpha^2 = (\text{MS}_A - \text{MS}_{AB} - \text{MS}_{AC} + \text{MS}_{ABC})/nbc$$
$$\sigma_\beta^2 = (\text{MS}_B - \text{MS}_{AB} - \text{MS}_{BC} + \text{MS}_{ABC})/nac$$
$$\sigma_\gamma^2 = (\text{MS}_C - \text{MS}_{AC} - \text{MS}_{BC} + \text{MS}_{ABC})/nab$$
$$\sigma_{\alpha\beta}^2 = (\text{MS}_{AB} - \text{MS}_{ABC})/nc$$
$$\sigma_{\alpha\gamma}^2 = (\text{MS}_{AC} - \text{MS}_{ABC})/nb$$
$$\sigma_{\beta\gamma}^2 = (\text{MS}_{BC} - \text{MS}_{ABC})/na$$
$$\sigma_{\alpha\beta\gamma}^2 = (\text{MS}_{ABC} - \text{MS}_e)/n$$
$$\sigma_e^2 = \text{MS}_e$$

13.9   UNEQUAL SAMPLE SIZES

Although most (but certainly not all) experiments are designed with the intention of having equal numbers of observations in each cell, the cruel hand of fate frequently intervenes to upset even the most carefully laid plans. Subjects fail to arrive for testing, animals die, data are lost, apparatus fails, and so on. When such problems arise, we are faced with several alternative solutions, with the choice depending on the nature of the data and the reasons why data are missing.

The difficulty we face when we have unequal sample sizes is that in this case the row, column, and interaction effects are no longer independent. The lack of independence produces some difficulty in interpretation.

Most textbooks have been concerned with three general types of solutions: the solution for proportional sample sizes, the unweighted-means solution, and the least-squares solution. We will postpone the last of these until Chapter 16 and deal in this chapter with only the proportional and unweighted-means solutions. Unfortunately, it is not possible to draw a clear distinction between these procedures. The **unweighted-means solution** is generally applicable to all situations, whereas the **proportional solution** can be used only when the sample sizes meet certain conditions. Even when those conditions are met, however, the choice between the two solutions depends primarily on the way in which we visualize the role of the sample sizes themselves. This last point will be elaborated in some detail after we examine the computations associated with the proportional solution.

Unweighted-means solution,
Proportional solution

Proportional cell frequencies

Suppose we selected two different classrooms and for reasons related to the particular experiment administered Treatment B_1 to one-half of the students in each classroom, Treatment B_2 to one-quarter of them, and Treatment B_3 to the remaining one-quarter. Further assume that there were 20 students in classroom A_1 and 32 students in classroom A_2. The resulting sample sizes would be

	B_1	B_2	B_3	n_i
A_1	10	5	5	20
A_2	16	8	8	32
n_j	26	13	13	$52 = N$

Note from this table that there is a certain proportionality among the cell frequencies. For example, $10 : 16 :: 5 : 8$, $10 : 5 : :16 : 8$, and so on. In general,

$$n_{ij} = \frac{n_i n_j}{N}$$

where n_i represents the number of subjects in row i, n_j represents the number of observations in column j, and n_{ij} represents the number of subjects in cell$_{ij}$ [e.g., $n_{12} = 20(13)/52 = 5$]. When this type of proportionality holds, *and the experimenter decides it is appropriate to let the sample sizes play a role*, analyzing the data is straightforward. We will simply return to the procedure discussed in Chapter 11 of dividing each squared term by its appropriate denominator *before* summing. Thus, letting T_{A_i} and T_{B_j} refer to the totals for row i and column j, respectively,

$$SS_A = \sum \left(\frac{T_{A_i}^2}{n_i}\right) - CF$$

$$SS_B = \sum \left(\frac{T_{B_j}^2}{n_j}\right) - CF$$

$$SS_{cells} = \sum \left(\frac{T_{ij}^2}{n_{ij}}\right) - CF$$

$$SS_{AB} = SS_{cells} - SS_A - SS_B$$

$$SS_{error} = SS_{total} - SS_{cells}$$

A simple example of this approach is presented in Table 13.10, where the entries are the cell totals. The individual observations have been omitted, but $SS_{total} = 1000$. The cell means are presented simply to clarify the meaning of the data.

TABLE 13.10
Illustration of calculations for proportional sample sizes

(a) Data

	Cell totals					**Cell Ns**			
	B_1	B_2	B_3	Total		B_1	B_2	B_3	Total
A_1	25	40	50	115	A_1	10	5	5	20
A_2	30	30	20	80	A_2	20	10	10	40
	55	70	70	195		30	15	15	60

	Cell means		
	B_1	B_2	B_3
A_1	2.5	8.0	10.0
A_2	1.5	3.0	2.0

(b) Computations

$SS_{total} = 1000$ (given)

$$SS_A \sim \sum \left(\frac{T_{A_i}^2}{n_i}\right) - \frac{G(\Sigma X)^2}{N} = \frac{115^2}{20} + \frac{80^2}{40} - \frac{195^2}{60} = 821.25 - 633.75$$

$$= 187.50$$

$$SS_B = \sum \left(\frac{T_{B_j}^2}{n_j}\right) - CF = \frac{55^2}{30} + \frac{70^2}{15} + \frac{70^2}{15} - 633.75 = 754.1667 - 633.75$$

$$= 120.417$$

$$SS_{cells} = \sum \left(\frac{T_{ij}^2}{n_{ij}}\right) - CF = \frac{25^2}{10} + \frac{40^2}{5} + \cdots + \frac{20^2}{10} - 633.75$$

$$= 1057.5 - 633.75 = 423.75$$

$$SS_{AB} = SS_{cells} - SS_A - SS_B = 423.75 - 187.50 - 120.417 = 115.833$$

$$SS_{error} = SS_{total} - SS_{cells} = 1000 - 423.75 = 576.25$$

TABLE 13.10 (Cont.) **(c) Summary Table**

Source	df	SS	MS	F
A	1	187.50	187.500	17.571*
B	2	120.417	60.208	5.642*
AB	2	115.833	57.916	5.427*
Error	54	576.250	10.671	
Total	59	1000.000		

*$p < .05$

It has generally been assumed that if our sample sizes exhibit the property of proportionality, as defined previously, the solution is straightforward. Unfortunately, this is not the case. Although it is often stated (Winer, 1971, p. 404) that with proportionality, row, column, and interaction effects are independent, this is not correct. The row and column effects are independent of each other, but they are not independent of the interaction effects. What this means in practical terms is that with this procedure the sample sizes play an active role in the result, and in fact we are really analyzing a set of weighted means. The sample sizes are treated as part of the treatment effect in that larger samples carry more weight in the analysis.

The issue of *weighted* versus *unweighted* means frequently causes confusion. Consider the following set of data, broken down by gender, from two schools. The dependent variable could be anything, but suppose that it is a body-fat score (as a measure of nutrition). Further assume that School I was found in a middle-class suburb (Junk-Food Heights), whereas School II came from an economically depressed urban neighborhood.

	Males		Females		Mean of Scores	Mean of Means
	$\overline{X}$	n	$\overline{X}$	n		
School I	155	10	110	20	125	132.5
School II	135	20	120	40	125	127.5

The traditional method of obtaining mean body-fat scores for each school (and the method employed by the solution in Table 13.10) is to add up the scores within each school and divide by the number of students in that school. But notice what this entails:

$$\overline{X}_{\text{School I}} = \frac{T_{\text{males}} + T_{\text{females}}}{N} = \frac{n_{\text{males}}\overline{X}_{\text{males}} + n_{\text{females}}\overline{X}_{\text{females}}}{N}$$

Weighted means

Here we see that the contribution made by the male and female means is a function of the sample sizes, and thus our value of 125 is a **weighted** combination of **means**. Using this system, we find that there is no difference between the two schools, and SS_{schools} obtained by the *proportional* approach to the analysis of variance would be exactly 0.

An alternative approach would be to give equal weight to male and female means, arguing that since males and females are equally represented in the general population and presumably in the populations of these schools, they should each make the same contribution to the school's mean, especially if that mean is going to be used to assess the students' nutrition. This can be accomplished by simply taking the mean of the means—for example, $(155 + 110)/2 = 132.5$. This represents a case of equally weighted

Unweighted means   means, called **unweighted means**. Using this approach, we see that the mean body-fat scores of the two schools differ by about five points. (In fact, with nonproportional data it is very easy to have $\text{School}_I < \text{School}_{II}$ for each gender, and yet have a greater overall mean for School_I.)

As has been said, the *proportional* approach to the analysis of variance compares weighted means (e.g., 125 versus 125). The method to be discussed in the next section ("*Unweighted-Means Solution*") can be thought of as an approximation to the comparison of unweighted means (e.g., 132.5 versus 127.5). (A more exact solution will be discussed in Chapter 16.)

Whether it is more appropriate to compare weighted means or unweighted means depends primarily on the nature of the experiment. If we were mainly interested in studying these two particular schools, and if males and females are really distributed (in the schools) in this peculiar way, then 125 body-fat units is our best estimate of each school's mean. However, if we are using these schools just because they are a convenient source of warm bodies, and if we assume that males and females are distributed about 50 : 50 in each community, then the unweighted means of 132.5 and 127.5 units are our best guesses as to the means of those communities (at least within the age range covered by our study). (In fact, with data such as these, the interaction is probably of more interest than the main effects.)

The decision as to which approach is more relevant is an important one, since using the unweighted-means method leads to tests of the form $H_0: \mu_1 = \mu_2$, whereas using the proportional approach leads to tests of the form $H_0: (n_1/N)\mu_1 = (n_2/N)\mu_2$. By and large, it generally makes much more sense to ignore the proportional nature of the frequencies and use an unweighted-means solution instead.

UNWEIGHTED-MEANS SOLUTION

When cell frequencies are not proportional, one appropriate method of analysis is the unweighted-means solution. As indicated, the term *unweighted means* is actually a misnomer, since what we really have are *equally weighted means*. As we saw in the last section, dividing each squared term by its own sample size as we go along [i.e., $\Sigma(T_i^2/n_i)$] amounts to weighting each mean in proportion to its sample size. In this section we will weight all means equally by using a form of average sample size (the harmonic mean of the n_{ij}).

We will take as our example data from a study by Klemchuk, Bond, and Howell (1990) on role-taking in children. In this study, children between the ages of 2 and 5 years were administered a battery of role-taking tasks. (For example, a stimulus card with a different picture on each side was placed upright between the experimenter and the subject, and the subject was asked to identify what the experimenter saw.) Subjects were classified into a group who had had no previous daycare experience and a group who had had extensive daycare experience (children who had had intermediate levels of daycare were not involved in this analysis). Children were also sorted into two age groups (2 to 3 years and 4 to 5 years). The investigators' hypothesis was that children with daycare experience would perform better on role-taking tasks than would children without daycare experience, because of the former group's greater opportunity for social development. It was expected that older children would outperform younger children and that there would be no Age by Daycare interaction. The dependent variable was a score on a role-taking factor, and it has no intuitive meaning other than that a higher score represents better performance. As you will see, the sample sizes are distinctly unequal. There is no logical reason why fewer older children had participated in some sort of daycare experiences—this is just the sort of result that we could happily have done without. With such unequal sample sizes, it is important to interpret the results with caution.

The data are presented in Table 13.11. Table 13.11a lists the raw data, the individual cell frequencies, the individual cell means, and the harmonic mean of the n_{ij} $(\bar{n}_h)$. The harmonic mean of k observations $(X_1, \ldots, X_k)$ is defined as

$$\bar{X}_h = \frac{k}{\dfrac{1}{X_1} + \dfrac{1}{X_2} + \dfrac{1}{X_3} + \cdots + \dfrac{1}{X_k}}$$

Corrected totals
Adjusted totals

From this point on, we will act as though every cell contained $\bar{n}_h$ observations. Thus, the number of subjects per row will be $\bar{n}_h$ times the number of cells in that row, the number of subjects per column will be $\bar{n}_h$ times the number of cells in that column, and the overall sample size will be $\bar{n}_h$ times the number of cells. The new values are shown in Table 13.11a$_2$. This section contains what we will call **corrected** or **adjusted totals**. If the mean of cell$_{11}$ is -1.209, and if we act as though each cell contained 7.925 observations, then the adjusted cell total must be $(\bar{X}_{ij})(\bar{n}_h) = -1.209 \times 7.925 = -9.581$. The same reasoning holds for all other totals in this table.

From here on, calculating main effects and the interaction proceeds just as in the equal-n case, substituting the adjusted totals for the actual totals and the harmonic mean of the sample sizes for n. The calculations are shown in Table 13.11b. Note that the error term (SS$_{error}$) is not obtained by subtraction; instead, we calculate SS$_{within\ cell}$ for each cell of the design and then sum these terms to obtain the sum of squares due to error. An alternative approach is to calculate MS$_{error}$ directly by taking a weighted average of the individual cell variances—that is, we weight each cell variance by its df, just as we did when we calculated a pooled variance estimate in Chapter 7.

The summary table appears in Table 13.11c, where it is apparent that the two main effects are significant. Thus, role-taking ability increases with age (hardly a surprising finding) and with daycare experience (an important finding). There is no interaction, indicating that the difference between Daycare and No-Daycare children is the same for each age group.

TABLE 13.11
Data from Klemchuk,
Bond, and Howell
(1990)

(a) Data

	Raw Data Age	
	Younger	Older
No Daycare	−0.139	−0.167
	−2.002	−0.285
	−1.631	0.851
	−2.173	−0.397
	0.179	0.351
	−0.829	−0.240
	−1.503	0.160
	0.009	−0.535
	−1.934	−0.102
	−1.448	0.273
	−1.470	0.277
	−1.545	0.714
	−0.137	
	−2.302	
Daycare	−1.412	0.859
	−0.681	0.782
	0.638	0.851
	−0.222	−0.158
	0.668	
	−0.896	
	−0.464	
	−1.659	
	−2.096	
	0.493	

	Cell Means			
	Young	Old	n_{ij}	
No Daycare	−1.2089	0.0750	14	12
Daycare	−0.5631	0.5835	10	4

$$\bar{n}_h = \frac{4}{\frac{1}{14} + \frac{1}{12} + \frac{1}{10} + \frac{1}{4}} = 7.925$$

(a_2) Adjusted Totals

	Adjusted Cell Totals		
	Young	Old	Sum
No Daycare	−9.581	0.594	−8.987
Daycare	−4.463	4.624	0.161
Sum	−14.044	5.218	−8.826

TABLE 13.11 (Cont.)

(b) Computations

$$SS_{Age} = \frac{\Sigma T_A^2}{d\bar{n}_h} - \frac{(\Sigma X)^2}{ad\bar{n}_h} = \frac{-14.044^2 + 5.218^2}{(2)(7.925)} - \frac{-8.826^2}{(2)(2)(7.925)}$$

$$= 14.162 - 2.457 = 11.704$$

$$SS_{Day} = \frac{\Sigma T_D^2}{a\bar{n}_h} - \frac{(\Sigma X)^2}{ad\bar{n}_h} = \frac{-8.987^2 + 0.161^2}{(2)(7.925)} - \frac{-8.826^2}{(2)(2)(7.925)}$$

$$= 5.097 - 2.457 = 2.640$$

$$SS_{cells} = \frac{\Sigma T_{ij}^2}{\bar{n}_h} - \frac{(\Sigma X)^2}{ab\bar{n}_h}$$

$$= \frac{-9.581^2 + .594^2 + -4.463^2 + 4.624^2}{7.925} - \frac{-8.826^2}{(2)(2)(7.925)}$$

$$= 16.839 - 2.457 = 14.382$$

$$SS_{AD} = SS_{cells} - SS_{Age} - SS_{Day} = 14.382 - 11.704 - 2.640 = 0.038$$

$$SS_{error}$$

	No Daycare		Daycare	
	Younger	Older	Younger	Older
n_{ij}	14	12	10	4
ΣX_{ij}	-16.925	0.900	-5.631	2.334
ΣX_{ij}^2	30.091	2.155	11.767	2.099
SS_{ij}	9.630	2.087	8.596	0.737

$$SS_{error} = \Sigma SS_{ij} = 9.630 + 2.087 + 8.596 + 0.737 = 21.050$$

(c) Summary Table

Source	df	SS	MS	F
Age	1	11.704	11.704	20.02*
Daycare	1	2.640	2.640	4.51*
AD	1	0.038	0.037	<1
Error	36	21.050	0.585	
Total	39			

*$p < .05$

Note that the summary table does not contain SS_{total}. The separate sums of squares do not usually sum to SS_{total} in the case of unequal sample sizes. I will expand this point considerably in Chapter 16, but for now I will simply state that when the sample sizes are unequal, the main effects and interaction all account for overlapping portions of the overall variation. If we were to add them together, we would be summing some parts of the variation two or more times.

The point of this example is to show that with the unweighted-means solution each cell mean contributes equally to the calculation of each of the sums of squares. We do not give greater weight to cells (or rows or columns) with larger sample sizes.

13.10   HIGHER-ORDER FACTORIAL DESIGNS

All of the principles concerning a two-way factorial design apply equally well to a three-way or higher-order design. With one additional piece of information, you should have no difficulty running an analysis of variance on any factorial design imaginable, although the arithmetic becomes increasingly more tedious as variables are added. We will take a simple three-way factorial as an example, since it is the easiest to use.

The only major way in which the three-way differs from the two-way is in the presence of more than one interaction term. To see this, we must first look at the underlying structural model for a factorial design with three variables:

$$X_{ijkl} = \mu + \alpha_i + \beta_j + \gamma_k + \alpha\beta_{ij} + \alpha\gamma_{ik} + \beta\gamma_{jk} + \alpha\beta\gamma_{ijk} + \varepsilon_{ijkl}$$

First-order interactions

Second-order interaction

In this model we have not only main effects, symbolized by α_i, β_j, and γ_k, but also two kinds of interaction terms. The two-variable or **first-order interactions** are $\alpha\beta_{ij}$, $\alpha\gamma_{ik}$, and $\beta\gamma_{jk}$, which refer to the interaction of variables A and B, A and C, and B and C, respectively. We also have a **second-order interaction** term, $\alpha\beta\gamma_{ijk}$, which refers to the joint effect of all three variables. The first-order interactions we have already examined in discussing the two-way. The second-order interaction can be viewed in several ways. Probably the easiest way to view the ABC interaction is to think of the AB interaction itself interacting with variable C. Suppose that we had two levels of each variable and plotted the AB interaction separately for each level of C. We might have the result shown in Figure 13.4. Notice that for C_1 we have one AB interaction, whereas for C_2 we have a different one. Thus, AB depends on C, producing an ABC interaction. This same kind of reasoning could be invoked using the AC interaction at different levels of B, or the BC interaction at different levels of A. The result would be the same.

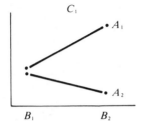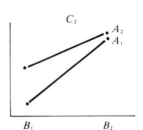

FIGURE 13.4
Plot of second-order interaction

As I have said, the three-way factorial is merely an extension of the two-way, with a slight twist. The twist comes about in obtaining the interaction sums of squares. In the two-way, we took an $A \times B$ table of cell totals, calculated SS_{cells}, subtracted the main effects, and were left with SS_{AB}. In the three-way, we have several interactions, but we will calculate them using techniques analogous to those employed earlier. Thus, to obtain SS_{BC} we will take a $B \times C$ table of cell totals (summing over A), obtain $SS_{cells\ BC}$, subtract the main effects of B and C, and end up with SS_{BC}. The same applies to SS_{AB} and SS_{AC}. We also follow the same procedure to obtain SS_{ABC}, but here we need to begin with an $A \times B \times C$ table of cell totals, obtain $SS_{cells\ ABC}$, and then subtract the main effects *and* the lower-order interactions to arrive at SS_{ABC}. In other words, for each interaction we start with a different table of cell totals, summing over the variable(s) in which we are not at the moment interested. We then obtain a SS_{cells} for that table and subtract from it any main effects and lower-order interactions that involve terms included in that interaction.

VARIABLES AFFECTING DRIVING PERFORMANCE

For an example, consider an experiment concerning the driving ability of two different types of drivers—inexperienced (A_1) and experienced (A_2). These people will drive on one of three types of roads—first class (B_1), second class (B_2), or dirt (B_3), under one of two different driving conditions—day (C_1) and night (C_2). Thus we have a $2 \times 3 \times 2$ factorial. The experiment will include four subjects per condition (for a total of 48 subjects), and the dependent variable will be the number of steering corrections in a one-mile section of roadway. The raw data are presented in Table 13.12a.

TABLE 13.12
Illustration of calculations for $2 \times 3 \times 2$ factorial design

(a) Data

Raw Data

	C_1			C_2		
	B_1	B_2	B_3	B_1	B_2	B_3
A_1	4	23	16	21	25	32
	18	15	27	14	33	42
	8	21	23	19	30	46
	10	13	14	26	20	40
A_2	6	2	20	11	23	17
	4	6	15	7	14	16
	13	8	8	6	13	25
	7	12	17	16	12	12

Tables of Cell Totals

ABC

	C_1			C_2			
	B_1	B_2	B_3	B_1	B_2	B_3	Total
A_1	40	72	80	80	108	160	540
A_2	30	28	60	40	62	70	290
Total	70	100	140	120	170	230	830

TABLE 13.12 (Cont.)

	AB					AC		

	B_1	B_2	B_3	Total		C_1	C_2	Total
A_1	120	180	240	540	A_1:	192	348	540
A_2	70	90	130	290	A_2:	118	172	290
Total	190	270	370	830	Total:	310	520	830

	BC			
	B_1	B_2	B_3	Total
C_1	70	100	140	310
C_2	120	170	230	520
Total	190	270	370	830

(b) Computations

$$SS_{total} = \sum X^2 - \frac{(\sum X)^2}{N} = 19{,}080 - \frac{830^2}{48} = 19{,}080 - 14{,}352.08 = 4727.92$$

$$SS_A = \frac{\sum T_{A_i}^2}{nbc} - CF = \frac{540^2 + 290^2}{24} - CF = 15{,}654.17 - 14{,}352.08 = 1302.08$$

$$SS_B = \frac{\sum T_{B_j}^2}{nac} - CF = \frac{190^2 + 270^2 + 370^2}{16} - CF = 15{,}368.75 - 14{,}352.08$$
$$= 1016.67$$

$$SS_C = \frac{\sum T_{C_k}^2}{nab} - CF = \frac{310^2 + 520^2}{24} - CF = 15{,}270.83 - 14{,}352.08 = 918.75$$

$$SS_{cell\ AB} = \frac{\sum T_{AB_{ij}}^2}{nc} - CF = \frac{120^2 + 180^2 + \cdots + 130^2}{8} - CF = 16{,}787.50$$
$$- 14{,}352.08 = 2435.42$$

$$SS_{AB} = SS_{cells\ AB} - SS_A - SS_B = 2435.42 - 1302.08 - 1016.67 = 116.67$$

$$SS_{cell\ AC} = \frac{\sum T_{AC_{ik}}^2}{nb} - CF = \frac{192^2 + \cdots + 172^2}{12} - CF = 16{,}789.67 - 14{,}352.08$$
$$= 2437.58$$

$$SS_{AC} = SS_{cells\ AC} - SS_A - SS_C = 2437.58 - 1302.08 - 918.75 = 216.75$$

$$SS_{cell\ BC} = \frac{\sum T_{BC_{jk}}^2}{na} - CF = \frac{70^2 + \cdots + 230^2}{8} - CF = 16{,}337.50 - 14{,}352.08$$
$$= 1985.42$$

$$SS_{BC} = SS_{cells\ BC} - SS_B - SS_C = 1985.42 - 1016.67 - 918.75 = 50.00$$

$$SS_{cells\ ABC} = \frac{\sum T_{ABC_{ijk}}^2}{n} - CF = \frac{40^2 + \cdots + 70^2}{4} - CF = 18{,}119.00 - 14{,}352.08$$
$$= 3766.92$$

$$SS_{ABC} = SS_{cell\ ABC} - SS_A - SS_B - SS_C - SS_{AB} - SS_{AC} - SS_{BC} = 3766.92$$
$$- 1302.08 - 1016.67 - 918.75 - 116.67 - 216.75 - 50.00 = 146.00$$

$$SS_{error} = SS_{total} - SS_{cells\ ABC} = 4727.92 - 3766.92 = 961.00$$

TABLE 13.12 (Cont.)   **(c) Summary Table**

Source	df	SS	MS	F
A (Experience)	1	1302.08	1302.08	48.78*
B (Road)	2	1016.67	508.33	19.04*
C (Conditions)	1	918.75	918.75	34.42*
AB	2	116.67	58.33	2.19
AC	1	216.75	216.75	8.12*
BC	2	50.00	25.00	<1
ABC	2	146.00	73.00	2.73
Error	36	961.00	26.69	
Total	47	4727.92		

*$p < .05$

The lower part of Table 13.12a contains all the necessary matrices of cell totals for the subsequent calculation of the interaction sums of squares. These matrices are obtained simply by summing across the levels of the irrelevant variable. Thus, the upper lefthand cell of the AB summary table contains the sum of all scores obtained under the treatment combination AB_{11}, regardless of the level of C (i.e., $ABC_{111} + ABC_{112}$).

Table 13.12b shows the calculations of the sums of squares. For the main effects, the sums of squares are obtained exactly as they would be for a one-way. For the first-order interactions, the calculations are just as they would be for a two-way, taking two variables at a time. The only new calculation is for the second-order interaction, and the difference is only a matter of degree. Here we first obtain the SS_{cells} for the three-dimensional matrix. This sum of squares represents all of the variation among the cell totals in the full-factorial design. From this, we must subtract all of the variation that can be accounted for by the main effects *and* by the first-order interactions. What remains is the variation that can be accounted for by only the joint effect of all three variables, namely SS_{ABC}.

The final sum of squares is SS_{error}. This is most easily obtained by subtracting $SS_{cells\ ABC}$ from SS_{total}. Since $SS_{cells\ ABC}$ represents all of the variation that can be attributable to differences among cells ($SS_{cells\ ABC} = SS_A + SS_B + SS_C + SS_{AB} + SS_{AC} + SS_{BC} + SS_{ABC}$), subtracting it from SS_{total} will leave us with only that variation within the cells themselves.

The summary table for the analysis of variance is presented in Table 13.12c. From this we can see that the three main effects and the $A \times C$ interaction are significant. None of the other interactions is significant.[†]

[†]You will notice that this analysis of variance included seven F values and thus seven hypothesis tests. With so many hypothesis tests, the familywise error rate would be quite high. Most people ignore the problem and simply test each F at a per-comparison error rate of $\alpha = .05$. However, if you are concerned about error rates, it would be appropriate to employ the equivalent of either the Bonferroni or multistage Bonferroni t procedure. This is generally only practical when you have the probability associated with each F, and can compare this probability against the probability required by the Bonferroni (or multistage Bonferroni) procedure. An interesting example of this kind of approach is found in Rosenthal and Rubin (1984).

SIMPLE EFFECTS

Since we have a significant interaction, the main effects of A and C should be interpreted with caution. To this end, the AC interaction has been plotted in Figure 13.5. When plotted, the data show that for the inexperienced driver night conditions produce considerably more steering corrections than do day conditions, whereas for the experienced driver the difference in the number of corrections made under the two conditions is relatively slight. Although the data do give us confidence in reporting a significant effect for A (the difference between experienced and inexperienced drivers), they should leave us a bit suspicious about differences due to variable C. At a quick glance, it would appear that there is a significant C effect for the inexperienced drivers, but possibly not for the experienced drivers. To examine this question more closely, we must consider the simple effects of C under A_1 and A_2 separately. This analysis is presented in Table 13.13, from which we can see that there is a significant effect between day and night condition not only for the inexperienced drivers, but also for the experienced drivers. (Note that we can again check the accuracy of our calculations; the simple effects should sum to $SS_C + SS_{AC}$.)

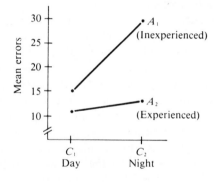

FIGURE 13.5
AC interaction for data in Table 13.12

TABLE 13.13
Simple effects for data in Table 13.12

(a) Data

	C_1	C_2	
A_1	192	348	540
A_2	118	172	290

(b) Computations

$$SS_{C \text{ at } A_1} = \frac{192^2 + 348^2}{12} - \frac{540^2}{24} = 13{,}164 - 12{,}150 = 1014.00$$

$$SS_{C \text{ at } A_2} = \frac{118^2 + 172^2}{12} - \frac{290^2}{24} = 3625.67 - 3504.17 = 121.50$$

(c) Summary Table

Source	df	SS	MS	F
C at A_1	1	1014.00	1014.00	37.99*
C at A_2	1	121.50	121.50	4.55*
Error	36	961.00	26.69	

*$p < .05$

TABLE 13.13 (Cont.)

(d) Decomposition of Sums of Squares

$$SS_{C\ at\ A_1} + SS_{C\ at\ A_2} = SS_C + SS_{AC}$$

$$1014.00 + 121.50 = 918.75 + 216.75$$

$$1135.50 = 1135.50$$

From this hypothetical experiment, we would conclude that there are significant differences among the three types of roadway, and between experienced and inexperienced drivers. We would also conclude that there is a significant difference between day and night conditions, for both experienced and inexperienced drivers.

SIMPLE INTERACTION EFFECTS

Simple main effects

Simple interaction effect

With the higher-order factorials, not only can we look at the effects of one variable at individual levels of some other variable (what we have called simple effects but what should more accurately be called **simple main effects**), but we can also look at the interaction of two variables at individual levels of some third variable. This we will refer to as a **simple interaction effect**.

Although our second-order interaction (ABC) was not significant, you might have a theoretical reason to expect an interaction between Experience (A) and Road (B) under night conditions, because driving at night is more difficult, but would expect no AB interaction during the day. As an example, I will break down the ABC interaction to get at those two simple interaction effects. (I should stress, however, that it is not good practice to test everything in sight just because it is possible to do so.)

In Figure 13.6 the AB interaction has been plotted separately for each level of C. It appears that there is no AB interaction under C_1, but there may be an interaction under C_2. We can test this hypothesis by calculating the AB interaction at each level of C, in a manner logically equivalent to the test we used for simple main effects. Essentially, all we need to do is treat the C_1 (day) and C_2 (night) data separately, calculating SS_{AB} for C_1 data and then for C_2 data. These simple interaction effects are then tested using MS_{error} from the overall analysis. This has been done in Table 13.14.

From the analysis of the simple interaction effects, it is apparent that the AB interaction is not significant for the day data, but it is for the night data. When night conditions (C_2) and dirt roads (B_3) occur together, differences between experienced (A_2) and inexperienced (A_1) drivers are magnified.

FIGURE 13.6
ABC interaction for data in Table 13.12

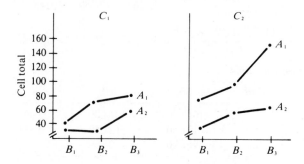

TABLE 13.14
Simple interaction effects for data in Table 13.12

(a) Data and Computations for $SS_{AB \text{ at } C_1}$

	C_1 Totals			
	B_1	B_2	B_3	Total
A_1	40	72	80	192
A_2	30	28	60	118
	70	100	140	310

$$SS_{A \text{ at } C_1} = \frac{192^2 + 118^2}{12} - \frac{310^2}{24} = 4232.33 - 4004.17 = 228.17$$

$$SS_{B \text{ at } C_1} = \frac{70^2 + 100^2 + 140^2}{8} - \frac{310^2}{24} = 4312.50 - 4004.17 = 308.33$$

$$SS_{\text{cells } AB \text{ at } C_1} = \frac{40^2 + \cdots + 60^2}{4} - \frac{310^2}{24} = 4617 - 4004.17 = 612.83$$

$$SS_{AB \text{ at } C_1} = SS_{\text{cells } AB \text{ at } C_1} - SS_{A \text{ at } C_1} - SS_{B \text{ at } C_1}$$
$$= 612.83 - 228.17 - 308.33 = 76.33$$

(b) Data and Computations for $SS_{AB \text{ at } C_2}$

	C_2 Totals			
	B_1	B_2	B_3	Total
A_1	80	108	160	348
A_2	40	62	70	172
	120	170	230	520

$$SS_{A \text{ at } C_2} = \frac{348^2 + 172^2}{12} - \frac{520^2}{24} = 12{,}557.33 - 11{,}266.67 = 1290.67$$

$$SS_{B \text{ at } C_2} = \frac{120^2 + 170^2 + 230^2}{8} - \frac{520^2}{24} = 12{,}025.00 - 11{,}266.67 = 758.33$$

$$SS_{\text{cells } AB \text{ at } C_2} = \frac{80^2 + \cdots + 70^2}{4} - \frac{520^2}{24} = 13{,}502.00 - 11{,}266.67 = 2235.33$$

$$SS_{AB \text{ at } C_2} = SS_{\text{cells } AB \text{ at } C_2} - SS_{A \text{ at } C_2} - SS_{B \text{ at } C_2}$$
$$= 2235.33 - 1290.67 - 758.33 = 186.33$$

(c) Summary Table

Source	df	SS	MS	F
AB at C_1	2	76.33	38.17	1.43
AB at C_2	2	186.33	93.17	3.49*
Error	36	961.00	26.69	

Although there is nothing to prevent someone from examining simple interaction effects in the absence of a significant higher-order interaction, cases for which this would make any logical sense are rare. If, however, the experimenter has a particular reason for looking at, for example, the AB interaction at each level of C, he is perfectly free to do so. On the other hand, if a higher-order interaction is significant, the experimenter should cast a wary eye on all lower-order effects and consider testing the important simple effects. However, to steal a line from Winer (1971, p. 442), "Statistical elegance does not necessarily imply scientifically meaningful inferences." Common sense is at least as important as statistical manipulations.

13.11 A COMPUTER EXAMPLE

As a final example of a two-way factorial and as an illustration of the output of two computer programs, consider the following learning experiment. An interesting phenomenon in the learning literature is called *reinstatement*: If we pair a tone and a shock until the tone comes to elicit a (conditioned) response, and if we then extinguish that response by presenting the tone alone, a single presentation of the (unpaired) shock will serve to "reinstate" the tone as a stimulus that will produce the conditioned response.

In the following experiment, we examine reinstatement when the animal is presented with either one, two, or three exposures of either a shock or a loud buzzer (which is aversive but has never been paired with the tone). The dependent variable is the magnitude of the (reinstated) response. The data are fictitious but might reasonably be expected to reflect the results of such an experiment.

	Number of Reinstatement Exposures		
	1	2	3
Shock	10	10	8
	8	12	9
	12	17	7
	15	14	9
Buzzer	10	11	5
	7	9	7
	6	10	7
	8	6	8

The results of the analysis using SPSS^X and EcStatic [a statistical package for microcomputers, Chalmer 1987] are presented in Exhibit 13.1. As you can see, the summary tables are essentially the same, but each program produces a somewhat different printout.

EXHIBIT 13.1
Computer analyses of
reinstatement data

(a) SPSS[X]

```
TITLE              'ANALYSIS OF REINSTATEMENT DATA'
FILE HANDLE        DATA /NAME = 'REINST.DAT'
DATA LIST          FILE = DATA/STIM 1 EXPOSURE 3 MAGNIT 4-5
ANOVA              MAGNIT BY STIM(1,2) BY EXPOSURE(1,3)
```

* * *   A N A L Y S I S   O F   V A R I A N C E   * * *

       MAGNIT
by   STIM
       EXPOSURE

Source of Variation	Sum of Squares	DF	Mean Square	F	Sig of F
Main Effects	109.792	3	36.597	7.965	0.002
STIM	57.042	1	57.042	12.260	0.003
EXPOSURE	52.750	2	26.375	5.669	0.012
2-Way Interactions	80.083	2	4.042	0.869	0.436
STIM EXPOSURE	80.083	2	4.042	0.869	0.436
Explained	117.875	5	23.575	5.067	0.020
Residual	83.750	18	4.653		
Total	201.625	23	8.766		

24 cases were processed.
0 cases (0.0 pct) were missing.

(b) EcStatic

```
        EcStatic - Breakdown  -  10/1/90 10:23 - File: EX1311.ECS
Dependent variable:     MAGNITUD        Magnitude of Response
  broken down by
  Row variable:         STIM            Shock of Buzzer
  Column variable:      EXPOSURE        Number of Reinstatement Exposures
```

Mean of MAGNITUD

	1	2	3	Total
1	11.250	13.250	8.2500	10.917
2	7.7500	9.0000	6.7500	7.8333
Total	9.5000	11.125	7.5000	9.3750

Valid cases: 24   Missing cases: 0

```
Dependent variable:     MAGNITUD        Magnitude of Response
  broken down by
  Row variable:         STIM            Shock of Buzzer
  Column variable:      EXPOSURE        Number of Reinstatement Exposures
```

S.D. of MAGNITUD

	1	2	3	Total
1	2.9861	2.9861	0.9574	3.1176
2	1.7078	2.1602	1.2583	1.8505
Total	2.9277	3.3139	1.3093	2.9608

Valid cases: 24   Missing cases: 0

Dependent variable: MAGNITUD   Magnitude of Response

Source	SS	DF	MS	F	Prob
STIM	57.0417	1	57.0417	12.2597	0.0025
EXPOSURE	52.7500	2	26.3750	5.6687	0.0123
STIM by EXPOSURE					
⇒ 8.0833		2	4.0417	0.8687	0.4364
Residual	83.7500	18	4.6528		
Total	201.6250	23	8.7663		

Valid cases: 24   Missing cases: 0

425

SPSS[X] shows only the summary table for the analysis of variance, although it would be possible to generate cell means and other statistics. One unique feature of SPSS[X] is that it shows the total variation explained by main effects, the total variation explained by interaction effects, and the total explained variation. EcStatic gives means and standard deviations (using a procedure called "breakdown") as well as the standard summary table. Programs such as EcStatic are intended to be *interactive*, meaning that you communicate directly with the computer and order analyses as they seem necessary. They are excellent for generating analyses in a logical progression from simple questions to more complex ones.

From each of these analyses, we see that there is a significant effect of the stimulus used (with the shock producing more reinstatement than the buzzer). Thus, it is not merely that all aversive events are equally effective in reinstating the response. There is also a significant effect due to the number of reinstatement exposures. Contrary to what we might expect, reinstatement does not increase monotonically with exposure. Rather, it increases at first and then decreases. Perhaps those who have received three unpaired exposures are beginning to learn that the aversive stimulus and the tone are not correlated.

KEY TERMS

Factors (introduction)

Two-way factorial design (introduction)

Factorial design (introduction)

Repeated-measures design (introduction)

Interaction (introduction)

2×5 factorial (introduction)

Cell (introduction)

Main effect (13.1)

Simple effect (13.1)

SS_{cells} (13.1)

"Disordinal" interactions (13.3)

Mixed-model designs (13.7)

Sampling fraction (13.7)

Unweighted-means solution (13.9)

Proportional solution (13.9)

Weighted means (13.9)

Unweighted means (13.9)

Corrected totals (13.9)

Adjusted totals (13.9)

First-order interactions (13.10)

Second-order interaction (13.10)

Simple main effects (13.10)

Simple interaction effect (13.10)

EXERCISES

13.1   In a more complete study of restaurant behavior than the one we discussed in Exercise 11.2, we observe restaurant patrons who sit as same-gender couples. We record the price of the entrée ordered by one person in each pair, and categorize subjects on the basis of their gender and whether or not they pay the bill. The data follow:

Host		Guest	
Male	Female	Male	Female
8.00	8.25	9.75	8.75
7.00	8.75	10.25	9.00
8.25	9.75	9.50	9.25
9.00	8.00	9.00	8.50
8.25	9.25	10.50	8.75

(a) Run a two-way analysis of variance on these data.

(b) Write the underlying structural model for the data in this experiment.

13.2   In a study of mother–infant interaction, mothers are rated by trained observers on the quality of their interactions with their infants. Mothers are classified on the basis of whether or not this was their first child (primiparous versus multiparous) and on the basis of whether this was a low-birthweight (LBW) infant or a normal-birthweight (NBW) infant. Mothers of LBW infants were further classified on the basis of whether or not they were under 18 years old. The data represent a score on a 12-point scale; a higher score represents better mother–infant interaction. Run and interpret the appropriate analysis of variance.

Primiparous			Multiparous			Primiparous			Multiparous		
LBW <18	LBW >18	NBW	LBW <18	LBW >18	NBW	LBW <18	LBW >18	NBW	LBW <18	LBW >18	NBW
4	6	8	3	7	9	7	6	2	7	2	10
6	5	7	4	8	8	4	2	5	1	1	9
5	5	7	3	8	9	5	6	8	4	9	8
3	4	6	3	9	9	4	5	7	4	9	7
3	9	7	6	8	3	4	5	7	4	8	10

13.3   In Exercise 13.2 the design may have a major weakness from a practical point of view. Notice the group of multiparous mothers under 18 years of age. Without regard to the data, would you expect this group to lie on the same continuum as the others?

13.4   Refer to Exercise 13.2. It seems obvious that the sample sizes do not reflect the relative frequency of age and parity characteristics in the population. Under what conditions would this be a relevant consideration, and under what conditions would it not be?

13.5   Use simple effects to compare the three groups of multiparous mothers in Exercise 13.2.

13.6   In a study of memory processes, animals were tested in a one-trial avoidance-learning task. The animals were presented with a fear-producing stimulus on the *learning* trial as soon as they stepped across a line in the test chamber. The dependent variable was the time it took them to step across the line on the *test* trial. Three groups of animals differed in terms of the area in which they had electrodes implanted in their cortex (neutral site, area A, or area B). Each group was further divided and given electrical stimulation either 50, 100, or 150 milliseconds after crossing the line and being presented with the fear-inducing stimulus. If the brain area that was stimulated is involved in memory, stimulation would be expected to interfere with memory consolidation and retard learning of the avoidance response, and the animal should not show any hesitancy in recrossing the line. The data on latency to recross the line are as follows:

Stimulation Area								
Neutral Site			Area A			Area B		
50	100	150	50	100	150	50	100	150
25	30	28	11	31	23	23	18	28
30	25	31	18	20	28	30	24	21
28	27	26	26	22	35	18	9	30
40	35	20	15	23	27	28	16	30
20	23	35	14	19	21	23	13	23

Run the analysis of variance.

13.7 Plot the cell means in Exercise 13.6.

13.8 For the study in Exercise 13.6, to what would α_1 refer (if A were used to represent Area)?

13.9 Use simple effects to clarify the results for the Area factor in Exercise 13.6. Show that these simple effects sum to the correct figure.

13.10 Use Fisher's LSD (protected t) test to compare the neutral site to each of the other areas in Exercise 13.6, ignoring length of stimulation. (*Hint*: Follow the procedures outlined in Chapters 11 and 12, but be sure that you take n as the number of scores on which the mean is based.)

13.11 Use simple effects to examine the effect of delay of stimulation in area A for the data in Exercise 13.6.

13.12 Refer to Exercise 11.3b. You will see that it forms a 2×2 factorial. Run the factorial analysis and interpret the results.

13.13 In Exercise 11.3 you ran a test between groups 1 and 3 combined versus groups 2 and 4 combined. How does that compare to testing the main effect of Location in Exercise 13.12? Is there any difference?

13.14 Make up a set of data for a 2×2 design that has two main effects but no interaction.

13.15 Make up a set of data for a 2×2 design that has no main effects but does have an interaction.

13.16 Describe a reasonable experiment for which the primary interest would be in the interaction effect.

13.17 Assume that in Exercise 13.2 the last three subjects in cell$_{12}$ (Primiparous, LBW > 18) and the last two subjects in cell$_{23}$ (Multiparous, NBW) refused to give consent for their data to be used. Rerun the analysis.

13.18 An experimenter was interested in hospital patients' responses to two different forms of physical therapy. For her own reasons, she thought that it was important to have greater precision in estimates of means for treatment B (we need not be concerned with why), and therefore she allocated two-thirds of the subjects to treatment B and one-third to treatment A. She ran the study at two different hospitals, one of which had more patients available. The data are given in terms of ratings of recovery of function:

	Treatment	
	A	B
Hospital 1	5	10
	8	12
	6	14
		12
		10
		8
Hospital 2	10	15
	12	28
		32
		34

Run the analysis for proportional data.

13.19 Run the unweighted-means analysis on the data in Exercise 13.18. Compare your results with those you obtained previously.

13.20 Calculate η^2 and $\hat{\omega}^2$ for Exercise 13.1.

13.21 Calculate η^2 and $\hat{\omega}^2$ for Exercise 13.2.

13.22 To study the effects of early experience on conditioning, an experimenter raised four groups of rats in the presence of (1) no special stimuli, (2) a tone stimulus, (3) a vibratory stimulus, and (4) both a tone and a vibratory stimulus. The rats were later classically conditioned using either a tone or a vibratory stimulus as the conditioned stimulus and one of three levels of foot shock as the unconditioned stimulus. This is a $4 \times 2 \times 3$ factorial design. The cell totals, rather than the raw data, follow. The $SS_{total} = 1646.00$ and $n_{ijk} = 5$. The dependent variable was the number of trials to a predetermined criterion.

	Conditioned Stimulus					
	Tone			Vibration		
	High	Med	Low	High	Med	Low
Control	11	16	21	19	24	29
Tone	25	28	34	21	26	31
Vibration	6	13	20	40	41	52
Tone and Vibration	22	30	30	35	38	48

Analyze the data and interpret the results.

13.23 The computer printout in Exhibit 13.2 is the summary table from an SPSS[X] analysis of the data in Exercise 13.18, using SPSS[X] Option 9.

  (a) Compare the values in the printout with the answers that you obtained in Exercises 13.18 and 13.19.

  (b) How would you interpret the sums of squares labeled "Main effects" and "Explained"?

EXHIBIT 13.2

Source of Variation	Sum of Squares	df	Mean Square	F	Signif of F
Main effects	750.012	2	375.006	16.673	0.000
Hospital	350.006	1	350.006	15.561	0.002
Treatment	350.006	1	350.006	15.561	0.002
2-way Interactions	107.339	1	107.339	4.772	0.051
HXT	107.339	1	107.339	4.772	0.051
Explained	948.183	3	316.061	14.052	0.000
Residual	247.417	11	22.492		
Total	1195.600	14	85.400		

COMPUTER EXERCISES

13.24 Create a data file and use any statistical package to run the analysis of variance in Exercise 13.18. (If you use SPSS^X, choose Option 9. If you use SAS, pay attention to the Type III sums of squares.) How do your results agree with those you obtained in Exercises 13.18 and 3.19?

13.25 Use any statistical package to run the two-way analysis of variance on Interval and Dosage for the data in Epineq.dat. Compare the results you obtain here with the results you obtained in Chapter 11, Exercises 11.28–11.31.

13.26 In Exercise 11.31 you calculated the average of the nine cell variances. How does that answer compare to the MS_{error} from Exercise 13.25?

13.27 Obtain the Newman–Keuls tests for Dosage from the analysis of variance in Exercise 13.25. Interpret these results.

13.28 The data for the three-way analysis of variance given in Table 13.12 are found on the instructor's disk. They are named Driving.dat. The first three entries in each record represent the coding for A (Experience), B (Road), and C (Conditions). The fourth entry is the dependent variable. Use any analysis of variance package to reproduce the summary table found in Table 13.12c.

13.29 Using the data from Exercise 13.28, reproduce the simple effects shown in Table 13.13.

CHAPTER FOURTEEN

REPEATED-MEASURES DESIGNS

OBJECTIVES *To discuss the analysis of variance by considering experimental designs in which the same subject is measured under all levels of one or more independent variables.*

CONTENTS

I n our discussion of the analysis of variance, we have concerned ourselves with experimental designs that have different subjects in the different cells. More precisely, we have been concerned with designs in which the cells are independent, or uncorrelated. (Under the assumptions of the analysis of variance, *independent* and *uncorrelated* are synonymous in this context.) Thus, if you think of a typical one-way analysis of variance with different subjects serving under the different treatments, you would probably be willing to concede that the correlations between treatments 1 and 2, 1 and 3, and 2 and 3 have an expectancy of zero:

Treatment 1	Treatment 2	Treatment 3
X_{11}	X_{21}	X_{31}
X_{12}	X_{22}	X_{32}
X_{13}	X_{23}	X_{33}
...	...	...
X_{1n}	X_{2n}	X_{3n}

However, suppose that in the design diagrammed here the same subjects were used in all three treatments. Thus, instead of $3n$ subjects measured once, we have n subjects measured three times. In this case, we would be hard put to believe that the intercorrelations of the three treatments would have expectancies of zero. On the contrary, the better subjects under treatment 1 would probably also perform well under treatments 2 and 3, and the poorer subjects under treatment 1 would probably perform poorly under the other conditions, leading to significant correlations among treatments.

Partition

Partialling out
Repeated-measures
designs

This lack of independence among the treatments would cause a serious problem if it were not for the fact that we can separate out, or **partition**, and remove the dependence imposed by repeated measurements on the same subjects. (To use a term that will become much more familiar in Chapter 15, we can say that we are **partialling out** effects that cause the dependence.) In fact, one of the main advantages of **repeated-measures designs** is that they allow us to reduce overall variability by using a common subject pool for all treatments, and at the same time allow us to remove subject differences from our error term, leaving the error components independent from treatment to treatment or cell to cell.

As an illustration, consider the highly exaggerated set of data on four subjects over three treatments that is presented in Table 14.1. Here the dependent variable is the number of trials to criterion on some task. If you look first at the treatment totals, you will see some slight differences, but nothing to get too excited about. There is so much variability within each treatment that it would at first appear that the totals differ only by chance. But look at the subject totals. It is apparent that subject 1 learns quickly under all conditions, and that subjects 3 and 4 learn remarkably slowly. These differences among the subjects are producing most of the differences *within* treatments, and yet they have nothing to do with the treatment effect. If we could remove these subject differences we would have a better (and smaller) estimate of error. At the same time, it is the subject differences that are creating the high positive intercorrelations among the treatments, and these too we will partial out by forming a separate term for subjects.

TABLE 14.1
Hypothetical data for simple repeated-measures designs

Subject	Treatment 1	Treatment 2	Treatment 3	Total
1	2	4	7	13
2	10	12	13	35
3	23	29	30	82
4	30	31	34	95
Total	65	76	84	225

One laborious way to do this would be to put all the subjects' contributions on a common footing by equating subject means without altering the relationships among the scores obtained by that particular subject. Thus, we could set $X'_{ij} = X_{ij} - \overline{X}_i$, where $\overline{X}_i$ is the mean of the ith subject. Now subjects would all have the same means

SS_{between subj} (SS_S)

SS_{within subj}

$(\overline{X}_i' = 0)$, and any remaining differences among the scores could be attributable only to error or to treatments. Although this approach is correct, it is not practical. An alternative, and easier, approach is to calculate a sum of squares between subjects (denoted as either **SS_{between subj}** or **SS_S**) and remove this from SS_{total} before we begin. This can be shown to be algebraically equivalent to the first procedure and is essentially the approach we will adopt.

The problem is represented diagrammatically in Figure 14.1. Here we partition the overall variation into variation between subjects and variation within subjects. Some of the variation within a subject is attributable to the fact that his scores come from different treatments, and some is attributable to error; this further partitioning of variation is shown in the third line of the figure. We will always think of a repeated-measures analysis as *first* partitioning the SS_{total} into $SS_{between subj}$ and **SS_{within subj}**. Depending on the complexity of the design, one or both of these partitions may then be further partitioned.

Partition of Sums of Squares

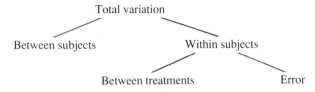

Partition of Degrees of Freedom

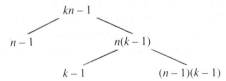

FIGURE 14.1
Partition of sums of squares

The following discussion of repeated-measures designs can only begin to explore the area. For historical reasons, the statistical literature has underemphasized the importance of these designs. As a result, they have been developed mostly by social scientists. By far the most complete coverage of these designs is found in Winer (1971). His treatment of repeated-measures designs is excellent and extensive, and much of this chapter reflects the influence of his work.

14.1   THE STRUCTURAL MODEL

Two structural models could underlie the analysis of data like those shown in Table 14.1. The simplest model is

$$X_{ij} = \mu + \pi_i + \tau_j + e_{ij}$$

where

μ = the grand mean

π_i = a constant associated with the ith person or subject

τ_j = a constant associated with the jth treatment

e_{ij} = the experimental error associated with the ith subject under the jth treatment

The variables π_i and e_{ij} are assumed to be independently and normally distributed around zero within each treatment. In addition, σ_π^2 and σ_e^2 are assumed to be homogeneous across treatments. With these assumptions it is possible to derive the expected mean squares shown in Model I of Table 14.2.

TABLE 14.2
Expected mean squares for simple repeated measures designs

Model I
$X_{ij} = \mu + \pi_i + \tau_j + e_{ij}$

Source	E(MS)
Subjects	$\sigma_e^2 + k\sigma_\pi^2$
Treatments	$\sigma_e^2 + n\sigma_\tau^2$
Error	σ_e^2

Model II
$X_{ij} = \mu + \pi_i + \tau_j + \pi\tau_{ij} + e_{ij}$

Source	E(MS)
Subjects	$\sigma_e^2 + k\sigma_\pi^2$
Treatments	$\sigma_e^2 + \sigma_{\pi\tau}^2 + n\sigma_\tau^2$
Error	$\sigma_e^2 + \sigma_{\pi\tau}^2$

An alternative and probably more realistic model is given by

$$X_{ij} = \mu + \pi_i + \tau_j + \pi\tau_{ij} + e_{ij}$$

Here we have added a Subject × Treatment interaction term to the model. The assumptions of the first model will continue to hold, and we will also assume the $\pi\tau_{ij}$ to be distributed around zero independently of the other elements of the model. This second model gives rise to the expected mean squares shown in Model II of Table 14.2.

14.2   *F* RATIOS

The expected mean squares in Table 14.2 indicate that the model we adopt influences the *F* ratios we employ. If we are willing to assume that there is no Subject × Treatment interaction, we can form the following ratios:

$$\frac{E(MS_{\text{between subj}})}{E(MS_{\text{error}})} = \frac{\sigma_e^2 + k\sigma_\pi^2}{\sigma_e^2}$$

and

$$\frac{E(MS_{\text{treat}})}{E(MS_{\text{error}})} = \frac{\sigma_e^2 + n\sigma_\tau^2}{\sigma_e^2}$$

Given an additional assumption that we will discuss, both of these lead to respectable *F* ratios that can be used to test the relevant null hypothesis.

Usually we are cautious about assuming that there is no Subject × Treatment interaction. As a result we usually prefer to work with the more complete model. [Tukey (1949) developed a test for additivity of effects that is useful in choosing between the two models. This test is discussed in Kirk (1968) and Winer (1962, 1971).]

The full model (which includes the interaction term) leads to the following ratios:

$$\frac{E(\text{MS}_{\text{between subj}})}{E(\text{MS}_{\text{error}})} = \frac{\sigma_e^2 + k\sigma_\pi^2}{\sigma_e^2 + \sigma_{\pi\tau}^2}$$

and

$$\frac{E(\text{MS}_{\text{treat}})}{E(\text{MS}_{\text{error}})} = \frac{\sigma_e^2 + \sigma_{\pi\tau}^2 + n\sigma_\tau^2}{\sigma_e^2 + \sigma_{\pi\tau}^2}$$

Although the resulting F for treatments is appropriate, the F for subjects is biased. If we did form this latter ratio and obtained a significant F, we would be fairly confident that subject differences really did exist. However, if the F were not significant, the interpretation would be ambiguous. A nonsignificant F would mean either that $k\sigma_\pi^2 = 0$ or that $k\sigma_\pi^2 > 0$ but $\leq \sigma_{\pi\tau}^2$. For this reason, we seldom test the effect due to Subjects. This represents no great loss, however, since we have little to gain by testing the Subject effect. The main reason for obtaining $\text{SS}_{\text{between subj}}$ in the first place is to absorb the correlations between treatments and thereby remove subject differences from the error term. A test on the Subject effect, if it were significant, would merely indicate that people are different—hardly a momentous finding.

14.3   THE COVARIANCE MATRIX

One of the assumptions required for any F ratio to be distributed as the central (tabled) F is that of compound symmetry of the covariance matrix.[†] To understand what this means, consider a matrix ($\hat{\Sigma}$) representing the covariances among the three treatments for the data given in Table 14.1.

$$\hat{\Sigma} = \begin{array}{c} \\ A_1 \\ A_2 \\ A_3 \end{array} \begin{array}{ccc} A_1 & A_2 & A_3 \\ \left[\begin{array}{ccc} 158.92 & 163.33 & 163.00 \\ 163.33 & 172.67 & 170.67 \\ 163.00 & 170.67 & 170.00 \end{array}\right] \end{array}$$

Main diagonal

Off-diagonal elements

On the **main diagonal** of this matrix are the variances within each treatment ($\hat{\sigma}_{A_j}^2$). Notice that they are all more or less equal, indicating that we have met the assumption of homogeneity of variance. The **off-diagonal elements** represent the covariances among the treatments (cov_{12}, cov_{13}, and cov_{23}). Notice that these are also more or less equal. The fact that they are also of the same magnitude as the variances is

[†] This assumption is overly stringent and will shortly be relaxed somewhat. It is nonetheless a sufficient assumption, and it is made often.

**Compound
symmetry**

**Covariance matrix
(Σ)**

Sphericity

irrelevant, reflecting merely the very high intercorrelations among treatments. A pattern of constant variances on the diagonal and constant covariances off the diagonal is referred to as **compound symmetry**. (Again, the relationship between the variances and covariances is irrelevant.) The assumption of compound symmetry of the (*population*) **covariance matrix (Σ)**, of which $\hat{\Sigma}$ is an estimate, represents a sufficient condition underlying the analysis of variance. The more general condition is known as **sphericity**, and you will often see references to that broader assumption. If we have compound symmetry we will meet the sphericity assumption, but it is possible to have sphericity without compound symmetry. Without this sphericity assumption, the F ratios may not have a distribution given by the distribution of F in the tables. Although this assumption applies to any analysis-of-variance design, when the cells are independent the covariances are always zero, and there is no problem—we merely need to assume homogeneity of variance. With repeated-measures designs, however, the covariances will not be zero and we need to assume that they are all equal. This has led some people (e.g., Hays, 1981) to omit serious consideration of repeated-measures designs. However, when we do have compound symmetry, the Fs are valid, and when we do not we can use either very good approximation procedures (to be discussed later in this chapter) or alternative methods that do not depend on assumptions about Σ. One alternative procedure that does not require any assumptions about the covariance matrix is **multivariate analysis of variance (MANOVA)**. This is a **multivariate procedure**, which essentially is one that deals with multiple dependent variables simultaneously. A brief introduction to multivariate analysis of variance for repeated-measures designs can be found in Section 14.12.

**Multivariate
analysis of variance
(MANOVA),**

**Multivariate
procedure**

14.4 ANALYSIS OF VARIANCE APPLIED TO RELAXATION THERAPY

As an example of a simple repeated-measures design, we will consider a study of the effectiveness of relaxation techniques in controlling migraine headaches. The data described here are fictitious, but they are in general agreement with data collected by Blanchard, Theobald, Williamson, Silver, and Brown (1978), who ran a similar, although more complex, study.

In this experiment we have recruited nine migraine sufferers and have asked them to record the frequency and duration of their migraine headaches. After 4 weeks of baseline recording during which no training was given, we had a 6-week period of relaxation training. (Each experimental subject participated in the program at a different time, so such things as changes in climate and holiday events, such as Christmas, should not systematically influence the data.) For our example we will analyze the data for the last 2 weeks of baseline and the last 3 weeks of training. The dependent variable is the duration (hours/week) of headaches in each of those 5 weeks. The data and the calculations are shown in Table 14.3.

TABLE 14.3
Analysis of data on
migraine headaches

(a) Data

Subject	Baseline		Training			Subject Totals
	Week 1	Week 2	Week 3	Week 4	Week 5	
1	21	22	8	6	6	63
2	20	19	10	4	4	57
3	17	15	5	4	5	46
4	25	30	13	12	17	97
5	30	27	13	8	6	84
6	19	27	8	7	4	65
7	26	16	5	2	5	54
8	17	18	8	1	5	49
9	26	24	14	8	9	81
Week totals:	201	198	84	52	61	596
Week means:	22.33	22.00	9.33	5.78	6.78	13.24

(b) Calculations

$$SS_{total} = \sum X^2 - \frac{(\sum X)^2}{N} = 21^2 + 20^2 + \cdots + 9^2 - \frac{596^2}{45}$$

$$= 11,060 - 7893.69 = 3166.31$$

$$SS_{subjects} = \frac{\sum T_S^2}{w} - \frac{(\sum X)^2}{N} = \frac{63^2 + \cdots + 81^2}{5} - \frac{596^2}{45}$$

$$= 8380.40 - 7893.69 = 486.71$$

$$SS_{weeks} = \frac{\sum T_W^2}{n} - \frac{(\sum X)^2}{N} = \frac{201^2 + \cdots + 61^2}{9} - \frac{596^2}{45}$$

$$= 10,342.89 - 7893.69 = 2449.20$$

$$SS_{error} = SS_{total} - SS_{subjects} - SS_{weeks}$$

$$= 3166.31 - 486.71 - 2449.20 = 230.4$$

(c) Summary Table

Source	df	SS	MS	F
Between subjects	8	486.71		
Weeks	4	2449.20	612.30	85.04*
Error	32	230.40	7.20	
Total	44	3166.31		

*$p < .05$

Look first at the data in Table 14.3a. Notice that there is a great deal of variability, but much of that variability comes from the fact that some people have more and/or longer-duration headaches than do others, which really has very little to do with the intervention program. As I have said, what we are able to do with a repeated-measures design but were not able to do with between-subjects designs is to remove this variability from SS_{total}, producing a smaller MS_{error} than we would otherwise have.

From Table 14.3 you can see that SS_{total} is calculated in the usual manner. Similarly, $SS_{subjects}$ and SS_{weeks} are calculated just as main effects always are [square the relevant totals, divide by the number of observations per total, and subtract $(\Sigma X)^2/N$]. Finally, the error term is obtained by subtracting $SS_{subjects}$ and SS_{weeks} from SS_{total}.

The summary table is shown in Table 14.3c. Notice that I have computed an F for weeks but not for subjects, for the reasons given earlier. The F value for weeks is based on 4 and 32 degrees of freedom, and $F_{.05}(4, 32) = 2.68$. We can therefore reject $H_0: \mu_1 = \mu_2 = \cdots = \mu_5$ and conclude that the relaxation program led to a reduction in the duration per week of headaches reported by subjects. Examination of the means in Table 14.3 reveals that during the last three weeks of training, the amount of time per week involving headaches was about one-third of what it was during baseline.

You may have noticed that no Subject × Weeks interaction is shown in the summary table. With only one score per cell, the interaction term *is* the error term, and in fact some people prefer to label it $S \times W$ instead of error. To put this differently, in the design discussed here it is impossible to separate error from any possible Subject × Weeks interaction, since they are completely confounded. As we saw in the discussion of structural models, both of these effects, if present, are combined in the expected mean square for error.

I spoke earlier of the assumption of compound symmetry. For the data in the example, the variance–covariance matrix follows, represented by the notation $\hat{\Sigma}$, where the ˆ is used to indicate that this is an estimate of the population variance–covariance matrix Σ.

$$\hat{\Sigma} = \begin{matrix} 21.000 & 11.750 & 9.250 & 7.833 & 7.333 \\ 11.750 & 28.500 & 13.750 & 16.375 & 13.375 \\ 9.250 & 13.750 & 11.500 & 8.583 & 8.208 \\ 7.833 & 16.375 & 8.583 & 11.694 & 10.819 \\ 7.333 & 13.375 & 8.208 & 10.819 & 16.945 \end{matrix}$$

Visual inspection of this matrix suggests that the assumption of compound symmetry is reasonable. The variances on the diagonal range from 11.5 to 28.5, whereas the covariances off the diagonal range from 7.333 to 16.375. Considering that we have only nine subjects, these values represent an acceptable level of constancy. (Keep in mind that the variances do not need to be equal to the covariances; in fact, they seldom are.) A statistical test of this assumption of compound symmetry is given in Winer (1971, p. 596) and would in fact show that we have no basis for rejecting the symmetry hypothesis. Box (1954b), however, showed that regardless of the form of Σ, a conservative test on null hypotheses in the repeated-measures analysis of variance is given by comparing F_{obt} against $F_{.05}(1, n - 1)$—that is, by acting as though we had only two treatment levels. This test is exceedingly conservative, however, and for most situations you will be better advised to evaluate F in the usual way. We will return to this problem later when we consider Greenhouse and Geisser's (1959) extension of Box's work.

As already mentioned, one of the major advantages or the repeated-measures design is that it allows us to reduce the error term by using the same subject for all treatments. Suppose for a moment that the data illustrated in Table 14.3 had actually been produced by three independent groups of subjects. In this case, we would not be able to pull out a subject term because $SS_{between\ subj}$ would be synonymous with SS_{total}. As a result, differences among subjects would be inseparable from error, and in fact SS_{error} would be the sum of what, for the repeated-measures design, are SS_{error} and $SS_{between\ subj}$ ($= 230.4 + 486.71 = 717.11$ on $32 + 8 = 40\ df$). This would lead to

$$F = \frac{MS_{weeks}}{MS_{error}} = \frac{612.30}{17.93} = 34.15$$

which, although still significant, is about one-half of what it was in Table 14.3.

To put it succinctly, subjects differ. When subjects are observed only once, these subject differences contribute to the error term. When subjects are observed repeatedly, we can obtain an estimate of the degree of subject differences and partial these differences out of the error term. In general, the greater the differences among subjects, the higher the correlations between pairs of treatments. The higher the correlations among treatments, the greater the relative power of repeated-measures designs.

We have been speaking of the simple case in which we have one independent variable (other than subjects) and test each subject on every level of that variable. In actual practice, there are many different ways in which we could design a study using repeated measures. For example, we could set up an experiment using two independent variables and test each subject under all combinations of both variables. Alternatively, each subject might serve under only one level of one of the variables, but under all levels of the other. If we had three variables, the possibilities are even greater. In this chapter we will discuss only a few of the possible designs. If you understand the designs discussed here, you should have no difficulty generalizing to even the most complex problems.

14.5   ONE BETWEEN-SUBJECTS VARIABLE   — Mixed design
AND ONE WITHIN-SUBJECTS VARIABLE

Consider the data presented in Table 14.4. These are the actual data from a study by King (1986). This study in some ways resembles the one on morphine tolerance by Siegel (1975) that we examined in Chapter 12. King investigated motor activity in rats following injection of the drug midazolam. The first time that this drug is injected, it typically leads to a distinct decrease in motor activity. Like morphine, however, a tolerance for midazolam develops rapidly. King wished to know whether that acquired tolerance could be explained on the basis of a conditioned tolerance, as in Siegel's work. He used three groups, collecting the crucial data (presented in Table 14.4) on only the last day, which was the test day. During pretesting, two groups of animals were repeatedly injected with midazolam over several days, whereas the Control group was injected with physiological saline. On the test day, one group—the

"Same" group—was injected with midazolam in the *same* environment in which it had earlier been injected. The "Different" group was also injected with midazolam, but in a *different* environment. Finally, the Control group was injected with midazolam for the first time. This Control group should thus show the typical initial response to the drug (decreased ambulatory behavior), whereas the Same group should show the normal tolerance effect—that is, they should decrease their activity little or not at all in response to the drug. If King is correct, however, the Different group should respond similarly to the Control group, because although they have had several exposures to the drug, they are receiving it in a novel environment and any conditioned tolerance will not have the necessary cues required for its elicitation. The dependent variable in Table 14.4 is a measure of ambulatory behavior, in arbitrary units, in each 5-minute interval of time.

TABLE 14.4
Ambulatory behavior by group and trials

(a) Data

		Intervals						Subject Total
		1	2	3	4	5	6	
Control		150	44	71	59	132	74	530
		335	270	156	160	118	230	1269
		149	52	91	115	43	154	604
		159	31	127	212	71	224	824
		159	0	35	75	71	34	374
		292	125	184	246	225	170	1242
		297	187	66	96	209	74	929
		170	37	42	66	114	81	510
	Total	1711	746	772	1029	983	1041	6282
Same		346	175	177	192	239	140	1269
		426	329	236	76	102	232	1401
		359	238	183	123	183	30	1116
		272	60	82	85	101	98	698
		200	271	263	216	241	227	1418
		366	291	263	144	220	180	1464
		371	364	270	308	219	267	1799
		497	402	294	216	284	255	1948
	Total	2837	2130	1768	1360	1589	1429	11,113
Different		282	186	225	134	189	169	1185
		317	31	85	120	131	205	889
		362	104	144	114	115	127	966
		338	132	91	77	108	169	915
		263	94	141	142	120	195	955
		138	38	16	95	39	55	381
		329	62	62	6	93	67	619
		292	139	104	184	193	122	1034
	Total	2321	786	868	872	988	1109	6944
	Interval Totals	6869	3662	3408	3261	3560	3579	24,339

TABLE 14.4 (Cont.)   **(b) Calculations**

$$SS_{total} = \sum X^2 - \frac{(\sum X)^2}{N} = 150^2 + 335^2 + \cdots + 122^2 - \frac{24,339^2}{144}$$

$$= 5,546,091 - 4,113,798.1 = 1,432,292.9$$

$$SS_{subj} = \frac{\sum T_S^2}{i} - \frac{(\sum X)^2}{N} = \frac{530^2 + 1269^2 + \cdots + 1034^2}{6} - \frac{24,339^2}{144}$$

$$= 4,784,335.2 - 4,113,798.1 = 670,537.1$$

$$SS_{groups} = \frac{\sum T_G^2}{ni} - \frac{(\sum X)^2}{N} = \frac{628^2 + 11,113^2 + 6944^2}{48} - \frac{24,339^2}{144}$$

$$= 4,399,613.1 - 4,113,798.1 = 285,815.0$$

$$SS_{intervals} = \frac{\sum T_I^2}{ng} - \frac{(\sum X)^2}{N} = \frac{6869^2 + 3662^2 + \cdots + 3579^2}{24} - \frac{24,339^2}{144}$$

$$= 4,513,534.6 - 4,113,798.1 = 399,736.5$$

$$SS_{cells} = \frac{\sum T_{ij}^2}{n} - \frac{(\sum X)^2}{N} = \frac{1711^2 + 746^2 + \cdots + 1109^2}{8} - \frac{24,339^2}{144}$$

$$= 4,880,169.6 - 4,113,798.1 = 766,371.5$$

$$SS_{I \times G} = SS_{cells} - SS_{groups} - SS_{intervals}$$

$$= 766,371.5 - 285,815.0 - 399,736.5 = 80,820.0$$

(c) Summary Table

Source	df	SS	MS	F
Between subjects	23	670,537.1		
Groups	2	285,815.0	142,907.5	7.80*
Ss w/in groups**	21	384,722.0	18,320.1	
Within subjects**	120	761,755.8		
Intervals	5	399,736.5	79,947.3	29.85*
I × G	10	80,820.0	8,082.0	3.02*
I × Ss w/in groups**	105	281,199.3	2,678.1	
Total	143	1,432,292.9		

* $p < .05$
** Term obtained by subtraction

Because the drug is known to be metabolized over a period of approximately 1 hour, King recorded his data in 5-minute blocks, or Intervals. We would expect to see the effect of the drug increase for the first few intervals and then slowly taper off. Our analysis uses the first six blocks of data. The design of this study can be represented diagrammatically as

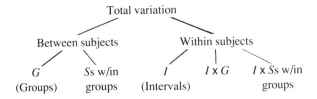

Here we have distinguished those effects that represent differences between subjects from those that represent differences within subjects. When we consider the between-subjects term, we can partition it into differences between groups of subjects (G) and differences between subjects in the same group (Ss w/in groups). The within-subject term can similarly be subdivided into three components—the main effect of Intervals (the repeated measure) and its interactions with the two partitions of the between-subject variation. You will see this partitioning represented in the summary table when we come to it.

PARTITIONING THE BETWEEN-SUBJECTS EFFECTS

Let us first consider the partition of the between-subjects term in more detail. From the design of the experiment, we know that this term can be partitioned into two parts. One of these parts is the main effect of Groups (G), since the treatments (Control, Same, and Different) involve different groups of subjects. This is not the only source of differences among subjects, however. We have eight different subjects within the control group, and differences among them are certainly between-subjects differences. The same holds for the subjects within the other groups. Here we are speaking of differences among subjects in the same group—that is, Ss within groups.

If we ignore intervals entirely (e.g., we simply collect our data over the entire session rather than breaking it down into 5-minute intervals), we can think of the study as producing the following data:

Control	Same	Different
530	1269	1185
1269	1401	889
604	1116	966
824	698	915
374	1418	955
1242	1464	381
929	1799	619
510	1948	1034
6282	11,113	6944

where the raw scores are the subject totals from Table 14.4. A one-way analysis of variance on the data in this form is directly analogous to the analysis that we will in fact apply to the between-subjects components of variance. Indeed, except for a constant representing the number of scores per subject (which cancels out in the end), the sums of squares for the simple one-way on these data would be the same as those in the actual analysis. The F that tests the main effect of Groups for these data would be equal to the one that we will obtain from the full analysis. Thus, the between-subjects partition of the total variation can be seen as essentially a separate analysis of variance, with its own error term (sometimes referred to as **error_{between}**) independent of the within-subject effects.

Error_{between}

PARTITIONING THE WITHIN-SUBJECTS EFFECTS

Next consider the within-subjects partition of SS_{total}. As we have already seen, this is itself partitioned into three terms. A comparison of the six intervals involves comparisons of scores from the same subject, and thus Intervals is a within-subjects term—it depends on differences within each subject. Since Intervals is a within-subjects term, the interaction of Intervals with Groups is also a within-subjects effect. The third term (Intervals $\times$ Ss within groups) is sometimes referred to as **error_{within}**, since it is the error term for the within-subjects effects. The $SS_{Intervals \times Ss\ w/in\ groups}$ term is actually the sum of the sums of squares for the $I \times S$ interactions calculated separately for each group. Thus, it can be seen as logically equivalent to the error term used in the previous design.

Error_{within}

THE ANALYSIS

Before considering the analysis in detail, it is instructive to look at the general pattern of results. Although there are not enough observations in each cell to examine the distributions in any serious way, it is apparent that on any given interval there is substantial variability within groups. For example, for the second interval in the control group, scores range from 0 to 270. There do not appear to be any extreme outliers, however, as often happens in this kind of research, and the variances within cells, although large, are approximately equal. You can also see that there are large individual differences, with some of the animals consistently showing relatively little ambulatory behavior and some showing a great deal. These are the kinds of differences that will be partialled out by our analysis. Looking at the Interval totals, you will see that, as expected, behavior decreased substantially after the first 5-minute interval and then increased slightly during the rest of the session. Finally, looking at the difference between the totals for the Control and Same group, you will see the anticipated tolerance effect, and looking at the different group you see that it is much more like the Control group than it is like the Same group. This is the result that King predicted.

Very little needs to be said about the actual calculations in Table 14.4b, since they are really no different from the usual calculations of main and interaction effects. Whether a factor is a between-subjects or within-subjects factor has no bearing on the calculation of its sum of squares, although it does affect its placement in the summary table and the ultimate calculation of the corresponding F.

In the summary table in Table 14.4c, the source column reflects the design of the experiment, with SS_{total} first partitioned into $SS_{between\ subj}$ and $SS_{w/in\ subj}$. Each of these sums of squares is further subdivided. You can also see from the ** next to some of the terms that we calculate three terms by subtraction ($SS_{w/in\,subj}$, $SS_{Ss\,w/in\,groups}$, and $SS_{I \times Ss\,w/in\,groups}$), based on the fact that sums of squares are additive and the whole must be equal to the sum of its parts. This simplifies our work considerably. Thus

$$SS_{w/in\,subj} = SS_{total} - SS_{between\,subj}$$

$$SS_{Ss\,w/in\,groups} = SS_{between\,subj} - SS_{groups}$$

$$SS_{I \times Ss\,w/in\,groups} = SS_{w/in\,subj} - SS_{intervals} - SS_{IG}$$

These last two terms will become error terms for the analysis.

The degrees of freedom are obtained in a relatively straightforward manner. For each of the main effects, the degrees of freedom are equal to the number of levels of the variable minus 1. Thus, for Subjects there are $24 - 1 = 23$ df, for Groups there are $3 - 1 = 2$ df, and for Intervals there are $6 - 1 = 5$ df. As for all interactions, the df for $I \times G$ are equal to the product of the df for the component terms. Thus, $df_{IG} = (6 - 1)(3 - 1) = 10$. The easiest way to obtain the remaining degrees of freedom is by subtraction:

$$df_{w/in\,subj} = df_{total} - df_{between\,subj}$$

$$df_{Ss\,w/in\,groups} = df_{between\,subj} - df_{groups}$$

$$df_{I \times Ss\,w/in\,groups} = df_{w/in\,subj} - df_{intervals} - df_{IG}$$

These df can also be obtained directly by considering what these terms represent. Within each subject, we have $6 - 1 = 5$ df. With 24 subjects, this amounts to $(5)(24) = 120$ $df_{w/in\,subj}$. Within each level of the Groups factor, we have $8 - 1 = 7$ df between subjects, and with three Groups we have $(7)(3) = 21$ $df_{Ss\,w/in\,groups}$. $I \times Ss$ w/in groups is really an interaction term, and as such its df are simply the product of df_I and $df_{Ss\,w/in\,groups} = (5)(21) = 105$.

Skipping over the mean squares, which are merely the sums of squares divided by their degrees of freedom, we come to F. From the column of F it is apparent that, as we anticipated, Groups and Intervals are significant. The interaction is also significant, reflecting the fact that the different group was at first intermediate between the Same and the Control group, but that by the second 5-minute interval it had come down to be equal to the Control group. This finding can be explained by a theory of conditioned tolerance. The really interesting finding is that, at least for the later intervals, simply injecting an animal in an environment different from the one in which it had been receiving the drug was sufficient to overcome the tolerance that had developed. These animals respond almost exactly as do animals who had never experienced midazolam. We will return to the comparison of Groups at individual Intervals later.

ASSUMPTIONS

For the F ratios actually to follow the F distribution we must invoke the usual assumptions of normality, homogeneity of variance, and compound symmetry of Σ, although the latter is again more stringent than necessary. For the *between-subjects* term(s), this means that we must assume that the variance of subject totals within any one level of A is the same as the variance of subject totals within every other level of A. If necessary, this assumption can be tested by calculating each of the variances and testing using either F_{max} on $(g, n - 1)$ df or, preferably, the test proposed by O'Brien (1981), which was referred to in Chapter 7. In practice, however, the analysis of variance is relatively robust against reasonable violations of this assumption (see Collier, Baker, & Mandeville, 1967; and Collier, Baker, Mandeville, and Hayes, 1967). Since the groups are independent, compound symmetry of the covariance matrix is assured if we have homogeneity of variance, since all off-diagonal entries will be zero.

For the *within-subjects* terms we must also consider the usual assumptions of homogeneity of variance and normality. The homogeneity of variance assumption in this case is that the $I \times S$ interactions are constant across the Groups, and here again this can be tested using F_{max} on g and $(n - 1)(i - 1)$ df. For the within-subjects effects, we must also make assumptions concerning the covariance matrix.

There are two assumptions on the covariance matrix (or matrices). Again, we will let $\hat{\Sigma}$ represent the matrix of variances and covariances among the levels of I (Intervals). Thus with six intervals,

$$\hat{\Sigma} = \begin{array}{cccccc} I_1 & I_2 & I_3 & I_4 & I_5 & I_6 \\ \hat{\sigma}_{11} & \hat{\sigma}_{12} & \hat{\sigma}_{13} & \hat{\sigma}_{14} & \hat{\sigma}_{15} & \hat{\sigma}_{16} \\ \hat{\sigma}_{21} & \hat{\sigma}_{22} & \hat{\sigma}_{23} & \hat{\sigma}_{24} & \hat{\sigma}_{25} & \hat{\sigma}_{26} \\ \hat{\sigma}_{31} & \hat{\sigma}_{32} & \hat{\sigma}_{33} & \hat{\sigma}_{34} & \hat{\sigma}_{35} & \hat{\sigma}_{36} \\ \hat{\sigma}_{41} & \hat{\sigma}_{42} & \hat{\sigma}_{43} & \hat{\sigma}_{44} & \hat{\sigma}_{45} & \hat{\sigma}_{46} \\ \hat{\sigma}_{51} & \hat{\sigma}_{52} & \hat{\sigma}_{53} & \hat{\sigma}_{54} & \hat{\sigma}_{55} & \hat{\sigma}_{56} \\ \hat{\sigma}_{61} & \hat{\sigma}_{62} & \hat{\sigma}_{63} & \hat{\sigma}_{64} & \hat{\sigma}_{65} & \hat{\sigma}_{66} \end{array}$$

For each Group we would have a separate variance–covariance matrix Σ_{G_i}. (Σ and Σ_{G_i} are estimated by $\hat{\Sigma}$ and $\hat{\Sigma}_{G_i}$, respectively.) For $MS_{I \times Ss\ w/in\ groups}$ to be an appropriate error term, we will first assume that the individual variance–covariance matrices (Σ_{A_i}) are the same for all levels of G. This can be thought of as an extension (to covariances) of the common assumption of homogeneity of variance.

The second assumption concerning covariances deals with the overall matrix Σ, where Σ is the pooled average of the Σ_{A_i}. (For equal samples sizes in each group, the entries in Σ will be the average of the corresponding entries in the individual Σ_{A_i} matrices.) A common and sufficient, but not necessary, assumption is that the matrix exhibits compound symmetry—meaning, as I said earlier, that all the variances on the main diagonal are equal, and all the covariances off the main diagonal are equal. Again, the variances do not have to equal the covariances, and usually will not. This assumption is in fact more stringent than necessary. All that we really need to assume is that the standard errors of the differences between pairs of Interval means are constant—in other words, that $\sigma^2_{\bar{I}_i - \bar{I}_j}$ is constant for all i and j ($j \neq i$). This sphericity requirement is met automatically if Σ exhibits compound symmetry, but other patterns of Σ will also have this property. For a more extensive discussion of the covariance assumptions, see Huynh and Feldt (1970) and Huynh and Mandeville (1979)—a particularly good discussion can be found in Edwards (1985, pp. 327–329, 336–339).

ADJUSTING THE DEGREES OF FREEDOM

Box (1954a) and Greenhouse and Geisser (1959) considered the effects of departure from this sphericity assumption on Σ. They showed that regardless of the form of Σ, the F ratio from the within-subjects portion of the analysis of variance will be approximately distributed as F on

$$(i - 1)\varepsilon, \ g(n - 1)(i - 1)\varepsilon$$

df for the Interval effect and

$$(g - 1)(i - 1)\varepsilon, \ g(n - 1)(i - 1)\varepsilon$$

df for the $I \times G$ interaction, where ε is estimated by

$$\hat{\varepsilon} = \frac{i^2(\bar{s}_{jj} - \bar{s})^2}{(i - 1)(\Sigma s_{jk}^2 - 2i\Sigma\bar{s}_j^2 + i^2\bar{s}^2)}$$

Here,

$\bar{s}_{jj}$ = the mean of the entries on the main diagonal of $\hat{\Sigma}$

$\bar{s}$ = the mean of all entries in $\hat{\Sigma}$

s_{jk} = the jkth entry in $\hat{\Sigma}$

$\bar{s}_j$ = the mean of all entries in the jth row of $\hat{\Sigma}$

Greenhouse and Geisser recommended that we at least adjust our degrees of freedom using $\hat{\varepsilon}$. They further showed that when all assumptions are met, $\varepsilon = 1$, and as we depart more and more from sphericity, ε approaches $1/(i - 1)$ as a minimum. They therefore suggested that a conservative test can be made by setting $\hat{\varepsilon} = 1/(i - 1)$, which reduces to setting the *df* for the test on I to

$$1, \ g(n - 1)$$

and the *df* for the $I \times G$ interaction to

$$(g - 1), \ g(n - 1)$$

This suggestion is so conservative that few people recommend its general adoption, preferring to calculate and use $\hat{\varepsilon}$. It does point out, however, that very large values of F are significant regardless of the form of Σ.

There is some suggestion that for large values of ε, even using $\hat{\varepsilon}$ to adjust the degrees of freedom can lead to a conservative test. Huynh and Feldt (1976) investigated this correction and recommended a modification of $\hat{\varepsilon}$ when there is reason to believe that the true value of ε lies near or above 0.75. Huynh and Feldt define

$$\tilde{\varepsilon} = \frac{ng(i - 1)\hat{\varepsilon} - 2}{(i - 1)[g(n - 1) - (i - 1)\hat{\varepsilon}]}$$

We then use $\hat{\varepsilon}$ or $\tilde{\varepsilon}$, depending on our estimate of the true value of ε. (Under certain circumstances, $\tilde{\varepsilon}$ will exceed 1, at which point it is set to 1.)

A test on the assumption of compound sphericity has been developed by Mauchly (1940) and evaluated by Huynh and Mandeville (1979) and by Keselman, Rogan,

Mendoza, and Breen (1980), who point to its extreme lack of robustness. Since you are unlikely ever to carry out this test by hand, it will not be presented here. However, it is available on BMDP2V, SPSS^X and SAS. Because tests of sphericity are likely to have serious problems when we need them the most, it has been suggested that we *always* use the correction to our degrees of freedom afforded by $\hat{\varepsilon}$ or $\tilde{\varepsilon}$, whichever is appropriate, or use a multivariate procedure to be discussed later. This is a reasonable suggestion and one worth adopting.

For our data, the F value for Intervals ($F = 29.85$) is such that its interpretation would be the same regardless of the value of ε, since the Interval effect will be significant even for the lowest possible df. If the assumption of sphericity is found to be invalid, however, alternative treatments would lead to different conclusions with respect to the $I \times G$ interaction. For King's data, the sphericity test, as found from BMDP2V, indicates that the assumption has been violated, and therefore it is necessary to deal with the problem resulting from this violation.

If we were to take Greenhouse and Geisser's (1959) conservative suggestion and set the degrees of freedom for the interaction at their minimum possible value $[g - 1, g(n - 1)]$, we would evaluate an F of 3.02 on 2 and 21 df. In this case, we would declare the interaction to be nonsignificant. Since we have the data, however, we can calculate $\hat{\varepsilon}$ and $\tilde{\varepsilon}$ and evaluate F on the appropriate df. The pooled variance–covariance matrix (averaged across the separate matrices) is presented in Table 14.5. (I have not presented the variance–covariance matrices for the several groups because they are roughly equivalent and because each of the elements of the matrix is based on only eight observations.)

From Table 14.5 we can see that our values of $\hat{\varepsilon}$ and $\tilde{\varepsilon}$ are .6569 and .8674, respectively. Since these are in the neighborhood of .75, we will follow Huynh and Feldt's suggestion and use $\tilde{\varepsilon}$. In this case, the degrees of freedom for the interaction are

$$(g - 1)(i - 1)(.8674) = 8.674$$

and

$$g(n - 1)(i - 1)(.8674) = 91.077$$

If we round these to 9 and 91 df, the critical value of $F_{.05}(9, 91) \simeq 2.00$, which means that we will reject the null hypothesis for the interaction. Thus, regardless of any problems with compound symmetry, all the effects in this analysis are significant.

TABLE 14.5
Variance–covariance matrix and calculation of $\hat{\varepsilon}$ and $\tilde{\varepsilon}$

	Interval						Row Mean
	1	2	3	4	5	6	
	6388.173	4696.226	2240.143	681.649	2017.726	1924.066	2991.330
	4696.226	7863.644	4181.476	2461.702	2891.524	3531.869	4271.074
	2240.143	4181.476	3912.380	2696.690	2161.690	3297.762	3081.690
$\hat{\Sigma} =$	681.649	2461.702	2696.690	4601.327	2248.600	3084.589	2629.093
	2017.726	2891.524	2161.690	2248.600	3717.369	989.310	2337.703
	1924.066	3531.869	3297.762	3084.589	989.310	5227.649	3009.208

TABLE 14.5 (Cont.)

$$\bar{s}_{jj} = \frac{6388.173 + 7863.644 + \cdots + 5227.649}{6} = 5285.090$$

$$\bar{s} = \frac{6388.173 + 4696.226 + \cdots + 989.310 + 5227.649}{36} = 3053.350$$

$$\sum s_{jk}^2 = 6388.173^2 + 4696.226^2 + \cdots 5227.649^2 = 416{,}392{,}330$$

$$\sum \bar{s}_j^2 = 2991.330^2 + \cdots + 3009.208^2 = 58{,}119{,}260$$

$$\hat{\varepsilon} = \frac{i^2(\bar{s}_{jj} - \bar{s})^2}{(i-1)(\Sigma s_{jk}^2 - 2i\Sigma \bar{s}_j^2 + i^2 \bar{s}^2)}$$

$$= \frac{36(5285.090 - 3053.350)^2}{(6-1)[416{,}392{,}330 - (2)(6)(58{,}119{,}260) + (36)(3053.350^2)]}$$

$$= \frac{179{,}303{,}883}{5[416{,}392{,}330 - 697{,}431{,}120 + 335{,}626{,}064]} = .6569$$

$$\tilde{\varepsilon} = \frac{ng(i-1)\hat{\varepsilon} - 2}{(i-1)[g(n-1) - (i-1)\hat{\varepsilon}]}$$

$$= \frac{(8)(3)(5)(.6569) - 2}{(5)[3(7) - (5)(.6569)]} = \frac{76.828}{5[21 - 5(.6569)]}$$

$$= .8674$$

SIMPLE EFFECTS

The Interval × Group interaction is plotted in Figure 14.2; the interpretation of the data is relatively clear. It is apparent that the Same group generally performs above the level of the other two groups—that is, the conditioned tolerance to midazolam leads to greater activity in that group than in the other groups. It is also clear that activity decreases noticeably after the first 5-minute interval (during which the drug is presumably having its effect). The interaction appears to be produced by the fact that the Different group is intermediate between the other two groups during the first interval, and also by the fact that the Same group continues declining until at least the fourth interval. Simple effects will prove useful in interpreting these results, especially in terms of examining group differences during the first and the last interval. Simple effects will also be used to test for differences between intervals within the control group, but only for purposes of illustration—it should be clear that Interval differences exist within each group.

As I have suggested earlier, the Greenhouse and Geisser and the Huynh and Feldt adjustments to degrees of freedom appear to do an adequate job of correcting for problems with the sphericity assumption when testing for overall main effects or interactions. However, a serious question about the adequacy of the adjustment arises when we consider within-subjects simple effects (Boik, 1981; Harris, 1985). The traditional approach to testing simple effects (see Howell, 1987) involves testing individual within-subjects contrasts against a pooled error term ($MS_{I \times Ss \text{ w/in groups}}$). If there are problems with the underlying assumption, this error term will sometimes underestimate and sometimes overestimate what would be the proper denominator for F, playing havoc with the probability of a Type I error. For that reason we are going to adopt a different, and in some ways simpler, approach.

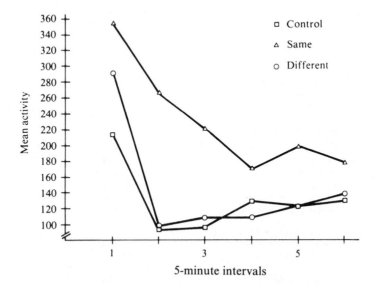

FIGURE 14.2
Interval × group interaction for data from Table 14.4

5-minute intervals

The approach we will take follows the advice of Boik in that a separate error term is derived for each tested effect. Thus, when we look at the simple effect of Intervals for the Control condition, the error term will speak specifically to that effect and will not pool other error terms that apply to other simple effects. We can test the Interval simple effects quite easily by running separate repeated-measures analyses of variance for each of the groups. For example, we can run a one-way repeated-measures analysis on Intervals for the Control group, as discussed in Section 14.4. We can then turn around and perform similar analyses on Intervals for the Same and Different groups separately. These analyses are shown in Table 14.6. In each case the Interval differences are significant, even after we correct the degrees of freedom using $\hat{\varepsilon}$ or $\tilde{\varepsilon}$, whichever is appropriate.

If you look at the within-subject analyses in Table 14.6 you will see that the average MS_{error} is $(2685.669 + 3477.571 + 1871.026)/3 = 2678.089$, which is $MS_{I \times Ss\,w/in\,groups}$ from the overall analysis found on page 441. Here these denominators for the F ratios are noticeably different from what they would have been had we used the pooled term, which is the traditional approach. You can also verify with a little work that the $MS_{Interval}$ terms for each analysis are the same as those that we would compute if we followed the usual procedures for obtaining simple effects mean squares.

For the between-subjects simple effects (e.g., Groups at Interval 1) the procedure is more complicated. Although we could follow the within-subject example and perform separate analyses at each Interval, we would lose considerable degrees of freedom unnecessarily. Here it is legitimate to pool error terms, and it is generally wise to do so.

(a) Interval at Control

Source	df	SS	MS	F
Between subjects	7	134,615.58		
Interval	5	76,447.25	15,289.45	5.69
Error	35	93,998.42	2685.67	
Total	47	305,061.25		

*$p < .05$; $\hat{\varepsilon} = .404$; $\tilde{\varepsilon} = .570$

(b) Interval at Same

Source	df	SS	MS	F
Between subjects	7	175,600.15		
Interval	5	193,090.85	38,618.17	11.10
Error	35	121,714.98	3477.57	
Total	47	490,405.98		

*$p < .05$; $\hat{\varepsilon} = .578$; $\tilde{\varepsilon} = 1.00$

(c) Interval at Different

Source	df	SS	MS	F
Between subjects	7	74,506.33		
Interval	5	211,018.42	42,203.68	22.56
Error	35	65,485.92	1871.03	
Total	47	351,010.67		

*$p < .05$; $\hat{\varepsilon} = .598$; $\tilde{\varepsilon} = 1.00$

For this example we will examine the simple effects of Group at Interval 1 and Group at Interval 6. The original data can found in Table 14.4 on page 440. The sum of squares for these effects are

$$SS_{G \text{ at Int. 1}} = \frac{1711^2 + 2837^2 + 2321^2}{8} - \frac{6869^2}{24} = 79,426.33$$

$$SS_{G \text{ at Int. 6}} = \frac{1041^2 + 1429^2 + 1109^2}{8} - \frac{3579^2}{24} = 10,732.00$$

Testing the simple effects of between-subjects terms is a little trickier. Consider for a moment the simple effect of Group at Interval 1. This is essentially a one-way analysis of variance with no repeated measures, since the Group totals now represent the sum of single—rather than repeated—observations on subjects. Thus, subject differences are confounded with experimental error. In this case, the appropriate error sum of squares is $SS_{\text{w/in cell}}$, where, from Table 14.4,

$$SS_{\text{w/in cell}} = SS_{Ss \text{ w/in group}} + SS_{I \times Ss \text{ w/in group}}$$

$$= 384,722.03 + 281,199.34 = 665,921.37$$

and

$$MS_{\text{w/in cell}} = \frac{SS_{\text{w/in cell}}}{df_{Ss \text{ w/in group}} + df_{I \times Ss \text{ w/in group}}}$$

$$= \frac{665{,}921.37}{21 + 105} = 5285.09$$

It may be easier for you to understand why we need this special $MS_{\text{w/in cell}}$ error term if you think about what it really represents. If you were presented with only the data for Interval 1 in Table 14.4 and wished to test the differences among the three groups, you would run a standard one-way analysis of variance, and the MS_{error} would be the average of the variances within each of the three groups. Similarly, if you had only the data from Interval 2, Interval 3, and so on, you would again average the variances within the three treatment groups. The $MS_{\text{w/in cell}}$ that we have just finished calculating is in reality the average of the error terms for these six different sets (Intervals) of data. As such, it is the average of the variance within each of the 18 cells.

We can now proceed to form our F ratios.

$$F_{G \text{ at Int. 1}} = \frac{MS_{G \text{ at Int. 1}}}{MS_{\text{w/in cell}}} = \frac{79{,}426.33/2}{5285.09} = 7.51$$

$$F_{G \text{ at Int. 6}} = \frac{MS_{G \text{ at Int. 6}}}{MS_{\text{w/in cell}}} = \frac{10{,}732/2}{5285.09} = 1.02$$

A further difficulty arises in the evaluation of F. Since $MS_{\text{w/in cell}}$ also represents the sum of two *heterogeneous* sources of error [as can be seen by examination of the $E(MS)$ for Ss w/in groups and $I \times Ss$ w/in groups), our F will not be distributed on 2 and 126 df. We will get ourselves out of this difficulty in the same way we did when we faced a similar problem concerning t in Chapter 7. We will simply calculate the relevant df against which to evaluate F—more precisely, we will calculate a statistic denoted as f' and evaluate F_{obt} against $F_{.05}(a - 1, f')$. In this case, the value of f' is given by Welch (1938) and Satterthwaite (1946) as

$$f' = \frac{(u + v)^2}{\dfrac{u^2}{df_u} + \dfrac{v^2}{df_v}}$$

where

$$u = SS_{Ss \text{ w/in groups}}$$

$$v = SS_{I \times Ss \text{ w/in groups}}$$

and df_u and df_v are the corresponding degrees of freedom. For our example,

$$u = 384{,}722.03 \qquad df_u = 21$$

$$v = 281{,}199.34 \qquad df_v = 105$$

$$f' = \frac{(384{,}722.03 + 281{,}199.34)^2}{\dfrac{384{,}722.03^2}{21} + \dfrac{281{,}199.34^2}{105}} = 56.84$$

Rounding to the nearest integer, $f' = 57$. Thus, our F is distributed on $(g - 1, f') = (2, 57)$ *df* under H_0. For 2 and 57 *df*, $F_{.05} \simeq 3.15$. Only the difference at Interval 1 is significant. By the end of 30 minutes, the three groups were performing at equivalent levels. It is logical to conclude that somewhere between the first and the sixth interval the three groups become nonsignificantly different, and many people test at each interval to find that point. However, I strongly recommend against this practice as a general rule. We have already run a number of significance tests, and running more of them serves only to increase the error rate. Unless there is an important theoretical reason to determine the point at which the group differences become nonsignificant—and I suspect that there are very few such cases—then there is nothing to be gained by testing each interval. Tests should be carried out to answer important questions, not to address idle curiousity or to make the analysis look "complete."

MULTIPLE COMPARISONS

Several studies have investigated the robustness of multiple-comparison procedures for testing differences among means on the within-subject variable. Maxwell (1980) studied a simple repeated-measures design with no between-subject component and advised adopting multiple-comparison procedures that do not use a pooled error term. We discussed such a procedure (the Games–Howell procedure) in Chapter 12.

Keselman and Keselman (1988) extended Maxwell's work to designs having one between-subject component and made a similar recommendation. In fact, they showed that when the Groups are of different sizes and sphericity is violated, experimentwise error rates can become very badly distorted. In the simple effects procedures that we have just considered, I recommended using separate error terms by running one-way repeated-measures analyses for each of the groups. For subsequent multiple-comparison procedures exploring those simple effects, especially with unequal sample sizes, it would probably be wise to employ the Games–Howell procedure using those separate covariance matrices. In other words, to compare Intervals 3 and 4 for the Control group, you would generate your error term using only the Interval 3 and 4 data from just the Control group.

14.6 TWO WITHIN-SUBJECTS VARIABLES

Occasionally, you will come across a study containing two variables in which every subject serves under all combinations of both variables, so there are no between-subjects variables. Since this design is merely a simplified version of the three within-subjects effects and no between-subjects effects design considered later in this chapter, it will not be discussed here. You can simply refer to the more complex analysis, ignoring all references there to variable C and its interactions.

14.7 TWO BETWEEN-SUBJECTS VARIABLES AND ONE WITHIN-SUBJECTS VARIABLE

The basic theory of repeated-measures analysis of variance has already been described in the discussion of the previous designs. However, experimenters commonly plan experiments with three variables, some or all of which represent repeated measures on the same subjects. We will briefly discuss the analysis of these designs. The calculations are basically very simple, since the sums of squares for main effects and interaction are obtained in the usual way and the error terms are obtained by subtraction.

We will not consider the theory behind these designs at any length. Essentially, it amounts to the extrapolation of what has already been said about the two-variable case. For an excellent discussion of the underlying statistical theory, see Winer (1971).

In a study of automobile driving somewhat different from the one in Chapter 13, assume that we want to examine driving behavior as a function of two times (T)—night (T_1) and day (T_2); three types of course (C)—special serpentine track (C_1), City streets (C_2), and open highway (C_3); and three sizes (S) of cars—small (S_1), medium (S_2), and large (S_3). For this design, assume that we will have independent groups of drivers for the Time (T) and Course (C) variables. This design is diagrammed as follows, where G_i represents the ith group of drivers.

	T_1			T_2		
	S_1	S_2	S_3	S_1	S_2	S_3
C_1	G_1	G_1	G_1	G_4	G_4	G_4
C_2	G_2	G_2	G_2	G_5	G_5	G_5
C_3	G_3	G_3	G_3	G_6	G_6	G_6

We will further assume that there are three subjects per group (to keep the arithmetic simple) and that the dependent variable is the number of steering errors.

The raw data and the necessary summary tables of cell totals are presented in Table 14.7a. In Table 14.7b are the calculations for the main effects and interactions. Here, as elsewhere, the calculations are carried out exactly as they are for any main effects and interactions.

The summary table for the analysis of variance is presented in Table 14.7c. In this table, the ** indicate terms that were obtained by subtraction. Thus,

$$SS_{\text{w/in subj}} = SS_{\text{total}} - SS_{\text{between subj}}$$

$$SS_{Ss\ \text{w/in group}} = SS_{\text{between subj}} - SS_T - SS_C - SS_{TC}$$

$$SS_{S \times Ss\ \text{w/in group}} = SS_{\text{w/in subj}} - SS_S - SS_{TS} - SS_{CS} - SS_{TCS}$$

These last two terms are the error terms for between-subjects and within-subjects effects, respectively. That these error terms are appropriate is shown by examining the expected mean squares presented in Table 14.8. For the expected mean squares of random and mixed models, see Kirk (1968, p. 293) or Winer (1971, p. 558).

TABLE 14.7
Data and calculations for two between-subjects variables and one within-subject variable

(a) Data

	S_1 Small	S_2 Medium	S_3 Large	T_{subj}	S_1 Small	S_2 Medium	S_3 Large	T_{subj}
		T_1 (Night)				T_2 (Day)		
C_1 (Track)	10	8	6	24	5	4	3	12
	9	8	5	22	4	3	3	10
	8	7	4	19	4	1	2	7
Total	27	23	15	65	13	8	8	29
C_2 (City)	9	7	5	21	4	3	3	10
	10	6	4	20	4	2	2	8
	7	4	3	14	3	3	2	8
Total	26	17	12	55	11	8	7	26
C_3 (Highway)	7	6	3	16	2	2	1	5
	4	5	2	11	2	3	2	7
	3	4	2	9	1	0	1	2
Total	14	15	7	36	5	5	4	14

	TC Cell Totals				**TS Cell Totals**		
	T_1	T_2	Total		T_1	T_2	Total
C_1	65	29	94	S_1	67	29	96
C_2	55	26	81	S_2	55	21	76
C_3	36	14	50	S_3	34	19	53
Total	156	69	225	Total	156	69	225

	CS Cell Totals			
	S_1	S_2	S_3	Total
C_1	40	31	23	94
C_2	37	25	19	81
C_3	19	20	11	50
Total	96	76	53	225

(b) Calculations

$$\text{SS}_{total} = \sum X^2 - \frac{(\Sigma X)^2}{N} = 1261 - 937.50 = 323.50$$

$$\text{SS}_{subj} = \frac{\Sigma T_{subj}^2}{s} - \frac{(\Sigma X)^2}{N} = \frac{24^2 + 22^2 + \cdots + 7^2 + 2^2}{3} - \frac{(\Sigma X)^2}{N}$$

$$= 1171.67 - 937.50 = 234.17$$

$$\text{SS}_T = \frac{\Sigma T_{T_i}^2}{ncs} - \frac{(\Sigma X)^2}{N} = 1077.67 - 937.50 = 140.17$$

TABLE 14.7 (Cont.)   **(b) Calculations (Cont.)**

$$SS_C = \frac{\Sigma T_{C_j}^2}{nts} - \frac{(\Sigma X)^2}{N} = 994.28 - 937.50 = 56.78$$

$$SS_S = \frac{\Sigma T_{S_k}^2}{ntc} - \frac{(\Sigma X)^2}{N} = 988.94 - 937.50 = 51.44$$

$$SS_{\text{cells } TC} = \frac{\Sigma T_{TC_{ij}}^2}{ns} - \frac{(\Sigma X)^2}{N} = 1139.89 - 937.50 = 202.39$$

$$SS_{TC} = SS_{\text{cells } TC} - SS_T - SS_C = 202.39 - 140.17 - 56.78 = 5.44$$

$$SS_{\text{cells } TS} = \frac{\Sigma T_{TS_{ik}}^2}{nc} - \frac{(\Sigma X)^2}{N} = 1145.89 - 937.50 = 208.39$$

$$SS_{TS} = SS_{\text{cells } TS} - SS_T - SS_S = 208.39 - 140.17 - 51.44 = 16.78$$

$$SS_{\text{cells } CS} = \frac{\Sigma T_{CS_{jk}}^2}{nt} - \frac{(\Sigma X)^2}{N} = 1054.50 - 937.50 = 117.00$$

$$SS_{CS} = SS_{\text{cells } CS} - SS_C - SS_S = 117.00 - 56.78 - 51.44 = 8.78$$

$$SS_{\text{cells } TCS} = \frac{\Sigma T_{TCS_{ijk}}^2}{n} - \frac{(\Sigma X)^2}{N} = 1219.67 - 937.50 = 282.17$$

$$SS_{TCS} = SS_{\text{cells } TCS} - SS_T - SS_C - SS_S - SS_{TC} - SS_{TS} - SS_{CS}$$

$$= 282.17 - 140.17 - 56.78 - 51.44 - 5.44 - 16.78 - 8.78 = 2.78$$

(c) Summary Table

Source	df	SS	MS	F
Between subjects	17	234.17		
T (Time)	1	140.17	140.17	52.89*
C (Course)	2	56.78	28.39	10.71*
TC	2	5.44	2.72	1.03
Ss w/in group	12	31.78**	2.65	
Within subjects	36	89.33**		
S (Size)	2	51.44	25.72	64.30*
TS	2	16.78	8.39	20.98*
CS	4	8.78	2.20	5.50*
TCS	4	2.78	0.70	1.75
S × Ss w/in group	24	9.55**	0.40	
Total	53	323.50		

*$p < .05$
**Term obtained by subtraction

From the column of F in the summary table in Table 14.7c, we see that all three main effects as well as the TS and CS interactions are significant. The presence of the two significant interactions suggests caution in interpreting the main effects.

Examination of the data suggests that nighttime conditions produced more errors than did daytime conditions (T_1 versus T_2), but that this difference decreased as the cars became larger and more stable (*TS*). There are still substantial differences even for large cars, and thus the main effect of *T* has meaning despite (or in addition to) the *TS* interaction. The main effect of *C* (Course) is of questionable importance in light of the pattern of the *CS* interaction. Here the analysis of simple effects will be instructive. The main effect of *S* (Size) is also thrown into question by the *CS* interaction, and again the analysis of simple effects would be profitable.

TABLE 14.8
Expected mean squares with *A, B,* and *C* fixed

Source	df	E(MS)
Between subjects	$tcn - 1$	
T	$t - 1$	$\sigma_e^2 + s\sigma_\pi^2 + ncs\sigma_\alpha^2$
C	$c - 1$	$\sigma_e^2 + s\sigma_\pi^2 + nts\sigma_\beta^2$
TC	$(t-1)(c-1)$	$\sigma_e^2 + s\sigma_\pi^2 + ns\sigma_{\gamma\beta}^2$
Ss w/in groups	$tc(n-1)$	$\sigma_e^2 + s\sigma_\pi^2$
Within subjects	$tcn(s-1)$	
S	$s-1$	$\sigma_e^2 + \sigma_{\gamma\pi}^2 + ntc\sigma_\gamma^2$
TS	$(t-1)(s-1)$	$\sigma_e^2 + \sigma_{\gamma\pi}^2 + nc\sigma_{\alpha\gamma}^2$
CS	$(c-1)(s-1)$	$\sigma_e^2 + \sigma_{\gamma\pi}^2 + nt\sigma_{\beta\gamma}^2$
TCS	$(t-1)(c-1)(s-1)$	$\sigma_e^2 + \sigma_{\gamma\pi}^2 + n\sigma_{\alpha\beta\gamma}^2$
$S \times$ Ss w/in groups	$tc(n-1)(s-1)$	$\sigma_e^2 + \sigma_{\gamma\pi}^2$
Total	$N-1$	

SIMPLE EFFECTS FOR COMPLEX REPEATED-MEASURES DESIGNS

In the previous example we saw that tests on within-subjects simple effects were occasionally disrupted by violations of the sphericity assumption, and we took steps to work around this problem. We will have much the same problem with this example.

We are again going to have to distinguish between simple effects on between-subject factors and simple effects on within-subject factors. We will start with between-subject simple effects.

We have three different between-subjects simple effects that we can examine; namely, the two simple main effects of Time and Course at Size$_i$ and the simple Time $\times$ Course interaction effect at Size$_i$. By far the easiest way to test these between-subject effects is to run separate two-way (Time $\times$ Course) analyses of variance at each level of Size. These three analyses will give you all three simple effects at each level of Size with only minor effort. You can then either accept the *F* values from those analyses, or you can pool the error terms from the three separate analyses and use that pooled error term in testing the mean square for the relevant effect. If these error terms are heterogeneous, you would be wise not to pool them. On the other hand, if they represent homogeneous sources of variance, they may be pooled, giving you more degrees of freedom for error.

The within-subject simple effects are handled in much the same way. For example, there is reason to look closely at the Time $\times$ Size interaction for each course. It would also be useful to look at Size differences at each type of course, and in doing so we need to include Time in our analysis so as not to inflate the error term. Such an analysis can easily be carried out by running a Size × Time repeated-measures analysis of variance at each level of Course. Here, however, we should not pool error terms across analyses because of concerns over sphericity.

The relevant analyses are presented in Table 14.9 for simple effects at one of the levels of the other variable. Tests at the other levels would be done in the same way. Although this table has more simple effects than we care about, they are presented to illustrate the way in which the tests were constructed. You would probably be foolish to consider all of the tests that result from this approach, because you would seriously inflate the experimentwise error rate. Decide what you want to look at before you run the analyses, and then stick to that decision. If you really want to look at a large number of simple effects, consider adapting one of the Bonferroni approaches discussed in Chapter 12.

TABLE 14.9
Simple effects for data in Table 14.7 (Only one example of each is included.)

(a) Between-Subject Effects (Time, Course, and T × C at $Size_1$)

Source	df	SS	MS	F
Time	1	80.222	80.222	55.54*
Course	2	43.000	21.500	14.88*
T × C	2	3.444	1.722	1.19
Error	12	17.333	1.444	
Total	17	144.000		

*$p < .05$

(b) Within-Subject Effects (Size, Time, and Size × Time at $Course_1$)

Source	df	SS	MS	F
Time	1	72.000	72.000	34.10*
Within subjects	12	32.667		
Size	2	24.111	12.056	43.40*
S × T	2	6.333	3.167	11.40*
Error	8	2.222	0.278	
Total	13	104.667		

*$p < .05$

14.8 TWO WITHIN-SUBJECTS VARIABLES AND ONE BETWEEN-SUBJECTS VARIABLE

The design we just considered can be seen as a straightforward extension of the case of one between- and one within-subjects variable. All that we needed to add to the summary table was another main effect and the corresponding interactions. However, when we examine a design with two within-subjects main effects, the problem becomes slightly more complicated because of the presence of additional error terms. To use a more generic notation, we will label the independent variables as A, B, and C.

Suppose that as a modification of the previous study we continued to use different subjects for the two levels of variable A, but we ran each subject under all combinations of variables B and C. This design can be diagrammed as

	A_1			A_2		
	C_1	C_2	C_3	C_1	C_2	C_3
B_1	G_1	G_1	G_1	G_2	G_2	G_2
B_2	G_1	G_1	G_1	G_2	G_2	G_2
B_3	G_1	G_1	G_1	G_2	G_2	G_2

Before we consider an example, we will examine the expected mean squares for this design. These are presented in Table 14.10 for the case of the fixed model. From the expected mean squares it is evident that we will have four error terms for this design. As before, the $MS_{Ss\ w/in\ groups}$ is used to test the between-subjects effect. When it comes to the within-subjects terms, however, B and the interaction of B with A are tested by $B \times Ss$ within groups; C and its interaction with A are tested by $C \times Ss$ within groups; and BC and its interaction with A are tested by $BC \times Ss$ within groups. Why this is necessary is apparent from the expected mean squares. It may be easier to appreciate what is happening, however, if we rewrite the source column of the summary table as in Table 14.11. Here we can see that each within-subjects effect is considered as interacting with the between-subjects term, and consequently with the partitions of the between-subjects variation. (These new terms are often called *dummy* terms since they play no real role in the analysis.) A similar kind of table could have been drawn up for the previous design, but there was no necessity for it. Here we must consider the form of Table 14.11 because it gives us a hint as to how we will compute our within-subjects error terms.

TABLE 14.10
Expected mean squares

Source	df	E(MS)
Between subjects	$an - 1$	
A	$a - 1$	$\sigma_e^2 + bc\sigma_\pi^2 + nbc\sigma_\alpha^2$
Ss w/in groups	$a(n - 1)$	$\sigma_e^2 + bc\sigma_\pi^2$
Within subjects	$na(bc - 1)$	
B	$b - 1$	$\sigma_e^2 + c\sigma_{\beta\pi}^2 + nac\sigma_\beta^2$
AB	$(a - 1)(b - 1)$	$\sigma_e^2 + c\sigma_{\beta\pi}^2 + nc\sigma_{\alpha\beta}^2$
$B \times Ss$ w/in groups	$a(b - 1)(n - 1)$	$\sigma_e^2 + c\sigma_{\beta\pi}^2$
C	$c - 1$	$\sigma_e^2 + b\sigma_{\gamma\pi}^2 + nab\sigma_\gamma^2$
AC	$(a - 1)(c - 1)$	$\sigma_e^2 + b\sigma_{\gamma\pi}^2 + nb\sigma_{\alpha\gamma}^2$
$C \times Ss$ w/in groups	$a(c - 1)(n - 1)$	$\sigma_e^2 + b\sigma_{\gamma\pi}^2$
BC	$(b - 1)(c - 1)$	$\sigma_e^2 + \sigma_{\beta\gamma\pi}^2 + nac\sigma_{\beta\gamma}^2$
ABC	$(a - 1)(b - 1)(c - 1)$	$\sigma_e^2 + \sigma_{\beta\gamma\pi}^2 + n\sigma_{\alpha\beta\gamma}^2$
$BC \times Ss$ w/in groups	$a(b - 1)(c - 1)(n - 1)$	$\sigma_e^2 + \sigma_{\beta\gamma\pi}^2$
Total	$N - 1$	

TABLE 14.11
Alternative partition
of total variation

Source	df
Between subjects	$an - 1$
A (groups)	$a - 1$
Subj w/in groups	$a(n - 1)$
Within subjects	$na(bc - 1)$
B	$b - 1$
$B \times S$	$(b - 1)(an - 1)$
AB	$(a - 1)(b - 1)$
$B \times S$s w/in groups	$a(b - 1)(n - 1)$
C	$c - 1$
$C \times S$	$(c - 1)(an - 1)$
AC	$(a - 1)(c - 1)$
$C \times S$s w/in groups	$a(c - 1)(n - 1)$
BC	$(b - 1)(c - 1)$
$BC \times S$	$(b - 1)(c - 1)(an - 1)$
ABC	$(a - 1)(b - 1)(c - 1)$
$BC \times S$s w/in groups	$a(b - 1)(c - 1)(n - 1)$
Total	$N - 1$

Direct computation of error terms in this design would be a most unpleasant undertaking. However, the calculation of the (dummy) terms $SS_{B \times S}$ and $SS_{C \times S}$ is relatively straightforward, since they are calculated just as is any interaction term. Because we know from Table 14.11 that $SS_{B \times S}$ is partitioned into SS_{AB} and $SS_{B \times Ss \text{ w/in groups}}$, then

$$SS_{B \times Ss \text{ w/in groups}} = SS_{B \times S} - SS_{AB}$$

The same reasoning holds for $SS_{C \times Ss \text{ w/in groups}}$ and $SS_{BC \times Ss \text{ w/in groups}}$. We do not need to calculate $SS_{BC \times S}$ directly, however, since it is readily obtained by subtraction:

$$SS_{BC \times S} = SS_{\text{w/in subj}} - SS_B - SS_{B \times S} - SS_C - SS_{C \times S} - SS_{BC}$$

AN ANALYSIS OF DATA ON CONDITIONED SUPPRESSION

Bouton and Swartzentruber (1985) investigated the degree to which a tone, which had previously been paired with shock, would suppress the rate of an ongoing bar-pressing response. Suppression was measured by taking the ratio of the number of bar presses during a 1-minute test period to the total number of bar presses during both a baseline period and the test period. For all groups, behavior was assessed in two Phases (a Shock and a No-shock phase) repeated over a series of four Cycles of the experiment.

It may be easier to understand the design of the study if you first glance at the layout of Table 14.12. During Phase I, Group A-B was placed in Box A. After a 1-minute baseline interval, during which the animal bar-pressed for food, a tone was presented for 1 minute and was followed by a mild shock. The degree of suppression of the bar-pressing response when the tone was present (a normal fear response) was recorded. The animal was then placed in Box B for Phase II of the cycle, where, after

1 minute of baseline bar-pressing, only the tone stimulus was presented. Since the tone was previously paired with shock, it should suppress bar-pressing behavior to some extent. Over a series of A-B cycles, however, the subject should learn that shock is never administered in Phase II and that Box B is therefore a "safe" box. Thus, for later cycles there should be less suppression on the no-shock trials.

TABLE 14.12
Analysis of conditioned suppression data[†]

(a) Data

		Cycle							
		1		2		3		4	
		Phase		Phase		Phase		Phase	
Group	I	II	I	II	I	II	I	II	Subject Total
A-B	01*	28	22	48	22	50	14	48	233
	21	21	16	40	15	39	11	56	219
	15	17	13	35	22	45	1	43	191
	30	34	55	54	37	57	57	68	392
	11	23	12	33	10	50	8	53	200
	16	11	18	34	11	40	5	40	175
	7	26	29	40	25	50	14	56	247
	0	22	23	45	18	38	15	50	211
	101	182	188	329	160	369	125	414	1868
A-A	1	6	16	8	9	14	11	33	98
	37	59	28	36	34	32	26	37	289
	18	43	38	50	39	15	29	18	250
	1	2	9	8	6	5	5	15	51
	44	25	28	42	47	46	33	35	300
	15	14	22	32	16	23	32	26	180
	0	3	7	17	6	9	10	15	67
	26	15	31	32	28	22	16	15	185
	142	167	179	225	185	166	162	194	1420
L-A-B	33	43	40	52	39	52	38	48	345
	4	35	9	42	4	46	23	51	214
	32	39	38	47	24	44	16	40	280
	17	34	21	41	27	50	13	40	243
	44	52	37	48	33	53	33	43	343
	12	16	9	39	9	59	13	45	202
	18	42	3	62	45	49	60	57	336
	13	29	14	44	9 ∴	50	15	48	222
	173	290	171	375	190	403	211	372	2185
Total	416	639	538	929	535	938	498	980	5473

[†] Lower scores represent greater suppression.
* Decimal points have been omitted.

TABLE 14.12 (Cont.) **(a_2) Subtables**

Phase × Cycle

	Cycle				
	1	2	3	4	Total
Phase I (Shock)	416	538	535	498	1987
Phase II (No-shock)	639	929	938	980	3486
Total	1055	1467	1473	1478	5473

Group × Cycle

	Cycle				
Group	1	2	3	4	Total
A-B	283	517	529	539	1868
A-A	309	404	351	356	1420
L-A-B	463	546	593	583	2185
Total	1055	1467	1473	1478	5473

Phase × Group

	Group			
	A-B	*A-A*	*L-A-B*	Total
Phase I (Shock)	574	668	745	1987
Phase II (No-shock)	1294	752	1440	3486
Total	1868	1420	2185	5473

Cycle × Subject

	Subject											
	1	2	3	4	5	6	7	8	9	10	11	12
Cycle 1	29	42	32	64	34	27	33	22	07	96	61	03
Cycle 2	70	56	48	109	45	52	69	68	24	64	88	17
Cycle 3	72	54	67	94	60	51	75	56	23	66	54	11
Cycle 4	62	67	44	125	61	45	70	65	44	63	47	20
	13	14	15	16	17	18	19	20	21	22	23	24
Cycle 1	69	29	03	41	76	39	71	51	96	28	60	42
Cycle 2	70	54	24	63	92	51	85	62	85	48	65	58
Cycle 3	93	39	15	50	91	50	68	77	86	68	94	59
Cycle 4	68	58	25	31	86	74	56	53	76	58	117	63

TABLE 14.12 (Cont.)

							Phase × Subject					
							Subject					
	1	2	3	4	5	6	7	8	9	10	11	12
Phase I	59	63	51	179	41	50	75	56	37	125	124	21
Phase II	174	156	140	213	159	125	172	155	61	164	126	30
	13	14	15	16	17	18	19	20	21	22	23	24
Phase I	152	85	23	101	150	40	110	78	147	43	126	51
Phase II	148	95	44	84	195	174	170	165	196	159	210	171

(b) Calculations

(Notation: Subjects; $n = 8$: Groups; $g = 3$: Phase; $p = 2$: Cycles; $c = 4$)

$$SS_{total} = \sum X^2 - \frac{(\Sigma X)^2}{N} = 20.8409 - 15.6009 = 5.2400$$

$$SS_{subjects} = \frac{\Sigma T_S^2}{pc} - \frac{(\Sigma X)^2}{N} = 17.6349 - 15.6009 = 2.0340$$

$$SS_{groups} = \frac{\Sigma T_G^2}{ncp} - \frac{(\Sigma X)^2}{N} = 16.0626 - 15.6009 = 0.4617$$

$$SS_{Ss\ w/in\ groups} = SS_{subj} - SS_G = 2.0340 - 0.4617 = 1.5723$$

$$SS_{cycle} = \frac{\Sigma T_C^2}{ngp} - \frac{(\Sigma X)^2}{N} = 15.8736 - 15.6009 = 0.2727$$

$$SS_{cells(CG)} = \frac{\Sigma T_{CG}^2}{np} - \frac{(\Sigma X)^2}{N} = 16.4400 - 15.6009 = 0.8391$$

$$SS_{C \times G} = SS_{cells(CG)} - SS_C - SS_G = 0.8391 - 0.2727 - 0.4617 = 0.1047$$

$$SS_{cells(CS)} = \frac{\Sigma T_{CS}^2}{p} - \frac{(\Sigma X)^2}{N} = 18.4885 - 15.6009 = 2.8876$$

$$SS_{C \times S} = SS_{cells(CS)} - SS_C - SS_S = 2.8876 - 0.2727 - 2.0340 = 0.5809$$

$$SS_{C \times Ss\ w/in\ groups} = SS_{C \times S} - SS_{CG} = 0.5809 - 0.1047 = 0.4762$$

$$SS_{phase} = \frac{\Sigma T_P^2}{ncg} - \frac{(\Sigma X)^2}{N} = 16.7712 - 15.6009 = 1.1703$$

$$SS_{cells(PG)} = \frac{\Sigma T_{PG}^2}{nc} - \frac{(\Sigma X)^2}{N} = 17.6383 - 15.6009 = 2.0374$$

$$SS_{P \times G} = SS_{cells(PG)} - SS_P - SS_G = 2.0374 - 1.1703 - 0.4617 = 0.4054$$

$$SS_{cells(PS)} = \frac{\Sigma T_{PS}^2}{c} - \frac{(\Sigma X)^2}{N} = 19.3999 - 15.6009 = 3.7990$$

$$SS_{P \times S} = SS_{cells(PS)} - SS_P - SS_S = 3.7990 - 1.1703 - 2.0340 = 0.5947$$

$$SS_{P \times Ss\ w/in\ groups} = SS_{PS} - SS_{PG} = 0.5947 - 0.4054 = 0.1893$$

TABLE 14.12 (Cont.)

$$SS_{cells(CP)} = \frac{\Sigma T_{CP}^2}{ng} - \frac{(\Sigma X)^2}{N} = 17.1181 - 15.6009 = 1.5172$$

$$SS_{C \times P} = SS_{cells(CP)} - SS_C - SS_P = 1.5172 - 0.2727 - 1.1703 = 0.0742$$

$$SS_{cells(CPG)} = \frac{\Sigma T_{CPG}^2}{n} - \frac{(\Sigma X)^2}{N} = 18.2173 - 15.6009 = 2.6164$$

$$SS_{C \times P \times G} = SS_{cells(CPG)} - SS_C - SS_P - SS_G - SS_{CP} - SS_{CG} - SS_{PG}$$

$$= 2.6164 - 0.2727 - 1.1703 - 0.4617 - 0.0742 - 0.1047 - 0.4054$$

$$= 0.1274$$

$$SS_{CP \times Ss\ w/in\ groups} = SS_{total} - \Sigma(\text{all other effects}) = 5.2400 - 0.4617 - 1.5723$$

$$- 0.2727 - 0.1047 - 0.4762 - 1.1703 - 0.4054$$

$$0.1893 - 0.0742 - 0.1274 = 0.3858$$

(c) Summary Table

Source	df	SS	MS	F
Between subjects	23	2.0340		
Groups	2	0.4617	0.2308	3.08
Ss w/in groups	21	1.5723	0.0749	
Within subjects	168	3.2060		
Cycle	3	0.2727	0.0909	11.96*
$C \times G$	6	0.1047	0.0175	2.30*
$C \times Ss$ w/in groups	63	0.4762	0.0076	
Phase	1	1.1703	1.1703	130.03*
$P \times G$	2	0.4054	0.2027	22.52*
$P \times Ss$ w/in groups	21	0.1893	0.0090	
$C \times P$	3	0.0742	0.0247	4.05*
$C \times P \times G$	6	0.1274	0.0212	3.48*
$CP \times Ss$ w/in groups	63	0.3858	0.0061	
Total	191	5.2400		

*$p < .05$

Group *L-A-B* was treated in the same way as Group *A-B* except that these animals previously had had experience with a situation in which a light, rather than a tone, had been paired with shock. Because of this previous experience, the authors expected the animals to perform slightly better (less suppression during Phase II) than did the other group, especially on the first cycle or two.

Group *A-A* was also treated in the same way as Group *A-B* except that both Phases were carried out in the same box—Box *A*. Because there were no differences in the test boxes to serve as cues (i.e., animals had no way to distinguish the no-shock from the shock phases), this group would be expected to show the most suppression during the No-shock phases.

Bouton and Swartzentruber predicted that overall there would be a main effect due to Phase (i.e., a difference between shock and no-shock Phases), a main effect due to Groups (*A-B* and *L-A-B* showing less suppression than *A-A*), and a main effect due to Cycles. They also predicted that each of the interactions would be significant. (One reason I chose to use this example, even though it is difficult to describe concisely, is that it is one of those rare studies in which all effects are predicted to be significant and meaningful.)

The data and analysis of variance for this study are presented in Table 14.12. The analysis has not been elaborated in detail because it mainly involves steps that you already know how to do. The results are presented graphically in Figure 14.3 for convenience, and for the most part they are clear-cut and in the predicted direction. Keep in mind that for these data a lower score represents more suppression—that is, the animals are responding more slowly. Calculating the sums of squares for the error terms may be somewhat easier to understand if you compare the summary table and Table 14.11. I have given an intermediate step so that if you have any question about how each term is calculated, you can work it out and compare your answer with mine. If your answer matches mine, you are almost certainly performing the calculations correctly.

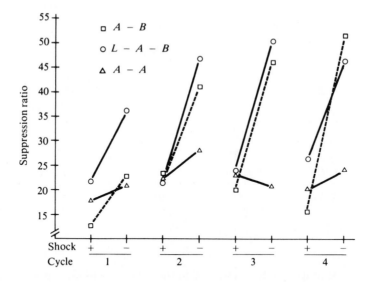

FIGURE 14.3
Conditioned
suppression data

From the summary table in Table 14.12c, it is clear that nearly all the predictions were supported. The only effect that was not significant was the main effect of Groups, but that effect is not critical because it represents an average across the shock and the no-shock phases, even though the experimenters had predicted little or no group differences in the shock phase. In this context, the Phase × Group interaction is of more interest, and it is clearly significant.

The presence of an interpretable three-way interaction offers the opportunity to give another example of the use of simple interaction effects. We would have predicted that all groups would show high levels of suppression of the shock trials on all Cycles, because anticipated shock is clearly disruptive. On no-shock trials, however, Groups *A-B* and *L-A-B* should show less suppression (higher scores) than Group *A-A*, and this latter difference should increase with Cycles. In other words, there should be a Groups × Cycles interaction for the no-shock trials, but no such interaction for the shock trials. The calculation of these simple effects is shown in Table 14.13. The calculation of the appropriate tests is carried out the same way it was earlier, by running a reduced analysis of variance at each level of the Phase variable. Here again we are using separate error terms to test the Shock and No-shock effects, thus reducing problems with the sphericity assumption. Since we still have a within-subjects term in each of our analyses, I have included $\hat{\varepsilon}$ and $\tilde{\varepsilon}$, although the conclusions would not be affected by adjusting the degrees of freedom in this case. (Again, just because the analyses also give simple effects due to Groups and Cycles is no reason to feel an obligation to interpret them. If they don't speak to issues raised by the experimental hypotheses, they should neither be reported nor interpreted unless you take steps to minimize the increase in the experimentwise error rate.)

TABLE 14.13
Simple interaction effects

(a) Within-Subject Effects (Group × Cycle at Phase = 1)

Source	df	SS	MS	F
Between subjects	23	1.2154		
Groups	2	0.0458	0.0229	<1
Ss w/in group	21	1.1696	0.0557	
Within subjects	72	0.5691		
Cycle	3	0.0404	0.0135	1.74
Cycle × Group	6	0.0416	0.0069	<1
Error	63	0.4871	0.0077	
Total	95	1.7845		

$\hat{\varepsilon} = .7971; \tilde{\varepsilon} = .9922$

(b) Within-Subject Effects (Group × Cycle at Phase = 2)

Source	df	SS	MS	F
Between subjects	23	1.4133		
Group	2	0.8213	0.4106	14.57*
Subj w/in group	21	0.5920	0.0282	
Within subjects	72	0.8719		
Cycle	3	0.3065	0.1022	17.03*
Cycle × Group	6	0.1905	0.0318	5.30*
Error	63	0.3749	0.0060	
Total	95	2.2852		

*$p < .05; \hat{\varepsilon} = .7583; \tilde{\varepsilon} = .9363$

From the simple interaction effects of Group × Cycle at each level of Phase, you can see that Bouton and Swartzentruber's predictions were upheld. There is no Cycle × Group interaction on Shock trials, but there is a clear interaction on No-shock trials.

14.9 THREE WITHIN-SUBJECTS VARIABLES

A design that is seldom discussed in the statistical literature but that occurs fairly frequently in practice is one in which every subject serves in every cell. Such designs seem to be particularly prevalent in research areas, such as perception, in which subjects are hard to find but, once found, are particularly dedicated (often they are the experimenter's children or coauthors).

This type of design can be conceptualized in two different ways. We can think of it as a repeated-measures design in which all variables are within-subjects variables. Alternatively, we can think of it as a factorial design in which "Subjects" is a variable—that is, $S \times A \times B \times C$—with one score per cell. We can conceptualize the design as a factorial because every subject is paired with every combination of every other variable. We assume Subjects to be a random variable, although in some cases this involves a major strain on the imagination (especially when the subjects are the experimenter's children).

There are two major possible models underlying this design, and the choice of a model will determine the error terms for the various F ratios. The simplest, but least realistic, model is

$$X_{ijkl} = \mu + \alpha_i + \beta_j + \gamma_k + \alpha\beta_{ij} + \alpha\gamma_{ik} + \beta\gamma_{jk} + \alpha\beta\gamma_{ijk} + \pi_l + e_{ijkl}$$

In this model the experimental variables (A, B, and C) and their interactions are all represented, as is the main effect of Subjects (π_l), but we assume that there are no interactions of the Subject variable with any of the other variables. If these interactions are present, they are confounded with error. If we are willing to adopt this model, which admittedly requires a strong element of faith, the expected mean squares are as given in Table 14.14 (variables A, B, and C are assumed to be fixed).

TABLE 14.14
Expected mean squares for simpler model

Source	df	E(MS)
S	$n - 1$	$\sigma_e^2 + abc\sigma_\pi^2$
A	$a - 1$	$\sigma_e^2 + nbc\sigma_\alpha^2$
B	$b - 1$	$\sigma_e^2 + nac\sigma_\beta^2$
C	$c - 1$	$\sigma_e^2 + nab\sigma_\gamma^2$
AB	$(a - 1)(b - 1)$	$\sigma_e^2 + nc\sigma_{\alpha\beta}^2$
AC	$(a - 1)(c - 1)$	$\sigma_e^2 + nb\sigma_{\alpha\gamma}^2$
BC	$(b - 1)(c - 1)$	$\sigma_e^2 + na\sigma_{\beta\gamma}^2$
ABC	$(a - 1)(b - 1)(c - 1)$	$\sigma_e^2 + n\sigma_{\alpha\beta\gamma}^2$
Residual (Error)	$(n - 1)(abc - 1)$	σ_e^2

A more reasonable model, but one that makes life somewhat more difficult, is given by

$$x_{ijkl} = \mu + \alpha_i + \beta_j + \gamma_k + \alpha\beta_{ij} + \alpha\gamma_{ik} + \beta\gamma_{jk} + \alpha\beta\gamma_{ijk} + \pi_l + \alpha\pi_{il} + \beta\pi_{jl} + \gamma\pi_{kl}$$

$$+ \alpha\beta\pi_{ijl} + \alpha\gamma\pi_{ikl} + \beta\gamma\pi_{jkl} + \alpha\beta\gamma\pi_{ijkl} + e_{ijkl}$$

This model presents a minor problem in that although it contains an error component e_{ijkl}, there is no way to obtain an independent estimate of that component. If Subjects is to be considered a variable, we have only one score per cell, and therefore no within-cell variance. The previous model assumed no interactions with Subjects and could thus use a residual term (that portion of SS_{total} not accounted for by the other terms in the model) as an estimate of error. This amounts to assuming, for example, that $\alpha\pi_{il} = 0$ and therefore $MS_{A \times S}$ can be taken as an estimate of experimental error (actually the residual would be the sum of *all* interactions with Subjects). In the present model, there will not be any residual for estimating error. All is not lost, however, as each of the interactions with Subjects can be shown to serve as a denominator for an F ratio. This can be seen from the expected mean squares for this model given in Table 14.15.

TABLE 14.15
Expected mean
squares for full model

Source	df	E(MS)
S	$n - 1$	
A	$a - 1$	$\sigma_e^2 + bc\sigma_{\alpha\pi}^2 + nbc\sigma_\alpha^2$
$A \times S$	$(a - 1)(n - 1)$	$\sigma_e^2 + bc\sigma_{\alpha\pi}^2$
B	$b - 1$	$\sigma_e^2 + ac\sigma_{\beta\pi}^2 + nac\sigma_\beta^2$
$B \times S$	$(b - 1)(n - 1)$	$\sigma_e^2 + ac\sigma_{\beta\pi}^2$
C	$c - 1$	$\sigma_e^2 + ab\sigma_{\gamma\pi}^2 + nab\sigma_\gamma^2$
$C \times S$	$(c - 1)(n - 1)$	$\sigma_e^2 + ab\sigma_{\gamma\pi}^2$
AB	$(a - 1)(b - 1)$	$\sigma_e^2 + c\sigma_{\alpha\beta\pi}^2 + nc\sigma_{\alpha\beta}^2$
$AB \times S$	$(a - 1)(b - 1)(n - 1)$	$\sigma_e^2 + c\sigma_{\alpha\beta\pi}^2$
AC	$(a - 1)(c - 1)$	$\sigma_e^2 + b\sigma_{\alpha\gamma\pi}^2 + nb\sigma_{\alpha\gamma}^2$
$AC \times S$	$(a - 1)(c - 1)(n - 1)$	$\sigma_e^2 + b\sigma_{\alpha\gamma\pi}^2$
BC	$(b - 1)(c - 1)$	$\sigma_e^2 + a\sigma_{\beta\gamma\pi}^2 + na\sigma_{\beta\gamma}^2$
$BC \times S$	$(b - 1)(c - 1)(n - 1)$	$\sigma_e^2 + a\sigma_{\beta\gamma\pi}^2$
ABC	$(a - 1)(b - 1)(c - 1)$	$\sigma_e^2 + \sigma_{\alpha\beta\gamma\pi}^2 + n\sigma_{\alpha\beta\gamma}^2$
$ABC \times S$	$(a - 1)(b - 1)(c - 1)(n - 1)$	$\sigma_e^2 + \sigma_{\alpha\beta\gamma\pi}^2$

It is evident from the expected mean squares that each effect to be tested has its own error term. Thus, every effect is tested by the interaction of that effect with the Subject effect. MS_S cannot be tested under this model, but this is seldom a problem.

The relationship between the two models becomes clearer when we see that $SS_{residual}$ in the first model can be seen as

$$SS_{residual} = SS_{A \times S} + SS_{B \times S} + SS_{C \times S} + SS_{AB \times S} + SS_{AC \times S} + SS_{BC \times S} + SS_{ABC \times S}$$

and thus represents a pooling of the several sources of error variance. If the assumption behind the first model (that the Subject variable does not interact with any of the other variables) is reasonable, then the residual or pooled error term is the appropriate denominator for all Fs. If the assumption is not reasonable, then using the residual term would provide a negatively biased (conservative) test. In general, the full model is preferred to the reduced model, although in some cases this leads to Fs on relatively few degrees of freedom. [Tukey (1949) developed a test for additivity for testing whether the reduced model is appropriate; see Winer (1971, p. 394) or Kirk (1968, p. 137).]

As an example of a study involving repeated measures on all variables, we will again use the driving data from Section 14.7, this time assuming that there were only three subjects, each subject serving in all cells. For convenience we will denote Time as A, Course as B, and Size as C. Subject effects are denoted by S. Since most of the calculations should be familiar by now, only the calculation of the $SS_{A \times S}$ term will be shown as an illustration. By this time, you should be able to carry out the rest of the calculations on your own.

From the raw data in Table 14.7 we find the following $A \times S$ table of cells totals for our revised design:

	A_1	A_2	Total
S_1	61	27	88
S_2	53	25	78
S_3	42	17	59
Total	156	69	225

We already know from Table 14.7 that $SS_A = 140.17$. For our new design,

$$SS_S = \frac{\Sigma T_{S_i}^2}{abc} - \frac{(\Sigma X)^2}{n} = 961.61 - 937.50 = 24.11$$

$$SS_{\text{cells } A \times S} = \frac{\Sigma T_{AS_{il}}^2}{bc} - \frac{(\Sigma X)^2}{n} = 1104.11 - 937.50 = 166.61$$

$$SS_{A \times S} = SS_{\text{cells } A \times S} - SS_A - SS_S = 166.61 - 140.17 - 24.11 = 2.33$$

TABLE 14.16
Summary table for design with repeated measures on all variables

Source	df	SS	MS	F
S	2	24.11		
A	1	140.17	140.17	119.80*
$A \times S$	2	2.33	1.17	
B	2	56.78	28.39	946.33*
$B \times S$	4	0.11	0.03	
C	2	51.44	25.72	91.86*
$C \times S$	4	1.12	0.28	
AB	2	5.44	2.72	2.08
$AB \times S$	4	5.23	1.31	
AC	2	16.78	8.39	38.14*
$AC \times S$	4	0.88	0.22	
BC	4	8.78	2.20	3.79
$BC \times S$	8	4.66	0.58	
ABC	4	2.78	0.70	1.94
$ABC \times S$	8	2.89	0.36	
Total	53	323.50		

*$p < .05$

The calculation of $SS_{A \times S}$ illustrates that the error terms in this design are calculated just as in any other interaction. The resulting summary table for the analysis is given in Table 14.16. From the summary table, we see that the three main effects (A, B, and C) are significant, as is the AC interaction. The analysis of simple effects follows the logic established in earlier designs.

14.10   OTHER CONSIDERATIONS

SEQUENCE EFFECTS

Sequence effects, Carryover effects

Repeated-measures designs are notoriously susceptible to **sequence effects** and **carryover** (practice) **effects**. Whenever the possibility that exposure to one treatment will influence the effect of another treatment exists, the experimenter should consider very seriously before deciding to use a repeated-measures design. In certain studies, carryover effects are desirable. In learning studies, for example, the basic data represent what is carried over from one trial to another. In most situations, however, carryover effects (and especially differential carryover effects) are considered a nuisance—something to be avoided.

Latin square

The statistical theory of repeated-measures designs assumes that the order of administration is randomized separately for each subject. In some situations, however, it makes more sense to assign testing sequences by means of a **latin square** or some other device. Although this violates the assumption of randomization, in some situations the gains outweigh the losses. What is important, however, is that random assignment, latin squares, and so on do not in themselves eliminate sequence effects. Ignoring analyses in which the data are analyzed by means of a latin square or a related statistical procedure, any system of assignment simply distributes sequence and carryover effects across the cells of the design, with luck lumping them into the error term(s). The phrase "with luck" implies that if this does not happen, the carryover effects will be confounded with treatment effects and the results will be very difficult, if not impossible, to interpret. For those students particularly interested in examining sequence effects, Winer (1971), Kirk (1968) and Cochran and Cox (1957) present excellent discussions of latin square and related designs.

UNEQUAL GROUP SIZES

One of the pleasant features of repeated-measures designs is that when a subject fails to arrive for an experiment, it usually means that that subject is missing from every cell in which he was to serve. This has the effect of keeping the cell sizes proportional, even if unequal. From this it follows that the solution for proportionally unequal sample sizes is possible, if the experimenter thinks the solution's treatment of sample sizes is appropriate. Otherwise, the unweighted-means solution is available, and probably preferable, for most cases. If you are so unlucky as to have a subject for whom you have partial data, the best procedure would probably be to eliminate that subject from the analysis. If, however, only one or two scores are missing, it is possible to replace them with estimates, and in many cases this is a satisfactory approach. For a discussion of this topic, see Federer (1955, pp. 125–126, 133ff).

MATCHED SAMPLES AND RELATED PROBLEMS

Randomized blocks designs

Matched samples

In discussing repeated-measures designs, we have spoken in terms of repeated measurements on the same subject. Although this represents the most common instance of the use of these designs, it is not the only one. The specific fact that a subject is tested several times really has nothing to do with the matter. Technically, what distinguishes repeated-measures designs (or, more generally, **randomized blocks designs**, of which repeated-measures designs are a special case) from the common factorial designs with equal *n*s is the fact that for repeated-measures designs, the off-diagonal elements of Σ do not have an expectancy of zero—that is, the treatments are correlated. Repeated use of the same subject leads to such correlations, but so does use of **matched samples** of subjects. Thus, for example, if we formed 10 sets of three subjects each, with the subjects matched on driving experience, and then set up an experiment in which the first subject under each treatment came from the same matched triad, we would have correlations among treatments and would thus have a repeated-measures design. Any other data-collection procedure leading to nonzero correlations (or covariances) could also be treated as a repeated-measures design.

14.11   A COMPUTER ANALYSIS USING A TRADITIONAL APPROACH

BMDP2V is a convenient package to use for running repeated-measures analyses. An abbreviated form of a BMDP analysis is shown in Exhibit 14.1 for the data from Table 14.4. Notice that the analysis contains a test of sphericity on the matrix of the orthogonal components of error and computes both the Greenhouse and Geisser $\hat{\varepsilon}$ and the Huynh and Feldt $\tilde{\varepsilon}$. (I have chosen to ignore the matrix of orthogonal components of error because of the complexity of the explanation, but the sphericity test on that matrix is a test of the necessary assumption of sphericity.) Alternatively, you can use one of the programs shown in Section 14.12 on MANOVA. Although the printout is somewhat more difficult to read, you do have the advantage of seeing the values for both the MANOVA and standard repeated-measures procedure. As long as you are looking at overall effects (or simple effects with separate error terms), I suggest relying on the standard design with correction for degrees of freedom.

EXHIBIT 14.1
BMDP2V analysis of
data from Table 14.4

PROGRAM INSTRUCTIONS

/PROGRAM	TITLE IS 'ANALYSIS OF KING"S DATA ON AMBULATION'.
/INPUT	VARIABLES ARE 7.
	FORMAT IS '(F1.0, 6F4.0)'.
	CASES ARE 24.
	FILE IS 'KING.DAT'.
/VARIABLE	NAMES ARE GROUP, I1, I2, I3, I4, I5, I6.
/DESIGN	DEPENDENT ARE I1, I2, I3, I4, I5, I6.
	LEVELS ARE 6.
	NAME IS INTERVAL.
	SYMMETRY.
	GROUPS = GROUP.
/END	

PROBLEM TITLE IS ANALYSIS OF KING"S DATA ON AMBULATION

SUMS OF SQUARES AND CORRELATION MATRIX OF THE
ORTHOGONAL COMPONENTS POOLED FOR ERROR 2 IN ANOVA TABLE BELOW.

83359.74107	1.000				
57596.75893	0.539	1.000			
66040.72917	0.007	-0.121	1.000		
48399.74107	-0.556	0.039	-0.128	1.000	
25802.34226	0.320	0.195	0.201	-0.309	1.000

SPHERICITY TEST APPLIED TO ORTHOGONAL COMPONENTS - TAIL PROBABILITY 0.0088

CELL MEANS FOR 1-ST DEPENDENT VARIABLE

					MARGINAL
GROUP =		*1	*2	*3	
INTERVAL					
I1	1	213.87500	354.62500	290.12500	286.20833
I2	2	93.25000	266.25000	98.25000	152.58333
I3	3	96.50000	221.00000	108.50000	142.00000
I4	4	128.62500	170.00000	109.00000	135.87500
I5	5	122.87500	198.62500	123.50000	148.33333
I6	6	130.12500	178.62500	138.62500	149.12500
MARGINAL		130.87500	231.52083	144.66667	169.02083
COUNT		8	8	8	24

STANDARD DEVIATIONS FOR 1-ST DEPENDENT VARIABLE

GROUP =		*1	*2	*3
INTERVAL				
I1	1	79.21118	89.91415	69.32210
I2	2	93.27341	109.68754	53.47563
I3	3	54.10308	69.88153	62.66236
I4	4	70.31346	78.10798	52.52754
I5	5	65.24117	66.22243	50.10275
I6	6	74.54708	83.59415	56.01514

ANALYSIS OF VARIANCE FOR 1-ST DEPENDENT VARIABLE - I1 I2 I3 I4 I5 I6

SOURCE	SUM OF SQUARES	D.F.	MEAN SQUARE	F	TAIL PROB.	GREENHOUSE GEISSER PROB.	HUYNH FELDT PROB.
MEAN	4113798.06250	1	4113798.06250	224.55	0.0000		
Group	285815.04167	2	142907.52083	7.80	0.0029		
1 ERROR	384722.06250	21	18320.09821				
Interval	399736.56250	5	79947.31250	29.85	0.0000	0.0000	0.0000
IG	80819.95833	10	8081.99583	3.02	0.0022	0.0092	0.0038
2 ERROR	281199.31250	105	2678.08869				

ERROR TERM	EPSILON FACTORS FOR DEGREES OF FREEDOM ADJUSTMENT	
	GREENHOUSE-GEISSER	HUYNH-FELDT
2	0.6569	0.8674

14.12   MULTIVARIATE ANALYSIS OF VARIANCE FOR REPEATED-MEASURES DESIGNS

Earlier in the chapter I said that the standard repeated-measures analysis of variance requires an assumption about the variance–covariance matrix known as *sphericity*, a specific form of which is known as *compound symmetry*. When we discussed $\hat{\varepsilon}$ and $\tilde{\varepsilon}$, we were concerned with correction factors that we could apply to the degrees of freedom to circumvent some of the problems associated with a failure of the sphericity assumption.

There is a considerable literature on repeated-measures analyses and their robustness in the face of violations of the underlying assumptions. Although there is not universal agreement that the adjustments proposed by Greenhouse and Geisser and by Huynh and Feldt are successful, the adjustments work reasonably well as long as we stick to overall main or interaction effects. Where we encounter serious trouble is when we try to run individual contrasts or simple effects analyses. Boik (1981) has shown that in these cases the repeated-measures analysis is remarkably sensitive to violations of the sphericity assumption unless we adopt separate error terms for each contrast. In several sections of this chapter I have indicated how to obtain those separate error terms.

A number of authors have suggested that we would be much further ahead if we used the multivariate analysis of variance (MANOVA) to analyze data having repeated measurements. MANOVA is considerably more complex and in some cases has less power, especially for studies with small numbers of observations, than a repeated-measures analysis, but it does not require the restrictive assumption of sphericity. Although not all authors agree that MANOVA is generally preferable to the standard repeated-measures analysis, psychologists can no longer continue to ignore that more complex approach in the hopes that it will go away. This section is designed to provide only an introduction to the topic, but I have included enough material to allow you to do meaningful analyses.

A multivariate analysis of variance is basically an analysis of variance that deals with more than one dependent variable at the same time. In the most common type of multivariate analysis of variance, we might wish to compare three groups differing with respect to the type of therapy they received, on four different measures of depression. In this case each subject has a score on each depression measure, and we want to treat those four scores in the same analysis rather than running a separate analysis of variance on each measure. A second example of MANOVA, and the one to be elaborated on in this chapter, is the specific case in which the multiple dependent variables are, originally, repeated measurements as we normally think of that term (e.g., trials). In particular, I am assuming that you have measured the same dependent variable at multiple points in time, and that you wish to deal primarily with how that variable changes over time.

Essentially you can think of MANOVA as extracting a linear combination of the dependent variables (which is optimal in some sense) and applying a standard analysis of variance to that linear composite. How those linear composites are obtained and how the significance test is evaluated is beyond the scope of this book, but I will attempt to provide a simple example to illustrate the basic approach. More complete coverage can be found in Harris (1985) and Tabachnik and Fidell (1989) (see particularly their chapter on profile analysis). A very good nontechnical discussion can be found in O'Brien and Kaiser (1985). Most of the textbook discussions are designed to provide a thorough understanding of the logic behind the tests and the possibilities that exist for structuring contrasts to ask meaningful questions. However, many of the standard computer programs have defaults that make setting up the analysis considerably easier than the discussions might lead you to expect. In particular, SAS, SPSS^X, and BMDP4V allow you to obtain the MANOVA results in what looks more like a standard repeated-measures summary table, without going through most of the calculations discussed below. (BMDP4V will even print out the results of the standard unadjusted approach, the Greenhouse and Geisser and Huynh and Feldt corrections, and the MANOVA procedure in the same summary table.) However, it is worth taking the time to understand the underlying process because you can run more powerful analyses if you carefully design them to address the questions of interest to you.

We will use the example of drug tolerance and ambulatory behavior found in Table 14.4. A tempting approach to the data would be to enter them into a data set with an entry representing group membership, and then to run a straightforward MANOVA on the data, treating the different intervals as different dependent variables. But this analysis would not really address the most important questions. It would simply ask if the three groups differed on the set of dependent variables. It would not get at differences among the different dependent variables (Intervals), nor would it get at the Group $\times$ Interval interaction, which is probably the most interesting effect. We are going to need to restructure the data in such a way as to get at all three effects.

One of the things we are most interested in with this experiment is change over time. Therefore, we will start by creating new variables that represent the amount of change from interval to interval. For example, define

$$\text{Diff}_1 = \text{Interval}_2 - \text{Interval}_1$$

$$\text{Diff}_2 = \text{Interval}_3 - \text{Interval}_2$$

$$\cdots$$

$$\text{Diff}_5 = \text{Interval}_6 - \text{Interval}_5$$

Each of these new change or difference variables measures how much change has taken place at each interval, and the set can be used to directly assess the Group $\times$ Interval interaction. Suppose that there is no interaction. Then each group will change just as much as any other group during a particular time period. The means on the original variables don't have to remain constant from interval to interval, and if there is an Interval effect, they won't. However, if there is no interaction, each group would be expected to show as much, or as little, change as every other group. In other words, in the absence of an interaction there would be no Group effect for the change scores. Group differences on the *change* scores really represent our test for interaction.

The difference scores also offer a test on the Interval effect. If there is no effect due to Interval, then we would expect the mean change from one interval to another to be 0.0. Thus, in the absence of an Interval effect, the grand mean of the change scores would be 0. All we need to do is test H_0: $\mu = 0$, where μ represents the Grand Mean. Such a test is provided by an F on the correction factor $[(\Sigma X)^2/N]$. In Section 11.11 we saw that such a test was found in BMDP by the MEAN effect. In other programs it is called the CONSTANT, or INTERCEPT, effect. In the SAS program that accompanies this example, the /Intercept command forces just such a test.

Using the difference scores, we have found ways to test both of the within-subjects terms. The only term left is the Group difference, which is our only between-subjects effect. As you might suspect, the Group effect is a test on group differences in the average score that each person received. In other words, we average over the six intervals. The simplest way to do this is to create one more variable called Average:

$$\text{Average} = \frac{\text{Interval}_1 + \text{Interval}_2 + \cdots + \text{Interval}_5 + \text{Interval}_6}{6}$$

Univariate

We now ask if there is a difference between the six groups on Average. This test requires a separate analysis, however. Since each subject has only one score (Average), we could use a simple **univariate** one-way analysis of variance. (An analysis of variance with only one dependent variable is often referred to as a univariate analysis, in contrast to the multivariate analysis of variance with multiple dependent variables.) However, for continuity I have used the MANOVA procedure. The final F value would be the same whichever was used.

A short SAS program to accomplish these analyses would look like the one in Exhibit 14.2. You can see that the additional variables are computed in the Data step. For a discussion of the MANOVA statement, see the SAS user's manual. The command "Nouni" appended to that statement suppresses the printing of univariate analyses for each of the three dependent variables. Without that command we would be presented with tests of group difference on Diff 1, Diff 2, ..., Diff 5 separately. I will say more about these univariate tests shortly.

EXHIBIT 14.2
MANOVA program for analysis of data in Table 14.4

```
Data KingData;
    Infile 'King.dat';
    Input Group   Int1   Int2   Int3   Int4   Int5   Int6;
    Diff1 = Int2 - Int1;    Diff2 = Int3 - Int2;    Diff3 = Int4 - Int3;
    Diff4 = Int5 - Int4;    Diff5 = Int6 - Int5;
    Average = (Int1 + Int2 + Int3 + Int4 + Int5 + Int6)/6;
Run;
Proc GLM Data = KingData;
    Class Group;
    Model  Diff1   Diff2   Diff3   Diff4   Diff5 = Group / Intercept Nouni;
    MANOVA H = _ALL_/Short;
Run;
Proc GLM Data = KingData;
    Class Group;
    Model Average = Group;
    Manova H = _ALL_/Short;
Run;
```

The results from this analysis are presented in very truncated form in Exhibit 14.3. For each effect you will see four separate test statistics, and for the interaction effect there are four different values of F, depending upon which statistic you chose. Although Harris (1985) has argued strongly for the greatest characteristic root (Roy's) statistic, the literature generally appears to support the use of Pillai's trace. In our case it doesn't really matter, because each of these would lead to the same conclusion. We will reject all three null hypotheses and conclude that there is a significant Group effect, a significant Interval effect, and a significant Group × Interval interaction. These are the same conclusions that we reached in conjunction with the analysis in Table 14.4, but the magnitudes of the F values for the within-subjects components are noticeably different. The F for Intervals has dropped from 29.85 to 19.11, whereas the F for the Group × Interval interaction has dropped from 3.02 to 2.17 (using Pillai's trace statistic). Earlier I pointed out that if we took the most conservative approach to possible violations of sphericity and evaluated the interaction on $(g - 1)$ and $g(n - 1)$ df, we would have declared it nonsignificant, whereas when we calculated $\hat{\varepsilon}$ and $\tilde{\varepsilon}$ the effect was significant. Here we have a test that does not depend on the validity of the sphericity assumption and it too tells us that the difference is significant. The finding is somewhat reassuring. Notice that the F on the between-subjects term is unchanged, as it should be. In fact, there is no reason why we could not have left off the final MANOVA command and run this as a straight analysis of variance, since there was only one dependent variable.

EXHIBIT 14.3
Output of MANOVA program for analysis of data in Table 14.4

(a) Test of Interval Effect

GENERAL LINEAR MODELS PROCEDURE

MANOVA TEST CRITERIA AND EXACT F STATISTICS FOR
THE HYPOTHESIS OF NO OVERALL INTERCEPT EFFECT

S=1   M=1.5   N=8

STATISTIC	VALUE	F	NUM DF	DEN DF	PR > F
WILKS' LAMBDA	0.1510417	19.110	5	17	0.0001
PILLAI'S TRACE	0.8489583	19.110	5	17	0.0001
HOTELLING-LAWLEY TRACE	5.620688	19.110	5	17	0.0001
ROY'S GREATEST ROOT	5.620688	19.110	5	17	0.0001

(b) Test of Group × Interval

MANOVA TEST CRITERIA AND F APPROXIMATIONS FOR
THE HYPOTHESIS OF NO OVERALL GROUP EFFECT

S=2   M=1   N=8

STATISTIC	VALUE	F	NUM DF	DEN DF	PR > F
WILKS' LAMBDA	0.3665217	2.216	10	34	0.0411
PILLAI'S TRACE	0.752845	2.173	10	36	0.0433
HOTELLING-LAWLEY TRACE	1.402677	2.244	10	32	0.0405
ROY'S GREATEST ROOT	1.109017	3.992	5	18	0.0130

NOTE: F STATISTIC FOR ROY'S GREATEST ROOT IS AN UPPER BOUND
F STATISTIC FOR WILKS' LAMBDA IS EXACT

(c) Test of Group Effect

MANOVA TEST CRITERIA AND EXACT F STATISTICS FOR
THE HYPOTHESIS OF NO OVERALL GROUP EFFECT

S=1   M=0   N=10

STATISTIC	VALUE	F	NUM DF	DEN DF	PR > F
WILKS' LAMBDA	0.5737521	7.801	2	21	0.0029
PILLAI'S TRACE	0.4262479	7.801	2	21	0.0029
HOTELLING-LAWLEY TRACE	0.7429131	7.801	2	21	0.0029
ROY'S GREATEST ROOT	0.7429131	7.801	2	21	0.0029

SIMPLE EFFECTS

In our previous analysis of these data, we looked at simple effects to try to understand better what the significant F values mean. We can do the same thing with MANOVA, and in some ways it is easier. Looking first at the interaction term, we can pull it apart in several different ways. In the first place we could run the MANOVA analysis separately for each of the groups, checking for an Interval effect. We could do this either by feeding in separate sets of data to each analysis or, for SAS, by adding "By Groups" in the Proc GLM statement. We would remove the Class statement and the word "Group " from the Model statement, leaving only a test of the intercept. Alternatively, we could examine the interaction by removing the "Nouni" statement from the MANOVA statement. This would provide us with separate univariate analyses of group differences for Diff 1, Diff 2, ..., Diff 5. To go even further, we could revert to the original variables (e.g., Int1) in place of the difference scores and ask for univariate analyses on them. Each of these analyses would give us meaningful information on the interaction.

son procedures on either variable. This is particularly easy on between-subjects variables such as Group because those effects are tested as in a standard analysis of variance.

In creating the variables labeled Diff 1, Diff 2, ..., Diff 5, I was using only one way of contrasting the levels of the original Interval variable. In effect I was using a set of contrasts of the form

$$[1 \quad -1 \quad 0 \quad 0 \quad 0 \quad 0]$$
$$[0 \quad 1 \quad -1 \quad 0 \quad 0 \quad 0]$$
$$[0 \quad 0 \quad 1 \quad -1 \quad 0 \quad 0]$$
$$\cdots$$

For example,

$$\text{Diff 1} = 1(\text{Int1}) - 1(\text{Int2}) + 0(\text{Int3}) + 0(\text{Int4}) + 0(\text{Int5}) + 0(\text{Int6})$$
$$\text{Diff 2} = 0(\text{Int1}) + 1(\text{Int2}) - 1(\text{Int3}) + 0(\text{Int4}) + 0(\text{Int5}) + 0(\text{Int6})$$

and so on. I could have broken the intervals up using a number of alternative contrast procedures. For example, I could have created new variables that would compare each interval with all of those that came after by using coefficients of the form

$$[5 \quad -1 \quad -1 \quad -1 \quad -1 \quad -1]$$
$$[0 \quad 4 \quad -1 \quad -1 \quad -1 \quad -1]$$
$$[0 \quad 0 \quad 3 \quad -1 \quad -1 \quad -1]$$
$$\cdots$$

or comparing each interval with the first by using the coefficients

$$[1 \quad -1 \quad 0 \quad 0 \quad 0 \quad 0]$$
$$[1 \quad 0 \quad -1 \quad 0 \quad 0 \quad 0]$$
$$[1 \quad 0 \quad 0 \quad -1 \quad 0 \quad 0]$$
$$\cdots$$

Each of these ways of forming contrasts would produce the same overall test statistics for main effects and interaction, but would speak to different questions when we look at the univariate tests. To see tests on these individual contrasts, we would simply ask for the univariate test statistics by dropping the "/Nouni" command.

THE SIMPLIFIED APPROACH

After explaining at some length how you can run your repeated-measures analysis of variance using transformed variables and MANOVA, I should point out that there is a simpler way. The problem with the simpler approach is that it does not provide you with a quick way of making tests on simple effects and contrasts. Moreover, such procedures are not available on all statistical packages.

It is not feasible to give worked examples using each statistical package, but Exhibit 14.4 shows the commands for running MANOVA on repeated measures using SAS, BMDP4V, and SPSS^X. In each case you should see the appropriate manual for more explanation. Each of these programs will give both the standard univariate tests and the multivariate ones for repeated measures and their interactions.

EXHIBIT 14.4
Simple programs for MANOVA analyses of repeated measures designs

(a) **SAS**

```
Data KingData;
      Infile 'Manova.dat';
      Input   Group  Int1  Int2  Int3  Int4  Int5  Int6;
Run;

Proc GLM Data = KingData;          /* This runs the overall analysis.*/
      Class Group;
      Model Int1 - Int6 = Group / Intercept Nouni;
      Repeated Interval 6 / Short;
Run;

Proc GLM Data = KingData;          /* This will do simple effects of Intervals at Group.*/
      By Group;
      Model Int1 - Int6 = Group / Intercept Nouni;
      Repeated Interval 6 ;
Run;
```

(b) **BMDP**

```
/Problem        Title is 'BMDP4V Analysis of King"s Data.'.
/Comment        'Requires BMDP4V'.
/Input          Variables are 7.
                Format is Free.
                Cases are 24.
                File is 'Manova.dat'.
/Variable       Names are  Group,  Int1,  Int2,  Int3,  Int4,  Int5,  Int6.
/Between        Factor is Group.
                Codes are 1, 2, 3.
                Names are  Control,  Same,  Different.
/Within         Factor is Interval.
                Codes are  1 to 6.
                Names are  Interval1,  Interval2,  Interval3,  Interval4,
                Interval5,   Interval6.
/Weights        Between are Equal.
                Within are Equal.
/End
Analysis        Procedure is Factorial./
```

EXHIBIT 14.4 (Cont.) **(c) SPSS^X**

Title	'SPSSX Run on King''s Data'
File Handle	Data/Name = 'Manova.dat'
Data List	File = Data Free/
	Group, Int1, Int2, Int3, Int4, Int5, Int6
Manova	Int1 to Int6 by Group (1,3)/
	WSFactor = Interval (6)/
	WSDesign = Interval

KEY TERMS

Partition (introduction)

Partialling out (introduction)

Repeated-measures designs (introduction)

$SS_{between subj}$ (SS_S) (introduction)

$SS_{within subj}$ (introduction)

Main diagonal (14.3)

Off-diagonal elements (14.3)

Compound symmetry (14.3)

Covariance matrix (Σ) (14.3)

Sphericity (14.3)

Multivariate analysis of variance (MANOVA) (14.3)

Multivariate procedure (14.3)

$Error_{between}$ (14.5)

$Error_{within}$ (14.5)

Sequence effects (14.10)

Carryover effects (14.10)

Latin square (14.10)

Randomized blocks designs (14.10)

Matched samples (14.10)

Univariate (14.12)

EXERCISES

14.1   It is at least part of the folklore that repeated experience with the Graduate Record Examination (GRE) leads to better scores, even without any intervening study. We obtain eight subjects and give them the GRE verbal exam every Saturday morning for 3 weeks. The data follow:

S	First	Second	Third
1	550	575	580
2	440	440	470
3	610	630	610
4	650	670	670
5	400	460	450
6	700	680	710
7	490	510	515
8	580	550	590

(a) Write the statistical model for these data.

(b) Run the analysis of variance.

(c) What, if anything, would you conclude about practice effects on the GRE?

14.2   Using the data from Exercise 14.1,

(a) delete the data for the third session and run a (matched-sample) *t* test between sessions 1 and 2.

(b) Now run a repeated-measures analysis of variance on the two columns you used in (a) and compare this F with the preceding t.

14.3 To demonstrate the practical uses of basic learning principles, a psychologist with an interest in behavior modification collected data on a study designed to teach self-care skills to severely retarded children. An experimental group received reinforcement for activities related to self-care. A second group received an equivalent amount of attention, but no reinforcement. The children were scored (blind) by a rater on a 10-point scale of self-sufficiency. The ratings were done in a baseline session and at the end of training. The data follow:

Experimental Group		Control Group		
Baseline	Training	Baseline	Training	
8	9	3	5	
5	7	5	5	
3	2	8	10	
5	7	2	5	
2	9	5	3	
6	7	6	10	
5	8	6	9	
6	5	4	5	
4	7	3	7	
4	9	5	5	

(handwritten annotations: $\Sigma D = -22$, $\Sigma D^2 = 104$, $\bar{D} = -2.2$, $s^2 = 6.1778$, $SD = 2.4855$; for control: $\Sigma D = -7$, $\Sigma D^2 = 63$, $\bar{D} = -.7$, $s^2 = 6.4556$, $SD = 2.5048$)

Run the appropriate analysis and state your conclusions.

14.4 An experimenter with only a modicum of statistical training took the data in Exercise 14.3 and ran an independent-groups t test instead, using the difference scores (training minus baseline) as the raw data.
(a) Run that analysis.
(b) Square the value of t and compare it to the Fs you obtained in Exercise 14.3.
(c) Explain why t^2 is not equal to F for Groups.

14.5 To understand just what happened in the experiment involving the training of severely retarded children (Exercise 14.3), our original experimenter evaluated a third group at the same times as he did the first two groups, but otherwise treated them just like all other residents of the training school. In other words, these children did not receive reinforcement, or even the extra attention that the control group did. Their data follow:

Baseline: 3 5 8 5 5 6 6 6 3 4
Training: 4 5 6 6 4 7 7 3 2 2

(a) Add these data to those in Exercise 14.3 and rerun the analysis.
(b) Plot the results.
(c) What can you conclude from the results you obtained in (a) and (b)?

14.6 For 2 years I carried on a running argument with my daughter concerning hand calculators. She wanted one. I maintained that children who use calculators never learn to do arithmetic correctly, whereas she maintained that they do. To settle the argument, we selected five of her classmates who had calculators and five who did not, and made a totally unwarranted assumption that the presence or absence of calculators was all that distinguished these children. We then gave each child three 10-point tests (addition, subtraction, and multiplication), which they were required to do in a very short time in their heads. The scores are as follows:

	Addition	**Subtraction**	**Multiplication**
Calculator owners	8 $\Sigma X = 38$ 7 $\Sigma X^2 = 294$ 9 $\bar{X} = 7.6$ 6 $s^2 = 1.3$ 8 $SD = 1.1402$	5 $\Sigma X = 25$ 5 $\Sigma X^2 = 133$ 7 $\bar{X} = 5$ 3 $s^2 = 2$ 5 $SD = 1.4142$	3 $\Sigma X = 10$ 2 $\Sigma X^2 = 24$ $\bar{X} =$ 3 $\bar{X} = 2$ 8.66 1 $s^2 = 1$ 1 $SD = 1$
Non–calculator owners	10 $\Sigma X = 41$ 7 $\Sigma X^2 = 347$ 6 $\bar{X} = 8.2$ 9 $s^2 = 2.7$ 9 $SD = 1.6432$	7 $\Sigma X = 31$ 6 $\Sigma X^2 = 195$ 5 $\bar{X} = 6.2$ 7 $s^2 = 0.7$ 6 $SD = .8367$	6 $\Sigma X = 33$ 5 $\Sigma X^2 = 231$ $\bar{X} =$ 5 $\bar{X} = 6.6$ 7 8 $s^2 = 3.3$ 9 $SD = 1.8166$

$\bar{X} = 7.9$ $\bar{X} = 5.6$ $\bar{X} = 4.3$

(a) Run the analysis of variance.

(b) Do the data suggest that I should have given in and bought my daughter a calculator? (I did anyway.)

$GM = 5.9333$

14.7 For the data in Exercise 14.6,
(a) calculate the variance–covariance matrices.
(b) calculate $\hat{\varepsilon}$ using your answers to (a).

14.8 From the results in Exercise 14.7, do we appear to have reason to believe that we have met the assumptions required for the analysis of repeated measures?

14.9 For the data in Exercise 14.6,
(a) calculate all possible simple effects after first plotting the results.
(b) test the simple effects, calculating test terms and adjusted degrees of freedom where necessary.

14.10 In a study of the way children and adults summarize stories, we selected 10 fifth graders and 10 adults. These were further subdivided into equal groups of good and poor readers (on the hypothesis that good and poor readers may store or retrieve story information differently). All subjects read 10 short stories and were asked to summarize the story in their own words immediately after reading it. All summaries were content analyzed, and the numbers of statements related to settings, goals, and inferred dispositions were recorded. The data are collapsed across the 10 stories:

Age	**Adults**			**Children**		
Items	Setting	Goal	Disp.	Setting	Goal	Disp.
Good readers	8	7	6	5	5	2
	5	6	4	7	8	4
	5	5	5	7	7	4
	7	8	6	6	4	3
	6	4	4	4	4	2
Poor readers	7	6	3	2	2	2
	5	3	1	2	0	1
	6	6	2	5	4	1
	4	4	1	4	4	2
	5	5	3	2	2	0

Run the appropriate analysis.

14.11   Refer to Exercise 14.10.
(a) Calculate the simple effect of reading ability for children.
(b) Calculate the simple effect of items for adult good readers.

14.12   Calculate the within-groups covariance matrices for the data in Exercise 14.10.

14.13   Suppose we had instructed our subjects to limit their summaries to 10 words. What effect might that have on the data in Exercise 14.10?

14.14   In an investigation of cigarette smoking, an experimenter decided to compare three different procedures for quitting smoking (tapering off, immediate stopping, and aversion therapy). She took five subjects in each group and asked them to rate (on a 10-point scale) their desire to smoke "right now" in two different environments (home versus work) both before and after quitting. Thus, we have one between-subjects variable (Treatment group) and two within-subjects variables (Environment and Pre/Post).

	Pre		Post	
	Home	Work	Home	Work
Taper	7	6	6	4
	5	4	5	2
	8	7	7	4
	8	8	6	5
	6	5	5	3
Immediate	8	7	7	6
	5	5	5	4
	7	6	6	5
	8	7	6	5
	7	6	5	4
Aversion	9	8	5	4
	4	4	3	2
	7	7	5	3
	7	5	5	0
	8	7	6	3

(a) Run the appropriate analysis of variance.
(b) Interpret the results.

14.15   Plot the results you obtained in Exercise 14.14.

14.16   Run simple effects on the data in Exercise 14.14 to clarify the results.

14.17   The abbreviated BMDP printout in Exhibit 14.5 represents the analysis of the data in Exercise 14.5.
(a) Compare this printout with the results you obtained in Exercise 14.5.
(b) What does a significant F for "MEAN" tell us?
(c) Relate $MS_{w/in\ cell}$ to the table of cell standard deviations.

14.18   The $SPSS^X$ printout in Exhibit 14.6 was obtained by treating the data in Exercise 14.10 *as though* all variables were between-subjects variables (i.e., as though the data represented a standard three-way factorial). Show that the error terms for the correct analysis represent a partition of the error term for the factorial analysis.

14.19   Outline the summary table for an $A \times B \times C \times D$ design with repeated measures on A and B and independent measures on C and D.

EXHIBIT 14.5   BMDP2V - ANALYSIS OF VARIANCE AND COVARIANCES WITH REPEATED MEASURES.

PROGRAM CONTROL INFORMATION

```
/PROBLEM        TITLE IS  'BMDP2V ANALYSIS OF EXERCISE 14.5'.
/INPUT          VARIABLES ARE  3.
                FORMAT IS  '(3F2.0)'.
                CASES ARE  30.
/VARIABLE       NAMES ARE  GROUP, PRE, POST.
/DESIGN         DEPENDENT ARE  2,3.
                LEVELS ARE  2.
                NAME IS  TIME.
                GROUP = 1.
/END
```

CELL MEANS FOR 1-ST DEPENDENT VARIABLE

		GROUP =	* 1.0000	* 2.0000	* 3.0000	MARGINAL
		TIME				
PRE	1		4.80000	4.70000	5.10000	4.86667
POST	2		7.00000	6.40000	4.60000	6.00000
MARGINAL			5.90000	5.55000	4.85000	5.43333
COUNT			10	10	10	30

STANDARD DEVIATIONS FOR 1-ST DEPENDENT VARIABLE

		GROUP =	* 1.0000	* 2.0000	* 3.0000
		TIME			
PRE	1		1.68655	1.76698	1.52388
POST	2		2.16025	2.45855	1.89737

ANALYSIS OF VARIANCE FOR 1-ST
DEPENDENT VARIABLE - PRE POST

	SOURCE	SUM OF SQUARES	DEGREES OF FREEDOM	MEAN SQUARE	F	TAIL PROBABILITY
	MEAN	1771.26667	1	1771.26667	322.48	0.0000
	GROUP	11.43333	2	5.71667	1.04	0.3669
1	ERROR	148.30000	27	5.49259		
	TIME	19.26667	1	19.26667	9.44	0.0048
	TG	20.63333	2	10.31667	5.06	0.0137
2	ERROR	55.10000	27	2.04074		

BMDP2V - ANALYSIS OF VARIANCE AND COVARIANCES WITH REPEATED MEASURES.
HEALTH SCIENCES COMPUTING FACILITY
UNIVERSITY OF CALIFORNIA, LOS ANGELES 90024

Computer exercises

14.20   Run a multivariate analysis of variance for the data in Exercise 14.10, incorporating tests on Setting versus Goal and Setting versus Disposition.

14.21   What do you gain and what do you lose by using MANOVA in Exercise 14.20 with respect to the tests you considered?

14.22   Use the BMDP4V program in Exhibit 14.4b to tie together the answers you received for main effects and interactions in Exercises 14.10 and 14.20. (*Hint*: Some of the names for the statistics will be different, but the numerical values will be the same.)

14.23   In the data file Stress.dat are data on the stress level reported by cancer patients and their spouses at two different times—shortly after the diagnosis and 3 months later. The data are also distinguished by the gender of the respondent. As usual, a "." indicates each missing data point.

EXHIBIT 14.6

```
FILE HANDLE   DATA/NAME = 'EX1410.DAT'
DATA LIST     FILE=DATA
              /READ 1-2 AGE 4-5 PART 7-8 SCORE 10-11
ANOVA         SCORE BY READ,AGE(1,2),PART(1,3)
```

* * * * * * * * *ANALYSIS OF VARIANCE* * * * * * * * * * *

SCORE
by READ
   AGE
   PART

* *

Source of Variation	Sum of Squares	DF	Mean Square	F	Sig of F
Main Effects	158.067	4	39.517	22.908	0.000
READ	68.267	1	68.267	39.575	0.000
AGE	29.400	1	29.400	17.043	0.000
PART	60.400	2	30.200	17.507	0.000
2-way Interactions	4.200	5	0.840	0.487	0.784
READ AGE	3.267	1	3.267	1.894	0.175
READ PART	0.933	2	0.467	0.271	0.764
AGE PART	0.000	2	0.000	0.000	1.000
3-way Interactions	8.533	2	4.267	2.473	0.095
READ AGE PART	8.533	2	4.267	2.473	0.095
Explained	170.800	11	15.527	9.001	0.000
Residual	82.800	48	1.725		
Total	253.600	59	4.298		

60 Cases were processed.
 0 Cases (0.0%) were missing.

(a) Use any statistical package to run a repeated-measures analysis of variance on the data with Gender and Role (patient versus spouse) as between-subject variables and Time as the repeated measure.

(b) Have the program print out cell means, and plot these means as an aid in interpretation.

(c) There is a significant three-way interaction in this analysis. Interpret it along with the main effects.

14.24 In Exercise 14.23 we ignored the fact that we often have pairs of subjects from the same family.

(a) What is wrong with doing this?

(b) What alternative analyses would you suggest?

14.25 In Exercise 14.23 you probably noticed that many observations at Time 2 are missing. (This is partly because for many patients it had not yet been 3 months since the diagnosis.)

(a) Compare the means *at Time 1* for those subjects who did, and who did not, have data at Time 2.

(b) If there are differences in (a), what would this suggest to you about the data?

Multiple Regression

Objectives *To show how we can predict a criterion variable on the basis of several predictor variables simultaneously, and to point out the problems inherent in this procedure.*

Contents

In Chapter 9 we considered the situation in which we have one criterion (Y) and one predictor (X) and wish to predict Y on the basis of X. In this chapter we will consider the case in which we still have only one criterion (Y) but have multiple predictors ($X_1, X_2, X_3, \ldots, X_p$), and want to predict Y on the basis of *simultaneous* knowledge of all p predictors. The situation we examined in Chapter 9 can be viewed as a special case of the one discussed in this chapter; alternatively, this chapter can be viewed as an extension of Chapter 9. We will continue to use many familiar concepts such as the correlation coefficient, the slope, the standard error of estimate, and $SS_{regression}$.

Scalar algebra   A standard approach to multiple regression in a book of this type uses the usual **scalar algebra** taught in high school. The main problem with that approach is that when there are more than two predictors, the arithmetic becomes appallingly laborious. Even with two predictors, the equations themselves provide little insight into what is actually going on when we solve a multiple-regression problem.

484

Matrix algebra

An alternative, and much better, approach taken by more advanced texts is to cast the problem in terms of **matrix algebra** and to sneak in a "quickie" chapter on matrices. Unfortunately, even the brightest and most diligent students come away from such a chapter with only the vaguest ideas of matrix theory.

A third approach, and the one to be adopted here, is to bow to reality and to recognize that almost all multiple-regression problems are solved by using readily available computer programs. What is important is not the calculations themselves but the alternative ways the problem can be approached and the interpretation of the results. Thus, what we need to concentrate on is not how the solution is actually obtained, but what the potential problems are and what interpretation can be assigned to the wealth of statistics printed out by any good regression program.

Rather than simplifying the discussion of multiple regression, the approach taken here actually complicates it. Generally, there can be little argument over formulas. On the other hand, questions about the optimal number of predictors, the use of regression diagnostics, the relative importance of various predictors, and the selection of predictors do not have universally accepted answers. Be forewarned that the opinions expressed in this chapter are only opinions, and are open to dispute—but then that is part of what makes statistics interesting. Excellent and readable advanced sources for the study of multiple regression are Cohen and Cohen (1975), Darlington (1990), and Draper and Smith (1981).

15.1 MULTIPLE LINEAR REGRESSION

The problem of multiple regression is that of finding a regression equation to predict Y (sometimes denoted X_0) on the basis of p predictors $(X_1, X_2, X_3, \ldots, X_p)$. Thus, we might wish to predict success in graduate school (Y) on the basis of undergraduate grade point average (X_1), Graduate Record Exam scores (X_2), number of courses taken in the major discipline (X_3), and some rating of "favorableness" of letters of recommendation (X_4). Similarly, we might wish to predict the time it takes to go from one point in a city to another on the basis of number of traffic lights (X_1), posted speed limit (X_2), presence or absence of "right turn on red" (X_3), and traffic density (X_4). These examples are both analyzed in the same way, although in the first we presumably care about predictions for individual applicants, whereas in the second we might be less interested in the prediction itself and more interested in the role played by each of the predictors.

THE·REGRESSION EQUATION

In Chapter 9 we started with the equation of a straight line ($\hat{Y} = bX + a$) and solved for the two unknowns (a and b) subject to the constraint that $\Sigma(Y - \hat{Y})^2$ is a minimum. In multiple regression we are going to do the same thing, although in this case we will solve the equation $\hat{Y} = b_0 + b_1 X_1 + b_2 X_2 + \cdots + b_p X_p$ where b_0 represents the intercept and $b_1, b_2, \ldots, b_p$ are the regression coefficients for the predictors $X_1, X_2, \ldots, X_p$, respectively. We will retain the restriction that $\Sigma(Y - \hat{Y})^2$ is to be minimized, since it still makes sense to find predicted values that come as close as possible to the obtained values of Y.[†] As mentioned earlier, the calculations required to estimate the b_i become more cumbersome as the number of predictors increases, and we will not discuss these calculations here. Instead, we will begin with a simple example and assume that the solution was obtained by any available computer program, such as Minitab, SPSS[X], or BMDP. This example will provide a general overview of multiple regression. Once we have that overview, we will step back and ask specific questions about the data themselves, the choice of variables to include in the model, and ways to index the importance of variables.

A number of years ago, the student association of a large university published an evaluation of over 100 courses taught during the preceding semester. Students in each course had completed a questionnaire in which they rated a number of different aspects of the course on a 5-point scale (1 = failure, very bad ... 5 = excellent, exceptional). The data in Table 15.1 are real data and represent mean scores on six variables for a random sample of 50 courses. These variables were (1) overall quality of lectures (Overall), (2) teaching skills of the instructor (Teach), (3) quality of the tests and exams (Exam), (4) instructor's perceived knowledge of the subject matter (Knowledge), (5) the student's expected grade in the course (Grade—F = 1, A = 5), and (6) the enrollment of the course (Enroll).

TABLE 15.1
Course-evaluation data

Overall	Teach	Exam	Knowledge	Grade	Enroll
3.4	3.8	3.8	4.5	3.5	21
2.9	2.8	3.2	3.8	3.2	50
2.6	2.2	1.9	3.9	2.8	800
3.8	3.5	3.5	4.1	3.3	221
3.0	3.2	2.8	3.5	3.2	7
2.5	2.7	3.8	4.2	3.2	108
3.9	4.1	3.8	4.5	3.6	54
4.3	4.2	4.1	4.7	4.0	99
3.8	3.7	3.6	4.1	3.0	51
3.4	3.7	3.6	4.1	3.1	47
2.8	3.3	3.5	3.9	3.0	73
2.9	3.3	3.3	3.9	3.3	25
4.1	4.1	3.6	4.0	3.2	37
2.7	3.1	3.8	4.1	3.4	83
3.9	2.9	3.8	4.5	3.7	70
4.1	4.5	4.2	4.5	3.8	16
4.2	4.3	4.1	4.5	3.8	14
3.1	3.7	4.0	4.5	3.7	12
4.1	4.2	4.3	4.7	4.2	20
3.6	4.0	4.2	4.0	3.8	18
4.3	3.7	4.0	4.5	3.3	260

[†]There are alternatives to the standard least squares criteria that often produce estimates that are in some ways superior to the estimates obtained by least squares. These procedures are less common, but many of them can be found in Rousseeuw and Leroy (1987).

TABLE 15.1 (Cont.)					
4.0	4.0	4.1	4.6	3.2	100
2.1	2.9	2.7	3.7	3.1	118
3.8	4.0	4.4	4.1	3.9	35
2.7	3.3	4.4	3.6	4.3	32
4.4	4.4	4.3	4.4	2.9	25
3.1	3.4	3.6	3.3	3.2	55
3.6	3.8	4.1	3.8	3.5	28
3.9	3.7	4.2	4.2	3.3	28
2.9	3.1	3.6	3.8	3.2	27
3.7	3.8	4.4	4.0	4.1	25
2.8	3.2	3.4	3.1	3.5	50
3.3	3.5	3.2	4.4	3.6	76
3.7	3.8	3.7	4.3	3.7	28
4.2	4.4	4.3	5.0	3.3	85
2.9	3.7	4.1	4.2	3.6	75
3.9	4.0	3.7	4.5	3.5	90
3.5	3.4	4.0	4.5	3.4	94
3.8	3.2	3.6	4.7	3.0	65
4.0	3.8	4.0	4.3	3.4	100
3.1	3.7	3.7	4.0	3.7	105
4.2	4.3	4.2	4.2	3.8	70
3.0	3.4	4.2	3.8	3.7	49
4.8	4.0	4.1	4.9	3.7	64
3.0	3.1	3.2	3.7	3.3	700
4.4	4.5	4.5	4.6	4.0	27
4.4	4.8	4.3	4.3	3.6	15
3.4	3.4	3.6	3.5	3.3	40
4.0	4.2	4.0	4.4	4.1	18
3.5	3.4	3.9	4.4	3.3	90

On the assumption that the best available rating of the course is the overall rating of the lectures (Overall), we will use that as the dependent variable (Y) and derive a regression equation predicting Y on the basis of the other five variables.

Before we consider the regression solution itself, we need to look at the distribution of each variable. These are shown as stem-and-leaf displays in Table 15.2. (Notice that the display for Enroll contains a discontinuity because the few very large enrollments require the scale to move from increasing in steps of 10 to increasing in steps of 100.) From these displays it is apparent that the criterion variable and four of the predictors are fairly well distributed. They are all more or less symmetric with a reasonable amount of variability. Notice that the center of each distribution is noticeably above 3.0, which was labeled on the scale as "average." Thus, there is some positive response bias in the data. This is an interesting result, but it should have no important effect on the multiple-regression solution; it will merely change the intercept from what it would be if each variable had a mean of 3.0. It is encouraging to notice that the distribution for scores on the instructors' Knowledge of their subject matter is particularly biased upward. It is nice to see that students think their instructors know the material, even when they think the instructor is a poor teacher. The Teach and Exam variables each have one score that is unusually low relative to the others, but these are not so low as to bring their accuracy into question. The Enroll variable is unusually distributed; 46 of the 50 courses have enrollments below about 100, whereas the other 4 have enrollments ranging from 220 to 800. We will consider these extreme values later.

TABLE 15.2
Stem-and-leaf displays for all variables for the data in Table 15.1

	Overall (Y)		Teach (X_1)		Exam (X_2)
1.		1.		1.	9
2*	1	2*		2*	
2t		2t	2	2t	
2f	5	2f		2f	
2s	677	2s	7	2s	7
2.	889999	2.	899	2.	8
3*	000111	3*	111	3*	
3t	3	3t	222333	3t	2223
3f	44455	3f	4444455	3f	455
3s	6677	3s	7777777	3s	6666666777
3.	88889999	3.	88888	3.	888889
4*	000111	4*	0000011	4*	00000111111
4t	22233	4t	22233	4t	222223333
4f	444	4f	4455	4f	4445
4s					
4.	8	4.	8		
5*					

	Knowledge (X_3)		Grade (X_4)		Enroll (X_5)
2*		2*		0	7
2t		2t		1	245688
2f		2f		2	0155577888
2s		2s		3	257
2.		2.	89	4	079
3*	1	3*	00011	5	00145
3t	3	3t	222222233333333	6	45
3f	55	3f	4445555	7	00356
3s	677	3s	6666777777	8	35
3.	8888999	3.	88889	9	0049
4*	000011111	4*	0011	1	00001
4t	2222333	4t	23	2	26
4f	4444555555555	4f		3	
4s	66777	4s		5	
4.	9	4.		5	
5*	0	5*		6	
				7	0
				8	0

Code: (Y to X_4)   3*|1 = 3.1   Code: X_5 9   0 = 90
                                                           1   0 = 100

(Underlined values would be shown as outliers in a boxplot.) Notice that the stems have been divided into five intervals per decade. The * stands for 0 and 1, t for 2 and 3, f stands for 4 and 5, s stands for 6 and 7, and . stands for 8 and 9.

Although each of these variables taken alone (with the possible exception of Enroll) is reasonably behaved, what is particularly noteworthy is the behavior of Course 3. This course accounts for the two extreme scores on the variables Teach and Exam, and also has the most extreme score on Enroll. It is important to keep this course in mind, as it may well contribute more than its share of influence to the final result. (A similar point was raised in Chapter 9 with respect to an example used there. Often an extreme point will pull the regression surface toward itself, especially when that point is extreme on several variables. On the other hand, such a point may fit neatly into the pattern of data points, merely representing an extreme case of a general pattern.) The influence of such scores can be examined in a number of ways, as we shall see shortly.

Validities

An abbreviated printout using the SAS Proc Corr and Proc Reg procedures is presented in Exhibit 15.1, parts of which will be explained as we go along. The first row of the intercorrelation matrix contains the correlations of each of the predictors with the criterion. [These correlations are often referred to as **validities**, since each is a measure of the degree to which the predictor (e.g., Teach) can be used as a valid predictor of the criterion (Overall).] From the matrix it is apparent that teaching skills (Teach) has the highest correlation with the rated quality of the lectures (.804, rounded to three decimal places). The instructor's apparent knowledge of the material and the quality of the exams come next in order of correlations with the criterion (.682 and .596, respectively), whereas the student's expected grade and the size of the class have relatively low correlations with the criterion (.301 and $-.240$, respectively). This last correlation runs counter to traditional folklore among faculty, who often assume that those instructors who teach large classes will suffer poor teaching evaluations. At least in terms of rating the quality of the lectures, Enroll, taken individually, played a nonsignificant role.

EXHIBIT 15.1
SAS **Proc Corr** and
Proc Reg analysis
of course-evaluation
data

```
PROGRAM:

Options nocenter;
Options ls = 80;
Options pagesize = 60;

Data Regres;
   Infile 'Albratros.dat';
   Input Overall Teach Exam Knowledg Grade Enroll;
Run;

Proc Corr;
Run;

Proc Reg Data = Regres;
   Model Overall = Teach Exam Knowledg Grade Enroll
                    /STB TOL VIF PCORR2 SCORR2 R INFLUENCE PARTIAL;
```

* *

OUTPUT:

CORRELATION ANALYSIS

Pearson Correlation Coefficients / Prob > |R| under Ho: Rho=0 / N = 50

	OVERALL	TEACH	EXAM	KNOWLEDG	GRADE	ENROLL
OVERALL	1.00000	0.80386	0.59558	0.68180	0.30080	-0.23960
	0.0	0.0001	0.0001	0.0001	0.0338	0.0938
TEACH	0.80386	1.00000	0.71970	0.52627	0.46913	-0.45112
	0.0001	0.0	0.0001	0.0001	0.0006	0.0010

EXHIBIT 15.1 (Cont.)

EXAM	0.59558	0.71970	1.00000	0.45147	0.61004	-0.55807
	0.0001	0.0001	0.0	0.0010	0.0001	0.0001
KNOWLEDG	0.68180	0.52627	0.45147	1.00000	0.22421	-0.12787
	0.0001	0.0001	0.0010	0.0	0.1175	0.3762
GRADE	0.30080	0.46913	0.61004	0.22421	1.00000	-0.33708
	0.0338	0.0006	0.0001	0.1175	0.0	0.0167
ENROLL	-0.23960	-0.45112	-0.55807	-0.12787	-0.33708	1.00000
	0.0938	0.0010	0.0001	0.3762	0.0167	0.0

Dependent Variable: OVERALL

Analysis of Variance

Source	DF	Sum of Squares	Mean Square	F Value	Prob > F
Model	5	13.93426	2.78685	27.184	0.0001
Error	44	4.51074	0.10252		
C Total	49	18.44500			

Root MSE	0.32018	R-square	0.7554
Dep Mean	3.55000	Adj R-sq	0.7277
C.V.	9.01923		

Parameter Estimates

Variable	DF	Parameter Estimate	Standard Error	T for HO: Parameter=0	Prob > |T|
INTERCEP	1	-1.194827	0.63116347	-1.893	0.0649
TEACH	1	0.763237	0.13292048	5.742	0.0001
EXAM	1	0.131981	0.16280257	0.811	0.4219
KNOWLEDG	1	0.488984	0.13653786	3.581	0.0008
GRADE	1	-0.184308	0.16549514	-1.114	0.2715
ENROLL	1	0.000525	0.00039008	1.347	0.1848

Variable	DF	Standardized Estimate	Squared Semi-partial Corr Type II	Squared Partial Corr Type II	Tolerance
INTERCEP	1	0.00000000			
TEACH	1	0.66197185	0.18325307	0.42835756	0.41818863
EXAM	1	0.10608414	0.00365270	0.01471655	0.32457355
KNOWLEDG	1	0.32506209	0.07128534	0.22570347	0.67463300
GRADE	1	-0.10547012	0.00689338	0.02741514	0.61968853
ENROLL	1	0.12424247	0.01008670	0.03961199	0.65344504

Variable	DF	Variance Inflation
INTERCEP	1	0.00000000
TEACH	1	2.39126540
EXAM	1	3.08096574
KNOWLEDG	1	1.48228740
GRADE	1	1.61371391
ENROLL	1	1.53035059

Collinearity

From the correlation matrix, we also see that some of the variables have reasonably high intercorrelations with each other. The perceived quality of the exams is related to the instructor's teaching skills ($r = .720$), to the student's expected grade ($r = .610$), and to the enrollment ($r = -.558$), the last correlation probably reflecting the kinds of exams given in large lecture classes. The fact that this variable is highly correlated with several of the other predictors is often referred to as **collinearity**, especially if the correlations are high. In this case the correlations suggest that Exam has much in common with several other variables and may have very little information that is unique to it. If so, when the other variables are included as predictors, Exam will have little new to offer in the way of explaining variability in the Overall rating.

Regression coefficients

The **regression coefficients** are given in Exhibit 15.1 under the heading "Parameter Estimates"; they can be interpreted in much the same way as a regression coefficient in simple regression—with one important difference that we will explain shortly. Letting b_0 represent the intercept and $b_1 - b_5$ represent the regression coefficients for the five predictors, we see from Exhibit 15.1, rounding to three decimal places, that

$$b_0 = -1.195$$
$$b_1 = 0.763$$
$$b_2 = 0.132$$
$$b_3 = 0.489$$
$$b_4 = -0.184$$
$$b_5 = 0.001$$

Thus, we can write

$$\hat{Y} = -1.195 + 0.763 \text{ Teach} + 0.132 \text{ Exam} + 0.489 \text{ Knowledge}$$
$$- 0.184 \text{ Grade} + 0.001 \text{ Enroll}$$

This is a standard regression equation and can be used to obtain a predicted value of Y (Overall) for any specific set of values of the predictors. For example, for Course 1, using the data from Table 15.1, we have

$$\hat{Y} = -1.195 + 0.763(3.8) + 0.132(3.8) + 0.489(4.5) - 0.184(3.5) + 0.001(21) = 3.733^{\dagger}$$

Since Course 1 actually obtained a mean Overall lecture rating of 3.4, our residual, or error of prediction, for that particular course is $e = Y - \hat{Y} = 3.4 - 3.733 = -0.373$. For Course 3, the one with the extreme observations,

$$\hat{Y} = -1.195 + 0.763(2.2) + 0.132(1.9) + 0.489(3.9) - 0.184(2.8) + 0.001(800) = 2.546$$

In this case, the actual Overall score was 2.6, for a residual of $2.6 - 2.546 = 0.054$. So the Course with extreme predictors was fit rather well. That is not to say, however, that we should be satisfied that extreme values are not a problem in this example. It may well be that this observation pulled the regression surface toward itself and thus fits well as a result.

From our regression equation, we can see that *if all other variables were held constant* the predicted value of Y would be higher by 0.763 units for every one-unit difference in Teach skills, and by 0.001 for every one-unit difference in Enroll. This does not necessarily mean that if two instructors differed by one unit on the Teach variable, they would differ by 0.763 units on the Overall course rating. The *predicted* values would differ by 0.763 units only if the two courses had equal ratings on all other variables. Moreover, this equation cannot be interpreted to indicate that if a given instructor were to spend time improving his Exam rating by one unit, the rated Overall quality of his lectures would improve by 0.132 units. First, such an assertion would imply a *causal* relationship, when none has necessarily been shown. Second, the

---

† Predicted values have been calculated with eight-digit accuracy to increase agreement with the computer printout.

pattern of interrelationships among the variables suggests that increasing the Exam rating might also be expected to alter the ratings on some of the other variables, which could in turn also affect the predicted score.

One common mistake is to treat the relative magnitudes of the b_i as an index of the relative importance of the individual predictors. By this (mistaken) logic, we might be tempted to conclude that Teach is a more important predictor than is Enroll, since its coefficient is appreciably larger. Although it might actually be the case that Teach is a more important predictor, we cannot draw such a conclusion based on the regression coefficients. The relative magnitudes of the coefficients are in part a function of the standard deviations of the corresponding variables. Since the standard deviation of Enroll is much larger than the standard deviation of the other variables, its regression coefficient (b_5) is almost certain to be small regardless of the importance of that variable.

It may be easier for you to appreciate this last point if you look at the problem somewhat differently. For one instructor to have a Teach rating one point higher than another instructor would be a major accomplishment, whereas having one additional student is a trivial matter. We hardly expect on a priori grounds that these two one-point differences will lead to equal differences in the predicted Overall rating, regardless of the relative importance of the two predictors.

STANDARDIZED REGRESSION COEFFICIENTS

Importance

As we shall see later, the question of the relative importance of variables has several different answers depending on what we mean by **importance**. One measure of importance should be mentioned here, however, since it is a legitimate statistic in its own right. Suppose that before we obtained our multiple-regression equation, we had standardized each of our variables. As you will recall, standardizing a variable sets its mean at 0 and its standard deviation at 1. Now all of our variables would have equal standard deviations (1) and a one-unit difference between two courses on one variable would be comparable to a one-unit difference between those courses on any other variable. If we now solved for our regression coefficients using the standardized variables, we would obtain

$$\hat{Y}_z = 0.662Z_1 + 0.106Z_2 + 0.325Z_3 - 0.105Z_4 + 0.124Z_5$$

Standardized regression coefficients

where Z is used to denote standardized variables. In this case, the regression coefficients are called **standardized regression coefficients** labeled "standardized estimate" by the SAS procedure, and denoted β_i. Thus

$$\beta_1 = 0.662$$
$$\beta_2 = 0.106$$
$$\beta_3 = 0.325$$
$$\beta_4 = -0.105$$
$$\beta_5 = 0.124$$

When variables have been standardized, the intercept (β_0) is equal to 0 and is not shown.

From the preceding values of β_i we can conclude that a one-unit difference between courses in Z_1 (the standardized Teach variable) (i.e., a difference of one standard deviation) with all other variables held constant will be associated with a difference in $\hat{Y}_Z$ of 0.662 units and therefore a difference in $\hat{Y}$ of 0.662 standard deviations. Comparable differences in Z_2 and Z_3 will be associated with differences in $\hat{Y}$ of 0.106 and 0.325 standard deviations, respectively. Although the relative magnitudes of the β_i are not necessarily the best indicators of "importance," they have a simple interpretation, are printed by most regression computer programs, and generally give at least a rough estimate of the relative contributions of the variables in the equation.

Lest you think you will be required to standardize the raw data in order to calculate the β_i, should the computer program not print them, there is an easier way. It can be shown quite easily that

$$\beta_i = \frac{b_i s_i}{s_0}$$

where s_0 is the standard deviation of the criterion. Going the other way,

$$b_i = \frac{\beta_i s_0}{s_i}$$

For our data,

$$\beta_1 = \frac{0.763(0.5321)}{0.6135} = 0.662$$

and

$$\beta_2 = \frac{0.132(0.4932)}{0.6135} = 0.106$$

15.2 STANDARD ERRORS AND TESTS OF REGRESSION COEFFICIENTS

Once we have a regression coefficient, standardized or not, we normally test it for statistical significance. If the coefficient relating Teach to Enroll is not significantly different from 0, then it will serve no useful purpose in the prediction of Enroll. As you might suspect, it doesn't matter whether we test the raw score regression coefficients (b_i) or the standardized coefficients (β_i). They are simply linear transformations of one another, and we would obtain the same test statistic in either case.

To test a regression coefficient (or most other statistics for that matter), we need to know the standard error of that statistic. The standard errors for the b_is are given in Exhibit 15.1. For example, the standard error of b_0, the intercept, is 0.63116, and the standard error for b_1 is 0.13292. As with other standard errors, the standard error of the regression coefficient refers to the variability of the statistic over repeated sampling. Suppose we repeated the course-evaluation study many times on different independent samples of students. Each replication would be expected to give us a slightly different value of b_1, although each of these would be an unbiased estimate of the true coefficient in the population, which we will denote as b_1^*. The many b_1s would be normally distributed about b_1^* with a standard deviation estimated by the standard error of $b_1 = 0.13292$.

We can use these standard errors to form a t test on the regression coefficients. Specifically,

$$t = \frac{b_j - b_j^*}{s_{b_j}}$$

on $N - p - 1$ degrees of freedom.[†]

Then to test $H_0 : b_j^* = 0$,

$$t = \frac{b_j}{s_{b_j}}$$

For a test on the regression coefficient of Teach, we have

$$t = \frac{0.76324}{0.13292} = 5.742$$

This is a standard Student's t on $N - p - 1 = 50 - 5 - 1 = 44$ df, and the critical value is found in Appendix t to be 2.02. Thus, we can reject H_0 and conclude that the regression coefficient in the population is not equal to 0. In other words, the predicted value of Y increases with increasing scores on Teach, and Teach thus makes a significant contribution to the prediction of Overall.

A corresponding test on the coefficient for Exam would produce

$$t = \frac{0.13198}{0.16280} = 0.811$$

This result is not significant, meaning that given the other four predictors, Exam does not contribute significantly to the prediction of Overall. We might consider dropping this predictor from our model, but there will be more on this issue later. It is important to recognize that a test on a variable is done in the context of all other variables in the equation. A variable might have a high individual correlation with the criterion, as does Exam, but have nothing useful to contribute once several other variables are included. That is the situation here.

Some computer programs prefer to print standard errors for, and test, standardized regression coefficients (β_j). It makes no difference which you do. Similarly, some programs provide an F test (on 1 and $N - p - 1$ df) instead of t. This F is simply the square of our t, so again it makes no difference which approach you take.

[†] A number of authors (e.g., Draper & Smith, 1981; Huberty, 1989) have pointed out that in general this is not exactly distributed as Student's t. However, it is generally treated as if it were, but one should not take the associated probability too literally.

15.3 RESIDUAL VARIANCE

We have just considered the standard error of the regression coefficient, recognizing that sampling error is involved in the estimation of the corresponding population regression coefficient. A somewhat different kind of error is involved in the estimation of the predicted Ys. In terms of course evaluation, we would hope that the Overall score is, at least in part, a function of such variables as Teach, Exam, and so on. (If we didn't think that, we would not have run the regression in the first place.) At the same time, we probably do not expect that the five variables we have chosen will predict Y perfectly, even if they could be measured, and the coefficients estimated, without error.

Residual variance, Residual error

Error will still be involved in the prediction of Y after we have taken all five of our predictors into account. This error is called **residual variance** or **residual error** and is defined as

$$\frac{\Sigma(Y - \hat{Y})^2}{N - p - 1}$$

and is denoted as $\mathrm{MS_{residual}}$ or $\mathrm{MS_{error}}$ or $s^2_{0.12345}$. In Exhibit 15.1 it is given as the error term in the analysis of variance summary table as 0.10252.

The concept of residual error is important because it is exactly the thing we hope to minimize in our study. We want our estimates of Y to be as accurate as possible. We will return to this concept later in the chapter.

The square root of $\mathrm{MS_{residual}}$ is called the *standard error of estimate* and has the same meaning as the standard error of estimate in Chapter 9. It is the standard deviation of the column of residual scores $(Y - \hat{Y})$. In Exhibit 15.1 it is denoted as Root MSE (which stands for "root mean square error").

15.4 DISTRIBUTION ASSUMPTIONS

So far we have made no assumptions about the nature of the distributions of our variables. The statistics b_i, β_i, and R (the multiple correlation coefficient) are legitimate measures independent of any distribution assumptions. Having said that, however, it is necessary to point out that certain assumptions will be necessary if we are to use these measures in several important ways. [It may be helpful to go back to Chapter 9 and quickly reread the brief discussions in the introduction (p. 221) and in Sections 9.7 and 9.12 (pgs. 243–244 and pgs. 255–256). Those sections explained the distinction between linear-regression models and bivariate-normal models and discussed the assumptions involved.]

To provide tests on the statistics we have been discussing, we will need to make one of two different kinds of assumptions, depending on the nature of our variables. If X_1, $X_2, \ldots, X_p$ are thought of as random variables, as they are in this example since we measure the predictors as we find them rather than fixing them in advance, we will

Multivariate normal

make the general assumption that the joint distribution of $Y, X_1, X_2, \ldots, X^p$ is **multivariate normal**. (This is the extension to multiple variables of the bivariate-normal distribution described in Section 9.12.) Although in theory this assumption is necessary for many of our tests, rather substantial departures from a multivariate-normal distribution are likely to be tolerable. First, our tests are reasonably robust. Second, in actual practice we are concerned not so much about whether R is significantly different from 0 as about whether R is large or small. In other words, with X_i random, we are not as interested in hypothesis testing as we were in the analysis of variance problems. Whether $R = .20$ is significant or not when it comes to prediction questions may be largely irrelevant, since it accounts for only 4% of the variation.

If the variables $X_1, X_2, \ldots, X_p$ are fixed variables, we will simply make the assumption that the conditional distributions of Y (i.e., the distribution of Y for specific levels of X_i) are normally and independently distributed. Here again moderate departures from normality are tolerable.

The fixed model and the corresponding assumption of normality in Y will be considered in Chapter 16. In this chapter we generally will be concerned with random variables. The multivariate-normal assumption is more stringent than is necessary for much of what follows, but it is sufficient. For example, the standard error of b_j does not require an assumption of multivariate normality. However, a person seldom wishes to find the standard error of b_j unless he or she wishes to test (or form confidence limits on) b_j, and this test requires the normality assumption. We will therefore impose this assumption on our data.

15.5 THE MULTIPLE CORRELATION COEFFICIENT

Multiple correlation coefficient $(R_{0.123...p})$

We will next consider the **multiple correlation coefficient $(R_{0.123...p})$**. The notation denotes the fact that the criterion (Y or X_0) is predicted from predictors 1, 2, 3 ... p simultaneously. When there is no confusion as to which predictors are involved, we generally drop the subscript and use plain old R.

R is defined as the correlation between the criterion (Y) and the best linear combination of the predictors. As such, R is really nothing but $r_{Y\hat{Y}}$, where

$$\hat{Y} = b_0 + b_1 X_1 + b_2 X_2 + \cdots + b_p X_p$$

Thus, if we wished, we could use the regression equation to generate $\hat{Y}$, and then correlate Y and $\hat{Y}$. Although no one would seriously propose calculating R in this way, it is helpful to realize that this is what the multiple correlation actually represents. In actual practice, R (or R^2) is printed out by every multiple-regression computer program. For our data, the multiple correlation between the criterion and the five predictors, taken simultaneously, is .869. (This value can be obtained from Exhibit 15.1 by taking the square root of R-Square = $\sqrt{.7554} = .869$.)

The coefficient R is a regular correlation coefficient and can be treated just like any other Pearson product-moment correlation. (This is obviously true, since $R = r_{Y\hat{Y}}$.) However, in multiple correlation (as is often the the case with simple correlation) we are more interested in R^2 than in R, because it can be directly interpreted in terms of percentage of accountable variation. Thus, $R^2 = .869^2 = .755$, and we can say that

75.5% of the variation in the overall quality of the lectures can be predicted on the basis of the five predictors. This is about 11 percentage points more than could be predicted on the basis of Teach, our best single predictor, alone.

Unfortunately, R^2 is not an unbiased estimate of the corresponding parameter in the population ($R^{*2}_{.123 \ldots p}$). The extent of this bias depends on the relative size of N and p. When $N = p + 1$, prediction is perfect and $R = 1$, regardless of the true relationship between Y and $X_1, X_2, \ldots, X_p$ in the population. (A straight line will perfectly fit any two points, a plane, like the three legs of a milking stool will perfectly fit any three points, and so on.) A relatively unbiased estimate of R^{*2} is given by

$$\text{est } R^{*2} = 1 - \frac{(1 - R^2)(N - 1)}{N - p - 1}$$

For our data,

$$\text{est } R^{*2} = 1 - \frac{(1 - .7554)(49)}{44} = .7277$$

This value agrees with the Adj R-sq printed by the SAS procedure in Exhibit 15.1.

It should be apparent from the definition of R that it can take on values only between 0 and 1. This follows both from the fact that it is defined as the positive square root of R^2, and from the fact that it can be viewed as $r_{Y\hat{Y}}$—we would hardly expect $\hat{Y}$ to be negatively correlated with Y.

TESTING THE SIGNIFICANCE OF R^2

We have seen how to ask if each of the variables is making a significant contribution to the prediction of Y by testing its regression coefficient (b_j). But perhaps a question that should be asked first is, Does the set of variables taken together predict Y at better than chance levels? I suggest that this question has priority because there is little point in looking at individual variables if no overall relationship exists.

The easiest way to test the overall relationship between Y and $X_1, X_2, \ldots, X_p$ is to test the multiple correlation coefficient for significance. This amounts to testing $H_0: R^* = 0$, where R^* represents the correlation coefficient in the population. By the nature of our test, it is actually easier to test R^2 than R, but that amounts to the same thing. The test on R^2 is recognizable as a simple extension from a test given in Chapter 9 when we had only one predictor. In this case we have p predictors and

$$F = \frac{(N - p - 1)R^2}{p(1 - R^2)}$$

is distributed as the standard F distribution on p and $N - p - 1$ degrees of freedom. [With only one predictor this reduces to the familiar $(N - 2)(r^2)/(1 - r^2)$.] For our data, $N = 50$, $p = 5$, and $R^2 = .7554$. Then

$$F = \frac{(50 - 5 - 1)(.7554)}{5(.2446)} = \frac{44(.7554)}{1.2230} = 27.184$$

This is the same F as that given in the summary table in Exhibit 15.1, although the

SAS printout uses the words "model" and "error" in place of the more common terms "regression" and "residual." An F of 27.184 on 5 and 44 df is obviously significant beyond $p = .05$, and we can therefore reject H_0: $R^* = 0$ and conclude that we can predict at better than chance levels.

SAMPLE SIZES

As you can tell from the formula for a relatively unbiased estimate of the population correlation coefficient and from the preceding formula for F, our estimate of the correlation depends on both the size of the sample (N) and the number of predictors (p). People often assume that if there is no relation between the criterion and the predictors, R should come out near 0. In fact, the expected value of R *for random data* is $p/(N - 1)$. Thus, with 5 predictors and 50 cases, an $R = .10$ would be the expected value. A rule of thumb that has been kicking around for years is that we should have *at least* 10 observations for every predictor. Harris (1985) points out, however, that he knows of no empirical evidence supporting this rule. It certainly fails in the extreme, because no one would be satisfied with 10 observations and 1 predictor. Harris advocates an alternative rule dealing not with the ratio of p to N, but with their difference. His rule is that N should exceed p by at least 50. Others have suggested the slightly more liberal $N \geq p + 40$. Whereas these two rules relate directly to the reliability of a correlation coefficient, Cohen and Cohen (1975) approach the problem from the direction of statistical power. They show that in the one-predictor case, to have power $= .80$ for a population correlation of .30 would require $N = 124$. With 5 predictors, a population correlation of .30 would require 187 subjects for the same degree of power. As you can see, a reasonable amount of power requires fairly large samples. Perhaps Darlington's (1990) rule of thumb is the best—"more is better."

15.6   GEOMETRIC REPRESENTATION OF MULTIPLE REGRESSION

Hyperspace, Regression surface

Any linear multiple-regression problem involving p predictors can be represented graphically in $p + 1$ dimensions. Thus, with one predictor we can readily draw a two-dimensional scatter diagram and fit a regression line through the points. With two predictors we can represent the data in three-dimensional space with a plane passing though the points. With more than three predictors, we would have to begin to think in terms of **hyperspace** (multidimensional space) with the **regression surface** (the analog of the regression line or plane) fitted through the points. People have enough trouble thinking in terms of three-dimensional space, without trying to handle hyperspaces, and so we will consider here only the two-predictor case. The generalization to the case of many predictors should be apparent, even if you cannot visualize the problem.

Figure 15.1 shows a three-dimensional plot of the following data. Each member of the data set is represented as the ball on top of a flagpole. The base of the flagpole is located at the point (X_1, X_2), and the height of the pole is Y.

$$Y \quad 1\ 2\ 1\ 3\ 5\ 3\ 3\ 3\ 4\ 6\ 5\ 7$$

$$X_1 \quad 3\ 3\ 3\ 3\ 3\ 4\ 4\ 5\ 5\ 5\ 7\ 7$$

$$X_2 \quad 0\ 1\ 2\ 4\ 7\ 1\ 4\ 4\ 6\ 7\ 5\ 7$$

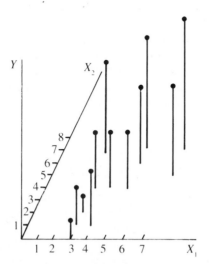

FIGURE 15.1
Three-dimensional representation of Y as a function of X_1 and X_2

In Figure 15.1, as you move from the lower left to the upper right, the heights of the flagpoles (and therefore the values of Y) increase. If you had the three-dimensional model represented by this figure, you could actually pass a plane through, or near, the points so as to give the best possible fit. Some of the flagpoles would stick up through the plane, and some would not reach it, but the points could be fit reasonably well by this plane. The vertical distances of the points from the plane, the distances $Y - \hat{Y}$, would be the residuals. Just as in the one-predictor case, the residuals represented the vertical distance of the points from the best-fitting line (or, in this three-dimensional case, the best-fitting plane).

We can derive one additional insight from this three-dimensional model. The plane we have been discussing forms some angle (in this case positive) with the axis X_1. In other words, the plane rises from left to right. The slope of that plane relative to X_1 is b_1. Similarly, the slope of the plane with respect to X_2 is b_2. The height of the plane at the point $(X_1, X_2) = (0, 0)$ is b_0.

FURTHER INTERPRETATION OF REGRESSION COEFFICIENTS

The regression coefficients we have been discussing (both β and b) are called *partial regression coefficients*; that is, b_1 is the coefficient for the regression of Y on X_1 when we *partial out* (remove, or hold constant) the effect of $X_2, X_3, \ldots, X_p$. As such, it should actually be denoted as $b_{01.23 \ldots p}$, although we employ the shorter notation except when confusion might otherwise result. Perhaps the easiest way to see what we mean by the "partialling out of X_2" is to consider Figure 15.1. If we look at only the data for $X_2 = 1$ (for example), we see that we could fit a straight line to the regression of Y on X_1. We do not need to consider X_2 because we are considering only those cases in which $X_2 = 1 =$ a constant. Similarly, we could look at only those cases in which $X_2 = 4$. For any one value of X_2, we have a regression for Y on X_1. The average of these is $b_{01.2}$. Now consider the values of Y and X_2 for only the cases in which $X_1 = 3$ (or 4, or 5, and so on). Here we have the regression of Y on X_2, with X_1 partialled out. The average of these coefficients is $b_{02.1}$.

One common mistake is to equate $b_{01.2}$ with b_{01}—that is, with the simple regression coefficient we would obtain if we regressed Y on X_1 *without regard to X_2*. That these coefficients cannot be equated can be seen in the simple extreme example shown in Figure 15.2. The raw data used to plot this figure are

$$Y \quad 2\ 1\ 4\ 3\ 6\ 5$$

$$X_1 \quad 1\ 2\ 3\ 4\ 5\ 6$$

$$X_2 \quad 2\ 2\ 4\ 4\ 6\ 6$$

Figure 15.2a represents the three-dimensional projection of Y on X_1 and X_2. Note that for any single value of X_2, the slope of the regression line of Y on X_1 is decidedly negative (in fact, $b_{01.2} = -1$). However, if you look at Figure 15.2b where Y is plotted against X_1, *ignoring X_2*, the slope is positive ($b_{01} = 0.829$). Thus, there is quite a difference between partialling out a variable and ignoring it. This is a deliberately extreme example, but it is an exaggeration of more typical cases. Only when X_1 and X_2 are independent ($r_{12} = 0$) will $b_{01.2}$ be equal to b_{01}.

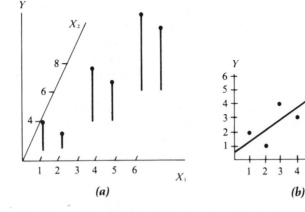

FIGURE 15.2
(a) Y as a function of X_1 and X_2
(b) Y plotted as a function of X_1 only

There is an alternative way of viewing partial regression coefficients. It is of no practical use in calculations, but it is very useful in understanding the process of partialling. Consider the partial regression coefficient $b_{01.2}$ for the data in Figure 15.2. As mentioned earlier, $b_{01.2} = -1$. Suppose that we regress Y on X_2 and obtain the values of $Y_i - \hat{Y}_i$ for this regression. These residual values would represent that part of Y that *cannot* be predicted by (is independent of) X_2. We will represent these residuals by the symbol Y_r. Now we regress X_1 on X_2 and generate the residuals $X_{1_i} - \hat{X}_{1_i}$. These represent the part of X_1 that is independent of X_2 and will be symbolized as X_{1r}. We now have two sets of residuals—the part of Y that is independent of X_2 and the part of X_1 that is independent of X_2. We have partialled X_2 out of Y and out of X_1. If we now regress Y_r on X_{1r}, the slope will be $b_{01.2}$. Moreover, the correlation between Y_r and X_{1r} is called the *partial correlation* of Y and X_1, with X_2 partialled out ($r_{01.2}$). Table 15.3 contains a simple illustration of what we have been discussing using the data from Figure 15.2a.

TABLE 15.3
Illustrative calculation of partial regression coefficient

	Data	
Y	X_1	X_2
2	1	2
1	2	2
4	3	4
3	4	4
6	5	6
5	6	6

Y on X_2			X_1 on X_2			Y_r on X_{1r}	
	$\hat{Y} = 1.0X_2 - 0.50$			$\hat{X}_1 = 1.0X_2 - 0.50$			
Y	$\hat{Y}$	Y_r	X_1	$\hat{X}_1$	X_{1r}	Y_r	X_{1r}
2	1.5	0.5	1	1.5	−0.5	0.5	−0.5
1	1.5	−0.5	2	1.5	0.5	−0.5	0.5
4	3.5	0.5	3	3.5	−0.5	0.5	−0.5
3	3.5	−0.5	4	3.5	0.5	−0.5	0.5
6	5.5	0.5	5	5.5	−0.5	0.5	−0.5
5	5.5	−0.5	6	5.5	0.5	−0.5	0.5

$$b_{Y_r X_{1r}} = \frac{\text{cov}_{Y_r X_{1r}}}{S_{X_{1r}}}$$

$$= \frac{-0.30}{0.30}$$

$$= -1 = b_{01.2}$$

15.7   PARTIAL AND SEMIPARTIAL CORRELATION

Two closely related correlations involve partialling out, or controlling for, the effects of one or more other variables. These correlations are the partial and semipartial correlation coefficients.

PARTIAL CORRELATION

Partial correlation
$r_{01.2}$

We have seen that a **partial correlation** $r_{01.2}$ is the correlation between two variables with one or more variables partialled out of both X and Y. More specifically, it is the correlation between the two sets of residuals formed from the prediction of the original variables by one or more other variables.

Consider an experimenter who wanted to investigate the relationship between earned income and success in college. He obtained measures for each variable and ran his correlation, which turned out to be significant. Elated with the results, he harangued his students with the admonition that if they did not do well in college they were not likely to earn large salaries. In the back of the class, however, was a bright student who realized that both variables were (presumably) related to IQ. She argued that people with high IQs tend to do well in college and also earn good salaries, and that the correlation between income and college success is an artifact of this relationship.

The simplest way to settle this argument is to calculate the partial correlation between Income and college Success with IQ partialled out of both variables. Thus, we regress income on IQ and obtain the residuals. These residuals represent the variation in Income that cannot be attributed to IQ. You might think of this as a "purified" income measure—purified of the influence of IQ. We next regress Success on IQ and again obtain the residuals, which here represent the portion of Success that is not attributable to IQ. We can now answer the important question: Can the variation in Income not explained by (independent of) IQ be predicted by the variation in Success that is also independent of IQ? The correlation between these two variables is the partial correlation of Income and Success, partialling out IQ.

The partial correlation coefficient is represented by $r_{01.23 \ldots p}$. The two subscripts to the left of the dot represent the variables being correlated, and the subscripts to the right of the dot represent those variables being partialled out of both.

A simple example illustrating the principle of partial correlation is presented in Table 15.4. Here you can see the calculation of the residuals and the correlation between the two sets of residuals. The partial correlation ($r_{01.2} = .738$) represents the independent contribution of variable X_1 toward the prediction of Y, partialling out X_2.

Hand calculation of partial correlation coefficients is exceedingly tedious, especially when you think of the potential number of partials we could have for any reasonably large value of p. That is why most regression problems are solved using computer software. However, we occasionally want the partial correlation between two variables with only one other partialled out. This can be calculated quite readily from the simple rs.

$$r_{01.2} = \frac{r_{01} - r_{02}r_{12}}{\sqrt{(1 - r_{02}^2)(1 - r_{12}^2)}}$$

For our example, $r_{01} = .757$; $r_{02} = .740$; and $r_{12} = .411$. Thus,

$$r_{01.2} = \frac{.757 - (.740)(.411)}{\sqrt{(1 - .740^2)(1 - .411^2)}} = .738$$

which agrees, within rounding error, with our previous calculation. The advantage of this formula is that you can easily calculate $r_{01.2}$ from a matrix of correlations even when you do not have access to the raw data.

TABLE 15.4
Illustrative calculation
of partial correlation
coefficient

Data		
Y	X_1	X_2
4	2	4
3	4	1
6	6	5
1	1	2
5	3	3

	Y on X_2			X_1 on X_2	
	$\hat{Y} = 0.90X_2 + 1.1$			$\hat{X}_1 = 0.50X_2 + 1.7$	
Y	$\hat{Y}$	$Y_r = Y - \hat{Y}$	X_1	$\hat{X}_1$	$X_{1r} = X_1 - \hat{X}_1$
4	4.7	−0.7	2	3.7	−1.7
3	2.0	1.0	4	2.2	1.8
6	5.6	0.4	6	4.2	1.8
1	2.9	−1.9	1	2.7	−1.7
5	3.8	1.2	3	3.2	−0.2

$$\Sigma Y_r = 0 \qquad \Sigma Y_r^2 = 6.70 \qquad\qquad \Sigma X_{1r} = 0 \qquad \Sigma X_{1r}^2 = 12.30$$

$$\Sigma Y_r X_{1r} = 6.70$$

$$r_{01.2} = r_{Y_r X_{1r}} = \frac{\text{cov}_{XY}}{S_{X_{1r}} S_{Y_r}} = \frac{1.675}{(1.294)(1.754)}$$

$$= .738$$

SEMIPARTIAL CORRELATION

**Semipartial
correlation $r_{0(1.2)}$**

A type of correlation that will prove exceedingly useful both here and in Chapter 16 is the **semipartial correlation $r_{0(1.2)}$**, sometimes called the *part* correlation. As the name suggests, a semipartial correlation is the correlation between the criterion and a partialled predictor variable. In other words, whereas the partial correlation ($r_{01.2}$) has variable 2 partialled out of both the criterion and predictor 1, the semipartial correlation $r_{0(1.2)}$ has variable 2 partialled out of only predictor 1. In this case, the semipartial correlation is simply the correlation between Y and the residual ($X_1 - \hat{X}_1 = X_{1r}$) of X_1 predicted on X_2. As such, it is the correlation of Y with that part of X_1 that is independent of X_2.[†] As an illustration, the computation of $r_{0(1.2)}$ by way of the

[†]You will note that we consider both partial and semipartial correlation but only mentioned the *partial* regression coefficient (b_j). This coefficient could equally well be called the *semipartial* regression coefficient.

residuals is presented in Table 15.5 for the data in Table 15.4. A much simpler method of computation exists, however. It can be shown that

$$r^2_{0(1.2)} = R^2_{0.12} - r^2_{02}$$

Using this formula, we can verify the calculation in Table 15.5. For those data, $R^2_{0.12} = .79389$, and $r^2_{02} = .54729$. Thus, rounding to 3 decimal places,

$$r^2_{0(1.2)} = .794 - .547 = .247$$

$$r_{0(1.2)} = \sqrt{r^2_{0(1.2)}} = \sqrt{.247} = .497$$

which agrees with the result in Table 15.5.

TABLE 15.5
Illustrative calculation of semipartial correlation coefficient $(\hat{X}_1 = 0.50X_2 + 1.7)$

Y	X_1	X_2	X_{1r}
4	2	4	−1.7
3	4	1	1.8
6	6	5	1.8
1	1	2	−1.7
5	3	3	−0.2

$\Sigma Y = 19$ $\quad \Sigma X_{1r} = 0.0$

$\Sigma Y^2 = 87$ $\quad \Sigma X^2_{1r} = 12.3$

$\Sigma YX_{1r} = 6.7$

The preceding formula for $r_{0(1.2)}$ affords an opportunity to explore further just what multiple-regression equations and correlations represent. Rearranging the formula we have

$$R^2_{0.12} = r^2_{02} + r^2_{0(1.2)}$$

This formula illustrates that the squared multiple correlation is the sum of the squared correlation between the criterion and one of the variables plus the squared correlation between the criterion and the part of the other variable that is independent of the first. Thus, we can think of R as being based on as much information as possible from one variable, any *additional, nonredundant* information from a second, and so on. In general

$$R^2_{0.123 \ldots p} = r^2_{01} + r^2_{0(2.1)} + r^2_{0(3.12)} + \cdots + r^2_{0(p.123 \ldots p-1)}$$

where $r^2_{0(3.12)}$ is the squared correlation between the criterion and variable 3, with variables 1 and 2 partialled out of 3. This way of looking at multiple regression will be particularly helpful when we consider the role of individual variables in predicting the criterion, and when we consider the least squares approach to the analysis of variance. As an aside, it should be mentioned that when the predictors are independent of one another, the preceding formula reduces to

$$R^2_{0.123 \ldots p} = r^2_{01} + r^2_{02} + r^2_{03} + \cdots + r^2_{0p}$$

since, if the variables are independent, there is no variance in common to be partialled out.

For the data on course evaluations, the squared semipartial and partial correlation coefficients were shown in Exhibit 15.1. These are the squared correlations partialling out all other variables in the model. For example, the squared semipartial correlation between Overall and Teach, partialling Exam, Knowledge, Grade, and Enroll from Teach, is .18325. This shows that Teach explains 18.3% of the variation in Overall once we have taken the other four variables into account.

The squared partial correlation between Overall and Teach, partialling the other four predictors, is .42836, showing that 42.8% of the variation in Overall that could not be explained by the other predictors can be accounted for by Teach. This point will be elaborated in the next section.

We do not need a separate significance test for semipartial or partial correlations, because we already have such a test in the test on the regression coefficients. If that test is significant, then corresponding β, partial, and semipartial coefficients are also significant. Therefore, from Exhibit 15.1 we also know that these coefficients for Teach are all significant. Keep in mind, however, that when we speak about the significance of a coefficient we are speaking of it within the context of the other variables in the model. For example, Exhibit 15.1 reveals that Exam does not make a significant contribution to the model. That does not mean that it would not contribute to any other model predicting Overall. (In fact, when used as the only predictor it predicts Overall at better than chance levels. See the matrix of intercorrelations.) It only means that once we have the other predictors in our model, Exam does not have any independent (or unique) contribution to make.

ALTERNATIVE INTERPRETATION OF PARTIAL AND SEMIPARTIAL CORRELATION

Venn diagrams

There is an alternative way of viewing the meaning of partial and semipartial that can be very instructive. This method is best presented in terms of what are called **Venn diagrams**.

Suppose that the box in Figure 15.3 is taken to represent all the variability in the criterion (Y) in a regression problem. We will set the area of the box equal to 100%— the percentage of the variation in Y to be explained. The circle labeled X_1 is taken to represent the percentage of the variation in Y that is explained by X_1. In other words, the area of the circle is equal to r_{01}^2. Similarly, the area of the circle labeled X_2 is the percentage of the variation in Y explained by X_2 and is equal to r_{02}^2. Finally, the overlap between the two circles represents the portion of Y that both X_1 and X_2 have in common. The area outside of either circle but within the box is the portion of Y that cannot be explained by either variable and is the residual variation. In this example you can see that 45% of the variation in Y can be explained by X_1 alone, 35% can be explained by X_2 alone, and 20% is shared by both X_1 and X_2.

The areas labelled B, C, and D, in Figure 15.4 represent portions of the variation in Y that can be accounted for by X_1 *and/or* X_2. (Area A represents the portion that cannot be explained by either variable or their combination, the residual variation.) Thus, the two predictors in our example account for 60% of the variation of Y: $B + C + D = 25 + 20 + 15 = 60$. The *squared semipartial correlation* between X_1 and Y, with X_2 partialled out of X_1, is the portion of the variation of Y that X_1

accounts for *over and above* the portion accounted for by X_2. As such, it is .25.

$$r_{0(1.2)}^2 = R_{0.12}^2 - r_{02}^2 = .60 - .35 = .25$$

The semipartial correlation is the square root of this quantity.

$$r_{0(1.2)} = \sqrt{.25} = .50$$

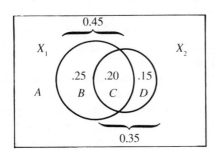

FIGURE 15.3
Venn diagram illustrating partial and semipartial correlation

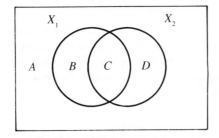

FIGURE 15.4
Venn diagram defining various correlational statistics

The *squared partial correlation* has a similar interpretation. Instead of being the additional percentage of Y that X_1 explains but that X_2 does not, which is the squared *semi*partial correlation, it is the additional amount that X_1 explains *relative to* the amount that X_2 left to be explained. For example, $r_{02}^2 = .35$ and $1 - r_{02}^2 = .65$,

$$r_{01.2}^2 = \frac{r_{0(1.2)}^2}{1 - r_{02}^2}$$

$$= \frac{.25}{.65} = .385$$

$$= \sqrt{.385}$$

$$= .620$$

Schematically, squared multiple, partial, and semipartial correlations can be represented as

$$r_{0(1.2)}^2 = B = \text{the squared semipartial correlation}$$

$$r_{01.2}^2 = \frac{B}{A + B} = \text{the squared partial correlation}$$

$$= \frac{r_{0(1.2)}^2}{1 - r_{0.2}^2}$$

In addition,

$$A = 1 - R_{0.12}^2 = \text{the residual (unexplained) variation in } Y$$

$$D = r_{0(2.1)}^2 = \text{the other squared semipartial correlation}$$

$$B + C + D = R_{0.12}^2 = \text{the squared multiple correlation coefficient}$$

$$B + C = r_{01}^2 = \text{the squared correlation between } Y \text{ and } X_1$$

$$C + D = r_{02}^2 = \text{the squared correlation between } Y \text{ and } X_2$$

15.8   SUPPRESSOR VARIABLES

Suppressor variable

Suppose we have a multiple-regression problem in which all variables are scored so as to correlate positively with the criterion. Since the scoring of variables is often arbitrary anyway, this presents no difficulty (if X is negatively related to Y, $C - X$ will be positively related to Y, where C is any constant). In such a situation, we would expect all the regression coefficients (β_i or b_i) to be positive. Occasionally, however, a regression coefficient in this situation will be (significantly) negative. Such a variable, if significant, is called a **suppressor variable**.

Suppressor variables seem, at first glance, to be unreasonable. We know that the simple correlation between the criterion and the variable is positive (by our definition), yet in the resulting regression equation an increment on this variable produces a decrement in $\hat{Y}$. Moreover, it can be shown that $R^2 = \Sigma\beta_i r_{0i}$. If r_{0i} is positive and β_i is negative, the product $\beta_i r_{0i}$ will be negative. Thus, by assigning β_i a negative value, the regression solution (which has the task of minimizing error) would *appear* to be reducing R^2. This does not fit with our preconceived ideas of what should be happening, and yet obviously there must be some logical explanation.

Space considerations do not allow an extensive discussion of the theory of suppressor variables, but it is important to illustrate one intuitively sensible explanation. For a more extensive discussion of suppressor variables, see Darlington (1968). Here we will merely take an example from Darlington (1990). Suppose a speeded history examination (a long exam with a short time in which to complete it) is used as a measure of some external criterion of knowledge of history. Although knowledge of history is presumably independent of reading speed, performance on the speeded test will not be. Thus, some of the variance in test scores will reflect differences in the reading speed of the students rather than differences in their actual knowledge. What we would really like to do is to penalize students who did well *only* because they read quickly, and help students who did poorly *only* because they read slowly. This is precisely what is accomplished by having reading speed serve as a suppressor variable. It is suppressing some of the error in the exam scores.

As Darlington points out, a variable will serve as a suppressor variable when it correlates more highly with Y_r than with Y (where Y_r represents the residual when predicting history knowledge from history score), and will not serve as a suppressor variable when it correlates more highly with Y than Y_r.

15.9 REGRESSION DIAGNOSTICS

In predicting course evaluations from variables that described the course and the instructor, we skipped an important step because of the need to first lay out some of the important concepts in multiple regression. It is now time to go back and fill that gap. Before throwing all of the observations and predictors into the model and asking computer software to produce an answer to be written up and interpreted, we need to look more closely at the data. We will do this using a variety of tools supplied by nearly all multiple-regression computer programs. Once we are satisfied with the data, we can then go on and use other available tools to help us decide which variables to include in the model.

The first step in examining the data has already been carried out in Table 15.2 with stem-and-leaf displays on all six variables. At that point we noted that most of the variables were fairly nicely distributed with few outliers. Teach and Exam each had one unusually low score, whereas Enroll had four quite high scores. This should alert us to the potential influence of those cases, but aside from correcting any obvious errors that we identify, we will go ahead with our first analysis.

Multivariate outliers

The fact that we don't have more outliers when we look at the variables individually does not necessarily mean that all is well. There is still the possibility of having **multivariate outliers**. A case might seem to have reasonable scores on each of the variables taken separately but have an unusual *combination* of scores on two or more variables. For example, it is not uncommon to be 6 feet tall, nor is it uncommon to weigh 115 pounds. But it clearly would be unusual to be 6 feet tall *and* weigh 115 pounds.

Having temporarily satisfied ourselves that the data set does not contain unreasonable data points and that the distributions are not seriously distorted, a useful second step is to conduct a preliminary regression analysis using all the variables, as we have done. I say "preliminary" because the point here is to use that analysis to examine the data rather than as an end in itself.

Instead of jumping directly into the course-evaluation data set, we will first investigate diagnostic tools with a smaller data set created to illustrate the use of those tools. These data are shown below and are plotted in Figure 15.5 using EXECUSTAT.

X: 1 1 3 3 3 4 5   5   7 6 10 13
Y: 1 2 3 5 7 6 8 10 10 5   4 14

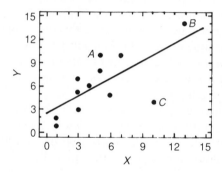

FIGURE 15.5
Scatterplot of *X* and *Y*

The three primary classes of diagnostic statistics, each of which is represented in Figure 15.5, are:

Distance

1. **Distance**, which is useful in identifying potential outliers in the dependent variable (Y).

Leverage (h_i)

2. **Leverage (h_i)**, which is useful in identifying potential outliers in the independent variables ($X_1, X_2, \ldots, X_p$).

Influence

3. **Influence**, which combines distance and leverage to identify unusually influential observations. An observation is influential if the location of the regression surface would change markedly depending on the presence or absence of that observation.

Our most common measure of distance is the residual ($Y_i - \hat{Y}_i$). It measures the vertical distance between any point and the regression line. Points *A* and *C* in Figure 15.5 have large residuals. Such points may represent random error, they may be data that are incorrectly recorded, or they may reflect unusual cases that don't really belong in this data set. (An example of this last point would arise if we were trying to predict physical reaction time as a function of cognitive processing features of a task, and our subjects included one individual who suffered from a neuromuscular disorder that seriously slowed his reaction time.) Residuals are a standard feature of all regression analyses, and you should routinely request and examine them in running your analyses.

Leverage (often denoted h_i, or "hat diag") measures the degree to which a case is unusual with respect to the predictor variables X_j. In the case of one predictor, leverage is simply a function of the deviation of the score on that predictor from the predictor mean. Point *B* in Figure 15.5 is an example of a point with high leverage because the X score for that point (13) is far from $\overline{X}$. Possible values on leverage range from a low of $1/N$ to a high of 1.0, with a mean of $(p + 1)/N$. Most programs for multiple regression compute and print the leverage of each observation if requested.

Points that are high on either distance or leverage do not necessarily have an important influence on the regression, but they have the potential for it. In order for a point to be high on influence, it must have relatively high values on both distance and leverage. In Figure 15.5, Point *B* is very high on leverage, but it has a relatively small residual. Point *A*, on the other hand, has a large residual but, since it is near the mean on X, has low leverage. Point *C* is high on leverage and has a large residual, suggesting that it is high on influence. The most common measure of influence is

Cook's D

known as **Cook's D**. It is a function of the sum of the squared *changes* in $\hat{Y}_i$ that would occur if the *i*th observation were removed from the data and the analysis rerun.

Exhibit 15.2 contains various diagnostic statistics for the data shown in Figure 15.5. These diagnostics were produced by a statistical package for microcomputers called NCSS, but similar statistics would be produced by almost any other program. (The entries have been reduced to two decimal digits for presentation, although calculations were carried out with 14-digit accuracy.)

To take the diagnostic statistics listed (on p. 510) in order, consider first the column headed Resid., which is a measure of distance. This column reflects what we can already see in Figure 15.5—that the 8th and 11th observations have the largest residuals. Considering that the Y values range only from 1 to 14, a residual of -5.89 seems substantial.

EXHIBIT 15.2
Diagnostic statistics
for data in Figure
15.5

	OBS	X	Y	PRED	RESID	RSTUDENT	HAT DIAG H	MSE	COOK'S D
	1	1	1	3.23	-2.23	-0.87	0.20	8.22	0.10
	2	1	2	3.23	-1.22	-0.47	0.20	8.71	0.03
	3	3	3	4.71	-1.71	-0.62	0.11	8.55	0.03
	4	3	5	4.71	0.29	0.10	0.11	8.91	0.00
	5	3	7	4.71	2.29	0.85	0.11	8.26	0.05
	6	4	6	5.45	0.55	0.19	0.09	8.88	0.00
	7	5	8	6.19	1.81	0.65	0.08	8.52	0.02
"A" →	8	5	10	6.19	3.81	1.49	0.08	7.16	0.09
	9	6	5	6.93	-1.93	-0.69	0.09	8.46	0.02
	10	7	10	7.77	2.33	0.86	0.11	8.24	0.05
"C" →	11	10	4	9.89	-5.89	-3.54	0.26	3.73	1.01
"B" →	12	13	14	12.11	1.89	0.98	0.54	8.06	0.55

If the data met the underlying assumptions, we would expect the values of Y to be normally distributed about the regression line. In other words, with a very large data set all of the Y values corresponding to a specific value of X would have a normal distribution. Five percent of these values would lie more than 1.96 adjusted standard errors from the regression line, and so on. (I use the word "adjusted" because the size of the standard error will depend in part on the degree to which X departs from the mean of X, as measured by h_i.) Within this context, it may be meaningful to ask if a point lies significantly far from the regression line. If so, we should be concerned about it. A t test on the magnitude of the residuals is given by the statistic RStudent, some-

Studentized residual   times called the **Studentized residual**. This can be interpreted as a standard t statistic on $(N - p - 1)$ degrees of freedom. Here we see that for case 11 RStudent = -3.54. This should give us pause because that is a substantial, and significant, deviation. It is often useful to think of RStudent less as a hypothesis-testing statistic and more as just an indicator of the magnitude of the residual. But significant or not, something that is 3.54 standard errors from the line is unusual and therefore noteworthy. We are not predicting that case well.

We now turn to leverage (h_i), shown in the column headed Hat Diag. Here we see that most observations have leverage values that fall between about 0.00 and 0.20. The mean leverage is $(p + 1)/N = 2/12 = 0.167$, and that is about what we would expect. Notice, however, that two cases have larger leverage; namely, cases 11 and 12. We have already seen that 11 has a large residual, so its modest leverage may make it an influential point. Case 12 has a leverage value nearly twice as large. However, it falls quite close to the regression line with a fairly small residual, and it is likely to be less influential.

Finally, we turn to the last two columns, which relate directly to the influence exerted by the individual observations. These two columns both deal with what we would expect if the observation in question were removed from the analysis. In the overall analysis, which is not shown, $MS_{residual}$ from the analysis of variance table was 8.025. This is a measure of the residual variance, or the variability in the data that cannot be predicted by X. The column headed MSE_i (which stands for mean square error and is synonymous with $MS_{residual}$) tells us what the residual variance would be if we deleted the corresponding case and reran the analysis. Thus, without the first case, $MS_{residual}$ would increase very slightly from 8.025 to 8.22. But note that if we set aside the 11th case, $MS_{residual}$ would drop by more than half, from 8.025 to 3.73.

Another way to look at influence is to calculate Cook's D, which is a function of residual, leverage (h_i), and $MS_{residual}$. Most of the values in the last column are quite small, but cases 11 and 12 are exceptions. In particular, observation 11 has a D exceeding 1.00. The sampling distribution of Cook's D is in dispute, and there is no general rule for what constitutes a large value; but values over 1.00 are unusual.

We can summarize the results shown in Exhibit 15.2 by stating that each of the three points labelled in Figure 15.5 is reflected in that table. Point A has a fairly, though not significantly, large residual but has small values for both leverage and influence. Point C has a large leverage, but Cook's D is not terribly high and its removal would not substantially reduce $MS_{residual}$. Point B has a large residual, a fairly large leverage, and a substantial Cook's D; its removal would provide a substantial reduction in $MS_{residual}$. This is the kind of observation that we should consider seriously. Although data should not be deleted merely because they are inconvenient and their removal would make the results look better, it is important to pay attention to observations such as case 11. There may be legitimate reasons to set that case aside and to treat it differently. Or it may in fact be erroneous. Because this is not a real data set, we cannot do anything further with it.

It may seem like overkill to compute regression diagnostics simply to confirm what anyone can see simply by looking at a plot of the data. However, we have looked only at a situation with one predictor variable. With multiple predictors there is no reasonable way to plot the data and visually identify influential points. In that situation you should at least create univariate stem-and-leaf displays, perhaps bivariate plots of each predictor against the criterion looking for peculiar distributions of points, and compute diagnostic statistics. From those statistics you can then target particular cases for closer study.

Returning briefly to the data on course evaluations, we can illustrate some additional points concerning diagnostic statistics. Exhibit 15.3 contains additional statistics taken from the SAS printout in Exhibit 15.1. These are a few of the statistics produced by the R and INFLUENCE options on the Model command.

	OBS	RESIDUAL	RSTUDENT	HAT DIAG H	COOK'S D
EXHIBIT 15.3					
Regression					
diagnostics for	1	-0.3734	-1.2010	0.0477	0.012
course-evaluation	2	0.2408	0.7921	0.1061	0.013
data	3	0.0536	0.2508	0.5644	0.014
	4	0.3488	1.1150	0.0401	0.009
	5	0.2576	0.9072	0.2167	0.038
	. . .	. . .	. . .	. . .	. . .
	13	0.3048	1.0094	0.1101	0.021
	14	-0.3945	-1.2875	0.0704	0.021
	15	0.8246	3.1489	0.1955	0.334
	16	-0.2025	-0.6549	0.0792	0.006
	. . .	. . .	. . .	. . .	. . .
	20	-0.0775	-0.2464	0.0562	0.001
	21	0.4141	1.3807	0.1045	0.036
	22	-0.1113	-0.3604	0.0836	0.002
	. . .	. . .	. . .	. . .	. . .
	41	-0.3467	-1.1104	0.0443	0.009
	42	0.1684	0.5409	0.0691	0.004
	43	-0.1564	-0.5116	0.1033	0.005
	44	0.6530	2.2351	0.0916	0.077
	45	-0.1624	-0.6928	0.4703	0.072
	46	0.0401	0.1297	0.0900	0.000
	. . .	. . .	. . .	. . .	. . .

You may recall that several observations had extreme scores on one or more variables. In particular, case 3 had unusually low ratings on Teach and Exam and a very high Enroll. It also had one of the lowest Overall ratings. Cases 4, 21, and 45 also had much larger Enrolls than usual. If we look at these cases in the diagnostic statistics above, we can see that none of them have very large residuals or leverage, and therefore they cannot have a high value for influence, as measured by Cook's D. (Case 3's leverage is larger than some, but is still not particularly large.) It is still possible, however, that the four courses with enrollments considerably larger than others make a disproportionate contribution to the regression. Recall that measures such as residuals or influence depend on how far that case departs from the regression surface. Cook's D in particular asks what the effect would be of removing a *single* case from the data set and rerunning the regression. When you have several cases that all depart in the same direction from the bulk of the data, removing one of them may have a minor effect because the rest are still there. If we have reason to think that large classes may differ in important ways from smaller ones and are worried about the potential effects of these outliers, it would make sense to rerun the analysis with those cases removed to see what effect this has. In fact, when you do so for the course data the value of R^2 is virtually unaffected (it goes from .7554 to .7580) and none of the regression coefficients (including that for Enroll) changes substantially.

One interesting case in these data is case 15, which has a Studentized residual (RStudent) of 3.1489, although it does not have particularly unusual values on any of the variables. Recall that RStudent is in fact a t statistic. At first glance this would seem like a significant value of t (on 44 degrees of freedom). However, keep in mind that we are computing 50 different t values here, and some of them can be expected to be significant by chance. We can apply a Bonferroni correction to this test statistic by using Appendix t' with $c = 50$ and $\alpha = .05$. With interpolation, the critical value of t' would be 3.525, and our test is not significant.

15.10 CONSTRUCTING A REGRESSION EQUATION

A major problem for anyone who has ever attempted to write a regression equation to predict some criterion concerns choosing the variables to be included in the model. We often suffer from having too many potential variables rather than too few. Although it would be possible to toss in all of the variables to see what would happen, this solution is neither practical nor wise.

Before we look at formal stepwise methods of constructing regression equations, we should first look at two (related) statistics that deal with the relationship among the potential predictor variables. If we want to use several variables to predict Y, presumably we would like each of those variables to bring something new to the task. If variables X_1 and X_2 are themselves very highly correlated, we won't learn much more from both of them than we would from either of them alone.

Exhibit 15.1 (p. 489) contains two columns of numbers that we have not yet discussed. The first is tolerance and the second is the variance inflation factor (VIF). **Toler-**

Tolerance

Cross-correlation

ance refers to the degree to which one predictor can itself be predicted by the other predictors in the model. To be more specific, if we let R_X refer to the correlation (sometimes called the **cross-correlation**) between one predictor and all other predictors, tolerance is defined as $(1 - R_X^2)$. Looking at Exhibit 15.1 we can see that with Teach as the criterion and Exam, Knowledge, Grade, and Enroll as the predictors, tolerance equals .41819 (rounded). Thus,

$$\text{Tolerance} = .41819 = (1 - R_X^2)$$

$$R_X^2 = (1 - .41819) = .58181$$

The squared multiple correlation predicting the Teach predictor from the other four predictors is .58. On the other hand, if we used one of the last three variables as the criterion and the others as predictors, the tolerance would be in the .60s and R_X^2 would be in the mid .30s.

Tolerance tells us two things. First, it tells us the degree of overlap among the predictors, helping us to see which predictors have information in common and which are relatively independent. Just because two variables substantially overlap in their information is not reason enough to combine them, but it does alert us to the possibility that their joint contribution might be less than we would like. Note that the only other significant variable in this model using all five predictors is Knowledge, which has, as it turns out, the highest tolerance and thus the least overlap with the others.

Singular

Second, the tolerance statistic alerts us to the potential problems of instability in our model. With very low levels of tolerance, the stability of the model and sometimes even the accuracy of the arithmetic can be in danger. In the extreme case where one predictor can be perfectly predicted from the others, we will have what is called a **singular** covariance (or correlation) matrix and most programs will stop without generating a model. If you see a statement in your printout that says that the matrix is singular or "not positive-definite," the most likely explanation is that one predictor has a tolerance of 0.00 and is perfectly correlated with others. In this case you will have to drop at least one predictor to break up that relationship. Such a relationship most frequently occurs when one predictor is the simple sum or average of the others, or where all p predictors sum to a constant.

Variance inflation factor (VIF)

The reciprocal of tolerance is called the **variance inflation factor (VIF)**, and it refers to the degree to which the standard error of b_j is increased because of the degree to which X_j is correlated with the other predictors. The higher the standard error of b_j, the more variable that coefficient will be from sample to sample and the less confidence we can have in the particular value that we obtained. We want stable regression coefficients, and therefore we want variables with low VIFs, or high tolerances. It is often worth eliminating a redundant variable from the model to achieve that goal.

SELECTION METHODS

There are many ways to construct some sort of "optimal" regression equation from a large set of variables. This section will briefly describe several of these approaches. But first we must raise the issue of whether this whole approach is generally appropriate. In many cases it is not.

If we assume that you have a large set of variables and a large number of data points, and are truly interested in a question of prediction (you want to predict who will do well at some job and have no particular theoretical axe to grind), then one of these methods may be for you. However, if you are trying to test some theoretical model by looking to see if certain variables are related to some outcome (e.g., can you predict adolescents' psychological symptoms on the basis of major stressful events, daily hassles, and parental stress), then choosing a model on the basis of some criterion such as the maximum R^2 or the minimum $MS_{residual}$ is not likely to be particularly helpful. In fact, it may be particularly harmful by causing you to focus on statistically derived models that fit only slightly, and perhaps nonsignificantly, better than some other more logically appropriate model. Conducting a stepwise analysis, for example, so as to report which of two competing psychological variables is second to enter the equation often adds a spurious form of statistical elegance to a poor theory. Solid arguments against the use of stepwise regression for the purpose of ordering variables by importance have been given by Huberty (1989), and Henderson and Denison (1989), in an excellent article that summarizes many of the important issues, imply that "stepwise regression" should be called "unwise regression."

On the assumption that you still want to construct a regression model using some form of variable-selection process, we will consider three alternative approaches: all subsets regression, backward elimination, and stepwise regression. A readable and much more thorough discussion of this topic can be found in Draper and Smith (1981, Chapter 6).

ALL SUBSETS REGRESSION

All subsets regression

The simplest of these methods at a conceptual level is called **all subsets regression** for the rather obvious reason that it looks at all possible subsets of the predictor variables. With three or four predictors and some patience you could conduct such an analysis by using any standard computer package to calculate multiple analyses. However, with a large number of variables the only way to go about this is to use a specialized program such as BMDP9R or SAS PROC RSQUARE. Either of these programs allows you to specify the largest and smallest number of predictors to appear in each subset and the number of subsets of each size. (For example, you can say, "Give me the eight models with the highest R^2s using five predictors.")

You can define "best" in several different ways; these ways do not always lead to the same models. You can select models on the basis of (1) the magnitude of R^2, (2) the magnitude of $MS_{residual}$, (3) a statistic called Mallow's C_p, and (4) a statistic called PRESS. The magnitudes of R^2 and $MS_{residual}$ have already been discussed. We search for that combination of predictors with the highest R^2 (or better yet, adjusted R^2) or that set that minimizes error. Mallow's C_p statistic compares the relative magnitudes of the error term in any particular model with the error term in the complete model with all predictors present (see Draper & Smith, 1981, p. 299). Since the error term in the reduced model must be greater than (or equal to) the error term in the full model, we want to minimize that ratio.

PRESS is a statistic similar to $MS_{residual}$ in that it looks at $\Sigma(Y_i - \hat{Y}_i)^2$, but in the case of PRESS the predictions are made from a data set that includes all cases *except* the one to be predicted. Ordering models on the basis of PRESS would generally, though not always, be similar to ordering them on the basis of $MS_{residual}$. The advantage of PRESS is that it is more likely to focus on influential data points (see Draper & Smith, 1981, p. 325.)

The major disadvantage of all subsets regression, aside from the enormous amount of computer time it could involve, is the fact that it has a substantial potential for capitalizing on chance. By fitting all possible models to the data, or at least the best of all possible models, you run the serious risk of selecting those models that best fit the peculiar data points that are unique to your data set. The final R^2 cannot reasonably be thought of as an unbiased estimate of the corresponding population parameter.

BACKWARD ELIMINATION

Backward elimination

The **backward elimination** procedure, as well as the stepwise regression procedure to follow, are generally lumped under the term *stepwise procedures* because they go about their task in a logical stepwise fashion. They both have the advantage of being easy to carry out interactively using standard regression procedures, although programs to carry them out automatically are readily available.

In the backward elimination procedure, we begin with a model that includes all of the predictors. Having computed that model, we examine the tests on the individual regression coefficients, or look at the partial or semipartial correlations and remove the variable that contributes the least to the model (assuming that its contribution is nonsignificant). We then rerun the regression without that predictor, again looking for the variable with the smallest contribution, remove that, and continue. Normally we continue until we come to a model in which all of the remaining predictors are significant, although alternative stopping points are possible. For example, we could plot R^2 or $MS_{residual}$ against the number of predictors in the model and stop when that curve shows a break in direction.

Most computer programs that use backward elimination or stepwise regression use some combination of terms called "F to enter," "F to remove," "p to enter," and "p to remove." To take just one of these, consider "p to remove." If we plan to remove predictors from the model if they fail to reach significance at $\alpha = .05$, then we set "p to remove" at .05. The "F to remove" would simply be the critical value of F corresponding to that level of p. (Those programs that calculate t statistics instead of F would simply make the appropriate change.) The situation is actually more complicated than I have made it seem (see Draper & Smith, 1981, p. 311), but for practical purposes it is as I have described.[†]

[†] As Draper and Smith (1981) point out, when we are testing *optimal* models the F statistics are not normal Fs and their probability values should not be interpreted as if they were. Thus, although both F and p form the basis of a legitimate ordering of potential variables, do not put too much faith in the actual probabilities. McIntyre, Montgomery, Srinwason, and Weitz (1983) address this problem directly and illustrate the liberal nature of the test. They also provide guidelines on more appropriate tests on stepwise correlation coefficients.

An important disadvantage of backward elimination is that it too capitalizes on chance. Since it begins with many predictors, it has the opportunity to identify and account for any suppressor relations among variables that can be found in the data. For example, if variables 7 and 8 have some sort of suppressor relationship between them, this method has a good chance of finding it and making those variables a part of the model. If that is a true relationship, then backward elimination has done what we want it to. On the other hand, if the relationship is spurious, we have just wasted extra variables explaining something that does not deserve explanation. Darlington (1990, p. 166) made this point about both backward elimination and all subsets regression. True suppressor relationships are fairly rare, but apparent ones are fairly common. Therefore, methods that systematically look for them, especially without accompanying hypothesis tests, may be misleading more often than simpler methods that ignore them.

STEPWISE REGRESSION

Stepwise regression

The **stepwise regression** method is more or less the reverse of the backward elimination method. However, since at each stage we do not have all of the other variables in the model and therefore immediately available to test as we did with backward elimination, we will go about it in a slightly different way.

Stepwise regression relies on the fact that

$$R_{0.123\ldots p}^2 = r_{01}^2 + r_{0(2.1)}^2 + r_{p(3.12)}^2 + \cdots$$

If we define variable 1 as that variable with the highest validity (correlation with the criterion), then the first step in the process involves only variable 1. We then calculate all semipartials of the form $r_{0(1,i)}$, $i = 2 \ldots p$. The variable (assume that it is X_2) with the highest (first-order) semipartial correlation with the criterion is the one that will produce the greatest increment in R^2. This variable is then entered and we obtain the regression of Y on X_1 and X_2. We now test to see whether that variable contributes significantly to the model containing two variables. We could either test the regression coefficient or the semipartial correlation directly, or test to see if there was a significant increment in R^2. The result would be the same. Because the test on the increment in R^2 will prove useful later, we will do it that way here.

A test on the difference between an R^2 based on f predictors and an R^2 based on r predictors (where the r predictors are a subset of the f predictors) is given by

$$F_{(f-r,N-f-1)} = \frac{(N - f - 1)(R_f^2 - R_r^2)}{(f - r)(1 - R_f^2)}$$

where R_f^2 is the r^2 for the full model $= R_{0.12}^2$, R_r^2 is the R^2 for the reduced model $= R_{0.1}^2$, f is the number of predictors in the full model, and r is the number of predictors in the reduced model.

This process is repeated until the addition of further variables produces no significant (by whatever criterion we wish to use) improvement. At each step in the process, before we add a new variable we first ask whether a variable that was added on an earlier step should now be removed on the grounds that it is no longer making a

Forward selection

significant contribution. If the test on a variable falls below "*F* to remove" (or above "*p* to remove"), that variable is removed before another variable is added. Procedures that do not include this step are often referred to as **forward selection** procedures.

An example of the use of the stepwise regression procedure is shown in Exhibit 15.4 for the data in Table 15.1. The solution was obtained using SPSS[X] with the STEP-WISE command. (Similar results would be obtained using BMDP2R or SAS PROC STEPWISE.) In SPSS[X] the STEPWISE command both adds variables in the forward direction *and* tests at each stage to see whether a variable that had previously been entered should now be removed. The SPSS[X] FORWARD command adds variables in a forward direction but does not remove any variable that has already been added. I do not recommend using that command unless you have a particular reason to do so.

EXHIBIT 15.4
Stepwise regression
for data in Table 15.1

```
1   0   Title          'Stepwise Regression for Course Evaluation Data'
2   0   File Handle    Data / Name = ' [D_Howell.book]Albatros.dat'
3   0   Data List      File = Data/
4   0                      Overall Teach Exam Knowledg Grade 1-20 Enroll 21-23
5   0   Regression     /Descriptives
6   0                  /Variables = all
7   0                  /Criterion PIN(.25) POUT(.30)
8   0                  /Dependent = Overall
9   0                  /Method = Stepwise
```

* * * *   M U L T I P L E   R E G R E S S I O N   * * * *

Listwise Deletion of Missing Data

	Mean	Std Dev	Label
OVERALL	3.550	.614	
TEACH	3.664	.532	
EXAM	3.808	.493	
KNOWLEDG	4.176	.408	
GRADE	3.486	.351	
ENROLL	88.000	145.059	

N of Cases =   50

Correlation:

	OVERALL	TEACH	EXAM	KNOWLEDG	GRADE	ENROLL
OVERALL	1.000	.804	.596	.682	.301	-.240
TEACH	.804	1.000	.720	.526	.469	-.451
EXAM	.596	.720	1.000	.451	.610	-.558
KNOWLEDG	.682	.526	.451	1.000	.224	-.128
GRADE	.301	.469	.610	.224	1.000	-.337
ENROLL	-.240	-.451	-.558	-.128	-.337	1.000

* * * *   M U L T I P L E   R E G R E S S I O N   * * * *

Equation Number 1   Dependent Variable . .   OVERALL
Beginning Block Number 1.   Method: Step 1

Variable(s) Entered on Step Number 1 . .   TEACH

Multiple R	.80386	Analysis of Variance			
R Square	.64620		DF	Sum of Squares	Mean Square
Adjusted R Square	.63882	Regression	1	11.91908	11.91908
Standard Error	.36872	Residual	48	6.52592	.13596

F =   87.66820   Signif F =   .0000

- - - - - - - - - Variables in the Equation - - - - - - - - - -   - - - - - - - - - Variables not in the Equation - - - - - - - - - -

Variable	B	SE B	Beta In	T	Sig T	Variable	Beta In	Partial	Min Toler	T	Sig T

EXHIBIT 15.4 (Cont.)

Variable	B	SE B	Beta In	T	Sig T	Variable				
TEACH	.926833	.098988	.803863	9.363	.0000	EXAM	.035361	.041275	.482038	.283	.7783
(Constant)	.154082	.366420		.421	.6760	KNOWLEDG	.357863	.511583	.723039	4.082	.0002
						GRADE	-.097856	-.145288	.779913	-1.007	.3192
						ENROLL	.154472	.231771	.796491	1.633	.1091

* *

Variable(s) Entered on Step Number 2 . .   KNOWLEDG

		Analysis of Variance			
Multiple R	.85953				
R Square	.73879		DF	Sum of Squares	Mean Square
Adjusted R Square	.72768	Regression	2	13.62703	6.81351
Standard Error	.32017	Residual	47	4.81797	.10251

      F = 66.46675   Signif F = .0000

---------- Variables in the Equation ----------   --------- Variables not in the Equation ---------

Variable	B	SE B	Beta In	T	Sig T	Variable	Beta In	Partial	Min Toler	T	Sig T
TEACH	.709690	.101084	.61553	7.021	.0000	EXAM	-.018910	-.025493	.431118	-.173	.8634
KNOWLEDG	.538326	.131884	.35786	4.082	.0002	GRADE	-.087527	-.151173	.593212	-1.037	.3051
(Constant)	-1.298356	.477335		-2.720	.0091	ENROLL	.107495	.185744	.573268	1.282	.2062

* * * * M U L T I P L E R E G R E S S I O N * * * *

Equation Number 1   Dependent Variable . . OVERALL

Variable(s) Entered on Step Number 3 . . ENROLL

		Analysis of Variance			
Multiple R	.86476				
R Square	.74780		DF	Sum of Squares	Mean Square
Adjusted R Square	.73136	Regression	3	13.79325	4.59775
Standard Error	.31800	Residual	46	4.65175	.10113

      F = 45.46600   Signif F = .0000

----------- Variables in the Equation -----------   ----------- Variables not in the Equation -----------

Variable	B	SE B	Beta	T	Sig T	Variable	Beta In	Partial	Min Toler	T	Sig T
TEACH	.775484	.112754	.672594	6.878	.0000	EXAM	.043445	.054586	.398124	.367	.7155
KNOWLEDG	.513828	.132376	.341578	3.882	.0003	GRADE	-.072471	-.125815	.510823	-.851	.3994
ENROLL	4.546E-04	3.546E-04	.107495	1.282	.2062						
(Constant)	-1.477127	.494180		-2.989	.0045						

End Block Number 1 PIN = .250 Limits reached.

In Exhibit 15.4 you can see that PIN (p to enter) was set to .25, meaning that a variable will be added if its regression coefficient would be significant at $\alpha = .25$. This was done primarily to make the example more complete. Normally, PIN would not be set much higher than .10. In this example, POUT (p to remove) was set at .30. It must be set higher than PIN to prevent a situation where a variable is continually added, then removed, then added again, ad infinitum.

Of the three variable selection methods discussed here, the stepwise regression method is probably the best. Both Draper and Smith (1981) and Darlington (1990) recommend it as perhaps the best compromise between finding an "optimal" equation for predicting future randomly selected data sets from the same population and finding an equation that predicts the maximum variance for the specific data set under consideration.

CROSS-VALIDATION

Cross-validation

The stumbling block for most multiple-regression studies is the concept of **cross-validation** of the regression equation against an independent data set. In cross-validation we might obtain data on 1000 subjects and then break the sample into two subsamples of 500 subjects each. For each sample we obtain a regression equation. We then apply the regression coefficients obtained from one sample against the data in the other sample to obtain predicted values of Y on a cross-validation sample ($\hat{Y}_{cv}$). Our interest then focuses on the question of the relationship between Y and $\hat{Y}_{cv}$ in the new subsample. If the regression equations have any reasonable level of validity, then the cross-validation correlation (R_{cv}—the correlation between Y and $\hat{Y}_{cv}$ predicted on the *other* sample's regression equation) should be high. If they do not, our solution does not amount to much. R_{cv}^2 will in almost all cases be less than R^2, since R^2 depends on a regression equation tailored for that set of data. Essentially, we have an equation that does its best to account for every bump and wiggle (including sampling error) in the data. We should not be surprised when it does not do as well in accounting for different bumps and wiggles in a different set of data. However, substantial differences between R^2 and R_{cv}^2 are an indication that our solution lacks appreciable validity. When our regression equation for the data from Table 15.1 (using Teach, Knowledge, and Enroll as predictors) was applied to a new set of 50 courses, the correlation of Y_i and $\hat{Y}_i$ derived from the regression equation in Exhibit 15.1 was .8181, representing an acceptable level of cross-validation, considering that the R for the original sample was .8691.

As Darlington (1990) pointed out, our adjusted R^2, defined as

$$\text{adj } R^2 = 1 - \frac{(1 - R^2)(N - 1)}{N - p - 1}$$

is an estimate of the correlation in the population between Y and a *population* regression equation for $\hat{Y}_i$. It is not (and in fact is an overestimation of) the expected correlation in a cross-validation sample. See Darlington (1990, p. 159f) for estimates of the cross-validation correlation.

15.11 THE "IMPORTANCE" OF INDIVIDUAL VARIABLES

When an investigator derives a regression equation to predict some criterion on the basis of several variables, it is logical for her to want to know which of the variables is most important in predicting Y. Unfortunately, that question has no simple answer, except in the unusual case in which the predictors are mutually independent. As we have seen, β_j (or β_j^2) is sometimes taken as a measure of importance. This is done on the grounds that β^2 can be interpreted as the *unique* contribution of each variable to the prediction of Y. Thus, X_1 has some variance in common with Y that is not shared by any of the other variables, and this variance is represented by β_1^2. The difficulty with this measure is that it has nothing to say about the portion of the variance of Y that X_1 shares with the other variables but that is in some sense part of the contribution of X_1 to the prediction of Y. Moreover, what does it mean to speak of the independent contribution of variables that are not independent?

Darlington (1990) has argued against using β_j as a measure of importance. β_j does represent the difference, in standard deviation units, between two cases that are equal on all other predictor variables but differ by one unit on X_j. However, this does not take into account the fact that when variables are highly correlated such cases will rarely, if ever, exist.

Multicollinearity

Basing a measure of importance on the β weights has the further serious drawback that when variables are highly correlated (a condition known as **multicollinearity**), the values of β are very unstable from sample to sample, although R^2 may change very little. Given two sets of data, it would not be particularly unusual to find

$$\hat{Y} = 0.50Z_1 + 0.25Z_2$$

in one case and

$$\hat{Y} = 0.25Z_1 + 0.50Z_2$$

in the other, with nearly equal values of R^2 associated with the two equations. If we now seek a measure of the contribution of each of the predictors in accounting for Y (as opposed to using regression to simply predict Y for a given set of data), we could come to quite different conclusions for the two data sets. Darlington (1968) presents an interesting discussion of this issue and concludes that β_i has only limited utility as a measure of "importance." An even stronger stand is taken by Cooley and Lohnes (1971), who point out that our estimate of β ultimately relies on our estimates of the elements of the intercorrelation matrix. Since this matrix contains $p + p(p - 1)/2$ intercorrelations that are all subject to sampling error, Cooley and Lohnes suggested that we must be exceedingly careful about attaching practical significance to the regression coefficients.

As an illustration of the variability of the regression coefficients, a second set of 50 courses, the same set as used for cross-validation, was drawn from the same source as that for the data in Table 15.1. In this case, R^2 was more or less the same as it had been for the first example ($R^2 = .70983$), but the regression equation looked quite different. In terms of standardized variables,

$$Z_{\hat{Y}} = 0.371 \text{ Teach} + 0.113 \text{ Exam} + 0.567 \text{ Knowledge} - 0.27 \text{ Grade} + 0.184 \text{ Enroll}$$

If you compare this equation with the one found from Exhibit 15.1, it is clear that there are substantial differences in some of the values of β_i.

Another measure of importance, which has much to recommend it, is the squared semipartial correlation between predictor i and the criterion (with all other predictors partialled out)—that is, $r^2_{0(i.12 \ldots p)}$. Darlington (1968) refers to this measure as the "usefulness" of a predictor. As we have already seen, this semipartial correlation squared represents the decrement in R^2 that would result from the elimination of the ith predictor from the model. When the main goal is prediction rather than explanation, this is probably the best measure of "importance." Fortunately, it is easy to obtain from most computer printouts, since

$$r^2_{0(i.123 \ldots p)} = \frac{F_i(1 - R^2_{0.123 \ldots p})}{N - p - 1}$$

where F_i is the F test on the individual β_i (or b_i) coefficients. (If your program uses t tests on the coefficient, $F = t^2$.) Since all terms but F_i are constant for $i = 1 \ldots p$, the F_is order the variables in the same way as do the squared semipartials, and thus can be used to rank order the variables in terms of their usefulness.

Darlington (1990) has made a strong case for not squaring the semipartial correlation when speaking about the importance of variables. His case is an interesting one. However, whether or not the correlations are squared will not affect the ordering of variables. (If you wish to argue persuasively about the absolute importance of a variable, you should read Darlington's argument.)

One final, and intriguing, proposal was offered by Cooley and Lohnes (1971). They proposed

$$\frac{r_{01}}{R_{0.123\ \ldots\ p}}$$

as a measure of the importance of the ith variable. It can be shown that this measure represents the correlation between X_i and $\hat{Y}$. As such, this measure has a certain intuitive appeal in that it is a direct measure of the degree to which variable i is related to the values actually predicted by the regression equation. The advantages and disadvantages of this measure have not been fully investigated, although Huberty (1989) has argued that it does little more than order variables by their validities. For an excellent discussion of measures of importance, see Harris (1985, 79ff).

One common, but unacceptable, method of ordering the importance of variables is to rank them by the order of their inclusion in a stepwise regression solution. The problem with this approach is that it ignores the interrelationships among the variables. Thus, the first variable to be entered is entered solely on the strength of its correlation with the criterion. The second variable entered is chosen on the basis of its correlation with the criterion after partialling the first variable but ignoring all others. The third is chosen on the basis of how it correlates with the criterion after partialling the first two variables, and so on. In other words, each variable is chosen on a different basis, and it makes little sense to rank them according to order of entry. To take a simple example, assume that variables 1, 2, and 3 correlate .79, .78, and .32 with the criterion. Assume further that variables 1 and 2 are correlated .95, whereas 1 and 3 are correlated .20. They will then enter the equation in the order 1, 3, and 2, with the last entry being nonsignificant. But in what sense do we mean to say that variable 3 ranks above variable 2 in importance? I would hate to defend such a statement to a reviewer—in fact, would be hard pressed even to say what I meant by importance in this situation. A similar point has been made well by Huberty (1989).

A considerable amount of work in psychology has been devoted to regression models of decision making and to the general problem of clinical versus actuarial prediction. An excellent, although dated, review of this literature is presented in Slovic and Lichtenstein (1971). This work represents a good example of the application of multiple regression to applied and theoretical problems in psychology.

15.12 USING APPROXIMATE REGRESSION COEFFICIENTS

I have pointed out that regression coefficients frequently show substantial fluctuations from sample to sample without producing drastic changes in R. This might lead someone to suggest that we might use rather crude approximations of these coefficients as a substitute for the more precise estimates obtained from the data. For example, suppose that a five-predictor problem produced the following regression equation:

$$\hat{Y} = 9.2 + 0.85X_1 + 2.1X_2 - 0.74X_3 + 3.6X_4 - 2.4X_5$$

We might ask how much loss we would suffer if we rounded these values to

$$\hat{Y} = 10 + 1X_1 + 2X_2 - 1X_3 + 4X_4 - 2X_5$$

The answer is that we would probably lose very little. Excellent discussions of this problem are given by Dawes and Corrigan (1974) and Wainer (1976, 1978).

This method of rounding off regression coefficients is more common than you might suppose. For example, the college admissions officer who quantifies the various predictors he has available and then weights the grade point average twice as highly as the letter of recommendation is really using crude estimates of what he thinks would be the actual regression coefficients. Similarly, many scoring systems for the Minnesota Multiphasic Personality Inventory (MMPI) are in fact based on the reduction of coefficients to convenient integers. Whether the use of these *diagnostic signs* produces results that are better than, worse than, or equivalent to the use of the usual linear regression equations is still a matter of debate. A dated but very comprehensive study of this question is presented in Goldberg (1965).

15.13   CURVILINEAR AND CONFIGURAL VARIABLES

We tend to think of multiple regression as being concerned solely with linear variables, although that is not necessarily the case. When we speak of *linear* multiple regression we are not referring to the fact that X_1 must be linear, but to the fact that the regression surface must be linear. Thus, in the one-predictor case, if we can draw a straight line representing the relationship between Y and X^2, we have a linear regression problem (although here the relationship between Y and X would be curvilinear). The same holds for the case of multiple regression. Thus, there is nothing to prevent us from writing a model of the form

$$\hat{Y} = b_0 + b_1 X_1 + b_2 X_2^2 + b_3 X_3^4 + b_4 X_4^{1/2}$$

Center

The only requirement is that our raw-data matrix must contain the values of X_1, X_2^2, X_3^3, and $X_4^{1/2}$, and not X_1, X_2, X_3, and X_4. In using models with exponential terms, it is often useful to **center** the data by subtracting the mean from each value of X_j. This is done because otherwise X_j and X_j^2 are likely to be highly correlated, thus introducing additional problems into the analysis.

A related problem is that presented by configural relationships among predictors. Thus, if we thought that X_1 and X_2 interacted with one another to produce a joint result, we might conceivably want a model of the form

$$\hat{Y} = b_0 + b_1 X_1 X_2 + b_2 X_3$$

Here again the raw data would consist of a column in which the entries were the products $X_1 X_2$ and a column in which the entries were X_3.

A particularly useful model in this regard resembles a standard analysis of variance model:

$$\hat{Y} = b_0 + b_1 X_1 + b_2 X_2 + b_3 X_1 X_2$$

Here X_1 and X_2 are analogous to the main effects of a two-way analysis of variance, whereas the $X_1 X_2$ term represents the interaction of those variables. The difference between this model and that for the analysis of variance is that its main effect and interaction terms are continuous rather than discrete variables. The interpretation of results would be similar, however. For an interesting discussion of such a model, see Finney, Mitchell, Cronkite, and Moos (1984). This paper includes a meaningful illustration examining depression as a function of stress, coping mechanisms, and their interaction. An important conclusion of this paper is that for the main effects to have a meaningful interpretation in the presence of an interaction, the variables X_1 and X_2 should be centered and expressed as deviations from their means. In other words, you should compute

$$X'_1 = X_1 - \overline{X}_1 \qquad \text{and} \qquad X'_2 = X_2 - \overline{X}_2$$

and run the analysis using the variables X'_1, X'_2, and $X'_1 X'_2$.

KEY TERMS

Scalar algebra (introduction)

Matrix algebra (introduction)

Validities (15.1)

Collinearity (15.1)

Regression coefficients (15.1)

Importance (15.1)

Standardized regression coefficients (15.1)

Residual variance (15.3)

Residual error (15.3)

Multivariate normal (15.4)

Multiple correlation coefficient ($R_{0.123 \dots p}$) (15.5)

Hyperspace (15.6)

Regression surface (15.6)

Partial correlation $r_{01.2}$ (15.7)

Semipartial correlation $r_{0(1.2)}$ (15.7)

Venn diagrams (15.7)

Suppressor variable (15.8)

Multivariate outliers (15.9)

Distance (15.9)

Leverage (h_i) (15.9)

Influence (15.9)

Cook's D (15.9)

Studentized residual (15.9)

Tolerance (15.10)

Cross correlation (15.10)

Singular (15.10)

Variance inflation factor (VIF) (15.10)

All subsets regression (15.10)

Backward elimination (15.10)

Stepwise regression (15.10)

Forward selection (15.10)

Cross-validation (15.10)

Multicollinearity (15.11)

Center (15.13)

EXERCISES

Note: Many of these exercises are based on a very small data set for reasons of economy of space and computational convenience. For actual applications of multiple regression, sample sizes should be appreciably larger than those used here.

15.1   A psychologist studying perceived "quality of life" in a large number of cities ($N = 150$) came up with the following equation using mean temperature (Temp), median income in $1000 (Income), per capita expenditure on social services (Socser), and population density (Popul) as predictors.

$$\hat{Y} = 5.37 - 0.01\,\text{Temp} + 0.05\,\text{Income} + 0.003\,\text{Socser} - 0.01\,\text{Popul}$$

(a) Interpret the regression equation in terms of the coefficients.
(b) Assume there is a city that has a mean temperature of 55 degrees, a median income of $12,000, spends $500 per capita on social services, and has a population density of 200 people per block. What is its predicted quality of life score?
(c) What would we predict in a different city that was identical in every way except that it spent $100 per capita on social services?

15.2   Refer to Exercise 15.1. Assume that

$$\beta = [-0.438 \quad 0.762 \quad 0.081 \quad -0.132]$$

Interpret the results.

15.3   For the values of β in Exercise 15.2, the corresponding standard errors are

$$[0.397 \quad 0.252 \quad 0.052 \quad 0.025]$$

Which, if any, predictor would you be most likely to drop if you wanted to refine your regression equation?

15.4   A large corporation is interested in predicting a measure of job satisfaction among its employees. They have collected data on 15 employees who each supplied information on job satisfaction, level of responsibility, number of people supervised, rating of working environment, and years of service. The data follow:

Satisfaction:	2 2 3 3 5 5 6 6 6 7 8 8 8 9 9
Responsibility:	4 2 3 6 2 8 4 5 8 8 9 6 3 7 9
No. Supervised:	5 3 4 7 4 8 6 5 9 8 9 3 6 9 9
Environment:	1 1 7 3 5 8 5 5 6 4 7 2 8 7 9
Years of Service:	5 7 5 3 3 6 3 2 7 3 5 5 8 8 1

Exhibit 15.5 is an abbreviated form of the printout from BMDP1R.
(a) Write out the regression equation using all five predictors.
(b) What are the β_is?

15.5   Refer to Exercise 15.4.
(a) Which variable has the largest semipartial correlation with the criterion, partialling out the other variables?
(b) The overall F in Exercise 15.4 is not significant, yet Environment correlates significantly ($r = .58$) with Y. How is this possible?

15.6   Calculate the adjusted R^2 for the data in Exercise 15.4.

EXHIBIT 15.5

DEPENDENT VARIABLE . . . .   1 SATIF
TOLERANCE 0.0100
ALL DATA CONSIDERED AS A SINGLE GROUP
MULTIPLE R   0.6974   STD. ERROR OF EST.   2.0572
MULTIPLE R-SQUARE   0.4864

ANALYSIS OF VARIANCE

	SUM OF SQUARES	DF	MEAN SQUARE	F RATIO	P(TAIL)
REGRESSION	40.078	4	10.020	2.367	0.12267
RESIDUAL	42.322	10	4.232		

VARIABLE		COEFFICIENT	STD. ERROR	STD. REG COEFF	T	P(2 TAIL)	TOLERANCE
INTERCEPT		1.66926					
RESPON	2	0.60516	0.428	0.624	1.414	0.188	0.263940
NUMSUP	3	-0.33399	0.537	-0.311	-0.622	0.548	0.205947
ENVIR	4	0.48552	0.276	0.514	1.758	0.109	0.600837
YRS	5	0.07023	0.262	0.063	0.268	0.794	0.919492

15.7 All other things being equal, the ability of two variables to predict a third will increase as the correlation between them decreases. Explain this fact in terms of semipartial correlation.

15.8 All other things being equal, the stability of any given regression coefficient across different samples of data is partly a function of how that variable correlates with other predictors. Explain this fact.

15.9 What does the Tolerance column in Exhibit 15.5 contribute to the answers to Exercises 15.7 and 15.8?

15.10 Using the data in Exercise 15.4, generate $\hat{Y}$ and show that $R_{0.1234} = r_{Y\hat{Y}}$.

15.11 Use Y and $\hat{Y}$ from Exercise 15.10 to show that MS_{residual} is $\Sigma(Y - \hat{Y})^2/(N - p - 1)$.

15.12 Using the following (random) data, demonstrate what happens to the multiple correlation when you drop out *cases* from the data set (e.g., use 15 cases, then 10, 6, 5, and 4).

$$Y \quad 5\ 0\ 5\ 9\ 4 \qquad 8\ 3\ 7\ 0\ 4 \qquad 7\ 1\ 4\ 7\ 9$$

$$X_1 \quad 3\ 8\ 1\ 5\ 8 \qquad 2\ 4\ 7\ 9\ 1 \qquad 3\ 5\ 6\ 8\ 9$$

$$X_2 \quad 7\ 6\ 4\ 3\ 1 \qquad 9\ 7\ 5\ 3\ 1 \qquad 8\ 6\ 0\ 3\ 7$$

$$X_3 \quad 1\ 7\ 4\ 1\ 8 \qquad 8\ 6\ 8\ 3\ 6 \qquad 1\ 9\ 7\ 7\ 7$$

$$X_4 \quad 3\ 6\ 0\ 5\ 1 \qquad 3\ 5\ 9\ 1\ 1 \qquad 7\ 4\ 2\ 0\ 9$$

15.13 Calculate the adjusted R^2 for the 15 cases in Exercise 15.12.

15.14 Refer to the first three variables from Exercise 15.4.
(a) Use any computer program to calculate the squared semipartial correlation and the squared partial correlation for Satisfaction as the criterion and No. Supervised as the predictor, partialling out Responsibility.
(b) Draw a Venn diagram to illustrate these two coefficients.

15.15 Refer to the first three variables in Exercise 15.4.
(a) Draw a figure comparable to Figure 15.1.
(b) Obtain the regression solution for these data and relate the solution to the figure.

15.16 The State of Vermont is divided into 10 Health Planning Districts—they correspond roughly to counties. The following data represent the percentage of live births of babies weighing under 2500 grams (Y), the fertility rate for females 17 years of age or younger (X_1), total high-risk fertility rate for females younger than 17 or older than 35 years of age (X_2), percentage of mothers with fewer than 12 years of education (X_3), percentage of births to unmarried mothers (X_4), and percentage of mothers not seeking medical care until the third trimester (X_5).

Y	X_1	X_2	X_3	X_4	X_5
6.1	22.8	43.0	23.8	9.2	6
7.1	28.7	55.3	24.8	12.0	10
7.4	29.7	48.5	23.9	10.4	5
6.3	18.3	38.8	16.6	9.8	4
6.5	21.1	46.2	19.6	9.8	5
5.7	21.2	39.9	21.4	7.7	6
6.6	22.2	43.1	20.7	10.9	7
8.1	22.3	48.5	21.8	9.5	5
6.3	21.8	40.0	20.6	11.6	7
6.9	31.2	56.7	25.2	11.6	9

A stepwise regression using BMDP2R is shown in Exhibit 15.6. (Only the first three steps are shown to conserve space. For purposes of this exercise, we will not let the lack of statistical significance worry us.)

(a) What are the values of R for the successive steps?

(b) From the definition of a partial correlation (in terms of Venn diagrams), show that the R^2 at step 2 is a function of R^2 at step 1 and the partial correlation listed under 1—variables not in equation.

EXHIBIT 15.6

```
   STEP NO.    1
VARIABLE ENTERED      3 X2
MULTIPLE R              0.6215
MULTIPLE R-SQUARE      0.3862
ADJUSTED R-SQUARE      0.3095
STD. ERROR OF EST.     0.5797
```

ANALYSIS OF VARIANCE

	SUM OF SQUARES	DF	MEAN SQUARE	F RATIO
REGRESSION	1.6917006	1	1.691701	5.03
RESIDUAL	2.6882995	8	0.3360374	

		VARIABLES IN EQUATION					•		VARIABLES NOT IN EQUATION			
VARIABLE	COEFFICIENT	STD. ERROR OF COEFF	STD. REG COEFF	TOLERANCE	F TO REMOVE	LEVEL	• VARIABLE	PARTIAL CORR.	TOLERANCE	F TO ENTER	LEVEL
(Y-INTERCEPT	3.529)						•				
X2 3	0.069	0.031	0.621	1.00000	5.03	1	• X1 2	-0.19730	0.25831	0.28	1
							• X3 4	-0.25039	0.43280	0.47	1
							• X4 5	0.00688	0.69838	0.00	1
							• X5 6	-0.59063	0.58000	3.75	1

```
   STEP NO.    2
VARIABLE ENTERED      6 X5
MULTIPLE R              0.7748
MULTIPLE R-SQUARE      0.6003
ADJUSTED R-SQUARE      0.4862
STD. ERROR OF EST.     0.5001
```

ANALYSIS OF VARIANCE

	SUM OF SQUARES	DF	MEAN SQUARE	F RATIO
REGRESSION	2.6294919	2	1.314746	5.26
RESIDUAL	1.7505082	7	0.2500726	

		VARIABLES IN EQUATION					•		VARIABLES NOT IN EQUATION			
VARIABLE	COEFFICIENT	STD. ERROR OF COEFF	STD. REG COEFF	TOLERANCE	F TO REMOVE	LEVEL	• VARIABLE	PARTIAL CORR.	TOLERANCE	F TO ENTER	LEVEL
(Y-INTERCEPT	2.949)						•				
X2 3	0.113	0.035	1.015	0.58000	10.47	1	• X1 2	-0.09613	0.24739	0.06	1
X5 6	-0.223	0.115	-0.608	0.58000	3.75	1	• X3 4	-0.05399	0.37826	0.02	1
							• X4 5	0.41559	0.53416	1.25	1

EXHIBIT 15.6 (Cont.)

STEP NO. 3
VARIABLE ENTERED 5 X4
MULTIPLE R 0.8181
MULTIPLE R-SQUARE 0.6694
ADJUSTED R-SQUARE 0.5041
STD. ERROR OF EST. 0.4913

ANALYSIS OF VARIANCE

	SUM OF SQUARES	DF	MEAN SQUARE	F RATIO
REGRESSION	2.9318295	3	0.9772765	4.05
RESIDUAL	1.4481706	6	0.2413618	

VARIABLES IN EQUATION

VARIABLE		COEFFICIENT	STD. ERROR OF COEFF	STD. REG COEFF	TOLERANCE	F TO REMOVE	LEVEL
(Y-INTERCEPT		1.830)					
X2	3	0.104	0.035	0.942	0.55484	8.93	1
X4	5	0.190	0.170	0.359	0.53416	1.25	1
X5	6	-0.294	0.130	-0.799	0.44362	5.14	1

VARIABLES NOT IN EQUATION

VARIABLE		PARTIAL CORR.	TOLERANCE	F TO ENTER	LEVEL
X1	2	-0.14937	0.24520	0.11	1
X3	4	0.14753	0.31072	0.11	1

15.17 In Exercise 15.16 what meaning attaches to R^* as far as the Vermont Department of Health is concerned?

15.18 In Exercise 15.16 the adjusted R^2 would actually be lower for five predictors than for three predictors. Why?

15.19 In Exercise 15.16 the fifth predictor has a very low correlation with the criterion ($r = .05$) and yet plays a significant role in the regression. Why?

15.20 For the data in Exercise 15.16, compute $\hat{Y} = 1X_2 + 1X_4 - 3X_5$. How well does this equation fit compared with the optimal equation? Why should this be the case?

15.21 For the data in Exercise 15.16, would it be safe to conclude that decreasing the number of mothers who fail to seek medical care before the third trimester is a good way to decrease the incidence of low-birthweight infants?

15.22 Create a set of data on 10 cases that illustrates leverage, distance, and influence. Use any standard regression program to produce statistics measuring these attributes.

15.23 Produce a set of data where the variance of Y values associated with large values of X is greater than the variance of Y values associated with small values of X. Then run the regression and plot the residuals on the ordinate against X on the abscissa. What pattern emerges?

COMPUTER EXERCISES

15.24 Use the data set Mireault.dat from Mireault (1990) to examine the relationship between current levels of depression and other variables. A reasonable model might propose that depression (DepressT) is a function of (1) the person's current perceived level of vulnerability to additional loss (PVLoss), (2) the person's level of social support (SuppTotl), and (3) the age at which the person lost a parent during childhood (AgeAtLos). Use any statistical package to evaluate the model outlined here. (Since only subjects in Group 1 lost a parent to death during childhood, your analysis will be restricted to that group.)

15.25 A compulsive researcher who wants to cover all possibilities might throw in the total score on perceived vulnerability (PVTotal) as well as PVLoss. (The total includes vulnerability to accidents, illness, and life-style related problems.)

(a) Run this analysis adding PVTotal to the variables used in Exercise 15.24.

(b) What effect did the inclusion of PVTotal have on R^2? What effect did it have on the standard error of the regression coefficient for PVLoss? If your program will also give you tolerance and VIF, what effect does the inclusion of PVTotal have on them?

     (c) What would you conclude about the addition of PVTotal to our model?

15.26 In Exercise 15.24 we posited a model in which depression was a function of perceived vulnerability, social support, and age at loss. An alternative, or additional, view might be that vulnerability itself is a function of social support and age at loss. (If you lost a parent when you were very young and you have little social support, then you might feel particularly vulnerable to future loss.)

     (a) Set up the regression problem for this question and run the appropriate analysis. (Use PVLoss, SuppTotl, and AgeAtLos.)

     (b) Interpret your results.

15.27 Draw one diagram to illustrate the relationships examined in Exercises 15.24 and 15.26. Use arrows to show predicted relationships, and write the *standardized* regression coefficients next to the arrows. (You have just run a simple path analysis.)

15.28 Notice that in the diagram in Exercise 15.27 SuppTotl has both a direct and an indirect effect on Depression. Its direct effect is the arrow that goes from SuppTotl to DepressT. The indirect effect (which here is not significant) comes from the fact that SuppTotl influences PVLoss, which in turn affects DepressT. Explain these direct and indirect effects in terms of semipartial regression coefficients.

15.29 Repeat the analysis of Exercise 15.24, requesting statistics on regression diagnostics.

     (a) What, if anything, do these statistics tell you about the data set?

     (b) Delete the subject with the largest measure of influence (usually indexed by Cook's D). What effect does that have for this particular data set?

15.30 It is useful to examine the effects of measurement reliability on the outcome of a regression problem. In Exercise 15.24 the variable PVLoss was actually a reasonably reliable variable. However, for purposes of illustration we can manufacture a new, and less reliable, measure from it by adding a bit of random error to PVLoss.

     (a) Create a new variable called UnrelLos with a statement *of the form*

$$\text{UnrelLos} = \text{PVLoss} + 7.5*\text{``random''}$$

[Here "random" is a random-number function available with most statistical programs. You will need to check the manual to determine the exact form of the statement. I used a multiplier of 7.5 on the assumption that the random-number function will sample from an $N(0, 1)$ population. Multiplying by 7.5 will increase the standard deviation of UnrelLos by 50% (see the variance sum law). You may want to play with other constants.]

     (b) Now repeat Exercise 15.24 using UnrelLos in place of PVLoss.

     (c) What effect does this new variable have on the contribution of the perceived vulnerability of loss to the prediction of DepressT? How has the regression coefficient changed? How has its standard error changed? How does a test on its statistical significance change? What changes occurred for the other variables in the equation?

CHAPTER SIXTEEN

ANALYSES OF VARIANCE AND COVARIANCE AS GENERAL LINEAR MODELS

OBJECTIVES *To show how the analysis of variance can be viewed as a special case of multiple regression; to present procedures for the treatment of unequal sample sizes; to present the analysis of covariance.*

CONTENTS

M ost people think of multiple regression and the analysis of variance as two totally separate statistical techniques that answer two entirely different sets of questions. In fact, this is not at all the case. In the first place they ask the same kind of questions, and in the second place they return the same kind of answers, although the answers may be phrased somewhat differently. The analysis of variance tells us that three treatments (X_1, X_2, and X_3) have different means ($\overline{X}_i$). Multiple regression tells us that means ($\overline{Y}_i$) are related to treatments (X_1, X_2, and X_3), which really amounts to the same thing. Furthermore, the analysis of variance produces a statistic (F) on the differences among means. The analysis of regression produces a statistic (F) on the significance of R. As we shall see shortly, these Fs are equivalent.

16.1 THE GENERAL LINEAR MODEL

Just as multiple regression and the analysis of variance are concerned with the same general type of question, so are they basically the same technique. In fact, the analysis

General linear model

of variance is a special case of multiple linear regression, which in turn is a special case of what is commonly referred to as the **general linear model**. The fact that the analysis of variance has its own formal set of equations can be attributed primarily to good fortune. It happens that when certain conditions are met (as they are in the analysis of variance), the somewhat cumbersome multiple-regression calculations are reduced to a few relatively simple equations. If it were not for this, there might not even be a separate set of procedures called the analysis of variance.

For the student interested solely in the application of statistical techniques, a word is in order in defense of even including a chapter on this topic. Why, you may ask, should you study what amounts to a cumbersome way of doing what you already know how to do in a simple way? Ignoring the cry of "intellectual curiosity," which is something that most people are loath to *admit* that they do not possess in abundance, there are several practical (applied) answers to such a question. First, this approach represents a relatively straightforward way of handling particular cases of unequal sample sizes. Second, it provides us with a simple, and intuitively appealing, way of running, and especially of understanding, an analysis of covariance—which is a very clumsy technique when viewed from the more traditional approach. Last, and most important, it represents a glimpse at the direction in which statistical techniques are moving. With the greatly extended use of powerful and fast computers, even desktop computers, many of the traditional statistical techniques are giving way to what were previously impractical procedures. The increase in the popularity of multivariate analysis of variance (with all of its attendant strengths and weaknesses) is a case in point. Other examples are such techniques as discriminant analysis, cluster analysis, and that old and much-abused standby, factor analysis. Unless you understand the relationship between the analysis of variance and the general linear model (as represented by multiple linear regression), and unless you understand how the data for simple analysis of variance problems can be cast in a multiple-regression framework, you will find yourself in the near future using more and more techniques about which you know less and less. This is not to say that t, χ^2, F, and so on are likely to disappear, but only that other techniques will be added, opening up entirely new ways of looking at data.

In the past 25 years, several excellent and very readable papers on this general topic have been written. The clearest presentation is still Cohen (1968). A paper by Overall and Spiegel (1969) is also worth seeing. Both of these papers appeared in the *Psychological Bulletin* and are therefore readily available. Other good discussions can be found in Overall (1972), Overall and Klett (1972). Overall, Spiegel, and Cohen (1975), and Carlson and Timm (1974). Appelbaum and Cramer (1974). Cramer and Appelbaum (1980), and Howell and McConaughy (1982) provide contrasting views on the choice of the underlying model and the procedures to be followed.

THE LINEAR MODEL

Consider first the traditional multiple-regression problem with a criterion (Y) and three predictors (X_1, X_2, and X_3). We can write the usual model

$$Y_i = b_0 + b_1 X_{1i} + b_2 X_{2i} + b_3 X_{3i} + e_i$$

or, in terms of *vector* notation

$$\mathbf{y} = \mathbf{b}_0 + b_1\mathbf{x}_1 + b_2\mathbf{x}_2 + b_3\mathbf{x}_3 + \mathbf{e}$$

where $\mathbf{y}$, $\mathbf{x}_1$, $\mathbf{x}_2$, and $\mathbf{x}_3$ are $(n \times 1)$ vectors (columns) of data. $\mathbf{e}$ is a $(n \times 1)$ vector of errors, and $\mathbf{b}_0$ is a $(n \times 1)$ vector whose elements are the intercept. This equation can be further reduced to

$$\mathbf{y} + \mathbf{X}\mathbf{b} + \mathbf{e}$$

where $\mathbf{X}$ is a $n \times (p + 1)$ matrix of predictors, the first column of which is 1s, and $\mathbf{b}$ is a $(p + 1) \times 1$ vector of regression coefficients.

Now consider the traditional model for a one-way analysis of variance:

$$Y_{ij} = \mu + \tau_j + e_{ij}$$

Here the symbol τ_j is simply a shorthand way of writing $\tau_1, \tau_2, \tau_3, \ldots, \tau_p$, where for any given subject we are interested in only that value of τ_j that pertains to the particular treatment in question. To see the relationship between this model and the traditional regression model, it is necessary to introduce the concept of a design matrix.

DESIGN MATRICES

Design matrix

A **design matrix** is a matrix of *coded*, or *dummy*, or *counter* variables representing group membership. The *complete* form of the design matrix (X) will have $p + 1$ columns, representing the mean (μ) and the p treatment effects. A subject is always scored 1 for μ, since μ is part of all observations. In all other columns, she is scored 1 if she is a member of the treatment associated with that column, and 0 otherwise. Thus, for three treatments with two subjects per treatment, the complete design matrix would be

$$\mathbf{X} = \begin{array}{c} \\ 1 \\ 2 \\ 3 \\ 4 \\ 5 \\ 6 \end{array} \begin{array}{cccc} S \quad \mu & A_1 & A_2 & A_3 \\ \left[\begin{array}{cccc} 1 & 1 & 0 & 0 \\ 1 & 1 & 0 & 0 \\ 1 & 0 & 1 & 0 \\ 1 & 0 & 1 & 0 \\ 1 & 0 & 0 & 1 \\ 1 & 0 & 0 & 1 \end{array}\right] \end{array}$$

Notice that subjects 1 and 2 (who received Treatment A_1) are scored 1 on μ and A_1, and 0 on A_2 and A_3, since they did not receive those treatments. Similarly, subjects 3 and 4 are scored 1 on μ and A_2, and 0 on A_1 and A_3.

We will now define the vector τ of treatment effects as $[\mu \quad \tau_1 \quad \tau_2 \quad \tau_3]$. Taking $\mathbf{X}$ as the design matrix, the analysis of variance model can be written in matrix terms as

$$\mathbf{y} = \mathbf{X}\tau + \mathbf{e}$$

which can be seen as being of the same form as the traditional regression equation. Expanding, we obtain

$$
\mathbf{y} = \begin{bmatrix} 1 & 1 & 0 & 0 \\ 1 & 1 & 0 & 0 \\ 1 & 0 & 1 & 0 \\ 1 & 0 & 1 & 0 \\ 1 & 0 & 0 & 1 \\ 1 & 0 & 0 & 1 \end{bmatrix} \times \begin{bmatrix} \mu \\ \tau_1 \\ \tau_2 \\ \tau_3 \end{bmatrix} + \begin{bmatrix} e_{11} \\ e_{21} \\ e_{12} \\ e_{22} \\ e_{13} \\ e_{23} \end{bmatrix}
$$

$$
\mathbf{y} = \qquad \mathbf{X} \qquad \times \quad \tau \;+\; \mathbf{e}
$$

which produces

$$
Y_{11} = \mu + \tau_1 + e_{11}
$$

$$
Y_{21} = \mu + \tau_1 + e_{21}
$$

$$
Y_{12} = \mu + \tau_2 + e_{12}
$$

$$
Y_{22} = \mu + \tau_2 + e_{22}
$$

$$
Y_{13} = \mu + \tau_3 + e_{13}
$$

$$
Y_{23} = \mu + \tau_3 + e_{23}
$$

For each subject we now have the model associated with her response. Thus, for the second subject in Treatment 2, $Y_{22} = \mu + \tau_2 + e_{22}$, and for the ith subject in Treatment j, we have $Y_{ij} = \mu + \tau_j + e_{ij}$, which is the usual analysis of variance model.

The point is that the design matrix allows us to view the analysis of variance in a multiple-regression framework, in that it permits us to go from

$$
Y_{ij} = \mu + \tau_j + e_{ij} \qquad \text{to} \qquad \mathbf{y} = \mathbf{Xb} + \mathbf{e}
$$

Moreover, the elements of $\mathbf{b}$ are the values of $\mu, \tau_1, \tau_2, \ldots, \tau_k$. In other words, these are the actual treatment effects in which we are interested.

The design matrix we have been using has certain technical difficulties that must be circumvented. First, it is redundant in the sense that if we are told that a subject is not in A_1 or A_2, we know without being told that she must be in A_3. This is another way of saying that there are only 2 df for treatments. For this reason we will eliminate the column headed A_3, leaving only $a - 1$ columns for the treatment effects. A second change is necessary if we want to use any computer program that obtains a multiple-regression equation by way of first calculating the intercorrelation matrix. The column headed μ has no variance, and therefore cannot enter into a standard multiple-regression program—it would cause us to attempt division by 0. Thus, it too must be eliminated. This is no real loss, since our ultimate solution will not be affected.

One further change will be made simply for the sake of allowing us to test the desired null hypotheses using the method to be later advocated for factorial designs. Since we have omitted a column dealing with the third (or ath) level of treatments, solutions given our modified design matrix would produce estimates of treatment effects in relation to $\overline{X}_3$ rather than in relation to $\overline{X}_{..}$. In other words, b_1 would turn out to be $(\overline{X}_1 - \overline{X}_3)$ rather than $(\overline{X}_1 - \overline{X}_{.})$. This problem can be eliminated, however, by a modification of the design matrix to make the mean $(\overline{X}_i)$ of each column of $\mathbf{X}$ equal to 0. Under this new system, a subject is scored 1 in column A_i if she is a member of Treatment A_i; she is scored -1 if she is a member of the ath (last) treatment; and she is scored 0 if neither of these conditions apply. (This restriction corresponds to the fixed-model analysis of variance requirement that $\Sigma\tau_i = 0$.)

These modifications have led us from

$$
\mathbf{X} = \begin{bmatrix} 1 & 1 & 0 & 0 \\ 1 & 1 & 0 & 0 \\ 1 & 0 & 1 & 0 \\ 1 & 0 & 1 & 0 \\ 1 & 0 & 0 & 1 \\ 1 & 0 & 0 & 1 \end{bmatrix} \text{ to } \begin{bmatrix} 1 & 1 & 0 \\ 1 & 1 & 0 \\ 1 & 0 & 1 \\ 1 & 0 & 1 \\ 1 & 0 & 0 \\ 1 & 0 & 0 \end{bmatrix} \text{ to } \begin{bmatrix} 1 & 0 \\ 1 & 0 \\ 0 & 1 \\ 0 & 1 \\ 0 & 0 \\ 0 & 0 \end{bmatrix} \text{ to } \begin{bmatrix} 1 & 0 \\ 1 & 0 \\ 0 & 1 \\ 0 & 1 \\ -1 & -1 \\ -1 & -1 \end{bmatrix}
$$

Although these look like major changes in that the last form of **X** appears to be far removed from where we started, it actually carries all the necessary information. We have merely eliminated redundant information, removed a constant term, and then caused the treatment effects to be given as deviations from $\overline{X}_{..}$.

16.2   ONE-WAY ANALYSIS OF VARIANCE

At this point a simple example is in order. Table 16.1 contains data for three subjects in each of four treatments. Table 16.1b shows the summary table for the corresponding analysis of variance, along with the value of η^2 (discussed in Chapter 11). Table 16.1c contains the estimated treatment effects $(\hat{\tau}_i)$ where $\hat{\tau}_i = \hat{\mu}_i - \hat{\mu}$. Since the fixed-model analysis of variance imposes the restriction that $\Sigma\tau_i = 0$, τ_4 is automatically defined by τ_1, τ_2, and τ_3.

TABLE 16.1
Illustrative calculations for simple one-way design with equal ns

(a) Data

	Treatment 1	Treatment 2	Treatment 3	Treatment 4
	8	5	3	6
	9	7	4	4
	7	3	1	9
Means	8	5	2.667	6.333
				GM = 5.5

(b) Summary Table

Source	df	SS	MS	F	η^2
Treatments	3	45.6667	15.222	4.46	.626
Error	8	27.3333	3.417		
Total	11	73.0000			

TABLE 16.1 (Cont.)   **(c) Estimated Treatment Effects**

$$\hat{t}_1 = \overline{X}_1 - GM = 8.0 - 5.5 = 2.5$$

$$\hat{t}_2 = \overline{X}_2 - GM = 5.0 - 5.5 = -0.5$$

$$\hat{t}_3 = \overline{X}_3 - GM = 2.67 - 5.5 = -2.83$$

Now let us approach the statistical treatment of these data by means of least-squares multiple linear regression. We will take as our criterion (Y) the raw data in Table 16.1. For the predictors we will use a design matrix of the form

$$\mathbf{X} = \begin{matrix} & \mathbf{A}_1 & \mathbf{A}_2 & \mathbf{A}_3 \\ \text{Treatment 1} & 1 & 0 & 0 \\ \text{Treatment 2} & 0 & 1 & 0 \\ \text{Treatment 3} & 0 & 0 & 1 \\ \text{Treatment 4} & -1 & -1 & -1 \end{matrix}$$

Here the elements of any one row are taken to apply to *all the subjects in that treatment*. The multiple-regression solution using the design matrix $\mathbf{X}$ as the matrix of predictors is presented in Table 16.2.

Notice the pattern of correlations in the intercorrelation matrix in Table 16.2. This type of pattern (constant off-diagonal correlations) will occur whenever there are equal numbers of subjects in the various treatments.

In the vector of regression coefficients, notice that b_1 (2.50) is equal to the estimated treatment effect of treatment 1 shown in Table 16.1. In other words, $b_1 = \hat{t}_1$. This also happens for b_2 and b_3. This fact necessarily follows from our definition of $\mathbf{X}$ and τ. Moreover, if we were to test the significance of b_i, we would simultaneously have a test on the hypothesis ($H_0: \tau_i = \mu_i - \mu = 0$). Notice further that the intercept (b_0) is equal to the grand mean ($\overline{Y}$). This follows directly from the fact that we scored the ath treatment as -1 on all coded variables. Using the (-1) coding, the mean of every column of $\mathbf{X}$ ($\overline{X}_i$) is equal to 0 and, as a result, $\Sigma b_i \overline{X}_i = 0$ and therefore $b_0 = \overline{Y} - \Sigma b_i \overline{X}_i = \overline{Y}$. This situation holds only in the case of equal ns, since otherwise $\overline{X}_i$ would not be 0 for all i. However, in all cases, b_0 is our best estimate of μ in a least squares sense.

The value of $R^2 = .626$ is equivalent to η^2, since they both estimate the percentage of variation in the dependent variable accounted for by variation among treatments. Furthermore, if we correct R^2 for shrinkage, the resulting value would be the squared **intraclass correlation coefficient**, occasionally used as a measure of accountable variation, especially for random models in which it is equivalent to $\hat{\omega}^2$.

Intraclass correlation coefficient

If we test R for significance, we have

$$F(p, N - p - 1) = \frac{R^2(N - p - 1)}{(1 - R^2)p}$$

$$F(3, 8) = \frac{.626(8)}{.374(3)} = 4.46$$

which is the same value of F as that we obtained in the analysis of variance.

TABLE 16.2
Regression solution
for data in Table 16.1

(a) Data

$$y = \begin{bmatrix} 8 \\ 9 \\ 7 \\ 5 \\ 7 \\ 3 \\ 3 \\ 4 \\ 1 \\ 6 \\ 4 \\ 9 \end{bmatrix} \quad X = \begin{bmatrix} 1 & 0 & 0 \\ 1 & 0 & 0 \\ 1 & 0 & 0 \\ 0 & 1 & 0 \\ 0 & 1 & 0 \\ 0 & 1 & 0 \\ 0 & 0 & 1 \\ 0 & 0 & 1 \\ 0 & 0 & 1 \\ -1 & -1 & -1 \\ -1 & -1 & -1 \\ -1 & -1 & -1 \end{bmatrix}$$

(b) Intercorrelation Matrix

$$\begin{bmatrix} 1.0 & 0.5 & 0.5 \\ 0.5 & 1.0 & 0.5 \\ 0.5 & 0.5 & 1.0 \end{bmatrix}$$

(c) Regression and Correlation Coefficients

$$b_1 = 2.5$$
$$b_2 = -0.5$$
$$b_3 = -2.83$$
$$b_0 = \bar{Y} - \Sigma b_i \bar{X}_i = 5.5 - 0 = 5.5$$
$$R^2 = .626$$
$$R = .791$$

Finally, we calculate the sums of squares:

$$SS_Y = (N - 1)s_Y^2 = 73.000 = SS_{total}$$

$$SS_{regression} = SS_Y R^2 = 73.0(.626) = 45.6667 = SS_{treat}$$

$$SS_{residual} = SS_Y(1 - R^2) = 73.0(.374) = 27.333 = SS_{error}$$

These three equations make it clear that there is complete correspondence between sums of squares in regression analysis and sums of squares in the analysis of variance. You can easily reproduce these results using any multiple-regression program.

The foregoing analysis has shown the marked similarity between the analysis of variance and multiple linear regression. This is primarily an illustration of the fact that there is no important difference between asking whether different treatments produce different means and asking whether means are a function of treatments. We are simply looking at two sides of the same coin.

We have discussed only the most common way of forming a design matrix. This matrix could take a number of other useful forms. For a good discussion of these, see Cohen (1968).

16.3   FACTORIAL DESIGNS

We can readily extend the analysis of regression to two-way and higher-order factorial designs, and doing so illustrates some important features of both the analysis of variance and the analysis of regression. We will consider first a two-way analysis of variance with equal ns.

THE FULL MODEL

The most common model for a two-way analysis of variance is

$$Y_{ijk} = \mu + \alpha_i + \beta_j + \alpha\beta_{ij} + e_{ijk}$$

As we did before, we can expand the α_i and β_j terms by using a design matrix. But then how should the interaction term be handled? The answer to this question relies on the fact that an interaction represents a multiplicative effect of the component variables. Suppose we consider the simplest case of a 2×2 factorial design. Letting the entries in each row represent the coefficients for all subjects in the corresponding cell of the design, we can write our design matrix as

$$\mathbf{X} = \begin{array}{c} \\ a_1b_1 \\ a_1b_2 \\ a_2b_1 \\ a_2b_2 \end{array} \begin{array}{ccc} A_1 & B_1 & AB_{11} \\ \left[\begin{array}{ccc} 1 & 1 & 1 \\ 1 & -1 & -1 \\ -1 & 1 & -1 \\ -1 & -1 & 1 \end{array} \right] \end{array}$$

The first column represents the main effect of A, and distinguishes between those subjects who received A_1 and those who received A_2. The next column represents the main effect of B, separating B_1 subjects from B_2 subjects. The third column is the interaction of A and B. Its elements are obtained by multiplying corresponding elements of columns 1 and 2. Thus, $1 = 1 \times 1$, $-1 = 1 \times -1$, $-1 = -1 \times 1$, and $1 = -1 \times -1$. Once again, we have as many columns per effect as we have degrees of freedom for that effect. We have no entries of 0 simply because with only two levels of each variable a subject must either be in the first or last level.

Now consider the case of a 2×3 factorial. With two levels of A and three levels of B, we will have $df_A = 1$, $df_B = 2$, and $df_{AB} = 2$. This means that our design matrix will require one column for A and two columns each for B and AB. This leads to the following matrix:

$$
\mathbf{X} = \begin{array}{c} a_1b_1 \\ a_1b_2 \\ a_1b_3 \\ a_2b_1 \\ a_2b_2 \\ a_2b_3 \end{array}
\begin{array}{ccccc}
A_1 & B_1 & B_2 & AB_{11} & AB_{12} \\
\left[\begin{array}{ccccc}
1 & 1 & 0 & 1 & 0 \\
1 & 0 & 1 & 0 & 1 \\
1 & -1 & -1 & -1 & -1 \\
-1 & 1 & 0 & -1 & 0 \\
-1 & 0 & 1 & 0 & -1 \\
-1 & -1 & -1 & 1 & 1
\end{array}\right]
\end{array}
$$

Column A_1 distinguishes between those subjects who are in treatment level A_1 and those in treatment level A_2. Column 2 distinguishes level B_1 subjects from those who are not in B_1, and Column 3 does the same for level B_2. Once again, subjects in the first $a - 1$ and first $b - 1$ treatment levels are scored 1 or 0 depending on whether or not they served in the treatment level in question. Subjects in the ath or bth treatment level are scored -1 for each column related to that treatment effect. The column labeled AB_{11} is simply the product of columns A_1 and B_1, whereas AB_{12} is the product of A_1 and B_2.

The analysis for a factorial design is more cumbersome than the one for a simple one-way design, since we wish to test two or more main effects and one or more interaction effects. If we consider the relatively simple case of a two-way factorial, however, you should have no difficulty generalizing it to more complex factorial designs. The basic principles are the same—only the arithmetic is messier.

As an illustration, we will consider the case of a 2×4 factorial with four subjects per cell. Such a design is analyzed by the conventional analysis of variance in Table 16.3, which also includes means, estimated effects, and values of η^2. From the summary table, it is apparent that the main effect of B is significant but that the effects of A and AB are not.

To analyze these data from the point of view of multiple regression, we begin with the following design matrix. Once again, the elements of each row apply to all subjects in the corresponding treatment combination.

$$
\mathbf{X} = \begin{array}{c} a_1b_1 \\ a_1b_2 \\ a_1b_3 \\ a_1b_4 \\ a_2b_1 \\ a_2b_2 \\ a_2b_3 \\ a_2b_4 \end{array}
\begin{array}{ccccccc}
A_1 & B_1 & B_2 & B_3 & AB_{11} & AB_{12} & AB_{13} \\
\left[\begin{array}{ccccccc}
1 & 1 & 0 & 0 & 1 & 0 & 0 \\
1 & 0 & 1 & 0 & 0 & 1 & 0 \\
1 & 0 & 0 & 1 & 0 & 0 & 1 \\
1 & -1 & -1 & -1 & -1 & -1 & -1 \\
-1 & 1 & 0 & 0 & -1 & 0 & 0 \\
-1 & 0 & 1 & 0 & 0 & -1 & 0 \\
-1 & 0 & 0 & 1 & 0 & 0 & -1 \\
-1 & -1 & -1 & -1 & 1 & 1 & 1
\end{array}\right]
\end{array}
$$

The first step in a multiple-regression analysis is presented in Table 16.4 using all seven predictors (A_1 to AB_{13}). The results have been reported to two or three decimal places, although the calculations were carried to eight significant digits. (This is true of all tables and equations in this chapter.)

TABLE 16.3
Sample data and summary table for 2×4 factorial design

(a) Data

	B_1	B_2	B_3	B_4	Means
A_1	5	2	8	11	
	7	5	11	15	
	9	7	12	16	
	8	3	14	10	8.93750
A_2	7	3	9	11	
	9	8	12	14	
	10	9	14	10	
	9	11	8	12	9.75000
Means	8.000	6.000	11.000	12.375	9.34375

(b) Summary Table

Source	df	SS	MS	F	η^2
A	1	5.282	5.282	<1	.014
B	3	199.344	66.448	11.452*	.537
AB	3	27.344	9.115	1.571	.074
Error	24	139.250	5.802		
Total	31	371.220			

*$p < .05$

(c) Estimated Treatment Effects

$$\hat{\mu} = GM = 9.34375$$

$$\hat{\alpha}_1 = \bar{A}_1 - GM = 8.9375 - 9.34375 = -0.40625$$

$$\hat{\beta}_1 = \bar{B}_1 - GM = 8.0000 - 9.34375 = -1.34375$$

$$\hat{\beta}_2 = \bar{B}_2 - GM = 6.0000 - 9.34375 = -3.34375$$

$$\hat{\beta}_3 = \bar{B}_3 - GM = 11.0000 - 9.34375 = 1.65625$$

$$\widehat{\alpha\beta}_{11} = \overline{AB}_{11} - \bar{A}_1 - \bar{B}_1 + GM = 7.25 - 8.9375 - 8.0000 + 9.34375 = -0.34375$$

$$\widehat{\alpha\beta}_{12} = \overline{AB}_{12} - \bar{A}_1 - \bar{B}_2 + GM = 4.25 - 8.9375 - 6.0000 + 9.34375 = -1.34375$$

$$\widehat{\alpha\beta}_{13} = \overline{AB}_{13} - \bar{A}_1 - \bar{B}_3 + GM = 11.25 - 8.9375 - 11.0000 + 9.34375 = 0.65625$$

TABLE 16.4
Regression solution using all predictors for data in Table 16.3

(a) Intercorrelation Matrix (R)

	A_1	B_1	B_2	B_3	AB_{11}	AB_{12}	AB_{13}
A_1	1.00	0	0	0	0	0	0
B_1	0	1.00	0.50	0.50	0	0	0
B_2	0	0.50	1.00	0.50	0	0	0
B_3	0	0.50	0.50	1.00	0	0	0
AB_{11}	0	0	0	0	1.00	0.50	0.50
AB_{12}	0	0	0	0	0.50	1.00	0.50
AB_{13}	0	0	0	0	0.50	0.50	1.00

TABLE 16.4 (Cont.)

(b) Regression Results

$$\mathbf{b} = [9.34 \quad -0.41 \quad -1.34 \quad -3.34 \quad 1.66 \quad -0.34 \quad -1.34 \quad 0.66]$$

$$R^2 = .625$$

$$R = .791$$

$$SS_{regression} = SS_Y(R^2) = (371.219)(.625) = 231.969$$

$$SS_{residual} = SS_Y(1 - R^2) = (371.219)(.375) = 139.250$$

(c) Summary Table for the Analysis of Variance for Regression

Source	df	SS	MS	F
Regression	7	231.969	33.138	5.711*
Residual	24	139.250	5.802	
Total	31	371.219		

*$p < .05$

Table 16.4 has several important features. First, consider the matrix **R**. Suppose that we simplify this matrix by defining the following sets of predictors: $A' = [A_1]$, $B' = [B_1, B_2, B_3]$, and $AB' = [AB_{11}, AB_{12}, AB_{13}]$. If we then rewrite the intercorrelation matrix, we have

$$
\begin{array}{c c}
& \begin{array}{ccc} A' & B' & AB' \end{array} \\
\begin{array}{c} A' \\ B' \\ AB' \end{array} &
\left[\begin{array}{ccc}
1.00 & 0.00 & 0.00 \\
0.00 & 1.00 & 0.00 \\
0.00 & 0.00 & 1.00
\end{array}\right]
\end{array}
$$

Notice that each of the effects is independent of the others. Such a pattern occurs only if there are equal numbers of subjects in each cell; this pattern is also what makes simplified formulas for the analysis of variance possible. The fact that this structure disappears in the case of unequal ns is what makes our life more difficult when we have missing subjects.

Next notice vector **b**. The first entry (b_0) is the grand mean, and the subsequent entries $(b_1, \ldots, b_7)$ are the estimates of the corresponding treatment effects. Thus, $b_1 = \hat{\alpha}_1$, $b_2 = \hat{\beta}_1$, and so on. Tests on these regression coefficients, which are not shown, would represent tests on the corresponding treatment effects. The fact that we have only the $(a - 1)(b - 1) = 3$ interaction effects presents no problem, due to the restriction that these effects must sum to 0 across rows and down columns. Thus, if $\alpha\beta_{12} = -1.34$, then $\alpha\beta_{22}$ must be $+1.34$. Similarly, $\alpha\beta_{14} = 0 - \Sigma\alpha\beta_{1j} = -\Sigma\alpha\beta_{1j} = 1.03$.

The value of $R^2 = .625$ represents the percentage of variation that can be accounted for by all the variables simultaneously. With equal ns, and therefore independent effects, it is equivalent to $\eta_A^2 + \eta_B^2 + \eta_{AB}^2$. The test on R^2 produces an F of 5.711 on 7 and 24 df, which, since it is significant $(p < .05)$, shows that there is a nonchance relationship between the treatment variables, considered all together, and the dependent variable (Y). (Here, and elsewhere, answers have been rounded to match computer results, which were based on more decimal places.)

Two more parallels can be drawn between Tables 16.3 and 16.4. First, notice that $SS_{regression} = SS_Y(R^2) = 231.969$. This is the variation that can be predicted by a linear combination of the predictors. This value is equal to $SS_A + SS_B + SS_{AB}$, although from Table 16.4 we cannot yet partition the variation among the separate sources. Finally, notice that $SS_{residual} = SS_Y(1 - R^2) = 139.250$, which is the error sum of squares in the analysis of variance. This makes sense when you recall that error is the variation that cannot be attributed to the separate or joint effects of the treatment variables.

REDUCED MODELS

At this point we know only the amount of variation that can be accounted for by all of the predictors simultaneously. What we wish to know is how this variation can be partitioned among A, B, and AB. This information can be readily obtained by computing several reduced regression equations.

Since in the subsequent course of the analysis we must compute several multiple correlation coefficients relating to the different effects, we will change our notation system and use the effect labels (α, β, and $\alpha\beta$) as subscripts. For the multiple regression just computed, the model contained variables to account for α, β, and $\alpha\beta$. Thus, we will designate the correlation coefficient (squared) as $R^2_{\alpha,\beta,\alpha\beta}$. If we dropped the last three predictors (AB_{11}, AB_{12}, and AB_{13}) we would be deleting those predictors carrying information concerning the interaction but would retain those predictors concerned with α and β. Thus, we would use the designation $R^2_{\alpha,\beta}$. If we used only A, AB_{11}, AB_{12}, and AB_{13} as predictors, the model would account for only α and $\alpha\beta$, and the resulting R^2 would be denoted $R^2_{\alpha,\alpha\beta}$.

For our particular example,

$$R^2_{\alpha,\beta,\alpha\beta} = R^2_{0.1234567}$$

$$R^2_{\alpha,\beta} = R^2_{0.1234}$$

$$R^2_{\alpha,\alpha\beta} = R^2_{0.1567}$$

$$R^2_{\beta,\alpha\beta} = R^2_{0.234567}$$

The left side of these equations represents a conventional notation system for the least-squares analysis of variance.

If the interaction term accounts for any of the variation, then removing the interaction predictors from the model should lead to a decrease in accountable variation. This decrease will be equal to the variation that can be attributable to the interaction. By this reasoning,

$$SS_{AB} = SS_{reg\alpha,\beta,\alpha\beta} - SS_{reg\alpha,\beta} = SS_Y(R^2_{\alpha,\beta,\alpha\beta}) - SS_Y(R^2_{\alpha,\beta})$$

where $SS_{reg\alpha,\beta,\alpha\beta}$ represents the sum of squares for regression using all predictors. A similar line of reasoning holds for SS_A and SS_B. Thus,

$$SS_A = SS_{reg\alpha,\beta,\alpha\beta} - SS_{reg\beta,\alpha\beta} = SS_Y(R^2_{\alpha,\beta,\alpha\beta}) - SS_Y(R^2_{\beta,\alpha\beta})$$

$$SS_B = SS_{reg\alpha,\beta,\alpha\beta} - SS_{reg\alpha,\alpha\beta} = SS_Y(R^2_{\alpha,\beta,\alpha\beta}) - SS_Y(R^2_{\alpha,\alpha\beta})$$

The relevant calculations are presented in Table 16.5; the calculations of the individual R^2s have been omitted. Students with access to a computer are urged to reproduce these results starting with the raw data.

TABLE 16.5
Regression solution
for data in Table 16.3

$$R^2_{\alpha,\beta,\alpha\beta} = .625$$

$$SS_{reg\alpha,\beta,\alpha\beta} = SS_Y(R^2_{\alpha,\beta,\alpha\beta}) = 231.969$$

$$SS_{residual} = SS_Y(1 - R^2) = 139.250$$

$$R^2_{\alpha,\beta} = .551$$

$$SS_{reg\alpha,\beta} = SS_Y(R^2_{\alpha,\beta}) = 204.625$$

$$R^2_{\beta,\alpha\beta} = .611$$

$$SS_{reg\beta,\alpha\beta} = SS_Y(R^2_{\beta,\alpha\beta}) = 226.687$$

$$R^2_{\alpha,\alpha\beta} = .088$$

$$SS_{reg\alpha,\alpha\beta} = SS_Y(R^2_{\alpha,\alpha\beta}) = 32.625$$

Summary Table

Source	df	SS	MS	F
A	1	5.282	5.282	<1
B	3	199.344	66.448	11.452*
AB	3	27.344	9.115	1.571
Error	24	139.250	5.802	
Total	31	371.219		

*$p < .05$

Looking first at the AB interactions, we see from Table 16.5 that when the interaction terms were deleted from the model, the proportion of accountable variation dropped from .625 to .551. This is a decrease of .074, which equals η^2_{AB} in Table 16.3. In terms of accountable variation, omitting the interaction terms produced a decrement of

$$SS_{reg\alpha,\beta,\alpha\beta} - SS_{reg\alpha,\beta} = 231.969 - 204.625 = 27.344$$

units of variation. This decrement can only be attributable to the predictive value of the interaction terms, and therefore

$$SS_{AB} = 27.344$$

By a similar line of reasoning, we can find the other sums of squares given in the summary table. Thus,

$$SS_A = 231.969 - 226.687 = 5.282$$

$$SS_B = 231.969 - 32.625 = 199.344$$

Notice that these values agree exactly with those obtained by the more traditional procedures. Notice also that the corresponding decrements in R^2 agree with the computed values of η^2.

Completely equivalent tests on the main effects and interaction can be made by testing the decrement in R^2 (rather than SS_{reg}) resulting from the deletion of a set of predictors. Thus, using the test statistic

$$F(f - r, N - f - 1) = \frac{(N - f - 1)(R_f^2 - R_r^2)}{(f - r)(1 - R_f^2)}$$

where f and r are the number of predictors in the full and reduced models, respectively, we obtain

$$F_A(1, 24) = \frac{(24)(.625 - .611)}{(1)(.375)} = 0.896$$

$$F_B(3, 24) = \frac{(24)(.625 - .088)}{(3)(.375)} = 11.452$$

$$F_{AB}(3, 24) = \frac{(24)(.625 - .551)}{(3)(.375)} = 1.571$$

These are the same values of F as those obtained by the more traditional procedures.

As Overall and Spiegel (1969) pointed out, the approach we have taken in testing the effects of A, B, and AB is not the only one we could have chosen. They presented two alternative models that might have been considered in place of this one. Fortunately, however, the different models all lead to the same conclusions in the case of equal sample sizes, since in this situation effects are independent of one another and therefore are additive. When we consider the case of unequal sample sizes, however, the choice of an underlying model will require careful consideration.

16.4   ANALYSIS OF VARIANCE WITH UNEQUAL SAMPLE SIZES

The least-squares approach to the analysis of variance is particularly useful for the case of factorial experiments with unequal sample sizes. However, special care must be used in selecting the particular restricted models that are employed in generating the various sums of squares.

Several different models could underlie an analysis of variance. Although in the case of equal sample sizes these models all lead to the same results, in the unequal n case they do not. This is because with unequal ns, the row, column, and interaction effects are no longer orthogonal and thus account for overlapping portions of the variance. Consider the Venn diagram in Figure 16.1. The area enclosed by the surrounding square will be taken to represent SS_{total}. Each circle represents the variation attributable to (or accounted for by) one of the effects. The area outside the circles but within the square represents SS_{error}. Finally, the total area enclosed by the circles represents

$SS_Y(R^2_{\alpha,\beta,\alpha\beta})$—the sum of squares for regression when all the terms are included in the model. If we had equal sample sizes, none of the circles would overlap, and each effect would be accounting for a separate, independent, portion of the variation. In that case, the decrease in $SS_{regression}$ resulting from deleting of an effect from the model would have a clear interpretation—it would be the area enclosed by the omitted circle and thus would be the sum of squares for the corresponding effect.

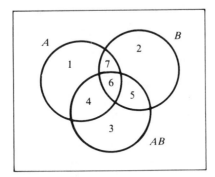

FIGURE 16.1
Venn diagram representing portions of overall variation

But what do we do when the circles overlap? If we were to take a model that included terms for A, B, and AB and compared it to a model containing only A and B terms, the decrement would not represent the area of the AB circle, since some of that area still would be accounted for by A and/or B. Thus, SS_{AB}, which we calculate as $SS_Y(R^2_{\alpha,\beta,\alpha\beta}) - SS_Y(R^2_{\alpha,\beta})$, represents only the portion of the enclosed area that is *unique* to AB—the area labelled with a "3." So far, all the models that have been proposed seriously are in agreement. SS_{AB} is that portion of the AB circle remaining after adjusting for A and B.

But now things begin to get a little sticky. Two major approaches have been put forth that differ in the way the remainder of the pie is allotted to A and B. These are Methods I and II of Overall and Spiegel (1969), and they have generated a voluminous literature debating their proper use and interpretation. Basically, the choice between them hinges on how we see the relationship between the sample size and the treatments themselves, or, more specifically, how we want to weight the various cell means to produce row and column means. Before exploring that issue, however, we must first examine the competing methods.

Method I

Method I is the method we used in the preceding section. In this case, each effect is adjusted for all other effects. Thus, we obtain SS_{AB} as $SS_Y(R^2_{\alpha,\beta,\alpha\beta} - R^2_{\alpha,\beta})$, SS_A as $SS_Y(R^2_{\alpha,\beta,\alpha\beta} - R^2_{\beta,\alpha\beta})$, and SS_B as $SS_Y(R^2_{\alpha,\beta,\alpha\beta} - R^2_{\alpha,\alpha\beta})$. In terms of Figure 16.1, each effect is defined as the part of the area that is unique to that effect. Thus, SS_A is represented by area "1," SS_B by area "2," and SS_{AB} by area "3."

Method II

Method II breaks up the pie differently. We continue to define SS_{AB} as area "3." But now that we have taken care of the interaction, we still have areas "1," "2," "4," "5," "6," and "7," which can be accounted for by the effects of A and/or B. Method II essentially redefines the full model as $R^2_{\alpha,\beta}$ and obtains $SS_A = SS_Y(R^2_{\alpha,\beta} - R^2_{\beta})$ and $SS_B = SS_Y(R^2_{\alpha,\beta} - R^2_{\alpha})$. Thus, A is allotted areas "1" and "4," whereas B is allotted areas "2" and "5." Methods I and II are summarized in Table 16.6.

TABLE 16.6
Alternative models
for solution of
nonorthogonal
designs

Method I

$$Y_{ijk} = \mu + \alpha_i + \beta_j + \alpha\beta_{ij} + e_{ijk}$$

Source	df	SS	Portion of Venn Diagram
A	$a - 1$	$SS_Y(R^2_{\alpha,\beta,\alpha\beta} - R^2_{\beta,\alpha\beta})$	1
B	$b - 1$	$SS_Y(R^2_{\alpha,\beta,\alpha\beta} - R^2_{\alpha,\alpha\beta})$	2
AB	$(a-1)(b-1)$	$SS_Y(R^2_{\alpha,\beta,\alpha\beta} - R^2_{\alpha,\beta})$	3
Error	$N - ab$	$SS_Y(1 - R^2_{\alpha,\beta,\alpha\beta})$	
Total	$N - 1$	SS_Y	

Method II

$$Y_{ijk} = \mu + \alpha_i + \beta_j + \alpha\beta_{ij} + e_{ijk} \text{ and } Y_{ijk} = \mu + \alpha_i + \beta_j + e_{ijk}$$

Source	df	SS	Portion of Venn Diagram
A	$a - 1$	$SS_Y(R^2_{\alpha,\beta} - R^2_{\beta})$	$1 + 4$
B	$b - 1$	$SS_Y(R^2_{\alpha,\beta} - R^2_{\alpha})$	$2 + 5$
AB	$(a-1)(b-1)$	$SS_Y(R^2_{\alpha,\beta,\alpha\beta} - R^2_{\alpha,\beta})$	3
Error	$N - ab$	$SS_Y(1 - R^2_{\alpha,\beta,\alpha\beta})$	
Total	$N - 1$	SS_Y	

Both these methods make a certain amount of sense when looked at from the point of view of the Venn diagram in Figure 16.1. However, the diagram is only a crude approximation and we have pushed it about as far as we can go.[†]

As Carlson and Timm (1974) argued, a more appropriate way to compare the models is to examine the hypotheses they test. These authors point out that Method I represents an estimation of treatment effects when cell means are weighted equally, and is particularly appropriate whenever we consider sample size to be independent of treatment conditions. A convincing demonstration of this is presented in Overall, Spiegel, and Cohen (1975). Carlson and Timm also showed that Method II produces estimates of treatment effects when row and column means are weighted by the sample sizes, but only when no interaction is present. When an interaction is present, simple estimates of row and column effects cannot be made, and, in fact, the null hypotheses actually tested are very bizarre indeed [see Carlson and Timm (1974) for a statement of the null hypotheses for Method II]. In that event Winer (1971), who seems to prefer Method II, falls back on Method I, although in fact that method represents an equal weighting of cells means. An excellent discussion of the hypotheses tested by different approaches is presented in Blair and Higgins (1978) and Blair (1978). As Cochran

---

[†] From this discussion you could easily get the impression that Method II will always account for more of the variation than Method I. This is not necessarily the case, since the degree of overlap represents the correlation between effects, and suppressor relationships might appear as "black holes," cancelling out accountable variation.

and Cox (1957) suggested, " the only complete solution of the 'missing data' problem is not to have them" (p. 82).

Howell and McConaughy (1982) argued that there are very few instances in which one would want to test the peculiar null hypotheses tested by Method II. The debate over the "correct" model will probably continue for some time, mainly because no one model is universally "correct," and because there are philosophical differences in the approaches to model specification [see Howell & McConaughy (1982) and Lewis & Keren (1977) versus Appelbaum & Cramer (1974) and O'Brien (1976)]. However, the conclusion to be drawn from the literature at present is that for the most common situations Method I is appropriate, since we usually want to test **equally weighted means**. This is method employed by BMDP2V and by SPSS^X Option 9. Method I sum of squares are the values labeled as Type III SS in SAS. It is also the method that is approximated by the *unweighted means solution* discussed in Chapter 13. (You may recall that in Chapter 13 I mentioned that the traditional label "unweighted means solution" really should be the "equally weighted means solution," since, using it, we are treating all means equally, regardless of the sample sizes.)

Equally weighted means

As an illustration of Method I, we will take the data used in the previous example but add four scores to produce unequal cell sizes. The data are given in Table 16.7, with the unweighted and weighted row and column means and the values resulting from the various regression solutions. The unweighted means are the mean of means (therefore, the mean of row$_1$ is the mean of the four cell means in that row). The weighted mean of row$_1$, for example, is really just the sum of the scores in row$_1$ divided by the number of scores in row$_1$.

An SPSS^X regression program might help to summarize the computations required to run this analysis and should illustrate the ease with which the analysis can be carried out. Such a program is shown in Exhibit 16.1.

From Table 16.7 we see that $R^2_{\alpha, \beta, \alpha\beta} = .532$, indicating that approximately 53% of the variation can be accounted for by a linear combination of the predictor variables. We do not know, however, how this variation is to be distributed among A, B, and AB. For that we need to form and calculate the reduced models.

TABLE 16.7
Illustrative calculations for nonorthogonal factorial design

	B_1	B_2	B_3	B_4	Unweighted Mean	Weighted Mean
A_1	5	2	8	11		
	7	5	11	15		
	9	7	12	16	8.975	8.944
	8	3	14	10		
		9		9		
A_2	7	3	9	11		
	9	8	12	14		
	10	9	14	10	9.625	9.778
	9	11	8	12		
			7	13		
Unweighted Mean	8.00	6.475	10.625	12.1		
Weighted Mean	8.00	6.333	10.556	12.1		

TABLE 16.7 (Cont.)　　　Full Model

$$R^2_{\alpha,\beta,\alpha\beta} = .532$$

$$SS_{\text{regression}} = SS_Y(R^2_{\alpha,\beta,\alpha\beta}) = 390.30559(.532) = 207.7055$$

$$SS_{\text{residual}} = SS_Y(1 - R^2_{\alpha,\beta,\alpha\beta}) = 390.30559(1 - .532) = 182.6001$$

Reduced Models

$$R^2_{\alpha,\beta} = .483$$

$$SS_{\text{regression}} = SS_Y(R^2_{\alpha,\beta}) = 390.30559(.483) = 188.430$$

$$R^2_{\beta,\alpha\beta} = .523$$

$$SS_{\text{regression}} = SS_Y(R^2_{\beta,\alpha\beta}) = 203.9500$$

$$R^2_{\alpha,\alpha\beta} = .076$$

$$SS_{\text{regression}} = SS_Y(R^2_{\alpha,\alpha\beta}) = 29.7499$$

EXHIBIT 16.1
SPSS^X program
indicating appropriate
regression
procedures.

```
TITLE          'ANALYSIS OF DATA IN TABLE 16.7'
FILE HANDLE    DATA/NAME = 'DATA.DAT'
DATA LIST      FILE=DATA/
               Y  A1  B1  B2  B3  AB11  AB12  AB13  1-24
REGRESSION     /DESCRIPTIVES /VARIABLES = ALL
               /DEPENDENT = Y  /ENTER A1 TO AB13
               /DEPENDENT = Y  /ENTER A1 TO B3
               /DEPENDENT = Y  /ENTER B1 TO AB13
               /DEPENDENT = Y  /ENTER A1, AB11 TO AB13
FINISH
```

TESTING THE INTERACTION EFFECTS

First, we delete the predictors associated with the interaction term and calculate $R^2_{\alpha,\beta}$. For these data, $R^2_{\alpha,\beta} = .483$, representing a drop in R^2 of about .05. If we examine the predictable sum of squares ($SS_{\text{regression}}$), we see that eliminating the interaction terms has produced a decrement in $SS_{\text{regression}}$ of

$$SS_Y(R^2_{\alpha,\beta,\alpha\beta}) = 207.7055$$

$$-SS_Y(R^2_{\alpha,\beta}) = \underline{188.4301}$$

$$SS_{AB} = 19.2754$$

This decrement is the sum of squares attributable to the AB interaction (SS_{AB}).

In the case of unequal ns, it is particularly important to understand what this term represents:

$$SS_{AB} = SS_Y(R^2_{\alpha,\beta,\alpha\beta}) - SS_Y(R^2_{\alpha,\beta})$$

$$= SS_Y(R^2_{\alpha,\beta,\alpha\beta} - R^2_{\alpha,\beta})$$

$$= SS_Y(R^2_{0(\alpha\beta \cdot \alpha,\beta)})$$

The final term in parentheses is the squared semipartial correlation between the criterion and the interaction effects, partialling out (adjusting for) the effects of A and B. In other words, it is the squared correlation between the criterion and the part of the AB interaction that is orthogonal to A and B. Thus, we can think of SS_{AB} as really being $SS_{AB(adj)}$, where the adjustment is for the effects of A and B. (In the equal-n case, the issue does not arise because A, B, and AB are independent, and therefore there is no overlapping variation to partial out.)[†]

TESTING THE MAIN EFFECTS

Since we are using Overall and Spiegel's Method I, we will calculate the main effects of A and B in a way that is directly comparable to our estimation of the interaction effect. Here, each main effect represents the sum of squares attributable to that variable after partialling out the other main effect and the interaction.

To obtain SS_A, we will delete the predictor associated with the main effect of A and calculate $R^2_{\beta, \alpha\beta}$. For these data, $R^2_{\beta, \alpha\beta} = .523$, producing a drop in R^2 of $.532 - .523 = .009$. In terms of the predictable sum of squares ($SS_{regression}$), the elimination of α from the model produces a decrement in $SS_{regression}$ of

$$SS_Y(R^2_{\alpha, \beta, \alpha\beta}) = 207.7055$$
$$-SS_Y(R^2_{\beta, \alpha\beta}) = \underline{203.9500}$$
$$SS_A = 3.7555$$

This decrement is the sum of squares attributable to the main effect of A.

By the same reasoning, we can obtain SS_B by comparing $SS_{regression}$ for the full model and for a model omitting β.

$$SS_Y(R^2_{\alpha, \beta, \alpha\beta}) = 207.7055$$
$$-SS_Y(R^2_{\alpha, \alpha\beta}) = \underline{29.7499}$$
$$SS_B = 177.9556$$

[†]Some people have trouble understanding the concept of nonindependent treatment effects. Perhaps an extreme example will help point out how a row effect could cause an *apparent* column effect, or vice versa. Consider the following two-way table. When we look at differences among means, are we looking at a difference due to A, B, or AB?

	B_1	B_2	**Means**
A_1	$\bar{X} = 10$ $n = 20$	$n = 0$	10
A_2	$n = 0$	$\bar{X} = 30$ $n = 20$	30
Means	10	30	

These results are summarized in Table 16.8, with the method by which they were obtained. Notice that the sums of squares do not sum to SS_{total}. This is as it should be, since the overlapping portions of accountable variation (segments "4," "5," "6," and "7" of Figure 16.1) are not represented anywhere. Also notice that SS_{error} is taken as the $SS_{residual}$ from the full model, just as in the case of equal sample sizes. Here again we define SS_{error} as the portion of the total variation that cannot be explained by any one or more of the independent variables.

TABLE 16.8
Calculation of sums of squares using Model I—the equally weighted means solution

Method I (Equally Weighted Means)

Source	df	SS
A	$a-1$	$SS_Y(R^2_{\alpha,\beta,\alpha\beta} - R^2_{\beta,\alpha\beta})$
B	$b-1$	$SS_Y(R^2_{\alpha,\beta,\alpha\beta} - R^2_{\alpha,\alpha\beta})$
AB	$(a-1)(b-1)$	$SS_Y(R^2_{\alpha,\beta,\alpha\beta} - R^2_{\alpha,\beta})$
Error	$N-ab$	$SS_Y(1 - R^2_{\alpha,\beta,\alpha\beta})$
Total	$N-1$	SS_Y

Summary Table for Analysis of Variance

Source	df	SS	MS	F
A	1	3.7555	3.7555	<1
B	3	177.9556	59.3185	9.10
AB	3	19.2754	6.4251	<1
Error	28	182.6001	6.5214	
Total	35	(390.3056)		

As I mentioned earlier, the unweighted-means solution presented in Chapter 13 is an approximation of the equally weighted means solution (Method I) given here. If you were to apply the equally weighted means solution to the data in Table 13.11, you would in fact find that the two solutions differ only in the second or third decimal place. The two solutions are not usually that close, although in my experience they seldom differ by very much. If I were faced with computing an analysis of variance on data with unequal sample sizes and could assume that the differences in sample sizes were independent of the treatments actually applied, and if I had only my hand calculator, I would almost certainly use the approach given in Chapter 13. However, if I analyzed the data using a standard computer program such as BMDP2V or SPSS[X] (and I almost *always* use Option 9 when I use SPSS[X] ANOVA), I would have the equally weighted means solution. The main reason for discussing that solution in this chapter is so that you will understand what the computer program is giving you and how it is treating the unequal sample sizes.

The very simple SAS program and its abbreviated output in Exhibit 16.2 illustrate that the Type III sums of squares from SAS PROC GLM do, in fact, produce the appropriate analysis of the data in Table 16.7.

EXHIBIT 16.2
Abbreviated SAS
analysis of the data in
Table 16.7

```
Options  nocenter:
Options ls = 80;
Options pagesize = 60;

Data Nonorth;
   Infile 'Tabl67.dat';
   Input  A B dv;
Run;

Proc GLM Data = Nonorth;
   Class A B;
   Model dv = A B A*B;
```

Source	DF	Type III SS	Mean Square	F Value	Pr > F
A	1	3.75555556	3.75555556	0.58	0.4543
B	3	177.95562457	59.31854152	9.10	0.0002
A*B	3	19.27550035	6.42516678	0.99	0.4139

16.5   THE ONE-WAY ANALYSIS OF COVARIANCE

**Analysis of
covariance**

An extremely useful tool for analyzing experimental data is the **analysis of covariance**. As normally presented within the context of the analysis of variance, the analysis of covariance appears to be unpleasantly cumbersome, especially so when there is more than one covariate. Within the framework of multiple regression, however, it is remarkably simple, requiring little, if any, more work than does the analysis of variance.

Suppose we wish to compare driving proficiency on three different sizes of cars to test the experimental hypothesis that small cars are easier to handle. We have available three different groups of drivers, but we are not able to match individual subjects on driving experience, which varies considerably within each group. Let us make the simplifying assumption, which will be discussed in more detail later, that the mean level of driving experience is equal across groups. Suppose further that using the number of steering errors as our dependent variable, we obtain the somewhat exaggerated data plotted in Figure 16.2. In this figure the data have been plotted separately for

Covariate

each group (size of car), as a function of driving experience (the **covariate**), and the separate regression lines have been superimposed.

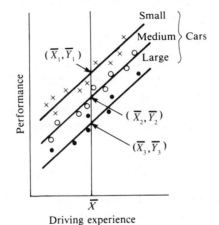

FIGURE 16.2
Hypothetical data
illustrating error-
reduction in analysis
of covariance

One of the most striking things about Figure 16.2 is the large variability in both performance and experience within each treatment. This variability is so great that an analysis of variance on performance scores would almost certainly fail to produce a significant effect. Most of the variability in performance, however, is directly attributable to differences in driving experience, which has nothing to do with what we wish to study. If we could somehow remove (partial out) the variance that can be attributed to experience (the covariate), we would have a clearer test of our original hypothesis. This is exactly what the analysis of covariance is designed to do, and this is precisely the situation in which it does its job best—its job in this case is to reduce the error term.

A more controversial use of the analysis of covariance concerns situations in which the treatment groups have different covariate (driving experience) means. Such a situation (using the same hypothetical experiment) is depicted in Figure 16.3, in which two of the treatments have been displaced along the X axis. At the point at which the three regression lines intersect the vertical line $X = \overline{X}$, you can see the values $\overline{Y}'_1$, $\overline{Y}'_2$,

Adjusted Y means

and $\overline{Y}'_3$. These are the **adjusted Y means** and represent our best guess as to what the Y means would have been if the treatments had not differed on the covariate. The analysis of covariance then tests whether these adjusted means differ significantly, again using an error term from which the variance attributable to the covariate has been partialled out.

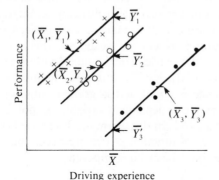

FIGURE 16.3
Hypothetical data
illustrating mean
adjustment in analysis
of covariance

Although the structure and procedures of the analysis of covariance are the same regardless of whether the treatment groups differ on the covariate means, the different ways of visualizing the problem as represented in Figures 16.2 and 16.3 are instructive. In the first case, we are simply reducing the error term. In the second case, we are both reducing the error term *and* adjusting the means on the dependent variable. We will have more to say about this distinction later in the chapter.

ASSUMPTIONS OF THE ANALYSIS OF COVARIANCE

Aside from the usual analysis of variance assumptions of normality and homogeneity of variance, we must add two more assumptions. First we will assume that whatever

Homogeneity of regression

the relationship between Y and the covariate (C), this relationship is linear.[†] Second, we will assume **homogeneity of regression**—that the regression coefficients are equal across treatments—$b_1^* = b_2^* = b_3^* = \cdots = b^*$. This is merely the assumption that the three lines in Figure 16.2 or 16.3 are parallel, and it is necessary to justify our substitution of one regression line (the pooled within-groups regression line) for the separate regression lines. As we shall see shortly, this assumption is testable. Note that no assumption has been made about the nature of the covariate; it may be either a fixed or a random variable.

CALCULATING THE ANALYSIS OF COVARIANCE

When viewed within the framework of multiple regression, the analysis of covariance is basically no different from the analysis of variance, except that we wish to partial out the effects of the covariate. As Cohen (1968) put it, "A covariate is, after all, nothing but an independent variable which, because of the logic dictated by the substantive issues of the research, assumes priority among the set of independent variables as a basis for accounting for Y variance" (p. 439).

If we want to ask about the variation in Y after the covariate (C) has been partialled out, and if the variation in Y can be associated with only C, the treatment effect (α), and error, then $R_{c,\alpha}^2$ represents the total percentage of accountable variation. If we now compare $R_{c,\alpha}^2$ with R_c^2, the difference will be the variation attributable to treatment effects *over and above* that attributable to the covariate.

We will take as an example a variation on the study by Conti and Musty (1984) presented in Chapter 11. As you may recall, in that study the authors were interested in examining the effects of different amounts of THC, the major active ingredient in marijuana, injected directly into the nucleus accumbens. The dependent variable was locomotor activity, which normally increases with the administration of THC by more traditional routes. Because of the nature of the experimental setting (all animals were observed under baseline conditions and then again after the administration of THC), activity should decrease in all animals as they become familiar and more comfortable with the apparatus. If THC has its effect through the nucleus accumbens, however, the effects of moderate doses of THC should partially compensate for this anticipated decrease, leading to relatively greater activity levels in the moderate-dose groups as compared to the low- or high-dose groups.

Conti and Musty (1984) actually analyzed postinjection activity as a percentage of preinjection activity, because that is the way such data are routinely analyzed in their field. An alternative procedure would have been to run an analysis of covariance on the postinjection scores, partialling out preinjection differences. Such a procedure would adjust for the fact that much of the variability in postinjection activity could be accounted for by variability in preinjection activity. It would also control for the fact that, by chance, there were group differences in the level of preinjection activity that could contaminate postinjection scores.

[†] Methods for handling nonlinear relationships are available but will not be discussed here.

As will become clear later, it is important to note here that all animals were assigned at random to groups. Therefore, we would *expect* equal group means on the preinjection phase. Any differences that do appear on the preinjection phase, then, are due to chance, and, *in the absence of any treatment effect*, we would expect that postinjection means, adjusted for chance preinjection differences, would be equal. The fact that subjects were assigned at random to treatments is what allows us to expect equal adjusted group means at postinjection (if H_0 is true), and this in turn allows us to interpret group differences at postinjection to be a result of real treatment differences rather than of some artifact of subject assignment.

The data and the design matrix for the Conti and Musty (1984) study are presented in Table 16.9. The raw data have been divided by 100 simply to make the resulting sums of squares manageable.[†] In the design matrix, only the first and last subject in each group are represented. Columns 6 though 9 of X represent the interaction of the covariate and the group variables. These columns are used to test the hypothesis of homogeneity of regression coefficients across groups:

$$H_0: b_1^* = b_2^* = b_3^* = b_4^* = b_5^*$$

The full model (including the interaction predictors) states that

$$Y_{ij} = \tau_j + c + \tau c_j + e_{ij}$$

where τ_j represents the treatment effect for the jth treatment, c represents the covariate, τc_j represents our term testing homogeneity of regression, and e_{ij} represents the error associated with the ith subject in treatment j.

TABLE 16.9
Pre- and postinjection data by group

	Control		0.1 μg		0.5 μg		1 μg		2 μg	
	Pre	Post	Pre	Post	Pre	Post	Pre	Post	Pre	Post
	4.34	1.30	1.55	0.93	7.18	5.10	6.94	2.29	4.00	1.44
	3.50	0.94	10.56	4.44	8.33	4.16	6.10	4.75	4.10	1.11
	4.33	2.25	8.39	4.03	4.05	1.54	4.90	3.48	3.62	2.17
	2.76	1.05	3.70	1.92	10.78	6.36	3.69	2.76	3.92	2.00
	4.62	0.92	2.40	0.67	6.09	3.96	4.76	1.67	2.90	0.84
	5.40	1.90	1.83	1.70	7.78	4.51	4.30	1.51	2.90	0.99
	3.95	0.32	2.40	0.77	5.08	3.76	2.32	1.07	1.82	0.44
	1.55	0.64	7.67	3.53	2.86	1.92	7.35	2.35	4.94	0.84
	1.42	0.69	5.79	3.65	6.30	3.84			5.69	2.84
	1.90	0.93	9.58	4.22					5.54	2.93
Means:	3.3770		5.3870		6.4944		5.0450		3.9430	
		1.0940		2.5860		3.9056		2.4850		1.5600

(Grand mean Pre = 4.8060; Grand mean Post = 2.2857)

[†] If the data had not been divided by 100, the resulting sums of squares and mean squares would be $100^2 = 10,000$ times their present size. The F and t values would be unaffected.

TABLE 16.9 (Cont.)

						Design Matrix					
	Cov	T1	T2	T3	T4	CT1	CT2	CT3	CT4		
	4.34	1	0	0	0	4.34	0	0	0		1.30
	...	...	...	...	...	...	...	...	...		...
	1.90	1	0	0	0	1.90	0	0	0		0.93
	1.55	0	1	0	0	0	1.55	0	0		0.93
	...	...	...	...	...	...	...	...	...		...
	9.58	0	1	0	0	0	9.58	0	0		4.22
	7.18	0	0	1	0	0	0	7.18	0		5.10
	...	...	...	...	...	...	...	...	...		...
$\mathbf{X} =$	6.30	0	0	1	0	0	0	6.30	0	$\mathbf{Y} =$	3.84
(47×9)	6.94	0	0	0	1	0	0	0	6.94	(47×1)	2.29
	...	...	...	...	...	...	...	...	...		...
	7.35	0	0	0	1	0	0	0	7.35		2.35
	4.00	−1	−1	−1	−1	−4.00	−4.00	−4.00	−4.00		1.44
	...	...	...	...	...	...	...	...	...		...
	5.54	−1	−1	−1	−1	−5.54	−5.54	−5.54	−5.54		2.93

The regression analysis of this model would produce

$$R^2_{t,c,tc} = .8238$$

If there is no significant difference in within-treatment regressions—that is, if the regression lines are parallel and thus the slopes of the regression lines that could be calculated for each group separately are homogeneous—called homogeneity of regression—the deletion of the interaction term should produce only a trivial decrement in the percentage of accountable variation. When we delete the CT terms, we have

$$R^2_{t,c} = .8042$$

The F test on this decrement is the usual F test on the difference between two models:

$$F(f - r, N - f - 1) = \frac{(N - f - 1)(R^2_{t,c,tc} - R^2_{t,c})}{(f - r)(1 - R^2_{t,c,tc})}$$

$$= \frac{(47 - 9 - 1)(.8238 - .8042)}{(4)(.1762)} = 1.03$$

Given an F of 1.03 on 4 and 37 degrees of freedom, we have no basis to reject the assumption of homogeneity of regression (common regression coefficients) within the five treatments. Thus, we can proceed with the analysis on the basis of the revised full model:

$$Y_{ij} = \mu + \tau_j + c + e_{ij}$$

This model will serve as the basis against which we compare reduced models.

The three sets of results of the multiple-regression solutions using the covariate and dummy treatment variables, just the treatment variables, and then just the covariates are presented in Table 16.10.

TABLE 16.10
Regression analyses

(a) Full Model

$$\hat{Y}_{ij} = 0.4347(\text{Pre}) - 0.5922(T1) + 0.0262(T2) + 0.8644(T3)$$
$$+ 0.0738(T4) + 0.2183$$

$$R^2_{\tau,c} = .8042$$

Analysis of Variance Summary Table for Regression				
Source	SS	df	MS	F
Regression	82.6435	5	16.5287	33.6726
Residual	20.1254	41	0.4909	
Total	102.7689	46	2.2341	

(b) Reduced Model—Omitting Treatment Predictors

$$\hat{Y}_{ij} = 0.5311(\text{Pre}) - 0.26667$$

$$R^2_c = .7144$$

Analysis of Variance Summary Table for Regression				
Source	SS	df	MS	F
Regression	73.4196	1	73.4196	112.5711
Residual	29.3493	45	0.6522	
Total	102.7689	46	2.2341	

(c) Reduced Model—Omitting Covariate (Pre)

$$\hat{Y}_{ij} = -1.2321(T1) + 0.2599(T2) + 1.5794(T3) + 0.1589(T4) + 2.3261$$
$$R^2_\tau = .4311$$

Analysis of Variance Summary Table for Regression				
Source	SS	df	MS	F
Regression	44.3028	4	11.0757	7.9564
Residual	58.4661	42	1.3921	
Total	102.7689	46	2.2341	

From Table 16.10 you can see that using both the covariate (Pre) and the group membership dummy variates $(T1 \ldots T4)$, the sum of squares for regression $(\text{SS}_{\text{regression}_{\tau,c}})$ is equal to 82.6435, which is the portion of the total variation that can be accounted for by these two sets of predictors. You can also see that the residual sum of squares $(\text{SS}_{\text{residual}})$ is 20.1254, which is the variability that cannot be predicted. In our analysis of covariance summary table, this will become the sum of squares for error.

When we remove the dummy group membership variates from the equation and use only the covariate (Pre) as a predictor, $SS_{regression}$ drops from 82.6435 to 73.4196. The difference between $SS_{regression}$ with and without the group membership predictors must be the amount of the sum of squares that can be attributable to treatment *over and above* the amount that can be explained by the covariate. For our data, this is

$$SS_{treat(adj)} = SS_{regression_{t,c}} - SS_{regression_c}$$

$$= 82.6435 - 73.4196$$

$$= 9.2239$$

This last value is called the *adjusted* treatment sum of squares for the analysis of covariance, because it has been adjusted for any effects of the covariate. In this case, it has been adjusted for the fact that the five groups differed on the pretest measure.

We need one additional term to form our analysis of covariance summary table, and that is the sum of squares to be attributed to the covariate. There are a number of different ways to define this term, but the most common is to define it analogously to the way the adjusted treatment effect was defined. We will attribute to the covariate that portion of the variation that cannot be defined by the treatment effect. In other words, we will take the model with both the covariate and treatment predictors and compare it to a model with only the treatment predictors. The difference in the two sums of squares due to regression will be the sum of squares that the covariate accounts for *over and above* what is accounted for by treatment effects. For our data, this is

$$SS_{covariate} = SS_{regression_{t,c}} - SS_{regression_t}$$

$$= 82.6435 - 44.3028$$

$$= 38.3407$$

We now have all the information necessary to construct the analysis of covariance summary table. This is presented in Table 16.11. Notice that in this table the error term is $SS_{residual}$ from the full model and the other sums of squares are as calculated before. Notice also that there is one degree of freedom for the covariate, since there is one covariate; there are $(k - 1) = (5 - 1) = 4$ df for the adjusted treatment effect; and there are $N - k - c = 41$ df for error (where k represents the number of groups and c represents the number of covariates).

ADJUSTED MEANS

Since $F_{.5}(1, 41) = 4.08 < F_{obt} = 4.698$, we would reject H_0: $\mu_1(adj) = \mu_2(adj) = \mu_3(adj) = \mu_4(adj) = \mu_5(adj)$ and conclude that there were significant differences among the treatment means after the effect of the covariate has been partialled out of the analysis. To interpret these differences, it would be useful to obtain the treatment means adjusted for the effects of the covariate. We are essentially asking for an estimate of what the postinjection treatment means would have been had the groups not differed on the preinjection means. The adjusted means are readily obtained from the regression solution using the covariate and treatments as predictors.

TABLE 16.11
Summary tables for
analysis of covariance

(a) General Summary Table for One-Way Analysis of Covariance

Source	df	SS
Covariate	c	$SS_{\text{regression}(\tau,c)} - SS_{\text{regression}(\tau)}$
Treat (adj)	$k - 1$	$SS_{\text{regression}(\tau,c)} - SS_{\text{regression}(c)}$
Error	$N - k - c$	$SS_{\text{residual}(\tau,c)}$
Total	$N - 1$	SS_Y

(b) Summary Table for Data in Table 16.9

Source	df	SS	MS	F
Covariate	1	38.3407	38.3407	78.108
Treat (adj)	4	9.2239	2.3060	4.698
Error	41	20.1254	0.4909	
Total	46	102.7689		

Full models: $\hat{Y}_{ij} = 0.4347(\text{Pre}) - 0.5922(T1) + 0.0262(T2)$

$+ 0.8644(T3) + 0.0738(T4) + 0.2183$

From the analysis of the revised full model, we obtained

$$\hat{Y}_{ij} = 0.4347(\text{Pre}) - 0.5922(T1) + 0.0262(T2) + 0.8644(T3) + 0.0738(T4) + 0.2183$$

Writing this in terms of means and representing adjusted means as $\overline{Y}'_j$, we have

$$\overline{Y}'_j, = 0.4347(\overline{\text{Pre}}) - 0.5922(T1) + 0.0262(T2) + 0.8644(T3) + 0.0738(T4) + 0.2183$$

where $\overline{\text{Pre}} = 4.8060$ (the mean preinjection score) and $T1$, $T2$, $T3$, and $T4$ are $(0, 1, -1)$ variables. (We substitute the mean Pre score for the individual Pre score because we are interested in the means for Y if all subjects had received the mean score on the covariate.) For our data, the adjusted means of the treatments are:

$\overline{Y}'_1 = 0.4347(4.8060) - 0.5922(1) + 0.0262(0) + 0.8644(0) + 0.0738(0) + 0.2183$

$= 1.7153$

$\overline{Y}'_2 = 0.4347(4.8060) - 0.5922(0) + 0.0262(1) + 0.8644(0) + 0.0738(0) + 0.2183$

$= 2.3336$

$\overline{Y}'_3 = 0.4347(4.8060) - 0.5922(0) + 0.0262(0) + 0.8644(1) + 0.0738(0) + 0.2183$

$= 3.1719$

$\overline{Y}'_4 = 0.4347(4.8060) - 0.5922(0) + 0.0262(0) + 0.8644(0) + 0.0738(1) + 0.2183$

$= 2.3813$

$\overline{Y}'_5 = 0.4347(4.8060) - 0.5922(-1) + 0.0262(-1) + 0.8644(-1)$

$+ 0.0738(-1) + 0.2183 = 1.9353$

The grand mean is

$$\overline{Y}' = 0.4347(4.8060) - 0.5922(0) + 0.0262(0) + 0.8644(0) + 0.0738(0) + 0.2183$$

$$= 2.3075$$

which is the mean of the adjusted means. (In a case in which we have equal sample sizes, the adjusted grand mean will equal the unadjusted grand mean.)[†]

Any individual comparisons among treatments would now be made using these adjusted means. In this case, however, we must modify our error term from that of the overall analysis of covariance. If we let $SS_{e(c)}$ represent the error sum of squares from an analysis of variance on the *covariate*, then Huitema (1980), in an excellent and readable book on the analysis of covariance, gives as a test of the difference between two adjusted means

$$F(1, N - a - 1) = \frac{(\overline{Y}'_j - \overline{Y}'_k)^2}{MS'_{error}\left[\left(\frac{1}{n_j} + \frac{1}{n_k}\right) + \frac{(C_j - C_k)^2}{SS_{e(c)}}\right]}$$

MS'_{error}

where **MS'_{error}** is the error term from the analysis of covariance. For an excellent discussion of effective error terms and comparisons among means, see Winer (1971, p. 771ff) and, especially, Huitema (1980).

As an example, suppose we wish to compare $\overline{Y}'_1$ and $\overline{Y}'_3$. From the preceding analysis, we either know or can compute

$$MS'_{error} = 0.4909$$

$$SS_{e(c)} = 202.938 \qquad \text{[calculation not shown]}$$

$$\overline{C}_1 = 3.3770 \qquad \overline{C}_3 = 6.4944$$

$$\overline{Y}'_1 = 1.7153 \qquad \overline{Y}'_3 = 3.1719$$

$$F(1, 41) = \frac{(1.7153 - 3.1719)^2}{0.4909\left[\left(\frac{1}{10} + \frac{1}{9}\right) + \frac{(3.3770 - 6.4944)^2}{202.938}\right]}$$

$$= \frac{2.1217}{0.1271} = 16.69$$

The critical value $[F_{.05}(1, 41)] = 4.08$. We would thus reject the null hypothesis that the adjusted means are equal in the population. Even after adjusting for the fact that the groups differed by chance on the pretest, we find significant posttest differences.

[†] An alternative approach to calculating adjusted means is to define

$$\overline{Y}'_j = \overline{Y}_j - b_w(\overline{C}_j - C.)$$

where $\overline{C}_j$ is the covariate mean for Group j, C. is the covariate grand mean, and b_w is the regression coefficient for the covariate from the complete model (here $b_w = 0.4347$). This more traditional way of calculating adjusted means makes it clear that the adjusted mean is some function of how deviant that group was on the covariate. The same values for the adjusted means will result from using either approach.

Exhibit 16.3 contains a sample BMDP program and output for the analysis of variance. This program was run using BMDP2V, but the same analysis could be conducted using other BMDP analysis of variance programs—in particular, BMDP4V, which is also used for multivariate analyses of variance.

EXHIBIT 16.3
BMDP program and output for analysis of Conti and Musty data

PROGRAM INSTRUCTIONS

```
/Problem        Title is 'BMDP2V Analysis of Conti-Musty Data.'
/Input          Variables are 3.
                Format is free.
                Cases are 47.
                File is 'Conticov.dat'.
/Variable       Names are Group, Pretest, PostTest.
/Design         Dependent is PostTest.
                Grouping is Group.
                Covariate is PreTest.
/End
```

PROBLEM TITLE IS
BMDP2V Analysis of Conti-Musty Data.

CELL MEANS   FOR 1-ST COVARIATE
- - - - - - - - - - - - - - - - - - - -

Group =	*1	*2	*3	*4	*5	MARGINAL
PreTest	3.37700	5.38700	6.49444	5.04500	3.94300	4.80596
COUNT	10	10	9	8	10	47

STANDARD DEVIATIONS   FOR 1-ST COVARIATE
- - - - - - - - - - - - - - - - - - - -

Group =	*1	*2	*3	*4	*5
PreTest	1.39629	3.44478	2.37814	1.68760	1.22075

CELL MEANS   FOR 1-ST DEPENDENT VARIABLE
- - - - - - - - - - - - - - - - - - - -

Group =	*1	*2	*3	*4	*5	MARGINAL
PostTest	1.09400	2.58600	3.90556	2.48500	1.56000	2.28574
COUNT	10	10	9	8	10	47

STANDARD DEVIATIONS   FOR 1-ST DEPENDENT VARIABLE
- - - - - - - - - - - - - - - - - - - -

Group =	*1	*2	*3	*4	*5
PosTest	0.58496	1.53317	1.47681	1.18739	0.87648

ANALYSIS OF VARIANCE FOR 1-ST DEPENDENT VARIABLE
PostTest

SOURCE	SUM OF SQUARES	D.F.	MEAN SQUARE	F	TAIL PROB.	REGRESSION COEFFICIENTS
Group	9.22387	4	2.30597	4.70	0.0033	
PreTest	38.34066	1	38.34066	78.11	0.0000	0.4347
1 ERROR	20.12545	41	0.49086			

ADJUSTED CELL MEANS   FOR 1-ST DEPENDENT VARIABLE
- - - - - - - - - - - - - - - - - - - -

Group =	*1	*2	*3	*4	*5
PostTest	1.71511	2.33344	3.17164	2.38110	1.93509

16.6   INTERPRETING AN ANALYSIS OF COVARIANCE

Interpreting an analysis of covariance can present certain problems, depending on the nature of the data and, more important, the design of the experiment. A thorough and readable discussion of most of these problems is presented by Huitema (1980). Other important sources for consideration of these problems are Anderson (1963), Evans and Anastasio (1968), Lord (1967, 1969), Maxwell and Cramer (1975), Reichardt (1979), Smith (1957), and Weisberg (1979). The geometric interpretation given by Maxwell, Delaney, and Manheimer (1985) is particularly good. I will present only a cursory examination of the difficulties that may arise.

The ideal application for an analysis of covariance is an experiment in which subjects are randomly assigned to treatments (or cells of a factorial design). In that situation, the *expected value* of each group or cell mean on the covariate is the same, and any differences can be attributed only to chance, assuming that the covariate was measured before the treatments were applied. In this situation, the analysis of covariance will primarily reduce the error term, but it will also, properly, remove any bias in the dependent variable means caused by chance group differences on the covariate. This was the situation in the Conti and Musty (1984) study that we have been discussing.

In a randomized experiment in which the covariate is measured after the treatment has been applied and has affected the covariate, interpreting the results of an analysis of covariance is difficult at best. In this situation the expected values of the group means on the covariates are not equal, even though the subjects were assigned randomly. It is difficult to interpret the results of the analysis because you are asking what the groups would have been like had they not differed on the covariate, when in fact the covariate differences may be an integral part of the treatment effect. This problem is particularly severe if the covariate was measured with error (i.e., if it is not perfectly

True-score analysis of covariance

reliable). In this case an alternative analysis, called the **true-score analysis of covariance**, may be appropriate if the other interpretive problems can be overcome. Such an analysis is discussed in Huitema (1980, Chapter 14).

When subjects are not assigned to the treatment groups at random, interpretating the analysis of covariance can be particularly troublesome. The most common example

Nonequivalent groups design

of this problem is what is called the **nonequivalent groups design**. In this design, two (or more) intact groups are chosen (e.g., schools or classrooms of children), a pretest measure is obtained from subjects in both groups, the treatment is applied to one of the groups, and the two groups are then compared on some posttest measure. Since subjects are not assigned to the groups at random, we have no basis for assuming that any differences that exist on the pretest are to be attributed to chance. Similarly, we have no basis for expecting the two groups to have the same mean on the posttest in the absence of a real treatment effect. Huitema (1980, pp. 149ff) gives an excellent demonstration that when the groups differ at the beginning of the experiment, the phenomenon of regression to the mean could lead to posttest differences even in the absence of a treatment effect. For alternative analyses that are useful under certain conditions, see Huitema (1980).

The problems of interpreting results of designs in which subjects are not randomly assigned to the treatment groups are not easily overcome. This is one of the reasons why random assignment is even more important than random selection of subjects. It is difficult to overestimate the virtues of randomization, both for interpreting data and for making causal statements about the relationship between variables. In what is probably only a slight overstatement of the issue, Lord (1967) remarked, "In the writer's opinion, the explanation is that with the data usually available for such studies, there is simply no logical or statistical procedure that can be counted on to make proper allowances for uncontrolled pre-existing differences between groups" (p. 305). (Lord was *not* referring to differences that arise by chance through random assignment.) Anderson (1963) made a similar point by stating, "One may well wonder exactly what it means to ask what the data would be like if they were not what they are" (p. 170). All of this is not to say that the analysis of covariance has no place in the analysis of data in which the treatments differ on the covariate. Anyone using covariance analysis, however, must think carefully about her data and the practical validity of the conclusions she draws.

16.7   THE FACTORIAL ANALYSIS OF COVARIANCE

The analysis of covariance applies to factorial designs just as well as it does to single-variable designs. Once again, the covariate may be treated as a variable that, because of methodological considerations, assumes priority in the analysis. In this chapter we will deal only with the case of equal cell sizes, but the generalization to unequal ns is immediate.

The logic of the analysis is straightforward and follows that used in the previous examples. The coefficient $R^2_{c,\alpha,\beta,\alpha\beta}$ is the percentage of variance attributable to a linear combination of the covariate, the main effects of A and B, and the AB interaction. Similarly, $R^2_{c,\alpha,\beta}$ is the percentage of variation attributable to a linear combination of the covariate and the main effects of A and B. The difference

$$R^2_{c,\beta,\alpha\beta} - R^2_{c,\alpha,\beta}$$

is the percentage of variation attributable to the AB interaction, with the covariate and the main effects partialled out. Since, with equal cell sizes, the two main effects and the interaction are all orthogonal, all that is *actually* partialled out is the covariate.

By the same line of reasoning,

$$R^2_{c,\alpha,\beta,\alpha\beta} - R^2_{c,\alpha,\alpha\beta}$$

represents the percentage of variation attributable to B, partialling out the covariate, and

$$R^2_{c,\alpha,\beta,\alpha\beta} - R^2_{c,\beta,\alpha\beta}$$

represents the percentage of variation attributable to the main effect of A, again partialling out the covariate.

The error term represents the variation remaining after controlling for A, B, AB, and the covariate. As such it is given by

$$SS_{error} = SS_Y(1 - R^2_{c,\alpha,\beta,\alpha\beta})$$

The general structure of the analysis is presented in Table 16.12. Notice that once again the error term loses a degree of freedom to each covariate. Since the independent variables and the covariate account for overlapping portions of the variance, their sums of squares will not sum to SS_{total}.

TABLE 16.12
Structure of the analysis of covariance

Source	df	SS
A (adj)	$a - 1$	$SS_Y(R^2_{c,\alpha,\beta,\alpha\beta} - R^2_{c,\beta,\alpha\beta})$
B (adj)	$b - 1$	$SS_Y(R^2_{c,\alpha,\beta,\alpha\beta} - R^2_{c,\alpha,\alpha\beta})$
AB (adj)	$(a - 1)(b - 1)$	$SS_Y(R^2_{c,\alpha,\beta,\alpha\beta} - R^2_{c,\alpha,\beta})$
Error	$N - ab - c$	$SS_Y(1 - R^2_{c,\alpha,\beta,\alpha\beta})$
Covariate	c	$SS_Y(R^2_{c,\alpha,\beta,\alpha\beta} - R^2_{\alpha,\beta,\alpha\beta})$
Total	$N - 1$	

As an example, consider a hypothetical study in which we wish to examine three methods of teaching map reading. For Method I, all teaching is done in the classroom, with no field experience at all. For Method II, one-half of the teaching takes place in the classroom and one-half of it takes place in the field. For Method III, all the teaching takes place in the field. Suppose further that we believe that it is important to consider where the people we are teaching grew up. We assume that people who were raised in the country have more experience with walking in the woods, climbing hills, and so on than do people who have lived all of their lives in the city, and this experience might prove useful in a course in map reading. Since we have a large number of subjects from which to select, we choose to draw equal numbers of subjects from rural and urban populations, and make this a second variable in our study. Finally, assume that in looking over our subjects we notice that there appears to be substantial variability in terms of years of formal schooling. It seems a reasonable assumption that the more formal education to which a person has been exposed, the better he or she might be expected to do in our course. This in turn will introduce substantial amounts of within-cell variance. In an attempt to remove the effects of this unwanted variance, we have chosen to use years of formal education as a covariate.

The data are presented in Table 16.13. The dependent variable (Y) is the final score on a 40-point map-reading exam, and the covariate (C) is the number of years of formal education. The data represent a 2×3 analysis of covariance with one covariate and four scores per cell.

Table 16.14 is an abbreviated form of the design matrix, showing only the entries for the first subject in every cell. Notice that the matrix contains a column for the covariate, the usual design matrix elements for the main effects of A and B and the AB interaction, and the interaction of the covariate with each of the treatment effects. The latter will be used to test the hypothesis H_0: $b_i^* = b_j^*$ (for all i, j), since the assumption of homogeneity of regression applies to any analysis of covariance.

TABLE 16.13
Data for the analysis
of covariance

Place of Residence		Teaching Methods						Row Means	
		B_1		B_2		B_3			
		Y	C	Y	C	Y	C	Y	C
Urban		5	8	15	10	28	11		
		12	10	10	13	26	8		
	A_1	16	12	26	15	13	6		
		28	15	23	17	12	5		
	Means	15.25	11.25	18.50	13.75	19.75	7.50	17.833	10.833
Rural		8	8	7	7	32	11		
		16	10	23	10	30	7		
	A_2	18	13	25	12	17	5		
		27	16	36	14	17	4		
	Means	17.25	11.75	22.75	10.75	24.00	6.75	21.333	9.750
Column Means		16.250	11.500	20.625	12.250	21.875	7.125	19.583	10.292

TABLE 16.14
Design matrix for the
analysis of covariance

$$
\mathbf{X} = \begin{bmatrix}
c & A_1 & B_1 & B_2 & AB_{11} & AB_{12} & CA_1 & CB_1 & CB_2 & CAB_{11} & CAB_{12} \\
8 & 1 & 1 & 0 & 1 & 0 & 8 & 8 & 0 & 8 & 0 \\
\cdots & \cdots & \cdots & \cdots & \cdots & \cdots & \cdots & \cdots & \cdots & \cdots & \cdots \\
10 & 1 & 0 & 1 & 0 & 1 & 10 & 0 & 10 & 0 & 10 \\
\cdots & \cdots & \cdots & \cdots & \cdots & \cdots & \cdots & \cdots & \cdots & \cdots & \cdots \\
11 & 1 & -1 & -1 & -1 & -1 & 11 & -11 & -11 & -11 & -11 \\
\cdots & \cdots & \cdots & \cdots & \cdots & \cdots & \cdots & \cdots & \cdots & \cdots & \cdots \\
8 & -1 & 1 & 0 & -1 & 0 & -8 & 8 & 0 & -8 & 0 \\
\cdots & \cdots & \cdots & \cdots & \cdots & \cdots & \cdots & \cdots & \cdots & \cdots & \cdots \\
7 & -1 & 0 & 1 & 0 & -1 & -7 & 0 & 7 & 0 & -7 \\
\cdots & \cdots & \cdots & \cdots & \cdots & \cdots & \cdots & \cdots & \cdots & \cdots & \cdots \\
11 & -1 & -1 & -1 & 1 & 1 & -11 & -11 & -11 & 11 & 11
\end{bmatrix}
\qquad
\mathbf{y} = \begin{bmatrix}
5 \\ \cdots \\ 15 \\ \cdots \\ 28 \\ \cdots \\ 8 \\ \cdots \\ 7 \\ \cdots \\ 32
\end{bmatrix}
$$

It is important to consider just what the interactions involving the covariate represent. Terms such as CA_1 carry information concerning the question of whether the regression lines for Y on C have the same slope for treatment A_1 as they do for treatment A_2. The terms CB_1 and CB_2 carry information on whether the slope of the regression line of Y on C within B_1 is the same as it is within B_2 and B_3. Finally, the terms CAB_{11} and CAB_{12} deal specifically with the within-cells regression lines—the regression line for the data in each cell of the design. Since our hypothesis concerns homogeneity of within-cells regression, we will ignore columns CA_1, CB_1, and CB_2 in favor of CAB_{11} and CAB_{12}. Although a good case might be made for considering all of these columns, we do not do so here because that would require sacrificing much-needed degrees of freedom for error. For a larger problem, the experimenter might consider the other columns, as they offer a test on the homogeneity of within-treatment (as opposed to within-cell) regression.

The first regression analysis is based on all predictors in X, except for the three we have just ruled out. From this analysis we obtain

$$R^2_{c,\alpha,\beta,\alpha\beta,c\alpha\beta} = .88031$$

Thus, 88% of the variation in this study can be accounted for by a model that includes the covariate, the main and interaction effects of A and B, and the CAB interaction. The first question concerns this CAB interaction. If we can delete these predictors from the model without any significant decrease in our ability to account for variation, then we can be satisfied that we have met the assumption of homogeneity of regression.

Rerunning the analysis using only the first six predictors, we obtain

$$R^2_{c,\alpha,\beta,\alpha\beta} = .82654$$

This decrement in R^2 is tested in the usual way:

$$F(f - r, N - f - 1) = \frac{(N - f - 1)(R^2_f - R^2_r)}{(f - r)(1 - R^2_f)}$$

$$F(2, 15) = \frac{(15)(.88031 - .82654)}{(2)(.11969)}$$

$$= 3.369$$

For 2 and 15 df, the critical value of $F_{.05}(2, 15) = 3.68$. Therefore, we will fail to reject H_0 and will conclude that we have no basis for assuming that there is not homogeneity of regression.

At this point, we can define our model as

$$\hat{Y} = b_0 + b_1 C + b_2 A_1 + b_3 B_1 + b_4 B_2 + b_5 AB_{11} + b_6 AB_{12}$$

or, in more traditional analysis of variance terms,

$$Y_{ijk} = \mu + c_k + \alpha_i + \beta_j + \alpha\beta_{ij} + e_{ijk}$$

This is our full model, against which we will evaluate the effects of deleting individual terms. For this model,

$$R^2_f = R^2_{c,\alpha,\beta,\alpha\beta} = .82654$$

$$SS_Y = 1681.833$$

$$SS_{reg(c,\alpha,\beta,\alpha\beta)} = SS_Y(R^2_{c,\alpha,\beta,\alpha\beta}) = 1390.107$$

$$SS_{residual} = SS_Y(1 - R^2_{c,\alpha,\beta,\alpha\beta}) = 291.727$$

To obtain an adjusted estimate of the variation attributable to the AB interaction, partialling out (or adjusting for) the covariate, we solve a reduced model that does not contain the interaction effects. This produces

$$R^2_{c,\alpha,\beta} = .75300$$

$$SS_{reg(c,\alpha,\beta)} = 1266.423$$

Since

$$SS_{AB}(adj) = SS_Y(R^2_{c,\alpha,\beta,\alpha\beta} - R^2_{c,\alpha,\beta}) = SS_{reg(c,\alpha,\beta,\alpha\beta)} - SS_{reg(c,\alpha,\beta)}$$

the adjusted variation attributable to the AB interaction is

$$SS_{AB}(\text{adj}) = 1390.107 - 1266.423 = 123.684$$

We can estimate the adjusted sums of squares for the main effects of A and B in a similar fashion. For $SS_B(\text{adj})$ we delete the B_j terms from the full model, producing

$$R^2_{c,\alpha,\alpha\beta} = .32570$$

$$SS_{\text{reg}(c,\alpha,\alpha\beta)} = 547.776$$

The adjusted sum of squares for B is then given by

$$SS_B(\text{adj}) = SS_{\text{reg}(c,\alpha,\beta,\alpha\beta)} - SS_{\text{reg}(c,\alpha,\alpha\beta)}$$

$$= 1390.107 - 547.776 = 842.331$$

To solve for the adjusted sum of squares for A, we delete the A_1 term from the design matrix. The produces

$$R^2_{c,\beta,\alpha\beta} = .68765$$

$$SS_{\text{reg}(c,\beta,\alpha\beta)} = 1156.514$$

Then

$$SS_A(\text{adj}) = SS_{\text{reg}(c,\alpha,\beta,\alpha\beta)} - SS_{\text{reg}(c,\beta,\alpha\beta)}$$

$$= 1390.107 - 1156.514 = 233.593$$

Finally, $SS_{\text{covariate}}$ represents the decrease in $SS_{\text{regression}}$ when we remove the covariate term from the complete model. This produces

$$R^2_{\alpha,\beta,\alpha\beta} = .1307$$

$$SS_{\text{reg}(\alpha,\beta,\alpha\beta)} = 219.833$$

Then

$$SS_{\text{covariate}} = SS_{\text{reg}(c,\alpha,\beta,\alpha\beta)} - SS_{\text{reg}(\alpha,\beta,\alpha\beta)}$$

$$= 1390.107 - 219.833 = 1170.274$$

Based on these calculations, we can now form the analysis of covariance summary table. This table is presented in Table 16.15 with the regression equation derived from the full model. From this table, it is apparent that all three effects are significant,

TABLE 16.15
Summary table for the analysis of covariance

Source	df	SS	MS	F
A_{adj}	1	233.593	233.593	13.613*
B_{adj}	2	842.331	421.165	24.543*
AB_{adj}	2	123.684	61.842	3.604*
Error	17	291.727	17.160	
Covariate	1	1170.274		
Total	23	(1681.833)		

Full Model

$$\hat{Y} = -7.681 + 2.649C - 3.185A_1 - 6.534B_1 - 4.146B_2 + 2.847AB_{11} - 2.914AB_{12}$$

although the interaction effect is borderline [$F_{.05}(2, 17) = 3.59$). Given the presence of a significant interaction, it would be especially prudent to plot the adjusted means and look at the simple effects.

ADJUSTED MEANS

The method of obtaining adjusted means is simply an extension of the method employed in the map-reading example. We want to know what the cell means would have been if the treatment combinations had not differed on the covariate.

From the full model, we have

$$\hat{Y} = -7.681 + 2.649C - 3.185A_1 - 6.534B_1 - 4.146B_2 + 2.847AB_{11} - 2.914AB_{12}$$

Since we want to know what the Y means would be if the treatments did not differ on the covariate, we will set $C = \bar{C} = 10.292$ for all treatments.

For all observations in cell$_{11}$, the appropriate row of the design matrix, with $C = \bar{C}$, is

$$10.292 \quad 1 \quad 1 \quad 0 \quad 1 \quad 0$$

Applying the regression weights and taking into account the intercept, we have

$$\hat{\bar{Y}}_{11} = -7.681 + 2.649(10.292) - 3.185(1) - 6.534(1) - 4.146(0)$$

$$+ 2.847(1) - 2.914(0)$$

$$= 12.711$$

Applying this procedure to all the cells, we obtain the following adjusted means:

	B_1	B_2	B_3	**Row Means**
A_1	12.711	9.338	27.145	16.398
A_2	13.387	21.536	33.381	22.768
Column Means	13.049	15.437	30.263	19.583

The row and column means can be found as the mean of means. Thus, for example,

$$\bar{A}_1' = \frac{\Sigma \overline{AB}_{1j}}{b}$$

Alternatively, since the regression coefficient for predictor A_1 (-3.185) is equal to the treatment effect ($\alpha_1 = \mu_{A_1} - \mu$), we can find $\bar{A}_1$ directly as

$$GM + \hat{\alpha}_1 = 19.583 - 3.185 = 16.398$$

TESTING ADJUSTED MEANS

The adjusted means are plotted in Figure 16.4. They illustrate the interaction and also the meaning that may be attached to the main effects. Further analyses of these data depend on the interests of the experimenter. The experimenter who is mainly interested in whether there are differences in effectiveness among the three training methods could stop right here. The main effect of methods (even considering the presence of an interaction), together with the adjusted means plotted in Figure 16.4, makes it clear that different methods do produce different degrees of learning. If, however, our experimenter wishes to show that (averaged across place of residence) Method III is better than the other two methods, he should then consider comparing $\bar{B}'_3$ with $\bar{B}'_1$ and $\bar{B}'_2$. This comparison requires some modification of the error term, to account for differences in the covariate. This adjustment was given by Winer (1971) as

$$\text{MS}''_{\text{error}} = \text{MS}'_{\text{error}} \left[1 + \frac{\dfrac{\text{SS}_{b(c)}}{b-1}}{\text{SS}_{e(c)}} \right]$$

where $\text{SS}_{b(c)}$ and $\text{SS}_{e(c)}$ represent the sum of squares attributable to B and error (respectively) in an analysis of variance performed on the *covariate*, and $\text{MS}'_{\text{error}}$ is the error term from the overall analysis of covariance.

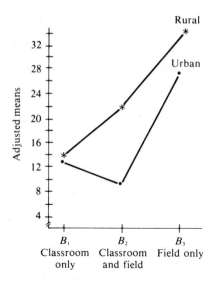

FIGURE 16.4
Adjusted cell means

For our data,

$$\text{MS}'_{\text{error}} = 17.16$$

$$\text{SS}_{b(c)} = 122.583$$

$$\text{SS}_{e(c)} = 166.750$$

Thus

$$\text{MS}''_{\text{error}} = 17.16 \left[1 + \frac{122.583/2}{166.750} \right] = 23.467$$

To compare the combination of $\bar{B}'_1$ and $\bar{B}'_2$ with $\bar{B}'_3$, we will first convert to adjusted totals, in line with the way similar comparisons were treated in Chapter 12.

$$T'_{B_1} = (\bar{B}'_1)(an) = 13.049(8) = 104.392$$

$$T'_{B_2} = (\bar{B}'_2)(an) = 15.437(8) = 123.496$$

$$T'_{B_3} = (\bar{B}'_3)(an) = 30.263(8) = 242.104$$

Then we use the standard formula for linear contrasts to get

$$L = 1(104.392) + 1(123.496) - 2(242.104) = -256.320$$

$$F(1, 17) = \frac{L^2}{n\Sigma a_i^2 MS''_{error}} = \frac{(-256.320)^2}{8(6)(23.468)} = 58.327$$

There can be no question that this difference is significant.

On the basis of this last result, our experimenter would conclude that Method III is better than the average of the other two methods and would most likely recommend adopting that method in the future teaching of map reading.

Another experimenter might be interested in examining the simple effects of teaching methods at each level of the residence variable. This would be especially interesting if one method appeared to be superior for the urban students and a second measure appeared to be superior for the rural students. If only one teaching method could be employed in the future (e.g., if urban and rural students must be taught all in one class), we would most likely choose the method that was higher *on the average*, which we have just shown to be Method III. If we can separate the students into two classes, however, we will wish to know which method is best for each group. If we want to examine these simple effects, we will again need to modify our error term in some way. This is necessary because we will be looking at the $\bar{B}_i$ at level A_1 only (for example), and the A_1 means on the covariate most likely will differ from the overall covariate mean. Probably the safest course in this case is to run separate analyses of covariance at each level of A. Although this method has the disadvantage of costing us degrees of freedom for error, it has the advantage of simplicity and eliminates the need to make discomforting assumptions in the adjustment of our error term.

If we were to run these separate analyses of covariance, we would find a significant effect of B at both levels of A. Thus, for B at A_1, $F(2, 8) = 8.444$, and for B at A_2, $F(2, 8) = 16.986$. Both of these Fs are significant at $p < .05$.

To complete our discussion of the tests we might wish to conduct, consider the experimenter who wants to compare two particular adjusted cell means (whether or not they are in the same row or column). The adjusted error term for this comparison was given by Winer (1971) as

$$MS''_{error} = \frac{2MS'_{error}}{n}\left[1 + \frac{\dfrac{SS_{cells(c)}}{ab - 1}}{SS_{e(c)}}\right]$$

where $SS_{cells(c)}$ is the sum of squares cells from an analysis of variance on the covariate.

You may wonder why we continually worry about adjusting the error term in making comparisons. The general nature of the answer is apparent when you recall what the confidence limits around the regression line looked like in Chapter 9. For $X = \bar{X}$, we were relatively confident about $\hat{Y}$. However, as X departed more and more from $\overline{X}$ we became less and less confident of our prediction, and consequently the confidence limits widened. If you now go back to Figure 16.3, you will see that the problem applies directly to the case of adjusted means. In that figure, $\overline{Y}_1'$ is a long way from $\overline{Y}_1$, and we would probably have relatively little confidence that we have estimated it correctly. On the other hand, we can probably have a reasonable degree of confidence in our estimate of $\overline{Y}_2'$. It is just this type of consideration that causes us constantly to adjust our error term.

The example we have used points up an important feature of the analysis of covariance—the fact that the covariate is just another variable that happens to receive priority. In designing the study, we were concerned primarily with evaluating three different teaching methods. However, we had two variables that we considered it necessary to control: place of residence and years of schooling. The first one (place of residence) we controlled by incorporating it into our design as an independent variable. The second (years of schooling) we controlled by treating it as a covariate. In many respects, these are two ways of treating the same problem. Although there are obvious differences in the way these two variables are treated, there are also important similarities. In obtaining $SS_{methods}$, we are actually partialling out *both* place of residence and the covariate. It is true that in the case of equal ns place of residence is orthogonal to methods, leaving nothing to partial out; but that is merely a technicality. In the case of unequal ns, the partialling out of both variables is a very real procedure. Although it is important not to lose sight of the fact that the analysis of covariance is a unique technique with its own additional assumptions, it is equally important to keep in mind that a covariate is just another variable. An experimenter with a different subject pool might easily find himself with methods and years of schooling as variables and place of residence as a covariate. One person's variable may be another person's covariate.

16.8   THE ANALYSIS OF COVARIANCE VERSUS THE ANALYSIS OF VARIANCE, AND OTHER ISSUES

It will be instructive to compare the analysis of covariance with an analysis of variance on the same data. Table 16.16 shows the results of the analysis of variance on the data presented in Table 16.13. This analysis contrasts sharply with the analysis of covariance presented in Table 16.15. First, the main effects and interaction sums of squares are markedly reduced. Second, the error term is substantially larger. The analysis of covariance has a considerably smaller error term because it has partialled out the portion of the within-cell variance that can be attributed to the covariate (years of schooling). In addition, the analysis of covariance has larger treatment effects because it has adjusted the means to account for mean differences on the covariate, which can be seen in the comparison of the unadjusted and adjusted means. This is an extreme example, but it serves to illustrate the two different influences an analysis of covariance has on our perception of the data.

TABLE 16.16
Summary table for
the analysis of
variance

Source	df	SS	MS	F
A	1	73.500	73.500	<1
B	2	139.583	69.792	<1
AB	2	6.750	3.375	<1
Error	18	1462.000	81.222	
Total	23	1681.833		

USING MULTIPLE COVARIATES

We have been concerned with the use of a single covariate. There is no theoretical or practical reason, however, why we must restrict ourselves in this way. For example, a study on the effectiveness of several different teaching methods might wish to treat IQ, Age, and Type of School (progressive or conservative) as covariates. When viewed from the point of view of multiple regression, this presents no particular problem, whereas when viewed within the traditional framework of the analysis of variance, the computational complexities for only a very few covariates would be overwhelming.

In the expression $R^2_{c, \alpha, \beta, \alpha\beta}$, β is really only a shorthand way of representing a set of predictors (e.g., $B_1, B_2, \ldots, B_b$). By the some token, c can be used to stand for a set of covariates $(C_1, C_2, \ldots, C_k)$. Thus, in terms of the more specific notation, $R^2_{c, \alpha, \beta, \alpha\beta}$ might really represent

$$R^2_{0.\text{IQ, Age, School}, A_1, B_1, B_2, AB_{11}, AB_{12}}$$

When seen in this light, the use of multiple covariates is no different from that of single covariates. If C represents the covariates IQ, Age, and School, then $SS_{AB}(\text{adj})$ remains

$$SS_Y(R^2_{c, \alpha, \beta, \alpha\beta} - R^2_{c, \alpha, \beta}) = SS_{\text{reg(IQ, Age, School}, A_1, B_1, B_2, AB_{11}, AB_{12})} - SS_{\text{reg(IQ, Age, School}, A_1, B_1, B_2)}$$

It should be apparent from the previous example that no restriction is placed on the nature of the covariate, other than that it is assumed to be linearly related to the criterion. It can be a continuous variable, as in the case of IQ and Age, or a discrete variable, as in the dichotomous classification of Schools as progressive and conservative.

A word of warning: Just because it is possible (and in fact easy) to use multiple covariates is not a good reason for adopting this procedure. Interpreting an analysis of covariance may be difficult enough (if not impossible) with only one covariate. The problems increase rapidly with the addition of multiple covariates. Thus, it might be easy to *say*, in evaluating several methods of teaching English, that such and such a method is better if groups are equated for age, IQ, type of school, parents' occupation, and so on. But the experimenter must then ask himself if such equated groups actually exist in the population. If they do not, he has just answered a question about what would happen in groups that could never exist, and it is unlikely that he will receive much applause for his efforts. Moreover, even if it is possible to form such groups, will they behave in the expected manner? The very fact that the students are now in homogeneous classes may itself have an effect on the dependent variable that could not have been predicted.

ALTERNATIVE EXPERIMENTAL DESIGNS

Stratification

The analysis of covariance is not the only way to handle data in which a covariate is important. Two common alternative procedures are also available: **stratification** (matched samples) and difference scores.

If we have available measures on the covariate and are free to assign subjects to treatment groups, then we can form subsets of subjects who are homogeneous with respect to the covariate, and then assign one member of each subset to a different treatment group. In the analysis of variance, we can then pull out an effect due to blocks (subsets) from the error term.

The use of matched samples and the analysis of covariance are almost equally effective when the regression of Y on C is linear. If ρ equals the correlation in the population between Y and C, and σ_e^2 represents the error variance in a straight analysis of variance on Y, then the use of matched samples reduces the error variance to

$$\sigma_e^2(1 - \rho^2)$$

The reduction due to the analysis of covariance in this situation was given by Winer (1971) as

$$\sigma_e^2(1 - \rho^2)\frac{(f_e)}{(f_e - 1)}$$

where f_e is the degrees of freedom for the error variance. Obviously, for any reasonable value of f_e, the two procedures are almost equally effective, assuming linearity of regression. If the relationship between Y and C is not linear, however, matching will be more effective than covariance analysis.

Difference scores

A second alternative to the analysis of covariance concerns the use of **difference scores**. If the covariate (C) represents a test score before the treatment is administered and Y a score on the same test after the administration of the treatment, the variable $C - Y$ is sometimes used as the dependent variable in an analysis of variance to control for initial differences on C. Obviously, this approach will work only if C and Y are comparable measures. We could hardly justify subtracting a test score (Y) from an IQ score (C). If the relationship between C and Y is linear and if $b_{CY} = 1.00$, the analysis of difference scores and the analysis of covariance will give the same estimates of the treatment effects. When b_{CY} is not equal to 1, the two methods will produce different results, and in this case it is difficult to justify the use of difference scores. In fact, for the Conti and Musty (1984) data on THC, if we took the *difference* between the Pre and the Post scores as our dependent variable, the results would be decidedly different ($F_{4,42} = 0.197$). In this case, the analysis of covariance was clearly a more powerful procedure. For a more complete treatment of this entire problem, see Harris (1963) and Huitema (1980).

KEY TERMS

General linear model (16.1)

Design matrix (16.1)

Intraclass correlation coefficient (16.2)

Method I (16.4)

Method II (16.4)

Equally weighted means (16.4)

Analysis of covariance (16.5)

Covariate (16.5)

Adjusted Y means (16.5)

Homogeneity of regression (16.5)

MS'_{error} (16.5)

True-score analysis of covariance (16.6)

Nonequivalent groups design (16.6)

Stratification (16.8)

Difference scores (16.8)

EXERCISES

16.1   The following hypothetical data were obtained from poor, average, and good readers on the number of eye fixations per line of text.

Poor	Average	Good
10	5	3
7	8	5
8	4	2
11	6	3
5	5	4

(a) Construct the design matrix for these data.

(b) Use any standard regression program to calculate a least-squares analysis of variance.

(c) Run the analysis of variance in the traditional manner and compare your answers.

16.2   For the data in Exercise 16.1,

(a) calculate treatment effects and show that the regression model reproduces these treatment effects.

(b) demonstrate that R^2 for the regression model is equal to η^2 for the analysis of variance.

16.3   Taking the data from Exercise 16.1, add the scores 5 and 8 to the Average group and the scores 2, 3, 3, and 5 to the Good group. Rerun the analysis for Exercise 16.1 using the more complete data.

16.4   Rerun the analysis of Exercise 16.2 for the amended data from Exercise 16.3.

16.5   A psychologist was concerned with the relationship between Gender, Socioeconomic Status (SES), and perceived Locus of Control. She took eight adults (age = 25 to 30 years) in each Gender–SES combination and administered a scale dealing with Locus of Control (a high score indicates that the individual feels in control of his or her everyday life).

	SES		
	Low	Average	High
Male	10	16	18
	12	12	14
	8	19	17
	14	17	13
	10	15	19
	16	11	15
	15	14	22
	13	10	20
Female	8	14	12
	10	10	18
	7	13	14
	9	9	21
	12	17	19
	5	15	17
	8	12	13
	7	8	16

(a) Run a traditional analysis of variance on these data.

(b) The following sums of squares have been computed on the data using the appropriate design matrix (α = Gender, β = SES):

$$SS_Y = 777.6667 \qquad SS_{reg(\alpha, \beta, \alpha\beta)} = 422.6667$$

$$SS_{reg(\alpha, \beta)} = 404.0000 \qquad SS_{reg(\beta, \alpha\beta)} = 357.3333$$

$$SS_{reg(\alpha, \alpha\beta)} = 84.000$$

Compute the summary table for the analysis of variance using these sums of squares.

16.6   Using the SES portion of the design matrix as our predictor, we find that $SS_{reg(\beta)} = 338.6667$.
(a) Why is this value the same as SS_{SES} in the answer to Exercise 16.5?
(b) Will this be the case in all analyses of variance?

16.7   When we take the data in Exercise 16.5 and delete the last two low-SES males, the last three average-SES males, and the last two high-SES females, we obtain the following sums of squares:

$$SS_Y = 750.1951 \qquad SS_{reg(\alpha, \beta, \alpha\beta)} = 458.7285$$

$$SS_{reg(\alpha, \beta)} = 437.6338 \qquad SS_{reg(\beta, \alpha\beta)} = 398.7135$$

$$SS_{reg(\alpha, \alpha\beta)} = 112.3392 \qquad SS_{reg(\alpha)} = 95.4511$$

$$SS_{reg(\beta)} = 379.3325$$

$$SS_{reg(\alpha\beta)} = 15.8132$$

Compute the analysis of variance using these sums of squares.

16.8   Using only the SES predictors for the data in Exercise 16.7, we find $SS_{reg(\beta)} = 379.3325$. Why is this not the same as SS_{SES} in Exercise 16.7?

16.9   For the data in Exercise 16.5, the complete model is

$$1.1667A_1 - 3.1667B_1 - 0.1667B_2 + 0.8333AB_{11} - 0.1667AB_{12} + 13.4167$$

Show that this model reproduces the treatment and interaction effects as calculated by the method shown in Table 16.3.

16.10   For the data in Exercise 16.7, the complete model is

$$1.2306A_1 - 3.7167B_1 + 0.3500B_2 + 0.4778AB_{11} + 0.5444AB_{12} + 13.6750$$

Show that this model reproduces the treatment and interaction effects calculated as in Table 16.3.

16.11   Using the following data. demonstrate that Method I (the method advocated in this chapter) really deals with unweighted means.

	B_1	B_2
A_1	5	11
	3	9
		14
		6
		11
		9
A_2	10	6
	11	2
	12	
	7	

16.12   Draw a Venn diagram representing the sums of squares in Exercise 16.5.

16.13   Draw a Venn diagram representing the sums of squares in Exercise 16.7.

16.14   If you have access to SPSS^X, use the data in Exercise 16.7 (and your answer to the question) to compare Options 7, 8, and 9 on SPSS^X ANOVA.

16.15   If you have access to SAS, use that program to analyze the data in Exercise 16.7. Add/SS1 SS2 SS3 SS4 to the end of your Model command and show that
   (a) Type I sums of squares adjust each term in the model only for those that come earlier in the model statement.
   (b) Type II sums of squares adjust main effects only for other main effect variables, while adjusting the interaction for each of the main effects.
   (c) Type III sums of squares adjust each term for all other terms in the model.
   (d) Type IV sums of squares in this case are equal to the Type III sums of squares.

16.16   In studying the energy consumption of families, we have broken them into three groups. Group 1 consists of those who have enrolled in a time-of-day electrical-rate system (the charge per kilowatt-hour of electricity is higher during peak demand times of the day). Group 2 is made up of those who inquired into such a system but did not use it, and Group 3 represents those who have shown no interest in the system. We record the amount of the electrical bill per month for each household as our dependent variable (Y). As a covariate, we take the electrical bill for that household for the same month last year (C). The data follow:

Group 1		Group 2		Group 3	
Y	C	Y	C	Y	C
58	75	60	70	75	80
25	40	30	25	60	55
50	68	55	65	70	73
40	62	50	50	65	61
55	67	45	55	55	65

(a) Set up the design matrix

(b) Run the analysis of covariance.

16.17   To refine the experiment described in Exercise 16.16, a psychologist added an additional set of households to each group. This group had a special meter installed to show them exactly how fast their electric bill was increasing. (The amount-to-date was displayed on the meter.) The data follow; the nonmetered data are the same as those in Exercise 16.16.

	Y	C	Y	C	Y	C
Nonmetered	58	75	60	70	75	80
	25	40	30	25	60	55
	50	68	55	65	70	73
	40	62	50	50	65	61
	55	67	45	55	55	65
Metered	25	42	40	55	55	56
	38	64	47	52	62	74
	46	70	56	68	57	60
	50	67	28	30	50	68
	55	75	55	72	70	76

(a) Run the analysis of covariance on these data—after first checking the assumption of homogeneity of regression.

(b) Draw the appropriate conclusions.

16.18   Compute the adjusted means for the data in Exercise 16.17.

16.19   Compute the energy *savings* per household for the data in Exercise 16.17 by subtracting this year's bill from last year's bill. Then run an analysis of variance on the savings scores and compare that to the analysis of covariance.

16.20   Use any statistical package to perform an analysis on the data from Klemchuk, Bond, and Howell (1990) in Table 13.11. Compare your answers to the answers in part c of that table. (If using SPSS^X, use Option 9. If using SAS GLM, examine Type III sums of squares.)

COMPUTER EXERCISES

16.21   Use the data set named Epinuneq.dat on the instructor's disk to examine the results of the study by Introini-Collison and McGaugh (1986). Using any statistical package, run a two-way analysis of variance with unequal sample sizes. What would you conclude from this analysis?

16.22 Using the data from Mireault (1990) in the file named Mireault.dat to run a two-way analysis of variance on the Global Symptom Index T score (GSIT) using Gender and Group as independent variables. Plot out the cell means and interpret the results.

16.23 Using the same data as in Exercise 16.22, run an analysis of covariance instead, using year in college (YearColl) as the covariate.
(a) Why would we want to consider YearColl as a covariate?
(b) How would you interpret the results?

16.24 In Exercise 16.23 we used YearColl as the covariate. Run an analysis of variance on YearColl, using Gender and Group as the independent variables. What does this tell us that is relevant to the preceding analysis of covariance?

CHAPTER SEVENTEEN

LOG-LINEAR ANALYSIS

OBJECTIVES *To present log-linear models as ways of exploring discrete data from experiments having multiple independent variables.*

CONTENTS

M ost of this book has been concerned with variables that are measured on a more-or-less continuous scale and for which the mean, or a related sample statistic, would be a typical measure of interest. However, many variables we deal with are measured discretely. For example, in Chapter 6 we looked at a classic study by Geller, Witmer, and Orebaugh (1976) in which a supermarket flier on "daily specials" was categorized both in terms of whether it contained a message about littering and where it was found at the end of the day (trashcan, litter, removed from store). In that particular example we were able to show that where a notice was left depended on whether it contained a message about littering. In other words, the two variables are not independent—they interact.

In the past, experimenters faced with multiple categorical variables routinely dealt with them two at a time, creating two-way contingency tables and computing the standard Pearson chi-square test statistic to check for independence. Recently, however, major efforts to develop procedures that deal with multiple categorical variables simultaneously have been undertaken. (I say "recently" because even though the important work in this field started with Leo Goodman at the University of Chicago in the 1960s, it generally takes at least 20 years for statistical procedures to work their way from initial development in the statistical journals, to occasional appearance in the experimental literature, to widespread acceptance. **Log-linear models** are just beginning to make it to the latter stage.)

Log-linear models

The presentation of log-linear models presents several challenges. In the first place such models are much easier to understand when presented as simple contingency tables with two dimensions (variables). However, the two-dimensional case is not handled appreciably better by log-linear models than by the standard approach, and the reader can easily be left wondering "So what?". Log-linear models come into their own with three-, four-, or higher-dimensional cases, but the explanation can become unpleasantly tortuous and opaque. For this reason we will start with the two-dimensional case, lay out most of the reasoning, and then move on to higher dimensions.

A second problem with log-linear models is that each author views them from a different perspective. If you skim several of the excellent books on such models, you might almost think that they were talking about different topics. Some authors are interested primarily in hypothesis testing, whereas others are interested primarily in model building. Some concentrate on examining individual effects, whereas others mention individual effects only in passing. Some concentrate on models in which all of the variables are treated as independent variables, whereas others focus on cases in which one or more variables are thought of as dependent variables and the others as independent variables. This chapter will try to steer a middle course, focusing on those aspects of the models that apply most directly to psychology and related disciplines. I recommend that the first time through you concentrate on the hypothesis testing aspects of log-linear models. Then go back and pay more serious attention to estimating treatment effects.

A number of excellent references on this subject are available. Some of the clearest are Agresti (1984, 1990—especially the former), Kennedy (1983), Marascuilo and Serlin (1990), Marascuilo and Busk (1987), and Green (1988). A quick introduction that lays out the important topics is Norusis (1985). An excellent presentation of the applications of standard computer software is given in Tabachnick and Fidell (1989). I have borrowed heavily from all of these sources.

SYMMETRIC AND ASYMMETRIC MODELS

In general, log-linear analysis treats independent and dependent variables alike, ignoring the distinction between them. We as experimenters, however, build our interpretation of the data in part on whether a variable is seen, by us, as independent or dependent.

To take a simple example, suppose that we have developed a scale of myths related to rape ("If a woman is raped she was probably partly responsible") and myths related to spouse abuse ("An abused wife is always free to leave her abuser"). Suppose further that our subjects have responded as Agree, Neutral, or Disagree with the items on both scales. If we want to look at the relation between rape myths and spouse abuse myths, neither variable would be dependent relative to the other. This would remain so if we added yet another dimension and categorized subjects in terms of other sorts of beliefs (e.g., just-world beliefs). Relations of this sort, in which all the variables are treated alike as dependent variables, are classed as **symmetric relationships**.

Symmetric relationships

Now suppose that we take another variable (Gender) and look to see if there are differences in rape myths between males and females. Here most people would see Gender as an independent variable and Rape Myth as a dependent variable. We

Assymmetric relationship

would account for Rape Myth as a function of Gender, but would be unlikely to account for Gender on the basis of Rape Myth. This is an **asymmetric relationship**.

Log-linear models apply to both symmetric and asymmetric models. The difference comes more in the interpretation than in the mathematics. When you have an asymmetric model, you will focus more on the dependent variable and its relations with independent variables. When the model is symmetric, you will spread your interest more widely. In addition, with asymmetric models you may choose to keep certain nonsignificant variables in the model on the basis of their role in the experiment. With symmetric models we are more even-handed.

Logit analysis, Logistic regression

One statistical technique that will not be examined here but that is closely related to log-linear models is **logit analysis**, or **logistic regression**. Logit analysis is often used when we have a design that closely resembles an analysis of variance (multiple independent variables and a clear dependent variable) and the dependent variable is a dichotomy. Logit analysis can be shown to be functionally and structurally equivalent to log-linear analysis of asymmetric models. The basic difference is that logit models make no attempt to account for the relations among independent variables, whereas log-linear models do. For a good discussion of logit analysis, see Agresti (1984).

17.1 TWO-WAY CONTINGENCY TABLES

We will begin with the simplest example of a 2 × 2 contingency table. Although log-linear analysis does not have a great deal more to offer than the standard Pearson chi-square approach in this situation, it will allow us to examine a number of important concepts in a simple setting. As we move to more complex situations we will leave more and more of the actual calculations to computer software, because such computations can become extremely cumbersome.

As an example we will use a study by Pugh (1983) on the "blaming-the-victim" issue in prosecutions for rape. Pugh's paper is an excellent example of how to use log-linear analysis to establish a statistical model to explain experimental results. But we will simplify the underlying experiment to create an example that is more useful for our purposes. The simplification involves collapsing over, and thereby ignoring, some experimental variables. (In general, we would not collapse across variables unless we were confident that they did not play a role or we were not interested in any role they did play.)

Pugh designed a study to examine what many have seen to be the disposition of jurors to base their judgments of defendants on the alleged behavior of the victim. Defense attorneys often adopt a strategy suggesting that the victim is in some way responsible for the crime, by attacking the victim's past behavior; the victim is "put on trial" instead of the defendant. Pugh's study varied the gender of the juror, the level of stigma attached to the victim, and the degree to which the juror could assign fault to the victim, and then looked at the degree to which the defendants were judged guilty or not guilty. For our first example we will collapse over two of those variables and look at the relationship between the degree to which the victim was believed to be "at fault" and the verdict. These data are shown in Table 17.1. (Expected frequencies for the standard test of the independence of these two variables are shown in parentheses.)

TABLE 17.1
Data from Pugh
collapsed across two
variables (1983)

		Verdict		
		Guilty	Not Guilty	Total
Fault	Low	153 (127.559)	24 (49.441)	177
	High	105 (130.441)	76 (50.559)	181
	Total	258	100	358

If we ran the standard Pearson chi-square test on these data, we would find, with a minor change in notation,

$$\chi_1^2 = \sum \frac{(O - E)^2}{E} = \sum \frac{(f_{ij} - F_{ij})^2}{F_{ij}} = 35.93$$

which is significant at $\alpha = .05$. The change in notation, equating f_{ij} with the observed frequency in cell$_{ij}$ and F_{ij} with the expected frequency in that cell, was instituted to bring the notation of this chapter more in line with the standard notation used with log-linear analysis.

If we calculate the likelihood ratio χ^2 (see Section 6.8) instead of Pearson's chi-square, we would have

$$\chi^2 = 2 \sum f_{ij} \ln\left(\frac{f_{ij}}{F_{ij}}\right)$$

$$= 2\left(153 \ln\frac{153}{127.559} + 24 \ln\frac{24}{49.441} + 105 \ln\frac{105}{130.441} + 76 \ln\frac{76}{50.559}\right)$$

$$= 37.3503$$

which is also approximated by the χ^2 distribution on one degree of freedom.[†] Again we would reject the null hypothesis of independence of rows and columns. We would conclude that in making a judgment of guilt or innocence the jurors base that judgment, in part, on the perceived fault of the victim.

The use of the chi-square test, whether using Pearson's statistic or the likelihood ratio statistic, focuses directly on hypothesis testing. (From this point on, all χ^2 statistics will be the likelihood ratio χ^2 unless otherwise noted.) But we can look at these data from a different perspective—the perspective of model building. We saw the modeling approach clearly in the analysis of variance where we associated a two-way factorial design with the model

---

[†]In this chapter we will frequently refer to natural logarithms. These are normally abbreviated either as ln or as $\log_e$. For notational convenience we will use ln throughout.

$$X_{ijk} = \mu + \alpha_i + \beta_j + \alpha\beta_{ij} + e_{ijk}$$

In the case of the analysis of variance, we first posited this model to underlie the obtained data and then used the model and its associated error term to develop tests of the components of that model. When the data analysis was complete, we let the model stand but made statements of the form, "There is a significant effect due to variable A and the $A \times B$ interaction, but there is no significant difference due to variable B."

In Chapter 15 on multiple regression we reversed the process. We used the data themselves to create a model rather than using an a priori model as in the analysis of variance. Using the backward solution, which is most relevant here, we continued to remove variables from our model so long as their removal did not produce a significant decrement in R^2 (or until we met some similar criterion). When we were done we were left with a model all of whose components contributed significantly to the prediction of Y.

In the case of log-linear models, we generally fall somewhere between these two approaches. We use a model-building approach, as in the regression situation, but the resultant model may, as in the analysis of variance, contain nonsignificant terms.

Consider Pugh's data and a variety of models that *might* be posited to account for those data.

EQUIPROBABILITY MODEL

At the simplest possible level, we might hypothesize that respondents distribute themselves among the four cells at random. In other words, p(Low, Guilty) = p(High, Guilty) = p(Low, Not Guilty) = p(High, Not Guilty) = .25. This model basically says that nothing interesting is going on in this study and one-quarter of the subjects (.25 × 358 = 89.5) would be expected to fall in each cell.

Using the likelihood ratio χ^2 to test this model, we have

Observed:	153	24	105	76
Expected:	89.5	89.5	89.5	89.5

$$\chi^2 = 2 \sum f_{ij} \ln\left(\frac{f_{ij}}{F_{ij}}\right)$$

$$= 2\left(153 \ln\frac{153}{89.5} + 24 \ln\frac{24}{89.5} + 105 \ln\frac{105}{89.5} + 76 \ln\frac{76}{89.5}\right)$$

$$= 109.5889$$

This can be evaluated as a χ^2 on $4 - 1 = 3$ df (the one restriction is that the cell totals must sum to N), and from Appendix χ^2 we find that $\chi^2_{3,.05} = 7.81$. Clearly, we can reject H_0, and conclude that this model does not fit the data. In other words, the individual cell frequencies cannot be fit by a model in which all cells are considered equally probable.

CONDITIONAL EQUIPROBABILITY MODEL

Our first model really had no variable contributing to the observed frequency (not differences due to Fault, not differences due to Verdict, and not differences due to the interaction of those variables). A second model, however, might hold that the individual cell frequencies represent differences due to assignment of Verdict, because noticeably more people were found guilty than were found innocent. By this model, $258/358 = 72.1\%$ of the observations fall in column 1 and 27.9% fall in column 2. Beyond that, however, observations are assumed to be equally likely to fall in rows 1 and 2. In other words, the null hypothesis states that once we have adjusted for the fact that more people were judged guilty than not guilty, assignment to Fault levels is equally probable. Put yet a third way, expected frequencies with levels of Fault are equiprobable, conditional on Verdict. By this model we would have the expected frequencies (shown in parentheses) contained in Table 17.2. (The expected frequencies in this model came from assuming that half of the column 1 total would fall in row 1 and half in row 2. Similarly for column 2.)

TABLE 17.2
Observed and expected frequencies for first conditional equiprobability model

		Verdict		
		Guilty	Not Guilty	Total
Fault	Low 153 (129)		24 (50)	177
	High 105 (129)		76 (50)	181
	Total 258		100	358

$$\chi^2 = 2 \sum f_{ij} \ln \left(\frac{f_{ij}}{F_{ij}} \right)$$

$$= 2 \left(153 \ln \frac{153}{129} + 24 \ln \frac{24}{50} + 105 \ln \frac{105}{129} + 76 \ln \frac{76}{50} \right)$$

$$= 37.3960$$

This model has $4 - 2 = 2$ degrees of freedom because we have imposed two restrictions—the cell frequencies in each column must sum to the expected frequency for that column. Since $\chi^2_{2,.05} = 5.99$, we will again reject H_0 and conclude that the model does not fit the observed data.

A second conditional equiprobability model could be created by assuming that cell frequencies are affected only by differences in levels of Fault. In this case probabilities are equal within each Fault condition but different between them. The expected frequencies in this case are given in Table 17.3.

This χ^2 has $4 - 2 = 2$ degrees of freedom for the same reason that the model in Table 17.2 did, and again the significant χ^2 shows that this model is an inadequate fit to the data. Thus, we have so far concluded that the data *cannot* be explained by assuming that observations fall in the four cells at random. Nor can they be explained by positing differences due simply to an unequal distribution across either Verdict or Fault. More would appear to be happening in the data. The next step would be to propose a model involving both Verdict and Fault operating independently of one another. This is the standard null model routinely tested by a chi-square test on a contingency table.

TABLE 17.3
Observed and expected frequencies for second conditional equiprobability model

	Verdict		
	Guilty	Not Guilty	Total
Fault Low 153 (88.5)		24 (88.5)	177
High 105 (90.5)		76 (90.5)	181
Total 258		100	358

$$\chi^2 = 2 \sum f_{ij} \ln \left(\frac{f_{ij}}{F_{ij}} \right)$$

$$= 2 \left(153 \ln \frac{153}{88.5} + 24 \ln \frac{24}{88.5} + 105 \ln \frac{105}{90.5} + 76 \ln \frac{76}{90.5} \right)$$

$$= 109.5442$$

Mutual independence model

We are now testing a model that assumes that two factors operate jointly, *but independently*, to produce expected cell frequencies. If the two variables are independent, then

$$F_{ij} = \frac{RT \times CT}{GT} = \frac{f_{i.} \times f_{.j}}{f_{..}}$$

where RT stands for the row total, CT for the column total, GT for the grand total, and the "dot notation" is used to show that we have collapsed across that dimension. This is the same formula for expected frequencies that we saw in Chapter 6.

We began this chapter by testing this hypothesis of independence. The expected frequencies and the likelihood ratio χ^2 are given on page 579. From those calculations we found that

$$\chi^2 = 37.3503$$

which is significant on 1 *df*. Thus, we can further conclude, and importantly so in this case, that a model that posits an independence between Fault and Verdict also does not fit the data. The only conclusion remaining is that the likelihood of a jury convicting a defendant of rape depends on an interaction between Fault and Verdict. Perceived guilt is, in part, a function of the blame that is attributed to the victim.

17.2 Model specification

The models we have been discussing can be represented algebraically as well as descriptively. The algebraic notation can seem awkward, but it allows us to learn a great deal more about the data. It is somewhat confusing because we start out with one set of parameters, represented as τ (tau), usually with a superscript, and then shortly convert to the natural logarithm of τ, represented as λ (lambda), with superscripts. Both of these statistics strongly resemble the grand mean (μ) and treatment effects (α, β, and $\alpha\beta$) that we saw in the analysis of variance. (You might think that we would be satisfied with one or the other, but in fact both have their uses.) I would urge you to read this next section fairly quickly just to see where we are heading, and then come back to it after you see how such parameter estimates are used in more complex models.

Geometric mean

In the simplest equiprobability model, all cell frequencies are explained by a single parameter τ, where τ is estimated by the **geometric mean** of the expected cell frequencies given by the model. In other words,

$$F_{ij} = \hat{\tau}$$

A geometric mean is the nth root of the product of n terms. In this case the geometric mean of the four expected frequencies is

$$\sqrt[4]{(89.5)(89.5)(89.5)(89.5)} = 89.5$$

which is not a very exciting result.

For the first conditional equiprobable model we have to go further. We again define $\hat{\tau}$ as the geometric mean of the expected cell frequencies in that model:

$$\hat{\tau} = \sqrt[4]{(129)(129)(50)(50)} = 80.3119$$

We also define $\hat{\tau}_1^V$ as the ratio of the geometric mean of the expected frequencies for the first Guilty column to the geometric mean of all the cells ($\hat{\tau}$). Then

$$\hat{\tau}_1^V = \frac{\sqrt{(129)(129)}}{\tau} = \frac{129}{80.3119} = 1.6062$$

You can think of $\hat{\tau}_i^V$ very much the way you thought of the treatment effect (α_i) in the analysis of variance. It is the contribution of row$_i$. But for the analysis of variance, α_i was the amount that was *added* to the grand mean to obtain the row mean. Here, on the other hand, $\hat{\tau}_i^V$ is the amount by which we *multiply* $\hat{\tau}$ to obtain the row's expected frequency. $\hat{\tau}_i^V = 1.6062$ says that the row expected frequency is 1.6062 times larger than the overall mean—or 160.62% of it. For the Not Guilty column,

$$\tau_2^V = \frac{\sqrt{(50)(50)}}{\tau} = \frac{50}{80.3119} = 0.6226$$

Then we can show that for this model

$$F_{ij} = \hat{\tau}\hat{\tau}_i^V$$

For cell 11 we would have $80.3119 \times 1.6062 = 129$, which has reproduced the expected frequency that we used in Table 17.2.

To go one step further, we can consider the independence model (Table 17.1), which contained both Fault and Verdict effects but not their interaction. Here

$$\hat{\tau} = \sqrt[4]{(127.559)(49.441)(130.441)(50.559)} = 80.3069$$

$$\hat{\tau}_1^V = \frac{\sqrt{(127.559)(130.441)}}{\tau} = \frac{128.9920}{80.3069} = 1.6062$$

$$\hat{\tau}_2^V = \frac{\sqrt{(49.441)(50.559)}}{\tau} = \frac{49.9969}{80.3069} = 0.6226$$

$$\hat{\tau}_1^F = \frac{\sqrt{(127.559)(49.441)}}{\tau} = \frac{79.4144}{80.3069} = 0.9889$$

$$\hat{\tau}_2^F = \frac{\sqrt{(130.441)(50.559)}}{\tau} = \frac{81.2094}{80.3069} = 1.0112$$

Then, for example,

$$F_{11} = \hat{\tau}\hat{\tau}_1^V \hat{\tau}_1^F = 80.3069 \times 1.6062 \times 0.9889 = 127.557$$

which agrees, within rounding error, with the actual expected value for the independence model. You should verify for yourself that in the general case, for the independence model

$$F_{ij} = \hat{\tau}\hat{\tau}_i^V \hat{\tau}_j^F$$

I have gone through the last few paragraphs to make a simple but very important point. In the analysis of variance we wrote an additive linear model for observations in each cell as

$$X_{ijk} = \mu + \alpha_i + \beta_j + \alpha\beta_{ij} + e_{ijk}$$

With log-linear models of categorical data, we have seen that we can write the independence model for expected cell *frequencies* as

$$F_{ij} = \hat{\tau}\hat{\tau}_i^V \hat{\tau}_j^F$$

This model is multiplicative rather than additive and doesn't look much like the analysis of variance model.[†] But if you recall your high-school algebra, you will remember that products become sums when you take logs. Thus, we can convert the preceding expression to

$$\ln(F_{ij}) = \ln(\hat{\tau}) + \ln(\hat{\tau}_i^V) + \ln(\hat{\tau}_j^F)$$

λ **(lambda)**

We can then substitute the symbol λ **(lambda)** to represent the natural log of τ and have

$$\ln(F_{ij}) = \lambda + \lambda_i^V + \lambda_j^F$$

which is an additive linear expression directly analogous to the model we had for the analysis of variance. This model is linear in the logs, hence the name *log-linear models.*

To summarize, in the analysis of variance we modeled expected cell means as the sum of the grand mean and row and column treatment effects. In log-linear models

---

[†] In the analysis of variance we have variation within cells and can thus calculate an error term. In log-linear models we are working with cell frequencies and will not have an error term. Therefore our models will have nothing comparable to e_{ijk}.

we model expected cell frequencies as the sum of the logs of row and column effects. The arithmetic is slightly different and we are modeling different things, but the logic is the same.

Given my new notation I can now go back and characterize the separate models by their underlying equations. The models are numbered in the order of their presentation.

1. Equiprobability model: $\ln(F_{ij}) = \lambda$
2. Conditional equiprobability model 1: $\ln(F_{ij}) = \lambda + \lambda_i^V$
3. Conditional equiprobability model 2: $\ln(F_{ij}) = \lambda + \lambda_j^F$
4. Mutual independence model: $\ln(F_{ij}) = \lambda + \lambda_i^V + \lambda_j^F$

If you think back to the analysis of variance you will realize that one possible model is missing. What about the complete interaction model?

5. $\ln(F_{ij}) = \lambda + \lambda_i^V + \lambda_j^F + \lambda_{ij}^{VF}$

In fact, such a model does exist. The interaction term (λ_{ij}^{VF}) is defined as what is left unexplained when we fit model 4 above. Thus,

$$\lambda_{ij}^{VF} = \ln(f_{ij}) - \ln(F_{ij}) = \ln(f_{ij}) - \lambda - \lambda_i^V - \lambda_j^F$$

Saturated model

This is a model in which every expected frequency is forced to be exactly equal to every obtained frequency, and χ^2 will be exactly 0.00. This is called the **saturated model**; a saturated model *always* fits the data perfectly.

Whereas in the analysis of variance we usually set up the complete model and *test* for interaction, the highest-order interaction in the log-linear analysis is not tested directly. The interaction model in the $R \times C$ case is basically the model that we adopt if the simpler additive model does not fit.

17.3 TESTING MODELS

The central issue in log-linear analysis is the issue of choosing an optimal model to fit the data. Within this context we have the five possible models we just discussed. These models are shown in Table 17.4 along with their associated likelihood ratio χ^2, degrees of freedom, and probability values.

TABLE 17.4
Five possible models for data in Table 17.1

Model	χ^2	df	p
1. $\ln(F_{ij}) = \lambda$	109.5889	3	$<.05$
2. $\ln(F_{ij}) = \lambda + \lambda_i^V$	37.3960	2	$<.05$
3. $\ln(F_{ij}) = \lambda + \lambda_j^F$	109.5442	2	$<.05$
4. $\ln(F_{ij}) = \lambda + \lambda_i^V + \lambda_j^F$	37.3503	1	$<.05$
5. $\ln(F_{ij}) = \lambda + \lambda_i^V + \lambda_j^F + \lambda_{ij}^{VF}$	0.00	0	—

From Table 17.4 we see that the first four models all have significant χ^2 values. This means that for each of these models there is a significant difference between observed and expected values; *none of them fits the obtained data.* From such results we must conclude that only a model that incorporates the interaction term can account for the results. (This is one of the few places in inferential statistics where we actually seek nonsignificant results.) Thus, as we have previously concluded, Fault and Verdict interact and, within the context of Pugh's experiment, we cannot model the data without taking this interaction into account. Since, for Pugh, Verdict is a dependent variable, we conclude that decisions about guilt or innocence are dependent on perceptions about Fault.

From the point of view of fitting models, these results suggest that we should conclude that

$$\ln(F_{ij}) = \lambda + \lambda_i^V + \lambda_j^F + \lambda_{ij}^{VF}$$

But when viewed from the perspective of the analysis of variance, something is missing in such a conclusion. In the analysis of variance we start out with (and generally retain) a model such as this, but we also test the individual elements of the model. In other words we ask, Within the complete model are there significant effects due to V, F, and their interaction? That is a question we haven't really asked. When we tested the model $\ln(F_{ij}) = \lambda + \lambda_j^F$ we were asking if such a model fit the data. We were not asking the equally important question, When we adjust for other effects is there a difference attributable to Fault?

There are two ways of asking these questions using log-linear models—the easy way and the harder way, paralleling what we did in the equal-n case of the analysis of variance in Chapter 16. The advantage of the more complicated way is that it generalizes to the process we will use on interactions in more complex designs.

Let's start with the easy way because it supplies a frame of reference. If you want to know whether there is a difference in the data attributable to Verdict (i.e., are there significantly more decisions of Guilty than Not Guilty), why not just ask that question directly by looking at the marginal totals? In other words, just run a one-dimensional likelihood ratio χ^2, as shown in Table 17.5. The $\chi^2 = 72.1929$ is a significant result on 1 df, and we would conclude that there is a difference in the number of cases judged guilty and not guilty.

TABLE 17.5
Test on differences
due to verdict

	Guilt	
	Guilty	Not Guilty
f_{ij}	258	100
F_{ij}	179	179

$$\chi^2 = 2 \sum f_{ij} \ln\left(\frac{f_{ij}}{F_{ij}}\right)$$

$$= 2\left(258 \ln\frac{258}{179} + 100 \ln\frac{100}{179}\right)$$

$$= 72.1929$$

Now let's ask the same question about low and high levels of Fault (see Table 17.6). This effect (0.0447) is clearly not significant—nor would Pugh have expected it to be given the design of the experiment.

TABLE 17.6
Test on differences
due to fault

	Fault	
	Low	High
f_{ij}	177	181
F_{ij}	179	179

$$\chi^2 = 2 \sum f_{ij} \ln \left(\frac{f_{ij}}{F_{ij}} \right)$$

$$= 2 \left(177 \ln \frac{177}{179} + 181 \ln \frac{181}{179} \right)$$

$$= 0.0447$$

The interaction itself we have already tested at the beginning of the chapter. There we found that $\chi^2 = 37.3503$, and we concluded that Fault and Verdict were not independent.

Now let's see how we can derive these tests from the log-linear models that we have already created. [In higher-order designs we can still test the effect of single variables (what the analysis of variance labels as main effects), but not interaction, in the way we just did. However, the model-comparison approach to be adopted generalizes to interaction effects as well.]

We have found that the simplest model [$\ln(F_{ij}) = \lambda$] produces a $\chi^2 = 109.5889$. When we added λ^V to this model, χ^2 dropped to 37.3960, reflecting the variation in cell frequencies attributable to Verdict. This drop ($109.5889 - 37.3960 = 72.1929$) is the χ^2 for Verdict, and its degrees of freedom equal the difference between the degrees of freedom in the two models ($3 - 2 = 1$). This is the same value we obtained in Table 17.5 when we compared the marginal frequencies. In other words, adjusting $\lambda + \lambda_i^V$ for λ yields the same result as basing our results on the marginals.

By a similar line of reasoning, we can note that going from $\ln(F_{ij}) = \lambda$ to $\ln(F_{ij}) = \lambda + \lambda_j^F$ reduces χ^2 from 109.5889 to 109.5442, for a decrease of 0.0447. This is the same as the marginal χ^2 on Fault that we obtained in Table 17.6.

Finally, we should note that when we go from a model of $\ln(F_{ij}) = \lambda + \lambda_i^V + \lambda_j^F$ to $\ln(F_{ij}) = \lambda + \lambda_i^V + \lambda_j^F + \lambda_{ij}^{VF}$, χ^2 drops from 37.3503 to 0.00. This drop (37.3503) is the same as the χ^2 for the interaction based on marginal frequencies. This equality will not generally hold for more complex designs unless we are looking at the highest-order interaction.

One other feature of log-linear models should be mentioned. The minimal model [$\ln(F_{ij}) = \lambda$] produced $\chi^2 = 109.5889$. The individual components of the saturated model had χ^2 values of 72.1929, 0.0447, and 37.3503. These sum to 109.5889. In other words, these likelihood ratio χ^2 values are additive. This would not have been the case had we computed the Pearson chi-square statistic instead.

At this point you should have an overview of parameter estimates. It would be smart to go back to the beginning of Section 17.2 and reread that section.

DIFFERENCES BETWEEN LOG-LINEAR MODELS AND THE ANALYSIS OF VARIANCE

Although I have frequently compared the analysis of variance models and log-linear models and pointed to the many real similarities between the two techniques, this comparison may at times lead to confusion. The purpose behind the models is not quite the same in the two situations. The analysis of variance models cell means, whereas log-linear analysis models cell frequencies.

To take a simple example, assume that we have an experiment looking at the effects of Previous Artistic Experience and Gender (two independent variables) on the quality of a written Composition (the dependent variable). First suppose that Composition is measured on a more-or-less continuous scale, that Artistic Experience and Gender are dichotomies, and that we have 20 male and 40 female subjects. Further assume that Gender has absolutely nothing to do with Composition. Then in an analysis of variance framework with Gender β_j included, our model would be

$$X_{ijk} = \mu + \alpha_i + \beta_j + \alpha\beta_{ij} + e_{ijk}$$

Here we would expect the main effect of Gender to be 0.00 because we have set the condition that Gender does not influence Composition. On the other hand, if in fact differences between the quality of Composition for males and females did exist, a significant main effect would appear. The presence or absence of an effect due to Gender relates to whether or not male and female subjects differ on the scores on Composition.

Now assume the same experiment, again with 20 males and 40 females, but this time record Composition scores as high, medium, and low and include Composition as a variable in our model. We fit a log-linear model to these data. This time even if there are no differences in Composition between males and females, we will still need to include Gender in our model, *and its effects will be significant.* The reason is quite simple. With our log-linear model we are *not* trying to model Composition; we are trying to model cell frequencies. We are trying to explain why there are more scores in some cells than in others. Those cells dealing with female subjects will be relatively larger than those cells with male subjects (all other things equal) because there are more female subjects. Similarly, if we had equal numbers of male and female subjects, even with huge differences in quality of Composition between the two sexes, the effect of Gender would be 0.00.

I point this out, and will come back to it again, because it is too easy and seductive to see Gender playing the same role in the two kinds of experiments. In fact, in asymmetric log-linear models the main effects associated with our independent variables (and their interactions with each other) are often of no interest whatsoever. They may merely reflect our sampling plan. They need to be included to model the data properly, but they do not have a substantive role. In such models it is the *interaction* of these variables with the dependent variables that is of interest (and that parallels main effects in the analysis of variance.)

17.4   ODDS AND ODDS RATIOS

Before moving to complex designs, there are two other basic concepts that are more easily explained with simple tables than with higher-order tables. Both of these concepts will become useful in what follows.

Conditional odds

Looking at our original data in Table 17.1, we note that in the low Fault condition 153 people were found guilty and 24 were found not guilty. Thus, the **conditional odds** of being judged guilty given that the victim was seen as low on Fault is $153/24 = 6.3750$. (This can be read to mean that in the low fault condition the odds in favor of being found guilty are 6.3750:1.) For every person who is found not guilty, 6.375 are found guilty. Or, you are 6.375 times more likely to be found guilty than to be found not guilty. However, the conditional odds of being found guilty given that the victim is seen as having a high degree of fault are only $105/76 = 1.3816$.

Odds ratio (Ω)

If there had been no interaction between Fault and Verdict, the odds of being found guilty would have been the same under the two conditions. Therefore, the *ratio* of the two odds would have been approximately 1.00. Instead, the ratio of the two conditional odds, the **odds ratio (Ω)**, is $6.3750/1.3816 = 4.6142$. A defendant is about 4.6 times more likely to be found guilty in the low fault condition than in the high fault condition.

An important feature of the odds ratio is that it is independent of the size of the sample, whereas χ^2 is not. A second advantage is that within the context of a 2×2 table, a test on the odds ratio, which we will not cover here, is equivalent to a likelihood ratio χ^2 test of independence. A third advantage of Ω is that its magnitude will not be artificially affected by the presence of unequal marginal distributions. In other words, if we doubled the number of cases in the high fault condition (but still held other things constant), χ^2 (either Pearson's or the likelihood ratio) and phi would change. Omega, however, would not be affected.

TREATMENT EFFECTS (LAMBDA)

As we have already seen, log-linear models have a nice parallel with the analysis of variance, and that parallelism extends to the treatment effects, here represented by λ. As you know, log-linear models work with the natural logs of frequencies rather than with the frequencies themselves.

Remember that for the fully saturated model $[\ln(F_{ij}) = \lambda + \lambda_i^V + \lambda_j^F + \lambda_{ij}^{FV}]$ the observed and expected frequencies are the same. Thus, we will start with the logs of the frequencies in each cell and treat these logs as the raw data, as shown in Table 17.7. Notice that I have also given the row and column marginal means and the grand mean.

For those of you who wondered why we used geometric means rather than arithmetic means earlier, the answer is not too complicated. The cell frequencies for row 1 were 153 and 24. Note that the mean for row 1 in Table 17.7 is really

$$\frac{\ln(153) + \ln(24)}{2} = 4.10424$$

The natural log of the geometric mean of row 1 is

$$\ln(\sqrt{(153)(24)}) = \ln(60.5970) = 4.10424$$

Remember that adding logs is equivalent to multiplying the raw scores, and dividing logs by a constant (C) is equivalent to taking the Cth root. Thus, taking the log of the geometric mean is equivalent to taking the mean of the logs. (Just thought you'd like to know.)

TABLE 17.7
Treatment effects for fully saturated model

		Verdict		
		Guilty	Not Guilty	Marginals
Fault	**High**	5.03043	3.17805	4.10424
	Low	4.65396	4.33073	4.49235
	Marginals	4.84220	3.75439	4.29830

Now recall that when we calculated treatment effects in the analysis of variance we took deviations of means. Thus,

$$\hat{\mu} = \overline{X}_{..} \qquad\qquad \lambda = 4.29830$$

$$\hat{\alpha} = \overline{X}_{i.} - \overline{X}_{..} \qquad\qquad \lambda_1^F = 4.10424 - 4.29830 = -0.19406$$

$$\hat{\beta}_j = \overline{X}_{.j} - \overline{X}_{..} \qquad\qquad \lambda_1^V = 4.84220 - 4.29830 = 0.54390$$

$$\hat{\alpha\beta}_{ij} = \overline{X}_{ij} - \overline{X}_{i.} - \overline{X}_{.j} + \overline{X}_{..} \qquad \lambda_{11}^{FV} = 5.03043 - 4.10424 - 4.84220 + 4.29830$$

$$= 0.38229$$

Note the parallelism. Further, $\Sigma\lambda_i^F = \Sigma\lambda_j^V = \Sigma_i\lambda_{ij}^{FV} = \Sigma_j\lambda_{ij}^{FV} = 0.00$. Thus we can calculate all of the rest of the effects directly.

$$\lambda_2^F = 0.19406$$

$$\lambda_2^V = -0.54390$$

$$\lambda_{12}^{FV} = -0.38229$$

$$\lambda_{21}^{FV} = -0.38229$$

$$\lambda_{22}^{FV} = 0.38229$$

17.5   THREE-WAY TABLES

Log-linear models come into their own once we move to contingency tables of more than two dimensions. These are the situations in which standard chi-square analyses are not able to reveal a full understanding of the data. In this section we will concentrate on three-way tables because they illustrate all of the essential points. Extrapolation to tables of higher dimensionality is direct. Good examples of the analysis and interpretation of four- and five-way tables can be found in Pugh (1983) and Tabachnick and Fidell (1989), respectively. [If you try to duplicate the results in Pugh's paper, instruct your program to add 0.5 to the cell frequencies in the four-way table before running any analyses. This is normally done anyway on a temporary basis when the program deals with the highest interaction to avoid problems of cell frequencies of zero; ln(0) is undefined. Pugh instructed BMDP4F to leave the 0.5 in while computing all tables.]

When we move beyond a simple $R \times C$ table, the calculations of expected frequencies, especially for interactions involving subsets of variables, become appreciably more complex. Such calculations are usually carried out by an iterative process in which initial estimates are continually refined until they meet some specified criterion. Most analyses at this level are solved by computers, and that is the approach adopted here. This chapter will focus on analyses computed by BMDP4F. Similar results would be obtained using SPSS^X or SYSTAT. PROC CATMOD in SAS can be used for log-linear analysis, but it uses a different algorithm and its parameter estimates and test statistics differ from those of SPSS^X and BMDP4F. (In two-way $R \times C$ tables they also differ from those computed by hand.)

ASSUMPTIONS

One of the pleasant things about log-linear models is the relative absence of assumptions. Like the more traditional chi-square test, log-linear analysis does not make assumptions about population distributions, although it does assume, as does Pearson's chi-square, that observations are independent. You may apply log-linear analysis in a wide variety of circumstances, including even the analysis of badly distributed (ill-behaved) continuous variables that have been classified into discrete categories.

The major problem with log-linear analysis is the same problem that we encountered with traditional chi-square. The expected frequencies have to be sufficiently large to allow the assumption that frequencies in each cell would be normally distributed over repeated sampling. In the case of chi-square, we set the rule that all (or at least most) of the expected frequencies should be at least 5. We also saw that serious departures from this rule were probably acceptable, as long as all expected frequencies exceeded 1 and 80% were greater than 5. However, in such cases we would have unacceptably low power. We have a similar situation with log-linear analysis. Once again we require that at least all cells have expected frequencies greater than 1 and that no more than 20% of the cells have expected frequencies less than 5. The biggest

Sparse matrices

problem comes with what are called **sparse matrices**, which are contingency tables with a large number of empty cells. In these cases you may wish to combine categories on the basis of some theoretical rationale, increase sample sizes, collapse across variables, or do whatever you can to increase the expected frequencies. Regardless of the effects such small cells have on the level of Type I errors, you are virtually certain to have very low levels of power.

HIERARCHICAL AND NONHIERARCHICAL MODELS

Most, but not all, analyses of log-linear models involve what are called hierarchical

Hierarchical model

models. You can think of a **hierarchical model** as one for which the presence of an interaction term requires the presence of all lower-order interactions and main effects involving the components of that higher-order interaction. For example, suppose that we had four variables, A, B, C, and D. If you include in the model the three-way interaction ACD, a hierarchical model would also have to include A, C, D, AC, AD, and CD, because each of these terms is a subset of ACD. Similarly, if your model included ABC and ABD, the model would actually include A, B, C, D, AB, AC, BC, AD, and BD. It need not include CD, ACD, BCD, or $ABCD$, because those are not components of either of the three-way interactions.

Hierarchical models are in many ways parallel to models used in the analysis of variance. If you turn to any of the models in Chapters 13, 14, and 16 you will note that they are all hierarchical—for a three-way analysis of variance all main effects and two-way interactions are included, along with the three-way interaction. Just as in the analysis of variance, the presence of a term in either analysis of variance or log-linear models does not necessarily mean that it will make a significant contribution. (If we design a study having exactly as many males as females, the contribution of Gender to a log-linear model will be precisely 0. We still usually include it in the model because of its influence on other expected frequencies.) BMDP4F, SPSS^X HILOGLINEAR, and SYSTAT TABLES handle only hierarchical models. On the other hand, SPSS^X LOGLINEAR, SAS PROC CATMOD, and SYSTAT LOGIT are capable of analyzing nonhierarchical models. We will deal only with hierarchical models in this chapter.

One of the convenient things about hierarchical designs is that they allow us to specify models very clearly and simply. Assume that we have four variables (A, B, C, and D). The notation ABC specifies a model that includes the ABC interaction, and, because we are speaking about hierarchical models, must also include A, B, C, AB, AC, and BC. We do not have to write out the latter to specify the model—ABC will suffice. Similarly, the label AB stands for a model that includes A, B, and AB, but not C or any interactions involving C. Finally, a model written as AB, ACD is really the model that involves A, B, C, D, AB, AC, AD, CD, and ACD, but not BC, BD, ABC, ABD, or BCD. In much of what follows we will characterize models by the interactions that define them (sometimes called their **defining set**, or **generating class**). Thus, when we shortly have a BMDP4F model listed as FM, MV, we are speaking about a model that includes M, F, V, FM, and MV.

Defining set,
Generating class

A THREE-WAY EXAMPLE

We will take as an example the study of rape by Pugh (1983). In the previous section we examined the relationship between Fault and Verdict. Pugh also attempted to manipulate a third variable (Moral) by varying the trial transcript to present the *victim* as someone with "high moral character," "low moral character," or "neutral" on this dimension. We now have three variables by which to categorize the data: Fault (F), Moral (M), and Verdict (V). Fault and Moral refer to characteristics attributed to the victim, whereas Verdict represents a judgment on the defendant. Fault and Verdict each have two levels, whereas Moral has three levels. Pugh's data collapsed across a fourth variable (Gender) are given in Table 17.8.

TABLE 17.8
Data from Pugh
collapsed across
gender (1983)

Verdict	Fault	Moral			Total
		High	Neutral	Low	
Guilty	Low	42	79	32	153
	High	23	65	17	105
	Total	65	144	49	258
Not Guilty	Low	4	12	8	24
	High	11	41	24	76
	Total	15	53	32	100
	Column Total	80	197	81	358

POSSIBLE MODELS

Our task is to try to explain the pattern of obtained cell frequencies in Table 17.8. We could ask a variety of possible questions in seeking an explanation, including the following:

1. Can the pattern of cell frequencies be explained by differences in the number of subjects in the three Moral conditions?

2. Can the pattern of cell frequencies be explained by differences in the number of people judged Guilty and Not Guilty?

3. Can the pattern be explained by a combination of the number of subjects in the three Moral conditions and a higher incidence of Guilty over Not Guilty?

4. Can the pattern be explained by an interaction of Moral and Verdict—for example, are there more judgments of Guilty when the victim is seen as being of "high moral character" and fewer when she is seen as being of "low moral character" or "neutral moral character"?

5. Can the pattern be explained by both the Moral × Verdict interaction *and* the difference in the number of cases where the victim was seen as high or low in Fault?

6. Can the pattern be explained by both a Moral × Verdict interaction *and* a Moral × Fault interaction?

7. Can the pattern be explained by a three-way interaction involving Fault, Moral, and Verdict?

Each of these possibilities—and there are a total of 18 if you count the hypothesis that the cell frequencies are random (equiprobable)—represents a possible underlying model. Our task will be to decide which of these models both fits the data and is parsimonious. (I already know that the saturated model, which by definition involves the highest-order interaction, will fit the data perfectly—but it is certainly not parsimonious.)

This list of questions corresponds directly to a list of different models. Letting F, M, and V stand for Fault, Moral, and Verdict, we can associate the first question with a model specified as M. To be more precise our underlying structural model, which is almost certainly much too simple, would be

$$\ln(F_{ijk}) = \lambda + \lambda^M$$

In the same way we can write out the other models, as shown in Table 17.9.

TABLE 17.9
Possible models for
data in Table 17.8

Question	Model	Specification
1	$\ln(F_{ijk}) = \lambda + \lambda^M$	M
2	$\ln(F_{ijk}) = \lambda + \lambda^V$	V
3	$\ln(F_{ijk}) = \lambda + \lambda^M + \lambda^V$	M, V
4	$\ln(F_{ijk}) = \lambda + \lambda^M + \lambda^V + \lambda^{MV}$	MV
5	$\ln(F_{ijk}) = \lambda + \lambda^F + \lambda^M + \lambda^V + \lambda^{MV}$	MV, F
6	$\ln(F_{ijk}) = \lambda + \lambda^F + \lambda^M + \lambda^V + \lambda^{MV} + \lambda^{FM}$	FM, MV
7	$\ln(F_{ijk}) = \lambda + \lambda^F + \lambda^M + \lambda^V + \lambda^{MV} + \lambda^{FM} + \lambda^{FV} + \lambda^{FMV}$	FMV

Notice once again that this is *not* an analysis of variance—that is, we are not trying to explain variability in a single dependent variable (Verdict) on the basis of two independent variables (Fault and Moral). It is easy to keep falling into that trap. We are trying to explain a pattern of observed cell frequencies, and the explanation may involve any or all of the variables (dependent or independent) and their interactions. Even where you have one clearly defined dependent variable and two clearly defined independent variables, part of the variability may involve just the independent variables—for example, higher frequencies in the Group 1 cells may be due to the often inconsequential fact that there were more subjects in Group 1.

EXAMINING THE SATURATED MODEL

In considering two-way tables, we defined a saturated model as one that includes all possible effects. The same holds for three-way and higher-order tables. Consider the model that can be designated as *FMV* or written as

$$\ln(F_{ijk}) = \lambda + \lambda^F + \lambda^M + \lambda^V + \lambda^{MV} + \lambda^{FM} + \lambda^{FV} + \lambda^{FMV}$$

This is the saturated model for our data. It includes all possible effects and exhausts the degrees of freedom available in the data. (One degree of freedom goes to estimating λ, one each to estimating F, V, and FV, and two each to estimating M, FM, MV, and FMV; M has three levels and thus two degrees of freedom for it and its interactions.) These total to 12, and since we have 12 cells there isn't anything left over.) If we knew the values of the various lambdas, and eventually we will, the resultant expected frequencies would equal the observed frequencies, leaving nothing else to be explained. For this reason we know without even looking at the data that the likelihood ratio χ^2 for this model will be exactly 0.00. We should not be any happier with this perfect fit than we are when we draw a straight line to fit perfectly any two points; and for the same reason—the model exhausts the degrees of freedom.

We do not fit a saturated model to data just because we hope that it will fit—we know that before we start. We usually fit it hoping that it will help us identify simpler models by revealing nonsignificant effects. If we could show, for example, that we could do just about as well by eliminating the three-way interaction and two of the two-way interactions, we would be well on our way to representing the data by a relatively simple model.

One of the reasons for starting with the saturated model is that you can then ask whether various levels of interaction are needed in the model. In Exhibit 17.1 you see a BMDP4F program, and in Exhibit 17.2 a portion of the printout that results. (Subsequent analyses will be based on this same program but with different "/FIT" paragraphs.)

EXHIBIT 17.1
BMDP4F program for log-linear analysis

/Problem	Title is 'BMDP4F on Moral*Fault*Verdict.'.
/Input	Variables are 4.
	Cases are 12.
	Format is Free.
	File is 'Loglin3.dat'.
/Variable	Names are Moral, Fault, Verdict, Freq.
/Category	Codes (Fault, Verdict) are 1, 2.
	Codes (Moral) are 1, 2, 3.
	Names (Fault) are Low, High
	Names (Verdict) are Guilty, NoGuilt.
	Names (Moral) are High, Neutral, Low.
/Table	Indices are Moral, Fault, Verdict.
	Count = Freq.
/Fit	Association is 3.
/Print	Lambda. Expected. Standardized. LRChi.
/End	

EXHIBIT 17.2
Simultaneous tests of model effects

***** THE RESULTS OF FITTING ALL K-FACTOR MARGINALS.
       SIMULTANEOUS TEST THAT ALL K+1 AND HIGHER FACTOR INTERACTIONS ARE ZERO.

K-FACTOR	D.F.	LR CHISQ	PROB.	PEARSON CHISQ	PROB.
0 - MEAN	11	191.92	0.00000	200.91	0.00000
1	7	48.93	0.00000	49.02	0.00000
2	2	0.26	0.88013	0.26	0.88021
3	0	0.	1.	0.	1.

***** SIMULTANEOUS TEST THAT ALL K-FACTOR INTERACTIONS ARE SIMULTANEOUSLY ZERO.
       THE CHI-SQUARES ARE DIFFERENCES IN THE ABOVE TABLE.

K-FACTOR	D.F.	LR CHISQ	PROB.	PEARSON CHISQ	PROB.
1	4	142.99	0.00000	151.88	0.00000
2	5	48.68	0.00000	48.77	0.00000
3	2	0.26	0.88013	0.26	0.88021

SIMULTANEOUS TESTS OF MODEL EFFECTS   The first item of interest in Exhibit 17.2 is the section showing the simultaneous tests on main effects and interactions. This section of Exhibit 17.2 tests the complexity of the required model. The first row of the *simultaneous* tests of all $K + 1$ and higher interactions asks if we need a model that includes any more than just the mean (λ). In our case it simultaneously tests the null hypotheses that λ^F, λ^M, λ^V, λ^{FM}, λ^{FV}, λ^{MV}, and λ^{FMV} are all 0. The test of this null hypothesis has $\chi^2 = 191.92$ on 11 *df*. This is significant at beyond the 0.00000 level, indicting that at least some of those terms are necessary—the cells are not all equal in the population.

The second line asks whether a model that includes only main effects is sufficient. It does this by testing the null hypothesis that λ^{FM}, λ^{FV}, λ^{MV}, and λ^{FMV} are all simultaneously 0. This χ^2 (48.93) is also significant, so we cannot be satisfied with a simple main effects model.

The third line asks whether some main effects and two-way interactions are sufficient by testing H_0: $\lambda^{FMV} = 0$. This χ^2 (0.26) is not significant, indicating that we are not going to need to include the three-way interaction in our model. That is a relief, because it is often difficult to explain a three-way interaction. More importantly, the saturated model is usually uninteresting.

The second half of Exhibit 17.2 asks similar questions, but it tests only the same order of interaction at any one point. The first line tests whether *any* or all of the main effects are significant; the second line tests whether *any* two-way interaction terms are significant; and the last line again tests the one three-way interaction. Again we see significance for main effects, tested simultaneously, and for two-way interactions, tested simultaneously, but not for the three-way interaction.

MARGINAL AND PARTIAL ASSOCIATIONS   The next step in identifying a model is shown in Exhibit 17.3. This exhibit presents tests of each effect within the context of the saturated model. These tests are carried out in two ways: as tests of partial association and as tests of marginal association. (For main effects and for the highest-order interaction, tests of partial and marginal association are equivalent, though BMDP4F only shows them in the Partial Association columns.)

EXHIBIT 17.3
Marginal and partial tests of association

***** ASSOCIATION OPTION SELECTED FOR ALL TERMS OF ORDER LESS THAN OR EQUAL TO 3

	PARTIAL ASSOCIATION			MARGINAL ASSOCIATION		
EFFECT	D.F.	CHISQUARE	PROB.	D.F.	CHISQUARE	PROB.
M.	2	70.75	0.0000			
F.	1	0.04	0.8326			
V.	1	72.19	0.0000			
FM.	2	2.56	0.2785	2	2.92	0.2325
MV.	2	8.41	0.0149	2	8.77	0.0125
FV.	1	36.99	0.0000	1	37.35	0.0000
FMV.	2	0.26	0.8801			

Marginal associations refer to effects calculated from marginal totals, collapsing across irrelevant variables. Thus, for example, if we took the Fault × Verdict subtable (shown in Table 17.1 on p. 579) and calculated the likelihood ratio $\chi^2 = 37.35$, we would obtain the entry given under the Marginal Association columns of Exhibit 17.3. Partial associations, on the other hand, adjust for other interactions. For example, the model containing all three two-way interaction terms (*FM*, *FV*, and *MV*) has a χ^2 value of 0.26 (see the top of Exhibit 17.2). When we eliminate *FV*, the model containing only *FM* and *FV* would have a χ^2 of 37.25. (This calculation will appear later, in Exhibit 17.5. χ^2 increased because the reduced model does not fit as well.) The difference in the fit of the two models (37.25 − 0.26 = 36.99) is the χ^2 for partial association of *FV*. Notice that this partial association χ^2 for *FV* (36.99) differs from the marginal association value (37.25) that we would calculate if we just computed a log-linear χ^2

on the $F \times V$ subtable. The same description of marginal and partial tests applies to the other two-way tables.

Starting at the bottom of Exhibit 17.3, we see that the contribution of FMV is not significant. The χ^2 of 0.26 is the difference between the saturated model (whose χ^2 value would be 0.00) and the hierarchical model containing all three two-way interactions, whose χ^2 value is 0.26. The difference ($0.26 - 0.00 = 0.26$) is the loss in fit attributable to deleting the three-way information. (This is the same information that we saw in Exhibit 17.2). This term could be dropped from our model without doing serious damage to the degree of fit.

Moving up the exhibit we see that both the partial and marginal tests on FV and MV are significant, meaning, in the case of the partial test, that when compared with a model containing FM, FV, and MV, a model without one or the other of these would represent a significantly poorer fit. Therefore, we do not want to drop either. However, both the partial and the marginal tests suggest that there would be little loss from dropping FM. Although you do not see it here, a χ^2 on a model including only FV and MV would be 2.81. With all three two-way interactions, χ^2 was 0.26. This difference $[2.81 - 0.26 = 2.56 \text{ (rounded)}]$ is the χ^2 shown in Exhibit 17.3 and it is not significant. It looks as if at least a tentative model would contain only FV and MV and would look like

$$\ln(F_{ijk}) = \lambda + \lambda^F + \lambda^M + \lambda^V + \lambda^{FV} + \lambda^{MV}$$

We will shortly explore that model further.

You might have noticed from Exhibit 17.3 that were we to look at the main effects, the effect for F is clearly not significant. We will not remove F from our model, however, because in order to maintain a hierarchical model we must have as a main effect any variable that contributes to an interaction that is included. Since F is part of FM, it must remain in the model.

A second point concerns the difference between partial and marginal association. In particular, what would we do if an interaction were significant as a partial association but not as a marginal association, or vice versa? Brown (1976) has addressed this issue and argued that if a variable is significant by *either* test it should remain in the model at least tentatively. This is the conservative, and safe, approach. We may decide later to remove the effect in question, but it should be left in to allow for closer examination.

17.6   DERIVING MODELS

We have just derived a model for our data using tests of partial and marginal association. Other approaches to model selection that usually, but not always, lead to the same model could have been used. We are going to look at some of those. Keep in mind that we are really covering much of the same ground that we have just covered, but from a different direction. Each different approach has the opportunity of shedding a bit more light on the interpretation of our data.

TESTING ALL POSSIBLE MODELS

One alternative way of arriving at a model using BMDP4F is to use the command "/FIT ALL." This command will fit all possible hierarchical models and print out a χ^2 test for goodness of fit for each.[†] Models whose χ^2 values are not significant provide an adequate fit between obtained and expected frequencies and are candidates for further study. Models whose χ^2 values are clearly significant can be eliminated as reasonable models. Exhibit 17.4 presents the output from the "/FIT ALL" command. From this table you can see that four models are nonsignificant at $\alpha = .05$. These are (FM, MV, FV), (FV, FM), (MV, FV), and (M, FV). The first one, (FM, MV, FV), we have already rejected in favor of the third, (MV, FV). The other two are what might be called borderline—they are not significant at $\alpha = .05$, but they are significant at $\alpha = .10$. One of these, (FV, FM), we did not even consider in the previous section because it would not include the MV interaction, whose removal led to a significant decrement at $\alpha = .0149$. In other words, the model might not be significant overall (its p value is .0791), but it fits significantly less well than (FM, MV, FV). As a result I would not be inclined to accept that model. The other borderline model, (M, FV), turns out to be unsatisfactory for similar reasons. To see this, note that χ^2 for M, $FV = 11.58$ on 6 df. The χ^2 for $(MV, FV) = 2.81$ on 4 df. The difference between these models is itself a χ^2 on degrees of freedom equal to the difference in df for the two models ($\chi^2_{\text{diff}} = 11.58 - 2.81 = 8.77$ on $6 - 4 = 2$ df. Since $\chi^2_{.05}(2) = 5.99$, the difference between these two models is significant, and therefore we lose important information when we drop the MV interaction. (One very good reason for using hierarchical models is that they allow us to test differences between models in this way.)

We want a model that (1) fits the data by having a nonsignificant χ^2 and (2) is not significantly different from some other, more complex, model. Our only real choice here is the model (MV, FV).

EXHIBIT 17.4
Test of all possible models

```
***** ALL MODELS ARE REQUESTED --
```

| | | LIKELIHOOD- | | PEARSON | |
MODEL	D.F.	RATIO CHISQ	PROB.	CHISQ	PROB.
M.	9	121.17	0.0000	109.51	0.0000
F.	10	191.88	0.0000	201.66	0.0000
V.	10	119.73	0.0000	125.38	0.0000
M, F.	8	121.12	0.0000	110.43	0.0000
F, V.	9	119.68	0.0000	125.03	0.0000
V, M.	8	48.98	0.0000	49.13	0.0000
M, F, V.	7	48.93	0.0000	49.02	0.0000
FM.	6	118.21	0.0000	105.99	0.0000
MV.	6	40.21	0.0000	38.64	0.0000
FV.	8	82.33	0.0000	84.99	0.0000
M, FV.	6	11.58	0.0720	11.63	0.0709
F, MV.	5	40.16	0.0000	38.60	0.0000
V, FM.	5	46.01	0.0000	45.02	0.0000
FM, MV.	3	37.25	0.0000	35.94	0.0000
MV, FV.	4	2.81	0.5898	2.80	0.5921
FV, FM.	4	8.66	0.0701	8.74	0.0680
FM, MV, FV.	2	0.26	0.8801	0.26	0.8802

[†]This technique will sometimes fail if the model is too complex and the calculations would require an unreasonable amount of computer resources.

Lest you think we have exhausted ways of identifying models, consider one further approach. Just as with multiple regression, there are stepwise procedures for model building in SPSS^X HILOGLINEAR and in BMDP4F. BMDP4F has more options, but both perform the standard backward solution that is generally recommended (although using different algorithms).

STEPWISE PROCEDURES

Exhibit 17.5 presents the BMDP4F solution. This analysis was generated by the following commands:

/FIT   Model = FMV.

Delete = Simple.

Step = 10.

Probability = .10.

The first statement tells the program what model to start from—it need not be the saturated model, although it is here. The second statement says to remove one effect at a time. Step = 10 simply gives the maximum number of steps allowed. The value is arbitrary, but the default is 0, which means that you will not get anywhere if you omit the Step command. Probability = .10 instructs the program to continue removing effects until a removal produces a result that is a significant decrement in χ^2 at $\alpha = .10$. The default is .05, but I would much prefer to stop too early than too late.

I will not go over the output systematically because you should be able to interpret it yourself. Two things, however, are worth pointing out. First of all, notice that Exhibit 17.5 gives both the significance level of the reduced model itself and the significance of the difference between that model and the preceding one. Both are important. Thus, the model FV, MV is nonsignificant at $p = .5898$ *and* is nonsignificantly different from FV, MV, FM ($p = .2785$). On the other hand, had we set α at .05, FV, M would have been nonsignificant, causing the program to continue, though it would have been significantly different from MV, FV and would not, therefore, be satisfactory. Using $p = .10$ we have once again identified (FV, MV) as the optimal model.

The second thing to point out is at the bottom of the exhibit. BMDP4F always seems to run one extra step. A reasonable person looking at this exhibit might conclude that the statement, "BEST MODEL FOUND IS—(FV, M," means that FV, M is the best model. In fact it is not. The program chooses the model from any given step with the highest p value (here $p = .0720$, but it could theoretically be .0001), declares that to be the best model, tests to see if it fails the $p \geq .10$ condition, discovers that it does fail, says "Oops!," and stops. The problem is that it doesn't bother to print out the "Oops!" The point is to ignore the final step in the stepwise solution. The best model here is really given by Step 2 as FV, MV.

If you had chosen to use SPSS^X instead of BMDP4F, you would have come to the same conclusion in this case. But in arriving at our model, BMDP4F followed the test of FV, MV with tests on FV, M and F, MV. SPSS^X, on the other hand, would have followed FV, MV with a test of MV and a test of FV. In other words, SPSS^X works by a different algorithm, with potentially quite different results. Moreover, had we chosen to set Probability $= .05$, BMDP4F would have produced FV, M as the final model, whereas SPSS^X would have stopped with FV, MV. (In fact, BMDP4F would have produced a model markedly different from our own preceding solutions using other approaches.)

EXHIBIT 17.5
Stepwise solution for an optimal model

MODELS FORMED BY DELETING TERMS FROM MODEL --
FMV.

MODEL	D.F.	LIKELIHOOD-RATIO CHISQ	PROB.	PEARSON CHISQ	PROB.
FV, MV, FM.	2	0.26	0.8801	0.26	0.8802
DIFF. DUE TO DELETING FMV.	2	0.26	0.8801		

STEP 1.   BEST MODEL FOUND IS --
FV, MV, FM.

FV, MV.	4	2.81	0.5898	2.80	0.5921
DIFF. DUE TO DELETING FM.	2	2.56	0.2785		
FV, FM.	4	8.66	0.0701	8.74	0.0680
DIFF. DUE TO DELETING MV.	2	8.41	0.0149		
MV, FM.	3	37.25	0.0000	5.94	0.0000
DIFF. DUE TO DELETING FV.	1	36.99	0.0000		

STEP 2.   BEST MODEL FOUND IS --
FV, MV.

FV, M.	6	11.58	0.0720	11.63	0.0709
DIFF. DUE TO DELETING MV.	2	8.77	0.0125		
F, MV.	5	40.16	0.0000	38.60	0.0000
DIFF. DUE TO DELETING FV.	1	37.35	0.0000		

STEP 3.   BEST MODEL FOUND IS --
FV, M.

STEPPING STOPS DUE TO CRITERION PROBABILITY (0.100).

We have seen three different ways to arrive at a final model. All of them eventually led to the same place (FV, MV) in this case, but each had something different to offer. (I recommend using all three. At the very least it gives you a better feel for the data. On occasion they can lead to different models.) And just to make life a little more interesting, we might take a fourth approach and keep a term in the model even if its removal would not lead to a significant decrease in χ^2. For example, in her analysis involving an additional variable, Gender, Pugh retained the Gender × Moral interaction because those marginal cell frequencies were fixed by the design of the experiment and she wanted to force the expected two-dimensional marginal totals to equal the observed totals. The interpretation of that interaction was of no interest, and she correctly ignored it in her discussion. (For the rationale behind this approach, see Bishop, Fienberg, & Holland, 1975. pp. 36, 70). With a large number of variables, we might also want to retain an effect because of its direct relation to the purpose of the experiment. This is particularly true when we have several models, all of which have roughly the same probability values. See Marascuilo and Busk (1987) for further discussion of model selection.

17.7   TREATMENT EFFECTS

Now that we have chosen a model, we can return to the treatment effect statistics that were discussed in conjunction with two-dimensional tables. Here we can see how they add to our understanding of the data. We can ask BMDP4F to fit our model, produce observed and expected frequencies, and calculate treatment effects (lambdas). Exhibit 17.6 contains this information on the model

$$\ln(F_{ijk}) = \lambda + \lambda^F + \lambda^M + \lambda^V + \lambda^{FV} + \lambda^{MV}$$

In this exhibit you first see the overall test of the model that we have seen before ($\chi^2 = 2.81$, $p = .5898$). Next you see the expected cell frequencies followed by a statistical test on the residuals (deviates)—the difference between observed and expected frequencies. This test is easy to compute because the standard error of a residual is simply the square root of the expected frequency. Thus,

$$z = \frac{\text{Observed} - \text{Expected}}{\sqrt{\text{Expected}}}$$

is conservatively a standard normal deviate (Agresti, 1990). Standardized deviates in excess of ± 1.96 should give cause for concern (our model did not fit that cell well), but since you are running a large number of such tests a Bonferroni correction would be in order. To do this, treat the deviates as though they were t values on an infinite number of degrees of freedom and use Appendix t' to adjust for the number of independent tests. For our example we have no significant deviations.

EXHIBIT 17.6
Estimates for optimal model

```
****************
*    MODEL 2    *
****************
```

				LIKELIHOOD-RATIO	
PEARSON MODEL	D.F.	CHI-SQUARE	PROB.	CHI-SQUARE	PROB.
FV, MV.	4	2.81	0.5898	2.80	0.5921

***** EXPECTED VALUES USING ABOVE MODEL

Verdict	Fault	Moral				TOTAL
		High	Neutral	Low		
Guilty	Low	38.5	85.4	29.1		153.0
	High	26.5	58.6	19.9		105.0
	TOTAL	65.0	144.0	49.0		258.0
NoGuilt	Low	3.6	12.7	7.7		24.0
	High	11.4	40.3	24.3		76.0
	TOTAL	15.0	53.0	32.0		100.0

EXHIBIT 17.6 (Cont.)   ***** STANDARDIZED DEVIATES = (OBS - EXP)/SQRT (EXP) FOR ABOVE MODEL

Verdict	Fault	Moral		
- - - - - -	- - - - -	High	Neutral	Low
Guilty	Low	0.6	-0.7	0.5
	High	-0.7	0.8	-0.7
NoGuilt	Low	0.2	-0.2	0.1
	High	-0.1	0.1	-0.1

ESTIMATES OF THE LOG-LINEAR PARAMETERS (LAMBDA) IN THE MODEL ABOVE

THETA (MEAN)   3.0826

***** ESTIMATES OF THE LOG-LINEAR PARAMETERS (LAMBDA) IN THE MODEL ABOVE

Moral		
High	Neutral	Low
-0.422	0.607	-0.185

***** RATIO OF THE LOG-LINEAR PARAMETER ESTIMATE TO ITS STANDARD ERROR

Moral		
High	Neutral	Low
-3.977	7.478	-1.975

***** ESTIMATES OF THE LOG-LINEAR PARAMETERS (LAMBDA) IN THE MODEL ABOVE

Fault	
Low	High
-0.194	0.194

***** RATIO OF THE LOG-LINEAR PARAMETER ESTIMATE TO ITS STANDARD ERROR

Fault	
Low	High
-2.915	2.915

***** ESTIMATES OF THE LOG-LINEAR PARAMETERS (LAMBDA) IN THE MODEL ABOVE

Verdict	
Guilty	NoGuilt
0.552	-0.552

***** RATIO OF THE LOG-LINEAR PARAMETER ESTIMATE TO ITS STANDARD ERROR

Verdict	
Guilty	NoGuilt
7.517	-7.517

EXHIBIT 17.6 (Cont.) ***** ESTIMATES OF THE LOG-LINEAR PARAMETERS (LAMBDA) IN THE MODEL ABOVE

Verdict	Moral		
	High	Neutral	Low
Guilty	0.251	0.018	-0.269
NoGuilt	-0.251	-0.018	0.269

***** RATIO OF THE LOG-LINEAR PARAMETER ESTIMATE TO ITS STANDARD ERROR

Verdict	Moral		
	High	Neutral	Low
Guilty	2.366	0.219	-2.877
NoGuilt	-2.366	-0.219	2.877

***** ESTIMATES OF THE LOG-LINEAR PARAMETERS (LAMBDA) IN THE MODEL ABOVE

Verdict	Fault	
	Low	High
Guilty	0.382	-0.382
NoGuilt	-0.382	0.382

***** RATIO OF THE LOG-LINEAR PARAMETER ESTIMATE TO ITS STANDARD ERROR

Verdict	Fault	
	Low	High
Guilty	5.744	-5.744
No Guilt	-5.744	5.744

Following the information about cell residuals is the information about the parameter estimates (lambdas). First we are told that the mean, denoted in the model by λ, is 3.0826. You may recall from the section on two-way models that this is simply the mean of the logs of the *expected* cell frequencies. If you do the arithmetic you will find this to be the case. You may also recall that if you take the mean of the natural logs of the expected frequencies under the "high moral character" condition (the logs of 38.5, 26.5, 3.6, and 11.4) and subtract the overall mean, you will have the treatment effect for that condition.

$$\frac{\ln(38.5) + \ln(26.5) + \ln(3.6) + \ln(11.4)}{4} = \frac{10.64235}{4} = 2.6606$$

$$\text{Mean}_{\text{moral high}} = 2.6606$$

$$\lambda_{\text{moral high}} = 2.6606 - 3.0826 = -0.4220$$

Now look at Exhibit 17.6 and you will see that the estimate of $\lambda_{\text{moral high}}$ high is in fact -0.422. This can be read to mean that averaged across Fault and Verdict, the expected frequency for the high moral condition is somewhat below average. This should not surprise us because the low and high moral conditions each had fewer than half the number of subjects as the neutral condition. Significance tests on the effects for

Moral are given next in the exhibit. Here the parameter estimates are divided by their standard errors to produce a standardized parameter estimate. These standardized estimates are normally distributed with a mean of 0 and a standard deviation of 1. Thus, values greater than ± 1.96 would be significantly different from 0, although we should use Bonferroni adjustments to make more precise statements about exact cut-off points. Clearly, there are significant differences due to Moral, as we would expect from the design of the study.

As you work through the exhibit you see all of the parameter estimates and their standardized values. Each effect has at least one significant parameter, including Fault. I mention Fault because earlier analyses had led to the expectation that it would not be significant because the number of subjects in the low and high fault conditions are similar (177 and 181). That variable does, however, appear to play a role in the model.

INTERPRETING THE MODEL

From the analysis we have just gone through, we can say quite a bit about our data. In the first place, the frequencies were a function of the level of the Moral variable, but since these frequencies were largely fixed by the experimenter, they are of no great interest. Similarly, the data reflect small, but significant, differences in the attribution of Fault to the victim, with slightly more subjects seeing the victim as high in fault. This again was in part attributable to the experimenter's sampling plan. What was not under the direct control of the experimenter, and is of more interest, is a significantly higher number of defendants judged guilty than judged not guilty. Collapsing across the other dimensions, the odds in favor of a guilty judgment are $258/100 = 2.58$.

When we look at the interactions we see that there is an interaction between Moral and Verdict. A guilty verdict is more likely when the victim is seen as of high moral character than when she is seen as of low moral character. Put another way, the odds in favor of a guilty verdict for the High, Neutral, and Low Moral conditions are $65/15 = 4.33$, $144/53 = 2.72$, and $49/32 = 1.53$, respectively. Whether a defendant is seen as guilty appears to depend on events beyond the alleged crime itself.

Finally, there is an interaction between Fault and Verdict. When the victim is seen as low in fault, the odds in favor of a guilty verdict are $153/24 = 6.38$. In the high fault condition, those same odds are $105/76 = 1.38$. (Thus, the odds ratio is $6.38/1.38 = 4.62$). A judgment of guilty is clearly dependent on the degree to which the victim is seen as being at fault. These data shed light on the tendency of defense attorneys to try to put the blame on the victim, in that they show that juries' judgments of guilt or innocence are influenced by attributions of fault and low moral character to the victim.

ORDINAL VARIABLES

So far we have treated our variables as if they were measured on a nominal scale, although Moral did have an ordinal scale of Low, Neutral, and High. If variables are measured on an ordinal scale, standard log-linear analysis does not use that information. Scrambling the levels of each variable would lead to the same statistical results.

Recently attention has focused on alternative treatments that allow us to use ordinal scaling of variables where it is available. Discussions of log-linear models with ordinal variables can be found in Green (1988) and Agresti (1984, 1990). SPSS^X LOG-LINEAR can accommodate the analysis.

KEY TERMS

Log-linear models (introduction)
Symmetric relationships (introduction)
Asymetric relationship (introduction)
Logit analysis (introduction)
Logistic regression (introduction)
Geometric mean (17.2)
λ (lambda) (17.2)

Saturated model (17.2)
Conditional odds (17.4)
Odds ratio $\{\Omega\}$ (17.4)
Sparse matrices (17.5)
Hierarchial model (17.5)
Defining set (17.5)
Generating class (17.5)

EXERCISES

All of the problems in this chapter will require solution by one or more computer programs. In most cases analyses by both SPSS^X and BMDP4F would be appropriate, because they produce somewhat different, and complementary, statistics.

Bell, Buerkel-Rothfuss, and Gore (1987) examined the relationships among aspects of idiomatic communication in 100 romantically involved heterosexual couples. Couples provided information on "any words, phrases, or nonverbal signs that they had created that had meaning to their relationship." These idioms were classified along several dimensions, but we will focus only on who invented the idiom and the function the idiom serves (confrontations, affection, labels for outsiders, nicknames, requests, sexual invitations, sexual references, and teasing insults.) (The title of the paper was "Did you bring the yarmulke for the Cabbage Patch kid?" I leave speculation as to its meaning to your imagination.)

The data follow:

Function	Inventor		
	Female Partner	Male Partner	Others/Unknown
Confrontation	14	10	6
Affection	27	41	11
Labels outsiders	23	43	11
Nickname—female	6	57	16
Nickname—male	68	11	10
Requests	12	21	3
Sexual invitation	26	41	13
Sexual reference	27	38	5
Teasing insults	35	62	10

This is only a two-dimensional table, but it allows you the opportunity to specify the model, test the fit of that model, and calculate treatment effects.

17.1   What are the possible models that could be hypothesized to underly the data matrix?

17.2   Test each of the alternative models using the likelihood ratio χ^2.

17.3   Compute and interpret λ coefficients for the complete model.

Hansen and Swanson (1983) collected data on the Strong-Campbell Interest Inventory for college majors. This example has been discussed at length by Marascuilo and Busk (1987). In this study, subjects were classified as female or male (Gender), and as satisfied or unsatisfied with their major (Satisfaction). In addition, a subject's major was classified as a direct or an indirect hit (Hit) depending on whether that major was clearly represented by an Occupational Scale of the Strong-Campbell. Finally, the Validity of the Strong-Campbell prediction was classified as excellent, moderate, or poor, depending on how well it fit the student's major. The latter two variables (Hit and Validity) can be thought of as dependent variables, whereas the first two (Gender and Satisfaction) are thought of as independent variables (See Marascuilo & Busk, 1987). (Obviously, there is some basis for arguing that Satisfaction can serve as a dependent variable, but the major focus is on the other dependent variables as a function of Satistifaction.) The data are presented below.

	Group	Hit Direct	Hit Indirect
Female	Satisfied		
	Excellent	35	8
	Moderate	14	0
	Poor	22	2
	Unsatisfied		
	Excellent	55	11
	Moderate	16	5
	Poor	68	9
Male	Satisfied		
	Excellent	16	8
	Moderate	8	4
	Poor	11	2
	Unsatisfied		
	Excellent	31	15
	Moderate	16	7
	Poor	53	12

17.4   Collapse the Hansen and Swanson data into a simple two-dimensional table of Gender × Hit and compute a likelihood ratio χ^2. Interpret the results.

17.5   If Hit is taken as a dependent variable, does the Strong-Campbell do a better job for Males than Females? Answer this question with respect to the odds and odds ratios for both genders.

17.6   Now collapse the same data into a Gender × Satisfaction table and compute a likelihood ratio χ^2. What would you conclude from this analysis?

17.7   Ignore the Hit dimension in Hansen and Swanson's data and compute a log-linear analysis on the three-dimensional table that results. Interpret your results.

17.8 Use all four dimensions of the Hansen and Swanson data and compute the complete log-linear analysis. Interpret your results.

17.9 Compare the statistics you obtained in each of the analyses on this data set. How do they change, or not change, as additional variables are entered into the analysis?

17.10 What difference does it make in Exercises 17.4–17.9 if you treat some of the variables as dependent and others as independent, as opposed to regarding all variables alike?

Dabbs and Morris (1990) investigated the effects of elevated testosterone levels in a representative sample of adult U.S. males (mean age 37). Subjects were classified as High (upper 10%) or Normal on testosterone, as high or low on socioeconomic status (SES), and as engaging (or not engaging) in adult delinquency (among many behaviors). Their data follow.

	Low SES		High SES	
Delinquent	Normal Testosterone	High Testosterone	Normal Testosterone	High Testosterone
Yes	190	62	53	3
No	1104	140	1114	70

17.11 Calculate the odds of being classed as an adult delinquent for each of the categories in the preceding table.

17.12 What are the odds ratios of delinquency for the four SES/Testosterone groups in the preceding table?

17.13 Apply a log-linear model to the data from Dabbs and Morris and interpret the results.

17.14 Dabbs and Morris collected data on a number of other variables, including childhood delinquency, hard-drug use, and many sex partners. Why would it be inappropriate to create a dimension labeled Behavior (adult delinquency, childhood delinquency, hard-drug use, many sex partners) and use that as an additional variable in the analysis? In other words, what is wrong with analyzing SES × Testosterone × Behavior × Delinquency?

This chapter was based heavily on a study by Pugh (1983) on the blaming-the-victim phenomenon in rape cases. The complete data from Pugh is given below, adding the Gender of the judge as the final variable.

Gender(G)	Stigma (S) (Moral Character)	Fault(F)	Verdict(V) Guilty	Verdict(V) Not Guilty
Male	High	Low	17	4
		High	11	7
Male	Neutral	Low	36	4
		High	23	18
Male	Low	Low	10	6
		High	4	18
Female	High	Low	25	0
		High	12	4
Female	Neutral	Low	43	8
		High	42	23
Female	Low	Low	22	2
		High	13	6

17.15   Run the complete analysis on these data. What effect does adding Gender to the analysis produce? You can compare your conclusions against the results given in Pugh's paper.

17.16   In her analysis, Pugh decided to drop Gender × Fault and Stigma × Fault on the basis of parsimony. Can you defend their exclusion from the final model?

CHAPTER EIGHTEEN

Nonparametric and Distribution-free Statistical Tests

OBJECTIVES *To present nonparametric (distribution-free) procedures, which can be used for testing hypotheses but which rely on less restrictive assumptions about populations than do previously discussed tests.*

Contents

Parametric tests

Nonparametric tests,

Distribution-free tests

Most of the statistical procedures we have discussed throughout this book have involved both estimation of one or more parameters of the distribution of scores in the population(s) from which the data were sampled and assumptions concerning the shape of that distribution. For example, the t test uses the sample variance (s^2) as an estimate of the population variance (σ^2) and also requires the assumption that the population from which the sample was drawn is normal. Tests such as the t test, which involve either assumptions about specific parameters or their estimation, are referred to as **parametric tests**.

There is a class of tests, however, that does not rely on parameter estimation and/or distribution assumptions. Such tests are usually referred to as **nonparametric tests** or **distribution-free tests**. By and large, if a test is nonparametric it is also distribution-free, and in fact it is the distribution-free nature of the test that is most valuable to us. Although the two names are often used interchangeably, the tests will be referred to here as *distribution-free tests*.

The argument over the value of distribution-free tests has gone on for many years, and it certainly cannot be resolved in this chapter. Many people believe that for most cases, parametric tests are sufficiently robust to make distribution-free tests unnecessary. Others, however, believe just as strongly in the unsuitability of parametric tests and the overwhelming superiority of the distribution-free approach. [Bradley (1968) is a forceful and articulate advocate for the latter group.] Regardless of the position you take on this issue, it is important that you be familiar with the most common distribution-free procedures and with their underlying rationale. These tests are too prevalent in the experimental literature to be ignored.

The major advantage generally attributed to distribution-free tests is also the most obvious—they do not rely on any very seriously restrictive assumptions concerning the shape of the sampled population(s). This is not to say that distribution-free tests do not make *any* distribution assumptions, but only that the assumptions they do require are far more general than those required for the parametric tests. The exact null hypothesis being tested may depend, for example, on whether or not two populations are symmetric or have a similar shape. None of these tests, however, makes an a priori assumption about the specific shape of the distribution; that is, the validity of the test is not affected by whether or not the distribution of the variable in the population is normal. A parametric test, on the other hand, usually includes some type of normality assumption, and, if that assumption is false, the conclusions drawn from that test may be inaccurate. Another characteristic of distribution-free tests that often acts as an advantage is the fact that many of them, especially the ones discussed in this chapter, are more sensitive to medians than to means. Thus, if the nature of your data is such that you are interested primarily in medians, then the tests presented here may be particularly useful to you.

Those who argue in favor of using parametric tests in every case do not deny that distribution-free tests are more liberal in the assumptions they require. They argue, however, that the assumptions normally cited as being required of parametric tests are overly restrictive in practice and that the parametric tests are remarkably unaffected by violations of distribution assumptions.

The major disadvantage generally attributed to distribution-free tests is their lower power relative to the corresponding parametric test. In general, when the assumptions of the parametric test are met, the distribution-free test requires more observations than does the comparable parametric test for the same level of power. Thus, for a given set of data, the parametric test is more likely to lead to rejection of a false null hypothesis than is the corresponding distribution-free test. Moreover, even when the distribution assumptions are violated to a moderate degree, the parametric tests are thought to maintain their advantage. A number of studies, however, have shown that for perfectly reasonable data sets distribution-free tests may have greater power than the corresponding parametric test in some cases.

It is often claimed that the distribution-free procedures are particularly useful because of the simplicity of their calculations. However, for an experimenter who has just invested 6 months in collecting her data, a difference of 5 minutes in computation time hardly justifies using a less desirable test.

Distribution-free tests have one other advantage. Since many of them rank the raw scores and operate on those ranks, they offer a test of differences in central tendency that are not affected by one or a few very extreme scores (outliers). An extreme score in a set of data actually can make the parametric test *less* powerful, because it inflates the variance, and hence the error term, as well as biasing the mean by shifting it toward the outlier (the latter may increase *or* decrease the mean difference).

This chapter will be concerned with five of the most important distribution-free methods. The first three are analogues of the *t* test—one for independent samples and two for matched samples. The next two tests are distribution-free analogues of the analysis of variance—the first for k independent groups and the second for k repeated measures. Four of these tests are members of a class known as **rank-randomization tests** because they deal with ranked data and take as the distribution of their test statistic, when the null hypothesis is true, the theoretical distribution of randomly distributed ranks. Since these tests convert raw data to ranks, the shape of the underlying distribution of scores in the population becomes less important. Thus, both the sets

Rank-randomization tests

1   4   5   6   7   12   (data that might have come from a normal distribution)

and

1   2   3   20   21   22   (data that might have come from a bimodal distribution)

reduce to the ranks

1   2   3   4   5   6

18.1   WILCOXON'S RANK-SUM TEST

Wilcoxon rank-sum test

One of the most common and best-known distribution-free tests is the **Wilcoxon rank-sum test** for two independent samples. This test is often thought of as the distribution-free analogue of the t test for two independent samples, although it tests a slightly different, and broader, null hypothesis. Its null hypothesis is the hypothesis that the two samples were drawn at random from identical populations (not just populations with the same mean), but it is especially sensitive to population differences in central tendency. Thus, rejection of H_0 is generally interpreted to mean that the two distributions had different central tendencies, but it is possible that rejection actually resulted from some other difference between the populations. Notice that when we gain one thing (freedom from assumptions) we pay for it with something else (loss of specificity).

The logical basis of Wilcoxon's rank-sum test is particularly easy to understand. Assume that we have two independent treatment groups, with n_1 observations in group 1 and n_2 observations in group 2. Further assume that the null hypothesis is *false* to a very substantial degree and that the population from which group 1 scores have been sampled contains values generally lower than the population from which group 2 scores were drawn. Then, if we were to rank all $n_1 + n_2 = N$ scores from lowest to highest without regard to group membership, we would expect that the lower ranks generally would fall to group 1 scores and the higher ranks to group 2 scores. Going one step further, if we were to sum the ranks assigned to each group, the sum of the ranks in group 1 would be expected to be appreciably smaller than the sum of the ranks in group 2.

Now consider the opposite case, in which the null hypothesis is *true* and the scores for the two groups were sampled from identical populations. In this situation if we were to rank all N scores without regard to group membership, we would expect some low ranks and some high ranks in each group, and the sum of the ranks assigned to group 1 would be roughly equal to the sum of the ranks assigned to group 2. These situations are illustrated in Table 18.1.

TABLE 18.1
Illustration of typical results to be expected under H_0 false and H_0 true

			H_0 False								
			Group 1						Group 2		
Raw Data	10	12	17	13	19	20	30	26	25	33	18	27
Ranks (R_i)	1	2	4	3	6	7	11	9	8	12	5	10
ΣR_i			23						55		
			H_0 True								
			Group 1						Group 2		
Raw Data	22	28	32	19	24	33	18	25	29	20	23	34
Ranks (R_i)	4	8	10	2	6	11	1	7	9	3	5	12
ΣR_i			41				37				

Wilcoxon based his test on the logic just described, using the sum of the ranks in one of the groups as his test statistic. If that sum is too small relative to the other sum, we will reject the null hypothesis. More specifically, we will take as our test statistic the sum of the ranks assigned to the *smaller* group, or, if $n_1 = n_2$, the *smaller* of the two sums. Given this value, we can use tables of the Wilcoxon statistic (W_S) to test the null hypothesis.

To take a specific example, consider the following hypothetical data on the number of recent stressful life events reported by a group of Cardiac Patients in a local hospital and a control group of Orthopedic Patients in the same hospital. It is well known that stressful life events (marriage, new job, death of spouse, and so on) are associated with illness, and it is reasonable to expect that many cardiac patients would have experienced more recent stressful events than would orthopedic patients (who just happened to break an ankle while tearing down a building or a leg while playing touch football). It would appear from the data that this expectation is borne out. Since we have some reason to suspect that life stress scores probably are not symmetrically distributed in the population (especially for cardiac patients, if our research hypothesis is true), we will choose to use a distribution-free test. In this case, we will use the Wilcoxon rank-sum test because we have two independent groups.

	Cardiac Patients						**Orthopedic Patients**				
Raw Data	32	8	7	29	5	0	1	2	2	3	6
Ranks	11	9	8	10	6	1	2	3.5	3.5	5	7

To apply Wilcoxon's test we first rank all 11 scores from lowest to highest, assigning tied ranks to tied scores (see the discussion on ranking in Chapter 10). The orthopedic group is the smaller of the two and, if those patients generally have had fewer recent stressful life events, then the sum of the ranks assigned to that group should be relatively low. Letting W_S stand for the sum of the ranks in the smaller group (the orthopedic group), we find

$$W_S = 2 + 3.5 + 3.5 + 5 + 7 = 21$$

We can evaluate the obtained value of W_S by using Wilcoxon's table (Appendix W_S) which gives the *smallest* value of W_S that we would expect to obtain by chance if the null hypothesis were true. From Appendix W_S we find that for $n_1 = 5$ subjects in the smaller group and $n_2 = 6$ subjects in the larger group (n_1 is *always* the number of subjects in the smaller group), the entry for $\alpha = .025$ (one-tailed) is 18. This means that for a difference between groups to be significant at the one-tailed .025 level, or the two-tailed .05 level, W_S must be less than or equal to 18. Since we found W_S to be equal to 21, we cannot reject H_0. (By way of comparison, if we ran a t test on these data, ignoring the fact that one sample variance is almost 50 times the other and that the data suggest that our prediction of the shape of the distribution of cardiac scores may be correct, t would be 1.52 on 9 df, a nonsignificant result.)

The entries in Appendix W_S are for a one-tailed test and will lead to rejection of the null hypothesis only if the sum of the ranks for the smaller group is sufficiently *small.* It is possible, however, that the larger ranks could be congregated in the smaller group, in which case if H_0 is false, the sum of the ranks would be larger than chance expectation rather than smaller. One rather awkward way around this problem would be to rank the data all over again, this time ranking from high to low. If we did this, then the smaller ranks would now appear in the smaller group and we could proceed as before. We do not have to go through the process of reranking data, however. We can accomplish the same thing by using the symmetric properties of the distribution of the rank sum by calculating a statistic called W_S'. The statistic W_S' is the sum of the ranks for the smaller group that we would have found if we had reversed our ranking and ranked from highest to lowest:

$$W_S' = 2\overline{W} - W_S$$

where $2\overline{W} = n_1(n_1 + n_2 + 1)$ and is shown in the table in Appendix W_S. We can then evaluate W_S' against the tabled value and have a one-tailed test on the *upper* tail of the distribution. For a two-tailed test of H_0 (which is what we normally want), we calculate W_S and W_S', enter the table with whichever is smaller, and double the listed value of α.

To illustrate W_S and W_S', consider the two sets of data in Table 18.2. Notice that the two data sets exhibit the same degree of *extremeness*, in the sense that for the first set four of the five lowest ranks are in group 1, and in the second set four of the five highest ranks are in group 1. Moreover, W_S for set 1 is equal to W_S' for set 2, and vice versa. Thus, if we establish the rule that we will calculate both W_S and W_S' for the *smaller* group and refer the *smaller* of W_S and W_S' to the tables, we will come to the same conclusion with respect to the two data sets.

TABLE 18.2
Sample data to
Wilcoxon's rank-sum
test

Set 1	Group 1				Group 2				
X	2	15	16	19	18	23	25	37	82
Ranks	1	2	3	5	4	6	7	8	9

$W_S = 11$
$W_S' = 29$

Set 2	Group 1				Group 2				
X	60	40	24	21	23	18	15	14	4
Ranks	9	8	7	5	6	4	3	2	1

$W_S = 29$
$W_S' = 11$

THE NORMAL APPROXIMATION

Appendix W_S is suitable for all cases in which n_1 and n_2 are less than or equal to 25. For larger values of n_1 and/or n_2, we can make use of the fact that the distribution of W_S approaches a normal distribution as sample sizes increase. This distribution has

$$\text{Mean} = \frac{n_1(n_1 + n_2 + 1)}{2}$$

and

$$\text{Standard error} = \sqrt{\frac{n_1 n_2(n_1 + n_2 + 1)}{12}}$$

Since the distribution is normal and we know its mean and standard deviation (the stand error), we can calculate z:

$$z = \frac{\text{Statistic} - \text{Mean}}{\text{Standard deviation}} = \frac{W_S - \dfrac{n_1(n_1 + n_2 + 1)}{2}}{\sqrt{\dfrac{n_1 n_2(n_1 + n_2 + 1)}{12}}}$$

and obtain from the tables of the normal distribution an approximation of the true probability of a value of W_S at least as low as the one obtained. (It is immaterial whether we use W_S or W_S' in this situation, since they will produce equal values of z, differing only in sign.)

To illustrate the computations for the case in which the larger ranks fall in the smaller groups and to illustrate the use of the normal approximation (although we do not really need to use an approximation for such small sample sizes), consider the data in Table 18.3. These data are hypothetical (but not particularly unreasonable) data on the birthweight (in grams) of children born to mothers who did not seek prenatal care until the third trimester and those born to mothers who received prenatal care starting in the first trimester.

TABLE 18.3
Hypothetical data on birthweight of infants born to mothers with different levels of prenatal care

Beginning of Care			
Third Trimester		First Trimester	
Birthweight	Rank	Birthweight	Rank
1680	2	2940	10
3830	17	3380	16
3110	14	4900	18
2760	5	2810	9
1700	3	2800	8
2790	7	3210	15
3050	12	3080	13
2660	4	2950	11
1400	1		
2775	6		

$$W_S = \sum(\text{ranks in group 2}) = 100$$

$$W_S' = 2\overline{W} - W_S = 152 - 100 = 52$$

$$= \frac{W_S - \dfrac{n_1(n_1 + n_2 + 1)}{2}}{\sqrt{\dfrac{n_1 n_2(n_1 + n_2 + 1)}{12}}}$$

$$= \frac{100 - \dfrac{8(8 + 10 + 1)}{2}}{\sqrt{\dfrac{8(10)(8 + 10 + 1)}{12}}}$$

$$= \frac{100 - 76}{\sqrt{126.6667}}$$

$$= 2.13$$

For the data in Table 18.3 the sum of the ranks in the smaller group equals 100. From Appendix W_S we find $2\overline{W} = 152$, and thus $W_S' = 2\overline{W} - W_S = 52$. Since 52 is smaller than 100, we enter Appendix W_S with $W_S' = 52$, $n_1 = 8$, and $n_2 = 10$. (n_1 is defined as the smaller sample size.) Since we want a two-tailed test, we will double the tabled value of α. The critical value of W_S (or W_S') for a two-tailed test at $\alpha = .05$ is 53, meaning that only 5% of the time would we expect a value of W_S or W_S' less than or equal to 53 if H_0 is true. Our obtained value of W_S' is 52, which thus falls in the rejection region, and we will reject H_0. We will conclude that mothers who do not receive prenatal care until the third trimester tend to give birth to smaller babies. This probably does not mean that not having care until the third trimester *causes* smaller babies, but only that variables associated with delayed care (e.g., young mothers, poor nutrition, or poverty) are also associated with lower birthweight.

The use of the normal approximation for evaluating W_S is illustrated in the bottom part of Table 18.3. Here we find that $z = 2.13$. From Appendix z we find that the probability of W_S as large as 100 or as small as 52 (a z as extreme as ± 2.13) is $2(.0166) = .33$. Since this value is smaller than our traditional cutoff of $\alpha = .05$, we will reject H_0 and again conclude that there is sufficient evidence to say that failing to seek early prenatal care is related to lower birthweight. Note that both the exact solution and the normal approximation lead to the same conclusion with respect to H_0. (It would be instructive for you to calculate t for the same set of data.)

THE TREATMENT OF TIES

When the data contain tied scores, any test that relies on ranks is likely to be somewhat distorted. Ties can be dealt with in several different ways. You can assign tied ranks to tied scores (as we have been doing), you can flip a coin and assign consecutive ranks to tied scores, or you can assign untied ranks in whatever way will make it hardest to reject H_0. In actual practice, most people simply assign tied ranks. Although that may not be the statistically best way to proceed, it is clearly the most common and is the method that we will use here.

THE NULL HYPOTHESIS

Wilcoxon's rank-sum test evaluates the null hypothesis that the two sets of scores were sampled from identical populations. This is broader than the null hypothesis tested by the corresponding t test, which dealt specifically with means (primarily as a result of the underlying assumptions that ruled out other sources of difference). If the two populations are assumed to have the same shape and dispersion, then the null hypothesis tested by the rank-sum test will actually deal with the central tendency (in this case the medians) of the two populations, and if the populations are also symmetric, the test will be a test of means. In any event, the rank-sum test is particularly sensitive to differences in central tendency.

THE MANN–WHITNEY U STATISTIC

Mann–Whitney U test

A common competitor to the Wilcoxon rank-sum test is the **Mann–Whitney U test**. We do not need to discuss the Mann–Whitney test at any length, however, because the two are equivalent tests, and there is a perfect linear relationship between W_S and U. The only reason for its inclusion here is that you may run across a reference to U, and therefore you should know what it is. Very simply,

$$U = \frac{n_1(n_1 + 2n_2 + 1)}{2} - W_S$$

From this formula we can see that for any given set of sample sizes, U and W_S differ by only a constant (as do their critical values). Since we have this relationship between the two statistics, we can always convert U to W_S and evaluate W_S using Appendix W_S.

18.2   WILCOXON'S MATCHED-PAIRS SIGNED-RANKS TEST

Wilcoxon is credited with developing not only the most popular distribution-free test for independent groups, but also the most popular test for matched groups (or paired scores). This test is the distribution-free analogue of the t test for related samples, and it tests the null hypothesis that two related (matched) samples were drawn either from identical populations or from symmetric populations with the same mean. More specifically, it tests the null hypothesis that the distribution of difference scores (in the population) is symmetric about zero. This is the same hypothesis tested by the corresponding t test when that test's normality assumption is met.

Wilcoxon matched-pairs signed-ranks test

The development of the logic behind the **Wilcoxon matched-pairs signed-ranks test** is as straightforward as it was for his rank-sum test and can be illustrated with a simple example. Assume that we want to test the often-stated hypothesis that a long-range program of running will reduce blood pressure. To test this hypothesis, we measure the blood pressure of a number of subjects, ask them to engage in a systematic program of running for 6 months, and again test their blood pressure at the end of that period. Our dependent variable will be the change in blood pressure over the 6-month interval. If running does reduce blood pressure, we would expect most of the subjects to show a lower reading the second time, and thus a positive pre–post difference. We also would expect that those whose blood pressure actually went up (and thus have a negative pre–post difference) would be only *slightly* higher. On the other hand, if running is worthless as a method of controlling blood pressure, then about one-half of the difference scores will be positive and one-half will be negative, and the positive differences will be about as large as the negative ones. In other words, if H_0 is really true, we would no longer expect most changes to be in the predicted direction with only small changes in the unpredicted direction.

As is illustrated in the following numerical example, in carrying out the Wilcoxon matched-pairs signed-ranks test we first calculate the difference score for each pair of measurements. We then rank all difference scores *without* regard to the sign of the difference, then assign the algebraic sign of the differences to the ranks themselves, and finally sum the positive and negative ranks separately. The test statistic (T) is taken as the smaller of the absolute values (i.e., ignoring the sign) of the two sums, and is evaluated against the tabled entries in Appendix T. (It is important to note that in calculating T we attach algebraic signs to the ranks only for convenience. We could just as easily, for example, circle those ranks that went with improvement and underline those that went with deterioration. We are merely trying to differentiate between the two cases.)

Assume that the study previously described produced the following data on systolic blood pressure before and after the 6-month training session:

Before:	130	170	125	170	130	130	145	160
After:	120	163	120	135	143	136	144	120
Difference ($B - A$):	10	7	5	35	−13	−6	1	40
Rank of Difference:	5	4	2	7	6	3	1	8
Signed Rank:	5	4	2	7	−6	−3	1	8

$$T_+ = \Sigma(\text{positive ranks}) = 27$$

$$T_- = \Sigma(\text{negative ranks}) = -9$$

The first two rows contain the subjects' blood pressures as measured before and after a 6-month program of running. The third row contains the difference scores, obtained by subtracting the "after" score from the "before." Notice that only two subjects showed a negative change—increased blood pressure. Since these difference scores do not appear to reflect a population distribution that is anywhere near normal, we have chosen to use a distribution-free test. In the fourth row, all the difference scores have been ranked without regard to the direction of the change; in the fifth row, the appropriate sign has been appended to the ranks to discriminate those subjects whose blood pressure decreased from those whose blood pressure increased. At the bottom of the table we see the sum of the positive and negative ranks (T_+ and T_-). Since T is defined as the smaller absolute value of T_+ and T_-, $T = 9$.

To evaluate T we refer to Appendix T, a portion of which is shown in Table 18.4. This table has a format somewhat different from that of the other tables we have seen. The easiest way to understand what the entries in the table represent is by way of an analogy. Suppose that to test the fairness of a coin you were going to flip it eight times and reject the null hypothesis, at $\alpha = .05$ (one-tailed), if there were too few heads. Out of eight flips of a coin there is no set of outcomes that has a probability of *exactly* .05 under H_0. The probability of one or fewer heads is .0352, and the probability of two or fewer heads is .1445. Thus, if we want to work at $\alpha = .05$, we can either reject for one or fewer heads, in which case the probability of a Type I error is actually .0352 (less than .05), or we can reject for two or fewer heads, in which case the probability of a Type I error is actually .1445 (very much greater than .05). The same kind of problem arises with T because it, like the binomial distribution that gave us the probabilities of heads and tails, is a discrete distribution.[†]

In Appendix T we find that for a one-tailed test at $\alpha = .025$ (or a two-tailed test at $\alpha = .05$) with $n = 8$, the entries are 3 0.0195 and 4 0.0273. This tells us that if we want to work at a (one-tailed) $\alpha = .025$, we can either reject H_0 for $T \leq 3$ (in which case α actually equals .0195) or we can reject for $T \leq 4$ (in which case the true value of α is .0273). Since we want a two-tailed test, the probabilities should be doubled to 3 0.0390 and 4 0.0546. Since we obtained a T value of 9, we would not reject H_0, whichever cutoff we chose. We will conclude therefore that we have no reason to doubt that blood pressure is unaffected by a short (6-month) period of daily running. It is going to take a lot more than 6 months to make up for a lifetime of dissipated habits.

[†] A similar situation arises for the Wilcoxon rank-sum test, but the standard tables for that test give only the conservative cutoff.

TABLE 18.4
Critical lower-tail values of T and their associated probabilities (abbreviated version of Appendix T)

	\multicolumn{8}{c}{Nominal α (One-Tailed)}
	\multicolumn{2}{c}{.05}	\multicolumn{2}{c}{.025}	\multicolumn{2}{c}{.01}	\multicolumn{2}{c}{.005}
N	T	α	T	α	T	α	T	α
5	0	.0313						
	1	.0625						
6	2	.0469	0	.0156				
	3	.0781	1	.0313				
7	3	.0391	2	.0234	0	.0078		
	4	.0547	3	.0391	1	.0156		
8	5	.0391	3	.0195	1	.0078	0	.0039
	6	.0547	4	.0273	2	.0117	1	.0078
9	8	.0488	5	.0195	3	.0098	1	.0039
	9	.0645	6	.0273	4	.0137	2	.0059
10	10	.0420	8	.0244	5	.0098	3	.0049
	11	.0527	9	.0322	6	.0137	4	.0068
11	13	.0415	10	.0210	7	.0093	5	.0049
	14	.0508	11	.0269	8	.0122	6	.0068
...	...		...		...		...	

TIES

Ties can occur in the data in two different ways. One way would be for a subject to have the same before and after scores, leading to a difference score of 0, which has no sign. In this case, we normally eliminate that subject from consideration and reduce the sample size accordingly, although this leads to some bias in the data.

In addition, we could have tied difference scores that lead to tied rankings. If both the tied scores are of the same sign, we can break the ties in any way we wish (or assign tied ranks) without affecting the final outcome. If the scores are of opposite signs, we normally assign tied ranks and proceed as usual.

THE NORMAL APPROXIMATION

When the sample size is larger than 50, which is the limit for Appendix T, a normal approximation is available to evaluate T. For larger sample sizes, we know that the sampling distribution is approximately normally distributed with

$$\text{Mean} = \frac{n(n+1)}{4} \quad \text{and} \quad \text{Standard error} = \sqrt{\frac{n(n+1)(2n+1)}{24}}$$

Thus we can calculate

$$z = \frac{T - \dfrac{n(n+1)}{4}}{\sqrt{\dfrac{n(n+1)(2n+1)}{24}}}$$

and evaluate z using Appendix z. The procedure is directly analogous to that used with the rank-sum test and will not be repeated here.

Another interesting example of the use of Wilcoxon's signed-ranks matched-pairs test is found in a study by Manning, Hall, and Gold (1990). These investigators were interested in studying the role of glucose in memory, in particular its effects on performance of memory tasks for elderly people. There has been considerable suggestion in the literature that subjects with poor glucose regulation show poor memory and decreased performance on other kinds of neuropsychological tests.

Manning et al. asked 17 elderly volunteers to perform a battery of tests early in the morning after having drunk an 8-ounce lemon-flavored drink sweetened with either glucose or saccharin. Subjects performed these tasks under both conditions, so we have matched sets of data. On one of these tasks, for which data were available on only 16 people, subjects were read a narrative passage and were asked for recall of that passage 5 minutes later. The dependent variable was not explicitly defined, but we will assume that it was the number of specific propositions recalled from the passage.

The data given in Table 18.5 were generated to produce roughly the same means, standard deviations, and test results as the data found by Manning et al. From Appendix T with $N = 16$ and a two-tailed test at $\alpha = .05$, we find that the critical value of T is 35 or 36, depending on whether you prefer to err on the liberal or conservative side. In either event, our value of $T_{\text{obt}} = 14.5$ is less than either and is therefore significant. This is the same conclusion that Manning et al. came to when they reported improved recall in the Glucose condition.

TABLE 18.5 Recall scores for elderly subjects after drinking a glucose or saccharin solution

Subject	1	2	3	4	5	6	7	8	9	10	11	12	13	14	15	16
Glucose	0	10	9	4	8	6	9	3	12	10	15	9	5	6	10	6
Saccharin	1	9	6	2	5	5	7	2	8	8	11	3	6	8	8	4
Difference	−1	1	3	2	3	1	2	1	4	2	4	6	−1	−2	2	2
Positive Ranks		3	12.5	8.5	12.5	3	8.5	3	14.5	8.5	14.5	16			8.5	8.5
Negative Ranks	−3												−3	−8.5		

$$T_+ = \Sigma(\text{positive ranks}) = 121$$

$$T_- = \Sigma(\text{negative ranks}) = 14.5$$

As an example of using the normal approximation, we can solve for the normal variate (z score) associated with a T of 14.5 for $N = 16$. In this case,

$$z = \frac{T - \dfrac{n(n+1)}{4}}{\sqrt{\dfrac{n(n+1)(2n+1)}{24}}} = \frac{14.5 - \dfrac{(16)(17)}{4}}{\sqrt{\dfrac{(16)(17)(33)}{24}}} = -2.77$$

which has a two-tailed probability under H_0 of .0056.

18.3   THE SIGN TEST

Sign test

The Wilcoxon matched-pairs signed-ranks test is an excellent distribution-free test for differences with matched samples. Unlike Student's t test, it makes less than maximum use of the data, in that it substitutes ranks for raw score differences, thus losing some of the subtle differences among the data points. When the assumptions of Student's t hold, it also has somewhat less power. When those assumptions do not hold, however, it may have greater power. A test that goes even further in the direction of gaining freedom from assumptions at the cost of power is the **sign test**. This test loses even more information by ignoring the values altogether and looking only at the sign of the differences. It also loses even more power. We discussed the test briefly in Chapter 6 but will give a second example here for completeness.

We can use the example from Manning et al. (1990) in the preceding section. It might be argued that this is a good candidate for such a test because the Wilcoxon was forced to rely on a large number of tied ranks. This argument is not all that persuasive because the results would have been the same no matter how you had broken the tied ranks, but it would be comforting to know that Manning et al.'s results are sufficiently solid that a sign test would also reveal their statistical significance.

The data from Manning et al. are repeated in Table 18.6. From these data you can see that 13 out of 16 subjects showed higher recall under the Glucose condition, whereas only 3 of the 16 showed higher recall under the Saccharine condition. The sign test consists simply of asking the question of whether a 3-to-13 split would be likely to occur if recall under the two conditions were equally good.

TABLE 18.6 Data from Manning et al. (1990)

Subject:	1	2	3	4	5	6	7	8	9	10	11	12	13	14	15	16
Glucose:	0	10	9	4	8	6	9	3	12	10	15	9	5	6	10	6
Saccharin:	1	9	6	2	5	5	7	2	8	8	11	3	6	8	8	4
Difference:	−1	1	3	2	3	1	2	1	4	2	4	6	−1	−2	2	2
Sign:	−	+	+	+	+	+	+	+	+	+	+	+	−	−	+	+

This text could be set up in several ways. We could solve for the binomal probability of 13 or more successes out of 16 trials given $p = .50$. From standard tables, or the binomial formula, we would find

$$p(13) = .0085$$
$$p(14) = .0018$$
$$p(15) = .0002$$
$$p(16) = .0000$$
$$\text{Sum}\quad .0105$$

Since the binomial distribution is symmetric for $p = .50$, we would then double this probability to obtain the two-tailed probability, which in this case is .021. Since this probability is less than .05, we would reject the null hypothesis and conclude that recall is greater in the Glucose condition.

We could also solve for this probability by using the normal approximation given in Chapter 5. We would again come to essentially the same result, differing only by the accuracy of the approximation.

Yet a third possibility, which is logically equivalent to the others, is to use a goodness of fix χ^2 test. In this case we would take 8.00 as our expected frequency for each cell, since if the two conditions lead to equal recall we would expect half of our 16 subjects to do better by chance under each condition. We would then set up the table

	Glucose	Saccharin
Observed	13	3
Expected	8	8

$$\chi^2 = \sum \frac{(O - E)^2}{E} = \frac{(13 - 8)^2}{8} + \frac{(3 - 8)^2}{8} = 6.25$$

The critical values of χ^2 on 1 df is 3.84, so we can reject H_0 and again conclude that the difference is significant. (The probability of $\chi^2 \geq 6.25$ is .0124, which agrees well enough, given the small sample size, with the exact binomial probability.) All three of these tests are more or less equivalent, and you can use whichever is most convenient.

18.4 KRUSKAL–WALLIS ONE-WAY ANALYSIS OF VARIANCE

Kruskal–Wallis one-way analysis of variance

The **Kruskal–Wallis one-way analysis of variance** is a direct generalization of the Wilcoxon rank-sum test to the case in which we have three or more independent groups. As such, it is the distribution-free analogue of the one-way analysis of variance discussed in Chapter 11. It tests the hypothesis that all samples were drawn from identical populations and is particularly sensitive to differences in central tendency.

To perform the Kruskal–Wallis test, we simply rank all scores without regard to group membership and then compute the sum of the ranks for each group. The sums are denoted by R_i. If the null hypothesis is true, we would expect the R_is to be more or less equal (aside from difference due to the size of the samples). A measure of the degree to which the R_i differ from one another is provided by

$$H = \frac{12}{N(N + 1)} \sum_{i=1}^{k} \frac{R_i^2}{n_i} - 3(N + 1)$$

where

k = the number of groups

n_i = the number of observations in group$_i$

R_i = the sum of the ranks in group$_i$

$N = \Sigma n_i$ = total sample size

H is then evaluated against the χ^2 distribution $k - 1$ df.

As an example, assume that the data in Table 18.7 represent the number of simple arithmetic problems (out of 85) solved (correctly or incorrectly) in 1 hour by subjects given a depressant drug, a stimulant drug, or a placebo. Notice that in the Depressant group three of the subjects were too depressed to do much of anything, and in the Stimulant group three of the subjects ran up against the limit of 85 available problems. These data are decidedly nonnormal, and we will use the Kruskal–Wallis test. The calculations are shown in the lower part of the table. The obtained value of H is 10.36, which can be treated as a χ^2 on $3 - 1 = 2$ df. The critical value of $\chi^2_{.05}(2)$ is found in Appendix χ^2, to be 5.99. Since $10.36 > 5.99$, we can reject H_0 and conclude that the three drugs lead to different rates of performance.

TABLE 18.7
Kruskal–Wallis test applied to data on problem solving

Depressant		Stimulant		Placebo	
Score	Rank	Score	Rank	Score	Rank
55	9	73	15	61	11
0	1.5	85	18	54	8
1	3	51	7	80	16
0	1.5	63	12	47	5
50	6	85	18		
60	10	85	18		
44	4	66	13		
		69	14		
R_i	35		115		40

$$H = \frac{12}{N(N+1)} \sum_{i=1}^{k} \frac{R_i^2}{n_i} - 3(N+1)$$

$$= \frac{12}{19(20)} \left(\frac{35^2}{7} + \frac{115^2}{8} + \frac{40^2}{4} \right) - 3(19+1)$$

$$= \frac{12}{380} (2228.15) - 60$$

$$= 70.36 - 60$$

$$= 10.36$$

$$\chi^2_{.05}(2) = 5.99$$

18.5   FRIEDMAN'S RANK TEST FOR k CORRELATED SAMPLES

Friedman's rank test for k correlated samples

The last test to be discussed in this chapter is the distribution-free analogue of the one-way repeated-measures analysis of variance, **Friedman's rank test for k correlated samples**. It was developed by the well-known economist Milton Friedman—in the days before he was a well-known economist. This test is closely related to a standard repeated-measures analysis of variance applied to ranks instead of raw scores. It is a test on the null hypothesis that the scores for each treatment were drawn from identical populations, and it is especially sensitive to population differences in central tendency.

Assume that we want to test the hypothesis that the judged quality of a lecture is related to the number of visual aids used. The experimeter obtains 17 people who frequently give lectures to local business groups on a variety of topics. Each lecturer delivers the same lecture to three different, but equivalent, audiences—once with no visual aids, once with a few transparencies to illustrate major points, and once with transparencies and flip charts to illustrate every point made. At the end of each lecture, the audience is asked to rate the lecture on a 75-point scale, and the mean rating across all members of the audience is taken as the dependent variable. Since the same lecturers serve under all three conditions, we would expect the data to be correlated. Terrible lecturers are terrible no matter how many visual aids they use. Hypothetical data are presented in Table 18.8, in which a higher score represents a more favorable rating. The ranking of the raw scores *within each subject* are shown in parentheses.

If the null hypothesis is true, we would expect the rankings to be randomly distributed within each lecturer. Thus, one lecturer might do best with no visual aids, another might do best with many aids, and so on. If this were the case, the sum of the rankings in each condition (column) would be approximately equal. On the other hand, if a few visual aids were to lead to the most popular lecture, then most lecturers would have their highest rating under that condition, and the sum of the rankings for the three conditions would be decidedly unequal.

To apply Friedman's test, we rank the raw scores for each lecturer separately and then sum the rankings for each condition. We then evaluate the variability of the sums by computing

$$\chi_F^2 = \frac{12}{Nk(k+1)} \sum_{i=1}^{k} R_i^2 - 3N(k+1)$$

where

$$R_i = \text{the sum of the ranks for the } i\text{th condition}$$

$$N = \text{the number of subjects (lecturers)}$$

$$k = \text{the number of conditions}$$

This value of χ_F^2 can be evaluated with respect to the standard χ^2 distribution on $k - 1$ *df*.

For the data in Table 18.8, $\chi_F^2 = 10.94$ on 2 *df*. Since $\chi_{.05}^2(2) = 5.99$, we will reject H_0 and conclude that the judged quality of a lecture differs as a function of the degree to which visual aids are included. The data suggest that some visual aids are helpful, but that too many of them can detract from what the lecturer is saying. [Note: The null hypothesis we have just tested says nothing about differences among subjects (lecturers), and in fact subject differences are completely eliminated by the ranking procedure.]

TABLE 18.8
Hypothetical data on
rated quality of
lectures

Lecturer	Number of Visual Aids		
	None	Few	Many
1	50(1)	58(3)	54(2)
2	32(2)	37(3)	25(1)
3	60(1)	70(3)	63(2)
4	58(2)	60(3)	55(1)
5	41(1)	66(3)	59(2)
6	36(2)	40(3)	28(1)
7	26(3)	25(2)	20(1)
8	49(1)	60(3)	50(2)
9	72(1)	73(2)	75(3)
10	49(2)	54(3)	42(1)
11	52(2)	57(3)	47(1)
12	36(2)	42(3)	29(1)
13	37(3)	34(2)	31(1)
14	58(3)	50(1)	56(2)
15	39(1)	48(3)	44(2)
16	25(2)	29(3)	18(1)
17	51(1)	63(2)	68(3)
	30	45	27

$$\chi_F^2 = \frac{12}{Nk(k+1)} \sum_{i=1}^{k} R_i^2 - 3N(k+1)$$

$$= \frac{12}{(17)(3)(4)}(30^2 + 45^2 + 27^2) - 3(17)(4)$$

$$= \frac{12}{204}(3654) - 204$$

$$= 214.94 - 204$$

$$= 10.94$$

KEY TERMS

Paramatric tests (introduction)

Nonparametric tests (introduction)

Distribution-free tests (introduction)

Rank-randomization tests (introduction)

Wilicoxon rank-sum test (18.1)

Mann–Whitney U test (18.1)

Wilcoxon matched-pairs signed-ranks test
(18.2)

Sign test (18.3)

Kruskal–Wallis one-way analysis of
variance (18.4)

Friedman's rank test for k correlated samples
(18.5)

EXERCISES

18.1   McConaughy (1980) has argued that younger children organize stories in terms of simple descriptive ("and then ...") models, whereas older children incorporate causal statements and social inferences. Suppose that we asked two groups of children differing in age to summarize a story they just read. We then counted the number of statements in the summary that can be classed as inferences. The data follow:

Younger Children:	0	1	0	3	2	5	2
Older Children:	4	7	6	4	8	7	

(a) Analyze these data using the two-tailed rank-sum test.
(b) What can you conclude?

18.2   Kapp, Frysinger, Gallagher, and Hazelton (1979) have demonstrated that lesions in the amygdala can reduce certain responses commonly associated with fear (e.g., decreases in heart rate). If fear is really reduced, then it should be more difficult to train an avoidance response in lesioned animals because the aversiveness of the stimulus will be reduced. Assume two groups of rabbits: one group has lesions in the amygdala, and the other is an untreated control group. The following data represent number of trials to learn an avoidance response for each animal:

Group with Lesions:	15	14	15	8	7	22	36	19	14	18	17
Control Group:	9	4	9	10	6	6	4	5	9		

(a) Analyze the data using the Wilcoxon rank-sum test (two-tailed).
(b) What can you conclude?

18.3   Repeat the analysis in Exercise 18.2 using the normal approximation.

18.4   Repeat the analysis in Exercise 18.2 using the appropriate one-tailed test.

18.5   Nurcombe and Fitzhenry-Coor (1979) have argued that training in diagnostic techniques should lead a clinician to generate (and test) more hypotheses in coming to a decision about a case. Suppose we take 10 psychiatric residents who are just beginning their residency and ask them to watch a videotape of an interview and to record their thoughts on the case every few minutes. We then count the number of hypotheses each resident includes in his or her written remarks. The experiment is repeated at the end of the residency with a comparable videotape. The data follow:

Subject:	1	2	3	4	5	6	7	8	9	10
Before:	8	4	2	2	4	8	3	1	3	9
After:	7	9	3	6	3	10	6	7	8	7

(a) Analyze the data using Wilcoxon's matched-pairs signed-ranks test.
(b) What can you conclude?

18.6   Refer to Exercise 18.5.
(a) Repeat the analysis using the normal approximation.
(b) How well do the two answers (18.5a and 18.6a) agree? Why do they not agree exactly?

18.7   It has been argued that first-born children tend to be more independent than later-born children. Suppose we develop a 25-point scale of independence and rate each of 20 first-born children and their second-born siblings using our scale. We do this when both siblings are adults, thus eliminating obvious age effects. The data on independence are as follows (a higher score means that the person is more independent):

Sibling Pair:	1	2	3	4	5	6	7	8	9	10	11	12	13	14	15	16	17	18	19	20
First Born:	12	18	13	17	8	15	16	5	8	12	13	5	14	20	19	17	2	5	15	18
Second Born:	10	12	15	13	9	12	13	8	10	8	8	9	8	10	14	11	7	7	13	12

(a) Analyze the data using Wilcoxon's matched-pairs signed-ranks test.

(b) What can you conclude?

18.8 Rerun the analysis in Exercise 18.7 using the normal approximation.

18.9 The results in Exercise 18.7 are not quite as clear-cut as we might like. Plot the differences as a function of the first-born's score. What does this figure suggest?

18.10 What is the difference between the null hypothesis tested by Wilcoxon's rank-sum test and the corresponding t test?

18.11 What is the difference between the null hypothesis tested by Wilcoxon's matched-pairs signed-ranks test and the corresponding t test?

18.12 One of the arguments put forth in favor of distribution-free tests is that they are more appropriate for ordinal-scale data. This issue was addressed earlier in the book in a different context. Give a reason why this argument is not a good one.

18.13 Why is rejection of the null hypothesis using a t test a more specific statement than rejection of the null hypothesis using the appropriate distribution-free test?

18.14 Three rival professors teaching English I all claim the honor of having the best students. To settle the issue, eight students are randomly drawn from each class and are given the same exam, which is graded by a neutral professor who does not know from which class the students came. The data follow:

Professor A:	82	71	56	58	63	64	62	53
Professor B:	55	88	85	83	71	70	68	72
Professor C:	65	54	66	68	72	78	65	73

Run the appropriate test and draw the appropriate conclusions.

18.15 A psychologist operating a group home for delinquent adolescents needs to show that it is successful at reducing delinquency. He samples nine adolescents living at home whom the police have identified as having problems, nine similar adolescents living in foster homes, and nine adolescents living in the group home. As an indicator variable, he uses truancy (number of days truant in the past semester), which is readily obtained from school records. On the basis of the following data, draw the appropriate conclusions.

Natural Home:	15	18	19	14	5	8	12	13	7
Foster Home:	16	14	20	22	19	5	17	18	12
Group Home:	10	13	14	11	7	3	4	18	2

18.16 As an alternative method of evaluating a group home, suppose that we take 12 adolescents who have been declared delinquent. We take the number of days truant (1) during the month before they are placed in the home, (2) during the month they live in the home, and (3) during the month after they leave the home. The data follow:

Adolescent:	1	2	3	4	5	6	7	8	9	10	11	12
Before:	10	12	12	19	5	13	20	8	12	10	8	18
During:	5	8	13	10	10	8	16	4	14	3	3	16
After:	8	7	10	12	8	7	12	5	9	5	3	2

Apply Friedman's test. What do you conclude?

18.17 What advantage does the study described in Exercise 18.16 have over the study described in Exercise 18.15?

18.18 It would be possible to apply Friedman's test to the data in Exercise 18.5. What would we lose if we did?

18.19 For the data in Exercise 18.5, we could say that 3 out of 10 residents used fewer hypotheses the second time and 7 used more. We could test this with χ^2. How would this differ from Friedman's test applied to those data?

18.20 The history of statistical hypothesis testing really began with a tea-tasting experiment (Fisher, 1935), so it seems fitting for this book to end with one. The owner of a small tearoom does not think that people really can tell the difference between the first cup made with a given tea bag and the second and third cups made with the same bag (perhaps that is why it is still a *small* tearoom). He chooses eight different brands of tea bags, makes three cups of tea with each, and then has a group of customers rate each cup on a 20-point scale (without knowing which cup is which). The data are shown here, with higher ratings indicating better tea.

Tea Brands	First Cup	Second Cup	Third Cup
1	8	3	2
2	15	14	4
3	16	17	12
4	7	5	4
5	9	3	6
6	8	9	4
7	10	3	4
8	12	10	2

Using Friedman's test, draw the appropriate conclusions.

APPENDICES

APPENDICES

APPENDIX: DATA SET

Howell and Huessy (1985) reported on a study of 386 children who had, and had not, exhibited symptoms of attention deficit disorder (ADD)—previously known as hyperkinesis or minimal brain dysfunction—during childhood. In 1965 teachers of all second-grade school children in a number of schools in northwestern Vermont were asked to complete a questionnaire for each of their students dealing with behaviors commonly associated with ADD. Questionnaires on these same children were again completed when the children were in the fourth and fifth grades and, for purposes of this data set only, those three scores were averaged to produce a score labeled ADDSC. The higher the score, the more ADD-like behaviors the child exhibited. At the end of ninth grade and again at the end of twelfth grade, information on the performances of these children was obtained from school records. Some of these variables are presented in the accompanying table for a sample of 88 of these students. These data offer the opportunity to examine questions about whether later behavior can be predicted from earlier behavior and to examine academically related variables and their interrelationships. The data are referred to in many of the exercises at the end of each chapter. A description of each variable follows.

ADDSC	Average of the three ADD-like behavior scores obtained in elementary school
GENDER	1 = male; 2 = female
REPEAT	1 = repeated at least one grade; 0 = did not repeat a grade
IQ	IQ obtained from a group-administered IQ test
ENGL	Level of English in ninth grade: 1 = college prep; 2 = general; 3 = remedial
ENGG	Grade in English in ninth grade: 4 = A; 3 = B; and so on
GPA	Grade point average in ninth grade
SOCPROB	Social problems in ninth grade: 1 = yes; 0 = no
DROPOUT	1 = dropped out before completing high school; 0 = did not drop out

APPENDIX: COMPUTER DATA SETS

Your course instructor has a disk containing a number of data sets. These represent a combination of data from actual studies, data that have been created to mimic the data from actual studies, data from examples in the book, and two sets of random numbers that have been generated to illustrate certain points.

All of these data sets are standard ASCII files, meaning that they can be read by virtually all computer programs and can be edited if necessary with standard editors available on any computer system. In particular, they can be edited by any word processor that can produce an ASCII file (sometimes referred to as a text file or a DOS file).

These data sets are the focus of a number of homework exercises in many different chapters. The descriptions that follow are intended to explain the study from which the data were drawn and to describe how the data are arranged in the data set. You should refer to these descriptions whenever you need to write programs to analyze the data.

ADD.dat   The data in this file come from a study by Howell and Huessy (1985). Those authors reported on a study of 386 children who had, or had not, exhibited symptoms of attention deficit disorder (ADD)—previously called hyperkinesis or minimal brain dysfunction— during childhood. In 1965 teachers of all second-grade school children in a number of schools in northwestern Vermont were asked to complete a questionnaire for each of their students dealing with behaviors commonly associated with ADD. Questionnaires on these same children were again completed when the children were in the fourth and fifth grades, and, for purposes of this data set only, those three scores were averaged to produce a score labeled ADDSC. The higher the score, the more ADD-like behaviors the child exhibited. At the end of ninth grade and again at the end of twelfth grade, information on the performance of these children was obtained from school records. Some of these variables are presented in ADD.dat for a sample of 88 of these students. The data offer the opportunity to examine questions about whether later behavior can be predicted from earlier behavior and to examine academically related variables and their interrelationships.

ADDSC	GENDER	REPEAT	IQ	ENGL	ENGG	GPA	SOCPROB	DROPOUT
45	1	0	111	2	3	2.60	0	0
50	1	0	102	2	3	2.75	0	0
49	1	0	108	2	4	4.00	0	0
55	1	0	109	2	2	2.25	0	0
39	1	0	118	2	3	3.00	0	0
68	1	1	79	2	2	1.67	0	1
69	1	1	88	2	2	2.25	1	1
56	1	0	102	2	4	3.40	0	0
58	1	0	105	3	1	1.33	0	0
48	1	0	92	2	4	3.50	0	0
34	1	0	131	2	4	3.75	0	0
50	2	0	104	1	3	2.67	0	0
85	1	0	83	2	3	2.75	1	0
49	1	0	84	2	2	2.00	0	0
51	1	0	85	2	3	2.75	0	0
53	1	0	110	2	2	2.50	0	0
36	2	0	121	1	4	3.55	0	0
62	2	0	120	2	3	2.75	0	0
46	2	0	100	2	4	3.50	0	0
50	2	0	94	2	2	2.75	1	1
47	2	0	89	1	2	3.00	0	0
50	2	0	93	2	4	3.25	0	0
44	2	0	128	2	4	3.30	0	0
50	2	0	84	2	3	2.75	0	0
29	2	0	127	1	4	3.75	0	0
49	2	0	106	2	3	2.75	0	0
26	1	0	137	2	3	3.00	0	0
85	1	1	82	3	2	1.75	1	1
53	1	0	106	2	3	2.75	1	0
53	1	0	109	2	2	1.33	0	0
72	1	0	91	2	2	0.67	0	0
35	1	0	111	2	2	2.25	0	0
42	1	0	105	2	2	1.75	0	0
37	1	0	118	2	4	3.25	0	0
46	1	0	103	3	2	1.75	0	0
48	1	0	101	1	3	3.00	0	0
46	1	0	101	3	3	3.00	0	0
49	1	1	95	2	3	3.00	0	0
65	1	1	108	2	3	3.25	0	0
52	1	0	95	3	3	2.25	1	0
75	1	1	98	2	1	1.00	0	1
58	1	0	82	2	3	2.50	0	1
43	2	0	100	1	3	3.00	0	0
60	2	0	100	2	3	2.40	0	0

ADDSC	GENDER	REPEAT	IQ	ENGL	ENGG	GPA	SOCPROB	DROPOUT
43	1	0	107	1	2	2.00	0	0
51	1	0	95	2	2	2.75	0	0
70	1	1	97	2	3	2.67	1	1
69	1	1	93	2	2	2.00	0	0
65	1	1	81	1	2	2.00	0	0
63	2	0	89	2	2	1.67	0	0
44	2	0	111	2	4	3.00	0	0
61	2	1	95	2	1	1.50	0	1
40	2	0	106	2	4	3.75	0	0
62	2	0	83	3	1	0.67	0	0
59	1	0	81	2	2	1.50	0	0
47	2	0	115	1	4	4.00	0	0
50	2	0	112	2	3	3.00	0	0
50	2	0	92	2	3	2.33	0	0
65	2	0	85	2	2	1.75	0	0
54	2	0	95	3	2	3.00	0	0
44	2	0	115	2	4	3.75	0	0
66	2	0	91	2	4	2.67	1	1
34	2	0	107	1	4	3.50	0	0
74	2	0	102	2	0	0.67	0	0
57	2	1	86	3	3	2.25	0	0
60	2	0	96	1	3	3.00	1	0
36	2	0	114	2	3	3.50	0	0
50	1	0	105	2	2	1.75	0	0
60	1	0	82	2	1	1.00	0	0
45	1	0	120	2	3	3.00	0	0
55	1	0	88	2	1	1.00	0	1
44	1	0	90	1	3	2.50	0	0
57	2	0	85	2	3	2.50	0	0
33	2	0	106	1	4	3.75	0	0
30	2	0	109	1	4	3.50	0	0
64	1	0	75	3	2	1.00	1	0
49	1	1	91	2	3	2.25	0	0
76	1	0	96	2	2	1.00	0	0
40	1	0	108	2	3	2.50	0	0
48	1	0	86	2	3	2.75	0	0
65	1	0	98	2	2	0.75	0	0
50	1	0	99	2	2	1.30	0	0
70	1	0	95	2	1	1.25	0	0
78	1	0	88	3	3	1.50	0	0
44	1	0	111	2	2	3.00	0	0
48	1	0	103	2	1	2.00	0	0
52	1	0	107	2	2	2.00	0	0
40	1	0	118	2	2	2.50	0	0

Variable Name	Columns	Description
ID	1–3	Subject identification number
ADDSC	5–6	ADD score averaged over 3 years
GENDER	8	1 = male; 2 = female
REPEAT	10	Number of school years repeated
IQ	12–14	IQ obtained from group-administered IQ test
ENGL	16	Level of English: 1 = college prep; 2 = general; 3 = remedial
ENGG	18	Grade in English: 4 = A, 3 = B, and so on
GPA	20–23	Grade point average in ninth grade
SOCPROB	25	Social problems: 0 = no, 1 = yes, 2 = many
DROPOUT	27	1 = Dropped out of school before finishing
		0 = Did not drop out

The first four lines of data are shown below.

```
1  45  1  0  111  2  3  2.60  0  0
2  50  1  0  102  2  3  2.75  0  0
3  49  1  0  108  2  4  4.00  0  0
4  55  1  0  109  2  2  2.25  0  0
```

Badcancr.dat   For a description of both the study behind these data and the data set, see the following section on Cancer.dat. The data in this file differ from those in Cancer.dat only by the inclusion of deliberate errors.

These data have been deliberately changed for purposes of an assignment. Errors have been added, and at least one variable has been distorted. The correct data are in Cancer.dat, which should be used for all *future* analyses. Virtually any program is likely to fail at first until errors are found and corrected, and even when it runs, impossible values will remain. The quickest way to find many of the errors is to print out the file and scan the columns.

The list of corrections to the data sets can be found on the disk in a file called Badcancr.err.

Cancer.dat   The data in this file come from a study by Compas (1990, personal communication) on the effects of stress in cancer patients and their families. Only a small portion of the data are shown here, primarily data related to behavior problems in children and psychological symptoms in the patient and her/his spouse. The file contains data on 89 families, and many of the data points are missing because of the time in the study at which these data were selected. This example does, however, offer a good opportunity to see preliminary data on important psychological variables.

The codebook (the listing of variables, descriptions, location, and legitimate values) for the data in Cancr.dat follows:

Variable	Description	Columns	Legal Values
FamNum	Family ID number	1–3	100–400

GSI Variables

Patient Variables

SexP	Gender of patient	5	1 = male; 2 = female
SomTP	Somaticism	8–9	41–80
DepTP	Depression T score	12–13	42–80
AnxTP	Anxiety T score	16–17	38–80
HosTP	Hostility T score	20–21	39–80
GSITP	Global Symptom Index T score	24–25	33–80

Spouse Variables

SexS	Gender of spouse	27	1 = male; 2 = female
SomTS	Somaticism T score	30–31	41–80
DepTS	Depression T score	34–35	42–80
AnxTS	Anxiety T score	38–39	38–80
HosTS	Hostility T score	42–43	39–80
GSITS	GSI T score	46–47	33–80

Child Behavior Checklist Variables

SexChild	Gender of child	49	1 = male; 2 = female
Intern	Internalizing subscale	51–52	0– 98
Extern	Externalizing subscale	54–55	0–102
TotBP	Total behavior problems	57–58	0–240
InternT	Internalizing T score	60–61	33–100
ExternT	Externalizing T score	63–64	30–100
TotBPT	Total behavior problem T score	66–67	30–100

Missing observations are represented with a period. The first four lines of data are shown below as an example.

```
101  2  62  50  52  39  52  1  42  44  41  40  42  .   .    .    .    .   .
104  1  56  65  55  40  57  2  53  73  68  67  71  1  11  12  28  58  57  60
105  1  56  57  67  65  61  2  41  67  63  66  65  2   7   7  15  47  48  45
106  2  41  61  64  53  57  1  60  60  59  67  62  1   6  10  15  49  52  48
```

Driving.dat These are the data from Table 13.12. The first three entries in each record represent the coding for A (Experience), B (Road), and C (Conditions). The fourth entry is the dependent variable. The first five entries follow.

```
1  1  1   4
1  1  1  18
1  1  1   8
1  1  1  10
1  1  2  21
```

Epineq.dat Epinuneq.dat Introini-Collison and McGaugh (1986) examined the hypothesis that hormones normally produced in the body can play a role in memory. Specifically, they looked at the effect of posttraining injections of epinephrine on retention of a previously learned discrimination. They first trained mice to escape mild shock by choosing the left arm of a Y-maze. Immediately after training they injected the mice with either 0.0, 0.3, or 1.0 mg/kg of epinephrine. They predicted that low doses of epinephrine would facilitate retention, whereas high doses would inhibit it.

Either 1 day, 1 week, or 1 month after original training, each mouse was again placed in the Y-maze. But this time, running to the right arm of the maze led to escape from shock. Presumably, the stronger the memory of the original training, the more it would interfere with the learning of this new task and the more errors the subjects would make.

This experiment has two data sets, named Epineq.dat and Epinuneq.dat. The original study used 18 animals in the three dosage groups tested after 1 day, and 12 animals in each group tested after intervals of 1 week and 1 month. Hypothetical data that closely reproduce the original results are contained in Epinuneq.dat, although five subjects having a 1-month recall interval have been deleted from the 1.0 mg/kg condition. A second data set was created with 12 observations in each of the 9 cells, and is called Epineq.dat. In both cases the need to create data that were integers led to results that are slightly conservative relative to the actual data. But the conclusions with respect to H_0 are the same.

For both data sets, there is a three-digit ID; dosage is coded (1, 2, or 3) in column 5; the retention interval is coded (1, 2, or 3) in column 7; and the number of errors in learning the second discrimination are coded in column 9. The first four lines of data follow:

01	1	1	0
02	1	1	3
03	1	1	4
04	1	1	2

Mireault.dat Mireault (1990) collected data from 381 college students, some of whom had lost a parent by death during their childhood. She had three groups of students. Group 1 was composed of subjects who had lost a parent. Group 2 was composed of subjects whose parents were still alive and married to each other. Group 3 consisted of students whose parents were divorced.

Mireault was interested in observing the effects of parental loss on the person's current level of symptomotology (as measured by the Brief Symptom Inventory, Derogatis, 1983) and on the individual's self-perceived vulnerability to future loss. In the interests of space, the data set includes only the total vulnerability measure, and not the subscales. There is also a single measure for social support. For all measures, a higher score represents more of the concept being measured.

The variables, and their location in the file, are listed below.

Variable Name	Columns	Description
ID	1–3	Subject identification number
Group	5	1 = loss; 2 = married; 3 = divorced
Gender	7	1 = male; 2 = female
YearColl	9	1 = first year; 2 = sophomore; and so on
College	11	1 = arts and sciences; 2 = health; 3 = engineering; 4 = business; 5 = agriculture
GPA	13	4 = A; 3 = B; 2 = C; 1 = D; 0 = F
LostPGen	15	Gender of lost parent
AgeAtLos	17–18	Age at parent's death
SomT	20–21	Somatization T score
ObsessT	23–24	Obsessive-compulsive T score
SensitT	26–27	Interpersonal sensitivity T score
DepressT	29–30	Depression T score
AnxT	32–33	Anxiety T score
HostT	35–36	Hostility T score
PhobT	38–39	Phobic anxiety T score
ParT	41–42	Paranoid ideation T score
PsyT	44–45	Psychoticism T score
GSIT	47–48	Global symptom index T score
PVTotal	50–52	Perceived vulnerability total score
PVLoss	54–56	Perceived vulnerability to loss
SuppTotl	58–60	Social support T score

Missing data are represented by a period. The first three lines of data are shown below as an example.

```
002  2  1  1  4  2  .   .  42  53  59  57  49  57  47  51  46  51  112  24  66
007  1  2  1  2  .  1  18  65  80  64  71  72  73  63  67  67  72  100  23  73
008  2  2  1  1  4  .   .  52  67  60  62  65  78  60  65  58  65  118  28  64
```

RandUnif.dat   The data in this file are 10,000 random numbers drawn from a uniformly distributed population with a mean of 50 and a standard deviation of 28.87. By that we mean that all values between the two extremes are equally likely, and a histogram of the data in the population would be flat. These data have been generated to allow you to play with the sampling distribution of the mean. By making small changes to the appropriate program, you can plot the sampling distribution of the mean and see that it behaves as the central limit theorem predicts. You can also see how the sampling distribution of the mean changes as the sample size changes, and you can plot the sampling distributions of other statistics besides the mean.

The data are arranged in 10 columns of two-digit numbers followed by a single digit, and there are 1000 rows in the data file. The 11th variable is either a 1 or a 2 and will be used to designate group membership. The data can be read most easily by a free format (i.e., an input statement in which you do not specify in what columns the data are to be found). The first four lines of the data file follow.

```
39  47  87   7  85   4  79  38   0  60  2
27  13  20  84  97  45  76  34  16  19  1
45  14  86  50  94  44  37  69  53  72  1
63  91  68  93  13  28  91  54  78  62  2
```

RandNorm.dat   The file is structured in nearly the same way as the preceding one, but the data were sampled from a normally distributed population instead of a uniform one. In this case the population mean is 50 and the population standard deviation is 10. The same analyses can be carried out using these data as you carried out using RandUnif.dat. The 11th column contains a variable named Group. Approximately half of the cases will have Group = 1; the other half will have Group = 2. (Group is assigned randomly.)

Random1.BMD Random1.Min Random1.SAS Random1.SPX   These files are not data files. Instead, they are simple programs written for four of the most frequently used statistical packages. The programs were written specifically to deal with the random data in RandUnif.dat and RandNorm.dat, but they can easily be adapted for other purposes. I suggest that you use them as a template for creating other programs.

Stress.dat   The data in this file are a subset of data being collected by Compas and his colleagues on stress and coping in cancer patients. The file contains the family number, the gender of the respondent (1 = Male; 2 = Female), the role of the respondent (1 = Patient; 2 = Spouse), and two stress measures (one obtained shortly after diagnosis and one 3 months later). The variables are in the following order: FamNum, Gender, Role, Time1, Time2. The first six cases follow:

```
101  2  1  2  .
101  1  2  2  .
104  1  1  4  .
104  2  2  5  .
105  1  1  3  4
105  2  2  5  4
```

APPENDIX χ^2: UPPER PERCENTAGE POINTS OF THE χ^2 DISTRIBUTION

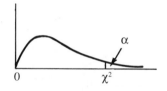

df	.995	.990	.975	.950	.900	.750	.500	.250	.100	.050	.025	.010	.005
1	0.00	0.00	0.00	0.00	0.02	0.10	0.45	1.32	2.71	3.84	5.02	6.63	7.88
2	0.01	0.02	0.05	0.10	0.21	0.58	1.39	2.77	4.61	5.99	7.38	9.21	10.60
3	0.07	0.11	0.22	0.35	0.58	1.21	2.37	4.11	6.25	7.82	9.35	11.35	12.84
4	0.21	0.30	0.48	0.71	1.06	1.92	3.36	5.39	7.78	9.49	11.14	13.28	14.86
5	0.41	0.55	0.83	1.15	1.61	2.67	4.35	6.63	9.24	11.07	12.83	15.09	16.75
6	0.68	0.87	1.24	1.64	2.20	3.45	5.35	7.84	10.64	12.59	14.45	16.81	18.55
7	0.99	1.24	1.69	2.17	2.83	4.25	6.35	9.04	12.02	14.07	16.01	18.48	20.28
8	1.34	1.65	2.18	2.73	3.49	5.07	7.34	10.22	13.36	15.51	17.54	20.09	21.96
9	1.73	2.09	2.70	3.33	4.17	5.90	8.34	11.39	14.68	16.92	19.02	21.66	23.59
10	2.15	2.56	3.25	3.94	4.87	6.74	9.34	12.55	15.99	18.31	20.48	23.21	25.19
11	2.60	3.05	3.82	4.57	5.58	7.58	10.34	13.70	17.28	19.68	21.92	24.72	26.75
12	3.07	3.57	4.40	5.23	6.30	8.44	11.34	14.85	18.55	21.03	23.34	26.21	28.30
13	3.56	4.11	5.01	5.89	7.04	9.30	12.34	15.98	19.81	22.36	24.74	27.69	29.82
14	4.07	4.66	5.63	6.57	7.79	10.17	13.34	17.12	21.06	23.69	26.12	29.14	31.31
15	4.60	5.23	6.26	7.26	8.55	11.04	14.34	18.25	22.31	25.00	27.49	30.58	32.80
16	5.14	5.81	6.91	7.96	9.31	11.91	15.34	19.37	23.54	26.30	28.85	32.00	34.27
17	5.70	6.41	7.56	8.67	10.09	12.79	16.34	20.49	24.77	27.59	30.19	33.41	35.72
18	6.26	7.01	8.23	9.39	10.86	13.68	17.34	21.60	25.99	28.87	31.53	34.81	37.15
19	6.84	7.63	8.91	10.12	11.65	14.56	18.34	22.72	27.20	30.14	32.85	36.19	38.58
20	7.43	8.26	9.59	10.85	12.44	15.45	19.34	23.83	28.41	31.41	34.17	37.56	40.00
21	8.03	8.90	10.28	11.59	13.24	16.34	20.34	24.93	29.62	32.67	35.48	38.93	41.40
22	8.64	9.54	10.98	12.34	14.04	17.24	21.34	26.04	30.81	33.93	36.78	40.29	42.80
23	9.26	10.19	11.69	13.09	14.85	18.14	22.34	27.14	32.01	35.17	38.08	41.64	44.18
24	9.88	10.86	12.40	13.85	15.66	19.04	23.34	28.24	33.20	36.42	39.37	42.98	45.56
25	10.52	11.52	13.12	14.61	16.47	19.94	24.34	29.34	34.38	37.65	40.65	44.32	46.93
26	11.16	12.20	13.84	15.38	17.29	20.84	25.34	30.43	35.56	38.89	41.92	45.64	48.29
27	11.80	12.88	14.57	16.15	18.11	21.75	26.34	31.53	36.74	40.11	43.20	46.96	49.64
28	12.46	13.56	15.31	16.93	18.94	22.66	27.34	32.62	37.92	41.34	44.46	48.28	50.99
29	13.12	14.26	16.05	17.71	19.77	23.57	28.34	33.71	39.09	42.56	45.72	49.59	52.34
30	13.78	14.95	16.79	18.49	20.60	24.48	29.34	34.80	40.26	43.77	46.98	50.89	53.67
40	20.67	22.14	24.42	26.51	29.06	33.67	39.34	45.61	51.80	55.75	59.34	63.71	66.80
50	27.96	29.68	32.35	34.76	37.69	42.95	49.34	56.33	63.16	67.50	71.42	76.17	79.52
60	35.50	37.46	40.47	43.19	46.46	52.30	59.34	66.98	74.39	79.08	83.30	88.40	91.98
70	43.25	45.42	48.75	51.74	55.33	61.70	69.34	77.57	85.52	90.53	95.03	100.44	104.24
80	51.14	53.52	57.15	60.39	64.28	71.15	79.34	88.13	96.57	101.88	106.63	112.34	116.35
90	59.17	61.74	65.64	69.13	73.29	80.63	89.33	98.65	107.56	113.14	118.14	124.13	128.32
100	67.30	70.05	74.22	77.93	82.36	90.14	99.33	109.14	118.49	124.34	129.56	135.82	140.19

Source: The entries in this table were computed by the author.

APPENDIX F: CRITICAL VALUES OF THE F DISTRIBUTION

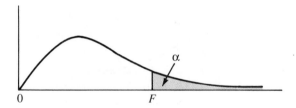

TABLE 1 $\alpha = .05$

	Degrees of Freedom for Numerator																
	1	2	3	4	5	6	7	8	9	10	15	20	25	30	40	50
1	161.4	199.5	215.8	224.8	230.0	233.8	236.5	238.6	240.1	242.1	245.2	248.4	248.9	250.5	250.8	252.6
2	18.51	19.00	19.16	19.25	19.30	19.33	19.35	19.37	19.38	19.40	19.43	19.44	19.46	19.47	19.48	19.48
3	10.13	9.55	9.28	9.12	9.01	8.94	8.89	8.85	8.81	8.79	8.70	8.66	8.63	8.62	8.59	8.58
4	7.71	6.94	6.59	6.39	6.26	6.16	6.09	6.04	6.00	5.96	5.86	5.80	5.77	5.75	5.72	5.70
5	6.61	5.79	5.41	5.19	5.05	4.95	4.88	4.82	4.77	4.74	4.62	4.56	4.52	4.50	4.46	4.44
6	5.99	5.14	4.76	4.53	4.39	4.28	4.21	4.15	4.10	4.06	3.94	3.87	3.83	3.81	3.77	3.75
7	5.59	4.74	4.35	4.12	3.97	3.87	3.79	3.73	3.68	3.64	3.51	3.44	3.40	3.38	3.34	3.32
8	5.32	4.46	4.07	3.84	3.69	3.58	3.50	3.44	3.39	3.35	3.22	3.15	3.11	3.08	3.04	3.02
9	5.12	4.26	3.86	3.63	3.48	3.37	3.29	3.23	3.18	3.14	3.01	2.94	2.89	2.86	2.83	2.80
10	4.96	4.10	3.71	3.48	3.33	3.22	3.14	3.07	3.02	2.98	2.85	2.77	2.73	2.70	2.66	2.64
11	4.84	3.98	3.59	3.36	3.20	3.09	3.01	2.95	2.90	2.85	2.72	2.65	2.60	2.57	2.53	2.51
12	4.75	3.89	3.49	3.26	3.11	3.00	2.91	2.85	2.80	2.75	2.62	2.54	2.50	2.47	2.43	2.40
13	4.67	3.81	3.41	3.18	3.03	2.92	2.83	2.77	2.71	2.67	2.53	2.46	2.41	2.38	2.34	2.31
14	4.60	3.74	3.34	3.11	2.96	2.85	2.76	2.70	2.65	2.60	2.46	2.39	2.34	2.31	2.27	2.24
15	4.54	3.68	3.29	3.06	2.90	2.79	2.71	2.64	2.59	2.54	2.40	2.33	2.28	2.25	2.20	2.18
16	4.49	3.63	3.24	3.01	2.85	2.74	2.66	2.59	2.54	2.49	2.35	2.28	2.23	2.19	2.15	2.12
17	4.45	3.59	3.20	2.96	2.81	2.70	2.61	2.55	2.49	2.45	2.31	2.23	2.18	2.15	2.10	2.08
18	4.41	3.55	3.16	2.93	2.77	2.66	2.58	2.51	2.46	2.41	2.27	2.19	2.14	2.11	2.06	2.04
19	4.38	3.52	3.13	2.90	2.74	2.63	2.54	2.48	2.42	2.38	2.23	2.16	2.11	2.07	2.03	2.00
20	4.35	3.49	3.10	2.87	2.71	2.60	2.51	2.45	2.39	2.35	2.20	2.12	2.07	2.04	1.99	1.97
22	4.30	3.44	3.05	2.82	2.66	2.55	2.46	2.40	2.34	2.30	2.15	2.07	2.02	1.98	1.94	1.91
24	4.26	3.40	3.01	2.78	2.62	2.51	2.42	2.36	2.30	2.25	2.11	2.03	1.97	1.94	1.89	1.86
26	4.23	3.37	2.98	2.74	2.59	2.47	2.39	2.32	2.27	2.22	2.07	1.99	1.94	1.90	1.85	1.82
28	4.20	3.34	2.95	2.71	2.56	2.45	2.36	2.29	2.24	2.19	2.04	1.96	1.91	1.87	1.82	1.79
30	4.17	3.32	2.92	2.69	2.53	2.42	2.33	2.27	2.21	2.16	2.01	1.93	1.88	1.84	1.79	1.76
40	4.08	3.23	2.84	2.61	2.45	2.34	2.25	2.18	2.12	2.08	1.92	1.84	1.78	1.74	1.69	1.66
50	4.03	3.18	2.79	2.56	2.40	2.29	2.20	2.13	2.07	2.03	1.87	1.78	1.73	1.69	1.63	1.60
60	4.00	3.15	2.76	2.53	2.37	2.25	2.17	2.10	2.04	1.99	1.84	1.75	1.69	1.65	1.59	1.56
120	3.92	3.07	2.68	2.45	2.29	2.18	2.09	2.02	1.96	1.91	1.75	1.66	1.60	1.55	1.50	1.46
200	3.89	3.04	2.65	2.42	2.26	2.14	2.06	1.98	1.93	1.88	1.72	1.62	1.56	1.52	1.46	1.41
500	3.86	3.01	2.62	2.39	2.23	2.12	2.03	1.96	1.90	1.85	1.69	1.59	1.53	1.48	1.42	1.38
1000	3.85	3.01	2.61	2.38	2.22	2.11	2.02	1.95	1.89	1.84	1.68	1.58	1.52	1.47	1.41	1.36

Degrees of Freedom for Denominator

Source: The entries in this table were computed by the author.

TABLE 2 $\alpha = .025$

	Degrees of Freedom for Numerator															
	1	2	3	4	5	6	7	8	9	10	15	20	25	30	40	50
1	647.8	799.5	864.2	899.6	921.8	937.1	948.2	956.7	963.3	968.6	984.9	993.1	998.1	1001	1006	1008
2	38.51	39.00	39.17	39.25	39.30	39.33	39.36	39.37	39.39	39.40	39.43	39.45	39.46	39.46	39.47	39.48
3	17.44	16.04	15.44	15.10	14.89	14.73	14.62	14.54	14.47	14.42	14.25	14.17	14.12	14.08	14.04	14.01
4	12.22	10.65	9.98	9.60	9.36	9.20	9.07	8.98	8.90	8.84	8.66	8.56	8.50	8.46	8.41	8.38
5	10.01	8.43	7.76	7.39	7.15	6.98	6.85	6.76	6.68	6.62	6.43	6.33	6.27	6.23	6.18	6.14
6	8.81	7.26	6.60	6.23	5.99	5.82	5.70	5.60	5.52	5.46	5.27	5.17	5.11	5.07	5.01	4.98
7	8.07	6.54	5.89	5.52	5.29	5.12	4.99	4.90	4.82	4.76	4.57	4.47	4.40	4.36	4.31	4.28
8	7.57	6.06	5.42	5.05	4.82	4.65	4.53	4.43	4.36	4.30	4.10	4.00	3.94	3.89	3.84	3.81
9	7.21	5.71	5.08	4.72	4.48	4.32	4.20	4.10	4.03	3.96	3.77	3.67	3.60	3.56	3.51	3.47
10	6.94	5.46	4.83	4.47	4.24	4.07	3.95	3.85	3.78	3.72	3.52	3.42	3.35	3.31	3.26	3.22
11	6.72	5.26	4.63	4.28	4.04	3.88	3.76	3.66	3.59	3.53	3.33	3.23	3.16	3.12	3.06	3.03
12	6.55	5.10	4.47	4.12	3.89	3.73	3.61	3.51	3.44	3.37	3.18	3.07	3.01	2.96	2.91	2.87
13	6.41	4.97	4.35	4.00	3.77	3.60	3.48	3.39	3.31	3.25	3.05	2.95	2.88	2.84	2.78	2.74
14	6.30	4.86	4.24	3.89	3.66	3.50	3.38	3.29	3.21	3.15	2.95	2.84	2.78	2.73	2.67	2.64
15	6.20	4.77	4.15	3.80	3.58	3.41	3.29	3.20	3.12	3.06	2.86	2.76	2.69	2.64	2.59	2.55
16	6.12	4.69	4.08	3.73	3.50	3.34	3.22	3.12	3.05	2.99	2.79	2.68	2.61	2.57	2.51	2.47
17	6.04	4.62	4.01	3.66	3.44	3.28	3.16	3.06	2.98	2.92	2.72	2.62	2.55	2.50	2.44	2.41
18	5.98	4.56	3.95	3.61	3.38	3.22	3.10	3.01	2.93	2.87	2.67	2.56	2.49	2.44	2.38	2.35
19	5.92	4.51	3.90	3.56	3.33	3.17	3.05	2.96	2.88	2.82	2.62	2.51	2.44	2.39	2.33	2.30
20	5.87	4.46	3.86	3.51	3.29	3.13	3.01	2.91	2.84	2.77	2.57	2.46	2.40	2.35	2.29	2.25
22	5.79	4.38	3.78	3.44	3.22	3.05	2.93	2.84	2.76	2.70	2.50	2.39	2.32	2.27	2.21	2.17
24	5.72	4.32	3.72	3.38	3.15	2.99	2.87	2.78	2.70	2.64	2.44	2.33	2.26	2.21	2.15	2.11
26	5.66	4.27	3.67	3.33	3.10	2.94	2.82	2.73	2.65	2.59	2.39	2.28	2.21	2.16	2.09	2.05
28	5.61	4.22	3.63	3.29	3.06	2.90	2.78	2.69	2.61	2.55	2.34	2.23	2.16	2.11	2.05	2.01
30	5.57	4.18	3.59	3.25	3.03	2.87	2.75	2.65	2.57	2.51	2.31	2.20	2.12	2.07	2.01	1.97
40	5.42	4.05	3.46	3.13	2.90	2.74	2.62	2.53	2.45	2.39	2.18	2.07	1.99	1.94	1.88	1.83
50	5.34	3.97	3.39	3.05	2.83	2.67	2.55	2.46	2.38	2.32	2.11	1.99	1.92	1.87	1.80	1.75
60	5.29	3.93	3.34	3.01	2.79	2.63	2.51	2.41	2.33	2.27	2.06	1.94	1.87	1.82	1.74	1.70
120	5.15	3.80	3.23	2.89	2.67	2.52	2.39	2.30	2.22	2.16	1.94	1.82	1.75	1.69	1.61	1.56
200	5.10	3.76	3.18	2.85	2.63	2.47	2.35	2.26	2.18	2.11	1.90	1.78	1.70	1.64	1.56	1.51
500	5.05	3.72	3.14	2.81	2.59	2.43	2.31	2.22	2.14	2.07	1.86	1.74	1.65	1.60	1.52	1.46
1000	5.04	3.70	3.13	2.80	2.58	2.42	2.30	2.20	2.13	2.06	1.85	1.72	1.64	1.58	1.50	1.45

Degrees of Freedom for Denominator

TABLE 3 $\alpha = .01$

Degrees of Freedom for Numerator

		1	2	3	4	5	6	7	8	9	10	15	20	25	30	40	50
	1	4048	4993	5377	5577	5668	5924	5992	6096	6132	6168	6079	6168	6214	6355	6168	6213
	2	98.50	99.01	99.15	99.23	99.30	99.33	99.35	99.39	99.40	99.43	99.38	99.48	99.43	99.37	99.44	99.59
	3	34.12	30.82	29.46	28.71	28.24	27.91	27.67	27.49	27.34	27.23	26.87	26.69	26.58	26.51	26.41	26.36
	4	21.20	18.00	16.69	15.98	15.52	15.21	14.98	14.80	14.66	14.55	14.20	14.02	13.91	13.84	13.75	13.69
	5	16.26	13.27	12.06	11.39	10.97	10.67	10.46	10.29	10.16	10.05	9.72	9.55	9.45	9.38	9.29	9.24
	6	13.75	10.92	9.78	9.15	8.75	8.47	8.26	8.10	7.98	7.87	7.56	7.40	7.30	7.23	7.14	7.09
	7	12.25	9.55	8.45	7.85	7.46	7.19	6.99	6.84	6.72	6.62	6.31	6.16	6.06	5.99	5.91	5.86
	8	11.26	8.65	7.59	7.01	6.63	6.37	6.18	6.03	5.91	5.81	5.52	5.36	5.26	5.20	5.12	5.07
	9	10.56	8.02	6.99	6.42	6.06	5.80	5.61	5.47	5.35	5.26	4.96	4.81	4.71	4.65	4.57	4.52
Degrees of Freedom for Denominator	10	10.04	7.56	6.55	5.99	5.64	5.39	5.20	5.06	4.94	4.85	4.56	4.41	4.31	4.25	4.17	4.12
	11	9.65	7.21	6.22	5.67	5.32	5.07	4.89	4.74	4.63	4.54	4.25	4.10	4.01	3.94	3.86	3.81
	12	9.33	6.93	5.95	5.41	5.06	4.82	4.64	4.50	4.39	4.30	4.01	3.86	3.76	3.70	3.62	3.57
	13	9.07	6.70	5.74	5.21	4.86	4.62	4.44	4.30	4.19	4.10	3.82	3.66	3.57	3.51	3.43	3.38
	14	8.86	6.51	5.56	5.04	4.69	4.46	4.28	4.14	4.03	3.94	3.66	3.51	3.41	3.35	3.27	3.22
	15	8.68	6.36	5.42	4.89	4.56	4.32	4.14	4.00	3.89	3.80	3.52	3.37	3.28	3.21	3.13	3.08
	16	8.53	6.23	5.29	4.77	4.44	4.20	4.03	3.89	3.78	3.69	3.41	3.26	3.16	3.10	3.02	2.97
	17	8.40	6.11	5.18	4.67	4.34	4.10	3.93	3.79	3.68	3.59	3.31	3.16	3.07	3.00	2.92	2.87
	18	8.29	6.01	5.09	4.58	4.25	4.01	3.84	3.71	3.60	3.51	3.23	3.08	2.98	2.92	2.84	2.78
	19	8.18	5.93	5.01	4.50	4.17	3.94	3.77	3.63	3.52	3.43	3.15	3.00	2.91	2.84	2.76	2.71
	20	8.10	5.85	4.94	4.43	4.10	3.87	3.70	3.56	3.46	3.37	3.09	2.94	2.84	2.78	2.69	2.64
	22	7.95	5.72	4.82	4.31	3.99	3.76	3.59	3.45	3.35	3.26	2.98	2.83	2.73	2.67	2.58	2.53
	24	7.82	5.61	4.72	4.22	3.90	3.67	3.50	3.36	3.26	3.17	2.89	2.74	2.64	2.58	2.49	2.44
	26	7.72	5.53	4.64	4.14	3.82	3.59	3.42	3.29	3.18	3.09	2.81	2.66	2.57	2.50	2.42	2.36
	28	7.64	5.45	4.57	4.07	3.75	3.53	3.36	3.23	3.12	3.03	2.75	2.60	2.51	2.44	2.35	2.30
	30	7.56	5.39	4.51	4.02	3.70	3.47	3.30	3.17	3.07	2.98	2.70	2.55	2.45	2.39	2.30	2.25
	40	7.31	5.18	4.31	3.83	3.51	3.29	3.12	2.99	2.89	2.80	2.52	2.37	2.27	2.20	2.11	2.06
	50	7.17	5.06	4.20	3.72	3.41	3.19	3.02	2.89	2.78	2.70	2.42	2.27	2.17	2.10	2.01	1.95
	60	7.08	4.98	4.13	3.65	3.34	3.12	2.95	2.82	2.72	2.63	2.35	2.20	2.10	2.03	1.94	1.88
	120	6.85	4.79	3.95	3.48	3.17	2.96	2.79	2.66	2.56	2.47	2.19	2.03	1.93	1.86	1.76	1.70
	200	6.76	4.71	3.88	3.41	3.11	2.89	2.73	2.60	2.50	2.41	2.13	1.97	1.87	1.79	1.69	1.63
	500	6.69	4.65	3.82	3.36	3.05	2.84	2.68	2.55	2.44	2.36	2.07	1.92	1.81	1.74	1.63	1.57
	1000	6.67	4.63	3.80	3.34	3.04	2.82	2.66	2.53	2.43	2.34	2.06	1.90	1.79	1.72	1.61	1.54

Source: The entries in this table were computed by the author.

APPENDIX *ncF*: CRITICAL VALUES OF THE NONCENTRAL *F* DISTRIBUTION

Power = 1 − (Table Entry)

df_e	α	0.50	1.0	1.2	1.4	1.6	1.8	2.0	2.2	2.6	3.0
						$df_t = 1$					
2	.05	0.93	0.86	0.83	0.78	0.74	0.69	0.64	0.59	0.49	0.40
	.01	0.99	0.97	0.96	0.95	0.94	0.93	0.91	0.90	0.87	0.83
4	.05	0.91	0.80	0.74	0.67	0.59	0.51	0.43	0.35	0.22	0.12
	.01	0.98	0.95	0.93	0.90	0.87	0.83	0.78	0.73	0.62	0.50
6	.05	0.91	0.78	0.70	0.62	0.52	0.43	0.34	0.26	0.14	0.06
	.01	0.98	0.93	0.90	0.86	0.81	0.75	0.69	0.61	0.46	0.31
8	.05	0.90	0.76	0.68	0.59	0.49	0.39	0.30	0.22	0.11	0.04
	.01	0.98	0.92	0.89	0.84	0.78	0.70	0.62	0.54	0.37	0.22
10	.05	0.90	0.75	0.66	0.57	0.47	0.37	0.28	0.20	0.09	0.03
	.01	0.98	0.92	0.87	0.82	0.75	0.67	0.58	0.49	0.31	0.17
12	.05	0.90	0.74	0.65	0.56	0.45	0.35	0.26	0.19	0.08	0.03
	.01	0.97	0.91	0.87	0.81	0.73	0.65	0.55	0.46	0.28	0.14
16	.05	0.90	0.74	0.64	0.54	0.43	0.33	0.24	0.17	0.07	0.02
	.01	0.97	0.90	0.85	0.79	0.71	0.61	0.52	0.42	0.24	0.11
20	.05	0.90	0.73	0.63	0.53	0.42	0.32	0.23	0.16	0.06	0.02
	.01	0.97	0.90	0.85	0.78	0.69	0.59	0.49	0.39	0.21	0.10
30	.05	0.89	0.72	0.62	0.52	0.40	0.31	0.22	0.15	0.06	0.02
	.01	0.97	0.89	0.83	0.76	0.67	0.57	0.46	0.36	0.19	0.08
∞	.05	0.89	0.71	0.60	0.49	0.38	0.28	0.19	0.12	0.04	0.01
	.01	0.97	0.88	0.81	0.72	0.62	0.51	0.40	0.30	0.14	0.05
df_e	α					$df_t = 2$					
2	.05	0.93	0.88	0.85	0.82	0.78	0.75	0.70	0.66	0.56	0.48
	.01	0.99	0.98	0.97	0.96	0.95	0.94	0.93	0.92	0.89	0.86
4	.05	0.92	0.82	0.77	0.70	0.62	0.54	0.46	0.38	0.24	0.14
	.01	0.98	0.96	0.94	0.92	0.89	0.85	0.81	0.76	0.66	0.54
6	.05	0.91	0.79	0.71	0.63	0.53	0.43	0.34	0.26	0.13	0.05
	.01	0.98	0.94	0.91	0.87	0.82	0.76	0.70	0.62	0.46	0.31
8	.05	0.91	0.77	0.68	0.58	0.48	0.37	0.28	0.20	0.08	0.03
	.01	0.98	0.93	0.89	0.84	0.78	0.70	0.61	0.52	0.34	0.19
10	.05	0.91	0.75	0.66	0.55	0.44	0.34	0.24	0.16	0.06	0.02
	.01	0.98	0.92	0.88	0.82	0.74	0.65	0.55	0.45	0.26	0.13
12	.05	0.90	0.74	0.64	0.53	0.42	0.31	0.22	0.14	0.05	0.01
	.01	0.98	0.91	0.86	0.80	0.71	0.61	0.51	0.40	0.22	0.09
16	.05	0.90	0.73	0.62	0.51	0.39	0.28	0.19	0.12	0.04	0.01
	.01	0.97	0.90	0.84	0.77	0.67	0.57	0.45	0.34	0.16	0.06
20	.05	0.90	0.72	0.61	0.49	0.36	0.26	0.17	0.11	0.03	0.01
	.01	0.97	0.90	0.83	0.75	0.65	0.53	0.42	0.31	0.14	0.04
30	.05	0.90	0.71	0.59	0.47	0.35	0.24	0.15	0.09	0.02	0.00
	.01	0.97	0.88	0.82	0.72	0.61	0.49	0.37	0.26	0.10	0.03
∞	.05	0.89	0.68	0.56	0.43	0.30	0.20	0.12	0.06	0.01	0.00
	.01	0.97	0.86	0.77	0.66	0.53	0.40	0.28	0.18	0.05	0.01

df_e	α	ϕ									
		0.50	1.0	1.2	1.4	1.6	1.8	2.0	2.2	2.6	3.0
df_e	α	\multicolumn{10}{c}{$df_t = 3$}									
2	.05	0.93	0.89	0.86	0.83	0.80	0.76	0.73	0.69	0.60	0.52
	.01	0.99	0.98	0.97	0.96	0.96	0.95	0.94	0.93	0.90	0.88
4	.05	0.92	0.83	0.77	0.71	0.63	0.55	0.47	0.39	0.25	0.14
	.01	0.98	0.96	0.94	0.92	0.89	0.86	0.82	0.77	0.67	0.55
6	.05	0.91	0.79	0.71	0.62	0.52	0.42	0.33	0.24	0.11	0.04
	.01	0.98	0.94	0.91	0.87	0.82	0.76	0.69	0.61	0.44	0.29
8	.05	0.91	0.76	0.67	0.57	0.46	0.35	0.25	0.17	0.06	0.02
	.01	0.98	0.93	0.89	0.84	0.77	0.68	0.59	0.49	0.30	0.16
10	.05	0.91	0.75	0.65	0.53	0.41	0.30	0.21	0.13	0.04	0.01
	.01	0.98	0.92	0.87	0.80	0.72	0.62	0.52	0.41	0.22	0.09
12	.05	0.90	0.73	0.62	0.50	0.38	0.27	0.18	0.11	0.03	0.01
	.01	0.98	0.91	0.85	0.78	0.69	0.58	0.46	0.35	0.17	0.06
16	.05	0.90	0.71	0.60	0.47	0.34	0.23	0.14	0.08	0.02	0.00
	.01	0.97	0.90	0.83	0.74	0.64	0.51	0.39	0.28	0.11	0.03
20	.05	0.90	0.70	0.58	0.45	0.32	0.21	0.13	0.07	0.01	0.00
	.01	0.97	0.89	0.82	0.72	0.60	0.47	0.35	0.24	0.08	0.02
30	.05	0.89	0.68	0.55	0.42	0.29	0.18	0.10	0.05	0.01	0.00
	.01	0.97	0.87	0.79	0.68	0.55	0.42	0.29	0.18	0.05	0.01
∞	.05	0.88	0.64	0.50	0.36	0.23	0.13	0.07	0.03	0.00	0.00
	.01	0.97	0.84	0.73	0.59	0.44	0.30	0.18	0.10	0.02	0.00
df_e	α	\multicolumn{10}{c}{$df_t = 4$}									
2	.05	0.94	0.89	0.87	0.84	0.81	0.77	0.74	0.70	0.62	0.54
	.01	0.99	0.98	0.97	0.97	0.96	0.95	0.94	0.93	0.91	0.88
4	.05	0.92	0.83	0.78	0.71	0.64	0.55	0.47	0.39	0.25	0.14
	.01	0.98	0.96	0.94	0.92	0.89	0.86	0.82	0.78	0.67	0.56
6	.05	0.92	0.79	0.71	0.62	0.52	0.41	0.31	0.23	0.10	0.04
	.01	0.98	0.94	0.91	0.87	0.82	0.76	0.68	0.60	0.43	0.28
8	.05	0.91	0.76	0.66	0.55	0.44	0.33	0.23	0.15	0.05	0.01
	.01	0.98	0.93	0.89	0.83	0.76	0.67	0.57	0.47	0.28	0.14
10	.05	0.91	0.74	0.63	0.51	0.39	0.27	0.18	0.11	0.03	0.01
	.01	0.98	0.92	0.86	0.79	0.70	0.60	0.49	0.37	0.19	0.07
12	.05	0.90	0.72	0.61	0.48	0.35	0.24	0.15	0.08	0.02	0.00
	.01	0.98	0.91	0.85	0.76	0.66	0.55	0.42	0.31	0.13	0.04
16	.05	0.90	0.70	0.57	0.44	0.31	0.19	0.11	0.06	0.01	0.00
	.01	0.97	0.89	0.82	0.72	0.60	0.47	0.34	0.23	0.08	0.02
20	.05	0.89	0.68	0.55	0.41	0.28	0.17	0.09	0.04	0.01	0.00
	.01	0.97	0.88	0.80	0.69	0.56	0.42	0.29	0.18	0.05	0.01
30	.05	0.89	0.66	0.52	0.37	0.24	0.14	0.07	0.03	0.00	0.00
	.01	0.97	0.86	0.77	0.64	0.50	0.35	0.22	0.13	0.03	0.00
∞	.05	0.88	0.60	0.45	0.29	0.17	0.08	0.04	0.01	0.00	0.00
	.01	0.96	0.81	0.68	0.53	0.36	0.22	0.11	0.05	0.01	0.00

Source: Abridged from M. L. Tiku (1967), Tables of the power of the *F* test, *Journal of the American Statistical Association*, 62, 525–539, with the permission of the author and the editors.

APPENDIX POLYNOMIAL: ORTHOGONAL POLYNOMIAL COEFFICIENTS

k	Polynomial	$X = 1$	2	3	4	5	6	7	8	9	10	Σa_i^2
3	Linear	-1	0	1								2
	Quadratic	1	-2	1								6
4	Linear	-3	-1	1	3							20
	Quadratic	1	-1	-1	1							4
	Cubic	-1	3	-3	1							20
5	Linear	-2	-1	0	1	2						10
	Quadratic	2	-1	-2	-1	2						14
	Cubic	-1	2	0	-2	1						10
	Quartic	1	-4	6	-4	1						70
6	Linear	-5	-3	-1	1	3	5					70
	Quadratic	5	-1	-4	-4	-1	5					84
	Cubic	-5	7	4	-4	-7	5					180
	Quartic	1	-3	2	2	-3	1					28
7	Linear	-3	-2	-1	0	1	2	3				28
	Quadratic	5	0	-3	-4	-3	0	5				84
	Cubic	-1	1	1	0	-1	-1	1				6
	Quartic	3	-7	1	6	1	-7	3				154
8	Linear	-7	-5	-3	-1	1	3	5	7			168
	Quadratic	7	1	-3	-5	-5	-3	1	7			168
	Cubic	-7	5	7	3	-3	-7	-5	7			264
	Quartic	7	-13	-3	9	9	-3	-13	7			616
	Quintic	-7	23	-17	-15	15	17	-23	7			2184
9	Linear	-4	-3	-2	-1	0	1	2	3	4		60
	Quadratic	28	7	-8	-17	-20	-17	-8	7	28		2772
	Cubic	-14	7	13	9	0	-9	-13	-7	14		990
	Quartic	14	-21	-11	9	18	9	-11	-21	14		2002
	Quintic	-4	11	-4	-9	0	9	4	-11	4		468
10	Linear	-9	-7	-5	-3	-1	1	3	5	7	9	330
	Quadratic	6	2	-1	-3	-4	-4	-3	-1	2	6	132
	Cubic	-42	14	35	31	12	-12	-31	-35	-14	42	8580
	Quartic	18	-22	-17	3	18	18	3	-17	-22	18	2860
	Quintic	-6	14	-1	-11	-6	6	11	1	-14	6	780

Appendix Power: Power as a Function of δ and Significance Level (α)

	α for Two-Tailed Test			
δ	.10	.05	.02	.01
1.00	.26	.17	.09	.06
1.10	.29	.20	.11	.07
1.20	.33	.22	.13	.08
1.30	.37	.26	.15	.10
1.40	.40	.29	.18	.12
1.50	.44	.32	.20	.14
1.60	.48	.36	.23	.17
1.70	.52	.40	.27	.19
1.80	.56	.44	.30	.22
1.90	.60	.48	.34	.25
2.00	.64	.52	.37	.28
2.10	.68	.56	.41	.32
2.20	.71	.60	.45	.35
2.30	.74	.63	.49	.39
2.40	.78	.67	.53	.43
2.50	.80	.71	.57	.47
2.60	.83	.74	.61	.51
2.70	.85	.77	.65	.55
2.80	.88	.80	.68	.59
2.90	.90	.83	.72	.63
3.00	.91	.85	.75	.66
3.10	.93	.87	.78	.70
3.20	.94	.89	.81	.73
3.30	.95	.91	.84	.77
3.40	.96	.93	.86	.80
3.50	.97	.94	.88	.82
3.60	.98	.95	.90	.85
3.70	.98	.96	.92	.87
3.80	.98	.97	.93	.89
3.90	.99	.97	.94	.91
4.00	.99	.98	.95	.92
4.10	.99	.98	.96	.94
4.20	—	.99	.97	.95
4.30	—	.99	.98	.96
4.40	—	.99	.98	.97
4.50	—	.99	.99	.97
4.60	—	—	.99	.98
4.70	—	—	.99	.98
4.80	—	—	.99	.99
4.90	—	—	—	.99
5.00	—	—	—	.99

Source: The entries in this table were computed by the author.

APPENDIX q: CRITICAL VALUES OF THE STUDENTIZED RANGE STATISTIC (q)

TABLE 1 $\alpha = .05$

Error df	\multicolumn{14}{c}{r = Number of Steps Between Ordered Means}
	2	3	4	5	6	7	8	9	10	11	12	13	14	15
1	17.97	26.98	32.82	37.08	40.41	43.12	45.40	47.36	49.07	50.59	51.96	53.20	54.33	55.36
2	6.08	8.33	9.80	10.88	11.74	12.44	13.03	13.54	13.99	14.39	14.75	15.08	15.38	15.65
3	4.50	5.91	6.82	7.50	8.04	8.48	8.85	9.18	9.46	9.72	9.95	10.15	10.35	10.53
4	3.93	5.04	5.76	6.29	6.71	7.05	7.35	7.60	7.83	8.03	8.21	8.37	8.52	8.66
5	3.64	4.60	5.22	5.67	6.03	6.33	6.58	6.80	7.00	7.17	7.32	7.47	7.60	7.72
6	3.46	4.34	4.90	5.31	5.63	5.90	6.12	6.32	6.49	6.65	6.79	6.92	7.03	7.14
7	3.34	4.16	4.68	5.06	5.36	5.61	5.82	6.00	6.16	6.30	6.43	6.55	6.66	6.76
8	3.26	4.04	4.53	4.89	5.17	5.40	5.60	5.77	5.92	6.05	6.18	6.29	6.39	6.48
9	3.20	3.95	4.42	4.76	5.02	5.24	5.43	5.60	5.74	5.87	5.98	6.09	6.19	6.28
10	3.15	3.88	4.33	4.65	4.91	5.12	5.30	5.46	5.60	5.72	5.83	5.94	6.03	6.11
11	3.11	3.82	4.26	4.57	4.82	5.03	5.20	5.35	5.49	5.60	5.71	5.81	5.90	5.98
12	3.08	3.77	4.20	4.51	4.75	4.95	5.12	5.26	5.40	5.51	5.62	5.71	5.79	5.88
13	3.06	3.74	4.15	4.45	4.69	4.88	5.05	5.19	5.32	5.43	5.53	5.63	5.71	5.79
14	3.03	3.70	4.11	4.41	4.64	4.83	4.99	5.13	5.25	5.36	5.46	5.55	5.64	5.71
15	3.01	3.67	4.08	4.37	4.60	4.78	4.94	5.08	5.20	5.31	5.40	5.49	5.57	5.65
16	3.00	3.65	4.05	4.33	4.56	4.74	4.90	5.03	5.15	5.26	5.35	5.44	5.52	5.59
17	2.98	3.63	4.02	4.30	4.52	4.70	4.86	4.99	5.11	5.21	5.31	5.39	5.47	5.54
18	2.97	3.61	4.00	4.28	4.50	4.67	4.82	4.96	5.07	5.17	5.27	5.35	5.43	5.50
19	2.96	3.59	3.98	4.25	4.47	4.64	4.79	4.92	5.04	5.14	5.23	5.32	5.39	5.46
20	2.95	3.58	3.96	4.23	4.44	4.62	4.77	4.90	5.01	5.11	5.20	5.28	5.36	5.43
24	2.92	3.53	3.90	4.17	4.37	4.54	4.68	4.81	4.92	5.01	5.10	5.18	5.25	5.32
30	2.89	3.49	3.84	4.10	4.30	4.46	4.60	4.72	4.82	4.92	5.00	5.08	5.15	5.21
40	2.86	3.44	3.79	4.04	4.23	4.39	4.52	4.64	4.74	4.82	4.90	4.98	5.04	5.11
60	2.83	3.40	3.74	3.98	4.16	4.31	4.44	4.55	4.65	4.73	4.81	4.88	4.94	5.00
120	2.80	3.36	3.69	3.92	4.10	4.24	4.36	4.47	4.56	4.64	4.71	4.78	4.84	4.90
∞	2.77	3.31	3.63	3.86	4.03	4.17	4.29	4.39	4.47	4.55	4.62	4.68	4.74	4.80

TABLE 2 $\alpha = .01$

| | r = Number of Steps Between Ordered Means | | | | | | | | | | | | | |
Error df	2	3	4	5	6	7	8	9	10	11	12	13	14	15
1	90.03	135.0	164.3	185.6	202.2	215.8	227.2	237.0	245.6	253.2	260.0	266.2	271.8	277.0
2	14.04	19.02	22.29	24.72	26.63	28.20	29.53	30.68	31.69	32.59	33.40	34.13	34.81	35.43
3	8.26	10.62	12.17	13.33	14.24	15.00	15.64	16.20	16.69	17.13	17.53	17.89	18.22	18.52
4	6.51	8.12	9.17	9.96	10.58	11.10	11.55	11.93	12.27	12.57	12.84	13.09	13.32	13.53
5	5.70	6.98	7.80	8.42	8.91	9.32	9.67	9.97	10.24	10.48	10.70	10.89	11.08	11.24
6	5.24	6.33	7.03	7.56	7.97	8.32	8.62	8.87	9.10	9.30	9.48	9.65	9.81	9.95
7	4.95	5.92	6.54	7.00	7.37	7.68	7.94	8.17	8.37	8.55	8.71	8.86	9.00	9.12
8	4.75	5.64	6.20	6.62	6.96	7.24	7.47	7.68	7.86	8.03	8.18	8.31	8.44	8.55
9	4.60	5.43	5.96	6.35	6.66	6.92	7.13	7.32	7.50	7.65	7.78	7.91	8.02	8.13
10	4.48	5.27	5.77	6.14	6.43	6.67	6.88	7.06	7.21	7.36	7.48	7.60	7.71	7.81
11	4.39	5.15	5.62	5.97	6.25	6.48	6.67	6.84	6.99	7.13	7.25	7.36	7.46	7.56
12	4.32	5.05	5.50	5.84	6.10	6.32	6.51	6.67	6.81	6.94	7.06	7.17	7.26	7.36
13	4.26	4.96	5.40	5.73	5.98	6.19	6.37	6.53	6.67	6.79	6.90	7.01	7.10	7.19
14	4.21	4.90	5.32	5.63	5.88	6.08	6.26	6.41	6.54	6.66	6.77	6.87	6.96	7.05
15	4.17	4.84	5.25	5.56	5.80	5.99	6.16	6.31	6.44	6.56	6.66	6.76	6.84	6.93
16	4.13	4.79	5.19	5.49	5.72	5.92	6.08	6.22	6.35	6.46	6.56	6.66	6.74	6.82
17	4.10	4.74	5.14	5.43	5.66	5.85	6.01	6.15	6.27	6.38	6.48	6.57	6.66	6.73
18	4.07	4.70	5.09	5.38	5.60	5.79	5.94	6.08	6.20	6.31	6.41	6.50	6.58	6.66
19	4.05	4.67	5.05	5.33	5.55	5.74	5.89	6.02	6.14	6.25	6.34	6.43	6.51	6.58
20	4.02	4.64	5.02	5.29	5.51	5.69	5.84	5.97	6.09	6.19	6.28	6.37	6.45	6.52
24	3.96	4.55	4.91	5.17	5.37	5.54	5.69	5.81	5.92	6.02	6.11	6.19	6.26	6.33
30	3.89	4.46	4.80	5.05	5.24	5.40	5.54	5.65	5.76	5.85	5.93	6.01	6.08	6.14
40	3.82	4.37	4.70	4.93	5.11	5.26	5.39	5.50	5.60	5.69	5.76	5.84	5.90	5.96
60	3.76	4.28	4.60	4.82	4.99	5.13	5.25	5.36	5.45	5.53	5.60	5.67	5.73	5.78
120	3.70	4.20	4.50	4.71	4.87	5.0	5.12	5.21	5.30	5.38	5.44	5.51	5.56	5.61
∞	3.64	4.12	4.40	4.60	4.76	4.88	4.99	5.08	5.16	5.23	5.29	5.35	5.40	5.45

Source: Abridged from H. L. Harter (1960), Tables of range and Studentized range, *Annuals of Mathematical Statistics, 31*, 1122–1147, with permission of the author and the publisher.

APPENDIX r': TABLE OF FISHER'S TRANSFORMATION OF r TO r'

r	r'	r	r'	r	r'	r	r'	r	r'
0.000	0.000	0.200	0.203	0.400	0.424	0.600	0.693	0.800	1.099
0.005	0.005	0.205	0.208	0.405	0.430	0.605	0.701	0.805	1.113
0.010	0.010	0.210	0.213	0.410	0.436	0.610	0.709	0.810	1.127
0.015	0.015	0.215	0.218	0.415	0.442	0.615	0.717	0.815	1.142
0.020	0.020	0.220	0.224	0.420	0.448	0.620	0.725	0.820	1.157
0.025	0.025	0.225	0.229	0.425	0.454	0.625	0.733	0.825	1.172
0.030	0.030	0.230	0.234	0.430	0.460	0.630	0.741	0.830	1.188
0.035	0.035	0.235	0.239	0.435	0.466	0.635	0.750	0.835	1.204
0.040	0.040	0.240	0.245	0.440	0.472	0.640	0.758	0.840	1.221
0.045	0.045	0.245	0.250	0.445	0.478	0.645	0.767	0.845	1.238
0.050	0.050	0.250	0.255	0.450	0.485	0.650	0.775	0.850	1.256
0.055	0.055	0.255	0.261	0.455	0.491	0.655	0.784	0.855	1.274
0.060	0.060	0.260	0.266	0.460	0.497	0.660	0.793	0.860	1.293
0.065	0.065	0.265	0.271	0.465	0.504	0.665	0.802	0.865	1.313
0.070	0.070	0.270	0.277	0.470	0.510	0.670	0.811	0.870	1.333
0.075	0.075	0.275	0.282	0.475	0.517	0.675	0.820	0.875	1.354
0.080	0.080	0.280	0.288	0.480	0.523	0.680	0.829	0.880	1.376
0.085	0.085	0.285	0.293	0.485	0.530	0.685	0.838	0.885	1.398
0.090	0.090	0.290	0.299	0.490	0.536	0.690	0.848	0.890	1.422
0.095	0.095	0.295	0.304	0.495	0.543	0.695	0.858	0.895	1.447
0.100	0.100	0.300	0.310	0.500	0.549	0.700	0.867	0.900	1.472
0.105	0.105	0.305	0.315	0.505	0.556	0.705	0.877	0.905	1.499
0.110	0.110	0.310	0.321	0.510	0.563	0.710	0.887	0.910	1.528
0.115	0.116	0.315	0.326	0.515	0.570	0.715	0.897	0.915	1.557
0.120	0.121	0.320	0.332	0.520	0.576	0.720	0.908	0.920	1.589
0.125	0.126	0.325	0.337	0.525	0.583	0.725	0.918	0.925	1.623
0.130	0.131	0.330	0.343	0.530	0.590	0.730	0.929	0.930	1.658
0.135	0.136	0.335	0.348	0.535	0.597	0.735	0.940	0.935	1.697
0.140	0.141	0.340	0.354	0.540	0.604	0.740	0.950	0.940	1.738
0.145	0.146	0.345	0.360	0.545	0.611	0.745	0.962	0.945	1.783
0.150	0.151	0.350	0.365	0.550	0.618	0.750	0.973	0.950	1.832
0.155	0.156	0.355	0.371	0.555	0.626	0.755	0.984	0.955	1.886
0.160	0.161	0.360	0.377	0.560	0.633	0.760	0.996	0.960	1.946
0.165	0.167	0.365	0.383	0.565	0.640	0.765	1.008	0.965	2.014
0.170	0.172	0.370	0.388	0.570	0.648	0.770	1.020	0.970	2.092
0.175	0.177	0.375	0.394	0.575	0.655	0.775	1.033	0.975	2.185
0.180	0.182	0.380	0.400	0.580	0.662	0.780	1.045	0.980	2.298
0.185	0.187	0.385	0.406	0.585	0.670	0.785	1.058	0.985	2.443
0.190	0.192	0.390	0.412	0.590	0.678	0.790	1.071	0.990	2.647
0.195	0.198	0.395	0.418	0.595	0.685	0.795	1.085	0.995	2.994

Source: The entries in this table were computed by the author.

APPENDIX t: PERCENTAGE POINTS OF THE t DISTRIBUTION

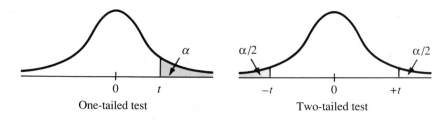

One-tailed test   Two-tailed test

	Level of Significance for One-Tailed Test								
	.25	.20	.15	.10	.05	.025	.01	.005	.0005
	Level of Significance for Two-Tailed Test								
df	.50	.40	.30	.20	.10	.05	.02	.01	.001
1	1.000	1.376	1.963	3.078	6.314	12.706	31.821	63.657	636.620
2	0.816	1.061	1.386	1.886	2.920	4.303	6.965	9.925	31.599
3	0.765	0.978	1.250	1.638	2.353	3.182	4.541	5.841	12.924
4	0.741	0.941	1.190	1.533	2.132	2.776	3.747	4.604	8.610
5	0.727	0.920	1.156	1.476	2.015	2.571	3.365	4.032	6.869
6	0.718	0.906	1.134	1.440	1.943	2.447	3.143	3.707	5.959
7	0.711	0.896	1.119	1.415	1.895	2.365	2.998	3.499	5.408
8	0.706	0.889	1.108	1.397	1.860	2.306	2.896	3.355	5.041
9	0.703	0.883	1.100	1.383	1.833	2.262	2.821	3.250	4.781
10	0.700	0.879	1.093	1.372	1.812	2.228	2.764	3.169	4.587
11	0.697	0.876	1.088	1.363	1.796	2.201	2.718	3.106	4.437
12	0.695	0.873	1.083	1.356	1.782	2.179	2.681	3.055	4.318
13	0.694	0.870	1.079	1.350	1.771	2.160	2.650	3.012	4.221
14	0.692	0.868	1.076	1.345	1.761	2.145	2.624	2.977	4.140
15	0.691	0.866	1.074	1.341	1.753	2.131	2.602	2.947	4.073
16	0.690	0.865	1.071	1.337	1.746	2.120	2.583	2.921	4.015
17	0.689	0.863	1.069	1.333	1.740	2.110	2.567	2.898	3.965
18	0.688	0.862	1.067	1.330	1.734	2.101	2.552	2.878	3.922
19	0.688	0.861	1.066	1.328	1.729	2.093	2.539	2.861	3.883
20	0.687	0.860	1.064	1.325	1.725	2.086	2.528	2.845	3.850
21	0.686	0.859	1.063	1.323	1.721	2.080	2.518	2.831	3.819
22	0.686	0.858	1.061	1.321	1.717	2.074	2.508	2.819	3.792
23	0.685	0.858	1.060	1.319	1.714	2.069	2.500	2.807	3.768
24	0.685	0.857	1.059	1.318	1.711	2.064	2.492	2.797	3.745
25	0.684	0.856	1.058	1.316	1.708	2.060	2.485	2.787	3.725
26	0.684	0.856	1.058	1.315	1.706	2.056	2.479	2.779	3.707
27	0.684	0.855	1.057	1.314	1.703	2.052	2.473	2.771	3.690
28	0.683	0.855	1.056	1.313	1.701	2.048	2.467	2.763	3.674
29	0.683	0.854	1.055	1.311	1.699	2.045	2.462	2.756	3.659
30	0.683	0.854	1.055	1.310	1.697	2.042	2.457	2.750	3.646
40	0.681	0.851	1.050	1.303	1.684	2.021	2.423	2.704	3.551
50	0.679	0.849	1.047	1.299	1.676	2.009	2.403	2.678	3.496
100	0.677	0.845	1.042	1.290	1.660	1.984	2.364	2.626	3.390
∞	0.674	0.842	1.036	1.282	1.645	1.960	2.326	2.576	3.291

Source: The entries in this table were computed by the author.

APPENDIX T: CRITICAL LOWER-TAIL VALUES OF T (AND THEIR ASSOCIATED PROBABILITIES) FOR WILCOXON'S MATCHED-PAIRS SIGNED-RANKS TEST

	Nominal α (One-Tailed)							
	.05		.025		.01		.005	
N	T	α	T	α	T	α	T	α
5	0	.0313						
	1	.0625						
6	2	.0469	0	.0156				
	3	.0781	1	.0313				
7	3	.0391	2	.0234	0	.0078		
	4	.0547	3	.0391	1	.0156		
8	5	.0391	3	.0195	1	.0078	0	.0039
	6	.0547	4	.0273	2	.0117	1	.0078
9	8	.0488	5	.0195	3	.0098	1	.0039
	9	.0645	6	.0273	4	.0137	2	.0059
10	10	.0420	8	.0244	5	.0098	3	.0049
	11	.0527	9	.0322	6	.0137	4	.0068
11	13	.0415	10	.0210	7	.0093	5	.0049
	14	.0508	11	.0269	8	.0122	6	.0068
12	17	.0461	13	.0212	9	.0081	7	.0046
	18	.0549	14	.0261	10	.0105	8	.0061
13	21	.0471	17	.0239	12	.0085	9	.0040
	22	.0549	18	.0287	13	.0107	10	.0052
14	25	.0453	21	.0247	15	.0083	12	.0043
	26	.0520	22	.0290	16	.0101	13	.0054
15	30	.0473	25	.0240	19	.0090	15	.0042
	31	.0535	26	.0277	20	.0108	16	.0051
16	35	.0467	29	.0222	23	.0091	19	.0046
	36	.0523	30	.0253	24	.0107	20	.0055
17	41	.0492	34	.0224	27	.0087	23	.0047
	42	.0544	35	.0253	28	.0101	24	.0055
18	47	.0494	40	.0241	32	.0091	27	.0045
	48	.0542	41	.0269	33	.0104	28	.0052
19	53	.0478	46	.0247	37	.0090	32	.0047
	54	.0521	47	.0273	38	.0102	33	.0054
20	60	.0487	52	.0242	43	.0096	37	.0047
	61	.0527	53	.0266	44	.0107	38	.0053
21	67	.0479	58	.0230	49	.0097	42	.0045
	68	.0516	59	.0251	50	.0108	43	.0051

APPENDIX T (Cont.)

	Nominal α (One-Tailed)							
	.05		**.025**		**.01**		**.005**	
N	T	α	T	α	T	α	T	α
22	75	.0492	65	.0231	55	.0095	48	.0046
	76	.0527	66	.0250	56	.0104	49	.0052
23	83	.0490	73	.0242	62	.0098	54	.0046
	84	.0523	74	.0261	63	.0107	55	.0051
24	91	.0475	81	.0245	69	.0097	61	.0048
	92	.0505	82	.0263	70	.0106	62	.0053
25	100	.0479	89	.0241	76	.0094	68	.0048
	101	.0507	90	.0258	77	.0101	69	.0053
26	110	.0497	98	.0247	84	.0095	75	.0047
	111	.0524	99	.0263	85	.0102	76	.0051
27	119	.0477	107	.0246	92	.0093	83	.0048
	120	.0502	108	.0260	93	.0100	84	.0052
28	130	.0496	116	.0239	101	.0096	91	.0048
	131	.0521	117	.0252	102	.0102	92	.0051
29	140	.0482	126	.0240	110	.0095	100	.0049
	141	.0504	127	.0253	111	.0101	101	.0053
30	151	.0481	137	.0249	120	.0098	109	.0050
	152	.0502	138	.0261	121	.0104	110	.0053
31	163	.0491	147	.0239	130	.0099	118	.0049
	164	.0512	148	.0251	131	.0105	119	.0052
32	175	.0492	159	.0249	140	.0097	128	.0050
	176	.0512	160	.0260	141	.0103	129	.0053
33	187	.0485	170	.0242	151	.0099	138	.0049
	188	.0503	171	.0253	152	.0104	139	.0052
34	200	.0488	182	.0242	162	.0098	148	.0048
	201	.0506	183	.0252	163	.0103	149	.0051
35	213	.0484	195	.0247	173	.0096	159	.0048
	214	.0501	196	.0257	174	.0100	160	.0051
36	227	.0489	208	.0248	185	.0096	171	.0050
	228	.0505	209	.0258	186	.0100	172	.0052
37	241	.0487	221	.0245	198	.0099	182	.0048
	242	.0503	222	.0254	199	.0103	183	.0050

APPENDIX T (Cont.)

N	.05		.025		.01		.005	
	T	α	T	α	T	α	T	α
38	256	.0493	235	.0247	211	.0099	194	.0048
	257	.0509	236	.0256	212	.0104	195	.0050
39	271	.0492	249	.0246	224	.0099	207	.0049
	272	.0507	250	.0254	225	.0103	208	.0051
40	286	.0486	264	.0249	238	.0100	220	.0049
	287	.0500	265	.0257	239	.0104	221	.0051
41	302	.0488	279	.0248	252	.0100	233	.0048
	303	.0501	280	.0256	253	.0103	234	.0050
42	319	.0496	294	.0245	266	.0098	247	.0049
	320	.0509	295	.0252	267	.0102	248	.0051
43	336	.0498	310	.0245	281	.0098	261	.0048
	337	.0511	311	.0252	282	.0102	262	.0050
44	353	.0495	327	.0250	296	.0097	276	.0049
	354	.0507	328	.0257	297	.0101	277	.0051
45	371	.0498	343	.0244	312	.0098	291	.0049
	372	.0510	344	.0251	313	.0101	292	.0051
46	389	.0497	361	.0249	328	.0098	307	.0050
	390	.0508	362	.0256	329	.0101	308	.0052
47	407	.0490	378	.0245	345	.0099	322	.0048
	408	.0501	379	.0251	346	.0102	323	.0050
48	426	.0490	396	.0244	362	.0099	339	.0050
	427	.0500	397	.0251	363	.0102	340	.0051
49	446	.0495	415	.0247	379	.0098	355	.0049
	447	.0505	416	.0253	380	.0100	356	.0050
50	466	.0495	434	.0247	397	.0098	373	.0050
	467	.0506	435	.0253	398	.0101	374	.0051

Nominal α (One-Tailed)

Source: The entries in this table were computed by the author.

APPENDIX t': CRITICAL VALUES OF BONFERRONI MULTIPLE COMPARISON TEST

TABLE 1 $\alpha = .05$

df	\multicolumn{9}{c}{Number of Comparisons}
	2	3	4	5	6	7	8	9	10
5	3.16	3.53	3.81	4.03	4.22	4.38	4.53	4.66	4.77
6	2.97	3.29	3.52	3.71	3.86	4.00	4.12	4.22	4.32
7	2.84	3.13	3.34	3.50	3.64	3.75	3.86	3.95	4.03
8	2.75	3.02	3.21	3.36	3.48	3.58	3.68	3.76	3.83
9	2.69	2.93	3.11	3.25	3.36	3.46	3.55	3.62	3.69
10	2.63	2.87	3.04	3.17	3.28	3.37	3.45	3.52	3.58
11	2.59	2.82	2.98	3.11	3.21	3.29	3.37	3.44	3.50
12	2.56	2.78	2.93	3.05	3.15	3.24	3.31	3.37	3.43
13	2.53	2.75	2.90	3.01	3.11	3.19	3.26	3.32	3.37
14	2.51	2.72	2.86	2.98	3.07	3.15	3.21	3.27	3.33
15	2.49	2.69	2.84	2.95	3.04	3.11	3.18	3.23	3.29
16	2.47	2.67	2.81	2.92	3.01	3.08	3.15	3.20	3.25
17	2.46	2.65	2.79	2.90	2.98	3.06	3.12	3.17	3.22
18	2.45	2.64	2.77	2.88	2.96	3.03	3.09	3.15	3.20
19	2.43	2.63	2.76	2.86	2.94	3.01	3.07	3.13	3.17
20	2.42	2.61	2.74	2.85	2.93	3.00	3.06	3.11	3.15
21	2.41	2.60	2.73	2.83	2.91	2.98	3.04	3.09	3.14
22	2.41	2.59	2.72	2.82	2.90	2.97	3.02	3.07	3.12
23	2.40	2.58	2.71	2.81	2.89	2.95	3.01	3.06	3.10
24	2.39	2.57	2.70	2.80	2.88	2.94	3.00	3.05	3.09
25	2.38	2.57	2.69	2.79	2.86	2.93	2.99	3.03	3.08
30	2.36	2.54	2.66	2.75	2.82	2.89	2.94	2.99	3.03
40	2.33	2.50	2.62	2.70	2.78	2.84	2.89	2.93	2.97
50	2.31	2.48	2.59	2.68	2.75	2.81	2.85	2.90	2.94
75	2.29	2.45	2.56	2.64	2.71	2.77	2.81	2.86	2.89
100	2.28	2.43	2.54	2.63	2.69	2.75	2.79	2.83	2.87
∞	2.24	2.39	2.50	2.58	2.64	2.69	2.73	2.77	2.81

TABLE 1 (Cont.)

df	\multicolumn{8}{c}{Number of Comparisons}
	15	20	25	30	35	40	45	50	55
5	5.25	5.60	5.89	6.14	6.35	6.54	6.71	6.87	7.01
6	4.70	4.98	5.21	5.40	5.56	5.71	5.84	5.96	6.07
7	4.36	4.59	4.79	4.94	5.08	5.20	5.31	5.41	5.50
8	4.12	4.33	4.50	4.64	4.76	4.86	4.96	5.04	5.12
9	3.95	4.15	4.30	4.42	4.53	4.62	4.71	4.78	4.85
10	3.83	4.00	4.14	4.26	4.36	4.44	4.52	4.59	4.65
11	3.73	3.89	4.02	4.13	4.22	4.30	4.37	4.44	4.49
12	3.65	3.81	3.93	4.03	4.12	4.19	4.26	4.32	4.37
13	3.58	3.73	3.85	3.95	4.03	4.10	4.16	4.22	4.27
14	3.53	3.67	3.79	3.88	3.96	4.03	4.09	4.14	4.19
15	3.48	3.62	3.73	3.82	3.90	3.96	4.02	4.07	4.12
16	3.44	3.58	3.69	3.77	3.85	3.91	3.96	4.01	4.06
17	3.41	3.54	3.65	3.73	3.80	3.86	3.92	3.97	4.01
18	3.38	3.51	3.61	3.69	3.76	3.82	3.87	3.92	3.96
19	3.35	3.48	3.58	3.66	3.73	3.79	3.84	3.88	3.93
20	3.33	3.46	3.55	3.63	3.70	3.75	3.80	3.85	3.89
21	3.31	3.43	3.53	3.60	3.67	3.73	3.78	3.82	3.86
22	3.29	3.41	3.50	3.58	3.64	3.70	3.75	3.79	3.83
23	3.27	3.39	3.48	3.56	3.62	3.68	3.72	3.77	3.81
24	3.26	3.38	3.47	3.54	3.60	3.66	3.70	3.75	3.78
25	3.24	3.36	3.45	3.52	3.58	3.64	3.68	3.73	3.76
30	3.19	3.30	3.39	3.45	3.51	3.56	3.61	3.65	3.68
40	3.12	3.23	3.31	3.37	3.43	3.47	3.51	3.55	3.58
50	3.08	3.18	3.26	3.32	3.38	3.42	3.46	3.50	3.53
75	3.03	3.13	3.20	3.26	3.31	3.35	3.39	3.43	3.45
100	3.01	3.10	3.17	3.23	3.28	3.32	3.36	3.39	3.42
∞	2.94	3.02	3.09	3.14	3.19	3.23	3.26	3.29	3.32

TABLE 2 $\alpha = .01$

df	\multicolumn{9}{c}{Number of Comparisons}
	2	3	4	5	6	7	8	9	10
5	4.77	5.25	5.60	5.89	6.14	6.35	6.54	6.71	6.87
6	4.32	4.70	4.98	5.21	5.40	5.56	5.71	5.84	5.96
7	4.03	4.36	4.59	4.79	4.94	5.08	5.20	5.31	5.41
8	3.83	4.12	4.33	4.50	4.64	4.76	4.86	4.96	5.04
9	3.69	3.95	4.15	4.30	4.42	4.53	4.62	4.71	4.78
10	3.58	3.83	4.00	4.14	4.26	4.36	4.44	4.52	4.59
11	3.50	3.73	3.89	4.02	4.13	4.22	4.30	4.37	4.44
12	3.43	3.65	3.81	3.93	4.03	4.12	4.19	4.26	4.32
13	3.37	3.58	3.73	3.85	3.95	4.03	4.10	4.16	4.22
14	3.33	3.53	3.67	3.79	3.88	3.96	4.03	4.09	4.14
15	3.29	3.48	3.62	3.73	3.82	3.90	3.96	4.02	4.07
16	3.25	3.44	3.58	3.69	3.77	3.85	3.91	3.96	4.01
17	3.22	3.41	3.54	3.65	3.73	3.80	3.86	3.92	3.97
18	3.20	3.38	3.51	3.61	3.69	3.76	3.82	3.87	3.92
19	3.17	3.35	3.48	3.58	3.66	3.73	3.79	3.84	3.88
20	3.15	3.33	3.46	3.55	3.63	3.70	3.75	3.80	3.85
21	3.14	3.31	3.43	3.53	3.60	3.67	3.73	3.78	3.82
22	3.12	3.29	3.41	3.50	3.58	3.64	3.70	3.75	3.79
23	3.10	3.27	3.39	3.48	3.56	3.62	3.68	3.72	3.77
24	3.09	3.26	3.38	3.47	3.54	3.60	3.66	3.70	3.75
25	3.08	3.24	3.36	3.45	3.52	3.58	3.64	3.68	3.73
30	3.03	3.19	3.30	3.39	3.45	3.51	3.56	3.61	3.65
40	2.97	3.12	3.23	3.31	3.37	3.43	3.47	3.51	3.55
50	2.94	3.08	3.18	3.26	3.32	3.38	3.42	3.46	3.50
75	2.89	3.03	3.13	3.20	3.26	3.31	3.35	3.39	3.43
100	2.87	3.01	3.10	3.17	3.23	3.28	3.32	3.36	3.39
∞	2.81	2.94	3.02	3.09	3.14	3.19	3.23	3.26	3.29

TABLE 2 (Cont.)

df	Number of Comparisons								
	15	20	25	30	35	40	45	50	55
5	7.50	7.98	8.36	8.69	8.98	9.24	9.47	9.68	9.87
6	6.43	6.79	7.07	7.31	7.52	7.71	7.87	8.02	8.16
7	5.80	6.08	6.31	6.50	6.67	6.81	6.94	7.06	7.17
8	5.37	5.62	5.81	5.97	6.11	6.23	6.34	6.44	6.53
9	5.08	5.29	5.46	5.60	5.72	5.83	5.92	6.01	6.09
10	4.85	5.05	5.20	5.33	5.44	5.53	5.62	5.69	5.76
11	4.68	4.86	5.00	5.12	5.22	5.31	5.38	5.45	5.52
12	4.55	4.72	4.85	4.96	5.05	5.13	5.20	5.26	5.32
13	4.44	4.60	4.72	4.82	4.91	4.98	5.05	5.11	5.17
14	4.35	4.50	4.62	4.71	4.79	4.87	4.93	4.99	5.04
15	4.27	4.42	4.53	4.62	4.70	4.77	4.83	4.88	4.93
16	4.21	4.35	4.45	4.54	4.62	4.68	4.74	4.79	4.84
17	4.15	4.29	4.39	4.47	4.55	4.61	4.66	4.71	4.76
18	4.10	4.23	4.33	4.42	4.49	4.55	4.60	4.65	4.69
19	4.06	4.19	4.28	4.36	4.43	4.49	4.54	4.59	4.63
20	4.02	4.15	4.24	4.32	4.39	4.44	4.49	4.54	4.58
21	3.99	4.11	4.20	4.28	4.34	4.40	4.45	4.49	4.53
22	3.96	4.08	4.17	4.24	4.31	4.36	4.41	4.45	4.49
23	3.93	4.05	4.14	4.21	4.27	4.33	4.37	4.42	4.45
24	3.91	4.02	4.11	4.18	4.24	4.29	4.34	4.38	4.42
25	3.88	4.00	4.08	4.15	4.21	4.27	4.31	4.35	4.39
30	3.80	3.90	3.98	4.05	4.11	4.15	4.20	4.23	4.27
40	3.69	3.79	3.86	3.92	3.98	4.02	4.06	4.09	4.13
50	3.63	3.72	3.79	3.85	3.90	3.94	3.98	4.01	4.04
75	3.55	3.64	3.71	3.76	3.81	3.85	3.88	3.91	3.94
100	3.51	3.60	3.66	3.72	3.76	3.80	3.83	3.86	3.89
∞	3.40	3.48	3.54	3.59	3.63	3.66	3.69	3.72	3.74

Source: The entries in this table were computed by the author.

APPENDIX t_d: CRITICAL VALUES OF DUNNETT'S t STATISTIC (t_d)

Error df	α	Two-Tailed Comparisons k = number of treatment means, including control								
		2	3	4	5	6	7	8	9	10
5	.05	2.57	3.03	3.29	3.48	3.62	3.73	3.82	3.90	3.97
	.01	4.03	4.63	4.98	5.22	5.41	5.56	5.69	5.80	5.89
6	.05	2.45	2.86	3.10	3.26	3.39	3.49	3.57	3.64	3.71
	.01	3.71	4.21	4.51	4.71	4.87	5.00	5.10	5.20	5.28
7	.05	2.36	2.75	2.97	3.12	3.24	3.33	3.41	3.47	3.53
	.01	3.50	3.95	4.21	4.39	4.53	4.64	4.74	4.82	4.89
8	.05	2.31	2.67	2.88	3.02	3.13	3.22	3.29	3.35	3.41
	.01	3.36	3.77	4.00	4.17	4.29	4.40	4.48	4.56	4.62
9	.05	2.26	2.61	2.81	2.95	3.05	3.14	3.20	3.26	3.32
	.01	3.25	3.63	3.85	4.01	4.12	4.22	4.30	4.37	4.43
10	.05	2.23	2.57	2.76	2.89	2.99	3.07	3.14	3.19	3.24
	.01	3.17	3.53	3.74	3.88	3.99	4.08	4.16	4.22	4.28
11	.05	2.20	2.53	2.72	2.84	2.94	3.02	3.08	3.14	3.19
	.01	3.11	3.45	3.65	3.79	3.89	3.98	4.05	4.11	4.16
12	.05	2.18	2.50	2.68	2.81	2.90	2.98	3.04	3.09	3.14
	.01	3.05	3.39	3.58	3.71	3.81	3.89	3.96	4.02	4.07
13	.05	2.16	2.48	2.65	2.78	2.87	2.94	3.00	3.06	3.10
	.01	3.01	3.33	3.52	3.65	3.74	3.82	3.89	3.94	3.99
14	.05	2.14	2.46	2.63	2.75	2.84	2.91	2.97	3.02	3.07
	.01	2.98	3.29	3.47	3.59	3.69	3.76	3.83	3.88	3.93
15	.05	2.13	2.44	2.61	2.73	2.82	2.89	2.95	3.00	3.04
	.01	2.95	3.25	3.43	3.55	3.64	3.71	3.78	3.83	3.88
16	.05	2.12	2.42	2.59	2.71	2.80	2.87	2.92	2.97	3.02
	.01	2.92	3.22	3.39	3.51	3.60	3.67	3.73	3.78	3.83
17	.05	2.11	2.41	2.58	2.69	2.78	2.85	2.90	2.95	3.00
	.01	2.90	3.19	3.36	3.47	3.56	3.63	3.69	3.74	3.79
18	.05	2.10	2.40	2.56	2.68	2.76	2.83	2.89	2.94	2.98
	.01	2.88	3.17	3.33	3.44	3.53	3.60	3.66	3.71	3.75
19	.05	2.09	2.39	2.55	2.66	2.75	2.81	2.87	2.92	2.96
	.01	2.86	3.15	3.31	3.42	3.50	3.57	3.63	3.68	3.72
20	.05	2.09	2.38	2.54	2.65	2.73	2.80	2.86	2.90	2.95
	.01	2.85	3.13	3.29	3.40	3.48	3.55	3.60	3.65	3.69
24	.05	2.06	2.35	2.51	2.61	2.70	2.76	2.81	2.86	2.90
	.01	2.80	3.07	3.22	3.32	3.40	3.47	3.52	3.57	3.61
30	.05	2.04	2.32	2.47	2.58	2.66	2.72	2.77	2.82	2.86
	.01	2.75	3.01	3.15	3.25	3.33	3.39	3.44	3.49	3.52
40	.05	2.02	2.29	2.44	2.54	2.62	2.68	2.73	2.77	2.81
	.01	2.70	2.95	3.09	3.19	3.26	3.32	3.37	3.41	3.44
60	.05	2.00	2.27	2.41	2.51	2.58	2.64	2.69	2.73	2.77
	.01	2.66	2.90	3.03	3.12	3.19	3.25	3.29	3.33	3.37
120	.05	1.98	2.24	2.38	2.47	2.55	2.60	2.65	2.69	2.73
	.01	2.62	2.85	2.97	3.06	3.12	3.18	3.22	3.26	3.29
∞	.05	1.96	2.21	2.35	2.44	2.51	2.57	2.61	2.65	2.69
	.01	2.58	2.79	2.92	3.00	3.06	3.11	3.15	3.19	3.22

Source: Reproduced from C. W. Dunnett (1964), New tables for multiple comparisons with a control, *Biometrics 20*, 482–491. With permission of The Biometric Society.

APPENDIX W_S: CRITICAL LOWER-TAIL VALUES OF W_S FOR RANK-SUM TEST FOR TWO INDEPENDENT SAMPLES ($N_1 \leq N_2$)

	N₁ = 1							N₁ = 2							
N_2	.001	.005	.010	.025	.05	.10	$2\overline{W}$	.001	.005	.010	.025	.05	.10	$2\overline{W}$	N_2
2							4						—	10	2
3							5						3	12	3
4							6					—	3	14	4
5							7					3	4	16	5
6							8					3	4	18	6
7							9				—	3	4	20	7
8						—	10				3	4	5	22	8
9						1	11				3	4	5	24	9
10						1	12				3	4	6	26	10
11						1	13				3	4	6	28	11
12						1	14			—	4	5	7	30	12
13						1	15		3	4	5	7	32	13
14						1	16		3	4	6	8	34	14
15						1	17		3	4	6	8	36	15
16						1	18		3	4	6	8	38	16
17						1	19		3	5	6	9	40	17
18					—	1	20	—	3	5	7	9	42	18
19					1	2	21	3	4	5	7	10	44	19
20					1	2	22	3	4	5	7	10	46	20
21					1	2	23	3	4	6	8	11	48	21
22					1	2	24	3	4	6	8	11	50	22
23					1	2	25	3	4	6	8	12	52	23
24					1	2	26	3	4	6	9	12	54	24
25	—	—	—	—	1	2	27	—	3	4	6	9	12	56	25

Note: For N₁ = 2, the columns are .001 | .005 | .010 | .025 | .05 | .10 | $2\overline{W}$ | N_2. The data above is aligned as: N₂=2: .10=—, $2\overline{W}$=10; N₂=3: .10=3, $2\overline{W}$=12; N₂=4: .05=—, .10=3, $2\overline{W}$=14; N₂=5: .05=3, .10=4, $2\overline{W}$=16; N₂=6: .05=3, .10=4, $2\overline{W}$=18; N₂=7: .025=—, .05=3, .10=4, $2\overline{W}$=20; N₂=8: .025=3, .05=4, .10=5, $2\overline{W}$=22; N₂=9: .025=3, .05=4, .10=5, $2\overline{W}$=24; N₂=10: .025=3, .05=4, .10=6, $2\overline{W}$=26; N₂=11: .025=3, .05=4, .10=6, $2\overline{W}$=28; N₂=12: .010=—, .025=4, .05=5, .10=7, $2\overline{W}$=30; N₂=13: .010=3, .025=4, .05=5, .10=7, $2\overline{W}$=32; N₂=14: .010=3, .025=4, .05=6, .10=8, $2\overline{W}$=34; N₂=15: .010=3, .025=4, .05=6, .10=8, $2\overline{W}$=36; N₂=16: .010=3, .025=4, .05=6, .10=8, $2\overline{W}$=38; N₂=17: .010=3, .025=5, .05=6, .10=9, $2\overline{W}$=40; N₂=18: .005=—, .010=3, .025=5, .05=7, .10=9, $2\overline{W}$=42; N₂=19: .005=3, .010=4, .025=5, .05=7, .10=10, $2\overline{W}$=44; N₂=20: .005=3, .010=4, .025=5, .05=7, .10=10, $2\overline{W}$=46; N₂=21: .005=3, .010=4, .025=6, .05=8, .10=11, $2\overline{W}$=48; N₂=22: .005=3, .010=4, .025=6, .05=8, .10=11, $2\overline{W}$=50; N₂=23: .005=3, .010=4, .025=6, .05=8, .10=12, $2\overline{W}$=52; N₂=24: .005=3, .010=4, .025=6, .05=9, .10=12, $2\overline{W}$=54; N₂=25: .001=—, .005=3, .010=4, .025=6, .05=9, .10=12, $2\overline{W}$=56.

	N₁ = 3							N₁ = 4							
N_2	.001	.005	.010	.025	.05	.10	$2\overline{W}$	.001	.005	.010	.025	.05	.10	$2\overline{W}$	N_2
3					6	7	21								
4				—	6	7	24			—	10	11	13	36	4
5				6	7	8	27		—	10	11	12	14	40	5
6			—	7	8	9	30		10	11	12	13	15	44	6
7			6	7	8	10	33		10	11	13	14	16	48	7
8		—	6	8	9	11	36		11	12	14	15	17	52	8
9		6	7	8	10	11	39	—	11	13	14	16	19	56	9
10		6	7	9	10	12	42	10	12	13	15	17	20	60	10
11		6	7	9	11	13	45	10	12	14	16	18	21	64	11
12		7	8	10	11	14	48	10	13	15	17	19	22	68	12
13		7	8	10	12	15	51	11	13	15	18	20	23	72	13
14		7	8	11	13	16	54	11	14	16	19	21	25	76	14
15		8	9	11	13	16	57	11	15	17	20	22	26	80	15

APPENDIX W_S (Cont.)

			$N_1 = 3$								$N_1 = 4$				
N_2	.001	.005	.010	.025	.05	.10	$2\overline{W}$	.001	.005	.010	.025	.05	.10	$2\overline{W}$	N_2
16	—	8	9	12	14	17	60	12	15	17	21	24	27	84	16
17	6	8	10	12	15	18	63	12	16	18	21	25	28	88	17
18	6	8	10	13	15	19	66	13	16	19	22	26	30	92	18
19	6	9	10	13	16	20	69	13	17	19	23	27	31	96	19
20	6	9	11	14	17	21	72	13	18	20	24	28	32	100	20
21	7	9	11	14	17	21	75	14	18	21	25	29	33	104	21
22	7	10	12	15	18	22	78	14	19	21	26	30	35	108	22
23	7	10	12	15	19	23	81	14	19	22	27	31	36	112	23
24	7	10	12	16	19	24	84	15	20	23	27	32	38	116	24
25	7	11	13	16	20	25	87	15	20	23	28	33	38	120	25

			$N_1 = 5$								$N_1 = 6$				
N_2	.001	.005	.010	.025	.05	.10	$2\overline{W}$	.001	.005	.010	.025	.05	.10	$2\overline{W}$	N_2
5		15	16	17	19	20	55								
6		16	17	18	20	22	60	—	23	24	26	28	30	78	6
7	—	16	18	20	21	23	65	21	24	25	27	29	32	84	7
8	15	17	19	21	23	25	70	22	25	27	29	31	34	90	8
9	16	18	20	22	24	27	75	23	26	28	31	33	36	96	9
10	16	19	21	23	26	28	80	24	27	29	32	35	38	102	10
11	17	20	22	24	27	30	85	25	28	30	34	37	40	108	11
12	17	21	23	26	28	32	90	25	30	32	35	38	42	114	12
13	18	22	24	27	30	33	95	26	31	33	37	40	44	120	13
14	18	22	25	28	31	35	100	27	32	34	38	42	46	126	14
15	19	23	26	29	33	37	105	28	33	36	40	44	48	132	15
16	20	24	27	30	34	38	110	29	34	37	42	46	50	138	16
17	20	25	28	32	35	40	115	30	36	39	43	47	52	144	17
18	21	26	29	33	37	42	120	31	37	40	45	49	55	150	18
19	22	27	30	34	38	43	125	32	38	41	46	51	57	156	19
20	22	28	31	35	40	45	130	33	39	43	48	53	59	162	20
21	23	29	32	37	41	47	135	33	40	44	50	55	61	168	21
22	23	29	33	38	43	48	140	34	42	45	51	57	63	174	22
23	24	30	34	39	44	50	145	35	43	47	53	58	65	180	23
24	25	31	35	40	45	51	150	36	44	48	54	60	67	186	24
25	25	32	36	42	47	53	155	37	45	50	56	62	69	192	25

APPENDIX W_S (Cont.)

	$N_1 = 7$							$N_1 = 8$							
N_2	.001	.005	.010	.025	.05	.10	$2\overline{W}$	.001	.005	.010	.025	.05	.10	$2\overline{W}$	N_2
7	29	32	34	36	39	41	105								
8	30	34	35	38	41	44	112	40	43	45	49	51	55	136	8
9	31	35	37	40	43	46	119	41	45	47	51	54	58	144	9
10	33	37	39	42	45	49	126	42	47	49	53	56	60	152	10
11	34	38	40	44	47	51	133	44	49	51	55	59	63	160	11
12	35	40	42	46	49	54	140	45	51	53	58	62	66	168	12
13	36	41	44	48	52	56	147	47	53	56	60	64	69	176	13
14	37	43	45	50	54	59	154	48	54	58	62	67	72	184	14
15	38	44	47	52	56	61	161	50	56	60	65	69	75	192	15
16	39	46	49	54	58	64	168	51	58	62	67	72	78	200	16
17	41	47	51	56	61	66	175	53	60	64	70	75	81	208	17
18	42	49	52	58	63	69	182	54	62	66	72	77	84	216	18
19	43	50	54	60	65	71	189	56	64	68	74	80	87	224	19
20	44	52	56	62	67	74	196	57	66	70	77	83	90	232	20
21	46	53	58	64	69	76	203	59	68	72	79	85	92	240	21
22	47	55	59	66	72	79	210	60	70	74	81	88	95	248	22
23	48	57	61	68	74	81	217	62	71	76	84	90	98	256	23
24	49	58	63	70	76	84	224	64	73	78	86	93	101	264	24
25	50	60	64	72	78	86	231	65	75	81	89	96	104	272	25

	$N_1 = 9$							$N_1 = 10$							
N_2	.001	.005	.010	.025	.05	.10	$2\overline{W}$	.001	.005	.010	.025	.05	.10	$2\overline{W}$	N_2
9	52	56	59	62	66	70	171								
10	53	58	61	65	69	73	180	65	71	74	78	82	87	210	10
11	55	61	63	68	72	76	189	67	73	77	81	86	91	220	11
12	57	63	66	71	75	80	198	69	76	79	84	89	94	230	12
13	59	65	68	73	78	83	207	72	79	82	88	92	98	240	13
14	60	67	71	76	81	86	216	74	81	85	91	96	102	250	14
15	62	69	73	79	84	90	225	76	84	88	94	99	106	260	15
16	64	72	76	82	87	93	234	78	86	91	97	103	109	270	16
17	66	74	78	84	90	97	243	80	89	93	100	106	113	280	17
18	68	76	81	87	93	100	252	82	92	96	103	110	117	290	18
19	70	78	83	90	96	103	261	84	94	99	107	113	121	300	19
20	71	81	85	93	99	107	270	87	97	102	110	117	125	310	20
21	73	83	88	95	102	110	279	89	99	105	113	120	128	320	21
22	75	85	90	98	105	113	288	91	102	108	116	123	132	330	22
23	77	88	93	101	108	117	297	93	105	110	119	127	136	340	23
24	79	90	95	104	111	120	306	95	107	113	122	130	140	350	24
25	81	92	98	107	114	123	315	98	110	116	126	134	144	360	25

N_2	$N_1 = 11$							$N_1 = 12$							N_2
	.001	.005	.010	.025	.05	.10	$2\overline{W}$	.001	.005	.010	.025	.05	.10	$2\overline{W}$	
11	81	87	91	96	100	106	253								
12	83	90	94	99	104	110	264	98	105	109	115	120	127	300	12
13	86	93	97	103	108	114	275	101	109	113	119	125	131	312	13
14	88	96	100	106	112	118	286	103	112	116	123	129	136	324	14
15	90	99	103	110	116	123	297	106	115	120	127	133	141	336	15
16	93	102	107	113	120	127	308	109	119	124	131	138	145	348	16
17	95	105	110	117	123	131	319	112	122	127	135	142	150	360	17
18	98	108	113	121	127	135	330	115	125	131	139	146	155	372	18
19	100	111	116	124	131	139	341	118	129	134	143	150	159	384	19
20	103	114	119	128	135	144	352	120	132	138	147	155	164	396	20
21	106	117	123	131	139	148	363	123	136	142	151	159	169	408	21
22	108	120	126	135	143	152	374	126	139	145	155	163	173	420	22
23	111	123	129	139	147	156	385	129	142	149	159	168	178	432	23
24	113	126	132	142	151	161	396	132	146	153	163	172	183	444	24
25	116	129	136	146	155	165	407	135	149	156	167	176	187	456	25

N_2	$N_1 = 13$							$N_1 = 14$							N_2
	.001	.005	.010	.025	.05	.10	$2\overline{W}$	.001	.005	.010	.025	.05	.10	$2\overline{W}$	
13	117	125	130	136	142	149	351								
14	120	129	134	141	147	154	364	137	147	152	160	166	174	406	14
15	123	133	138	145	152	159	377	141	151	156	164	171	179	420	15
16	126	136	142	150	156	165	390	144	155	161	169	176	185	434	16
17	129	140	146	154	161	170	403	148	159	165	174	182	190	448	17
18	133	144	150	158	166	175	416	151	163	170	179	187	196	462	18
19	136	148	154	163	171	180	429	155	168	174	183	192	202	476	19
20	139	151	158	167	175	185	442	159	172	178	188	197	207	490	20
21	142	155	162	171	180	190	455	162	176	183	193	202	213	504	21
22	145	159	166	176	185	195	468	166	180	187	198	207	218	518	22
23	149	163	170	180	189	200	481	169	184	192	203	212	224	532	23
24	152	166	174	185	194	205	494	173	188	196	207	218	229	546	24
25	155	170	178	189	199	211	507	177	192	200	212	223	235	560	25

N_2	$N_1 = 15$							$N_1 = 16$							N_2
	.001	.005	.010	.025	.05	.10	$2\overline{W}$	.001	.005	.010	.025	.05	.10	$2\overline{W}$	
15	160	171	176	184	192	200	465								
16	163	175	181	190	197	206	480	184	196	202	211	219	229	528	16
17	167	180	186	195	203	212	495	188	201	207	217	225	235	544	17
18	171	184	190	200	208	218	510	192	206	212	222	231	242	560	18
19	175	189	195	205	214	224	525	196	210	218	228	237	248	576	19
20	179	193	200	210	220	230	540	201	215	223	234	243	255	592	20
21	183	198	205	216	225	236	555	205	220	228	239	249	261	608	21
22	187	202	210	221	231	242	570	209	225	233	245	255	267	624	22
23	191	207	214	226	236	248	585	214	230	238	251	261	274	640	23
24	195	211	219	231	242	254	600	218	235	244	256	267	280	656	24
25	199	216	224	237	248	260	615	222	240	249	262	273	287	672	25

APPENDIX W_S (Cont.)

N_2			$N_1 = 17$								$N_1 = 18$				
	.001	.005	.010	.025	.05	.10	$2\overline{W}$	.001	.005	.010	.025	.05	.10	$2\overline{W}$	N_2
17	210	223	230	240	249	259	595								
18	214	228	235	246	255	266	612	237	252	259	270	280	291	666	18
19	219	234	241	252	262	273	629	242	258	265	277	287	299	684	19
20	223	239	246	258	268	280	646	247	263	271	283	294	306	702	20
21	228	244	252	264	274	287	663	252	269	277	290	301	313	720	21
22	233	249	258	270	281	294	680	257	275	283	296	307	321	738	22
23	238	255	263	276	287	300	697	262	280	289	303	314	328	756	23
24	242	260	269	282	294	307	714	267	286	295	309	321	335	774	24
25	247	265	275	288	300	314	731	273	292	301	316	328	343	792	25

N_2			$N_1 = 19$								$N_1 = 20$				
	.001	.005	.010	.025	.05	.10	$2\overline{W}$	.001	.005	.010	.025	.05	.10	$2\overline{W}$	N_2
19	267	283	291	303	313	325	741								
20	272	289	297	309	320	333	760	298	315	324	337	348	361	820	20
21	277	295	303	316	328	341	779	304	322	331	344	356	370	840	21
22	283	301	310	323	335	349	798	309	328	337	351	364	378	860	22
23	288	307	316	330	342	357	817	315	335	344	359	371	386	880	23
24	294	313	323	337	350	364	836	321	341	351	366	379	394	900	24
25	299	319	329	344	357	372	855	327	348	358	373	387	403	920	25

N_2			$N_1 = 21$								$N_1 = 22$				
	.001	.005	.010	.025	.05	.10	$2\overline{W}$	.001	.005	.010	.025	.05	.10	$2\overline{W}$	N_2
21	331	349	359	373	385	399	903								
22	337	356	366	381	393	408	924	365	386	396	411	424	439	990	22
23	343	363	373	388	401	417	945	372	393	403	419	432	448	1012	23
24	349	370	381	396	410	425	966	379	400	411	427	441	457	1034	24
25	356	377	388	404	418	434	987	385	408	419	435	450	467	1056	25

N_2			$N_1 = 23$								$N_1 = 24$				
	.001	.005	.010	.025	.05	.10	$2\overline{W}$	.001	.005	.010	.025	.05	.10	$2\overline{W}$	N_2
23	402	424	434	451	465	481	1081								
24	409	431	443	459	474	491	1104	440	464	475	492	507	525	1176	24
25	416	439	451	468	483	500	1127	448	472	484	501	517	535	1200	25

N_2			$N_1 = 25$				
	.001	.005	.010	.025	.05	.10	$2\overline{W}$
25	480	505	517	536	552	570	1275

Source: Table 1 in L. R. Verdooren (1963), Extended tables of critical values for Wilcoxon's test statistic, *Biometrika, 50,* 177–186, with permission of the author and the editor.

Appendix Z: The Normal Distribution (z)

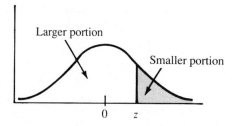

z	Mean to z	Larger Portion	Smaller Portion	y	z	Mean to z	Larger Portion	Smaller Portion	y
.00	.0000	.5000	.5000	.3989	.36	.1406	.6406	.3594	.3739
.01	.0040	.5040	.4960	.3989	.37	.1443	.6443	.3557	.3725
.02	.0080	.5080	.4920	.3989	.38	.1480	.6480	.3520	.3712
.03	.0120	.5120	.4880	.3988	.39	.1517	.6517	.3483	.3697
.04	.0160	.5160	.4840	.3986	.40	.1554	.6554	.3446	.3683
.05	.0199	.5199	.4801	.3984	.41	.1591	.6591	.3409	.3668
.06	.0239	.5239	.4761	.3982	.42	.1628	.6628	.3372	.3653
.07	.0279	.5279	.4721	.3980	.43	.1664	.6664	.3336	.3637
.08	.0319	.5319	.4681	.3977	.44	.1700	.6700	.3300	.3621
.09	.0359	.5359	.4641	.3973	.45	.1736	.6736	.3264	.3605
.10	.0398	.5398	.4602	.3970	.46	.1772	.6772	.3228	.3589
.11	.0438	.5438	.4562	.3965	.47	.1808	.6808	.3192	.3572
.12	.0478	.5478	.4522	.3961	.48	.1844	.6844	.3156	.3555
.13	.0517	.5517	.4483	.3956	.49	.1879	.6879	.3121	.3538
.14	.0557	.5557	.4443	.3951	.50	.1915	.6915	.3085	.3521
.15	.0596	.5596	.4404	.3945	.51	.1950	.6950	.3050	.3503
.16	.0636	.5636	.4364	.3939	.52	.1985	.6985	.3015	.3485
.17	.0675	.5675	.4325	.3932	.53	.2019	.7019	.2981	.3467
.18	.0714	.5714	.4286	.3925	.54	.2054	.7054	.2946	.3448
.19	.0753	.5753	.4247	.3918	.55	.2088	.7088	.2912	.3429
.20	.0793	.5793	.4207	.3910	.56	.2123	.7123	.2877	.3410
.21	.0832	.5832	.4168	.3902	.57	.2157	.7157	.2843	.3391
.22	.0871	.5871	.4129	.3894	.58	.2190	.7190	.2810	.3372
.23	.0910	.5910	.4090	.3885	.59	.2224	.7224	.2776	.3352
.24	.0948	.5948	.4052	.3876	.60	.2257	.7257	.2743	.3332
.25	.0987	.5987	.4013	.3867	.61	.2291	.7291	.2709	.3312
.26	.1026	.6026	.3974	.3857	.62	.2324	.7324	.2676	.3292
.27	.1064	.6064	.3936	.3847	.63	.2357	.7357	.2643	.3271
.28	.1103	.6103	.3897	.3836	.64	.2389	.7389	.2611	.3251
.29	.1141	.6141	.3859	.3825	.65	.2422	.7422	.2578	.3230
.30	.1179	.6179	.3821	.3814	.66	.2454	.7454	.2546	.3209
.31	.1217	.6217	.3783	.3802	.67	.2486	.7486	.2514	.3187
.32	.1255	.6255	.3745	.3790	.68	.2517	.7517	.2483	.3166
.33	.1293	.6293	.3707	.3778	.69	.2549	.7549	.2451	.3144
.34	.1331	.6331	.3669	.3765	.70	.2580	.7580	.2420	.3123
.35	.1368	.6368	.3632	.3752	.71	.2611	.7611	.2389	.3101

APPENDIX Z (Cont.)

z	Mean to z	Larger Portion	Smaller Portion	y	z	Mean to z	Larger Portion	Smaller Portion	y
.72	.2642	.7642	.2358	.3079	1.17	.3790	.8790	.1210	.2012
.73	.2673	.7673	.2327	.3056	1.18	.3810	.8810	.1190	.1989
.74	.2704	.7704	.2296	.3034	1.19	.3830	.8830	.1170	.1965
.75	.2734	.7734	.2266	.3011	1.20	.3849	.8849	.1151	.1942
.76	.2764	.7764	.2236	.2989	1.21	.3869	.8869	.1131	.1919
.77	.2794	.7794	.2206	.2966	1.22	.3888	.8888	.1112	.1895
.78	.2823	.7823	.2177	.2943	1.23	.3907	.8907	.1093	.1872
.79	.2852	.7852	.2148	.2920	1.24	.3925	.8925	.1075	.1849
.80	.2881	.7881	.2119	.2897	1.25	.3944	.8944	.1056	.1826
.81	.2910	.7910	.2090	.2874	1.26	.3962	.8962	.1038	.1804
.82	.2939	.7939	.2061	.2850	1.27	.3980	.8980	.1020	.1781
.83	.2967	.7967	.2033	.2827	1.28	.3997	.8997	.1003	.1758
.84	.2995	.7995	.2005	.2803	1.29	.4015	.9015	.0985	.1736
.85	.3023	.8023	.1977	.2780	1.30	.4032	.9032	.0968	.1714
.86	.3051	.8051	.1949	.2756	1.31	.4049	.9049	.0951	.1691
.87	.3078	.8078	.1922	.2732	1.32	.4066	.9066	.0934	.1669
.88	.3106	.8106	.1894	.2709	1.33	.4082	.9082	.0918	.1647
.89	.3133	.8133	.1867	.2685	1.34	.4099	.9099	.0901	.1626
.90	.3159	.8159	.1841	.2661	1.35	.4115	.9115	.0885	.1604
.91	.3186	.8186	.1814	.2637	1.36	.4131	.9131	.0869	.1582
.92	.3212	.8212	.1788	.2613	1.37	.4147	.9147	.0853	.1561
.93	.3238	.8238	.1762	.2589	1.38	.4162	.9162	.0838	.1539
.94	.3264	.8264	.1736	.2565	1.39	.4177	.9177	.0823	.1518
.95	.3289	.8289	.1711	.2541	1.40	.4192	.9192	.0808	.1497
.96	.3315	.8315	.1685	.2516	1.41	.4207	.9207	.0793	.1476
.97	.3340	.8340	.1660	.2492	1.42	.4222	.9222	.0778	.1456
.98	.3365	.8365	.1635	.2468	1.43	.4236	.9236	.0764	.1435
.99	.3389	.8389	.1611	.2444	1.44	.4251	.9251	.0749	.1415
1.00	.3413	.8413	.1587	.2420	1.45	.4265	.9265	.0735	.1394
1.01	.3438	.8438	.1562	.2396	1.46	.4279	.9279	.0721	.1374
1.02	.3461	.8461	.1539	.2371	1.47	.4292	.9292	.0708	.1354
1.03	.3485	.8485	.1515	.2347	1.48	.4306	.9306	.0694	.1334
1.04	.3508	.8508	.1492	.2323	1.49	.4319	.9319	.0681	.1315
1.05	.3531	.8531	.1469	.2299	1.50	.4332	.9332	.0668	.1295
1.06	.3554	.8554	.1446	.2275	1.51	.4345	.9345	.0655	.1276
1.07	.3577	.8577	.1423	.2251	1.52	.4357	.9357	.0643	.1257
1.08	.3599	.8599	.1401	.2227	1.53	.4370	.9370	.0630	.1238
1.09	.3621	.8621	.1379	.2203	1.54	.4382	.9382	.0618	.1219
1.10	.3643	.8643	.1357	.2179	1.55	.4394	.9394	.0606	.1200
1.11	.3665	.8665	.1335	.2155	1.56	.4406	.9406	.0594	.1182
1.12	.3686	.8686	.1314	.2131	1.57	.4418	.9418	.0582	.1163
1.13	.3708	.8708	.1292	.2107	1.58	.4429	.9429	.0571	.1145
1.14	.3729	.8729	.1271	.2083	1.59	.4441	.9441	.0559	.1127
1.15	.3749	.8749	.1251	.2059	1.60	.4452	.9452	.0548	.1109
1.16	.3770	.8770	.1230	.2036	1.61	.4463	.9463	.0537	.1092

APPENDIX Z (Cont.)

z	Mean to z	Larger Portion	Smaller Portion	y	z	Mean to z	Larger Portion	Smaller Portion	y
1.62	.4474	.9474	.0526	.1074	2.07	.4808	.9808	.0192	.0468
1.63	.4484	.9484	.0516	.1057	2.08	.4812	.9812	.0188	.0459
1.64	.4495	.9495	.0505	.1040	2.09	.4817	.9817	.0183	.0449
1.65	.4505	.9505	.0495	.1023	2.10	.4821	.9821	.0179	.0440
1.66	.4515	.9515	.0485	.1006	2.11	.4826	.9826	.0174	.0431
1.67	.4525	.9525	.0475	.0989	2.12	.4830	.9830	.0170	.0422
1.68	.4535	.9535	.0465	.0973	2.13	.4834	.9834	.0166	.0413
1.69	.4545	.9545	.0455	.0957	2.14	.4838	.9838	.0162	.0404
1.70	.4554	.9554	.0446	.0940	2.15	.4842	.9842	.0158	.0396
1.71	.4564	.9564	.0436	.0925	2.16	.4846	.9846	.0154	.0387
1.72	.4573	.9573	.0427	.0909	2.17	.4850	.9850	.0150	.0379
1.73	.4582	.9582	.0418	.0893	2.18	.4854	.9854	.0146	.0371
1.74	.4591	.9591	.0409	.0878	2.19	.4857	.9857	.0143	.0363
1.75	.4599	.9599	.0401	.0863	2.20	.4861	.9861	.0139	.0355
1.76	.4608	.9608	.0392	.0848	2.21	.4864	.9864	.0136	.0347
1.77	.4616	.9616	.0384	.0833	2.22	.4868	.9868	.0132	.0339
1.78	.4625	.9625	.0375	.0818	2.23	.4871	.9871	.0129	.0332
1.79	.4633	.9633	.0367	.0804	2.24	.4875	.9875	.0125	.0325
1.80	.4641	.9641	.0359	.0790	2.25	.4878	.9878	.0122	.0317
1.81	.4649	.9649	.0351	.0775	2.26	.4881	.9881	.0119	.0310
1.82	.4656	.9656	.0344	.0761	2.27	.4884	.9884	.0116	.0303
1.83	.4664	.9664	.0336	.0748	2.28	.4887	.9887	.0113	.0297
1.84	.4671	.9671	.0329	.0734	2.29	.4890	.9890	.0110	.0290
1.85	.4678	.9678	.0322	.0721	2.30	.4893	.9893	.0107	.0283
1.86	.4686	.9686	.0314	.0707	2.31	.4896	.9896	.0104	.0277
1.87	.4693	.9693	.0307	.0694	2.32	.4898	.9898	.0102	.0270
1.88	.4699	.9699	.0301	.0681	2.33	.4901	.9901	.0099	.0264
1.89	.4706	.9706	.0294	.0669	2.34	.4904	.9904	.0096	.0258
1.90	.4713	.9713	.0287	.0656	2.35	.4906	.9906	.0094	.0252
1.91	.4719	.9719	.0281	.0644	2.36	.4909	.9909	.0091	.0246
1.92	.4726	.9726	.0274	.0632	2.37	.4911	.9911	.0089	.0241
1.93	.4732	.9732	.0268	.0620	2.38	.4913	.9913	.0087	.0235
1.94	.4738	.9738	.0262	.0608	2.39	.4916	.9916	.0084	.0229
1.95	.4744	.9744	.0256	.0596	2.40	.4918	.9918	.0082	.0224
1.96	.4750	.9750	.0250	.0584	2.41	.4920	.9920	.0080	.0219
1.97	.4756	.9756	.0244	.0573	2.42	.4922	.9922	.0078	.0213
1.98	.4761	.9761	.0239	.0562	2.43	.4925	.9925	.0075	.0208
1.99	.4767	.9767	.0233	.0551	2.44	.4927	.9927	.0073	.0203
2.00	.4772	.9772	.0228	.0540	2.45	.4929	.9929	.0071	.0198
2.01	.4778	.9778	.0222	.0529	2.46	.4931	.9931	.0069	.0194
2.02	.4783	.9783	.0217	.0519	2.47	.4932	.9932	.0068	.0189
2.03	.4788	.9788	.0212	.0508	2.48	.4934	.9934	.0066	.0184
2.04	.4793	.9793	.0207	.0498	2.49	.4936	.9936	.0064	.0180
2.05	.4798	.9798	.0202	.0488	2.50	.4938	.9938	.0062	.0175
2.06	.4803	.9803	.0197	.0478	2.51	.4940	.9940	.0060	.0171

APPENDIX Z (Cont.)

z	Mean to z	Larger Portion	Smaller Portion	y	z	Mean to z	Larger Portion	Smaller Portion	y
2.52	.4941	.9941	.0059	.0167	2.81	.4975	.9975	.0025	.0077
2.53	.4943	.9943	.0057	.0163	2.82	.4976	.9976	.0024	.0075
2.54	.4945	.9945	.0055	.0158	2.83	.4977	.9977	.0023	.0073
2.55	.4946	.9946	.0054	.0154	2.84	.4977	.9977	.0023	.0071
2.56	.4948	.9948	.0052	.0151	2.85	.4978	.9978	.0022	.0069
2.57	.4949	.9949	.0051	.0147	2.86	.4979	.9979	.0021	.0067
2.58	.4951	.9951	.0049	.0143	2.87	.4979	.9979	.0021	.0065
2.59	.4952	.9952	.0048	.0139	2.88	.4980	.9980	.0020	.0063
2.60	.4953	.9953	.0047	.0136	2.89	.4981	.9981	.0019	.0061
2.61	.4955	.9955	.0045	.0132	2.90	.4981	.9981	.0019	.0060
2.62	.4956	.9956	.0044	.0129	2.91	.4982	.9982	.0018	.0058
2.63	.4957	.9957	.0043	.0126	2.92	.4982	.9982	.0018	.0056
2.64	.4959	.9959	.0041	.0122	2.93	.4983	.9983	.0017	.0055
2.65	.4960	.9960	.0040	.0119	2.94	.4984	.9984	.0016	.0053
2.66	.4961	.9961	.0039	.0116	2.95	.4984	.9984	.0016	.0051
2.67	.4962	.9962	.0038	.0113	2.96	.4985	.9985	.0015	.0050
2.68	.4963	.9963	.0037	.0110	2.97	.4985	.9985	.0015	.0048
2.69	.4964	.9964	.0036	.0107	2.98	.4986	.9986	.0014	.0047
2.70	.4965	.9965	.0035	.0104	2.99	.4986	.9986	.0014	.0046
2.71	.4966	.9966	.0034	.0101	3.00	.4987	.9987	.0013	.0044
2.72	.4967	.9967	.0033	.0099	· · ·	· · ·	· · ·	· · ·	· · ·
2.73	.4968	.9968	.0032	.0096	3.25	.4994	.9994	.0006	.0020
2.74	.4969	.9969	.0031	.0093	· · ·	· · ·	· · ·	· · ·	· · ·
2.75	.4970	.9970	.0030	.0091	3.50	.4998	.9998	.0002	.0009
2.76	.4971	.9971	.0029	.0088	· · ·	· · ·	· · ·	· · ·	· · ·
2.77	.4972	.9972	.0028	.0086	3.75	.4999	.9999	.0001	.0004
2.78	.4973	.9973	.0027	.0084	· · ·	· · ·	· · ·	· · ·	· · ·
2.79	.4974	.9974	.0026	.0081	4.00	.5000	1.0000	.0000	.0001
2.80	.4974	.9974	.0026	.0079					

Source: The entries in this table were computed by the author.

References

Achenbach, T. M. (1991a). *Manual for the Child Behavior Checklist/4–18 and 1991 profile*. Burlington, VT: University of Vermont Department of Psychiatry.

Achenbach, T. M. (1991b). *Manual for the Youth Self-Report and 1991 profile*. Burlington, VT: University of Vermont Department of Psychiatry.

Achenbach, T. M., McConaughy, S. H., & Howell, C. T. (1987). Child/Adolescent behavioral and emotional problems: Implications of cross-informant correlations for situational specificity. *Psychological Bulletin, 101*, 213–232.

Agresti, A. (1984). *Analysis of ordinal categorical data*. New York: Wiley.

Agresti, A. (1990). *Categorical data analysis*. New York: Wiley.

Anderson, N. H. (1963). Comparison of different populations: Resistance to extinction and transfer. *Psychological Review, 70*, 162–179.

Appelbaum, M. I., & Cramer, E. M. (1974). Some problems in the nonorthogonal analysis of variance. *Psychological Bulletin, 81*, 335–343.

Bell, R. A., Buerkel-Rothfuss, N. L., & Gore, K. E. (1987). "Did you bring the yarmulke for the Cabbage Patch kid?": The idiomatic communication among young lovers. *Human Communication Research, 14*, 47–67.

Bishop, Y. M. M., Fienberg, S. E., & Holland, P. W. (1975). *Discrete multivariate analysis: Theory and practice*. Cambridge, MA: MIT Press.

Blair, R. C. (1978). I've been testing some statistical hypotheses .... Can you guess what they are? *Journal of Educational Research, 72*, 116–118.

Blair, R. C., & Higgins, J. J. (1978). Tests of hypotheses for unbalanced factorial designs under various regression/coding method combinations. *Educational and Psychological Measurement, 38*, 621–631.

Blair, R. C., & Higgins, J. J. (1980). A comparison of the power of Wilcoxon's rank-sum statistic to that of Student's *t* statistic under various nonnormal distributions. *Journal of Educational Statistics, 5*, 309–335.

Blair, R. C., & Higgins, J. J. (1985). Comparison of the power of the paired samples *t* test to that of Wilcoxon's signed-ranks test under various population shapes. *Psychological Bulletin, 97*, 119–128.

Blanchard, E. B., Theobald, D. E., Williamson, D. A., Silver, B. V., & Brown, D. A. (1978). Temperature biofeedback in the treatment of migraine headaches. *Archives of General Psychiatry, 35*, 581–588.

Bohj, D. S. (1978). Testing equality of means of correlated variates with missing data on both responses. *Biometrika, 65*, 225–228.

Boik, R. J. (1981). A priori tests in repeated measures designs: Effects of nonsphericity. *Psychometrika, 46*, 241–255.

Boneau, C. A. (1960). The effects of violations of assumptions underlying the *t* test. *Psychological Bulletin, 57*, 49–64.

Bouton, M., & Swartzentruber, D. (1985). Unpublished raw data, University of Vermont.

Box, G. E. P. (1953). Non-normality and tests on variance. *Biometrika, 40*, 318–335.

Box, G. E. P. (1954a). Some theorems on quadratic forms applied in the study of analysis of variance problems: I. Effect of inequality of variance in the one-way classification. *Annals of Mathematical Statistics, 25*, 290–302.

Box, G. E. P. (1954b). Some theorems on quadratic forms applied in the study of analysis of variance problems: II. Effect of inequality of variance and of correlation of errors in the two-way classification. *Annals of Mathematical Statistics, 25*, 484–498.

Bradley, D. R., Bradley, T. D., McGrath, S. G., & Cutcomb, S. D. (1979). Type I error rate of the chi-square test of independence in $R \times C$ tables that have small expected frequencies. *Psychological Bulletin, 86*, 1290–1297.

Bradley, J. V. (1963). *Studies in research methodology: IV. A sampling study of the central limit theorem and the robustness of one-sample parametric tests* (AMRL Tech. Rep. No. 63–29). Aerospace Medical Research Laboratories, Wright-Patterson Air Force Base, OH.

Bradley, J. V. (1964). *Studies in research methodology: VI. The central limit effect for a variety of populations and the robustness of z, t, and F* (AMRL Tech. Rep. No. 64–123). Aerospace Medical Research Laboratories, Wright-Patterson Air Force Base, OH.

Bradley, J. V. (1968). *Distribution-free statistical tests.* Englewood Cliffs, NJ: Prentice-Hall.

Brown, M. B. (1976). Screening effects in multidimensional contingency tables. *Applied Statistics, 25,* 37.

Brown, M. B., & Forsythe, A. B. (1974). The ANOVA and multiple comparisons for data with heterogeneous variances. *Biometrics, 30,* 719–724.

Camilli, G., & Hopkins, K. D. (1978). Applicability of chi-square to 2 × 2 contingency tables with small expected cell frequencies. *Psychological Bulletin, 85,* 163–167.

Camilli, G., & Hopkins, K. D. (1979). Testing for association in 2 × 2 contingency tables with very small sample sizes. *Psychological Bulletin, 86,* 1011–1014.

Campbell, A., Converse, P. E., & Rogers, W. L. (1976). *The quality of American life.* New York: Russel Sage Foundation.

Carlson, J. E., & Timm, N. H. (1974). Analaysis of nonorthogonal fixed-effects designs. *Psychological Bulletin, 81,* 563–570.

Carmer, S. G., & Swanson, M. R. (1973). An evaluation of ten multiple comparison procedures by Monte Carlo methods. *Journal of the American Statistical Association, 68,* 66–74.

Chalmer, B. (1990). *Ecstatic: A statistical package.* Montpelier, VT: Someware in Vermont.

Chambers, J. M., Cleveland, W. S., Kleiner, B., & Tukey, P. A. (1983). *Graphical methods for data analysis.* Belmont, CA: Wadsworth.

Clark, K. B., & Clark, M. K. (1939). The development of consciousness of self in the emergence of racial identification in Negro pre-school children. *Journal of Social Psychology, 10,* 591–599.

Cleveland, W. S. (1984). Graphical methods for data presentation: Full scale breaks, dot charts, and multibased logging. *American Statistician, 38,* 270–280.

Cleveland, W. S., & McGill, R. (1984). Graphical perception: Theory, experimentation, and application to the development of graphical methods. *Journal of the American Statistical Association, 79,* 531–554.

Cochran, W. G., & Cox, G. M. (1957). *Experimental designs* (2nd ed.). New York: Wiley.

Cohen, J. (1960). A coefficient of agreement for nominal scales. *Educational and Psychological Measurement, 10,* 37–46.

Cohen, J. (1962). The statistical power of abnormal-social psychological research: A review. *Journal of Abnormal and Social Psychology, 65,* 145–153.

Cohen, J. (1965). Some statistical issues in psychological research. In B. B. Wolman (ed.), *Handbook of Clinical Psychology.* New York: McGraw-Hill.

Cohen, J. (1968). Multiple regression as a general data-analytic system. *Psychological Bulletin, 70,* 426–443.

Cohen, J. (1969). *Statistical power analysis for the behavioral sciences* (1st Ed.) Hillsdale, N.J.: Erlbaum.

Cohen, J. (1973). Eta-squared and partial eta-squared in fixed factor ANOVA designs. *Educational and Psychological Measurement, 33,* 107–112.

Cohen, J. (1988). *Statistical power analysis for behavioral sciences* (2nd ed.). New York: Academic Press.

Cohen, J., & Cohen, P. (1975). *Applied multiple regression/correlation analysis for the behavioral sciences.* Hillsdale, NJ: Erlbaum.

Collier, R. O., Jr., Baker, F. B., & Mandeville, G. K. (1967). Tests of hypothesis in a repeated measures design from a permutation viewpoint. *Psychometrika, 32,* 15–24.

Collier, R. O., Jr., Baker, F. B., Mandeville, G. K., & Hayes, T. F. (1967). Estimates of test size for several test procedures based on conventional variance ratios in the repeated measures design. *Psychometrika, 32,* 339–353.

Compas, B. E., Howell, D. C., Phares, V., Williams, R. A., & Giunta, C. (1989). Risk factors for emotional/behavioral problems in young adolescents: A prospective analysis of adolescent and parental stress symptoms. *Journal of Consulting and Clinical Psychology, 57,* 732–740.

Compas, B. E., Howell, D. C., Phares, V., Williams, R. A., & Ledoux, N. (1989). Parent and child stress and symptoms: An integrative analysis. *Developmental Psychology, 25,* 550–559.

Conti, L., & Musty, R. E. (1984). The effects of delta-9-tetrahydrocannabinol injections to the nucleus accumbens on the locomotor activity of rats. In S. Aquell et al. (Eds.), *The cannabinoids: Chemical, pharmacologic, and therapeutic aspects.* New York: Academic Press.

Cooley, W. W., & Lohnes, P. R. (1971). *Multivariate data analysis.* New York: Wiley.

Craik, F. I. M., & Lockhart, R. S. (1972). Levels of processing: A framework for memory research, *Journal of Verbal Learning and Verbal Behavior, 11*, 671–684.

Cramer, E. M., & Appelbaum, M. I. (1980). Nonorthogonal analysis of variance—Once again. *Psychological Bulletin, 87*, 51–57.

Cramér, H. (1946). *Mathematical methods of statistics.* Princeton, NJ: Princeton University Press.

Dabbs, J. M., Jr., & Morris, R. (1990). Testosterone, social class, and antisocial behavior in a sample of 4462 men. *Psychological Science, 1*, 209–211.

Darley, J. M., & Latané, B. (1968). Bystander intervention in emergencies: Diffusion of responsibility. *Journal of Personality and Social Psychology, 8*, 377–383.

Darlington, R. B. (1968). Multiple regression in psychological research and practice. *Psychological Bulletin, 69*, 161–182.

Darlington, R. B. (1990). *Regression and linear models.* New York: McGraw-Hill.

Dawes, R. M., & Corrigan, B. (1974). Linear models in decision making. *Psychological Bulletin, 81*, 95–106.

DeCarni, J. S. (1984). Balancing Type I risk and loss of power in ordered Bonferroni procedures. *Journal of Educational Psychology, 76*, 1035–1037.

Delucchi, K. L. (1983). The use and misuse of chi-square: Lewis and Burke revisited. *Psychological Bulletin, 94*, 166–176.

Derogatis, L. R. (1983). *SCL-90-R administration, scoring, and procedures manual* (vol 1.). Towson, MD: Clinical Psychometric Research.

Dodd, D. H., & Schultz, R. F., Jr. (1973). Computational procedures for estimating magnitude of effect for some analysis of variance designs. *Psychological Bulletin, 79*, 391–395.

Doob, A. N., & Gross, A. E. (1968). Status of frustrator as an inhibitor of horn-honking responses. *Journal of Social Psychology, 76*, 213–218.

Draper, N. R., & Smith, H. (1981). *Applied regression analysis* (2nd ed.). New York: Wiley.

Dunn, O. J. (1961). Multiple comparisons among means, *Journal of the American Statistical Association, 56*, 52–64.

Dunnett, C. W. (1955). A multiple comparison procedure for comparing several treatments with a control. *Journal of the American Statistical Association, 50*, 1096–1121.

Dunnett, C. W. (1964). New tables for multiple comparisons with a control. *Biometrics, 20*, 482–491.

Dwyer, J. H. (1974). Analysis of variance and the magnitude of effects: A general approach. *Psychological Bulletin, 81*, 731–737.

Edwards, A. L. (1985). *Experimental design in psychological research* (5th ed.). New York: Harper & Row.

Eron, L. D., Huesmann, L. R., Lefkowitz, M. M., & Walden, L. O. (1972). Does television violence cause aggression? *American Psychologist, 27*, 253–263.

Evans, S. H., & Anastasio, E. J. (1968). Misuse of analysis of covariance when treatment effect and covariate are confounded. *Psychological Bulletin, 69*, 225–234.

Eysenck, M. W. (1974). Age differences in incidental learning. *Developmental Psychology, 10*, 936–941.

Federer, W. T. (1955). *Experimental design: Theory and application.* New York: Macmillan.

Finney, J. W., Mitchell, R. E., Cronkite, R. C., & Moos, R. H. (1984). Methodological issues in estimating main and interactive effects: Examples from coping/social support and stress field. *Journal of Health and Social Behavior, 25*, 85–98.

Fisher, R. A. (1921). On the probable error of a coefficient of correlation deduced from a small sample. *Metron, 1*, 3–32.

Fisher, R. A. (1935). *The design of experiments.* Edinburgh: Oliver & Boyd.

Fisher, R. A., & Yates, F. (1953). *Statistical tables for biological, agricultural, and medical research* (4th ed.). Edinburgh: Oliver & Boyd.

Fleiss, J. L. (1969). Estimating the magnitude of experimental effects. *Psychological Bulletin, 72*, 273–276.

Fowler, R. L. (1985). Point estimates and confidence intervals in measures of association. *Psychological Bulletin, 98*, 160–165.

Frigge, M., Hoagland, D. C., & Iglewicz B. (1989). Some implementations of the boxplot. *American Statistician, 43*, 50–54.

Galton, F. (1886). Regression towards mediocrity in hereditary stature. *Journal of the Anthropological Institute, 15*, 246–263.

Games, P. A. (1978a). A three-factor model encompassing many possible statistical tests on independent groups. *Psychological Bulletin, 85*, 168–182.

Games, P. A. (1978b). A four-factor structure for parametric tests on independent groups. *Psychological Bulletin*, *85*, 661–672.

Games, P. A., & Howell, J. F. (1976). Pairwise multiple comparison procedures with unequal *n*'s and/or variances: A Monte Carlo study. *Journal of Educational Statistics*, *1*, 113–125.

Games, P. A., Keselman, H. J., & Rogan, J. C. (1981). Simultaneous pairwise multiple comparison procedures for means when sample sizes are unequal. *Psychological Bulletin*, *90*, 594–598.

Geller, E. S., Witmer, J. F., & Orebaugh, A. L. (1976). Instructions as a determinant of paper disposal behaviors. *Environment and Behavior*, *8*, 417–439.

Glass, G. V., McGaw, B., & Smith, M. L. (1981). *Meta-analysis in social research*. Beverly Hills, CA: Sage.

Goldberg, L. R. (1965). Diagnosticians versus diagnostic signs: The diagnosis of psychosis versus neurosis from the MMPI. *Psychological Monographs*, *79* (9, Whole No. 602).

Green, J. A. (1988). Loglinear analysis of cross-classified ordinal data: Applications in developmental research. *Child Development*, *59*, 1–25.

Greenhouse, S. W., & Geisser, S. (1959). On methods in the analysis of profile data. *Psychometrika*, *24*, 95–112.

Gross, J. S. (1985). Weight modification and eating disorders in adolescent boys and girls. Unpublished doctoral dissertation, University of Vermont.

Guilford, J. P., & Fruchter, B. (1973). *Fundamental statistics in psychology and education*. New York: McGraw-Hill.

Hansen, J. C., & Swanson, J. L. (1983). Stability of interests and the predictive and concurrent validity of the 1981 Strong-Campbell Interest Inventory for college majors. *Journal of Counseling Psychology*, *30*, 194–201.

Harris, C. W. (Ed.). (1963). *Problems in measuring change*. Madison, WI: University of Wisconsin Press.

Harris, R. J. (1985). *A primer of multivariate statistics* (2nd ed.). New York: Academic Press.

Harter, H. L. (1960). Tables of range and Studentized range. *Annals of Mathematical Statistics*, *31*, 1122–1147.

Hays, W. L. (1963). *Statistics for psychologists*. New York: Holt, Rinehart & Winston.

Hays, W. L. (1973). *Statistics for the social sciences* (2nd ed.). New York: Holt, Rinehart & Winston.

Hays, W. L. (1981). *Statistics* (3rd ed.). New York: Holt, Rinehart & Winston.

Hedges, L. V. (1982). Estimation of effect size from a series of independent experiments. *Psychological Bulletin*, *92*, 490–499.

Henderson, D. A., & Denison, D. R. (1989). Stepwise regression in social and psychological research. *Psychological Reports*, *64*, 251–257.

Hindley, C. B., Filliozat, A. M., Klackenberg, G., Nicolet-Meister, D., & Sand, E. A. (1966). Differences in age of walking for five European longitudinal samples. *Human Biology*, *38*, 364–379.

Hoaglin, D. C., Mosteller, F., & Tukey, J. W. (1983). *Understanding robust and exploratory data analysis*. New York: Wiley.

Hochberg, Y., & Tamhane, A. C. (1987). *Multiple comparison procedures*. New York: Wiley.

Holm, S. (1979). A simple sequentially rejective multiple test procedure. *Scandinavian Journal of Statistics*, *6*, 65–70.

Holmes, T. H., & Rahe, R. H. (1967). The social readjustment rating scale. *Journal of Psychosomatic Research*, *11*, 213.

Holway, A. H., & Boring, E. G. (1940). The moon illusion and the angle of regard. *American Journal of Psychology*, *53*, 509–516.

Hotelling, H. (1931). The generalization of Student's ratio. *Annals of Mathematical Statistics*, *2*, 360–378.

Howell, D. C. (1987). *Statistical methods for psychology* (2nd ed.). Boston: PWS-KENT.

Howell, D. C. (1989). *Fundamental Statistics for the Behavioral Sciences* (2nd ed.). Boston: PWS-KENT.

Howell, D. C., & Huessy, H. R. (1981). Hyperkinetic behavior followed from 7 to 21 years of age. In M. Gittelman (Ed.), *Intervention strategies with hyperactive children* (pp. 201–214). White Plains, NY: M. E. Sharpe.

Howell, D. C., & Huessy, H. R. (1985). A fifteen-year follow-up of a behavioral history of Attention Deficit Disorder (ADD). *Pediatrics*, *76*, 185–190.

Howell, D. C., & McConaughy, S. H. (1982). Nonorthogonal analysis of variance: Putting the question before the answer. *Educational and Psychological Measurement*, *42*, 9–24.

Hraba, J., & Grant, G. (1970). Black is beautiful: A re-examination of racial preference and identification. *Journal of Personality and Social Psychology*, *16*, 398–402.

Huberty, C. J. (1989). Problems with stepwise methods—better alternatives. In B. Thompson (Ed.) *Advances in Social Science Methodology* (Vol. 1) (43–70). Greenwich, CT: JAI Press.

Huitema, B. E. (1980). *The analysis of covariance and alternatives.* New York: Wiley.

Huynh, H., & Feldt, L. S. (1970). Conditions under which mean square ratios in repeated measurement designs have exact F-distributions. *Journal of the American Statistical Association, 65,* 1582–1589.

Huynh, H., & Feldt, L. S. (1976). Estimation of the Box correction for degrees of freedom from sample data in the randomized block and split plot designs. *Journal of Educational Statistics, 1,* 69–82.

Huynh, H., & Mandeville, G. K. (1979). Validity conditions in repeated measures designs. *Psychological Bulletin, 86,* 964–973.

Introini-Collison, I., & McGaugh, J. L. (1986). Epinephrine modulates long-term retention of an aversively-motivated discrimination task. *Behavioral and Neural Biology, 45,* 358–365.

Kapp, B., Frysinger, R., Gallagher, M., & Hazelton, J. (1979). Amygdala central nucleus lesions: Effects on heart rate conditioning in the rabbit. *Physiology and Behavior, 23,* 1109–1117.

Katz, S., Lautenschlager, G. J., Blackburn, A. B., & Harris, F. H. (1990). Answering reading comprehension items without passages on the SAT. *Psychological Science, 1,* 122–127.

Kaufman, L., & Rock, I. (1962). The moon illusion, I. *Science, 136,* 953–961.

Kendall, M. G. (1948). *Rank correlation methods.* London: Griffin.

Kennedy, J. J. (1983). *Analyzing qualtitative data: Introductory log-linear analysis for behavioral research.* New York: Praeger.

Kenny, D. A., & Judd, C. M. (1986). Consequences of violating the independence assumption in analysis of variance. *Psychological Bulletin, 99,* 422–431.

Keppel, G. (1973). *Design and analysis: A researcher's handbook.* Englewood Cliffs, NJ: Prentice-Hall.

Keselman, H. J. (1974). The statistic with the smaller critical value. *Psychological Bulletin, 81,* 130–131.

Keselman, H. J., Games, P. A., & Rogan, J. C. (1979). Protecting the overall rate of Type I errors for pairwise comparisons with an omnibus test statistic. *Psychological Bulletin, 86,* 884–888.

Keselman, H. J., & Kesselman, J. C. (1988). Repeated measures multiple comparison procedures: Effects of violating multisample sphericity in unbalanced designs. *Journal of Educational Statistics, 13,* 215–226.

Keselman, H. J., & Rogan, J. C. (1977). The Tukey multiple comparison test: 1953–1976. *Psychological Bulletin, 84,* 1050–1056.

Keselman, H. J., Rogan, J. C., Mendoza, J. L., & Breen, L. J. (1980). Testing the validity conditions of repeated measures F tests. *Psychological Bulletin, 87,* 479–481.

King, D. A. (1986). Associative control of tolerance to the sedative effects of a short-acting benzodiazepine. Unpublished doctoral dissertation, University of Vermont.

Kirk, R. E. (1968). *Experimental design: Procedures for the behavioral sciences.* Belmont, CA: Brooks/Cole.

Klemchuk, H. P., Bond, L. A., & Howell, D. C. (1990). Coherence and correlates of level 1 perspective taking in young children. *Merrill-Palmer Quarterly, 36,* 369–387.

Koele, P. (1982). Calculating power in analysis of variance. *Psychological Bulletin, 92,* 513–516.

Kohr, R. L., & Games, P. A. (1974). Robustness of the analysis of variance, the Welch procedure, and a Box procedure to heterogeneous variances. The *Journal of Experimental Education, 43,* 61–69.

Lane, D. M., & Dunlap, W. P. (1978). Estimating effect size: Bias resulting from the significance criterion in editorial decisions. *British Journal of Mathematical and Statistical Psychology, 31,* 107–112.

Langlois, J. H., & Roggman, L. A. (1990). Attractive faces are only average. *Psychological Science, 1,* 115–121.

Larzelere, R. E., & Mulaik, S. A. (1977). Single-sample tests for many correlations. *Psychological Bulletin, 84,* 557–569.

Latané, B., & Dabbs, J. M., Jr. (1975). Sex, group size, and helping in three cities. *Sociometry, 38,* 180–194.

Levene, H. (1960). Robust tests for the equality of variance. In I. Olkin (Ed.), *Contributions to probability and statistics.* Palo Alto, CA: Stanford University Press.

Lewis, C., & Keren, G. (1977). You can't have your cake and eat it too: Some considerations of the error term. *Psychological Bulletin, 84,* 1150–1154.

Lewis, D., & Burke, C. J. (1949). The use and misuse of the chi-square test. *Psychological Bulletin, 46,* 433–489.

Lewis, H. B., & Franklin, M. (1944). An experimental study of the role of ego in work. II. The significance of task-orientation in work. *Journal of Experimental Psychology, 34*, 195–215.

Lord, F. M. (1953). On the statistical treatment of football numbers. *American Psychologist, 8*, 750–751.

Lord, F. M. (1967). A paradox in the interpretation of group comparisons. *Psychological Bulletin, 68*, 304–305.

Lord, F. M. (1969). Statistical adjustments when comparing pre-existing groups. *Psychological Bulletin, 72*, 336–337.

Manning, C. A., Hall, J. L., & Gold, P. E. (1990). Glucose effects on memory and other neuropsychological tests in elderly humans. *Psychological Science, 1*, 307–311.

Marascuilo, L. A., & Busk, P. L. (1987). Loglinear models: A way to study main effects and interactions for multidimensional contingency tables with categorical data. *Journal of Counseling Psychology, 34*, 443–455.

Marascuilo, L. A., & Serlin, R. C. (1990). *Statistical methods for the social and behavioral sciences.* New York: Freeman.

Marks, E. (1982). A note on a geometric interpretation of the correlation coefficient. *Journal of Educational Statistics, 7*, 233–237.

Mauchly, J. W. (1940). Significance test for sphericity of a normal *n*-variate distribution. *Annals of Mathematical Statistics, 11*, 204–209.

Maxwell, S. E. (1980). Pairwise multiple comparisons in repeated measures designs. *Journal of Educational Statistics, 5*, 269–287.

Maxwell, S., & Cramer, E. M. (1975). A note on analysis of covariance. *Psychological Bulletin, 82*, 187–190.

Maxwell, S. E., Delaney, H. D., & Manheimer, J. M. (1985). ANOVA of residuals and ANCOVA: Correcting an illusion by using model comparisons and graphs. *Journal of Educational Statistics, 10*, 197–209.

McConaughy, S. H. (1980). Cognitive structures for reading comprehension: Judging the relative importance of ideas in short stories. Unpublished doctoral dissertation, University of Vermont.

McIntyre, S. H., Montgomery, D. B., Srinwason, V., & Weitz, B. A. (1983). Evaluating the statistical significance of models developed by stepwise regression. *Journal of Marketing Research, 10*, 1–11.

McNemar, Q. (1969). *Psychological statistics* (4th ed.). New York: Wiley.

Melzer, K. M. (1975). Components of the judgmental process: Effects of cue presentation on IQ estimates. Unpublished master's thesis, University of Vermont.

Miller, G. H., & Gerstein, D. R. (1983). The life expectancy of nonsmoking men and women. *Public Health Reports, 98*, 343–349.

Miller, R. G., Jr. (1981). *Stimultaneous statistical inference* (2nd ed.). New York: McGraw-Hill.

Mireault, G. C. (1990). Parent death in childhood, perceived vulnerability, and adult depression and anxiety. Unpublished M. A. thesis, University of Vermont.

Mood, A. M. (1950). *Introduction to the theory of statistics.* New York: McGraw-Hill.

Mood, A. M., & Graybill, F. A. (1963). *Introduction to the theory of statistics* (2nd ed.). New York: McGraw-Hill.

Myers, J. L. (1979). *Fundamentals of experimental design* (3rd ed.). Boston: Allyn & Bacon.

Neyman, J., & Pearson, E. S. (1933). On the problem of the most efficient tests of statistical hypotheses. *Philosophic Transactions of the Royal Society of London (Series A), 231*, 289–337.

Norton, D. W. (1953). Study reported in E. F. Lindquist, *Design and analysis of experiments in psychology and education.* New York: Houghton Mifflin.

Norusis, M. J. (1985). *SPSS^X advanced statistics guide.* New York: McGraw-Hill.

Nurcombe, B., & Fitzhenry-Coor, I. (1979, October). Decision making in the mental health interview: I. An introduction to an education and research problem. Paper delivered at the Conference on Problem Solving in Medicine, Smuggler's Notch, Vermont.

Nurcombe, B., Howell, D. C., Rauh, V. A., Teti, D. M., Ruoff, P., & Brennan, J. (1984). An intervention program for mothers of low-birthweight infants: Preliminary results. *Journal of the American Academy of Child Psychiatry, 23*, 319–325.

O'Brien, R. G. (1976). Comment on "Some problems in the nonorthogonal analysis of variance." *Psychological Bulletin, 83*, 72–74.

O'Brien, R. G. (1981). A simple test for variance effects in experimental designs. *Psychological Bulletin, 89*, 570–574.

O'Brien, R. G., & Kaiser, M. K. (1985). MANOVA method for analyzing repeated measures designs: An extensive primer. *Psychological Bulletin, 97*, 316–333.

O'Grady, K. E. (1982). Measures of explained variation: Cautions and limitations. *Psychological Bulletin, 92*, 766–777.

O'Neil, R., & Wetherill, G. B. (1971). The present state of multiple comparison methods. *Journal of the Royal Statistical Society (Series B), 33*, 218–250.

Overall, J. E. (1972). Computers in behavioral science: Multiple covariance analysis by the general least squares regression method. *Behavioral Science, 17*, 313–320.

Overall, J. E. (1980). Power of chi-square tests for 2×2 contingency tables with small expected frequencies. *Psychological Bulletin, 87*, 132–135.

Overall, J. E., & Klett, C. J. (1972). *Applied multivariate analysis.* New York: McGraw-Hill.

Overall, J. E., & Spiegel, D. K. (1969). Concerning least squares analysis of experimental data. *Psychological Bulletin, 72*, 311–322.

Overall, J. E., Spiegel, D. K., & Cohen, J. (1975). Equivalence of orthogonal and nonorthogonal analysis of variance. *Psychological Bulletin, 82*, 182–186.

Ozer, D. J. (1985). Correlation and the coefficient of determination. *Psychological Bulletin, 97*, 307–315.

Pearson, K. (1900). On a criterion that a given system of deviations from the probable in the case of a correlated system of variables is such that it can reasonably be supposed to have arisen in random sampling. *Philosophical Magazine, 50*, 157–175.

Pitman, E. J. G. (1939). A note on normal correlation. *Biometrika, 31*, 9–12.

Pugh, M. D. (1983). Contributory fault and rape convictions: Loglinear models for blaming the victim. *Social Psychology Quarterly, 46*, 233–242.

Reichardt, C. S. (1979). The statistical analysis of data from nonequivalent control group designs. In T. D. Cook & D. T. Campbell (Eds.), *Quasi-experimentation: Design and analysis issues for field settings* (pp. 147–205). Boston: Houghton Mifflin.

Reilly, T. P., Drudge, O. W., Rosen, J. C., Loew, D. E., & Fischer, M. (1985). Concurrent and predictive validity of the WISC-R, McCarthy Scales, Woodcock-Johnson, and academic achievement. *Psychology in the Schools, 22*, 380–382.

Robson, D. S. (1959). A simple method for constructing orthogonal polynomials when the independent variable is unequally spaced. *Biometrics, 15*, 187–191.

Rosenthal, R. (1978). Combining results of independent studies. *Psychological Bulletin, 85*, 185–193.

Rosenthal, R. (1990). How are we doing in soft psychology? Comment in *American Psychologist, 45*, 775–777.

Rosenthal, R., & Rubin, D. B. (1982). A simple, general purpose display of magnitude of experimental effect. *Journal of Educational Psychology, 74*, 166–169.

Rosenthal, R., & Rubin, D. B. (1984). Multiple contrasts and ordered Bonferroni procedures. *Journal of Educational Psychology, 76*, 1028–1034.

Rousseeuw, P. J., & Leroy, A. M. (1987). *Robust regression and outlier detection.* New York: Wiley.

Ryan, B. F., Joiner, B. L., & Ryan, T. A. (1985). *Minitab handbook* (2nd ed.). Boston: Duxbury Press.

Ryan, T. A. (1959). Multiple comparisons in psychological research. *Psychological Bulletin, 56*, 26–47.

Satterthwaite, F. E. (1946). An approximate distribution of estimates of variance components. *Biometrics Bulletin, 2*, 110–114.

Scheffé, H. A. (1953). A method for judging all possible contrasts in the analysis of variance. *Biometrika, 40*, 87–104.

Scheffé, H. A. (1959). *The analysis of variance.* New York: Wiley.

Shaffer, J. P. (1986). Modified sequentially rejective multiple test procedures. *Journal of the American Statistical Association, 81*, 826–831.

Siegel, S. (1975). Evidence from rats that morphine tolerance is a learned response. *Journal of Comparative and Physiological Psychology, 80*, 498–506.

Sgro, J. A., & Weinstock, S. (1963). Effects of delay on subsequent running under immediate reinforcement. *Journal of Experimental Psychology, 66*, 260–263.

Slovic, P., & Lichtenstein, S. (1971). Comparison of Bayesian and regression approaches to the study of information processing in judgment. *Organizational Behavior and Human Performance, 6*, 649–744.

Smith, H. F. (1957). Interpretation of adjusted treatment means and regression in analysis of covariance. *Biometrics, 13*, 282–308.

Smith, M. L. (1980). Sex bias in counseling and psychotherapy. *Psychological Bulletin, 87*, 392–407.

Smith, M. L., & Glass, G. V. (1977). Meta-analysis of psychotherapy outcome studies. *American Psychologist, 32,* 752–760.

Snedecor, G. W., & Cochran, W. G. (1967). *Statistical methods* (6th ed.). Ames, IA: Iowa State University.

Steiger, J. H. (1980). Tests for comparing elements of a correlation matrix. *Psychological Bulletin, 87,* 245–251.

Stevens, S. S. (1951). Mathematics, measurement, and psychophysics. In S. S. Stevens (Ed.), *Handbook of Experimental psychology* (pp. 1–49). New York: Wiley.

Strube, M. J. (1985). Combining and comparing significance levels from nonindependent hypothesis tests. *Psychological Bulletin, 97,* 334–341.

Tabachnick, B. G., & Fidell, L. S. (1989). *Using multivariate statistics.* New York: Harper & Row.

Tiku, M. L. (1967). Tables of the power of the *F* test. *Journal of the American Statistical Association, 62,* 525–539.

Tolman, E. C., Ritchie, B. F., & Kalish, D. (1946). Studies in spatial learning: I. Orientation and the short cut. *Journal of Experimental Psychology, 36,* 13–24.

Tomarken, A. J., & Serlin, R. C. (1986). Comparison of ANOVA alternatives under variance heterogeneity and specific noncentrality structures. *Psychological Bulletin, 99,* 90–99.

Toothaker, L. (1991). *Multiple comparisons for researchers.* Newbury Park, CA: Sage.

Tufte, E. R. (1983). *The visual display of quantitative information.* Cheshire, CT: Graphics Press.

Tukey, J. W. (1949). One degree of freedom for nonadditivity. *Biometrics, 5,* 232–242.

Tukey, J. W. (1953). The problem of multiple comparisons. Unpublished manuscript, Princeton University.

Tukey, J. W. (1977). *Exploratory data analysis.* Reading, MA: Addison-Wesley.

U.S. Department of Commerce. (1977). *Social indicators, 1976.* (Document #C3.2: S01/2/976). Washington, DC: U.S. Government Printing Office.

Vaughan, G. M., & Corballis, M. C. (1969). Beyond tests of significance: Estimating strength of effects in selected ANOVA designs. *Psychological Bulletin, 72,* 204–223.

Velleman, P., & Hoaglin, D. (1981). *Applications, basics, and computing of exploratory data analysis.* Boston: Duxbury Press.

Verdooren, L. R. (1963). Extended tables of critical values for Wilcoxon's test statistic. *Biometrika, 50,* 177–186.

Vermont Department of Health. (1982). *1981 Annual report of vital statistics in Vermont.* Burlington, VT.

Visintainer, M. A., Volpicelli, J. R., & Seligman, M. E. P. (1982). Tumor rejection in rats after inescapable or escapable shock. *Science, 216,* 437–439.

Wagner, B. M., Compas, B. E., & Howell, D. C. (1988). Daily and major life events: A test of an integrative model of psychosocial stress. *American Journal of Community Psychology, 61,* 189–205.

Wainer, H. (1976). Estimating coefficients in linear models: It don't make no nevermind. *Psychological Bulletin, 83,* 213–217.

Wainer, H. (1978). On the sensitivity of regression and regressors. *Psychological Bulletin, 85,* 267–273.

Wainer, H. (1984). How to display data badly. *American Statistician, 38,* 137–147.

Wainer, H., & Thissen, D. (1981). Graphical data analysis. *Annual Review of Psychology, 32,* 191–241.

Walker, H. M. (1940). Degrees of freedom. *Journal of Educational Psychology, 31,* 253–269.

Weisberg, H. I. (1979). Statistical adjustments and uncontrolled studies. *Psychological Bulletin, 86,* 1149–1164.

Welch, B. L. (1938). The significance of the difference between two means when the population variances are unequal. *Biometrika, 29,* 350–362.

Welch, B. L. (1947). The generalization of Student's problem when several difference population variances are involved. *Biometrika, 34,* 29–35.

Welch, B. L. (1951). On the comparison of several mean values: An alternative approach. *Biometrika, 38,* 330–336.

Welkowitz, J., Ewen, R. B., & Cohen, J. (1991). *Introductory statistics for the behaviorial sciences* (4th ed.). New York: Academic Press.

Wilcox, R. R. (1986). Critical values for the correlated *t*-test when there are missing observations. *Communications in Statistics, Simulation and Computation. 15,* 709–714.

Wilcox, R. R. (1987a). New designs in analysis of variance. *Annual Review of Psychology, 38,* 29–60.

Wilcox, R. R. (1987b). *New statistical procedures for the social sciences.* Hillsdale, NJ: Erlbaum.

Williams, E. J. (1959). The comparison of regression variables. *Journal of the Royal Statistical Society (Series B), 21,* 396–399.

Winer, B. J. (1962). *Statistical principles in experimental design.* New York: McGraw-Hill.

Winer, B. J. (1971). *Statistical principles in experimental design* (2nd ed.). New York: McGraw-Hill.

Yates, F. (1934). Contingency tables involving small numbers and the χ^2 test. Supplement. *Journal of the Royal Statistical Society (Series B)*, *1*, 217–235.

Younger, M. S. (1985). *A first course in linear regression* (2nd ed.). Boston: Duxbury Press.

Yuen, K. K., & Dixon, W. J. (1973). The approximate behavior and performance of the two-sample trimmed *t*. *Biometrika*, *60*, 369–374.

Zeigarnik, B. (1927). Das Behalten erledgiter und unerledgiter Handliegen (The memory of completed and uncompleted actions). *Psychologische Forschung*, *9*, 1–85.

Zemsky, R. (1989). *Structure and coherence: Measuring the undergraduate curriculum.* Washington, DC: Association of American Colleges.

Answers to Selected Exercises

Chapter 1

1.1. The entire student body of your college or university would be considered a population under any circumstances in which you want to generalize *only* to the student body of your college or university and no further.

1.3. The students of your college or university are a nonrandom sample of U.S. students, for example, because all U.S. students do not have an equal chance of being included in the sample.

1.5. Independent variables: first-grade students who attended kindergarten versus those who did not; seniors, masters, submasters, and juniors as categories of marathon runners. Dependent variables: social-adjustment scores assigned by first-grade teachers; time to run 26.2 miles.

1.7. Continuous variables: length of gestation; typing speed in words/minute; number of books in the library collection.

1.9. The planners of a marathon race would like to know the average times of senior, master, submaster, and junior runners so they can plan appropriately.

1.11. Categorical data: **(a)** The number of Brown University students in an October, 1984, referendum voting for and the number voting against the university's stockpiling suicide pills in case of nuclear disaster. **(b)** The number of students in a small midwestern college who are white, African-American, Hispanic-American, Asian, or other. **(c)** One year after an experimental program to treat alcoholism, the number of participants who are "still on the wagon," "drinking without having sought treatment," or "again under treatment."

1.13. Children's IQ scores in an inner-city elementary school could be reported directly (a measurement variable), or they could be categorized as retarded (IQs < 70), slow (70–90), average (90–110), above average (110–130), or gifted (> 130).

1.15. For adults of a given height and gender, weight is a ratio scale of body weight, but it is at best an ordinal scale of physical health.

1.17. Speed is probably a much better index of motivation than of learning.

1.19. **(a)** The final grade point average for low-achieving students taking courses that interested them could be compared with the averages of low-achieving students taking courses that do not interest them. **(b)** The frequency of sexual intercourse could be compared for happily versus unhappily married couples.

Chapter 2

2.1. **(b)** Unimodal and positively skewed

2.3. The problem with making a stem-and-leaf display of the data in Exercise 2.1 is that almost all the values fall on only two leaves if we use the usual tens' digits for stems. And things are not much better even if we double the number of stems.

2.4. **(a)** The scores for adults are noticeably smaller.

2.13. The shape of the distribution of the number of movies attended per month for the next 200 people you meet would be positively skewed with a peak at zero movies per month and a sharp drop-off to essentially baseline by about five movies per month.

2.17. **(a)** 9, 2 **(b)** 57

2.19. **(a)** 3249, 377 **(b)** 5.789 **(c)** 2.406 **(d)** The units of measurement are squared musicality scores in Exercise 2.19b and musicality scores in Exercise 2.19c.

2.21. **(a)** $\Sigma(X + Y) = (10 + 9) + (8 + 9) + \cdots + (7 + 2) = 19 + 17 + \cdots + 9 = 134 = 77 + 57 = \Sigma X + \Sigma Y$ **(b)** $\Sigma XY = 10(9) + 8(9) + \cdots + 7(2) = 460$; $\Sigma X \Sigma Y = (77)(57) = 4389$ **(c)** $\Sigma CX = \Sigma 3X = 3(10) + 3(8) + \cdots + 3(7) = 231 = 3(77) = C\Sigma X$ **(d)** $\Sigma X^2 = 10^2 + 8^2 + \cdots + 7^2 = 657$; $(\Sigma X)^2 = 77^2 = 5929$

2.24. Adults say "and then" less frequently than children do.

2.27. Invented data: 1 9 10 15 15; mean = median = 10; mode = 15.

2.34. The numerical codes for the levels of GENDER and ENGL are arbitrary. ($\overline{X} - 1$) for GENDER would be the *proportion* of subjects who were female.

2.37. Range = 30; variance = 20.214; standard deviation = 4.496.

2.39. The two standard deviations are roughly the same, although the range for the children is about twice the range for the adults.

2.40. The interval $\overline{X} \pm 2s_X = 9.908$ to 27.892 includes 96% of the scores.

2.45. -0.893, 0.535, -1.846, 0.535, -0.417, 1.012, 1.012, 0.059

2.46. Standardized scores; the first is a score 0.893 standard deviations below the mean; the second is a score 0.536 standard deviations above the mean.

2.52. Coefficient of variation = 0.35071. In Exercise 2.33 the coefficient is given as a percentage.

2.53. The instructor's disk has a list of deliberate errors in Badcancr.Err.

CHAPTER 3

3.3. (a) 68% (b) 50% (c) 84%

3.5. $z = (950 - 975)/15 = -1.67$; only 4.75% of the time would we expect a count as low as 950, given what we know about the distribution.

3.7. The answers to (b) and (c) of Exercise 3.6 will be equal when the two distributions have the same standard deviation.

3.9. (a) $z = 1.28$; $X = \overline{X} + 1.28(400) = 2512$
(b) $z = -1.645$; $X = \overline{X} - 1.645(400) = 1342$

3.11. Multiply the raw scores by 10/7 to raise the standard deviation to 10, and then add 11.43 points to each new score to bring the mean up to 80.

3.15. $2.05 = (X - 50)/10$; $X = 70.50$

CHAPTER 4

4.1. (a) The null hypothesis was that last night's game was actually an NHL hockey game. (b) On the basis of that null hypothesis, you expected that each team would earn somewhere between zero and six points. You then looked at the actual points and concluded that they were way out of line with what you would expect if this were an NHL hockey game. You therefore rejected the null hypothesis.

4.3. You would draw a very large number of samples. For each sample you would calculate the mode, the range, and their ratio (M). You would then plot the resulting values of M.

4.5. Is the car at the stop sign going to stay there (H_0) or dart out in front of you (H_1)?

4.7. The word "distribution" refers to the set of values obtained for any set of observations or measurements. The phrase "sampling distribution" is reserved for the distribution of outcomes (either theoretical or empirical) of a sample statistic.

4.9. A Type I error would be concluding that you had been shortchanged when in fact you had not been.

4.11. You would adopt a one-tailed test (using the right-hand tail) if you wanted to detect being shortchanged but were not concerned about receiving too much money. In that case, you would not reject the null hypothesis no matter how much excess change you received (you would not care whether the restaurant was being cheated). If you chose the wrong tail, however, you would be looking out for the restaurant's interests and ignoring your own.

4.13. $z = (490 - 650)/50 = -3.2$; $p = .0007$; the probability that a student drawn at random from those properly admitted would have a GRE score as low as 490 is .0007. It would be reasonable to suspect that the fact that his mother was a member of the board of trustees played a role in his admission.

4.15. The distribution would drop away smoothly to the right for the same reason that it always does—there are very few high-scoring people. It would drop away to the left because fewer of the borderline students would be admitted (no matter how high the borderline is set).

CHAPTER 5

5.1. (a) Analytic: If two tennis players are exactly equally skillful—so that the outcome of their match is random—the probability is .50 that Player A will win their upcoming match. (b) Relative frequency: If in past matches Player A has beaten Player B on 13 of the 17 occasions on which they played, then Player A has a probability of $13/17 = .76$ of winning their upcoming match. (c) Subjective: Player A's coach feels that he has a probability of .90 of winning his upcoming match with Player B.

5.3. (a) $p = 1/9 = .111$ that you will win second prize given that you do not win first prize. (b) $p = (2/10)(1/9) = (.20)(.111) = .022$ that he will win first and you second. **(c)** $p = (1/10)(2/9) = (.10)(.22) = .022$ that you will win first and he second. **(d)** p(that you are first and he second $[= .022]) + p$(that he is first and you second $[= .022]) = p$(that you and he will be first and second) $= .044$.

5.5. Conditional probabilities were involved in Exercise 5.3a.

5.7. Conditional probabilities: What is the probability that skiing conditions will be good on Wednesday, *given* that they are good today?

5.9. $p = (2/13)(3/13) = (.154)(.231) = .036$

5.11. The continuous distribution of children's learning abilities are often treated as discrete by school systems that divide children into those needing special education versus those who should attend regular classes. Often, schools further divide the regular classes into fast, average, and slow tracks.

5.13. $p = 10/300 = .03$

5.15. **(a)** $z = (50 - 52.6)/12.42 = -0.21$; p(larger portion) $= .5832$. **(b)** 45% exceed 50, 56% ≥ 50

5.17. p(dropout|ADDSC ≥ 60) $= 7/25 = .28$

5.19. p(dropout) $= 10/88 = .11$; p(dropout|ADDSC ≥ 60) $= .28$; students are much more likely to drop out of school if they scored at or above ADDSC $= 60$ in elementary school.

5.21. The probability of 6 or more correct (out of 10) if $p = .20$ is only .0064. Thus, if 6 of the 10 were correct, you would conclude that they were not operating at chance (some cheating is going on!).

5.23. 24

5.25. $1/60 = .017$

5.27. 15

5.29. $z = (22 - 30(.60))/\sqrt{30(.60)(.40)} = 1.49$; we cannot reject H_0 at $\alpha = .05$.

CHAPTER 6

6.1. $\chi^2 = 11.33$ on 2 df; reject H_0 and conclude that students do not enroll at random.

6.3. $\chi^2 = 2.4$ on 4 df; do not reject H_0 that the child's sorting behavior is in line with the theory.

6.5. $\chi^2 = 29.35$ on 1 df; reject H_0 and conclude that the children did not choose dolls at random (at least with respect to color).

6.7. $\chi^2 = 34.184$ on 1 df; reject H_0 and conclude that the distribution of choices between Black and White dolls was different in the two studies. Choice is *not* independent

of Study. We are no longer asking whether one color of doll is preferred over the other color, but whether the *pattern* of preference is constant across studies. In analysis of variance terms, we are dealing with an interaction.

6.9. **(a)** The chi-square test tests the null hypothesis that the type of diagnosed problem is independent of the mental health center at which a person seeks help. **(b)** $\chi^2 = 10.305$ on 4 df. **(c)** Reject H_0 and conclude that the two variables are not independent—the mental health clinic and the diagnosis are not independent.

6.11. **(a)** Take a group of subjects at random and sort them by gender and by life-style (categorized three ways). **(b)** Deliberately take an equal number of males and females and ask them to specify a preference among three types of life-style. **(c)** Deliberately take 10 males and 10 females and have them divide into two teams of 10 players each.

6.13. **(a)** $\chi^2 = 16.094$ on 7 df. **(b)** Reject H_0. **(c)** Since nearly one-half of the cell frequencies are less than five, you should feel very uncomfortable. One approach would be to combine adjacent columns.

6.15. $\chi^2 = 8.85$ on 2 df. Reject H_0. The ability to reject a tumor is affected by the shock condition.

6.17. $\chi^2 = 8.64$ on 1 df. Reject H_0. Helping behavior is not independent of the gender of the bystander.

6.19. $\chi^2 = 5.08$ on 1 df. Reject H_0.

6.21. We would be asking whether the students are evenly distributed among the eight categories. What we really tested in Exercise 6.13 was whether that distribution, *however it appeared*, was the same for those who later took remedial English as it was for those who later did not take remedial English.

6.23. **(a)** $\chi^2 = 9.00$ on 1 df; reject H_0. **(b)** If watching Monday Night Football really changes people's opinions (in a negative direction), then of those people who change, more should change from positive to negative than vice versa, which is what happened.

6.25. **(b)** Five is the observed frequency; 14.3% of the deliveries in 1 day occur for distances of 50 miles; 16.7% of the letters mailed from 50 miles away were delivered in 1 day; 4.8% of the observations fall in this cell. **(c)** The probability of a value of χ^2 greater than or equal to 12.89583 is exactly .0447.

6.27. $C = 0.17$, which is not significant. $C_{max} = \sqrt{1/2} = 0.707$.

6.29. **(a)** $\phi_C = 0.31$ **(b)** $C = .39$ **(c)** There is a significant, although nonlinear, relationship between income and financial security.

6.33. 5.50, 1.60, 0.44

6.35. $0.11/0.29 = 0.379$. Men in the Normal group are only 0.379 times as likely to exhibit adult delinquency as men in the High Testosterone group.

6.37. **(a)** 92.5% **(b)** 83.2% **(c)** The behaviors were much more likely to be absent then present. **(d)** Reduce the agreement on Present and increase the agreement on Absent by the corresponding amount.

6.39. **(c)** We would not be able to clearly separate differences due to the parent's gender from differences due to the subject's gender.

CHAPTER 7

7.5. The data do not address the issue because (1) they are not a random sample, and (2) we have no definition of what is meant by "a terrible state" nor whether SAT scores measure it.

7.7. The answers (rejection of H_0) are the same in Exercises 7.4 and 7.6 although we rejected much more emphatically in the latter case than in the former. This difference in the values of z obtained was due to the considerable difference in sample sizes.

7.9. $H_0: \mu = 500; H_1: \mu \neq 500$

7.11. In this case, it is not an important finding because the difference is so small. Even if $\mu = 503$ instead of 500, it makes no particular difference to anyone—it hardly qualifies as a sign of major improvement in GRE scores, especially since it is based on a selected sample.

7.13. H_0 could not be rejected because there was a fair amount of variability and N was relatively low.

7.15. $500.3 \leq \mu \leq 505.7$

7.17. **(a)** $t = 20.70$. The students were not responding at chance levels. **(b)** No. It is still possible that better students had higher scores then poorer students.

7.19. No. The answer is not clear, because the physical-guidance condition always followed the imitation condition. Improvement may reflect just the passage of time or the delayed effects of imitation.

7.21. $0.07 \leq \mu_D \leq 3.67$

7.23. $t = -0.35$ on 14 df; do not reject H_0.

7.25. If we wanted to study the effectiveness of two methods of treating breast cancer (radical versus limited mastectomy), we could not use the same subjects, since

the effects of each treatment would obviously carry over to the other.

7.27. **(a)** $H_0: \mu_1 = \mu_2$. There is no difference between the two groups. **(b)** $H_1: \mu_1 \neq \mu_2$. The population means are different. **(c)** $t = 8.89$; reject H_0. **(d)** Students do significantly better on a test when they have read the material!

7.29. A significant difference was not found in Exercise 7.28 because of the large amounts of variability in each group.

7.31. **(a)** $H_0: \mu_1 - \mu_2 = 0$. People receiving training in creative problem solving do not generate more possible solutions than do people who do not receive training. **(b)** $H_1: \mu_1 \neq \mu_2$. There is a difference in the number of solutions generated by the two groups. **(c)** $t = 2.477$ on 16 df. **(d)** There is a significant difference between the two groups in terms of the mean number of generated solutions.

7.33. $t = 4.54$ on 16 df; reject H_0.

7.35. The differential dropout rate may be very important. Only half as many people were able to complete Program A as completed Program B.

7.37. $-3.036 \leq \mu_1 - \mu_2 \leq 5.342$

7.39. $t = 1.66$ on 86 df; do not reject H_0.

7.41. ADDSC in elementary school is quite a good predictor of GPA in ninth grade.

7.43. $t = 2.13$ on 8 df; do not reject H_0.

CHAPTER 8

8.1. **(a)** 0.250 **(b)** 2.50 **(c)** .71

8.3. $N = 99, 126, 169$ (I have rounded up since N is always an integer.)

8.7. **(a)** $N = 38.72 \simeq 39$ subjects per group.
(b) $N = 84.5 \simeq 85$ subjects per group.

8.9. Power $= .51$

8.11. The first one. Since he found a significant difference with an experiment having relatively little power, he is presumably dealing with a fairly large effect.

8.15.

Effect Size	d	One-Sample t	Two-Sample t
Small	.20	289	1156
Medium	.50	47	186
Large	.80	19	74

8.17. Not unless we choose the wrong tail for our one-tailed test. In that case, the power will be approximately zero.

8.19. (a) Power = .24, .71, and .999 assuming $N = 50$ for both groups.

CHAPTER 9

9.3. $r = .35$

9.5. 4.67, 3.33, -4.67

9.8. $r = .74$. 55% of variation in grades can be accounted for by variation in the number of problems completed.

9.9. $t = 4.64$ on 18 df; reject H_0.

9.11. (a) Power = .17 **(b)** 197

9.13. $s_{Y \cdot X} = 0.580$

9.15. The incidence of birthweight < 2500 grams would be 8.36.

9.17. $\hat{Y} = 80.156$

9.19. $0.327 \le b^* \le 0.623$

9.21. $\hat{Y} = 90.701$, which is equal to $\overline{Y}$.

9.23. The regression equation for faculty shows that the best estimate of starting salary for faculty is $15,000 (the intercept in the equation). For every additional year of service, salary increases on average by $900 (the slope). For administrative staff, the best estimate of starting salary is $10,000 (the intercept), but every year of additional service increases the salary by an average of $1,500 (the slope). They will be equal at $8\frac{1}{3}$ years of service.

9.25. Power $\simeq .58$

9.29. $z = 2.52$; reject H_0.

9.33. (a) The intercorrelations vary between approximately .40 and .80. **(b)** The separate scales are definitely not independent.

9.35. We cannot also break down the regressions by the gender of the child because our sample sizes would be extremely small.

CHAPTER 10

10.1. (b) $r_{pb} = -.540$; $t = -2.722$. **(c)** Performance in the morning is significantly related to people's perceptions of their peak periods.

10.3. It looks as though morning people vary their performance across time, but evening people are uniformly poor.

10.5. $t = 2.725$. This is equal to the t test on r_{pb}.

10.7. $\hat{Y} = 0.202X + 0.093$; when $X = \overline{X} = 2.903$, $\hat{Y} = 0.68 = \overline{Y}$.

10.9. (b) $\phi = .256$ **(c)** $t = 1.27$, not significant.

10.11. (a) $\phi = .628$ **(b)** $\chi^2 = 12.62$, $p < .05$.

10.13. (a) $\tau = .886$ **(b)** $z = 4.60$, $p < .05$

10.15. $\tau = .733$

CHAPTER 11

11.1.

Source	df	SS	MS	F
Group	2	2100.0	1050.000	40.127*
Error	15	392.5	26.167	
Total	17	2492.5		

*$p < .05$ [$F_{.05}(2, 15) = 3.68$]

11.3. (a)

Source	df	SS	MS	F
Group	3	655.1429	218.3810	10.778*
Error	24	486.2857	20.2619	
Total	27	1141.4286		

*$p < .05$ [$F_{.05}(3, 24) = 3.01$]

(b)

Source	df	SS	MS	F
Group	1	51.5714	51.5714	1.230 ns
Error	26	1089.8572	41.9176	
Total	17	1141.4286		

[$F_{.05}(1, 26) = 4.23$]

This F tests the null hypothesis that the display of a product in a prominent place is no different from the display in the usual place, disregarding the popularity of the brands.

11.5. (a)

Source	df	SS	MS	F
Group	1	1.260	1.260	0.867 ns
Error	10	14.532	1.453	
Total	11	15.792		

[$F_{.05}(1, 10) = 4.96$]

(b) $t(\text{unpooled}) = -0.883 = \sqrt{0.780}$. **(c)** $t(\text{pooled}) = -0.931 = \sqrt{0.867}$. **(d)** The pooled t.

11.6. $\eta^2 = .196$, $\hat{\omega}^2 = .087$. We would assume a fixed model. The levels were clearly not chosen at random.

11.7. We would assume that the levels of the independent variable are fixed. It is unlikely that randomly chosen variables would just happen to fall 15 days apart.

11.9. We would conclude that there may be a problem with our assumption of homogeneity of variance. More important, such a result would suggest that capitalizing key words has substantially different effects on different people.

11.10. (a)

Source	df	SS	MS	F
Group	2	413.433	206.717	4.82*
Error	12	514.512	42.876	
Total	14	927.945		

$*p < .05 \ [F_{.05}(2, 12) = 3.89]$

There are still significant differences between groups. Notice that most of the entries have been halved, including the F, but not including MS_{error}.

11.11. (b) The sum of squares labeled "MEAN" is the correction factor. The F for this effect is a test of the null hypothesis that the grand mean (μ) is 0.

11.13. $X_{ij} = \mu + \tau_j + e_{ij}$ where $\mu = $ grand mean, τ_j is the effect for the jth treatment, and e_{ij} is the unit of error for the ith subject in treatment j.

11.15. $X_{ij} = \mu + \tau_j + e_{ij}$ where $\mu = $ grand mean, τ_j is the effect of the jth treatment, and e_{ij} is the unit of error for the ith subject in treatment j.

11.17.

Source	df	SS	MS	F
Group	7	44.557	6.365	7.27*
Error	264	231.282	0.876	
Total	271	275.839		

$*p < .05 \ [F_{.05}(7, 264) = 2.06]$

11.19. $t = \sqrt{4.261} = 2.064$, $df' = 78.573$. These agree almost exactly with the results given in Chapter 7.

11.23. $\eta^2 = .16$; $\hat{\omega}^2 = .14$

11.25. Transforming time to speed involves a reciprocal transformation. The effect of the transformation is to decrease the relative distance between large values.

CHAPTER 12

12.1. (a)

Source	df	SS	MS	F
Treatments	4	816.00	204.00	36.429**
1, 2 versus, 3, 4, 5	1	682.67	682.67	121.905**
1 versus 2	1	90.00	90.00	16.071**
3, 4 versus 5	1	3.33	3.33	<1
3 versus 4	1	40.00	40.00	7.143*
Error	20	112.00	5.60	
Total	24	928.00		

$*p < .05 \ [F_{.05}(1, 20) = 4.35, F_{.05}(4, 20) = 2.87]$
$**p < .01 \ [F_{.01}(1, 20) = 8.10, F_{.01}(4, 20) = 4.43]$

(b) a_i: $\quad 3 \ \ 3 \ -2 \ -2 \ -2 \qquad c_i$: $\ \ 0 \ \ 0 \ \ 1 \ \ 1 \ -2$
$ b_i$: $\quad 1 \ -1 \ \ 0 \ \ 0 \ \ 0 \qquad d_i$: $\ \ 0 \ \ 0 \ \ 1 \ -1 \ \ 0$

$\Sigma a_i b_i = (3)(1) + (3)(-1) + (-2)(0) + (-2)(0)$
$\qquad + (-2)(0) = 0$

$\Sigma a_i c_i = (3)(0) + (3)(0) + (-2)(1) + (-2)(1)$
$\qquad + (-2)(-2) = 0$

$\Sigma a_i d_i = (3)(0) + (3)(0) + (-2)(1) + (-2)(-1)$
$\qquad + (-2)(0) = 0$

$\Sigma b_i c_i = (1)(0) + (-1)(0) + (0)(1) + (0)(1)$
$\qquad + (0)(-2) = 0$

$\Sigma c_i d_i = (0)(0) + (0)(0) + (1)(1) + (1)(-1) + (-2)(0) = 0$

(c) $682.67 + 90.00 + 3.33 + 40.00 = 816.00$

12.3. For $\alpha = .05$: $PC = \alpha = .05$; $PE = 2\alpha = .10$; $FW = 1 - (1 - \alpha)^2 = .0975$.

12.5. $q = -1.976$; $t \sqrt{2} = -1.976$

12.7. $t' = -5.86$; reject H_0.
$\qquad t' = -6.77$; reject H_0.

12.9. For the larger contrast, compare $t = -6.77$ against $t'_{\alpha/2}$ (on 15 df and two comparisons) = 2.49. Reject H_0. Then compare the next contrast ($t = -5.86$) against $t_{\alpha/2}$ (on 15 df and one comparison) = 2.131 (from Student's t table). Again reject H_0.

12.11. Tukey$_a$ $w_5 = w_4 = w_3 = w_2 = 3.973$
Tukey$_b$ $w_5 = 3.973$; $w_4 = 3.855$; $w_3 = 3.678$ $w_2 = 3.393$

For the Tukey$_b$ analysis, we find the same pattern of significant differences as we did for Exercise 12.8. For the Tukey$_a$ analysis, we have the same pattern of differences.

12.13. We use the same procedures as we did in Exercise 12.12, except q_r is taken as the average of q_r and q_{max_r} for the WSD and as q_{max} for the HSD. The results are the same as those for Exercise 12.12.

12.15. The variances are approximately equal and so are the sample sizes, so we will use the harmonic mean of the n_i, which is 9.3264.

	Control 34.00	2 μg 38.10	1 μg 48.50	0.1 μg 50.80	0.5 μg 60.33	r	q_r	W_r
34.00	—	4.1	14.5	16.8	26.33*	5	4.04	20.51
38.10		—	10.4	12.7	22.23*	4	3.79	19.24
48.50			—	2.3	11.83	3	3.44	17.46
50.80				—	9.53	2	2.86	14.52

$$W_r = q_r \sqrt{\frac{MS_{error}}{\bar{n}_h}} = q_r \sqrt{\frac{240.35}{9.3264}} = q_r(5.0765)$$

The 0.5 μg group is different from the control group and the 2 μg group. All other differences are not significant. The maximum FW is $2(0.05) = .10$.

12.17. Combine the data from the appropriate groups to form two sets, calculate t, and refer t to the Bonferroni t' tables.

12.19. $SS_{linear} = 178.479$; $F = 0.74$; no significant linear trend. $SS_{quad} = 2134.888$; $F = 8.88$; significant quadratic trend.

CHAPTER 13

13.1. (a)

Source	df	SS	MS	F
Host/Guest	1	3.828	3.828	10.43*
Gender	1	0.078	0.078	<1
$H \times S$	1	3.403	3.403	9.27*
Error	16	5.875	0.367	
Total	19	13.184		

*$p < .05$ [$F_{.05}(1, 16) = 4.49$]

(b) $X_{ijk} = \mu + \alpha_i + \beta_j + \alpha\beta_{ij} + \varepsilon_{ijk}$

13.3. It is hard to believe that mothers who are less than 18 years old and have had at least their second child do not differ in many respects from the rest of the mothers.

13.5. $SS_{size\,at\,Mult.} = 97.267$; $F = 12.483$; $p < .05$

13.9.

$S_{area\,at\,50} = 357.733$		$F = 6.10*$	
$S_{area\,at\,100} = 363.333$		$F = 6.20*$	
$S_{area\,at\,150} = 6.933$		$F < 1$	
	$\overline{728.000} = SS_{area} + SS_{DXA}$		

*$p < .05$

13.11. $F = 4.35$ on 2 and 36 df; reject H_0.

13.13. The Location effect in the one-way and the Location effect in the two-way have the same df, SS, and MS. However, the F is different because when we combined the groups we inflated the error term. (*Note:* The one-way on four groups and the 2×2 produce the same error term.)

13.17.

Source	df	SS	MS	F
Parity	1	11.2356	11.2356	2.69
Size/Age	2	85.8261	42.9130	10.26*
$P \times S$	2	15.4540	7.7270	1.85
Error	49	205.0034	4.1837	
Total	54			

*$p < .05$ [$F_{.05}(2, 49) = 4.04$]

13.19.

Source	df	SS	MS	F
Hospital	1	350.0052	350.0052	15.56*
Treatment	1	350.0052	350.0052	15.56*
$H \times T$	1	107.3391	107.3391	4.77
Error	11	247.4167	22.4924	
Total	14			

*$p < .05$ [$F_{.05}(1, 11) = 4.84$]

13.21. $\eta_p^2 = .04$; $\eta_w^2 = .29$; $\eta_{pw}^2 = .05$; $\hat{\omega}_p^2 = .03$; $\hat{\omega}_w^2 = .26$; $\hat{\omega}_{pw}^2 = .03$

CHAPTER 14

14.1. (a) $X_{ij} = \mu + \pi_i + \tau_j + \pi\tau_{ij} + e_{ij}$ or $X_{ij} = \mu + \pi_i + \tau_j + e'_{ij}$

(b)

Source	df	SS	MS	F
Between subjects	7	189,112.5		
Within subjects	16	5400.0		
Session	2	1918.75	959.375	3.858*
Error	14	3481.25	248.661	
Total	23	194,512.5		

*$p < .05$ [$F_{.05}(2, 14) = 3.74$]

(c) There is a significant difference among the session totals, with scores increasing as a function of experience.

14.3.

Source	df	SS	MS	F
Between subjects	19	106.475		
Groups	1	1.225	1.225	<1
Ss within groups	18	105.250	5.847	
Within subjects	20	83.500		
Trials	1	38.025	38.025	15.259*
$T \times G$	1	0.625	0.625	<1
$T \times Ss$ within groups	18	44.850	2.492	
Total	39	189.975		

*$p < .05$ [$F_{.05}(1, 18) = 4.41$]

There is a significant change from baseline to training, but it does not occur differentially between the two groups and there are no overall differences between groups.

14.5.

Source	df	SS	MS	F
Between subjects	29	159.733		
Groups	2	11.433	5.716	1.04
Ss within groups	27	148.300	5.492	
Within subjects	30	95.000		
Trials	1	19.267	19.267	9.44*
$T \times G$	2	20.633	10.316	5.06*
$T \times Ss$ within groups	27	55.100	2.040	
Total	59	254.733		

*$p < .05$ [$F_{.05}(1, 27) = 4.22$; $F_{.05}(2, 27) = 3.36$]

(c) Reinforcement or attention are sufficient to produce a change from baseline performance, but the additional control group demonstrates that this change is real and not one that would have happened anyway.

14.7. (b) $\hat{e} = .771$

14.9. (a) and **(b)**

$SS_{\text{group at add}} = 0.9$		$F < 1$
$SS_{\text{group at subt}} = 3.6$		$F = 1.96$
$SS_{\text{group at mult}} = 52.9$		$F = 28.86*$
$SS_{\text{prob at calc}} = 78.533$		$F = 57.49*$
$SS_{\text{prob at noncalc}} = 11.200$		$F = 8.20*$

*$p < .05$ [$F_{.05}(2, 16) = 3.63$]

14.11. (a) $SS_{\text{reading at child}} = 50.7$; $F = 12.675*$.
(b) $SS_{\text{items at adult good}} = 4.133$; $F = 3.52*$.

14.13. There would be a very decided lack of independence among items because an increase in one category would necessitate a decrease in another—that is, the subject would have less opportunity to draw from all categories.

14.17. (b) The F for MEAN is a test on $H_0: \mu = 0$. **(c)** $MS_{\text{within cell}}$ is the average of the cell variances.

CHAPTER 15

15.1. (a) A difference of $+1$ degree in temperature (all other things being equal) is associated with a difference of -0.01 in perceived quality of life. A difference of $1000 in median income is associated with a $+0.05$ difference in perceived quality of life (again, all other variables held constant). There is a similar interpretation for the other values of b. The intercept has no practical interpretation here. **(b)** 4.92 **(c)** 3.72

15.3. Temperature ($t = -1.104$)

15.5. (a) Environment **(b)** The gain in prediction from adding the additional variables is more than offset by the loss in power due to the increase in p relative to N.

15.7. As the correlation between them decreases, the higher will be the squared semipartial correlation of each variable with the criterion. Thus, each will add more previously unexplained variation.

15.9. Numsup and Respon are fairly well correlated with the other predictors, whereas YRS is nearly independent of them.

15.13. $R_{\text{adj}}^2 = \text{est } R^{2*} = -.158$. Since a squared coefficient cannot be negative, declare it undefined and nonsignificant.

15.17. It has no meaning in that we have the data for the population of interest (the 10 districts).

15.19. It plays an important role through its correlation with the residual components of the other variables.

15.21. Within the context of a multiple-regression equation, we cannot look at one variable alone. The slope for one variable is only the slope for that variable when all other variables are held constant.

15.25. (b) The value of R^2 was virtually unaffected. However, the standard error of the regression coefficient for PVLoss increased from 0.105 to 0.178. Tolerance for PVLoss decreased from .981 to .345, whereas VIF increased from 1.019 to 2.900. **(c)** PVTotal should not be included in the model because it is redundant.

CHAPTER 16

16.1. (c)

Source	df	SS	MS	F
Treatments	2	57.733	28.867	9.31*
Error	12	37.200	3.100	
Total	14	94.933		

*$p < .05$ [$F_{.05}(2, 12) = 3.89$]

16.3. (a)

Source	df	SS	MS	F
Treatments	2	79.010	39.505	14.919*
Error	18	47.657	2.648	
Total	20	126.667		

*$p < .05$ [$F_{.05}(2, 18) = 3.55$]

16.5.

Source	df	SS	MS	F
Gender	1	65.333	65.333	7.73*
SES	2	338.667	169.333	20.03*
$G \times S$	2	18.667	9.333	1.10
Error	42	355.000	8.452	
Total	47	777.667		

*$p < .05$ [$F_{.05}(1, 42) = 4.08$; $F_{.05}(2, 42) = 3.23$]

16.7.

Source	df	SS	MS	F
Gender	1	60.015	60.015	7.21*
SES	2	346.389	173.195	20.80*
$G \times S$	2	21.095	10.547	1.27
Error	35	291.467	8.328	
Total	40			

*$p < .05$ [$F_{.05}(1, 35) = 4.12$; $F_{.05}(2, 35) = 3.27$]

16.9. $\hat{\mu} = 13.4167$; $\alpha_1 = 1.167$; $\beta_1 = -3.167$; $\beta_2 = -0.167$; $\alpha\beta_{11} = 0.833$; $\alpha\beta_{12} = -0.167$.

16.11. If we are actually dealing with unweighted means, SS_A and SS_B will be 0 because means of means are all 7 for rows and columns.

16.17. (a)

Source	df	SS	MS	F
Covariate	1	2304.801	2304.801	103.375*
Metering	1	172.697	172.697	7.746*
Treatment	2	1120.872	560.436	25.137*
$M \times T$	2	8.246	4.123	<1
Error	23	512.799	22.296	
Total	29	4796.700		

*$p < .05$ [$F_{.05}(1, 23) = 4.28$; $F_{.05}(2, 23) = 3.42$]

(b) After adjusting for last year's usage, there are significant differences between the time-of-day groups in terms of usage and between the metered group and the others. There is no interaction between the two independent variables.

16.19.

Source	df	SS	MS	F
Metering	1	197.633	197.633	5.64*
Treatment	2	1086.467	543.233	15.50*
$M \times T$	2	6.066	3.033	<1
Error	24	841.200	35.050	
Total	29	2131.366		

*$p < .05$ [$F_{.05}(1, 24) = 4.26$; $F_{.05}(2, 24) = 3.40$]

CHAPTER 17

17.1.

$\ln(F_{ij}) = \lambda$	Equiprobability
$\ln(F_{ij}) = \lambda + \lambda^F$	Conditional equiprobability on Function
$\ln(F_{ij}) = \lambda + \lambda^I$	Conditional equiprobability on Inventor
$\ln(F_{ij}) = \lambda + \lambda^F + \lambda^I$	Independence
$\ln(F_{ij}) = \lambda + \lambda^F + \lambda^I + \lambda^{FI}$	Saturated model

17.3. (1) $\lambda = 2.8761 =$ mean of $\ln(\text{cell}_{ij})$ (2) $\lambda^{\text{Inventor}} = 0.199$ 0.540 -0.739. The effect for Female Partner is 0.199. The $\ln$(frequencies in row 1) are slightly above average. (3) $\lambda^{\text{Function}} = -0.632$ 0.260 0.222 -0.007 0.097

−0.667 0.303 −0.029 0.452. The effect of Confrontation is −0.632. Confrontation contributes somewhat less than its share of idiosyncratic expressions. (4)
$$\lambda^{\text{Inventor} \times \text{Function}} = \begin{matrix} 0.196 & -0.039 & \dots & 0.249 & 0.028 \\ -0.481 & 0.038 & \dots & 0.250 & 0.259 \\ 0.286 & 0.001 & \dots & -0.500 & -0.287 \end{matrix}$$
The unique effect of $cell_{11}$ is 0.196. It contributes slightly more than would be predicted from the row and column totals alone.

17.5. For females the odds in favor of a direct hit are 6.00, whereas for males they are only 2.8125. This leaves an odds ratio of 6.00/2.8125 = 2.1333. A female is 2.1333 times more likely to have a direct hit than a male.

17.7. Letting S represent Satisfaction, G represent Gender, and V represent Validity, and with 0.50 added to all cells because of small frequencies, the optimal model is

$$\ln(F_{ij}) = \lambda + \lambda^G + \lambda^S + \lambda^V + \lambda^{SV}$$

For this model, $\chi^2 = 4.53$ on 5 df; $p = .4763$.

17.11.

	Low SES		High SES	
	Normal Testosterone	High Testosterone	Normal Testosterone	High Testosterone
Odds delinquent	0.1721	0.4429	0.0476	0.0429

17.13. The optimal model for the Dabbs and Morris (1990) data is

$$\ln(F_{ij}) = \lambda + \lambda^S + \lambda^D + \lambda^T + \lambda^{SD} + \lambda^{ST} + \lambda^{DT}$$

The χ^2 for this model is 3.52 on 1 df, for $p = .0607$. The removal of any term would lead to a significant decrement in the fit of the model.

17.15. When you add Gender to the analysis of Pugh's data, it contributes significantly to the fit of the model. Pugh forced the Gender × Stigma interaction into the model, even though its removal did not significantly affect the fit of the model, because the sampling plan for the study was based on those variables. She settled on the

There are other models that fit nearly as well, and for the specific arguments you should refer to her paper.

CHAPTER 18

18.1. (a) $W_S = 23$; $W_{.025} = 27$. (b) Reject H_0 and conclude that older children include more inferences in their summaries.

18.3. $z = -3.15$; reject H_0.

18.5. (a) $T = 8.5$; $T_{.025} = 8$; do not reject H_0. (b) We cannot conclude that we have evidence supporting the hypothesis that there is a reliable increase in hypothesis generation and testing over time. (Here is a case in which alternative methods of breaking ties could lead to different conclusions.)

18.8. (a) $T = 46$; $T_{.025} = 52$. (b) Reject H_0 and conclude that first-born children are more independent.

18.9. The difference between the pairs is heavily dependent on the score for the first born.

18.11. The Wilcoxon matched-pairs signed-ranks test tests the null hypothesis that paired scores were drawn from identical populations or from symmetric populations with the same mean (and median). The corresponding t test tests the null hypothesis that the paired scores were drawn from populations with the same mean and assumes normality.

18.13. Rejection of the H_0 by a t test is a more specific statement than rejection using the appropriate distribution-free test because by making assumptions about normality and homogeneity of variance, the t test refers specifically to population means.

18.15. $H = 6.757$; reject H_0.

18.17. The study in Exercise 18.16 has an advantage over the one in Exercise 18.15 in that it eliminates the influence of individual differences (differences in overall level of truancy from one person to another).

18.19. These are equivalent tests in this case.

18.20. $\chi_F^2 = 9.00$. We reject H_0 and conclude that people do not like tea made with used tea bags.

INDEX